CASES AND MATERIALS ON
STATE AND LOCAL GOVERNMENT LAW

Eighth Edition

■ ■ ■

Richard Briffault
Joseph P. Chamberlain Professor of Legislation
Columbia University School of Law

Laurie Reynolds
Prentice H. Marshall Professor of Law
University of Illinois College of Law

AMERICAN CASEBOOK SERIES®

WEST
ACADEMIC
PUBLISHING

American Casebook Series is a trademark registered in the U.S. Patent and Trademark Office.

COPYRIGHT © 1975, 1980, 1987, 1992 WEST PUBLISHING CO.
© West, a Thomson business, 2001, 2004
© 2009 Thomson/Reuters
© 2016 LEG, Inc. d/b/a West Academic
    444 Cedar Street, Suite 700
    St. Paul, MN 55101
    1-877-888-1330

West, West Academic Publishing, and West Academic are trademarks of West Publishing Corporation, used under license.

Printed in the United States of America

ISBN: 978-0-314-28501-0

To Mrs. P, O, and J, R.B.

To my three Loves, L.R.

PREFACE

This is an exciting time to study state and local government law. The federal system as a whole is in ferment, and states and local governments are playing a large and growing role in providing public services, in regulating private economic activity, and in addressing controversial social questions. States and localities are experimenting with new forms of service delivery, new institutional structures, new means of raising money, new types of interlocal arrangements, and new public policies. They face a host of difficult challenges, including problems of interlocal inequality, assuring democratic accountability, and addressing the problems of metropolitan regions. Lawyers will continue to play crucial roles in this complex process—drafting legislation, litigating cases, and advising clients, as they help individuals, community organizations, firms, and governments negotiate the increasingly complex world of state and local government law.

Building on its predecessors, the Eighth Edition of our casebook will provide law students with a knowledge of the legal doctrines, institutions, processes, theories, and analytical tools that will enable them to succeed as state and local government lawyers. Like its predecessors, this edition is founded on the authors' belief that the study of state and local government law requires an understanding of case law, of the often-conflicting theories and normative concerns that have driven the development of that case law, of the distinctive institutions that mark the state and local sphere, and of the real-world problems that state and local governments face. This edition will continue to provide students with a critical introduction to the many important functions performed by states and local governments, and to the role that law and legal institutions play in structuring state and local activities and promoting effective and accountable governance at the state and local level.

The Eighth Edition closely resembles the three most recent editions in both content and style. However, the many changes that continue to reshape, and roil, the field are well-reflected in this new edition, including recent academic work on local redistribution and urban economics (Chapter I); new material on the role of special districts and quasi-private governments (Chapter II); the latest trends in local government formation and boundary change (Chapter III); the local role and state-local conflicts in such diverse areas as the promotion of public health and the regulation of firearms, fracking, marijuana, and employee wages and benefits (Chapter IV); new state efforts to come to grips with school finance reform (Chapter V); tax increment financing, and state and local efforts to deal with fiscal distress, including municipal bankruptcy (Chapter VI); and controversies surrounding municipal tort liability, juvenile curfews and order maintenance policing (Chapter VII).

Chapter I provides both an important analytical framework for understanding the often bewildering variety of local governments in our system and an introduction to the longstanding constitutional, political, and legal debate which has framed many of the central issues of local government law: the question of which level of government should undertake which functions, and what issues and concerns need to be considered in order to answer that question. Drawing on both classic sources like Madison and Tocqueville and contemporary legal scholars, Chapter I provides a stimulating foundation for the study of such legal questions as local government formation and annexation, home rule and state-local conflicts, interlocal relations and regional governance, and state and local finances and services. This chapter also analyzes state constitutions and the differences between the federal and state constitutions. This section will be a useful basis for study of the role state constitutional law plays in shaping many of the issues considered in later chapters.

Chapter II examines the federal constitutional status of local governments. At a time of renewed and intense Supreme Court attention to federalism, the constitutional position of local governments is of great importance. Indeed, the Court's views of local government have produced constitutional decisions in areas of great local concern, including land use and education. The Court's cases also provide a useful pedagogical device for examining the conceptions of local government that have been central to our legal system. All of local government law has been shaped by the multiple and, at times, conflicting visions of local government as arm of the state, as local democracy, and as quasi-proprietary firm. As we indicate, these different visions have shaped, and are captured by, the Supreme Court's application of the one person, one vote doctrine to local governments. This chapter, thus, has the additional benefit of providing an analysis of the structure of political representation at the local level.

Chapter III addresses local government formation and boundary change. It provides students with an understanding of the significance of the creation or expansion of a new local government, both for local residents and for residents of the surrounding area. At a time of rapid population growth and accompanying boundary issues in many metropolitan areas, this chapter offers a nuanced examination of the many legal, fiscal, social, and institutional concerns that go into the vitally important questions of local government formation and boundary change.

Chapter IV examines state-local relations, with particular attention to local home rule. It includes several new cases and notes that enable students to consider the connection between local home rule and the authority of local governments to experiment with innovative policies in a range of controversial areas. The final section distills many of the complex issues presented when questions of local power and state-local conflicts arise into a succinct and useful study aid.

Chapter V examines interlocal relations and metropolitan area problems. At a time when urban sprawl, deteriorating regional infrastructure, interlocal conflicts, interlocal differences in the financing and quality of basic services like education, and regional governance are hotly debated across the country, we believe that a state and local government law book must give the legal issues that frame these questions greater attention. Chapter V considers a wide range of recent cases, statutes, institutional innovations and legal and social writings concerning interlocal conflicts, interlocal cooperation, and the possibilities of metropolitan area regional governance.

The treatment of state and local finance in Chapter VI includes a number of new, cutting-edge issues. Longstanding state constitutional public purpose requirements have been increasingly challenged by state and local economic development programs that provide direct aid to private enterprises. Voter initiatives and other state constitutional innovations have imposed new legal restrictions on state and local taxation and debt. The ever-rising demand for state and local services, however, has sparked the creation of a host of revenue-raising and borrowing devices, and expanded the role of special districts and public authorities in order to avoid those constraints. This point-counterpoint of restriction and evasion has generated an extensive body of challenging case law, and has proved to be of vital importance to the financing of state and local governments at a time when states and localities have taken on an even greater role in providing public services. The Great Recession of 2007–09 imposed new levels of financial stress on states and local governments, leading to new forms of state intervention in local affairs and the most significant municipal bankruptcy in our history. A new section of this chapter examines the legal and policy issues raised by state and local fiscal distress.

Building on Chapter VI's treatment of the financing of state and local government, Chapter VII turns to the business of government. This includes the legal obligations that attach when government provides services, municipal tort liability, and the fundamental questions of when government is obligated to provide services and of how norms of equal treatment apply to service delivery. Chapter VII also looks at the scope of local regulatory authority by examining some of the constitutional constraints that apply to one of the most important manifestations of the local police power—the maintenance of public order.

The authors of the Eighth Edition are indebted to numerous individuals who contributed to its preparation. Professor Briffault thanks several generations of Columbia Law students for their stimulating class participation, which was of extraordinary help in developing his thinking about state and local government law, and Columbia Law School for its generous administrative support. He would particularly like to thank Max Hirsch of the Columbia Class of 2014 and Sasha Zheng of the Columbia Class of 2016 and his invaluable assistant Taylor Cook for all the work they did that helped make the Eighth Edition possible. Professor Reynolds wishes to thank Jackie Walters for many hours of secretarial assistance and cheerful help explaining the mysterious world of Word; her research assistants Erin Solomon, Jillian Schmitz, and Mike Kozlowski, all fabulous University of Illinois law students; and the many other students who contributed, either with their research assistance or as members of the classes in which earlier versions of these materials were tested.

RICHARD BRIFFAULT
LAURIE REYNOLDS

March 2016

ACKNOWLEDGMENTS

The authors gratefully acknowledge the generosity of the following authors and publishers. They have allowed us to reprint portions of their work in this book. The works are listed here in alphabetical order by last name of the first author.

Lynn Baker, Conditional Federal Spending After Lopez, 95 Columbia Law Review 1911 (1995).

Richard Briffault, Our Localism, Part I: The Structure of Local Government Law, 90 Columbia Law Review 1 (1990).

Richard Briffault, Our Localism, Part II: Localism and Legal Theory, 90 Columbia Law Review 346 (1990).

Richard Briffault, Who Rules at Home: One Person/One Vote and Local Governments, 60 University of Chicago Law Review 339 (1993).

Richard Briffault, What About the "Ism?" Normative and Formal Concerns in Contemporary Federalism, 47 Vanderbilt Law Review 1313 (1994).

Richard Briffault, The Local Government Boundary Problem in Metropolitan Areas, 48 Stanford Law Review 1115 (1996).

Richard Briffault, A Government of Our Time: Business Improvement Districts and Urban Governance, 99 Columbia Law Review 365 (1999).

Mark Brown, The Failure of Fault Under Section 1983, 84 Cornell Law Review 1503 (1999).

J. Peter Byrne, Are Suburbs Unconstitutional? (reviewing Suburbs Under Siege: Race, Space, and Audacious Judges), 85 Georgetown Law Journal 2265 (1997). Reprinted by permission of the publisher, Georgetown Law Journal © 1997.

Robert C. Ellickson, "Controlling Chronic Misconduct in City Spaces: Of Panhandlers, Skid Rows, and Public-Space Zoning", 105 Yale Law Journal 1165 (1996). Reprinted by permission of the Yale Law Journal Company and William S. Hein Company from The Yale Law Journal, Vol. 105.

Richard Thompson Ford, Beyond Borders: A Partial Response to Richard Briffault, 48 Stanford Law Review 1173 (1996).

Kathyrn A. Foster, The Political Economy of Special Purpose Government (1997). Reprinted by permission of Georgetown University Press.

Gerald E. Frug, The City as a Legal Concept, 93 Harvard Law Review 1057 (1980). Reprinted by permission of the author and Harvard Law Review Association.

Ester Fuchs, Mayors and Money: Fiscal Policy in New York and Chicago (1992), University of Chicago Press.

John Jeffries, In Praise of the Eleventh Amendment and Section 1983, 84 Virginia Law Review 47 (1998).

Neal Katyal, Judges as Advicegivers, 50 Stanford Law Review 1709 (1998).

Debra Livingston, Police Discretion and the Quality of Life in Public Places: Courts, Communities, and the New Policing, 97 Columbia Law Review 551 (1997).

Deborah Merritt, Three Faces of Federalism: Finding a Formula for the Future, 47 Vanderbilt Law Review 1563 (1994).

John Stuart Mill, Considerations on Representative Government, pp. 294–95 (Amherst, NY: Prometheus Books), 1991. Reprinted by permission of the publisher.

Martha Minow, School Finance: Does Money Matter?, 28 Harvard Journal on Legislation 395 (1991). Permission granted © 1991 by the President and Fellows of Harvard College and the Harvard Journal on Legislation.

Arthur O'Sullivan, Terri A. Sexton, and Steven M. Sheffrin (eds.), Property Taxes and Tax Revolts: The Legacy of Proposition 13 (Cambridge University Press, 1995). Reprinted by permission of Cambridge University Press.

Neil R. Peirce, Citistates: How Urban American Can Prosper in a Competitive World (1993). Reprinted by permission of Seven Locks Press.

Laurie Reynolds, Rethinking Municipal Annexation Powers, 24 Urban Lawyer 247 (1992). Copyright © 1992 American Bar Association. Reprinted by permission.

Stewart Sterk, Controlling Legislative Shortsightedness: The Effectiveness of Constitutional Debt Limitations, 1991 Wisconsin Law Review 1301.

Jon Teaford, City Versus State: The Struggle for Legal Ascendancy, 17 American Journal of Legal History 60 (1973).

Charles M. Tiebout, A Pure Theory of Local Expenditures, 64 Journal of Political Economy 64, p. 416 (1956). Reprinted by permission of the University of Chicago Press.

Richard F. Wagner and Warren E. Weber, Competition, Monopoly, and the Organization of Government in Metropolitan Areas, 18 Journal of Law and Economics 661 (1975).

Gregory R. Weiher, The Fractured Metropolis: Political Fragmentation and Metropolitan Segregations. State University of New York Press, 1991.

Joan Williams, The Invention of the Municipal Corporation: A Case Study in Legal Change, 34 American Law Review 369 (1985). Reprinted by permission of the author and the American University Law Review.

Robert Williams, State Constitutional Law Processes, 24 William and Mary Law Review 169 (1983). Reprinted by permission of the William and Mary Law Review.

James Q. Wilson, Broken Windows: The Police and Neighborhood Safety; Atlantic Monthly, March, 1982 at 29.

Edward A. Zelinsky, Metropolitanism, Progressivism, and Race, 98 Columbia Law Review 665 (1998).

SUMMARY OF CONTENTS

TABLE OF CONTENTS

TABLE OF CASES

The principal cases are in bold type.

CASES AND MATERIALS ON
STATE AND LOCAL GOVERNMENT LAW
Eighth Edition

CHAPTER I

INTRODUCTION TO THE STUDY OF STATE AND LOCAL GOVERNMENT LAW

■ ■ ■

A. INTRODUCTION

Writing in Federalist Number 45, James Madison predicted that the states would dominate the new federal union. The powers of the federal government were "few and defined," limited primarily to "external objects, as war, peace, negotiation, and foreign commerce." By contrast, the states would continue to control "all the objects which, in the ordinary course of affairs, concern the lives, liberties and properties of the people, and the internal order, improvement, and prosperity of the State." The states would have a greater role in governance and more direct contact with, and therefore enjoy more affection from, the people than would the smaller and more distant national government. Madison assumed the principal problem of federalism would be protecting a fragile federal government from the states, not protecting the states from the federal government.

Madison may have been poor-mouthing the prospects for the federal government in order to allay concerns about the Constitution's shift of power from state to national hands. Yet, for most of American history, the federal government, as Madison predicted, played only a limited role in peacetime domestic life, and most government power was exercised at the state and local levels. As late as 1927, on the eve of the Great Depression, federal spending accounted for barely one-sixth of total domestic government—federal, state, and local—spending, with the federal government providing few services directly to the people and only a modest amount of financial assistance to state and local governments. *See* J. Richard Aronson & John L. Hilley, Financing State and Local Governments 17 (Brookings Inst., 4th ed. 1986).

Since the 1920s, this situation has changed dramatically. The emergence of a national—and increasingly global—economy, two world wars, the rise of the United States to superpower status, and the ongoing cultural and technological transformations of our society have been accompanied by a tectonic shift in power to the federal government. During the second and third quarters of the twentieth century, the federal government came to play an enormous role in regulating the economy, promoting social welfare, enforcing political and civil rights, and protecting the environment. Federal institutions—the President, Congress, the Supreme Court and the lower federal courts, federal administrative agencies—became the focus of legal education as well. In most law schools today, constitutional law, administrative law, and other public law courses concentrate on the federal constitution and federal law. States and local governments may appear when they are on the receiving end of federal action, but states and local governments are only rarely the subjects of law school study.

Yet, states and local governments continue to play a significant role in American governance. As in Madison's day, for most people "the ordinary course of affairs" remains largely the domain of state and local governments. The rules that structure civil society—contract law, tort law, property and land use law, criminal law, family law, the incorporation of businesses, the regulation of the professions—are developed, implemented, and enforced primarily at the state and local levels. So, too, most public services that affect people in their homes and families—public schools, policing and the incarceration of offenders, public safety, the provision of clean water and the removal of solid wastes and sewage, maintenance of roads and streets, public parks, public hospitals and emergency medical services—are provided by states and localities, not the federal government. The vast majority of the opportunities for participation in political life—such as running for office, campaigning for or against a ballot proposition, or appearing before such critical governing institutions as the school board, the planning and zoning commission, or a town meeting—are at the state and local level, too.

In the twenty-first century, dramatic events continue to underscore the central place of states and local governments in our federal system. The new century began with the 2000 Presidential election and the bitter post-election battle over Florida's 25 electoral votes, which reminded us that there is no *national* presidential election. Instead we undertake 50—actually, 51 including the District of Columbia—separate and simultaneous state elections. The winner is determined not by the national popular vote, but by the states' electoral votes, which are based in part on state population but also provide representation for the states as states. The process of collecting, tabulating, and recounting presidential votes is conducted by state and local officials, pursuant to state rules. Local officials also decide such basic features of the electoral system as the type of voting machinery used, the design of the ballot, the decision whether to undertake a manual recount, the discretion whether to accept a technically flawed absentee ballot, and the question of whether a dangling or dimpled chad is sufficient to mark the intent of a voter. To be sure, as the Supreme Court's decision in *Bush v. Gore*, 531

U.S. 98 (2000), indicates, there are federal constitutional rules that crucially constrain state and local decision-making. And Congress has taken modest steps to improve voting systems nationwide, such as the Help America Vote Act of 2002. But the 2000 election was a stunning reminder of how states and local governments play a crucial role in filling our most important national office.

One year later, September 11, 2001 highlighted the crucial role of the states and especially local governments in dealing with issues of public safety and security. Although September 11th was an attack on our nation, most of the domestic response involved local governments. New York City police, firefighters, and emergency medical personnel responded to the attacks on the World Trade Center, and local public health and safety workers from the District of Columbia and various Virginia and Maryland counties battled the consequences of the terrorist attack on our most important federal military installation, the Pentagon. Much of the subsequent public effort to increase the security of public buildings, public spaces, and vulnerable infrastructure facilities has involved state and local security officers. In detecting and pursuing terrorists and preventing future terrorist attacks, the 600,000 local police officers are likely to play at least as great a role as the FBI and its 11,000 agents. This is not simply a matter of numbers—although the enormous difference in the magnitude of the local versus federal police forces is surely relevant. Local police forces are likely to have far greater knowledge of local conditions and dangers, including access to informants and awareness of unusual or suspicious incidents. *See generally* Matthew C. Waxman, National Security Federalism in the Age of Terror, 64 Stan. L. Rev. 289 (2013); Richard Briffault, Facing the Urban Future After September 11, 2001, 34 Urb. Law. 563 (2002).

If September 11th stands as a successful example of intergovernmental cooperation, Hurricane Katrina will be remembered for, among other things, the uncoordinated failure of all levels of government. Some have suggested that the governments' failures were a direct result of federalism, whose doctrinal respect of state autonomy was reflected in the federal government's decision to leave primary disaster response in the hands of the lowest levels of government. New Orleans' Comprehensive Emergency Management Plan conferred authority on the mayor to order and supervise a mandatory evacuation, but city officials failed to evacuate over 70,000 individuals. Similarly, the State of Louisiana failed to order a timely evacuation, a decision which ultimately resulted in hundreds of deaths and the suffering of thousands. For its part, the federal government explained its failure to pre-deploy resources in anticipation of Katrina's arrival on its National Response Plan's limitation of federal pre-deployment to events for which there is no prior notice, such as a sudden nuclear or radiological attack.

Federal, state and local governments have used the tragedy to rethink the traditional disaster response. For example, the federal government's plan now explicitly allows federal pre-deployment intervention and resource allocation in anticipation of a disaster, thus allowing it to be proactive rather than merely react to local requests. This changed system may more effectively integrate the local knowledge and expertise evidenced on September 11th with the resources and logistical expertise of the federal government underutilized during Katrina. Regardless of the changes made to the nation's disaster response system, state and local governments will continue to play a critical role in emergency preparedness. For extensive analysis of the intergovernmental relations aspect of Katrina, *see* Daniel A. Farber, et al, Disasters and the Law: Katrina and Beyond (Aspen Pub., 2d ed. 2009).

The shortcomings of local law enforcement drew national attention in a series of highly publicized incidents in 2014 and 2015 involving the deaths of unarmed African-American men in confrontations with local police officers in Ferguson, Missouri; Staten Island, New York; Baltimore, Maryland; and elsewhere. These cases underscored the intensely local nature of much of our criminal justice system. Our criminal laws are primarily state laws, but decisions concerning policing practices are made by local governments; decisions whether to indict are made by locally elected prosecutors and locally empanelled grand juries. Yet, these decisions can have national repercussions. It is too soon to determine the longer-term consequences of these events, but it is certain that much of the criminal justice system will continue to be administered and enforced at the local level.

The continued significance of the states and local governments is not simply a lingering aftermath of an earlier era. The centralizing trend that marked much of the twentieth century has plateaued, and the federal system has witnessed a modest tilt away from the federal government and back to the states and localities. This can be seen in several different ways—in the enhanced state and local share of the public workforce and public spending; the central role of states and local governments in providing basic public services like primary and secondary education, public safety, transportation, and water supply and public utilities; and in the many policy initiatives that have sprung from the states and localities.

In 2014, the federal government civilian workforce was 2,726,000—down 12% from the roughly 3.1 million federal civilian employees in the late 1980s, and, remarkably, smaller than the federal civilian workforce of 1966. By contrast, the combined state and local workforce in 2013 consisted of more than 16 million full-time-equivalent employees—or nearly six times the federal workforce. And while the federal workforce has been stagnant, the state and local workforce has been growing. The number of state and local employees in 2013 was 11% higher than in 1990—and roughly double the state and local workforce of 1966. United States Census Bureau, 2013 Annual Survey of Public Employment and Payroll.

The state and local share of total government spending is also on the rise. In 1980, federal spending was 78% greater than state and local spending, but by 2013 that number had been reduced to 47%. If federal spending on defense and foreign affairs, interest on the national debt, and the two major social insurance programs—Medicare and Social Security— are subtracted from the federal total, so that the focus is on domestic regulation and public services, then state and local spending actually dominates federal spending—by roughly 2:1. Moreover, approximately 17% of federal spending consists of grants-in-aid to state and local governments. Looking at just the non-defense, non-international affairs, non-Medicare, non-Social Security and non-interest-on-the-debt portion of the federal budget, grants-in-aid came to 30% of federal spending in 1980 and 47% of federal spending in 2012. Yet, even as a significant and rising share of the federal discretionary domestic budget is devoted to state and local aid, states and local governments have not become appreciably more dependent on federal funds. Federal aid amounted to 22% of state and local spending in 1980, and 24% in 2012. Economic Report of the President, February 2015, at Tables B-22 to B-4. To a considerable degree, states and local governments fund education, public welfare, highways, hospitals, public safety, water supply, solid waste disposal and wastewater treatment, and other basic programs that are their primary responsibilities in our federal system.

States and localities are also major players in addressing a wide range of domestic policy issues. This is reflected in the unprecedented leadership role assumed by the state attorneys general in shaping national policy on tobacco; the initiatives underway in nearly a dozen states to tackle the sprawling pattern of urban growth; the states' exploration of new forms of school finance, HMO regulation, income assistance, and health insurance for the uninsured; the combination of voter-initiated and legislatively-adopted measures addressing campaign finance, redistricting, voting, and government ethics; and the state and local legislative and judicial decisions re-examining family and marriage relationships. States and local governments have been particularly active in addressing such "hot button" issues as abortion and reproductive rights; firearms regulation and gun owners' rights; wages and workplace conditions; the regulation of hydraulic fracturing ("fracking"); the treatment of immigrants; and the legalization of marijuana use for medical or recreational purposes. Reflecting the diversity of opinions within the United States, different states will adopt very different policies, *see, e.g.,* Law Center to Prevent Gun Violence, "Tracking State

Gun Laws: 2014 Developments" (noting that in 2013–14, states adopted 64 laws strengthening gun regulation and 70 laws weakening so that on balance eight states significantly toughened their laws and four states significantly weakened them); Guttmacher Institute, State Center, "Laws Affecting Reproductive Health and Rights: 2013 State Policy Review" (in 2013, 39 states enacted 141 laws related to reproductive health and rights); and Jenni Bergal, "Many Cities Are Creating Policies Apart from Their States," Pew Charitable Trusts, Stateline, Jan. 15, 2015 (discussing local minimum wage and sick leave laws and fracking regulations that have triggered state opposition). In these and other areas, states and localities are important, independent policy-makers within the federal system. Indeed, their role may be growing as political polarization contributes to policy gridlock in Washington. Moreover, states and local governments are often viewed more favorably by the public. In a 2013 survey, 63% of respondents expressed a favorable opinion of their local government—a number virtually unchanged over two decades; 57% expressed a favorable view of their state government; but only 28% had a favorable view of the federal government. *See* Pew Research Center, State Governments Viewed Favorably as Federal Rating Hits New Low, April 15, 2013.

This casebook provides a foundation for the study of state and local government law. For us, the key word is "government." We do not examine state and local law generally. So much American law is state and local law—ranging from criminal and tort law to land use, domestic relations, and corporate and insurance law—that a course on state and local law would consume most of your three years in law school. Rather, we focus on state and local government—that is, the organization and structure of states and local governments; the procedures that determine how they make law, impose taxes, and provide services; the criteria for the allocation of policy-making and service responsibilities between states and local governments; and the rules that determine the relationships between states and local governments, and among local governments within states and metropolitan areas. Although we will consider some substantive state and local policies, our primary concern will be the institutions, rules, and processes that affect how those policies are made.

This chapter is intended to furnish you with an introduction to some of the basic facts, issues, and legal considerations affecting the study of states and local governments. Section A provides basic information about the states and, especially, local governments. Local governments are key players in the state-local system and provide most of the public services that the American people receive. Yet they are little-studied and poorly understood. This section introduces you to the many different types of local governments and to the roles they play in American governance. Section B is an introduction to the debate over localism that has become central to the study of state and local government law in recent decades. State and local government law gives considerable attention to the determination of which level of government ought to exercise a particular power or provide a particular service and to the definition of the relationships among the various levels of government. The localism debate has helped to focus the values and concerns that shape the allocation of powers and responsibilities among and between states and local governments. Section C then provides a brief introduction to state constitutional law. State constitutional provisions play a central role in state and local government law. Indeed, state constitutions are often pivotal in disputes involving state-local relations (Chapter IV); the state and local provision of elementary and secondary education (Chapter V); state and local finance (Chapter VI); and the privatization of state and local public services (Chapter VII). Yet, in contrast to the federal constitution, state constitutions receive little attention in American law schools. Section C examines how state constitutions differ in theory, in form, and in substance from the federal constitution.

B. STATES AND LOCAL GOVERNMENTS

1. THE STATES

The states are easily grasped. There are exactly fifty of them and they are the basic component elements of the United States. Although not all American land or residents are found within the states—the District of Columbia, the Commonwealth of Puerto Rico, and territories such as American Samoa, Guam, the Northern Marianas Islands, and the Virgin Islands are also parts of the United States—the federal government is structurally constituted out of the United States. As the Supreme Court has observed, "[t]he Constitution, in all its provisions, looks to an indestructible Union, composed of indestructible States." Texas v. White, 74 U.S. 700, 725 (1868). No state may be deprived of its equal suffrage in the Senate, U.S. Const., Art. V, and no state may be created out of the territory of another state without its consent, U.S. Const., Art. IV, § 3. Under the Guarantee Clause, Art. IV, § 4 the United States is committed to protecting the states from invasion and domestic violence.

The states have inherent law-making autonomy. The states are in no sense arms of the federal government. They are not like federal administrative agencies or regional offices; the federal government does not appoint state officers. Moreover, the states can legislate without having to demonstrate any authorization from the federal Constitution or by the federal government. The states have residual power over all aspects of government not granted to the federal government or not constrained by the Constitution or by the federal government acting pursuant to the Constitution. To be sure, the federal Constitution does impose significant restrictions on the scope of state law-making authority, and Congress acting pursuant to the Constitution's grants of power to the federal government can impose further limitations on the states. Nonetheless, the states continue to possess and exercise broad police power authority over their territory and their citizens.

As already suggested, the vast majority of law in the United States, affecting such diverse fields as contracts, civil obligations and torts, criminal law, property, family relationships, health care, insurance, and business behavior, is state law. So, too, the states play a preeminent role in the provision of criminal and civil justice, the building and maintenance of our physical infrastructure, and the financing or direct provision of such basic services as primary and secondary education; public higher education; highways and transportation; public health and hospitals, and health insurance; income assistance to the poor; environmental protection and the regulation of natural resources; and the incarceration of offenders.

2. LOCAL GOVERNMENTS

Most law students come to this course reasonably familiar with the states. There are only fifty states, and many of us can name them all. The number of states is quite stable, as are state boundary lines. All but five states were admitted to the union before the start of the twentieth century, and the last two states, Alaska and Hawaii, were admitted in 1959, or well over a half-century ago. The states are comparable to each other in powers, constitutional status, internal organization, and authority over their citizens even if they differ significantly in territorial size and population. The place of the states in American federalism is reasonably well understood, even if, as Chief Justice John Marshall once observed, tension between the federal and state governments "is perpetually arising, and will probably continue to arise, as long as our system exists." M'Culloch v. Maryland, 17 U.S. 316, 405 (1817).

Local governments are quite a different story. There are more than 90,000 of them and they differ dramatically in powers, status, organization, function, authority, and mode of creation across the country and, indeed, within a particular state. There is not even a consistent terminology for local governments; different states include such diverse local units as parishes, boroughs, and townships, as well as the more common forms of local government like county or city. Unlike the states, local governments may—and frequently do—overlap each other's territory. Unlike the states, local governments are frequently created, modified territorially, or abolished. Unlike the states, local governments lack inherent law-making authority. So, too, while the federal Constitution makes frequent reference to the states, the federal Constitution is entirely silent on the subject of local governments. As a result, although this book gives little direct attention to the constitutional status or powers of the states or to the formation of state governments, Chapters II, III, and IV address the federal constitutional status of local governments; local government formation and boundary change; and state-local relationships.

Local governments are crucial to the state-local system. Nearly three-quarters of the aggregate total of state and local employees are actually employed by local governments. So, too, the overwhelming majority of state and local elected officials serve at the local level. The states may be formally responsible for the provision of most domestic public services, but local governments play the key role in actually delivering such basic services as education, policing, fire prevention, street and road maintenance, mass transit, and sewage and solid waste removal. Local governments are also the dominant actors in our intergovernmental system in regulating land use and in community development. A considerable portion of state spending is used not for the provision of state programs but consists, instead, of grants to local governments to help them finance local services and activities.

This section is intended to provide you with a basic understanding of the different types of local governments and of the different roles local governments play within the state-local system.

Local governments can be analyzed along two different dimensions: (a) top-down v. bottom-up, and (b) general purpose v. special purpose.

a.   Top-Down v. Bottom-Up

Most local governments are agents with two principals—their state government and their local constituents. As we will see in Chapters II and IV, as a matter of legal theory, local governments are creatures of their states, established to discharge state functions locally. On the other hand, local governments are more than simply administrative arms of the state government. Local government law is not administrative law. Typically, local governments are structured in such a way as to give local constituents a critical role in directing their activities and shaping their performance. This may involve local popular election of local government officials; appointment of some local officials by other, locally elected officials; or a requirement that the state appoint only local residents to the governance of the local unit. Local autonomy may also result from the powers and discretion accorded to the local government. Local governments, thus, also have a bottom-up or local control aspect, as well as a top-down or state control aspect.

Although most local governments are subject to control by both their states and local constituents, the mix of state and local control may vary for different categories of local governments. The differences can be seen when three traditional forms of local government—the county, the city, and the township—are considered.

Historically, the classic top-down local government was the **county**. Descended from the old English shire, the county traditionally provided basic state services at the local level. Thus, the county was responsible for public prosecutions, recording deeds, keeping birth, death, and other public records, assessing property for tax purposes, registering voters, maintaining public roads, and providing poor relief and health care for the indigent. Most states are entirely divided up into counties. (Alaska uses the term "borough" for its counties, and Louisiana uses the term "parish" for its counties.) The principal exceptions are Virginia, where most of the cities are outside the jurisdiction of a county, and Baltimore, Maryland and St. Louis, Missouri, which are outside the jurisdiction of a county. In Connecticut and Rhode Island the county exists as a territorial unit but there are no county governments. In approximately forty cities—including Boston, Denver, Honolulu, New York, Philadelphia, and San Francisco—city and county governments are combined.

In most states, the county structure is relatively stable, with counties only rarely created or destroyed, and county borders rarely changed. Indeed, in many states, the current county structure dates back to the state's entry into the Union. In 2014, there were 3,028 counties, or virtually the same as the 3,052 in the middle of the twentieth century.

Traditionally, the county was a regulatory and service-providing body, not a law- or policy-making one. Indeed, often there was neither a county executive nor a county legislature; instead, the county government may have consisted of a group of independent officials, such as the Assessor, the Coroner or Medical Examiner, the Register of Deeds, the Board of Elections, the Sheriff, and the District Attorney. Although locally-elected and thus to a considerable extent locally accountable, their function was to discharge state services locally. Counties were particularly important in providing basic services in rural and small town areas.

Beginning in the mid-twentieth century, however, counties, particularly those in urban areas, began to take on broader responsibilities and to assume a policy-making role. Frequently encompassing central cities, smaller outlying cities, and suburbs, counties are often well-situated to provide area-wide services in metropolitan regions. Many states have provided for stronger county governments, including elected executives and legislatures, and they have increased county functions to include such area-wide activities as housing, mass transit, airports, parks and recreation, water supply and sewage, planning, zoning and regional governance.

Counties differ dramatically in population. The smallest county, Loving County, Texas, had just 71 inhabitants in 2010, while Los Angeles County, California, surpassed 10.1 million in 2014. Although the average county had a population of 100,000 in 2012, there were 703 counties that each had fewer than 10,000 people. On the other hand, the 146 largest counties accounted for a majority of the U.S. population.

In 2012, counties spent $383 billion providing a range of public services, including operating and maintaining infrastructure—highways, roads, bridges, transit, airports, water systems, sewage and solid waste management—and providing education and libraries, public health services and hospitals, parks, police and fire protection, corrections, and courts. U.S. Census, 2012 Census of Governments. There were more than 19,000 county elected officials and 3.3 million county employees. *See* National Association of Counties, Why Counties Matter, July 2013.

This process of county development has unfolded quite unevenly, both across the country and within particular states. *See* Jonathan Walters, "Cry, the Beleaguered County," Governing 31 (August 1996). Nevertheless, it seems fair to say that many counties, particularly those in urban areas, are increasingly bottom-up (that is, locally accountable, policy-making bodies) as well as top-down units carrying out state functions locally. For a recent analysis of the role of counties in providing services to unincorporated areas, *see* Michelle Wilde Anderson, Mapped Out of Local Democracy, 62 Stan. L. Rev. 931, 979–1012 (2010), and for a critique of the role of the county in land use regulation, *see* Michelle Wilde Anderson, Sprawl's Shepherd: The Rural County, 100 Cal. L. Rev. 365 (2012).

The classic bottom-up local unit is the **city** or **municipal corporation**, which, depending on the terminology used in a particular state, may also include the borough (but not the Alaskan "borough," which is really a county), the town (but not the New England town), and the village. The city is closely associated with the idea of urbanness, that is, with greater population and especially greater population density. As a result, cities have a greater need for regulation and services—police, fire, sanitation, traffic control, public health, water, sewage disposal, land use, social services—than do lightly populated rural areas. The traditional county government was considered adequate to the needs of rural areas, but the more densely populated city requires the additional services and regulation of a municipal government.

The city also relies on the concept of **incorporation**. Like a private business corporation or a not-for-profit corporation, a municipality is incorporated when local people seek a new local entity to provide the services and undertake the functions they believe are necessary to deal with the consequences of population growth and density. Typically, the municipal government includes an elected legislative or policy-making body and an elected executive or appointed manager.

The number of municipal corporations is far more fluid than the number of counties. There were 19,508 municipal corporations in 2012—a 2701 (or 16%) increase over the 16,807 municipal corporations in 1952. This increase reflects both population growth and dramatic population movements. Municipal corporations are also able to change their boundaries and increase their population through the annexation of unincorporated land. (Municipal incorporation and boundary change are examined in Chapter III).

Although municipal corporations account for only 3.5% of the United States' total land area, in 2012 nearly 200 million people, or 62.7% of the population, lived in cities. U.S. Census Bureau, Population Trends in Incorporated Places, 2000–2013. Like counties, cities vary widely in their population. The vast majority of cities—16,494 (or about 85% of the total)—have fewer than 10,000 inhabitants, but these smaller cities account for only 14% of the city population and 9.1% of the total U.S. population. By contrast, the 77 cities with populations of 250,000 or more had a total population of 67 million, and the 203 cities with populations of 100,000 or more were home to 99 million people, or half the urban population. *Id.* Cities are far more densely populated than unincorporated areas. The average population density for cities in 2013 was 1593.5 people per square mile, or 46 times greater than the population density of 34.6 per square mile in unincorporated areas. Moreover, population density tends to increase with city size. The population density of cities of 1 million people or more was, on average, 7,192.3 per square mile. Although the aggregate municipal population was less than the aggregate county population, in 2012 municipal governments spent $544 billion, or $160 billion more than counties did, reflecting the greater service provision responsibilities of municipal governments.

Unlike the county, the municipal corporation involves either local creation or state creation in response to local demands. Traditionally the municipality had greater powers to provide services and greater discretion, although the rise of the metropolitan county and the expansion of county powers has blurred this distinction in some states. Like all local governments, the municipal corporation also has top-down elements, since it relies on state law for its incorporation, territory, and powers. Incorporation also means that most city residents—exceptions include people who live in the cities in Virginia that are legally outside counties and people living in cities that have merged their governments with those of their counties—are subject to the jurisdiction of two local governments, their city and their county.

Combining the top-down and bottom-up elements of cities and counties are what the United States Census Bureau calls "**town or township governments**." These entities are located in just twenty states, concentrated in New England, the Middle Atlantic states, and the Midwest. (The New England states, New York, and Wisconsin use the term "town" while the other states use the term "township.") In these states, all or most of the counties or the parts of counties outside of incorporated municipalities are typically subdivided into towns or townships, much as the state is divided into counties. Thus, they are top-down in that they are created by the state generally and not in response to local demand or local population needs. In New England and in the Middle Atlantic states, however, they are frequently found in densely populated urban areas and perform many municipal-type regulatory and service functions. In New England, they may be governed by town meetings, which makes them intensely bottom-up in orientation. By contrast, in the Midwest, many township governments perform only a very limited range of services for predominantly rural areas. There they resemble old-fashioned top-down counties.

There were 16,519 town or township governments in 2012, and, like the number of counties, the number of towns and townships is relatively stable, dropping only slightly from the total of 17,202 in 1952. Town and township governments play only a modest role in local governance in the United States as a whole. Indeed, township expenditures amounted to just $50 billion in 2012, mostly on elementary and secondary education, highways, police and fire protection, water, sewerage, solid waste management, and parks.

b.   General Purpose v. Special Purpose

Local governments may also be categorized according to their range of activities and functions. Although no local government has the full range of powers of a state, counties, cities and townships are all considered to be **general purpose** governments in that they have relatively broad responsibilities over a significant number of areas—public safety, public health, land use, streets, highways and transportation. Indeed, as we will see in Chapter IV, many municipalities and even some counties have been given general authority, albeit usually subordinate to the state, to exercise the police power and pass legislation to promote the local health, safety, and general welfare within their territorial jurisdiction.

By contrast, a significant number of local governments are given very narrowly defined authority and may undertake only one or a very limited number of functions. These are known as **special purpose** local governments, and they are actually the most common form of local government in the United States today. The most widespread special purpose government is the independent **school district**. A school district is independent when it is not operated as part of another government, such as a city. In 2012, there were 12,880 independent school districts in the United States. The Census Bureau lumps all other forms of special purpose government into the category of "**special district governments**." There were 38,266 special districts in 2012, or more than the total number of municipalities and towns and townships combined— and far more than the total number of municipal governments and counties. The special district has also been the most rapidly growing form of local government in the United States over the last half-century. The number of special districts in 2012 was more than triple the 12,340 counted in 1952.

The vast majority of special districts perform a single function, such as fire protection (5,865 districts), water supply (3,522), housing and community development (3,399), and drainage and flood control (3,438).There are also special districts devoted to soil and water conservation, sewerage, cemeteries, libraries, health and hospitals, parks and recreation, highways, air transportation, solid waste management, parking facilities, public utility services, industrial development, and financial assistance to other local governments. Approximately 3,000 special districts are multi-function districts that engage in two or more activities, particularly involving sewerage, water supply, and natural resources. Special districts other than school districts spent approximately $206 billion in 2012. That represented a more than 70% increase from just ten years earlier. Independent school districts spent $500 billion but because school districts are heavily funded by state aid and appropriations from general purpose local governments, school district expenditures may not be an appropriate measure of the importance of school districts in the state and local government system.

Special districts may be created for a variety of reasons. These include giving them independence from general purpose cities or counties; tailoring the territorial scope of the government to the proper dimensions of its function or activity; avoiding certain state constitutional restrictions that apply to cities or counties; and obtaining some of the infrastructure and service benefits of local government without having to incur the full costs of general purpose local government.

The independent local school district nicely exemplifies the use of the district to separate a function or service from the rest of local government, and thereby take its finances and decision-making "out of politics"—or at least out of the partisan politics of city or county government. Other special districts were created as a condition for the receipt of certain forms of federal or state aid in order to assure that the aid was channeled directly to the targeted program and did not provide general support for city or county governments. As Professor Kathryn A. Foster, a leading scholar of special districts, has observed:

> Under President Franklin D. Roosevelt, a foe of big city administrators and staunch advocate of the neutral public authority, the federal government instituted numerous programs that stipulated creation of independent agencies as a condition of receiving federal funding. Hundreds of special purpose governments, notably soil conservation districts and public housing authorities, formed in response to federal funding enticements.

Kathryn A. Foster, The Political Economy of Special-Purpose Government 18 (Georgetown Univ. Press 1997). *See also id.* (noting the role of federal or state fiscal incentives in the creation of special purpose health, planning, air quality control, resource conservation, economic development, airport, transit, and sewer districts).

Many natural resource, park, utility, and transportation special districts reflect the second purpose—matching the scope of the government to the scope of the problem. Flood control, irrigation, water supply, electricity, airports, and commuter rail systems may be most efficiently provided over a broad territorial area. To require that the entire area constitute a single general purpose local government would produce a local government of considerable territory and population and, thus, eliminate many of the benefits of small size associated with local government. Superimposing a special purpose district on existing cities, counties, and townships facilitates area-wide services while preserving the independence of smaller general purpose local governments. (The role of special purpose districts in regional governance is considered more fully in Chapter V.) The use of special districts to fine-tune the territorial scope of local government services is not limited to large regions. Some districts, like downtown business improvement districts, may be created in order to provide special or additional services, financed by additional taxes, within a general purpose local government.

A third reason for the widespread growth of special districts is the evasion of state constitutional restrictions on local government taxation and debt. As we will see in Chapter VI, state constitutions typically restrict taxing and borrowing by cities and counties. These constitutions, however, may fail to address special district revenue-raising. In part because special districts are often financed by fees or charges for specific services rather than general taxes, state courts often exempted special districts from these restrictions. "To local officials, the special district offered a legal, easy-to-implement means for circumventing municipal debt and tax constraints." *See* Foster, *supra*, at 17. Many of these districts are coterminous with existing cities or counties and may be controlled by appointees of those general purpose governments. *See id.* at 20. For a critical evaluation of the role of special districts in avoiding state fiscal limits, *see* Steven L. Schwarcz, The Use and Abuse of Special-Purpose Entities in Public Finance, 97 Minn. L. Rev. 369 (2012).

Finally, special districts may be created to provide physical improvements, basic services, or some of the regulatory benefits of municipal government, such as the subdivision of land and the provision of development-related infrastructure, without having to bear the full costs and restrictions of a full-fledged general purpose government. These include community services districts in California, community development districts and stewardship districts in Florida, and municipal utility districts in Texas. The role of special purpose districts in facilitating development and undertaking some of the traditional functions of municipal government appears to have grown in recent decades. *See id.* at 20; Nancy Burns, The Formation of American Local Governments: Private Values in Public Institutions 98–100 (Oxford Univ. Press 1994). For a comprehensive treatment of this new role for special districts, *see* Nadav Shoked, Quasi-Cities, 93 B.U. L. Rev. 1921 (2013). *See also* Sara C. Galvan, Wrestling with MUDs to Pin Down the Truth About Special Districts, 75 Fordham L. Rev. 3041 (2007). As you will see later in this book, whether a government is a special district or general purpose government can affect such basic issues as the rules and procedures for local government formation, voting rights, taxing authority, and regulatory power.

Like general purpose governments, special districts combine top-down and bottom-up elements. They may be created by the state, by local constituents pursuant to state enabling legislation, or by other local governments. Those with locally elected or appointed governing bodies have a stronger bottom-up aspect. Unlike general purpose local governments, some special purpose districts, particularly those that are regional in scope, may be governed by state-appointed boards of directors, which reinforces their top-down element. Moreover, unlike general purpose governments, many bottom-up special districts are designed to be accountable to and controlled not by the local population generally but by discrete local groups, such as local landowners or users of the service provided by the special district. In these districts, representation in district governance may be tied to land values or assessment payments. The constitutional interests raised by state laws that make special districts politically accountable to specialized local constituencies are considered more fully in Chapter II.

C. THE VERTICAL DISTRIBUTION OF POWER QUESTION

A repeatedly recurring problem in our system of multiple levels of government is the question of which level of government is to be responsible for which functions and activities. Indeed, a central issue for American federalism is the determination of the criteria for deciding which level of government is to be given what powers and responsibilities. The issue goes well beyond the allocation of particular powers and functions. It has implications for such issues as the relationships between different levels of government, the relationships among governments on the same level, the rules for creating new governments, the rules for sharing power, and the rules for resolving conflicts among governments.

The distribution of power among the different levels of government is a central issue for this course with a deeply normative dimension. The statesmen, judges, and scholars—including lawyers, economists, and political scientists—who have entered the debate over more than two centuries have argued over what values ought to inform the issue as well as the quasi-empirical questions of how well different levels of government advance different values, and how much power different levels of government actually wield.

What follows are excerpts from five writers who have addressed the different benefits and costs of placing power at different levels of government. The first two texts—Madison's Federalist #10, and Tocqueville's Democracy in America—are classics of American political science. The third, Charles Tiebout's mid-twentieth century article, *A Pure Theory of Local Expenditures*, is the foundation of economic analysis of local power. The final two articles reflect the efforts of contemporary legal scholars to come to grips with a variety of arguments concerning local autonomy, or what has been called "localism."

JAMES MADISON
THE FEDERALIST, NUMBER 10
(1787)

Among the numerous advantages promised by a well constructed Union, none deserves to be more accurately developed than its tendency to break and control the violence of faction. The friend of popular governments never finds himself so much alarmed for their character and fate, as when he contemplates their propensity to this dangerous vice. He will not fail, therefore, to set a due value on any plan which, without violating the principles to which he is attached, provides a proper cure for it. . . .

By a faction, I understand a number of citizens, whether amounting to a majority or a minority of the whole, who are united and actuated by some common impulse of passion, or of interest, adverse to the rights of other citizens, or to the permanent and aggregate interests of the community.

There are two methods of curing the mischiefs of faction: the one, by removing its causes; the other, by controlling its effects.

There are again two methods of removing the causes of faction: the one, by destroying the liberty which is essential to its existence; the other, by giving to every citizen the same opinions, the same passions, and the same interests.

It could never be more truly said than of the first remedy, that it was worse than the disease. Liberty is to faction what air is to fire, an aliment without which it instantly expires. But it could not be less folly to abolish liberty, which is essential to political life, because it nourishes faction, than it would be to wish the annihilation of air, which is essential to animal life, because it imparts to fire its destructive agency.

The second expedient is as impracticable as the first would be unwise. As long as the reason of man continues fallible, and he is at liberty to exercise it, different opinions will be formed. As long as the connection subsists between his reason and his self-love, his opinions and his passions will have a reciprocal influence on each other; and the former will be objects to which the latter will attach themselves. The diversity in the faculties of men, from which the rights of property originate, is not less an insuperable obstacle to a uniformity of interests. The protection of these faculties is the first object of government. From the protection of different and unequal faculties of acquiring property, the possession of different degrees and kinds of property immediately results; and from the influence of these on the sentiments and views of the respective proprietors, ensues a division of the society into different interests and parties.

The latent causes of faction are thus sown in the nature of man; and we see them everywhere brought into different degrees of activity, according to the different circumstances of civil society. A zeal for different opinions concerning religion, concerning government, and many other points, as well of speculation as of practice; an attachment to different leaders ambitiously contending for pre-eminence and power; or to persons of other descriptions whose fortunes have been interesting to the human passions, have, in turn, divided mankind into parties, inflamed them with mutual animosity, and rendered them much more disposed to vex and oppress each other than to co-operate for their common good. So strong is this propensity of mankind to fall into mutual animosities, that where no substantial occasion presents itself, the most frivolous and fanciful distinctions have been sufficient to kindle their unfriendly passions and excite their most violent conflicts. But the most common and durable source of factions has been the various and unequal distribution of property. Those who hold and those who are without property have ever formed distinct interests in society. Those who are creditors, and those who are debtors, fall under a like discrimination. A landed interest, a manufacturing interest, a mercantile interest, a moneyed interest, with many lesser interests, grow up of necessity in civilized nations, and divide them into different classes, actuated by different sentiments and views. The regulation of these various and interfering interests forms the principal task of modern legislation, and involves the spirit of party and faction in the necessary and ordinary operations of the government.

. . . . It is in vain to say that enlightened statesmen will be able to adjust these clashing interests, and render them all subservient to the public good. Enlightened statesmen will not always be at the helm. Nor, in many cases, can such an adjustment be made at all without taking into view indirect and remote considerations, which will rarely prevail over the immediate interest which one party may find in disregarding the rights of another or the good of the whole.

The inference to which we are brought is, that the CAUSES of faction cannot be removed, and that relief is only to be sought in the means of controlling its EFFECTS.

If a faction consists of less than a majority, relief is supplied by the republican principle, which enables the majority to defeat its sinister views by regular vote. It may clog the administration, it may convulse the society; but it will be unable to execute and mask its violence under the forms of the Constitution. When a majority is included in a faction, the form of popular government, on the other hand, enables it to sacrifice to its ruling passion or interest both the public good and the rights of other citizens. To secure the public good and private rights against the danger of such a faction, and at the same time to preserve the spirit and the form of popular government, is then the great object to which our inquiries are directed. . . .

By what means is this object attainable? Evidently by one of two only. Either the existence of the same passion or interest in a majority at the same time must be prevented, or the majority, having such coexistent passion or interest, must be rendered, by their number and local situation, unable to concert and carry into effect schemes of oppression. If the impulse and the opportunity be suffered to coincide, we well know that neither moral nor religious motives can be relied on as an adequate control. . . . From this view of the subject it may be concluded that a pure democracy, by which I mean a society consisting of a small number of citizens, who assemble and administer the government in person, can admit of no cure for the mischiefs of faction. A common passion or interest will, in almost every case, be felt by a majority of the whole; a communication and concert result from the form of government itself; and there is nothing to check the inducements to sacrifice the weaker party or an obnoxious individual. Hence it is that such democracies have ever been spectacles of turbulence and contention; have ever been found incompatible with personal security or the rights of property; and have in general been as short in their lives as they have been violent in their deaths. Theoretic politicians, who have patronized this species of government, have erroneously supposed that by reducing mankind to a perfect equality in their political rights, they would, at the same time, be perfectly equalized and assimilated in their possessions, their opinions, and their passions.

A republic, by which I mean a government in which the scheme of representation takes place, opens a different prospect, and promises the cure for which we are seeking. Let us examine the points in which it varies from pure democracy, and we shall comprehend both the nature of the cure and the efficacy which it must derive from the Union.

The two great points of difference between a democracy and a republic are: first, the delegation of the government, in the latter, to a small number of citizens elected by the rest; secondly, the greater number of citizens, and greater sphere of country, over which the latter may be extended.

The effect of the first difference is, on the one hand, to refine and enlarge the public views, by passing them through the medium of a chosen body of citizens, whose wisdom may best discern the true interest of their country, and whose patriotism and love of justice will be least likely to sacrifice it to temporary or partial considerations. Under such a regulation, it may well happen that the public voice, pronounced by the representatives of the people, will be more consonant to the public good than if pronounced by the people themselves, convened for the purpose. On the other hand, the effect may be inverted. Men of factious tempers, of local prejudices, or of sinister designs, may, by intrigue, by corruption, or by other means, first obtain the suffrages, and then betray the interests, of the people. The question resulting is, whether small or extensive republics are more favorable to the election of proper guardians of the public weal; and it is clearly decided in favor of the latter by two obvious considerations:

In the first place, it is to be remarked that, however small the republic may be, the representatives must be raised to a certain number, in order to guard against the cabals of a few; and that, however large it may be, they must be limited to a certain number, in order to guard against the confusion of a multitude. Hence, the number of representatives in the two cases not being in proportion to that of the two constituents, and being proportionally greater in the small republic, it follows that, if the proportion of fit characters be not less in the large than in the small republic, the former will present a greater option, and consequently a greater probability of a fit choice.

In the next place, as each representative will be chosen by a greater number of citizens in the large than in the small republic, it will be more difficult for unworthy candidates to practice with success the vicious arts by which elections are too often carried; and the suffrages of the people being more free, will be more likely to centre in men who possess the most attractive merit and the most diffusive and established characters.

It must be confessed that in this, as in most other cases, there is a mean, on both sides of which inconveniences will be found to lie. By enlarging too much the number of electors, you render the representatives too little acquainted with all their local circumstances and lesser interests; as by reducing it too much, you render him unduly attached to these, and too little fit to comprehend and pursue great and national objects. The federal Constitution forms a happy combination in this respect; the great and aggregate interests being referred to the national, the local and particular to the State legislatures.

The other point of difference is, the greater number of citizens and extent of territory which may be brought within the compass of republican than of democratic government; and it is this circumstance principally which renders factious combinations less to be dreaded in the former than in the latter. The smaller the society, the fewer probably will be the distinct parties and interests composing it; the fewer the distinct parties and interests, the more frequently will a majority be found of the same party; and the smaller the number of individuals composing a majority, and the smaller the compass within which they are placed, the more easily will they concert and execute their plans of oppression. Extend the sphere, and you take in a greater variety of parties and interests; you make it less probable that a majority of the whole will have a common motive to invade the rights of other citizens; or if such a common motive exists, it will be more difficult for all who feel it to discover their own strength, and to act in unison with each other. Besides other impediments, it may be remarked that, where there is a consciousness of unjust or dishonorable purposes, communication is always checked by distrust in proportion to the number whose concurrence is necessary.

Hence, it clearly appears, that the same advantage which a republic has over a democracy, in controlling the effects of faction, is enjoyed by a large over a small republic, is enjoyed by the Union over the States composing it. Does the advantage consist in the substitution of representatives whose enlightened views and virtuous sentiments render them superior to local prejudices and schemes of injustice? It will not be denied that the representation of the Union will be most likely to possess these requisite endowments. Does it consist in the greater security afforded by a greater variety of parties, against the event of any one party being able to outnumber and oppress the rest? In an equal degree does the increased variety of parties comprised within the Union, increase this security. Does it, in fine, consist in the greater obstacles opposed to the concert and accomplishment of the secret wishes of an unjust and interested majority? Here, again, the extent of the Union gives it the most palpable advantage.

The influence of factious leaders may kindle a flame within their particular States, but will be unable to spread a general conflagration through the other States. A religious sect may degenerate into a political faction in a part of the Confederacy; but the variety of sects dispersed over the entire face of it must secure the national councils against any danger from that source. A rage for paper money, for an abolition of debts, for an equal division of property, or for any other improper or wicked project, will be less apt to pervade the whole body of the Union than a particular member of it; in the same proportion as such a malady is more likely to taint a particular county or district, than an entire State.

In the extent and proper structure of the Union, therefore, we behold a republican remedy for the diseases most incident to republican government. And according to the degree of pleasure and pride we feel in being republicans, ought to be our zeal in cherishing the spirit and supporting the character of Federalists.

ALEXIS DE TOCQUEVILLE
DEMOCRACY IN AMERICA

(12th ed. 1848, G. Lawrence trans. 1966, J.P. Mayer ed. 1969)

. . . [T]he strength of free peoples resides in the local community. Local institutions are to liberty what primary schools are to science; they put it within the people's reach; they teach people to appreciate its peaceful enjoyment and accustom them to make use of it. Without local institutions a nation may give itself a free government, but it has not got the spirit of liberty. . . .

The New England township combines two advantages which, whenever they are found, keenly excite men's interest; they are independence and power. . . .

It is important to appreciate that, in general, men's affections are drawn only in directions where power exists. . . . The New Englander is attached to his township not so much because he was born there as because he sees the township as a free, strong, corporation of which he is part and which is worth the trouble to direct. . . . [I]f you take power and independence from a municipality, you may have docile subjects but you will not have citizens.

. . . . It is in the township, the center of the ordinary business of life, that the desire for esteem, the pursuit of substantial interests, and the taste for power and self-advertisement are concentrated; these passions, so often troublesome elements in society, take on a different character when exercised so close to home and, in a sense, within the family circle.

. . . . The New Englander is attached to his township because it is strong and independent; he has an interest in it because he shares in its management; he loves it because he has no reason to complain of his lot; he invests his ambition and his future in it; in the restricted sphere within his scope, he learns to rule society; he gets to know the formalities without which freedom can advance only through revolutions, and becoming imbued with their spirit, develops a taste for order, understands the harmony of powers, and in the end accumulates clear, practical ideas about the nature of his duties and the extent of his rights.

* * *

County and township are not constituted everywhere in the same way, but one can say that the organization of township and county in the United States everywhere depends on the same idea, viz., that each man is the best judge of his own interest and the best able to satisfy his private needs. So township and county are responsible for their special interests. The state rules but does not administer. One finds exceptions to that principle, but no contradictory principle.

The first consequence of this doctrine was for the inhabitants themselves to choose all the administrators of town and county or at least for them to be chosen exclusively from among them. . . . Administrative power is spread among a multitude of people.

* * *

A central power, however enlightened and wise one imagines it to be, can never alone see to all the details of the life of a great nation. It cannot do so because such a task exceeds human strength. When it attempts unaided to create and operate so much complicated machinery, it must be satisfied with very imperfect results or exhaust itself in futile efforts.

. . . . Centralization easily imposes an aspect of regularity on day-to-day business; it can regulate the details of social control skillfully; check slight disorders and petty offenses; maintain the status quo of society, which cannot properly be called either decadence or progress; and keep society in that state of administrative somnolence which administrators are in the habit of calling good order and public tranquility. In a word, it excels at preventing, not doing. . . .

Europeans, accustomed to the close and constant presence of officials interfering in almost everything, find it difficult to get used to the different machinery of municipal administration. Generally speaking, we may say that those little details of social regulation which make life smooth and comfortable are neglected in America but the guarantees essential to man as a member of society exists there as everywhere. In America the force behind the state is much less well regulated, less enlightened, and less wise but it is a hundred times more powerful than in Europe. . . .

Granting, for the sake of argument, that the villages and counties of the United States would be more efficiently administered by a central authority from outside . . . I will, if you insist, admit that there would be more security in America and that social resources would be more wisely and judiciously employed, if the administration of the whole country were concentrated in one pair of hands. But the *political* advantages derived by the Americans from a system of decentralization would make me prefer that to the opposite system. . . .

I think that provincial institutions are useful for all peoples, but none have a more real need for them than those whose society is democratic.

In an aristocracy one can always be sure that a certain degree of order will be maintained in freedom.

The ruling class has much to lose, and order is an important interest for the rulers.

It is also fair to say that in an aristocracy the people are always defended from the excesses of despotism, for there are always organized forces ready to resist a despot.

A democracy without provincial institutions has no guarantee against such ills.

How can liberty be preserved in great matters among a multitude that has never learned to use it in small ones?

How can tyranny be resisted in a country where each individual is weak and where no common interest unites individuals?

Those who fear license and those who are afraid of absolute power should both, therefore, desire the gradual growth of provincial liberties.

* * *

Despotism, by its very nature suspicious, sees the isolation of men as the best guarantee of its own permanence. So it usually does all it can to isolate them. . . .

Equality puts men side by side without a common link to hold them firm. Despotism raises barriers to keep them apart. It disposes them not to think of their fellows and turns indifference into a sort of public virtue.

Despotism, dangerous at all times, is therefore particularly to be feared in ages of democracy.

. . . The Americans have used liberty to combat the individualism born of equality, and they have won.

The lawgivers of America did not suppose that a general representation of the whole nation would suffice to ward off [individualism,] a disorder at once so natural to the body social of a democracy and so fatal. They thought it also right to give each part of the land its own political life so that there should be an infinite number of occasions for the citizens to act together and so that every day they should feel that they depended on one another.

That was wise conduct.

The general business of a country keeps only the leading citizens occupied. It is only occasionally that they come together in the same places, and since they often lose sight of one another, no lasting bonds form between them. But when the people who live there have to look after the affairs of a district, the same people are always meeting, and they are forced, in a manner, to know and adapt themselves to one another.

It is difficult to force a man out of himself and get him to take an interest in the affairs of the whole state, for he has little understanding of the way in which the fate of the state can influence his own lot. But if it is a question of taking a road past his property, he sees at once that this small public matter has a bearing on his greatest private interests, and there is no need to point out to him the close connection between his private profit and the general interest.

Thus, far more may be done by entrusting citizens with the management of minor affairs than by handing over control of great matters, toward interesting them in the public welfare and convincing them that they stand constantly in need of one another in order to provide for it.

Some brilliant achievement may win a people's favor at one stroke. But to gain the affection and respect of your immediate neighbors, a long succession of little services rendered and of obscure good deeds, a constant habit of kindness and an established reputation for disinterestedness, are required.

Local liberties, then, which induce a great number of citizens to value the affection of their kindred and neighbors, bring men constantly into contact, despite the instincts which separate them, and force them to help one another. . . .

The free institutions of the United States and the political rights enjoyed there provide a thousand continual reminders to every citizen that he lives in society. At every moment they bring his mind back to this idea, and that it is the duty as well as the interest of men to be useful to their fellows. . . . At first it is of necessity that men attend to the public interest, afterward by choice. What had been calculation becomes instinct. By dint of working for the good of his fellow citizens, he in the end acquires a habit and taste for serving them.

NOTES AND QUESTIONS

1.   *The Vertical Distribution of Power and the Tyranny of the Majority*. Both Madison and Tocqueville raise several concerns that are implicated by the vertical distribution of power: the prevention of tyranny, the quality of government decision-making, and the benefits of political participation. Madison presents two reasons for concentrating power at a higher level of government, that is, one encompassing greater population and territory than a smaller or lower one. First, he suggests that the upper level of government is likely to enjoy better leadership. There are only a certain number of "fit characters" in any society, but a larger polity has fewer leadership positions to fill, relative to its population, than a decentralized one. Consequently, an "extended" republic "will present a greater option, and consequently a greater possibility of a fit choice." Second, he argues it is more difficult for a tyrannical majority—indeed, *any* majority—to coalesce and dominate in a larger government than in a smaller one. Madison's central insight is that in a society based on popular sovereignty, majority rule can result in tyranny over the minority. In his view, the best way to prevent the tyranny of the majority without interfering with liberty is to create institutional barriers that make it difficult for majorities to form and act. This argument has become central to American constitutionalism and canonical in contemporary debates over centralization and decentralization. It continues to play a central role in arguments about the distribution of power. *See, e.g.,* Clayton P. Gillette, In Partial Praise of Dillon's Rule, Or, Can Public Choice Theory Justify Local Government Law?, 67 Chi-Kent L. Rev. 959 (1991) (suggesting that limits on local autonomy are appropriate because local governments are prone to domination by special interests). Popular columnists critical of local policing, occupational licensing, and land use regulatory policies have also drawn on the Madisonian assessment of the potential for abuse of power at the local level. *See, e.g.,* Franklin Foer, The Autocrat Next Door, The New Republic, Sept. 15, 2014; Jonathan Chait, Why the Worst Governments in America Are Local Governments, New York Magazine, Sept. 7, 2014.

2.   *Decentralization and the Quality of Local Government Officials*. Madison's first argument, that upper level governments are more likely to attract "representatives whose enlightened views and virtuous sentiments

render them superior to local prejudices," has a more elitist character, and is less often made today. It was, however, a central concern for the nineteenth century English political philosopher, John Stuart Mill. Indeed, Mill sought limits on the decentralization of power because of his concern about the quality of local administration:

> The greatest imperfection of popular local institutions, and the chief cause of the failure which so often attends them, is the low calibre of the men by whom they are almost always carried on. That these should be of a very miscellaneous character is, indeed, part of the usefulness of the institution; it is that circumstance chiefly which renders it a school of political capacity and general intelligence. But a school supposes teachers as well as scholars: the utility of the instruction greatly depends on its bringing inferior minds into contact with superior. . . . The school, moreover, is worthless, and a school of evil instead of good, if, through the want of due surveillance, and of the presence within itself of a higher order of characters, the action of the body is allowed, as it so often is, to degenerate into an equally unscrupulous and stupid pursuit of the self-interest of its members.

John Stuart Mill, Considerations on Representative Government 294–95 (1861 Prometheus Books ed. 1991). Do you think this is an appropriate concern in considering the distribution of powers between states and local governments? Given the enormous differences in the populations of our local governments—ranging from cities and counties with millions of people to some with just a few hundred or less—should we be more concerned about government quality when decentralization involves granting power to very small local units? Do you think Madison and Mill underestimate the ability of local people to deal with local matters? Or do you agree with Tocqueville that a little inefficiency in administration is a small price to pay for the other benefits of decentralization?

3. *Local Government as School of Democracy.* Madison feared that in a democratic society a consolidated majority could tyrannize the minority. Tocqueville expressed the concern that the equality and individualism that accompany democracy can make it difficult for people to cooperate and, thus, make them easy targets for despotism. He determined that the strong local governments he found in Jacksonian America, particularly the New England township, provided a solution to that danger. Tocqueville found that by giving Americans an interest and an opportunity to participate in self-government—and, thus, a "habit and taste" for working together concerning public matters—local government strengthened Americans' commitment to their own freedom. In his view, local government was a sort of "primary school" of democracy. Interestingly, Mill used a similar metaphor, noting that participation in local government "may be called the public education of the citizens." On Representative Government, *supra*, at 288. Thomas Jefferson, similarly, emphasized democracy's dependence on the training in citizenship provided by local self-government: By "giving to every citizen, personally, a

part in the administration of the public affairs," "and in the offices nearest and most interesting to him," local government "will attach him by his strongest feelings to the independence of his country and its republican Constitution." Thomas Jefferson, Letter to Samuel Kercheval, July 12, 1816.

For Tocqueville, as for Jefferson, the critical value of local government is that it makes people "citizens," that is, active participants in self-governance who, due to that participation, become committed to maintaining and defending self-government. As we will see when we look at the more recent work of Professor Frug, Tocqueville's commitment to political participation as the critical benefit of local autonomy and a vital contribution to the preservation of democracy is central to contemporary thinking about the vertical distribution of power. Do you think Tocqueville's localism is responsive to Madison's concern about the tyranny of the local majority?

Other political theorists have stressed the benefits of political participation in educating people about the issues, processes, and institutions of self-government. It has been suggested that participation equips people with the "individual attitudes and psychological qualities" that make self-government possible while providing an opportunity for "practice in democratic skills and procedures." Carole Pateman, Participation and Democratic Theory 42 (Cambridge Univ. Press 1970). *See also* Jane Mansbridge, Beyond Adversary Democracy 4 (U. Chi. Press 1980).

4. *Local Government and Local Politics.* As several scholars have noted, the decentralization question cannot be fully addressed without some attention to the differences in the nature of politics and political institutions at different levels of governments. *See, e.g.,* David Schleicher, Local Government Law's "Law and ___" Problem, 40 Fordham Urb. L.J. 1951, 1965–69 (2013). Many local governments are dominated by political machines, *see, e.g.,* Jessica Trounstine, Political Monopolies in American Cities (U. Chi. Press 2008), or suffer from a lack of competitive politics, *see, e.g.,* David Schleicher, Why Is There No Partisan Competition in City Council Elections?: The Role of Election Law, 23 J. L. & Pol. 419 (2007). City legislatures are typically organized on a unicameral basis, whereas Congress and all but one state legislature are bicameral. Unlike elections for federal and most state offices, elections for many local offices are nonpartisan, that is, the ballot does not indicate any party affiliation for the candidates. In addition, in an effort to keep local issues separate from federal and state politics, many municipal elections are held during odd-numbered years or in months other than November. As a result, turnout in local elections is typically far lower than in elections for federal or state office. *See, e.g.,* Alan Greenblatt, The Elections No One Cares About, Governing, Aug. 11, 2015; Sarah F. Anzia, Partisan Power Play: The Origins of Local Election Timing as an American Political Institution, 26 Stud Am. Pol. Dev. 24 (2012). Many local governments do not have an elected chief executive but are instead run by a commission that combines executive and legislative functions or under the council-manager system in which an elected council selects a professional city manager to direct city operations. On the other hand, some large cities

have "strong mayor" governments in which the mayor wields far more power relative to the legislature than does the chief executive in the federal and most state governments. *See, e.g.,* Richard C, Schragger, Can Strong Mayors Empower Weak Cities? On the Power of Local Executives in a Federal System, 115 Yale L.J. 2542 (2006). Initiatives and referenda can also have a significant impact on local decision-making. *See, e.g.,* Clayton Gillette, Plebiscites, Participation and Collective Action in Local Government Law, 86 Mich. L. Rev. 930 (1988).

Scholars have debated the significance of these distinctive features of local governments. Professor Paul Diller has suggested that the streamlined legislative structure, strong mayors, and the lack of party competition, along with the smaller scale of local governments and the attendant lower costs of local campaigning and lobbying, have contributed to the ability of local governments to innovate. *See* Paul Diller, Why Do Cities Innovate in Public Health? Implications of Scale and Structures, 91 Wash. U. L. Rev. 1219 (2014). Professor David Schleicher argues that the lack of party competition in most big cities contributes to corruption. *See* David Schleicher, I Would But I Need the Eggs: Why Neither Exit Nor Voice Substantially Limits Big City Corruption, 42 Loy. U. Chi. L.J. 277, 284–89 (2011). Perhaps the key point is that the implications of the vertical distribution of power for liberty and democracy need to be considered in light of the different institutions that exist at different levels of government. So, too, the differences in size and scale of different levels of government could be factored into the design of the political institutions for those different governments.

CHARLES M. TIEBOUT
A PURE THEORY OF LOCAL EXPENDITURES
64 J. Pol. Econ. 416 (1956)

One of the most important developments in the area of "applied economic theory" has been the work of Musgrave and Samuelson in public finance theory. . . . The two writers agree . . . that no "market type" solution exists to determine the level of expenditures on public goods. . . . The core problem with which both Musgrave and Samuelson deal concerns the mechanism by which consumer-voters register their preferences for public goods. . . . As things now stand, there is no mechanism to force the consumer-voter to state his true preferences. . . .

Musgrave and Samuelson implicitly assume that expenditures are handled at the central government level. . . . However, the provision of such governmental services as police and fire protection, education, hospitals, and courts does not necessarily involve federal activity. Many of these goods are provided by local governments. . . . Hence an important question arises whether at this level of government any mechanism operates to insure that expenditures on these public goods approximate the proper level.

Consider for a moment the case of the city resident about to move to the suburbs. What variables will influence his choice of municipality? If he has children, a high level of expenditures on schools may be important. Another person may prefer a community with a community golf course. The availability and quality of such facilities and services as beaches, parks, police protection, roads, and parking facilities will enter into the decisionmaking process. Of course, non-economic variables will also be considered. . . .

The consumer-voter may be viewed as picking that community which best satisfies his preference pattern for public goods. This is a major difference between central and local provision of public goods. At the central level the preferences of the consumer-voter are given, and the government tries to adjust to the pattern of these preferences, whereas at the local level various governments have their revenue and expenditure patterns more or less set. Given these revenue and expenditure patterns, the consumer-voter moves to that community whose local government best satisfies his number of preferences. The greater the number of communities and the greater the variance among them, the closer the consumer will come to fully realizing his preference position.

The implications of the preceding argument may be shown by postulating an extreme model. Here the following assumptions are made:

   1.   Consumer-voters are fully mobile and will move to that community where their preference patterns, which are set, are best satisfied.

   2.   Consumer-voters are assumed to have full knowledge of differences among revenue and expenditure patterns and to react to these differences.

   3.   There are a large number of communities in which the consumer-voters may choose to live.

   4.   Restrictions due to employment opportunities are not considered. It may be assumed that all persons are living on dividend income.

   5.   The public services supplied exhibit no external economies or diseconomies between communities.

Assumptions 6 and 7 to follow are less familiar and require brief explanations:

   6.   For every pattern of community services set by, say, a city manager who follows the preferences of the older residents of the community, there is an optimal community size. This optimum is defined in terms of the number of residents for which

this bundle of services can be produced at the lowest average cost. . . .

7.   The last assumption is that communities below the optimum size seek to attract new residents to lower average costs. Those above optimum size do just the opposite. Those at an optimum try to keep their populations constant.

. . . . Clearly, communities below the optimum size, through chambers of commerce or other agencies, seek to attract new residents. . . . The case of the city that is too large and tries to get rid of residents is more difficult to imagine. . . . Nevertheless, economic forces are at work to push people out of it. Every resident who moves to the suburbs to find better schools, more parks, and so forth, is reacting, in part, against the pattern the city has to offer.

The case of the community which is at the optimum size and tries to remain so is not hard to visualize. Again proper zoning laws, implicit agreements among realtors, and the like are sufficient to keep the population stable.

Except when this system is in equilibrium, there will be a subset of consumer-voters who are discontented with the patterns of their community. Another set will be satisfied. Given the assumptions about mobility and the other assumptions listed previously, movement will take place out of the communities of greater than optimal size and into the communities of less than optimal size. The consumer-voter moves to the community that satisfies his preference pattern.

The act of moving or failing to move is crucial. Moving or failing to move replaces the usual market test of willingness to buy a good and reveals the consumer-voter's demand for public goods. Thus each locality has a revenue and expenditure pattern that reflects the desires of its residents. . . .

Each city manager now has a certain demand for n local public goods. In supplying these goods, he and $m-1$ other city managers may be considered as going to a national market and bidding for the appropriate units of service of each kind: so many units of police for the ith community; twice that number for the jth community; and so on. The demand on the public goods market for each of the n commodities will be the sum of the demands of the m communities. In the limit . . . this total demand will approximate the demand that represents the true preferences of the consumer-voters—that is, the demand they would reveal, if they were forced, somehow, to state their true preferences. In this model, there is no attempt on the part of local governments to 'adapt to' the preferences of consumer-voters. Instead, those local governments that attract the optimum number of residents may be viewed as being 'adopted by' the economic system.

. . . . We are maximizing within the framework of the resources available. . . . On the production side, it is assumed that communities are forced to keep production costs at a minimum either through the efficiency of city managers or through competition from other communities. . . . [O]n the demand side . . . [j]ust as the consumer may be visualized as walking to a private market place to buy his goods, the prices of which are set, we place him in the position of walking to a community where the prices (taxes) of community services are set. Both trips take the consumer to market. There is no way in which the consumer can avoid revealing his preferences in a spatial economy. Spatial mobility provides the local public-goods counterpart to the private market's shopping trip.

Relaxing assumption 5 has some interesting implications. There are obvious external economies and diseconomies between communities. My community is better off if its neighbor sprays trees to prevent Dutch elm disease. On the other hand, my community is worse off if the neighboring community has inadequate law enforcement.

In cases in which the external economies and diseconomies are of sufficient importance, some form of integration may be indicated. Not all aspects of law enforcement are adequately handled at the local level. The function of the sheriff, the state police, and the FBI—as contrasted with the local police—may be cited as resulting from a need for integration. In real life the diseconomies are minimized in so far as communities reflecting the same socioeconomic preferences are contiguous. Suburban agglomerations such as Westchester, the North Shore, and the Main Line are, in part, evidence of those external economies and diseconomies.

Assumptions 1 and 2 should be checked against reality. Consumer-voters do not have perfect knowledge and set preferences, nor are they perfectly mobile. The question is how do people actually react in choosing a community. . . . Such studies as have been undertaken seem to indicate a surprising awareness of differing revenue and expenditure patterns. The general disdain with which proposals to integrate municipalities are met seems to reflect, in part, the fear that local revenue-expenditure patterns will be lost as communities are merged into a metropolitan area.

. . . . Policies that promote residential mobility and increase the knowledge of the consumer-voter will improve the allocation of government expenditures in the same sense that mobility among jobs and knowledge relevant to the location of industry and labor improve the allocation of private resources.

NOTES

1.   *The Political and Economic Cases for Local Autonomy Contrasted.* Both Madison and Tocqueville were concerned with the consequences of

political participation within local governments. Madison saw the danger of majority tyranny, whereas Tocqueville found the benefits of an education in democracy. In contrast, Tiebout has little or nothing to say about the inner workings of local government. His focus is not on participation *within* local government—or "voice"—but on movement *between* local governments, or "exit." A local resident participates not by "voicing" her preferences concerning local issues or local representatives in local elections but by remaining in a locality, or "exiting" from one locality to another, depending on her preferences concerning the different packages of services, regulations and taxes offered by different local communities. *Cf.* Albert Hirschman, Exit, Voice, and Loyalty: Response to Decline in Firms, Organizations, and States (Harvard Univ. Press 1970). The local government is less a polity and more a firm—one of a number of firms in a metropolitan area market place. The benefit of decentralization is not political participation—Tiebout refers not to citizens but to consumer-voters—but the increased likelihood that one's preferences for the mix of government services, regulations and taxes will be maximized when one can choose among a multiplicity of local governments rather than be limited to the offerings of one national government or a small number of state governments.

Tiebout's model is highly stylized. Few people have perfect information, are perfectly mobile, or live on dividend income. Many local government actions have external effects. But it is certainly the case that in most metropolitan areas there are a large number of local governments relatively near each other and within commuting range of one's job. In 1987, the typical metropolitan area had 113 local governments, including forty-seven general purpose governments, with the profusion of local governments even greater in areas like metropolitan Chicago (over 1250 local governments); Pittsburgh (nearly 300 local governments); Seattle (more than 300 local governments); and Baltimore (350 local governments). *See* Richard Briffault, The Local Government Boundary Problem in Metropolitan Areas, 48 Stan. L. Rev. 1115, 1120 (1996). A person could choose a home among dozens—in some areas, hundreds—of different local governments without having to change jobs or move out of the region. Although few people live on dividend income, as Tiebout's assumption 4 requires, their jobs do not require that they remain in a particular community.

Empirical work has tended to confirm some of the implications of the Tiebout model. If households in fact "shop" for the optimal package of local taxes and public services, then increases in the quality of the tax-service package ought to result in increases in local property values, and studies have found that such "capitalization" does occur, particularly in suburban areas. *See* Wallace E. Oates, The Effects of Property Taxes and Local Public Spending on Property Values: An Empirical Study of Tax Capitalization and the Tiebout Hypothesis, 77 J. Pol. Econ. 957 (1969); Wallace E. Oates, The Many Faces of the Tiebout Model, *in* The Tiebout Model at Fifty: Essays in Public Economics in Honor of Wallace Oates (William A. Fischel ed., Lincoln Inst. of Land Policy 2006). On the other hand, there is evidence that people move (or fail to move) for many reasons other than the quality of local government services or the tax-service package: "[R]ace, socio-economic class, shared friendships/kin networks, social perceptions, and geographic distance" from one's former home and from work matter, too. Kenneth A. Stahl, Mobility and Community in Urban Policy: An Essay on *Great American City* by Robert J. Sampson, 46 Urb. Lawyer 625, 629 (2014).

2. *Implications for Local Decision-Making.* Tiebout treats local governments as relatively passive participants in the metropolitan area marketplace; in his model the principal moving part is the consumer-voter who moves or declines to move from one locality to another. The economic approach to local government, however, has evolved to include arguments that consumer-voters influence local government actions. A consumer-voter is free to move from a locality that taxes her at a rate higher than she wants to pay to fund services she does not want. As a result, a locality whose public policies are inconsistent with the preferences of too many of its residents or potential residents will lose population and tax revenue. The locality is likely to respond by cutting taxes and altering its policies. *See, e.g.,* Robert Bish & Vincent Ostrom, Understanding Urban Government: Metropolitan Reform Reconsidered 53 (AEI Press 1973). Indeed, given their dependence on local tax bases to fund their programs, local governments may be seen as competing with each other, like private firms, for taxpayers. *See, e.g.,* Vincent Ostrom, Robert Bish, and Elinor Ostrom, Local Government in the United States 206 (ICS Press 1988). Such interlocal competition may provide local governments with an incentive to provide services more cheaply and more efficiently. According to Professor Fischel, in residential suburbs, homeowners are deeply invested in the value of their homes and accordingly press their local governments to adopt tax, service, and regulatory policies that will protect property values. *See* William A. Fischel, The Homevoter Hypothesis: How Home Values Influence Local Government Taxation, School Finance, and Land Use Policies (Harvard Univ. Press 2001). Local governments can use their zoning and land use regulatory policies to keep up land values and, thus, hold down the property tax per resident. *See* Bruce W. Hamilton, Zoning and Property Taxation in a System of Local Governments, 12 Urb. Studies 205 (1975). Big cities also use the tools at their disposal—such as land use rules, tax breaks, and other economic development incentives—to attract business investment that will increase urban property values. *See, e.g.,* John R. Logan and Harvey L, Molotch, Urban Fortunes: The Political Economy of Place (U. Cal. Press 1987) (developing concept of "city as a growth machine").

3. *The Tiebout Model and Redistributive Programs at the Local Level.* One implication of the Tiebout model is that local governments will—and should—focus on programs like public safety, good schools, clean streets, basic infrastructure and other amenities and avoid redistributive tax and spending programs to aid the poor, which ought to be undertaken only by higher levels of government. *See, e.g.,* Paul E. Peterson, City Limits (U. Chicago Press 1981). The combination of small size and large numbers of

localities within a metropolitan area means, in the words of urban economist Edward Glaeser, "[t]he mobility of the prosperous limits the ability of any city government to play Robin Hood." Edward Glaeser, Triumph of the City 61 (Penguin Press 2011). According to Professor Glaeser, "the city can succeed only by providing a business-friendly environment." *Id.* at 242. The anti-local-redistribution implication of the "orthodox theory of urban finance," Clayton P. Gillette, Local Redistribution and Local Democracy: Interest Groups and the Courts 31 (Yale Univ. Press 2011), has been challenged. Many cities do engage in some redistributive activity, including redistributive taxes, regulation, and spending on welfare, housing, health care and homelessness assistance that benefit low income people. Indeed, local governments have a "prodigious history" of redistribution dating back to the poor relief programs of the colonial era. Minor Myers III, A Redistributive Role for Local Government, 36 Urb. Law. 754, 771 (2004). Professor Gillette suggests that some localities may have a "taste" for redistribution, with people choosing to move to such communities, Local Redistribution, *supra*, at 41; that some forms of local redistribution, such as health care, may have local economic benefits, *id.* at 90; and, most importantly, that the economic and other advantages firms and high-income residents derive from being in certain cities make them willing to absorb some redistributive costs, *id.* at 96–101. Similarly, Professor Schragger has argued that although typically "[m]obile capital drives the law and politics of local government," thereby limiting the ability of cities to engage in redistribution, some cities may be able to leverage the locational advantages they enjoy and the stickiness of some forms of investment to engage in some redistributive activity so that "the potential contours of local economic policy are less constrained than usually thought." Schragger, Mobile Capital, Local Economic Regulation, and the Democratic City, 123 Harv. L. Rev. 482, 488 (2009). He points in particular to local land use regulations that require developers to provide neighborhood amenities and local laws favorable to labor. *Id.* at 509–17. *See also* Schragger, Is a Progressive City Possible? Reviving Urban Liberalism for the Twenty-First Century, 7 Harv. L. & Pol. Rev. 231 (2013).

4. *The Tiebout Model and Agglomeration Economics.* In making their arguments for the possibility of local redistribution, both Professors Gillette and Schragger rely on the concept of "agglomeration economics," the study of why firms and residents concentrate in cities despite the greater expense of doing business there and the costs resulting from congestion. As Professor Glaeser has explained, cities are essentially defined by "the absence of physical space between people and companies. They are proximity, density, closeness." Triumph of the City, *supra*, at 6. Cities exist and grow (or decline) primarily for economic reasons. In his article, The City as Law and Economic Subject, 2010 U. Ill. L. Rev. 1507 (2010), Professor David Schleicher explains that cities attract residents and firms because of the economic benefits they provide, including reduced transportation costs for goods; the advantages of large labor and consumption markets, including opportunities for specialization and the insurance provided by more job options if one business fails; and information spillovers, both within and across industries. *See id.* at

1515–1529. He argues there is considerable tension between agglomeration economics and Tiebout's focus on interlocal mobility as a means of determining local public services. People and businesses move from one locality to another (or fail to do so) primarily to "obtain agglomeration gains," not because of local government policies. *Id.* at 1534. Agglomeration effects can reduce the likelihood of "exit" because of preferences concerning local government policies as people and businesses may choose to stay put because of the economic gains of remaining in place, or the losses they would suffer if they moved, even if they dislike the actions of their local governments. *Id.* at 1535–40. Conversely, to the extent that people or firms do follow Tiebout and relocate away from their economically optimal location for public policy reasons, this can have negative economic effects, and not just for those who move but for the residents and firms who remain in the moved-away-from city who lose the economic benefit of close proximity to those who have moved. *Id.* at 1540–45. So, too, the restrictive local land use regulations that are associated with the Tiebout model's interest in keeping up local property values and holding down tax rates can interfere with agglomeration benefits by dispersing instead of concentrating people and business. *Id.*

Agglomeration economics does not refute the Tiebout Model's significance for local government law. Sorting efficiency can coexist with agglomeration economics when local government powers, and varying local policies, do not interfere with the ability of people and businesses to make locational decisions based on economic advantage. *Id.* at 1557–58. *See also* Schleicher, Local Government Law's "Law and ___ Problem," *supra*, 40 Fordham Urb. L. J. at 1963 (agglomeration economics "supplements without displacing" Tiebout). The combination of large numbers of relatively small local governments near each other and the relatively easy ability of at least some businesses and residents to move among them does provide a basis for people and firms to increase their satisfaction with, to influence, and to constrain, local government policies. Moreover, agglomeration economics is focused on "cities," whereas local government law focuses on all local governments, including some that are quite small, have low population density, and are primarily residential. It is not clear how far the agglomeration analysis applies to all local governments. But agglomeration economics, along with other factors such as the stickiness of investments and the social ties of people to their communities that inhibit movement, certainly operate to constrain Tiebout's sorting model and thus the efficiency benefits—in terms of the matching of people to public policies—of decentralization. So, too, agglomeration economics points towards to the economic costs that can result when local governments, responding to local preferences, adopt measures that can interfere with agglomeration benefits.

5. *Implications for Metropolitan Area Governance.* Tiebout's model assumes considerable local control over service delivery decisions, regulation, and taxation. It also has implications for the organization of metropolitan areas. Although many urbanists had long decried the "fragmentation" and "overlap" of metropolitan areas composed of dozens, if not hundreds, of

general and special purpose local governments and had called for metropolitan area regional governments, the Tiebout model suggests that, by offering metropolitan area residents multiple local government alternatives and promoting interlocal competition, fragmentation and overlap are strengths, not weaknesses. *See, e.g.,* Robert L. Bish, The Public Economy of Metropolitan Areas (Markham Pub. Co. 1971); Robert B. Parks & Ronald J. Oakerson, Metropolitan Organization & Governance: A Local Public Economy Approach, 25 Urb. Aff. Q. 18 (1989); Richard E. Wagner & Warren E. Weber, Competition, Monopoly, and the Organization of Government in Metropolitan Areas, 18 J.L. & Econ. 661 (1975); Vincent Ostrom, Charles E. Tiebout, and Robert Warren, The Organization of Government in Metropolitan Areas: A Theoretical Inquiry, 55 Am. Pol. Sci. Rev. 831 (1961). Conversely, to the extent that, as described in Note 4, *supra,* local policies interfere with economically efficient location decisions by residents and firms, there are economic arguments for some metropolitan area limits on local decision-making, We will consider the question of metropolitan area governance more extensively in Chapter V.

GERALD E. FRUG
THE CITY AS A LEGAL CONCEPT
93 Harv. L. Rev. 1057 (1980)

.... It is tempting to relate the cities' lack of power to the so-called "crisis of the cities." But exactly what this crisis is, or why we should care about it, is uncertain. It may be the need to improve the quality of life for those—often poor, often black or Hispanic—who live in the nation's major cities, or the need to encourage greater concentrations of people because of the energy shortage and the environmental damage caused by the suburbanization of the countryside, or the need to preserve city institutions important to the nation as a whole, such as trade or cultural centers.

Yet if the "crisis of the cities" means no more than these kinds of problems, an increase in city power does not seem necessary for their solution. Indeed, many of these problems might be solved more quickly if local autonomy were prohibited altogether, and cities were administered by federal officials authorized to implement a national urban policy. The need for city power does not rest on the view that local autonomy is the only, or even the most efficient, way to solve local problems.

In fact, if we focus on cities as they are presently organized and managed, we will not see the argument for city power. Cities as they currently exist should not simply be made more powerful. Rather, the argument for city power rests on what cities have been and what they could become. Cities have served—and might again serve—as vehicles to achieve purposes which have been frustrated in modern American life. They could respond to what Hannah Arendt has called the need for "public freedom"—the ability to participate actively in the basic societal decisions that affect one's life. This conception of freedom—a positive activity designed to create one's way of life—differs markedly from the currently popular idea of freedom as merely "an inner realm into which men might escape at will from the pressures of the world," of a "liberum arbitrium which makes the will choose between alternatives."

The basic critique of the development of Western society that has emerged since the beginning of the nineteenth century has emphasized the limited ability of individuals to control their own lives. This development is sometimes attributed to the growth of bureaucracy; an individual's work is increasingly controlled by a distant, hierarchic chain of command, and an individual's political destiny is determined by distant government officials. Others attribute the development to the evolution of the capitalist system to a stage in which the few individuals who control the bulk of productive property directly make the economic decisions, and indirectly make the political decisions, that shape society's future. Still others emphasize the organization of society to conform to the utilitarian view of the individual as merely a consumer of satisfactions so that economic freedom is defined as the ability to choose from an array of products and jobs, political freedom as the ability to choose among political candidates, and intellectual freedom as the ability to choose opinions from the "marketplace of ideas." There is little opportunity, in each case, for the individual to create his own material life, determine his own political future, or form his own ideas from personal experience. For our purposes, the important point is that all of these critiques stress the need for the individual to gain control over those portions of his life now determined by others.

Since absolute individual self-determination is pure fantasy, these critiques have focused on a more limited objective: reorganizing society to increase the degree of individual involvement in societal decisions. One step towards meeting that objective is the reduction of the scale of decisionmaking, since limited size appears to be a prerequisite to individual participation in political life or at the workplace. Reestablishing the definition of political democracy as popular involvement in the decisionmaking process, rather than as merely providing a choice of candidates at an election, is possible only at the local level. Similarly, some Marxists have argued that socialist control of economic life requires decentralized decisionmaking to avoid substituting the power of a centralized status hierarchy for the power of those who control the means of production. As the tradition from Aristotle to Rousseau emphasizes, individual involvement in decisionmaking is impossible except on a small scale.

More than a reduction in the size of decisionmaking units is necessary, however, before popular participation in societal decisionmaking can be realized. There must also be a genuine transfer of power to the decentralized units. No one is likely to participate in the decisionmaking of an entity of any size unless that participation will make a difference in his life. Power and participation are inextricably linked: a sense of powerlessness tends to produce apathy rather than participation, while the existence of power encourages those able to participate in its exercise to do so.

The idea of communal decisionmaking will appear utopian to some. Indeed it is, if we define utopia, as did Karl Mannheim, as a vision of the world derived from unrealized and unfulfilled tendencies in current society that threaten to break through the existing order and cause its transformation. The idea of freedom as popular participation in the exercise of power has been a persistent and persistently revolutionary idea in Western social thought. It was, according to some scholars, the purpose of the American revolution until the reaction against mass democracy in the 1780's; it was also, according to others, the central core of Marxism prior to the Leninist addition of the priority of organization.

What makes the concept of popular participation so unrealistic to us is not only its frightening unfamiliarity, but also our conviction that all decisionmaking requires specialization, expertise, and a chain of command. For us, small units are organized just as large ones—as hierarchic bureaucracies. Cities are just another version of bureaucratic government managed by elected politicians, and small businesses tend to be structured as if they were larger ones. We find it difficult to conceive how communal decisionmaking might work, how people could be induced to participate, and how knowledge could be sufficiently widespread and decisionmaking sufficiently orderly to be possible. Popular participation seems to us to be chaos; it challenges not only our idea of property rights and sovereign power, but also our idea of the possible ways of organizing human activity. Yet even Lenin and Max Weber, both of whom believed in the necessity of bureaucracy in the modern world, recognized that democracy presents an alternative to bureaucracy as a method of decisionmaking. Moreover, descriptions of the governing of Athens by forty thousand citizens, the control of industry by Yugoslavian workers, and the management of Israeli kibbutzim by their members suggest the viability of this alternative vision of the possibilities for organizing human behavior.

Another objection to communal decisionmaking, an objection as old as Plato's, is that it appeals to the worst instincts of individuals and leads to a despotism of ignorance and prejudice. But the proponents of popular participation, themselves relying on Greek theory, suggest that involvement in power itself changes the individuals who participate, giving them a practical notion of the needs of social life and an interest in the welfare of their community. In the 1830's, de Tocqueville saw the then-widespread participation in local government as the essential strength of American democracy. John Dewey, almost a century later, viewed the demise of participatory local government as the central evil of the modern era. Popular participation seemed to him the only method of replacing reliance on mass propaganda with personally acquired information, and of creating the sense of a common venture necessary for any meaningful definition of the "public interest." Hannah Arendt argued that no one can be truly free or happy without recapturing the meaning of freedom as active participation in public decisionmaking and the meaning of happiness as public happiness, the sharing of public power. Freedom is cheapened, she argued, by defining it merely as a source of protection for our private lives, rather than as a creative form of control over our lives. For these critics, popular participation is the source of values, the creation of morality, not its elimination.

It should be emphasized that participatory democracy on the local level need not mean the tyranny of the majority over the minority. Cities are units within the state, not the state itself; cities, like all individuals and entities within the state, could be subject to state-created legal restraints that protect individual rights. Nor does participatory democracy necessitate the frustration of national political objectives by local protectionism; participatory institutions, like others in society, could still remain subject to general regulation to achieve national goals. The liberal image of law as mediating between the need to protect the individual from communal coercion and the need to achieve communal goals could thus be retained even in the model of participatory democracy.

We need not decide here whether this alternative vision of society would improve the human condition. Certainly Rousseau's model of popular participation can be characterized as both the full expression and full suppression of individualism. Yet any denial of the possibility of such a vision of democracy in a country which professes democratic ideals must be explained, and the creation of powerless cities is just such a denial. Participatory democracy exists today only as a faint echo, discernible in the remnants of the New England town meetings and in the sense that, somehow, the bureaucratic governments of most localities are still more accessible, controllable, and amenable to popular direction than is the federal bureaucracy. The question becomes, then, one of establishing how the powerlessness of cities is a factor in preventing the emergence of participatory democracy.

It is not that cities are the only form in which participatory democracy is possible in American society. The Populist movement can be viewed as an experiment in popular participation. In addition, some writers have suggested that private corporations are vehicles for creating new forms of human association based upon the communal tie created by the pursuit of common goals. Such an idea has many possible meanings, ranging from socialism on the one hand to business management based on the infusion of communal values on the other. But surely a more likely source of participatory democracy has always been the cities, in part because of the tradition of local participatory democracy from the colonial era to as recently as de Tocqueville's time.

Why are cities today governed as bureaucracies, rather than as experiments in participatory democracy? The answer cannot simply be that they are too large, because when city powerlessness first became a legal principle, there were only two cities in the United States with over one hundred thousand people. Moreover, many cities—even without our special definition of the word—remain as small today as Athens was in classical times. Instead, the answer must be sought in the development of our liberal ideology which makes the idea of participatory democracy seem so bizarre, so dangerous, and so unworkable that most state constitutions prohibit its emergence. Complementing this is the relationship depicted above between participation and powerlessness. Since significant powers have been withheld from cities, the idea of cities' becoming experiments in popular democracy is unattractive. Individual participation in powerless institutions fails to provide individuals with the opportunity to shape their lives in a meaningful manner. Thus, state control has prevented cities from becoming experiments in participatory democracy while simultaneously making them unlikely targets for attempts at popular control.

City powerlessness, then, diminishes the possibility of developing a form of human association based on participation in public power. City power would not ensure the success of such a form of association, but it could be an important ingredient of it. Indeed, a powerful city is desirable only if it becomes transformed, modifying its functions and organization and, perhaps, its boundaries, to engender greater participation in its decisionmaking.

RICHARD BRIFFAULT
OUR LOCALISM, PART II: LOCALISM AND LEGAL THEORY
90 Colum. L. Rev. 346 (1990)

Contemporary normative discourse about the proper scope of local autonomy is dominated by two theories which—although they proceed from distinctive premises, are phrased in different rhetoric and represent separate scholarly traditions—converge on the general proposition that local autonomy should be protected and enhanced. The two arguments emphasize different fundamental values: participation in public life in the one and efficiency in the provision of public sector goods and services in the other. Similarly, the theories rely on contrasting metaphors for the central mechanism of local public life: "voice" in the one case and "exit" in the other. Yet the two tales told by political and economic theorists share a common commitment to localism. . . .

. . . . Frug asserts that localities are legally powerless. This is important to his argument since otherwise it would be difficult to account for the low level of popular participation in local politics. . . . Yet a fundamental premise of the Tiebout hypothesis is that localities possess substantial discretion over local taxing, spending and regulatory decisions. Although this premise usually passes unstated, Tiebout's theory would make no sense without it, since it is this discretion that allows local governments to respond to consumer-voter preferences. Mobile citizens and multiple local governments would have little economic significance if each locality simply executed the decisions of a higher level government or if local decisions were regularly superseded by state or federal action.

. . . . [T]he economists' assumptions come far closer to capturing the scope of local legal authority than does Frug's assertion of city powerlessness. Local governments have substantial autonomy in deciding the size and distribution of local budgets, setting tax rates and regulating local land use. The states generally grant localities broad discretion, and as a rule state courts and legislatures have been reluctant to interfere with local autonomy in these important areas. State incorporation and annexation laws facilitate the formation of new governments with the full panoply of local powers while inhibiting the expansion of older governments or the consolidation of localities into metropolitan or regional units. In short, the economists' basic premise about local legal power captures local government law in practice; Frug's assertion of "city powerlessness" does not.

Tiebout's assumptions about the number of local governments and the mobility of people also have considerable contemporary validity. Focusing only on general-purpose governments, one study of the twenty-five largest urbanized areas found that in twenty-one areas there were twenty or more local governments; in twelve areas there were more than fifty local governments; in six areas there were more than one hundred local governments. Another researcher found that in only two metropolitan areas did the central city account for as much as half the metropolitan area population and in most cases the central city's share of population was forty percent or less. Nor was there a concentration of land or population in a relatively small number of large suburbs. Instead, most urbanized areas are fragmented into numerous general-purpose jurisdictions, and "most people who live in large metropolitan areas do have several local governments in whose jurisdiction they could realistically live." As for mobility, since the 1950s approximately twenty percent of American households have moved each year. Over a five-year period nearly half of all families change their residence at least once.

Although the majority of moves are to new homes within a few miles of the original residence, many moves, including some involving relatively short distances, entail changes in political jurisdiction.

The large number of local governments and the mobility of local residents lessen both the significance, if not the likelihood, of local political participation in two ways. First, the impact of participation is reduced when the multiplicity of local governments and the resultant interlocal competition narrow the scope of local politics. Second, the multiplicity of local governments and the interlocal mobility of people together undermine the notion that local communitarian feelings will inspire residents of local governments to greater participation than is likely to occur at the state or national level. The bonds linking transient residents to their localities may be weak, and the sense of belonging to a particular place may be attenuated by the multiple linkages each resident has to other jurisdictions.

Although Frug puts the case for participation primarily in terms of the psychological and emotional benefits of individual involvement in political life, latent in his theory is the assumption that city power will somehow transform local politics in the direction of greater social justice. His specific proposals—that cities operate banks, insurance companies and other financial institutions, provide housing, create food cooperatives and run profit-making businesses—reflect the idea that such municipal activity would radically transform local political life and provide a basis for empowering workers, the poor and consumers. . . .

But it is highly unlikely that greater local participation would have such a transformative effect. The multiplicity of localities and the mobility of people and capital that Tiebout describes and that exist today seriously erode the capacity of most cities to undertake new programs that would impose costs on already straitened local budgets and that are likely to be perceived as benefitting the poor or municipal workers at the expense of business and middle-and upper-income interests. Corporate and upper-income residents are the city residents most sensitive to changes in local taxes and the quality of urban services. It is relatively easy for affluent people and businesses who feel dissatisfied with municipal tax and spending policies to leave the city, become residents of adjacent communities and continue to have ready access to the city as a place to work, shop, sell and enjoy recreational and cultural amenities. Officials in city governments know this, and the range of political choices available to them is accordingly constrained. . . .

Developments in transportation, communication and production technologies have increased the ease of movement of both people and capital. The locational advantages cities once possessed, in terms of the presence of large markets and proximity to rivers and railroads, are of decreasing significance in the age of aviation, computers and the electronic and telephonic transmission of data and documents. As a result, interlocal competition for businesses and affluent residents has intensified, city tax bases have become more fragile and cities' fiscal capacities to carry out their current public service functions, let alone implement progressive innovations, are more severely stressed. . . . Cities already have sufficient legal authority to intervene broadly in economic life, take on traditional business functions and pursue ambitious social programs. But the economic constraints on urban politics deriving from the multiplicity of local governments and the mobility of people and businesses are structural, and they make the municipal pursuit of private capital a far more likely prospect than the adoption of a program of municipal socialism.

Beyond narrowing the range of local political choices, the multiplicity of local governments and the mobility of people casts doubt on the assumption, fundamental to participation theory, that local autonomy and the spirit of community are mutually reinforcing—that participation will be stronger in local governments because localities are communities. . . . For participationists, local governments are communities—places where an individual's activities and experiences are bound up with those of her neighbors, where repeated interactions and daily communications breed interdependence, shared feelings and values and a public-spirited commitment to the community's well-being. This sense of community is said to provide an incentive to participate in local affairs and to ease participation by providing residents with an awareness of how much they have in common, thereby facilitating community decision making.

But the connection between today's local governments and the spirit of community is tenuous. One cannot, of course, find a standard metric to gauge the sense of community. If, however, as some urban sociologists contend, "the single most important variable leading to stronger social bonds is length of residence"—more than social class or stage of life—then the high rate of interlocal mobility suggests that community bonds within localities cannot be very strong. We are a mobile society, and the ease and frequency of relocation necessarily reduces the sense of common needs, mutual values and shared lives "community" ordinarily connotes.

Furthermore, the large number of localities in each metropolitan area is a significant reminder that people are regularly involved in more than one locality in the course of their daily lives. We are not just a mobile society; we are also a commuter society. Most people no longer reside in the locality in which they work, and they no longer confine their weekly travel, shopping, social, cultural or other routine activities to the community in which they reside. The statement of a southern California woman—" 'I live in Garden Grove, work in Irvine, shop in Santa Ana, go to the dentist in Anaheim . . . and used to be president of the League of Women Voters in Fullerton.' "—is emblematic of the multi-jurisdictional lives most metropolitan area residents lead. Some sense of interdependence and common experience, of shared values and mutual knowledge and sympathy, no doubt remains. Clearly, however, this sense cannot be as strong as participation theorists contend when so many communities are composed of newcomers, transients and people whose attention is often focused on issues and events outside the local jurisdiction. Participation theory, like the law, treats an individual as a member of only one local community—the one in which he or she currently resides. But other localities—places of work, schooling or shopping; places through which a person passes during the diurnal commute; places of former residence—may play an important role in the individual's life, thereby reducing interest in and involvement with the person's current home locality.

Despite their numerous contacts with other local governments, people remain intensely concerned with issues pertaining to their jurisdiction of residence. It is this locality that makes tax, regulatory and spending decisions that directly affect the value of one's home, the character of one's neighbors and the quality and cost of basic public services. Still, the mystic quality with which the term "community" often invests these shared interests—the hint of some organic unity of the individual and the place—is hard to sustain. The strong identification of the citizen with the local community that characterized the Greek polis, the high-medieval city and the New England town has given way to a society in which daily life is spread over a number of places. The role of any one locality in the life of the individual, the personal commitment to that locality and one's fellow feeling for other local residents must be correspondingly reduced.

The role of mobility and the multiplicity of local governments in limiting the sense of community as an incentive to and a benefit of participation do not require us to reject participation as a political value or to deny the importance of the local setting as a focus of participation. But we can question whether participation would be greatly advanced by further local autonomy and whether the benefits of the increment in participation would be worth the costs additional local autonomy would impose. . . .

The Tiebout hypothesis describes the contemporary urban setting better than does Frug's theory. But the descriptive power of economic localism does not translate into a satisfactory normative justification for the enhancement of local power or even for the current broad scope of local autonomy. . . .

For Tiebout, the central mechanism of citizen-government relations is departure. The individuals who drive the system and make it work are the ones who leave, are likely to leave or have recently arrived; their significance to the local polity derives from their marginal status. Although the interlocal competition for taxpayers and investors indicates that there is considerable descriptive power in this view of local government, it is unclear why we should *want* a local government system in which the critical actors are those with the weakest ties to the locality and the critical decisions do not involve the structure of local decision making, the substance of local policies or the process of local political activity, but rather the decision whether or not to exit. . . .

Interjurisdictional movement is not cost-free. It is constrained by a variety of economic and social factors that tend to affect poorer people more than affluent ones. First, there are the out-of-pocket costs of relocation—of picking up, selling a home or otherwise disinvesting from one's original locality, searching for a new place to live, transporting one's self and family and finding and paying for a new home. Second, most people can only reside where they have access to work. Thus, corporate investment decisions and local zoning regulations that determine the location of jobs, the education and skills requirements that determine who will be eligible for those jobs and the costs of commuting from home to workplace all limit ease of movement. Poorer, less educated potential movers will have fewer options and will be forced to bear more costs if they attempt to move.

Similarly, people can only reside where they can afford to reside. Suburban exclusionary ordinances, such as large-lot zoning and the exclusion of multifamily and subsidized housing, drive up the cost of housing in many jurisdictions, denying many potential movers a meaningful choice of places to live. Access to jobs and access to homes are often interrelated. Suburban zoning decisions often make the communities adjacent to new manufacturing facilities, office and industrial parks or corporate headquarters economically inaccessible to all but relatively affluent people, effectively refusing poorer people both housing and employment opportunities or forcing them to endure long commutes as the price of a job.

Economic factors are not the only restrictions on movement. People are tied to their home jurisdictions by bonds of emotion and sentiment. A home is not just a house but a place with friends, family and neighbors. The home jurisdiction is not just a political unit but a familiar and dependable environment, the setting of one's daily routine, a source of physical and psychic security and a component of one's sense of personal identity. Although patterns of mobility and commutation strain the notion of community, sentimental attachments to place do exist, and the severing of personal ties is a cost of relocation and a restriction on interlocal movement.

Residents are, to some degree, grounded by social forces. The relocation decisions of businesses and investors, by contrast, are usually less constrained by feelings of community or attachments to neighborhood. The economic costs of shifting capital from one place to another are also less than the costs of relocation for residents. Investors can transfer wealth across local boundaries instantaneously. Although investment in plants and equipment is less mobile, firms can cut back on maintenance and decline to modernize old plants, while gradually shifting new investments to new settings.

Thus, investors of capital and owners of businesses, rather than residents, are the prime beneficiaries of the system of multiple jurisdictions and ease of movement. They can consider a broader array of jurisdictions as sites for investment than are available to individuals as possible new homes. These interjurisdictional shifts in investment will, in turn, determine the location of jobs, the patterns of residential migration, local economic and fiscal prosperity (or decline) and the ability of localities to provide programs that respond to the needs of local residents.

The relative mobility of capital and, to a lesser degree, of more affluent residents is central to the dynamics of the contemporary interlocal competition for new investment and new taxpayers. The operational significance of mobility and the multiplicity of jurisdictions in shaping local government behavior cannot be denied. But it is hard to see why, given the system's built-in economic discrimination and its preference for capital over residential consumer-voters, capital mobility and jurisdictional multiplicity should constitute a normative justification for the preservation, let alone the extension, of local autonomy. A metropolitan marketplace for municipal services in which local "firms" cater primarily to the interests of businesses and wealthy residents may enable investors and the affluent to maximize the satisfaction of their preferences for local services, taxes and regulation. Clearly, however, such a system provides fewer benefits for residents whose mobility is constrained by the economic and social costs of moving and by local exclusionary regulations.

The importance of economic and social inequalities in calling into question the normative value of the Tiebout hypothesis cuts deeper than the class-and wealth-based distinctions in ability to move. The economic model assumes that the tax, service and regulatory differences among localities are the result of variations in "tastes." In theory, one locality may prefer a municipal swimming pool, another might favor parks, a third might opt for new roads and a fourth might decide to lower taxes and spend less on local services. In fact, however, local taxing and spending decisions are often based not simply on idiosyncratic tastes but also on the stark differences in local fiscal capacity that divide localities within each metropolitan area.

. . . . [I]n state after state the level of local spending on education and the quality of local schools correlated with local taxable wealth, not just with local tax rates. Wealthy communities generally spend much more per capita on their schools, but can still tax their residents at much lower rates than poorer communities, which typically tax at high rates but can still manage only relatively low levels of school spending. The small per-student amounts of school spending in poorer jurisdictions were a result not of the lack of a "taste" for education among residents of that locality, but rather of the inadequacy of local taxable resources. Other studies have found that the quantity and quality of other local services also vary directly with local fiscal capacity.

. . . . Local fiscal capacity is not so much a matter of local preferences as the result of the siting decisions of industrial, commercial and financial firms and of broader regional, national or international economic developments. Although local governments regularly seek to influence the locational and investment decisions of private firms, and may have some impact at the margin, for the most part local fiscal resources are dependent on decisions over which local governments have little control. Local wealth thus is often not a result of local decisions but rather of external forces. . . .

[E]conomic localism reflects and reinforces existing interpersonal and interlocal inequalities. By accepting the preexisting distribution of wealth, economic localism prefers the interests of businesses and investors over those of individuals and families, those of the affluent over those of the poor and those of localities with healthy tax bases over those of localities with limited fiscal capacity. The local government system may be efficient, but if the amelioration of inequality is to remain an important value in our legal and political culture, then economic localism cannot provide a sufficient normative basis for protecting, let alone extending, local autonomy.

. . . . Both [political and economic] models assume that the consequences of local actions are borne primarily within the acting locality—internalized, in the economists' term. . . . Yet . . . [t]oday, local borders cut across densely packed and economically and socially intertwined metropolitan areas, virtually guaranteeing that there will be externalities and that some people, namely nonresidents, will be excluded from participating in the decisions of one of the region's many local governments though they are intimately affected by these decisions.

. . . . Local boundaries do not simply define the size of the locality; they also determine who is left out. If local boundaries corresponded to divisions between relatively self-contained and self-sufficient communities, marked by tight economic, political and social bonds, distant or at least relatively detached from their neighbors, then the exclusionary aspect of boundaries might not be significant. Each person could then reside in and be a member of the locality that had the dominant impact on her life. But today most localities are not self-contained or self-sufficient. Nor are local boundaries typically drawn with a concern to promote efficient local operations or to include within local borders all those people with a strong stake in local decisions. Local borders enclose only small fractions of interdependent urbanized areas. As a result, local decisions regularly impose externalities on people outside the local polity who are not entitled to participate in the local decision-making process. . . .

Legal theory must take into account the suburbanization of local government, especially the impact of suburbanization on the nature of participation at the local level. The suburbs are essential to the analysis of local participation because suburbs are the future—indeed, the present—of American local governments. Moreover, suburbs constitute the principal case for participatory localism today. Suburbs are generally smaller in population and area than the larger cities, so suburban residents have a greater opportunity for direct involvement in local decisions. The legal and fiscal resources of more affluent suburbs may enable them to be more successful in attaining local goals, thus satisfying the concern that participation will occur only where governments are effectively empowered. Indeed, there is some evidence that citizens do participate more in suburbs than in cities and that suburban governments are more responsive to their residents. . . . Suburbs, although small, are not microcosms of metropolitan areas or reflections of regional diversity. Instead, suburbs are often highly specialized by economic function, race and ethnicity and class and income of residents. . . . [C]ontemporary metropolitan areas are characterized by a close connection between interpersonal and interjurisdictional economic inequality. . . .

Suburban politics is the politics of residence. Suburban residents share a bit of territory and, perhaps, common social and cultural values growing out of their relationship to the local territory. . . . In this setting, public life is often focused on the protection of private life and the insulation of home and family from broader public concerns. . . . Localism in this setting enables residents to believe that their range of concerns is, and ought to be, limited by local boundary lines. Poverty, crime, deteriorating school systems and the lack of affordable housing outside the home community are defined as the private, local problems of other communities and not as subjects of public concern. Local participation may drive communities apart, intensify the sense of interlocal difference and reduce the possibilities of fashioning regional solutions to regional problems.

This objection to local autonomy derives not from the potential internal oppressiveness of local majorities that troubled Madison, but rather from the function-, race-and income-segregated nature of the contemporary polis. The suburb can be a very private polis, both in terms of the issues that are the focus of local politics and the desire to avoid extralocal problems. The fragmentary nature of localities and the interlocal differences in personal wealth and municipal fiscal capacity mean that local autonomy will be worth a great deal more to some localities than others. Interlocal ethnic and class differences shape local decision making, leading to the adoption of land-use, tax and spending policies that perpetuate inequities and maintain residential separation. The private nature of local public values leads to the narrowing of local politics, the disclaiming of responsibility for problems beyond local borders and the rejection of interlocal cooperation on matters of social significance. They tend to lead as well to the pursuit of localist objectives at higher levels of government.

Local autonomy, thus, should be seen as normatively ambiguous. . . . In empowering some, local autonomy disempowers others. Given the political economy of contemporary metropolitan areas and the resulting implications for local politics, the contention that greater local power and a categorically localist resolution of questions of local government law would enhance the quality of American political life and create new opportunities for the advancement of a progressive political agenda simply cannot be justified.

NOTES AND QUESTIONS

1. *City Powerlessness?* In his travels across Jacksonian America, Tocqueville found that local governments enjoyed considerable autonomy. Writing nearly a century and a half later, Professor Frug made "city powerlessness" a central assumption of his analysis of local government law. He concluded that nineteenth century developments in the law of state-local relations had effectively stripped local governments of the autonomy they had enjoyed in Tocqueville's time and that subsequent developments, such as "home rule," had effectively failed to remedy the loss of local power.

Professor Briffault, in turn, argues that although, as a matter of black-letter law, local governments have limited powers vis-a-vis their states, and, typically, lose in head-to-head, state-local conflicts, local governments enjoy far greater autonomy in practice than Professor Frug acknowledged: "In most states, local governments operate in major policy areas without significant external legislative, administrative or judicial supervision. Local governments have considerable fiscal and policy-making responsibility and extensive regulatory authority." Richard Briffault, Our Localism, Part I: The

Structure of Local Government Law, 90 Colum.L.Rev. 1, 112 (1990). Indeed, he suggests that in many areas "state legislatures make only limited use of their formal authority to pre-empt local lawmaking in areas of fundamental local concern. The states have been reluctant to supersede local land use regulations, redistribute local resources, redraw local boundaries or control local government formation decisions. . . . The state's legal power to prevail in state-local conflicts is less significant than the fact that such conflicts are relatively infrequent. . . . [T]here is considerable local autonomy emanating from the states' delegation of fiscal and regulatory authority with both the practice of state legislatures of leaving local governments alone and the tendency of state courts to elevate that practice to the level of a legally protected interest. Local power may be tacit or de facto, rather than a product of formal, constitutional arrangement, but it is nevertheless very real." *See id.* at 113–14. Local governments may not have all the powers adequate to local needs, but that appears to be attributable more to the variations in wealth and fiscal capacity among localities than to general legal limitations on local government. *See id.* at 114. Other scholars have been more skeptical about the scope of local powers. In their survey of the differing legal structures of seven major cities, Professors Frug and Barron, concluded that cities are limited in their ability to control land use, improve their schools, and raise revenue. Gerald E. Frug and David J. Barron, City Bound: How States Stifle Urban Innovation (Cornell U. Press 2008).

The legal rules governing state-local relations and addressing state-local conflicts are examined in Chapter IV.

2. *The Benefits of Small Size.* Whereas Madison feared that small size facilitated the power of majority factions—and raised questions about the ability to attract capable people for local administration—Professor Frug and other political participationists have made the small size of local governments a critical part of the argument for local autonomy. Small size is said to "facilitate the deliberative process, the exchange of information and ideas that is at the heart of participation. Face-to-face interaction is possible only in small units. Furthermore, people in small units are believed to understand more about the issues at stake and know more about each other, both of which may facilitate public-spirited decision-making. It is often assumed that people in smaller units are likely to have common interests and to share values and norms, and that, as a result, they may be willing to put aside individual self-interest for the local city's common good. In other words, localities may have a greater sense of community, which, it is assumed, will facilitate participatory decision-making. Participation, in turn, is said to reinforce the sense of community that promotes greater local participation." Richard Briffault, Our Localism: Part II, Local Government and Legal Theory, 90 Colum. L. Rev. 346, 396 (1990). *See generally* Jane Mansbridge, Beyond Adversary Democracy, *supra,* at 270–73, 281–85; Clayton P. Gillette, Plebiscites, Participation, and Collective Action in Local Government Law, 86 Mich. L Rev. 930, 964–68, 984–85 (1988).

The economic argument for local autonomy also finds some value to small size. The costs of government include the costs of political transactions—the time and effort involved in the bargaining, debate and interactions that are necessary for a collective body to reach a decision—and the costs to individuals of government decisions that go against them. These costs relate to the size of the polity. The larger the group, and the more interactions within it, the more time and effort a collective decision will require. Moreover, larger units are likely to be more heterogeneous. In heterogeneous units, more people are likely to have divergent preferences, while in smaller, more homogeneous units, there may be less internal disagreement. *See* Briffault, Our Localism, Part II, *supra*, 90 Colum. L. Rev. at 402–03.

Of course, not all local governments are small. As noted earlier in this chapter, many cities and counties have hundreds of thousands, even millions, of people. While still smaller than most states, they are considerably larger than the townships of Tocqueville's era. As the political scientist Robert Dahl once put it from a participationist perspective, "[t]o regard the government of New York [City] as a local government is to make nonsense of the term." Robert Dahl, The City in the Future of Democracy, 61 Am. Pol. Sci. Rev. 953, 968 (1967). A challenge for local government law is the development of principles of local governance and state-local relations that make sense in light of the enormous variation in local circumstances, such as differences in population.

Some scholars have suggested that for big cities the benefits of small size may be obtained from some decentralization of power within cities to neighborhoods. *See, e.g.,* Kenneth A. Stahl, Neighborhood Empowerment and the Future of the City, 161 U. Pa. L. Rev. 939 (2013); Robert C. Ellickson, New Institutions for Old Neighborhoods, 48 Duke L.J. 75 (1998); George W. Liebmann, Devolution of Power to Community and Block Associations, 25 Urb. Law. 335 (1993). Some cities provide for some formal sublocal governance structures. *See generally*, Kenneth Miller, Legal Neighborhoods, 37 Harv. Envt'l L. Rev. 105 (2013); Richard Briffault, The Rise of Sublocal Structures in Urban Governance, 82 Minn. L. Rev. 503 (1997). Neighborhoods and communities can also participate in urban governance in more informal ways. *See* Nadav Shoked, The New Local, 100 Va. L. Rev. 1323 (2014). As a result, neighborhood institutions and groups can bring some of the elements of intercity and suburban "exit" and "voice" options to big cities. Of course, the same cautions and concerns about the consequences of decentralization from states to cities apply to further decentralization within cities.

3.   *Small Size, Local Borders and Local Parochialism.* As Professor Briffault notes, the small size of local governments is accomplished by the creation of local government boundaries. But boundaries are as important for what and who they exclude as for what and who they include. In contemporary metropolitan areas, with multiple local governments virtually on top of each other, local government decisions can have effects beyond their borders. Moreover, the division of the metropolitan region into numerous

independent, largely residential local governments—with their own tax bases, locally-funded services, and local regulatory regimes—leads to areas of great local wealth and areas of great local poverty. Thus, central to Professor Briffault's skepticism about localism are concerns about local parochialism and interlocal inequality. He would give a greater role to the states: "The states are larger and far more politically, economically and socially complex than are individual localities. States are usually more demographically diverse, and include both businesses and homes. They consist of many localities, cities as well as suburbs. . . . Moreover, the states have greater resources than most local governments. . . . Because they include many localities, the states can internalize a wider range of decisions and can take a regional perspective on regional problems." *See* Briffault, Our Localism, Part II, *supra*, 90 Colum. L. Rev. at 447–48. In effect, he would reframe the question of state-local relations as a problem, in many metropolitan areas, of interlocal relations, with the state playing a key role in mediating interlocal conflicts and effecting interlocal redistribution.

Professor Richard Thompson Ford has expressed a similar concern about local parochialism and interlocal inequality, but, like Professor Frug, he places great value on the participatory and community self-governance benefits of local decision-making. He would avoid the "Hobson's Choice" of state versus local by making local borders more "permeable," as by allowing nonresidents to vote in local elections, thus "open[ing] local politics to interested nonresidents, creat[ing] more fluid polities and more flexible citizen identities." Richard Thompson Ford, Beyond Borders: A Partial Reply to Richard Briffault, 48 Stan. L. Rev. 1173, 1175, 1185–86, 1188–89 (1996). Professor Frug has made similar proposals to open local governments more to the interests of their neighbors without subjecting them to greater state power. *See* Jerry Frug, Decentering Decentralization, 60 U. Chi. L. Rev. 253 (1993). For criticism of this attempt to avoid the Hobson's Choice, *see* Briffault, The Local Government Boundary Problem in Metropolitan Areas, 48 Stan. L. Rev. *supra* at 1151–64. Looking to the history of efforts to promote local home rule, Professor Barron has suggested that decentralization has never been about "local autonomy per se" but has reflected more substantive concerns about enabling cities to address particular issues in urban governance, and so could address local parochialism through programs to promote interlocal cooperation rather than returning power to the state. *See* David J. Barron, Reclaiming Home Rule, 116 Harv. L. Rev. 2255 (2003).

As you read the materials on local boundaries (Chapter III), state-local conflicts (Chapter IV), and metropolitan area governance (Chapter V), you should consider how state and local government law may best capture the participatory and efficiency benefits of local decision-making while addressing the problems of local parochialism and interlocal wealth differences.

D. THE STATE CONSTITUTION

One unusual feature of this course is that you will be examining state constitutions and considering questions of state constitutional law. State constitutions generally receive little attention in most American law schools, or in American life generally. *See* U.S. Advisory Commission on Intergovernmental Relations, State Constitutions in the Federal System 7 (1989) (only 44% of Americans know that their state has its own constitution). But state constitutional provisions play a central role in state and local government law. Indeed, state constitutions are often pivotal in disputes involving state-local relations (Chapter IV); the state and local provision of elementary and secondary education (Chapter V); state and local finance (Chapter VI); and the privatization of state and local public services (Chapter VII).

State constitutions resemble the United States Constitution in two fundamental ways. First, much as the federal constitution creates the structure of the federal government, a state constitution establishes the basic structural framework for its state. A central feature of American federalism is that the federal constitution does not create the states or design their governments. It is the state constitution that provides for the basic component parts of state government, allocates powers among these components, and determines how these parts interact. Second, state constitutions, like the federal, establish fundamental rights that limit the scope of governmental authority. Most state constitutions contain provisions that are similar to the federal due process and equal protection clauses and the provisions in the Bill of Rights. Useful recent treatments of state constitutional law include Robert F. Williams, The Law of American State Constitutions (Oxford Univ. Press 2010); John J. Dinan, The American State Constitutional Tradition (Univ. Press of Kansas 2006); G. Alan Tarr, Understanding State Constitutions (Princeton Univ. Press 1998); Symposium, A Wave of Change: Celebrating the 50th Anniversary of Michigan's Constitution and the Evolution of State Constitutionalism, 60 Wayne L. Rev. 1 (2014); Symposium, The Law of American State Constitutions, 45 N. Eng. L. Rev. 901 (2011); Symposium, State Constitutional Law Steps Out of the Shadows, 59 U. Kan. L. Rev. 897 (2011).

On the other hand, state constitutions differ from the federal constitution in three significant ways—***theory***, ***form***, and ***substance***.

1. THE THEORY OF THE STATE CONSTITUTION: GRANT V. LIMITATION

Federal and state constitutions differ at the level of theory. The United States government enjoys only those powers granted to it by the federal constitution. Expansive interpretations of such open-ended provisions as the necessary and proper clause, the commerce clause, and the spending power have given the federal government broad authority, but still, in theory, all federal powers must be expressly or impliedly granted by the federal constitution. By contrast, state governments acting through their state legislatures are presumed to have broad, residual, plenary governmental powers. State constitutions are seen not as granting powers to state governments but, instead, as limiting the powers the states inherently possess. According to Dean Daniel B. Rodriguez, "the keystone of state constitutionalism [is] that state constitutions are documents of limit, rather than grant." Daniel B. Rodriguez, The Political Question Doctrine in State Constitutional Law, 43 Rutgers L.J. 573, 586 (2013). As the Michigan Supreme Court once put it, "the legislative power of the people through their agent the legislature is limited only by the [state] Constitution, which is not a grant of power but a limitation on the exercise of power." Oakland County Taxpayers' League v. Board of Supervisors, 94 N.W.2d 875 (Mich.1959). The potential practical significance of the grant/limitation distinction is nicely illustrated in the following case.

GANGEMI V. BERRY

Supreme Court of New Jersey
134 A.2d 1 (1957)

HEHER, J.

The question at issue here is the constitutional sufficiency of the provisions of L.1953, c. 211, N.J.S.A. 19:57—1 et seq., styled the "Absentee Voting Law (1953)," purporting to authorize civilian absentee voting at elections held in New Jersey.

May 14, 1957, there was an election in Jersey City to choose five members of the city commission, constituted the local governing body. * * * It is conceded that Berry's "plurality was produced by the civilian absentee votes"; and thus the decisive question is whether the statutory direction to that end is in contravention of the State's organic law.

* * * Section 3 of the statute, N.J.S.A. 19:57–3, includes within the class entitled to vote by absentee ballot a "civilian absentee voter who expects to be or may be absent outside the State or the United States on the day on which an election is held or who may be within the State on the day of any election but because of illness or physical disability will be unable to cast his ballot at the polling place in his election district on the day of the election, provided he is a registered voter, and is not otherwise disqualified by law from voting in such election." * * *

The contention is that this purposed exercise of the legislative function is in excess of the "grant of power" contained in Article II, paragraph 4 of the 1947 State Constitution, and therefore void. . . .

The particular provision of the Constitution is in these terms:

4.   In time of war no elector in the military service of the State or in the armed forces of the United States shall be deprived of his vote by reason of absence from his election district. The Legislature may provide for absentee voting by members of the armed forces of the United States in time of peace. The Legislature may provide the manner in which and the time and place at which such absent electors may vote, and for the return and canvass of their votes in the election district in which they respectively reside.

* * * Acknowledging the "well-recognized distinction" between State and Federal Constitutions . . . it is nevertheless insisted that here we are concerned with a constitutional grant rather than a limitation of power, and where "*granting* as distinguished from *limiting* provisions [are] involved, this rule, to which the Court below axiomatically adhered, [is] not properly applicable," citing State v. Carrigan, 82 N.J.L. 225, 82 A. 524 (Sup.Ct.1912) * * *

We seek for the sense and meaning of the particular constitutional provision, related to the context and the essential character of the instrument itself. The government of the United States is one of enumerated powers; and in its very nature the State Constitution is not a grant but a limitation of the exercise of the sovereign power inherent in the people, subject to the limitations imposed by the grant to the general government and, as well, those so fundamental in the social compact as to be necessarily implied. * * * By Article IV, section I, paragraph 1 of the 1947 State Constitution, the people vested full sovereign authority in the Legislature, save as otherwise therein provided. * * * The theory of our political system is that the ultimate sovereignty is in the people, "from whom springs all legitimate authority"; * * * Cooley's Constitutional Limitations (8th ed.), 81, 175 et seq.; 180, note.

> "[The people], in framing the constitution, committed to the legislature the whole lawmaking power of the state, which they did not expressly or impliedly withhold. Plenary power in the legislature for all purposes of civil government is the rule. A prohibition to exercise a particular power is an exception. In inquiring, therefore, whether a given statute is constitutional, it is for those who question its validity to show that it is forbidden." People ex rel. Wood v. Draper, 15 N.Y. 532, 543 (App.Ct.1857), Denio, Ch. J. The American legislatures "have the same unlimited power in regard to legislation which resides in the British parliament, except where they are restrained by written constitutions. That must be conceded, I think, to be a fundamental principle in the political organizations of the

American states. We cannot well comprehend how, upon principle, it should be otherwise. The people must of course, possess all legislative power originally. They have committed this in the most general and unlimited manner to the several state legislatures, saving only such restrictions as are imposed by the constitution of the United States, or of the particular state in question." Thorpe v. Rutland and Burlington Railroad Co., 27 Vt. 140 (Sup.Ct.1854), Redfield, Ch. J. * * *

The 1947 Constitution does not in terms affirmatively prohibit civilian absentee voting; and the purpose so to do is not revealed as a matter of negative inference. The preceding paragraph 3 of Article II of the Constitution insures the right of suffrage to every citizen of the given age and residence qualifications. In regard to absentee voting, paragraph 4 treats electors absent in military service as in the one category, but differently as to imperative right depending upon whether the military service is rendered in time of war or in time of peace. * * *

Be that as it may, there is no good reason to suppose that by this express inclusion of a provision for military absentee voting in time of peace, * * * it was designed to exclude all civilian absentee voting by legislative authority. The one does not *per se* imply the other. So to hold would do violence to reason and logic. Such a curtailment of basic legislative power, granted by Article IV, paragraph 1 of the Constitution, cannot be made to rest upon vague and uncertain implication. . . .

NOTES

1. *Conflicting Interpretive Principles.* The grant/limitation distinction has implications for the interpretation of state constitutional provisions. In *Gangemi,* the New Jersey Supreme Court cautioned that the well-known maxim of interpretation, "expressio unius est exclusio alterius"—roughly, the mention of one thing implies the exclusion of another—is of limited applicability to state constitutions:

> The rule "is not to be applied with the same rigor in construing a state constitution as a statute" * * * only those things expressed in such positive affirmative terms as plainly imply the negative of what is not mentioned will be considered as inhibiting the powers of the legislature. * * * [State v. Martin, 30 S.W. 421 (Ark.1895)]. The implication must be clear and compelling, a necessary consequence, not a conjectural or purely theoretical concept.

134 A.2d at 6.

Indeed, *expressio unius* is in tension with the notion of the state constitution as a limitation on otherwise plenary powers. Several state supreme courts have concluded that *expressio unius* is inapplicable to state constitutional interpretation. *See, e.g.,* Dean v. Kuchel, 230 P.2d 811

(Cal.1951) (constitutional provision of a Fish and Game Commission does not preclude the legislature from creating a separate board to manage a fish and game conservation program); Eberle v. Nielson, 306 P.2d 1083 (Idaho 1957) (constitutional provision authorizing payment of per diem and travel expenses of state legislators in connection with attending legislative sessions does not preclude statute authorizing additional payments for expenses in connection with service on legislative committees). *See also* Independent School Dist., Cassia Co. v. Pfost, 4 P.2d 893 (Idaho 1931) (constitutional enumeration of certain types of taxation does not preclude legislative adoption of additional forms of taxation). The "grant-not-limitation" principle continues to be invoked in cases concerning the nature of constitutional authority for legislative action. *See, e.g.,* State v. Thiel, 343 P.3d 1110, 1117 (Idaho 2015) ("Our State Constitution is a limitation, not a grant of power, and the [l]egislature has plenary power in all matters, except those prohibited by the Constitution."); Cave Creek Unified School Dist. v. Ducey, 308 P.3d 1152, 1156 (Ariz. 2013) ("Our state constitution, unlike the federal constitution, does not grant power but instead limits the exercise and scope of legislative authority"); Idaho Press Club, Inc. v. State Legislature, 132 P.3d 397, 399–400 (Idaho 2006) ("Because the Constitution is not a grant of power, there is no reason to believe that a Constitutional provision enumerating powers of a branch of government was intended to be an exclusive list. The branch of government would inherently have powers that were not included in the list").

2.   *Negative Implications from State Provisions.* State courts, however, have on occasion treated the explicit grant of a particular power as impliedly denying similar but unmentioned powers. This has occurred, for example, when the state constitution provides for certain offices and spells out the qualifications for election to those offices. Courts have frequently found that the constitutional criteria were intended to be exclusive. *See* Reale v. Board of Real Estate Appraisers, 880 P.2d 1205, 1206–07 (Colo. 1994). The *Reale* Court determined that the "grant-not-limitation" principle "supports the conclusion that the legislature does not have the power to impose additional qualifications" for holding the office of county assessor, on the theory that for the constitution "to specify the qualifications for this office limits, by implication, the legislature's power to impose additional qualifications." *Id.* at 1208. Courts have also found negative implications of specific grants of power in other settings. In Gallenthin Realty Dev., Inc. v. Borough of Paulsboro, 924 A.2d 447 (N.J. 2007), the New Jersey Supreme Court considered the provision of the New Jersey Constitution authorizing governmental takings of private property for public use. The constitution's Blighted Areas Clause specified that the taking of blighted areas for purposes of redevelopment satisfies the public use requirement. *Gallenthin* determined that the Blighted Areas Clause impliedly limited the taking power so that a borough's plan to take unimproved but not blighted land was impermissible.

Given the background assumption of the state legislature's plenary authority many specific delegations of power by the state constitution to the legislature are unnecessary. As a result, "[i]n order to give effect to such special authorizations . . . courts have often given them the full effect of negative implication, relying sometimes on the canon of construction *expressio unius est exclusio alterius. . . .*" Frank P. Grad, The State Constitution: Its Function and Form for Our Time, 54 Va. L. Rev. 928, 964 (1968). Narrow state judicial interpretation of state constitutional provisions can have the effect of muddying the grant/limitation distinction. As Professor Williams has noted, "[t]he general characterization of state constitutions as documents of limitation is correct but oversimplified. Many provisions in modern state constitutions were adopted to overcome earlier ·judicial interpretations of the constitution prohibiting the exercise of the power in question. Such provisions are grants of power, or at least the removal of limitations." Robert F. Williams, State Constitutional Law Processes, 24 Wm. & Mary L. Rev. 169, 178–79 (1983).

2. THE FORM OF THE STATE CONSTITUTION: LENGTH, FREQUENCY OF REVISION, AND "STATUTORY" DETAIL

A second major distinction between the federal and state constitutions is one of form. State constitutions tend to look and feel different from the federal constitution. To the reader accustomed to the broad sweep and majestic general principles of the federal constitution, state constitutions often seem more "statutory" than "constitutional." The length and detail may be, in part, a reflection of the nature and scope of state responsibilities. State governments have primary, frontline responsibility for defining basic rights and rules of civil society; protecting life, liberty and property; providing education; administering justice; regulating business activity; and other basic governmental activities.

The length of state constitutions is also a function of the relative frequency—compared with the federal constitution—with which state constitutions are amended. These amendments add length and detail. Moreover, to the extent that the "document of limitation" doctrine gives negative implications to some amendments, further amendments may be needed to remove the limitations unintentionally imposed by a prior amendment.

a. Length

The United States Constitution is approximately 7,300 words long. As of January 1, 2014, the shortest state constitution—that of Vermont— was 8,565 words; the longest, Alabama's, was a remarkable 376,006 words. The constitutions of the three most populous states—California, Florida, and Texas—were all in excess of 50,000 words, as were the constitutions of Arkansas, Colorado, Louisiana, Missouri, Ohio, and

Oklahoma. *See* Council of State Governments, The Book of the States 2014 at Table 1.1.

b.   Frequency of State Constitutional Change

The United States has operated under the same constitution since 1787. It has been amended 27 times. By contrast, the fifty states have had 144 constitutions, or nearly three per state. Louisiana has had eleven constitutions, Georgia ten, South Carolina seven, and Alabama, Florida and Virginia have each had six constitutions. Three states have had five constitutions; eight states four; four states three; and ten states two. Only nineteen states have operated under just one constitution, and only one of those—Massachusetts—is one of the original thirteen states. Indeed, the Massachusetts Constitution of 1780 has the distinction of being older than the federal Constitution. However, it has also been amended 120 times. Indeed, not only do states frequently change their constitutions, but they even more frequently amend the ones they have. At the start of 2014, the states' current constitutions had been amended nearly 7,400 times, or approximately 148 amendments per state. Alabama led the way with 880 amendments. California, South Carolina, and Texas have each amended their current constitutions more than 480 times. Even the newest state constitution—the Rhode Island constitution of 1986—has been amended 12 times in less than thirty years. Book of the States 2014, *supra*.

One factor contributing to the frequency of state constitutional change (and the resulting lengthy constitutions) is the relative ease of amendment. An amendment to the federal constitution requires the approval of two-thirds of each house of Congress followed by ratification by three-quarters of the states. Most state constitutional amendments also require legislative approval by a supermajority, followed by a ratification process, but ratification usually involves approval by the voters of the state as a whole rather than a "federalist" approval by a supermajority of subunits. This may make ratification less onerous. In addition, seventeen states empower the voters to amend the state constitution with voter-initiated measures that do not require legislative approval. Many state constitutions also provide for the convening of constitutional conventions with elected delegates who propose revisions for general voter approval. Some states have established constitutional commissions charged with making recommendations for constitutional change. The vast majority of state constitutional amendments, even in the states with the voter initiative, however, are initiated by the legislature.

c. "Statutory" Detail

The principal difference between the federal and state constitutional amendment processes is not the rigors of ratification but the number of proposals passed by the legislatures and submitted for ratification. State legislatures, as well as state constitutional conventions, state constitutional commissions charged with considering constitutional amendments, and voter initiatives, simply submit an enormous number of proposals for constitutional change. This reflects and reinforces the detailed, statute-like nature of state constitutions.

More than a century ago, Lord Bryce, the famous British commentator on American government, found that the state constitutions of the late nineteenth century included "a great deal of matter which is in no distinctive sense constitutional law but general law, . . . matter therefore which seems out of place in a constitution because it is better fit to be dealt with in ordinary statutes." Lord Bryce, The American Commonwealth, Vol. I (1891) at 116. Although state constitutional reformers have long sought to purge their constitutions of statutory detail, state constitutions continue to address such non-fundamental matters as casino gambling, lotteries, bonds for veterans housing, liquor by the drink, and the eradication of the boll weevil. Oklahoma's constitution provides that "the flash test . . . for all kerosene oil for illuminating purposes shall be 115 degrees Fahrenheit; and the specific gravity test for all such oil shall be 40 degrees Baumé." Okla. Const. art 20, § 2. New York's constitution includes provisions dealing with the tolls on the Erie Canal and the ski trails in the Adirondack Park. N.Y. Const., Arts. XIV, XV.

The length and frequency of revision of state constitutions are intertwined with the detailed quasi-statutory nature of state constitutions. State constitutions are far more enmeshed in the conflicts of state politics and the substance of state government than is the federal constitution in the federal government. In the states, policy battles are frequently fought through the constitution rather than through ordinary legislation. The result is a longer, more detailed constitution that has a more direct effect on the ordinary operations of state government, as well as a constitution that requires additional amendments when the political balance within a state changes and a new majority wants new policies.

3. SUBSTANCE: SOME SUBSTANTIVE DIFFERENCES BETWEEN THE FEDERAL AND STATE CONSTITUTIONS

Although the states have enormous freedom with respect to the content of state constitutions and the design of state governments, most states resemble each other and the federal government in basic structure.

Thus, all fifty states have adopted the separation of powers, with three separate branches of government. Indeed, some state constitutions, in addition to providing for three branches of government, also contain a distinct textual provision calling for the separation of powers. All fifty states have an independently elected governor and an independently elected legislature. In 49 states the legislature is bicameral; in many states the members of the upper house of the legislature serve for longer terms than members of the lower house. All fifty states also have an independent judiciary, and in all fifty states the courts engage in judicial review of state legislation. State bill of rights provisions frequently resemble those of the federal constitution, too.

Still, in the areas of governmental structure and fundamental rights, many state constitutions include provisions that differ significantly from those in the federal constitution, or have no federal constitutional counterpart at all. Many of these involve additional constraints on state legislatures. As the basic theory of state constitutional law is the plenary power of the legislature and the role of the constitution as a document of limitation, it is perhaps not surprising that state constitutions focus on limiting the legislature. In addition, unlike the federal constitution, many state constitutions impose affirmative duties on the legislature to undertake substantive policies and programs. These, too, can be construed as limitations on the legislature since they deny the legislature the discretion not to undertake the programs mandated by the constitution. Some highlights of the differences between the federal constitution and state constitutions include:

a.   Elected Judiciary

Federal judges are appointed and, once confirmed by the Senate, enjoy life tenure, but most state constitutions provide that most state judges are elected rather than appointed. In eighteen states, judges face retention elections; that is, they are initially appointed to their positions but must be approved by the voters in order to retain their positions. In another nineteen states, judges are selected through partisan elections. For an analysis of the emergence of the elective judiciary, *see* Jed Shugerman, The People's Courts: The Rise of Judicial Elections and Judicial Power in America (Harvard Univ. Press 2012). In addition, nearly all state judges serve either for fixed terms or until a mandatory retirement age, and so do not have life tenure.

It has been suggested an elected judiciary mitigates, if it does not eliminate altogether, the so-called countermajoritarian difficulty, that is, the concern that judicial review and invalidation of legislation adopted by popularly elected legislators is in fundamental tension with democracy. *See* Helen Hershkoff, Positive Rights and State Constitutions: The Limits of Federal Rationality Review, 112 Harv. L. Rev. 1131, 1157–61 (1999).

Where judges are also elected, they can reasonably argue that they are representative of and accountable to the people. On the other hand, it has also been argued that elected judges who must win re-election if they are to remain in office may be "reluctant to enforce unpopular rights." *Id. See also* Jeffrey S. Sutton, What Does—and Does Not—Ail State Constitutional Law, 59 U. Kan. L. Rev. 687, 700 (2011) (the impact of judicial elections on state constitutional law "should not be overstated"). The increasing cost of judicial elections raises troubling ethical considerations concerning the relationship between judicial campaign finance and judicial decisions. *See, e.g.,* Michael S. Kang and Joanna Shepherd, The Partisan Price of Justice: An Empirical Analysis of Campaign Contributions and Judicial Decisions, 86 N.Y.U. L. Rev. 69 (2011); Roy A. Schotland, Elective Judges' Campaign Financing: Are State Judges' Robes the Emperor's Clothes of American Democracy? 2 J.L. & Pol. 57 (1985).

In contrast with the federal judiciary, which is restricted to the adjudication of "cases and controversies," many states authorize their state supreme courts to give advisory opinions concerning the constitutionality of proposed legislation or executive actions. *See, e.g.,* Opinion of the Justices, 112 A.2d 926 (Me. 2015) (responding to request from governor concerning powers of the attorney general); In re Request for an Opinion of the Justices of the Delaware Supreme Court Regarding House Bills Nos. 134 and 135 of the 146th General Assembly, 37 A.3d 860 (Del. 2012) (governor sought opinion concerning constitutionality of bills passed that would change the handling of certain traffic offenses); Opinion of the Justices, 69 So.3d 847 (Ala. 2011) (opinion sought concerning constitutionality of tax law change), The combination of judicial elections and the authority to deliver advisory opinions prior to the enactment of legislation places state judges more directly into the states' political processes.

b. Legislative Procedure

Most state constitutions contain detailed provisions regulating the structure and operations of state legislatures. Typical procedural limitations include: requirements that titles of legislative acts provide general notice of their contents; requirements that all bills be referred to committees; requirements that a bill be before the legislature for a certain number of days or read aloud a certain number of times before the legislature may act on it; restrictions on the alteration of a bill during the process of legislative consideration; prohibitions on an act containing more than a single subject; limitations on the methods of amending existing statutes; and limitations on the enactment of special laws. *See* G. Alan Tarr, Understanding State Constitutions 16–17, 118–21 (Princeton Univ. Press 1998). These provisions have no parallel in the federal constitution, which simply designates the presiding officers of the houses of Congress, requires that a journal be kept, and provides that each house "may determine the rules of its proceedings." U.S. Const., art. I, § 5.

We will consider the ban on special legislation, and, especially, its implications for state-local relations in Chapter IV. For now it is worth noting that the central theme of many of these state constitutional provisions is the promotion of an orderly and deliberative legislative process, with greater accountability to the public for legislative actions. The single-subject requirement, for example, reflects a desire to prevent logrolling—or the practice of aggregating legislative proposals no one of which would command a legislative majority in order to create a majority that would vote for the entire bill—as well as to make it more difficult to package a less popular proposal with a more popular one, and thus, effectively, enact the former on the strength of the latter. *See* Millard H. Ruud, "No Law Shall Embrace More than One Subject," 42 Minn. L. Rev. 389 (1958). *See also* Martha Dragich, State Constitutional Restrictions on Legislative Procedure: Rethinking the Analysis of Original Purpose, Single Subject, and Clear Title Challenges, 38 Harv. J. Legis. 103 (2001). State courts, however, have varied considerably in their willingness to enforce the constitutional rules affecting legislative procedure, with many presuming that final legislative action complies with constitutional requisites. *See, e.g.,* Robert F. Williams, State Constitutional Limits on Legislative Procedure: Legislative Compliance and Judicial Enforcement, 17 Publius: The Journal of Federalism 91 (1987). The single-subject rule has been particularly difficult to enforce given the difficulty of determining what exactly is a "subject." As Professor Gillette has observed, "[t]he question of what qualifies as a single subject has generated all the mischief that one would anticipate from such a vague standard." Clayton P. Gillette, Expropriation and Institutional Design in State and Local Government Law, 80 Va. L. Rev. 625, 657 (1994). State courts have enforced the single subject rule against laws that combine multiple, tenuously related subjects. *See, e.g.,* Thompson v. State, 708 So.2d 315 (Fla.App.1998); People v. Cervantes, 723 N.E.2d 265 (Ill.1999); State v. Mabry, 460 N.W.2d 472 (Iowa 1990); Porten Sullivan Corp. v. State, 568 A.2d 1111 (Md.1990); Simmons-Harris v. Goff, 711 N.E.2d 203 (Ohio 1999). But a court may pull back when invalidating a statute on single-subject grounds appears particularly disruptive. *See, e.g.,* Arangold Corp. v. Zehnder, 718 N.E.2d 191 (Ill. 1999).

c. Legislative Term Limits

Although the federal constitution limits the number of terms a president may serve, there are no term limits for members of Congress. Fifteen states, however, limit the number of terms state legislators can serve. Legislative term limits are a comparatively recent development in state constitutional law. The first limits were adopted by voter initiatives in 1990 in California, Colorado, and Oklahoma. *See, e.g.*, Legislature of the State of California v. Eu, 816 P.2d 1309 (Cal.1991) (rejecting federal constitutional challenges to California's term limits). *See also* Massey v. Secretary of State, 579 N.W.2d 862 (Mich. 1998) (upholding Michigan term limits). Over the next decade, a total of 21 states adopted legislative term limits, but in four states they were thrown out by the state supreme courts, *see, e.g.,* League of Women Voters v. Secretary of the Commonwealth, 681 N.E.2d 842 (Mass. 1997) (finding that the voter initiative may not be used to alter the qualifications for holding state office), and in two states in which limits were adopted by legislation they were subsequently repealed. No new states have adopted term limits since 2000, although states with term limits have modified them. *See* National Conference of State Legislatures, Term Limits: An Overview. [1] Term limits vary between six and twelve years, and also differ with respect to whether the limits are on consecutive terms or on lifetime service. Term limits have had a particular effect on legislative leadership. In states without term limits, leaders often serve for fifteen, twenty, or more years. In term-limited legislatures, members become leaders earlier in their careers and leadership changes more frequently. For an assessment of the impact of term limits on state governments, *see* Karl T. Kurtz, Bruce Cain, and Richard Niemi (eds.) Institutional Change in American Politics: The Case of Term Limits (U. Mich. Press 2007).

d. Plural Executive

The federal constitution creates only two executive branch officers—the president and the vice president. In contrast, most states provide for numerous independently elected state officials, many of whom exercise executive functions independently of the governor. In all but seven states, for example, the voters elect the attorney general, and in two of the other states, the attorney general is selected by an institution other than the governor. (The attorney general is elected by the state legislature in Maine, and appointed by the judges of the state supreme court in Tennessee.) The governor and attorney general, who may be of different parties, may clash over questions of legal policy. Twice in 2003 state supreme courts were forced to address conflicts between an attorney general and another top state executive official over legislative reapportionment. In Perdue v. Baker, 586 S.E.2d 606 (Ga. 2003), the Georgia Supreme Court held that the state attorney general had the authority to appeal to the United States Supreme Court a decision of a lower federal court invalidating a state redistricting plan even though the state's governor had ordered the attorney general not to appeal. The court

---

[1] A state's effort to limit the number of terms the members of Congress elected from that state may serve was held unconstitutional in U.S. Term Limits, Inc. v. Thornton, 514 U.S. 779 (1995).

refused to extend that holding several years later, when it reached the opposite result in In the Interest of I.S., 607 S.E.2d 546 (Ga. 2005), on the grounds that the issue in the case was not "of significant public concern." Colorado also allowed the attorney general to file suit against the governor's wishes. In People ex rel. Salazar v. Davidson, 79 P.3d 1221 (Colo. 2003), the Colorado Supreme Court held that the state attorney general had the authority to sue the state's secretary of state to block implementation of a congressional redistricting plan that the governor had just signed into law. Indeed, the Colorado Supreme Court agreed with the attorney general on the merits and struck down the plan. In addition to the independent attorney general, forty-one states have an independently elected treasurer or comptroller. Other officials who in some states are elected independently include the secretary of state, the commissioner of education, the commissioner of insurance, and the commissioner of agriculture. For assessments of the states' experience with the plural executive, see William P. Marshall, Break Up the Presidency? Governors, State Attorneys General, and Lessons From the Divided Executive, 115 Yale L.J. 2446 (2006); Vikram David Amar, Lessons From California's Recent Experience With Its Non-Unitary (Divided) Executive: Of Mayors, Governors, Controllers, and Attorneys General, 59 Emory L.J. 469 (2009).

e.   Item Veto

The federal constitution enables the president to veto proposed legislation, but the president must veto an entire bill if he is to veto it at all. By contrast, 43 states allow the governor to veto "items" or "parts" of bills, although in every state but one that provides for this power the item veto is limited to appropriation bills. The item veto has given rise to considerable dispute over what constitutes an "item," and, to a lesser degree, over what constitutes an appropriation bill. In one, admittedly extreme, case, the Wisconsin Supreme Court held that the governor could veto individual letters from words and individual digits from numbers so long as "what remains after the veto [is] a complete and workable law" and the result is "germane" to the bill originally passed by the legislature. State ex rel. Wisconsin Senate v. Thompson, 424 N.W.2d 385 (Wis. 1988). A subsequently enacted constitutional amendment prohibited the governor from vetoing individual letters from words but left in place the power to veto individual numbers. In the spring of 2008, Wisconsin amended its item veto provision once again, this time to provide that the governor may not use his veto pen to "create a new sentence by combining parts of two or more sentences" of the bill sent to him by the legislature.

The item veto reflects three basic policies of state constitutional law: "the rejection of legislative logrolling; the imposition of fiscal restrictions on the legislature; and the strengthening of the governor's role in budgetary matters." Richard Briffault, The Item Veto in State Courts, 66 Temple L. Rev. 1171, 1177 (1993). Congress's attempt to give the president item veto power through federal legislation rather than a constitutional amendment was invalidated by the Supreme Court in Clinton v. City of New York, 524 U.S. 417 (1998).

f.   Direct Democracy

The federal government is representative in form: the people elect representatives who then do the governing. Apart from voting for candidates, citizens have no direct role in the ongoing processes of government.

Most state constitutions, however, provide for some direct role for the people in governing. In every state but one (Delaware), popular approval in a referendum is necessary to ratify changes to the constitution. Many state constitutions condition the issuance of state or local debt on voter approval. (The rules governing state and local debt are considered in Chapter VI.) Twenty-one states also permit voter-initiated referenda on new legislation: if a petition initiating a referendum obtains the requisite number of signatures, the effectiveness of the legislation that is the subject of the petition is blocked until the matter is submitted to the voters for their consideration. Most importantly, sixteen states provide for direct voter initiation of amendments to the state constitution, with two other states providing for voter initiation of amendments for legislative consideration ("indirect initiative"). Twenty-two states authorize direct or indirect voter initiation of legislation. In addition, twenty states authorize citizens to initiate the recall of state elected officials prior to the expiration of their terms, and many more allow recall of local government officials. People all over the world became more aware of state recall provisions in October 2003 when the voters of California used the recall to remove Governor Gray Davis from office and to elect in his place Arnold Schwarzenegger.

Direct democracy, particularly voter-initiated legislation and constitutional amendments, has had an enormous impact on the states that provide for it. Although provisions for the voter initiative date back to the early years of the twentieth century, the initiative did not start to become significant until the late 1970s. Today, in states like California, Colorado, Washington, and Oregon it is a central part of the political process. The voter initiative played a critical role in the adoption and spread of legislative term limits and in the imposition of limits on state and local taxation and spending, as we will see in Chapter VI. Voter initiatives have also focused on other aspects of the political process, such as reapportionment and campaign finance reform. Moreover,

> [i]n recent years, the focus of constitutional initiatives in several
> states has shifted from questions of governmental structure,

responsiveness, and expense to questions of substantive policy. Highly contentious economic and social issues avoided by legislatures have come to dominate the agenda, exacerbating splits among the populace. Thus Florida has had initiatives in tort liability, gambling, the rights of gays, and the creation of an official language; Colorado on the rights of gays and parental rights; and California on affirmative action and the rights of immigrants.

Tarr, Understanding State Constitutions, *supra*, at 160–61.

Direct democracy, particularly the voter initiative, has proven highly controversial. Advocates argue that direct democracy enables the voters to break through partisan and special interest group domination of legislatures and can lead to the adoption of measures that promote the public interest and that reflect the interests and views of state voters. Moreover, by giving citizens the opportunity to participate in self-governance, direct democracy, proponents contend, can reduce voter malaise and energize the electorate. Critics argue that direct democracy results in inferior legislation since it eliminates legislative expertise, provides no opportunity for revision of initiative proposals once they have been put before the voters, and fragments the legislative process into separate consideration of different proposals which may have interlinked effects. They assert that direct democracy is actually less democratic than representative democracy since voter turnout in ballot proposition elections tends to be lower than turnout for the election of representatives, with the resulting electorate skewed in favor of better educated and higher income voters. They also contend that by eliminating the possibility for deliberation and compromise within the legislature direct democracy especially burdens minorities. Moreover, the growing cost of ballot proposition campaigns and the increasing participation of well-funded special interests in initiative elections has arguably diminished the ability of the initiative to advance public-regarding measures. For reviews of the arguments concerning direct democracy and consideration of its effects on state government, *see* David B. Magleby, Direct Legislation: Voting on Ballot Propositions in the United States (Johns Hopkins Univ. Press 1984); Thomas E. Cronin, Direct Democracy: The Politics of Initiative, Referendum, and Recall (Harvard Univ. Press 1989); Elisabeth R. Gerber, The Populist Paradox: Interest Group Influence and the Promise of Direct Legislation (Princeton Univ. Press 1999); Sherman J. Clark, A Populist Critique of Direct Democracy, 112 Harv. L. Rev. 434 (1998); Hans A. Linde, Taking Oregon's Initiative Toward a New Century, 34 Willamette L. Rev. 391 (1998); Dale A. Oesterle, The South Dakota Referendum on Abortion: Lessons from a Popular Vote on a Controversial Right, 116 Yale L.J. Pocket Part 122 (2006); Craig M. Burnett, Elizabeth Garrett, and Matthew D. McCubbins,

The Dilemma of Direct Democracy, 9 Elec. L.J. 305 (2010); Peter Conti-Brown, Direct Democracy and State Fiscal Crises: The Problem of Too Much Law, 7 Duke J. Const. L. & Pub. Pol'y 43 (2012); Symposium, A More Perfect Union? Democracy in the Age of Ballot Initiatives, 97 Minn. L. Rev. 1549 (2013). *See also* Peter Schrag, Paradise Lost: California's Experience, America's Future 129–255 (New Press 1998) (contending that many of California's problems are connected to the significant use of initiatives in making public policy in that state).

g.   Fundamental Rights

All state constitutions contain provisions declaring and protecting fundamental rights. Some of these provisions are similar, if not virtually identical to, the Bill of Rights and other fundamental rights provisions of the federal constitution. Nevertheless, differences in textual detail, state history and tradition, or a state court's constitutional doctrines can result in a state court giving a more expansive interpretation to a state constitutional provision concerning free speech, criminal procedure, or equal protection than the federal courts have given to the provision's federal analogue. United States Supreme Court Justice William Brennan famously urged state courts to use their constitutions to enhance civil liberties and to go beyond the Supreme Court's protection of individual rights. *See* William J. Brennan, State Constitutions and the Protection of Individual Rights, 90 Harv. L. Rev. 489 (1977). Brennan's call for an activist state judicial vindication of individual rights appears to have had some success. One survey of state constitutional law found that whereas in 1950–69, state judges relied on their constitutions to provide greater protection of individual rights than that afforded under federal guarantees in only 10 cases, more than 300 such decisions were handed down between 1970 and 1986. *See* G. Alan Tarr, The New Judicial Federalism in Perspective, 72 Notre Dame L. Rev. 1097, 1112 (1997). The appropriate role of state supreme courts and the civil rights and civil liberties provisions of state constitutions in the protection of individual rights remains controversial. *Compare* James Gardner, The Failed Discourse of State Constitutionalism, 90 Mich. L. Rev. 761 (1992) (criticizing the legitimacy of an autonomous state constitutionalism) *with* Paul W. Kahn, Interpretation and Authority in State Constitutionalism, 106 Harv. L. Rev. 1147 (1993) (calling for a "vigorous state constitutionalism" in which state courts are actively involved in the "ongoing debate about the meaning of the rule of law in a democratic political order").

In addition to the civil rights and civil liberties provisions that parallel those in the federal constitution, some state constitutions have fundamental rights protections that lack a counterpart in the federal document. Thus, some state constitutions ban gender discrimination, establish a right of privacy, provide for a right to open government, guarantee open access to the courts, create a right to environmental quality, or declare the rights of victims of crimes. In 2013, a plurality of the Pennsylvania Supreme Court relied on the "environmental rights amendment" of that state's constitution—which creates a right to clean air, pure water and the preservation of certain environmental values, and imposes a duty on the state to conserve and maintain public natural resources for the benefit of future generations—in striking down state laws that preempted local legislation in order to promote fracking for shale gas. *See* Robinson Township v. Commonwealth, 83 A.3d 901 (Pa. 2013). The state-local conflict over fracking regulation is addressed in Chapter IV.

h.   Substantive Programs and Policies

Perhaps the most striking distinction between the federal and state constitutions is the inclusion of multiple substantive programs and policy measures in many state constitutions. Unlike the federal constitution, all state constitutions give detailed attention to government finance by imposing detailed rules and procedures concerning state and local borrowing, taxing, and spending. (We shall consider these in Chapter VI.) Every state constitution also contains an education article that requires the state to establish a system of free public schools. These have become the basis for litigation in many states challenging the constitutionality of the state's school financing scheme. (We shall consider the state education articles and the school finance reform litigations in Chapter V.)

Less widespread, many state constitutions also contain provisions concerning poverty, shelter and income assistance to the needy. Article XVII of the New York Constitution, for example, provides that "aid, care and support of the needy are public concerns and shall be provided by the state and by such of its subdivisions, and in such manner and by such means, as the legislature may from time to time determine." Although the provision was adopted, in part, to overcome doubts concerning the authority of the legislature to spend money on social welfare programs, and although the provision gives the legislature considerable discretion concerning the amount of aid and the definition of the needy, New York's highest court has held that the state constitution "unequivocally prevents the Legislature from simply refusing to aid those whom it has classified as needy." Tucker v. Toia, 371 N.E.2d 449, 452 (N.Y. 1977). Similarly, the Montana constitution states that the "legislature shall provide for such economic assistance and social and rehabilitative services as may be necessary for those inhabitants who, by reasons of age, infirmities, or misfortune may have need for the aid of society." The Montana Supreme Court relied on that provision to invalidate a state law eliminating general assistance payments to able-bodied childless adults. *See* Butte Community Union v. Lewis, 712 P.2d 1309 (Mont.1986).

Other policy areas addressed in state constitutions include: the regulation of business corporations; environmental preservation and the regulation of natural resources; the provision of civil service protections for state and local employees (the implications of civil service provisions for the privatization of state and local service delivery are considered in Chapter VII); civil litigation and tort reform; and lotteries and casino gambling. Each of these provisions operates to mandate or preclude substantive government regulatory or service-delivery programs by taking at least some basic decisions concerning these programs out of the domain of the legislature and placing them in the state constitution.

CHAPTER II

LOCAL GOVERNMENT IN THE AMERICAN CONSTITUTIONAL ORDER

■ ■ ■

The states are fundamental elements of the American constitutional system. The Constitution protects the territorial integrity of the states, and it requires the federal government to guarantee the states a republican form of government and protect them from invasion and domestic violence. The federal government is constituted out of the states, with Senators elected from the states, members of the House of Representatives elected from districts drawn within the states, and the President chosen by an Electoral College composed of electors selected by the states. Amending the Constitution requires the participation of the states through the ratification process. Most importantly, the Constitution treats the states as autonomous actors, with inherent law-making authority, and not as agents of the national government. The constitutional status of local governments is far more uncertain. The Constitution is utterly silent on the subject of local government. It gives local units no role in the national government, and says nothing about their powers or their relationship to the states. Formally, at least, the United States is a two-tier federal-state system rather than a three-tier federal-state-local system. Yet, as we have noted in Chapter I, by providing most public services, engaging in substantial amounts of regulation, and affording significant opportunities for grass-roots political participation, local governments have long played an important part in American governance. The tension between the Constitution's formal silence and local government's de facto significance structures federal judicial consideration of the legal status of local governments.

As you will see in this Chapter, three strands run through the federal courts' consideration of the place of local governments in our constitutional order.

The first treats local governments as state instrumentalities. As mere agents of the states, localities have no federal constitutional rights against their states. So, too, people have no federal constitutional right to local self-government. Instead, the states have plenary powers with respect to the organization and power of local units. This state-centered approach is the dominant conception of local government under our federal constitutional system, but it has been challenged by an alternative, more locally oriented vision.

The second major approach combines attention to the de facto autonomy local governments actually enjoy in practice with a normative commitment to the belief that local self-governance plays an important role in our democratic political system. Although nominally creatures of the state, local governments are polities that enable communities of local people to articulate and implement a local vision of the public interest. This approach has been particularly important in cases involving voting rights in local elections. If a local government is merely an agent of the state, then voting in local elections should have little constitutional significance. The vision of local government as an autonomous, democratic polity, however, has led the Supreme Court to emphasize the importance of democratic voting rules—universal suffrage and equally weighted votes—in local elections. This more localist orientation has also been found in other cases which have implicitly relied on the constitutional value of local autonomy to distinguish local government action from state action and to sustain the authority of local governments to promote local values. In these cases, the local government is less an agent of the state and more an extension of the people who constitute the local community.

The third strand treats local government as a quasi-proprietary firm, akin to a business corporation. This approach has deep historical roots and a growing contemporary significance. Like the democratic model, the quasi-proprietary theme assumes that local governments act on behalf of local constituents rather than the state. But the quasi-proprietary model assumes a different vision of local constituents and local interests. Local constituents are seen more as consumers or investors than as members of a democratic community, and local services are treated as relatively private—providing distinct benefits to particular local taxpaying constituents—rather than broadly public. As a matter of federal constitutional doctrine, this approach, like the democratic model, has also been particularly important in cases involving the vote in local elections. It is probably not surprising that voting rights cases are a critical focus for the conflict over the constitutional status of local governments, since the question of who may vote in local elections is inevitably intertwined with the issue of who controls local governments and determines the interests they advance. Although the Supreme Court has held that the one person, one vote doctrine applies to local elections, the Court has carved out a significant exception that encompasses many special district elections. Coupled with the expanding role of special districts in providing local services (*see* the discussions in Chapter III and Chapter V), the exemption of many special districts from democratic voting rules raises important questions of political accountability at the local level.

As you read this Chapter, consider the difficulty the courts have had in situating local governments in our constitutional order. How have the many roles that local governments play and the enormous variety in their population, territorial scope, legal powers and governmental function complicated the ability of courts to determine the constitutional status of local governments? Does any one of these models provide the best way for thinking about local government? Or does each get at a truth about the role of local government in our system—that local governments can be simultaneously agents of the state, local democratic polities, and local service providers for local constituents?

A. LOCAL GOVERNMENT AS AGENT OF THE STATE

HUNTER v. CITY OF PITTSBURGH

Supreme Court of the United States
207 U.S. 161 (1907)

MR. JUSTICE MOODY * * * delivered the opinion of the court:

The plaintiffs in error seek a reversal of the judgment of the supreme court of Pennsylvania, which affirmed a decree of a lower court, directing the consolidation of the cities of Pittsburgh and Allegheny. This decree was entered by authority of an act of the general assembly of that state, after proceedings taken in conformity with its requirements. The act authorized the consolidation of two cities, situated with reference to each other as Pittsburgh and Allegheny are, if, upon an election, the majority of the votes cast in the territory comprised within the limits of both cities favor the consolidation, even though, as happened in this instance, a majority of the votes cast in one of the cities oppose it. * * * This procedure was followed by the filing of a petition by the city of Pittsburgh; by an election, in which the majority of all the votes cast were in the affirmative, although the majority of all the votes cast by the voters of Allegheny were in the negative; and by a decree of the court, uniting the two cities. * * *

[T]he plaintiffs in error, who were citizens, voters, owners of property, and taxpayers in Allegheny, * * * claimed that the act of assembly was in violation of the Constitution of the United States. * * *

There were two claims of rights under the Constitution of the United States which were clearly made in the court below and as clearly denied. They appear in the second and fourth assignments of error. Briefly stated, the assertion in the second assignment of error is that the act of assembly impairs the obligation of a contract existing between the city of Allegheny and the plaintiffs in error, that the latter are to be taxed only for the governmental purposes of that city, and that the legislative attempt to subject them to the taxes of the enlarged city violates article 1, § 9, ¶ 10, of the Constitution of the United States.[1] This assignment does not rest upon the theory that the charter of the city is a contract with the state, a proposition frequently denied by this and other courts. It rests upon the novel proposition that there is a contract between the citizens and taxpayers of a municipal corporation and the corporation itself, that the citizens and taxpayers shall be taxed only for the uses of that corporation, and shall not be taxed for the uses of any like corporation with which it may be consolidated. It is not said that the city of Allegheny expressly made any such extraordinary contract, but only that the contract arises out of the relation of the parties to each other. It is difficult to deal with a proposition of this kind except by saying that it is not true. No authority or reason in support of it has been offered to us, and it is utterly inconsistent with the nature of municipal corporations, the purposes for which they are created, and the relation they bear to those who dwell and own property within their limits. This assignment of error is overruled.

Briefly stated, the assertion in the fourth assignment of error is that the act of assembly deprives the plaintiffs in error of their property without due process of law, by subjecting it to the burden of the additional taxation which would result from the consolidation. The manner in which the right of due process of law has been violated, as set forth in the first assignment of error and insisted upon in argument, is that the method of voting on the consolidation prescribed in the act has permitted the voters of the larger city to overpower the voters of the smaller city, and compel the union without their consent and against their protest. The precise question thus presented has not been determined by this court * * * although its solution by principles long settled and constantly acted upon is not difficult. This court has many times had occasion to consider and decide the nature of municipal corporations, their rights and duties, and the rights of their citizens and creditors. [citations omitted] We think the following principles have been established by them and have become settled doctrines of this court, to be acted upon wherever they are applicable. Municipal corporations are political subdivisions of the state, created as convenient agencies for exercising such of the governmental powers of the state as may be intrusted to them. For the purpose of executing these powers properly and efficiently they usually are given the power to acquire, hold, and manage personal and real property. The number, nature, and duration of the powers conferred upon these corporations and the territory over which they shall be exercised rests in the absolute discretion of the state. Neither their charters, nor any law conferring governmental powers, or vesting in them property to be used for governmental purposes, or authorizing them to hold or manage such

---

[1] [Editors' Note: The Court is presumably referring to Article 1, § 10, ¶ 1 of the Constitution, which provides that "No State shall . . . pass any . . . Law impairing the Obligation of Contracts." There is no article 1, § 9, ¶ 10 in the United States Constitution.]

property, or exempting them from taxation upon it, constitutes a contract with the state within the meaning of the Federal Constitution. The state, therefore, at its pleasure, may modify or withdraw all such powers, may take without compensation such property, hold it itself, or vest it in other agencies, expand or contract the territorial area, unite the whole or a part of it with another municipality, repeal the charter and destroy the corporation. All this may be done, conditionally or unconditionally, with or without the consent of the citizens, or even against their protest. In all these respects the state is supreme, and its legislative body, conforming its action to the state Constitution, may do as it will, unrestrained by any provision of the Constitution of the United States. Although the inhabitants and property owners may, by such changes, suffer inconvenience, and their property may be lessened in value by the burden of increased taxation, or for any other reason, they have no right, by contract or otherwise, in the unaltered or continued existence of the corporation or its powers, and there is nothing in the Federal Constitution which protects them from these injurious consequences. The power is in the state, and those who legislate for the state are alone responsible for any unjust or oppressive exercise of it.

* * * It will be observed that, in describing the absolute power of the state over the property of municipal corporations, we have not extended it beyond the property held and used for governmental purposes. Such corporations are sometimes authorized to hold and do hold property for the same purposes that property is held by private corporations or individuals. The distinction between property owned by municipal corporations in their public and governmental capacity and that owned by them in their private capacity, though difficult to define, has been approved by many of the state courts * * * and it has been held that, as to the latter class of property, the legislature is not omnipotent. If the distinction is recognized it suggests the question whether property of a municipal corporation owned in its private and proprietary capacity may be taken from it against its will and without compensation. Counsel for plaintiffs in error assert that the city of Allegheny was the owner of property held in its private and proprietary capacity, and insist that the effect of the proceedings under this act was to take its property without compensation and vest it in another corporation, and that thereby the city was deprived of its property without due process of law, in violation of the 14th Amendment. But no such question is presented by the record, and there is but a vague suggestion of facts upon which it might have been founded. * * * The question is entirely outside of the record and has no connection with any question which is raised in the record.

The judgment is affirmed.

NOTES AND QUESTIONS

1. *The Consolidation of Allegheny and Pittsburgh.* In the 1900 census, Pittsburgh, with 322,000 people, had well over twice the population of Allegheny, which had just 133,000 people. Allegheny, however, had a more advanced physical infrastructure. According to the complaint in the case, Allegheny had "improved its streets, established its own system of electric lighting; and . . . established a satisfactory water supply" while Pittsburgh was "largely in debt" and was contemplating major new capital investments to improve its water supply and provide electric lighting. Plaintiffs described Pittsburgh's plans for "the further expenditure of various sums of money for the acquirement of advantages and property which the citizens of Allegheny now practically own and enjoy but which the citizens of Pittsburgh do not, and to acquire which would largely increase the indebtedness of the city of Pittsburgh." Moreover, they asserted, "if the city of Allegheny should be annexed to the city of Pittsburgh, the taxpayers of Allegheny . . . who now own and possess these advantages and privileges" would have to pay higher taxes "without any material benefit to them whatever."

2. *Hunter and Municipal Consolidation.* In *Hunter* the state authorized the consolidation of two municipalities on the affirmative vote of a majority of the voters of the two cities taken together, without requiring the separate approval of the voters of each city. Could a state make consolidation contingent on the approval of separate majorities of voters in each of the cities? *Cf.* Town of Lockport v. Citizens for Community Action, 430 U.S. 259 (1977) (upholding state requirement that change in county charter requires the approval of separate majorities of city and noncity residents). Could a state dispense with any local vote at all? *See, e.g.*, Carlyn v. City of Akron, 726 F.2d 287 (6th Cir.1984); Berry v. Bourne, 588 F.2d 422 (4th Cir.1978). For a discussion of how *Hunter* continues to frame judicial treatment of challenges to state laws affecting local government formation and boundary changes, *see* City of Herriman v. Bell, 590 F.3d 1176 (10th Cir. 2010). These issues are discussed in greater detail in Chapter III.

3. *What Contract?* The Allegheny residents argued that the consolidation of their city with Pittsburgh violated the Contracts Clause. But what contract did they claim the state law impaired? It was not the charter issued by the state that incorporated the city, but, rather, a metaphoric contract between Allegheny and its taxpayers that the latter will only be taxed for the purposes of Allegheny. Why didn't they argue that consolidation would unconstitutionally "impair" the contract between Pennsylvania and Allegheny embodied in the city's corporate charter?

The answer to that question grows out of one of the earliest Supreme Court cases to address the legal status of local governments, the famous Dartmouth College Case, Trustees of Dartmouth College v. Woodward, 17 U.S. (4 Wheat.) 518 (1819). In *Dartmouth College*, the Supreme Court distinguished between a charter issued by a state to a private entity, which it held to be protected by the Contracts Clause from a subsequent state impairment, and a charter issued to a local government. According to Chief Justice Marshall, "the framers of the constitution did not intend to restrain the States in the regulation of their civil institutions, adopted for internal government." 17 U.S. at 629. Local governments are "instruments of government, created for its purposes." The power of state government to alter local governments is not affected by the presence of a charter. "The right to change them is not founded on their being incorporated, but on their being the instruments of government, created for its purposes. . . . The incorporating act neither gives nor prevents this control." *Id.* at 638.

4.   *Hunter and the Right to Local Self-Government. Hunter* was decided at a time when American scholars and judges were actively debating whether there is a constitutionally protected right to local self-government. The leading treatise on municipal corporations, authored by Judge John Dillon of the Iowa Supreme Court, prefigured *Hunter* in asserting that local governments are mere creatures of the states, entirely subject to state authority. J. Dillon, Treatise on the Law of Municipal Corporations (1st ed. 1872). By contrast, Judge Thomas Cooley of the Michigan Supreme Court, in an opinion that combined analysis of his state's constitution with a consideration of "the historical facts regarding local government in America" and general considerations of political liberty found that some form of local autonomy was protected by the Michigan constitution: "The state may mould local institutions according to its views of policy and expediency; but local government is a matter of absolute right; and the state cannot take it away." People ex rel. Le Roy v. Hurlbut, 24 Mich. 44 (1871). Other scholars, noting that in many of the early colonies and along the frontier, local governments were organized by settlers acting independently of colonial or territorial governments, argued that, descriptively at least, local governments were not simply creatures of the states but were institutions created by local people. *See, e.g.,* Amasa Eaton, The Right to Local Self-Government (pts 1–3), 13 Harv.L.Rev. 441, 570, 638 (1900); (pts 4–5), 14 Harv.L.Rev. 20, 116 (1900); Eugene McQuillin, The Law of Municipal Corporations (1st ed. 1911).

Hunter came down on the Dillon side of the debate with respect to federal constitutional law, effectively eliminating the idea that there is a federal constitutionally protected right to local self-government, and treating questions of local governance as matters for state determination. *Hunter* does not address state constitutional law, but the case appears to have affected the thinking of most state courts as well. For a review of the history of this debate, *see* Gerald E. Frug, The City as a Legal Concept, 93 Harv.L.Rev. 1057, 1109–1117 (1980). For an assessment of Judge Cooley's theory of local government, *see* David J. Barron, The Promise of Cooley's City: Traces of Local Constitutionalism, 147 U.Pa.L.Rev. 487 (1999). The right to local self-government concept in state constitutional law is discussed in Chapter IV.

More than a century after it was decided, *Hunter* continues to be the subject of scholarly debate. For a critical treatment of *Hunter*'s failure to recognize that localities are not simply instrumentalities of their states but "also act as units of representative democracy," *see* Kathleen S. Morris, The

Case for Local Constitutional Enforcement, 47 Harv. Civ. Rts-Civ. Lib. L. Rev. 1 (2012). Morris points out that "today, most state constitutions delegate to localities considerable authority to determine their own powers and functions," *id.* at 31, but, she contends, "*Hunter* has contributed powerfully to a national political and legal culture that devalues and underutilizes local public entities." *Id.* at 35. For a pragmatic defense of *Hunter* as appropriately "maintaining state flexibility over the powers and contours of its municipalities," *see* Josh Bendor, Municipal Constitutional Rights: A New Approach, 31 Yale L. & Pol'y Rev. 389, 396 (2013). Bendor's argument is that "[a]s demography, the economy, and technology change, the state might sensibly want to change the powers or boundaries of its municipalities. If municipal powers or boundaries are constitutionally cognizable contracts or property, state flexibility is inhibited. *Hunter* prevents such powers and boundaries from being set in stone by the Constitution." *Id.* at 412. Bendor, however, finds *Hunter* to be overly broad and would allow municipalities to assert constitutional claims when that would not affect "state policy flexibility." *See id.* at 424–27.

5.   *Hunter and Plenary State Power.* The Supreme Court applied *Hunter*'s principle of plenary state power in City of Trenton v. State of New Jersey, 262 U.S. 182 (1923). New Jersey had granted a private company a franchise to take water from the Delaware River without limit and without having to pay a fee. The private company subsequently sold that right to the City of Trenton. Thereafter, the state imposed a fee on the city's use of the water. The Court determined that even if the private water works company had a Contracts Clause or Due Process Clause claim against the state with respect to the fee, the municipality could have no such claim: "The power of the State, unrestrained by the contract clause or the Fourteenth Amendment over the rights and property of cities held and used for 'governmental purposes' cannot be questioned." *Id.* at 188. A few years later, in Williams v. Mayor & City Council of Baltimore, 289 U.S. 36 (1933), the Court held that local governments could not mount a Fourteenth Amendment challenge to a state law exempting a specific railroad from local property taxes. Writing for a unanimous Court, Justice Cardozo brusquely ruled: "A municipal corporation, created by a state for the better ordering of government, had no privileges or immunities under the federal constitution which it may invoke in opposition to the will of its creator." *Id.* at 40. Ysura v. Pocatello Education Ass'n, 555 U.S. 353 (2009) provides a more recent example of the continuing influence of *Hunter*'s vision of local governments as essentially arms of their states. *Ysura* addressed a First Amendment suit against an Idaho law that permitted public employees to elect to have a portion of their wages deducted by their employer to pay union dues but prohibited the use of payroll deductions for use by unions for political activities. The unions accepted the state's ability to adopt such a rule for its own employees but challenged the state's ability to impose the ban on the payroll systems of local governments. Although such state interference in the inner workings of a private corporation would raise a serious First Amendment question, the Court, in an opinion by Chief Justice Roberts, found the analogy to private corporations

"misguided." "A private corporation enjoys constitutional protections" but a locality "is a subordinate unit of government created by the State to carry out delegated governmental functions." The local payroll systems received no subsidy from the state and managed their own day-to-day operations independent of the state. But "[g]iven the relationship between the State and its political subdivisions . . . it is immaterial how the State allocates funding or management responsibilities between the different levels of government." *Id.* at 363–64. Justice Breyer, in a separate opinion concurring in part and dissenting in part, was troubled by the First Amendment implications of the state law, but agreed with the majority that municipalities are "ordinarily treat[ed] . . . as creatures of the state," *id.* at 365, so that the First Amendment outcome ought to be the same for both the state and its localities. Justice Souter, dissenting on other grounds, also agreed "that the lower echelons of Idaho government are creatures of the State exercising state power in discharging what are ultimately state responsibilities," *id.* at 376. Only Justice Stevens, who disagreed with the majority's First Amendment analysis, found any basis for treating local governments differently. As he observed, "[a]ll States do not treat their subdivisions the same, and those differences are sometimes consequential," *id.* at 374. The primary focus of Justice Stevens's dissent, however, was on what he concluded was the state's intent to make it more difficult for unions to finance political speech, not the constitutional status of the state-local relationship.

6.   *Hunter and Municipal "Private" Property.* The final paragraph of *Hunter* draws a distinction between property owned by a municipality in its "public and governmental" capacity—which is not protected by the Constitution from state taking—and property owned by a municipality in its "private and proprietary capacity," *id.* at 181, which may be so protected. This notion of municipal "private" property reflects the roots of American local government in the English municipal corporation. Growing out of a feudal society which drew "no sharp distinction" between public and private, English "corporate boroughs exercised both public and private powers." Joan Williams, The Invention of the Municipal Corporation: A Case Study in Legal Change, 34 Am.U.L.Rev. 369, 373 (1985). "At one extreme, the charter established a court structure and granted regulatory authority to the town officers. At the other extreme, boroughs performed roles that the law today considers 'private'," *id.* at 379, such as control over access to various trades and crafts, the operation of markets, and property-like ownership of real estate within the community. *See also* Jon C. Teaford, The Municipal Revolution in America: Origins of Modern Urban Government 1650–1825 (U. Chi. Press 1975) at 3–15. Hendrik Hartog's classic study, Public Property and Private Power: The Corporation of the City of New York in American Law, 1730–1870 (1983) describes the corporate origins of the City of New York and, especially, the colonial era city's use of its quasi-private powers over the lands it owned to shape the city's development.

After the American Revolution and, especially, in the first half of the nineteenth century, courts increasingly emphasized the public aspect of local governments and de-emphasized their quasi-private side. One consequence of this, as *Dartmouth College* suggests, was to strengthen the legal position of state governments, as the hierarchically superior public entities, relative to their local governments. Nevertheless, as *Hunter* indicates, courts continued to find that local governments have a private aspect, too. Thus, in a late nineteenth century case that appears to have directly influenced *Hunter*'s final paragraph, the Massachusetts Supreme Judicial Court held that the state could not force the City of Boston to transfer title to a cemetery without compensation since the city held the property in a proprietary capacity:

> The city of Boston is possessed of much ... property which ... is held for the benefit of the public, but in other respects is held more like the property of a private corporation.... [T]he city has not acted strictly as an agent of the state government ... but rather with special reference to the benefit of its own inhabitants.... [T]he cemetery falls within the class of property which the city owns in its private or proprietary character, as a private corporation might own it, and that its ownership is so protected under the [federal and state constitutions], so that the legislature has no power to require its transfer without compensation.

Proprietors of Mount Hope Cemetery v. City of Boston, 33 N.E. 695, 698 (1893).

Mount Hope implied that a broad range of Boston's property, including its system of waterworks, its parks, its market, its hospital, and its library, might be considered proprietary and thus protected by the federal and state constitutions from state interference. In the twentieth century, however, the notion of local "proprietary" property appeared to have narrowed in cases involving constitutional claims against the states. For example, as discussed in Note 5, the Supreme Court in Trenton v. New Jersey, *supra*, treated a municipal waterworks as governmental property. *See also* City of Cambridge v. Commissioner of Public Welfare, 257 N.E.2d 782 (1970) (city liens that supported claims under an old age assistance program are "governmental," not "proprietary," and, thus, not protected from elimination by state law); City of Worcester v. Commonwealth, 185 N.E.2d 633 (Mass.1962) (city denied compensation for school and park land taken for state highway purposes; property was "governmental" and not "proprietary"); City of New Rochelle v. State, 198 N.E.2d 41 (N.Y. 1964) (city denied compensation for sewage and drainage system property taken as part of construction of highway system; the property served a governmental function). *See generally* Sands & Libonati, Local Government Law § 3.15 (waterworks, parks, wharves, and ferry franchises treated as governmental property). The governmental/proprietary distinction continues to be significant in other areas, including local voting rights, considered later in this Chapter, and municipal tort liability, *see* Chapter VII. It is worth noting that the Supreme Court has held that the provision of the Takings Clause of the United States Constitution that requires the payment of just compensation when government takes "private property" for public use also applies when the federal government takes property owned by states or local governments. United States v. 50 Acres of Land, 469 U.S. 24, 31 (1984).

GOMILLION V. LIGHTFOOT
Supreme Court of the United States
364 U.S. 339 (1960)

MR. JUSTICE FRANKFURTER delivered the opinion of the Court.

This litigation challenges the validity, under the United States Constitution, of Local Act No. 140, passed by the Legislature of Alabama in 1957, redefining the boundaries of the City of Tuskegee. Petitioners, Negro citizens of Alabama who were, at the time of this redistricting measure, residents of the City of Tuskegee, * * * claim * * * that enforcement of the statute, which alters the shape of Tuskegee from a square to an uncouth twenty-eight-sided figure, will constitute a discrimination against them in violation of the Due Process and Equal Protection Clauses of the Fourteenth Amendment to the Constitution and will deny them the right to vote in defiance of the Fifteenth Amendment.

The respondents moved for dismissal of the action for failure to state a claim upon which relief could be granted and for lack of jurisdiction of the District Court. The court granted the motion, stating, "This Court has no control over, no supervision over, and no power to change any boundaries of municipal corporations fixed by a duly convened and elected legislative body, acting for the people in the State of Alabama." 167 F.Supp. 405, 410. On appeal, the Court of Appeals for the Fifth Circuit, affirmed the judgment, one judge dissenting. 270 F.2d 594. We brought the case here since serious questions were raised concerning the power of a State over its municipalities in relation to the Fourteenth and Fifteenth Amendments.

At this stage of the litigation we are not concerned with the truth of the allegations, that is, the ability of petitioners to sustain their allegations by proof. The sole question is whether the allegations entitle them to make good on their claim that they are being denied rights under the United States Constitution. The complaint, charging that Act 140 is a device to disenfranchise Negro citizens, alleges the following facts: Prior to Act 140 the City of Tuskegee was square in shape; the Act transformed it into a strangely irregular twenty-eight-sided figure as indicated in the diagram appended to this opinion. The essential inevitable effect of this redefinition of Tuskegee's boundaries is to remove from the city all save only four or five of its 400 Negro voters while not removing a single white voter or resident. The result of the Act is to deprive the Negro petitioners discriminatorily of the benefits of residence in Tuskegee, including, inter alia, the right to vote in municipal elections.

These allegations, if proven, would abundantly establish that Act 140 was not an ordinary geographic redistricting measure even within familiar abuses of gerrymandering. If these allegations upon a trial remained uncontradicted or unqualified, the conclusion would be irresistible, tantamount for all practical purposes to a mathematical demonstration, that the legislation is solely concerned with segregating white and colored voters by fencing Negro citizens out of town so as to deprive them of their pre-existing municipal vote.

* * * The respondents invoke generalities expressing the State's unrestricted power—unlimited, that is, by the United States Constitution—to establish, destroy, or reorganize by contraction or expansion its political subdivisions, to wit, cities, counties, and other local units. We freely recognize the breadth and importance of this aspect of the State's political power. To exalt this power into an absolute is to misconceive the reach and rule of this Court's decisions in the leading case of *Hunter v. Pittsburgh*, 207 U.S. 161, and related cases relied upon by respondents.

* * * [*Hunter* and the other] cases that have come before this Court regarding legislation by States dealing with their political subdivisions fall into two classes: (1) those in which it is claimed that the State, by virtue of the prohibition against impairment of the obligation of contract (Art. I, § 10) and of the Due Process Clause of the Fourteenth Amendment, is without power to extinguish, or alter the boundaries of, an existing municipality; and (2) in which it is claimed that the State has no power to change the identity of a municipality whereby citizens of a pre-existing municipality suffer serious economic disadvantage.

Neither of these claims is supported by such a specific limitation upon State power as confines the States under the Fifteenth Amendment. As to the first category, it is obvious that the creation of municipalities—clearly a political act—does not come within the conception of a contract under the *Dartmouth College* case. 4 Wheat. 518. As to the second, if one principle clearly emerges from the numerous decisions of this Court dealing with taxation it is that the Due Process Clause affords no immunity against mere inequalities in tax burdens, nor does it afford protection against their increase as an indirect consequence of a State's exercise of its political powers.

* * * [A] correct reading of the seemingly unconfined dicta of *Hunter* and kindred cases is not that the State has plenary power to manipulate in every conceivable way, for every conceivable purpose, the affairs of its municipal corporations, but rather that the State's authority is unrestrained by the particular prohibitions of the Constitution considered in those cases.

The *Hunter* opinion itself intimates that a state legislature may not be omnipotent even as to the disposition of some types of property owned by municipal corporations, 207 U.S., at 178–181. Further, other cases in this Court have refused to allow a State to abolish a municipality, or alter its boundaries, or merge it with another city, without preserving to the creditors of the old city some effective recourse for the collection of debts owed them. * * *

This line of authority conclusively shows that the Court has never acknowledged that the States have power to do as they will with municipal corporations regardless of consequences. Legislative control of municipalities, no less than other state power, lies within the scope of relevant limitations imposed by the United States Constitution. The observation in *Graham v. Folsom*, 200 U.S. 248, 253, becomes relevant: "The power of the State to alter or destroy its corporations is not greater than the power of the State to repeal its legislation." In that case, which involved the attempt by state officials to evade the collection of taxes to discharge the obligations of an extinguished township, Mr. Justice McKenna, writing for the Court, went on to point out, with reference to the *Mount Pleasant* and *Mobile* cases:

> "It was argued in those cases, as it is argued in this, that such alteration or destruction of the subordinate governmental divisions was a proper exercise of legislative power, to which creditors had to submit. The argument did not prevail. It was answered, as we now answer it, that such power, extensive though it is, is met and overcome by the provision of the Constitution of the United States which forbids a State from passing any law impairing the obligation of contracts * * * "

200 U.S., at 253–254.

If all this is so in regard to the constitutional protection of contracts, it should be equally true that, to paraphrase, such power, extensive though it is, is met and overcome by the Fifteenth Amendment to the Constitution of the United States, which forbids a State from passing any law which deprives a citizen of his vote because of his race. The opposite conclusion, urged upon us by respondents, would sanction the achievement by a State of any impairment of voting rights whatever so long as it was cloaked in the garb of the realignment of political subdivisions.

The respondents find another barrier to the trial of this case in *Colegrove v. Green*, 328 U.S. 549. In that case the Court passed on an Illinois law governing the arrangement of congressional districts within that State. The complaint rested upon the disparity of population between the different districts which rendered the effectiveness of each individual's vote in some districts far less than in others. This disparity came to pass solely through shifts in population between 1901, when Illinois organized its congressional districts, and 1946, when the complaint was lodged. During this entire period elections were held under the districting scheme devised in 1901. The Court affirmed the dismissal of the complaint on the ground that it presented a subject not meet for adjudication. The decisive facts in this case, which at this stage must be taken as proved, are wholly different from the considerations found controlling in *Colegrove*.

That case involved a complaint of discriminatory apportionment of congressional districts. The appellants in *Colegrove* complained only of a dilution of the strength of their votes as a result of legislative inaction over a course of many years. The petitioners here complain that affirmative legislative action deprives them of their votes and the consequent advantages that the ballot affords. When a legislature thus singles out a readily isolated segment of a racial minority for special discriminatory treatment, it violates the Fifteenth Amendment. In no case involving unequal weight in voting distribution that has come before the Court did the decision sanction a differentiation on racial lines whereby approval was given to unequivocal withdrawal of the vote solely from colored citizens. Apart from all else, these considerations lift this controversy out of the so-called "political" arena and into the conventional sphere of constitutional litigation.

* * * According to the allegations here made, the Alabama Legislature has not merely redrawn the Tuskegee city limits with incidental inconvenience to the petitioners; it is more accurate to say that it has deprived the petitioners of the municipal franchise and consequent rights and to that end it has incidentally changed the city's boundaries. While in form this is merely an act redefining metes and bounds, if the allegations are established, the inescapable human effect of this essay in geometry and geography is to despoil colored citizens, and only colored citizens, of their theretofore enjoyed voting rights. That was not *Colegrove v. Green*.

When a State exercises power wholly within the domain of state interest, it is insulated from federal judicial review. But such insulation is not carried over when state power is used as an instrument for circumventing a federally protected right * * *.

For these reasons, the principal conclusions of the District Court and the Court of Appeals are clearly erroneous and the decision below must be

Reversed.

MR. JUSTICE WHITTAKER, concurring.

I concur in the Court's judgment, but not in the whole of its opinion. It seems to me that the decision should be rested not on the Fifteenth

Amendment, but rather on the Equal Protection Clause of the Fourteenth Amendment to the Constitution. I am doubtful that the averments of the complaint, taken for present purposes to be true, show a purpose by Act No. 140 to abridge petitioners' "right * * * to vote," in the Fifteenth Amendment sense. It seems to me that the "right * * * to vote" that is guaranteed by the Fifteenth Amendment is but the same right to vote as is enjoyed by all others within the same election precinct, ward or other political division. And, inasmuch as no one has the right to vote in a political division, or in a local election concerning only an area in which he does not reside, it would seem to follow that one's right to vote in Division A is not abridged by a redistricting that places his residence in Division B if he there enjoys the same voting privileges as all others in that Division, even though the redistricting was done by the State for the purpose of placing a racial group of citizens in Division B rather than A.

But it does seem clear to me that accomplishment of a State's purpose—to use the Court's phrase—of "fencing Negro citizens out of" Division A and into Division B is an unlawful segregation of races of citizens, in violation of the Equal Protection Clause of the Fourteenth Amendment * * *; and, as stated, I would think the decision should be rested on that ground—which, incidentally, clearly would not involve, just as the cited cases did not involve, the *Colegrove* problem.

NOTES AND QUESTIONS

1.   *Tuskegee and the Gomillion Litigation.* Tuskegee, the seat of Macon County, Alabama had an unusually high percentage of African Americans registered to vote for a city in the deep South before the enactment of the 1965 Voting Rights Act. Tuskegee was the home of both the Tuskegee Institute (now Tuskegee University)—the center of higher education established for African Americans by Booker T. Washington in the nineteenth century— and of a hospital opened by the federal government in the 1920s for black veterans of World War I. Both institutions were staffed by African Americans and "provided a pool of educated, middle-class blacks who challenged political apartheid in later years." Jonathan L. Entin, Of Squares and Uncouth Twenty-Eight-Sided Figures: Reflections on *Gomillion v. Lightfoot* After Half a Century, 50 Washburn L.J. 133, 134–35 (2010). Charles G. Gomillion, the lead plaintiff, was a sociology professor at Tuskegee Institute. The expansions of the Institute and the VA hospital after World War II, combined with the growing civil rights movement, the persistent efforts of black Tuskegee residents to register to vote, litigation, and the support of one sympathetic white member of the Macon County Board of Registrars led to a significant increase in black voter registration in the late 1940s and early 1950s. *See id.* at 135–38. By 1955, blacks were forty percent of the city's electorate and one-third of the voters of Macon County, so that "they effectively could control the outcome of any election in which whites were divided." *Id.* at 138. At that point a white state senator from

Macon County moved the Tuskegee gerrymandering bill—which also managed to remove Tuskegee Institute from Tuskegee—through the legislature, which approved it unanimously and without debate in July 1957. *Id.* Although the *Gomillion* decision undid the gerrymander, considerable additional litigation was necessary before racially discriminatory local registration practices were ended. *See id.* at 141–43.

2. *What Constitutional Provision Was Violated?* Justice Frankfurter, in his opinion for the Court, concluded that as Act 140 effectively denied virtually all of Tuskegee's African-American residents the right to vote in Tuskegee elections, Alabama had violated the Fifteenth Amendment's prohibition on racial discrimination in voting. However, as Justice Whittaker correctly pointed out, the right to vote in a local election is normally a right of local residents. (The Supreme Court subsequently affirmed this connection between voting and residency in Holt Civic Club v. City of Tuscaloosa, 439 U.S. 60 (1978), discussed in Section B of this Chapter.) Due to Act 140, the plaintiffs were no longer residents of Tuskegee, thus they had no legal right to vote in Tuskegee elections. Moreover, nothing in Act 140 precluded the plaintiffs from incorporating a new municipality consisting of the areas that had been gerrymandered out of Tuskegee and then voting in the new locality's elections. Nor did Act 140 bar them from voting in the elections of Macon County, the county in which the areas detached from Tuskegee by Act 140 were located.

For Justice Whittaker, the constitutional vice of Act 140 was not that it denied black Tuskegeeans the right to vote because of their race in violation of the Fifteenth Amendment, but that it intentionally took the plaintiffs out of Tuskegee because of their race, thus violating the Fourteenth Amendment's ban on racial discrimination. *Gomillion* has frequently been cited in Fourteenth Amendment cases, leading Justice O'Connor to conclude in Shaw v. Reno, 509 U.S. 630, 645 (1993), that the Court has come to accept "the correctness of Justice Whittaker's view."

Justice Frankfurter may have sought to ground *Gomillion* in the Fifteenth Amendment in order to avoid creating a precedent for use of the Fourteenth Amendment in gerrymandering cases. Justice Frankfurter was the author of Colegrove v. Green, and as his effort to distinguish *Colegrove* in this case suggests, strongly opposed judicial review of legislative districting. Two years later, over Justice Frankfurter's strong dissent, the Supreme Court held that legislative districting was subject to judicial review under the Fourteenth Amendment. In so doing, the Court specifically invoked *Gomillion. See* Baker v. Carr, 369 U.S. 186, 229–31 (1962). Alternatively, Justice Frankfurter's focus on the Fifteenth Amendment may more accurately reflect what the case was really about—the racial struggle over political power in Tuskegee in the 1950s. Justice Whittaker may have been formally correct in linking the local vote to residency within the locality, and, thus focusing on the Fourteenth Amendment violation of a law that draws lines based on race. But Justice Frankfurter realistically recognized that Tuskegee's black residents continued to remain a part of Tuskegee, considered as an economic and social community, even after they had been excluded from its legal limits.

3. *State Power over Local Government Creation and the Establishment Clause.* In Board of Education of Kiryas Joel Village School Dist. v. Grumet, 512 U.S. 687 (1994), the Supreme Court found that the New York legislature's special creation of a school district for the specific benefit of the devoutly religious Satmar Hasidic Jewish community residing in the village of Kiryas Joel violated the Establishment Clause of the First Amendment. Children in the village were educated in parochial schools, but those schools did not provide special educational services to handicapped children. The handicapped children of Kiryas Joel were sent to public schools in the district that included the village (and many other communities) in order to receive special educational services, but their parents alleged that the children experienced fear and trauma in leaving their community and interacting with people whose ways were so different from theirs. New York responded by creating a new school district coterminous with the village of Kiryas Joel. The Supreme Court held that the act creating the district was "tantamount to an allocation of political power on a religious criterion." *Id.* at 690. Two subsequent efforts by the state legislature to facilitate the formation of a school district for Kiryas Joel were held unconstitutional by the New York Court of Appeals. *See* Grumet v. Cuomo, 681 N.E.2d 340 (N.Y.1997); Grumet v. Pataki, 720 N.E.2d 66 (N.Y.1999). It is worth noting that the Supreme Court distinguished between the formation of the Kiryas Joel school district and the preceding incorporation of the Village of Kiryas Joel. When the Satmars first settled in the area, it was an undeveloped subdivision of the town of Monroe. When a zoning dispute arose between the Satmar community and the town, the Satmars presented the town board with a petition to form a new village within the town, "a right that New York's Village Law gives almost any group of residents who satisfy certain procedural niceties." 512 U.S. at 2485. After extended negotiations the proposed boundaries were drawn so as to include "just the . . . acres owned and inhabited entirely by Satmars" and the village was then incorporated. *Id.* Despite the attention given to religious affiliation in the drawing of the new village's boundaries, the Court observed there was no constitutional issue because the process of incorporation involved only "the application of a neutral state law designed to give almost any group of residents the right to incorporate." *Id.* at 2491 n. 7. For further discussion, *see* Richard Thompson Ford, Geography and Sovereignty: Jurisdictional Formation and Racial Segregation, 49 Stan. L. Rev. 1365, 1383–86 (1997); Kenneth A. Stahl, Local Government, "One Person, One Vote," and the Jewish Question, 49 Harv. Civ. Rts.-Civ. Lib. L. Rev. 1, 41–44 (2014).

4. *State Power over Local Governments and the Rights of Bondholders.* As *Gomillion* indicates, if a state abolished a local government but failed to provide some mechanism to protect the interests of investors who had bought the bonds of the former locality, such a state action would probably constitute an impairment of the obligation of the locality's contracts in violation of the

Contracts Clause. *Cf.* Port of Mobile v. Watson, 116 U.S. 289, 305 (1886). After *Hunter*, local residents may not have a contract-like interest in the continued existence of their local government, but local bondholders have a constitutionally protected interest in the ability of the local government bond issuer to satisfy its contractual commitments. The impact of the Contracts Clause on state and local debt obligations is more fully examined in Chapter VI.

5. *Constitutional Constraints on State Power to Alter Local Decisions.* In Washington v. Seattle School District No. 1, 458 U.S. 457 (1982), the Supreme Court held that a state statute that prohibited local school boards from busing children to promote desegregation was unconstitutional. *Washington* acknowledged that "States traditionally have been accorded the widest latitude in ordering their internal governmental processes," *id.* at 476, and that "school boards, as creatures of the State, obviously must give effect to policies announced by the state legislature." *Id.* at 475. But the Court found that shifting power over busing from the local district to the state "worked a major reordering of the State's educational decisionmaking process" with respect to a racially significant matter, *id.* at 479. The statute

> remove[d] the authority to address a racial problem—and only a racial problem—from the existing decisionmaking body, in such a way as to burden minority interests. Those favoring the elimination of *de facto* school segregation now must seek relief from the state legislature, or from the statewide electorate. Yet authority over all other student assignments decisions, as well as over most other areas of educational policy, remains vested in the local school board.

Id. at 474. As a result, the state law violated the Equal Protection Clause.

Similarly, in Romer v. Evans, 517 U.S. 620 (1996), the Supreme Court invalidated a Colorado constitutional amendment that prohibited all legislative, executive, or judicial action at any level of state or local government designed to protect homosexuals. "The impetus for the amendment and the contentious campaign that preceded its adoption came in large part from [gay rights] ordinances that had been passed in various Colorado municipalities" including Aspen, Boulder and Denver. *Id.* at 623–24. In finding that the amendment's broad prohibition of measures designed to protect homosexuals from discrimination violated the Equal Protection Clause, *Romer* effectively reinstated the power of Colorado local governments to adopt and enforce gay rights ordinances.

In both *Washington* and *Romer*, the Supreme Court assumed that the state had broad authority as a matter of federal constitutional law to constrain or veto local decisions. The constitutional infirmity of the laws invalidated in those cases, however, resulted from the particular mix of state actions: the state's delegation of some powers to localities combined with its withdrawal of other powers unconstitutionally burdened individual (not local government) rights. For an argument that *Romer* has broader implications for a federal constitutional protection of local autonomy, *see* Lawrence

Rosenthal, Romer v. Evans as the Transformation of Local Government Law, 31 Urb. Law. 257 (1999).

Schuette v. Coalition to Defend Affirmative Action, 134 S.Ct, 1623 (2014) considered the implications of *Washington* for an Equal Protection Clause challenge to an amendment to the Michigan constitution, adopted by voter initiative, that barred Michigan's public institutions of higher education from implementing any race-conscious admissions policy, thereby taking away from the boards of trustees of those institutions the authority, which they had previously enjoyed, to adopt such policies. The Court rejected the challenge. The plurality opinion, for three justices, held that *Washington* was distinguishable as in that case "the state action in question . . . had the serious risk, if not the purpose, of causing specific injuries on account of race" because it appeared that racial segregation in the Seattle school system may have been "the partial result of school board policies" so that the state's action interfered with a remedy for unconstitutional segregation. *Id.* at 1633. The plurality rejected a broader reading of *Washington* that would have subjected to strict judicial scrutiny state actions that make it more difficult for racial minorities than for other groups to achieve government policies that are in their interest. The plurality, however, did not question *Washington*'s determination that a state's alteration of the powers of a locality could be invalidated under the Equal Protection Clause. In his concurrence, Justice Scalia, joined by Justice Thomas, would have overturned *Washington*, in part because of what those justices saw as *Washington*'s inconsistency with *Hunter's* "rule of structural state sovereignty," which he described as the "the near-limitless sovereignty of each State to design its governing structure as it sees fit." *Id.* at 1645–47. Nonetheless, the plurality, a separate concurrence by Justice Breyer, and the opinion joined by the two dissenters indicate that *Washington*'s recognition of a constitutional constraint on a state's power over its local governments continues to command significant support on the Court.

ROGERS V. BROCKETTE

United States Court of Appeals
588 F.2d 1057 (5th Cir.1979)

GOLDBERG, J.

Since 1966 the federal government has subsidized breakfasts for school children. Participation in this school breakfast program is voluntary, but Congress left it unclear whether the choice to participate is to be made by the individual school, the local school board, or the state. A Texas state statute requires certain school districts to participate. One of those districts, the Garland Independent School District (GISD), resisted and filed this suit in federal district court for declaratory and injunctive relief. * * *

Texas asserts that GISD has no standing to bring this suit. * * * Texas * * * cites a series of Supreme Court decisions which seem to hold that a municipality[19] cannot sue the state that created it. In some of these cases the state altered the municipality's boundaries or consolidated different municipalities; *Hunter v. Pittsburgh*, 207 U.S. 161 (1907), is usually considered the leading example. In other cases, of which *Trenton v. New Jersey*, 262 U.S. 182 (1923) is typical, the state attempted to modify a grant or charter it had previously given to the municipality. Invariably federal courts have ruled against the municipality's claim that the state actions violated the municipality's rights under the contract clause, *see, e.g., Railroad Comm'n v. Los Angeles R.R.*, 280 U.S. 145 (1929); *Hunter v. Pittsburgh*, 207 U.S. 161 (1907); *City of Safety Harbor v. Birchfield*, 529 F.2d 1251, 1254–55 (5th Cir.1976) or the just compensation clause, *see, e.g., City of Trenton v. New Jersey*, 262 U.S. 182 (1923), or the due process, *see, e.g., id.; Northwestern School Dist. v. Pittenger*, 397 F.Supp. 975, 979 (W.D.Pa.1975), or equal protection clauses, *See, e.g. Williams v. Mayor of Baltimore*, 289 U.S. 36 (1933); *City of Newark v. New Jersey*, 262 U.S. 192 (1923); *Williams v. Eggleston*, 170 U.S. 304 (1898). * * * While these cases do not always speak of standing, the Supreme Court has said that "(being) but creatures of the State, municipal corporations have no standing to invoke the contract clause or the provisions of the Fourteenth Amendment of the Constitution in opposition to the will of their creator." *Coleman v. Miller*, 307 U.S. 433, 441 (1939). And these decisions are frequently said to establish that a municipality has no standing to sue the state that created it. * * * Some of the language in the opinions is indeed broad enough to support this interpretation. *See, e.g., Williams v. Mayor of Baltimore*, 289 U.S. 36, 40 (1933) ("A municipal corporation, created by a state for the better ordering of government, has no privileges or immunities under the Federal Constitution which it may invoke in opposition to the will of its creator."); *City of Trenton v. New Jersey*, 262 U.S. 182, 187 (1923) ("(A) municipality is merely a department of the state, and the state may withhold, grant or withdraw powers or privileges as it sees fit. However great or small its sphere of action, it remains the creature of the state exercising and holding powers and privileges subject to the sovereign will."). *See also Hunter v. Pittsburgh*, 207 U.S. 161, 178–79 (1907).

We believe, however, that these decisions, properly interpreted, do not require us to deny GISD standing in this case. The Supreme Court itself said, in a somewhat different context from that facing us here, that "a correct reading of the seemingly unconfined dicta of *Hunter* and kindred cases is not that the State has plenary power to manipulate in every conceivable way, for every conceivable purpose, the affairs of its

---

[19] For purposes of this analysis, the Garland Independent School District may be treated as a municipality * * * because the reasoning of the cases cited by Texas applies to all political subdivisions created by a state.

municipal corporations, but rather that the State's authority is unrestrained by the particular prohibitions of the Constitution considered in those cases." *Gomillion v. Lightfoot*, 364 U.S. 339, 344 (1960). We agree. We think these cases are substantive interpretations of the constitutional provisions involved; we do not think they hold that a municipality never has standing to sue the state of which it is a creature. In fact, correctly interpreted, these cases do not deal with "standing," in the sense in which we use the term, at all. We reach these conclusions for several reasons. * * *

As we read them, the *Hunter* and *Trenton* line of cases are simply faithful to this principle of *Dartmouth College*. They hold that the Constitution does not interfere in the internal political organization of states. Decisions in the *Hunter* and *Trenton* line dealing with claims under the equal protection or due process clauses extend this principle to the fourteenth amendment. In some respects the Court has retreated from this absolute position, *see, e.g. Gomillion v. Lightfoot*, 364 U.S. 339 (1960) * * * but these retreats are not our present concern. Our point is that *Hunter*, *Trenton*, and allied cases are substantive holdings that the Constitution does not interfere in states' internal political organization. They are not decisions about a municipality's standing to sue its state. * * *

The opinions in the *Hunter* and *Trenton* line do occasionally but by no means uniformly speak of "standing," and deny that a municipality has "standing" to sue the state. But when those cases were decided, "standing" generally meant something somewhat different from what it means today. A party had standing or a "right to sue" if it was correct in its claim on the merits that the statutory or constitutional provision in question protected its interests; standing was not seen as a preliminary or threshold question. * * * In speaking of "standing," cases in the *Hunter* and *Trenton* line meant only that, on the merits, the municipality had no rights under the particular constitutional provisions it invoked. * * *

NOTES AND QUESTIONS

1.   *The No-Standing Rule. Rogers* points up a central ambiguity in the *Hunter* doctrine—whether *Hunter* simply states a substantive constitutional rule that local governments lack constitutional rights against their states, or whether the rule goes further and denies them standing to sue their states. The United States Court of Appeals for the Ninth Circuit adheres to the no-standing rule. *See, e.g.*, Palomar Pomerado Health System v. Belshe, 180 F.3d 1104 (9th Cir.1999); Burbank-Glendale-Pasadena Airport Authority v. City of Burbank, 136 F.3d 1360, 1363–64 (9th Cir.1998). Other courts have expressed uncertainty about whether the "no-standing" rule applies. *See, e.g.*, Amato v. Wilentz, 952 F.2d 742, 754–55 (3d Cir.1991) (applying rule but noting that judicial support is declining); City of Charleston v. Public Serv.

Comm'n of West Virginia, 57 F.3d 385, 389–90 (4th Cir.1995) (status of "no-standing" rule is uncertain; declining to resolve the question since plaintiff municipality would lose on the merits); South Macomb Disposal Auth. v. Township of Washington, 790 F.2d 500, 504 (6th Cir.1986) ("[t]here may be occasions in which a political subdivision is not prevented, by virtue of its status as a subdivision of the state, from challenging the constitutionality of state legislation"). The Tenth Circuit, relying in part on *Rogers*, determined that although a "municipality may not bring a constitutional challenge against its creating state when the constitutional provision that supplies the basis for the complaint was written to protect individual rights"—such as the Contracts Clause, Due Process Clause, or the Equal Protection Clause—a municipality does have standing to assert a constitutional provision designed to protect "collective or structural rights," such as the Supremacy Clause. Branson School District RE–82 v. Romer, 161 F.3d 619, 627–30 (10th Cir.1998). *Accord*, City of Hugo v. Nichols, 656 F.3d 1251 (10th Cir. 2011). Of course, it is not always clear what counts as a structural claim. *City of Hugo* essentially limited municipal standing to Supremacy Clause cases in which the source of the claimed substantive right is a federal statute; the court denied the municipality standing to sue under the Dormant Commerce Clause. *Id.* at 1255–63. The dissent, however, contended that the Dormant Commerce Clause is structural because it deals with the allocation of power between the federal government and the states. *Id.* at 1271–75.

It is uncertain if the Supreme Court continues to adhere to the no-standing rule. In both *Washington v. Seattle School District No.1*, *supra*, and *Romer v. Evans*, *supra*, local governments were among the victorious plaintiffs. At no time did the Court suggest that the local government plaintiffs lacked standing to raise the constitutional claims against their states. On the other hand, the Court never discussed the question of local government standing at all. Because several individual plaintiffs indisputably met the Court's standing requirements, local government standing was not essential to the Court's jurisdiction. Shortly before the *Washington* decision, the Supreme Court, over the dissent of Justices White and Marshall, declined to grant a writ of certiorari to a decision of the Ninth Circuit invoking the no-standing rule in dismissing a local government's constitutional claim. *See* City of South Lake Tahoe v. California Tahoe Regional Planning Agency, 449 U.S. 1039 (1980). *See also* Board of Education of Central School Dist. No. 1 v. Allen, 392 U.S. 236, 241 & n.5 (1968) (noting the standing issue had arisen in an Establishment Clause lawsuit by a local school board against the state's commissioner of education, but accepting the board's standing because it was not challenged by the state and because individual members of the school board had standing because they were at risk of expulsion from office if they refused to comply with the state law they challenged); Indian Oasis-Baboquivari v. Kirk, 91 F.3d 1240, 1243–44 (9th Cir.1996), *reh'g en banc granted*, 102 F.3d 999 (9th Cir.1996), *appeal dismissed*, 109 F.3d 634 (9th Cir.1997) (en banc)(rejecting the argument that *Washington sub silentio* overruled the no-standing rule).

For a review of the standing question, and a federalism-based argument against a local government's standing to raise a federal claim against its state, *see* Alexander Willscher, Comment, The Justiciability of Municipal Preemption Challenges to State Law, 67 U.Chi.L.Rev. 243 (2000). For an argument that local governments should have standing to raise procedural due process claims against their states, *see* Michael A. Lawrence, Do 'Creatures of the State' Have Constitutional Rights?: Standing for Municipalities to Assert Procedural Due Process Claims Against the State, 47 Vill. L. Rev. 93 (2002). For an argument that local governments have standing to bring suits against their states to vindicate individual rights generally, *see* Samuel P. Tepperman-Gelfant, Note, Constitutional Capacity: The Role of Local Governments in Protecting Individual Rights, 41 Harv. C.R.-C.L. Rev. 219 (2006). *See also* David Barron, Why (and When) Cities Have a Stake in Enforcing the Constitution, 115 Yale L.J. 2218 (2006) (arguing that cities should have the authority to challenge the constitutionality of state laws in court when that would expand the scope of local policy-making discretion); Josh Bendor, Municipal Constitutional Rights: A New Approach, 31 Yale L. Pol'y Rev. 389, 411–19 (2014) (arguing that *Hunter* is a rule of substantive constitutional law, not standing).

2.   *Congressional Authority to Empower Local Governments.* In *Rogers* and in many of the cases involving local government standing to sue, the local government's federal constitutional claim was really a federal statutory claim constitutionalized by the Supremacy Clause. In these cases, Congress granted some authority to a local government that was arguably in tension with a state restriction on that local government's power, and the locality claimed the state law violated the Supremacy Clause. Can Congress, through the Commerce Clause, the Spending Power or some other federal constitutional source of power, provide a local government with authority above and beyond the authority granted by the locality's state? According to Judge Kozinski, concurring separately in a Ninth Circuit case reaffirming that circuit's commitment to the no-standing rule: "There is a plausible argument that Congress may not interfere with the functioning of state officials and instrumentalities by endowing them with powers and duties that conflict with their responsibilities under state law." Burbank-Glendale-Pasadena Airport Authority v. City of Burbank, 136 F.3d 1360, 1365 (9th Cir.1998). *See also* Willscher, *supra*, 67 U.Chi.L. Rev. at 252–58 (empowering local governments to sue their states would interfere with states' internal political organization).

The Supreme Court has at least twice acted as though the federal government can provide a local government more power than it has received from its own state, although the Court did not flatly so hold in either case. City of Tacoma v. Taxpayers of Tacoma, 357 U.S. 320 (1958), addressed the question of whether the grant by the Federal Power Commission ("FPC") of a license to the City of Tacoma, Washington to operate a power project on the Cowlitz River gave the city the authority to take by eminent domain a fish hatchery owned and operated by the state of Washington. Taking the hatchery was essential to the project because a reservoir created by one of the project's dams would inundate the hatchery. In a suit brought by the city to establish the validity of the bonds to be used to finance the project, the Washington Supreme Court held that as a matter of state law the city lacked the authority to condemn state lands unless the state expressly granted the city that power, which Washington had not done. City of Tacoma v. Taxpayers of Tacoma, 307 P.2d 567 (Wash. 1957). The state court then rejected the "momentous and novel theory of constitutional government" that "the Federal government may endow a state-created municipality with powers greater than those given it by its creator, the state legislature." *Id.* at 577. The United States Supreme Court reversed, effectively allowing Tacoma to go ahead with the bond issue and the taking of the state hatchery. But the Court did so on procedural grounds without directly addressing the question of federal authority to empower a local government. According to the Court, the question of the city's authority to exercise eminent domain over the state hatchery had been raised by the state in the initial FPC licensing proceeding, in which the state had opposed the license, and the FPC had concluded the city had the necessary authority under state law. The Court found the state had raised the issue again in its unsuccessful petition to the federal court of appeals seeking review of the FPC's grant of the license. *Cf.* State of Washington Department of Game v. Federal Power Commission, 207 F.2d 391 (9th Cir.1953) (upholding FPC's grant of license to Tacoma to operate a dam).With the state's petition for certiorari in the initial licensing dispute having been denied, the Supreme Court concluded the effort to raise the question again was an "impermissible collateral attack[ ]," 357 U.S. at 341, on the earlier determination. In a brief concurrence Justice Harlan rather cryptically added that he did "not understand the Court to suggest that the Federal Power Act endowed the [FPC] and the Court of Appeals with authority to decide any issues of state law *if such law were deemed controlling.*" *Id.* at 342 (emphasis supplied). One of the authors of this book has written that although the holding turned on the question of issue preclusion, the Court's opinion gave little attention to formal state control over local government and instead "focused on the strong federal interests in enabling local construction of the dam," which fell within the federal government's jurisdiction over navigable waters and "reflected strong federal interests in interstate commerce, national defense, flood control, and the generation of electric power." Laurie Reynolds, A Role for Local Government Law in Federal-State-Local Disputes, 43 Urb. Law. 977, 989–90 (2011).

In Lawrence County v. Lead-Deadwood School Dist. No. 40–1, 469 U.S. 256 (1985), the Supreme Court held that a federal law superseded a state statutory limit on local government discretion. *Lawrence County* involved the federal Payment in Lieu of Taxes ("PILOT") Act, which provides for federal payments to local governments to offset the revenue loss resulting from the presence of federal properties (which are exempt from taxation) within those localities. The federal statute provided that each local unit that received payments under the Act "may use the payment for any governmental purpose." South Dakota required local governments to distribute all federal and state payments in the same way they were obligated by the state to distribute locally-raised tax revenues. A South Dakota school district contended this required a county receiving PILOT funds to make a specific payment to the district. The Supreme Court, however, concluded that the state restriction was preempted by federal law. After a careful review of the legislative history, the Court concluded that Congress definitely intended "to vest discretion in local governments over the expenditure" of the PILOT moneys, *id.* at 264. The Court acknowledged the state's argument that "because of concerns of federalism, the Federal Government may not intrude lightly into the State's efforts to provide fiscal guidance to its subdivisions," but the Court gave the federalism argument short shrift, noting the "Federal Government . . . has not presumed to dictate the manner in which the counties may spend *state* in-lieu-of-tax payments. Rather, it has merely imposed a condition on its disbursement of federal funds." *Id.* at 269–70 (emphasis in original). The Court went on to assume that the federal power to place conditions on the use of federal funds extended to giving local governments more spending discretion than the state had authorized:

> It is far from a novel proposition that pursuant to its power under the Spending Clause, Congress may impose conditions on the receipt of federal funds, absent some independent constitutional bar. In our view, Congress was sufficiently clear in its intention to funnel [PILOT] moneys directly to local governments, so that they might spend them for governmental purposes without substantial interference.

Id. In dissent, then-Justice Rehnquist, joined by Justice Stevens, looked to *Hunter*'s "settled doctrine" that municipal corporations are simply state instrumentalities. They concluded that "in light of the long history of treatment of counties as being by law totally subordinate to the States which have created them," *id.* at 273, the better reading of the statute was that Congress had not intended to displace state control over how local governments spend the PILOT funds. Strikingly, the *Lawrence County* majority did not even mention *Hunter*.

However, *Hunter*'s treatment of local governments as arms of their states played a central role in the next case.

NIXON V. MISSOURI MUNICIPAL LEAGUE

Supreme Court of the United States
541 U.S. 125 (2004)

JUSTICE SOUTER delivered the opinion of the Court.

Section 101(a) of the Telecommunications Act of 1996, 110 Stat. 70, 47 U.S.C. § 253, authorizes preemption of state and local laws and regulations expressly or effectively "prohibiting the ability of any entity" to provide telecommunications services. The question is whether the class of entities includes the State's own subdivisions, so as to affect the power

of States and localities to restrict their own (or their political inferiors')
delivery of such services. We hold it does not.

In 1997, the General Assembly of Missouri enacted the statute
codified as § 392.410(7) of the State's Revised Statutes: "No political
subdivision of this state shall provide or offer for sale, either to the public
or to a telecommunications provider, a telecommunications service or
telecommunications facility used to provide a telecommunications service
for which a certificate of service authority is required pursuant to this
section."

* * * The municipal respondents, including municipalities, municipal
organizations, and municipally owned utilities, petitioned the Federal
Communications Commission * * * for an order declaring the state
statute unlawful and preempted under 47 U.S. C § 253 * * *.

[T]he FCC refused to declare the Missouri statute preempted * * *.
The agency concluded that "the term 'any entity' in section 253(a) . . .
was not intended to include political subdivisions of the state, but rather
appears to prohibit restrictions on market entry that apply to
independent entities subject to state regulation." The FCC also adverted
to the principle of *Gregory v. Ashcroft,* 501 U.S. 452 (1991), that Congress
needs to be clear before it constrains traditional state authority to order
its government. But at the same time the Commission rejected
preemption, it also denounced the policy behind the Missouri statute, and
the Commission's order carried two appended statements (one by
Chairman William E. Kennard and Commissioner Gloria Tristani, and
one by Commissioner Susan Ness) to the effect that barring
municipalities from providing telecommunications substantially disserved
the policy behind the Telecommunications Act.

The municipal respondents appealed to the Eighth Circuit, where a
panel unanimously reversed the agency disposition, with the explanation
that the plain-vanilla "entity," especially when modified by "any,"
manifested sufficiently clear congressional attention to governmental
entities to get past *Gregory.* * * * We now reverse. * * *

The Eighth Circuit trained its analysis on the words "any entity," left
undefined by the statute, with much weight being placed on the modifier
"any." But concentration on the writing on the page does not produce a
persuasive answer here. While an "entity" can be either public or private
* * * there is no convention of omitting the modifiers "public and private"
when both are meant to be covered. * * * Nor is coverage of public entities
reliably signaled by speaking of "any" entity; "any" can and does mean
different things depending upon the setting. * * * To get at Congress's
understanding, what is needed is a broader frame of reference, and in this
litigation it helps if we ask how Congress could have envisioned the
preemption clause actually working if the FCC applied it at the municipal

respondents' urging. * * * We think that the strange and indeterminate results of using federal preemption to free public entities from state or local limitations is the key to understanding that Congress used "any entity" with a limited reference to any private entity when it cast the preemption net.

In familiar instances of regulatory preemption under the Supremacy Clause, a federal measure preempting state regulation in some precinct of economic conduct carried on by a private person or corporation simply leaves the private party free to do anything it chooses consistent with the prevailing federal law. If federal law, say, preempts state regulation of cigarette advertising, a cigarette seller is left free from advertising restrictions imposed by a State, which is left without the power to control on that matter. On the subject covered, state law just drops out.

But no such simple result would follow from federal preemption meant to unshackle local governments from entrepreneurial limitations. The trouble is that a local government's capacity to enter an economic market turns not only on the effect of straightforward economic regulation below the national level (including outright bans), but on the authority and potential will of governments at the state or local level to support entry into the market. Preemption of the state advertising restriction freed a seller who otherwise had the legal authority to advertise and the money to do it if that made economic sense. But preempting a ban on government utilities would not accomplish much if the government could not point to some law authorizing it to run a utility in the first place. And preemption would make no difference to anyone if the state regulator were left with control over funding needed for any utility operation and declined to pay for it. In other words, when a government regulates itself (or the subdivision through which it acts) there is no clear distinction between the regulator and the entity regulated. Legal limits on what may be done by the government itself (including its subdivisions) will often be indistinguishable from choices that express what the government wishes to do with the authority and resources it can command. That is why preempting state or local governmental self-regulation (or regulation of political inferiors) would work so differently from preempting regulation of private players that we think it highly unlikely that Congress intended to set off on such uncertain adventures. * * *

[C]onsider how preemption would apply to a state statute authorizing municipalities to operate specified utilities, to provide water and electricity but nothing else. The enumeration would certainly have the effect of prohibiting a municipally owned and operated electric utility from entering the telecommunications business (as Congress clearly meant private electric companies to be able to do), and its implicit prohibition would thus be open to FCC preemption. But what if the FCC did preempt the restriction? The municipality would be free of the statute, but freedom is not authority, and in the absence of some further, authorizing legislation the municipality would still be powerless to enter the telecommunications business. There is, after all, no argument that the Telecommunications Act of 1996 is itself a source of federal authority granting municipalities local power that state law does not. * * *

Or take the application of § 253 preemption to municipalities empowered by state law to furnish services generally, but forbidden by a special statute to exercise that power for the purpose of providing telecommunications services. If the special statute were preempted, a municipality in that State would have a real option to enter the telecommunications business if its own legislative arm so chose and funded the venture. But in a State next door where municipalities lacked such general authority, a local authority would not be able to, and the result would be a national crazy quilt. We will presumably get a crazy quilt, of course, as a consequence of state and local political choices arrived at in the absence of any preemption under § 253, but the crazy quilt of this hypothetical would result not from free political choices but from the fortuitous interaction of a federal preemption law with the forms of municipal authorization law.

Finally, consider the result if a State that previously authorized municipalities to operate a number of utilities including telecommunications changed its law by narrowing the range of authorization. Assume that a State once authorized municipalities to furnish water, electric, and communications services, but sometime after the passage of § 253 narrowed the authorization so as to leave municipalities authorized to enter only the water business. The repealing statute would have a prohibitory effect on the prior ability to deliver telecommunications service and would be subject to preemption. But that would mean that a State that once chose to provide broad municipal authority could not reverse course. A State next door, however, starting with a legal system devoid of any authorization for municipal utility operation, would at the least be free to change its own course by authorizing its municipalities to venture forth. The result, in other words, would be the federal creation of a one-way ratchet. A State or municipality could give the power, but it could not take it away later. Private counterparts could come and go from the market at will, for after any federal preemption they would have a free choice to compete or not to compete in telecommunications; governmental providers could never leave (or, at least, could not leave by a forthright choice to change policy), for the law expressing the government's decision to get out would be preempted.

The municipal respondents' answer to the one-way ratchet, and indeed to a host of the incongruities that would follow from preempting governmental restriction on the exercise of its own power, is to rely on § 253(b), which insulates certain state actions taken "on a competitively neutral basis." Respondents contend that a State or municipality would be able to make a competitively neutral change of mind to leave the telecommunications market after deciding earlier to enter it or authorize entry.

But we think this is not much of an answer. The FCC has understood § 253(b) neutrality to require a statute or regulation affecting all types of utilities in like fashion, as a law removing only governmental entities from telecommunications could not be. An even more fundamental weakness in respondents' answer is shown in briefs filed by *amici* City of Abilene and Consumer Federation of America. We have no reason to doubt them when they explain how highly unlikely it is that a state decision to withdraw would be "neutral" in any sense of the word. There is every reason to expect just the contrary, that legislative choices in this arena would reflect the intent behind the intense lobbying directed to those choices, manifestly intended to impede, not enhance, competition. After all, the notion that the legislative process addressing governmental utility authority is susceptible to capture by competition-averse private utilities is fully consistent with (and one reason for) the FCC's position that statutes like Missouri's disserve the policy objects of the Telecommunications Act of 1996. Given the unlikely application of § 253(b) to state or local choices driven by policy, not business failure, the fair conclusion is that § 253(a), if read respondents' way, would allow governments to move solely toward authorizing telecommunications operation, with no alternative to reverse course deliberately later on.

In sum, § 253 would not work like a normal preemptive statute if it applied to a governmental unit. It would often accomplish nothing, it would treat States differently depending on the formal structures of their laws authorizing municipalities to function, and it would hold out no promise of a national consistency. We think it farfetched that Congress meant § 253 to start down such a road in the absence of any clearer signal than the phrase "ability of any entity." * * *

The municipal respondents' position holds sufficient promise of futility and uncertainty to keep us from accepting it, but a complementary principle would bring us to the same conclusion even on the assumption that preemption could operate straightforwardly to provide local choice, as in some instances it might. Preemption would, for example, leave a municipality with a genuine choice to enter the telecommunications business when state law provided general authority and a newly unfettered municipality wished to fund the effort. But the liberating preemption would come only by interposing federal authority between a State and its municipal subdivisions, which our precedents teach, "are created as convenient agencies for exercising such of the governmental powers of the State as may be entrusted to them in its absolute discretion." Hence the need to invoke our working assumption that federal legislation threatening to trench on the States' arrangements for conducting their own governments should be treated with great skepticism, and read in a way that preserves a State's chosen disposition of its own power, in the absence of the plain statement *Gregory* requires. What we have said already is enough to show that § 253(a) is hardly forthright enough to pass *Gregory:* "ability of any entity" is not limited to one reading, and neither statutory structure nor legislative history points unequivocally to a commitment by Congress to treat governmental telecommunications providers on par with private firms. The want of any "unmistakably clear" statement to that effect would be fatal to respondents' reading.

JUSTICE STEVENS, dissenting.

* * * The Court begins its analysis by asking us to imagine how § 253 might apply to "a state statute authorizing municipalities to operate specified utilities, to provide water and electricity but nothing else" * * *. Certainly one might plausibly interpret § 253, as the Court does, to forbid States' refusals to provide broader authorization or to provide necessary capital as impermissible prohibitions on entry. And as the Court observes, such an interpretation would undeniably produce absurd results; it would leave covered entities in a kind of legal limbo, armed with a federal-law freedom to enter the market but lacking the state-law power to do so. But we need not—and in my opinion, should not—interpret § 253 in this fashion. We should instead read the statute's reference to state and local laws that "prohibit or have the effect of prohibiting the *ability* of any entity," § 253(a), to enter the telecommunications business to embody an implicit understanding that the only "entities" covered by § 253 are entities otherwise able to enter the business—*i.e.,* entities both authorized to provide telecommunications services and capable of providing such services without the State's direct assistance. In other words, § 253 prohibits States from withdrawing municipalities' pre-existing authority to enter the telecommunications business, but does not command that States affirmatively grant either that authority or the means with which to carry it out.

Of course, the Court asserts that still other absurd results would follow from application of § 253 pre-emption to state laws that withdraw a municipality's pre-existing authority to enter the telecommunications business. But these results are, on closer examination, perhaps not so absurd after all. The Court first contends that reading § 253 in this manner will produce a "national crazy quilt" of public telecommunications authority, where the possibility of municipal participation in the telecommunications market turns on the scope of the authority each State has already granted to its subdivisions. But as the Court acknowledges, permitting States such as Missouri to prohibit municipalities from providing telecommunications services hardly will help the cause of national consistency. That the "crazy quilt" the Court describes is the product of political choices made by Congress rather than state legislatures renders it no more absurd than the "crazy quilt" that will result from leaving the matter of municipal entry entirely to individual States' discretion.

The Court also contends that applying § 253 pre-emption to bar withdrawal of authority to enter the telecommunications market will result in "the federal creation of a one-way ratchet" * * * But nothing in § 253 prohibits States from scaling back municipalities' authority in a general way. A State may withdraw comprehensive authorization in favor of enumerating specific municipal powers, or even abolish municipalities altogether. Such general withdrawals of authority may very well "have the effect of prohibiting" municipalities' ability to enter the telecommunications market just as enforcement of corporate governance and tax laws might "have the effect of prohibiting" other entities' ability to enter. But § 253 clearly does not pre-empt every state law that "has the effect" of restraining entry. It pre-empts only those that constitute *nonneutral* restraints on entry. A general redefinition of municipal authority no more constitutes a prohibited nonneutral restraint on entry than enforcement of other laws of general applicability that, practically speaking, may make it more difficult for certain entities to enter the telecommunications business.

As I read the statute, the one thing a State may not do is enact a statute or regulation specifically aimed at preventing municipalities or other entities from providing telecommunications services. This prohibition would certainly apply to a law like Missouri's, which "advertise[s][its] prohibitory agenda on [its] fac[e]." But it would also apply to a law that accomplished a similar result by other means—for example, a law that permitted only private telecommunications carriers to receive federal universal service support or access to unbundled network elements. * * *

NOTES AND QUESTIONS

1.   *Preemption of a Restriction vs. Empowerment.* An important theme in Justice Souter's opinion is that because Missouri's local governments ultimately trace their powers back to the state the preemption of the state law prohibition on municipal provision of telecommunications will be ineffective without some affirmative grant of authority by the state to local governments. Justice Stevens responded to Justice Souter by pointing to the authority of at least some Missouri localities to provide telecommunications services prior to the enactment of the Missouri law being challenged. Justice Stevens' argument resembles the approach taken by the Court in *Gomillion*

v. Lightfoot, supra, Washington v. Seattle School District No. 1, supra, and other cases that found that although the state normally has very broad authority over local boundaries or powers certain departures by the state from a preexisting baseline can give rise to an inference of discriminatory intent and be subject to constitutional challenge. Does a similar approach of focusing on the state's withdrawal of authority it had previously granted address Justice Souter's argument, or do those cases differ because they involved individual rights as well as the state-local distribution of power?

2.   *Federalism and State-Local Relations. Nixon,* which did not discuss or cite *Lawrence County,* affirms the continuing importance of the *Hunter* principle, this time in the context of a question of statutory interpretation. *Nixon*'s reliance on *Gregory v. Ashcroft* may also be significant. *Gregory* held that when a case presents the question of whether a generally-worded federal law displaces state law concerning the operations of state government "we must be absolutely certain that Congress intended such an exercise." 501 U.S. at 464. *Gregory* dealt specifically with whether the Age Discrimination in Employment Act's prohibition of a mandatory retirement age applies to state judges. The Court found that rules concerning qualification to serve as a judge relate to the state's core concern with the "structure of its government," "a decision of the most fundamental sort for a sovereign entity." *Id.* at 460. By invoking *Gregory*'s clear statement requirement, *Nixon* implicitly takes the view that local government is a part of the structure of state government and that control of state-local relations is a fundamental issue of state governance. *Nixon* does not hold that Congress could not displace state control over local telecommunications activity; but it does require as a matter of federalism that no such federal regulation will be found unless federal law clearly so provides.

In an article published before the *Nixon* decision, Professor Roderick M. Hills, Jr. suggested that the federalism values that generally support state control over local government are advanced by federal action that provides local governments with additional powers. *See* Roderick M. Hills, Jr., Dissecting the State: The Use of Federal Law to Free State and Local Officials from State Legislatures' Control, 97 Mich.L.Rev. 1201, 1234–52 (1999). Professor Hills contended that both federalism and local self-government have value in decentralizing power and promoting intergovernmental competition. He argued that *Hunter*'s state supremacy doctrine generally serves the interest in local self-governance because the states are likely to be better than Congress at creating local governments and allocating power among them. But, Professor Hills noted, state legislatures, like Congress, may also try to centralize power, and federal grants to local governments can offset centralization at the state level. He called for a "presumption of institutional autonomy," which would allow the federal government to delegate authority and grant powers to local governments unless the state expressly objects to the federal law.

Professor Hills further distinguished between state laws that are "revenue-enhancing," that is, which seek to divert federal funds to state ends, and state laws that simply impose "regulatory limits" on local government behavior. He contends that courts ought to presume that states would waive their revenue-enhancing constraints on local governments rather than forego a federal grant, but that there should be no such presumption with respect to state regulatory limits. In his view, *Lawrence County* was rightly decided since the South Dakota law in question was state revenue-enhancing rather than regulatory. *See id.* at 1245–46.

What do you think? Is the federal provision of powers to local governments inconsistent with *Hunter*'s federalist vision of state-local relations? Can Professor Hills' "presumption of institutional autonomy" reconcile ultimate state supremacy over local governments with the benefits of local self-governance? Does his distinction between state "revenue-enhancing" measures and state "regulatory limits" on local government provide a workable means of determining when the federal government can add to local powers and when it cannot? Does it provide a means of reconciling *Lawrence County* as a revenue-enhancement case with *Nixon* as a "regulatory limits" case? Or do the two cases really reflect different judicial philosophies about the appropriate approach to federal laws that benefit local governments more than their states would want?

3.   *The Place of State Law in Resolving the Federal Authority Question.* Professor Reynolds has faulted the Court for failing to attend to the actual powers state law delegates to local governments. Although the Supreme Court in *Nixon* assumed that without the federal law local governments in Missouri would lack the authority to provide telecommunications services, Professor Reynolds pointed out that Missouri, like many other states, provides its municipalities with home rule, which gives them "substantial regulatory initiative and independence. . . . The prohibition versus enabling distinction, then, though it may make some sense for non-home rule entities, has no relevance for home rule governments." Reynolds, A Role for Local Government Law in Federal-State-Local Disputes, 43 Urb. Law. 977, 1006 (2011). She argued that the Court's consideration of the state sovereignty interest ought to be "informed by the ways in which the states themselves have shaped and modified their powers of their political subdivisions." *Id.* at 995. This would involve a case-by-case consideration of the scope of local authority under state law—which can vary from state to state, and among the different types of local governments within a state—rather than "bright line" presumptions about federal power or state sovereignty. *See id.* at 1011– 12. (The meaning and scope of home rule are considered in Chapter IV.) Taking this approach, she concluded that the Court got both *Nixon* and *Lead-Deadwood* wrong: Missouri had given its municipalities considerable policy-making discretion, while South Dakota's counties "received very narrow and detailed listings of specific powers by state statute." *Id.* at 1009.

4.   *Telecommunications Policy and Local Government.* The *Nixon* litigation is also a reminder of the role that local governments have sought to play in the telecommunications arena, whether by trying to draw revenue from private providers that use municipal rights of way, *see, e.g.,* Puerto Rico

Telephone Co., Inc. v. Municipality of Guayanilla, 450 F.3d 9 (1st Cir. 2006) (invalidating under the federal Telecommunications Act a municipal ordinance imposing a 5% gross receipts tax on telecommunications providers); or by offering their own services, including municipal broadband or Wi-Fi services. For a discussion of municipal efforts in this area, and the complex legal issues they raise, *see, e.g.,* Jeff Stricker, Casting a Wide 'Net: How and Why State Laws Restricting Municipal Broadband Networks Must Be Modified, 81 Geo. Wash. L. Rev. 589 (2013); Olivier Sylvain, Broadband Localism, 73 Ohio St. L.J. 795 (2012). In this rapidly developing area, in March 2015, the Federal Communications Commission issued an order preempting state statutes in North Carolina and Tennessee that had the effect of prohibiting municipal provision of broadband services. In the Matter of City of Wilson, North Carolina (FCC 15–25, March 12, 2015). The FCC determined its position was not inconsistent with *Nixon* because it was relying on a different provision of the Telecommunications Act, section 706, which directs it to promote advanced telecommunications services. Moreover, the municipalities in the two states had the authority to provide telecommunication services under state law; the FCC's action targeted only the additional restrictions North Carolina applied only to municipal providers and a specific geographic restriction adopted by Tennessee. The FCC's action has led to proposals in Congress to deny the agency the power to preempt such state laws.

5.   *Local Governments Unprotected by State Immunities.* A different challenge to *Hunter's* "agent-of-the-state" approach to state-local relations comes from a number of Supreme Court decisions holding that local governments do not benefit from various immunities that shelter the states. The Eleventh Amendment's sovereign immunity principle, which precludes Congress from authorizing suits against a state for money damages without the state's consent, does not protect most local governments. *See, e.g.,* Northern Ins. Co. of N.Y. v. Chatham County, 547 U.S. 189 (2006); Mt. Healthy City School Dist. v. Doyle, 429 U.S. 274 (1977); Lincoln County v. Luning, 133 U.S. 529 (1890). The Eleventh Amendment cases are unusual in that they provide a locality with the incentive to claim close control by the state as a basis for protection against lawsuits. Most of the disputes involving the scope of the Eleventh Amendment have involved school districts. In *Mount Healthy,* the Supreme Court held that as a matter of Ohio law, which gives school boards extensive authority to issue bonds and levy taxes, an Ohio school district is "more like a county or city than it is an arm of the State" and thus enjoys no Eleventh Amendment immunity. 429 U.S. at 280. *Mount Healthy* turned on Ohio law and did not clearly hold that all school districts are outside the scope of Eleventh Amendment immunity, but most federal and state courts have found that their state school districts enjoy sufficient autonomy in practice that they cannot take advantage of the state's Eleventh Amendment protection. *See, e.g.,* Walker v. Jefferson Co. Bd. of Educ., 771 F.3d 748 (11th Cir. 2014) (Alabama school boards are not "arms of the state" for purposes of Eleventh Amendment immunity); Rose R. v. Connelly, 889 F.2d 435 (2d Cir. 1989) (Connecticut school districts); Cash v. Granville Co.

Board of Educ., 242 F.3d 219, 226 (4th Cir. 2001) (North Carolina school districts); Duke v. Grady Municipal Schools, 127 F.3d 972 (10th Cir. 1997) (New Mexico school districts). Courts in California, however, have found that due to a combination of school finance reform, controls on local taxation, and other state laws, "the state [is] so entangled with the operations of California's local school districts" and so closely controls district revenues, that local school districts are like "wholly owned subsidiaries" of the state and protected by the Eleventh Amendment against suits for damages. *See* Association of Mexican-American Educators v. State, 231 F.3d 572, 582 (9th Cir. 2000). *Milliken v. Bradley*, discussed in the next section of this chapter, provides further insight into the disputed status of school districts. School finance reform as an issue in state-local relations is discussed in Chapter V.

Similarly, a state is not a "person" within the meaning of 42 U.S.C. § 1983, and thus cannot be sued for the civil rights violations that are actionable under that statute, *see* Will v. Michigan Department of State Police, 491 U.S. 58 (1989), but a local government is a "person" suable under the federal civil rights law. Monell v. New York City Dept. of Social Services, 436 U.S. 658 (1978). The Supreme Court has also found, as a matter of statutory interpretation, that the Sherman Act does not apply to the states, Parker v. Brown, 317 U.S. 341 (1943), but the "state action" exemption does not automatically extend to local governments, *see, e.g.*, Community Communications Co. v. City of Boulder, 455 U.S. 40 (1982). The potential antitrust liability burden on local governments, however, has been mitigated by the Local Government Antitrust Act of 1984, which eliminated money damages in antitrust suits against local governments.

B. THE AMERICAN POLIS: LOCAL GOVERNMENT AS AUTONOMOUS, DEMOCRATIC POLITY

AVERY V. MIDLAND COUNTY

Supreme Court of the United States
390 U.S. 474 (1968)

MR. JUSTICE WHITE delivered the opinion of the Court.

Midland County has a population of about 70,000. The Commissioners Court is composed of five members. One, the County Judge, is elected at large from the entire county, and in practice casts a vote only to break a tie. The other four are Commissioners chosen from districts. The population of those districts, according to the 1963 estimates that were relied upon when this case was tried, was respectively 67,906; 852; 414; and 828. This vast imbalance resulted from placing in a single district virtually the entire city of Midland, Midland County's only urban center, in which 95% of the county's population resides.

The Commissioners Court is assigned by the Texas Constitution and by various statutory enactments with a variety of functions. According to the commentary to Vernon's Texas Statutes, the court:

> "is the general governing body of the county. It establishes a courthouse and jail, appoints numerous minor officials such as the county health officer, fills vacancies in the county offices, lets contracts in the name of the county, builds roads and bridges, administers the county's public welfare services, performs numerous duties in regard to elections, sets the county tax rate, issues bonds, adopts the county budget, and serves as a board of equalization for tax assessments."

The court is also authorized, among other responsibilities, to build and run a hospital, * * * an airport, * * * libraries. * * * It fixes boundaries of school districts within the county, * * * may establish a regional public housing authority, * * * and determines the districts for election of its own members. * * *

In *Reynolds v. Sims,* * * * the Equal Protection Clause was applied to the apportionment of state legislatures. Every qualified resident, *Reynolds* determined, has the right to a ballot for election of state legislators of equal weight to the vote of every other resident, and that right is infringed when legislators are elected from districts of substantially unequal population. The question now before us is whether the Fourteenth Amendment likewise forbids the election of local government officials from districts of disparate population. * * * [W]e hold that it does.

The Equal Protection Clause reaches the exercise of state power however manifested, whether exercised directly or through subdivisions of the State. * * * Although the forms and functions of local government and the relationships among the various units are matters of state concern, it is now beyond question that a State's political subdivisions must comply with the Fourteenth Amendment. The actions of local government are the actions of the State. A city, town, or county may no more deny the equal protection of the laws than it may abridge freedom of speech, establish an official religion, arrest without probable cause, or deny due process of law.

When the State apportions its legislature, it must have due regard for the Equal Protection Clause. Similarly, when the State delegates lawmaking power to local government and provides for the election of local officials from districts specified by statute, ordinance, or local charter, it must insure that those qualified to vote have the right to an equally effective voice in the election process. If voters residing in oversize districts are denied their constitutional right to participate in the election of state legislators, precisely the same kind of deprivation occurs when the members of a city council, school board, or county governing board are elected from districts of substantially unequal population. If the five senators representing a city in the state legislature may not be elected from districts ranging in size from 50,000 to 500,000, neither is it permissible to elect the members of the city council from those same districts. In either case, the votes of some residents have greater weight than those of others; in both cases the equal protection of the laws has been denied.

That the state legislature may itself be properly apportioned does not exempt subdivisions from the Fourteenth Amendment. While state legislatures exercise extensive power over their constituents and over the various units of local government, the States universally leave much policy and decisionmaking to their governmental subdivisions. Legislators enact many laws but do not attempt to reach those countless matters of local concern necessarily left wholly or partly to those who govern at the local level. What is more, in providing for the governments of their cities, counties, towns, and districts, the States characteristically provide for representative government—for decisionmaking at the local level by representatives elected by the people. And, not infrequently, the delegation of power to local units is contained in constitutional provisions for local home rule which are immune from legislative interference. In a word, institutions of local government have always been a major aspect of our system, and their responsible and responsive operation is today of increasing importance to the quality of life of more and more of our citizens. We therefore see little difference, in terms of the application of the Equal Protection Clause and of the principles of *Reynolds v. Sims*, between the exercise of state power through legislatures and its exercise by elected officials in the cities, towns, and counties.

We are urged to permit unequal districts for the Midland County Commissioners Court on the ground that the court's functions are not sufficiently "legislative." The parties have devoted much effort to urging that alternative labels—"administrative" versus "legislative"—be applied to the Commissioners Court. As the brief description of the court's functions above amply demonstrates, this unit of local government cannot easily be classified in the neat categories favored by civics texts. The Texas commissioners courts are assigned some tasks which would normally be thought of as "legislative," others typically assigned to "executive" or "administrative" departments, and still others which are "judicial." In this regard Midland County's Commissioners Court is representative of most of the general governing bodies of American cities, counties, towns, and villages. One knowledgeable commentator has written of "the states' varied, pragmatic approach in establishing governments." R. Wood, in Politics and Government in the United States 891–892 (A. Westin ed. 1965). That approach has produced a staggering number of governmental units—the preliminary calculation by the Bureau of the Census for 1967 is that there are 81,304 "units of government" in the United States—and an even more staggering diversity. Nonetheless, while special-purpose organizations abound and in many States the allocation of functions among units results in instances of overlap and vacuum, virtually every American lives within what he and his neighbors regard as a unit of local government with general responsibility and power for local affairs. In many cases citizens reside within and are subject to two such governments, a city and a county.

The Midland County Commissioners Court is such a unit. While the Texas Supreme Court found that the Commissioners Court's legislative functions are "negligible," * * * the court does have power to make a large number of decisions having a broad range of impacts on all the citizens of the county. It sets a tax rate, equalizes assessments, and issues bonds. It then prepares and adopts a budget for allocating the county's funds, and is given by statute a wide range of discretion in choosing the subjects on which to spend. In adopting the budget the court makes both long-term judgments about the way Midland County should develop—whether industry should be solicited, roads improved, recreation facilities built, and land set aside for schools—and immediate choices among competing needs.

The Texas Supreme Court concluded that the work actually done by the Commissioners Court "disproportionately concern[s] the rural areas." * * * Were the Commissioners Court a special-purpose unit of government assigned the performance of functions affecting definable groups of constituents more than other constituents, we would have to confront the question whether such a body may be apportioned in ways which give greater influence to the citizens most affected by the organization's functions. That question, however, is not presented by this case, for while Midland County authorities may concentrate their attention on rural roads, the relevant fact is that the powers of the Commissioners Court include the authority to make a substantial number of decisions that affect all citizens, whether they reside inside or outside the city limits of Midland. The Commissioners maintain buildings, administer welfare services, and determine school districts both inside and outside the city. The taxes imposed by the court fall equally on all property in the county. Indeed, it may not be mere coincidence that a body apportioned with three of its four voting members chosen by residents of the rural area surrounding the city devotes most of its attention to the problems of that area, while paying for its expenditures with a tax imposed equally on city residents and those who live outside the city. And we might point out that a decision not to exercise a function within the court's power—a decision, for example, not to build an airport or a library, or not to participate in the federal food stamp program—is just as much a decision affecting all citizens of the county as an affirmative decision.

The Equal Protection Clause does not, of course, require that the State never distinguish between citizens, but only that the distinctions that are made not be arbitrary or invidious. The conclusion of Reynolds v. Sims was that bases other than population were not acceptable grounds for distinguishing among citizens when determining the size of districts used to elect members of state legislatures. We hold today only that the Constitution permits no substantial variation from equal population in drawing districts for units of local government having general governmental powers over the entire geographic area served by the body.

Holding

This Court is aware of the immense pressures facing units of local government, and of the greatly varying problems with which they must deal. The Constitution does not require that a uniform straitjacket bind citizens in devising mechanisms of local government suitable for local needs and efficient in solving local problems. Last Term, for example, the Court upheld a procedure for choosing a school board that placed the selection with school boards of component districts even though the component boards had equal votes and served unequal populations. *Sailors v. Board of Education*, 387 U.S. 105 (1967). The Court rested on the administrative nature of the area school board's functions and the essentially appointive form of the scheme employed. In *Dusch v. Davis*, 387 U.S. 112 (1967), the Court permitted Virginia Beach to choose its legislative body by a scheme that included at-large voting for candidates, some of whom had to be residents of particular districts, even though the residence districts varied widely in population.

The *Sailors* and *Dusch* cases demonstrate that the Constitution and this Court are not roadblocks in the path of innovation, experiment, and development among units of local government. We will not bar what Professor Wood has called "the emergence of a new ideology and structure of public bodies, equipped with new capacities and motivations. . . ." R. Wood, 1400 Governments, at 175 (1961). Our decision today is only that the Constitution imposes one ground rule for the development of arrangements of local government: a requirement that units with general governmental powers over an entire geographic area not be apportioned among single-member districts of substantially unequal population.

MR. JUSTICE FORTAS, dissenting.

I agree that application of the Equal Protection Clause of the Constitution, decreed by this Court in the case of state legislatures, cannot stop at that point. Of course local governmental units are subject to the commands of the Equal Protection Clause. * * * That much is easy. The difficult question, and the one which the Court slights, is: What does the Equal Protection Clause demand with regard to local governmental units?

* * * [One person, one vote] is appropriate to the selection of members of a State Legislature. The people of a State are similarly affected by the action of the State Legislature. Its functions are comprehensive and pervasive. They are not specially concentrated upon the needs of particular parts of the State or any separate group of citizens. As the Court in *Reynolds* said, each citizen stands in "the same relation" to the State Legislature. Accordingly, variations from substantial population equality in elections for the State Legislature take away from the individual voter the equality which the Constitution mandates. They amount to a debasement of the citizen's vote and of his citizenship.

But the same cannot be said of all local governmental units, and certainly not of the unit involved in this case. Midland County's Commissioners Court has special functions—directed primarily to its rural area and rural population. Its powers are limited and specialized, in light of its missions. Residents of Midland County do not by any means have the same rights and interests at stake in the election of the Commissioners. * * *

The Court in this case concedes that in a "special-purpose unit of government," the rights of certain constituents may be more affected than the rights of others. It implies that the one man, one vote rule may not apply in such cases. * * * But it says that we do not here have to confront the implications of such a situation. I do not agree.

I submit that the problem presented by many, perhaps most, county governments (and by Midland County in particular) is precisely the same as those arising from special-purpose units. The functions of many county governing boards, no less than the governing bodies of special-purpose units, have only slight impact on some of their constituents and a vast and direct impact on others. They affect different citizens residing within their geographical jurisdictions in drastically different ways.[5]

* * * The population of Midland County is chiefly in a single urban area. That urban area has its own municipal government which, because of home rule, has relative autonomy and authority to deal with urban problems. In contrast, the Midland County government, like county governments generally, acts primarily as an administrative arm of the State. It provides a convenient agency for the State to collect taxes, hold

---

[5] If these complexities do not exist in a given case (that is, if the functions of the governing unit involved have an essentially equal impact upon all the citizens within its geographical jurisdiction), then the one man, one vote rule would apply as it did in *Reynolds*. Some city councils, for example, are in effect miniature state legislatures. Some county governing units have geographical jurisdiction which is co-extensive with a city or which includes only reasonably homogeneous rural areas.

elections, administer judicial and peace-keeping functions, improve roads, and perform other functions which are the ordinary duties of the State. The powers of the Commissioners Court, which is the governing body of Midland County, are strictly limited by statute and constitutional provision. Although a mere listing of these authorizing statutes and constitutional provisions would seem to indicate that the Commissioners Court has significant and general power, this impression is somewhat illusory because very often the provisions which grant the power also circumscribe its exercise with detailed limitations.

For example, the petitioner cites Art. VIII, § 9, of the Texas Constitution and Article 2352 of the Texas Civil Statutes as granting the Commissioners Court authority to levy taxes. Yet, at the time this suit was tried, Art. VIII, § 9, provided that no county could levy a tax in excess of 80 cents on $100 property valuation. And Article 2352 allocated that 80 cents among the four "constitutional purposes" mentioned in Art. VIII, § 9 (not more than 25 cents for general county purposes, not more than 15 cents for the jury fund, not more than 15 cents for roads and bridges, and not more than 25 cents for permanent improvements).

Another example is the authority to issue bonds. It is true, as the majority notes, that the Commissioners Court does have this authority. Yet Title 22 of the Texas Civil Statutes sets up a detailed code concerning how and for what purposes bonds may be issued. Significantly, Article 701 provides that county bonds "shall never be issued for any purpose" unless the bond issue has been submitted to the qualified property-taxpaying voters of the county.

More important than the statutory and constitutional limitations, the limited power and function of the Commissioners Court are reflected in what it actually does. * * * [I]t is apparent that the Commissioners are primarily concerned with rural affairs, and more particularly with rural roads. * * * As the Texas Supreme Court stated:

> "Theoretically, the commissioners court is the governing body of the county and the commissioners represent all the residents, both urban and rural, of the county. But developments during the years have greatly narrowed the scope of the functions of the commissioners court and limited its major responsibilities to the nonurban areas of the county. It has come to pass that the city government with its legislative, executive and judicial branches, is the major concern of the city dwellers and the administration of the affairs of the county is the major concern of the rural dwellers." * * *

Moreover, even with regard to those areas specifically delegated to the county government by statute or constitutional provision, the Commissioners Court sometimes does not have the power to make decisions. Within the county government there are numerous departments which are controlled by officials elected independently of the Commissioners Court and over whom the Commissioners Court does not exercise control. The Commissioners view themselves primarily as road commissioners. * * *

As the Texas Supreme Court stated, "the county commissioners court is not charged with the management and control of all of the county's business affairs. * * * The various officials elected by all the voters of the county have spheres that are delegated to them by law and within which the commissioners court may not interfere or usurp." * * * These officials, elected on a direct, one man, one vote, countywide basis, include the Assessor and Collector of Taxes, the County Attorney, the Sheriff, the Treasurer, the County Clerk, and the County Surveyor. The County Judge, who is the presiding officer of the Commissioners Court, is also elected on a countywide basis. Other county officials and employees are appointed by the Commissioners Court.

The elected officials are generally residents of the city, probably because of its preponderant vote. * * * It is apparent that the city people have much more control over the county government than the election of the Commissioners Court would indicate. Many of the county functions which most concern the city, for example, tax assessment and collection, are under the jurisdiction of officials elected by the county at large.

In sum, the Commissioners Court's functions and powers are quite limited, and they are defined and restricted so that their primary and preponderant impact is on the rural areas and residents. The extent of its impact on the city is quite limited. To the extent that there is direct impact on the city, the relevant powers, in important respects, are placed in the hands of officials elected on a one man, one vote basis. Indeed, viewed in terms of the realities of rights and powers, it appears that the city residents have the power to elect the officials who are most important to them, and the rural residents have the electoral power with respect to the Commissioners Court which exercises powers in which they are primarily interested.

* * * Midland County's Commissioners Court has its primary focus in nonurban areas and upon the nonurban people. True, the county's revenues come largely from the City of Midland. But the Commissioners Court fixes the tax rate subject to the specific limitations provided by the legislature. It must spend tax revenues in the categories and percentages which the legislature fixes. Taxes are assessed and collected, not by it, but by an official elected on a county-wide basis. It is quite likely that if the city dwellers were given control of the Commissioners Court, they would reduce the load because it is spent primarily in the rural area. This is a state matter. If the State Legislature, in which presumably the city

dwellers are fairly represented (*Reynolds v. Sims*), wishes to reduce the load, it may do so. But unless we are ready to adopt the position that the Federal Constitution forbids a State from taxing city dwellers to aid their rural neighbors, the fact that city dwellers pay most taxes should not determine the composition of the county governing body. We should not use tax impact as the sole or controlling basis for vote distribution. It is merely one in a number of factors, including the functional impact of the county government, which should be taken into account in determining whether a particular voting arrangement results in reasonable recognition of the rights and interests of citizens. Certainly, neither tax impact nor the relatively few services rendered within the City of Midland should compel the State to vest practically all voting power in the city residents to the virtual denial of a voice to those who are dependent on the county government for roads, welfare, and other essential services.

NOTES AND QUESTIONS

1.   *One Person, One Vote and the Variety of Local Governing Bodies.* As the Court notes, most local governments do not abide by the tidy separation of powers characteristic of federal and state governments. In many jurisdictions there may be no one local governing body. Instead, there may be a profusion of boards, commissions, and authorities that combine legislative and executive authority over various governmental functions. Should each of these entities be subject to one person, one vote? Consider New York City's Board of Estimate, a body of elected officials that managed the city's property, granted franchises, exercised zoning authority, and shared power with the City Council over the city's budget, but which had no general legislative authority. The Supreme Court determined that the Board's powers were "general enough" and had "sufficient impact" throughout the city that one person, one vote applied. Board of Estimate v. Morris, 489 U.S. 688, 697 (1989). For a general overview of the application of the one person, one vote doctrine to local governments, *see* Richard Briffault, Who Rules at Home? One Person/One Vote and Local Governments, 60 U. Chi. L. Rev. 339 (1993).

2.   *One Person, One Vote and the Representation of Territorial Subunits.* Many local governments include smaller local units within their borders. A county may include cities, towns, or villages. A large city may include boroughs or community districts. The one person, one vote doctrine requires that representation in local governing bodies be based on population rather than on political subdivisions. Accommodating local legislative district lines to smaller local or sublocal boundaries can justify relatively minor deviations from population equality, *see, e.g.*, Abate v. Mundt, 403 U.S. 182 (1971) (permitting 11.9% deviation from equality in apportionment of seats in county legislature to enable legislative district lines to correspond to town boundaries within the county), but the one person, one vote principle greatly

limits the ability to provide for the representation of smaller local governments within larger ones.

The priority of population equality over the representation of subunits was confirmed by Board of Estimate v. Morris, *supra*. The New York City Board of Estimate consisted of three officials elected on a city-wide basis, who cast two votes apiece, and New York City's five borough presidents, who cast one vote each. The largest borough, Brooklyn, however, had more than six times the population of the smallest, Staten Island. The borough borders reflected topographical boundaries and historic political subdivision lines (each borough corresponded to a county of New York State), and the boroughs provided a form of sublocal government within New York City. Moreover, a majority of the votes on the Board were vested in the officials elected on a city-wide basis. Although the residents of Staten Island were overrepresented relative to a perfect equality standard, they came nowhere near to dominating the Board, unlike the rural voters in *Avery*. Nonetheless, the Board of Estimate overrepresented some New Yorkers relative to others, and the Supreme Court held the Board's voting structure unconstitutional. New York City subsequently abolished the Board and redistributed its powers.

The application of one person, one vote to local governments has implications for the creation of governance structures to address metropolitan area problems. *See* Robert G. Dixon, Jr., Rebuilding the Urban Political System: Some Heresies Concerning Citizen Participation, Community Action, Metros, and One Man-One Vote, 58 Geo. L.J. 955, 974–84 (1970). As a practical matter, a state may be reluctant to create a regional government without the consent of the residents of the affected local governments. Residents of smaller localities may fear their voices and their interests will be lost in a regional entity unless they are given extra representation. *See, e.g.*, Cunningham v. Municipality of Metropolitan Seattle, 751 F.Supp. 885 (W.D.Wash.1990) (invalidating metropolitan area special district because of overrepresentation of certain cities). *Cunningham* is examined at greater length in Chapter V. Moreover, all participants may view the pre-existing local government as the primary focus of their interests in local governance and thus may seek to provide for representation of their constituent local units in the regional entity. The inability to create a federal structure in which the principle of population equality is tempered by a concern for some parity of representation for the pre-existing units may, thus, create a political barrier to the creation of a regional governance structure. Parity aside, one person, one vote may make it difficult even to use component localities as districts for elections to a regional body if the local units have substantially different populations.

Avery suggested some mechanisms that regional or other large local governments can use to assure representation of component subunits. The Court cited with approval its earlier decisions in Dusch v. Davis, 387 U.S. 112 (1967) and Sailors v. Board of Education of Kent County, 387 U.S. 105 (1967); those cases upheld local arrangements providing for the representation of subunits. *Dusch* involved elections to a local council in which all council members were elected at large, but some were required to be residents of territorial subunits that varied widely in population. As the subunits were used "'merely as the basis of residence for candidates, not for voting or representation,'" 387 U.S. at 115, one person, one vote did not apply. *Sailors* involved the two-step election of members of a county school board. Local voters first elected their local boards, which in turn sent delegates to a meeting at which members of the county school board were elected. At the county board election, however, votes were allocated on a "one local school board, one vote" basis. Since the selection of the county board members did not involve a popular vote, the Court found that the one person, one vote principle did not apply. *Dusch*'s candidate-residence districts (in which voters of the entire regional body participate in the election of the subunit representatives) are relatively uncommon in local elections, but their use for appointive local government positions is more frequent. As one person, one vote applies only to offices filled by popular election, a regional body can be composed of representatives of smaller localities, with each locality having an equal number of representatives regardless of population if the representatives are appointed to the regional board by the component localities. *See, e.g.*, City of St. Albans v. Northwest Regional Planning Comm. 708 A.2d 194 (Vt. 1998) (sustaining regional planning commission composed of representatives appointed by member municipal governments, with each commissioner having one vote, despite differences in populations of appointing communities); Burton v. Whittier Regional Vocational Technical School Dist., 587 F.2d 66 (1st Cir.1978).

3. *General Government or Special Purpose District?* Justice Fortas agreed with the majority that one person, one vote ought to apply to local governments that, like states, "have an essentially equal impact upon all the citizens" in the locality. 390 U.S. at 500 n. 5 (Fortas, J., dissenting). Similarly, the majority suggested that for "a special-purpose unit of government assigned the performance of functions affecting definable groups of constituents more than other constituents," *id.* at 484–85, those more affected by the government's decision might be given a greater electoral voice than those less affected. The heart of the disagreement between Justice White and Justice Fortas, then, was not the principle of whether one person, one vote applied to local governments at all but how that principle applied to the Midland County commissioners court. Was the commissioners court a general purpose local government for the entire territory within the county's boundaries, or was it instead a special purpose government for the rural areas? On the one hand, the court had broad authority over the entire county. On the other, the residents of the City of Midland received most of their services from the city government which was elected by Midland City voters. Moreover, Justice Fortas contended that due to various state constraints on county spending and borrowing, the commissioners court had relatively little authority with respect to county-wide matters.

Is Justice Fortas right in concluding that, given the primary focus of the commissioners court in managing rural roads, rural voters could be given the primary voice in commissioners court elections? Or is Justice White correct in suggesting that the commissioners court's concentration on rural matters despite its much broader powers was not a *justification* for continued rural domination but, instead, the *consequence* of the malapportionment that gave rural voters the dominant position in commissioners court elections? Should the case have come out differently if the commissioners court's sole power was to manage county roads which were located predominantly in rural areas?

Subsequently, in Kramer v. Union Free School District No. 15, 395 U.S. 621 (1969), the Supreme Court held that elections to a local school board were subject to the one person, one vote requirement. In Hadley v. Junior College District of Metropolitan Kansas City, 397 U.S. 50 (1970), the Court extended the one person, one vote rule to elections to a junior college district board.

4.   *What About the Rural Voters*? As Justice Fortas pointed out, one consequence of the decision is to dramatically reduce the voice of rural voters in commissioners court elections. Is there any constitutional mechanism for protecting the influence of rural voters in county elections? Would the rural voters be better off if a separate county were created for them? What would they lose by the formal division of Midland County into separate urban and rural counties?

5.   *Local Taxation and the Local Vote.* Justice Fortas dismissed the significance of the fact that under the Midland apportionment most of the county's taxes were paid by urban voters, but tax rates and the use of tax dollars were effectively controlled by rural voters. As he points out, the state legislature, which was elected on a one person, one vote basis, could redistribute tax dollars from urban to rural voters directly. Why cannot the state effect the same redistribution through the allocation of representation on the county commissioners court?

CITY OF PHOENIX V. KOLODZIEJSKI

Supreme Court of the United States
399 U.S. 204 (1970)

MR. JUSTICE WHITE delivered the opinion of the Court:

Does the Federal Constitution permit a State to restrict to real property taxpayers the vote in elections to approve the issuance of general obligation bonds?

This question arises in the following factual setting: On June 10, 1969, the City of Phoenix, Arizona, held an election to authorize the issuance of $60,450,000 in general obligation bonds as well as certain revenue bonds. Under Arizona law, property taxes were to be levied to service this indebtedness, although the city was legally privileged to use other revenues for this purpose. The general obligation bonds were to be issued to finance various municipal improvements, with the largest amounts to go for the city sewer system, parks and playgrounds, police and public safety buildings, and libraries. Pursuant to Arizona constitutional and statutory provisions, only otherwise qualified voters who were also real property taxpayers were permitted to vote on these bond issues. All of the bond issues submitted to the voters were approved by a majority of those voting. * * *

In *Cipriano v. City of Houma*, [395 U.S. 701] the denial of the franchise to nonproperty owners in elections on revenue bonds was held to be a denial of the Fourteenth Amendment rights of the nonproperty owners since they, as well as property owners, are substantially affected by the issuance of revenue bonds to finance municipal utilities. It is now argued that the rationale of *Cipriano* does not render unconstitutional the exclusion of nonproperty owners from voting in elections on general obligation bonds.

The argument proceeds on two related fronts. First, it is said that the Arizona statutes require that property taxes be levied in an amount sufficient to service the general obligation bonds, the law thus expressly placing a special burden on property owners for the benefit of the entire community. Second, and more generally, whereas revenue bonds are secured by the revenues from the operation of particular facilities and these revenues may be earned from both property owners and nonproperty owners, general obligation bonds are secured by the general taxing power of the issuing municipality. Since most municipalities rely to a substantial extent on property tax revenues which will be used to make debt service payments if other revenue sources prove insufficient, general obligation bonds are in effect a lien on the real property subject to taxation by the issuing municipality. Whatever revenues are actually used to service the bonds, an unavoidable potential tax burden is imposed only on those who own realty since that property cannot be moved beyond the reach of the municipality's taxing power. Hence, according to appellants, the State is justified in recognizing the unique interests of real property owners by allowing only property taxpayers to participate in elections to approve the issuance of general obligation bonds.

holding

*

* * * The differences between the interests of property owners and the interests of nonproperty owners are not sufficiently substantial to justify excluding the latter from the franchise. This is so for several reasons.

First, it is unquestioned that all residents of Phoenix, property owners and nonproperty owners alike, have a substantial interest in the public facilities and the services available in the city and will be substantially affected by the ultimate outcome of the bond election at issue in this case. Presumptively, when all citizens are affected in important ways by a governmental decision subject to a referendum, the Constitution does not permit weighted voting or the exclusion of otherwise qualified citizens from the franchise. * * *

Second, although Arizona law ostensibly calls for the levy of real property taxes to service general obligation bonds, other revenues are legally available for this purpose. According to the parties' stipulation in this case, it is anticipated with respect to the instant bonds, as has been true in the past, that more than half of the debt service requirements will be satisfied not from real property taxes but from revenues from other local taxes paid by nonproperty owners as well as those who own real property. Not only do those persons excluded from the franchise have a great interest in approving or disapproving municipal improvements, but they will also contribute, as directly as property owners, to the servicing of the bonds by the payment of taxes to be used for this purpose.

Third, the justification for restricting the franchise to the property owners would seem to be strongest in the case of a municipality which, unlike Phoenix, looks only to property tax revenues for servicing general obligation bonds. But even in such a case the justification would be insufficient. Property taxes may be paid initially by property owners, but a significant part of the ultimate burden of each year's tax on rental property will very likely be borne by the tenant rather than the landlord since, as the parties also stipulated in this case, the landlord will treat the property tax as a business expense and normally will be able to pass all or a large part of this cost on to the tenants in the form of higher rent. Since most city residents not owning their own homes are lessees of dwelling units, virtually all residents share the burden of property taxes imposed and used to service general obligation bonds. Moreover, property taxes on commercial property, much of which is owned by corporations having no vote, will be treated as a cost of doing business and will normally be reflected in the prices of goods and services purchased by nonproperty owners and property owners alike.

While in theory the expected future income from real property, and hence property values in a municipality, may depend in part on the predicted future levels of property taxes, the actual impact of an increase in property taxes is problematical. Moreover, to the extent that property values are directly affected by the additional potential tax burden entailed in the bond issue, any adverse effect would normally be offset at least in substantial part by the favorable effects on property values of the improvements to be financed by the bond issue.

It is true that a general obligation bond may be loosely described as a "lien" on the property within the jurisdiction of the municipality in the sense that the issuer undertakes to levy sufficient taxes to service the bond. In theory, if the economy of the issuing city were to collapse, the

levy of sufficiently high property taxes on property producing little or no income might result in some cases in defaults, foreclosures, and tax sales. Nothing before us, however, indicates that the possibility of future foreclosures to meet bond obligations significantly affects current real estate values or the ability of the concerned property owner to liquidate his holdings to avoid the risk of those future difficulties; the price of real estate appears to be more a function of the health of the local economy than a reflection of the level of property taxes imposed to finance municipal improvements. In any event, we are not convinced that the risk of future economic collapse that might result in bond obligations becoming an unshiftable, unsharable burden on property owners is sufficiently real or substantial to justify denying the vote in a current bond election to all those nonproperty owners who have a significant interest in the facilities to be financed, who are now indirectly sharing the property tax burden, and who will be paying other taxes used by the municipality to service its general obligation bonds.

We thus conclude that, although owners of real property have interests somewhat different from the interests of nonproperty owners in the issuance of general obligation bonds, there is no basis for concluding that nonproperty owners are substantially less interested in the issuance of these securities than are property owners. That there is no adequate reason to restrict the franchise on the issuance of general obligation bonds to property owners is further evidenced by the fact that only 14 States now restrict the franchise in this way; most States find it possible to protect property owners from excessive property tax burdens by means other than restricting the franchise to property owners. The States now allowing all qualified voters to vote in general obligation bond elections do not appear to have been significantly less successful in protecting property values and in soundly financing their municipal improvements. Nor have we been shown that the 14 States now restricting the franchise have unique problems that make it necessary to limit the vote to property owners.

NOTES AND QUESTIONS

1. *Who Bears the Tax Burden—And Should It Matter in Determining the Local Vote?* The City of Phoenix argued that since property taxes were to be levied to pay the debt service on general obligation bonds, it was reasonable to limit the vote on bond issues to taxpayers. As the Court pointed out, however, much of the revenue Phoenix collected to pay its debts came from other local taxes, including taxes paid by residents not subject to the property tax. Should the case have come out differently if Phoenix's general obligation bonds were serviced solely by property tax payments?

The Phoenix property tax is formally paid by Phoenix property owners, but Justice White contended that "a significant part of the ultimate burden" of the property tax is passed along by residential property owners to their tenants and by commercial property owners to Phoenix residents who consume goods and services produced by the commercial taxpayers. The ability of residential landowners to shift the burden to their tenants, however, is affected by competition in the rental market. If there were an excess supply of rental units, landowners might be unable to pass along any additional property taxes resulting from the bond issue. Similarly, the ability of Phoenix producers to pass along a tax increase imposed on commercial property will be affected by competition between Phoenix producers and producers from outside the city. Who should have the burden of proving that the property tax is passed along to nonproperty owners—the plaintiffs challenging the state law, or the City arguing for a restriction on the franchise to property taxpayers?

Even if it turns out that property taxpayers bear most of the burden of the property tax, should that affect the outcome of the case? As the Court noted, nontaxpayers would *benefit* from the facilities to be financed by the bond issue. Why isn't benefit as important as tax burden in determining who is entitled to vote in a local election?

2. *Can Taxpayers Get a Greater Voice?* Assuming that the bond issue affects both taxpayers and nontaxpaying residents, but that the taxpayers are somewhat more affected, would it be constitutional to create a mechanism in which both groups participate but the taxpayers get an extra voice? Arguably, that is what Arizona law provided for. Taxpayers and nontaxpayers participated on a one person, one vote basis in the election of the Phoenix city council which proposed the bond issue; taxpayers then voted on the bond issue itself. If all residents are entitled to vote on a bond issue, could a city require the separate approval of both taxpayers and nontaxpayers before a bond could be issued? *See* Hill v. Stone, 421 U.S. 289 (1975) (invalidating Texas "dual box" voting technique for bond elections; election scheme failed to meet compelling state interest test).

Professor Robert C. Ellickson criticized *City of Phoenix* and the constitutional ban on laws that would limit the local franchise to property taxpayers. Although he agrees that universal suffrage, without regard to property ownership, ought to be the rule for federal and state elections, he argues that property taxpayers are particularly affected by local government decisions, with local taxes capitalized into land values. Although he would not mandate limiting the franchise to property owners, he would allow localities that option. *See* Robert C. Ellickson, Cities and Homeowners Associations, 130 U.Pa.L.Rev. 1519, 1539–63 (1982). For critical reviews of Ellickson's proposal, *see* Frank Michelman, Universal Resident Suffrage: A Liberal Defense, 130 U.Pa.L.Rev. 1581 (1982); Gerald E. Frug, Cities and Homeowners Associations: A Reply, 130 U.Pa.L.Rev. 1589 (1982).

3. *Parent Power in School Board Elections?* In Kramer v. Union Free School Dist., 395 U.S. 621 (1969), the Court invalidated a New York law that limited the right to vote in school board elections to the owners or renters of

taxable property within the school district and to the parents of children enrolled in the district's schools. The effect of the law was to disenfranchise the plaintiff, an otherwise eligible voter who had no children, lived with his parents, and neither owned nor leased taxable property in the district. The Court held that a restriction on the local franchise would be subject to strict judicial scrutiny and would be sustained only if narrowly drawn to advance a compelling state interest. The state asserted it had a compelling interest in limiting the franchise to the portion of the community primarily interested in and affected by school board elections, that is, parents and the direct and indirect payers of the property tax. The Court declined to reach the question of whether limiting the franchise to the "primarily interested" constituency, 395 U.S. at 632, is a compelling state interest for a voting rule because it found that the state had failed to align the franchise precisely with the primarily interested group. According to the Court, the plaintiff, although neither a parent nor a local taxpayer, was "substantially interested in and significantly affected by" school board decisions. *Id.* at 630. The Court, however, failed to explain how the plaintiff was interested in or affected by the election since he neither used the district's services nor paid for them. Is the Court stating that all area residents are necessarily affected by the local elementary and secondary school system and, thus, ought to have the right to vote in local school board elections?

Somewhat paradoxically, *Kramer*'s protection of the school district franchise subsequently operated to limit a state's experimentation with school-based governance. In Fumarolo v. Chicago Board of Education, the Illinois Supreme Court held that *Kramer* required it to invalidate the franchise and representation provisions of the 1988 Chicago School Reform Act, which provided for the creation of local school councils for each of Chicago's schools. These councils were given powers over the hiring of the principal, the recommendation of textbooks, disciplinary and attendance policies, and the review of the principal's expenditure plan. Each council was to consist of ten members, with six elected by parents, two elected by the school's teachers, and two elected by community residents. The court found that given a council's broad powers over education within its school, the one person, one vote rule applied. Due to the exclusion of nonparent residents from voting for most of a council's seats, the Act was unconstitutional. Fumarolo v. Chicago Board of Educ., 566 N.E.2d 1283 (Ill. 1990). In response to *Fumarolo*, the Illinois legislature revised the law to enable all residents to vote for all members of a council, while still reserving six seats on the council (out of eight) for parents. The United States Court of Appeals for the Seventh Circuit upheld the law, reasoning that due to the very limited powers of the local schools councils their elections did not trigger the one person, one vote requirement. Pittman v. Chicago Board of Educ., 64 F.3d 1098 (7th Cir.1995). Should a state or locality be able to give parents a greater vote than other residents in local school board elections? Is the question of a greater vote for parents comparable to, or different from, the question of a greater vote for taxpayers?

HOLT CIVIC CLUB V. CITY OF TUSCALOOSA
Supreme Court of the United States
439 U.S. 60 (1978)

MR. JUSTICE REHNQUIST delivered the opinion of the Court.

Holt is a small, largely rural, unincorporated community located on the northeastern outskirts of Tuscaloosa, the fifth largest city in Alabama. Because the community is within the three-mile police jurisdiction circumscribing Tuscaloosa's corporate limits, its residents are subject to the city's "police [and] sanitary regulations." * * * Holt residents are also subject to the criminal jurisdiction of the city's court, * * * and to the city's power to license businesses, trades, and professions. * * * Tuscaloosa, however, may collect from businesses in the police jurisdiction only one-half of the license fee chargeable to similar businesses conducted within the corporate limits.

In 1973 appellants, an unincorporated civic association and seven individual residents of Holt, brought this statewide class action in the United States District Court for the Northern District of Alabama, challenging the constitutionality of these Alabama statutes. They claimed that the city's extraterritorial exercise of police powers over Holt residents, without a concomitant extension of the franchise on an equal footing with those residing within the corporate limits, denies residents of the police jurisdiction rights secured by the Due Process and Equal Protection Clauses of the Fourteenth Amendment.

* * *

Appellants focus their equal protection attack on * * * the statute fixing the limits of municipal police jurisdiction and giving extraterritorial effect to municipal police and sanitary ordinances. Citing *Kramer v. Union Free School Dist.*, 395 U.S. 621 (1969), and cases following in its wake, appellants argue that the section creates a classification infringing on their right to participate in municipal elections. The State's denial of the franchise to police jurisdiction residents, appellants urge, can stand only if justified by a compelling state interest.

* * * From * * * our * * * voting qualifications cases a common characteristic emerges: The challenged statute in each case denied the franchise to individuals who were physically resident within the geographic boundaries of the governmental entity concerned. *See, e.g., Hill v. Stone*, 421 U.S. 289 (1975) (invalidating provision of the Texas Constitution restricting franchise on general obligation bond issue to residents who had "rendered" or listed real, mixed, or personal property for taxation in the election district); *Harper v. Virginia Board of Elections*, 383 U.S. 663 (1966) (invalidating Virginia statute conditioning the right

to vote of otherwise qualified residents on payment of a poll tax); *cf.* *Turner v. Fouche*, 396 U.S. 346 (1970) (invalidating Georgia statute restricting county school board membership to *residents* owning real property in the county). No decision of this Court has extended the "one man, one vote" principle to individuals residing beyond the geographic confines of the governmental entity concerned, be it the State or its political subdivisions. On the contrary, our cases have uniformly recognized that a government unit may legitimately restrict the right to participate in its political processes to those who reside within its borders. [citations omitted]

Appellants' argument that extraterritorial extension of municipal powers requires concomitant extraterritorial extension of the franchise proves too much. The imaginary line defining a city's corporate limits cannot corral the influence of municipal actions. A city's decisions inescapably affect individuals living immediately outside its borders. The granting of building permits for high rise apartments, industrial plants, and the like on the city's fringe unavoidably contributes to problems of traffic congestion, school districting, and law enforcement immediately outside the city. A rate change in the city's sales or ad valorem tax could well have a significant impact on retailers and property values in areas bordering the city. The condemnation of real property on the city's edge for construction of a municipal garbage dump or waste treatment plant would have obvious implications for neighboring nonresidents. Indeed, the indirect extraterritorial effects of many purely internal municipal actions could conceivably have a heavier impact on surrounding environs than the direct regulation contemplated by Alabama's police jurisdiction statutes. Yet no one would suggest that nonresidents likely to be affected by this sort of municipal action have a constitutional right to participate in the political processes bringing it about. And unless one adopts the idea that the Austinian notion of sovereignty, which is presumably embodied to some extent in the authority of a city over a police jurisdiction, distinguishes the direct effects of limited municipal powers over police jurisdiction residents from the indirect though equally dramatic extraterritorial effects of purely internal municipal actions, it makes little sense to say that one requires extension of the franchise while the other does not.

Given this country's tradition of popular sovereignty, appellants' claimed right to vote in Tuscaloosa elections is not without some logical appeal. We are mindful, however, of Mr. Justice Holmes' observation in *Hudson Water Co. v. McCarter*, 209 U.S. 349, 355 (1908):

"All rights tend to declare themselves absolute to their logical extreme. Yet all in fact are limited by the neighborhood of principles of policy which are other than those on which the particular right is founded, and which become strong enough to hold their own when a certain point is reached. . . . The boundary at which the conflicting interests balance cannot be determined by any general formula in advance, but points in the line, or helping to establish it, are fixed by decisions that this or that concrete case falls on the nearer or farther side."

The line heretofore marked by this Court's voting qualifications decisions coincides with the geographical boundary of the governmental unit at issue, and we hold that appellants' case, like their homes, falls on the farther side.

Thus stripped of its voting rights attire, the equal protection issue presented by appellants becomes whether the Alabama statutes giving extraterritorial force to certain municipal ordinances and powers bear some rational relationship to a legitimate state purpose. * * *

Government, observed Mr. Justice Johnson, "is the science of experiment," *Anderson v. Dunn*, 6 Wheat. 204, 226 (1821), and a State is afforded wide leeway when experimenting with the appropriate allocation of state legislative power. This Court has often recognized that political subdivisions such as cities and counties are created by the State "as convenient agencies for exercising such of the governmental powers of the State as may be entrusted to them." *Hunter v. Pittsburgh*, 207 U.S. 161, 178 (1907). *See also, e.g., Sailors v. Board of Education*, 387 U.S., at 108; *Reynolds v. Sims*, 377 U.S. 533, 575 (1964). In *Hunter v. Pittsburgh*, the Court discussed at length the relationship between a State and its political subdivisions, remarking: "The number, nature and duration of the powers conferred upon [municipal] corporations and the territory over which they shall be exercised rests in the absolute discretion of the State." 207 U.S., at 178. While the broad statements as to state control over municipal corporations contained in *Hunter* have undoubtedly been qualified by the holdings of later cases such as *Kramer v. Union Free School Dist., supra,* we think that the case continues to have substantial constitutional significance in emphasizing the extraordinarily wide latitude that States have in creating various types of political subdivisions and conferring authority upon them.

The extraterritorial exercise of municipal powers is a governmental technique neither recent in origin nor unique to the State of Alabama. *See* R. Maddox, Extraterritorial Powers of Municipalities in the United States (1955). In this country 35 States authorize their municipal subdivisions to exercise governmental powers beyond their corporate limits. Comment, The Constitutionality of the Exercise of Extraterritorial Powers by Municipalities, 45 U. Chi. L. Rev. 151 (1977). Although the extraterritorial municipal powers granted by these States vary widely, several States grant their cities more extensive or intrusive powers over bordering areas than those granted under the Alabama statutes.[8]

In support of their equal protection claim, appellants suggest a number of "constitutionally preferable" governmental alternatives to Alabama's system of municipal police jurisdictions. For example, exclusive management of the police jurisdiction by county officials, appellants maintain, would be more "practical." From a political science standpoint, appellants' suggestions may be sound, but this Court does not sit to determine whether Alabama has chosen the soundest or most practical form of internal government possible. Authority to make those judgments resides in the state legislature, and Alabama citizens are free to urge their proposals to that body. *See, e.g., Hunter v. Pittsburgh,* 207 U.S., at 179. Our inquiry is limited to the question whether "any state of facts reasonably may be conceived to justify" Alabama's system of police jurisdictions * * * and in this case it takes but momentary reflection to arrive at an affirmative answer.

The Alabama Legislature could have decided that municipal corporations should have some measure of control over activities carried on just beyond their "city limit" signs, particularly since today's police jurisdiction may be tomorrow's annexation to the city proper. Nor need the city's interests have been the only concern of the legislature when it enacted the police jurisdiction statutes. Urbanization of any area brings with it a number of individuals who long both for the quiet of suburban or country living and for the career opportunities offered by the city's working environment. Unincorporated communities like Holt dot the rim of most major population centers in Alabama and elsewhere, and state legislatures have a legitimate interest in seeing that this substantial segment of the population does not go without basic municipal services

---

8 * * * Cities in many States are statutorily authorized to zone extraterritorially, [citing Arizona, Michigan, and North Dakota statutes], a power not afforded Alabama municipalities. * * *

We do not have before us, of course, a situation in which a city has annexed outlying territory in all but name, and is exercising precisely the same governmental powers over residents of surrounding unincorporated territory as it does over those residing within its corporate limits. *See Little Thunder v. South Dakota,* 518 F.2d 1253 (C.A.8 1975). Nor do we have here a case like *Evans v. Cornman,* [398 U.S. 419 (1970)] where NIH [National Institute of Health, a federal enclave in Maryland] residents were subject to such "important aspects of state powers" as Maryland's authority "to levy and collect [its] income, gasoline, sales, and use taxes" and were "just as interested in and connected with electoral decisions as * * * their neighbors who [lived] off the enclave." 398 U.S., at 423, 424, 426.

Appellants have made neither an allegation nor a showing that the authority exercised by the city of Tuscaloosa within the police jurisdiction is no less than that exercised by the city within its corporate limits. The minute catalog of ordinances of the city of Tuscaloosa which have extraterritorial effect set forth by our dissenting Brethren * * * is as notable for what it does not include as for what it does. While the burden was on appellants to establish a difference in treatment violative of the Equal Protection Clause, we are bound to observe that among the powers not included in the "addendum" to appellants' brief referred to by the dissent are the vital and traditional authorities of cities and towns to levy ad valorem taxes, invoke the power of eminent domain, and zone property for various types of uses.

such as police, fire, and health protection. Established cities are experienced in the delivery of such services, and the incremental cost of extending the city's responsibility in these areas to surrounding environs may be substantially less than the expense of establishing wholly new service organizations in each community.

Nor was it unreasonable for the Alabama Legislature to require police jurisdiction residents to contribute through license fees to the expense of services provided them by the city. The statutory limitation on license fees to half the amount exacted within the city assures that police jurisdiction residents will not be victimized by the city government.

"Viable local governments may need many innovations, numerous combinations of old and new devices, great flexibility in municipal arrangements to meet changing urban conditions." *Sailors v. Board of Education*, 387 U.S., at 110–111. This observation in Sailors was doubtless as true at the turn of this century, when urban areas throughout the country were temporally closer to the effects of the industrial revolution. Alabama's police jurisdiction statute, enacted in 1907, was a rational legislative response to the problems faced by the State's burgeoning cities. Alabama is apparently content with the results of its experiment, and nothing in the Equal Protection Clause of the Fourteenth Amendment requires that it try something new.

MR. JUSTICE BRENNAN, with whom MR. JUSTICE WHITE and MR. JUSTICE MARSHALL join, dissenting.

* * * Our decisions before today have held that bona fide residency requirements are an acceptable means of distinguishing qualified from unqualified voters. * * * The Court holds today, however, that the restriction of the franchise to those residing within the corporate limits of the city of Tuscaloosa is such a bona fide residency requirement. * * * The Court thus insulates the Alabama statutes challenged in this case from the strict judicial scrutiny ordinarily applied to state laws distributing the franchise. In so doing, the Court cedes to geography a talismanic significance contrary to the theory and meaning of our past voting-rights cases.

We have previously held that when statutes distributing the franchise depend upon residency requirements, state-law characterizations of residency are not controlling for purposes of the Fourteenth Amendment. *See, e.g.*, *Evans v. Cornman*, 398 U.S. 419 (1970); *Carrington v. Rash*, 380 U.S. 89 (1965). Indeed, *Dunn v. Blumstein*, [405 U.S. 330 (1972)], was careful to exempt from strict judicial scrutiny only bona fide residency requirements that were "appropriately defined and uniformly applied." 405 U.S., at 343. The touchstone for determining whether a residency requirement is "appropriately defined" derives from the purpose of such requirements, which, as stated in *Dunn*, is "to preserve the basic conception of a political community." *Id.*, at 344. At the heart of our basic conception of a "political community," however, is the notion of a reciprocal relationship between the process of government and those who subject themselves to that process by choosing to live within the area of its authoritative application. *Cf. Avery v. Midland County*, 390 U.S. 474, 485 (1968). Statutes such as those challenged in this case, which fracture this relationship by severing the connection between the process of government and those who are governed in the places of their residency, thus undermine the very purposes which have led this Court in the past to approve the application of bona fide residency requirements.

There is no question but that the residents of Tuscaloosa's police jurisdiction are governed by the city.[10] Under Alabama law, a

---

[10] Appellants have included in their brief an unchallenged addendum listing the ordinances of the city of Tuscaloosa, Code of Tuscaloosa (1962, Supplemented 1975), that have application in its police jurisdiction:

"*Licenses*:

    4–1 ambulance

    9–4, 9–18, 9–33 bottle dealers

    19–1 junk dealers

    20–5 general business license ordinance

    20–67 florists

    20–102 hotels, motels, etc.

    20–163 industry

"*Buildings*:

    10–1 inspection service enforces codes

    10–10 regulation of dams

    10–21 Southern Standard Building Code adopted

    10–25 building permits

    13–3 National Electrical Code adopted

    14–23 Fire Prevention Code adopted

    14–65 regulation of incinerators

    14–81 discharge of cinders

    Chapter 21A mobile home parks

    25–1 Southern Standard Plumbing Code adopted

    33–79 disposal of human wastes

    33–114, 118 regulation of wells

"*Public Health:*

    5–4 certain birds protected

    5–4C, 42, 55 dogs running at large and bitches in heat prohibited

    14–4 no smoking on buses

    14–15 no self-service gas stations

    15–2 regulation of sale of produce from trucks

    15–4 food establishments to use public water supply

    15–16 food, meat, milk inspectors

    15–37 thru 40 regulates boardinghouses

    15–52 milk code adopted

    17–5 mosquito control

municipality exercises "governing" and "lawmaking" power over its police jurisdiction. * * * Residents of Tuscaloosa's police jurisdiction are subject to license fees exacted by the city, as well as to the city's police and sanitary regulations, which can be enforced through penal sanctions effective in the city's municipal court. * * * The Court seems to imply, however, that residents of the police jurisdiction are not governed enough to be included within the political community of Tuscaloosa, since they are not subject to Tuscaloosa's powers of eminent domain, zoning, or ad valorem taxation. * * * But this position is sharply contrary to our previous holdings. In *Kramer v. Union Free School Dist.*, 395 U.S. 621 (1969), for example, we held that residents of a school district who neither

---

"*Traffic Regulations*:

    22–2 stop & yield signs may be erected by chief of police

    22–3 mufflers required

    22–4 brakes required

    22–5 inspection of vehicle by police

    22–6 operation of vehicle

    22–9 hitchhiking in roadway prohibited

    22–9.1 permit to solicit funds on roadway

    22–11 impounding cars

    22–14 load limit on bridges

    2–15 police damage stickers required after accident

    22–25 driving while intoxicated

    22–26 reckless driving

    22–27 driving without consent of owner

    22–33 stop sign

    22–34 yield sign

    22–38 driving across median

    22–40 yield to emergency vehicle

    22–42 cutting across private property

    22–54 general speed limit

    22–72 thru 78 truck routes

"*Criminal Ordinances*:

    23–1 adopts all state misdemeanors

    23–7.1 no wrecked cars on premises

    23–15 nuisances

    23–17 obscene literature

    23–20 destruction of plants

    23–37 swimming in nude

    23–38 trespass to boats

    26–51 no shooting galleries in the police jurisdiction or outside fire limits (downtown area)

    28–31 thru 39 obscene films

"*Miscellaneous*:

    20–120 thru 122 cigarette tax

    24–31 public parks and recreation

    26–18 admission tax

    Chapter 29 regulates public streets

    30–23 taxis must have meters."

owned nor leased taxable real property located within the district, or were not married to someone who did, or were not parents or guardians of children enrolled in a local district school, nevertheless were sufficiently affected by the decisions of the local school board to make the denial of their franchise in local school board elections a violation of the Equal Protection Clause. Similarly, we held in *Cipriano v. City of Houma*, 395 U.S. 701 (1969), that a Louisiana statute limiting the franchise in municipal utility system revenue bond referenda to those who were "property taxpayers" was unconstitutional because all residents of the municipality were affected by the operation of the utility system. *See Phoenix v. Kolodziejski*, 399 U.S. 204 (1970).

The residents of Tuscaloosa's police jurisdiction are vastly more affected by Tuscaloosa's decisionmaking processes than were the plaintiffs in either *Kramer* or *Cipriano* affected by the decisionmaking processes from which they had been unconstitutionally excluded. * * * A municipality, for example, may use its police powers to regulate, or even to ban, common professions and businesses. * * * The Court today does not explain why being subjected to the authority to exercise such extensive power does not suffice to bring the residents of Tuscaloosa's police jurisdiction within the political community of the city. Nor does the Court in fact provide any standards for determining when those subjected to extraterritorial municipal legislation will have been "governed enough" to trigger the protections of the Equal Protection Clause. * * *

The Court argues, however, that if the franchise were extended to residents of the city's police jurisdiction, the franchise must similarly be extended to all those indirectly affected by the city's actions. This is a simple non sequitur. There is a crystal-clear distinction between those who reside in Tuscaloosa's police jurisdiction, and who are therefore subject to that city's police and sanitary ordinances, licensing fees, and the jurisdiction of its municipal court, and those who reside in neither the city nor its police jurisdiction, and who are thus merely affected by the indirect impact of the city's decisions.

NOTES AND QUESTIONS

1. *Extraterritoriality*. As the Court notes, many states grant some municipalities powers to provide public services and regulate conduct outside municipal boundaries. These extraterritorial powers may include zoning, prohibition of nuisances, licensing and regulation of businesses, criminal law enforcement, and general health and safety regulation. Extraterritorial powers may advance the interests of the municipality by allowing it to regulate activities just beyond its borders that may have direct effects on the health, safety, or development of the municipality. Extraterritoriality may reflect state policies designed to facilitate central city expansion and limit the formation of new municipalities on the urban fringe by strengthening the

power of the core city over fringe development and by reducing the incentive for fringe areas to incorporate in order to obtain urban services. Extraterritoriality may be a way of providing the necessary regulation and services to fringe areas that have neither the population nor the resources to support their own municipal government. As in *Holt Civic Club*, courts are generally deferential to state legislative decisions to grant some municipalities extraterritorial authority. *See, e.g.*, Mixon v. State of Ohio, 193 F.3d 389, 404–06 (6th Cir.1999) (sustaining Ohio law reorganizing the Cleveland School District by allowing the Mayor of the City of Cleveland to appoint all members of the school board even though four other communities in addition to the City of Cleveland are within the district; upheld, even when considered as a form of extraterritorial authority, as a reasonable response to the state's interest in improving public schools). However, courts may require that municipalities claiming extraterritorial authority demonstrate that such authority has been expressly granted by the state. *See, e.g.*, Seigles, Inc. v. City of St. Charles, 849 N.E.2d 456 (Ill. App. 2006) (extraterritorial application of municipal lumber tax ordinance invalid in absence of express grant of extraterritorial authority by the state legislature).

Extraterritorial authority reflects the state's use of local government to accomplish its own ends and to benefit the municipality given extraterritorial authority. But extraterritoriality separates local government power from local representation. The residents of Holt, for example, were subject to regulation by a government they had no voice in electing. From their perspective, Tuscaloosa was not so much their local government as an arm of the state providing them with local services and regulation. Their voice in local governance was indirect, through their participation in the election of the state government officials that ultimately structured and controlled local government in Alabama. The argument that such a limited voice was sufficient to protect the interest in local self-government was rejected in *Avery* but accepted in *Holt Civic Club*. Can the two cases be reconciled?

2.   *A Question of Boundaries. Holt Civic Club* holds that constitutional protection of the right to vote in local elections extends only to those who reside within local boundaries. But even if one accepts the constitutional validity of that principle, how does that principle resolve the case? *Holt Civic Club* does not involve the claim of a right to vote in a local government election by residents of a nearby community indirectly affected by local decision-making. The people of Holt were directly subject to Tuscaloosa's police jurisdiction. The state of Alabama had drawn two sets of boundary lines—one setting the Tuscaloosa corporate limits and the other creating the police jurisdiction. Given Tuscaloosa's formal authority over Holt, why aren't the boundaries of the police jurisdiction the critical boundaries for determining residency for purposes of voting in local elections? The legal issues surrounding the government's delineation of boundaries between and among local government units are discussed more extensively in Chapter III.

3.   *Extraterritoriality v. De Facto Governance. Holt* emphasized the relatively limited authority that the City of Tuscaloosa exercised over its

police jurisdiction, finding this was not "a situation in which a city has annexed outlying territory in all but name." Other courts have also looked to the limited nature of the extraterritorial power in upholding extraterritorial authority. *See, e.g.*, Schmidt v. City of Kenosha, 571 N.W.2d 892 (Wis.App.1997). In note 8 of the *Holt* majority opinion, the Court pointed to ad valorem (property) taxation, zoning, and eminent domain as the kind of extraterritorial powers that support the claim of de facto governance. Yet in practice extraterritorial authority often includes eminent domain, Municipalities have long been granted the power to create and control necessary infrastructure facilities—reservoirs and water supply, sewage and solid waste disposal plants, utilities—beyond their borders and to use eminent domain to secure the necessary land. *See* Richard Briffault, *Town of Telluride v. San Miguel Valley Corp.: Extraterritoriality and Local Autonomy*, 86 Denver U. L. Rev. 1311, 1316 (2009); Town of Telluride v. San Miguel Valley Corp., 185 P.3d 161 (Colo. 2008) (treating extraterritorial eminent domain as one of a municipality's home rule powers and sustaining exterritorial condemnation for "open space, parks, and recreation"); Reed v. City of Idaho Falls, 742 F.3d 1100 (9th Cir. 2013) (finding that state of Idaho has expressly granted cities extraterritorial eminent domain power for purposes of constructing cemeteries, and constructing and maintaining airports, but not for constructing electric transmission lines). *Telluride v. San Miguel Valley Corp.* is a principal case examined in Chapter IV. Extraterritorial zoning and land use regulation also occur, despite the voting rights and interlocal planning coordination issues such extraterritorial activity raises. *See* Andrew P. Gulotta, Darkness on the Edge of Town: Reforming Extraterritorial Planning and Zoning in Illinois to Ensure Regional Effectiveness and Representation, 28 St. Louis U. Pub. L. Rev. 495 (2009); Town of Northville v. Village of Sheridan, 655 N.E.2d 22 (Ill. App. 1995) (relying on *Holt* to reject claim of Northville residents that because they were subject to Sheridan's extraterritorial zoning they were entitled to vote in Sheridan's municipal elections). Extraterritorial taxation, however, is rarely authorized, Briffault, *supra,* 86 Denver U. L. Rev, at 1313–18.

Two decisions by the United States Court of Appeals for the Third Circuit concerning relationships between New Jersey school districts nicely illustrate the indeterminacy of the extraterritoriality/de facto governance distinction. In English v. Board of Educ. of Boonton, 301 F.3d 69 (3d Cir.2002) and Board of Educ. of Branchburg v. Livingston, 312 F.3d 614 (3d Cir.2002), the court considered the right to vote implications of a so-called send-receive relationship in which one school district that does not maintain a high school sends its high school age students to a neighboring district which does operate a high school. The sending district pays its students' "actual costs" and is able to send one representative to the receiving district's school board; that representative may vote only on high school issues. The receiving district's residents elect the other nine school board members. In the *Boonton* and *Branchburg* cases, over time the sending districts had grown faster than the receiving districts and actually accounted for a majority of the receiving districts' high school student populations. Although these arrangements were originally entered into voluntarily, many of their terms were governed by state law, and the relationship was difficult to sever. Residents of the sending districts sued, claiming that the voting rules violated their constitutional rights. They contended that because a receiving district exercises complete control over the high school education of the children from a sending community, *Holt* should not apply. The Third Circuit, however, disagreed, finding that the sending community's residents "are subject to the extraterritorial powers of the Boonton board only with respect to their high school-aged children. For matters concerning K–8 education, the residents of Lincoln Park [the sending community] exercise exclusive control through their own school board elected solely by Lincoln Park residents." 301 F.3d at 79. Similarly, in the *Branchburg* case, Branchburg, the sending community, "is free to control the education of its children from K–8, and the reach of Somerville's [the receiving district] powers over Branchburg is limited exclusively to the High School. . . . [T]his is not a situation where the powers of Somerville are coextensive with regard to both Somerville and Branchburg residents." 312 F.3d at 623. *Branchburg* also dismissed the significance of the fact that although the send-receive relationship was originally entered into voluntarily it became extremely difficult to terminate. *Id.* at 623–24. Do you agree with the Third Circuit that in assessing whether the receiving district was the de facto school district for the sending district that the proper focus was the full K–12 educational program, rather than just high school? The *Boonton* and *Branchburg* cases are discussed more fully in Chapter V.

4. *Local Voting and Local Residency.* In Kramer v. Union Free School District, *supra*, the Supreme Court held that restrictions on the local franchise would be subject to strict judicial scrutiny. The Court indicated, however, that requirements that a voter be an adult, a United States citizen, and a local resident were constitutional—either those requirements would not be subjected to strict scrutiny, or they satisfied it. Why is local residency a valid criterion for the local vote? In a contemporaneous case, the Court observed that bona fide residency requirements are "necessary to preserve the basic conception of a political community." Dunn v. Blumstein, 405 U.S. 330, 343–44 (1972). Do you agree? Why or why not?

Several local government scholars have challenged the connection between local residency and the local vote. Pointing to the impacts of local government decisions on nearby communities, and to the regular movements of metropolitan area workers and shoppers across local boundaries, Professors Jerry Frug and Richard Thompson Ford have argued that local elections ought to be open to all residents of the metropolitan region. *See* Richard Thompson Ford, The Boundaries of Race: Political Geography in Legal Analysis, 107 Harv.L.Rev. 1841, 1909–10 (1994); Jerry Frug, Decentering Decentralization, 60 U.Chi.L.Rev. 253, 329–30 (1993). They have presented proposals in which each regional voter would be entitled to cast a number of votes in local elections; the voter could then decide in which locality or localities to cast his or her votes. According to Professor Ford, by providing for broader "democratic inclusion," this electoral reform would ameliorate the "evils of parochialism and insularity." 107 Harv.L.Rev. at 1909. For a criticism of these proposals on the grounds that they would undermine the local conditions conducive to political participation, and would especially threaten local self-determination for central cities, *see* Richard Briffault, The Local Government Boundary Problem in Metropolitan Areas, 48 Stan.L.Rev. 1115, 1156–62 (1996).

5. *Local Residency and Second Homes*. In practice, the principal challenge to the link between local residency and local voting comes from the growing number of Americans who maintain homes in two or more localities. Unless these second-home residents elect to declare their second home to be their primary residence, they are typically considered to be nonresidents and barred from voting in their second-home jurisdiction. Yet, in many beach or mountain resort communities a significant fraction of local property taxes are paid by property owners who reside in the community on weekends or during vacation periods. As a result, "[f]rom Cape Cod to Colorado, second-home owners are clamoring—usually with the help of their lawyers—for a limited franchise. They want a voice in how their tax dollars are spent and in how much year-rounders may charge them for services they seldom use." Blaine Harden, Summer Residents Want Year-Round Voice, New York Times, May 30, 2000, at A1 (noting that in Southhampton, N.Y. three-quarters of village property taxes are paid by summer residents). Should someone be able to vote in local elections in two communities if she maintains homes in both communities? For a criticism of allowing part-time residents to vote in their second-home locality, *see* Amitai Etzioni, Summer-Share Citizenship?, New York Times, June 1, 2000, at A29. For an argument that bona fide second-home residents ought to be allowed to vote in local elections wherever they reside, *see* Ashira Pelman Ostrow, Note, Dual Resident Voting: Traditional Disfranchisement and Prospects for Change, 102 Colum. L. Rev. 1954 (2002). The United States Court of Appeals for the Second Circuit rejected such an argument, finding that the state could constitutionally limit someone to one voting residence, *see* Wit v. Berman, 306 F.3d 1256 (2d Cir.2002). *Wit* is discussed more fully in Chapter III.

If the franchise is extended to second-home residents, do other residents have a claim that their voting rights have been unconstitutionally diluted? The issue has arisen in several cases; the courts typically hold that the extension of the franchise to those who do not have a constitutional right to vote is subject only to the rational basis test, not strict scrutiny. The ownership of taxable property has been held to give nonresidents sufficient interest in local affairs to make it rational to include them in the local political process. *See, e.g.*, May v. Town of Mountain Village, 132 F.3d 576 (10th Cir.1997); Bjornestad v. Hulse, 281 Cal.Rptr. 548 (1991) (franchise in water district extended to residents and all nonresident property owners including commercial entities); Snead v. City of Albuquerque, 663 F.Supp. 1084 (D.N.M.1987), *aff'd*, 841 F.2d 1131, *cert. denied*, 485 U.S. 1009 (1988) (right to vote in city bond issue election extended to all residents and to residents of the surrounding county who owned property in the city but did not live in the city); Glisson v. Mayor & Councilmen of Town of Savannah Beach, 346 F.2d 135 (5th Cir.1965). *But cf.* Brown v. Board of Commissioners of Chattanooga, 722 F.Supp. 380, 399 (E.D.Tenn.1989) (unconstitutional to extend the franchise to nonresidents who own "trivial" fractional interests in local property).

6. *The Right to Vote in Overlapping School Districts.* An issue comparable to that presented by the enfranchisement of nonresidents arose in a series of cases concerning city and county boards of education, where one school system operates in a city and the second operates in the county in which the city is located. The city residents are primarily served by the city school system, and they vote in city school board elections. But they may be enfranchised to vote in county school board elections, too. The county residents who live outside the city contended that city resident voting in county school board elections unconstitutionally threatens to undermine the non-city residents' ability to govern their own local educational institutions. The courts generally held that city residents may be allowed to vote in county school board elections provided there was some objective city interest in county school operations, such as some student crossovers between the two systems, city contribution to county school finances, or shared city-county facilities. *Compare* Board of County Commissioners of Shelby County v. Burson, 121 F.3d 244 (6th Cir.1997) (city voting in county school board election unconstitutional where city made no contribution to county schools and student crossover was minimal) *with* Duncan v. Coffee County, 69 F.3d 88 (6th Cir.1995) (city voting constitutional where city made significant financial contribution to rural schools). *See also* Davis v. Linville, 864 F.2d 127 (11th Cir.1989); Sutton v. Escambia County Board of Educ., 809 F.2d 770 (11th Cir.1987); Hogencamp v. Lee County Board of Educ., 722 F.2d 720 (11th Cir.1984); Phillips v. Andress, 634 F.2d 947 (5th Cir.1981); Creel v. Freeman, 531 F.2d 286 (5th Cir.1976), *cert. denied* 429 U.S. 1066 (1977). *But cf.* Locklear v. North Carolina State Board of Elections, 514 F.2d 1152 (4th Cir.1975) (using strict scrutiny rather than rational basis test). *See also* Collins v. Town of Goshen, 635 F.2d 954 (2d Cir.1980) (upholding law permitting all residents of town to vote in water district elections including those who lived outside the water district; franchise extension satisfied rational basis test because the town had provided financial assistance to the district.)

MILLIKEN v. BRADLEY

Supreme Court of the United States
418 U.S. 717 (1974)

MR. CHIEF JUSTICE BURGER delivered the opinion of the Court.

On September 27, 1971, the District Court issued its findings and conclusions on the issue of segregation, finding that "Governmental actions and inaction at all levels, federal, state and local, have combined, with those of private organizations, such as loaning institutions and real estate associations and brokerage firms, to establish and to maintain the pattern of residential segregation throughout the Detroit metropolitan area." * * *

Accordingly, the District Court proceeded to order the Detroit Board of Education to submit desegregation plans limited to the segregation problems found to be existing within the city of Detroit. At the same time, however, the state defendants were directed to submit desegregation plans encompassing the three-county metropolitan area[10] despite the fact that the 85 outlying school districts of these three counties were not parties to the action and despite the fact that there had been no claim that these outlying districts had committed constitutional violations. * * *

On March 28, 1972, the District Court issued its findings and conclusions on the three Detroit-only plans submitted by the city Board and the respondents. It found that the best of the three plans "would make the Detroit school system more identifiably Black * * * thereby increasing the flight of Whites from the city and the system." * * * From this the court concluded that the plan "would not accomplish desegregation * * * within the corporate geographical limits of the city." * * * Accordingly, the District Court held that it "must look beyond the limits of the Detroit school district for a solution to the problem," and that "[school] district lines are simply matters of political convenience and may not be used to deny constitutional rights." * * *

[O]n June 14, 1972, the District Court issued its ruling on the "desegregation area" and related findings and conclusions. The court acknowledged at the outset that it had "taken no proofs with respect to the establishment of the boundaries of the 86 public school districts in the counties [in the Detroit area], nor on the issue of whether, with the exclusion of the city of Detroit school district, such school districts have committed acts of de jure segregation." Nevertheless, the court designated 53 of the 85 suburban school districts plus Detroit as the "desegregation area" and appointed a panel to prepare and submit "an effective desegregation plan" for the Detroit schools that would encompass the entire desegregation area. * * *

---

[10] At the time of the 1970 census, the population of Michigan was 8,875,083, almost half of which, 4,199,931, resided in the tri-county area of Wayne, Oakland, and Macomb. Oakland and Macomb Counties abut Wayne County to the north, and Oakland County abuts Macomb County to the west. These counties cover 1,952 square miles, Michigan Statistical Abstract (9th ed. 1972), and the area is approximately the size of the State of Delaware (2,057 square miles), more than half again the size of the State of Rhode Island (1,214 square miles) and almost 30 times the size of the District of Columbia (67 square miles). Statistical Abstract of the United States (93d ed. 1972). The populations of Wayne, Oakland, and Macomb Counties were 2,666,751; 907,871; and 625,309, respectively, in 1970. Detroit, the State's largest city, is located in Wayne County. In the 1970–1971 school year, there were 2,157,449 children enrolled in school districts in Michigan. There are 86 independent, legally distinct school districts within the tri-county area, having a total enrollment of approximately 1,000,000 children. In 1970, the Detroit Board of Education operated 319 schools with approximately 276,000 students.

On June 12, 1973, a divided Court of Appeals, sitting en banc, affirmed in part, vacated in part, and remanded for further proceedings. * * * The Court of Appeals held, first, that the record supported the District Court's findings and conclusions on the constitutional violations committed by the Detroit Board, * * * and by the state defendants. * * * It stated that the acts of racial discrimination shown in the record are "causally related to the substantial amount of segregation found in the Detroit school system," * * * and that "the District Court was therefore authorized and required to take effective measures to desegregate the Detroit Public School System." * * *

The Court of Appeals also agreed with the District Court that "any less comprehensive a solution than a metropolitan area plan would result in an all black school system immediately surrounded by practically all white suburban school systems, with an overwhelmingly white majority population in the total metropolitan area." * * *

Accordingly, the Court of Appeals concluded that "the only feasible desegregation plan involves the crossing of the boundary lines between the Detroit School District and adjacent or nearby school districts for the limited purpose of providing an effective desegregation plan." * * * It reasoned that such a plan would be appropriate because of the State's violations, and could be implemented because of the State's authority to control local school districts. * * *

[T]he District Court's * * * analytical starting point was its conclusion that school district lines are no more than arbitrary lines on a map drawn "for political convenience." Boundary lines may be bridged where there has been a constitutional violation calling for interdistrict relief, but the notion that school district lines may be casually ignored or treated as a mere administrative convenience is contrary to the history of public education in our country. No single tradition in public education is more deeply rooted than local control over the operation of schools; local autonomy has long been thought essential both to the maintenance of community concern and support for public schools and to quality of the educational process. * * * Thus, in *San Antonio School District v. Rodriguez*, 411 U.S. 1, 50 (1973), we observed that local control over the educational process affords citizens an opportunity to participate in decisionmaking, permits the structuring of school programs to fit local needs, and encourages "experimentation, innovation, and a healthy competition for educational excellence."

The Michigan educational structure involved in this case, in common with most States, provides for a large measure of local control,[20] and a

---

[20] Under the Michigan School Code of 1955, the local school district is an autonomous political body corporate, operating through a Board of Education popularly elected. Mich. Comp. Laws §§ 340.27, 340.55, 340.107, 340.148, 340.149, 340.188. As such, the day-to-day affairs of the school district are determined at the local level in accordance with the plenary power to acquire

review of the scope and character of these local powers indicates the extent to which the interdistrict remedy approved by the two courts could disrupt and alter the structure of public education in Michigan. The metropolitan remedy would require, in effect, consolidation of 54 independent school districts historically administered as separate units into a vast new super school district. Entirely apart from the logistical and other serious problems attending large-scale transportation of students, the consolidation would give rise to an array of other problems in financing and operating this new school system. Some of the more obvious questions would be: What would be the status and authority of the present popularly elected school boards? Would the children of Detroit be within the jurisdiction and operating control of a school board elected by the parents and residents of other districts? What board or boards would levy taxes for school operations in these 54 districts constituting the consolidated metropolitan area? What provisions could be made for assuring substantial equality in tax levies among the 54 districts, if this were deemed requisite? What provisions would be made for financing? Would the validity of long-term bonds be jeopardized unless approved by all of the component districts as well as the State? What body would determine that portion of the curricula now left to the discretion of local school boards? Who would establish attendance zones, purchase school equipment, locate and construct new schools, and indeed attend to all the myriad day-to-day decisions that are necessary to school operations affecting potentially more than three-quarters of a million pupils? * * *

Of course, no state law is above the Constitution. School district lines and the present laws with respect to local control, are not sacrosanct and if they conflict with the Fourteenth Amendment federal courts have a duty to prescribe appropriate remedies. *See, e.g., Wright v. Council of the City of Emporia,* 407 U.S. 451 (1972); *United States v. Scotland Neck Board of Education,* 407 U.S. 484 (1972) (state or local officials prevented from carving out a new school district from an existing district that was in process of dismantling a dual school system); *cf. Haney v. County Board of Education of Sevier County,* 429 F.2d 364 (C.A.8 1970) (State contributed to separation of races by drawing of school district lines); *United States v. Texas,* 321 F.Supp. 1043 (E.D.Tex.1970), *aff'd,* 447 F.2d

---

real and personal property, §§ 340.26, 340.77, 340.113, 340.165, 340.192, 340.352; to hire and contract with personnel, §§ 340.569, 340.574; to levy taxes for operations, § 340.563; to borrow against receipts, § 340.567; to determine the length of school terms, § 340.575; to control the admission of nonresident students, § 340.582; to determine courses of study, § 340.583; to provide a kindergarten program, § 340.584; to establish and operate vocational schools, § 340.585; to offer adult education programs, § 340.586; to establish attendance areas, § 340.589; to arrange for transportation of nonresident students, § 340.591; to acquire transportation equipment, § 340.594; to receive gifts and bequests for educational purposes, § 340.605; to employ an attorney, § 340.609; to suspend or expel students, § 340.613; to make rules and regulations for the operation of schools, § 340.614; to cause to be levied authorized millage, § 340.643a; to acquire property by eminent domain, § 340.711 et seq.; and to approve and select textbooks, § 340.882.

441 (C.A.5 1971), *cert. denied sub nom. Edgar v. United States*, 404 U.S. 1016 (1972) (one or more school districts created and maintained for one race). But our prior holdings have been confined to violations and remedies within a single school district. We therefore turn to address, for the first time, the validity of a remedy mandating cross-district or interdistrict consolidation to remedy a condition of segregation found to exist in only one district.

The controlling principle consistently expounded in our holdings is that the scope of the remedy is determined by the nature and extent of the constitutional violation. * * * Before the boundaries of separate and autonomous school districts may be set aside by consolidating the separate units for remedial purposes or by imposing a cross-district remedy, it must first be shown that there has been a constitutional violation within one district that produces a significant segregative effect in another district. Specifically, it must be shown that racially discriminatory acts of the state or local school districts, or of a single school district have been a substantial cause of interdistrict segregation. Thus an interdistrict remedy might be in order where the racially discriminatory acts of one or more school districts caused racial segregation in an adjacent district, or where district lines have been deliberately drawn on the basis of race. In such circumstances an interdistrict remedy would be appropriate to eliminate the interdistrict segregation directly caused by the constitutional violation. Conversely, without an interdistrict violation and interdistrict effect, there is no constitutional wrong calling for an interdistrict remedy.

The record before us, voluminous as it is, contains evidence of de jure segregated conditions only in the Detroit schools; indeed, that was the theory on which the litigation was initially based and on which the District Court took evidence. * * * With no showing of significant violation by the 53 outlying school districts and no evidence of any interdistrict violation or effect, the court went beyond the original theory of the case as framed by the pleadings and mandated a metropolitan area remedy. * * *

The constitutional right of the Negro respondents residing in Detroit is to attend a unitary school system in that district. Unless petitioners drew the district lines in a discriminatory fashion, or arranged for white students residing in the Detroit District to attend schools in Oakland and Macomb Counties, they were under no constitutional duty to make provisions for Negro students to do so. The view of the dissenters, that the existence of a dual system in *Detroit* can be made the basis for a decree requiring cross-district transportation of pupils, cannot be supported on the grounds that it represents merely the devising of a suitably flexible remedy for the violation of rights already established by our prior decisions. It can be supported only by drastic expansion of the constitutional right itself, an expansion without any support in either constitutional principle or precedent.

* * * The Court of Appeals * * * held the State derivatively responsible for the Detroit Board's violations on the theory that actions of Detroit as a political subdivision of the State were attributable to the State. Accepting, *arguendo*, the correctness of this finding of state responsibility for the segregated conditions within the city of Detroit, it does not follow that an interdistrict remedy is constitutionally justified or required. With a single exception, * * * there has been no showing that either the State or any of the 85 outlying districts engaged in activity that had a cross-district effect. The boundaries of the Detroit School District, which are coterminous with the boundaries of the city of Detroit, were established over a century ago by neutral legislation when the city was incorporated; there is no evidence in the record, nor is there any suggestion by the respondents, that either the original boundaries of the Detroit School District, or any other school district in Michigan, were established for the purpose of creating, maintaining, or perpetuating segregation of races. There is no claim and there is no evidence hinting that petitioner outlying school districts and their predecessors, or the 30-odd other school districts in the tricounty area—but outside the District Court's "desegregation area"—have ever maintained or operated anything but unitary school systems. * * *

MR. JUSTICE WHITE, with whom MR. JUSTICE DOUGLAS, MR. JUSTICE BRENNAN, and MR. JUSTICE MARSHALL join, dissenting.

* * * Despite the fact that a metropolitan remedy, if the findings of the District Court accepted by the Court of Appeals are to be credited, would more effectively desegregate the Detroit schools, would prevent resegregation, and would be easier and more feasible from many standpoints, the Court fashions out of whole cloth an arbitrary rule that remedies for constitutional violations occurring in a single Michigan school district must stop at the school district line. Apparently, no matter how much less burdensome or more effective and efficient in many respects, such as transportation, the metropolitan plan might be, the school district line may not be crossed. Otherwise, it seems, there would be too much disruption of the Michigan scheme for managing its educational system, too much confusion, and too much administrative burden.

I am * * * mystified as to how the Court can ignore the legal reality that the constitutional violations, even if occurring locally, were committed by governmental entities for which the State is responsible and that it is the State that must respond to the command of the Fourteenth Amendment. An interdistrict remedy for the infringements that occurred in this case is well within the confines and powers of the

State, which is the governmental entity ultimately responsible for desegregating its schools. The Michigan Supreme Court has observed that "[the] school district is a State agency," *Attorney General ex rel. Kies v. Lowrey*, 131 Mich. 639, 644, 92 N.W. 289, 290 (1902), and that " '[education] in Michigan belongs to the State. It is no part of the local self-government inherent in the township or municipality, except so far as the legislature may choose to make it such. The Constitution has turned the whole subject over to the legislature. * * * ' " *Attorney General ex rel. Zacharias v. Detroit Board of Education*, 154 Mich. 584, 590, 118 N.W. 606, 609 (1908).

* * * The Court draws the remedial line at the Detroit school district boundary, even though the Fourteenth Amendment is addressed to the State and even though the State denies equal protection of the laws when its public agencies, acting in its behalf, invidiously discriminate. The State's default is "the condition that offends the Constitution," * * * and state officials may therefore be ordered to take the necessary measures to completely eliminate from the Detroit public schools "all vestiges of state-imposed segregation." * * * I cannot understand, nor does the majority satisfactorily explain, why a federal court may not order an appropriate interdistrict remedy, if this is necessary or more effective to accomplish this constitutionally mandated task. * * *

The result reached by the Court certainly cannot be supported by the theory that the configuration of local governmental units is immune from alteration when necessary to redress constitutional violations. In addition to the well-established principles already noted, the Court has elsewhere required the public bodies of a State to restructure the State's political subdivisions to remedy infringements of the constitutional rights of certain members of its populace, notably in the reapportionment cases. In *Reynolds v. Sims*, 377 U.S. 533 (1964), for example, which held that equal protection of the laws demands that the seats in both houses of a bicameral state legislature be apportioned on a population basis, thus necessitating wholesale revision of Alabama's voting districts, the Court remarked:

> "Political subdivisions of States—counties, cities, or whatever—
> never were and never have been considered as sovereign entities.
> Rather, they have been traditionally regarded as subordinate
> governmental instrumentalities created by the State to assist in
> the carrying out of state governmental functions." *Id.*, at 575.

And even more pointedly, the Court declared in *Gomillion v. Lightfoot*, 364 U.S. 339, 344–345 (1960), that "[legislative] control of municipalities, no less than other state power, lies within the scope of relevant limitations imposed by the United States Constitution."

Nor does the Court's conclusion follow from the talismanic invocation of the desirability of local control over education. Local autonomy over school affairs, in the sense of the community's participation in the decisions affecting the education of its children, is, of course, an important interest. But presently constituted school district lines do not delimit fixed and unchangeable areas of a local educational community. If restructuring is required to meet constitutional requirements, local authority may simply be redefined in terms of whatever configuration is adopted, with the parents of the children attending schools in the newly demarcated district or attendance zone continuing their participation in the policy management of the schools with which they are concerned most directly. * * *

MR. JUSTICE MARSHALL, with whom MR. JUSTICE DOUGLAS, MR. JUSTICE BRENNAN, and MR. JUSTICE WHITE join, dissenting.

* * * Under Michigan law a "school district is an agency of the State government." *School District of the City of Lansing v. State Board of Education*, 367 Mich. 591, 600, 116 N.W.2d 866, 870 (1962). It is "a legal division of territory, created by the State for educational purposes, to which the State has granted such powers as are deemed necessary to permit the district to function as a State agency." *Detroit Board of Education v. Superintendent of Public Instruction*, 319 Mich. 436, 450, 29 N.W.2d 902, 908 (1947).

* * *

The State's control over education is reflected in the fact that, contrary to the Court's implication, there is little or no relationship between school districts and local political units. To take the 85 outlying local school districts in the Detroit metropolitan area as examples, 17 districts lie in two counties, two in three counties. One district serves five municipalities; other suburban municipalities are fragmented into as many as six school districts. Nor is there any apparent state policy with regard to the size of school districts, as they now range from 2,000 to 285,000 students.

Centralized state control manifests itself in practice as well as in theory. The State controls the financing of education in several ways. The legislature contributes a substantial portion of most school districts' operating budgets with funds appropriated from the State's General Fund revenues raised through statewide taxation.[6] The State's power over the purse can be and is in fact used to enforce the State's powers over local districts. In addition, although local districts obtain funds through local property taxation, the State has assumed the responsibility to ensure

---

6   * * * The State contributed an average of 34% of the operating budgets of the 54 school districts included in the original proposed desegregation area. In 11 of these districts, state contributions exceeded 50% of the operating budgets.

equalized property valuations throughout the State. The State also establishes standards for teacher certification and teacher tenure; determines part of the required curriculum; sets the minimum school term; approves bus routes, equipment, and drivers; approves textbooks; and establishes procedures for student discipline. The State Superintendent of Public Instruction and the State Board of Education have the power to remove local school board members from office for neglect of their duties.

Most significantly for present purposes, the State has wide-ranging powers to consolidate and merge school districts, even without the consent of the districts themselves or of the local citizenry. *See, e.g., Attorney General ex rel. Kies v. Lowrey*, 131 Mich. 639, 92 N.W. 289 (1902), aff'd, 199 U.S. 233 (1905). Indeed, recent years have witnessed an accelerated program of school district consolidations, mergers, and annexations, many of which were state imposed. Whereas the State had 7,362 local districts in 1912, the number had been reduced to 1,438 in 1964 and to 738 in 1968. By June 1972, only 608 school districts remained. Furthermore, the State has broad powers to transfer property from one district to another, again without the consent of the local school districts affected by the transfer.

* * * The actions of the State itself directly contributed to Detroit's segregation. Under the Fourteenth Amendment, the State is ultimately responsible for the actions of its local agencies. And, finally, given the structure of Michigan's educational system, Detroit's segregation cannot be viewed as the problem of an independent and separate entity. Michigan operates a single statewide system of education, a substantial part of which was shown to be segregated in this case.

* * * Nor should it be of any significance that the suburban school districts were not shown to have themselves taken any direct action to promote segregation of the races. Given the State's broad powers over local school districts, it was well within the State's powers to require those districts surrounding the Detroit school district to participate in a metropolitan remedy. The State's duty should be no different here than in cases where it is shown that certain of a State's voting districts are malapportioned in violation of the Fourteenth Amendment. *See Reynolds v. Sims*, 377 U.S. 533 (1964). Overrepresented electoral districts are required to participate in reapportionment although their only "participation" in the violation was to do nothing about it. Similarly, electoral districts which themselves meet representation standards must frequently be redrawn as part of a remedy for other over-and under-inclusive districts. No finding of fault on the part of each electoral district and no finding of a discriminatory effect on each district is a prerequisite to its involvement in the constitutionally required remedy. By the same logic, no finding of fault on the part of the suburban school districts in

this case and no finding of a discriminatory effect on each district should be a prerequisite to their involvement in the constitutionally required remedy.

It is the State, after all, which bears the responsibility under *Brown* of affording a nondiscriminatory system of education. The State, of course, is ordinarily free to choose any decentralized framework for education it wishes, so long as it fulfills that Fourteenth Amendment obligation. But the State should no more be allowed to hide behind its delegation and compartmentalization of school districts to avoid its constitutional obligations to its children then it could hide behind its political subdivisions to avoid its obligations to its voters. *Reynolds v. Sims, supra*, at 575. *See also Gomillion v. Lightfoot*, 364 U.S. 339 (1960).

NOTES AND QUESTIONS

1. *State Agents or Local Actors?* The district court found, and the court of appeals agreed, that racial segregation in the Detroit schools was attributable to various actions of the Detroit board of education and of the state of Michigan. If the state government was both directly involved in the segregation of the Detroit school system and vicariously responsible for the Detroit system's operations, why were the Michigan school districts outside the Detroit school district considered to be beyond the nature and extent of the violation? Why is it important that there was no proof that those districts engaged in any action affecting segregation in Detroit?

How much of the disagreement between the majority and the dissents turns on their differing appraisals of just how much legal autonomy Michigan's school districts enjoyed? Why does the extent of local autonomy matter in determining whether a federal court could create a metropolitan area remedy for segregation in the Detroit schools?

The question of state vicarious liability for the actions of its local governments remains a disputed one. *See, e.g.,* Reynolds v. Giuliani, 506 F.3d 183 (2d Cir. 2007) (reversing district court finding of vicarious liability). For an assessment of the issue, *see* Note, The State's Vicarious Liability for the Actions of the City, 124 Harv. L. Rev. 1036 (2011).

2. *Local Autonomy as a Federal Constitutional Value.* What arguments does the Court give for why local autonomy is an important value, or how local autonomy would be threatened by the metropolitan remedy?

In San Antonio Independent School District v. Rodriguez, 411 U.S. 1 (1973), the Court described the benefits of Texas's decision to require local school districts to finance a substantial portion of their expenses out of local resources:

> [Local financing] permits and encourages a large measure of participation in and control of each district's schools at the local level. In an era that has witnessed a consistent trend toward

centralization of the functions of government, local sharing of responsibility for public education has survived. . . .

The persistence of attachment to government at the lowest level where education is concerned reflects the depths of commitment of its supporters. In part, local control means . . . the freedom to devote more money to the education of one's children. Equally important, however, is the opportunity it offers for participation in the decisionmaking process that determines how those local tax dollars will be spent. Each locality is free to tailor local programs to local needs. Pluralism also affords some opportunity for experimentation, innovation, and a healthy competition for educational excellence.

Id. at 49–50.

For an analysis of the part arguments about local control have played in school finance reform litigation, *see* Richard Briffault, The Role of Local Control in School Finance Reform, 24 Conn.L.Rev. 773 (1992). For a discussion of school finance reform litigation, *see* Chapter V.

3.   *Regional Remedies. Milliken* does not reject all regional remedies for segregation. The Court indicated that an interdistrict remedy would have been appropriate if the state had manipulated the boundaries of the Detroit school district or the adjacent suburban districts to promote segregation. In Hills v. Gautreaux, 425 U.S. 284 (1976), the Court upheld a lower court's order requiring the federal Department of Housing and Urban Development (HUD), which had practiced racial discrimination in its siting of public housing projects in Chicago, to site future housing in the suburbs. The Court reasoned that because HUD had authority to operate in the Chicago housing market, which extended beyond the Chicago city limits, the larger boundary of the housing market determined the territorial scope of the remedy. Moreover, the remedial order against HUD did not impair the zoning autonomy of Chicago's suburbs, since HUD had no authority to build housing without a local application or approval. Unlike the *Milliken* remedy, the *Gautreaux* order

would not consolidate or in any way restructure local governmental units. The remedial decree would neither force suburban governments to submit public housing proposals to HUD nor displace the rights and powers accorded to local government entities under federal or state housing statutes or existing land-use laws.

Id. at 305–06.

For a critical assessment of *Milliken* and of the long-term consequences of the Supreme Court's rejection of a metropolitan desegregation remedy, *see* Myron Orfield, *Milliken, Meredith,* and Metropolitan Segregation, 62 U.C.L.A. L. Rev. 364 (2015).

4.   *Reasoning from One Person, One Vote.* In a footnote, the *Milliken* majority responded to the dissenters' argument concerning the lack of local school board autonomy by stating: "Since the Court has held that a resident

of a school district has a fundamental right protected by the Federal Constitution to vote in a district election, it would seem incongruous to disparage the importance of the school district in a different context [citing *Kramer v. Union Free School Dist. No. 15*]." 418 U.S. 717, 746 n. 21. Is that persuasive? Conversely, Justice White's and Justice Marshall's dissenting opinions rely on the Court's earlier holding in *Reynolds v. Sims* that localities cannot be used as units of representation in the state legislature even though the states are used as units of representation in Congress. Similarly, they argued, because the Detroit suburban schools are mere arms of the state, they should be included in the remedy because of the state's violations. Is that argument persuasive?

VILLAGE OF BELLE TERRE V. BORAAS

Supreme Court of the United States
416 U.S. 1 (1974)

MR. JUSTICE DOUGLAS delivered the opinion of the Court.

Belle Terre is a village on Long Island's north shore of about 220 homes inhabited by 700 people. Its total land area is less than one square mile. It has restricted land use to one-family dwellings excluding lodging houses, boarding houses, fraternity houses, or multiple-dwelling houses. The word "family" as used in the ordinance means, "one or more persons related by blood, adoption, or marriage, living and cooking together as a single housekeeping unit, exclusive of household servants. A number of persons but not exceeding two (2) living and cooking together as a single housekeeping unit though not related by blood, adoption, or marriage shall be deemed to constitute a family."

Appellees the Dickmans are owners of a house in the village and leased it in December 1971 for a term of 18 months to Michael Truman. Later Bruce Boraas became a colessee. Then Anne Parish moved into the house along with three others. These six are students at nearby State University at Stony Brook and none is related to the other by blood, adoption, or marriage. When the village served the Dickmans with an "Order to Remedy Violations" of the ordinance, the owners plus three tenants thereupon brought this action under 42 U. S. C. § 1983 for an injunction and a judgment declaring the ordinance unconstitutional. The District Court held the ordinance constitutional, 367 F.Supp. 136, and the Court of Appeals reversed, one judge dissenting, 476 F.2d 806. * * *

This case brings to this Court a different phase of local zoning regulations from those we have previously reviewed. *Euclid v. Ambler Realty Co.*, 272 U.S. 365, involved a zoning ordinance classifying land use in a given area into six categories. Appellee's tracts fell under three classifications: U-2, which included two-family dwellings; U-3, which included apartments, hotels, churches, schools, private clubs, hospitals, city hall and the like; and U-6, which included sewage disposal plants, incinerators, scrap storage, cemeteries, oil and gas storage and so on. Heights of buildings were prescribed for each zone; also, the size of land areas required for each kind of use was specified. The land in litigation was vacant and being held for industrial development; and evidence was introduced showing that under the restricted-use ordinance the land would be greatly reduced in value. The claim was that the landowner was being deprived of liberty and property without due process within the meaning of the Fourteenth Amendment.

The Court sustained the zoning ordinance under the police power of the State. * * * The main thrust of the case in the mind of the Court was in the exclusion of industries and apartments, and as respects that it commented on the desire to keep residential areas free of "disturbing noises"; "increased traffic"; the hazard of "moving and parked automobiles"; the "depriving children of the privilege of quiet and open spaces for play, enjoyed by those in more favored localities." *Id.*, at 394. The ordinance was sanctioned because the validity of the legislative classification was "fairly debatable" and therefore could not be said to be wholly arbitrary. *Id.*, at 388.

Our decision in *Berman v. Parker*, 348 U.S. 26, sustained a land-use project in the District of Columbia against a landowner's claim that the taking violated the Due Process Clause and the Just Compensation Clause of the Fifth Amendment. The essence of the argument against the law was, while taking property for ridding an area of slums was permissible, taking it "merely to develop a better balanced, more attractive community" was not, *id.*, at 31. We refused to limit the concept of public welfare that may be enhanced by zoning regulations. * * *

The present ordinance is challenged on several grounds: that it interferes with a person's right to travel; that it interferes with the right to migrate to and settle within a State; that it bars people who are uncongenial to the present residents; that it expresses the social preferences of the residents for groups that will be congenial to them; that social homogeneity is not a legitimate interest of government; that the restriction of those whom the neighbors do not like trenches on the newcomers' rights of privacy; that it is of no rightful concern to villagers whether the residents are married or unmarried; that the ordinance is antithetical to the Nation's experience, ideology, and self-perception as an open, egalitarian, and integrated society.

We find none of these reasons in the record before us. It is not aimed at transients. *Cf. Shapiro v. Thompson*, 394 U.S. 618. It involves no procedural disparity inflicted on some but not on others such as was presented by *Griffin v. Illinois*, 351 U.S. 12. It involves no "fundamental" right guaranteed by the Constitution, such as voting, *Harper v. Virginia Board*, 383 U.S. 663; the right of association, *NAACP v. Alabama*, 357

U.S. 449; the right of access to the courts, *NAACP v. Button*, 371 U.S. 415; or any rights of privacy, *cf. Griswold v. Connecticut*, 381 U.S. 479; *Eisenstadt v. Baird*, 405 U.S. 438, 453–454. We deal with economic and social legislation where legislatures have historically drawn lines which we respect against the charge of violation of the Equal Protection Clause if the law be " 'reasonable, not arbitrary' " (quoting *Royster Guano Co. v. Virginia*, 253 U.S. 412, 415) and bears "a rational relationship to a [permissible] state objective." *Reed v. Reed*, 404 U.S. 71, 76.

It is said, however, that if two unmarried people can constitute a "family," there is no reason why three or four may not. But every line drawn by a legislature leaves some out that might well have been included. That exercise of discretion, however, is a legislative, not a judicial, function.

It is said that the Belle Terre ordinance reeks with an animosity to unmarried couples who live together. There is no evidence to support it; and the provision of the ordinance bringing within the definition of a "family" two unmarried people belies the charge.

The ordinance places no ban on other forms of association, for a "family" may, so far as the ordinance is concerned, entertain whomever it likes.

The regimes of boarding houses, fraternity houses, and the like present urban problems. More people occupy a given space; more cars rather continuously pass by; more cars are parked; noise travels with crowds.

A quiet place where yards are wide, people few, and motor vehicles restricted are legitimate guidelines in a land-use project addressed to family needs. This goal is a permissible one within *Berman v. Parker, supra*. The police power is not confined to elimination of filth, stench, and unhealthy places. It is ample to lay out zones where family values, youth values, and the blessings of quiet seclusion and clean air make the area a sanctuary for people.

MR. JUSTICE MARSHALL, dissenting.

I am in full agreement with the majority that zoning is a complex and important function of the State. It may indeed be the most essential function performed by local government, for it is one of the primary means by which we protect that sometimes difficult to define concept of quality of life. I therefore continue to adhere to the principle of *Euclid v. Ambler Realty Co.*, 272 U.S. 365 (1926), that deference should be given to governmental judgments concerning proper land-use allocation. * * *

I would also agree with the majority that local zoning authorities may properly act in furtherance of the objectives asserted to be served by the ordinance at issue here: restricting uncontrolled growth, solving traffic problems, keeping rental costs at a reasonable level, and making the community attractive to families. The police power which provides the justification for zoning is not narrowly confined. * * * And, it is appropriate that we afford zoning authorities considerable latitude in choosing the means by which to implement such purposes. But deference does not mean abdication. This Court has an obligation to ensure that zoning ordinances, even when adopted in furtherance of such legitimate aims, do not infringe upon fundamental constitutional rights.

* * * Zoning officials properly concern themselves with the uses of land—with, for example, the number and kind of dwellings to be constructed in a certain neighborhood or the number of persons who can reside in those dwellings. But zoning authorities cannot validly consider who those persons are, what they believe, or how they choose to live, whether they are Negro or white, Catholic or Jew, Republican or Democrat, married or unmarried.

My disagreement with the Court today is based upon my view that the ordinance in this case unnecessarily burdens appellees' First Amendment freedom of association and their constitutionally guaranteed right to privacy. * * * The choice of household companions—of whether a person's "intellectual and emotional needs" are best met by living with family, friends, professional associates, or others—involves deeply personal considerations as to the kind and quality of intimate relationships within the home. That decision surely falls within the ambit of the right to privacy protected by the Constitution. * * *

The instant ordinance discriminates on the basis of just such a personal lifestyle choice as to household companions. It permits any number of persons related by blood or marriage, be it two or twenty, to live in a single household, but it limits to two the number of unrelated persons bound by profession, love, friendship, religious or political affiliation, or mere economics who can occupy a single home. Belle Terre imposes upon those who deviate from the community norm in their choice of living companions significantly greater restrictions than are applied to residential groups who are related by blood or marriage, and compose the established order within the community.[4] The village has, in effect, acted to fence out those individuals whose choice of lifestyle differs from that of its current residents.

This is not a case where the Court is being asked to nullify a township's sincere efforts to maintain its residential character by

---

[4] "Perhaps in an ideal world, planning and zoning would be done on a *regional* basis, so that a given community would have apartments, while an adjoining community would not. But as long as we allow zoning to be done community by community, it is intolerable to allow one municipality (or many municipalities) to close its doors at the expense of surrounding communities and the central city." *Appeal of Girsh*, 437 Pa. 237, 245 n. 4, 263 A. 2d 395, 399 n. 4 (1970).

preventing the operation of rooming houses, fraternity houses, or other commercial or high-density residential uses. Unquestionably, a town is free to restrict such uses. Moreover, as a general proposition, I see no constitutional infirmity in a town's limiting the density of use in residential areas by zoning regulations which do not discriminate on the basis of constitutionally suspect criteria. This ordinance, however, limits the density of occupancy of only those homes occupied by unrelated persons. It thus reaches beyond control of the use of land or the density of population, and undertakes to regulate the way people choose to associate with each other within the privacy of their own homes. * * *

Because I believe that this zoning ordinance creates a classification which impinges upon fundamental personal rights, it can withstand constitutional scrutiny only upon a clear showing that the burden imposed is necessary to protect a compelling and substantial governmental interest, *Shapiro v. Thompson*, 394 U.S. 618, 634 (1969). And, once it be determined that a burden has been placed upon a constitutional right, the onus of demonstrating that no less intrusive means will adequately protect the compelling state interest and that the challenged statute is sufficiently narrowly drawn, is upon the party seeking to justify the burden. * * *

A variety of justifications have been proffered in support of the village's ordinance. It is claimed that the ordinance controls population density, prevents noise, traffic and parking problems, and preserves the rent structure of the community and its attractiveness to families. As I noted earlier, these are all legitimate and substantial interests of government. But I think it clear that the means chosen to accomplish these purposes are both overinclusive and underinclusive, and that the asserted goals could be as effectively achieved by means of an ordinance that did not discriminate on the basis of constitutionally protected choices of lifestyle. The ordinance imposes no restriction whatsoever on the number of persons who may live in a house, as long as they are related by marital or sanguinary bonds—presumably no matter how distant their relationship. Nor does the ordinance restrict the number of income earners who may contribute to rent in such a household, or the number of automobiles that may be maintained by its occupants. In that sense the ordinance is underinclusive. On the other hand, the statute restricts the number of unrelated persons who may live in a home to no more than two. It would therefore prevent three unrelated people from occupying a dwelling even if among them they had but one income and no vehicles. While an extended family of a dozen or more might live in a small bungalow, three elderly and retired persons could not occupy the large manor house next door. Thus the statute is also grossly overinclusive to accomplish its intended purposes. * * *

NOTES AND QUESTIONS

1.   *Local Autonomy and Local Zoning*. Land use regulation is one of the most important powers wielded by local governments. Land use is probably the area in which the local share of power—relative to the federal and state shares—is greatest. In upholding the power to zone in Euclid v. Ambler Realty Co., 272 U.S. 365 (1926), the Supreme Court recognized how zoning empowers relatively small localities, including those that occupy only a small fraction of a metropolitan region:

> It is said that the Village of Euclid is a mere suburb of the City of Cleveland; that the industrial development of that city has now reached and in some degree extended into the village and, in the obvious course of things, will soon absorb the entire area for industrial enterprises; that the effect of the ordinance is to divert the natural development elsewhere. . . . But the village, though physically a suburb of Cleveland, is politically a separate municipality, with powers of its own and authority to govern itself as it sees fit within the limits of the organic law of its creation and the State and Federal Constitutions.

272 U.S. at 389.

2.   *Local Autonomy, Individual Rights, and Community Character*. The central issue in *Belle Terre* was the standard of review to be applied to the local ordinance. Justice Marshall, dissenting, found that the ordinance infringed on fundamental rights; he argued for application of strict judicial scrutiny. The majority, by contrast, found that the ordinance had no impact on fundamental rights and could be sustained under the rational basis test. But Justices Douglas and Marshall also appeared to disagree over the value of the locality's interest in maintaining its character as a community of traditional families. The majority celebrated Belle Terre's ability to "lay out zones" for "family values." Justice Marshall, however, only considered the local interests in controlling density, noise, and traffic—not family character—in assessing whether there was an adequate justification for the ordinance. Suppose, like Justice Marshall, you concluded that the ordinance did affect a fundamental right, such as the choice of living companions in one's home. Could you find that the locality's interest in creating and maintaining a traditional family character would still justify the ordinance notwithstanding its impact on that fundamental right? *Cf.* Frank Michelman, Political Markets and Community Self-Determination: Competing Judicial Models of Local Government Legitimacy, 53 Ind.L.J. 145 (1977–78) (suggesting that the Court found that the ordinance did not affect fundamental individual rights in order to avoid weighing the conflict between individual and community interests in self-determination).

3.   *The Constitutional Consequences of Small Community Size*. Justice Douglas seems to stress Belle Terre's small size. How important do you think that was in explaining the outcome of the case? One of the authors of this casebook has suggested that Belle Terre's small size contributed to

the Court's broader evocation of local government as a kind of moat protecting home and family from the crime, congestion, and alien influences of the outside world. The local government in Belle Terre was an extension of the home, not an arm of the state, a defender of the family rather than an oppressor of individual liberty. The locality's exclusion of people who practiced an alternative lifestyle was unobjectionable because it was seen as an action similar to that of a family choosing not to welcome an unwanted guest into its home.

Richard Briffault, Our Localism: Part II—Localism and Legal Theory, 90 Colum.L.Rev. 346, 383 (1990).

In his dissent from a Supreme Court opinion invalidating a local ordinance banning all live entertainment—and aimed at nude, nonobscene dancing at an "adult" bookstore—Chief Justice Burger, joined by then-Justice Rehnquist, implied that "a small borough" ought to be given considerable leeway in regulating to protect community character:

> The residents of this small enclave chose to maintain their town as a placid, 'bedroom' community of a few thousand people. To that end, they passed an admittedly broad regulation prohibiting certain forms of entertainment. Because I believe that a community of people are—within limits—masters of their own environment, I would hold that, as applied, the ordinance is valid.

> At issue here is the right of a small community to ban an activity incompatible with a quiet, residential atmosphere. * * * Mount Ephraim is a small community on the periphery of two major urban centers where this kind of entertainment may be found acceptable. The fact that nude dancing has been totally banned in this community is irrelevant. 'Chilling' this kind of show business in this tiny residential enclave can hardly be thought to show that the appellants' 'message' will be prohibited in nearby—and more sophisticated—cities.

> The fact that a form of expression enjoys some constitutional protection does not mean that there are not times and places inappropriate for its exercise. The towns and villages of the Nation are not, and should not be, forced into a mold cast by this Court.

Schad v. Borough of Mount Ephraim, 452 U.S. 61, 85, 85–87 (1981) (Burger, C.J., dissenting).

Given the large number of small localities in any metropolitan area, should it be possible for some localities to adopt "community character" zoning rules even if the state could not impose such a rule on a state-wide or region-wide basis? Would it be appropriate to permit some localities to adopt such a rule, if a state or regional agency limited the number of such localities so that there would be some other localities open to people with nontraditional lifestyles? Would it be appropriate to permit small towns like

Belle Terre and Mount Ephraim to adopt regulations that are more protective of community interests and more intrusive on individual rights as long as big cities like New York City and Philadelphia are subject to the constitutional norms that apply to states and the federal government? *Cf.* Mark D. Rosen, The Surprisingly Strong Case for Tailoring Constitutional Principles, 153 U. Pa. L. Rev. 1513 (2005) (suggesting that the meaning of constitutional principles may be "tailored" according to the level of government, taking into account differences in geographic scope, exit costs, difficulties in assembling majorities, and governmental functions and responsibilities); Christopher Serkin, Local Property Law: Adjusting the Scale of Property Protection, 107 Colum. L. Rev. 883, 906 (2007) (arguing for local tailoring of Takings Clause doctrine).

4.   *Local Regulation of Living Arrangements.* In other cases, the Supreme Court has curtailed the ability of local governments to use zoning to affect living arrangements or the type of people who may live in a community. Moore v. City of East Cleveland, 431 U.S. 494 (1977), distinguished *Belle Terre* to invalidate an ordinance that limited occupancy of a dwelling unit to members of a single nuclear family. The effect of the ordinance was to make it illegal for a grandmother to live with her son and two grandsons. Justice Powell, writing for a plurality that included Justices Brennan, Marshall, and Blackmun, found that unlike the Belle Terre ordinance, which affected only unrelated individuals, the East Cleveland law "slic[ed] deeply into the family itself." *Id.* at 498. He concluded that the city's interests in preventing overcrowding, minimizing traffic and parking congestion, and avoiding burdening the school system were only marginally served by the ordinance and could not justify the intrusion into family living arrangements. In City of Cleburne v. Cleburne Living Center, 473 U.S. 432 (1985), the Court invalidated, under the rational basis test, a local zoning ordinance that required a special use permit for a group home for the mentally retarded, although no special use permit was required for apartment houses, multiple dwellings, boarding houses, apartment hotels, dormitories, hospitals, or nursing homes for convalescents or the aged. The district court had found that the permit requirement had rested, in part, on the negative attitudes and fears of area residents about the mentally retarded. The Supreme Court expressed its disapproval:

> But mere negative attitudes, or fear, unsubstantiated by factors which are properly cognizable in a zoning proceeding, are not permissible bases for treating a home for the mentally retarded differently from apartment houses, multiple dwellings, and the like.

473 U.S. at 448. *See also* City of Edmonds v. Oxford House, Inc., 514 U.S. 725 (1995) (federal statute prohibiting housing discrimination against the handicapped preempts use of local "family-only" zoning ordinances to bar group homes.)

Belle Terre continues to be followed in cases involving challenges to single-family zoning ordinances. *See, e.g.,* City of Baton Rouge/Parish of East

Baton Rouge v. Myers, 14 So.2d 320 (La. 2014) (sustaining ordinance defining "family" as two unrelated individuals; two or more individuals related by blood, marriage or adoption; or four people "living together by joint agreement and occupying a single housekeeping unit with single culinary facilities on a non-profit, cost sharing basis" provided the owner lives on the premises); McMaster v. Columbia Bd. of Zoning Apps., 719 S.E.2d 660 (S.C. 2011). Several state supreme courts, however, have determined that *Belle Terre*-style ordinances that prohibit groups of unrelated people from living together violate their state constitutions. *See, e.g.*, City of Santa Barbara v. Adamson, 610 P.2d 436 (Cal. 1980); McMinn v. Town of Oyster Bay, 488 N.E.2d 1240 (N.Y.1985); Charter Township of Delta v. Dinolfo, 351 N.W.2d 831 (Mich.1984); State v. Baker, 405 A.2d 368 (N.J.1979).

    5.   *College Towns.* Courts seem to be more sympathetic to *Belle Terre*-style ordinances when, as in *Belle Terre* itself, they have been adopted by communities dealing with college student populations. Indeed, college towns have frequently prevailed when state constitutional challenges have been brought against their ordinances restricting the number of unrelated people living together. *See, e.g.*, Ames Rental Property Ass'n v. City of Ames, 736 N.W.2d 255 (Ia. 2007) (upholding ordinance restricting housing in certain zoning districts to any number of related people but no more than three unrelated people in city which is home of Iowa State University); Anderson v. Provo City Corp., 108 P.3d 701 (Utah 2005) (upholding ordinance governing residential neighborhoods near Brigham Young University that prohibited nonresident homeowners from renting out "accessory" apartments in their basements or upper floors); City of Brookings v. Winker, 554 N.W.2d 827 (S.D.1996) (upholding ordinance adopted by city which is the home of South Dakota State University barring more than three unrelated people from living in a residential unit); State v. Champoux, 555 N.W.2d 69 (Neb.App.1996) (upholding ordinance adopted by city which is the home of University of Nebraska which barred more than three unrelated people from living together in an area zoned for families). The Iowa Supreme Court in *Ames* acknowledged that the three-unrelated-persons rule did not precisely match the goals of quiet, traffic safety, and population stability at which it aimed but concluded that the ordinance was a "reasonable attempt to address concerns by citizens who fear living next door to the hubbub of an 'Animal House.'" 736 N.W.2d at 262. The court agreed with the City that when groups of unrelated persons live together as roommates the arrangements typically are relatively short term and involve young adults.

> These persons tend not to establish roots in the community nor do they provide playmates for their neighbors' children. Moreover, large numbers of young adults living together typically attract friends, which create additional noise and traffic. By limiting the number of unrelated persons who may live together, Ames's ordinance furthers the City's goal of creating family-oriented neighborhoods that are safe and quiet for young children.

Id. at 261. The three dissenters concluded that the ordinance was both underinclusive—in failing to address the problems posed by "raucous," transient or multiple-car-owning families—while burdening the poor and the elderly who are "those most likely to live with roommates." Are these laws more appropriate in the university town setting, or are the *Ames* dissenters (and Justice Marshall in *Belle Terre)* right in contending that cities should be required to regulate noise, traffic, and density directly rather than "by intruding into . . . citizens' homes and differentiating, classifying, and eventually barring . . . citizens from the community solely based on the type of relationship a person has to the other persons residing in their home"? *Id.* at 265. *See also* Adams v. Town of Brunswick, 987 A.2d 502 (Me. 2010) (sustaining municipal decision to allow landowner to renovate building to facilitate occupancy by eleven Bowdoin College students in two units; "the Town had no legitimate interest in the relationship between the individual tenants, because the Ordinance's definition of "household" is not restricted by relationship, but rather by living arrangement: if the group of people occupying an apartment do so as a collective enterprise in a unit providing independent kitchen, bathroom and sleeping facilities, then their occupancy qualifies as a residential use, whether they are college students or college professors").

C. LOCAL GOVERNMENT AS QUASI-PROPRIETARY FIRM

BALL V. JAMES

Supreme Court of the United States
451 U.S. 355 (1981)

JUSTICE STEWART delivered the opinion of the Court.

The public entity at issue here is the Salt River Project Agricultural Improvement and Power District, which stores and delivers untreated water to the owners of land comprising 236,000 acres in central Arizona. The District, formed as a governmental entity in 1937, subsidizes its water operations by selling electricity, and has become the supplier of electric power for hundreds of thousands of people in an area including a large part of metropolitan Phoenix. Nevertheless, the history of the District began in the efforts of Arizona farmers in the 19th century to irrigate the arid lands of the Salt River Valley, and, as the parties have stipulated, the primary purposes of the District have always been the storage, delivery, and conservation of water.

As early as 1867, farmers in the Salt River Valley attempted to irrigate their lands with water from the Salt River. In 1895, concerned with the erratic and unreliable flow of the river, they formed a "Farmers Protective Association," which helped persuade Congress to pass the Reclamation Act of 1902, 32 Stat. 388, 43 U. S. C. § 371 *et seq.* Under that

Act, the United States gave interest-free loans to help landowners build reclamation projects. The Salt River Project, from which the District developed, was created in 1903 as a result of this legislation. In 1906, Congress authorized projects created under the Act to generate and sell hydroelectric power, 43 U. S. C. § 522, and the Salt River Project has supported its water operations by this means almost since its creation. The 1902 Act provided that the water users who benefitted from the reclamation project had to agree to repay to the United States the costs of constructing the project, and the Salt River Valley Water Users Association was organized as an Arizona corporation in 1903 to serve as the contracting agent for the landowners. The Association's Articles, drafted in cooperation with the Federal Reclamation Service, gave subscribing landowners the right to reclamation water and the power to vote in Association decisions in proportion to the number of acres the subscribers owned. The Articles also authorized acreage-proportionate stock assessments to raise income for the Association, the assessments becoming a lien on the subscribing owners' land until paid. For almost 15 years, the Federal Reclamation Service operated and maintained the project's irrigation system for the landowners; under a 1917 contract with the United States, however, the Association itself took on these tasks, proceeding to manage the project for the next 20 years.

The Association faced serious financial difficulties during the Depression as it built new dams and other works for the project, and it sought a means of borrowing money that would not overly encumber the subscribers' lands. The means seemed to be available in Arizona's Agricultural Improvement District Act of 1922, which authorized the creation of special public water districts within federal reclamation projects. * * * Such districts, as political subdivisions of the State, could issue bonds exempt from federal income tax. Nevertheless, many Association members opposed creating a special district for the project, in part because the state statute would have required that voting power in elections for directors of the district be distributed per capita among landowners, and not according to the acreage formula for stock assessments and water rights. In 1936, in response to a request from the Association, the state legislature amended the 1922 statute. Under the new statutory scheme, which is essentially the one at issue in this case, the legislature allowed the district to limit voting for its directors to voters, otherwise regularly qualified under state law, who own land within the district, and to apportion voting power among those landowners according to the number of acres owned. * * * The Salt River Project Agricultural Improvement and Power District was then formed in 1937, its boundaries essentially the same as the Association's. Under the 1937 agreement, the Association made the District its contracting agent, and transferred to the District all its property, and the Association in turn agreed to continue to operate and maintain the Salt River Project.

Under the current agreement, the District itself manages the power and water storage work of the project, and the Association, as agent for the District, manages water delivery. As for financing, the statute now permits the special districts to raise money through an acreage-proportionate taxing power that mirrors the Association's stock assessment scheme, * * * or through bonds secured by liens on the real property within the District, though the bonds can simultaneously be secured by District revenues. * * *

This lawsuit was brought by a class of registered voters who live within the geographic boundaries of the District, and who own either no land or less than an acre of land within the District. The complaint alleged that the District enjoys such governmental powers as the power to condemn land, to sell tax-exempt bonds, and to levy taxes on real property. It also alleged that because the District sells electricity to virtually half the population of Arizona, and because, through its water operations, it can exercise significant influence on flood control and environmental management within its boundaries, the District's policies and actions have a substantial effect on all people who live within the District, regardless of property ownership. Seeking declaratory and injunctive relief, the appellees claimed that the acreage-based scheme for electing directors of the District violates the Equal Protection Clause of the Fourteenth Amendment.

Reynolds v. Sims * * * held that the Equal Protection Clause requires adherence to the principle of one-person, one-vote in elections of state legislators. *Avery v. Midland County*, 390 U.S. 474, extended the *Reynolds* rule to the election of officials of a county government, holding that the elected officials exercised "general governmental powers over the entire geographic area served by the body." 390 U.S., at 485. The Court, however, reserved any decision on the application of *Reynolds* to "a special-purpose unit of government assigned the performance of functions affecting definable groups of constituents more than other constituents." 390 U.S., at 483–484. In *Hadley v. Junior College District*, 397 U.S. 50, the Court extended *Reynolds* to the election of trustees of a community college district because those trustees "exercised general governmental powers" and "[performed] important governmental functions" that had significant effect on all citizens residing within the district. 397 U.S., at 53–54. But in that case the Court stated: "It is of course possible that there might be some case in which a State elects certain functionaries whose duties are so far removed from normal governmental activities and so disproportionately affect different groups that a popular election in compliance with *Reynolds* * * * might not be required * * *." *Id.*, at 56.

The Court found such a case in *Salyer* [*Land Co. v. Tulare Lake Basin Water Storage District*, 410 U.S. 719 (1973)]. The Tulare Lake Basin Water Storage District involved there encompassed 193,000 acres,

85% of which were farmed by one or another of four corporations. * * * Under California law, public water districts could acquire, store, conserve, and distribute water. * * * The costs of the project were assessed against each landowner according to the water benefits the landowner received. * * * At issue in the case was the constitutionality of the scheme for electing the directors of the district, under which only landowners could vote, and voting power was apportioned according to the assessed valuation of the voting landowner's property. The Court recognized that the Tulare Lake Basin Water Storage District did exercise "some typical governmental powers," including the power to hire and fire workers, contract for construction of projects, condemn private property, and issue general obligation bonds. *Id.*, at 728, and n. 7. Nevertheless, the Court concluded that the district had "relatively limited authority," because "its primary purpose, indeed the reason for its existence, is to provide for the acquisition, storage, and distribution of water for farming in the Tulare Lake Basin." *Id.*, at 728 (footnote omitted). The Court also noted that the financial burdens of the district could not but fall on the landowners, in proportion to the benefits they received from the district, and that the district's actions therefore disproportionately affected the voting landowners. *Id.*, at 729. The *Salyer* Court thus held that the strictures of *Reynolds* did not apply to the Tulare District, and proceeded to inquire simply whether the statutory voting scheme based on land valuation at least bore some relevancy to the statute's objectives.[8] The Court concluded that the California Legislature could have reasonably assumed that without voting power apportioned according to the value of their land, the landowners might not have been willing to subject their lands to the lien of the very assessments which made the creation of the district possible. 410 U.S., at 731.

* * * [T]he services currently provided by the Salt River District are more diverse and affect far more people than those of the Tulare Lake Basin Water Storage District. Whereas the Tulare District included an area entirely devoted to agriculture and populated by only 77 persons, the Salt River District includes almost half the population of the State, including large parts of Phoenix and other cities. Moreover, the Salt River District, unlike the Tulare District, has exercised its statutory power to generate and sell electric power, and has become one of the largest suppliers of such power in the State. Further, whereas all the water delivered by the Tulare District went for agriculture, roughly 40% of the water delivered by the Salt River District goes to urban areas or is used for nonagricultural purposes in farming areas. Finally, whereas all

---

8 In *Kramer v. Union Free School District No.* 15, 395 U.S. 621, 627, the Court stated that the exclusion of otherwise qualified voters from a particular election must be justified by some compelling state interest. But in considering whether the voting scheme for the Tulare Lake Basin Water Storage District bore some relevancy to the purpose for which the scheme was adopted, *Salyer* imposed no such requirement.

operating costs of the Tulare District were born by the voting landowners through assessments apportioned according to land value, most of the capital and operating costs of the Salt River District have been met through the revenues generated by the selling of electric power. Nevertheless, a careful examination of the Salt River District reveals that, under the principles of the *Avery*, *Hadley*, and *Salyer* cases, these distinctions do not amount to a constitutional difference.

First, the District simply does not exercise the sort of governmental powers that invoke the strict demands of *Reynolds*. The District cannot impose ad valorem property taxes or sales taxes. It cannot enact any laws governing the conduct of citizens, nor does it administer such normal functions of government as the maintenance of streets, the operation of schools, or sanitation, health, or welfare services.

Second, * * * even the District's water functions, which constitute the primary and originating purpose of the District, are relatively narrow. The District and Association do not own, sell, or buy water, nor do they control the use of any water they have delivered. The District simply stores water behind its dams, conserves it from loss, and delivers it through project canals. It is true * * * that as much as 40% of the water delivered by the District goes for nonagricultural purposes. But the distinction between agricultural and urban land is of no special constitutional significance in this context. The constitutionally relevant fact is that all water delivered by the Salt River District, like the water delivered by the Tulare Lake Basin Water Storage District, is distributed according to land ownership, and the District does not and cannot control the use to which the landowners who are entitled to the water choose to put it. As repeatedly recognized by the Arizona courts, though the state legislature has allowed water districts to become nominal public entities in order to obtain inexpensive bond financing, the districts remain essentially business enterprises, created by and chiefly benefitting a specific group of landowners. * * * As in *Salyer*, the nominal public character of such an entity cannot transform it into the type of governmental body for which the Fourteenth Amendment demands a one-person, one-vote system of election.

Finally, neither the existence nor size of the District's power business affects the legality of its property-based voting scheme. As this Court has noted in a different context, the provision of electricity is not a traditional element of governmental sovereignty, *Jackson v. Metropolitan Edison Co.*, 419 U.S. 345, 353, and so is not in itself the sort of general or important governmental function that would make the government provider subject to the doctrine of the *Reynolds* case. In any event, since the electric power functions were stipulated to be incidental to the water functions which are the District's primary purpose, they cannot change the character of that enterprise. The Arizona Legislature permitted the District to generate and sell electricity to subsidize the water operations, which were the beneficiaries intended by the statute. A key part of the *Salyer* decision was that the voting scheme for a public entity like a water district may constitutionally reflect the narrow primary purpose for which the district is created. In this case, the parties have stipulated that the primary legislative purpose of the District is to store, conserve, and deliver water for use by District landowners, that the sole legislative reason for making water projects public entities was to enable them to raise revenue through interest-free bonds, and that the development and sale of electric power was undertaken not for the primary purpose of providing electricity to the public, but "to support the primary irrigation functions by supplying power for reclamation uses and by providing revenues which could be applied to increase the amount and reduce the cost of water to Association subscribed lands."

The appellees claim, and the Court of Appeals agreed, that the sheer size of the power operations and the great number of people they affect serve to transform the District into an entity of general governmental power. But no matter how great the number of nonvoting residents buying electricity from the District, the relationship between them and the District's power operations is essentially that between consumers and a business enterprise from which they buy. Nothing in the *Avery*, *Hadley*, or *Salyer* cases suggests that the volume of business or the breadth of economic effect of a venture undertaken by a government entity as an incident of its narrow and primary governmental public function can, of its own weight, subject the entity to the one-person, one-vote requirements of the *Reynolds* case.

The functions of the Salt River District are therefore of the narrow, special sort which justifies a departure from the popular-election requirement of the *Reynolds* case. And as in *Salyer*, an aspect of that limited purpose is the disproportionate relationship the District's functions bear to the specific class of people whom the system makes eligible to vote. The voting landowners are the only residents of the District whose lands are subject to liens to secure District bonds. Only these landowners are subject to the acreage-based taxing power of the District, and voting landowners are the only residents who have ever committed capital to the District through stock assessments charged by the Association. The *Salyer* opinion did not say that the selected class of voters for a special public entity must be the only parties at all affected by the operations of the entity, or that their entire economic well-being must depend on that entity. Rather, the question was whether the effect of the entity's operations on them was disproportionately greater than the effect on those seeking the vote.

As in the *Salyer* case, we conclude that the voting scheme for the District is constitutional because it bears a reasonable relationship to its statutory objectives. Here, according to the stipulation of the parties, the subscriptions of land which made the Association and then the District possible might well have never occurred had not the subscribing landowners been assured a special voice in the conduct of the District's business. Therefore, as in *Salyer*, the State could rationally limit the vote to landowners. Moreover, Arizona could rationally make the weight of their vote dependent upon the number of acres they own, since that number reasonably reflects the relative risks they incurred as landowners and the distribution of the benefits and the burdens of the District's water operations. * * *

JUSTICE WHITE, with whom JUSTICE BRENNAN, JUSTICE MARSHALL, and JUSTICE BLACKMUN join, dissenting.

* * * The District involved here clearly exercises substantial governmental powers. The District is a municipal corporation organized under the laws of Arizona and is not, in any sense of the word, a private corporation. Pursuant to the Arizona Constitution, such districts are "political subdivisions of the State, and vested with all the rights, privileges and benefits, and entitled to the immunities and exemptions granted municipalities and political subdivisions under this Constitution or any law of the State or of the United States." Ariz. Const., Art. 13, § 7. Under the relevant statute controlling agricultural improvement districts, the District is "a public, political, taxing subdivision of the state, and a municipal corporation to the extent of the powers and privileges conferred by this chapter or granted generally to municipal corporations by the constitution and statutes of the state, including immunity of its property and bonds from taxation." Ariz. Rev. Stat. Ann. § 45–902 (1956). The District's bonds are tax-exempt, and its property is not subject to state or local property taxation. This attribute clearly indicates the governmental nature of the District's function. The District also has the power of eminent domain, a matter of some import. The District has also been given the power to enter into a wide range of contractual arrangements to secure energy sources. Inherent in this authorization is the power to control the use and source of energy generated by the District, including the possible use of nuclear power. Obviously, this broad authorization over the field of energy transcends the limited functions of the agricultural water storage district involved in *Salyer*.

Like most "private" utilities, which are often "natural monopolies," * * * private utilities in Arizona are subject to regulation by public authority. The Arizona Corporation Commission is empowered to prescribe "just and reasonable rates" as well as to regulate other aspects of the business operations of private utilities. *See* Ariz. Rev. Stat. Ann. § 40–321 (1974). The rate structure of the District now before us, however, is not subject to control by another state agency because the District is a municipal corporation and itself purports to perform the public function of protecting the public interest that the Corporation Commission would otherwise perform. *See* Ariz. Const., Art. 13, § 7, Art. 15, § 2. *See also Rubenstein Construction Co. v. Salt River Project Agricultural Improvement & Power Dist.*, 76 Ariz. 402, 265 P. 2d 455 (1953) (Salt River Project is not a public service corporation and therefore statute forbidding certain business practices did not apply). Its power to set its own rates and other conditions of service constitutes important attributes of sovereignty. When combined with a consideration of the District's wide-ranging operations which encompass water for agricultural and personal uses, and electrical generation for the needs of hundreds of thousands of customers, it is clear that the District exercises broad governmental power. With respect to energy management and the provision of water and electricity, the District's power is immense and its authority complete. * * *

The area within the District, once primarily rural, now encompasses eight municipalities and a major part of the city of Phoenix. Its original purpose, the supply of irrigation water, now provides only a tiny fraction of its gross income. For the fiscal year ending April 30, 1980, the District had a total operating income of approximately $450 million, 98% of which was derived from the generation of electricity and its sale to approximately 240,000 consumers. * * * The District is now the second largest utility in Arizona. Furthermore, as of April 30, 1980, the District had outstanding long-term debt of slightly over $2 billion. Approximately $1.78 billion, or about 88%, of that debt are in the form of revenue bonds secured solely by the revenues from the District's electrical operations. All of the District's capital improvements since 1972 have been financed by revenue bonds, and the general obligation bonds, now representing a small fraction of the District's long-term debt, are being steadily retired from the District's general revenues. It must also be noted that at the present time, 40% of the water delivered by the District is used for nonagricultural purposes—25% for municipal purposes and 15% to schools, playgrounds, parks, and the like.

With these facts in mind, it is indeed curious that the Court would attempt to characterize the District's electrical operations as "incidental" to its water operations, or would consider the power operations to be irrelevant to the legality of the voting scheme. The facts are that in *Salyer* the burdens of the Water District fell entirely on the landowners who were served by the District. * * * Unlike the situation in *Salyer*, the financial burden of supplying irrigation water has been shifted from the landowners to the consumers of electricity. At the very least, the structure of the District's indebtedness together with the history of the District's operations compels a finding that the burdens placed upon the lands within the District are so minimal that they cannot possibly serve as a basis for limiting the franchise to property owners. * * *

It is apparent in this case that landowning irrigators are getting a free ride at the expense of the users of electricity. It would also seem apparent that except for the subsidy, utility rates would be lower. Of course, subsidizing agricultural operations may well be in the public interest in Arizona, but it does not follow that the amount of the subsidy and the manner in which it is provided should be totally in the hands of a select few.

To conclude that the effect of the District's operations in this case is substantially akin to that in *Salyer* ignores reality. As recognized in *Salyer*, there were "no towns, shops, hospitals, or other facilities designed to improve the quality of life within the district boundaries, and it does not have a fire department, police, buses, or trains." 410 U.S., at 729. In short, there was nothing in the Water Storage District for its operations to affect except the land itself. The relationship between the burdens of the District and the land within the District's boundaries was strong. Here, the District encompasses one of the major metropolitan areas in the country. The effects of the provision of water and electricity on the citizens of the city are as major as they are obvious. There is no strong relationship between the District's operation and the land qua land. The District's revenues and bonds are tied directly to the electrical operation. Any encumbrance on the land is at best speculative. Certainly, any direct impact on the land is no greater than in *Phoenix v. Kolodziejski*, 399 U.S. 204 (1970), where we rejected the same argument presented today. Simply put, the District is an integral governmental actor providing important governmental services to residents of the District. To conclude otherwise is to ignore the urban reality of the District's operations.

Underlying the Court's conclusion in this case is the view that the provision of electricity and water is essentially private enterprise and not sufficiently governmental—that the District "simply does not exercise the sort of governmental powers that invoke the strict demands" of the Fourteenth Amendment because it does not administer "such normal functions of government as the maintenance of streets, the operation of schools, or sanitation, health, or welfare services." * * * This is a distinctly odd view of the reach of municipal services in this day and age. Supplying water for domestic and industrial uses is almost everywhere the responsibility of local government, and this function is intimately connected with sanitation and health. Nor is it any more accurate to consider the supplying of electricity as essentially a private function. The United States Government and its agencies generate and sell substantial amounts of power; and in view of the widespread existence of municipal utility systems, it is facetious to suggest that the operation of such utility systems should be considered as an incidental aspect of municipal government. Nor will it do, it seems to me, to return to the proprietary-governmental dichotomy in order to deliver into wholly private hands the control of a major municipal activity which acts to subsidize a limited number of landowners.

NOTES AND QUESTIONS

1.   *Special Purpose Districts.* There are more than 38,000 independent special purpose districts in the United States, and the special district is perhaps our most common and rapidly growing form of local government. *See, e.g.,* David L. Chicoine & Norman Walzer, Governmental Structure and Local Public Finance 8–16 (Oelgeschlager, Gunn & Hain, Inc. 1985); Douglas R. Porter, et al., Special Districts: A Useful Technique for Financing Infrastructure 1–9 (Urban Land Inst., 2d ed. 1990). *See generally* Kathryn A. Foster, The Political Economy of Special-Purpose Government (Georgetown Univ. Press 1997). More than 3,500 special purpose districts deal with water management functions, including drainage, irrigation, flood control and water management functions. Christopher R. Berry, Imperfect Union: Representation and Taxation in Multilevel Governments, 31–34 (Cambridge U. Press. 2009). Many are quite large in size, with roughly ten percent crossing two or more counties. *Id.* at 42. The formation of special districts is discussed in Chapter III.E; legal issues surrounding the creation of special districts that are regional in scope are explored in Chapter V.

2.   *One Acre, One Vote. Ball* does not simply uphold the limitation of the franchise in these special districts to landowners; it upholds the allocation of votes according to acreage. Although property ownership as a qualification for voting has a long history, votes were generally not allotted according to the value of the property owned. Under the Arizona statute invalidated in *City of Phoenix v. Kolodziejski, supra,* each taxpayer cast a single, equally-weighted vote. The traditional role of property ownership requirements was to establish that the voter had an economic stake in the community and a measure of political independence. The voting schemes sustained in *Salyer* (which allocated votes according to assessed valuation) and *Ball* are more akin to those of business corporations than to those of municipalities. In *Salyer,* the use of assessment-weighted voting actually tended to cancel out the participation of most landowners because one corporation owned enough property in the district to command a majority of the votes, and the four largest owners together garnered approximately eighty-five percent of the votes.

3.   *"Nominal" Public Entity.* What does the Court mean when it describes the Salt River district as a "nominal" public entity? The district had a sufficiently "public character" that it could avoid state taxes, sell tax-exempt bonds, condemn property, and be exempt from the oversight of the state agency regulating private utilities. Indeed, it was sufficiently public that the Court assumed that the Fourteenth Amendment applied to its voting arrangements, although one person, one vote was not required. What made it only "nominally" public? And if it was only "nominally" public, what was it actually?

4. *Rural and Urban. Salyer* was the first case in which the Court found a "special limited purpose district" to be exempt from one person, one vote. With only fifty-nine adults living on its 193,000 acres, the Tulare Lake Basin district was a rural area whose population was far below the minimum California required as a precondition for municipal incorporation. *See* Cal.Govt.Code § 56043. *Salyer* emphasized "[t]here are no towns, shops, hospitals, or other facilities designed to improve the quality of life within the district boundaries." 410 U.S. at 729. In effect, there was no local community appropriate for democratic self-government. The Salt River district at issue in *Ball* was quite another matter: At the time of the litigation, the district was, in terms of revenues and expenditures, one of the five largest special districts in the United States, *see* Comment, Voter Restrictions in Special Districts: A Case Study of the Salt River Project, 1969 Law & Soc. Order (Ariz.St.L.J.) 636, 658. Moreover, it had a broad impact over the Phoenix metropolitan area—"vastly more influence over the lives of the people of Phoenix than do most conventional governments." Joel Garreau, Edge City: Life on the New Frontier 193 (Anchor Books 1991).

5. *Disproportionate Impact?* In *Salyer*, the landowners bore the district's full financial costs. In *Ball*, however, most of the district's revenues came from the sale of electric power to nonlandowner residents. In what way were district landowners disproportionately affected by the district's operations? How does *Ball*'s analysis of disproportionate impact square with the analysis used in *City of Phoenix?* Does the difference in the nature of the government activities affected by the vote justify the difference in the Court's approach to the use of disproportionate impact in the allocation of the right to vote?

6. *Taxation vs. Assessment.* The Salt River district, like the Tulare Lake Basin district, lacked the power to tax real property. Instead, both districts were empowered to impose assessments on land in the district. The differences between property taxation and assessments are discussed more fully in Chapter VI, but, briefly, an assessment is a charge against land for a service or improvement provided to the land by the community. The landowner may not be required to pay an assessment greater than the benefit he or she receives, and the community may not be able to collect more in assessments than the cost of the project the assessments finance. By contrast, the property tax may be redistributive—the taxpayer may be required to pay more in taxes than he or she receives in services—and may be used by the community to finance programs in addition to those that benefit property. Both taxation and assessment, however, are coercive. The assessment, like the property tax, can be imposed without the consent of the payer. Moreover, the assessment, like the tax, has long been used by general purpose governments, as well as special purpose governments, to finance the construction and maintenance of public improvements. How does a district's use of the assessment rather than the property tax make it less public and more proprietary?

7.   *Special Districts and the Voting Rights Act.* The voting rules of the Salt River District were subject to legal challenge once again when African-American plaintiffs who lived within the boundaries of the district claimed that the district's property ownership requirement for voting violates Section 2 of the Voting Rights Act as only forty percent of African-American heads of household within the district owned homes, compared with sixty percent of white heads-of-households. Section 2 of the Voting Rights Act prohibits any state "or political subdivision" from using any voting qualification, prerequisite to voting or standard "in a manner which results in a denial or abridgement of the right . . . to vote on account of race or color." The United States Court of Appeals for the Ninth Circuit found that the district is a "political subdivision" within the meaning of the Voting Rights Act, relying in part on the Act's legislative history and on the district's status under Arizona law. Smith v. Salt River Project Agricultural Improvement & Power Dist., 109 F.3d 586, 592–94 (9th Cir.1997). But the court concluded that under the circumstances—including the lack of any history of intentional discrimination in district elections and the state's "important interest in landowner-based voting"—the land ownership requirement was not discriminatory. *See id.* at 596.

8.   *Characterizing Special Purpose Districts.* Not all special districts are exempt from the one person, one vote requirement. The *Salyer* and *Ball* decisions indicate that the earlier decisions in *Kramer* and *Hadley* applying one person, one vote to a school board and a junior college board of trustees are still good law. What distinguishes the two sets of districts? Is water supply less important than education? Is water supply less of a governmental, and more of a proprietary, activity than education? Is a garbage collection district, Lane v. Town of Oyster Bay, 564 N.Y.S.2d 655 (N.Y.Sup.Ct.1990) or a tunnel improvement district, Chesser v. Buchanan, 568 P.2d 39 (Colo.1977), or a district that provides water pollution abatement and public transportation functions, Cunningham v. Municipality of Metropolitan Seattle, 751 F.Supp. 885 (W.D.Wash.1990), more akin to a school district or to a water supply district for deciding local voting rights? *Cf.* Finke v. State ex rel. McGrath, 65 P.3d 576, 581 (Mont.2003) (election to authorize a "municipal jurisdictional area" or "county jurisdictional area" which would be responsible for the enforcement of building codes cannot be limited to record owners of real property, but is subject to one person, one vote; "the application and enforcement of building codes is an issue of public safety that affects all persons living in the affected area, not only record owners of real property"). How important should it be that a district is financed solely by assessments?

9.   *Voting Rights and the Financing of Physical Infrastructure.* Determining whether voting in a special district is to be determined by democratic or quasi-proprietary norms is particularly difficult when the district is used to finance—but not operate or control—physical infrastructure. In State v. Frontier Acres Community Development District, 472 So.2d 455 (Fla.1985), the Florida Supreme Court sustained a state

statute providing for the election, on a one acre/one vote basis, of the board of supervisors of a community development district. The district is basically a device for developers to finance streets, drainage, and sewers on the urban fringe to improve the marketability of their developments. The Florida court determined that the district's powers "implement the single, narrow legislative purpose of ensuring that future growth in this State will be complemented by an adequate community infrastructure." *Id.* at 457. For more on the role of special districts in funding, constructing, and operating public infrastructure, *see* Janice C. Griffith, Special Tax Districts to Finance Residential Infrastructure, 39 Urb. Law. 959 (2007).

In Southern California Rapid Transit District v. Bolen, 822 P.2d 875 (Cal. 1992), a divided California Supreme Court upheld a state law allowing only property owners to vote in a referendum on imposing assessments that would be used to fund part of the costs of construction of a rapid transit line. The Southern California Rapid Transit District ("SCRTD") was authorized to create special benefit assessment districts to defray part of the costs of construction of a planned rapid transit line connecting downtown Los Angeles to North Hollywood. On the theory that the rail system would specially benefit landowners within a certain distance of the new rail stations, the SCRTD created two districts and sought to impose special assessments on commercial property in the districts. The assessments were subject to a property owner referendum, with votes allotted according to the assessed valuation of the property in the district.

The three judges of the court of appeal—and the California Supreme Court dissenters—argued that the case was controlled by *Kramer* and *City of Phoenix*: "[P]ublic transportation, like public education, is an issue affecting all citizens." 269 Cal.Rptr. 147, 155 (1990). Thus, a restriction on the referendum franchise should be subject to strict scrutiny. Following *City of Phoenix*, although the assessment would be imposed on commercial landowners, these judges assumed that the assessment payers would be able to shift the burden to their tenants and also noted that the entire community would benefit from the facility funded by the assessment. Thus, as in *City of Phoenix*, the franchise could not be limited to the assessment payers.

The five-member majority of the California Supreme Court, however, found that the election concerned not the SCRTD, but the special assessment districts, which "lack virtually any of the incidents of government." 822 P.2d at 883. The "narrow purpose" of the assessment district was not the governmental function of transportation but simply "the recoupment of some of the added economic value conferred on commercial property resulting from its proximity to the transit station." *Id.* at 884. With a special assessment district seen as simply a quasi-proprietary investment vehicle, a restriction on the franchise in an assessment district election was subject only to the rational basis test. Limiting the franchise to those required to pay the assessment (and linking the number of votes to assessed valuation) passed that test. How would you have decided this dispute?

Some infrastructure development districts may serve for some period of time as de facto general purpose governments for their communities. Florida provides for the eventual transition of the governance of its community development districts from elections based on a one acre, one vote basis to one person, one vote depending on district size, the attainment of certain population milestones, or the decision to impose the ad valorem property tax, Fla. Stat. Ann. 190.006, but Florida also uses "stewardship districts," which are created by special act, and do not have a clear path from landowner to resident governance. *See, e.g.,* Ave Maria Stewardship Community District Act, Florida Laws 2004–461, Fla. Stat. Ann. 165–0615; Nadav Shoked, Quasi-Cities, 93 B.U.L. Rev. 1971, 1972–74 (2013) (noting that in the Ave Maria Stewardship Community District, the "government levied taxes, issued municipal bonds, and condemned private property—all in order to support schools, roads, water supply, sewage, garbage removal, city parks, and urban planning" but that residents lacked the right to vote). *See also id.* at 2004–05 (discussing Florida's Reedy Creek Improvement District, which has development and planning powers identical to Florida municipalities and was created at the request of the Disney Corporation to keep Disney World outside of city and county zoning and development rules).

KESSLER V. GRAND CENTRAL DISTRICT MANAGEMENT ASSOCIATION, INC.

United States Court of Appeals
158 F.3d 92 (2d Cir.1998)

KEARSE, CIRCUIT JUDGE:

To promote commercial development in urban areas, the New York State ("State") legislature has authorized municipalities in the State to establish business improvement districts ("BIDs"). In a BID, owners of nonexempt real property pay a periodic assessment to the municipality, over and above their ordinary municipal taxes. That assessment money is used to fund the construction of capital improvements to land in the district and the provision of certain services intended to promote business activity in the district. * * *

For each BID, there must be established a not-for-profit corporation called a "district management association," which is charged with "carrying out such activities as may be prescribed in the [district] plan." * * *

The Grand Central BID was established in 1988, and its territory was extended in June 1995 * * *. As extended, the Grand Central BID encompasses 337 properties on sections of 75 blocks in midtown Manhattan, including the Grand Central Terminal railroad station. There are 242 owners of property within the GCBID. That property includes approximately 71 million square feet of commercial space, constituting approximately 19% of the total commercial space in Manhattan. The office space in the GCBID "exceeds the entire space inventory of the Central Business District in such cities as Houston, San Francisco, Dallas, Denver, and Boston." * * * The GCBID also contains approximately 897,000 square feet of residential space, occupied by approximately 930 residents.

The District Plan authorizes the construction of capital improvements (the "Improvements") and the provision of additional services (the "Services") in the GCBID. The Improvements include the renovation of sidewalks and crosswalks; the planting of trees; the installation of new lighting, street signs, bus shelters, news kiosks, and trash receptacles; contributions to the renovation of Grand Central Terminal; and "the creation of a restaurant facility" on 42nd Street. The Services "may include any services required for the enjoyment and protection of the public and the promotion and enhancement of the District," including [security, sanitation, tourist information, social services for homeless persons, special maintenance and repair, public events, retail improvements.]

Pursuant to a contract between the City Department of Business Services and [the Grand Central District Management Association, Inc., ("GCDMA")] dated July 30, 1993 (the "Contract"), GCDMA became the Grand Central BID's management association. * * * To carry out the District Plan, GCDMA, through its operating entity, Grand Central Partnership, Inc., employs approximately 63 security guards, most of whom are unarmed. These guards "patrol the streets and sidewalks of the District" and "attempt[ ] to obtain compliance with City regulations controlling vending, sidewalk obstructions, noise generation, and air pollution." They are "tied into [the New York City Police Department's] communications network" and act "in cooperation with [the New York City Police Department] and the building staffs of private property-owners." (Id.) GCDMA employs "sanitation" workers, who perform functions such as sweeping sidewalks and streets, as well as removing graffiti, washing sidewalks, caring for trees and plants, "poster removal, cleaning street signs, and repainting street furniture." These workers bag trash, which is in due course collected by the City's Department of Sanitation in the normal course of its refuse removal duties. GCDMA also provides other services to improve the attractiveness of the district, such as giving free assistance to retailers in removing old signs and designing new signs and facades; and it provides assistance in complying with applicable City ordinances.

In addition, GCDMA contributes to the funding and operation of a 24-hour "outreach, assessment and referral" facility for homeless persons that provides services such as job training. Other GCDMA Services include operating tourist information booths in the district and sponsoring events, such as an alcohol-free New Year's Eve celebration, in the district's public spaces. GCDMA "retains the flexibility to eliminate or add to" the Services listed in the District Plan.

The primary source of funding for the Grand Central BID is an assessment that the City levies against and collects from all industrial, commercial, and residential property within the district. * * *

The Act provides that the assessment is to be "determined, levied and collected in the same manner, at the same time and by the same officers, as general municipal taxes are levied and collected." N.Y. Gen. Mun. Law § 980–j(b). * * *

The Act provides that the board of directors of the management association of a BID is to consist of representatives of owners and tenants within the [BID], provided, however, that not less than a majority of its members shall represent owners and provided further that tenants of commercial space and dwelling units within the [BID] shall also be represented on the board, along with, in a municipality "having a population of one million or more," [four representatives selected by designated elected city officials.] Thus, while the management association's board is to include representatives of both property owners and tenants, the owners have the right to elect a majority of the directors.

[Under GCDMA's bylaws, the Board of Directors is composed of 31 directors elected by the owners of commercial property; 16 directors elected by commercial tenants; 1 director elected by residential tenants; and 4 City government representatives.]

Plaintiffs are [nonproperty-owning, noncommercial] residents of the Grand Central BID. They live in an apartment building at 372 Fifth Avenue, which was added to the GCBID in June 1995. * * * As amended, their complaint asserted that the "system of voting" for GCDMA Board members "privileges one class of district members over another without regard to actual number or place of residence" and that because residents are consigned to a permanent minority status on the Board even though they are numerically superior to the class of owners of property within the district, they are deprived of any meaningful opportunity to advance their interests concerning GCDMA activities. * * * Plaintiffs contended that GCDMA provides general services to the whole district, funded by a general mandatory tax, and that its functions are neither narrow in scope nor limited in purpose and thus give it the character of local government. They sought, inter alia, a declaration that the system of representation on the Board * * * violates the Equal Protection Clause by denying to the plaintiffs, who are residential tenants in the district, representation on the basis of the principle of one person, one vote * * * and they requested a permanent injunction ensuring plaintiffs equal voting rights.

* * * [W]e conclude that although a few of GCDMA's functions are of the type that the City also performs, GCDMA's responsibilities and

powers are so circumscribed that GCDMA cannot be said to exercise the core powers of sovereignty typical of a general purpose governmental body. We also conclude that both the burdens and the benefits of GCDMA activities disproportionately impact property owners, and that the voting system for GCDMA's Board is reasonably related to the goals warranting the establishment of a BID.

1.   THE GCBID'S LIMITED PURPOSE

* * * [T]he purpose of the Grand Central BID is the promotion of business. Its geographic area is a swath of midtown Manhattan devoted overwhelmingly to commercial use (the ratio of commercial space to residential space is more than 70 to 1), and its goal is to attract and keep businesses by assisting property owners to achieve the remunerative use of that commercial space.

The greater diversity of the projects undertaken by GCDMA, as compared to the projects in *Salyer*, is a result of the substantial differences in the nature and use of the property to be benefitted. While *Salyer* involved 193,000 acres of rural land devoted almost exclusively to agricultural use, the GCBID encompasses all or parts of 75 city blocks, in which the businesses are diverse and the premises concentrated. While owners of agricultural land often have no greater concern than their need for adequate water supplies, *see, e.g., Salyer*, 410 U.S. at 721–22, the problems of property owners in the GCBID, which includes some of the * * * most heavily developed land in the nation, are necessarily more complex, involving the need to maintain a lively, safe, and attractive commercial center through which millions of people pass daily. The greater complexity of the latter problems leads to greater complexity of the functions of the managing agent in devising solutions and coordinating programs.

Yet the complexity of the projects aimed at promoting business in the GCBID should not obscure the fact that the promotion of business is a limited purpose. The GCBID, like the water districts at issue in *Salyer* and *Ball*, is not concerned with the provision of general public services such as schools, housing, hospitals, jails, firefighting, transportation, utilities, or zoning. And although * * * some of GCDMA's functions are of a public welfare nature, its functions as a matter of law cannot supplant the fundamental obligations of the City.

2.   GCDMA'S LACK OF SOVEREIGN POWER

Not only does the purpose of the Grand Central BID not encompass many traditional governmental functions, the GCDMA lacks the powers normally enjoyed by a governmental body. GCDMA does not have the power, for example, to impose income taxes or sales taxes. Nor, indeed, does GCDMA levy or collect the assessments needed to fund the GCBID. Those functions are performed by the City, which holds the moneys until they are disbursed—either to GCDMA, or perhaps to another entity if the City is displeased with GCDMA's performance and elects to contract with a new manager. * * *

Further, GCDMA has no authority to enact or enforce any laws governing the conduct of persons present in the district. It cannot, for example, make or enforce any environmental or other sanitation regulations. Although it employs workers who bag trash, remove graffiti, and engage in other area-beautification projects, it performs no inspections in matters of health and safety, and neither the Act nor the District Plan gives it any power to issue citations for violations of City building or zoning codes.

And although GCDMA employs security guards, its guards have no authority to perform typical law enforcement functions. The guards are not authorized by the Act or the District Plan to, for example, make arrests, conduct investigations, obtain warrants for searches, or detain suspects. Except for specially licensed supervisors, GCDMA's security personnel are not armed. Their tools are communications equipment tying them into the City's police network to enable them to summon law enforcement personnel from the City police department.

In short, GCDMA itself cannot meaningfully alter the conduct of persons present in the district.

3.   GCDMA'S LIMITED ROLE AND RESPONSIBILITY

Plaintiffs contend, however, that application of the one-person-one-vote principle is warranted because of GCDMA's functions in the area of security, sanitation, and social services. While these are types of services that are often provided by local governments, we conclude that the fact that GCDMA also provides them is insufficient to subject it to the one-person-one-vote requirement because (a) by law GCDMA's responsibility for these functions is at most secondary to that of the City, (b) GCDMA's activities in these areas are quantitatively dwarfed by those of the City, and (c) the services performed by GCDMA are qualitatively different from core municipal functions.

As a matter of law GCDMA does not have primary responsibility for providing security, sanitation, or social services within the district. * * * [T]he City itself has—and by law must retain—the primary responsibility for providing security, sanitation, and social services in the GCBID.

Moreover, the City's provision of these services is far more extensive than the limited activities of GCDMA. For example, while GCDMA employs some 63 security guards, most of them unarmed, the District is served primarily by three City police precincts which it overlaps. Further, as discussed above, the GCDMA security guards do not act as policemen. Although they patrol the district in the expectation that their visible presence will deter the incidence of serious crime, if law enforcement is needed, GCDMA security personnel call in the City police.

As to social services, while GCDMA contributes to the funding of a single outreach facility for homeless persons, the City has an entire Department devoted to assisting the homeless. Indeed, even if GCDMA had a more extensive role in the outreach facility and even if the facility provided the homeless with more extensive services, such as temporary housing, those facts alone would not transform GCDMA into a general governmental body, any more than it makes public bodies out of religious or other charitable organizations that offer such services.

Further, most of the so-called "sanitation" activities in which GCDMA engages are not focused on matters of public health. For example, GCDMA sanitation workers bag loose trash, but they do not cart it away. It remains the responsibility of the City's Department of Sanitation to perform the ordinary municipal refuse removal service. Rather, the physical [i]mprovements, such as installing better street lights and more attractive trash bins and illuminating Grand Central Terminal at night, as well as many of the [s]ervices, such as removing graffiti and old posters, cleaning street signs, and assisting merchants to design and install new signs and facades, are simply efforts to improve the physical appearance of the district. We cannot conclude that these activities reflect the exercise of general governmental authority.

Other GCDMA activities, such as the operation of information booths for tourists, the planned opening of a restaurant near Grand Central Terminal, and the sponsorship of public events are also nothing more than efforts to make the district more attractive to tourists and other consumers. None of these activities are indicative of general governmental authority.

4.   THE CITY'S CONTROL OVER GCDMA

[E]ven the activities that GCDMA performs are subject to close City control. For example, under the Act, the total annual amount to be spent on improvements, maintenance, and operation must be set out in the District Plan, and the Plan limits the amount and type of expenditures GCDMA may make. The Plan cannot be implemented unless it is approved by the City Council; nor can the total annual amount to be expended be increased unless the City amends the District Plan. * * * GCDMA cannot increase the rate of the assessment above the maximum rate which is set by the City.

It is true that once the City approves a maximum annual budget amount for GCDMA, GCDMA may continue spending at that level in each succeeding year, and property will continue being assessed at the corresponding rate in each succeeding year, with no requirement of continued City approval. But that fact does not subject GCDMA elections to the one-person-one-vote rule, for even "the power to levy and collect special assessments * * * does not create * * * general governmental authority." *Ball*, 451 U.S. at 366 n.11.

* * * In addition, the City has considerable supervisory authority over GCDMA's expenditure of whatever money GCDMA does receive from the City. GCDMA was required to submit to the City annually a detailed explanation of its past year's expenditures and a planned budget for the upcoming year. It is also required to submit to the City design plans and specifications for all proposed Improvements and must submit a schedule for their completion. The parties further agree that GCDMA has no independent authority to make physical improvements within the BID without the approval of the relevant City agencies. And while GCDMA has somewhat greater latitude in its provision of the[s]ervices, under the Contract its performance of the [s]ervices is subject to the review and reasonable direction and control of the Commissioner, who has the right to "inspect" GCDMA's [s]ervices and, if he finds them unsatisfactory, to order that they be properly performed. If GCDMA does not comply with the order, the City may withhold funds from GCDMA and have someone other than GCDMA perform the [s]ervices. Finally, we note that the City had the right, if displeased with GCDMA's performance, to refuse to renew the Contract—a right it has now exercised.

In sum, in light of (a) the BID's limited goal of improving the area for business, (b) the fact that GCDMA is not the primary provider of the limited security, sanitation, or social services it performs, and (c) the City's control over GCDMA's performance with respect to the functions it performs, we conclude that here, as in *Salyer* and *Ball*, the district's manager has relatively limited authority and does not exercise the sort of governmental powers that normally triggers the one-person-one-vote principle.

* * * Since the GCBID is a special-purpose district that affects property owners disproportionately, the Constitution requires only that the weighted voting system for electing GCDMA's Board bear a reasonable relationship to the purposes of the GCBID. Plaintiffs have made no attempt to argue that GCDMA's weighted voting system lacks such a reasonable relationship, and we think such a relationship is obvious. The need for cooperative action among property owners is clear. Projects such as the [i]mprovements to land in the district, the sweeping of streets, and the provision of additional security personnel are projects that redound to the benefit of many property owners; but for that very reason, these are projects that no owner would likely undertake individually. The GCBID allows property owners to pool their resources to accomplish mutually beneficial projects to increase the attractiveness of district property for commercial purposes.

In *Ball,* the Supreme Court found that weighted voting had the requisite reasonable relationship by virtue of the fact that the creation of the district "might well have never occurred had not the subscribing landowners been assured a special voice in the conduct of the District's business." 451 U.S. at 371. * * * Here too, if a sufficient number of property owners in the district had objected, they could have prevented the establishment of the GCBID. *See* N.Y. Gen. Mun. Law §§ 980–e(b), 980–f(b)(1). Indeed, if a sufficient number object in the future, the GCBID will be dissolved. *See id.* § 980–n(a). Since only property owners are assessed to fund GCDMA's activities, the State legislature could reasonably have concluded that property owners, unless given principal control over how the money is spent, would not have consented to having their property subject to the assessment. The guarantee that property owners will have majority representation on the Board is thus reasonably related to the goal of promoting commercial activity in the GCBID.

WEINSTEIN, J., dissenting:

* * * The virtual exclusion of the plaintiffs' voice from the governance of their own Business Improvement District is an unacceptable derogation of the one person, one vote principle. These "cities within cities" are performing an increasing number of important governmental functions in our country. The GCDMA spends millions of municipally raised tax dollars every year to provide a wide range of governmental functions, including security, sanitation, capital improvements, social services, promotion of tourism, transportation control, and public events. In performing these services the GCDMA exercises a degree of policy-making authority and discretion which rivals that of any municipal agency. There is no basis in law, therefore, for holding that the GCDMA is free to exclude its own residents from meaningfully participating in the BID's administration through the vote for the board. While BIDs may not fit neatly within the traditional definition of a government entity, this fact alone does not exempt them from the fundamental requirements of our republican form of government. All residents of the Grand Central BID are entitled to a meaningful voice in governance. The one person, one vote mandate of the Fourteenth Amendment requires it, as does our fundamental sense of democracy.

As in both *Hadley* and *Avery,* the GCDMA performs important governmental functions which directly impact the lives of all those who live and work within its jurisdiction. Some of the services, such as security, sanitation, social services, capital improvement, maintenance of public roads, and promotion of tourism, are traditional functions of government. In fact, the GCDMA provides a far broader range of traditional governmental services than that provided by the board of trustees in *Hadley.*

The GCDMA is also subject to the one person, one vote requirement because of the substantial discretion it enjoys in determining which services will be provided within the district and how and when they will be performed. As in *Hadley* and *Avery*, the GCDMA has the freedom to shape and tailor the provision of municipal services in the district according to its own policy and legislative preferences. The fact that the residential tenants may wish to effectuate a different set of policies than those of the GCDMA's board is more, not less, reason to open up the GCDMA to fair elections.

* * * The GCDMA decides, for example, such matters as how many security guards will patrol the district, where they will patrol, which kinds of behavior they will monitor, and the manner in which they will conduct themselves on the streets. It decides how to supervise and discipline its security force, and whether to implement procedures or safeguards to help ensure that those who have been charged with protecting the public do not infringe upon the personal rights of individuals. The GCDMA decides which streets within the district will be the cleanest, the most well lit, and the most closely patrolled. It decides who within the district will get "extra" street lights, trash collection, assistance in upgrading and cleaning facades and signs, and graffiti removal. The GCDMA decides whether to operate homeless shelters within the district and, if so, where, how many and what types of services these centers will provide. It decides where tourist information centers will be located and where within the district the taxi stands will located. It also plays the leading role in determining when and where millions of dollars of city money and tax exempt bond proceeds will be used to make capital improvements within the district. * * *

* * * The Grand Central BID provides a far wider range of governmental services than the water districts in *Salyer* and *Ball*. The general services provided by the GCDMA have a dramatic impact upon all groups and residents within the district. Its activities are far more typical of general local governmental services than of those involved in *Salyer* and *Ball*. In *Ball* the Court reasoned that the water district at issue did not fall within the one person, one vote requirement because the district did not perform normal governmental activities such as "the maintenance of streets, the operation of schools, or sanitation, health, or welfare services." *Ball*, 451 U.S. at 366. * * * In the instant case, the GCDMA performs at least three of these paradigmatic governmental functions. In addition, the GCDMA provides other "core" governmental functions to the district such as the provision of security. * * *

The services the GCDMA provides affect all those who live within the district. Everyone, residents, tenants, owners, and businesspeople alike, derives benefits from the proper maintenance, upkeep, and beautification of the district. Everyone within the district derives benefits from the existence of clean, safe, and well lit streets and sidewalks, from the successful operation of social services programs and from the efficient flow of pedestrian and vehicular traffic. Everyone, tenants and owners alike, suffers from the detriments of a poorly organized or inefficiently operated BID. Everyone within the district is subject to the potential difficulties which result from inadequate or irresponsible supervision of security, sanitation, or social service programs.

In an effort to distinguish itself from those public bodies which have been held subject to the one person, one vote requirement, appellee GCDMA attempts to denigrate the quasi-public nature of BIDs such as the GCDMA and portray itself as just another "private, non-profit entity." *See* Brief of Defendant-Appellee Grand Central District Management Association, Inc. at 2. This characterization is disingenuous.

The broad array of services the GCDMA provides must be construed as "municipal" services partly because they are made possible by a special municipal "tax" specifically collected by the City of New York for the purpose of funding the GCDMA's activities. There is nothing voluntary about these assessments which all property owners within the district must pay to fund the GCDMA. Those who wish to avoid supporting the GCDMA are subject to the full weight of the City's coercive collection powers.

* * * If BIDs such as the GCDMA are not held to the one person, one vote requirement of the Fourteenth Amendment, there is a significant risk that a substantial portion of this country's urban population will be effectively prevented from controlling much of local government.

Cities today are utilizing BIDs in increasing numbers and experimenting with their use in new and different circumstances. * * * While it is true that the District Plan provides that general municipal services will not be reduced within the district as a result of the GCDMA's presence, there is nothing to prevent the City from reducing the services it provides on a City wide basis as a result of its reliance on the City's growing number of BIDs. BIDs decrease both the need and the incentive for the City to expand or maintain the general municipal services it provides to the City as a whole. * * * As more BIDs are created, the level of general services may decline still further, and even more BIDs will be needed to provide traditional public services to more favored areas and groups. * * *

When BIDs multiply in number and expand into new and innovative uses, they constitute an ever larger portion of the public sphere. Unless BID boards are elected in a democratic fashion, the result of this trend may be the effective disenfranchisement of a substantial percentage of our urban population.

Appellees argue that this loss of voting power is justified because BIDs provide services which are only "supplemental" to the municipal services provided by the City. Yet, there appears to be no principled way to distinguish services which are "supplemental" from those which are "essential." Virtually every municipal service is "supplemental" in the sense that city residents can survive with a reduction in the service. Trash may be collected several times a day in a BID, but it need not be collected as often in non-BID areas if the only requirement is that the City provide the most "basic" service. As larger and larger numbers of New Yorkers come under the umbrella of BIDs, on what basis shall it be determined that a service is sufficient to constitute the minimum floor for non-BID residents? Today the GCDMA spends some $12 million per year on the provision of services. How high must that figure rise until their services are important enough to qualify for constitutional scrutiny?

NOTES AND QUESTIONS

1.   *Business Improvement Districts.* Business improvement districts emerged in the 1980s and are now used widely to provide supplemental security, sanitation, and street maintenance services in cities throughout the United States. Most BIDs also provide direct assistance to businesses through programs that market the products of district businesses, recruit and retain firms within the district, and attract tourists, conventioneers, and consumers. A few, like the Grand Central BID, provide social services, too. Although particularly associated with the midtown and downtown areas of major cities such as New York City—which had 72 BIDs at the start of 2016—many BIDs have been established along small commercial strips within big cities, small towns, and suburbs. As in New York, most BIDs are primarily financed by supplemental assessments on property within the district, although some states provide for BIDs that are financed by surcharges on business taxes, such as the business license fee or occupation tax. As in New York, most BIDs are managed by boards that are elected primarily by property owners within the district, subject to oversight by city government. *See generally* Richard Briffault, A Government for Our Time? Business Improvement Districts and Urban Governance, 99 Colum.L.Rev. 365 (1999). For a collection of scholarly critiques of BIDs and case studies of sixteen BIDs in Philadelphia, *see* Symposium: Business Improvement Districts and the Evolution of Urban Governance, 3 Drexel L. Rev. 1 (2010).

Although not subject to one person, one vote, BIDs and their governing boards have generally been found to be subject to the rules that apply to public bodies. In *Epstein v. Hollywood Entertainment District II BID,* 104 Cal. Rptr. 2d 857 (Cal. App. 2001), a California appeals court held that the Hollywood Entertainment District Property Owners Association ("POA")—the private, nonprofit corporation that managed the Hollywood BID—was subject to California's open meetings law. *Accord,* Kennedy v. Montclair Center Corp. BID, 220 N.J. 269 (2014). A second question that has sometimes emerged is whether BID assessments are subject to state restrictions on taxation. That issue is addressed in Chapter VI.

2.   *The Grand Central District.* At the time of the *Kessler* litigation, the Grand Central BID raised and spent more money than any other BID in the country:

> The BID ha[d] undertaken an extensive program of security, sanitation, social services and assistance to business, as well as an ambitious capital program of street improvements. It has been a leader on issues of urban design and public amenities, installing hundreds of benches, bicycle racks, news racks, street signs, directions for tourist destinations, planters and trees.
>
> Grand Central is not only the largest BID in the country; it has been the most controversial. Its debt-financed capital program was an early source of city concern. [I]n 1995 the BID was embroiled in a contretemps, which eventually cost it a half-million-dollar federal grant, over inappropriately mingling security and social service functions in its homeless outreach program. A federal district court subsequently found that the BID's use of formerly homeless and jobless people, who were paid a "training" stipend rather than the minimum wage, to perform a variety of clerical, administrative, maintenance, food service and outreach work in its homeless services program violated the Fair Labor Standards Act and New York's minimum wage law. Its internal management practices were sharply criticized by a City Comptroller's audit. The BID's management, known as the Grand Central Partnership, also manages two other large midtown BIDs—34th Street and Bryant Park—thereby creating the impression that the BID wields undue power. The BID's management often stressed its private nature, and appeared to purposely push the envelope of independence from public control.

Briffault, A Government for Our Time?, *supra*, 99 Colum. L. Rev. at 431–32. For a critical assessment of the Grand Central BID, *see* David J. Kennedy, Note, Restraining the Power of Business Improvement Districts: The Case of the Grand Central Partnership, 15 Yale L. & Pol'y Rev. 283 (1996). *See also* Daniel R. Garodnick, Comment, What's the BID Deal? Can the Grand Central Business Improvement District Serve a Special Limited Purpose?, 148 U. Pa. L. Rev. 1733 (2000). For a more positive treatment, *see* Brian R. Hochleutner, Note, BIDs Fare Well: The Democratic Accountability of Business Improvement Districts, 78 N.Y.U. L. Rev. 374 (2003).

3.   *BIDs and Intracity Service Inequalities.* In his dissenting opinion, Judge Weinstein expressed the concern that the rise of BIDs will lead to public service inequalities within major cities. As areas with BIDs receive greater services—financed out of district assessments—compared to other areas, Weinstein predicted that the growing use of BIDs would provide an

incentive for cities to reduce their baseline level of services, thereby increasing the degree of inequality between BID and nonBID areas. By contrast, defenders of BIDs assert that the districts can help bolster city finances by making downtowns and other commercial districts more competitive with suburban malls and developments in outlying areas as sites for offices, stores, and entertainment and cultural activities. As a result, they argue, property values and property tax revenues are enhanced. *See, e.g.,* The Benefits of Business Improvement Districts (Furman Center for Real Estate and Urban Policy, Policy Brief July 2007) (finding that BIDs have a large, positive impact on commercial property values, although the major impact is in areas with larger BIDs while smaller BIDs have less discernible impact). BIDs also benefit other residents of nonBID areas, who come into the business districts to work, shop, seek entertainment or enjoy public amenities. Moreover, "BID functions are restricted, and BID budgets are just a small fraction of city taxes, with assessment levels often tightly limited by state law. There are huge categories of local government expenditures that are entirely outside the bailiwick of BIDs." Briffault, *supra,* 99 Colum.L.Rev. at 467. The degree of intracity service inequality attributable to BID activities is currently quite modest, although it could grow.

4.   *BIDs in Residential Neighborhoods.* Although BIDs are reserved for areas where the primary property uses are business-related, the districts could become a model for collecting assessments and providing supplemental services, such as additional policing or park improvements, in residential neighborhoods. *See* Robert C. Ellickson, New Institutions for Old Neighborhoods, 48 Duke L.J. 75 (1998), for a proposal for small-scale residential "block-level improvement districts." Could the right to vote for the board of such a "residential improvement district" be limited to taxpaying landowners within the district?

5.   *Kessler and the Determination of Special District Status.* The Grand Central BID operates in the heart of the urban center, and provides many services—including public safety, street maintenance, and sanitation—that closely resemble the services provided by municipal governments. In what sense, then, is it a special limited purpose district? The court appears to have given great weight to the BID's relatively limited power with respect to the matters within its authority. The United States Court of Appeals for the Seventh Circuit took a similar approach to an innovative form of school governance in Pittman v. Chicago Board of Education, 64 F.3d 1098 (7th Cir.1995). The court upheld an Illinois law which reserved most of the seats on elected Chicago local schools councils for parents—as opposed to other members of the community—by emphasizing the councils' limited powers. Although the councils were empowered to select school principals and approve a plan for the expenditure of funds allocated to their schools by the city's board of education, the councils had no taxing authority, borrowing authority, or control over the size of their schools' budgets: "The governing body of the public schools of Chicago is the Board of Education of the City of Chicago, not these local councils. Vital public education may be, but these

councils . . . do not control it. The interest of the public at large in the councils is therefore attenuated." *Id.* at 1103. The Seventh Circuit also emphasized the value of permitting experimentation in the forms of school governance:

> "It is common knowledge that the public schools of Chicago are a troubled institution. A change in the method of their governance may or may not bring about an improvement. * * * There is a nationwide movement toward the decentralization and privatization of governmental functions, and the parent-centered local school councils are one manifestation of that movement. They are an experiment, and may fail, but federal courts * * * ought not to snuff them out."

Id.

6.   *BIDs and the Three Models of Local Governments.* The business improvement district combines features of each of the three models of local government that we have studied in this Chapter and, thus, nicely illustrates the difficulty of situating local government in our constitutional order. First, the BID is a creature of an upper-level government. The laws that provide for the creation of BIDs and regulate their powers and governance are state laws, reflecting a state policy of authorizing such districts to promote the economic well-being of urban downtowns. To a considerable extent, however, the relevant upper-level government is the city which creates the BID and oversees its operations. In that sense, the city-BID relationship is yet another instance of the multiple layering of local governments we discussed in Chapter I.

Second, the Grand Central BID is to some an extent a local polity. With a governing board dominated by representatives elected from within the district, it relies primarily on revenues collected from the district to finance physical improvements and such basic local services as security and sanitation. Although there is extensive city oversight of its operations, the BID also enjoys considerable autonomy with respect to its program.

Finally, the BID exemplifies the quasi-proprietary model. Governed by a board legally dominated by assessment payers, financed by an assessment imposed primarily on business property owners, its mandate is to promote business interests within the district.

Indeed, the *Kessler* litigation illustrates the tension between the democratic and quasi-proprietary models of local control and the difficulty, under current Supreme Court doctrine, of determining whether a special district is subject to the one person, one vote requirement that is the hallmark of the democratic locality. It also suggests that the democratic-proprietary conflict may be intertwined with the state agent-local control conflict. How did the Second Circuit resolve the case? Did the court say the BID was not engaged in governmental activities? Or did it say that due to City control over the BID, the BID did not have governmental power with respect to those activities? How did the court deal with Judge Weinstein's argument that, whatever the City's supervisory authority in theory, the BID enjoys considerable autonomy in practice? Does the question of the scope of BID autonomy and the nature of voting rights in BID elections resemble the issue of the scope of county autonomy and the nature of voting rights in county elections in *Avery*? Are *Kessler* and *Avery* consistent?

Should BIDs and other special districts which rely on special assessments to provide local services but have less than the full powers of a general purpose local government—and operate in an area where there is also a general purpose local government—be subject to democratic voting rules? Would you require such a rule if the result would be the de facto elimination of such districts and the additional services they provide?

Given the wide range of services that BIDs provide, how can the exemption of BIDs from one person, one vote be reconciled with the constitutional requirement that general purpose governments—cities and counties—must be governed according to democratic rules? Even if *Kessler* and *Avery* can be reconciled doctrinally on the assumption that the Second Circuit was correct in finding that the BID enjoys relatively limited discretion with respect to the services it provides, does the existence of BIDs and other special service districts which tie voting control to tax payments eat away at the norm of democratic control of local government? Or does the current combination of state and local oversight and general purpose government and special district voting rules provide an appropriate accommodation for state experimentation with different forms of local governance, local democracy, and inducements to taxpayers to fund higher quality urban services?

7. *Quasi-Public Private Governments.* Water storage districts, infrastructure development districts, and business improvement districts are often treated as quasi-private governments, exempted from many of the rules, such as one person, one vote elections that apply to local governments generally. But there is no doubt that they are public entities. The courts in the cases you have read subjected the districts in *Ball* and *Kessler* to the Fourteenth Amendment's equal protection clause—which applies only to state actors—although because of their particular characteristics the constitutional requirements applied to them differently than to other governments. In addition to these quasi-private public governments, there are also many private entities with quasi-public characteristics that have implications for local governance.

Roughly one in five Americans—that is, more than 66 million people— live in private residential communities in which, by virtue of their home ownership, they are required to pay assessments to an association to which they belong that provides certain basic services and maintains certain amenities and facilities they use and enforces contractual restrictions that affect the appearance, design and use of their homes. *See* Community Associations Inst. ("CAI"), National and State Statistical Review for 2014. The terminology for these communities varies from state to state, and according to the formal legal structure of the community, but they are typically known as common interest communities (CICs) or common interest developments (CIDs). The entities that collect the assessments, provide the services, maintain the facilities, and enforce the restrictions are called variously homeowners associations, property owners associations, community associations, condominium associations, or residential community associations (RCAs). *See* Evan McKenzie, Beyond Privatopia: Rethinking Residential Private Government 3–4 (Urban Inst. Press 2011). Although many of these RCAs consist of single high-rise buildings in older urban areas, more than half (51%–55% according to the CAI 2014 statistical review) are "territorial," that is, they include single-family homes or attached townhouses plus streets, parking lots, open space, recreational facilities such as golf courses or swimming pools, and sewer and drainage systems. *See* United States Advisory Comm. on Intergovernmental Relations, Residential Community Associations: Private Governments in the Intergovernmental System? 11–12 (1989) (drawing the "territorial"/"nonterritorial" distinction).

Typically, these territorial RCAs are created as part of planned developments. The developer sells off individual units to homebuyers but transfers control of the rest of the development to a not-for-profit corporation (the RCA), which is governed by a board of directors elected by the homeowners. All the units are subject to various covenants, conditions and restrictions ("CC&Rs") which can restrict how the units are used, regulate their external appearance, authorize assessments, and empower the RCA board to enforce the CC&Rs. Although the product of private contracts, these entities have regulatory powers, service delivery responsibilities, financing authority, and governance structures that resemble those of public local governments.

Private residential communities are particularly widespread in the Sunbelt states of Florida, Texas, California, North Carolina, Georgia, Arizona, and Nevada, as well as in suburban areas of northern states like Illinois and New Jersey. Their growth is often promoted by local governments, which may condition the approval of a new housing development on the developer's commitment to create an RCA which will assume responsibility to provide certain basic services—road and sidewalk maintenance, trash pickup, street lighting, open space maintenance and landscaping, stormwater management, snow removal—for the community, financed by assessments imposed on homeowners in the community. *See, e.g.,* McKenzie, *supra*, at 75–77; Steven Siegel, The Public Role in Establishing Private Residential Communities: Towards a New Formulation of Local Government Land Use Policies That Eliminates the Legal Requirements to Privatize New Communities in the United States, 38 Urb. Law. 859, 887–89 (2006). Such requirements allow local governments to benefit from the increased tax base resulting from new development while avoiding some of the costs of providing additional municipal services. Some governments formally or informally recognize the role of RCAs in local governance. The state of New Jersey and some local governments provide for municipal payments or tax credits to RCAs to offset their costs in providing what are essentially local government services. *See* McKenzie, *supra*, at 78, 100. Others have established relationships with their RCAs with respect to issues like crime or emergency preparedness. *Id.* at 79–80. Private community restrictions and requirements concerning the use and design of private homes and activities in common areas are often more intrusive than public zoning and land use regulations and have led to contentious disputes between communities and residents. *See, e.g.,* Paul Boudreaux, Homes, Rights, and Private Communities, 20 U. Fla. J.L. & Pub. Pol'y 479 (2009) (discussing lawn sodding requirements, restrictions on paint color, the size of backyard patios, and the number of permissible guests). Community restrictions on expressive activity—displays of political yard signs, flying flags, distributing political literature or soliciting support for political activity—have been especially controversial. If the First Amendment applied to RCA actions, these restrictions would likely be held unconstitutional, but courts have usually held the RCAs are private, not state actors, and so not subject to constitutional requirements. *Id. See, e.g.,* Golden Gateway Center v. Golden Gateway Tenants Ass'n, 29 P.3d 797 (Cal. 2001); Midlake on Big Boulder Lake Condo Ass'n v. Cappuccio, 673 A.2d 340 (Pa. 1996); Brock v. Watergate Mobile Home Park Ass'n, 502 So.2d 1380 (Fla. App. 1987); Quail Creek Property Owners Ass'n v. Hunter, 538 So.2d 1238 (Fla. App. 1989); Goldberg v. 400 East Ohio Condominium Ass'n, 12 F.Supp.32d 820 (N.D. Ill. 1998); Westphal v. Lake Lotawana Ass'n, Inc., 95 S.W.3d 144 (Mo. App. 2003). *But cf.* Committee for a Better Twin Rivers v. Twin Rivers Homeowners' Ass'n, 929 A.2d 1060 (N.J. 2007) (holding that private community restriction on political signs violated New Jersey constitution's protection of free expression, which is not limited to state actors); Mazdabrook Commons Homeowners' Ass'n v. Khan, 46 A.3d 507 (N.J. 2012) (same); Dublirer v. 2000 Linwood Avenue Owners, Inc., 103 A.3d 249 (N.J. 2014) (private cooperative's ban on posting notices and distributing written campaign materials violates New Jersey constitution's protection of free speech rights). Similarly, the right to vote for directors of the RCA is not based on one person, one vote, but is typically limited to homeowners (thereby excluding tenants), and based on one unit, one vote. *See* Robert C. Ellickson, Cities and Homeowners Associations, 130 U. Pa. L. Rev. 1519 (1982).

Building on Supreme Court cases that found state action in privately-owned "company towns," Marsh v. Alabama, 326 U.S. 501 (1946), judicial enforcement of racially restrictive covenants, Shelley v. Kraemer, 334 U.S. 1 (1948), or significant state participation and involvement in the actions of private entities, Burton v. Wilmington Parking Auth., 365 U.S. 715 (1961), some scholars and advocates have developed theories for treating at least some RCAs as state actors for at least some purposes. *See, e.g.,* Steven Siegel, The Constitution and Private Government: Toward the Recognition of Constitutional Rights in Private Residential Communities, 6 Wm. & M. Bill Rts. J. 461 (1998). But the Court has limited the *Marsh* "company town" doctrine to settings in which private property "has taken on all the attributes of a town," including a business district, Hudgens v. NLRB, 424 U.S. 507, 516

(1976); and courts have been reluctant to extend either *Shelley* or *Burton* to the RCA context. *But see* Gerber v. Longboat Harbour North Condo., Inc., 724 F. Supp. 884 (M.D. Fla.1989) (finding state action in judicial enforcement of RCA ban on a homeowner flying an American flag); Park Redlands Covenant Control Comm. v. Simon, 226 Cal.Rptr. 199 (Cal. App. 1986) (finding state action where city was closely involved in imposing challenged restriction). Instead judicial review of the actions of RCAs has been governed by the common law of property or legislation specifically addressing RCAs and common interest communities. *See, e.g.,* Nahrstedt v. Lakeside Village Condominium Ass'n, Inc., 878 P.2d 1275 (Cal. 1994).

Although RCAs combine elements of both public and private and, like business improvement districts, could be considered a form of local government, in this book we will follow the practice of most courts and commentators and treat them as a means of property ownership or land use control to be studied in courses on property or land use regulation rather than in local government law. For students interested in reading further on the quasi-public aspects of RCAs, *see* (in addition to the sources already cited), Robert H. Nelson, Private Neighborhoods and the Transformation of Local Government (Urban Inst. Press 2005); David T. Beito, Peter Gordon & Alexander Tabarrok, eds., The Voluntary City: Choice, Community, and Civil Society (U. Mich. Press 2002); Edward J. Blakely and Mary Gail Snyder, Fortress America: Gated Communities in the United States (Brookings Inst. 1997); Evan McKenzie, Privatopia: Homeowner Associations and the Rise of Private Residential Government (Yale U. Press. 1994); Stephen E. Barton & Carol J. Silverman, eds., Common Interest Communities: Private Governments and the Public Interest (IGS Press 1994); Robert Jay Dilger, Neighborhood Community Associations in American Governance (NYU Press 1992).

CHAPTER III

LOCAL GOVERNMENT FORMATION AND BOUNDARY CHANGE

■ ■ ■

Boundaries are the lines that mark the limits of a local government's territorial jurisdiction. In so doing, boundaries may serve a variety of functions. Boundaries can determine the scope of a local government's regulatory authority, the area in which it provides services, its revenue base, and its electoral constituency. These aspects of local government are not ineluctably tied to boundaries. As Holt Civic Club v. City of Tuscaloosa, 439 U.S. 60 (1978), discussed in Chapter II, pointed out, local governments may be authorized to exercise some powers beyond their boundaries. But typically boundaries play the major role in shaping local legal authority, local finances, and the local polity itself.

In this chapter, we will examine the legal principles that shape local government formation and boundary change. The introductory section examines the central role boundaries play in local government law. Only when the significance of local boundaries is understood can the rules governing the creation and alteration of local boundaries be effectively analyzed. The next two sections consider the creation and modification of the territorial scope of the local governments that fall within the democratic model described in Chapter II, particularly municipalities. Specifically, we focus on incorporation, annexation, and dissolution. Issues central to the study of local government—the tension between local autonomy and the interests of broader areas, and the relationship between local democracy and regional equity—are presented most sharply in the context of municipal formation and boundary change. The fourth section analyzes the role that the right to vote plays in questions affecting local boundaries. The final section briefly examines the creation and expansion of special purpose districts.

A.   THE SIGNIFICANCE OF LOCAL BOUNDARIES

GREGORY WEIHER
THE FRACTURED METROPOLIS: POLITICAL FRAGMENTATION AND METROPOLITAN SEGREGATION
(SUNY Press 1991)

The first function of boundaries is geographic. They demarcate discrete panels of land. The differences between sub-units in urban areas are first understood by understanding that they are different places.

If the matter were to end with geography, there would be little to inspire comment. It is because geographic boundaries incorporate a number of other functions that they are interesting. The most obvious among these is the political function. Boundaries in urban areas wed geographic expanses to political authority. Hence municipalities, for instance, are not only places but public agencies with certain legal powers and responsibilities—the power to tax, the power to spend, power over land use, the responsibility to provide services, and so on. The political boundary is a compound symbol of political authority exercised in a finite geographic area.

Political boundaries also perform economic functions. Geographic and economic functions interact because firms are typically located in discrete places. A number of economic effects—employment * * *, the distribution of goods and services—are mediated by geographic factors. The political, economic, and geographic functions interact because political units generally exercise a monopoly over certain sources of tax revenue within their jurisdiction. Hence, the number and nature of firms located within a boundary greatly affects the types and levels of public services that political units are able to provide. In turn, the policies adopted by political units and imposed in particular places influence the location decision of firms. * * *

Finally, political boundaries perform social functions. They define populations, and, as with politics and economics, they structure the interaction of population and geography. Political boundaries become identified with the people who live within them. These people may be socioeconomically, racially, ethnically, religiously, or culturally distinctive. The existence of a boundary gives this social distinctiveness a geographic component. The identity of the population in such a specifically defined place is not only religious, cultural, racial or ethnic, but geographic as well. The individuals which comprise such a population are, among other things, the people that live in *that* place.

1.   LOCAL BOUNDARIES AND THE RIGHT TO VOTE IN LOCAL ELECTIONS

Boundaries usually determine the local electorate. Typically, only those people who reside within local boundaries are entitled to vote in local elections. The leading case is Holt Civic Club v. City of Tuscaloosa, 439 U.S. 60 (1978), discussed in Chapter II, in which the Supreme Court rejected a constitutional challenge to an Alabama law that allowed the City of Tuscaloosa to engage in extraterritorial regulation but limited the vote in Tuscaloosa elections to residents who lived within Tuscaloosa's borders. The Court acknowledged that even though the city was authorized to exercise some of its powers beyond its borders, the state could "legitimately restrict" the right to vote in city elections to those who reside within the city's boundaries. *Id.* at 68–69. The next case raises another dispute over local voting rights, this one involving the interests of people have residences in more than one locality.

WIT V. BERMAN

United States Court of Appeals
306 F.3d 1256 (2d Cir.2002)

WINTER, CIRCUIT JUDGE.

Harold M. Wit and Donald C. Ebel appeal from the dismissal of their complaint by Judge Hellerstein for failure to state a claim. *See* Fed.R.Civ.P. 12(b)(6). The complaint alleged a violation of appellants' rights to equal protection of the laws under the federal and state constitutions. We affirm, holding that the New York State Election Law ("Election Law") does not impermissibly deny citizens who have homes in multiple communities the right to vote in multiple local elections.

BACKGROUND

Each appellant has maintained a home in New York City for over forty years. Each pays income and property taxes in the City, owns real property there, is listed in the New York City telephone directory, uses his New York City residence for personal financial statements, and spends a considerable portion of every year living there. In addition, each appellant meets other qualifications—age and citizenship—to register to vote in New York City.

Appellants were once registered to vote in New York City and voted there. However, for some years, both have also lived, and have been registered voters in, the towns of East Hampton and Southampton, respectively. Appellants are currently barred from voting in New York City because they are also registered to vote in the Hamptons. Each alleges that, if they were not registered to vote in the Hamptons, they would be allowed to register in New York City.

Under New York law, one must be a resident of an electoral district to register as a voter in that district. "Residence" is defined in the Election Law as *"that place* where a person maintains a fixed, permanent and principal home and to which he, wherever temporarily located, always intends to return." N.Y. Elec. Law § 1–104(22) (emphasis added). Section 17–104 of the Election Law provides that any person who "[r]egisters or attempts to register as an elector in more than one election district for the same election" is guilty of a felony. N.Y. Elec. Law § 17–104(2), (5). Other sections of the Election Law also impose felony penalties on those who knowingly attempt to register "when not qualified" and on those who attempt to vote in an election "more than once." N.Y. Elec. Law § 17–132(1), (3), (9).

* * *

DISCUSSION

* * * Where a statute invidiously discriminates in granting the right to vote, we apply strict scrutiny in our review. *See Kramer v. Union Free School Dist. No. 15,* 395 U.S. 621, 626–28, 89 S.Ct. 1886, 23 L.Ed.2d 583 (1969). However, although voting is of the most fundamental significance under our constitutional structure ... [i]t does not follow ... that the right to vote in any manner and the right to associate for political purposes through the ballot are absolute. *Burdick v. Takushi,* 504 U.S. 428, 433, 112 S.Ct. 2059, 119 L.Ed.2d 245 (1992) (citation omitted). As the Court elaborated in *Burdick:*

> Election laws will invariably impose some burden upon individual voters. Each provision of a code, "whether it governs the registration and qualifications of voters, the selection and eligibility of candidates, or the voting process itself, inevitably affects—at least to some degree—the individual's right to vote and his right to associate with others for political ends." Consequently, to subject every voting regulation to strict scrutiny and to require that the regulation be narrowly tailored to advance a compelling state interest ... would tie the hands of States seeking to assure that elections are operated equitably and efficiently.

Id. (citation omitted) (quoting *Anderson v. Celebrezze,* 460 U.S. 780, 788, 103 S.Ct. 1564, 75 L.Ed.2d 547 (1983)). The *Burdick* Court went on to state that where voting rights are subjected to "severe" restrictions, regulations must be "narrowly drawn to advance a state interest of compelling importance," *id.* at 434, 112 S.Ct. 2059 (quoting *Norman v. Reed,* 502 U.S. 279, 289, 112 S.Ct. 698, 116 L.Ed.2d 711 (1992)), but that where a state election law provision imposes only "reasonable, nondiscriminatory restrictions" upon the rights of voters, "the State's important regulatory interests are generally sufficient to justify" the restrictions. *Id.* (quoting *Anderson,* 460 U.S. at 788, 103 S.Ct. 1564). For reasons discussed *infra,* we uphold the provisions of the Election Law challenged by appellants because those provisions impose only "reasonable, nondiscriminatory restrictions" and advance important state regulatory interests.

An Equal Protection claim must be based on impermissible differential treatment. * * * The differential treatment alleged here is that, because appellants are otherwise qualified under New York law to register in both New York City and the Hamptons, the provision of the Election Law prohibiting them from registering in two places treats them differently than the qualified voters in the election district in which they are not registered. To put it another way, appellants are not allowed to vote in New York City solely because they are registered in the Hamptons. Were they to give up their registration in the Hamptons, they could register in New York City. Therefore, they argue, they are being treated differently than others qualified to vote in the City. Because there is in their view no permissible governmental interest justifying this differential treatment, they conclude that they have been denied their rights under the Equal Protection Clause. We disagree.

* * * New York's rule against voting in two election districts reflects a critical aspect of the concept of domicile. The principal usefulness of the concept is that it resolves jurisdictional issues in circumstances in which exclusivity is desirable or necessary, such as probating an estate. Although one may be legally domiciled in different places for different legal purposes, a person is deemed to have only a single domicile for the particular legal purpose for which the concept is then being used. * * *

For purposes of voting in New York, domicile is defined as "that place" where one has the fixed, permanent, and principal home to which, even with extended periods of living elsewhere, one intends to return. N.Y. Elec. Law § 1–104(22) * * *. When a person's domicile determines where that person can vote, therefore, it must be a single electoral district.

The domicile test for determining where citizens may vote dominates the election laws of most states. *See* William H. Danne, Jr., Annotation, *Residence of Students for Voting Purposes,* 44 A.L.R.3d 797 § 2 (1972) (observing that "[i]t is a matter of virtually uniform recognition" that, where state constitutional and statutory provisions limit the right to vote to the residents of a given geographical area, "the term residence should be equated with the concept of domicil"); Restatement (Second) of Conflict of Laws § 11(1) cmt. k (1989) (noting that "residence" is generally interpreted as being the equivalent of "domicil" when used in state statutes relating to voting).

The reasons for the reliance upon domicile are quite pertinent to the issue before us. At first blush, it may seem that domicile plays such a key role because it is a close proxy for determining the election district in which a voter has the greatest stake in the outcome of elections. This is an oversimplification, however.

Particularly in modern times, domicile is very often a poor proxy for a voter's stake in electoral outcomes because many of an individual voter's varied interests are affected by outcomes in elections in which they do not vote. Some, or even many, voters may reasonably perceive that their primary political concerns are affected more by outcomes in elections in which they do not vote than by outcomes in elections in which they do vote. There are endless examples of the bad fit between domicile and a voter's interest in electoral outcomes. For example, a person who works in a factory, or owns one, located in a municipality other than where the person lives, has interests in that municipality's tax, traffic, law enforcement, and other policies. To take an interstate example, many voters in New England believe that their lives are directly affected by environmental policies in the mid-west industrial states.

However, while one may mount ethereal arguments against the single-domicile-registration rule, the administrative problems that interests-based rules would cause for thousands of registrars of voters render those rules virtually unthinkable. Voter registration is generally a nondiscretionary function of local government carried out by low level officials. Absent meaningful guidance, some registrars (even in the same precinct) would use a "whatever-you-say" approach, others will adopt a "show-me-beyond-a-reasonable-doubt" stance, while yet others will resort to *ad hoc, ad hominem,* or whimsical standards.

Given the need for workable standards, determination of where one may vote based on interests in electoral outcomes is not a manageable rule. Honoring the desires of voters to vote in other districts based on their expression of subjective interests in the political decisions of those other districts would essentially lead to a "vote-in-however-many-districts-you-please" rule. Such a rule would be truly chaotic, save for the small measure of order that corruption would bring to it. An objective test of voter interests is equally unworkable. At the very least, it would involve an ever-changing analysis by registrars of the merits of political issues—e.g., does an employee of a firm in one city who lives in another have a sufficient interest in the traffic and tax policies of the former to vote there, or is there sufficiently harmful acid rain in Vermont as a result of loose environmental standards in Ohio to justify a Vermonter voting in Ohio—and would also be chaotic.

Domicile as a rule may have its philosophical defects, therefore, but it has enormous practical advantages over the alternatives. It almost always insures that a voter has *some* stake in the electoral outcome in the domiciliary district and almost always does not involve large numbers of disputes over where one may vote. The domicile rule informs would-be voters where they may vote, a vital function that encourages registration and voting. Moreover, it gives voters the notice required for the enforcement of criminal laws against individuals voting in places where they are not eligible. *See* N.Y. Elec. Law § 17–132.

* * * To be sure, domicile as a test entails administrative difficulties at the margins. The domicile of students is an example. *See, e.g., Auerbach,* 765 F.2d at 351; Danne, Jr., *Residence of Students for Voting Purposes* § 2, *supra.* So too is the registration of the homeless. *See, e.g., Pitts v. Black,* 608 F.Supp. 696, 709–10 (S.D.N.Y.1984). However, these difficulties are slight compared to those that abandonment of the domicile rule and its one domicile/one electoral district restriction might entail.

Appellants are members of a class of persons that gives rise to administrative difficulties under the domicile rule. Their problem is the opposite of the homeless problem—because appellants have multiple homes, there is doubt as to which home is "that place" for domiciliary purposes. New York has responded to this administrative difficulty in a pragmatic way. New York courts have held that, rather than compel persons in appellants' circumstances to establish to the satisfaction of a registrar of voters or a court that one home or the other is their principal, permanent residence, they can choose between them. * * * This pragmatic approach lessens the burdens on registrars, who in most cases need only verify an address, and on people like appellants, who otherwise might be turned down at both places and have to go to court in order to be able to vote anywhere. New York's solution to the multiple home problem is, therefore, quite favorable to appellants and hardly one that can be said to disadvantage them.

* * * The need to avoid these problems, which can grow from a tangle to a morass to outright chaos, is probably the reason that domicile remains the dominant American method of determining where persons may vote. New York's granting to persons such as appellants the benefit of the doubt by using a one-or-the-other rule does not undermine the important governmental interests served by the domicile rule and allows appellants to choose freely, rather than compelling them to establish their domicile in only one place. The one-or-the-other rule does not in any sensible use of the word "discriminate" against appellants. Indeed, the Election Law's permissive approach allows appellants to align their strongest, personal political interests with the appropriate voting location. In light of this enhancement of appellants' voting power, the fact that the Election Law does not go further by multiplying appellants' voting power in light of their claimed multiple local interests is not a compelling ground for a claim of discriminatory treatment. *Cf. McDonald*

v. Bd. of Election Comm'rs of Chi., 394 U.S. 802, 811, 89 S.Ct. 1404, 22 L.Ed.2d 739 (1969) (declining to invalidate a remedial election law on the ground that it "has not gone still further," noting that such legislation need not "strike at all evils at the same time").

NOTES AND QUESTIONS

1. *Voting for Nonresidents.* The result in this case comports with the general rule that the state may limit local voting rights to one place of residence irrespective of the number of properties a citizen owns. For a similar result, *see* Massad v. City of New London, 652 A.2d 529 (Conn.App.1995). Although nonresidents who own land within a locality have argued that they have a distinctive stake in local governance—their property is subject to local taxation—they have been unsuccessful in establishing such a right in the courts. *See* Neilson v. City of California City, 35 Cal.Rptr.3d 453 (Cal.App.2005), in which the court upheld the city's decision to exclude non-residents from voting on a proposed flat rate real property parcel tax, even though nonresident landowners would constitute the primary source of revenue from that tax. The court reasoned that the city could have rationally determined that local residents had a greater interest in local affairs. The plaintiff in *Nielsen* brought another challenge to the California tax in 2008, this time based on an equal protection theory. The suit was also unsuccessful, *see* Nielsen v. City of California City, 2008 WL 2588067 (Cal.App.2008).

This view has come under fire from scholars who have noted the broad impact a local government can have on property owners who do not claim domicile in the jurisdiction. Some academic commentary, in fact, has called for the abolition of the residency requirement in local elections. *See, e.g.,* Richard Thompson Ford, Beyond Borders: A Partial Response to Richard Briffault, 48 Stan.L.Rev. 1173, 1188–89 (1996); Richard Thompson Ford, The Boundaries of Race: Political Geography in Legal Analysis, 107 Harv.L.Rev. 1841, 1909–1910 (1994); Jerry Frug, Decentering Decentralization, 60 U.Chi.L.Rev. 253, 329–30 (1993). Professors Frug and Ford raise important questions about the nexus between residency and voting in contemporary metropolitan areas where people often have interests, activities, and concerns in more than one local jurisdiction. A student note argues for the right to vote in multiple local elections based on bona fide resident status, irrespective of whether the voter is eligible to vote in other municipalities as well. *See* Ashira Pelman Ostrow, Note, Dual Resident Voting: Traditional Disenfranchisement and Prospects for Change, 102 Colum. L. Rev. 1954 (2002). The argument is based on fundamental principles of democratic, representative government, such as the consent of the governed and the illegitimacy of taxation without representation. Does the principle have a stopping point? In other words, would someone with five homes, who claimed equal attachment and residency interests to all five jurisdictions, be entitled to vote in five municipal elections?

2.   *Pragmatic Government Interest or Preference for the Wealthy?* Can the New York statute be challenged because of the way in which it favors citizens with money? That is, under the statute, a citizen is able to choose to be a resident in any local jurisdiction where he or she owns a residence, irrespective of whether that residence qualifies as the citizen's domicile. Those who can only afford one home, of course, do not have the similar ability to "municipality shop." The court alludes to this problem when it notes that the New York law is, in fact, "quite favorable" to citizens who own more than one home. On the other hand, could it be argued that by denying residents the right to vote in their second-home community, where their homes are subject to local property taxation, the law enables the local voting majority to exploit them? What about the homeless?

3.   *Voters' Stake in Municipal Elections.* The court noted that domicile requirements generally allow the government to verify that voters have some stake in the electoral outcome. Can you think of any other voting restrictions that the government can impose in furtherance of that goal? Remember that in *City of Phoenix v. Kolodziejski* (considered in Chapter II), the city did not prevail on the argument that limiting the vote on a bond issue to property owners was justified by their allegedly greater stake in the bond issue vote. How does domicile differ from property ownership?

4.   *Granting the Vote to Nonresidents. Wit v. Berman* holds only that the government cannot be forced to extend the right to vote to citizens in a multiplicity of municipal jurisdictions. What if the government chooses to grant local voting rights to property owners who do not claim the locality as their domicile? In some jurisdictions nonresident landowners have been allowed to vote in local elections. Courts have generally upheld such an expansion of the local franchise against challenges by local residents that allowing nonresidents to vote unconstitutionally dilutes the residents' vote. *See, e.g.*, May v. Town of Mountain Village, 132 F.3d 576 (10th Cir.1997); Glisson v. Mayor of Savannah Beach, 346 F.2d 135 (5th Cir.1965); Snead v. City of Albuquerque, 663 F.Supp. 1084 (D.N.M.1987); Bjornestad v. Hulse, 281 Cal.Rptr. 548, 563–64 (Cal.Ct.App.1991).

5.   *Scrutinizing Claims of Residency.* Note that the New York statute upheld in *Wit* allowed individuals with multiple homes the discretion to choose their place of residency. Not all states are so deferential to individual choice. *Compare* In re Nomination Petition of Driscoll, 847 A.2d 44 (Pa. 2004), in which the court articulated a very different attitude about residence for election purposes: "A person cannot, for purposes of the Election Code, simply declare a new residence or domicile by purchasing or renting a home in one location; that person must also have an intent to live in the new residence permanently, and if the person is married and not separated from his spouse, he and his spouse must both intend to live in the new residence permanently." Domicile challenges acquire heightened importance when the electorate is very small; in *In re Nov. 2, 2010 General Election*, 423 N.J.Super. 190 (N.J.App. 2011), only one vote separated the winner from the runner-up.

6.   *The Problem with Counties.* Although *Avery v. Midland County*, discussed in Chapter II, clearly established one person, one vote requirements for general purpose county legislatures, the typical county's dual service base may cause disputes over the scope of the right to vote. That is, because it provides some services on a countywide basis (e.g., court system, correctional facilities, airports, environmental protection) and some services only to the unincorporated areas of the county (e.g., zoning, police, fire-rescue, roads, parks, garbage collection), residents in the unincorporated areas may object to city residents' power to vote for the legislative body that will have a greater influence on them than on people living in the city. Short of creating two totally distinct county governments, one to provide county wide services and one to service the unincorporated areas, is the lack of congruity between the electorate, the service base, and the taxing base inevitable? For an interesting case in which the court rejected the challenges of the residents in the unincorporated area of Miami-Dade County, *see* Levy v. Miami-Dade County, 254 F.Supp.2d 1269 (S.D.Fla. 2003).

2.   LOCAL BOUNDARIES AND LOCAL REVENUE

CITY OF PITTSBURGH V.
COMMONWEALTH OF PENNSYLVANIA

Supreme Court of Pennsylvania
559 A.2d 513 (1989)

ZAPPALA, J.

The gravamen of this controversy is the inability of the City to collect its 1.125 percent wage tax from non-City residents who work within the City's boundaries. * * *

Under § 6902 of [the Local Tax Enabling Act] LTEA, political subdivisions, such as the City of Pittsburgh, may levy, assess and collect taxes for general revenue purposes from persons within their boundaries. * * * Section 6908(3) limits the rate of taxation a municipality may assess against an individual on wages, salaries, commissions, and other earned income to one percent. Finally, § 6914 requires that a non-resident taxpayer be given credit by the municipality in which that taxpayer works for any taxes paid to the municipality in which he lives.

The City of Pittsburgh * * * is a home rule community. * * * Notwithstanding the adoption of a Home Rule Charter, LTEA controls the rate of tax permissible with regard to non-residents. As indicated, the maximum rate permissible under § 6908(3) of LTEA is one percent.

It is this taxation scheme that the City and Mayor are attacking as unconstitutionally impermissible. In support of their position, the Appellants rely upon *Danyluk v. Johnstown*, 406 Pa. 427, 178 A.2d 609 (1962) and *Leonard v. Thornburgh*, 507 Pa. 317, 489 A.2d 1349 (1985).

In *Danyluk*, we held that the City of Johnstown's attempt to tax non-residents violated the uniformity provision of our constitution. The City had attempted to avoid this obvious result by formulating the assessment as an occupation tax. In actuality, the City was attempting to levy a direct tax on non-residents.

> [Such a] tax is imposed because of the protection which a governmental unit affords to persons residing therein, and is designed primarily to require contribution from all residents for the services rendered them by the taxing authority. Consequently, per capita, capitation or head taxes can be imposed only upon residents of the particular political subdivision since residence alone furnishes the contact necessary to render a person amenable to the direct levy.

The Appellants now argue that *Danyluk* supports its position because in that case we looked unfavorably upon residency as a classification. Although the premise upon which the Appellants' argument is based is an accurate interpretation of *Danyluk*, its conclusion is not. In *Danyluk* we rejected an attempt to levy a direct tax on non-residents concluding that non-residents and residents do not receive the same benefits from the appropriate taxing authorities. In fact, we held contrary to the appellants' interpretation concluding that residency is a legitimate basis for imposing a direct levy. Accordingly, the Appellants' reliance upon *Danyluk* is misplaced.

More recently, in *Leonard v. Thornburgh, supra,* we reviewed the City of Philadelphia's Wage Ordinance No. 1716 and its different treatment of residents and non-residents. The City of Philadelphia had adopted a wage tax rate of 4 5/16 percent for non-residents in accordance with the Philadelphia Non-resident Wage Tax Cap Act. This rate was almost 1.5 percent lower than that rate levied against city residents. A city resident filed suit arguing that the Philadelphia Non-resident Wage Tax Cap Act and Ordinance 1716 were unconstitutional in that the tax was not uniformly applied to residents and non-residents. * * * [W]e concluded that residents and non-residents utilize city services to different extents, non-residents, in some instances, not at all. As such, residents and non-residents are not similarly situated in this context. Furthermore, we were deeply concerned about the inability of non-residents to protect themselves in the assessment of an appropriate wage tax. We surmised that to avoid abuse of unprotected non-residents, the legislature capped the maximum rate a non-resident could be taxed.

As with *Danyluk*, the City has misconstrued our holding and discussion in *Leonard*. *Leonard* does not mean that the legislature must permit taxation of non-residents if it permits taxation of residents. All *Leonard* holds is that if the legislature adopts legislation allowing the levying of taxes on non-residents, that classification must be reasonable. The fact that non-residents utilize city services without paying their "fair share" is an argument properly addressed to the legislature not this Court. To suggest that *Leonard* requires the legislature to adopt legislation to permit taxation of non-residents comparable to residents is incorrect.

NOTES AND QUESTIONS

1. *Local Taxation of Nonresidents.* Boundaries are central to local finances. Local governments raise most of their revenue from sources—such as property, sales, and incomes—within their borders. As we shall see in Chapter IV's discussion of home rule and Chapter VI's treatment of local taxation, relatively few localities actually have the power to tax incomes, and most local income taxes are limited to local residents and to incomes earned within the locality. *See* Helen F. Ladd & John Yinger, America's Ailing Cities: Fiscal Health and the Design of Urban Policy 132–34 (Johns Hopkins Univ. Press 1989). Only a few states have followed Pennsylvania's decision to permit local taxation of the locally earned incomes of nonresidents. Congress has followed the majority and has prohibited the District of Columbia from imposing a tax on nonresidents working in the city. The District, its mayor, and the City Council filed suit challenging the prohibition. The D.C. Circuit rejected claims based on the Constitution's equal protection and uniformity clauses. *See* Banner v. United States, 428 F.3d 303 (D.C. Cir. 2005).

When a local government has the power to tax nonresidents, the local boundary line remains crucial in determining the scope of local taxing authority and the rate a taxpayer will have to pay. In the main case, Pittsburgh challenged the state's determination that the city could tax its nonresidents only at a lower rate than the one established for Pittsburgh residents. Previous cases in Pennsylvania, and in some other states, had determined that municipalities cannot levy higher income tax rates on commuters than on residents. The courts in those cases rejected the cities' claims that the decision to tax the commuters' income at a higher rate than the residents' properly reflected the fact that city residents, unlike commuters, pay a number of other municipal taxes and fees that go towards funding the services enjoyed by all, residents and nonresidents alike. *See* Danyluk v. Bethlehem Steel Co., 178 A.2d 609 (Pa. 1962); County of Alameda v. City and County of San Francisco, 97 Cal.Rptr. 175 (Cal.App. 1971).

This nexus between local boundaries and local revenues has important implications for local finances. When nonresidents commute to city jobs, they may use city streets, city police, city parks, and city sanitation and fire prevention services. These services are funded by city taxes, which nonresidents generally do not pay. To be sure, as *Pittsburgh* noted, commuters probably do not use city services as much as residents do, so it might not be fair to tax residents and nonresidents equally. Moreover, commuters who hold down city jobs and shop in city stores probably contribute indirectly to city coffers by increasing the value of commercial property subject to city property taxation. Nevertheless, tying local finances to the property and residents within local borders tends to constrict the local tax base. One consequence is that local governments have a financial incentive for territorial expansion—to enhance the local tax base by adding residents who may be a part of the city as an economic unit, but not a part of the city as a legal unit.

What about tax exemptions for local residents? An Illinois court upheld a local transfer tax exemption for residents who purchased a new home within the municipality. The tax revenue in this case was earmarked for local schools and reflected popular sentiment that newcomers did not contribute sufficiently to local schools. *See* Ratjerowski v. Sycamore, 940 N.E.2d 682 (Ill.Ct.App. 2010).

2.   *State Taxation of Nonresidents.* The importance of boundaries in determining the scope of the government's revenue-raising power extends to state borders as well. In many metropolitan areas, large numbers of people live in one state and work in another. At the interstate level, the Commerce Clause and the Privileges and Immunities Clause of the Constitution become applicable. In the context of state income tax laws, applicable constitutional guarantees have been interpreted as requiring "substantial equality" of treatment between residents and nonresidents. *See* Austin v. New Hampshire, 420 U.S. 656 (1975).

3.   *State Residency as a Classification in Local Income Taxation.* A New York law, invalidated by the state's highest court in City of New York v. State, 730 N.E.2d 920 (N.Y. 2000), imposed a local nonresident income tax on commuters from other states. Thus, New York state residents who commuted to New York City did not pay the tax on the income they earned there, while commuters from other states did. The interstate discrimination was fatal to the tax, as the court held that the Privileges and Immunities protection extended to local taxes as well.

The commuter tax issue is a contentious one between the state government and the City of New York. Under state law, cities of more than one million people can tax the income of their own residents. They have no such power over nonresidents. Until 1999, however, the New York State Legislature had authorized a commuter income tax in New York City. The .45% tax was applied equally to all nonresidents working in the city, regardless of state of residency. In 1999, the commuter tax was repealed by the legislature for in-state commuters. That led to the judicial decision noted above, and in response, the entire tax was repealed. In more recent decisions, the New York court has refined its stance, clarifying that the state may tax out-of-state telecommuters as though they did all their work in the city of their employment. *See* Zelinsky v. Tax Appeals Tribunal of State, 801 N.E.2d 840 (N.Y. 2003).

When the tax was repealed in 1999, the loss to the city was estimated at $360 million per year. The state government again rejected the commuter tax in 2003, when it was part of a financial package designed to close the city's $3.4 billion deficit. Supporters of the tax say that all those who partake of the city's services should have to pay some small percentage of the cost of maintaining those services. Opponents argue that commuters already support the city by contributing to the productivity of businesses that generate billions in tax revenue. They also fear that reinstating the commuter tax will have a negative impact on overall job creation and the retention of nonresident employees.

3. LOCAL BOUNDARIES AND LOCAL SERVICES

A central function of local government is the provision of services— such as police, fire protection, garbage collection, water, and sewerage—to local residents. In many jurisdictions, local governments may provide those services only within local boundaries. Some states, however, expressly authorize their localities to engage in extra-local service delivery. This raises the issue of whether a local government can use extra-local services to advance the locality's interests in territorial growth or revenues. A related question concerns whether a locality can discriminate between residents and nonresidents in the delivery of services *within* local boundaries, such as by charging a nonresident a higher fee to use a city park. The following materials explore these questions.

BAKIES V. CITY OF PERRYSBURG
Supreme Court of Ohio
843 N.E.2d 1182 (2006)

O'DONNELL, J.

The principal issue presented in this appeal concerns whether a municipality may, through either a written agreement or by ordinance, require extraterritorial water and sewer customers to annex their property to the municipality or face termination of their utility service.

* * *

During the 1970s and 1980s, the city of Perrysburg, located in Wood County, which operated its own water district, contracted with the Wood County Board of Commissioners to provide water and sewer services to unincorporated areas within the county.

In 1975, the Cavalear Development Company sought to develop Willowbend subdivision, a proposed upscale residential development in Perrysburg Township, adjacent to the city of Perrysburg. In order to provide water and sewer service to Willowbend, Cavalear contracted with Wood County to pay for extension of a water line. The contract further specified that the water would be provided subject to the rules and regulations of the city of Perrysburg.

In his brief filed in our court, Richard Smith stated that he purchased property and built a home in Willowbend in 1978, Perrysburg extended water and sewer services to his property without requiring any written agreement, and he has continuously received such services, paying extraterritorial rates since that time.

Subsequent to that arrangement, Perrysburg began to enact ordinances with respect to its water service. In 1983, it provided by ordinance that following that date, extraterritorial customers had to agree to petition for annexation of their property immediately or agree to do so when their property became contiguous to any part of the city.

Then, in 1988, because of large population growth in areas adjacent to the city and in an effort to achieve organized growth, Perrysburg declared its intention to annex all adjacent urbanized areas and all adjacent low-density areas when it became reasonably certain that urbanization of those areas would occur. To carry out this policy, Perrysburg mandated that all current extraterritorial customers execute an agreement to annex their property and exert all efforts to obtain annexation. Smith never took any action in response to any of this legislation.

Ten years later, in 1998, Gregory and Karen Bakies purchased a home in the Willowbend subdivision and signed a contract for water service with the city of Perrysburg in which they agreed to cooperate with Perrysburg's annexation plans or face termination of their service.

Subsequently, the city of Perrysburg and Perrysburg Township agreed to designate areas where the township would consent to annexation. Following that agreement, in June 2002, Perrysburg mailed letters to approximately 260 property owners in Perrysburg Township requesting that they sign a petition for annexation pursuant to either a previously signed agreement for water and sewer service or pursuant to applicable ordinances of the city of Perrysburg. The Bakieses received a letter, but refused to sign the annexation petition, and as a result, Perrysburg notified them that their water and sewer service would be terminated. Smith also refused to sign and received a similar notice of termination of his service.

The Bakieses filed a complaint in common pleas court, seeking injunctive relief to prevent Perrysburg from terminating their water and sewer services; subsequently, they filed an amended complaint adding Smith as an additional party.

* * * Following that preliminary hearing, the court granted a preliminary injunction preventing Perrysburg from terminating water or sewer service for 60 days and scheduled the matter for further proceedings.

Perrysburg thereafter answered the amended complaint and counterclaimed, seeking a declaration as to the enforceability of the Bakieses' agreement and an order compelling them to immediately sign an annexation petition. It also moved for summary judgment and submitted a deposition of Perrysburg Mayor Jody Holbrook describing the city's plans to annex portions of Perrysburg Township. Several factors, including an agreement with Perrysburg Township, proximity to the city's corporation limits, tax revenue, and the city's ability to provide services more cost-effectively, influenced which properties it selected for annexation. The mayor also testified that Perrysburg would benefit because the annexations would generate revenue for the city by increasing the city's tax base, which would far exceed the revenue Perrysburg gained from selling water. He further testified that township residents would also benefit from the annexations because the city of Perrysburg could provide better and more effective services for residents than the township, as evidenced by its parks, recreation, and fire and police services, among others.

Several months later, the court granted Perrysburg's motion for summary judgment, declared the Bakieses' contract for delivery of water and sewer services valid and enforceable, and ordered the Bakieses and Smith to sign the annexation petition within 60 days.

The homeowners appealed to the Sixth District Court of Appeals, which affirmed the judgment of the trial court * * *

The homeowners appealed to this court, and we granted discretionary review. * * *

The Bakieses' written contract

The Bakieses complain that Perrysburg cannot require consent to annexation as a condition of continued service for existing extraterritorial customers, urging that the Ohio Supreme Court has permitted municipalities to require annexation only for the extension of water service to extraterritorial customers. Perrysburg, however, contends that absent a contractual obligation, a municipality has no duty to continue to supply water and sewer services to extraterritorial customers.

Thus, the issue presented here relates to whether a municipality that has historically provided water and sewer service for extraterritorial customers is permitted to require annexation of the extraterritorial property as a condition of continued service to those customers.

Section 6, Article XVIII, of the Ohio Constitution authorizes a municipality to sell surplus water or sewer services outside its territorial boundaries. Further, in State ex rel. Indian Hill Acres, Inc. v. Kellogg (1948), 149 Ohio St. 461, 37 O.O. 137, 79 N.E.2d 319, we considered Cincinnati's obligation to extraterritorial consumers of city water and held that in the absence of a contract, "the municipality may sell and dispose of its surplus products in such quantities and in such manner as the council thereof determines to be in the best interest of the municipality and its inhabitants." *Id.* at paragraph three of the syllabus.

In addition, in Fairway Manor, Inc. v. Summit Cty. Bd. of Commrs. (1988), 36 Ohio St.3d 85, 89, 521 N.E.2d 818, we stated:

"Municipally owned public utilities have no duty to sell their products, including water, to extraterritorial purchasers absent a contractual obligation. * * * Even where there is a contract, but the contract provides no termination date, either party to the agreement may terminate it upon reasonable notice. Thus, it can be seen that a municipality does not assume a duty to continue supplying water in perpetuity to extraterritorial customers merely by virtue of having once agreed to supply it. * * * The municipality has the sole authority to decide whether to sell its water to extraterritorial purchasers."

In [previous cases], we recognized that a municipality has no obligation to continue to provide water to extraterritorial customers in the absence of contract. Although the Bakieses attempt to distinguish a municipality's authority to impose conditions at the time it extends service from its ability to impose conditions upon continued service, our precedent does not make that distinction. We therefore reaffirm the principle that absent a contractual obligation, a municipality has no duty to continue to supply water to extraterritorial customers. Further, the Bakieses signed a written contract with Perrysburg agreeing to cooperate with annexation or face termination of their service.

Accordingly, we conclude that a contract between a municipality and an extraterritorial water and sewer customer in which the customer agrees to annex property or face termination of service is a valid and enforceable contract.

Smith's oral contract

Smith claims that Perrysburg has provided him with water and sewer service since 1978 pursuant to an oral agreement whereby Perrysburg provides service conditioned on timely payment therefor and that Perrysburg cannot now unilaterally alter the terms of that agreement. Perrysburg contends, however, that Smith has failed to prove the existence of any such agreement.

* * * [W]e agree with the court of appeals that the record does not evidence the terms of any oral contract involving his water and sewer services. It does, however, reflect that Perrysburg enacted ordinances in 1983 and 1998 notifying extraterritorial users of conditions for continued receipt of services, and Smith's continued receipt of services after those enactments subjected him to the provisions of those ordinances. * * *

Constitutionality of Perrysburg ordinances

Finally, the Bakieses and Smith urge that conditions imposed by Perrysburg ordinances for the sale of water to extraterritorial users are unreasonable, arbitrary, and capricious and lack a rational relationship to the health, safety, and welfare of its citizens. * * *

Section 4, Article XVIII of the Ohio Constitution empowers any municipality to acquire, construct, own, lease, and operate any public utility within or without its corporate limits to serve the municipality and its inhabitants. Section 6, Article XVIII further authorizes a municipality owning or operating a public utility to sell and deliver surplus utility product to others.

* * * [W]e conclude that ordinances requiring extraterritorial customers to agree to annexation in exchange for continuation of services are a valid exercise of the police power of a municipality, that such a requirement is not unreasonable, arbitrary, or capricious, and that it bears a rational relationship to the health, safety, and welfare of the municipality's citizens. The homeowners here have failed to advance any basis upon which we could conclude otherwise.

Perrysburg, on the other hand, has demonstrated a legitimate basis for selecting the homes owned by the Bakieses and Smith for annexation—including tax revenue, proximity to Perrysburg's corporate limit, and its prior agreement with Perrysburg Township. Perrysburg further demonstrated that annexation would create a larger tax base, which would increase its general revenue and reduce the strain on city services caused by adjacent urbanized areas of Perrysburg Township. And it would benefit township residents by providing better and more cost-effective services such as parks, recreation, and police and fire services to residents.

Judgment affirmed.

NOTES AND QUESTIONS

1. *Extraterritorial Service Provision.* The *Bakies* opinion states the clear majority rule that a municipality has no duty to provide services beyond local boundaries, and that when a municipality does so it has wide latitude in establishing the terms under which such extraterritorial service is provided. Nevertheless, some courts will impose limits on the scope of a municipality's discretion in determining the conditions of extraterritorial service provision. Those issues are discussed in Chapter VII.

2. *Municipal Services as Leverage for Annexation.* As we will see later in this chapter, many states condition a locality's ability to annex new territory on the consent of the residents of the area to be annexed. One incentive for people outside the city to consent to annexation is that they will be able to receive better services if they agree to become part of the city. If,

however, nonresidents can receive city services without annexation, that incentive disappears. A city might be tempted to provide services outside city borders in order to obtain additional revenues from service delivery fees, but that would mean losing an inducement to annexation. In *Bakies,* the city found a way of providing nonresidents with services (and obtaining utility fees) without sacrificing the ability to use city services as an incentive to accept annexation. Did Perrysburg's policy unfairly vitiate the consent the state required as a condition for annexation? Or was it a legitimate technique for providing nonresidents with desirable services while preserving the city's long term interests? *See also* Blackwell v. City of St. Charles, 726 F.Supp. 256 (E.D.Mo.1989) (rejecting various federal constitutional challenges to local policy of tying extra-local service provision to agreement to support future annexations); Robarge v. City of Greenville, 675 S.E.2d 788 (S.C. 2009) (upholding city's requirement that water users agree to annexation). In Yakima County (West Valley) Fire Pro. Dist. No. 12 v. City of Yakima, 858 P.2d 245 (Wash. 1993), the court upheld the same "annexation for water" requirement but noted that the landowners had failed to present evidence of "economic duress" or "lack of meaningful choice." Do the facts in *Bakies* suggest arguments along those lines? *Bakies* goes further than any of the cases cited above, because the Perrysburg policy applied to existing, rather than merely new, service customers.

3.   *Municipal Service Provision and the Right to Vote.* In Hussey v. City of Portland, 64 F.3d 1260 (9th Cir.1995), *cert. denied,* 516 U.S. 1112 (1996), the court invalidated a Portland ordinance that required nonresidents to consent to annexation as a condition for receiving a reduction in the city's sewer system connection charge. The court reasoned that consent to annexation was the constitutional equivalent of voting, and that conditioning the subsidy on support for annexation "severely and unreasonably interferes with the right to vote." *Id.* at 1265. "While Portland's stated goals of promoting stability of neighborhoods and aligning service and tax boundaries are certainly legitimate, they are not compelling. Portland is free to charge residents of unincorporated areas its estimated actual cost of servicing them. Moreover, it is not necessary that Portland link its subsidy to a person's vote. . . . The Portland ordinance has, in effect, created a classic Prisoners' Dilemma, thereby subverting the process through which citizens consent to be governed." *Id.* The *Hussey* case is also discussed in Note 3 after *Sacramento v. LAFCO,* in Section D of this Chapter.

4.   *Limiting Municipal Leverage.* While courts may look kindly on municipal requirements of annexation in exchange for receipt of municipal services, what if the municipality tries to use the provision of services to extract other types of concessions? In MT Development, LLC v. City of Renton, 165 P.3d 427 (Wash. App. 2007), the court invalidated a city's requirement that extraterritorial service recipients comply with residential density limits imposed by the city. Because the municipality had no extraterritorial zoning powers, the court concluded that the city had violated its duty to be reasonable in the imposition of conditions on extraterritorial

service. Do you agree? Should it have mattered that the location was within the municipality's potential annexation area?

4. SCOPE OF REGULATION

In the absence of an express delegation of extraterritorial authority by the state, local powers are generally confined within local boundaries. Many states, however, have adopted legislation expressly granting some local governments, typically municipalities, some powers in discrete zones of unincorporated territory immediately outside municipal borders. These powers may include zoning, prohibiting nuisances, licensing and regulating businesses, enforcing criminal laws, and general health and safety regulation. *See* Comment, The Constitutionality of the Exercise of Extraterritorial Powers by Municipalities, 45 U.Chi.L.Rev. 151 (1977). The grant of such extraterritorial authority typically reflects state policies designed to control development on the urban fringe or to provide basic regulation to fringe areas that lack the population to support their own municipal governments. Extraterritorial regulatory authority may also be associated with municipal expansion, with municipal exercise of extraterritorial authority serving as a halfway step towards the ultimate absorption of the extraterritorial zone. As previously noted in Chapter II, in Holt Civic Club v. City of Tuscaloosa, 439 U.S. 60 (1978), the Supreme Court upheld the power of states to grant their municipalities extraterritorial authority.

B. MUNICIPAL INCORPORATION

Counties and county boundaries tend to be relatively stable over time. In 1952, there were 3,052 counties in the United States; in 2014, the number of counties was 3,028—a very modest change. When states do create, alter or abolish counties, they typically act by special laws concerned with the counties in question rather than by general laws that articulate general rules and procedures for county formation and county boundaries.

The number and boundaries of municipalities are far more fluid, and the law governing municipal formation and boundary change consequently is far more important. Between 1952 and 2012, there was a net increase of more than 2700 municipalities—or roughly 16%—in the United States.

The creation of a new municipality is known as "incorporation"—the term invokes the distinctive legal status of a city, borough or village as a municipal *corporation*. Most states provide for the incorporation of new municipalities by general laws. These laws differ in substantive criteria and procedural requirements. Yet all state incorporation laws have to address the same fundamental questions: Should a new local government be created in the area proposed for incorporation? Are the boundaries proposed the right ones? Who should participate in the process for deciding whether to create a new municipality and where to place its boundaries? Which institution or institutions should make the ultimate decision?

WHITE V. LORINGS
Supreme Court of Arkansas
623 S.W.2d 837 (1981)

PURTLE, J.

A petition to incorporate the town of Wrightsville pursuant to the provisions of Ark. Stat. Ann. § 19–101, et seq. was rejected by the Pulaski County Court. The appeal to circuit court resulted in a trial de novo in which the petition was again rejected. On appeal to this court the appellants urged that * * * the trial court erred in holding that much of the area proposed to be incorporated is agricultural or open and vacant and would not derive any benefit from incorporation, but would be subject to taxation. * * *

Ark. Stat. Ann. § 19–101 * * * requires that 150 qualified voters residing within the described territory may petition to be incorporated.

Ark. Stat. Ann. § 19–102 provides for a hearing by the county court on a petition for incorporation. It specifically provides that affidavits for and against a petition may be prepared for, submitted to and examined by the court. About the only limit placed in this provision is that the county court may not increase the area proposed for incorporation but may delete portions of land proposed for incorporation.

Ark. Stat. Ann. § 19–106 provides for a hearing in circuit court when the decision of a county court is appealed. * * * The statute provides that the court shall not approve the incorporated area if it finds: (1) that the area does not contain the requisite number of inhabitants; or, (2) that a majority have not signed the petition; or, (3) that the area is unreasonably large or unreasonably small; or, (4) that the lands are not properly and sufficiently described.

The * * * trial court * * * found that much of the area to be incorporated is agricultural or open and vacant land and would not derive any benefit from incorporation but would be subject to taxation. Obviously, the court was taking into consideration the statutes which provide for annexation of territory to an already existing town. Indeed, Ark. Stat. Ann. § 19–307.1 provides that lands used only for agricultural or horticultural purposes and where the highest and best use of certain lands is for agricultural or horticultural purposes shall not be annexed. There has never been such a provision in the statutes governing the original incorporation of towns and cities. * * * [Another] reason the court gave for denying the incorporation was that the area to be incorporated is unreasonably large. The area was described as containing approximately two square miles and 919 inhabitants. From looking at the aerial map and the map prepared by the land surveyor it is obvious that most of the land is occupied and developed.

* * * Although there is no definition for "unreasonably large" or "unreasonably small," we have to use common sense in passing judgment upon such matters. In considering an approximately two square mile area containing more than 900 people with its own post office, school and over 400 other buildings, we are of the opinion that the area does not fall within the definition of unreasonably large. Therefore, the court should have allowed the incorporation.

HICKMAN, J., dissenting.

* * * [T]he majority's judgment * * * ignores the fact that Arkansas law gives the trial court some discretion in granting or denying a petition to incorporate. Ark. Stat. Ann. § 19–103 reads:

If the County Court shall be satisfied, after hearing such petition, * * * it shall * * * be deemed right and proper, in the judgment and discretion of the Court, that said petition shall be granted. * * *

This language can only mean that incorporation is not automatic, to be granted if form only is satisfied—if enough names are on a petition and if a map is filed. It is always a question of whether it is "right and proper" to grant an incorporation petition. * * * It is not right and proper to incorporate solely to tax land. * * * Whether land is suited for "municipal purposes" is a consideration. Agricultural and timber lands are not such lands. Another consideration is whether the proposed limits of the town are unreasonably large. * * *

From the testimony of the witnesses one cannot help but conclude that there were other solid reasons for not granting the petition. Michael Garman testified that he had lived in Wrightsville twenty-nine years and was a property owner. He opposed incorporation because of lack of planning; he did not see how the "town" could be supported; he did not know where the money was coming from and, furthermore, he knew that not all the citizens of Wrightsville wanted incorporation. It was stipulated that Nell Higgins, Betty Flowers, George B. Walton, J. B. Morgan, Lon Lorings and Charles Washington would testify to the same effect.

A proponent of the plan, Charles Tatum, who owns a liquor store in Wrightsville and helped conduct the questionable survey, said he favored incorporation because they needed improvements: Police protection, fire protection, recreation, health services, streets and water. But he seemed to have no conception of how those improvements would be paid for. * * *

The lower courts found the area "unreasonably large," a finding that I cannot say is clearly wrong, not if the fact finders are given any say in the matter. But the majority, totally ignoring the prerogatives of the lower courts and totally ignoring the legal discretionary power of those courts, has substituted its judgment for that of the lower courts. * * * Obviously the lower courts were not satisfied in this case that it was right and proper to grant incorporation for any number of valid reasons, all of which have been recognized by us as legitimate reasons for denying incorporation.

NOTES AND QUESTIONS

1. *The Judicial Role in Incorporation.* A state legislature's choice of incorporation procedures is well within the scope of sovereign control over the formation of local government units as most famously described in *Hunter v. Pittsburgh*, in Chapter II. On that basis, the South Dakota Supreme Court rejected a challenge to the procedures of its state incorporation statute. Kraft v. Meade County, 726 N.W.2d 237 (S.D. 2006). State statutes display a wide range in terms of the level of judicial involvement they envision. In some states, substantive discretionary decisions are required, as *White v. Lorings* indicates. In others, though, the court's involvement is limited to certification of the fulfillment of purely objective criteria. *See* In re Fitzgerald, 140 S.W.3d 380 (Tex. 2004), in which the trial judge had refused to certify an incorporation election on the grounds that the area to be incorporated was primarily rural. The supreme court ordered the judge to certify the election, noting that the statute limited judicial involvement to verifying that the petition was properly filed and that the area to be incorporated contained between 201 and 4,999 inhabitants. The courts in Mississippi seem to take a middle ground, noting that although state law limits judicial involvement to determining compliance with technical criteria, such as number of signatures on a petition, that limited role does not remove judicial independence to examine, for instance, whether the voter rolls actually show the number of qualified voters in an area. *See* Fletcher v. Diamondhead Incorporators, 77 So. 3d 92 (Miss. 2012). In general, the level of judicial involvement will depend on how the state's statute addresses the questions discussed in the next four notes, that is, need, capacity, preference, and boundaries.

2. *The Question of Need.* Incorporation creates a municipal government where one did not exist before. To be sure, the unincorporated area proposed to become the town of Wrightsville was subject to the jurisdiction of Pulaski County. But an incorporated municipality typically wields powers of taxation and regulation that are greater than those available to a county. The people within the new municipality gain the powers to provide themselves additional public services and to make collective decisions concerning local matters. In short, they can govern themselves at the municipal level. This also raises the danger of new impositions on local residents. Most local decisions—the election of local officials, the actions of local legislative bodies, votes in local referenda—are

by majority rule. Some local tax or regulatory decisions may burden a local minority. More generally, the operations of a new local government can place new costs on all local residents.

A central question that all municipal incorporation laws seek to answer is whether the potential benefits of local collective action outweigh, and thereby justify, the dangers. This is often posed as the question of whether the area needs a new local government. Some states frame this question in terms of relatively simple and straightforward standards, such as the requirement of a minimum population, a minimum density, or the devotion of a significant portion of the land within the proposed municipality to residential, commercial, industrial or related uses. *See, e.g.*, U.S. Advisory Commission on Intergovernmental Relations, State Laws Governing Local Government Structure and Administration 22–23 (1993) (forty states require a minimum population as a condition for incorporation); Ga.Rev.Stat. § 36–31–3. Other states ask whether the land in question is "urban" or suitable for urban development or whether the residents of the area need more services than the existing county government can provide.

3.   *The Question of Capacity.* Related to the question of the need for municipal government is the issue of whether the area in question has the resources to support a new government. Residents of an area may need or want additional services, but those services will have to be funded out of a local tax base. This may involve not simply the operational costs of providing new police, sanitation or road maintenance services, but also the costs of establishing a city government, creating a municipal government infrastructure, and managing new city agencies. Thus, some states require, as a precondition to incorporation, some evidence that the population be "large and stable enough to support" a new government, Alaska Stat. § 29.05.031(a)(1), or that the new municipality be able "to provide customary municipal services within a reasonable time," Iowa Code § 368.17(1). Six states require a minimum ad valorem tax base.

One way potential new municipalities deal with the question of capacity is by purchasing municipal services from the county, existing cities, or special service districts. This practice was pioneered by the Southern California community of Lakewood which, when it incorporated in the 1950s, purchased all of its basic services from Los Angeles County. The so-called Lakewood Plan provoked an explosion of incorporation activity in Southern California; between 1954 and 1961, twenty-five communities incorporated and then contracted to purchase most municipal services from the county government.

Not all states, however, accept the Lakewood model for municipal incorporation. The Iowa Supreme Court sustained a lower court decision finding that a proposed municipality's plan to purchase most basic services from the county, townships, or private businesses meant that the proposal failed the state's statutory requirement that a new municipality provide customary municipal services within a reasonable time. *See* Citizens of Rising Sun v. Rising Sun City Development Committee, 528 N.W.2d 597 (Iowa

1995). Do you think the requirement that a municipality furnish customary municipal services means that those services must be provided by municipal employees, rather than by private firms or by other governments pursuant to contracts with the new municipality? Why? Or why not?

4. *The Question of Local Preferences.* One way of determining whether there is sufficient need for, and capacity to finance, new municipal services and regulation is to ask the residents of the area proposed for incorporation what they think. The desires of the people living in the area for which a new municipal government is proposed are a critical element in nearly all incorporation statutes. In most states, some significant fraction of local residents or local landowners is needed to initiate the incorporation process by signing petitions. In many states, a referendum in which residents of the area proposed for annexation must approve the proposal is also necessary.

To the extent that the issues posed by an incorporation concern local needs and local resources, there may be much to be said for leaving the question to local residents. Many courts have treated the local desire for municipal government, as revealed by the incorporation request, as virtually dispositive of the question of local benefit from incorporation. *See* Daniel R. Mandelker, Standards for Municipal Incorporation on the Urban Fringe, 36 Tex.L.Rev. 271, 276–89 (1958). When local people want to incorporate is there any reason a state should impose additional substantive standards or procedural requirements?

5. *The Question of Boundaries.* One reason that another institution—a court, an administrative body, or both—may be asked to review a proposed incorporation even if a majority of the residents in the area proposed for incorporation support the proposal is the question of boundaries. Before a new municipality is created out of unincorporated territory, there may be no obvious definition of its boundaries or no standard for determining where the borders ought to be located. Incorporation proponents may face conflicting goals of making the locality small—to focus the proposal on the residents most likely to support incorporation and thereby win the consent the proposal needs—and of making it large so as to include more taxable land and land for future growth. Moreover, the issue of boundaries is not simply a matter of optimal size but of avoiding potential conflicts concerning regulation or services within the new locality. Some states require that the local population be "interrelated and integrated as to its social, cultural, and economic activities," Alaska Stat. § 29.05.031(a)(1), that the "entire territory of the proposed village or city shall be reasonably homogeneous and compact," Wisc. Stats. § 66.016(1)(a) or that there be "a body of citizens whose residences are contiguous to and all of which form a homogeneous settlement or community," Ala. Code § 11–41–1. It may be that Arkansas's requirement that an area not be "unreasonably large" reflects this concern as well.

Arkansas asks not just whether an area is unreasonably large but whether it is "unreasonably small." This criterion may reflect some concern about the area's capacity to fund municipal services. But it may also indicate an intent to avoid creating a municipality that is only a fragment of the relevant geographic area. As the next set of cases indicate, a new municipality can have an impact on the people outside its borders as well as those residing within its boundaries.

IN RE INCORPORATION OF THE BOROUGH
OF BRIDGEWATER

Commonwealth Court of Pennsylvania
488 A.2d 374 (1985)

PALLADINO, J.

The proposed borough, also known as "Toby Farms", consists of ninety-two acres, and lies within Chester Township in Delaware County. Pursuant to Section 202 of The Borough Code, the Petition, signed by a majority of the freeholders residing in the proposed borough, was filed with the Court of Common Pleas (trial court) on July 5, 1979. Exceptions to the Petition were filed by Chester Township and the Chester-Upland School District.

* * * [T]he Township entered a motion requesting the trial court to proceed under the amended version of Section 202, which required the trial court to appoint a five-member Borough Advisory Committee (Committee).[2] A Committee was established, it held several hearings, and submitted its report to the trial court on July 29, 1982. The Committee concluded that the disadvantages of creating the Borough of Bridgewater outweighed the advantages, and recommended that the borough should not be incorporated. Two members of the Committee dissented and filed a minority report. * * *

Of the factors considered by the trial court, we find several to be significant. The current racial composition of the Township is 59% white and 41% non-white. The composition of the proposed borough would be 82.5% white and 17.4% non-white. The remaining portion of the Township would be 26.6% white and 73% non-white. The trial court found that the motivation for the proposed Borough was to segregate it from the rest of the Township.

Additionally, the trial court listed the several debts accumulated by the Township and concluded that the proposed Borough sought to escape

---

[2] After a petition for incorporation has been filed, subsection (b) of Section 202 requires that:

(b) The court shall establish a Borough Advisory Committee which shall consist of two residents of the proposed borough, two residents of the existing governmental unit or units recommended by the respective governing body of the unit or units and not residing within the proposed borough and one resident of the county not residing in either area who shall serve as the chairman of the committee. Such a committee shall be established when a petition is received by the court for the creation of a borough * * *.

supporting the financially troubled Township. In addition to its debts, the portion of the Township which would remain intact after the proposed incorporation would carry the responsibility for all of the low-income housing currently supported by the entire Township.

The proposed Borough is comprised wholly of privately owned residential units, with little or no existing or potential area for commercial or industrial growth. While acknowledging that the proposed Borough would probably be able to take care of itself financially, by imposing a real estate tax, the trial court held that the remainder of the Township would be deprived of the "support and balance which is essential to preserve and develop a complete, integrated and, yet, diverse community of population interests, and uses; all of which are essential to the stability and growth of a suburban municipality."

We cannot fault the trial court in its concern for preserving the diversity of the Township necessary to support it financially and socially. Therefore, we hold that the trial court properly exercised its discretion under Section 202 in denying the Petition to Incorporate.

IN RE INCORPORATION OF BOROUGH OF NEW MORGAN

Supreme Court of Pennsylvania
590 A.2d 274 (1991)

FLAHERTY, J.

This case arose when Morgantown Properties, a limited partnership, filed a petition to incorporate a tract of land it owned in Berks County. The proposed borough consisted of 3,700 acres, part of which is located in Caernarvon Township, and part of which is located in Robeson Township. Morgantown Properties is the sole owner of the entire tract of land to be incorporated, and there are only six occupied homes in the proposed borough. Morgantown's proposal is to develop the land with a landfill, a trash-to-steam plant, a tourist attraction which it calls a Victorian Village, a golf course, a cultural center, a mixed use center, commercial areas, agricultural areas, and open space areas.

Pursuant to the Borough Code, the Court of Common Pleas of Berks County established a Borough Advisory Committee consisting of two residents of the proposed borough, one resident of Caernarvon Township, one resident of Robeson Township, and a fifth member who was a resident of Berks County, but did not reside in either affected township or in the proposed borough. * * * After conducting more than 100 hours of hearings, the committee voted three to two in favor of incorporation.

* * * The first of the appellants' claims is that Morgantown's motive for the incorporation was to avoid the townships' zoning regulations, that this is an impermissible motive, and, therefore, that its application for

incorporation should have been denied. The Commonwealth Court case cited by the appellants in support of this claim, *In re Incorporation of Borough of Bridgewater*, 87 Pa.Cmwlth. 599, 488 A.2d 374 (1985), stands for the proposition that incorporation of a borough may be denied when it is demonstrated that the applicant's motive is racial segregation. The case does not stand for the broad proposition that incorporation may be denied when the applicant has an "improper motive." Indeed, the legislature has been silent on the matter of motive, and Pennsylvania cases have turned on motive only where racial discrimination was at issue. Absent, therefore, fundamental constitutional concerns or other direction from the General Assembly, we do not understand inquiry into motive of the applicant to be appropriate.

Even if it were, however, and even if avoiding existing land use regulations were deemed an improper motive, appellants have failed to show improper motive. The majority of the advisory committee found:

> Applicant is basically motivated by a desire to establish an independent governmental agency which will complement the conceptual theme of cohesive combination of related but unique land and development uses unfettered by unreasonable governmental restraints.

The majority report concluded:

> [T]he incorporation . . . is not intended to circumvent existing land use controls but will encourage large scale economic development to an otherwise dormant segment of the Townships.

* * * These findings are supported by the record and were adopted by the trial court.

* * * In short, the appellants have failed to demonstrate that Morgantown's motivation was to avoid existing zoning and land use restrictions, but even if they had demonstrated this, neither the statute nor our caselaw prohibits such avoidance. In fact, the entire incorporation process is predicated on the applicant's notion that the proposed borough's regulations, whatever they are, are preferable to those of the existing governments from which the proposed borough is derived.

* * * [T]he appellants claim that the disadvantages of incorporation to Caernarvon and Robeson Townships outweigh the advantages to New Morgan. The essence of the appellants' argument here is that if one looks to the future, the townships will lose approximately $2,600,000 in lost tax revenue and fees to be paid for hosting a solid waste disposal facility, and in any event, the townships will be burdened, if the plan is carried out, by substantially increased traffic and expense for road maintenance.

This claim is without merit. First, in considering the loss of taxes and fees, the proper focus is those which may be presently lost, not those which may be lost in the future. The present loss of $9,917 to Caernarvon Township and $1,265 to Robeson Township are not losses of sufficient dimension to turn the balance against approval of Morgantown's application. Second, balancing the disadvantage to the townships of increased road maintenance against the need for incorporation, the balance rests in favor of incorporation, for the maintenance of roads leading to the proposed borough is a relatively minor matter as against the advantages of incorporation.

For the foregoing reasons, the order of Commonwealth Court is affirmed.

McDERMOTT, J.

I dissent * * * from the view that an improper motive is confined only to attempts to racially segregate. * * * The majority would find no possibility of improper motive even if the sole purpose were to avoid local zoning regulations. If applicants are dissatisfied with local zoning laws, they ought not lightly be allowed to start their own municipality to evade those laws. The surrounding municipalities ought not be required to surrender their sovereignty or their land for what amounts to commercial fiefs or zoning raiders. Certainly to gerrymander a new governmental unit between two existing communities to evade zoning regulations is destructive of the "harmonious whole" and the legitimate expectations of settled, self-supporting communities, and to my mind improper motive.

LARSEN J., joins this dissenting opinion.

IN RE INCORPORATION OF THE BOROUGH OF CHILTON

Commonwealth Court of Pennsylvania
646 A.2d 13 (1994)

SMITH, J.

* * * In September 1990, Robert M. Mumma II, his wife Susan Mumma, Gemini Equipment Company, Double M Development Company, and the Wellington Heights Properties Owners Association by Martin L. Grass and Mark G. Caldwell (collectively Appellees) filed a petition with the trial court proposing to incorporate the Borough from land located within [Monaghan] Township, the Appellees being a majority of the freeholders residing within the limits of the proposed Borough. * * *

The proposed Borough is largely undeveloped land owned by Appellees consisting of approximately 492 acres located entirely within the Township along the Yellow Breeches Creek and is presently farmland with a mansion and a few tenant houses located on the property. The principal residence is occupied by the Mummas and their child. No adjoining landowners requested inclusion in the petition to incorporate. The proposal would cut off part of the Township from the main body of the Township, thereby creating a small peninsula, and in December 1992, the proposed Borough was populated by three adults.

The proposed Borough would contain a planned residential community featuring an eighteen-hole championship golf course and club house. Surrounding the golf course would be approximately 350 dwelling units, mostly single-family dwellings. In order to avoid the requirement of providing for a mix of uses, the Borough would not adopt a zoning ordinance. Land uses would be controlled through deed restrictions and architectural standards which would control building type, size, materials, and use. The proposed residential use is targeted at high income persons, with the average price of a home estimated to be $215,000.

In its majority report recommending against incorporation, the [Borough Advisory] Committee focused mainly on two reasons for its recommendation: the proposed Borough would be unable to function as a borough and comply with other requirements by law, in particular the Borough Code and the Pennsylvania Election Code * * * for an indefinite and possibly prolonged time following incorporation; and plans for the proposed Borough are only speculation, with no assurance that they would be carried out as presented to the Committee. The Committee expressed concern that the "vague and speculative plan" for the Borough would never be implemented and determined that for these reasons and others, the incorporation would not be in the public interest.

The Committee concluded that the proposed Borough was clearly not a "harmonious whole," being largely vacant farm, orchard, and wood land: as a result, there is no existing development that could presently support the formation of a borough. The Committee further concluded that no evidence was presented to indicate that the present services provided by the Township were inadequate to meet the present needs of the area proposed for incorporation; incorporation would not presently have an adverse effect upon the tax base of the Township; however, because the land proposed for incorporation is undeveloped there are no common interests or problems that could better be addressed by a separate government; and the necessity for creation of another local government does not exist. The Committee also expressed concern that incorporation of a borough with fewer voters than required under the Election Code to fill all of the borough offices would be a result that is absurd, unreasonable, and impossible of execution.

On October 26, 1992, the trial court * * * rejected the Committee's conclusions [and] * * * held that the proposed Borough would be a harmonious whole, was desirable as defined by statute, and the request to incorporate must be submitted to a vote of the electorate of the proposed borough. * * * Appellants appealed to this Court. * * *

Throughout its opinion, the trial court expressed reservations and reluctance in coming to its conclusion to allow incorporation. After noting that formation of a new municipality goes against the trend toward regionalization in order to more economically provide necessary municipal services, the trial court stated that resolution of this conflict "is not the perogative [sic] of the Court. * * * The role of the Court is merely to interpret and enforce the law as the Legislature has written it." * * * In response to the report of the York County Planning Commission Director, which noted that the objective of Appellees' plans was to create an "elitist enclave" of very affluent individuals thus resulting in economic segregation, the trial court stated that "[t]his is probably the most compelling argument raised by the opponents of the proposed Borough. However it is really an argument for why the present law should be changed, rather than an argument as to whether this Borough is 'desirable' within the context of the present law." * * *

After stating its belief that "it would have been far better had this development occurred within the Township," the trial court observed: "The creation of new boroughs, for whatever reason, only expands the problems which flow from the existence of too many separate municipalities. For many economic and social reasons it would be better if municipal services were regionalized, rather than further fragmented." * * * Further, the trial court noted that the proposal to form a borough by a wealthy developer in order to avoid existing regulations "just doesn't seem right." Nevertheless, the court concluded that the proposed borough would be a "harmonious whole" and formation of the borough would be "desirable" as that term is defined by the Borough Code. * * *

Pennsylvania's appellate courts have made it clear that the proper analysis of borough incorporation petitions requires the court to look beyond the three statutory provisions of Section 202(c) of the Borough Code. It is thus evident that the trial court incorrectly believed it was constrained by the statutory language and was without authority to adopt the recommendation of the Committee to reject the petition for incorporation, despite the trial court's clearly expressed misgivings in reaching its conclusion.

* * * Of particular concern to the Committee and to this Court is the potential incorporation of a borough with few residents and no guarantee that the proposed plans will be carried out. Section 201 of the Borough Code, 53 P.S. § 45201, was recently amended by the legislature:

§ 45201. Areas may be incorporated

The courts of common pleas may incorporate any contiguous area within their jurisdiction, not already incorporated or a part of an incorporated municipality *and having a population of at least 500 residents*, as a borough, which, after having been so incorporated, shall be a body corporate and politic by the name which shall be decreed by the court. [Emphasis added]

* * * [T]he minimum resident requirement applies to applications and petitions presented on or after March 25, 1992 except in counties of the fifth class, where the act shall apply to applications and petitions presented on or after the effective date of the act. Although the minimum resident requirement is not directly applicable in the present case, this Court nevertheless believes it is important to note the legislative change.

[The amendment] represents evidence of a trend away from the incorporation of boroughs with few residents as has been allowed in the past, and this concern is heightened in cases such as the present where the petitioners have neither embarked on a course of development nor made substantial contributions to commencement of the development. The instant proposal stands in contrast to [*Canterbury Village, Inc. Appeal*, 462 A.2d 865 (Comm.Ct.1983)] in which the petition for incorporation was granted where there was a small resident population, but the landowner had already installed complete road, water, and sewer systems, including a sewage treatment plant, and had executed contracts for fire, police, and garbage collection.

In [*Glen Mills Schools Appeal*, 558 A.2d 592 (Comm.Ct.1989)] this Court articulated its concern regarding a situation in which one landowner wants to separate and govern itself, which left this Court to ponder—

[H]ow far would it go: colleges, universities, sundry institutions, corporations, larger land owners, perhaps smaller too, would break-off at will from Townships and into multi-separate boroughs. Each borough going its own way to create a mix of perhaps harmonious, perhaps antagonistic, but incongruous zoning or development patterns, and as well conflicting and often inconsistent services. The potential for exclusion, exploitation and overreaching becomes real and ever present * * *

In the end we have not come so far in our evolving history to now go backward toward creating what would ultimately become feudal-like estates. This is certainly not the acceptable or reasonable basis and approach to local government.

Id. at 595. In light of these considerations, the trial court erred in failing to exercise its discretion and to adopt the recommendations of the Committee and the York County director of planning. Accordingly, the trial court's order is reversed.

NOTES AND QUESTIONS

1.   *Race, Ethnicity and Local Boundaries*. As *Bridgewater* indicates, the placement of local government boundaries can affect the racial composition of a community—or rather, of two communities, the newly created municipality and the area out of which the municipality has been carved. Racial, ethnic, and class concerns have long played an important role in local government formation, as members of a particular group have sought to use municipal borders to separate themselves from people of other groups. *See, e.g.*, Taylor v. Township of Dearborn, 120 N.W.2d 737, 742–43 (Mich.1963); Village of Inkster v. Wayne County Supervisors, 108 N.W.2d 822, 825 (Mich.1961); NAACP v. Town of Hilton Head, 335 S.E.2d 806 (S.C.1985); Symposium, The White Curtain: Racially Disadvantaging Local Government Boundary Practices, 54 J. Urb. L. 679–1073 (1977); Kenneth Jackson, Crabgrass Frontier: The Suburbanization of the United States 150–51 (Oxford Univ. Press 1985); Nancy Burns, The Formation of American Local Governments: Private Values in Public Institutions 35–37, 83–86 (Oxford Univ. Press 1994). Boundaries can determine who will be the majority—and who will be the minority—within any community and can, thus, affect the quantity and quality of local services, the scope of local finances, and the nature of local regulatory policy.

The Supreme Court has held that a state's intentional use of race or religious criteria to determine the boundaries of a locality is unconstitutional, *see* Gomillion v. Lightfoot, 364 U.S. 339 (1960); Board of Educ. of Kiryas Joel Village School Dist. v. Grumet, 512 U.S. 687 (1994). But it is less clear how the Constitution applies when local residents seek to utilize a general incorporation statute to create a new municipality whose boundaries happen to include people who are predominantly of one racial or ethnic group. In *Kiryas Joel*, the Court invalidated a local school district created by a special act of the New York state legislature in order to assure that a "religious enclave" of Satmar Hasidic Jews who lived in the Village of Kiryas Joel could have control over their own school district. A few years earlier local residents, using the mechanism provided by the state's general village formation legislation, had incorporated the Village of Kiryas Joel. The "boundaries of the village of Kiryas Joel were drawn to include just the 320 acres owned and inhabited entirely by Satmars." 512 U.S. at 691. Yet, the Supreme Court stressed that although the state's intentional use of a religious criterion in establishing a school district was unconstitutional, "this conclusion does not imply that any political subdivision that is coterminous with the boundaries of a religiously homogeneous community suffers from the same constitutional infirmity." *Id.* at 702 n.6. Creation of the village "involv[ed] . . . the application of a neutral state law designed to give almost any group of residents the right to incorporate." *Id.* at 703 n.7. Is the Court's distinction between special state legislation and local residents' use of general incorporation legislation persuasive to you?

2.   *Incorporation to Avoid Other Local Governments*. As *New Morgan* indicates, one goal of incorporation may be to reduce or eliminate the role of

another local government in the area. In most states, a municipality cannot annex territory that is part of another municipality. An unincorporated area may incorporate primarily to avoid annexation by another entity. Indeed, such *defensive incorporation* has been a major cause of the proliferation of small municipalities on the fringe of large cities. Some states have limited defensive incorporation by prohibiting new incorporations within a certain distance (typically one to six miles) of an existing municipality without that municipality's consent. *See, e.g.*, Ariz.Rev.Stat. § 9–101.01(A); Ark.Stat.Ann. § 14–38–101; Ga.Rev.Stat. § 36–31–2; Il.St.Ch. 65 § 5/2–2–6; Mo.St. 72.130. These areas constitute *growth zones* for existing municipalities. *See also* U.S. Advisory Commission on Intergovernmental Relations, State Laws Governing Local Government Structure and Administration 22–23 (1993) (sixteen states require a new municipality to be a minimum distance from existing local units). Residents and voters challenged the Arizona provision, arguing that the requirement that nearby municipalities consent to incorporations violated the equal protection clause and the constitutionally based right to vote. The Ninth Circuit rejected the constitutional challenges, concluding that the law appropriately furthered the state's interests in protecting the interests of existing municipalities and in reducing the proliferation of local units of government. *See* Green v. Tucson, 340 F.3d 891 (9th Cir.2003).

Incorporation may also be a means to reduce the authority of overlying local governments, such as a county or township, in the newly incorporated area. Depending on the law of the particular state, incorporation may shift control over land use regulation or reduce the ability of an overlying government to raise revenues within the incorporated area.

Should incorporation in order to achieve a substantive change in local policy—such as land use regulation—be considered an illegitimate basis for the creation of a new local government, or is incorporation a legitimate means of achieving local political goals? Should it matter whether the proponents are local residents with distinctive views that differ from those in power in the surrounding area or whether, instead, they are developers seeking approval for a new commercial venture? Should it matter if the goal of the incorporators is simply to narrow the area in which their local tax dollars are spent?

3. *External Effects and Statutory Criteria.* As these cases indicate, municipal incorporation is not simply a matter of increasing the amount of government in a previously unincorporated area. Municipal incorporation involves a determination of *which* government, and which borders, will have jurisdiction over a particular area. The incorporation decision may, thus, involve consideration of the impact on the surrounding area—the county or township from which the new municipality is effectively subtracted; nearby cities that might have annexed the land; and the governance of the relevant metropolitan region. Some state statutes explicitly include the impact of incorporation on the surrounding area as a criterion for approval of an incorporation. *See, e.g.*, Kans.Rev.Stat. § 15–121(8) ("effect of the proposed action, and of alternative actions, on adjacent areas, and on the local

governmental structure of the entire urban community"); Ohio Rev. Code § 707.07 (incorporation must consider the "general good" of the community, including both the area to be incorporated and the surrounding area); 53 Pa.Stat. § 45202(c)(3) ("the financial or tax effect on the proposed borough and existing governmental unit or units"); Utah Code Ann. § 10–2–106 ("the fiscal impact on unincorporated areas, other municipalities, special districts, and other governmental entities in the county"); Wisc.Stat. § 66.016(2)(c) ("[t]he impact, financial and otherwise, upon the remainder of the town from which the territory is to be incorporated").

In other states, the statutory criteria may be less explicit but judicial decisions require that the impact of an incorporation on nearby municipalities or the surrounding area be taken into account. *See, e.g.*, City of Pascagoula v. Scheffler, 487 So.2d 196, 202 (Miss.1986) (interpreting Mississippi statutory standard of "serving public convenience and necessity" to include consideration of "whether incorporation affects an existing city within three miles . . . whether a community has a separate identity . . . ; whether natural geographical boundaries separate an area from other municipalities"). Judicial awareness of the implications of municipal incorporation for the surrounding area may also lead to a greater willingness to permit individuals and governments outside the proposed municipality's boundaries to participate in, and challenge, the incorporation process. *See, e.g.*, Vashon Island Committee for Self-Government v. Washington State Boundary Review Board, 903 P.2d 953 (Wash.1995); City of Madison v. Town of Fitchburg, 332 N.W.2d 782 (Wis.1983). *But see* In re Petition for Incorporation of the Village of Holiday City, 639 N.E.2d 42 (Ohio 1994) (neither township nor township residents living outside the area to be incorporated had standing to challenge incorporation decision).

4. *The Decision-Makers.* Incorporation involves not just substantive criteria but procedures and institutions. In *White v. Lorings*, the process consisted of a petition followed by judicial review for compliance with relatively minimal statutory criteria. In the Pennsylvania cases, the process involved a petition, review by an ad hoc borough advisory committee composed of residents of the borough and residents of the affected surrounding area, court action, and a referendum in the area sought to be incorporated. Other states utilize other institutions and procedures. In some states, the decision on incorporation is for the county legislature. *See e.g.*, Kans.Rev.Stat. § 15–123. In others, a county-level committee must review and approve a proposed new municipal incorporation. *See, e.g.*, Cal.Gov't Code § 56826 (local agency formation commission). In some states, such as Minnesota and Wisconsin, a statewide commission must review, and may reject, proposed incorporations. *See also* 1000 Friends of Oregon v. Wasco County Court, 703 P.2d 207 (Ore.1985) (new incorporations in Oregon subject to review by Land Use Board of Appeals for consistency with state land use policies). Many states combine several steps, such as petition, review by an administrative body, judicial review of the administrative decision, and a referendum.

Generally, the creation of a special county or state commission to review the formation of new local governments reflects a state policy to assure that a new government is in the interests of the region as a whole and to place "substantial obstacles in the path of the incorporation of a city or a village which falls within the metropolitan area." Town of Pleasant Prairie v. Department of Local Affairs, 334 N.W.2d 893, 900 (Wisc.1983). The increasing—albeit still limited—role of administrative bodies may also reflect a growing recognition that an assessment of the complex mix of political, economic, fiscal, demographic, geographic, land use, transportation and other factors that go into determining whether a particular area is ripe for municipal government—and whether it ought to have its own government or be part of an existing government or of a larger area—is less a matter of legal principle and more a matter of pragmatic policy analysis. It is unclear, however, whether administrative agencies have had a significant impact on the pace of incorporation. For a critical appraisal of the role of California's local agency formation commissions (LAFCOs), see Gary Miller, Cities by Contract: The Politics of Municipal Incorporation 103 (MIT Press 1981) ("The LAFCO boards do not do anything that was not previously done elsewhere; they simply represent a different balance of power by creating an extra review step in the incorporation process"). For a more positive assessment of the Minnesota and Wisconsin boundary review commissions, see Richard Briffault, Our Localism: Part I—The Structure of Local Government Law, 90 Colum.L.Rev. 1, 83 (1990) (boundary review commissions dramatically reduced the number of incorporations in those states).

C. ANNEXATION AND BOUNDARY CHANGE

Annexation is the territorial expansion of a municipal corporation though the addition of new land. Consolidation, or merger, is the combination of one or more local governments into a single local entity. Detachment—also known as secession, deannexation or disconnection—is the removal of territory from an existing municipality. The various forms of boundary change raise some of the basic issues, already considered in the analysis of municipal incorporation, posed by the organization of local governments: is an area appropriate for the more intensive governance that results from inclusion in a municipality? What is the appropriate size of a local government? Should two geographic areas be treated as distinct units for political and legal purposes, or should they be united in one government? What should be the roles of local residents, courts, legislatures, and administrative agencies in making these decisions? Indeed, incorporation and boundary change issues may often be intertwined; frequently an alternative to incorporation of a new municipality is annexation by an existing one. Boundary change decisions play an especially important role in determining the governance of contemporary metropolitan areas.

1. ANNEXATION

Annexation is by far the most common form of boundary change. Between 1990 and 1995, approximately 1,138,000 people were added to American municipalities by more than 30,000 annexations. The total amount of land annexed—3600 square miles—was nearly twice the size of the state of Delaware. The cities of Portland, Oregon and San Antonio, Texas each added more than 40,000 people by annexation, and cities in North Carolina, Texas, and California have been particularly active in adding new territory through annexation. *See* Joel Miller, Boundary Changes, 1990–1995 in International City Management Ass'n, Municipal Year Book 1997, at 35.

There are five principal methods of annexation: (i) by state legislative act; (ii) by municipal action (ordinance or resolution); (iii) by petition of the residents or landowners in the area to be annexed; (iv) by judicial determination; and (v) by regional or statewide boundary review commissions. *See* Advisory Commission on Intergovernmental Relations, State and Local Roles in the Federal System 360–82 (1982). Direct statutory action to add new territory to an existing municipality was a common form of boundary change in the nineteenth century but is relatively rare today. Instead, most states have enacted general laws that permit annexation without direct legislative action. Many states provide multiple annexation mechanisms that combine several different techniques. An annexation may be initiated by a city or by a petition of landowners in an area outside the city, and then be subject to review by a court or boundary commission. A referendum in the area to be annexed may also be required.

Annexation is frequently an uncontested and virtually unnoticed fact of life for many municipalities, but occasionally it becomes the scene of high drama, intensified emotions, and protracted litigation. The interested groups in an annexation decision are essentially the same as those with a stake in an incorporation: residents and owners in the territory proposed for annexation; the annexing city; the county or subcounty unit in which the territory to be annexed is located; and perhaps nearby cities which would also like to annex the land.

Consider the following observations about municipal annexation disputes:

> Annexation battles are typically fought in one of two contexts: when neighboring municipalities are competing for the same piece of land; or when a municipality is seeking to annex land from its unincorporated environs. In the first type of battle, occurring mainly in developed areas where municipalities are frequently adjacent or nearly so, the result will determine which municipal governments will win the prize of annexation. . . . In

most states, the first municipality to initiate annexation proceedings will be the victor.

In the second type of annexation conflict, the stakes are somewhat different. The result will determine whether the land will become part of a municipal government's jurisdiction at all or, in the alternative, remain in the unincorporated county. This conflict most frequently involves residential subdivisions whose owners prefer to remain in the county with its lower tax rates, even though to the uninformed observer, the subdivision already forms part of the municipality whose annexation it is resisting.

Unfortunately, most state annexation procedures do not adequately respond to the variety of interests at issue in the two very different contexts. . . .

Laurie Reynolds, Rethinking Municipal Annexation Powers, 24 Urb. Law. 247, 249–50 (1992).

The following cases raise some of these questions.

IN THE MATTER OF THE ENLARGEMENT AND EXTENSION OF THE MUNICIPAL BOUNDARIES OF THE CITY OF JACKSON, MISSISSIPPI

Supreme Court of Mississippi
691 So.2d 978 (1997)

ROBERTS, J.

Jackson, Mississippi's mayor, Kane Ditto, recommended to the City Council that the City annex a total of 24.25 square miles of territory [of the unincorporated area known as Byram] made up of two tracts of land lying south and southwest, respectively, of Jackson's existing corporate limits. * * * On April 21, 1992, the City Council adopted an ordinance approving the proposed annexation, and a petition of annexation was filed in * * * Chancery Court. * * * Final judgment in favor of the City of Jackson was filed on June 4, 1993. * * *

While "[a]nnexation is a legislative affair," confirmation of annexations is in the province of the chancery court. * * * The role of the judiciary in annexations is limited to one question: whether the annexation is reasonable. * * * Courts are "guided" in this determination of reasonableness by twelve factors previously set forth by this Court. * * *

The twelve indicia of reasonableness are: (1) the municipality's need to expand, (2) whether the area sought to be annexed is reasonably within a path of growth of the city, (3) potential health hazards from sewage and waste disposal in the annexed areas, (4) the municipality's financial ability to make the improvements and furnish municipal services promised, (5) need for zoning and overall planning in the areas, (6) need for municipal services in the areas sought to be annexed, (7) whether there are natural barriers between the city and the proposed annexation area, (8) past performance and time element involved in the city's provision of services to its present residents, (9) economic or other impact of the annexation upon those who live in or own property in the proposed annexation area, (10) impact of the annexation upon the voting strength of protected minority groups, (11) whether the property owners and other inhabitants of the areas sought to be annexed have in the past, and in the foreseeable future unless annexed will, because of their reasonable proximity to the corporate limits of the municipality, enjoy economic and social benefits of the municipality without paying their fair share of taxes, and (12) any other factors that may suggest reasonableness. * * *

These twelve factors are not separate, independent tests which are conclusive as to reasonableness. * * * Rather, these factors are "mere indicia of reasonableness." "[T]he ultimate determination must be whether the annexation is reasonable under the totality of the circumstances." * * * In making this determination, the annexation must be viewed "from the perspective of both the city and the landowners" of the proposed annexation area. * * *

There was considerable undisputed evidence presented at trial that the population of the City of Jackson is decreasing and, that although there is considerable vacant, developable land within the City, applications for both residential and commercial building permits have decreased considerably over the last few years. While it is true that this Court has allowed annexations even though there is no significant population growth and/or a relatively high percentage of undeveloped land within the existing city limits, this presence of these factors should, at the very least, be an impediment to annexation. * * *

Evidence shows 40.15 square miles of vacant land within the City in 1990. The City's population has declined from 202,888 in 1983 to 196,637 in 1990 with an outmigration from Jackson of 26,532 people. Mayor Ditto admitted at trial that Jackson had no need to expand to accommodate "anticipated growth within its boundaries." The City admits in its brief that it is not trying to annex Byram because it has outgrown its existing boundaries, but argues that there are other factors that indicate its need to expand.

Michael Bridge, the Objectors' expert in urban and regional development, testified * * * concerning the effect of a large amount of vacant and developable land within a city:

> When you have vacant developable land that's not put into productive urban use, then it essentially tends to be a drain on the economy and the fiscal structure of the city. Vacant land—

normally to go from developed area to vacant land to another developed area, you have to have roads. The utilities have to extend through that vacant area. So the city is in a position where they have expended in many instances significant resources to extend infrastructure into vacant areas and through vacant areas, and if the area does not develop or is not encouraged to develop, then it becomes a drain on the city because they have to extend those lines further and further. Those are not in productive uses. When those vacant lands go into productive uses, then they tend to strengthen the tax base. The converse, when you continually stretch the rubber band, you know, ultimately it will break. The concept of strengthening the tax base by ignoring the vacant land resources within the existing city is on the simplest basis just totally wrong.

* * * The City at trial and in its brief has not been at all hesitant to state that it wants the revenues annexation would provide by expanding its tax base. Numerous witnesses testified at trial that the City was in need of expanding its tax base in order to continue providing the same level of services. Although it has been held that a city's need to maintain or expand its tax base, especially as growth and development occurs on its perimeters, is a factor to be considered when determining the reasonableness of a proposed annexation, * * * this Court has in the past, been very critical of annexations which are in effect "tax grabs." * * *

From studying the record and briefs, especially the testimony of city officials, we believe that the City of Jackson's primary motivation for the proposed annexation is to expand its tax base. Whether or not the taxes garnered by annexing Byram would be beneficial to the City of Jackson when compared to the expenditures that would result from the annexation is debatable. Bridge testified for the Objectors that it would not.

> * * * The City of Jackson probably has a real need to do some investing within their community to enhance the development of their properties within the city. It would be cheaper to do that than to go outside of the existing borders of the city and continually stretch that rubber band by extending, extending, extending infrastructure and services and facilities. . . .

> I think the City of Jackson is going to see some potential tax benefits in the first few years, but as the need for services—as the citizens start knocking on the door expecting the promises as set forth in the annexation ordinance to be fulfilled, you're going to see an increasing burden placed upon the city. * * * I think the city's going to have problems.

We tend to agree with Mr. Bridge's assessment. Before the City of Jackson annexes more land and residents for which it has had to extend infrastructure and provide services, it should make an effort to extend that infrastructure to the vacant, developable land within the existing boundaries and take steps to encourage development in those areas.

The City of Jackson maintains that if the city experiences a decline it will have an adverse affect on the entire metropolitan area, including the proposed annexation area. * * * It is a fact that Jackson is the capital of the state and its largest city, and for these and other reasons the City's prosperity affects more than just the city itself. These things are validly taken into consideration; however, it is not a "super-factor" whereby whatever Jackson wants, Jackson gets. * * * We believe the chancellor placed too much importance on this so-called "Jackson factor."

The City failed to prove that the current services in the proposed annexation area are inadequate. * * * Instead, all residents who testified expressed concern about a decrease in the level of services, especially police protection, if annexation occurred. Furthermore, it should be noted that the proposal for improvements and extension of services presented to the Court by the City was merely the product of department head and planner recommendations, and the City Council had not approved any of the improvements the witnesses for the City testified that the City intended to make in the proposed annexation area. * * *

The Objectors concede that "theoretically Jackson has the financial ability to make the expenditures it proposes." However, they argue that the City's desire or will to make promised improvements should be considered in light of the City's past performance of failing to furnish the promised improvements to the 1976 and 1989 annexed areas.

The Objectors produced a number of Jackson residents, mostly from the 1976 annexation area, who testified unfavorably about the level of services provided by the City. Their main complaints dealt with the City's police and fire protection, road maintenance and sewer service. There was testimony concerning slow response time of the Jackson Police Department and their failure to sufficiently investigate crimes. There was also testimony concerning the lack of fire hydrants and insufficient water flow to adequately fight fires in South Jackson.

The only municipal service that the chancellor held that the proposed annexation area was in need of was sewer service. As to all other municipal services, she found only that they would be enhanced by annexation. When current services are adequate, the fact that annexation may enhance municipal services should not be given much relevance, * * * especially as here, where the evidence of the likelihood of enhanced service is greatly conflicting. * * *

All these and other factors have a significant bearing on the reasonableness of the proposed annexation, and we find that at this time the City of Jackson's proposed annexation is unfair to the residents of the proposed annexation area and fails to meet the test of reasonableness. The proof before this Court does not sustain the chancellor's decision and, accordingly, we reverse.

PRATHER, J., dissenting.

I respectfully dissent. In my view, the chancellor's ruling was supported by substantial evidence and should be affirmed. * * * One particular concern I have is with regard to the City's need to expand its tax base. The objectors would have this Court place little if any importance on this issue, but, it is clearly essential that the City be able to gain revenue from those citizens who so often enjoy the benefits of its services. * * *

This Court has held that City of Jackson's need to maintain or expand its tax base, especially as growth and development occurs on its perimeters, is a factor to be considered under the "need to expand" factor. In *Matter of Extension of Boundaries of City of Jackson*, 551 So. 2d 861 (Miss.1989), this Court wrote that:

> Jackson's need for an expanded tax base is reasonable as well. As a matter of fact, recent years reflect a gradual recession of Jackson's (economic) life blood to the various surrounding communities. These communities have experienced meteoric growth, most of them with a planned development. They have drained off and continue to drain off the life of the city's flow of wealth in people, culture and dollars. Indeed, the very statistics recited by the Court below are the product of the flight of so many persons from Jackson's corporate limits, not so far as to deprive themselves of full access to the economic, social and cultural benefits Jackson has to offer but only so far as to sever their relationship with Jackson's assessor and tax collector. Barring a wholly unanticipated act of altruism by Ridgeland, Madison, Flowood, Pearl, Richland, Florence or Clinton—not to mention unincorporated western Rankin County, Jackson faces the certainty of a slow but sure erosion of its tax base by the unilateral actions of these selfish former citizens.

City of Jackson, 551 So. 2d at 865. The words of this Court in *City of Jackson* are equally applicable today. I find it ironic that representatives of areas which have grown largely out of a desire to avoid taxation for the services which they enjoy in City of Jackson should accuse the City of attempting a "tax grab" out of considerations of greed.

In the case of *City of Jackson*, the need for tax dollars is more a matter of survival than greed. As the home of many government buildings, City of Jackson is faced with the burden of having much of its real estate occupied by tax-exempt entities, and the City has recently seen a flight of important tax-paying businesses to surrounding areas. This Court has given some, but, in my view, insufficient, consideration to City of Jackson's need for physical expansion outside of its current boundaries, but the welfare of our capital city depends upon more than available land. Tax-paying citizens are indeed the lifeblood of a modern city, and allowing City of Jackson the physical area it needs to expand while depriving it of the economic lifeblood it needs to survive would be tantamount to allowing the City to wither on the vine.

This majority decision presents a challenge to the leadership of the metro communities of the greater Jackson area to develop inter-governmental co-operative activities that improve the infrastructure of the entire area and advance the general welfare of the cooperating people. By appropriate action of their joint governing bodies, the municipalities of the metro area should seek to exercise powers common to them, or seek statutory legislation for such action, to enhance services, facilities, or other projects. Co-operative intergovernmental relationships of all of the metro municipalities engender the improvement of the quality of service for the entire area as most of the workforce comes into City of Jackson to earn their livelihood.

Although revenue considerations constitute one of City of Jackson's most pressing problems at this time, the fact remains that the majority's opinion will also serve to place in jeopardy one of City of Jackson's two remaining paths of growth. The chancellor noted that City of Jackson's ability to expand towards the east, north, northeast, and west have been cut off by surrounding communities, and the majority's opinion places the area to the south/south-west in increasing danger of being cut off as well. It is clear that Byram lies in one of City of Jackson's few remaining potential paths of growth, and this Court noted in *City of Jackson* that it need only be shown that the area to be annexed is, "in a path of growth, not necessarily the most urgent or even the city's primary path of growth." *City of Jackson*, 551 So. 2d at 865.

* * * I find unpersuasive the objectors' argument that the City has no need to expand based on the fact that it is not experiencing a population growth. In previous cases, this Court has allowed annexations in cases in which there was no significant population growth and/or a relatively high percentage of undeveloped land within the existing city limits. * * *

This Court should not permit the annexation without a showing that the citizens in the annexation area would receive value for their tax dollars. * * * In this regard, the chancellor found that the increased taxes that would be imposed on residents in the annexation area would be offset by increased services and a reduction in fire insurance premiums and water rates. As both parties agree, the City of Jackson has the financial ability to make improvements and furnish necessary services. Although the City's past performance in its previous annexed areas has at times been less than exemplary, the evidence does show that City of Jackson has provided numerous services and improvements in annexed areas.

A continuation in City of Jackson's decline will have an adverse effect on the entire metropolitan area, including the proposed annexation area. If the annexation is denied, there will most likely be a renewed effort to incorporate the proposed annexation area which, if successful, would effectively cut off one of the City of Jackson's two remaining paths of growth. In my view, the chancellor properly gave serious consideration to the needs of our capital city in concluding the annexation to be reasonable, and I would affirm her ruling. Accordingly, I dissent.

BANKS, J., joins this opinion.

NOTES AND QUESTIONS

1. *Annexation and Self-Determination.* A central theme in the law of annexation is self-determination in the area sought to be annexed. In roughly half the states that authorize annexation by general law, the annexation of unincorporated land requires the consent of the voters in the area to be annexed. As the *Jackson* case indicates, even where involuntary annexation is permissible, courts may be sensitive to local self-determination by residents on the outskirts of a city in deciding whether a proposed annexation is "reasonable."

The large role played by self-determination in the area to be annexed appears to reflect both a belief that, as a matter of political liberty, the people of an area ought to be able to determine whether that area will be part of a municipal government, and respect for the kinds of concerns that might motivate the residents of an outlying area to oppose becoming part of an adjacent city. As the dissenter in a previous—but successful—annexation effort by Jackson, Mississippi put it:

> I have not seen a decision which adequately explains why cities have the right to grow by absorbing those who do not wish to be absorbed. These hapless souls are not consulted. They are merely selected to provide additional revenues to be expended by those who have been elected by others and for purposes which probably will benefit, primarily, those who took them in. When cities are concerned we abandon the hallowed concept of democracy that the just powers of the government are derived from the consent of the governed. Nations which extend their boundaries without the consent of the occupants of the new territory are condemned as aggressors. Cities are merely vibrant and growing, even if every citizen brought in is screaming in protest.

City of Jackson v. City of Ridgeland, 551 So.2d 861, 869 (Miss.1989). Although some members of the Mississippi Supreme Court may be sympathetic to this view, the court rejected out of hand the suggestion that it require annexation elections. *See* Poole v. City of Pearl, 908 So.2d 728 (Miss. 2005).

Like some of the political theorists discussed in Chapter I, judges in local government boundary cases may be sympathetic to the values of smaller governments:

> [M]any of the people like to live in their small towns where they can know the mayor, city council members and other officials personally, and where they can live their lives, as they see it, relatively free from regulation and have a direct voice in such municipal matters as zoning or the granting of a liquor license.

> Where financial considerations are a primary motive in opposing annexations, frequently they involve a conscious desire to accept fewer municipal services as a trade off for lower taxes. For example, many of the smaller communities, both incorporated and unincorporated, keep taxes rather low by utilizing volunteer fire departments, part-time police forces, septic tanks instead of sewers, no city manager or engineer, etc. From this point of view, the prevention of annexation enables those with limited financial resources better to own their own homes. To such people terms like "metro government" and "annexation" are calls to a holy war of resistance.

Moorman v. Wood, 504 F.Supp. 467, 469 (E.D.Ky.1980). For more discussion of the right to vote in connection with boundary changes generally, see Section D of this chapter.

2. *Annexation and the Central City.* Although self-determination for the people on a city's outskirts plays a leading role in the law of annexation today, that was not always the case. As urban historian Kenneth Jackson has noted, "[w]ithout exception, the adjustment of local boundaries has been the dominant method of population growth in every American city of consequence." Kenneth Jackson, Crabgrass Frontier, *supra,* at 140. In the nineteenth and early twentieth centuries, many states associated their economic growth and prestige with the growth of their large cities, and adopted laws that permitted cities to add new land as urban populations moved beyond the city limits. *See* Jon Teaford, City and Suburb: The Political Fragmentation of Metropolitan America 77 (Johns Hopkins Univ. Press 1979). According to Professor Jackson, "[t]he predominant view in the nineteenth century was the doctrine of forcible annexation. No small territory could be allowed to retard the development of the metropolitan community." Crabgrass Frontier, *supra,* at 147.

As the twentieth century progressed this view changed in many states, particularly in the Northeast and the Midwest, which began to require local approval for new annexations. These changes coincided with other economic, demographic and legal developments which made outlying areas resistant to joining cities and more inclined to preserve their independence. Over time, suburban areas, which in the nineteenth and early twentieth centuries were frequently poorer than the cities, became more affluent relative to the cities. Ethnic and racial differences between cities and suburbs grew. And states developed new local government structures, such as special districts and interlocal agreements, which enabled outlying areas to obtain high quality public services without accepting annexation to the city.

Today, the argument for facilitating city annexation has less to do with the prestige of the state—although the *Byram* case indicates that some members of the Mississippi Supreme Court had special concerns about the state capital—and more about the needs of and fairness to the central city. As one court in North Carolina, whose annexation law allowed involuntary annexation until major statutory revisions were adopted in 2012, put it:

> It is common knowledge and experience that residents of areas adjacent to our cities and towns which are subject to annexation under the laws of our State enjoy a great many city services financed by city taxpayers without paying city property taxes themselves. Most of those outside residents work in the city, shop in the city, use all manner of office facilities in the city, use in-city health care facilities, park and recreational facilities and programs and while doing so use city streets, city law enforcement and fire protection services, city garbage and refuse collection services, city parking facilities and city water and sewer services. They also receive planning, zoning and inspection services from the city. With the possible exception of parking fees, inspection fees, and in some instances fees for the use of recreational facilities and perhaps some other isolated costs, these outside residents pay nothing for these services financed by taxes paid by residents of our cities. Fairness dictates that there comes a time when these residents must join in bearing the costs of those services. . . .

> Annexation brings forth a higher level of debate than perhaps any other activity of municipal government. By the imposition of stringent standards and guidelines and procedural safeguards, the legislature has attempted to ensure fairness in balancing the benefits of city services with the burden of paying for them.

In re Annexation Ordinance #D–21927, 278 S.E.2d 224, 233 (N.C.1981).

Professor Reynolds has argued that "annexation of the fringe would merely confirm the reality that these developments are already a part of the city they surround." *Rethinking Municipal Annexation Powers*, 24 Urb. Law. 247, 257 (1992). Or, as former Albuquerque Mayor David Rusk, put it: "The real city is the total metropolitan area—city and suburb." David Rusk, Cities Without Suburbs 5 (Woodrow Wilson Center Press, 2d ed. 1995).

In his book, Mayor Rusk notes that today most population and employment growth is on the urban fringe. These areas draw people and jobs out of the cities and then attract much of the new growth that comes into a metropolitan area. Rusk asserts that cities need to expand their boundaries in order to benefit from this growth. His research finds that cities that are capable of expanding their boundaries have less concentrated poverty, less racial segregation, and narrower city-suburb income differentials than cities whose boundaries are frozen. For the opposite view, *see* Clayton P. Gillette, Voting With Your Hands: Direct Democracy in Annexation, 78 S.Cal. L. Rev. 835 (2005).

3. *Annexation and City Need.* A central argument in Rusk's book is that because most developed cities lack vacant land to accommodate new residents within their borders, urban growth requires the addition of new territory. In the *Byram* case, the Byram residents argued that Jackson had enough vacant land to accommodate additional population growth within the city. Even if you believe that city needs ought to play a larger role—and suburban preferences a smaller one—in the annexation decision, does the presence of developable land within the city eliminate the growth justification for annexation? Is a city's need for a bigger tax base sufficient by itself to justify annexation over the objections of the residents of the area to be annexed? Does the argument that Jackson and Byram are already part of one economic and social unit—albeit not a legal unit—provide the justification? Or does that argument fail to take into account the Tiebout hypothesis, discussed in Chapter I, that there is a value in having multiple local governments in a metropolitan area?

As a postscript to the Byram resistance to Jackson's annexation, the residents of this unincorporated community filed for incorporation subsequent to the court's ruling in the main case. In 2009, the Mississippi Supreme Court upheld the incorporation, rejecting Jackson's various legal challenges. *See* Jackson v. Byram Incorporators, 16 So.3d 662 (Miss. 2009).

4. *Annexation Without Consent.* A number of states, particularly in the South and the West, do permit at least some cities—typically more populous cities or cities enjoying home rule—to annex territory without consent of the area to be annexed. The power of unilateral annexation may be limited to territory that is contiguous; urban in character or ready for urban development; and within a certain distance of the city. Some states require that a municipality seeking to annex must establish its ability to provide municipal services. *See, e.g.,* Iowa Code § 368.17(4) (municipality must establish that it "will be able to provide to the territory [proposed for annexation] substantial municipal services and benefits not previously enjoyed by such territory"). *See also* Dickinson County v. City Development Committee, 521 N.W.2d 466 (Iowa 1994) (annexation invalid because city failed to establish ability to provide services to territory it sought to annex); Town of Sellersburg v. Proposed Annexation, 677 N.E.2d 608 (Ind.App.1997) (same); City of Pacific v. Metro Development Corp., 922 S.W.2d 59 (Mo.App.1996) (same).

Professor Reynolds, who strongly supports the ability of cities to annex without the consent of people in the area to be annexed, argues that a "vital component[ ] in a statutory scheme granting enhanced municipal annexation abilities" is to assure the extension of municipal services to the annexed area. Reynolds, *supra*, 24 Urb.L. at 280. The concern about whether annexed residents would receive improved municipal services clearly worried the *Byram* court, too.

Legislative developments suggest that the trend is once again away from involuntary annexation. In 2012, the North Carolina legislature changed annexation procedures to provide that a 2/3 negative vote of the people to be annexed would block a municipal annexation. The Tennessee legislature has also adopted limits to what had been broad municipal annexation powers. Though a municipality may still involuntarily annex developed land within its urban growth boundaries, if local opponents can establish in court that the "health, safety, and welfare of the citizens and property owners . . . will not be materially retarded in the absence of such annexation," judicial invalidation will result. *See* Tenn.Code Ann. § 6–58–111(b).

5. *Involuntary Annexation or Consolidation?* Nebraska law takes involuntary annexation further than any other state. As the state's only "city of the metropolitan class," Omaha has the power to annex any adjoining city with a population below 10,000. In the 1990s, Omaha began to consider annexation of nearby Elkhorn and its approximately 8,000 residents. Supporters argued that annexation was necessary to prevent Elkhorn from cutting off Omaha's westward expansion and that the region as a whole would benefit from a strong central city. As Omaha's intentions became known, Elkhorn undertook an aggressive annexation policy with the goal of reaching a population of 10,000 and the immunity from annexation it would bring. In early March 2005, Omaha annexed unincorporated land between Elkhorn and Omaha, as well as the entire territory of Elkhorn. The state supreme court upheld the annexation, *see* Elkhorn v. Omaha, 725 N.W.2d 792 (Neb. 2007), rejecting statutory and constitutional arguments, including the argument that Omaha's actions resulted in a consolidation or merger of two existing municipalities, and that under state law, consolidations require voter approval of both municipalities.

6. *Annexation and the Counties.* Annexation can have a significant impact on the county or subcounty unit—such as a township—in which the annexing city and the annexed area are located. As with a new incorporation, an annexation can reduce—and in some cases effectively eliminate—some county powers or revenues. On the other hand, in some states the impact on the county may be minimal.

In Virginia, the city-county conflict is often acute since municipal incorporation and annexation completely withdraws the affected territory from the surrounding county. As many counties also assumed the role of primary service provider to large areas of highly developed, yet unincorporated, land, annexation could impair the county government's ability to serve the unincorporated remainder. Annexation battles were fierce, expensive, and lengthy. As a result, the Virginia legislature adopted a unique statutory provision conferring complete or partial immunity from annexation on various Virginia counties. Va.Code Ann. § 15.2–3300 et seq. For an explanation of the context in which this statute was passed, and an analysis of the law's provisions, *see* Robert E. Spicer, Jr., Comment, Annexation in Virginia: The 1979 Amendments Usher in a New Era in City-County Relations, 17 U.Rich.L.Rev. 819 (1983); Note, Annual Survey of Developments in Virginia Law—Municipal Corporations, 66 Va.L.Rev. 327 (1980).

Professor Reynolds has suggested that as a quid pro quo for facilitating annexation states should address the financial impact of annexation on counties or townships to assure that they can continue to meet the needs of their remaining territory. She notes that some states require the annexing municipality to pay to the unit of government that is losing territory a decreasing share of its lost revenue over a specified period of time. Reynolds, *supra*, 24 Urb. Law. at 299–301. Do you agree that there is still a need for compensation to other local governments if the annexation's impact on those units is taken into account when the annexation is approved?

DAUGHERTY V. CITY OF CARLSBAD
Court of Appeals of New Mexico
905 P.2d 1120 (1995)

BLACK, J.

Based on a petition by Intervenors, the Carlsbad City Council adopted Ordinance 93–16, which annexed approximately 141 acres of land into the City of Carlsbad (City). Plaintiffs, who also own land within the annexed parcels, filed an appeal in the district court, challenging the annexation. * * *

The facts are undisputed. Intervenors, Richard Forrest, Sr. and Richard Forrest, Jr., Gene R. Taylor, Tommy Wilson, Collett Ryan and Sherry Campbell filed a petition seeking annexation of a tract of land that they owned (Forrest Property). The Forrest Property itself did not touch the City limits and the Intervenors proposed linking their property to the City limits by a twenty-three acre irregular-shaped strip of land owned by Plaintiffs. The combined tracts adjoin the Carlsbad City limits on the west.

The City filed a motion for summary judgment attaching an affidavit of Gary Robertson, a land surveyor, and an assistant to the City Engineer. After setting forth the various City boundaries, he stated that "the Tract annexed by the City Council of the City of Carlsbad on 9/28/93 by Ordinance No. 93–16 shares a common boundary with and is therefore 'Contiguous to' the then existing City of Carlsbad upon a common boundary extending for at least 930.30 feet." Plaintiffs responded to the City's motion and filed a cross motion for summary judgment. Plaintiffs Jesse Rayroux and Louise Tracy filed affidavits in support of their motion. Tracy averred that her land is "unimproved, raw land," and Rayroux stated that his land "is devoted to agricultural purposes." Both stated that, although annexation would subject their lands to City ordinances, neither of them would receive any "economic, commercial, proprietary, or aesthetic advantage by the annexation." They further testified that the land annexed "is not likely to be used by the City to advance any of its governmental functions, or to benefit the City in any economic, commercial, proprietary, or aesthetic, manner." Based on the agreement of both sides, the district court found that there was no issue of material fact. The district court stated that "there exists only an issue of law, as follows: What constitutes 'contiguous' pursuant to 3–7–17 N.M.S.A.(A) 1978." The district court concluded that the annexed tract was contiguous as a matter of law. * * *

Plaintiffs challenge the annexation on the ground that the Forrest Property was not contiguous to the City limits, as required by Section 3–17–7. Plaintiffs argue that the City cannot make the Forrest Property contiguous by annexing the "shoestring" comprised of Plaintiff's property.

* * * In establishing the petition procedure, the Legislature created a process legally distinct from * * * annexation * * * initiated by the municipal government desiring the annexation. * * * In such a context, a neutral third party may well have been thought necessary to protect citizens from the potentially arbitrary abuse of governmental power. The petition method, however, may only be initiated by the owners of property contiguous to the municipality, and not by the city itself. In this situation, there is less danger that the municipality will use its governmental power arbitrarily to obtain what it wants. The Legislature therefore established the city as the arbitrator of what is essentially a political dispute between competing groups of citizens. Under the petition procedure, "the legislature intended to delegate its authority to a legislative body and required a legislative decision-making process—the enactment of an ordinance—to make the decision effective." *Dugger v. City of Santa Fe*, 114 N.M. 47, 52, 834 P.2d 424, 429 (Ct. App.), *writ quashed,* 113 N.M. 744, 832 P.2d 1223 (1992). Therefore, "unlike the two administrative methods, the petition method does not expressly include criteria that, if met, require a municipality to approve an annexation petition." *Id.*

* * * [An annexation initiated by a city is subject to review by an administrative agency—the boundary review commission—which is itself subject to judicial review.] In reviewing a decision of the boundary commission, * * * the court should "determine [w]hether the administrative body acted fraudulently, arbitrarily or capriciously, whether the order was supported by substantial evidence and, generally,

whether the action of the administrative body was within the scope of its authority." * * * The petition process, on the other hand, is not administrative but legislative. *Dugger*, 114 N.M. at 51, 834 P.2d at 428. We "limit judicial review of an ordinance passed pursuant to express legislative authority to the constitutional validity of the statute or its application." *Id.* at 53, 834 P.2d at 430. Therefore, when such an annexation comes up for judicial review, "there is no independent inquiry into the wisdom, policy, or justness of the legislative action." *Id.* The judiciary merely determines whether the municipality has complied with the plain meaning of the legislation and whether the legislation is itself constitutional. * * *

The failure of the New Mexico Legislature to require that petitioners show more than proof of physical contiguity creates a temptation for judicial intervention when annexation might appear to produce poor urban planning or an apparent lack of suitable community cohesiveness. Such intervention, however, deprives the process of predictability and does not produce provably better results than the political process established by our Legislature. * * *

The district court found that the annexed tract in dispute is contiguous to the City. The district court properly refused Plaintiffs' invitation to analyze the economic or political benefits or burdens bestowed upon their land by the annexation.

HARTZ, J., (dissenting)

I respectfully dissent. The law governing municipal annexations requires that annexed territory be contiguous to the municipality. In my view, the contiguity requirement cannot be evaded by means of a sham or subterfuge, and the record in this case establishes that contiguity was accomplished by such means. * * *

The statutory provision at issue is NMSA 1978, Section 3–7–17(A) (Repl. Pamp. 1987), which states:

Whenever a petition:

> (1) seeks the annexation of territory contiguous to a municipality;

> (2) is signed by the owners of a majority of the number of acres in the contiguous territory;

> (3) is accompanied by a map which shall show the external boundary of the territory proposed to be annexed and the relationship of the territory proposed to be annexed to the existing boundary of the municipality; and

(4) is presented to the governing body, the governing body shall by ordinance express its consent to or rejection of the annexation of such contiguous territory.

When an annexation is challenged as being in violation of this provision, I would think that the court's role would be to interpret the statutory language, determine whether the annexation complied with the statutory requirements, and overturn the annexation if it did not comply.

I cannot agree with the apparent view of the majority that these tasks can be avoided by simply characterizing the municipality's decision to annex as "legislative" action. This characterization is a mischaracterization resulting from reading too much into our decision in *Dugger*. * * *

In *Dugger* the city had rejected a petition to annex certain territory. We pointed out that under the petition method of annexation the legislature had not set forth criteria whose satisfaction required the municipality to consent to the annexation. Unlike annexation by the two other statutory methods, which provided that annexation must take place if certain facts were established, the statute governing annexation by petition permitted a municipality to reject the petition for any reason. Because the legislature had imposed no standards governing *rejection* of a petition, it was appropriate to refer to such a rejection as a "political" or "legislative" matter, subject only to review for constitutionality.

But it does not follow that municipal *consent* to a petition for annexation is reviewable only for constitutionality. Although the legislature imposed no restrictions on a municipality's *rejection* of a petition for annexation, it did set standards that must be satisfied before the municipality could *consent* to the petition. The petition must be valid (that is, comply with statutory requirements) before the municipality can consent to it, whereas the validity of the petition is irrelevant if the municipality rejects annexation. Thus, the analysis that led the *Dugger* court to state that the decision to reject a petition is solely a "legislative" or "political" determination does not apply to consent to a petition. *Dugger* had no occasion to consider the scope of review of a municipality's consent to annexation. Nothing in *Dugger* suggests that the courts should ignore specific statutory requirements that must be satisfied before a municipality can consent to a petition for annexation.

* * * The legislature permits annexation only of contiguous territory. We must decide the meaning of the statutory requirement and whether the requirement has been satisfied in this case.

On its face, the contiguity requirement is a straightforward one. I see no reason to give the word "contiguous" a meaning other than its ordinary meaning of "bordering" or "adjacent." My research of the case law has not revealed a special meaning of the word "contiguous" in the context of municipal annexation. In particular, it does not appear that "contiguous" has been generally held to incorporate such notions as "community of interest."

One's initial reaction may be that adoption of this definition ends virtually all dispute regarding application of the statutory requirement. If the annexed territory borders or adjoins the municipality, then presumably the contiguity requirement is met, regardless of any other features of the annexation. But adoption of such an approach could eviscerate the contiguity requirement. This conclusion follows from a consideration of the procedure for annexation by petition.

A municipality may annex territory if the territory is contiguous to the municipality and the owners of a majority of the acreage of the territory sign a petition seeking annexation. * * * What if the owner of a parcel not contiguous to the municipality wishes to be annexed by the municipality and the governing body of the municipality shares in the desire? No problem. Just include in the petition a little bit of land owned by others. The land would be a strip leading from the municipality to the non-contiguous parcel. Even if the owner or owners of the connecting strip oppose the annexation, their total acreage can be kept below the acreage of the non-contiguous parcel simply by making the connecting strip sufficiently narrow. Consequently, the owners of the majority of the acreage to be annexed would favor annexation. Because of this possibility, the contiguity requirement becomes a paper tiger. It imposes no constraint on an annexation if the governing body of the municipality and the owner of the non-contiguous parcel want the annexation to take place.

To avoid such evisceration of the contiguity requirement, the annexation statute must be read as prohibiting an annexation when contiguity is achieved by a sham or subterfuge. There is nothing remarkable in so reading the annexation statute. * * * Several courts apparently have rejected annexations on just this ground. * * *

The "sham" rule prohibits an annexation if what the municipality is really doing is annexing a non-contiguous parcel by using a connecting strip which is included in the annexation solely for the purpose of achieving contiguity. Although application of the rule may sometimes be difficult, there is no reason why application of the rule should involve the courts in municipal policy-making. The issue is not whether there is a *good* municipal purpose for annexing the connecting strip; it is only whether there is a plausible municipal purpose other than achieving contiguity. (I should add, however, that there is no reason to require a municipal purpose if the owners of the connecting strip approve of the annexation. In that event there is no sham or subterfuge: The owners of the connecting strip could petition for annexation; and once their land was annexed, there would be no contiguity problem with annexing the parcel that had been non-contiguous.) * * *

What is remarkable in this case is that Carlsbad has offered absolutely no municipal purpose for annexing the property owned by Plaintiffs. Plaintiffs' affidavits are uncontradicted in their assertions that no purpose is served by annexing their land. * * * Thus, on this record a finding of sham or subterfuge is required. Although remand might now be appropriate to enable the City to show a municipal purpose (assuming that the City could not have anticipated the adoption of a "sham" rule), the majority's decision makes it unnecessary to consider that issue.

NOTES AND QUESTIONS

1. *The Role of the Courts in the Annexation Process.* As with incorporation, the role of the courts in the annexation process ranges from the narrowly ministerial to the broadly discretionary. Where the state statute contains objective and technical requirements—such as number of signatures on a petition or a description of the territory affected—the courts may limit their role to simply determining whether the statutory requirements have been met. In State ex rel. Pan American Production Co. v. Texas City, 303 S.W.2d 780, 782 (Tex.1957), app. dismissed, 355 U.S. 603 (1958), the court stated that approach quite clearly: "[T]he conclusion of the petitioners here that the annexation ordinance was unreasonable and arbitrary is only to say that it was unreasonable and arbitrary because the land was not suitable, and had no relation to the City's needs, and it was for the purpose only of acquiring additional revenue and could afford no benefit to the owners of the property annexed. The decisions of this State have repeatedly held that such facts do not warrant intervention or review by the courts." *See also* Paulding County v. City of Hiram, 240 S.E.2d 71, 74 (Ga.1977) ("judicial oversight is not appropriately exercised where the annexation statute specifies all of the circumstances governing annexation"). *But cf.* Cottonwood City Electors v. Salt Lake County Board of Commissioners, 499 P.2d 270 (Utah 1972) (County Commission has discretion to deny incorporation petition that satisfies the only criteria—population and petition signatures—mentioned in the statute).

In many states, however, annexation statutes require courts to play a more substantial role. The Mississippi statute requires the court hearing the annexation petition to determine whether annexation is "reasonable and is required by the public convenience and necessity . . ." Miss.St.Ann. § 21–1–33. As you saw in the *Byram* case, however, the Mississippi courts have identified twelve "indicia of reasonableness," in much the same way as a statute might dictate. The Mississippi Supreme Court rejected a challenge to the statute, upholding the reasonableness standard against the claim that the law was unconstitutionally vague. *See* In re Extension of the Boundaries of Hattiesburg, 840 So.2d 69 (Miss. 2003). It later refused to add additional criteria to the twelve indicia, stressing that it was a matter for legislative action. *See* In re City of Brookhaven, 957 So.2d 382 (Miss. 2007). Over the past decade, the legislature has considered approximately a dozen proposals to change state annexation law, but none has been adopted. As a result, the Mississippi courts continue their application of the twelve factors, which results in lengthy qualitative assessments of local conditions and predictions about the future. *See, e.g.,* In re Boundaries of Biloxi, 109 So.3d 529 (Miss. 2013), in which the court divided a parcel of land into three smaller pieces, allocating it between the annexing city and the objecting county.

In Virginia, an annexation is considered by a special annexation court which determines "the necessity for and expediency of annexation." Va. Code Ann. § 15.2–3209. Some state courts have developed "the rule of reason" to engage in more searching review of municipal annexations, to prevent, in their words, "arbitrary, unreasonable, unjust, and unnecessary" annexations. Portland General Electric Co. v. City of Estacada, 241 P.2d 1129, 1135 (Or.1952). Wisconsin, the leading proponent of the rule of reason, has identified three substantive criteria that must be met before the reviewing court can uphold the challenged annexation as proper: "(1) reasonable boundaries, (2) demonstrable need for the property, and (3) no indication that the City otherwise abused its discretion." Town of Delavan v. City of Delavan, 500 N.W.2d 268, 276 (Wis.1993). Still other state courts seem to adopt a middle ground in which they apply a "fairly debatable" standard to evaluate whether the annexing unit acted within the scope of its delegated authority. Birmingham v. Mead Corp., 372 So.2d 825, 828 (Ala.1979).

In *Daugherty*, the New Mexico Supreme Court indicated that the level of judicial review would vary according to the type of annexation in question: Annexations initiated by a city would receive rigorous review but courts would be highly deferential to an annexation initiated by landowners in the area to be annexed. In the second situation, the court found that "there is less danger that the municipality will use its governmental power arbitrarily to obtain what it wants." That may be true, but doesn't a landowner-initiated annexation create the danger that some landowners will use the governmental power of annexation "arbitrarily to obtain" what they want but what others in the area do not want? Should the level of review depend on whether the annexation is initiated by the annexing city or by landowners in the annexation area?

2.   *Contiguity: Purpose and Meaning.* Nearly all states limit municipal annexation powers to land that is contiguous to—that is, physically touching—the annexing city. The rare exception is North Carolina which permits annexation of noncontiguous land within three miles of the city, with the consent of the residents of the annexed area. Contiguity is a nearly universal precondition for municipal incorporation as well. It may be easier for a local government to provide services to contiguous territory, and people who live in contiguous territory may be more likely to "share the sense of community that presumably explains the reasons for gravitating to a common locality." Clayton P. Gillette, Expropriation and Institutional Design in State and Local Government Law, 80 Va.L.Rev. 625, 672–73 (1994).

However, as *Daugherty* indicates, "[t]echnical or literal contiguity . . . can be realized through the most tenuous attachments to an annexed area." *Id.* at 673. Local government lawyers refer to strip, barbell, balloon, stem, spoke, spoke and stem, shoestring, saucepan, cherry stem, or flag annexations to describe the shapes that result when a city or landowners use narrow corridors of land to link the annexing city to relatively distant areas seeking to be annexed. State courts are divided over whether the statutory contiguity requirement is satisfied by technical continuity. *Carlsbad* and Paulding County v. City of Hiram, 240 S.E.2d 71, 74 (Ga.1977), found that technical contiguity was enough. Other courts invalidate annexations that are contiguous only in a technical sense. *See, e.g.*, Sarpy v. Papillion, 765 N.W.2d 456 (Neb. 2009) ("arms" of the proposed annexation were sufficiently contiguous for annexation, while "tails" were not); Cornhusker Pub. Power Dist. v. City of Schuyler, 699 N.W.2d 352 (Neb. 2005) (narrow thirty-foot strip does not meet statutory requirement that land be "substantially adjacent"); In re De-Annexation from the City of Seminole, 102 P.3d 120 (Okla. 2004) (three-foot strip not sufficient to establish contiguity); People ex rel. Cherry Valley Fire Protection Dist. v. City of Rockford, 256 N.E.2d 653, 658 (Ill.App.1970) (annexed land must have a "substantial common boundary; a common border of reasonable length or width; or must touch or adjoin one another in a reasonable substantial physical sense").

Some state legislatures have attempted to deal with the problem by defining contiguity in their annexation laws. *See, e.g.*, Ariz.Rev.Stat.Ann. § 9–471(H) (annexed territory is contiguous only if (i) it adjoins the external boundary of the annexing city or town for at least three hundred feet; (ii) is at least two hundred feet wide at all points; and (iii) the distance from the point where the annexor's boundary adjoins the annexed territory to the furthest point of the annexed territory is no more than twice the width of the annexed territory); Nev.Rev.Stat.Ann. § 268.618 (annexed land is contiguous if at least 15% of its boundaries is coterminous with the annexor's boundaries).

3. *Annexation Boundaries and the Manufacture of Consent.* One reason strip annexations may occur is that state law makes annexation contingent on the consent of the annexation area. Indeed, concern about the manipulation of the boundaries of a proposed annexation is not limited to whether the boundaries violate contiguity. "The issue of arbitrary boundary-drawing generally arises when landowners or electors opposed to annexation are excluded from the proposed area so as to ensure the success of the annexation. . . . However certain strategic inclusions of property can also result in the drawing of an arbitrary boundary." Town of Menasha v. City of Menasha, 488 N.W.2d 104, 108–09 (Wis.App.1992). Some courts are relatively deferential to proposed annexation boundaries, but others are not. In In re Petition for Annexation of 948.885 Acres, 665 N.E.2d 1165 (Ohio App.1995), the court concluded that a statutory requirement that an annexation serve "the general good" "must involve more than a determination of what a simple majority of the owners in the annexation area desire." *Id.* at 1169. On that basis, the court invalidated an annexation petition although

the petition had been signed by the requisite percentage of property owners. The supreme court of Alabama similarly invalidated a proposed annexation by the city of Birmingham when it found that "[t]here can be no doubt that Birmingham arranged the boundary lines and predetermined the result of the election by eliminating most of the opposition." Birmingham v. Community Fire District, 336 So.2d 502, 504 (Ala. 1976). Is such annexation gerrymandering a problem? Is there reason to share Professor Gillette's concern about the ability of courts to distinguish between bad and good boundaries? What is wrong with boundaries that include supporters and exclude opponents of annexation? Is this simply another way of achieving the "community of interest" which is considered so desirable in the incorporation context?

4.   *The Prior Jurisdiction Rule.* In some instances, two or more nearby municipal governments will have annexation designs on the same tract of land. In most states, such disputes are resolved by the so-called "prior jurisdiction rule," which rewards the municipality that initiated annexation proceedings first. *See, e.g.,* City of Tualatin v. City of Durham, 439 P.2d 624 (Ore.1968); *see generally,* 2 Eugene McQuillan, Municipal Corporations § 7.22a (3d ed. 1987) (discussion of jurisdictional priority); Joni W. Crichlow, Comment, Competitive Annexation Among Municipalities: North Carolina Adopts the Prior Jurisdiction Rule, 63 N.C.L.Rev. 1260 (1985). Do the advantages of this clear, objective rule outweigh the potential disadvantages of rewarding quick action? The supreme court of Mississippi abolished the prior jurisdiction rule as "antiquated" in In the Matter of the Enlargement and Extension of the Municipal Boundaries of the City of D'Iberville, 867 So.2d 241 (Miss. 2004).

5.   *Municipal Refusal to Annex.* In *Daugherty,* the New Mexico Supreme Court relied in part on an earlier New Mexico case, Dugger v. City of Santa Fe, 834 P.2d 424 (N.M.Ct.App.1992), which upheld a city's absolute discretion to refuse to annex, even though the annexation had been proposed by the residents or landowners seeking to be annexed and satisfied all other statutory criteria. Municipal authority to decline to annex is well established. Indiana, however, authorizes court-ordered annexation even without the consent of a municipality:

> The court . . . shall order the proposed annexation to take place only if the evidence introduced by the parties establishes that: (1) essential municipal services and facilities are not available to the residents of the territory sought to be annexed; (2) the municipality is physically and financially able to provide municipal services to the territory sought to be annexed; (3) the population density of the territory sought to be annexed is at least three (3) persons per acre; and (4) the territory sought to be annexed is contiguous to the municipality. If the evidence does not establish all four of the preceding factors, the court shall deny the petition and dismiss the proceeding.

Ind. Code Ann. § 36–4–3–5 (Burns 1981 & Supp.1991).

In an article urging the statutory adoption of broad municipal annexation powers, Professor Reynolds endorsed the Indiana legislature's decision that the power to compel annexation should be available both to municipal governments and to owners of contiguous, urbanized territory. In her view, this assures that urban land comes within the jurisdiction of a municipal government and provides a needed check on what would otherwise be unlimited municipal discretion to refuse to annex urbanized land that may be in need of municipal services. Reynolds, *supra*, 24 Urb. Law. at 284–86.

As others have documented, if municipalities have absolute discretion to refuse to annex, they may use that power to exclude from their borders outlying territory inhabited by low-income or minority residents. *See* Symposium, The White Curtain: Racially Disadvantaging Local Government Boundary Practices, 54 U.Det.J.Urb.L. 681 (1977). Indeed, the term "municipal underbounding" has been used to describe what occurs when communities, particularly but not exclusively in the South, expand their borders but avoid including communities of color on the urban fringe. *See* Charles S. Aiken, Race as a Factor in Municipal Underbounding, 77 Annals Ass'n Am. Geographers 564 (1987); Daniel T. Lister, et al., Municipal Underbounding? Annexation and Racial Exclusion in Small Southern Towns, 72 Rural Soc. 47 (2007). This practice can create poor, unincorporated minority enclaves with little or no access to basic public services, such as water, sewers, or police protection. *See, e.g.*, James Dao, Ohio Town's Water at Last Runs Past a Color Line, N.Y. Times, Feb. 17, 2004, at A2 (describing Zanesville, Ohio's longstanding refusal to provide water to nearby African American community). *See also* Shaila Dewan, In County Made Rich by Golf, Some Enclaves are Left Behind, N.Y. Times, June 7, 2005, at A1. This may occur even when the town has extraterritorial regulatory authority over these unincorporated areas. *See* U.N.C. Center for Civil Rights, Invisible Fences: Municipal Underbounding in Southern Moore County (2006).

6. *The Role of Administrative Agencies.* In a number of states, administrative agencies have been created to review incorporations, annexations and other forms of local boundary changes. These boundary review commissions are generally reactive in nature. They lack the power to initiate annexations, but they can veto annexations initiated by municipalities or petitioning landowners. Moreover, boundary commissions typically do not displace other mechanisms, such as the referendum of voters living in the area to be annexed, designed to protect local landowners. Rather, they add another step in the annexation process. *See, e.g.*, Alaska Stat. § 29.06.040(c)(1) (annexation approved by commission must still obtain majority vote of residents in area to be annexed); Or.Rev.Stat. § 199.505 (annexation approved by commission must be submitted to vote upon petition of 10% of landowners); Minn.Stat.Ann. § 414.031.5 (election required unless annexation proceeding was "initiated by . . . a majority of the property owners within the area to be annexed"); Cal.Gov't Code § 57078 (commission must terminate annexation proceedings if a majority of voters or owners protest).

The commissions provide greater assurance that the interests of the entire area affected by an annexation will be taken into account, but they leave in place the principle of local consent to boundary change. In Interlake Sporting Assoc. v. Washington State Boundary Review Board, 146 P.3d 904 (Wash. 2006), the court invalidated the review board's proposed annexation as having attempted an improper end run around the statutory requirement of voter approval for most annexations.

7.   *When Does a Carrot Become a Stick?* The owners of approximately 515 acres in the outskirts of Dubuque, Iowa, approached the city for annexation. Voluntary annexation proceedings were not possible, because the annexation of those 515 acres would create islands of unincorporated property, which is prohibited by state law. As a result, Dubuque began to pursue the annexation of the approximately 700 acres that constitute the islands. In an effort to entice the property owners, Dubuque offered some benefits: (1) a five-year partial exemption from property taxes; (2) reduced sewer hook-up charges; (3) reduced water connection charges; and (4) a promise to consider road widening and improvements.

Dubuque sent a letter offering those terms to each property owner, explaining that only those who agreed to annex would be entitled to the benefits, and establishing a six-day period for the owners' response. Twenty-one property owners signed the agreement. That left eight owners of about 65 acres of land, all of whom then turned to the nearby town of Asbury and petitioned for annexation. Asbury agreed and filed for voluntary annexation with the City Development Board, a state administrative agency with jurisdiction over annexation petitions. About two weeks later, Dubuque filed a petition for annexation of the entire 700 acres. The City Development Board directed the cities to work towards a compromise, but none was forthcoming. The Board then dismissed Asbury's petition, because it would have created several prohibited islands.

Dubuque's petition for annexation included the land of the non-consenting owners. Under Iowa's "80/20 law," however, the petition still qualified as a "voluntary annexation." Under that provision, a city-initiated annexation will be considered voluntary if the owners of at least 80% of the property consent, and if the inclusion of the non-consenting property is necessary to avoid creating an island, or to create more uniform boundaries. The Iowa Supreme Court upheld the annexation by Dubuque and rejected the challenges of the non-consenting owners, *see* City of Dubuque v. Iowa Dist. Court for Dubuque County, 725 N.W.2d 449 (Iowa 2006). What arguments would you have made?

2.   ANNEXATION AGREEMENTS

The following case involves a challenge to an Illinois law that specifically authorizes annexation agreements between municipalities and the owners of non-contiguous land. The statute was adopted by the legislature in response to the Illinois Supreme Court's holding in *Village of Lisle v. Action Outdoor Advertising Co.*, 544 N.E.2d 836 (Ill.App.1989), which had limited the territorial reach of annexation agreements to land that the municipality could actually annex at the moment the agreement was entered into, that is, land contiguous to the municipality. The Illinois law now provides in relevant part:

> § 11–15.1–1. The corporate authorities of any municipality may enter into an annexation agreement with one or more of the owners of record of land in unincorporated territory. That land may be annexed to the municipality in the manner provided in Article 7 at the time the land is or becomes contiguous to the municipality. The agreement shall be valid and binding for a period of not to exceed 20 years from the date of its execution. Lack of contiguity to the municipality of property that is the subject of an annexation agreement does not affect the validity of the agreement whether approved by the corporate authorities before or after the effective date of this amendatory Act of 1990.

> § 11–15.1–2.1. Annexation agreement; municipal jurisdiction.(a) * * * [P]roperty that is the subject of an annexation agreement adopted under this Division is subject to the ordinances, control, and jurisdiction of the annexing municipality in all respects the same as property that lies within the annexing municipality's corporate limits.

The next case involves a legal challenge to the revised statute.

VILLAGE OF CHATHAM V. COUNTY OF SANGAMON

Supreme Court of Illinois
837 N.E.2d 29 (Ill.2005)

JUSTICE FREEMAN delivered the opinion of the court:

At issue is whether the Village of Chatham, Illinois, or the County of Sangamon, Illinois, has zoning and building code jurisdiction over unincorporated lands that are subject to annexation agreements between the property owners and the Village. * * *

Various persons who owned property in unincorporated Sangamon County reached agreements with the Village for the future annexation of their properties. The property owners and associated contractors obtained permits from the Village and began construction upon the properties. On March 8, 2002, the County sent letters to the property owners and the Village regarding the construction, asserting building code jurisdiction over the properties. In letters to the property owners, the County's zoning and building administrator noted that the County had not issued construction permits to the owners and requested that the owners contact the County as soon as possible. In the letter to the Village, the County stated that it had noticed construction taking place in areas "pre-annexed" to the Village, where the property owners had not obtained building permits from the County. The County asked the Village to refer to the County all applications for building permits in unincorporated areas and all questions regarding zoning of unincorporated areas.

In response, the Village filed an action for declaratory judgment. The Village sought a determination that the Village, and not the County, has zoning and building code jurisdiction in areas subject to annexation agreements with the Village, and an injunction preventing the County from making demands on contractors and interfering with the Village's annexation agreements. * * *

[The trial court granted summary judgment for the Village, and the appellate court affirmed.] We now affirm the judgment of the appellate court. * * *

B. *Police Power*

The County * * * maintains that division 15.1 is an invalid exercise of the police power. The County notes that "while lands cannot be annexed to a municipality until they are contiguous to the corporate boundaries of the municipality, the Division permits unlimited power of a municipality to assert zoning and building code and other jurisdiction * * * over lands covered by an agreement that may be many miles and hundreds of miles away from the municipality, thus defeating the sound land use principles of unity and continuity in the extension of corporate jurisdiction." The County argues "the Division will permit a landowner to bargain with unlimited municipalities across the State for the best zoning deal available, even though annexation may never be able to occur as a practical matter, thus permitting municipalities with no valid government interest in the zoning to bargain away the public interest of those legitimately concerned with the zoning of the lands." The County concludes that division 15.1 does not bear a reasonable relationship to public health, safety, morals and general welfare or convenience.

[The court applied the standard rational basis review, presumption of validity, and deference to legislative judgment to conclude that the statute was within the scope of the police power. *See City of Carbondale v. Brewster*, 398 N.E.2d 829 (Ill. 1979).]

* * *

Also instructive is this court's opinion in *City of Belleville*, 84 Ill.2d 1, 48 Ill.Dec. 723, 417 N.E.2d 125. As discussed above, the court invalidated several ordinances which purported to annex property because the statute at issue required contiguity at the time the petitions for annexation were filed. In doing so, the court observed:

"We realize that this construction requires a municipality desirous of annexing several parcels, only one of which is contiguous to the municipality, to annex each parcel at separate times. In some situations this requirement may appear cumbersome. We can only conclude that the General Assembly has imposed this limitation to prevent a municipality from conducting a wholesale annexation of successive parcels of property where each parcel, other than the first, is not contiguous to, and is more remote from, the original corporate limits. Since this is peculiarly a legislative judgment, we will not interfere with it." *City of Belleville,* 84 Ill.2d at 11, 48 Ill.Dec. 723, 417 N.E.2d 125.

Although the court invalidated the ordinances which purported to annex property, the court upheld the validity of an ordinance which authorized an annexation agreement for *property noncontiguous to the municipality,* but did not attempt to annex the property. Thus, the *City of Belleville* court recognized that the legislature has broad discretion to determine what the interests of the public welfare require and what measures are necessary to secure such interest. Also, the court determined that the legislature may authorize an annexation agreement for property which is noncontiguous to a municipality. * * *

We do not believe that the legislature has abused its discretion in determining what the interests of the public welfare require and what measures are necessary to secure such interest. The orderly development of municipalities is a matter clearly impacting upon the public health, safety, and welfare. Further, as this court observed in *City of Belleville,* 84 Ill.2d at 12, 48 Ill.Dec. 723, 417 N.E.2d 125: "The purpose of the contiguity requirement is to permit the natural and gradual extension of municipal boundaries to areas which 'adjoin one another in a reasonably substantial physical sense.'" That purpose will be met fully, however, at *the time the property is annexed.* Division 15.1 clearly requires contiguity for effective annexation of property. Section 11–15.1–1 provides: "That land may be annexed to the municipality in the manner provided in Article 7 at the time the land is or becomes contiguous to the municipality." 65 ILCS 5/11–15.1–1 (West 2002). Article 7 also requires contiguity of property being annexed. *See* 65 ILCS 5/7–1–8 (West 2002).

The County expresses strong disagreement with *the timing utilized by the legislature.* The legislature has determined that a municipality may exercise certain jurisdiction over property which is subject to an annexation agreement as of *the time the agreement is entered into,* rather than *the time of annexation.* This is a determination, however, which is best left to the discretion of the legislature in the exercise of its police power. We see no reason to reconsider our decisions in *Meegan,* 52 Ill.2d 354, 288 N.E.2d 423, and *City of Belleville,* 84 Ill.2d 1, 48 Ill.Dec. 723, 417 N.E.2d 125, and to countermand the legislature's determination of the interests of the public welfare.

NOTES AND QUESTIONS

1. *Annexation Agreements.* In many states, either through the adoption of express state enabling legislation or by judicial recognition of local regulatory discretion, local governments are empowered to negotiate the terms under which annexation will occur. Known generally as annexation agreements, these devices allow the city and landowner to reach a particularized, parcel-sensitive agreement about aspects of development that might otherwise be beyond the scope of the government's regulatory powers. In a typical annexation agreement, both the owner of the land to be annexed and the annexing government make specific promises respecting the land's status and development upon annexation. The government may promise to rezone the annexed property, to provide stipulated city services, or to give tax or other fiscal incentives. In exchange, the landowner/developer will serve the city's interest by promising, for instance, to provide funds for a local school district, to pay the capital costs of certain city infrastructure, or to waive its tax-exempt status. Some state courts have invalidated annexation agreements as an unlawful contracting away of the police power, *see, e.g.,* Louisville v. Fiscal Court of Jefferson County, 623 S.W.2d 219 (Ky.1981), but judicial acceptance of the annexation agreement as a proper exercise of local discretionary control is the more usual response. *See, e.g.,* Geralnes B.V. v. City of Greenwood Village, 583 F.Supp. 830 (D.Colo.1984); City of Leeds v. Town of Moody, 319 So.2d 242 (Ala.1975); Perl-Mack Enters. v. City & County of Denver, 568 P.2d 468 (Colo.1977); Beshore v. Town of Bel Air, 206 A.2d 678 (Md.1965); In re Joint Resolution of Watertown, 375 N.W.2d 582 (Minn.Ct.App.1985); Derrenger v. City of Billings, 691 P.2d 1379 (Mont.1984); Miller v. City of Port Angeles, 691 P.2d 229 (Wash.App.1984); Town of Brockway v. City of Black River Falls, 702 N.W.2d 418 (Wis. App. 2005). The opinion of the Colorado Supreme Court in City of Colorado Springs v. Kitty Hawk Dev. Co., 392 P.2d 467 (1964), exemplifies the dominant pragmatic attitude about annexation agreements:

> A municipality is under no legal obligation in the first instance to annex contiguous territory, and may reject a petition for annexation for no reason at all. It follows then that if the municipality elects to accept such territory solely as a matter of its discretion, it may impose such conditions by way of agreement as it sees fit. If the party seeking annexation does not wish to annex under the conditions imposed, he is free to withdraw his petition to annex and remain without the city. Annexation can take place only when the minds of the city and the owners of the land contiguous to the city agree that the property shall be annexed and upon the terms upon which such annexation can be accomplished.

Id. at 472.

California, in addition to Illinois, has enacted formal substantive and procedural guidelines for the negotiation of annexation agreements. *See, e.g.,* Illinois (65 ILCS 5/11–15.1–1 et seq.), and California (Cal.Gov't Code

§§ 65864 et seq.). Is the need for local discretion better served with general statutory requirements?

2. *Annexation "in all but name?"* In Holt Civic Club v. City of Tuscaloosa, 439 U.S. 60 (1978), examined in Chapter II, the Supreme Court rejected the claim that the city's exercise of extraterritorial jurisdiction improperly denied the non-residents of their right to vote. In footnote 8 of that opinion, though, the Court was careful to note that it was not dealing with a situation "in which a city has annexed outlying territory in all but name, and is exercising precisely the same governmental powers over residents of surrounding unincorporated territory as it does over those residing within its corporate limits." Do the residents of the land subject to Chatham's annexation agreement have a one person, one vote challenge to the Illinois law's extension of broad governmental powers over land not currently within the municipality's jurisdiction? Note that the law states that land involved in an annexation agreement "is subject to the ordinances, control, and jurisdiction of the annexing municipality in all respects the same as property that lies within the annexing municipality's corporate limits."

3. *Parade of Horribles or Realistic Concern?* In the main case, the county argued that the statute would make it possible for a city to enter into an annexation agreement with landowners whose land was many, indeed hundreds, of miles away from the municipality's border. Is the court's response to that concern satisfactory? Is the political process itself now the only check? If so, will that be satisfactory? For instance, what if a city, in need of a new landfill, enters into an annexation agreement with a landowner who owns a large tract 15 or 20 miles away in the middle of rural, unincorporated territory. Under the statute, can't the city zone the land to allow the construction of the landfill without consideration of the county's interests and/or its zoning regulations? The result in the *Chatham* case seems contrary to two important policies articulated in the Illinois Supreme Court's earlier opinion in *Lisle*: (1) "the fundamental notion of a municipal corporation is that of unity and continuity, not separated or segregated areas;" and (2) annexation should further "the encouragement of expanding urban areas and to do so uniformly, economically, efficiently, and fairly . . ." *Village of Lisle*, 544 N.E.2d at 839.

3. OTHER FORMS OF BOUNDARY CHANGE

Other forms of municipal boundary change include consolidation (or merger) of two or more municipalities; detachment (or deannexation or secession) of land from an existing municipality; and disincorporation of a municipality. None of these changes is very common. In the 1980s, there were just 34 mergers of incorporated local units, and in the first half of the 1990s an additional 34 mergers were reported—out of a total of more than 19,000 municipal governments. *See* Joel Miller, Boundary Changes, 1990–1995, in International City Management Association, Municipal Year Book 1997 at 38. These consolidations included two mergers of a city with a county as well as the mergers of cities, or villages, with each other. Consolidations, like incorporations and annexations, may result from general state enabling legislation, in which case they typically require the separate consent of both pre-existing municipalities as well as an agreement of the consolidated municipality to assume the debts and liabilities of its predecessors. More commonly than incorporations or mergers, a consolidation may also result from a special state legislative act in which case the separate consents of the affected municipalities—or municipality and county—are not required. The role of consolidation, especially city-county consolidations, in the governance of metropolitan areas will be considered more fully in Chapter V.

Disincorporation (or dissolution) is only slightly more common than consolidation, but its consequences can be much more extreme. More than 130 municipalities have dissolved since 2000, usually for financial reasons. *See* Michelle Wilde Anderson, *Dissolving* Cities, 121 Yale L.J. 1364 (2012). These actions typically involve very small communities. Disincorporation may result in the surrounding county or township assuming greater responsibilities in the area of the former municipality, or in annexation by an adjacent municipality. Disincorporation may be contingent on some provision for payment of the former municipality's debts and obligations. *See, e.g.,* Mont.Code Ann. § 7–2–4916; N.M.Stat.Ann. § 3–4–4.

Detachments—also known as deannexations, disconnections, or secessions—are more common than consolidations or disincorporations, although still much less common than annexations. In the period from 1980 through 1986, the land area involved in detachments was about 4.4% of the land area involved in annexations, and the population affected was about 1,800 persons annually, or less than one percent of the population in annexed areas. *See* Joel C. Miller, Municipal Annexation and Border Change, in Municipal Year Book 1988, at 59–60. Secessions are typically initiated by residents or landowners in the area that would like to secede from a city, although a detachment may result from the decision of a city to release land from its control. *See, e.g.,* Lee v. City of Villa Rica, 449 S.E.2d 295 (Ga.1994).

Most secessions involve only modest losses of territory from relatively small communities. In the 1990s, however, there were calls for secession in substantial portions of some of the nation's largest cities, including the borough of Staten Island in New York City and the San Fernando Valley in Los Angeles. *See, e.g.,* Richard Briffault, Voting Rights, Home Rule, and Metropolitan Governance: The Secession of Staten Island as a Case Study in the Dilemmas of Local Self-Determination, 92 Colum.L.Rev. 775, 777 (1992). The New York legislature went so far as to authorize a referendum on Staten Island to determine the extent of sentiment for secession. When more than 80% of Staten Island voters expressed support for secession, the state created a charter commission to draft a charter for an independent city of Staten Island. Staten Islanders eventually approved the charter by an overwhelming vote. Other New York City residents were not allowed to participate in the referendum, and the City of New York announced its opposition to the secession. The state has, so far, declined to authorize independence for the borough without the consent of New York City.

In Southern California, the San Fernando Valley, Hollywood and the Harbor Area attempted to secede from the City of Los Angeles. The Local Agency Formation Commission (LAFCO) for Los Angeles County, which oversees the secession and incorporation process, concluded that Hollywood and the San Fernando Valley met the statutory and financial requirements of secession. Gerald Frug, Is Secession from the City of Los Angeles a Good Idea?, 49 UCLA L. Rev. 1783 (2002); see also Cal. Gov't Code §§ 56650–56815 (providing the mechanism for secession, including the requirement that all secessions be revenue neutral for the ceding municipality). One study found that the revenue-neutral provision, which requires that newly incorporated areas compensate the former government for any losses in tax revenue, would have forced the San Fernando Valley to pay Los Angeles $68 million a year. Patty McCormac, The Price of Cityhood, San Diego Union-Tribune, July 27, 2003 at N1. The San Fernando Valley and Hollywood secession questions were on the November 2002 ballot for all Los Angeles County voters. In order for secession to succeed, voters in both the area hoping to secede and in Los Angeles as a whole would have to approve. Valley residents wishing to secede prevailed in the Valley by a slim margin of 50.7% of the vote, but Hollywood residents voted against secession, and Los Angeles voters overwhelmingly rejected both secession proposals. Sue Fox & Patrick McGreevy, After Defeat at the Polls, Valley Cityhood Leaders Consider Strategies and Take Heart in Local Win, L.A. Times, Nov. 7, 2002 at B1. Although the Valley lost its bid for secession, the campaign did put a new emphasis on service delivery issues in the area and on the need for the City to decentralize government in certain areas. Id.

Secession raises many of the issues posed by incorporation and annexation—indeed, secession is often the first step in a two-step process in which, following detachment, the territory will either incorporate as a new municipality or seek annexation to an existing city. See, e.g., Carlyn v. City of Akron, 726 F.2d 287 (6th Cir.1984); Moorman v. Wood, 504 F.Supp. 467 (E.D.Ky.1980); West Point Island Civic Ass'n v. Township Comm., 255 A.2d 237 (N.J.1969). Like incorporation or annexation, a secession may be driven by a dispute over zoning, taxes, or services, or by the sense that a neighborhood is a distinctive community that ought to have its own government rather than be a part of the larger municipality.

In general, municipalities have little or no protection from state legislation authorizing secession. *See, e.g.*, Kel-Kan Inv. Corp. v. Village of Greenwood, 428 So.2d 401 (La.1983); City of Freemont v. Kotas, 781 N.W.2d 456, 461(Neb. 2010) (because detachment is a matter of statewide concern, local city council found to be without power to enact local ordinance). But state laws may require a decision-maker, such as a court considering a secession petition, to give special attention to the impact of the secession on the seceded-from municipality. Illinois, for example, prohibits disconnection if it shall "result in the isolation of any part of the municipality from the remainder of the municipality," "unreasonably disrupt[ ]" the municipality's "growth prospects and plan and zoning ordinances," cause "substantial disruption . . . to existing municipal service facilities," or cause the municipality to be "unduly harmed through loss of tax revenue in the future." 65 ILCS 5/7–3–6. Of course, as the next two cases indicate, statutes or judicial rules providing that the impact of a secession on the existing municipality be taken into account do not determine how a court will balance the benefit to a seceding area against the harm to the municipality that would lose territory in a secession.

HARRIS TRUST & SAVINGS BANK V. VILLAGE OF BARRINGTON HILLS

Supreme Court of Illinois
549 N.E.2d 578 (Ill.1989)

MORAN, C.J.

Harris Trust & Savings Bank, Faith Lutheran Church of Meadowdale, Caryl C. Wilder, Jonathan T. Wilder and Phillip E. Bash (collectively, plaintiffs) originally filed a petition in the circuit court of Cook County pursuant to section 7–3–6 of the Illinois Municipal Code to disconnect certain property from the defendant, the village of Barrington Hills (village). * * * Following a bench trial, the plaintiffs' petition was denied because the trial court found that disconnecting the property would unreasonably disrupt the growth prospects and plan and zoning ordinances of the village. Plaintiffs appealed and the appellate court reversed * * *. The village's petition for leave to appeal was allowed and the City of Chicago, City of Elgin, Village of Long Grove, Lake County and Illinois Municipal League were granted leave to file briefs as amici curiae * * * in support of the village. * * *

The village covers nearly 27 square miles, 25% of which is forest preserves and other permanent open space, and over 90% of the village, including the preserves and open spaces, is zoned R–1 (single-family residence district), which requires a minimum lot size of five acres. Plaintiffs are the owners of record of approximately 95 acres situated on the village's western limit at its border with Carpentersville. The property, resembling an inverted "L," is located on the south side of Helm Road about a quarter of a mile east of Route 25. It has 1,800 feet of frontage on Helm Road, a maximum depth of 2,600 feet, and is surrounded on the north, south and west by Carpentersville. To the east are three lots of five acres or more and the Helm Woods Forest Preserve, which is owned by the Kane County Forest Preserve District. The Dundee Township Park District also owns a park that is contiguous with the parcel's southeast corner. * * * The parcel is zoned R-1 and is used for farming, and includes three houses, a church and parsonage.

At trial both sides presented expert witnesses. Plaintiffs' experts were John Coleman and Steven Lenet. Coleman, a realtor and real estate appraiser, stated the impact of disconnection would be minimal because the residential properties to the east were all developed and the Kane County forest preserve would not be affected at all. * * *

Lenet, a land-use consultant, testified that disconnection would not unreasonably disrupt the plan or zoning ordinances nor would it unreasonably disrupt the village's growth prospects, because under the current zoning only 14 or 15 lots could be developed. * * *

[Donald] Klein, executive director of the Barrington Area Council of Governments, said disconnection was simply a way of avoiding the planning and zoning process. He said disconnection would unreasonably disrupt: the village's growth prospects, because it would fragment its western edge; the planning ordinance, because planning implies continuity and disconnection would upset that continuity; and the zoning ordinance, because disconnection would fragment the village limits. * * *

[Lane] Kendig, a land-use consultant, stated disconnection would unreasonably disrupt the village's growth prospects because it would remove the property from the village, thereby making it unavailable for village growth, and would undermine the land market in the village. He said that disconnection would unreasonably disrupt the village's plan because it would alter the boundaries and character of the village, and the village would be threatened by incremental disconnections. He stated that disconnection would unreasonably disrupt the zoning ordinance because it would result in a zoning change, but without going through the zoning process. He said the property as zoned could be developed, if the property and homes were designed to minimize the impact of the smaller homes and lot sizes of Carpentersville.

On cross-examination, Kendig said the threat disconnection posed was in serving as a precedent for future disconnections. He admitted, however, that there had been two prior judicial disconnections over the past 25 years; that those cases were known within the village and there had been no rush to disconnect. * * *

It is * * * well settled that the legislature has the power to fix and control the territory and boundaries of municipal corporations. * * * The legislature has provided various methods for altering municipal boundaries, including provisions for the disconnection of property.

* * * The requirements for this type of petition are set forth in the statute. * * * The parties agreed that all, but factor four, of the statute had been met. Factor four looks to the disruption that disconnection will have on the growth prospects and plan and zoning ordinances of the municipality.

* * * [B]y using "the term 'growth prospects,' the legislature did not intend that courts should look to development that would occur in the remaining part of the municipality but for * * * disconnection." * * * Neither the future development of the site nor the future development of the village are proper considerations under this prong of the statute. * * *

In ruling on the plaintiffs' petition, the trial court relied upon the fact that disconnection would adversely affect the land market in the village as a reason to deny it. The appellate court found that the trial court erred in considering market reaction to the disconnection.

The only evidence presented to support the village's claim that market reaction would "unreasonably" disrupt its growth prospects and plan and zoning ordinances was the testimony of two of its witnesses. No evidence, economic or otherwise, was presented to support that assertion. * * * Therefore, the trial court's finding was against the manifest weight of the evidence.

Nevertheless, the village argues that there was "plenty" of evidence in the record to support the trial court's finding. The record reveals plaintiffs' experts testified that disconnection would not unreasonably disrupt the village's growth prospects and plan and zoning ordinances, as only 14 to 15 lots could be developed, the property was separated from the village by the Helm Woods Forest Preserve, and disconnection would only minimally impact the surrounding area. The village's experts opposed disconnection because it would: alter or fragment the village's character and boundaries; circumvent the zoning process; or serve as precedent for future disconnections.

The legislature has recognized that some disruption to a municipality's growth prospects and plan and zoning ordinances may occur as a result of a disconnection. That alone is no reason to deny a disconnection petition. The test created by the legislature is whether disconnection will "unreasonably disrupt" the growth prospects and plan and zoning ordinances of the municipality.

It states a truism that disconnection will alter the village's borders and, following disconnection, the property will not support any growth within the municipality. Similarly, disconnection of one parcel does not serve as precedent for any other disconnection petition. Each case must turn on its own facts and merits. Moreover, this is a disconnection case not a zoning case. Consequently, those considerations should not enter into the analysis when examining a disconnection petition.

Here, the village has planned and zoned its growth prospects for large lot residential development, limiting population and other nongeographic growth. Also, the subject property is zoned R-1, as is over 90% of the 27 square mile village. As the map highlights, the site is surrounded by Carpentersville and virtually isolated from the village by the Helm Woods Forest Preserve, which would buffer any disruption to the village. Applying the "unreasonable disruption" test to the facts of this case leads to the compelling conclusion that disconnection will not unreasonably disrupt the village's growth prospects and plan and zoning ordinances.

RYAN v. MAYOR & COUNCIL OF DEMAREST

Supreme Court of New Jersey
319 A.2d 442 (1974)

CLIFFORD, J.

Beechwood Farms is a development of * * * thirty "beautiful homes, large estates," bisected by the borderline between the Borough of Demarest and the Borough of Alpine in Bergen County. Sixteen of the homes are consequently in Demarest and fourteen are in Alpine.

The plaintiffs here are fourteen of the sixteen Beechwood Farms homeowners whose properties lie in Demarest. On January 4, 1971 they filed a petition with the Mayor and Council of Demarest * * * requesting consent to deannexation of that part of the development which is located in that Borough so that "said lands may become part of the Borough of Alpine." On May 17, 1971 the Council adopted a resolution refusing to grant its consent, declaring that deannexation "would be contrary to the best interest of the Borough of Demarest and its general public and welfare * * *." Plaintiffs then filed a complaint * * * to compel the Council to grant its consent. * * *

As indicated Demarest and Alpine are adjacent boroughs. Demarest is about 2 square miles and had a population in 1970 of 6,262; Alpine is about 5.3 square miles and had a population of 1,344. At the time of trial Demarest was 90% residential; it had a shopping center but no industry. Alpine was almost entirely residential with no stores, other than an antique shop, and some gasoline stations.

In 1971 Demarest's total tax assessment was about $45.5 million, while Alpine's was about $27.6 million. The tax rate that year was $4.70 per $100 of valuation in Demarest and $2.67 per $100 in Alpine. * * *

The exclusive development of Beechwood Farms has a Beechwood Farms Association which charges dues to its members and which maintains a swimming pool, fishing lake and picnic grounds for their use. The residents perceive themselves as a community, despite the fact that they straddle the two Boroughs.

The Demarest section of Beechwood Farms lies on the eastern boundary of the Borough. It is separated from the rest of Demarest by Aldecress Country Club and Holy Angels Academy. In order to get to the business section of Demarest or other residential sections of the Borough, one must cross over into Alpine, pass briefly through the Borough of Cresskill and return to Demarest. The development lies about two miles from the center of the Borough.

It is undisputed that the Beechwood Farms homes located in Demarest are much more expensive than the average home elsewhere in the Borough. In 1971 the development accounted for only 16 homes out of approximately 1,547 homes in Demarest or 1.03% of the total. Nevertheless, it provided $959,000 in assessed valuation in the Borough or 2.11% of the total valuation, including commercial property. The Beechwood Farms homes provided $45,100 to Demarest in property taxes. It is also undisputed that the property taxes for the same homes would be significantly lower if they were located in Alpine.

At trial, the technical sufficiency of the petition and compliance with the statute were conceded by the defendant Borough. The only issue was whether the refusal of Demarest to consent to deannexation was arbitrary and unreasonable under *West Point Island Civic Association v. Township Committee of Dover Township*, [54 N.J. 339 (1969)]. * * *

The defendant municipality called as witnesses the borough accountant, the mayor, and the borough engineer. Their testimony revealed that the elimination of sixteen homes would not produce any reduction in the municipality's operating costs—that is, Demarest could not hire one fewer policeman, fireman or road man after deannexation. The operating costs would remain fairly constant. Likewise, there would be no substantial economy in the budget of the grammar schools as a result of deannexation, although Demarest would save $9,600 to $12,000 in costs for the high school students (different cost figures were supplied by the accountant and the mayor) and there would be a saving in county taxes. These savings would not offset the loss of revenue. In the final analysis, the tax rate for the remainder of Demarest would be increased as a result of the deannexation of Beechwood Farms.

Mayor Ringelstein stated that in reaching its decision the Council considered both the loss in revenue in the upcoming fiscal year and the total loss over the next ten to twenty years and concluded that deannexation would result in an economic hardship. * * *

According to the Mayor, residents of Beechwood Farms had been active in Demarest social and community activities such as Little League and had participated in municipal and political activities. The movement for deannexation began only when it became apparent that Demarest would be required to have a bond issue to finance a sewer system which the State Board of Health has ordered the Borough to install. The borough engineer testified the sewer system was undergoing installation at the time of trial. * * *

It was in this posture of the proofs that the trial judge concluded that the effect of deannexation would be "insignificant" and "not of any injury * * * to the municipality." Accordingly, he gave judgment to plaintiffs and ordered Demarest to "adopt a resolution in the form necessary to indicate its consent to the Petition for Annexation * * *." The Appellate Division's affirmance was predicated on agreement with the finding that deannexation would not "specifically injure the municipality or its social and economic well-being."

The trial judge demonstrated a full understanding of all facets of the holding in the *West Point Island* case, but we are satisfied that he and the Appellate Division misapplied to this case the law set forth therein. * * *

West Point Island held that the municipality's consent to deannexation is neither a purely ministerial act nor a purely political judgment reviewable only upon a showing of fraudulent abuse of discretion. Rather, the word "consent" implies a voluntary act, not a statutory compulsion, and the municipality has discretion to withhold its consent to the deannexation. However, the discretionary authority is subject to close judicial scrutiny to prevent arbitrary and unreasonable action, *West Point Island Civic Association v. Township Committee of Dover Township, supra*, 54 N.J. at 345–346, and if the municipality in which the land is located is to object to deannexation, it "must come forward" with "proof of specific injury." *Id.* at 348. * * * Proof of either economic or social injury, substantial in nature, is sufficient to satisfy the municipality's burden of coming forward with the evidence and there need not be a showing of both. It is likewise conceivable that there be both economic and social detriment, neither of which standing alone would be considered "substantial" but the total of which taken together would work a substantial injury on the community were deannexation allowed. * * *

[T]he ultimate burden of proving that the municipality acted in an arbitrary or unreasonable manner remains with the plaintiffs, the side challenging the invalidity of the withholding of consent. * * *

Comparison with *West Point Island*'s facts, where consent to deannexation was ordered, is instructive. There the island, a part of Dover Township, was located across Barnegat Bay, east of the mainland of the Township, and connected by a short bridge to Lavallette, the municipality to which the residents sought to be annexed. The island was "isolated from the schools as well as the governmental, business and shopping areas of Dover Township." The residents looked to Lavallette "as the focus of community interest and activity." Under these circumstances it was held that Dover Township would not suffer any social injury as a result of deannexation. Likewise, the Court found no economic injury to the Township from deannexation; the loss in revenue was offset by an equivalent reduction in the cost of municipal services.

Here, however, Beechwood Farms is not isolated from the remainder of Demarest as West Point Island was isolated from Dover Township. The geography and logistics of the situation do not compel the conclusion that the land in question more naturally belongs to the municipality to which deannexation is sought. In an area of the state where many small municipalities intertwine with one another, we cannot say that Alpine is the natural focus of social activity for the residents of Beechwood Farms in the same way that Lavallette was unquestionably the natural focus of West Point Island due to the most unusual geography in that case. While the residents may prefer to live in Alpine, they did participate in Demarest's political, social and church activities.

It is also acknowledged that Beechwood Farms constitutes an affluent community whose presence adds prestige to the Borough of Demarest. This is not an inconsiderable factor in determining whether social detriment would result from deannexation, nor can it be lightly dismissed as mere "snob appeal" and thus unworthy of consideration.

The evidence also makes it clear that deannexation would indeed cause economic hardship to Demarest. While the testimony does not lend itself to a precise computation of the loss of revenue above the cost of services for the development other than has been set forth ante, it is certain that the owners of these exclusive and expensive homes contributed substantially more to the Borough than they cost in services. What is clearly inferable from the record * * * is that plaintiffs sought deannexation primarily because it would save them considerable money, the property tax rate in Alpine being significantly lower than in Demarest, where they feared an additional burden because of sewer installation. The municipal fathers quite properly considered the amount of both the long term and the short term loss of revenue in determining that the proposed deannexation would mean economic injury to the Borough.

Thus, we conclude that the Borough of Demarest did meet its burden of coming forward with reasons why deannexation would be injurious to it. It showed injury to both the social and economic well-being of the municipality. Its justifications for refusal to consent have much more substance than the mere "sentimental resistance" which was found in the Township of Dover in the West Point Island case.

* * * [W]e have considered the problem of what kind of evidence is relevant to the issue of "social detriment," at the same time acknowledging that "economic injury" is relatively easy to recognize and quantify. In undertaking briefly to address this problem we would stress the point that whatever factors are alluded to are in no way intended to be all-inclusive, for in the final analysis the governing body and the trial judge will have to bring to bear their own knowledge, experience and perceptions in determining what, in the context of deannexation, would inflict social injury upon the well-being of a community. With that cautionary note in mind we would suggest that social detriment might be found in a community's being deprived of the petitioner's participation in the religious, civic, cultural, charitable and intellectual activities of the municipality; their meaningful interaction with other members of the community and their contribution to its prestige and social standing; the part they play in general scheme of their municipality's social diversity; and, conceivably, the wholesome effect their presence has on racial integration. These are, of course, values which undergo change with the times and are accorded different weight depending in part on the composition of the community and its governing body. We repeat that in listing them, we are recognizing only some of the appropriate considerations.

Lastly, we take note of what plaintiffs contend is the legislative intention manifest in the annexation statute, N.J.S.A. 40:43–26. That act represents, it is argued, "a long history of legislative recognition that municipal boundaries are largely a matter of historical accident, and that more effective home rule can be achieved by adjusting the boundaries from time to time to conform with the community of interests of the residents of particular areas."

* * * [W]e [do not] perceive that the statute in question encourages the adjustment of municipal boundaries "from time to time" dependent upon the changing "community of interests" of the residents. We find in the statute an intention on the part of the Legislature to give precedence to a more significant policy, that of preservation of municipal boundaries and maintenance of their integrity against challenge prompted by short-term or even frivolous considerations such as "tax shopping" or avoidance

of assessments. It is exactly for this reason that there must be secured the governing body's consent, which may be withheld in the reasonable exercise of its discretion. That safeguard stands in support of the intended policy of the legislature.

NOTES AND QUESTIONS

1.   *Balancing the Costs and Benefits of Secession.* Both *Barrington Hills* and *Ryan* acknowledged that the deannexation or disconnection in question could have a negative effect on the seceded-from community. But both courts also determined that "some harm" was not by itself enough to justify barring the proposed secession. *Barrington Hills*, construing the Illinois statute, required an "unreasonable disruption" of a village before it would reject the secession. *Ryan* looked to whether there was a *substantial* impact on the social and economic well-being of the existing municipality. Was the negative impact of deannexation on the Borough of Demarest demonstrably more substantial than the impact of the proposed disconnection on the Village of Barrington Heights? Did the disconnection proponents in *Barrington Hills* make a better case for their need for secession than did the deannexation proponents in *Ryan*? Or do the results simply reflect differences in judicial policy preferences?

Municipal attorneys in Illinois were dismayed by *Barrington Hills*. One brief account described it as the "last nail in the coffin" and predicted that "legislative action is needed to prevent chaos in planning and zoning. . . ." Susan G. Connelly, Disconnection from Municipalities after Barrington Hills, 79 Ill.B.J. 450 (1991). Since 1990, four reported opinions in Illinois have ordered disconnection against a municipality's wishes. *See* Falcon Funding, LLC v. City of Elgin, 924 N.E.2d 1216 (Ill. App. 2010); Austin Bank of Chicago v. Village of Barrington Hills, 919 N.E.2d 88 (Ill. App. 2009); Vo-Land, LLC v. Village of Bartlett, 919 N.E.2d 1 (Ill. App. 2009); La Salle National Trust v. Village of Mettawa, 616 N.E.2d 1297 (Ill.App.1993).

2.   *Social Well-Being. Ryan*, following the earlier *West Point Island* case, held that one of the criteria for reviewing a municipality's denial of a deannexation petition was whether the deannexation would have a negative impact on the social well-being of a community. What does that mean? Does the secession of a more affluent neighborhood, or a particular racial or ethnic group, have a negative impact on the well-being of the community? Is the court indicating a preference for socially heterogeneous localities? Is that in tension with incorporations that look to "homogeneity" or a "community of interest" within the territory?

3.   *Deannexation as a Threat.* The availability of disconnection for disgruntled property owners may motivate cities to provide adequate services to territory within their jurisdiction. In that way, it may temper the municipality's zeal to annex. As the Mississippi Supreme Court noted in a case allowing deannexation for land that had been annexed ten years earlier: "The deannexation process should serve as a reminder to the municipality

that even if annexation is approved, the responsibility to provide the promised services is a serious one. . . . Although the court may grant annexation when a city petitions it with a reasonable plan, the court must be just as quick to grant deannexation when the city does not deliver on services promised in the plan." In re The Exclusion of Certain Territory from City of Jackson, 698 So.2d 490, 494 (Miss.1997). Arkansas' detachment statute actually codifies that bargaining strategy. It explicitly authorizes landowners who are not receiving desired services to detach and subsequently annex to another adjacent municipality that will provide the services. *See* Ark. Code Ann. § 14–40–2002. The supreme court of Arkansas construed the law somewhat narrowly in Maumelle v. Jeffrey Sand Co., 120 S.W.3d 55 (Ark. 2003), when it held that the statutory provision did not give the complaining landowners the right to detach from a municipality in which services were provided, albeit not by the municipality itself, but rather from a regional special district. A year later, the court applied the law more generously, when it upheld detachment from a municipality that had met its statutory obligation to commit to the provision of services but had not done so within a reasonable time. *See* Rockport v. Malvern, 155 S.W.3d 9 (Ark. 2004).

4.   *Beyond Deannexation to Dissolution.* Though the phenomenon of municipal dissolution may be limited, empirical research shows that in addition to the 130 municipalities that have dissolved since 2000, many more are on the brink. The legal rules governing this process are rooted in 19th century technical requirements and procedures, generally unaffected by the fact that dissolutions typically tell one of two very different stories. Dissolution may be the first step towards a broader regional consolidation (as it was in Jacksonville, Florida), and it may also be the first step in a process whereby wealthy enclaves "dump" poor taxpayers and residents and then form their own homogeneous municipal islands by reincorporating a new municipality (as it almost was in Miami). To understand the human reality that is dependent on and changed by these arcane legal rules, *see* Michelle Wilde Anderson, *Dissolving Cities*, 126 Yale L.J. 1364 (2012).

D.   BOUNDARY CHANGE AND THE RIGHT TO VOTE

BOARD OF SUPERVISORS OF SACRAMENTO COUNTY v. LOCAL AGENCY FORMATION COMMISSION OF SACRAMENTO COUNTY

Supreme Court of California
838 P.2d 1198 (Cal.1992)

MOSK, JUSTICE.

Residents of an unincorporated area of Sacramento County seek to incorporate into a city. Government Code section 57103 provides that only the voters residing in the territory to be incorporated may vote to confirm the incorporation. The Court of Appeal found this law unconstitutional as applied, holding that it violates the guaranty of equal protection of the laws. We conclude that the law is constitutional, both on its face and as applied to the incorporation at issue.

The case before us illustrates the tension between California's financially beleaguered counties and the desire of residents of unincorporated areas to form cities and draw local government closer to home. * * * The counties fear that if tax-rich districts form cities, the counties will be deprived of revenue and their financial position further weakened. On the other hand, community residents and landowners often prefer to govern their local affairs insofar as possible, and cityhood provides them with greater opportunities for self-determination than does residence or ownership in a more amorphous unincorporated area. The evolution of cities is a natural process when population grows and communities begin to form their own identities.

Acknowledging the tension between fiscal concerns and the desire for self-government, the Legislature enacted the Cortese-Knox Local Government Reorganization Act of 1985. * * *

In 1986 persons in the unincorporated Sacramento County community of Citrus Heights, containing a population of approximately 69,000, collected enough valid signatures to qualify an incorporation petition to the Sacramento County Local Agency Formation Commission (commission), which by law supervises municipal incorporations in the county. * * * [The commission] approved a resolution setting forth the incorporation proposal. The resolution contained a provision designed to mitigate the financial impact on the county: the proposed city limits were relocated to exclude a sales-tax-rich shopping center. Requests for reconsideration of that resolution followed, in part on the ground that the boundaries still unfairly impacted the county's tax base. The commission adopted a new resolution that moved another shopping center outside the proposed city limits, and then, to further mitigate the county's financial loss, amended that resolution to require that the new city's receipt of property taxes be phased in more slowly. In accordance with section 57103, the commission ordered a confirming election to be held only within the territory of the proposed city.

This lawsuit followed. Plaintiffs include the Sacramento County Board of Supervisors, the Sacramento County Deputy Sheriffs' Association, and Sacramentans to Save our Services. The latter party alleged that it is an unincorporated umbrella organization of some 40 social and community service, labor, law enforcement, and business organizations, many of which receive county funds. Displeased, among other things, with the law's limitation of the confirming election to the voters in the territory to be incorporated, plaintiffs challenged the limitation's constitutionality on the ground that section 57103 denies them equal protection of the laws. * * *

The Cortese-Knox Act requires that every unconsolidated county have a local agency formation commission (see § 56325), appointed by local lawmaking bodies (*ibid.*), to "review and approve or disapprove with or without amendment, wholly, partially, or conditionally, proposals for changes of organization or reorganization. . . ." (§ 56375, subd. (a).) A change of organization includes the incorporation of a city with at least 500 registered voters from unincorporated county land. * * *

A local agency formation commission ordinarily is a five-member body that includes two county representatives from the board of supervisors (board), two city representatives "each of whom shall be a city officer" (defined in § 56025 as a mayor or city council member), and one member of the general public chosen by the other four. * * * The panel must be enlarged to include two representatives of special districts if the commission of any county (1) orders special districts to be represented thereon, and (2) adopts regulations affecting the "functions and services" of such districts. * * *

The commission cannot act on an incorporation petition unless signed by not less than 25 percent of the registered voters residing in the territory of the proposed city or by not less than 25 percent of the landowners, which latter group must also own not less than 25 percent of the assessed land value. * * *

Only after these hurdles have been surmounted does the commission have the power to approve or disapprove an incorporation in whole or in part. But the Cortese-Knox Act does not give the commission carte blanche to approve incorporations. Its discretion is limited by requirements, among others, that the incorporation be consistent with the act's intent; that the commission have reviewed the comprehensive fiscal analysis prepared under section 56833.1, the Controller's report prepared under section 56833.3, the report of the commission executive officer (an individual defined in § 56038), and the testimony presented at a public hearing; and that the proposed city likely will be fiscally sound for three fiscal years following its incorporation (§ 56375.1).

The commission cannot ratify an incorporation petition without a public hearing. (§§ 56836, subd. (b), 56069, 56021, subd. (a).) The county is given notice of the hearing (§ 56835, subd. (e)), and its presence is assured in any event because of the law's requirement that board members serve on the commission. In reviewing an incorporation proposal, the commission is required to consider a multitude of factors.[7]

---

[7]   These include but are not limited to:

    "(a) Population, population density; land area and land use; per capita assessed valuation; topography [and] natural boundaries . . . ; proximity to other populated

An incorporation proposal also triggers an elaborate inquiry into the reapportionment of property tax revenues. (§ 56842.)

The commission may make its approval conditional on a virtually limitless array of factors (see § 56844, subd. (v)), which are set forth in detail in sections 56843 and 56844.[8]

After the commission has completed its inquiry and issued a resolution approving or disapproving the proposal (see §§ 56851–56852), a county, or others affected by the decision, may request reconsideration (§ 56857, subd. (a)). Several such requests were made in this case, and, as noted above, the commission acted on them (see § 56858), modifying its resolutions to mitigate the impact of the incorporation of Citrus Heights on the county's finances.

Once the commission has issued its final resolution, the matter is in the hands of the "conducting authority," which in this case is the Sacramento County Board of Supervisors (§ 56029, subd. (d)(1)). The board must conduct a public hearing on the proposal. (§§ 57025, subd. (a), 57050.) If more than 50 percent of the voters in the territory to be incorporated protest the incorporation, the board must end the proceedings. (§§ 57077, subd. (a)(1), 57078, subd. (b); see § 56043.) Otherwise it must order the incorporation, subject to the voters' "confirmation."

As the foregoing recitation reveals, the voters' role under the Cortese-Knox Act in confirming an incorporation is rather like that of the masons who place a keystone at the apex of a high and intricate arch. The voters' approval is an essential piece, but as we have shown, by the time the question reaches the electorate the incorporation proposal will already have undergone a labyrinthine process containing elaborate safeguards designed to protect the political and economic interests of affected local governments, residents, and landowners. * * *

The question we confront * * * is whether section 57103 impinges on the right to vote in a manner that requires the application of strict

---

areas; the likelihood of significant growth in the area, and in adjacent incorporated and unincorporated areas, during the next 10 years.

"(b) . . . [T]he present cost and adequacy of governmental services . . . ; probable future needs for those services. . . .

"(c) The effect of the proposed action . . . on adjacent areas, on mutual social and economic interests, and on the local governmental structure of the county. . . .

"(g) Consistency with city or county general and specific plans. . . .

"(i) The comments of any affected local agency [including a city or county: see §§ 56014, 56054]." (§ 56841.)

[8] These include reimbursement for the acquisition or use of public property (§ 56844, subd. (a)), apportionment of bond obligations between the county and the proposed city (*id.*, subd. (c)), the incurring of new debt (*id.*, subd. (f)), property transfers (*id.*, subd. (h)), employee discharges and modification or termination of employment contracts (*id.*, subd. (l)), and the transfer of authority and responsibility among any affected cities and counties for the administration of special tax and special assessment districts (*id.*, subd. (u)).

scrutiny. As will appear, the statute does not compel that standard of review.

We agree that section 57103 touches on the right to vote. As it happens, the right to vote does not include a right to compel the state to provide any electoral mechanism whatever for changes of municipal organization. Such line-drawing is a function that the Legislature may reserve to itself. * * * But when the state has provided for the voters' direct input, the equal protection clause requires that those similarly situated not be treated differently unless the disparity is justified. * * *

The mere fact, however, that a state law touches on the right to vote does not necessarily require the application of strict scrutiny. * * * As we now undertake to explain by reviewing federal precedent, section 57103's impact in the case before us falls well short of the "real and appreciable," for individual interests in voting are much attenuated by the state's plenary power to oversee and regulate the formation of its political subdivisions, and the same power entitles the state to identify as differing in degree the interests of those who may vote under section 57103 and those who may not.

In our federal system the states are sovereign but cities and counties are not; in California as elsewhere they are mere creatures of the state and exist only at the state's sufferance. * * * Accordingly, the United States Supreme Court has long recognized the states' plenary power to create and dissolve their political subdivisions. In *Hunter v. Pittsburgh* (1907) 207 U.S. 161, * * * residents of Allegheny, threatened with absorption by much larger Pittsburgh, challenged a Pennsylvania law authorizing the two cities' consolidation if a majority of the total votes cast in a referendum approved consolidation. One ground for the challenge was that the law was "in violation of the law of the land, it being * * * unequal * * * in that it permits the qualified electors of the larger city to overpower and outnumber those of the lesser city, and to annex the lesser city without the vote or consent of a majority of the qualified electors of the lesser city." (207 U.S. at p. 168, internal quotation marks omitted.) * * *

The federal high court, noting that "[m]unicipal corporations are political subdivisions of the State," concluded, "The number, nature and duration of the powers conferred upon these corporations and the territory over which they shall be exercised rests in the absolute discretion of the State. * * * The State, therefore, at its pleasure may modify or withdraw all such powers, * * * expand or contract the territorial area, unite the whole or a part of it with another municipality, [or] repeal the charter and destroy the corporation * * * with or without the consent of the citizens, or even against their protest. * * * Although the inhabitants * * * may by such changes suffer inconvenience [or] * * * the burden of increased taxation, * * * there is nothing in the Federal Constitution which protects them from these injurious consequences. The power is in the State and those who legislate for the State are alone responsible for any unjust or oppressive exercise of it." (*Hunter v. Pittsburgh, supra*, 207 U.S. at pp. 178–179). * * *

In *Lockport v. Citizens for Community Action* (1977) 430 U.S. 259, the court faced a constitutional challenge to a New York law that forbade the implementation of a new Niagara County charter unless approved by concurrent majorities of both the city and noncity residents of the county. The unincorporated-area residents, though fewer in number, voted against the new charter; thus it was defeated even though a majority of the total votes cast favored it.

The concurrent-majority requirement was challenged on equal protection grounds. In deciding the question, the United States Supreme Court, though implicitly deciding the different classes of county resident were similarly situated because living in the county and affected by any charter change, * * * applied the rational basis test. The court stated that if there "is a genuine difference in the relevant interests of the groups that the state electoral classification has created" then an "enhancement of minority voting strength" is permissible unless it "nonetheless amounts to invidious discrimination in violation of the Equal Protection Clause." * * * In other words, if the state's citizens have different interests, then an electoral classification for a referendum that reorganizes local government will survive an equal protection challenge unless it works a purely arbitrary result.

Applying that test, the high court held that "the State's identification of the distinctive interests of the residents of the cities and towns within a county rather than their interests as residents of the county as a homogeneous unit" arose from "the realities of the distribution of governmental powers in New York, and is consistent with our cases that recognize * * * the wide discretion the States have in forming and allocating governmental tasks to local subdivisions . . . " (*Lockport, supra*, 430 U.S. at pp. 268–269). Thus the state could decide that city and noncity residents possessed genuinely different relevant interests. And the court held that the classification was not arbitrary and hence did not violate equal protection principles. (Id. at pp. 272–273).

Lockport recognizes the high degree of deference due to a voting-based classification when a state undertakes the essentially political task of apportioning power among its local governmental subdivisions— "constituent units that in a sense compete to provide similar governmental services" (430 U.S. at p. 272, 97 S.Ct. at p. 1055).

To be sure, *Lockport* did not decide what standard of deference applies when voters with a more diffuse interest in an incorporation are excluded from voting to confirm the result of a legislative scheme that tries to balance competing interests in the politically freighted incorporation process. To our knowledge, the United States Supreme Court has never addressed this question. But we conclude that we should not apply strict scrutiny. Under *Lockport, supra*, 430 U.S. 259, 97 S.Ct. 1047, the residents in the area to be incorporated and the remaining residents of Sacramento County possess, on the face of the law, genuinely different relevant interests. Thus, though the right to vote is perforce implicated whenever the state specifies that certain people may vote and others may not, we conclude that the essence of this case is not the fundamental right to vote, but the state's plenary power to set the conditions under which its political subdivisions are created. For that reason, the impairment of the right to vote is insufficiently implicated to demand the application of strict scrutiny. * * *

We conclude that under applicable precedent we should apply a deferential standard in evaluating the classification set forth on the face of section 57103. The Legislature's traditional power to regulate the formation of political subdivisions allows it to decide that the county residents living outside the territory to be incorporated have a lesser degree of interest in the proposed incorporation than those within, in which case the classification must be denied effect only if it lacks a rational basis. * * *

In section 56001 the Legislature announced a policy "to encourage orderly growth and development . . . essential to the social, fiscal, and economic well-being of the state," and stated that "the logical formation and determination of local agency boundaries is an important factor in promoting orderly development. * * * [T]he Legislature further finds and declares that this policy should be effected by the logical formation and modification of the boundaries of local agencies."

The foregoing sufficiently shows a legitimate purpose in enacting section 57103. And we conclude that section 57103 is fairly related to the Legislature's declared purpose, for, if large, relatively disinterested majorities could veto incorporations decided through the Cortese-Knox Act's elaborate process, the result might well hinder orderly growth and development. Thus there is no invidious discrimination of the type referred to in *Lockport, supra*. * * *

The act accommodates competing local governmental and private interests, narrowly channeling the commission's ultimate determination before the territory's voters consider the decision. The election merely asks the affected residents to confirm that they desire self-government. To deny the Legislature the authority to let the potentially incorporating territory's voters have the final say in the matter would be to lessen political participation, not increase it. We do not believe that result is required by our federal and state Constitutions.

NOTES AND QUESTIONS

1.   *The Constitution and Boundary Change.* In Chapter II, we gave considerable attention to Hunter v. City of Pittsburgh, 207 U.S. 161 (1907), as the fountainhead of the "state instrumentality model" of local government. *Hunter* continues to shape this field, *see, e.g.,* Jordan v. Town of Morningside, 30 Fed. Appx. 144 (4th Cir.2002) ("our review of municipal annexations under the Fourteenth Amendment is tightly circumscribed, recognizing that the state is vested with the exclusive power to make annexation decisions and that the state's exercise of that power generally does not give rise to federal constitutional claims"); Morgan v. City of Florissant, 147 F.3d 772 (8th Cir.1998)(noting that whereas laws imposing restrictions on the vote are subject to strict judicial scrutiny, laws providing for "the drawing and redrawing of state political subdivisions" are subject only to rational basis review). We also noted that later cases limited *Hunter's* plenary state power principle. It is unconstitutional for a state to draw local government boundary lines for a racially discriminatory purpose, *see* Gomillion v. Lightfoot, 364 U.S. 339 (1960), or to promote the interests of a religious community, *see* Board of Educ. of Kiryas Joel Village School Dist. v. Grumet, 512 U.S. 687 (1994). Most importantly for considering the right to vote on boundary changes, cases such as Avery v. Midland County, 390 U.S. 474 (1968) and Kramer v. Union Free School Dist. No. 15, 395 U.S. 621 (1969), determined that limitations on voting in local elections are subject to review under the Equal Protection Clause of the U.S. Constitution. The states have no obligation to provide for a vote in any local incorporation or boundary matter. *See* Niere v. St. Louis County, 305 F.3d 834 (8th Cir.2002), in which the court upheld a state law that authorized disincorporation of a municipality by petition. *Accord*, Green v. City of Tucson, 340 F.3d 891, 896 (9th Cir.2003) ("there is no inherent right to vote on municipal incorporation under the federal constitution"). Nevertheless, states typically do include an election as one step in the process of boundary change, and they frequently do so under rules that provide the franchise to some groups and deny it to others. These distinctions may be subject to federal constitutional challenge.

Two kinds of issues with respect to the local vote on incorporation and boundary change have arisen. One involves territorial discrimination: the electors in some areas get to vote but electors in other areas arguably affected by the boundary change do not. If the regulations "unreasonably deprive some residents in a geographically defined governmental unit from voting in a unit wide election," they will receive strict scrutiny. *See* Lemons v. Bradbury, 538 F.3d 1098, 1104 (9th Cir. 2008). The other involves the practice of many states of giving a special voice to landowners, such as by limiting the power to initiate a boundary change to landowners or by requiring the separate consents of both landowners and residents. Strict scrutiny will apply if the challenged regulations are deemed to "dilut[e] the voting power of some qualified voters within the electoral unit." *Id.* These territorial and landowner issues are considered in the next two notes.

2.   *Territorial Distinctions.* Boundary change decisions can affect many territorially distinct groups of voters. In an incorporation, voters in the area sought to be incorporated could be allowed to vote, but voters from the surrounding county would not be given the vote. This was the voting rule in the *Sacramento* case. In an annexation, a referendum could be held in an annexation area but not in the annexing city or surrounding county. Similarly, in a secession, the approval of the voters in the area seeking secession but not in the rest of the seceded-from city could be required. Even if voters in all relevant areas are enfranchised, there may be different rules for aggregating the votes. Is the relevant electorate all the participating voters, so that the test is whether the boundary change wins among the voters overall? Or can a state provide for concurrent majorities—that is, separate approvals in each area—so that the boundary action could be blocked if one group of voters is opposed even though the voters in the aggregate supported it?

Sacramento relied heavily on Town of Lockport v. Citizens for Community Action, 430 U.S. 259 (1977) in determining that the standard for reviewing state territorial distinctions in the allocation of the right to vote concerning a boundary change is the rational basis test, not strict judicial scrutiny. *Lockport* was not actually a boundary change case. Rather, it involved a referendum on a proposal to revise the charter of New York's Niagara County to transform it from a weak county to a strong county format, with a new administrative structure and enhanced regulatory capacity. Under the New York Constitution, such a change requires the approval of concurrent majorities of county voters who live in cities and county voters who live outside cities. The proposal twice won the approval of city voters and a majority of all county voters, but each time it was rejected by a majority of non-city voters and, thus, failed. City voters contended that the concurrent majority rule unconstitutionally diluted their votes, but a unanimous Supreme Court disagreed.

The Court likened the county reorganization, which strengthened the county government and weakened other local units, to "the structural decision to annex or consolidate," 430 U.S. at 271, which could have a differential impact on the "separate and potentially opposing interests" of city and non-city voters. The Court then assumed that in an annexation or consolidation proceeding a state could require separate consents from the voters of each affected unit even if that meant that the smaller group was outweighing the vote of the two units together. Without expressly stating that a state could require separate consents, the Court emphasized the "wide discretion the States have in forming and allocating governmental tasks to local subdivisions." *Id.* Citing *Hunter*, the Court indicated it would defer to a state's determination "that the residents of the annexing city and the residents of the area to be annexed formed sufficiently different constituencies with sufficiently different interests." *Id.*

One year after *Lockport*, the Supreme Court in *Holt Civic Club* rejected the voting rights claim of residents of Tuscaloosa's extraterritorial zone. The two cases, taken together, suggest that strict scrutiny of territorial distinctions with respect to the local vote "stops at the local jurisdictional boundary line and . . . the states . . . have considerable discretion in selecting the determinative boundary line. When the residents of one jurisdiction are entitled to vote on a boundary change, but the residents of other jurisdictions affected are not, strict scrutiny will not apply to this interjurisdictional discrimination. The issue will be treated not as a matter of voting rights but as a question of state boundary change policy." Richard Briffault, Who Rules at Home?: One Person/One Vote and Local Governments, 60 U.Chi.L.Rev. 339, 392 (1993). *See, e.g.*, St. Louis County v. City of Town & Country, 590 F.Supp. 731, 737–39 (E.D.Mo.1984); Moorman v. Wood, 504 F.Supp. 467, 472–76 (E.D.Ky.1980); City of New York v. State, 562 N.E.2d 118, 120–21 (N.Y.1990). In a similar vein, the Utah Supreme Court upheld the voting scheme of its amended annexation statute, which was intended to make it easier for towns that straddle county lines to consolidate within the borders of one county. *See* Grand County v. Emery County, 52 P.3d 1148 (Ut. 2002).

Sacramento represents a change in the approach the California Supreme Court has taken to this question. In earlier cases, the California high court had held that limiting the right to vote to just one area affected by a boundary change would be subject to strict judicial scrutiny. *See* Fullerton Joint Union High Sch. Dist. v. State Bd. of Educ., 654 P.2d 168 (Cal.1982); Citizens Against Forced Annexation v. Local Agency Formation Comm'n, 654 P.2d 193 (Cal.1982).

Sacramento gave considerable attention to the role of the Sacramento LAFCO in representing the interests of the county as a whole and in assuring the reasonableness of the incorporation of Citrus Heights. Should the limitation of the vote in an incorporation referendum to residents of the area seeking incorporation—thereby excluding residents of the surrounding county—be sustained in the absence of some mechanism like the LAFCO for representing the interests of those other county residents?

Another way in which a state can require that the concerns of surrounding residents be taken into account in the consideration of a proposed municipal incorporation is by making the consent of nearby municipalities a prerequisite for incorporation. Arizona law prohibits a new incorporation unless all existing municipalities with a population of 5,000 or more within six miles of the proposed municipality give their prior consent. In 1997, the residents of the community of Tortolita overwhelmingly petitioned for incorporation, but three nearby municipalities refused to consent and thereby blocked the incorporation. The residents of Tortolita sued, claiming that the consent requirement violated their right to vote. The United States Court of Appeals for the Ninth Circuit agreed that the petition procedure for direct incorporation was "sufficiently similar to voting to be treated as such for equal protection purposes," Green v. City of Tucson, 340

F.3d 891, 897 (9th Cir.2003), but then held that the statute still passed constitutional muster. The court noted that the statute treated all residents of the proposed city of Tortolita equally with respect to the right to petition, so that the statute "discriminates between different electoral units based on their proximity to existing municipalities, rather than between voters in any single electoral unit." *Id.* at 900. Relying on *Holt Civic Club*, the court applied rational basis review and upheld the statute: "Municipal incorporation of areas on the fringes of existing cities and towns, if left unchecked, can lead to intergovernmental conflict over resources and development. . . . Arizona has rationally chosen to prevent such intermunicipal conflict by giving existing municipalities a veto over the incorporation of neighboring areas." *Id.* at 903.

   3. *Landowners vs. Residents.* The second constitutional issue concerning the right to vote on boundary changes grows out of the widespread practice of giving a special voice to local landowners. California's Knox-Cortese Act provides that the incorporation process may be started by a petition of not less than 25 percent of the landowners in the proposed city, provided they own not less than 25 percent of the assessed land value. Although California also provides a mechanism for non-landowning residents to initiate the incorporation process, in some states only landowners may initiate an incorporation or annexation. In *Daugherty v. Carlsbad*, for example, the annexation petition was a landowner petition, not a residents' petition. In other states, a landowner protest can stop an incorporation or annexation that would otherwise take place.

   The largest portion of local revenues typically comes from the tax on land, and a major function of local government is to regulate land. Nevertheless, it would be unconstitutional to limit the vote in a municipal election to landowners, *see, e.g.*, Cipriano v. City of Houma, 395 U.S. 701 (1969); City of Phoenix v. Kolodziejski, 399 U.S. 204 (1970) or even to require concurrent majorities of local voters and local landowners, *see* Hill v. Stone, 421 U.S. 289 (1975). It would be unconstitutional to require that a school board member or a member of a local airport commission be a landowner, *see* Turner v. Fouche, 396 U.S. 346, 362–64 (1970) (property ownership requirement for school board membership not rationally related to any legitimate state interest); Chappelle v. Greater Baton Rouge Airport Dist., 431 U.S. 159 (1977) (same for airport district). Similarly, it is unconstitutional to require that the members of a commission appointed to propose a plan for local government reorganization be landowners, *see* Quinn v. Millsap, 491 U.S. 95 (1989) (no rational basis for limiting board membership to landowners; landowners do not have a better understanding of local problems or a stronger long-term stake in the community). If landowners cannot be given a preferred position in the ongoing political processes of existing localities, is it constitutional to give them a special voice in the creation or expansion of local governments?

   (a) It is clear that a state boundary change law that provides for a referendum limited to landowners, gives extra votes to landowners, or requires the separate consent of landowners, is unconstitutional. *See*

Hayward v. Clay, 573 F.2d 187 (4th Cir.1978) (invalidating law conditioning annexation on the affirmative vote of the majority of landowners in the annexation area as well as on the approval of a majority of voters in the annexation area and the annexing city); Mayor & Council of City of Dover v. Kelley, 327 A.2d 748 (Del.1974) (law weighting votes in annexation according to the assessed valuation of real estate owned by each eligible voter unconstitutional).

(b) On the other hand, most courts that have considered the issue have held that laws giving only landowners the power to petition to initiate an incorporation or boundary change are constitutional. *See, e.g.,* Carlyn v. City of Akron, 726 F.2d 287 (6th Cir.1984); Berry v. Bourne, 588 F.2d 422 (4th Cir.1978); Adams v. City of Colorado Springs, 308 F.Supp. 1397 (D.Colo.), *aff'd mem* 399 U.S. 901 (1970) Goodyear Farms v. City of Avondale, 714 P.2d 386 (Ariz.1986); Charter Township of Bloomfield v. Oakland County Clerk, 654 N.W.2d 610 (Mich. App. 2002); Torres v. Village of Capitan, 582 P.2d 1277 (N.M.1978). The courts in these cases emphasized that a petition is not an election and that "[w]ithout an election, the voting rights cases are not directly applicable," *Goodyear*, 714 P.2d at 389. In addition, in these cases the ultimate decision was made either by the annexing city or by the county legislature. "The petitioners are mere supplicants and have no power or right to require annexation." *Goodyear*, 714 P.2d at 391. "[T]he important fact is that the action of the freeholders in signing the request for annexation does not authorize annexation. Annexation depends wholly on the favorable vote of the governing body of the annexing city. This is the crucial action." *Berry*, 588 F.2d at 424. The Arizona Supreme Court found that limiting the power to initiate annexation to landowners was reasonable because "property owners face more of an increased financial burden. . . . The legislature intended that the permanency associated with a property owner be present in a signer of an annexation petition." *Goodyear*, 714 P.2d at 392.

In *Goodyear*, Justice Feldman of the Arizona Supreme Court disagreed with the consensus view, contending in dissent that strict scrutiny should apply to the annexation petition process and that there was no rational basis for limiting the petition process to landowners. On the first point, he argued that although a "state does not have to deal with popular opinion at all in the annexation process . . . when the state chooses to do so . . . [it] must deal with all the people equally." As annexation affects "the nature of the governmental entity that is to exercise power over one's person and one's family," the petition process, although not "electoral . . . is one of fundamental importance in its impact upon residents." *Id.* at 393. He also denied that property owners are more affected by annexations, as the burden of property taxes can be passed on to consumers through increased rents and higher prices. *Id.* at 394. Who do you think has the stronger argument?

In Hussey v. City of Portland, 64 F.3d 1260 (9th Cir.1995), the United States Court of Appeals for the Ninth Circuit held that a consent on an annexation petition is the "constitutional equivalent" of voting. *Id.* at 1263. The case involved an Oregon law which provided that annexation could be accomplished either (i) by an election, with the consent of a majority of the ballots cast, or (ii) by the combination of the written consent of a majority of all voters registered in the territory to be annexed and of the written consent of the owners of a majority of the land in that territory—the so-called "double majority" method. The case considered whether Portland could condition the provision of subsidized sewer system hook-ups to nonresidents on their advance consent to annexation. The court concluded that "because the consent forms are analytically like votes, and are a substitute for them, legally they must be treated like votes," *id.* at 1265, and found the consent requirement unconstitutional. The court did not directly consider the constitutionality of the double majority requirement itself, although its statement that "Portland may pursue annexation either by calling for an election . . . or by the consent of a double majority of landowners and registered voters," *id.*, suggests that the court was not troubled by the double majority requirement. If giving written consent to annexation is the "constitutional equivalent" of voting, then how can the double majority requirement be constitutional?

In Grant County Fire Protection Dist. No. 5 v. City of Moses Lake, 83 P.3d 419 (Wash. 2004) (on rehearing en banc), the Washington Supreme Court upheld a pair of state laws permitting annexation on the written consent of the owners of a supermajority of the land, as measured by assessed valuation, and without an election. The court rejected challenges based on the Washington Constitution's Privileges and Immunities Clause, Wash. Const., Art. I, § 12. *Grant County* involved two annexations. The first, by a code city, followed a Washington statute that permitted annexation if (i) initiated by a notice of intent signed by the owners of at least 10% of the assessed value of the proposed annexation area and with the approval of the city council of the annexing city, and (ii) approved by signatures on the petition of owners of at least 60% of the area's assessed valuation. The other annexation followed the procedure applicable to a non-code city: (i) initiation by a petition signed by the owners of at least 10% of the assessed value of the proposed annexation area or by at least 10% of the total number of property owners; (ii) review, with modification and approval, by the Washington State Boundary Review Board, and by the city council of the annexing city, and (iii) final approval by the petition signatures of the owners of 75% of the assessed valuation in the annexation area. In both cases, the annexing cities had obtained the necessary property owners' consents in advance, in exchange for the provision of extraterritorial utility services. In an earlier decision in this case, the Washington Supreme Court had held that the provision of a landowner-dominated petition process as an alternative to voter approval did not unconstitutionally infringe upon the right to vote. Expressly disagreeing with the Ninth Circuit's *Hussey* decision, the court had concluded that the process "rationally related to the objective of giving all affected parties a voice in the annexation process." *See* 42 P.3d at 405. With regard to the privileges and immunities issue, the court concluded that the statute did not involve a fundamental attribute of citizenship, but merely reflected the legislature's plenary power to adjust the boundaries of its municipal corporations. As such, the Privileges and Immunities Clause was not violated. *See* 83 P.3d at 429–30.

(c)   The supreme courts of California and Washington have held that state laws that permit a landowner petition to block an election are unconstitutional. *See* Curtis v. Board of Supervisors, 501 P.2d 537 (Cal.1972); City of Seattle v. State, 694 P.2d 641 (Wash.1985). In each case, the state statutory scheme provided for a petition to initiate the process; review by a boundary review board (*Seattle*) or county commission (*Curtis*); and referendum in the area proposed for annexation (*Seattle*) or incorporation (*Curtis*). In both cases, though, the owners of a sizable fraction of the assessed valuation in the area (75% in *Seattle* and 51% in *Curtis*) could block the election and thus prevent the annexation or boundary change. Both courts concluded that by giving property owners the power to halt an election, the relevant state laws burdened the right to vote and were, thus, subject to strict scrutiny. Both courts determined that because incorporation or annexation will affect all residents in the area, including those who do not own property as well as those who do, the state could have no compelling interest in giving landowners the power to block an election by voters.

(d)   What happens if a state law provides that some fraction of property owners (measured by their share of assessed valuation in the relevant area) is necessary to initiate a boundary change, but that the ultimate decision is reserved for the electorate in the area? Is the preferred position for property owners in the initiation process subject to rational basis review—as the petitioners are "mere supplicants" in the language of the *Goodyear* court—or strict scrutiny, since property owner opposition can block an election? The Fourth Circuit considered this issue in Muller v. Curran, 889 F.2d 54, 55–56 (4th Cir.1989). The case involved a challenge to Maryland's incorporation procedure, which established a three step process of (i) petition; (ii) county council consideration; (iii) referendum in which all registered voters in the area proposed for incorporation can vote. The statute required that the petition be signed by 20% of the registered voters in the area and also by the owners of 25% of the assessed value of real property in the area. The Fourth Circuit held that this procedure was analogous to the property owner veto in *Seattle* and *Curtis*, and to the requirement of concurrent majorities of property owners and voters in *Hayward*, and thus invalidated the Maryland law. The court distinguished its earlier decision in Berry v. Bourne, 588 F.2d 422 (4th Cir.1978), which had upheld a law limiting the power to initiate an annexation to landowners. Crucial to the court's distinction was the observation that, although the law in *Berry* conferred power on landowners, it did not involve an election. The Maryland law in *Muller*, in contrast, was found invalid because it "permits a popular vote to be blocked by property owners. That is so because the county council cannot schedule such a vote unless a given percentage of the property owners authorize it." 889 F.2d at 56–57.

Do you agree with the Fourth Circuit that requiring property owner support for an incorporation or annexation should be subject to strict scrutiny when the ultimate decision is made by the general electorate but not when it is made by a city or county legislature? Is it odd that the procedure that combines a special landowner role with a greater popular voice is more constitutionally objectionable than one that provides for no local popular voice? Or does that follow from the logic of the limited nature of the federal constitutional interest in boundary change, which is the equal protection of the vote?

NOTE ON ANNEXATIONS AND THE VOTING RIGHTS ACT

Local government boundary changes are also subject to federal scrutiny under the Voting Rights Act of 1965, 42 U.S.C. § 1973 et seq. Section 2 of the Act prohibits any "standard, practice, or procedure" that "results in a denial or abridgement of the right . . . to vote on account of race or color" or language minority status. 42 U.S.C. § 1973(a). Section 2 applies to claims of "vote dilution," that is to voting rules and procedures that do not interfere with the casting of ballots but that, under certain circumstances, make it more difficult for the minority groups protected by the Act to win elections. It also applies an effects, not an intent, standard. Section 2 has been important in suits challenging racial gerrymandering or the use of at-large elections in which a single jurisdiction-wide majority can win all the contested seats.

In Section 5 of the Act, Congress established a special procedure for voting law changes in certain states and localities that had had a history of racial discrimination in voting. Changes in those states had to be "precleared" by either the Attorney General or the federal district court for the District of Columbia, with the burden on the jurisdiction of proving that the change did not have a discriminatory purpose or effect. The Supreme Court held that Section 5 applied to local government boundary changes, including annexations:

> Changing boundary lines by annexations which enlarge the city's number of eligible voters also constitutes the change of a 'standard, practice, or procedure with respect to voting.' Clearly, revision of boundary lines has an effect on voting in two ways: (1) by including certain voters within the city and leaving others outside, it determines who may vote in the municipal election and who may not; (2) it dilutes the weight of the votes of the voters to whom the franchise was limited before the annexation, and 'the right of suffrage can be denied by a debasement or dilution of the weight of a citizen's vote just as effectively as by wholly prohibiting the free exercise of the franchise.' Reynolds v. Sims, 377 U.S. 533, 555 (1964). Moreover, § 5 was designed to cover changes having a potential for racial discrimination in voting, and such potential inheres in a change in the composition of the electorate affected by an annexation.

Perkins v. Matthews, 400 U.S. 379, 388 (1971).

In Shelby County v. Holder, 570 U.S. ___, 133 S.Ct. 2612 (2013), the Supreme Court struck down section 4 of the Voting Rights Act, which provided the standard for determining which states and local governments are subject to preclearance. The Court determined that the statutory criteria, which looked to the percentages of minority residents who were registered to vote or who voted in the presidential elections of 1964, 1968 and 1972. Although Congress, when it renewed the Act in 2006, concluded that those voting rates, when combined with the use of certain illegal tests, appropriately measured whether a jurisdiction should be subject to preclearance, the Court disagreed and held the coverage formula to be unconstitutional. Section 5 remains on the books, but without a constitutional coverage formula there are no longer any jurisdictions subject to preclearance. The section 5 cases dealing with annexations, however, may still be relevant to section 2 challenges to local boundary changes.

Annexations can present difficult voting rights issues. An annexation of populated territory dilutes the voting strength of the members of the pre-annexation locality. Unless the annexed territory has the same racial composition as the annexing locality, the annexation will alter the voting strength of racially identifiable groups. Yet annexations are often undertaken for reasons other than affecting voting strength. A central city with a large black population might annex adjacent white-majority suburbs. The annexation could increase the city's tax base, permit improved services, and created a more integrated city. But the annexation would also reduce the voting strength of the city's black population.

City of Richmond v. United States, 422 U.S. 358 (1975), concerned an annexation by Richmond, Virginia of 23 square miles of suburban Chesterfield County. Before the annexation the city was 52% black; afterwards, it was 42% black. Richmond was governed by a nine-member city council elected on a city-wide at-large basis. In the elections immediately before and immediately after the 1969 annexation, three of the council members were black. When Richmond sought preclearance of the annexation, the Attorney General objected because he found that the annexation substantially increased the proportion of whites in the city and thereby tended to dilute black voting strength. Richmond brought a declaratory judgment suit in District of Columbia district court for preclearance. While the case was pending, the city and the Attorney General reached an agreement for a district election system. The city was divided into nine wards, including four with substantial black majorities, and a fifth with a 41% black minority. The Attorney General and the city submitted the plan to the district court in the form of a consent judgment. The district court rejected the plan, finding that the annexation was motivated by a racially invidious purpose—to prevent blacks from acquiring political control of the city. The Supreme Court, however reversed, determining that "[a]s long as the ward system fairly reflects the strength of the Negro community as it exists after the annexation, we cannot hold . . . that such an annexation is nevertheless barred by § 5." 422 U.S. at 371. Several years later, the Court upheld the denial of preclearance to actions of the City of Port Arthur, Texas, consolidating itself with two smaller cities and then annexing additional territory. The boundary changes reduced the black proportion of the city's population. Although the city modified its electoral system from all at-large to a mix of at-large and district seats, the Supreme Court found that "the post-expansion electoral system did not sufficiently dispel the adverse impact of the expansions on the relative political strength of the black community." City of Port Arthur v. United States, 459 U.S. 159, 166 (1982).

City of Pleasant Grove v. United States, 479 U.S. 462 (1987), involved the application of section 5 to a different type of annexation problem. Pleasant Grove, Alabama was an all-white municipality that sought to annex two empty parcels of land. It would be hard to say—given the absence of black voters in either the pre-or post-annexation city—that the annexation had a discriminatory effect. But the Attorney General denied preclearance because he found the city's refusal to annex an adjacent black community that had petitioned for inclusion showed it had applied a discriminatory annexation standard. The Supreme Court affirmed the denial of preclearance: "[T]he failure to annex [black] areas, while the city was simultaneously annexing non-black areas, is highly significant in demonstrating that the city's annexation here was purposefully designed to perpetuate Pleasant Grove as an enlarged enclave of white voters." *Id.* at 470 (quoting the brief for the United States).

The result in *Pleasant Grove* was to prevent annexation of the uninhabited parcels. Could the Voting Rights Act be used to compel a white city to annex a black area? Probably not: "Although [the Supreme Court's cases] permit a court to order a city not to annex white areas, thus diluting the black minority's vote within the city, they do not permit a court to order the city to annex the black areas. . . . A city does not dilute minority votes by refusing for racial reasons to annex. It dilutes minority votes by annexing non-minority areas . . . or de-annexing minority areas." Burton v. City of Belle Glade, 966 F.Supp. 1178, 1186 (S.D.Fla.1997), *aff'd*, 178 F.3d 1175 (11th Cir.1999). *See also* Holder v. Hall, 512 U.S. 874, 884 (1994) ("[W]e think it quite improbable to suggest that a § 2 dilution challenge could be brought to a town's existing political boundaries (in an attempt to force it to annex surrounding land) by arguing that the current boundaries dilute a racial group's voting strength in comparison to the proposed new boundaries.") (Opinion of Justice Kennedy, joined by Chief Justice Rehnquist). To be sure, a federal district court in Alabama in a selective annexation case brought under the Voting Rights Act approved a consent decree that required a municipality to agree to annex two black neighborhoods (if the residents of the areas agreed) in exchange for permission to annex five white areas whose annexation had been previously vetoed by the Justice Department under Section 5 of the Voting Rights Act. *See* Dillard v. City of Foley, 926 F.Supp. 1053 (M.D. Ala. 1996). But as a consent decree, that order was agreed to by the city and, thus, technically not imposed by the court. Nevertheless, the

Voting Rights Act imposes some federal constraint on the ability of municipalities to engage in racially selective boundary-line redrawing.

E. SPECIAL DISTRICTS

As we noted in Chapter I, special districts vary enormously in size, scope, function and relationship to general purpose governments. Some special districts provide a range of infrastructure services over a wide metropolitan area; these regional special districts are more fully considered in Chapter V. Others provide just a single service within a neighborhood in one county or city. Due to this extensive variation in the nature of special districts, states generally do not have a single mechanism for creating special districts. Indeed a state may have in place multiple statutory schemes for special district formation. *See* Kathyrn A. Foster, The Political Economy of Special-Purpose Government 11 (Georgetown Univ. Press 1997) (finding that California alone has 206 general statutes enabling 55 types of special districts performing 55 different service functions). *See also* Douglas R. Porter et al., Special Districts: A Useful Technique for Financing Infrastructure 13–16 (Urb. Land Inst., 2d ed. 1990) (describing methods of creating water, sewer and road districts in Florida, California, New Jersey, Pennsylvania, Virginia and Texas).

Recognizing the broad variation in state systems of special district formation, we can sketch out a few general patterns. First, special districts may be created by a special act of the state legislature. This is likely to be the mechanism for creating districts of regional scope, such as those that finance and operate port development or transportation systems in metropolitan areas, or irrigation and flood control systems in regional watersheds. Some districts, such as the Port Authority of New York and New Jersey, or the Delaware River and Bay Authority, may even cross state lines. These require special acts of the legislatures of all the affected states, as well as approval by Congress pursuant to the Compact Clause of the United States Constitution.

Second, many districts are created by local governments pursuant to general state enabling legislation. As we will see in Chapter VI, state restrictions on municipal or county taxation and borrowing have encouraged municipalities and counties to create special districts that are coterminous with a general purpose government but are not subject to the state constitution's fiscal limits. General purpose local governments may also enter into agreements with each other, pursuant to state enabling legislation, to create special districts to provide services, such as waste removal or supply of electricity, to the cooperating localities. Other coterminous special districts may result from the mandate of the state or the decision of a city or county to spin off the operation of a particular service, like parks, hospitals, or public schools, from the general purpose government to a quasi-autonomous entity responsible for that service.

Third, many districts are created pursuant to general enabling legislation that authorizes local residents, landowners, or taxpayers to initiate the district creation process. This form of special district creation most resembles municipal incorporation, involving landowner or resident petitions, review by a city or county, possible additional review by a court or boundary commission, and, perhaps, a requirement of voter approval at the end of the process. Districts created pursuant to resident or landowner initiative may provide more intensive water, sewer or utility services to unincorporated areas within a county, or, like the business improvement districts discussed in Chapter II, additional public safety, sanitation, and economic development services within a city. Districts such as Florida's Community Development Districts, Fla.Stat.Ann. § 190 et seq., and Texas' Municipal Utility Districts, Vernon's Tex.Code Ann., Water Code, ch. 54 et seq., are frequently used by developers to finance the installation of new urban infrastructure in unincorporated areas. *See* Marion Perrenod, Special Districts, Special Purposes; Fringe Governments and Urban Problems in the Houston Area (Texas A. & M. Univ. Press 1984). The regional impact of special districts in metropolitan areas will be discussed in Chapter V.

In terms of special district powers, the power to tax is a fundamental defining characteristic. Approximately forty percent of special districts lack the power to tax property. Most of these districts are primarily regional special districts, such as transportation or port authorities, or districts coterminous with the cities or counties that have created them. These districts rely primarily on user fees, bond revenues, intergovernmental assistance, or other taxes, such as the sales tax, which may be imposed by other governments with the proceeds earmarked for the district.

Conversely, sixty percent of special districts do have the power to levy taxes on property, and two-thirds of these districts are sublocal districts intended to provide new or higher levels of services in addition to those provided by an overlying general purpose government. The formation of these districts is likely to involve resident or landowner participation—whether through the requirement of a petition, referendum vote, or the opportunity to protest the district after it has been approved by the city, county, or appropriate administrative agency.

STATE FARM MUTUAL AUTOMOBILE INS. CO.
V. CITY OF LAKEWOOD

Supreme Court of Colorado
788 P.2d 808 (1990)

JUSTICE ROVIRA delivered the Opinion of the Court.

* * * This appeal stems from a petition to organize the Academy Park Metropolitan District[2] (district) encompassing a tract of land of approximately 230 acres situated entirely within the municipality of Lakewood, a home rule city. Petitioners Donald L. Lawhead, Richard M. Reynolds, Walter V. Rayner, Walter A. Koelbel, Jr., and Walter A. Koelbel, as joint tenants, own approximately 1/5 of an acre of unimproved land within the proposed district, which was deeded to them by Koelbel and Company. Petitioner Chris M. Saros also owns a parcel of unimproved property within the proposed district. The six petitioners will be referred to as "the Koelbel group."

State Farm Mutual Automobile Insurance Company, P.C.M.T. Partnership, Tishman West Management Corporation, ROC-Denver, Inc., and Martin Marietta Corporation (opponents) own developed property within the proposed district.

In September 1984, the Koelbel group submitted an initial petition[3] to organize the district to the Lakewood City Council (city council). The proposed district would provide sanitation services, parks and recreational services, street improvements and traffic safety controls, and transportation services and facilities. General obligation bonds would be issued to finance the district, to be paid by the levy of *ad valorem* taxes.

The record discloses that some, but not all, of the real property owners within the district were notified of the submission of the initial petition to the city council. * * * However, public notice of the hearing on the initial petition was published in the local newspaper for three successive weeks. On December 10, 1984, the city council held a hearing on the petition. Proponents and opponents of the proposed district, including the parties to this case, were given an opportunity to speak on the merits of the petition. After the hearing, the city council adopted a resolution, by a vote of 8 to 3, approving the initial petition. * * *

---

[2] A metropolitan district is defined in section 32–1–103, 13 C.R.S. (1984 Supp.), as "a special district which provides for the inhabitants thereof any two or more of the following services: (a) Fire protection; (b) Mosquito control; (c) Parks and recreation; (d) Safety protection; (e) Sanitation; (f) Street improvement; (g) Television relay and translation; (h) Transportation; (i) Water."

[3] In forming a special district, a petition to organize must be submitted for approval by both a local governing body and the district court. For clarity, we will refer to the "initial petition" when discussing the petition which is submitted to local government, and the "petition for organization" when discussing the petition which is submitted to the district court.

The opponents * * * alleged that they were denied both procedural and substantive due process. They asserted a denial of procedural due process in that proper notice of the hearing was not given and they did not have a hearing before a fair and impartial tribunal. Further, the city council's failure to adopt standards to guide its determination, and the lack of applicable standards in the Act, deprived them of due process of law. * * *

The district court * * * held that because the city council's action was legislative, no procedural due process violation existed. Further, the lack of standards to guide the city council's discretion did not deny due process because the council was obligated to make its decision in accordance with the reasonableness standard which controls the exercise of all police power, and because the subsequent procedural steps in the district formation process provide additional safeguards. * * * The opponents appeal the judgment of the district court.

II

A

In order to determine these issues, the procedures for establishing a special district must be examined. A special district is a quasi-municipal corporation organized to provide specific services to the inhabitants of such districts. The Act, §§ 32–1–101 to –1307, 13 C.R.S. (1984 Supp.), provides procedures for the formation and dissolution of a special district and delineates the powers that may be exercised by such district. * * *

If the proposed district is situated exclusively within the boundaries of an existing municipality, * * * the Act requires only that the petition be approved by resolution of the governing body of the municipality before it is submitted to the district court [for approval]. The Act does not detail the information which is required to be submitted in the initial petition, nor does it contain any standards against which the petition must be judged by the governing body. Further, the Act does not require notice or a public hearing as a prerequisite to approval of the initial petition by resolution. Finally, the Act does not provide for judicial review of the municipality's decision to approve or disapprove an initial petition. * * *

B

Here, the proposed district is situated entirely within the boundaries of the City of Lakewood. Therefore, the Act only required that the city council approve the initial petition by resolution before a petition for organization could be submitted to the district court. * * *

The predominant consideration in determining whether a governmental body has exercised a quasi-judicial function is the nature of the decision rendered and the process by which the decision is reached. * * * Quasi-legislative action is usually reflective of some public policy relating to matters of a permanent or general character, is not normally restricted to identifiable persons or groups, and is usually prospective in nature. Further, quasi-legislative action requires the balancing of questions of judgment and discretion, is of general application, and concerns an area usually governed by legislation. * * *

Quasi-judicial action, on the other hand, generally involves a determination of the rights, duties, or obligations of specific individuals on the basis of the application of presently existing legal standards or policy considerations to past or present facts developed at a hearing conducted for the purpose of resolving the particular interests in question. * * * The existence of a statute or ordinance mandating notice and a hearing is evidence that the governmental decision is to be regarded as quasi-judicial.

Here, the city council made a political decision as to whether the City would perform certain services or would give its initial approval to the creation of a metropolitan district to perform such services. This decision is reflective of public policy and requires the balancing of questions of judgment and discretion. Further, the decision is prospective in nature, affects a large area within the municipality, and concerns a subject usually governed by legislation. Moreover, the city council's action did not involve a determination of the rights, duties, or obligations of specific individuals by applying presently existing legal standards or policy considerations to past or present facts. The city council's action did not create a special district, and thus had no immediate effect on anyone's rights and liabilities. Further, the decision does not pertain only to the immediate parties, as quasi-judicial acts typically do. Nor was the city council required, by statute or ordinance, to apply presently existing legal standards or policy considerations to past or present facts developed at the hearing. Finally, although the city council made provisions for notice and a public hearing, it was not required to do so by statute or preexisting ordinance. * * *

III

The opponents allege that the city council's action and certain portions of the Act violate the due process provision of both the Colorado and the United States Constitutions.

A

The opponents first contend that they were denied due process because they were not afforded adequate notice of the city council hearing and were not afforded a meaningful opportunity to be heard. The short answer to this contention is that when a municipal body is acting in a quasi-legislative rather than a quasi-judicial capacity, there is no constitutional requirement for notice and a hearing. *Cottrell v. City & County of Denver,* 636 P.2d 703 (Colo.1981). Therefore, the granting of notice and an opportunity to be heard by the city council was gratuitous, and not constitutionally required.

Nor does the lack of notice and hearing requirements in the statute deprive the opponents of due process of law. The General Assembly has plenary power to create quasi-municipal corporations such as those provided for in the Act. *Aurora v. Aurora Sanitation Dist.,* 112 Colo. 406, 149 P.2d 662 (1944); *People v. Lee,* 72 Colo. 598, 213 P. 583 (1923). Creation of such quasi-municipal bodies may be accomplished by several methods. First, the legislature may establish a district directly. Second, the legislature may provide for the formation of a district only upon the happening of events which are future and uncertain, such as approval by local government or by vote of the people.

Whether owners of land have any right to participate in the formation or administration of a quasi-municipal corporation is a political question only. *People v. Lee,* 72 Colo. 598, 213 P. 583 (1923). The legislature is not constitutionally required to provide landowners with notice, the right to be heard, the right to vote, or the right to appeal on the issue of the establishment of a quasi-municipal corporation or on the issue of whether a city council should give preliminary approval to a petition to form a special district. * * *

B

The opponents next contend that they were deprived of due process because the Act contains no standards to limit and channel the city council's discretion in approving the initial petition. Their argument is twofold: First, they argue that the statute is an unconstitutional delegation of legislative authority and, second, that the lack of standards in the statute violates due process.

Under the non-delegation doctrine, legislation must provide sufficient "standards and safeguards and administrative standards and safeguards, in combination, to protect against unnecessary and uncontrolled exercise of discretionary power." *Cottrell,* 636 P.2d at 703. At the time this case arose, the Act did not contain any standards which the governing body of a municipality must consider in deciding whether to approve an initial petition for the organization of a special district. Nor had the city council enacted any guidelines for approval or disapproval of a petition at that time. * * *

The trial court found that the Act contained implicit standards by which the city council was to make its determination. As an exercise of its police power, the city council was obligated "to act reasonably to promote and preserve the public peace, health and safety." Further, the trial court found that the subsequent procedural steps provided sufficient safeguards "to protect against unnecessary and uncontrolled exercise of discretionary power." *Cottrell,* 636 P.2d at 703. We agree.

The decision on how best to provide necessary services to the inhabitants of a municipality is an exercise of the police power. When police power is delegated, it is often impracticable for the General Assembly to fix rigid standards to guide the city council without destroying the flexibility necessary to effectuate legislative goals in dealing with complex economic and social problems. *People v. Lowrie,* 761 P.2d 778 (Colo.1988); *Elizondo v. Motor Vehicle Div.,* 194 Colo. 113, 570 P.2d 518 (1977). Thus, when police power is involved, we have held that "reasonableness" is a sufficient standard to guide the exercise of such power. *Cottrell,* 636 P.2d at 703; *Asphalt Paving Co. v. Board of County Comm'rs,* 162 Colo. 254, 425 P.2d 289 (1967).

Further, the subsequent procedural steps required in the formation of the district provide substantial protections to persons adversely affected by the city council's action. The district court must determine whether the petition to organize is in order, which includes a determination as to whether a sufficient percentage of the taxpaying electorate has signed the petition, and the legitimacy of those signatures. § 32–1–305(1), 13 C.R.S. (1984 Supp.). Moreover, landowners may request exclusion of their real property before the district court, and such property may be excluded from the special district if the court determines that it is in the best public interest to do so. § 32–1–305(3), 13 C.R.S. (1984 Supp.). Finally, the question of whether the district should be organized must be submitted to a vote by the taxpaying electorate. This election, in effect, is a review of the city council's decision by those who will be affected by the formation of the special district. We believe that the trial court was correct in finding that the standards implicit in the Act, in conjunction with the subsequent procedural steps provided, provide adequate safeguards against the dangers of an overly broad delegation of legislative power. * * *

The judgment of the district court is affirmed.

NOTES AND QUESTIONS

1. *Judicial Review of the Formation of Special Districts.* As the Colorado opinion in *Lakewood* illustrates, judicial review of the formation of special districts is relatively limited, even when the new district has taxing powers. *See also* Sheldon v. Town of Highlands, 536 N.E.2d 1141 (N.Y.1989) (state's creation of a local sewer improvement district is a legislative act; landowner not entitled to notice and hearing prior to enactment).

Courts may invalidate the formation of a special district where the relevant local government failed to comply with statutory requirements, *see, e.g.,* Foote Clinic, Inc. v. City of Hastings, 580 N.W.2d 81 (Neb.1998) (resolution adopted by city council to create business improvement district failed to specify the improvements to be made by the BID and the estimated costs of those improvements), or if the jurisdictional prerequisites for the formation of the district do not exist. *Cf.* City of Scottsdale v. McDowell Mountain Irrigation & Drainage Dist., 483 P.2d 532, 537–38 (Ariz.1971) (en banc) (remanding for a determination of whether an irrigation district may be formed in an urbanized area where the sole purpose of irrigation would be to water city lawns). A landowner or taxpayer may also challenge her inclusion in a limited purpose taxing district on the theory that she would be required to pay taxes to support district operations but would not receive any benefit from the district's operations. *See* Myles Salt Co. v. Board of Comm'rs, 239 U.S. 478 (1916).

2. *Special Districts and the Problem of Self-Determination.* Special districts created by petition are subject to the same problems of manufacturing consent that we saw in our discussion of annexation. In *Lakewood,* the objecting property owner, State Farm Insurance Co., was probably unhappy about the way in which its neighbors could force it into a special district over which it has no control and no input. For one thing, the final step in the creation of the special district is a general election vote of all residents in the district, but State Farm, a corporate entity, will have no vote. Once the district is up and running, moreover, it will exercise a wide range of powers. Though the district directors in Colorado are elected, *see* Colo. Stat. § 32–1–305.5, in many states special districts are run by unelected officials. Does that matter to the legal analysis? Does it suggest that heightened judicial scrutiny might generally be appropriate for challenges to special district formation?

3. *Growth of Special Districts.* Special districts are the most rapidly growing and most numerous form of local government in the United States. Special districts, however, have been criticized on a number of grounds: (1) they may be unaccountable to the electorate; (2) they are typically invisible to the general populace; (3) they may be immune from land use regulations and free to disregard local concerns; (4) they may allow the municipal government to create a new unit of government for purposes of removing a contentious policy issue from the general local political debate; (5) they may allow the municipality to avoid tort liability; and (6) they may be a convenient way for a municipality to circumvent state debt and/or taxing limitations. *See* Laurie Reynolds, Intergovernmental Cooperation, Metropolitan Equity, and the New Regionalism, 78 Wash.L. Rev. 93, 140–43 (2003). If the special district can be criticized on so many grounds, what do you think accounts for its spectacular growth?

4. *Impact of Special Districts on Municipal Powers and Autonomy.* The creation of a special district can affect municipal formation and annexation. Special districts may enable newly urbanizing areas to receive the additional local public services or infrastructure that growing populations require without actually forming or joining a municipal government. *See, e.g.,* Burns, *supra,* The Formation of American Local Governments at 78–80. This allows special district residents to receive—and be charged for—only those services they want, and to avoid the more extensive taxation and regulation, such as zoning and land use controls, that can result when they are subject to the

jurisdiction of a municipal government. In the many states where incorporation or annexation requires the consent of the residents affected, the availability of the special district option may enable residents to vote against annexation or incorporation without having to forego the services that municipal governments can provide. The proliferation of special districts may also remove many issues from the scope of the municipality's power, thus rendering it less important to the average citizen. Consider, for instance, the list of activities available to the metropolitan special district in *Lakewood*, as detailed in footnote 2 in the case. That list encompasses many traditional municipal governmental functions. Professor Reynolds elaborates on these criticisms in Local Governments and Regional Governance, 39 Urb. Law. 483 (2007). Increasingly, special districts are being created to provide services that cities once provided exclusively. *See* Barbara Coyle McCabe, Special-District Formation among the States, 32 State and Local Gov. Rev. 121, 124 (2000). Can you identify other consequences for municipal governments that might flow from the proliferation of these special districts?

5.   *Dissolving Special Districts.* Dissolution of a special district may be a non-event, resulting in the transfer of ownership of large infrastructure and service responsibilities from one district to another, or from a special district to a municipality or other local government unit, but it may also have stark political and social consequences. Such was the case in Memphis, when the Memphis School Board voted in 2011 to dissolve. Under the state law then in effect, the dissolution meant that the surrounding Shelby County would assume responsibility for Memphis's 103,000 students. 87% of those students were African American or Latino, and nearly 90% in poverty. Shelby County's 48,000 students were majority white and much wealthier. A swift state legislative response sought to authorize county residents to block the merger, but a federal district court invalidated that first legislative solution as special legislation. *See* Bd. of Educ. of Shelby County v. Memphis Bd. of Educ., 911 F.Supp.2d 631 (W.D. Tenn. 2012). Subsequently, the Tennessee legislature repealed a pre-existing law that would have prohibited the county's suburbs from forming their own school districts. *See* Tenn.Code Ann. § 49–2–502(b)(3). By 2014, all of the county's incorporated municipalities had withdrawn from the Shelby County school system and formed their own districts.

CHAPTER IV

STATE-LOCAL RELATIONS

▪ ▪ ▪

A. INTRODUCTION: THE CONFLICT BETWEEN PLENARY STATE POWER AND LOCAL AUTONOMY

The legal relationship between the states and their local governments is probably the most hotly contested issue in all of local government law. As a matter of black-letter principles, the states enjoy complete hegemony over their local governments. In Chapter II, we considered the status of local governments under federal constitutional law. We found that local governments generally lack constitutional rights against their states and that there is no federal constitutional right to local self-government. But we also saw that an important strand of federal jurisprudence recognizes the widespread existence and importance of local self-government and values the practice of local autonomy. This Chapter returns to the state-local relationship, and to the interest of local people in local self-government, but it shifts the focus from federal law to state constitutional and statutory arrangements. We will see that in the state setting too, the state-local relationship has been shaped by this long-standing duel between the themes of plenary state power and local self-government.

For the states, as well as for the federal constitution, the dominant theme has been plenary state power. As one of the co-authors of this book explained,

> The formal legal status of a local government in relation to its state is summarized by the three concepts of 'creature,' 'delegate' and 'agent.' The local government is a creature of the state. It exists only by an act of the state, and the state, as creator, has plenary power to alter, expand, contract or abolish at will any or all local units. The local government is a delegate of the state, possessing only those powers the state has chosen to confer upon it. Absent any specific limitation in the state constitution, the state can amend, abridge or retract any power it has delegated, much as it can impose new duties or take away old privileges. The local government is an agent of the state, exercising limited powers at the local level on behalf of the state. A local

government is like a state administrative agency, serving the state in its narrow area of expertise, but instead of being functional specialists, localities are given jurisdictions primarily by territory, although certain local units are specialized by function as well as territory.

Richard Briffault, Our Localism, Part I—The Structure of Local Government Law, 90 Colum.L.Rev. 1, 7–8 (1990).

This approach to state-local relations has had two consequences. First, state governments have plenary power to alter or abolish local powers, displace local actions, and eliminate local governments. In the absence of a specific state constitutional provision, localities generally lack state constitutional protection from the hostile actions of their states. Second, even when state governments create local governments and give them power to act, state courts have tended to read local powers narrowly. In the absence of a specific grant to undertake a particular action, local governments were presumed to lack power to act.

This dominant plenary state power approach, however, has repeatedly been challenged by scholars, judges, and lawmakers who support greater legal protection for local autonomy. First, as a matter of legal history, some American local governments exercised broad powers and relative independence from colonial governments in the seventeenth and eighteenth centuries. See, e.g., Hendrik Hartog, Public Property and Private Power: The Corporation of the City of New York in American Law, 1730–1870 (Cornell Univ. Press 1983); Joan C. Williams, The Invention of the Municipal Corporation: A Case Study in Legal Change, 34 Am.U.L.Rev. 369 (1985); James E. Herget, The Missing Power of Local Governments: A Divergence Between Text and Practice in Our Early State Constitutions, 62 Va.L.Rev. 999 (1976). Indeed, on the colonial frontier, local governments may have helped to create colonial "state" governments rather than the other way around. See Amasa M. Eaton, The Right to Local Self-Government, 13 Harv.L.Rev. 441 (1900). Moreover, in some states some local governments continued to enjoy a measure of autonomy well into the nineteenth century.

Second, some judges concluded that the widespread practice of local autonomy and the importance of local self-government in American democracy require that some aspects of local decision-making be protected from state interference, notwithstanding the principle of plenary state power. In one famous nineteenth century decision, the Michigan Supreme Court invalidated a state law which would have replaced the locally selected members of the boards of water and sewer commissioners of the city of Detroit with state appointees. Although the state's action did not violate any specific provision of the state constitution, the Court concluded:

"But when we recur to the history of the country, and consider the nature of our institutions, and of the government provided for by this constitution, the vital importance which in all the states has so long been attached to local municipal governments by the people of such localities, and their rights of self-government, as well as the general sentiment of hostility to everything in the nature of control by a distant central power in the mere administration of such local affairs, and ask ourselves the question, whether it was probably the intention of the convention in framing, or the people in adopting, the constitution, to vest in the legislature the appointment of all local officers, or to authorize them to vest it elsewhere than in some of the authorities of such municipalities, and to be exercised without the consent, and even in defiance of the wishes of the proper officers who would be accountable rather to the central power than to the people over whose interests they are to preside—thus depriving the people of such localities of the most essential benefits of self-government enjoyed by other political divisions of the state—when we take all these matters into consideration, the conclusion becomes very strong that nothing of this kind could have been intended by the provision. And this conviction becomes stronger when we consider the fact that this constitution went far in advance of the old one, in giving power to the people which had formerly been exercised by the executive, and in vesting, or authorizing the legislature to vest, in municipal organizations a further power of local legislation than had before been given to them. We cannot, therefore, suppose it was intended to deprive cities and villages of the like benefit of the principle of local self-government enjoyed by other political divisions of the state."

People ex rel. Le Roy v. Hurlbut, 24 Mich. 44, 65–66 (1871).

In an important concurring opinion, Judge Thomas Cooley, who subsequently became one of the leading American constitutional law scholars of the late nineteenth century, first recognized that "the accepted theory of state constitutional law" provides for plenary state power over local governments. He urged, however, that the critical role of local "independence and self-control" in protecting civil and political rights required the courts to read some protection for local autonomy into the state constitution: "The state may mould local institutions according to its views of policy or expediency; but local government is a matter of absolute right; and the state cannot take it away." *Id.* at 96, 107–08.

The *Hurlbut* decision and Judge Cooley's concurring conclusion that state constitutions implicitly protect local self-government have been distinctly minority judicial approaches. *Compare* People ex rel. Wood v.

Draper, 15 N.Y. 532 (1857); Mayor & City Council of Baltimore v. State, 15 Md. 376 (1859). *See* Jon Teaford, City Versus State: The Struggle for Legal Ascendancy, 17 Am.J.Leg.Hist. 51, 65 (1973). Indeed, the doctrine of an *inherent* state constitutional right of local autonomy was consistently repudiated by courts and commentators. *See, e.g.,* Howard Lee McBain, The Doctrine of an Inherent Right of Local Self-Government, 16 Colum.L.Rev. 190 (1916). But Cooley's concern that local autonomy ought to receive some recognition in state constitutional law did come to play a central role in the legal evolution of the state-local relationship, and Cooley's analysis continues to be of interest to local government law scholars, *see* David J. Barron, The Promise of Cooley's City: Traces of Local Constitutionalism, 147 U.Penn.L.Rev. 487 (1999).

Building on Cooley's views concerning the connection between local self-government and political freedom, as well as on many of the other arguments for broader local autonomy articulated in Chapter I, the states have repeatedly amended their constitutions and adopted legislation intended to strengthen the legal status of local governments relative to their states. These provisions have taken two forms. One, considered in Section B, has sought to protect local governments from certain specific forms of state interference. These amendments have banned specific types of state legislation that were especially burdensome for local governments. The second, considered in Section C, has replaced the traditional rule of narrow judicial construction of local powers with the principle of "home rule," establishing broad local government power to act even in the absence of specific state authority. Some home rule measures have also sought to protect local governments from state actions that interfere with local initiatives.

With the enactment of restrictions on state power and, especially, the adoption of home rule, local autonomy has now joined plenary state power in the state law of state-local relations. Most states now provide for both plenary state power and some home rule, although the scope of local home rule varies dramatically from state to state. A system that combines both plenary state power and home rule is bound to produce legal clashes; Section D examines the general issue of how state courts consider these state-local conflicts. Finally, Section E concludes with a study aid intended to help you sort out the knotty questions of state-local relations.

B. STATE CONSTITUTIONAL LIMITATIONS ON STATE SUPREMACY

State constitutions limit state governments in many ways. This section focuses on three provisions found in many state constitutions that limit the power of the states over their local governments. Two of these measures—the prohibitions on special state commissions that perform municipal functions, and on special or local legislation—date back to the middle decades of the nineteenth century. They have been described as important, albeit limited, precursors to the development of home rule. *See* Howard Lee McBain, The Law and the Practice of Municipal Home Rule 45–48, 64–106 (Colum. Univ. Press 1916). The third—the restriction on unfunded mandates—is a late twentieth century development. As you read the cases that follow, consider whether these are appropriate restrictions on state legislative power and desirable protections for local governments.

1. THE PROHIBITION ON SPECIAL COMMISSIONS

SPECHT V. CITY OF SIOUX FALLS

Supreme Court of South Dakota
526 N.W.2d 727 (1995)

AMUNDSON, JUSTICE.

The 1992 South Dakota Legislature enacted SDCL ch. 34–11B authorizing municipalities to establish a regional emergency medical services authority (EMS authority). After public hearings, the Sioux Falls City Commission (Commission) passed Resolution 408–92 creating the Sioux Falls Regional Emergency Medical Services Authority (SFREMSA). * * *

On July 30, 1993, Michael Specht and the Sioux Falls Fire Fighters Association (Specht) [challenged the constitutionality of the city commission's resolution and of the state law authorizing the formation of the authority]. * * * Specht argued SFREMSA and its enabling statutory scheme (SDCL ch. 34–11B) violates Article III, § 26,[3] because it creates a special commission whose powers, defined by SDCL ch. 34–11B, involve an improper delegation of municipal functions. * * *

A. Is SFREMSA Engaging in a "Municipal Function"?

* * * This court has never ruled what constitutes a nondelegable "municipal function" under Article III, § 26. Here, the trial court specifically found that "municipalities are better able to govern ambulance and emergency medical services because of the wide diversity between communities and . . . resources within [those] communities." The trial court found that municipalities have historically performed and are better able to perform ambulance and emergency medical service. We agree. The trial court also observed that although oversight and

---

[3] "The Legislature shall not delegate to any special commission, private corporation or association, any power to make, supervise or interfere with any municipal improvement, money, property, effects, whether held in trust or otherwise, or levy taxes, or to select a capital site, or to perform any municipal functions whatever." S.D. CONST. ART. III, § 26.

regulation of ambulance service and prehospital emergency care may affect some interests of people beyond the boundaries of Sioux Falls, its main concern is a city-wide function protecting the local interest only.

* * * City argues that, since the statutes allow more than one municipality to participate in an EMS authority, it is not a municipal function. This argument rings hollow. The fact that the statutory scheme allows only municipal corporations to participate in such EMS authorities supports the trial court's conclusion that this is a municipal function.

City further alleges that SFREMSA is not engaged in a municipal function because the state issues licenses to EMS authorities, like it does to physicians, surgeons, practitioners of healing arts, physicians' assistants, advanced life support personnel, registered and practical nurses, medical assistants, respiratory care practitioners, ambulances, and hospitals. We are not persuaded by such argument. Were we to adopt City's position, the only true "municipal function" would be one that is independent of state license or regulation. Just because people subject to these regulations are required to obtain licenses from the state does not render the function nonmunicipal. Therefore, we affirm the trial court's holding that SFREMSA is engaged in a municipal function.

B. SFREMSA is a "Special Commission" Prohibited by Article III, § 26.

* * * City cites *Tribe v. Salt Lake City Corporation*, 540 P.2d 499, 502–03 (Utah 1975), where the Utah Supreme Court defined a special commission as "some body or group separate and distinct from municipal government." City's reliance on this case is misplaced. SDCL ch. 34–11B defines an EMS authority as "an *independent* public body." (Emphasis added.) SFREMSA by statute, and City's definition of "special commission," are one and the same. Therefore this argument lacks merit.

Further, as noted by the trial court, the effect was that the legislature was creating a special commission; it did not appoint the commission, but it defined its powers. Unfortunately, the legislation does not provide specific standards to guide the EMS authority in the broad exercise of its power.

C.   The SFREMSA is Not Subject to Local Control or Oversight.

As the trial court found, the most significant constitutional problem with the legislation "is the extent to which [it] will intrude upon the ability of the [municipality's citizens] to control through their elected officials the substantive policies that affect them uniquely."

City also asserts the trial court erred in finding SFREMSA not subject to local control, asserting that it is accountable because municipal corporations are not required to create an EMS authority. This argument is confusing. Whether or not a community creates an EMS authority is irrelevant and completely distinct from whether SFREMSA is accountable for its actions. We agree this entity is optional, but must examine its amenability to local control after it has been created. Our review indicates that once commissioned, the SFREMSA is beyond the control or supervision of any outside source.

City argues that SFREMSA is accountable to the citizens because the commissioners of the authority are appointed by the City Commission for a definite term. This argument is fatally flawed however, because SDCL ch. 34–11B has no provision for removing commissioners. Theoretically, commissioners can remain in their appointed positions forever. The trial court found that City had no power to remove the commissioners once appointed, or to control the taxing authority of those commissioners once the taxing authority had been granted. City has not effectively disputed this finding.

Another example of Commission's power is that its authority cannot be decreased unless all the commissioners consent to same in conjunction with the city commissioners. SDCL 34–11B–12. Furthermore, Commission's authority to act cannot be diminished if "the authority has any bonds outstanding * * * unless one hundred percent of the holders of the bonds consent in writing." *Id*. Related to this issue, Specht also points out that SDCL 34–11B–31 allows SFREMSA to sell bonds without an election. This ability to unilaterally sell municipal bonds contradicts SDCL 6–8B–2, which requires a sixty percent majority vote in favor of issuance before a public body may so act. By dispensing with the election requirement, the public has no control over this bonding authority.

Additionally, City is not free to withdraw from SFREMSA if it is in debt; yet SFREMSA is permitted to borrow money for any of its purposes, without any independent supervision or permission. SDCL 34–11B–12 & 31. Consequently, City is subject to SFREMSA's unsupervised, unaccountable financial practices.

City, in reality, has little or no control over the SFREMSA after its creation. From that point on, SFREMSA has the statutory authority to become a self-propelled, unaccountable, bureaucratic freight train.

NOTES AND QUESTIONS

1. *Origins and Purpose of the Ban on Special Commissions.* The prohibition of state creation of special commissions to perform municipal functions can be found in the constitutions of eight states—California, Colorado, Montana, New Jersey, Pennsylvania, South Dakota, Utah and Wyoming. The ban is a reaction to a particularly notorious mid- and late-nineteenth century state abuse in which states took control of a critical local function away from a major city and vested it in a state-appointed commission. In 1857, for example, the New York state legislature transferred

control of the New York City police force to a state-created Metropolitan Police District—"an act which was vigorously protested and so violently resisted that its enforcement led to violence and bloodshed in the city." McBain, Law and Practice of Municipal Home Rule, *supra*, at 7. "State legislators in Michigan, Massachusetts, Maryland, and Missouri followed suit and assumed control of police departments in Detroit, Boston, Baltimore, St. Louis and Kansas City." Teaford, *supra*, 17 Am. J. Leg. Hist. at 65. Michigan's *Hurlbut* litigation, discussed in the introduction of this Chapter, involved a Michigan law that took control of Detroit's water and sewer systems away from the city and vested it in a state-created commission. "And in 1870 lawmakers in [Pennsylvania] even assumed management of the construction of Philadelphia's City Hall, extending state supervision to an unprecedented extreme." *Id.*

These so-called "ripper bills" reflected the intense ethnic conflicts between the growing, increasingly immigrant-dominated urban centers of New York, Boston, Baltimore, and Detroit and the more rurally-oriented state governments. With city services an important source of patronage, ripper bills were also clearly driven by partisan concerns. *See generally* David O, Porter, The Ripper Clause in State Constitutional Law: An Early Urban Experiment—Parts I and II, 1969 Utah L.Rev. 287, 450.

"The special commission ban was intended to protect the structural integrity of municipalities by barring the transfer of municipal services or activities to agencies not a part of local government." Briffault, Our Localism, *supra,* 90 Colum.L.Rev. at 9–10. In some states, a particular purpose of the special commission ban was to protect the local fisc since the commissions were often empowered to incur expenditures that the municipalities were required to finance. Thus, as the Pennsylvania Supreme Court has observed, the special commission provision of that state's constitution was "intended to prevent independent commissions from exercising municipal powers that may result in the expenditure of tax dollars." Pennsylvania School Boards Ass'n, Inc. v. Commonwealth Ass'n of School Administrators, 805 A.2d 476, 480 (Pa. 2002).

The effect of the special commission ban, however, has been restricted by the need for courts to determine, against the backdrop of plenary state power, that the agency created by the state is a "special commission" and not some other governmental body, and that it has been empowered to perform a distinctly "municipal" function.

2.   *Defining Special Commission.* How does the *Specht* court decide that SFREMSA is a "special commission" and not just an extension of the government of the City of Sioux Falls? Given the historic focus of the special commission ban on state ripper legislation, isn't it somewhat incongruous to apply the ban to an agency that is actually created by a city government? Under the South Dakota law, Sioux Falls could not be compelled to delegate its ambulance and EMS to SFREMSA; instead, its action appears to have been voluntary. Are you persuaded by the court's concerns about the city's

lack of power to remove SFREMSA commissioners, its limited authority over SFREMSA, and its limited freedom to withdraw from the Authority? Should the facts of local discretion and control be relevant to whether the entity is a prohibited special commission? What about the voluntary nature of SFREMSA's formation? If the purpose of the constitutional protection is to prevent state interference with local autonomy, what justifies judicial invalidation of an entity that doesn't create the evil sought to be avoided by the provision?

In Municipal Building Authority of Iron County v. Lowder, 711 P.2d 273 (Utah 1985), the Utah Supreme Court gave great weight to the fact that the Iron County Building Authority was created by Iron County, using the Utah Municipal Building Authority Act, to finance and construct a new county jail in rejecting the claim that the authority was an unconstitutional special commission. The court assumed that providing a jail is a traditional municipal function, *id.* at 281, but determined that the Act did not impose a "special commission" because it did not involve "the evils at which" the constitutional provision was aimed. *Id.* The court noted that the Act gave local governments the discretion to create local building authorities and did not impose an authority. Moreover, the county governing body had "total control" over the authority, with the county's commissioners serving ex officio as trustees of the authority so that "[l]ocal control is thus retained over a locally created entity." *Id.* at 282. Although the authority had the power to issue bonds to finance construction of the new jail, it did not have power to impose a tax, and the bonds would be an obligation of the authority, not the county taxpayers. The county would lease the jail from the authority and its lease payments would be used to pay off the bonds, but the county was free to terminate the lease. How does this compare with the arrangement in *Specht*? As the court explained, the county had created the building authority to circumvent state constitutional provisions imposing a debt ceiling and requiring voter approval of a county bond issue as that requirement did not apply to the building authority. Instead of criticizing this end-run around the constitution, the court justified the Utah Municipal Building Authority Act was "a means for financing needed capital improvements without being restricted" by the "financial straitjacket imposed" by the constitutional constraints. *Id.* at 277, 281. The court made clear it was construing the special commission ban "narrowly so as to facilitate flexibility in local government finance." *Id.* at 281. State constitutional limits on local borrowing and the use of building authorities as a judicially-accepted means of evading them are considered more fully in Chapter VI.

3. *Defining Municipal Function.* The second definitional challenge to applying the special commission ban is whether the state-created entity performs a municipal function. How did *Specht* decide that ambulance and emergency medical services are municipal functions that could not be turned over to an agency not directly controlled by a city? The court relies on the finding of the trial court that "municipalities have historically performed and

are better able to perform ambulance and emergency medical service." Is this a question better resolved by courts or legislatures?

Note that the "R" in SFREMSA refers to "regional." Presumably some of the agency's services were provided outside the Sioux Falls city limits. The court notes that the trial court observed that SFREMSA's services "may affect some interests of people beyond the boundaries of Sioux Falls." Should the presence of some extra-local interest have been given greater weight by the court? Does the court's action make it more difficult for a South Dakota municipality that has been providing ambulance and emergency medical services to its own residents to share those services—and control over the provision of those services—with residents of its region?

In other cases, courts have given greater deference to the state's determination that a service, even though previously performed by a municipality, is not necessarily a municipal function for purposes of the special commission ban. This is particularly likely if the agency in question operates on a state-wide or regional basis. In City of West Jordan v. Utah State Retirement Board, 767 P.2d 530 (Utah 1988), the Utah Supreme Court concluded that the state retirement board, which administers the retirement plans of all municipal employees, does not perform a municipal function. Describing an "increasing [judicial] willingness to recognize that many functions traditionally performed by municipalities may be sufficiently infused with a state, as opposed to an exclusively local, interest . . . " the court eschewed a bright line test in favor of a balancing approach. The relevant factors in that inquiry "include but are not limited to, the relative abilities of the state and municipal governments to perform the function, the degree to which the performance of the function affects the interests of those beyond the boundaries of the municipality, and the extent to which the legislation under attack will intrude upon the ability of the people within the municipality to control through their elected officials the substantive policies that affect them uniquely." Id. at 534. Apply this test to the facts of Specht.

See also Regional Transportation District v. Colorado Department of Labor and Employment, 830 P.2d 942, 946–47 (Colo.1992) (regional transport authority does not exercise a municipal function but instead deals with "economic and social issues of concern to the entire state"); Tribe v. Salt Lake City Corporation, 540 P.2d 499 502 (Utah 1975) (each individual project of a redevelopment agency occurs within a particular locality, but "it is a local operation of an act of general statewide scope"). Should the aggregation of local problems convert a local function into a statewide function that is immune from special commission challenge? How else can a court reconcile the special legislation prohibition with the increasing interrelatedness and complexities of local problems?

4. *Special Commissions and Binding Arbitration of Municipal Employment Disputes.* The special commission ban has had some effect in limiting the ability of the states to regulate the municipal employment relationship. Several courts have applied the special commission provision to

invalidate state laws attempting to establish binding arbitration commissions for municipal employees, *see* Greeley Police Union v. City Council of Greeley, 553 P.2d 790 (Colo.1976); City of Sioux Falls v. Sioux Falls Firefighters, Local 814, 234 N.W.2d 35 (S.D.1975). *Cf.* County of Riverside v. Superior Court, 66 P.3d 718 (Cal. 2003) (finding that state law requiring counties to submit to binding arbitration of economic issues that arise during negotiations with unions representing firefighters or law enforcement officers violates provision of the state constitution prohibiting the delegation to a "private person or body power to . . . interfere with county or municipal corporation . . . money . . . or perform a municipal function.") *But see* Pennsylvania School Boards Ass'n, Inc. v. Commonwealth Ass'n of School Administrators, 805 A.2d 476 (Pa. 2002) (finding that state law conferring on certain school administrators power to compel binding arbitration to resolve collective bargaining impasses does not violate special commission ban because it delegates only the "administrative" power to determine contract terms and not any "legislative" power, such as taxation); Cadue v. Moore, 646 A.2d 450 (Pa. Cmwlth Ct. 1994) (county salary board can set salary increases but cannot compel county commissioners to perform the legislative acts of appropriating funds or levying taxes). Compare binding arbitration commissions with SFREMSA. Which presents a more convincing case of a special commission?

2. THE BAN ON SPECIAL LEGISLATION

Most state constitutions contain provisions prohibiting the enactment of special or local legislation. These provisions date back to the middle decades of the nineteenth century, and they reflect multiple goals. As one early twentieth century court eloquently put it:

> This constitutional limitation is based upon the theory that the state is a unit, to be governed, throughout its length and breadth, on all subjects of common interest, by the same laws and that these laws should be general in their application and uniform in their operation. When it was adopted the evil effects of special legislation, enacted at the behest of private individuals or local communities, were well understood and appreciated. The makers of the [1859 Kansas] Constitution were confronted with the experience of the older states, which had demonstrated that Legislatures were wholly unable to withstand the constant demands for private grants of power and special privilege. * * *

> The inherent vice of special laws is that they create preferences and establish irregularities. As an inevitable consequence, their enactment leads to improvident and ill-considered legislation. The members whose particular constituents are not affected by a proposed special law become indifferent to its passage. It is customary, on the plea of legislative courtesy, not to interfere with the local bill of another member; and members are elected, and reelected on account of

their proficiency in procuring for their respective districts special privileges in the way of local or special laws. The time which the legislature would otherwise devote to the consideration of measures of public importance is frittered away in the granting of special favors to private or corporate interests or to local communities. Meanwhile, in place of a symmetrical body of statutory law on subjects of general and common interest to the whole people, we have a wilderness of special provisions, whose operation extends no further than the boundaries of the particular school district or township or county to which they were made to apply. * * * Worse still, rights and privileges, which should only result from the decree of a court of competent jurisdiction after a full hearing and notice to all parties in interest, are conferred upon individuals and private corporations by special acts of the Legislature, without any pretense of investigation as to the merits, or of notice to adverse parties.

Anderson v. Board of Comm'rs of Cloud County, 95 P. 583, 584, 586 (Kan.1908). For a contemporaneous history of the enactment of state constitutional restrictions on special legislation, *see* Charles Chauncy Binney, Restrictions Upon Local and Special Legislation in State Constitutions (1894). For a twenty-first century account, *see* Robert M. Ireland, The Problem of Local, Private and Special Legislation in the Nineteenth Century United States, 46 Am. J. Legal Hist. 271 (2004).

In other words, the prohibition of special legislation was intended to promote legislation based on broad general principles; to lead legislators to focus on the public interest of the state as a whole rather than on idiosyncratic local or private interests; to protect legislators' time from distraction by private or local matters; to promote greater equality of legal treatment; and to reduce the unfairness inherent in special legislative deals. *See* Anthony Schutz, State Constitutional Restrictions on Special Legislation as Structural Restraints, 40 J. Legis. 39, 57–61 (2013) (explaining that special laws receive inadequate legislative scrutiny, take time that would be better applied to broader problems, and provide no assurance that a bill on the same subject with the same facts would receive the same treatment.)

Special legislation also lends itself to "logrolling," that is, vote trading among legislators, each of whom is pushing his or her own special bill. The Indiana Supreme Court emphasized the anti-logrolling aspect of the special act prohibitions in a case invalidating a state law creating a special voting rule for annexations in just one county in the state:

"[T]hese anti-logrolling provisions are grounded in the view that as long as a law affects only one small area of the state, voters in most areas will be ignorant of and indifferent to it. As a result,

> many legislators will be tempted, some would say expected, to
> support the proposals of the legislators from the affected area,
> even if they deem the proposal to be a bad policy that they could
> not support if it affected their own constituents."

Municipal City of South Bend v. Kimsey, 781 N.E.2d 683, 686 (Ind. 2003).
See also Clayton P. Gillette, Expropriation and Institutional Design in
State and Local Government Law, 80 Va.L.Rev. 625, 642–57 (1994)
(emphasizing the role of the special legislation ban in preventing
legislative logrolling).

The ban on special legislation is not focused just on local
governments. Indeed, for some states it functions as an equal protection
clause as well as a rule of state-local relations. *See* Pennsylvania
Turnpike Comm'n v. Commonwealth, 899 A.2d 1085, 1094 (Pa. 2006) (the
state's special act ban "has been recognized to be analogous to federal
principles of equal protection of the law . . . and, thus, special legislation
claims and equal protection claims have been reviewed under the same
jurisprudential rubric. . . . The common constitutional principle . . . is that
like persons in like circumstances should be treated similarly by the
sovereign"). *See also* Justin Long, State Constitutional Prohibitions on
Special Laws, 60 Clev. St. L. Rev. 719, 732–36 (2012) (criticizing state
courts for generally treating special legislation bans like the equal
protection clause and typically applying rational basis review). *But cf.*
Republic Investment Fund I v. Town of Surprise, 800 P.2d 1251, 1256
(Ariz. 1990) (distinguishing between equal protection and special/local
law challenges; suggesting that the equal protection clause proscribes
unreasonable discrimination *against* a class, whereas the special law ban
is aimed at preventing the granting of special benefits). But by limiting
the ability of the states to tailor laws to particular local governments, the
special act ban may have also been intended to prevent the states from
singling out particular local governments for targeted interferences.

One difficulty with the prohibition on special legislation grows out of
the tension between the aspiration to uniform statewide treatment and
the reality of enormous differences—in needs, conditions, and
preferences—among the many local governments across a state.
Legislation that may deal appropriately with a situation in a large city
may be unwise for a smaller municipality. Indeed, the state ban on
special legislation is typically subject to the qualification that local laws
are barred only when a state-wide law may be made applicable, and
courts routinely permit state legislatures to limit the scope of laws to
particular localities or areas when that is justified by a state-wide
interest. Thus, the central issue when a state law affecting a particular
local government is challenged as special legislation is whether the terms
of the law targeting the particular locality reflect a principled

determination of the scope of the problem in question or, instead, an unprincipled locally-targeted response to a broader problem.

TOWN OF SECAUCUS V.
HUDSON COUNTY BOARD OF TAXATION

Supreme Court of New Jersey
628 A.2d 288 (1993)

HANDLER, J.

This case asks the Court to resolve the question whether a statute * * * that exempts the City of Bayonne from paying its share of taxes committed to the operation of the Hudson County Vocational School violates * * * the prohibition on special legislation, article IV, section 7, paragraph 9(6) * * * of the New Jersey Constitution. * * *

I

The City of Bayonne, located in Hudson County, has operated a vocational-educational program since 1931. Originally, Bayonne implemented that program through a separate vocational high school. In the 1960s, however, Bayonne created a comprehensive high school that fully integrated the vocational program into its general high school curriculum. Bayonne's vocational-education program, which has been widely praised, allows vocational students to participate fully in school activities and attend many classes with general education high school students.

In 1972, the Board of Education of the Hudson County Vocational School (hereafter "HCVS" or "county vocational school") passed a resolution authorizing the acquisition of a building for a new county vocational school. The following year, a $2 million budget was proposed for the operation of HCVS, and in 1974 HCVS began operating from its own facility. Realizing that the Bayonne vocational program, by that time in existence more than forty years, would not be discontinued, and wanting to spare Bayonne the double expense of supporting its own and the county's vocational programs, State legislators from Hudson County proposed legislation exempting Bayonne from contributing to the maintenance of the county vocational school.

The terms of the original legislation, proposed as Senate Bill 74 in the 1972 Legislative Session, were quite broad. Those terms provided that

> each municipality included within a school district maintaining a system of vocational education approved for the purposes of federal or state allotment of vocational funds by the Commissioner of Education under the regulations of the State Board of Education shall be exempt from assessment, levy or

collection of taxes based on any apportionment of amounts appropriated for the use of a county vocational school district.

The effect of the original legislation would have exempted virtually every municipality with a vocational-education program from contributing to the support of its county's vocational school. Recognizing that, Senate Education Committee amendments to Senate Bill 74 significantly narrowed the scope of the exemption in order to exempt only Bayonne from the general obligation to support county vocational-educational programs. That narrowing was achieved by limiting the effect of the legislation in two ways. First, the amendments restricted the municipalities affected only to those in a "county of the first class having a population of not more than 700,000 according to the 1970 Federal Census." * * * In 1973, N.J.S.A. 40A:6–1 defined a first class county as "a county having a population of more than 600,000." By that criterion, Bergen County (1970 population 897,148), Essex County (1970 population 932,526), and Hudson County (1970 population 607,839) qualified as first class counties. Only Hudson, however, met the amended statute's population requirement for the tax exemption.

Second, the amendments required that in order for a municipality to qualify for the exemption, its vocational program would have to have been in existence, as a program approved by the State Board of Education for state or federal funding, for at least twenty years. Because, among the Hudson County municipalities, only Bayonne had a vocational education program in existence and approved by the State for at least twenty years, the amended statute applied only to Bayonne. The statement to the bill, from the Senate Education Committee, left no doubt about the intent of the legislation: "This bill, as amended, would exempt the City of Bayonne from any assessment of taxes due to the cost of supporting the county vocational school in Hudson County". * * *

To implement the mandate of N.J.S.A. 18A:54–37, Hudson County devised a two-tier tax system for assessing the county tax burden on its municipalities. The system, administered by defendant Hudson County Board of Taxation (HCBT), provided a higher rate (which included the costs of operating the county vocational school) for eleven of Hudson County's twelve municipalities, including plaintiff, Secaucus, and a lower rate (which excluded the costs of operating the county vocational school) for Bayonne. * * *

Secaucus, as one of the eleven Hudson County municipalities subjected to the higher tax rate, brought a complaint * * * against Hudson County and HCBT. * * *

The New Jersey Constitution provides that:

"9. The Legislature shall not pass any private, special or local laws:

(6) Relating to taxation or exemption therefrom. [N.J. Const. art. IV, § 7, ¶ 9(6)]"

From a constitutional standpoint, a law is regarded as special legislation " 'when, by force of an inherent limitation, it arbitrarily separates some persons, places or things from others upon which, but for such limitation, it would operate. The test of a special law is the appropriateness of its provisions to the objects that it excludes.' "

* * * Taken in a light most favorable to the constitutionality of the statute, two possible interpretations of N.J.S.A. 18A:54–37 on their face reveal a legitimate legislative purpose. First, N.J.S.A. 18A:54–37 may be conceived most generally as a tax relief statute designed to lessen the burden on those municipalities that maintain their own vocational education programs. * * *

A second purpose of N.J.S.A. 18A:54–37 may be to promote the development of local, high-quality vocational educational programs within densely-populated communities. In achieving that objective, the statute would have the added benefit of reducing the strain on county vocational schools.

After careful scrutiny of the specific facts of this case and the statute under challenge, how N.J.S.A. 18A:54–37 realizes either of those purposes is difficult to see.

In the first case, if alleviating the problem of double contribution for municipalities that maintain their own vocational programs is the real purpose of N.J.S.A. 18A:54–37, the population-density and longevity requirements of the statute make little sense. At least twenty municipalities within the state, and at least one other municipality within Hudson County (Kearny), maintain their own vocational-education programs. As Secaucus noted, to the extent that the burden from double contribution is not any less for municipalities that have maintained local vocational programs for fewer than twenty years, the longevity requirement of N.J.S.A. 18A:54–37 seems particularly ill-suited to the goal of tax relief.

In the second case, if the goal of N.J.S.A. 18A:54–37 is to encourage the development of high-quality vocational-education programs within densely-populated municipalities, thereby reducing the strain on county vocational schools, to exclude municipalities either in the most-populous counties, i.e. Essex and Bergen, or in less but densely-populated counties like Union and Middlesex, does not seem reasonable. Nonetheless, the statute excludes Essex and Bergen on the basis of their excessive populations (over 700,000), and excludes densely-populated Union and Middlesex counties because they are not designated first-class counties.

That "[a] classification based on population does not automatically render a law unconstitutional special legislation" is well settled. * * * This Court has recognized the rational "nexus between accountability and population."

* * * In this case, we are cognizant of the fact that Hudson County is unique in terms of the density and urbanization of its population, having almost twice as many residents per square mile (12,108.1) as the next most densely-populated county, Essex County (6,701.7). From that fact, it is possible to conjecture that the Legislature had a special interest in encouraging the development of local vocational education programs in the State's most densely populated areas. Nevertheless, that possibility seems remote, if not illusory. That concern has never been advanced as a possible legislative purpose or concern. Further, from the perspective of making educational services available to as many students as feasible, the encouragement of excellent vocational schools by individual school districts would make as much sense for less densely-populated areas as those more densely-populated. However, as already noted, the particular limitations embodied in N.J.S.A. 18A:54–37 go well beyond population size and density.

The requirement that the local vocational program be in operation for at least twenty years—the so-called "longevity" requirement—works to exclude other municipalities, in areas just as densely populated as Bayonne, from the benefit of the statute. To accept the classifications contained in N.J.S.A. 18A:54–37 as having a rational basis, one must imagine that the Legislature had some reasonable ground for encouraging the development of local vocational programs only in the most-densely-populated county in the state with a total population below 700,000, *and* that the Legislature had reasonable grounds for concluding that only those programs in existence for at least twenty years were of sufficient quality to be worthy of financial encouragement through tax relief. Those conclusions seem to us to stretch credulity beyond reasonable limits.

The dissent finds the statute rational because it pursues a very different mode of analysis of the classifications embodied in the statute. First, the dissent disaggregates the population and longevity requirements. With respect to the twenty-year approval requirement, the dissent simply refuses to "second-guess" the legislature and finds the longevity requirement rational. * * * The dissent then finds the population requirements, if not rational, at least harmless because "[t]he list of approved vocational programs reveals that no municipality either in Bergen or Essex Counties maintains such a program." * * *

As noted earlier * * * the original terms of what became N.J.S.A. 18A:54–37 would have achieved the broad and entirely rational purpose of tax relief for all those municipalities that operated their own vocational-education programs. The bill was amended, however, to be directed toward a class of one: Bayonne. * * *

When, in 1981, the population of Hudson County fell below 600,000, thus jeopardizing its status as a county of the first class, the Legislature responded by redefining county of the first class with new total population and population-density requirements. The population-density requirement had the effect of keeping Middlesex County, which by 1980 had a population larger than that of Hudson County, from becoming a county of the first class. At the same time it redefined a first-class county, the Legislature amended N.J.S.A. 18A:54–37 so that its population ceiling of 700,000 would track the most recent decennial census. The effect of those amendments was to continue to guarantee that only Bayonne would derive the benefit of the statute's exemption.

True, a statute is not unconstitutional as special legislation merely because its effect is limited to a particular municipality. * * * Nevertheless, the classification by which a statute limits its effects must be grounded in a rational basis. * * * When a statute has the effect of addressing the needs of a particular community or serving a particular legislative purpose, the Court looks to, inter alia, whether "other municipalities could, and from time to time have, come within its scope." * * *

In this case, even if one could justify rationally the total population and population-density requirements of N.J.S.A. 18A:54–37, we cannot conceive of a rational basis for excluding other municipalities that may satisfy the population requirements of N.J.S.A. 18A:54–37 on the basis of the fact that their vocational programs have not been approved by the State for at least twenty years.

The history of N.J.S.A. 18A:54–37 makes clear not only that the classifications embodied within it lacked a reasonable basis, but that no other municipality—partly due to the statute's subsequent amendment—has come within its scope or derived its benefit. Kearny, which implemented its vocational-education program in 1980, would come within the statute's scope in the year 2000. Were that to occur the statute would have been in operation almost three decades before a municipality other than Bayonne came within its scope.

Based on the foregoing analysis, we conclude that N.J.S.A. 18A:54–37, as it actually operates, does not represent a reasonable legislative classification. Accordingly, we find that N.J.S.A. 18A:54–37 violates the prohibition on special legislation of article IV, section 7, paragraph 9 of the New Jersey Constitution. * * *

NOTES AND QUESTIONS

1.   *Problem-Solving vs. Principles.* What was the flaw in New Jersey's attempt to allow the City of Bayonne to preserve its successful vocational-educational program, while avoiding double taxation in Bayonne and generally providing for vocational education at the county level? Note that the statutory exemption was proposed by state legislators from Hudson County, the only county affected by Bayonne's exemption. If Hudson County's representatives found this to be an appropriate compromise and were able to persuade the rest of the legislature, why should the court veto it? After *Town of Secaucus*, is it possible for New Jersey to provide tax relief for Bayonne? What would such a law look like? Would it be an improvement over the law invalidated in this case? For a study of this case, *see* Thomas M. Palisi, Comment, Town of Secaucus v. Hudson County Board of Taxation: An Analysis of the Special Legislation and Tax Uniformity Clauses of the New Jersey Constitution, 47 Rutgers L.Rev. 1229 (1995).

2.   *Classification by Population.* A critical element of the New Jersey law was its limitation of tax relief to municipalities in "a county of the first class having a population of not more than 700,000," with counties of the first class in turn defined in terms of population. Classification by population is a widespread state legislative response to prohibitions on special legislation. Population classifications reflect the assumptions that local circumstances, concerns and needs are affected by local population, so that it may be reasonable to limit the operation of certain laws to cities or counties of a certain size. Large, densely populated cities, in particular, may require or benefit from laws that differ from those applicable in smaller localities. *Cf.* Gallardo v. State, 336 P.3d 717, 721–22 (Ariz. 2014) (rejecting special act challenge to law adding two at-large members to the governing board of any community college district located in a county with a population of at least three million people; the legislature "could have rationally concluded" that adding seats to the governing boards of only the most populous districts "would promote better governance and representation"); City of Enid v. Public Emp. Rels. Bd. 133 P.3d 281, 288 (Okla. 2006) (rejecting special act ban challenge to state law requiring municipal employers, defined as municipalities with populations greater than 35,000, to engage in collective bargaining with their employees; limiting the law to larger cities was reasonable because they have greater administrative and financial capacity to undertake collective bargaining than the exempted smaller cities). However, even laws targeted on the largest localities may be found to violate the special legislation ban if there is an insufficient relationship between the purpose of the act and population size. *See, e.g.,* Knoop v. City of Little Rock, 638 S.W.2d 670 (Ark. 1982) (invalidating law that required cities with populations over 100,000 and a city manager form of government to elect the mayor by majority vote; the court was unable to find "any reasonable basis" for linking city size to electoral rules); In re Marxus B., 13 P.3d 290 (Ariz. Ct. App. 2000) (law, applicable only to counties with populations of more than 500,000, making it a crime for a minor to knowingly carry or possess on his

person a firearm in any public place is an unconstitutional special law; "there is no indication that the minors or parents in Maricopa and Pima counties are more irresponsible with firearms than are those in other counties;" legislature's decision to provide greater protection for residents of those counties was "unexplainable").

Population classes are more subject to challenge if they involve relatively narrow bands of intermediate-size cities and counties. *See, e.g.*, In re Village of Vernon Hills, 658 N.E.2d 365 (Ill.1995) (invalidating a law dealing with fire protection districts in counties with a population of between 500,000 and 750,000). In *Town of Secaucus*, the tax relief measure was targeted not simply at first class counties, e.g., counties with a population greater than 600,000, but counties of the first class having a population of not more than 700,000. By excluding the two largest first class counties, this created an odd class composed solely of municipalities in the third largest county in the state. As the court indicated, if the purpose of the measure was to promote vocational-education programs in densely populated counties, it did not seem reasonable to exclude the two most populous counties. Similarly, the Missouri Supreme Court had little difficulty striking down a law that applied to fire protection districts "wholly within first class counties with more than 198,000 but fewer than 199,200 inhabitants." Jefferson County Fire Protection Districts Ass'n v. Blunt, 205 S.W.3d 866 (Mo. 2006). In an opinion written by the same judge and handed down on the same day, however, the Missouri Supreme Court sustained a state law requiring competitive bidding for expenditures of more than $5000 undertaken by the executive of a county with a charter form of government and with more than 600,000 but fewer than 700,000 inhabitants. Jackson County v. State, 207 S.W.3d 608 (Mo. 2006). The *Jackson County* Court noted that the range of the competitive bidding law was considerably broader than in the *Jefferson County* case. The court concluded there was a "rational basis for the classification"—the state had only three counties with a charter form of government, and the other two had already placed checks on their executive's spending in their charters. *See id.* at 612. Do you think that the *Town of Secaucus* court would have agreed that this provided a rational basis?

It is usually not a problem if only one city or county falls within the population class in question provided that the class is formally *open* or *elastic*, that is, other cities or counties could grow into the class, even if, as a practical matter, that is unlikely. *See, e.g.*, Gallardo, *supra*, 336 P.2d at 724–26 (upholding expanded community college governing board in counties of at least three million people even though there was only one such county in the state; other counties could grow into the class "even though none will likely do so in the near future"); Maryland Dep't of the Environment v. Days Cove Reclamation Co., Inc., 27 A.3d 565 (Md. App. 2011) (law prohibiting the issuance of landfill permits within close proximity of certain waterways that immediately affected only one company not a closed class because the statute applies prospectively so other companies could be affected in the future); CLEAN v. State, 928 P.2d 1054 (Wash.1996) (upholding state law establishing procedures for the construction and financing of a baseball stadium in counties of more than one million inhabitants; although Washington had only one such county, other counties might grow to that size in the future). *See also* Jackson County, *supra*, 207 S.W.2d at 611–12 (classifications based on populations are "open-ended" and thus generally presumed to be constitutional); Jefferson County, *supra*, 205 S.W.3d at 870–71 (presumptive constitutionality of open-ended population class is overcome when the classification is "so narrow that as a practical matter others could not fall into that classification)." Even if a law was adopted in response to a particular problem in a particular locality it may be saved from a special act challenge if the class is open and the problem addressed could arise in other localities. *See, e.g.*, City of Greenwood Village v. Petitioners for Proposed City of Centennial, 3 P.3d 427 (Colo. 2000) (upholding Colorado law holding an annexation proceeding in abeyance pending a conflicting incorporation proceeding involving a proposed city of over 75,000 inhabitants; although the "catalyst" for the law's adoption was an annexation-incorporation battle over the proposed City of Centennial, the court found the law to be "generic in its application," "applicable to other foreseeable situations," and not to "deal with a class of one"). A class can be considered closed if the measure of population is tied to a specific census, or to an action that had to be taken either before enactment of the statute or within a short time thereafter. *See, e.g.*, City of Springfield v. Sprint Spectrum L.P., 203 S.W.3d 177 (Mo. 2006) (invalidated statute that exempted certain municipalities from a statewide limit on their authority to impose business license taxes on telephone companies because it applied only to those municipalities that had taken affirmative steps to collect the tax prior to the statute's enactment); Republic Investment Fund I v. Town of Surprise, *supra*, 800 P.2d at 1259 ("A classification limited to a population as of a particular census or date is a typical form of a defective closed class; such an act is a form of identification, not of classification, because it is impossible for entities to enter or exit the class with changes in population").

Notice how in the principal case the state of New Jersey combined multiple conditions to define a statutory class which, while technically open, consisted solely of Bayonne.

Courts frequently search for a reasonable relationship between the purpose of the law and the city or county population classification. *Compare* CLEAN v. State, *supra*, at 1064 ("the relationship between the population of an area and its ability to put fans in the seats of the stadium is obvious") *with* State ex rel. City of Charleston v. Bosely, 268 S.E.2d 590, 596 (W.Va.1980) (invalidating law enabling cities with a population larger than 50,000 to tax hotel occupancy; "[i]f one municipality is to be given the authority to tax in order to further civic development, all municipalities should be given that authority"). Was there any connection between Bayonne's status as a city in a less populous first-class county that had provided a vocational-education program for a period that satisfied the statute's longevity requirement and the asserted goal of promoting municipal vocational education or providing tax relief for municipalities that provide vocational education?

3. *Factor by Factor or Composite Review*? An important question in special legislation cases that involve classes defined by more than one factor is whether the reasonableness of the factors should be considered in the aggregate or separately. Justice Stein, dissenting in *Secaucus*, considered the rationality of each individual factor. The exemption from taxation was available to those cities that: (1) were located in a first-class county with populations of not more than 700,000; and (2) had vocational school programs in operation for at least twenty years. Because each factor standing alone was based on a rational distinction, the dissent found it irrelevant that the factors combined in such a way as to make Bayonne the only city eligible for the exemption.

Like the *Secaucus* majority, the Washington Supreme Court invalidated a state law that authorized the establishment of community councils on island communities located in counties (1) composed entirely of islands and (2) having an unincorporated population greater than 30,000:

> [W]e find ourselves unable to articulate any rational basis why other populated island communities are excluded from the scope of the community council act. The purpose sought to be achieved by the statute is as applicable to island communities which belong to mainland counties as it is to island communities which belong to counties comprised entirely of islands.

Island County v. State, 955 P.2d 377, 384 (Wash.1998).

In contrast, the Illinois Supreme Court, in The Chicago National League Ball Club, Inc. v. Thompson, 483 N.E.2d 1245 (Ill.1985), rejected a challenge to an amendment to the noise pollution provisions of Illinois environmental laws, which applied noise emission standards to sports stadia that met the following four criteria: (1) located in cities with more than a million inhabitants; (2) held nighttime sporting events; (3) held professional sporting events; and (4) had not held nighttime sporting events prior to 1982. The court examined each legislative criterion individually and found a rational basis for each one. By adopting a factor by factor approach, the court was able to avoid dealing with the coincidence that these factors combined in such a way as to prohibit nighttime games at only one stadium in the state of Illinois. The individual assessment of factors makes it more likely that the court will accept state legislation narrowly targeted at one or a small number of localities. If the factors are reasonable, then why is narrow targeting a problem? Or is narrow targeting inherently in tension with the ban on special legislation?

4. *Protection from Burdens or Prohibition of Benefits*? Should it matter whether the locality that is the subject of a special state law is benefitted or burdened by the law? Following the logic of the special commission ban, courts might be more inclined to strike down state laws that impose burdens

on individual local governments or interfere with local autonomy while tolerating laws that provide special benefits. Would such a distinction be workable in practice? Did the New Jersey law at issue in *Town of Secaucus* provide an acceptable benefit to Bayonne, or did it impose a burden on the other municipalities in Hudson County? Did the law at issue in the Jackson County case discussed in Note 2 requiring competitive bidding for expenditures above $5000 in chartered counties benefit or burden those counties? If a law authorizing landowners to petition for deannexation applies only to a limited class of municipality, does that law burden the municipalities where deannexation petitions are authorized (and implicitly benefit municipalities not covered) or does it benefit the landowners who can petition for deannexation? *See* Long, State Constitutional Prohibitions on Special Laws, *supra*, 60 Clev. St. L. Rev. at 737–39 (discussing decision of Arizona Supreme Court in Republic Investment Fund I, *supra*).

5. *Special Legislation or "Pilot Program"?* Can a state law dealing with a statewide problem but narrowly focused on a small number of local governments be saved from a special legislation challenge on the theory that the legislature could experiment with a "pilot program" before regulating the entire state? The Pennsylvania Supreme Court held that it could in Harrisburg School District v. Zogby, 828 A.2d 1079 (Pa. 2003). *Harrisburg* dealt with an amendment to Pennsylvania's Educational Empowerment Act ("PEEA") which allows the mayors of certain medium-sized cities to assume control of failing school districts. Under the PEEA, the governing board in any school district found by the state Department of Education to be "failing" is, after a period of time, subject to replacement by a "board of control" appointed by the state Secretary of Education. Another provision of the PEEA provided a different mechanism for replacing a school board. In "a school district of the second class with a history of low test performance which is coterminous with the city of the third class which contains the permanent seat of government," the mayor of that city was authorized to appoint and remove members of the board of control. Due to the permanent-seat-of-government criterion, this class had but a single member—the Harrisburg School District—and for that reason the Pennsylvania Supreme Court found the measure violated the state constitution's ban on special legislation. Harrisburg School District v. Hickok, 761 A.2d 1132 (Pa. 2000). The legislature then revised the special provision to authorize mayoral control in "a school district of the second class which has a history of extraordinarily low performance, which is coterminous with a city of the third class that has opted under the 'Optional Third Class City Charter Law' . . . to be governed by a mayor-council form of government and which has a population in excess of 45,000." Under Pennsylvania law, a school district of the second class has a population of between 30,000 and 250,000; cities of the third class are those with populations under 250,000. Although the impetus for the amendment was the empowerment of the mayor of Harrisburg, the effect of the new law was to extend the opportunity for mayoral take-over to a handful of other small cities.

The Commonwealth Court held that notwithstanding the expansion of the affected class, the law still violated the special act ban:

> "The number and oddness of the distinctions that mix and match a class of school with a particular subclass of a third class city that itself is a particular subclass of a home rule municipality that is further narrowed by a population classification that itself is a subclass of population classification used to determine classes of city indicates that the object of the legislation was to winnow down the number of school districts so that it would apply to a very, very, very small number. While that, in and of itself, does not make the legislation violative of [the special legislation ban] the absence of any apparent 'rhyme or reason' for the factors used indicates that they were artificial and irrelevant to remedying the situation in districts with 'extraordinarily low [state assessment] scores.'"

Harrisburg School Dist. v. Hickok ("Hickok II"), 781 A.2d 221, 228 (Pa. Cmwlth. 2001).

The Pennsylvania Supreme Court reversed. The court began by reframing the purpose of the ban on special legislation as "not so much to prohibit the General Assembly from undertaking limited, remedial measures as part of a long-term strategy to fulfill its duties connected with the public interest, but to end the practice of favoritism." 828 A.2d at 1088. The court then proceeded to find a reasonable connection between each piece of the statutory definition and the statutory purpose of ameliorating conditions in failing school districts. The focus on urban districts was appropriate because "the Legislature could reasonably have believed that social issues interrelated with education, such as crime, poverty, and a weak tax base, are more severe in urban districts than in rural ones and sufficiently so to warrant special treatment." *Id.* at 1090. "The Legislature could reasonably have sought to limit the program initially to cities with a mayor-led government in which the mayor is accountable to the same local electorate that makes up the school district" because this "has the benefit of providing the individual who retains ultimate authority over the board of control (i.e., the mayor) with the greatest political incentive to ensure that effective means are implemented to improve the performance of the school district." *Id.* The further limit to home rule cities was also reasonable because the legislature "could reasonably have concluded that . . . such conditions would lend themselves to the mayor 'hav[ing] significant input into the development and implementation of any school district improvement plan adopted.'" *Id.*

> "Finally, although as noted by the Commonwealth Court, these restrictions collectively narrow the class of school districts [affected] . . . to a small number, we believe it was rational for the General Assembly to seek to limit the program's initial reach to a small group of districts before prescribing the same procedures more generally throughout the state. Such is consistent with the codified legislative findings, which indicate that the effectiveness of a

> mayor-led system of school governance should be assessed under the
> act's 'pilot program' before being made more generally available.
> Moreover, there is nothing improper about this method of attacking
> social problems of statewide dimension, as the Legislature is free,
> for reasons of necessity or otherwise, to address such issues
> incrementally."

Id. at 1090–91. Although the court denied the dissent's charge that it had
created a "pilot program exception" to the constitutional ban on special
legislation, the court's opinion seems intended to make the case that a
reasonably designed pilot program, which is also an open class, should be
sustained. Should the legislature be limited to the choice of either
authorizing mayoral takeovers of broad classes of failing schools or not
authorizing such takeovers, or should a law permitting takeovers in a narrow
and oddly defined class of school districts be seen as a permissible form of
experimentation and incrementalism?

The Pennsylvania Supreme Court declined to extend *Zogby* in West
Mifflin Area School Dist. v. Zahorchak, 4 A.3d 1042 (Pa. 2010). That case
considered a challenge to a law authorizing the state secretary of education to
require certain school districts to accept high school students and give a
hiring priority for furloughed high school teachers from (i) a third class school
district (ii) in which a public high school is not maintained, (iii) which for five
consecutive years has operated under a special board of control (due to
financial problems), (iv) has been placed by the secretary "on the educational
empowerment list" due to a history of low test performance, (v) has, with the
approval of the secretary, curtailed its educational program by eliminating its
high school, and (vi) has not arranged for the assignment of its high school
pupils to another school district. Only one school district in Pennsylvania, the
Duquesne City District, met all the criteria in the statute. The three school
districts that, due to their proximity to Duquesne, would be required by the
statute to accept students and furloughed teachers asserted the measure was
an invalid special law. The intermediate court of appeals upheld the statute
under *Zogby*, finding that its criteria are "similar to those that were held to
be rational considerations in *Zogby*" and "relate rationally to the objective of
identifying school districts that have had educational shortcomings and have
ongoing severe financial problems and providing assistance if necessary when
such a district eliminates its high school program." 956 A.2d 1040, 1049
(Cmwlth Ct. Pa 2008). The state supreme court, however, reversed, finding
the statute created an unconstitutional "class of one member that is closed or
substantially closed to future membership." 4 A.3d at 1048. There were only
five other school districts that had ever been placed on the "empowerment
list," which had been closed in 2004, and none of those operated under a
special board of control. As a result, "the practical effect" of the statute "was,
and was always intended to be, to provide a remedy solely for the adverse
circumstances obtaining within the Duquesne City School District upon
elimination of its high school." *Id.* at 1049. Acknowledging that the law "may
embody a salutary program aimed at resolving certain problems that arose

within the Duquesne City School District in the summer of 2007, and that efforts by the General Assembly to ameliorate such difficulties are consistent with its obligation" under the state constitution to provide a system of public education, the court nonetheless concluded that the measure was an unconstitutional special law. *Id.* What should the Pennsylvania legislature have done to address the Duquesne high school situation?

EMERALD ISLE V. STATE
Supreme Court of North Carolina
360 S.E.2d 756 (1987)

FRYE, JUSTICE.

* * * The Town of Emerald Isle * * * is a municipality located on Bogue Banks, Carteret County, North Carolina, and has approximately eight miles of frontage on the Atlantic Ocean and Bogue Sound. * * *

In 1982, the Town obtained a permit from the State and constructed a vehicular ramp over the sand dunes and accreted lands at the western end of Inlet Drive at a point where the paved surface of Inlet Drive had eroded away. The vehicular ramp was constructed on accreted lands within the extended bounds of the right-of-way of Inlet Drive. After completion of the ramp, vehicles could travel westerly over Inlet Drive and the vehicular ramp to the beach areas within Blocks 53 and 54. Pedestrians were also allowed access to the beaches through the right-of-way.

The Town's Beach Access Ordinance regulates the entrance and travel of vehicles on the beaches. Under its terms, vehicles are allowed to gain access to the Emerald Isle beaches through certain designated access points, and once access is gained vehicular travel is limited to certain marked streets and areas of the beach.

On 16 June 1983, the North Carolina General Assembly enacted Chapter 539 of the 1983 Session Laws. * * *

In essence, the act directs the Department of Natural Resources, in cooperation with the Town of Emerald Isle, to acquire real property (in the vicinity of Bogue Inlet) which surrounds the vehicle access ramp. The Department is also directed to build facilities for public pedestrian beach access to the property. Once the facilities are completed, the act prohibits motor vehicular traffic in the four blocks adjacent to the facilities and limits the use of the existing vehicle access ramp to public service and emergency vehicles and pedestrians.

Plaintiff Town of Emerald Isle, along with the four individual plaintiffs, property owners and taxpayers of the Town of Emerald Isle, two of whom possess beach access permits issued by the Town authorizing vehicular access to the ocean and inlet beaches, brought this declaratory judgment action to challenge the constitutionality of 1983 N.C.Sess.Laws, ch. 539, § 1. * * *

Plaintiffs first contend that the act violates Article XIV, section 3 of the North Carolina Constitution. This portion of our constitution provides, in pertinent part, that "no special or local act shall be enacted concerning the subject matter directed or authorized to be accomplished by general or uniformly applicable laws." The act in question, according to plaintiffs, is a local act.

* * * This Court, in *Adams v. Dept. of N.E.R.* and *Everett v. Dept. of N.E.R.*, 295 N.C. 683, 249 S.E.2d 402 (1978), set forth the test for distinguishing general laws from local acts, stating that

> the distinguishing factors between a valid general law and a prohibited local act are the related elements of reasonable classification and uniform application. A general law defines a class which reasonably warrants special legislative attention and applies uniformly to everyone in the class. On the other hand, a local act unreasonably singles out a class for special legislative attention or, having made a reasonable classification, does not apply uniformly to all members of the designated class. In sum, the constitutional prohibition against local acts simply commands that when legislating in certain specified fields the General Assembly must make rational distinctions among units of local government which are reasonably related to the purpose of the legislation. A law is general if "any rational basis reasonably related to the objective of the legislation can be identified which justifies the separation of units of local government into included and excluded categories."

Ferrell, Local Legislation in the North Carolina General Assembly, 45 N.C.L.Rev. 340, 391 (1967).

* * * We find that the traditional reasonable classification analysis previously applied by this Court in determining what constitutes a "local act" in *Adams* is ill-suited to the question presented in this case, since by definition a particular public pedestrian beach access facility must rest in but one location. Furthermore, assuming the legislature acts within its authority when it establishes such facilities by legislative action, we find it unnecessary to require it to do so by crafting tortured classifications.

The primary purpose of the constitutional limitation on legislative enactments of local acts is to allow the General Assembly an opportunity to devote more time and attention to legislation of state-wide interest and concern. * * * Accordingly we find that, instead of applying a reasonable classification analysis, our attention should focus on the extent to which the act in question affects the general public interests and concerns. In doing so, we are aware that "a statute will not be deemed private merely because it extends to particular localities or classes of persons." *Yarborough v. Park Commission*, 196 N.C. 284, 291, 145 S.E. 563, 568 (1928).

We believe that a legislative enactment establishing particular public beach access facilities in order to promote the general public welfare of the State does not constitute a local act within the meaning of Art. XIV, § 3 of the North Carolina Constitution. Specifically, we hold that the act in question, the purpose of which is to establish pedestrian beach access facilities for general public use in the vicinity of Bogue Inlet, is not a local act. As this Court recognized in *Adams*, the coastal areas of North Carolina are among the State's most valuable resources. That Court found, in essence, that the need to preserve and enhance the enormous recreational and esthetic value of the coastal area was of such significance to the public welfare as to justify special legislative treatment.

The stipulated facts in this case disclose that the ocean front and inlet beaches within the Town of Emerald Isle are frequented on a regular basis by numerous sport fishermen operating vehicles on the beaches. These beach areas adjacent to Bogue Inlet in particular are noted for excellent fishing, and annually attract numerous fishermen. Because no parking is available within two miles of the vehicle access ramp in this area, many of the fishermen are forced to drive along the beaches in order to gain access to the fishing areas.

Chapter 539, however, creates a public facility in the vicinity of Bogue Inlet. By directing the establishment of public pedestrian beach access facilities including parking areas, pedestrian walkways, and restroom facilities, the legislature by this act has sought to promote the general public welfare by preserving the beach area for general public pedestrian use. We do not believe that Art. XIV, § 3 of the North Carolina Constitution was intended to deprive the legislature of its authority to so act in the interest of promoting the general public welfare.

Furthermore, plaintiffs present before this Court nothing which suggests the absence of a rational basis for the General Assembly's selection of the Bogue Inlet area as the site for public pedestrian beach access facilities proposed by the act. Additionally, we find nothing in the record to support a conclusion that the site was chosen on an improper basis or in any arbitrary manner or that the particular site is unsuited for the intended purpose. We hold therefore that Chapter 539, which provides for the establishment and maintenance of public pedestrian beach access facilities in the vicinity of Bogue Inlet, is a general law and not a local act. * * * Since the act is general law and not a local act, it does not violate Art. XIV, § 3 of the North Carolina Constitution. * * *

NOTES AND QUESTIONS

1. *Comparing Secaucus and Emerald Isle.* The courts in the two main cases approached the challenged statutes from very different perspectives. Which opinion strikes the better balance of judicial enforcement of the norm against special legislation with legislative discretion to fine-tune legislation? Can the two opinions be reconciled?

Consider also the approach of the Colorado Supreme Court, when it stated: "[T]he determination whether a general law can be made applicable to a situation is 'a discretionary determination to be made by the legislature, which is not reviewable by the court unless a palpable abuse of discretion is shown.'" City of Littleton v. Board of County Comm'rs of Arapahoe County, 787 P.2d 158, 163 (Colo.1990). Which of the approaches better enables the court to identify and invalidate legislation that impermissibly singles out a certain municipality or other political subdivision? Your answer may depend on whether you think it likely that the legislatures in these cases were responding to unique conditions or, in the alternative, that the challenged acts represented nothing more than an unsavory "horse trade" that did not reflect a rational consideration of the overall general welfare of the state.

2. *Site-Specific Legislation.* Is a matter affecting the land around one vehicle access ramp in one town necessarily a local matter, or can there be a broader state interest in the site as well? Assume the court is right in concluding that the state law did address a question of state concern—the general public's access to the beach, which happened to require passing through a particular town—and not a local matter. But North Carolina has an extensive coastline with beach access not limited solely to the town of Emerald Isle. Should the principles that animate the special act ban— promoting generally applicable legislation, avoiding special deals, extricating the state legislature from the details of local regulation—have required North Carolina to adopt a more general law, addressing access to the state's beaches generally, rather than a law aimed solely at one access ramp in one town?

Site-specific laws may involve unique local conditions or natural resources. In Schrader v. Florida Keys Aqueduct Auth., 840 So.2d 1050 (Fla. 2003), the Florida Supreme Court upheld a state law that authorized local governments in Monroe County and only Monroe County to pass wastewater laws more restrictive than those provided for in the rest of the state. Monroe County is home to the Florida Keys, which the state had previously designated an "area of critical state concern." The court explained that "[i]f particular physical conditions exist in only a portion of a state, enactments with reference thereto nonetheless may be general laws." *Id.* at 1055. The nearshore waters of the Florida Keys are "a vital natural resource of the state" and have a "direct relationship with industries of statewide importance such as tourism and seafood," so that the "actual impact" of the law "far exceeds the limited geographic area of Monroe County." *Id.* at 1056.

Of course, the claim that there is something unique about a specific site will not always be accepted. Compare *Emerald Isle* with City of New Bern v. New Bern-Craven County Board of Education, 450 S.E.2d 735, 739 (N.C.1994), in which the North Carolina Supreme Court invalidated a state law that attempted to resolve a conflict between a city and a county over building code enforcement by shifting the responsibility for code enforcement "from [one] city to [one] county. Such a legislated change could be effected as easily in . . . any other city in the state. These acts therefore are not site-specific, and thus the *Emerald Isle* general public interest method of analysis is unsuited to this case."

Similarly, in Williams v. Blue Cross Blue Shield of N.C., 581 S.E.2d 415 (N.C. 2003), the North Carolina Supreme Court invalidated as a special law a state statute, enacted at Orange County's request, authorizing the County to adopt its own comprehensive employment discrimination ordinance. "This legislation is not site-specific as in *Emerald Isle*," *id.* at 184, because there was "no evidence in the record to suggest that employment practices in Orange County differ in any significant way from the employment practices in other North Carolina counties." *Id.* at 187. *See also* Martin Memorial Medical Ctr, Inc. v. Tenet HealthSystem Hospitals, Inc., 875 So.2d 797, 803 (Fla. App. 2004) (Florida statute authorizing the state health care agency to exempt hospitals in five counties from certificate-of-need review for the establishment of open-heart surgery programs an invalid special law; *Schrader, supra,* and similar site-specific cases distinguished as "dealing with protected water bodies, water resource management, and transportation systems that had impacts far exceeding the limited geographic area identified in the laws themselves").

3. THE REGULATION OF UNFUNDED MANDATES

Unfunded mandates occur when states require local governments to provide or expand existing local services, or to otherwise assume costly new responsibilities, without providing their localities with the funds to cover the resulting costs. In addition to the sheer financial burden these measures impose on local governments and local taxpayers, mandates have been criticized for blurring the lines of accountability by making it unclear to the public exactly which level of government is responsible for a particular program—the state government that requires it or the local government that is compelled to implement it. Moreover, the power to mandate costly local action may produce governmental inefficiency. The state reaps the political benefit of requiring a program that is popular with some groups but does not incur the cost of paying for that program. As a result, it may be too quick to authorize new programs without actually comparing costs and benefits. Finally, mandates impair local autonomy by treating local governments as mere instruments for carrying out state programs rather than as polities that can determine their own programs.

The last three decades of the twentieth century witnessed growing efforts at the state level to curtail state mandates on local governments. Starting with Maryland's adoption of a "fiscal note" requirement in 1968, by the early 1990s well over a majority of states had adopted state constitutional amendments, statutes or legislative rules requiring that when a state legislature considers the adoption of a bill that would mandate new or additional local costs, "the costs of each legislative mandate be attached to the bill under consideration for the purpose of providing legislators adequate notice of the costs being imposed on subordinate governments." Robert M.M. Shaffer, Comment, Unfunded State Mandates and Local Governments, 64 U.Cinn.L.Rev. 1057, 1065 (1996). Although fiscal notes do not limit the ability of the states to impose new mandates, the assumption behind the requirement is that a greater awareness of the costs of mandates would fuel political opposition to new mandates. It is not clear whether the fiscal note requirements have had much effect. Starting with California in 1979, several states went beyond fiscal notes to require that state governments actually reimburse local governments for the costs of complying with new mandates. By the mid-1990s, seventeen states had enacted such reimbursement requirements. In many states, the mandate restrictions were adopted as part of voter initiatives to limit local, or state and local, taxation. In other words, in these states the motivation behind the mandate restriction was less to increase local autonomy than to limit taxing and spending. Nevertheless, in attempting to protect local governments from state fiscal impositions, mandate reimbursement requirements tend to promote local autonomy.

Although the basic concept of a mandate, and of the problem unfunded state mandates pose for local governments, is clear, it is often uncertain whether a particular measure constitutes a mandate. The next case illustrates the difficulty.

COUNTY OF LOS ANGELES V. STATE

Supreme Court of California
729 P.2d 202 (1987)

GRODIN, JUSTICE. We are asked in this proceeding to determine whether legislation enacted in 1980 and 1982 increasing certain workers' compensation benefit payments is subject to the command of article XIIIB of the California Constitution that local government costs mandated by the state must be funded by the state. * * *

I

On November 6, 1979, the voters approved an initiative measure which added article XIIIB to the California Constitution. That article imposed spending limits on the state and local governments and provided in section 6 (hereafter section 6):

"Whenever the Legislature or any state agency mandates a new program or higher level of service on any local government, the state shall provide a subvention of funds to reimburse such local government for the costs of such program or increased level of service, except that the Legislature may, but need not, provide such subvention of funds for the following mandates: [¶] (a) Legislative mandates requested by the local agency affected; [¶] (b) Legislation defining a new crime or changing an existing definition of a crime; or [¶] (c) Legislative mandates enacted prior to January 1, 1975, or executive orders or regulations initially implementing legislation enacted prior to January 1, 1975."

No definition of the phrase "higher level of service" was included in article XIIIB, and the ballot materials did not explain its meaning.

The genesis of this action was the enactment in 1980 and 1982, after article XIIIB had been adopted, of laws increasing the amounts which employers, including local governments, must pay in workers' compensation benefits to injured employees and families of deceased employees. * * * No appropriation for increased state-mandated costs was made in this legislation.

Test claims seeking reimbursement for the increased expenditure mandated by these changes were filed with the State Board of Control in 1981 by the County of San Bernardino and the City of Los Angeles. The board rejected the claims, after hearing, stating that the increased maximum workers' compensation benefit levels did not change the terms or conditions under which benefits were to be awarded, and therefore did not, by increasing the dollar amount of the benefits, create an increased level of service. The first of these consolidated actions was then filed by the County of Los Angeles, the County of San Bernardino, and the City of San Diego. * * * They * * * sought a declaration that because the State of California and the board were obliged by article XIIIB to reimburse them, they were not obligated to pay the increased benefits until the state provided reimbursement. * * *

III

* * * In construing the meaning of the constitutional provision, our inquiry is * * * focused on * * * what the voters meant when they adopted article XIIIB in 1979. To determine this intent, we must look to the language of the provision itself. * * * In section 6, the electorate commands that the state reimburse local agencies for the cost of any "new program or higher level of service." * * *

[I]t is apparent that the subvention requirement for increased or higher level of service is directed to state mandated increases in the services provided by local agencies in existing "programs." But the term "program" itself is not defined in article XIIIB. What programs then did the electorate have in mind when section 6 was adopted? We conclude that the drafters and the electorate had in mind the commonly understood meanings of the term—programs that carry out the governmental function of providing services to the public, or laws which, to implement a state policy, impose unique requirements on local governments and do not apply generally to all residents and entities in the state.

The concern which prompted the inclusion of section 6 in article XIIIB was the perceived attempt by the state to enact legislation or adopt administrative orders creating programs to be administered by local agencies, thereby transferring to those agencies the fiscal responsibility for providing services which the state believed should be extended to the public. In their ballot arguments, the proponents of article XIIIB explained section 6 to the voters: "Additionally, this measure: (1) Will not allow the state government to *force programs* on local governments without the state paying for them." (Ballot Pamp., Proposed Amend. to Cal. Const. with arguments to voters, Spec. Statewide Elec. (Nov. 6, 1979) p. 18.) In this context the phrase "to force programs on local governments" confirms that the intent underlying section 6 was to require reimbursement to local agencies for the costs involved in carrying out functions peculiar to government, not for expenses incurred by local agencies as an incidental impact of laws that apply generally to all state residents and entities. Laws of general application are not passed by the Legislature to "force" programs on localities.

The language of section 6 is far too vague to support an inference that it was intended that each time the Legislature passes a law of general application it must discern the likely effect on local governments and provide an appropriation to pay for any incidental increase in local costs. We believe that if the electorate had intended such a far-reaching construction of section 6, the language would have explicitly indicated that the word "program" was being used in such a unique fashion. * * *

Were section 6 construed to require state subvention for the incidental cost to local governments of general laws, the result would be far-reaching indeed. Although such laws may be passed by simple majority vote of each house of the Legislature (art. IV, § 8, subd. (b)), the revenue measures necessary to make them effective may not. * * * Revenue bills must be passed by two-thirds vote of each house of the Legislature. (art. IV, § 12, subd. (d).) Thus, were we to construe section 6 as applicable to general legislation whenever it might have an incidental effect on local agency costs, such legislation could become effective only if passed by a supermajority vote. Certainly no such intent is reflected in the language or history of article XIIIB or section 6.

We conclude therefore that section 6 has no application to, and the state need not provide subvention for, the costs incurred by local agencies in providing to their employees the same increase in workers' compensation benefits that employees of private individuals or organizations receive. Workers' compensation is not a program administered by local agencies to provide service to the public. Although local agencies must provide benefits to their employees either through insurance or direct payment, they are indistinguishable in this respect from private employers. In no sense can employers, public or private, be considered to be administrators of a program of workers' compensation or to be providing services incidental to administration of the program. Workers' compensation is administered by the state through the Division of Industrial Accidents and the Workers' Compensation Appeals Board. (*See* Lab.Code, § 3201 et seq.) Therefore, although the state requires that employers provide workers' compensation for nonexempt categories of employees, increases in the cost of providing this employee benefit are not subject to reimbursement as state-mandated programs or higher levels of service within the meaning of section 6. * * *

NOTES AND QUESTIONS

1. *Local Government Services or Local Government Costs?* The California Supreme Court determined that the mandates restriction applies only to state requirements of new local services or programs, not to state measures that have the effect of driving up a local government's costs in providing current services. What if the unfunded mandates provision had been adopted in California before the creation of the workers compensation program? Would the court's rationale exempt it from the mandates prohibition? If not, how can the court exempt the increase in benefits? Compare the court's holding with Boone County Court v. State, 631 S.W.2d 321 (Mo. 1982), in which the Missouri court held that a state law mandating a pay increase for tax collectors in counties of the second class fell afoul of the Hancock Amendment, a voter-initiated measure that combined limits on state and local taxation and spending with a provision that "[a] new activity or service or an increase in the level of any activity or service beyond that required by existing law shall not be required by the general assembly or any state agency of counties or other political subdivisions, unless a state appropriation is made and disbursed to pay the county or other political subdivision for any increased costs." Mo.Const., Art. X, § 21. The court rejected the state's contention that the pay increase did not constitute a directive to increase the "service" or "activity" provided by county tax collectors: "[T]his argument addresses the wrong question because the concern is the increased activity required of the county rather than of the individual collector." *Id.* 631 S.W.2d at 326. Should the mandates

reimbursement requirement apply to any state measure that increases local costs, or should a court limit it to those state laws that require local governments to undertake new services, expand existing services, or reduce existing levels of state funding for existing services? Why?

Following the *Boone County* decision Missouri voters amended their constitution to provide that a law authorizing an increase in compensation for county officers "shall not be construed as requiring a new activity or service or an increase in the level of any activity or service within the meaning of this constitution." Mo. Const., Art. VI, § 11. Subsequently, the Missouri Supreme Court determined that a state requirement that counties contribute to the pensions of county prosecuting attorneys was not an unconstitutional unfunded mandate. Missouri Prosecuting Attorneys v. Barton County, 311 S.W.3d 737 (Mo. 2010).

The California Supreme Court adhered closely to *County of Los Angeles* when, in City of Sacramento v. State, 785 P.2d 522 (Cal. 1990), it held that a state law extending mandatory coverage under the state's unemployment insurance law to state and local governments and to nonprofit corporations did not violate the ban on unfunded mandates. *City of Sacramento* reiterated the court's emphasis on the fact that the law did not apply "uniquely" to local governments: "Most private employers in the state already were required to provide unemployment protection to their employees. Extension of this requirement to local governments, together with the state and nonprofit corporations, merely makes the local agencies 'indistinguishable in this respect from private employers.'" *Id.* at 530–31. *See also* Schmidt v. Department of Education, 490 N.W.2d 584, 604 (Mich. 1992) (change in state reimbursement for local share of social security taxes does not implicate a change in "activity or service" within the meaning of Michigan constitutional ban on unfunded mandates). Should it be relevant that a state directive applies to employers generally, and not just to local governments? Does the broad application of the law tend to assure that its costs and benefits would have been more fully aired and that any political opposition would have been brought before the legislature? Evaluate whether it is appropriate to apply the mandates requirement to the following state-imposed requirements on local governments: compliance with anti-discrimination laws, handicap access laws, and general public health and safety laws—such as the regulation of workplace conditions or the imposition of controls on environmental pollution by water and sewer systems. On the one hand, these laws can involve costly new requirements that can eat up considerable portions of local budgets. On the other hand, they may be seen less as a crafty state move to shift fiscal burdens to localities than as an effort to hold local governments to the same standards of accountability as other employers and organizations. *Cf.* David E. Dana, The Case for Unfunded Environmental Mandates, 69 So. Cal.L.Rev. 1 (1995).

2. *Local Policy Autonomy or Local Service Costs?* A California court of appeal decision emphasized that the focus of that state's ban on unfunded mandates is on compelled local service costs, not the protection of local

autonomy. In County of Los Angeles v. Commission on State Mandates, 2 Cal.Rptr.3d 419 (Cal. App. 2003), the court held that a state law requiring local law enforcement agencies to devote two hours to domestic violence training—out of the twenty-four hours required every two years under the state's "Peace Officer Standards and Training (POST)" certification program—was not a mandate within the meaning of the state constitution. The domestic violence provision did not increase the total number of hours required under the POST program. "Adding domestic violence training obviously may displace other courses. . . . [W]hile the County may lose some flexibility in tailoring its training programs, such loss of flexibility does not rise to the level of a state mandated reimbursable program." *Id.* at 435–36.

Many state programs that rely on local action for implementation may impose costs that seem only incidental to the state's purposes, but are nonetheless burdensome for localities. In San Diego Unified School Dist. v. Commission on State Mandates, 94 P.3d 589 (Cal. 2004), for example, the California Supreme Court found that a new state education law mandating the suspension or expulsion of students for certain offenses—such as possession of a firearm on school grounds—constituted a "new program or higher level of service" within the meaning of the state constitution's mandates provision. As a result, the state would be required to pay for the costs of the due process hearings triggered by the law. Similarly, in Brooks v. State, 128 S.W.3d 844 (Mo. 2004), the Missouri Supreme Court concluded that a new state law directing county sheriffs to fingerprint and conduct criminal background checks on all applicants for a permit to carry a concealed firearm fell within the state's constitutional provision prohibiting the state from "requiring any new or expanded activities by counties and other political subdivisions without full state financing." *See also* Adair v. State, 680 N.W.2d 386 (Mich. 2004) (requiring school districts to create and maintain student data on an ongoing basis following state-specified data-gathering procedures and to transmit those data over the Internet to the state as part of the state's program on educational performance and information raises a "colorable claim" under Michigan's constitutional restriction on mandates).

As some of these cases indicate, the education system has been a fertile source of mandates disputes. With the state ultimately responsible for the public school system and able to determine the basic elements of what constitutes an education, but local school districts actually responsible for delivering that education, it is not surprising that states and localities quarrel over when an education measure is a mandate. *Compare* Rolla 31 School Dist. v. State, 837 S.W.2d 1 (Mo. 1992) (new state requirement that school districts provide special education and related services for disabled three- and four-year-olds a "mandate" within the meaning of the Hancock Amendment) *with* Breitenfeld v. School Dist. of Clayton, 399 S.W.3d 816, 828–32 (Mo. 2013) (law requiring a school district that loses accreditation with state board of education to pay tuition for any resident pupil who attends an accredited school in another district in the same or adjoining county not a "mandate" on either the paying district or the district required to accept pupils; whereas the law in *Rolla 31* increased the level of services required of districts, the pupil transfer law merely "reallocate[s] responsibilities for educating some children among school districts").

3. *Mandate or Reversion?* State unfunded mandate restrictions generally apply to new state directives, not the continuation of prior obligations. At times, however, it may be difficult to determine whether a change in state law imposes a new obligation or simply triggers a preexisting requirement. Thus, California had at one time required a local school district to contribute part of the cost of educating pupils from the district at state schools for the severely handicapped. In 1979, the legislature repealed that requirement and assumed full state responsibility. In 1980, the restriction on unfunded mandates was added to the California Constitution, and in 1981 the state reinstated the old requirement of local school district contribution to the costs of educating the severely handicapped at state schools. The California Supreme Court rejected the state's argument that the local obligation was not "new" and held, instead, that it fell squarely within the anti-mandate provision's purpose of preventing the state from "compelling" local governments "to accept financial responsibility in whole or in part for a program which was funded entirely by the state before advent" of the anti-mandates amendment. Lucia Mar Unified School Dist. v. Honig, 750 P.2d 318 (Cal. 1988). Similarly, in County of San Diego v. State, 931 P.2d 312 (Cal. 1997), the California Supreme Court found that the state had imposed an unfunded mandate on the counties when it reduced its financial support for county medical services for a category of medically indigent adults. In the late 1970's the state had covered those costs as part of its Medi-Cal program. In 1982, those medically indigent adults were removed from that program, but the state had committed to provide the counties with the funds necessary to cover their costs, which it did until tight state budgets in the early 1990s led the state to cut its funding for the program. The state argued that because state law had long imposed on counties a residual duty to care for the medically indigent, the cutbacks in state support were not a new mandate. However, because at the time the anti-mandates measure was adopted the state paid all the costs of medical care for the medically indigent, state cutbacks that "trigger the counties' responsibility to provide medical care as providers of last resort" imposed a mandate. *See id.* at 330. With these two California cases, compare Town of Nelson v. New Hampshire Department of Transportation, 767 A.2d 435 (N.H. 2001), in which the court held that the state's reclassification of a certain road from a state highway—maintained by state funds—to a town highway, to be maintained by the town, without providing the town with additional funds was not a mandate because towns had been responsible for the maintenance of the local roads within their borders long prior to New Hampshire's adoption of its anti-mandates measure:

> "In this case, the State has not created any new program nor required that the town accept any new responsibility. It has simply

decided that a road which now serves only local traffic will no longer be part of the State-maintained highway system. That the contested segments now serve only local traffic may be a new development; the town's responsibility for maintaining roads that serve only local traffic is not new."

Id. at 438. *See also* David J. Barron & Gerald E. Frug, Defensive Localism: A View from the Field, 21 J.L. & Pol'y 261, 277 (2005) (finding that in Massachusetts state courts have permitted the state legislature to condition existing funds on new mandates).

4. *The Scope and Effectiveness of State Unfunded Mandate Restrictions.* Nearly every unfunded mandate provision has some exemption, exception or exclusion. The following are just a few examples of the types of provisions that are frequently not subject to the requirement of reimbursement: laws promulgated to comply with a federal mandate (La. Const., Art. 6, § 14); laws defining a new crime or changing an existing definition of a crime (Cal. Const., Art. 13B, § 6); laws modifying school finance requirements (Colo. St. § 29–1–304.5); laws requiring funding of pension benefits (Fla. Const., Art. 7 § 18); laws that impose similar obligations on both government and non-government entities (N.J. Const., Art. 8, § 2, ¶ 5); laws implementing the state constitution (*id.*); laws that protect the public from local government misconduct (R.I. Stat. § 45–13–10 (1997)); laws regulating elections and public meetings (*id.*). Do you see any consistent themes in these exemptions?

Mandate reimbursements may also exempt costly conditions imposed as a condition for local eligibility for state grants. Such conditions may be seen by the courts as voluntary rather than mandatory, even if the scheme of conditioning state aid on costly local actions involves "hard choices" for the locality. *See* School Committee of Lexington v. Commissioner of Educ., 492 N.E.2d 736, 738 (Mass.1986). Some state mandate restrictions are substantially weakened by the requirement that the state must "share" in the cost of new mandates without specifying a required contribution. *E.g.*, Hawaii Const., Art. 8, § 5 (1997); Tenn. Const., Art. 2, § 24 (1997). Other state mandate measures permit state governments to satisfy the reimbursement requirement by diverting existing state aid to the mandated program rather than adding to the total of state assistance to the locality. *See* Mahaffey v. Attorney General, 564 N.W.2d 104, 112 (Mich.App.1997) (Michigan mandate restriction "requires only that a state appropriation be made to pay the local governmental unit for any increased costs" but does not prevent funding "out of an existing appropriation"). In addition, mandate restrictions generally do not apply to state laws reallocating state contributions, or local funding obligations among different local governments, such as counties, cities, and school districts. *See, e.g.,* County of Sonoma v. Commission on State Mandates, 101 Cal.Rptr.2d 784 (Cal.App. 2000) (state law reallocating property tax revenues from counties to school districts not a mandate); City of San Jose v. State of California, 53 Cal.Rptr.2d 521 (Cal.App. 1996) (statute reallocating part of county jail costs to cities not a mandate).

These measures also require determinations of how much a new mandate will cost and whether new state funding will cover the costs. *Cf.* Oakland County v. State of Michigan, 566 N.W.2d 616 (Mich.1997) (remand for calculation of whether state child care fund amendment reduced state-financed proportion of mandated county foster care costs). State courts have been relatively deferential to state legislative determinations of compliance with the requirements of the anti-mandate restrictions. State courts may also rely on standing, ripeness, and mootness principles to avoid conflicts with state legislatures over mandates. One commentator linked the courts' apparent reluctance to enforce limits on state mandates to the courts' longstanding assumption of broad state power and suspicion of local autonomy, as well as to the courts' sympathy for the substantive policy goals of many mandated programs. *See* Robert M.M. Shaffer, Unfunded State Mandates, *supra*, 64 U.Cinn.L.Rev. at 1076–88. For a skeptical assessment of limits on state-to-local mandates, *see* Edward A. Zelinsky, The Unsolved Problem of the Unfunded Mandate, 23 Ohio No. U. L. Rev. 741, 776–81 (1997).

C. DETERMINING THE SCOPE OF LOCAL POWER

1. FROM DILLON'S RULE TO HOME RULE

For nearly a century and a half the benchmark for determining whether a local government had the power to provide a particular service, undertake a particular program, or adopt a particular regulation has been Dillon's Rule. Named after Judge John F. Dillon of the Iowa Supreme Court, who first authored the rule in his Commentaries on the Law of Municipal Corporations shortly after the Civil War, Dillon's Rule provides:

> A municipal corporation possesses and can exercise only the following powers: (1) those granted in *express words*; (2) those *necessarily or fairly implied* in or incident to the powers expressly granted; (3) those *essential* to the accomplishment of the declared objects and purposes of the corporation—not simply convenient, but indispensable. Any fair, reasonable, substantial doubt concerning the existence of power is resolved by the courts against the corporation, and the power is denied.

Dillon's Rule is the counterpart to the rule of plenary state legislative power in establishing the background norms of state-local relations. Where the norm of plenary state power provides that the states have broad authority to modify or curtail local powers and supersede local enactments, Dillon's Rule assumes that even when a state creates a local government, gives it powers, and gets out of the local government's way, the locality still has very limited authority to act. *See also* Southern Constructors, Inc. v. Loudon Co. Bd. of Educ., 58 S.W.3d 706, 711–12

(Tenn. 2001) (Dillon's Rule of strict construction of local powers arises out of "constitutional realities of local government in this state;" localities lack inherent right of local self-government and all local power is the result of a delegation by the state). As one of the authors of this book has explained:

> Dillon's Rule operates as a standard of delegation, a canon of construction and a rule of limited power. It reflects the view of local governments as agents of the state by requiring that all local powers be traced back to a specific delegation: whenever it is uncertain whether a locality possesses a particular power, a court should assume that the locality *lacks* that power. By denying localities broad authority, Dillon's Rule limits the number of entities that may regulate private activity. Only through a clear and express state delegation may a locality obtain power to govern.

Briffault, Our Localism, *supra*, 90 Colum.L.Rev. at 8 (emphasis in original).

Judge Dillon authored his rule in response to a series of mid-nineteenth century cases in which local governments used public funds to provide financial assistance to railroads and other private enterprises. When those private enterprises ran into difficulty, the localities had to make good on the assurances they had provided to private investors. *See, e.g.*, Joan C. Williams, The Invention of the Municipal Corporation: A Case Study in Legal Change, 34 Am. U. L. Rev. 369, 437 (1985). Dillon saw cities, with their turbulent electorates and their special interest politics, as particularly susceptible to corruption. Dillon "sought to protect private property not only against abuse by democracy, but also against abuse by private economic power." Gerald Frug, The City as a Legal Concept, 90 Harv.L.Rev. 1057, 1110 (1980). By limiting local powers and requiring explicit state authorization for new local programs, Dillon would protect local taxpayers from the costs of local autonomy.

Dillon's Rule was widely followed from the late nineteenth century well into the twentieth century. In cases where the scope of local power was challenged by private individuals subject to local regulation, the Rule operated to limit local power to act. Early Estates, Inc. v. Housing Board of Review of City of Providence, 174 A.2d 117 (R.I.1961), nicely illustrates the narrowing effect of Dillon's Rule on local action. *Early Estates* involved a Rhode Island law that authorized the city of Providence to adopt an ordinance "for the establishment and enforcement of minimum standards for dwellings." The statute defined minimum standards to include "minimum standards governing the conditions, maintenance, use and occupancy of dwellings and dwelling premises deemed necessary to make said dwellings and dwelling premises safe, sanitary, and fit for human habitation." Providence adopted a housing ordinance that required, *inter alia*, the installation of hot water for all kitchens and bathrooms. When a landlord subject to the ordinance claimed that the hot water requirement exceeded the scope of the state enabling law, the Rhode Island Supreme Court, applying a classic Dillon's Rule analysis, agreed:

> In the absence of an express grant of legislative authority, the determination of the issue . . . depends wholly upon the question whether the statutory language . . . indicates a clear legislative intent to delegate the power in question. . . . Is the requirement of hot water facilities related to the 'uncleanliness' of dwellings and dwelling premises? . . .

[handwritten: Main point of Dillon's Rule]

> [C]an it reasonably be said that by empowering the [city] council to enact minimum standards necessary to make dwellings and dwelling premises 'fit for human habitation,' the legislature meant that the installation of hot water facilities is necessary to achieve the desired purpose? Can it be said that dwellings and dwelling premises lacking such facilities are unfit for human habitation?

> Prior to the enactment of [the Rhode Island enabling law], in the absence of contractual obligations to the contrary there was no duty on a property owner to provide hot water facilities under the law of this state. After careful consideration it is our opinion that the act contains no language indicating a legislative intent to enact an ordinance requiring the installation of hot water facilities. The requirement of those facilities is not necessarily related to sanitation or public health and welfare, nor is such requirement reasonably necessary to make dwellings and dwelling premises fit for human habitation.

Id. at 119.   *[handwritten: necessary v reasonably related]*

Note the court's view that hot water must be "necessary" to and not simply reasonably related to promoting health and safety. Note also the court's concern that a broader reading of the enabling act would allow a local government to change the common law without an express directive from the legislature. The narrow reading of state-granted local powers and the desire to limit the power to change legal rules to the state are hallmarks of the Dillon's Rule approach to state-local relations. As Chief Judge Randall Shepard of the Indiana Supreme Court put it, "[u]nder the Dillon Rule, a person who simply found himself on the wrong side of some local action could easily challenge that action by essentially asserting that it was *ultra vires*. . . . The resulting legal landscape handcuffed municipal corporations, preventing them from taking a wide range of governmental

*[handwritten: * important]*

[handwritten: beyond one's legal power or authority]

actions we might find common place today." Kole v. Faultless, 963 N.E.2d 493, 496 (Ind. 2012).

Dillon's Rule has long been criticized. Indeed, local governments have sought to undo Dillon's Rule virtually from the time Judge Dillon articulated it. They have prodded their states to adopt constitutional amendments or statutory provisions that provide at least some local governments with broad powers to act even in the absence of specific state authorization. This expansion of local decision-making authority is known as home rule. As early as 1875, Missouri amended its constitution to provide St. Louis, its largest city, with home rule, and California followed suit in 1879 with a similar constitutional amendment for its then-largest city, San Francisco. Home rule became a significant factor in shaping state-local relations over the course of the twentieth century. By 1990, forty-eight states provided a measure of home rule for at least some of their cities. In addition, thirty-seven states provided for home rule for some of their counties. *See* U.S. Advisory Commission on Intergovernmental Relations, State Laws Governing Local Government Structure and Administration 20–21 (1993). Home rule provisions, which may be adopted either pursuant to state constitutional amendment or statutory enabling legislation, often expressly provide that local powers are to be "liberally construed." Such a rule of liberal construction is an express rejection of Dillon's Rule. Even without providing home rule for all its localities, a state may pass a statute requiring the liberal construction of local powers, *see, e.g.*, N.C. Gen. Stat. § 160A–4, or explicitly abrogating Dillon's Rule, *see, e.g.*, Ind. Code. Ann. § 36–1–3–4(a).

Dillon's Rule, however, continues to be of importance. Not all states provide for home rule, and in many states, home rule extends to only some cities (usually the more populous ones) and counties (usually the more urbanized ones), not to all. For the remaining localities, Dillon's Rule may continue to shape the interpretation of local powers.

MARBLE TECHNOLOGIES, INC. v. CITY OF HAMPTON

Supreme Court of Virginia
690 S.E.2d 84 (2010)

KINSER, JUSTICE.

This appeal involves the Chesapeake Bay Preservation Act, Code §§ 10.1–2100 through –2115 (the Act), and its implementing regulations. The dispositive issue asks whether the General Assembly expressly or impliedly authorized a locality to utilize as a criterion for designating Chesapeake Bay Preservation Areas within its jurisdiction whether particular land is among the "lands designated as part of the Coastal

Barrier Resources System," which is created by the Coastal Barrier Resources Act, 16 U.S.C. §§ 3501 through 3510 (the federal Act). * * *

The Act requires, inter alia, "the counties, cities, and towns of Tidewater Virginia [to] incorporate general water quality protection measures into their comprehensive plans, zoning ordinances, and subdivision ordinances." To further the Act's implementation, the General Assembly established the Chesapeake Bay Local Assistance Board (the Board), and authorized the Board to "promulgate regulations which establish criteria for use by local governments to determine the ecological and geographic extent of Chesapeake Bay Preservation Areas," that is, the "area delineated by a local government in accordance with [the Board's] criteria" and thereby made subject to the Act's restrictions. A Chesapeake Bay Preservation Area consists "of a Resource Protection Area [RPA] and a Resource Management Area."

Pursuant to this authority, the Board promulgated criteria for a locality to utilize in designating lands within its jurisdiction to be included in an RPA. The Board's regulation establishes these relevant criteria:

A.   At a minimum, Resource Protection Areas shall consist of lands adjacent to water bodies with perennial flow that have an intrinsic water quality value due to the ecological and biological processes they perform or are sensitive to impacts which may cause significant degradation to the quality of state waters. In their natural condition, these lands provide for the removal, reduction or assimilation of sediments, nutrients and potentially harmful or toxic substances in runoff entering the bay and its tributaries, and minimize the adverse effects of human activities on state waters and aquatic resources.

B.   The Resource Protection Area shall include:

   1.   Tidal wetlands;

   2.   Nontidal wetlands connected by surface flow and contiguous to tidal wetlands or water bodies with perennial flow;

   3.   Tidal shores;

   4.   Such other lands considered by the local government to meet the provisions of subsection A of this section and to be necessary to protect the quality of state waters; and

   5.   A buffer area not less than 100 feet in width located adjacent to and landward of the components listed in

subdivisions 1 through 4 above, and along both sides of any water body with perennial flow.

As directed by Code § 10.1–2109, the City of Hampton (the City) amended its zoning ordinance in 1990, creating Article Ten of the City's Zoning Code, which is entitled "Chesapeake Bay Preservation District," "to implement the Chesapeake Bay Preservation Act at the local level." City Zoning Ordinance § 17.3–60. In January 2008, the City took the action at issue in this appeal, amending its definition of the buffer area of an RPA. Now the buffer area is defined as "[a] variable width buffer area not less than one hundred (100) feet in width. . . . The variable width buffer area shall also include lands designated as part of the Coastal Barrier Resources System not otherwise listed as a Resource Protection Area Feature where present." City Zoning Ordinance § 17.3–62(16)(iv). The City also amended its buffer area requirements for RPAs to incorporate the new definition. City Zoning Ordinance § 17.3–64(2)(b)(iii)(3).

Marble Technologies, Inc. and Shri Ganesh, LLC (collectively, the plaintiffs), own two separate parcels of land located in the "Grand View" section of the City. According to the plaintiffs, the "developable area" of their parcels was not included in an RPA or its buffer area prior to the 2008 amendment to the City zoning ordinance. Following the amendment, the plaintiffs' parcels fell entirely "within the RPA portion of the City's Chesapeake Bay Preservation District" because the parcels are included in the Coastal Barrier Resources System. The plaintiffs contend that their parcels are thus subject to additional development restrictions.

Shortly after the amendment's passage, the plaintiffs filed a complaint seeking "declaratory and injunctive relief prohibiting the City's enforcement of the amendment as it applies to the [p]laintiffs' property." The plaintiffs alleged, among other things, that the City had "exceeded its authority in violation of Virginia law and Dillon's [R]ule." * * *

In support of their motion for summary judgment, the plaintiffs argued that the 2008 zoning "[a]mendment impermissibly permits the federal government to alter the City's zoning scheme without further action of the City Council in violation of the Dillon Rule," as the General Assembly has not "express[ly] or implicit[ly] grant[ed localities the] authority to delegate any portion of" the responsibility for designating RPAs within the locality's jurisdiction. The plaintiffs maintained that because the General Assembly authorized only localities to designate lands subject to the Act's restrictions, the City did not have authority to incorporate land into an RPA by referencing the Coastal Barrier Resources System. The City, however, maintained that the General Assembly had "expressly and implicitly grant[ed] the City the power to enact the challenged ordinances," which must be "presumed valid and constitutional." * * *

The issue we decide is whether the General Assembly expressly and/or impliedly authorized localities, through the Act or the regulations passed pursuant thereto, to utilize as a criterion for designating lands to be included in an RPA whether particular land is part of the federal Act's Coastal Barrier Resources System. * * *

Contrary to the City's argument that the zoning amendment at issue, as the legislative enactment of a locality, must be presumed valid unless proven to be clearly unreasonable, arbitrary, or capricious, "the Dillon Rule is applicable to determine in the first instance, from express words or by implication, whether a power exists at all. If the power cannot be found, the inquiry is at an end." (citations omitted).

The Dillon Rule provides that "municipal corporations have only those powers that are expressly granted, those necessarily or fairly implied from expressly granted powers, and those that are essential and indispensable." * * * This is so because "[a] municipal corporation has no element of sovereignty. It is a mere local agency of the state, having no other powers than such as are clearly and unmistakably granted by the law-making power." *Whiting v. Town of West Point,* 88 Va. 905, 906, 14 S.E. 698, 699 (1892); *see Hunter v. City of Pittsburgh,* 207 U.S. 161, 178, 28 S.Ct. 40, 52 L.Ed. 151 (1907) ("Municipal corporations are political subdivisions of the State, created as convenient agencies for exercising such of the governmental powers of the State as may be entrusted to them."). Thus, "[i]f there is a reasonable doubt whether legislative power exists, the doubt must be resolved against the local governing body." (citations omitted).

In applying the Dillon Rule, we first examine the plain terms of the legislative enactment to determine whether the General Assembly expressly granted a particular power to the municipal corporation. * * * If the power is not expressly granted, we then "determine whether the power . . . is necessarily or fairly implied from the powers expressly granted by the statute." * * * "To imply a particular power from a power expressly granted, it must be found that the legislature intended that the grant of the express also would confer the implied." * * *

With these principles in mind, we proceed to the question before us: whether the General Assembly expressly or impliedly authorized the City to use as a criterion for designating RPAs in its jurisdiction whether particular land is included in the Coastal Barrier Resources System pursuant to the federal Act. The General Assembly expressly authorized counties, cities, and towns "to exercise their police and zoning powers to protect the quality of state waters consistent with the provisions" of the Act. Code § 10.1–2108. That authority, however, is limited to using the criteria created by the Board. The provisions of Code § 10.1–2100(A)(ii) direct localities to "define and protect" Chesapeake Bay Preservation Areas "in accordance with criteria established by the Commonwealth." The Act, in Code § 10.1–2109(A) and (C), mandates that localities "use the criteria developed by the Board to determine the extent of the Chesapeake Bay Preservation Area within their jurisdictions," and directs "[z]oning in Chesapeake Bay Preservation Areas [to] comply with all criteria set forth in or established pursuant to [Code] § 10.1–2107," which is the provision empowering the Board to develop "criteria for use by local governments to determine the ecological and geographic extent of Chesapeake Bay Preservation Areas." Code § 10.1–2107(A). The provisions of Code § 10.1–2111 reiterate that "[l]ocal governments shall employ the criteria promulgated by the Board to ensure that the use and development of land in Chesapeake Bay Preservation Areas shall be accomplished in a manner that protects the quality of state waters consistent with the provisions of [the Act]." And the definition given the term "Chesapeake Bay Preservation Area" is that of "an area delineated by a local government in accordance with criteria established pursuant to § 10.1–2107." Code § 10.1–2101. Thus, we conclude the General Assembly expressly authorized localities to designate lands subject to the Act within their jurisdictions pursuant to the Board's criteria. * * *

[T]he Board's criteria mandate that certain lands be included in an RPA and authorize the inclusion of "other lands" that both "meet the provisions of subsection A" and are "necessary to protect the quality of state waters." After designating lands encompassed by subsections B(1) through (4), the locality must designate a "buffer area not less than 100 feet in width located adjacent to and landward of the components listed" in subsections B(1) through (4) and "along both sides of any water body with perennial flow."

The foregoing review demonstrates that the General Assembly, acting through the Board, neither expressly nor impliedly granted localities the authority to designate RPAs based on criteria established by the federal government. Instead, the designations must be based on criteria established by the Board. * * * And, the Board's criteria do not include "lands designated as part of the Coastal Barrier Resources System not otherwise listed as a Resource Protection Area Feature." City Zoning Ordinance § 17.3–62(16)(iv).

The City argues that its inclusion of lands covered by the federal Act in the buffer area is authorized by the "other lands" component. This argument is without merit. First, the Board's regulation treats lands designated under subsection B's "other lands" provision as separate from the buffer area, which is "located adjacent to and landward of the components listed in subdivisions 1 through 4." Second, the regulations do not authorize a "variable width buffer area" within a particular locality, but only authorize localities to designate uniform buffer areas of "not less than 100 feet in width." The central reason why the City's argument is unavailing, however, is because the Board's criteria do not mention the federal Act or imply that a parcel's inclusion pursuant to the federal Act, as land the development of which the federal government does not want to encourage through "Federal expenditures and financial assistance," has any bearing upon, much less serves as a determinative factor when, designating land as part of an RPA.

rationale

Thus, the City ordinance, which makes inclusion in the Coastal Barrier Resources System a criterion for designating lands part of an RPA, violates the General Assembly's express mandate that a locality "use the criteria developed by the Board to determine the extent of the Chesapeake Bay Preservation Area within [its] jurisdiction[ ]." Accordingly, the City's 2008 zoning amendments challenged in this appeal are void insofar as they include lands in its RPAs on the basis of the federal Act's applicability.

holding

NOTES AND QUESTIONS

1.   *Dillon's Rule in Theory and Practice. Marble Technologies* indicates that Dillon's Rule's narrow construction of local powers is grounded in the *Hunter v. City of Pittsburgh* theory of local government as subordinate state instrumentality. In theory, a state could combine the creature-of-the-state vision of local government with a rule of liberal construction of local powers. As we will see later in this Chapter, that is the main effect of home rule. But for the Virginia court the rule of narrow construction seems to flow directly out of the subordinate status of local governments. Several other courts, even as they acknowledge modern critiques of Dillon's Rule, have taken a similar approach. *See, e.g.,* City of Montpelier v. Barnett, 49 A.3d 120, 129 (Vt. 2012) ("[f]or better or for worse, this rule expresses the . . . commitment to the state as the centralized source of political power"); Olesen v. Town of Hurley, 691 N.W.2d 324, 328–29 (S.D. 2004) (a "city, as such, has no inherent powers, and none of the attributes of sovereignty" and so Dillon's Rule requires a "reasonably strict construction" of state enabling legislation"); Southern Constr., Inc. v. Loudon Co. Bd. of Educ., 58 S.W.2d 706, 712 (Tenn. 2001) ("It is from this rationale—that local governments have no inherent right to autonomous self-government—that the rule of strict construction arises on this state").

Marble Technologies also nicely illustrates Dillon's Rule in action. The court rejects any presumption in favor of the City's action. It makes no argument that the measure is unreasonable, arbitrary, or capricious, that it is in conflict with state law or policy, or that it has invaded a field the state has reserved for itself. Nor was there an argument that including lands covered by the federal Coastal Barrier Resources System was in any way inconsistent with the state's Chesapeake Bay preservation program. Rather, the problem was that the state had not expressly or impliedly authorized its local governments to incorporate the federal criteria into their resource protection programs. Accord, City of Montpelier v. Barnett, *supra*, 49 A.3d at 136 ("To begin with, Dillon's Rule creates a presumption against finding a grant of power to the municipality").

Dillon's Rule is frequently invoked in Virginia. That does not always result in the invalidation of local measures, and the Virginia Supreme Court has often upheld innovative local actions. *See, e.g.*, City Council of Alexandria v. Lindsey Trusts, 520 S.E.2d 181 (Va.1999) (explicit power to terminate certain uses necessarily implies the power to regulate them); City of Chesapeake v. Gardner Enterprises, 482 S.E.2d 812 (Va.1997) (explicit power to regulate existing structures on certain lots implies power to regulate new construction); Resource Conservation Management v. Board of Supervisors of Prince William County, 380 S.E.2d 879 (Va.1989) (power to zone implies power to prohibit the use of landfills); Stallings v. Wall, 367 S.E.2d 496 (Va.1988) (upholding city's firearm registration ordinance). *Cf.* Cohen v. Board of Water Commissioners, 585 N.E.2d 737 (Mass.1992) (explicit powers to regulate water supply and collect payments for water usage supports implication of power to require water meters). On the other hand, Dillon's Rule has also frequently been invoked as a basis for curtailing local authority. *See, e.g.*, Board of Zoning Appeals v. Board of Supervisors, 666 S.E.2d 315 (Va.2008) (in absence of specific grant of authority, zoning appeals board lacks power to bring declaratory judgment action); Arlington County v. White, 528 S.E.2d 706 (Va.2000) (county lacks authority to treat unmarried domestic partners of its employees as "dependents" eligible for employee dependent health benefits); Board of Supervisors of Augusta County v. Countryside Investment Co., 522 S.E.2d 610 (Va.1999) (state law allowing counties to impose requirements for subdivision of land did not authorize denial of subdivision approval on basis that development would destroy county's rural environment); City of Richmond v. Confrere Club of Richmond, 387 S.E.2d 471 (Va.1990) (city council lacked authority to delegate to city director of finance the power to suspend organization's bingo and raffle permit); Cupp v. Board of Supervisors of Fairfax County, 318 S.E.2d 407 (Va.1984) (statute authorizing counties to zone did not confer power to require developers to donate land for road construction); Tabler v. Board of Supervisors of Fairfax County, 269 S.E.2d 358 (Va.1980) (state law authorizing counties to enact ordinances regulating garbage and litter did not confer power to require purchasers of disposable bottles to pay a cash deposit).

2.   *Dillon's Rule as Residual Rule.* Although many states have rejected Dillon's Rule for certain categories of local government, such as cities or counties, and for certain local powers, Dillon's Rule is often the residual rule for construing the powers of other local governments. The Tennessee Supreme Court made this point in *Southern Constructors, supra,* which addressed whether a school district has the authority to arbitrate disputes arising out of a school construction contract. The court noted that Tennessee by statute provides for the liberal construction of municipal powers; that

constitutional and statutory provisions grant charter counties "broad authority for the regulation of their own local affairs;" and that constitutional and statutory provisions enable municipal governments "to adopt and operate under home rule authority," 58 S.W.3d at 712–14. The state, however, had neither made a broad grant of authority to school boards nor provided for a rule of liberal construction for school board powers. As a result, Dillon's Rule applied to school boards, although the court determined that the power given to boards to enter into construction contracts impliedly authorized them to arbitrate disputes. *Id.* at 716–17. Subsequently, the Tennessee Supreme Court repeatedly invalidated school board contracts, finding the boards lacked authority to bind their districts to certain contract terms. Although technically limiting school board authority, those cases were in practice victories for the boards which, by arguing for a limited construction on their powers, were able avoid certain contractual obligations. *See* Elijah Swiney, John Forrest Dillon Goes to School: Dillon's Rule in Tennessee Ten Years After *Southern Constructors*, 79 Tenn. L. Rev. 103, 123–24 (2011). *See also* Hugh Spitzer, "Home Rule" vs. "Dillon's Rule" for Washington Cities, 38 Seattle Univ. L. Rev. 809, 856 (2015) (noting that although the state constitution and statutes vest home rule powers in many Washington cities, "Washington should be considered a 'Dillon's Rule state' for its special purpose districts, noncharter counties, and the state's nine noncode cities and sixty-nine towns"); Tri-Power Resources, Inc. v. City of Carlyle, 967 N.E.2d 811, 813 (Ill. App. 2012) (non-home-rule municipalities in Illinois are subject to Dillon's Rule). Professor Spitzer has also pointed to the "persistence of Dillon's Rule rhetoric" in Washington Supreme Court cases even in disputes involving home rule cities. 38 Seattle Univ. L. Rev. at 858.

3.   *Dillon's Rule and the Uncertain Scope of Local Powers.* Local governments do not always lose Dillon's Rule cases. The real problem with Dillon's Rule is the *indeterminate scope* of local authority. Localities simply may not know what their powers are, and local decisions are subject to an unpredictable determination of whether an action is fairly implied from or incident to explicitly granted powers. Courts, too, are often divided over whether a particular local power can be inferred from a state grant of authority. For example, the justices of the North Carolina Supreme Court divided over whether a county has authority under the state's zoning enabling act to condition approval of new residential construction on developers' paying a fee to subsidize new school construction. *See* Lanvale Properties LLC v. County of Cabares, 731 S.E.2d 142 (N.C. 2012). The dissenting justices found the county's action supported by the broad language of the zoning enabling act, as well as by specific references in the act to the use of zoning to "facilitate the efficient and adequate provision of . . . schools" and to impose temporary moratoria because of concerns about the adequacy of public school facilities, *id.* at 175–76, 179–81; but the majority concluded that "the legislative powers of county governments in these areas are not as broad as the dissent characterizes them" and that conditioning development approvals on the payment of an impact fee went well beyond the express or implied grants in the zoning enabling act, *id.* at 152–58. Similarly, the judges

in Pennsylvania split over the question of whether the state's Municipal Planning Code ("MPC"), which authorizes municipalities to adopt and revise zoning and subdivision land development ordinances, empowers a township to adopt a moratorium on development while it revises its land use plan. The trial court and the intermediate appellate court found that although the MPC did not expressly grant the moratorium power, such power was "incidental as essential and necessary for the effectuation of a municipality's power to regulate land use under the MPC." Naylor v. Township of Hellam, 773 A.3d 770, 773 (Pa. 2001). A divided state supreme court, however, reversed, finding that the power to "*suspend* land development has historically been viewed . . . as a power distinct from and not incidental to any power to *regulate* land development." *Id.* at 405 (emphasis in original). Some other state courts have upheld the local power to enact development moratoria even in the absence of express state statutory authorization. *See also* Olesen v. Town of Hurley, *supra,* 691 N.W.2d at 328–29 ("City's express power to sell alcohol by the glass does not imply a necessary power to operate a restaurant"), *id.* at 332 (dissenting justice finds that "express power to sell alcohol by the glass confers upon it the implied and necessary powers to do what is necessary to operate the municipal bar within reasonable limits," including the sale of food). As a result of this uncertainty, Dillon's Rule "sends local governments to State legislatures seeking grants of additional power; it causes local officials to doubt their power, and it stops local government programs from developing fully." U.S. Advisory Comm'n on Intergovernmental Relations, State Constitutional and Statutory Restrictions Upon the Structural, Functional, and Personnel Powers or Local Government 24 (1962).

STATE OF UTAH V. HUTCHINSON

Supreme Court of Utah
624 P.2d 1116 (1980)

STEWART, JUSTICE:

Defendant, a candidate for the office of Salt Lake County Commissioner, was charged with having violated § 1–10–4, Revised Ordinances of Salt Lake County, which requires the filing of campaign statements and the disclosure of campaign contributions. * * *

A complaint charged defendant in two counts: (1) failure to report the name and address of a $6,000 contributor to his election campaign, and (2) failure to file supplemental campaign disclosures of the discharge of campaign debts and obligations.

Defendant filed a motion in a city court to dismiss the complaint on the ground that the ordinance was in violation of the Utah Constitution. The court granted the motion and held that Salt Lake County was without constitutional or statutory authority to enact the ordinance under which defendant was charged and dismissed the complaint.

An appeal was taken to a district court which affirmed the dismissal. That court wrote a memorandum decision observing that ". . . it may be true that our Utah Supreme Court has not been completely consistent in every case on this issue, (but) the majority of the (Utah Supreme Court) cases have indicated that grants of powers to cities or counties are to be strictly construed to the exclusion of implied powers not reasonably necessary in carrying out the purposes of the expressed powers granted." * * *

Concededly, the district court was correct in holding that the Legislature has not expressly authorized enactment of an ordinance requiring disclosure of campaign contributions in county elections. However, the Legislature has conferred upon cities and counties the authority to enact all necessary measures to promote the general health, safety, morals, and welfare of their citizens. Section 17–5–77, U.C.A. (1953), as amended, provides:

> The board of county commissioners may pass all ordinances . . . not repugnant to law . . . necessary and proper to provide for the safety, and preserve the health, promote the prosperity, improve the morals, peace and good order, comfort and convenience of the county and the inhabitants thereof, . . . and may enforce obedience to such ordinances . . . by fine in any sum less than $300 or by imprisonment not to exceed six months, or by both such fine and imprisonment

The Legislature has made a similar grant of power to the cities.

The specific issue in this case is whether § 17–5–77 by itself provides Salt Lake County legal authority to enact the ordinance for disclosure of campaign contributions, or whether there must be a specific grant of authority for counties to enact measures dealing with disclosures of campaign financing to sustain the ordinance in question. Defendant claims that the powers of municipalities must be strictly construed and that because Salt Lake County did not have specific, delegated authority to enact the ordinance in issue, the ordinance is invalid.

The rule requiring strict construction of the powers delegated by the Legislature to counties and municipalities is a rule which is archaic, unrealistic, and unresponsive to the current needs of both state and local governments and effectively nullifies the legislative grant of general police power to the counties. Furthermore, although the rule of strict construction is supported by some cases in this State, it is inconsistent with other cases decided by this Court—a situation that permits choosing from among conflicting precedents to support a particular result.

Dillon's Rule, which requires strict construction of delegated powers to local governments, was first enunciated in 1868. The rule was widely adopted during a period of great mistrust of municipal governments and has been viewed as "the only possible alternative by which extensive governmental powers may be conferred upon our municipalities, with a measurable limit upon their abuse."

The courts, in applying the Dillon Rule to general welfare clauses, have not viewed the latter as an independent source of power, but rather as limited by specific, enumerated grants of authority. * * * More recently, however, reasoned opinion regarding the validity of the rule has changed. * * *

As pointed out in Frug, The City As A Legal Concept, 93 Harvard L.Rev. 1059, 1111 (1980):

> Most troubling of all to Dillon, cities were not managed by those "best fitted by their intelligence, business experience, capacity and moral character." Their management was "too often both unwise and extravagant." A major change in city government was therefore needed to achieve a fully public city government dedicated to the common good. (Footnotes omitted.)

If there were once valid policy reasons supporting the rule, we think they have largely lost their force and that effective local self-government, as an important constituent part of our system of government, must have sufficient power to deal effectively with the problems with which it must deal. In a time of almost universal education and of substantial, and sometimes intense, citizen interest in the proper functioning of local government, we do not share the belief that local officials are generally unworthy of the trust of those governed. Indeed, if democratic processes at the grassroots level do not function well, then it is not likely that our state government will operate much better. * * *

The fear of local governments abusing their delegated powers as a justification for strict construction of those powers is a slur on the right and the ability of people to govern themselves. Adequate protection against abuse of power or interference with legitimate statewide interests is provided by the electorate, state supervisory control, and judicial review. Strict construction, particularly in the face of a general welfare grant of power to local governments, simply eviscerates the plain language of the statute, nullifies the intent of the Legislature, and seriously cripples effective local government.

There are ample safeguards against any abuse of power at the local level. Local governments, as subdivisions of the State, exercise those powers granted to them by the State Legislature * * * and the exercise of a delegated power is subject to the limitations imposed by state statutes and state and federal constitutions. A state cannot empower local governments to do that which the state itself does not have authority to do. In addition, local governments are without authority to pass any ordinance prohibited by, or in conflict with, state statutory law. * * * Also, an ordinance is invalid if it intrudes into an area which the Legislature has preempted by comprehensive legislation intended to blanket a particular field.

In view of all these restraints and corrective measures, it is not appropriate for this Court to enfeeble local governments on the unjustified assumption that strict construction of delegated powers is necessary to prevent abuse. The enactment of a broad general welfare clause conferring police powers directly on the counties was to enable them to act in every reasonable, necessary, and appropriate way to further the public welfare of their citizens.

The ultimate limitation upon potential abuses by local governments is the people themselves. It is their vigilance and sound judgment by which all democratic governments in the end, are restricted and directed. Officials who abuse the powers with which they have been entrusted ought not to be, and usually are not, long tolerated.

In short, we simply do not accept the proposition that local governments are not to be trusted with the full scope of legislatively granted powers to meet the needs of their local constituents. On the contrary, the history of our political institutions is founded in large measure on the concept at least in theory if not in practice that the more local the unit of government is that can deal with a political problem, the more effective and efficient the exercise of power is likely to be.

* * *

The wide diversity of problems encountered by county and municipal governments are not all, and cannot realistically be, effectively dealt with by a state legislature which sits for sixty days every two years to deal with matters of general importance. Thus the manner in which the Legislature operates militates in favor of a rule of judicial construction which permits localities to deal with their problems by local legislative action.

The general welfare provision, § 17–5–77, grants county commissioners of each county two distinct types of authority. In the first instance, power is given to implement specific grants of authority. Second, the counties are granted an independent source of power to act for the general welfare of its citizens. Thus § 17–5–77 provides authority to "pass all ordinances and rules and make all regulations, not repugnant to law, necessary for carrying into effect or discharging the powers and duties conferred by this title. . . ." The second part of that section empowers counties to pass ordinances that are "necessary and proper to provide for the safety, and preserve the health, promote the prosperity, improve the morals, peace and good order, comfort and convenience of the county and the inhabitants thereof, and for the protection of property therein."

Nothing in § 17–5–77 or in Title 17 suggests that the general welfare clause should be narrowly or strictly construed. Its breadth of language demands the opposite conclusion. * * *

* * * When the State has granted general welfare power to local governments, those governments have independent authority apart from, and in addition to, specific grants of authority to pass ordinances which are reasonably and appropriately related to the objectives of that power, i. e., providing for the public safety, health, morals, and welfare. * * * And the courts will not interfere with the legislative choice of the means selected unless it is arbitrary, or is directly prohibited by, or is inconsistent with the policy of, the state or federal laws or the constitution of this State or of the United States. Specific grants of authority may serve to limit the means available under the general welfare clause, for some limitation may be imposed on the exercise of power by directing the use of power in a particular manner. But specific grants should generally be construed with reasonable latitude in light of the broad language of the general welfare clause which may supplement the power found in a specific delegation.

Broad construction of the powers of counties and cities is consistent with the current needs of local governments. The Dillon Rule of strict construction is antithetical to effective and efficient local and state government. If at one time it served a valid purpose, it does so no longer. The complexities confronting local governments, and the degree to which the nature of those problems varies from county to county and city to city, has changed since the Dillon Rule was formulated. Several counties in this State, for example, currently confront large and serious problems caused by accelerated urban growth. The same problems however, are not so acute in many other counties. Some counties are experiencing, and others may soon be experiencing, explosive economic growth as the result of the development of natural resources. The problems that must be solved by these counties are to some extent unique to them. According a plain meaning to the legislative grant of general welfare power to local governmental units allows each local government to be responsive to the particular problems facing it.

Local power should not be paralyzed and critical problems should not remain unsolved while officials await a biennial session of the Legislature in the hope of obtaining passage of a special grant of authority. Furthermore, passage of legislation needed or appropriate for some counties may fail because of the press of other legislative business or the disinterest of legislators from other parts of the State whose constituencies experience other, and to them more pressing, problems. In granting cities and counties the power to enact ordinances to further the general welfare, the Legislature no doubt took such political realities into consideration.

holding

We therefore hold that a county has the power to preserve the purity of its electoral process. The county was entitled to conclude that financial disclosure by candidates would directly serve the legitimate purpose of achieving the goal that special interests should not be able to exercise undue influence in local elections without their influence being brought to light. * * *

In sum, the Dillon Rule of strict construction is not to be used to restrict the power of a county under a grant by the Legislature of general welfare power or prevent counties from using reasonable means to implement specific grants of authority. County ordinances are valid unless they conflict with superior law; do not rationally promote the public health, safety, morals and welfare; or are preempted by state policy or otherwise attempt to regulate an area which by the nature of the subject matter itself requires uniform state regulation. Of course a specific power delegated to municipalities may imply a restriction upon the manner of exercise of that power, but the restriction on the exercise of such power is to be construed to permit a reasonable discretion and latitude in attaining the purpose to be achieved.

home rule

MAUGHAN, JUSTICE (dissenting):

The analysis of the majority opinion utilizes the familiar technique of erecting a straw man, in this case, the abstract principle of law identified as Dillon's Rule, and throttling it with the evocative shibboleth of local control. The majority then interprets Section 17–5–77 as a carte blanche delegation of the state police power to local government, unless there be a specific and direct conflict between state and local law. This interpretation is inconsistent with the multiple statutes, wherein the legislature confers specific powers and duties on local government, and distorts the nature of the police power.

The State is the sole and exclusive repository of the police power, neither the federal nor local government has any such inherent power. The police power is awesome, for it confers the right to declare an act a crime and to deprive an individual of his liberty or property in order to protect or advance the public health, safety, morals, and welfare. The decision of whether a problem should be deemed one of local concern and should be regulated under the police power should initially be decided by the legislature representing all the citizens of this state. The legislature may then elect to delegate the power to local government to deal with the specific area of concern. It is equally a legislative judgment to deny delegating this power to local government.

The palliative suggested by the majority opinion that local citizens can change the law by electing new officials provides no relief for the individual previously convicted and avoids the basic issue of whether the police power has, in fact, been delegated under the specific circumstance.

All exercise of the police power by local government is derivative, none is inherent, and it is the exclusive prerogative of the State to establish the conditions under which it will be exercised. If local government discerns a condition which merits control through the police power, this matter should be submitted to the legislature so that representatives of the entire state may resolve whether the problem should be addressed on a local level.

* * * There are no constitutional provisions conferring the police power concerning local matters on counties or non-chartered cities. These corporate political bodies have no inherent powers and none of the elements of sovereignty; they cannot go beyond the powers granted them and must exercise such powers in a reasonable manner. The exercise of the police power is an attribute of state sovereignty, a portion of which it may delegate, but not to relinquish, to municipalities, which have none of the elements of sovereignty.

* * * In the matter at hand, there is no express grant conferring authority on Salt Lake County to enact a corrupt practices act concerning local elected officials. Such authority cannot be implied from the general welfare clause of Section 17–5–77 since it does not have a sufficiently direct, substantial, immediate effect on the specific general welfare interests set forth therein.

NOTES AND QUESTIONS

1. *Judicial Abrogation of Dillon's Rule.* As *Hutchinson* illustrates, Dillon's Rule may be abrogated by judicial action as well as by a state constitutional amendment or legislative command. The court relied on Utah Code Section 17–5–77, which generally authorizes local governments to enact "all necessary measures" to promote the local health, safety, morals, and welfare. This is known as a general welfare or police power grant. Courts in other states have also treated legislative adoption of a general welfare clause in the grant of powers to municipalities or counties as a basis for a broad construction of local powers. *See, e.g.*, Birkenfeld v. City of Berkeley, 550 P.2d 1001 (Cal.1976); Leavenworth Club Owners Assoc. v. Atchison, 492 P.2d 183 (Kan.1971); Krolick v. Lowery, 302 N.Y.S.2d 109 (N.Y.App.1969). *See also* Homebuilders Assoc. of Charlotte v. City of Charlotte, 442 S.E.2d 45, 49–50 (N.C.1994) (state statute declaring it "the policy of the General Assembly" that cities "should have adequate authority to execute the powers, duties, privileges, and immunities conferred upon them" and state-granted powers and city charters "shall be broadly construed and grants of power shall be construed to include any additional and supplementary powers that are reasonably necessary or expedient to carry them into execution and effect" held to abrogate Dillon's Rule). Can Dillon's Rule possibly co-exist with a state's adoption of a general welfare clause? If so, how?

2.   *Debating Dillon's Rule.* The clash between the majority and dissent in *Hutchinson* may represent the best modern judicial debate over Dillon's Rule. Why, according to the court, should local power be read expansively? If the rule of narrow construction is eliminated, what protections does the court find against local abuses? If local governments are particularly subject to special interest manipulation, as Professor Gillette has suggested, are the protections cited by the *Hutchinson* court likely to be adequate? *See* Clayton Gillette, In Partial Praise of Dillon's Rule, or Can Public Choice Theory Justify Local Government Law?, 67 Chi-Kent L.Rev. 959 (1991). On the other hand, is there any reason to believe that local governments are more subject to special interest manipulation than states? In the absence of adequate empirical data, should we presume that local governments are less trustworthy than, or as trustworthy as, their states? Why? *Cf.* Richard Briffault, Home Rule, Majority Rule, and Dillon's Rule, 67 Chi-Kent L.Rev. 1011 (1991) (criticizing Gillette's attempt to justify Dillon's Rule as an effort to limit the ability of special interests to manipulate localities). Should a court determine whether Dillon's Rule or a more expansive view of local power ought to apply by considering the views presented in Chapter I with respect to the vertical distribution of power? Is it possible to resolve the question without considering those views?

Is the *Hutchinson* dissent arguing that local governments are particularly untrustworthy? Or does the concern about the "awesome" nature of the police power reflect a deeper distrust of all government action? Does the Dillon's Rule approach, by requiring the state to decide police power questions, operate to restrict the scope of public power? Should those who distrust government action generally favor or oppose local autonomy? For a partial defense and a call for only a "limited overhaul" of Dillon's Rule in light of challenges to the Rule in Nevada, *see* Louis V. Csoka, The Dream of Greater Municipal Autonomy: Should the Legislature or the Courts Modify Dillon's Rule, A Common Law Restraint on Municipal Power? 29 N.C. Cent. L.J. 194 (2007).

Is abrogation of Dillon's Rule in the absence of an express directive from a state's constitution or statutes an appropriate action for courts? The Tennessee Supreme Court in *Southern Constructors, supra,* discussed *Hutchinson* at some length but concluded that as the Tennessee constitution vested all law-making power in the state legislature, the legislature "has the sole and plenary authority to determine whether, and under what circumstances, portions of that power should be delegated to local governments. . . . [A]bsent some indication to the contrary, the General Assembly must be presumed to have endowed local governments with only as much authority as it has granted through the language of delegation." 58 S.W. 3d at 711–12. On the other hand, given that Dillon's Rule is a judicially-adopted common-law-like rule reflecting late nineteenth century views of local governments, why shouldn't twenty-first century courts feel free to adopt a rule of construction of local governments power that reflects contemporary concerns?

2. HOME RULE

a. Defining "Home Rule"

The constitutional amendments and statutory provisions authorizing home rule vary enormously from state to state, and may provide different types of home rule powers for different categories or sizes of local governments within a single state. So, too, judicial construction of home rule has been neither uniform nor consistent, but has instead been marked by variations from state to state and often within a state.

Broadly speaking, home rule may be classified in two ways—in terms of the nature of home rule powers being exercised, and in terms of the legal framework of the home rule measure.

(1) Home Rule Powers: Initiative and Immunity

Home rule may be said to involve two powers:

(a) to enable local governments to undertake actions over a range of important issues without having to run to the state for specific authorization. This portion of home rule, in other words, undoes Dillon's Rule and gives local governments power to engage in policy-making concerning local matters.

(b) to protect local government decisions concerning local actions from displacement by state law. This portion of home rule, building on the nineteenth century special commission and special act bans, seeks to limit plenary state power with respect to local matters.

Professor Gordon L. Clark has observed that local autonomy involves both the capacity to *initiate* actions and the provision of a "sphere of local *immunity*" from the state. Clark, Judges and the Cities: Interpreting Local Autonomy 7 (U. Chi. Press 1985). Both initiative and immunity are central themes in the development and interpretation of home rule as well, as the Louisiana Supreme Court described:

Local governmental autonomy or home rule . . . may exist only to the extent that the state constitution endows a local governmental entity with two interactive powers, viz., the power to initiate local legislation and the power of immunity from control by the state legislature. . . .

The first power, initiation, refers to a local government's ability to initiate legislation and regulation in the absence of express state legislative authorization. For example, if local governments have the power to regulate with respect to land use and zoning, then they are also able to initiate plans and designs for the formal spatial configuration of local economic activities. . . . The power of immunity, on the other hand, is essentially the power of localities to act without fear of the supervisory authority of the state government. Immunity exists to the extent that the local entity is insulated from state control. For example, a certain degree of immunity would result from a constitutional provision barring the legislature from changing local ordinances except by general law or by a supermajority vote. This basic distinction between the power of initiation and the power of immunity provides an interpretive key to comprehending diverse state constitutional home rule provisions.

City of New Orleans v. Board of Commissioners of the Orleans Levee District, 640 So.2d 237, 242 (La.1994).

(2) Home Rule: The Legal Forms

Early versions of home rule sought to provide home rule municipalities with both initiative and immunity powers with respect to "local" or "municipal affairs." Indeed, in applying Missouri's pioneer home rule provision the United States Supreme Court referred to the city of St. Louis as an "imperium in imperio" or a government within a government. St. Louis v. Western Union Tel. Co., 149 U.S. 465, 468 (1893). The term "imperio" continues to be used to describe this original home rule system.

In theory, by combining initiative and immunity, imperio home rule provisions establish extensive local autonomy. In practice, however, the scope of that autonomy is often quite limited. With basic terms like "local" or "municipal" usually left undefined, imperio home rule provisions effectively turn the substantive scope of home rule into a question for the courts. In many state courts, the Dillon's Rule philosophy lingered, leading to narrow judicial construction of local home rule power. State courts were particularly hostile to municipal claims that home rule immunized certain local acts from state regulation. Yet, with the same language used to establish both local initiative and local immunity functions under state law, narrow judicial interpretations of "local" or "municipal" in immunity cases sometimes led to equally narrow judicial readings of the same language in local initiative cases. As a result, in the middle years of the twentieth century, home rule advocates sought a new formula that would reduce the judicial role, and strengthen local initiative, even at the price of conceding the power of the state to displace local actions. The Louisiana Supreme Court, in *Orleans Levee District, supra,* reviewed this history:

Early constitutional amendments attempted to provide a measure of home rule by enabling localities to legislate with respect to "municipal affairs." Ohio Const. art. XVIII, § 3 (adopted 1912) ("all powers of local self-government"); Cal. Const. art. XI, § 6 (adopted 1896) ("municipal affairs"); Wis.

Const. art. XI, § 3 (adopted 1924) ("local affairs and government"). These constitutional provisions granted both the power of initiation in regard to "local affairs" and the power of immunity from state regulation in this sphere. Court decisions interpreting this type of state-local test were inconsistent, however, and generally reflected either hostility toward home rule or undue deference to legislative intervention. [citation omitted] The degree of local autonomy that home rule advocates believed they had gained through constitutional amendments was eroded by court decisions characterizing many interests as "state" interests and thus beyond the scope of local regulation.

In 1953, the American Municipal Association (later, the National League of Cities (NLC)) sought to remedy the deficiency of the state-local test by proposing a model state constitutional provision under which all delegable legislative powers would be granted to the local government, subject to the legislature's power to deny local government's exercise of authority by state statute. American Municipal Ass'n, Model Constitutional Provisions for Municipal Home Rule, § 6 (1953). In 1968, the National Municipal League (NML) amended the NLC model to provide more immunity by providing that "[a] . . . city may exercise any legislative power . . . not denied . . . by general law." National Municipal League, Model State Constitution § 8.02 (6th ed. 1963). Some states following the NML model required that the legislature must expressly *deny* or *prohibit*, in order to override, a local government's particular exercise of legislative power. Mont. Const. art. XI, § 6 (adopted 1972); N.M. Const. art X, § 6 D (adopted 1970); Alaska Const. art. X, § 11 (adopted 1956).

640 So.2d at 242–43.

The NLC/NML home rule formulation is sometimes referred to as "legislative" home rule. This designation does not indicate the source of home rule authority; indeed, NLC or NML home rule authorizations are usually amendments to state constitutions and not the products of state legislation. Rather, the "legislative" label refers to the theory underlying the NLC/NML approach—to shift the determination of whether a matter is "local" or "municipal" from the courts to the state legislature. Legislative home rule presumes that a home rule local government has a power to act unless and until the power is taken away from the locality by the state legislature acting pursuant to general law. In other words, NLC/NML home rule creates a presumption in favor of home rule initiative but at the price of providing no home rule immunity.

In practice, many state home rule provisions blur these theoretically sharp distinctions and combine both imperio and NLC or NML language. *See* George D. Vaubel, Toward Principles of State Restraint Upon the Exercise of Municipal Power in Home Rule, 20 Stetson L. Rev. 845 (1991). The following state constitutional provisions are illustrative:

Alaska Constitution Art. 10, § 11

A home rule borough or city may exercise all legislative powers not prohibited by law or by charter.

California Constitution Art. 11, § 5(a)

It shall be competent in any city charter to provide that the city governed thereunder may make and enforce all ordinances and regulations in respect to municipal affairs, . . . and in respect to other matters they shall be subject to general laws. City charters . . . with respect to municipal affairs shall supersede all laws inconsistent therewith.

Iowa Constitution Art. III, § 38A

Municipal corporations are granted home rule power and authority, not inconsistent with the laws of the general assembly, to determine their local affairs and government, except that they shall not have power to levy any tax unless expressly authorized by the general assembly.

The rule or proposition of law that a municipal corporation possesses and can exercise only those powers granted in express words is not a part of the law of this state.

New Mexico Constitution Art. 10, § 6 (D)

A municipality which adopts a charter may exercise all legislative powers and perform all functions not expressly denied by general law or charter. This grant of powers shall not include the power to enact private or civil laws governing civil relationships except as incident to the exercise of an independent municipal power, nor shall it include the power to provide for a penalty greater than the penalty provided for a petty misdemeanor. No tax imposed by the governing body of a charter municipality, except a tax authorized by general law, shall become effective until approved by a majority vote in the charter municipality.

Which are the imperio provisions? Which are the NML provisions? Which constitutions combine elements of both?

Although the particular constitutional or statutory language affects the development of home rule, no choice of words or magic label can guarantee that courts will follow the intended path. For that reason, the classification of home rule provisions as imperio or legislative may seem somewhat academic. Deferential courts in imperio states may allow as much local experimentation and initiative as courts in legislative home rule states. *Cf.,* Terrance Sandalow, The Limits of Municipal Power Under Home Rule: A Role for the Courts, 48 Minn.L.Rev. 643 (1964) (finding that even in imperio home rule states courts often read local powers generously). Conversely, courts in legislative home rule states may interpret the scope of local initiative narrowly even in the absence of legislative prohibition.

To be sure, a court in a legislative home rule state is less likely to uphold a local ordinance that conflicts with state laws. A court sympathetic to local autonomy, however, may strain to avoid finding a conflict or may find a basis for determining that the state measure is beyond the scope of the state legislature's authority. *See, e.g.,* State ex rel. Haynes v. Bonem, 845 P.2d 150 (N.M.1992) (state statute requiring that in a city governed by an elected commission the commission must consist of five members is not a "general law" because it does not relate to a matter of statewide concern and thus does not displace a city's determination to provide for a seven-member commission, even though the state home rule amendment limits local autonomy to matters not inconsistent with general law). Even in imperio states, however, courts tend to read general grants of local power to act with respect to local or municipal affairs narrowly when local and state laws come into conflict—although specific constitutional provisions declaring that particular subjects fall within the scope of local authority are more likely to be enforced even in the face of conflicting state laws. *See, e.g.,* Sonoma County Organization of Public Employees v. County of Sonoma, 591 P.2d 1 (Cal.1979) (invalidating, partly on home rule grounds, state grant of funds to local governments conditioned on local adoption of certain limits on cost of living increases; California constitution specifically provides that the compensation of the officers and employees of chartered cities and counties falls within local home rule authority). Finally, on a more pragmatic, political level, the contours of home rule power in a particular state are also likely to be influenced by a wide range of extra-legal factors, including the attitudes of state legislators, the initiative of municipal officers themselves, and general civic culture in the state.

Although not dispositive, the imperio and legislative home rule concepts are still useful tools in the doctrinal analysis of home rule questions. They help to distinguish between home rule provisions that are aimed primarily at expanding local initiative from those that seek to provide immunity from state displacement, too. For analyses of the history and development of home rule, *see* Hugh Spitzer, "Home Rule" vs. Dillon's Rule for Washington Cities, 38 Seattle U. L. Rev. 809 (2015); Symposium: Home Rule, 86 Denver U. L. Rev. 1239–1473 (2009); Paul

Diller, The Partly Fulfilled Promise of Home Rule in Oregon, 87 Ore. L. Rev. 939 (2008); Richard Briffault, Home Rule for the Twenty-First Century, 36 Urb. Law. 253 (2004); David Barron, Reclaiming Home Rule, 116 Harv. L. Rev. 2255 (2003); George D. Vaubel, Toward Principles of State Restraint Upon the Exercise of Municipal Power in Home Rule, 22 Stetson L.Rev. 643 (1993) and 20 Stetson L.Rev. 5 (1991); Kenneth Vanlandingham, Constitutional Municipal Home Rule Since the AMA (NLC) Model, 17 Wm. & Mary L.Rev. 1 (1975); Kenneth Vanlandingham, Municipal Home Rule in the United States, 10 Wm. & Mary L.Rev. 269 (1968).

b. The Initiative Function (Home Rule as a "Sword")

ILLINOIS RESTAURANT ASSOCIATION V. CITY OF CHICAGO

U.S. District Court
492 F.Supp.2d 891 (N.D. Ill. 2007)

MANNING, J.

Foie gras, or "fatty liver," is produced using the French practice of gavage, which involves feeding ducks or geese with the goal of fattening their livers. The practice dates back to at least Roman times, when Pliny the Elder wrote of the practice of feeding geese dried figs to enlarge their livers. Pliny the Elder, Natural History, Book VIII, Ch. 77 (Teubner ed.1909). In the nineteenth century, the debate over the propriety of the practice continued, as Jean Anthelme Brillat-Savarin sided with the geese and ducks, writing that "[t]hey have not only been deprived of the means of reproduction, but they have been kept in solitude and darkness, and forced to eat until they were led to an unnatural state of fatness." Physiologie du goût (The Physiology of Taste), sec. III (1825). On the other hand, his contemporary, Charles Gerard, called the goose "an instrument for the output of a marvelous product, a kind of living hothouse in which there grows the supreme fruit of gastronomy." Charles Gérard, L'Ancienne Alsace à table (1862).

The debate rages on today, as the City of Chicago entered the fray in 2006 by enacting an ordinance banning the sale of foie gras at food dispensing establishments in the City. The Illinois Restaurant Association and Allen's New American Café sued the City in state court, claiming that the foie gras ordinance exceeded the City's police powers under the Illinois Constitution. The City removed this action after the plaintiffs amended their complaint to add a Commerce Clause claim arising under the federal Constitution. The City's motion to dismiss for failure to state a claim is before the court. For the following reasons, the court finds that the foie gras ordinance is consistent with the Illinois and United States Constitutions. Thus, the City's motion to dismiss for failure to state a claim is granted in its entirety. * * *

Foie gras is not produced in Chicago or Illinois. Instead, it is produced domestically at farms in California and New York and is produced and imported into the United States from farms in Canada and France. The production of foie gras in these out-of-state and foreign locations is lawful, and imported foie gras is subject to federal tariffs and other federal regulations allowing its importation for sale into the United States. Furthermore, the United States Department of Agriculture ("USDA") has found that foie gras is safe for human consumption. *Id.*

The parties offer differing characterizations of the City Council's motives for passing the Ordinance. According to the plaintiffs, the City Council has never advanced any health, consumer protection, or fraud bases as justification for the Ordinance and no such justifications exist. Instead, the Ordinance is a "moral statement" which was passed "because of the purportedly inhumane manner in which foie gras is *produced.*"

On the other hand, the City points to the "WHEREAS" clauses of the Ordinance, which note the City Council's recognition that "the media has shed light on the unethical practices of the care and preparation of the livers of birds." The City Council specifically focused upon the practice during which "[b]irds, in particular geese and ducks, are inhumanely force fed, via a pipe inserted through their throats several times a day, in order to produce a rare delicacy, foie gras, for restaurant patrons." * * *

The City Council also recognized that the City "is home to many famous restaurants offering the finest cuisine and dining experiences to their customers," and that "[m]illions of people visit Chicago every year, attending cultural events and dining in our legendary restaurants." The City Council then expressed its view that "[t]he people of Chicago and those who visit here have come to expect, and rightfully deserve, the highest quality in resources, service and fare" and concluded that "[b]y ensuring the ethical treatment of animals, who are the source of the food offered in our restaurants, the City of Chicago is able to continue to offer the best in dining experiences." The City then passed the Ordinance.

* * *

The plaintiffs contend that the Ordinance exceeds the City's home rule powers because it is not aimed at a legitimate local problem and has an impermissible extraterritorial effect since it is meant to affect the production process of foie gras, which only occurs outside Chicago. Under the Illinois Constitution of 1970, "a home rule unit may exercise any power and perform any function pertaining to its government and affairs including, but not limited to, the power to regulate for the protection of the public health, safety, morals and welfare. . . ." Ill. Const. Art. VII, § 6(a). The City "is a home rule unit of local government under the 1970 Illinois Constitution." Thus, the Ordinance does not violate the Illinois Constitution if it is within the scope of the City's broad home rule powers.

The court begins with an overview of home rule. The Illinois Supreme Court has emphasized that home rule units have expansive powers. ("Section 6(a) gives home rule units the broadest powers possible"). Because home rule powers are "broad and imprecise in order to allow for great flexibility," a home rule unit's powers and functions "shall be construed liberally." Ill. Const.1970 art. VII, § 6(m). Moreover, a home rule unit "has broad discretion to determine not only what the public interest and welfare require, but to determine the measures needed to secure such interest."

Because a home rule unit's powers are so broad, the constitutionality of its ordinances does not turn on a court's assessment of their wisdom or desirability. Nevertheless, an ordinance enacted by a home rule unit must address a local problem, as opposed to a problem arising at the state or national level. * * * A problem can be local in nature even if it is also a state or national issue. *See Scadron v. City of Des Plaines,* 153 Ill.2d 164, 175, 180 Ill.Dec. 77, 606 N.E.2d 1154 (Ill.1992) (regulation of outdoor advertising promoted traffic safety and aesthetics and thus was a permissible use of home rule power even though "the proliferation of billboards may be a national and State problem").

When determining whether an ordinance has a sufficient local angle for the purposes of home rule, the court must consider "[1] the nature and extent of the problem, [2] the units of government which have the most vital interest in its solution, and [3] the role traditionally played by local and statewide authorities in dealing with it." *Kalodimos v. Village of Morton Grove,* 103 Ill.2d 483, 501, 83 Ill.Dec. 308, 470 N.E.2d 266 (1984). With these basic principles in mind, the court turns to the plaintiffs' overlapping claims that the Ordinance is not aimed at a local problem and has an impermissible extraterritorial effect.

1.   The Nature and Extent of the Problem

The Ordinance addresses sales of foie gras in Chicago and thus addresses a local aspect of the more general question as to whether foie gras should be available at the state or national level. *See Village of Bolingbrook v. Citizens Utilities Co. of Illinois,* 158 Ill.2d at 139–41, 198 Ill.Dec. 389, 632 N.E.2d 1000 (despite existence of state laws governing the disposal of waste and sewage, Bolingbrook's ordinance assessing fines based on the disposal of certain sewage was a proper exercise of its home rule powers because it had the authority to regulate within its boundaries). This is so even though foie gras sales are lawful elsewhere, as the fact that conduct is lawful outside the jurisdiction does not bar a home rule unit from enacting legislation which controls conduct inside its borders. *Kalodimos v. Village of Morton Grove,* 103 Ill.2d at 503–05, 83 Ill.Dec. 308, 470 N.E.2d 266 (Morton Grove's handgun ban addressed local problem because it did not regulate conduct outside of its boundaries).

Similarly, the federal government's regulation of the safety of foie gras consumption does not preempt regulation of sales at the local level because Chicago is not enacting legislation directed at whether foie gras is fit for consumption. *See id.* at 503, 83 Ill.Dec. 308, 470 N.E.2d 266 (local governments may enact their own solutions to problems "in the face of less stringent or conflicting State regulation, following a determination that the State's expression of interest in the subject as evidenced by its statutory scheme did not amount to an express attempt to declare the subject one requiring exclusive State control"); *Scadron v. City of Des Plaines,* 153 Ill.2d at 186, 180 Ill.Dec. 77, 606 N.E.2d 1154 ("home rule units may exercise any nonexclusive power concurrently with the state, provided such power has not been specifically limited").

Moreover, the Ordinance states that because the vast majority of Americans oppose foie gras production, banning foie gras will enhance the reputation of restaurants in Chicago. Contrary to the plaintiffs' position, the City's expressed desire to use a foie gras ban to make a statement about the methods used to produce foie gras is a local interest since local political bodies traditionally enact legislation reflecting the perceived desires of their constituency, and the Ordinance reflects the City Council's belief that a majority of Chicagoans want to ban foie gras sales in Chicago. *See City of Evanston v. Create, Inc., 421 N.E.2d 196* ("the local governing body can create an ordinance specifically suited for the unique needs of its residents and is keenly and uniquely aware of the needs of the community it serves").

The Ordinance thus reflects the City Council's judgment that banning the sale of foie gras would benefit the City and advance the morals of the community. The court cannot sit as a superlegislature and determine if, in its judgment, the City Council was correct. *Chicago Nat. League Ball Club, Inc. v. Thompson,* 108 Ill.2d at 364, 91 Ill.Dec. 610, 483 N.E.2d 1245 ("the legislature has broad discretion to determine not only what the public interest and welfare require, but to determine the measures needed to secure such interest"); *Village of Glenview v. Ramaker,* 282 Ill.App.3d 368, 371, 217 Ill.Dec. 921, 668 N.E.2d 106 (1st Dist.1996) (declining to strike down an ordinance prohibiting residents from keeping swine within village because, among other things, "[c]ourts will not disturb an exercise of police power merely because there is room for a difference of opinion about the wisdom or necessity of its exercise"). In other words, the Ordinance's constitutionality does not depend on whether the court or the parties agree as to its wisdom. *See id.* The plaintiffs' numerous arguments regarding the desirability of a foie gras ban are, therefore, beside the point.

2. Who Has the Most Vital Interest in the Problem and Who Traditionally Deals With The Problem

The court next considers whether the Chicago City Council is the unit of government with the most vital interest in solving the problem at the heart of the Ordinance. Because the Ordinance regulates food which may be served in Chicago restaurants and sold in Chicago grocery stores, the Chicago City Council clearly meets this standard. It is also the proper authority to address the problem because it is uniquely situated to govern the conduct of Chicago business establishments. *Id.*

This is true even if Chicago's ban has effects outside the jurisdiction (such as reducing the national consumption of foie gras), because, as discussed above, a law's potential extraterritorial effects do not cancel out its local aspects and render Chicago powerless to address a perceived local problem. *See Kalodimos v. Village of Morton Grove,* 103 Ill.2d at 504–05, 83 Ill.Dec. 308, 470 N.E.2d 266 (Morton Grove's ban of operable handguns addressed the local interest of controlling guns even though it had the secondary effect of causing people carrying guns to route themselves around Morton Grove). In addition, the City's home rule powers enable it to prohibit the sale of foie gras even though it cannot regulate the production of foie gras outside its borders. *See id.* ("The grant of home rule powers contemplates that different communities which perceive a problem differently may adopt different measures to address the problem, provided that the legislature has taken no affirmative steps to circumscribe the measures that may be taken and that the measures taken are reasonable"). In this regard, the court notes that the Ordinance governs the sale of foie gras in Chicago, and does not regulate the treatment of ducks or geese located in the United States or elsewhere.

Accordingly, for the above reasons, the court finds that despite the Ordinance's extraterritorial effects, it is a valid exercise of Chicago's home rule powers under the Illinois Constitution because it is aimed at a sufficiently local problem. [The court also held that the ordinance did not violate the Commerce Clause of the United States Constitution.]

NOTES AND QUESTIONS

1. *Aftermath.* Although it passed the Chicago City Council by the lopsided vote of 48–1 and drew widespread praise from animal rights groups, the foie gras ordinance stirred "overwhelming controversy and backlash from restaurant owners. Many Chicago restaurants passionately opposed the ban, going so far as to protest the law by creating and openly serving specialty items featuring foie gras; some restaurants even threw foie gras parties on the day the law took effect." Joshua I. Grant, Hell to the Sound of Trumpets: Why Chicago's Ban on Foie Gras Was Constitutional and What It Means for the Future of Animal Welfare Laws, 2 Stan. J. Animal L. & Pol'y 52, 66–67 (2009). Although he did not oppose or veto the ordinance, Chicago Mayor

Richard M. Daley openly criticized it as "the silliest law" the City Council had ever passed, and two years later helped maneuver its repeal. The repeal proposal was referred to the Council's Rules Committee, instead of the Health Committee, which had approved the foie gras ban, and then taken up on the Council floor, without having had a committee hearing, "a rare occurrence at the City Council. Alderman Moore, the original sponsor of the ban, objected to the absence of a hearing and attempted to exercise his right to postpone the vote. Mayor Daley ruled him out of order and when Alderman Moore tried to debate the merits of the bill, Mayor Daley ruled that the issue was not debatable. As Alderman Moore shouted objections . . . Mayor Daley ordered the City Council Clerk to call roll and continue with the vote." The repeal passed by a vote of 37–6, with six abstentions. *Id.* at 68. The Chicago foie gras ban did, however, considerably raise the salience of the issue of whether the force-feeding process by which foie gras is produced is inhumane.

Prior to Chicago's ordinance, California had enacted a ban on the sale of products that are the result of force feeding birds to enlarge their livers beyond normal size, but delayed the ban's effective date until 2012. When the law came into effect it was challenged as unconstitutional under the Commerce Clause. Like the Chicago federal district court, the United States Court of Appeals for the Ninth Circuit rejected the argument. Ass'n des Eleveurs de Canards et d'Oies du Quebec v. Harris, 729 F.3d 937 (9th Cir. 2013). But a federal district court subsequently found the ban preempted by the federal Poultry Products Inspection Act. Ass'n des Eleveurs de Canards et d'Oies du Quebec v. Harris, 2015 WL 191375 (C.D. Cal. 2015).

2. *What Is a Local Problem?* Illinois gives its home rule units—every municipality with a population of more than 25,000, smaller municipalities that elect by referendum to become home rule units, and counties that elect their chief executives—a very broad grant of authority to act. Art. VII, § 6(a) of the state constitution provides that a home rule unit may "exercise any power and perform any function pertaining to its government and affairs." But, as the court explains, that still requires some determination of what matters pertain to local government and affairs. In this case, foie gras was produced outside Chicago, and there was no argument that foie gras consumption posed a health or consumer protection issue. Moreover, foie gras was sold and consumed all over the United States, and Chicago did not suggest that there was anything unique about the sale or consumption of foie gras *in Chicago* that made this a particularly Chicago problem. So, in what sense was this an appropriate matter for local regulation? *See also* Scadron v. City of Des Plaines, 606 N.E.2d 1154, 1158 (Ill. 1992) ("[s]imply because the proliferation of billboards may be a national or state problem, it does not then immediately follow that the problems posed by billboard advertising is of no concern to home rule municipalities").

Under home rule local governments often address local problems that are not uniquely local or particular to the city or county taking action. For example, local governments have taken the initiative on a range of public health matters not distinctively local, becoming, in the words of one study, "public health policy-makers." Lainie Rutkow, Jennifer L. Pomerantz, and Sara O. Rodman, Local Governments and the Food System: Innovative Approaches to Public Health Law and Policy, 22 Annals of Health Law 355, 358 (2013). With respect to smoking and tobacco regulations, localities were among the first governments in the United States to ban smoking in indoor public places like restaurants and bars; to restrict tobacco-related billboard advertising; to restrict the sale and marketing of tobacco products to minors; and to require retail vendors of cigarettes to prominently post graphic warning signs. *See* Paul Diller, Why Do Cities Innovate in Public Health? Implications of Scale and Structure, 91 Wash. U. L. Rev. 1219, 1225–36 (2014). As will be discussed later in this Chapter, some of these local actions were challenged as in conflict with and thus preempted by federal or state law. Subject to the possibility of preemption, it is now widely accepted that this is an area fit for local regulation. Moreover, many local initiatives in this area have been taken up by higher levels of government. *See id.* Similarly, local governments have played a leading role in addressing obesity, including the adoption of bans on trans fats and menu labeling requirements. *See id.* at 1236–43. These local laws "propelled regulatory changes nationwide," with menu labeling ultimately becoming part of federal public health policy. *Id.* at 1237. When challenged in court, the principal legal issue has been preemption, not whether these subjects are appropriate for local action. *See, e.g.,* New York State Restaurant Ass'n v. New York City Board of Health, 556 F.3d 114 (2d Cir. 2009) (rejecting preemption challenge to New York City law requiring certain restaurants to post calorie information on their menus and menu boards). *Cf.* New York Statewide Coalition of Hispanic Chambers of Commerce v. New York City Dep't of Health, 23 N.Y.3d 681 (2014) (invalidating New York City's "portion cap" rule for sugary drinks on administrative law grounds; city board of health lacked power to adopt the rule in absence of authorization from city council). *See also* Elizabeth Daigneau, Should Localities Be Allowed to Ban Pesticides?, Governing (March 2014) (Takoma Park, Maryland adopts ordinance banning 23 cosmetic lawn pesticides).

3.   *Extraterritorial Effects.* In considering the Chicago foie gras ban, the Illinois Supreme Court gave attention to whether the measure would have extraterritorial effects. Indeed, the plaintiffs contended that the measure had an extraterritorial purpose—to affect, and presumably ultimately end, the production process of foie gras, which occurs only outside Chicago. Extraterritorial effects are often invoked as a basis for denying local authority to act. However, it will often be difficult to cabin the effects of a local decision entirely within local borders. How did the court resolve the extraterritorial effect issue? Extraterritorial effects, and the relative weight of local and nonlocal interests, will also be taken into account when courts consider whether a local measure is in tension with state laws on the same subject.

4.   *Other Constraints on Home Rule Initiative.* In addition to whether a matter is distinctively local or has extraterritorial effects, courts have looked

at other considerations in deciding whether a local ordinance falls within the scope of the home rule grant. Local governments generally cannot regulate a state institution, such as the court system, Ampersand, Inc. v. Finley, 338 N.E.2d 15 (Ill. 1975) (invalidating ordinance that directed the clerk of the circuit court for the county to collect a $2 filing fee in civil cases to support the county law library; held to be a condition on the right to litigate in the courts, which is beyond home rule power), Isaac v. Los Angeles, 77 Cal.Rptr.2d 752 (Cal.App.1998) (determination of lien priorities not a local matter); Gloudeman v. St. Francis, 422 N.W.2d 864 (Wis.App.1988) (notice requirements for enforcement of ordinance not a local matter), or a regional institution, such as a sanitary district, Metropolitan Sanitary Dist. v. City of Des Plaines, 347 N.E.2d 716 (Ill. 1976) (home rule city cannot compel sanitary district to obtain a city permit in order to build a sewage treatment plant within its borders as the proposed plant would serve six other municipalities). Courts may also find that other provisions of a state constitution take a matter out of local hands. *See, e.g.,* Biggers v. City of Bainbridge Island, 169 P.3d 14 (Wash. 2007) (plurality opinion) (state constitution reserves control of the shoreline to the state so home rule power does not give city authority to impose a moratorium on shoreline development within its borders); City of Lima v. State, 909 N.E.2d 616 (Ohio 2009) (state constitutional provision giving legislature power to provide "for the comfort, health, safety, and general welfare of all employe[e]s" precludes local governments from claiming home rule authority to adopt residency requirements for local public employees). But the most important constraint on local power to act is the existence of state laws that either expressly preclude local action or are inconsistent with the local measure. This issue of state preemption did not arise in the Chicago foie gras dispute as there was no even arguably relevant state law on the subject. However, there is frequently state law on or related to the same subject as a local home rule ordinance, so the question of preemption commonly arises. As it often involves consideration of some of the same issues—the nature of the local interest and the extent of extraterritorial impact of local regulation—as are implicated by local power to act, the two questions are often intertwined. The analysis of state-local conflict and preemption will be taken up later in this Chapter.

5. *Home Rule Action on Controversial Issues.* Some of the most controversial uses of home rule powers have involved so-called "hot button" issues where the circumstances or political preferences of local residents, particularly in big cities, diverge significantly from those of the rest of the state. Two such areas have been local regulation of firearms, and local measures dealing with gay and lesbian rights.

(a) *"Firearm Localism."* In his article, Firearm Localism, 123 Yale L.J. 82 (2013), Professor Joseph Blocher observed that America has "two gun cultures"—a rural culture in which people grow up with guns, have positive views about the use and possession of guns, and oppose gun control; and an urban culture in which high rates of gun-related crime and concerns about gun safety have resulted in considerable support for gun control. *Id.* at 90–107. This has meant that although strong gun laws are only rarely enacted at the federal and state levels, many local governments have adopted stringent gun regulations. That, in turn, has led to many legal disputes under both state and federal law concerning local power to act in this area.

In the leading case of Kalodimos v. Village of Morton Grove, 470 N.E.2d 266 (Ill. 1984), the Illinois Supreme Court sustained Morton Grove's ban on the possession of handguns within the village. The court found that the handgun ban fell within the home rule power to regulate for local public health, safety, morals and welfare, and was not preempted by state laws regulating firearms. Other local measures have focused on the possession of assault weapons. *See, e.g.,* Richmond Boro Gun Club, Inc. v. City of New York, 896 F.Supp. 276 (E.D.N.Y. 1995) (upholding local law criminalizing the possession or transfer of certain assault weapons); Robertson v. City and County of Denver, 874 P.2d 325 (Colo. 1994) (upholding most of ordinance banning manufacture, sale or possession of assault weapons); Citizens for a Safer Community v. City of Rochester, 627 N.Y.S.2d 193 (Sup. Ct., Monroe Co. 1994) (upholding ordinance banning possession and sale of semi-automatic rifles and shotguns); Arnold v. City of Cleveland, 616 N.E.2d 163 (Ohio 1993) (upholding ordinance banning possession and sale of assault weapons). These courts found such prohibitions to grow out of the local power "to promote the health, safety, and security" of its citizens. *Robertson, supra,* 874 P.2d at 332. *Accord, Arnold, supra,* 616 N.E.2d at 172 ("the legislation is a reasonable regulation, promoting the welfare and safety of the people of Cleveland"). Local governments have also used traditional local powers, like zoning or business licensing, to regulate gun ownership or sale: "Through their zoning power, localities have prohibited gun shows and gun dealers from operating in or near residentially-zoned areas, schools zones, and 'safety zones.' Local control over business licensing has been used to require gun dealers to maintain appropriate levels of liability insurance, follow specific safety and security standards and establish fees to recover the costs of processing applications, monitoring permit holders, and enforcing ordinance provisions." Darwin Farrar, In Defense of Home Rule: California's Preemption of Local Firearms Regulation, 7 Stan. L. & Pol. Rev. 51, 56 (1995–96) (discussing actions of California localities).

On the other hand, some local firearm regulations have been held to be preempted by state gun laws. *See, e.g.,* Ortiz v. Commonwealth, 681 A.2d 152 (Pa. 1996) (Philadelphia and Pittsburgh ordinances regulating assault weapons preempted by state legislation expressly prohibiting local laws concerning "ownership, possession, transfer or transportation of firearms"). In other words, even if home rule authority could be interpreted to permit local regulation of guns, state laws expressly barring local gun regulation will preempt local initiatives. *See also* Farrar, *supra,* 7 Stan. L. & Pol. Rev. at 54–57 (describing and criticizing California state preemption of local firearms regulation). State preemption, rather than local authority to act in the absence of state law, has been a principal issue in many cases. *See, e.g.,*

Fiscal v. City & County of San Francisco, 70 Cal.Rptr.3d 324 (Cal. App. 2008); Ohioans for Concealed Carry v. City of Clyde, 896 N.E.2d 967 (Ohio 2008). *But see* Calguns Foundation, Inc. v. County of San Mateo, 160 Cal.Rptr.3d 698 (Cal. App. 2013) (state concealed weapon licensing statute did not preempt county ordinance prohibiting guns in parks and recreational areas). Due to aggressive lobbying by the National Rifle Association, more states have adopted laws that preempt local firearms regulation. *See* Joe Palazzolo, Ashby Jones, and Patrick O'Connor, City Gun Laws Hit Roadblock, Wall St. J., Feb. 5, 2013. A number of local governments have also brought tort actions against firearms manufacturers and dealers. Relying on a range of negligence, failure to warn, nuisance, and product liability theories, these suits seek compensatory damages to cover the law enforcement, emergency medical costs, and other costs incurred due to crimes committed with guns, as well as injunctive relief to change the way in which guns are manufactured and marketed. These suits have had little success, and have faced preemption problems. *See, e.g.,* Sturm, Ruger & Co. v. City of Atlanta, 560 S.E.2d 525, 530 (Ga. App. 2002) (city's suit against gun manufacturers and trade associations for negative design and failure to warn preempted by state law; "[t]hat the City has filed a lawsuit rather than passing an ordinance does not make this any less a usurpation of State power. The City may not do indirectly that which it cannot do directly"); Morial v. Smith & Wesson Corp., 785 So.2d 1 (La. 2001). For a discussion of the Atlanta and New Orleans cases, *see* Eric Womack, A Revolution in Local Government Law: Recognizing the Home Rule Implications of Municipality Suits Against Gun Manufacturers, 5 N.Y.U. J. Legis. & Pub. Pol. 255 (2001). *See also* City of Philadelphia v. Beretta U.S.A. Corp., 126 F. Supp.2d 882 (E.D.Pa. 2000) (Pennsylvania law preempting local regulation of firearms also barred municipality from suing gun industry in its role of parens patriae, that is, on behalf of its citizens); Ganim v. Smith & Wesson Corp., 780 A.2d 98 (Conn. 2001) (City of Bridgeport lacks standing to sue firearms manufacturers, trade associations, and retail sellers because the injuries sustained by the municipality are "too remote, indirect, or derivative" of the injuries of others to support a claim). *But cf.* City of Boston v. Smith & Wesson Corp., 12 Mass. L. Rptr. 225 (Mass. Super. 2000) (Boston's budget costs in dealing with gun violence gave it standing to bring product liability and nuisance claims against gun manufacturers; Massachusetts Firearms Act did not preempt the lawsuit since that statute applied only to regulation and not to tort claims; city subsequently voluntarily terminated the action); City of Cincinnati v. Beretta U.S.A. Corp., 768 N.E.2d 1136 (Ohio 2002) (city could bring nuisance, negligence, and product liability claims against handgun manufacturers to recover costs of city services responding to gun violence; case ultimately dropped due to high litigation costs). Congress enacted the Protection of Lawful Commerce in Arms Act of 2005, codified at 15 U.S.C. §§ 7901–03; to block these suits. *See* City of New York v. Beretta U.S.A. Corp., 524 F.3d 384 (2d. Cir. 2008). For critical appraisals of municipal tort litigation against gun manufacturers, *see* Joseph W. Cleary, Municipalities versus Gun Manufacturers: Why Public Nuisance Claims Just

Do Not Work, 31 U. Balt. L. Rev. 273 (2002); Lawrence S. Greenwald and Cynthia A. Shay, Municipalities' Suits Against Gun Manufacturers—Legal Folly, 4 J. Health Care L. & Pol. 13 (2000).

The legal landscape for local regulation of firearms was transformed by the decisions of the United States Supreme Court in District of Columbia v. Heller, 554 U.S. 570 (2008), which determined that the Second Amendment of the United States Constitution protects the individual right to possess a gun, and McDonald v. City of Chicago, 561 U.S. 742 (2010), which applied the Second Amendment to the states and local governments and invalidated ordinances passed by Chicago and the village of Oak Park, a Chicago suburb, banning the possession of handguns in the home. This effectively overruled the earlier Seventh Circuit decision rejecting a Second Amendment challenge to the Morton Grove handgun ban that was the subject of Illinois's home rule handgun regulation case, Quilici v. Village of Morton Grove, 695 F.2d 261 (1982), cert. den. 464 U.S. 863 (1983). However, Heller also stated that the Second Amendment does not ban all firearms restrictions. As a result, although it created new issues for and restrictions on local gun regulations, Heller did not end all local efforts to regulate guns. See, e.g. Friedman v. City of Highland Park, 784 F.3d 406 (7th Cir. 2015) (local ordinance prohibiting possession, sale, or manufacture of semi-automatic assault weapons and large capacity magazines does not violate Second Amendment); Jackson v. City and County of San Francisco, 746 F.3d 953 (9th Cir. 2014), cert. den. 135 S.Ct. 2799 (2015) (upholding ordinance regulating handgun storage and ammunition sales). See also J.B. Wogan, Cities Find New Ways to Go After Gun Violence, Governing, Sept. 2014.

Not all local governments are anti-gun. Responding to Morton Grove's handgun ban, Kennesaw, Georgia in 1982 adopted a requirement that every household own at least one firearm with ammunition. Nucla, Colorado adopted a similar requirement in 2013, and Virgin, Utah has a comparable rule. See Lauren Loftus, Life in the small Colorado town that requires a gun in every household, The Washington Post, Aug. 28, 2014; Keith Wagstaff, 5 towns that have considered making gun ownership mandatory, The Week, March 6, 2013.

(b) *Domestic Partnership Ordinances.* Same-sex relationships is another area in which local norms and preferences, particularly in large urban centers, may differ sharply from statewide attitudes. Before the decision of the Massachusetts Supreme Judicial Court in Goodridge v. Department of Public Health, 798 N.E.2d 941 (2003) in 2003, no state recognized same-sex marriage. Local governments, however, took a pioneering role in this area. Although family law, including the definition of marriage, is considered a state matter, *see, e.g.,* Li v. State, 110 P.3d 91 (Ore. 2006) (county lacked authority to issue marriage license to same-sex couple), many cities and counties adopted ordinances providing for domestic partnership registries in which same-sex couples, unable to marry, could register as domestic partners. In addition to the symbolic recognition of their union, there were certain concrete benefits, including visitation rights in city hospitals and jails, and employment benefits for the same-sex partners of local government employees. Many local governments also adopted employment discrimination measures protecting gays and lesbians. *See* Michael A. Woods, The Propriety of Local Government Protections of Gays and Lesbians from Discriminatory Employment Practices, 52 Emory L.J. 515, 554–55 (2003).

Many of these measures were challenged as beyond the scope of local home rule power and/or preempted by state law. *See, e.g.,* Devlin v. City of Philadelphia, 862 A.2d 1234 (Pa. 2004); Tyma v. Montgomery County, 801 A.2d 148 (Md. 2002); Heinsma v. City of Vancouver, 29 P.3d 709 (Wash. 2001); Lowe v. Broward County, 766 So.2d 1199 (Fla. Dist. Ct. App. 2000), *rev. den.,* 789 So.2d 346 (Fla. 2001); Crawford v. City of Chicago, 710 N.E.2d 91 (Ill.App.) *app. den.,* 720 N.E.2d 1090 (Ill.1999); Slattery v. City of New York, 686 N.Y.S.2d 683 (N.Y. Sup.Ct. 1999), *aff'd* 697 N.Y.S.2d 603 (N.Y. App. Div. 1999); Connors v. City of Boston, 714 N.E.2d 335 (Mass. 1999); Schaefer v. City & County of Denver, 973 P.2d 717 (Colo.App.1998); City of Atlanta v. Morgan, 492 S.E.2d 193 (Ga. 1997); Lilly v. City of Minneapolis, 527 N.W.2d 107 (Minn.App. 1995). *See also* Arlington County v. White, 528 S.E.2d 706 (Va. 2000) (application of Dillon's Rule to county effort to treat domestic partners as "dependents" of county employees). The principal questions for these courts were whether formal recognition of domestic partnership infringed on the state's exclusive control over marriage, and whether state laws dealing with the provision of employment benefits to municipal employees precluded local governments from adding new categories of beneficiaries or redefining the concept of "dependent" to include a same-sex partner. The courts that sustained these measures generally emphasized the limited nature of domestic partnership, *see, e.g., Devlin, supra,* 862 A.2d at 1243 ("we do not believe that the City's mere designation of 'Life Partnership' as a 'marital status' demonstrates that it was equating Life Partnership with state-sanctioned marriage. . . . Life Partnership is simply not the functional equivalent of marriage"); *Tyma, supra,* 801 A.2d at 158 (Montgomery County did not "by its terms or implication, restrict, modify or alter any rights incident to a marriage recognized in this State or give one domestic partner rights, beyond the employment benefits enumerated, against the other"); *Crawford, supra,* 710 N.E.2d at 98 n. 11 (Chicago domestic partnership ordinance does not purport "to create a marital status or marriage as those terms are commonly defined"). They also focused on the home rule interest in determining local public employee benefits. *See, e.g., Devlin, supra,* 862 A.2d at 1245–46 ("the City's provision of benefits to Life Partners is not legislation in an area of state-wide concern, but rather is a matter affecting merely the *personnel* and *administration* of the offices local to Philadelphia and which are no concern to citizens elsewhere") (emphasis in original; internal quotations omitted); *Heinsma, supra,* 29 P.3d at 566 (invoking the rule that "grants of municipal power are to be construed liberally, rather than narrowly" in deciding that city could treat domestic partner as "dependent"). On the other hand, where the court found that the state clearly intended a definition of dependent limited to spouses and minor children, the city's efforts to extend benefits to the domestic partners of employees was deemed preempted. *See Lilly, supra; Connors, supra.*

In other contexts, some state courts have also upheld local antidiscrimination ordinances that are more expansive than state antidiscrimination laws, *see, e.g.,* Laborers' Int'l Union, Local 478 v. Burroughs, 541 So.2d 1160 (Fla.1989) (state anti-discrimination law that applies only to employers with fifteen or more employees does not preclude county from adopting anti-discrimination ordinance applying to employers of five or more employees); New York State Club Ass'n, Inc. v. City of New York, 505 N.E.2d 915 (N.Y. 1987) (state law that excludes private clubs from ban on discrimination in places of public accommodations does not preempt local ordinance applying anti-discrimination ban to clubs with more than four hundred members that provide regular meal service, and regularly receive payment for or on behalf of nonmembers in connection with their trade or business). *See also* Bloom v. City of Worcester, 293 N.E.2d 268 (Mass.1973) (city may establish commission to receive complaints concerning housing and employment discrimination despite existence of comparable state commission); Hutchinson Human Relations Commission v. Midland Credit Management, Inc., 517 P.2d 158 (Kan.1973) (upholding local antidiscrimination ordinance); Marshall v. Kansas City, 355 S.W.2d 877 (Mo.1962) (upholding local ordinance banning discrimination in places of public accommodations); Holiday Universal Club v. Montgomery County, 508 A.2d 991 (Md.App.1986) (same); *but see* McCrory Corp. v. Fowler, 570 A.2d 834 (Md.1990) (county ordinance banning employment discrimination beyond scope of home rule grant).

In February 2004, Mayor Gavin Newsom of San Francisco opened a new chapter in the story of the local role in addressing the rights of gays and lesbians when he ordered the county clerk to issue marriage licenses to same-sex couples. In the twenty-nine days before the California Supreme Court ordered the city to stop issuing such licenses, San Francisco officials performed over 3,500 same-sex marriages. The mayor did not claim that San Francisco had the authority, under California's home rule amendment, to adopt an ordinance setting its own marriage requirements. Rather, the mayor contended that the California marriage law violated state constitutional guarantees of equal protection and due process. San Francisco's action inspired officials in other cities, including San Jose and Santa Cruz in California and in New Paltz, New York, Multnomah and Benton Counties in Oregon, Sandoval County, New Mexico, and Asbury Park, New Jersey, to issue marriage licenses to same-sex couples. *See* Richard C. Schragger, Cities as Constitutional Actors: The Case of Same-Sex Marriage, 21 J. L. & Pol. 147, 148–49 (2005). The California Supreme Court determined that Mayor Newsom exceeded the scope of his authority in issuing marriage licenses to same-sex couples, and held that those marriages were invalid. *See* Lockyer v. City & County of San Francisco, 95 P.3d 459 (Cal. 2004). Four years later, however, the California Supreme Court held that the state's prohibition of same-sex marriage violated the state constitution. *See In re*

Marriage Cases, 183 P.3d 384 (Cal. 2008). Subsequently, the United States Supreme Court came to the same position. Obergefell v. Hodges, 135 S.Ct. 2584 (2015). For an assessment of the role of localities as "agents of constitutional change" with respect to the rights of gays and lesbians, *see* Michèle Finck, The Role of Localism in Constitutional Change: A Case Study, 30 J. L. & Pol. 53 (2014).

NEW MEXICANS FOR FREE ENTERPRISE V. CITY OF SANTA FE

Court of Appeals of New Mexico
126 P.3d 1149 (2005)

FRY, J.

Plaintiffs New Mexicans for Free Enterprise, the Santa Fe Chamber of Commerce, and several local business owners challenge an ordinance enacted by the City of Santa Fe mandating certain city-based businesses to pay a minimum wage higher than the current state and federal minimum hourly wage. Plaintiffs contend that the ordinance is beyond the power of a home rule municipality to enact * * *. We conclude that a home rule municipality may set a minimum wage higher than that required by the state Minimum Wage Act * * *.

In 2002, the City passed the first version of the ordinance setting a minimum wage above that of the federal and state minimum wages for its own workers, contractors doing substantial business with the City, and other businesses directly receiving city benefits. The City also established a Living Wage Roundtable that was directed to "explore and develop" an amendment to the 2002 ordinance that would mandate a living wage for the entire city. The Roundtable reviewed a substantial amount of information regarding local wages, cost of living, the daily challenges faced by both workers and employers in Santa Fe, and the costs and benefits of minimum wage requirements. The Roundtable consisted of nine members representing both labor and business management.

The Roundtable presented majority and minority recommendations to the city council, with management members writing the minority report. The majority recommended, among other things, amending the ordinance to impose minimum wage requirements on all employers citywide, except those with fewer than ten employees. * * * The city council then held public hearings on the amended ordinance proposed by the Roundtable majority, and received input from over 150 speakers on both sides of the issue. * * * On the night that the council was to vote on the amendments to the ordinance, the council expanded the small business exemption by requiring compliance by only those businesses with twenty-five or more workers. The councilor making the proposal noted that expanding the exemption for small businesses would approximately cut in half the number of private businesses impacted while reducing the percentage of Santa Fe low-wage workers benefitting from the higher wage from around 75 percent to around 58 percent. * * * The ordinance as amended requires for-profit businesses or non-profit entities that are registered or licensed in Santa Fe and that employ twenty-five or more workers (either full-time or part-time) to pay a minimum hourly wage of $8.50. *Id.* § 1.5(A)(4), (C). This wage increases to $9.50 in 2006 and to $10.50 in 2008; thereafter, the hourly wage is to be increased in tandem with increases in the Consumer Price Index. *Id.* § 1.5(B). Employers receive an hourly wage credit for employer-provided health care and childcare. *Id.* § 1.5(B). Tips are included in the wage calculation if the employee customarily receives at least $100 per month in tips. *Id.* The ordinance made a violation of its terms a misdemeanor and included provisions for enforcement by the city manager as well as by private, civil actions against an employer.

In passing the amendments to the ordinance, the council issued legislative findings, including a finding that many workers in Santa Fe earn wages insufficient to support themselves and their families and that the community bore the burden when workers could not meet basic needs such as housing, food, shelter, and health care. The council also found that the cost of living in Santa Fe is 18 percent higher than the national average, while average earnings in Santa Fe are 23 percent below the national average. In finding that Santa Fe housing is substantially more expensive than in most of New Mexico and that low-wage workers must spend a disproportionate portion of their income for housing in Santa Fe, the city council concluded:

> A.   The public welfare, health, safety and prosperity of Santa Fe require wages and benefits sufficient to ensure a decent and healthy life for workers and their families.
>
> . . . .
>
> D.   Minimum wage laws promote the general welfare, health, safety and prosperity of Santa Fe by ensuring that workers can better support and care for their families through their own efforts and without financial governmental assistance.
>
> . . . .
>
> I.   It is in the public interest to require certain employers benefiting [sic] from city actions and funding, and from the opportunity to do business in the city, to pay employees a minimum wage, a "living wage[,]" adequate to meet the basic needs of living in Santa Fe. * * *

New Mexico adopted its current version of home rule in 1970 by constitutional amendment. Home rule "was to enable municipalities to conduct their own business and control their own affairs, to the fullest possible extent, in their own way ... upon the principle that the municipality itself knew better what it wanted and needed than did the state at large." "[I]n New Mexico, ... a home rule municipality no longer has to look to the legislature for a grant of power to act, but only looks to legislative enactments to see if any express limitations have been placed on their power to act." The home rule amendment, in pertinent part, states:

> D. A municipality which adopts a charter may exercise all legislative powers and perform all functions not expressly denied by general law or charter. This grant of powers shall not include the power to enact private or civil laws governing civil relationships except as incident to the exercise of an independent municipal power.
>
> E. The purpose of this section is to provide for maximum local self-government. A liberal construction shall be given to the powers of municipalities.

N.M. Const. art. X, § 6(D), (E)

By its phrase "may exercise all legislative powers and perform all functions not expressly denied," the home rule amendment was clearly intended to devolve onto home rule municipalities remarkably broad powers. In addition, the express purpose and liberal construction clauses make clear that the home rule amendment is intended to provide chartered municipalities with the utmost ability to take policymaking initiative. *See Home Rule Manual for N.M. Municipalities,* ch. III, § 17 (noting that New Mexico's home rule provision is "probably among the more liberal in the nation" in terms of granting power to municipalities).

Plaintiffs contend that the ordinance is a private or civil law governing the civil relationship of employer and employee because it "seeks to establish legal duties between private businesses and their private employees, and it establishes a new cause of action against private businesses that do not pay the wage." We agree. While there are no bright-line divisions between public law and private law, Terrance Sandalow, *The Limits of Municipal Power Under Home Rule: A Role for the Courts,* 48 Minn. L.Rev. 643, 674 [hereinafter Sandalow], private law has been defined as consisting "of the substantive law which establishes legal rights and duties between and among private entities, law that takes effect in lawsuits brought by one private entity against another." Gary T. Schwartz, *The Logic of Home Rule and the Private Law Exception,* 20 UCLA L.Rev. 671, 688 [hereinafter Schwartz] (internal footnotes omitted). That definition certainly applies to the ordinance, which sets a mandatory minimum wage term for labor contracts between private parties that the employee may enforce by bringing a civil action against the employer. The fact that the city administrator may punish violation of the ordinance as a misdemeanor does not convert the ordinance into "public law" nor does it alter the basic nature of the ordinance, which is to set and enforce a key contract term between private parties. *See Marshal House, Inc. v. Rent Review & Grievance Bd. of Brookline,* 357 Mass. 709, 260 N.E.2d 200, 206 (1970) (noting that public enforcement is not dispositive of the private law nature of an ordinance). The relationship between private employer and employee has been described as a civil relationship because it is governed by the civil law of contracts. *See New Orleans Campaign for a Living Wage v. City of New Orleans,* 02–0991 at p. 11, 825 So.2d at 1117 (Weimer, J., concurring) (concluding that a private employee-employer relationship is both a private and civil relationship and that a minimum wage ordinance is attempting to regulate that relationship). We conclude that the ordinance is a private or civil law governing civil relationships within the meaning of the home rule amendment.

Although the ordinance is a private law, nonetheless the home rule amendment permits a municipality to enact such a law if it is "incident to the exercise of an independent municipal power." N.M. Const. art. X, § 6(D). Both commentators and courts have noted the ambiguity of this independent power exemption. For example, Professor Schwartz observed that while its "precise legal meaning can be questioned . . . [it] clearly attempts to express the idea that cities have a substantial stake in private law insofar as that law may advance or support the cities' 'independent' (i.e. public law) programs or enactments." Schwartz, *supra,* at 718 (internal footnote omitted).

Also noting the vagueness of the private law exception overall, the Massachusetts Supreme Judicial Court held in *Marshal House, Inc.* that for an ordinance to fall within the independent power exemption, a municipality must point to an "individual component of the municipal police power" that provides it authority to act; otherwise, the private law exception might have "a very narrow range of application." 260 N.E.2d at 206–07. The court held that the municipality failed to do this in connection with a provision establishing a rent-control and review board. The court rejected the municipality's claims that its objective in controlling rents was to provide for the public welfare. *Id.* While the court recognized the link between affordable housing and the public welfare, it stated that "[r]ent control, however, is also an objective in itself designed to keep rents at reasonable levels." *Id.* at 206. The court held that "it would be, in effect, a contradiction (or circuitous) to say that a by-law the *principal objective* . . . of which is *to control rent payments,* is also merely incidental to the exercise of an independent municipal power to control rents." *Id.* at 207 (emphasis added).

Plaintiffs urge us to follow *Marshal House, Inc.* by requiring that the City point to an "individual component" of its police power providing the power to pass the ordinance. We decline to adopt the reasoning in *Marshal House, Inc.* for two reasons. First, the court in that case provided a specious answer to the question "What is the object of the regulation?" by concluding the object was "to control rent payments." There, the stated "principal objective" of the municipality was not to control rent payments as an end itself, but to provide for the general health and welfare of residents by providing sufficient affordable housing. Second, because New Mexico municipalities have been delegated a generic police and general welfare power, we think that forcing a municipality to point to an "individual component" of its police power puts an unduly restrictive gloss on the exemption and reads words into the home rule amendment that are not there.

The exemption refers to an "independent municipal power," which we conclude means any power other than home rule. There is no indication in the phrase "independent municipal power" that such a power must be in some way particularized or tailored; as long as there is a power granted by the legislature that is independent from home rule power, that is enough. We take the view that as long as a municipality can point to a power that the legislature has delegated to it, and the regulation of the civil relationship is reasonably incident to, and clearly authorized by that power, the exemption can apply.

The only additional limitation on a municipality's power, which we have gleaned from the commentators, is the need for uniformity that informs any consideration of the private law exception and independent powers exemption. *See* Howard McBain, *The Law and the Practice of Municipal Home Rule* (1916) 673 (noting that, "[b]y common understanding such general subjects as crime, domestic relations, wills and administration, mortgages, trusts, contracts, real and personal property, insurance, banking, corporations and many others have never been regarded by any one, least of all by the cities themselves, as appropriate subjects of local control"); Schwartz, *supra,* at 720–47 (proposing three underlying rationales for the private law exception, including "the need to retain uniformity in private law"); Sandalow, *supra,* at 678–79 (stating that "chaos would ensue" if all home rule municipalities could "adjust contract, property and the host of other legal relationships between private individuals"). Given this concern for uniformity, we conclude there are two prerequisites to a municipality's regulation of a civil relationship. Where a municipality has been given powers by the legislature to deal with the challenges it faces, those may be sufficiently independent municipal powers to allow regulation of a civil relationship as long as (1) the regulation of the civil relationship is reasonably "incident to" a public purpose that is clearly within the delegated power, and (2) the law in question does not implicate serious concerns about non-uniformity in the law. This rule allows a home rule municipality to regulate a civil relationship as far as necessary within its delegated powers to address local public concerns, while preventing the harm at which the private law exception is primarily aimed. * * * This rule is also sufficiently flexible to allow a fact-intensive evaluation of any given municipal action by balancing the municipality's pursuit of the public interest to address local issues against the need for stability and uniformity in the law across the state. *See* Schwartz, *supra,* at 747 (describing some non-uniformity as "a price we willingly pay in order to achieve the benefits of local democracy"). This rule is consistent with the home rule amendment and Municipal Code, both of which provide for liberal construction in favor of granting power to cities for a "maximum local self-government." N.M. Const. art. X, § 6(E); § 3–15–13(B) (repeating this rule of construction).

In light of this holding, we apply the rule and evaluate (1) whether the ordinance's regulation of the civil relationship is reasonably "incident to" a public purpose that is clearly within the legislature's delegation of specific, independent powers, and (2) whether the ordinance implicates serious concerns about non-uniformity in the law. With respect to public purpose within a municipality's delegated powers, the legislature has given all municipalities the power to provide for the general welfare of their residents by the general welfare clause in Section 3–17–1(B). In addition, the legislature has given all municipalities the police power to "protect generally the property of its municipality and its inhabitants" and to "preserve peace and order within the municipality" by Section 3–18–1(F) and (G). While these are separate powers, they may be treated as one. We consider these powers to be independent municipal powers within the meaning of the home rule amendment because they are powers delegated to municipalities completely independent from the home rule amendment.

The connection between wages and the general welfare of workers is well established in American jurisprudence and is clearly within the police power of a state to regulate. *Rui One Corp. v. City of Berkeley,* 371 F.3d 1137, 1150 (9th Cir.2004) (stating that "[t]he power to regulate wages and employment conditions lies clearly within a state's or a municipality's police power"); *New Orleans Campaign for a Living Wage,* 02–0991, at p. 13, 825 So.2d at 1098 (affirming that the power to set a minimum wage is an exercise of the police power) * * * * [W]e conclude that setting a minimum wage is unquestionably a public purpose and that such legislation is within the police and general welfare power of a New Mexico municipality.

As to whether the City is acting incident to the exercise of an independent municipal power, there is little conclusive authority on the subject. In *Marshal House, Inc.,* the court held that regulating the landlord-tenant relationship by setting the rental price term was a direct, rather than incidental, regulation of the relationship, yet it would have allowed regulation of the relationship for safety or health codes, such as fire prevention or hallway lighting, which it viewed as incidental to the police power.

The rationale of *Marshal House, Inc.,* appears to allow comparatively minor intrusions by an ordinance into a civil relationship, but bars greater intrusions. Yet we fail to see how regulating a private relationship in terms of health and building safety codes is "indirect" while regulating a more central or important aspect, such as the rental term in *Marshal House, Inc.,* is "direct." Such a principle would lead to arcane inquiries into the relative importance of different aspects of an agreement. Is building safety or rent more important to the landlord-tenant relationship? Is worker health and safety less critical than wages or hours? We read "incident to an exercise of an independent municipal power" as simply limiting the circumstances in which a municipality may pass a private or civil law, not as barring certain types of private or civil law or limiting the degree of their intrusion into the relationship. *Id.* We conclude that as long as the intrusion into the private relationship is in pursuit of the public interest and clearly within the independent municipal power, that is sufficient to permit the municipality to pass a private or civil law regulating that relationship as long as the law does not generate non-uniformity issues. We focus on whether there is a public purpose or objective for the exercise of the independent municipal power. Here, there clearly is a public purpose as described by the myriad authorities holding that a minimum wage protects the general welfare of the community.

Amicus Association of Commerce and Industry of New Mexico, echoing the reasoning in *Marshal House, Inc.,* argues that the City's regulation of wages is "both the specific purpose and the direct result" of the power to enact private law. We disagree. The object of this legislation is not to regulate private wages as an end in itself or to set comprehensive "reasonable wages" in the City, but rather to provide for the general welfare of workers and taxpayers in the City. The City has thus pursued a public program to ensure that workers can meet their basic needs and avoid becoming a burden on the community. The City is in no way singling out private employers or burdening them as an end in itself. The ordinance is analogous to many types of other health and safety ordinances that may impact private and civil relationships, but which are aimed at the health, welfare, or safety of renters, workers, or consumers. *See, e.g.,* Santa Fe, N.M., Environmental Regulations: Prohibition of Smoking [in] Places of Employment ch. X, § 6.6 (1999) (mandating that private employers in the city provide a smoke-free workplace); Santa Fe,

N.M., Fair Housing: Discrimination in Sales or Rental of Housing ch. VII, § 14.8 (1999) (prohibiting discrimination in the sale or rental of private housing within the city); Santa Fe, N.M., Environmental Regulations: Premises to be Free from Litter and Refuse ch. X, § 1.14 (requiring private property owners to keep their premises free of litter and refuse).

We now turn to the second prong of the rule permitting regulation of a civil relationship and consider whether the ordinance seriously implicates concerns about non-uniformity. Commentators and courts have expressed concern about home rule municipalities creating a patchwork quilt of law that would hamper business transactions and unfairly upset parties' expectations, and we have concluded that this is the primary evil at which the private law exception is aimed. We view the inquiry, then, as whether the ordinance disrupts or confuses New Mexico law to an unacceptable degree.

The nature of the ordinance is central in determining whether it implicates serious concerns about non-uniformity. For example, substantial disorder and confusion would result if the City rejected the Uniform Commercial Code, adopted a contributory negligence regime, or if it imposed heightened burdens on corporate boards of directors for companies doing business in the City. Leaving aside potential conflicts with state law (which will often bar such local laws), these types of private or civil law changes would frustrate and confuse even the most diligent consumer, businessperson, or lawyer. Those contracting with city parties, corporations doing business there, or those injured by tortfeasors in the City would have little reason to know of these special rules and each would cause notice, compliance, and choice of law issues. Our task is to determine whether such issues are so pervasive that the ordinance disrupts or confuses New Mexico law.

Here, the ordinance does not raise serious concerns about non-uniformity in the way that any of the prior examples would. Any concerns about inefficiency in terms of high notice and compliance costs are allayed by the limited application of the ordinance—it applies only to employers who are registered or licensed in the City. We presume that those entities with more than twenty-five employees seeking city business licenses are doing so purposefully (and with at least some deliberation), and we doubt that they are unaware of such a high-profile ordinance. In addition, the burden on a regional or national business of discovering and applying a higher wage for city workers is modest at most. Presumably, extra-local businesses can identify their own locations and workers licensed in the City and set their hourly wage.

Given modern technology and administration, the cost of discovering and complying with the City's law is minimal. We would be much more concerned if the City were attempting to set a minimum wage term for any contracts for labor "entered into" within the City or for any "labor provided" in the City. Such provisions would raise more serious questions regarding the cost of discovering and complying with the ordinance and the overall disruption of employment contract terms. In light of the ordinance's requirements, we doubt that the ordinance will generate confusion in the law of contracts in New Mexico, produce great inefficiency among the businesses that are required to comply with the ordinance, or cause choice of law problems. Thus, the ordinance does not implicate any serious concerns about generating non-uniformity in New Mexico law.

We emphasize that our conclusion is informed by the circumstances of this case, in which the City has made a showing that it was addressing a serious local problem and where the particular regulation of the employer/employee relationship has long been considered a reasonable exercise of the police power. * * * We disagree with Plaintiffs' contention that allowing a home rule municipality to rely on its police power to enact private or civil law governing civil relationships would render the private law exception in the home rule amendment "meaningless." We conclude that our construction is a straightforward application of the language in the home rule amendment as well as consistent with the model version of the private law exception.

NOTE ON THE "PRIVATE LAW" EXCEPTION

The "private or civil law" exception language of the New Mexico constitution tracks a proviso in the National Municipal League home rule model:

> This grant of home rule powers shall not include the power to enact private or civil law governing civil relationships except as incident to an exercise of an independent county or city power.

The principle that home rule authority does not extend to the enactment of "private or civil law governing civil relationships," however, long predates the NML model. In a frequently quoted dictum, Benjamin Cardozo, then Chief Judge of the New York Court of Appeals, observed:

> There are other affairs exclusively those of the state, such as the law of domestic relations, of wills, of inheritance, of contracts, of crimes not essentially local (for example, larceny or forgery), the organization of courts, the procedure therein. None of these things can be said to touch the affairs that a city is organized to regulate, whether we have reference to history or to tradition or to the existing forms of charters.

Adler v. Deegan, 167 N.E. 705, 713 (N.Y.1929) (Cardozo, C.J., concurring). Relying on Cardozo's statement, Chief Judge Vanderbilt of the New Jersey Supreme Court also observed:

Matters that because of their nature are inherently reserved for the State alone and among which have been the master and servant and landlord and tenant relationships, matters of descent, the administration of estates, creditors' rights, domestic relations, and many other matters of general and statewide significance, are not proper subjects for local treatment under the authority of the general statutes . . . In Paul v. Gloucester County, 50 N.J.L. 585, 601–602, 15 A. 272, 280, 1 L.R.A. 86 (E. & A. 1888), our former Court of Errors and Appeals noted this inherent characteristic of some subjects of governmental concern saying:

"The limitation upon legislative power is in the subject itself, and not in the nature or character of the political subdivision of the state to which the grant is made.

Can the right to declare what the law of attachment shall be, or how the action of ejectment shall be conducted or what the law of descent shall be, be committed to a city any more than to a county?"

Wagner v. Mayor & Municipal Council of City of Newark, 132 A.2d 794, 800–01 (N.J.1957).

Courts have relied on the private law exception to invalidate local ordinances imposing rent control, *see* Wagner v. Newark, *supra*; City of Miami Beach v. Fleetwood Hotel, Inc., 261 So.2d 801 (Fla.1972); Marshal House, Inc. v. Rent Review & Grievance Board, 260 N.E.2d 200 (Mass.1970); regulating landlord-tenant relations, *see* City of Bloomington v. Chuckney, 331 N.E.2d 780 (Ind.App.1975); regulating the conversion of residential rental units to condominiums, *see* Bannerman v. City of Fall River, 461 N.E.2d 793 (Mass.1984); CHR General, Inc. v. City of Newton, 439 N.E.2d 788 (Mass.1982); and prohibiting employment discrimination, *see* McCrory Corp. v. Fowler, 570 A.2d 834 (Md.App.1990).

The private law exception is controversial. Several state courts have denied that it curtails home rule in their states, *see, e.g.*, Sims v. Besaw's Café, 997 P.2d 201 (Ore.App. *en banc* 2000) (upholding local power to create a cause of action for discrimination based on sexual orientation); City of Evanston v. Create, Inc., 405 N.E.2d 1350 (Ill.App.1980), *aff'd,* 421 N.E.2d 196 (Ill.1981) (upholding local landlord-tenant regulation); Birkenfeld v. City of Berkeley, 550 P.2d 1001 (Cal.1976) (upholding local rent control ordinance). Indeed, the leading study of the private law exception found few courts actually upholding or applying the exception, although the author acknowledged that this may be because few localities seek to create private law. *See* Gary T. Schwartz, The Logic of Home Rule and the Private Law Exception, 20 UCLA L.Rev. 671, 702–03 (1973).

The private law exception presents several difficult and intertwined questions: What is "private law"? Why provide a special exception for local ordinances dealing with private law if the matter in question is otherwise a local concern? And, for the states that have adopted the NML language, when is a local private law measure "incident to an exercise of an independent county or city power?" According to Professor Schwartz, private law "consists of the substantive law which establishes legal rights and duties between and among private entities." *See id.* at 687. As the quotes from Chief Judges Cardozo and Vanderbilt suggest, private law has long been equated with the heart of the traditional first-year of law school common law curriculum— contracts, torts, property—along with such upper-year subjects as domestic relations, trusts and estates, and commercial law. As the Maryland court that rejected a county anti-discrimination ordinance determined, such questions as whether contributory negligence is a bar to a negligence action, whether contracts must be supported by consideration, and whether the parol evidence rule applies are all matters of private law that are beyond the scope of local action. *See McCrory Corp., supra.*

Yet, as Professor Schwartz has pointed out, in practice it is often difficult to distinguish between the "private" law of contracts, torts, and property, and "public" health and safety ordinances that indirectly affect tort, contract and property rights. City ordinances "have regularly played a major role in private personal injury litigation," with the defendant's violation of city safety codes frequently treated as establishing negligence. *See* 20 U.C.L.A. L. Rev., *supra*, at 704. So, too, courts have considered whether a landlord's violation of a municipal housing code provides a tenant with a defense against an eviction action, and have looked to local zoning ordinances in the determination of property rights. Many jurisdictions have treated ordinances barring discrimination in employment, housing, and public accommodations as public, police power matters rather than as regulations of contracts or property. In his critique of the private law exception, Professor Diller argues that the public-private distinction is "untenable" and has become more so over time: "[P]ublic regulation of formerly private realms has only increased . . . including significant changes in landlord-tenant and consumer protection law. . . . Further, the protean nature of the private law category invites unrestrained judicial policymaking, as almost any form of government regulation will touch a private law subject in some way." Paul A. Diller, The City and the Private Right of Action, 64 Stan. L. Rev. 1109, 1121 (2012).

Even if a clear and determinate distinction could be drawn between public regulation and private law, why should such a distinction be drawn and used to limit the scope of local home rule power? To be sure, allowing local regulation of such matters can result in multiple, varying local rules. With people and goods regularly crossing local government borders, this can create costs of compliance. But a purpose of home rule is to permit local legal variation in light of different local needs, circumstances, and preferences. Is there reason to believe that local private laws have either greater costs or fewer benefits than local public regulation? As Professor Schwartz notes, in practice, the question of local power to adopt so-called private or civil laws as a matter of home rule initiative is often obviated by the existence of extensive state laws on private law subjects. Thus, in most jurisdictions the local initiative question with respect to private or civil law-making will likely be conflated with the issues of whether the local initiative is in conflict with and preempted by state laws. The issue of local authority, however, may be significant in areas where there are no state statutes and state law consists of judge-made common law rather than state legislation. In a state that has not codified a particular property, tort, or contract rule but, instead, relies on case law, should a home rule locality be able to adopt an ordinance specifying a different rule for real property, accidents, or contracts entered into within the locality—at least until its rule is preempted by a conflicting state statute?

Professor Diller argues that in practice the private law exception operates less to deny local governments authority over certain subjects and more as a rule in some states to limit the ability of localities to authorize private citizens to bring suits to enforce local measures regulating private behavior, such as rent control ordinances, housing codes, and laws against discrimination in housing, employment or public accommodations. *See* Diller, *supra*, 64 Stan. L. Rev. at 1129–34, 1162–67. He is critical of even this more limited use of the private law exception as inconsistent with promoting effective rule compliance and vindicating community norms.

NOTE ON LOCAL LIVING WAGE ORDINANCES

In 1994, following the efforts of "an alliance of churches, labor unions, and low-wage service workers," Baltimore, Maryland adopted an ordinance establishing a "living wage," that is, a minimum wage greater than the federally- or state-determined minimum wage, for the employees of businesses who hold contracts with the city worth more than a threshold amount. "The success of the Baltimore living wage campaign in passing the ordinance touched off a living wage movement that has resulted in the passage of eighty-three living wage ordinances in cities and counties throughout the United States." Rachel Harvey, Labor Law: Challenges to the Living Wage Movement: Obstacles in a Path to Economic Justice, 14 U. Fla. J. L. & Pub. Pol. 229, 229–30 (2003). By 2011, 140 municipalities had adopted local living wage laws. *See* Local Living Wage Laws and Coverage, National Employment Law Project (2011). Many counties have also adopted living wage measures. *See, e.g.,* Daniel Beekman, Washington State's King County Approves Living Wage Legislation, McClatchy News, Oct. 7, 2014. Most living wage ordinances limit their focus to companies that have received some benefit from the locality, such as a government contract above a threshold amount. Some have defined city benefit broadly to include city tax abatements, tax credits, loan forgiveness, bond financing, grants, and other forms of public aid. Other ordinances apply to lessees of city property. *See* William Quigley, Full-Time Workers Should Not Be Poor: The Living Wage Movement, 70 Miss. L.J. 889, 929–930 (2001) (describing living wage ordinances in St. Louis, Oakland, Los Angeles, Houston, and Gary, Indiana). Living wage proponents contend that by raising wages paid by firms that do business with local government or receive local government benefits, the living wage can combat poverty and promote urban economic development. *See* Harvey, *supra*, at 243–50. Critics, by contrast, have contended that by forcing up local labor costs, living wage ordinances can interfere with local economic development, *see, e.g.,* Georgette Poindexter, Economic Development and Community Activism, 32 Urb. Law. 401 (2000) (critiquing San Antonio living wage ordinance), and that it may also increase the costs of municipal contracts to local taxpayers. As noted, living wage ordinances have generally focused on firms that either do business with a local government or receive benefits from local government. This has tended to insulate living wage requirements from legal challenge since the requirements can be seen as voluntarily accepted conditions for doing business with the locality. *See* Harvey, *supra,* at 256–57 (discussing federal courts' rejection of a challenge to Berkeley, California's living wage ordinance). Can localities go further and raise the minimum wage for all firms doing business within the locality? In 2002, New Orleans voters amended the city charter to raise the minimum wage to one dollar above the federal minimum wage. This was immediately challenged as in violation of a state law, adopted in 1997, prohibiting local governments from establishing a minimum wage rate for private employers. The trial court held that the state law was an unconstitutional interference with New Orleans' home rule, but the Louisiana Supreme Court reversed, holding that the state law was a proper exercise of the state's police power, so that the local law was preempted. New Orleans Campaign for a Living Wage v. City of New Orleans, 825 So.2d 1098 (La. 2002).

The decision of the New Mexico appellate court in *New Mexicans for Free Enterprise,* thus, was the first precedent for the authority of a local government to adopt a living wage applicable to private employers. As in the New Orleans litigation, an important issue in the Santa Fe case was preemption. The New Mexico Constitution includes a rule of express preemption—a local ordinance will not be deemed preempted unless a state law "expressly denies" local power to act. The state's minimum wage law did not expressly prohibit local minimum wage ordinances, and the higher local minimum was not inconsistent with the state minimum wage. As we will see in the preemption section of this chapter, *infra,* not all states or state courts are as reluctant to find preemption. A handful of other jurisdictions, including Berkeley and San Francisco, California, Madison, Wisconsin, and Washington, D.C. have living wage ordinances applicable to some significant portion of the private workforce, *see* Darin M. Dalmat, Bringing Economic Justice Closer to Home: The Legal Viability of Local Minimum Wage Laws Under Home Rule, 39 Colum. J.L. & Soc. Probs. 93, 100 (2005). *See also* Rubalcava v. Martinez, 70 Cal.Rptr.3d 225 (Cal. App. 2007) (Los Angeles living wage ordinance). For a thoughtful exploration of the legal and policy issues raised by local living wage ordinances, *see* Clayton P. Gillette, Local Redistribution, Living Wage Ordinances, and Judicial Intervention, 101 Nw. U. L. Rev. 1057 (2007).

Local living wage measures raise several interesting legal questions. Do home rule localities have the power to adopt minimum wage ordinances as a matter of home rule initiative, or are they precluded by the so-called civil law exception? Even if they do, does the state have the authority to bar such local actions, as some states now do? *See* Harvey, *supra*, at 254 (noting Utah law banning local governments from setting minimum wages higher than the state minimum wage; an Oregon law limiting local living wage laws to firms that have a contract with the locality or have received local subsidies or tax abatements; and efforts to adopt similar legislation in other states). *See also* "Voters in Arizona cities may enact 'living wage' laws," http://tucson.com, June 30, 2015 (opinion of state attorney general that state law precluding local living wage laws violates state constitution).

Local governments have also taken a leading role in the movement to require businesses to give their employees paid sick leave, a right not guaranteed by federal law or available in most states. San Francisco, in 2006, was the first government to require paid sick leave, followed by the District of Columbia and Milwaukee in 2008, Seattle in 2011, and Portland, Oregon, New York City, and Jersey City in 2013, and additional cities and counties thereafter. As of July 2015, eighteen cities and counties and the District of Columbia had adopted paid sick leave requirements—which may include leave time to care for ill family members—for at least firms with a threshold number of employees, if not most firms. *See* State and Local Action on Paid Sick Days, Nat'l P'ship for Women & Families (July 2015). Four states—Connecticut, California, Massachusetts, and Oregon—have followed the local lead. *Id.* On the other hand, a number of states have pushed back against their localities on this issue. In 2011, Wisconsin adopted legislation preempting the Milwaukee measure, and as of early 2015, eleven states had passed laws prohibiting local governments from mandating sick leave for employers within their jurisdiction. *See* Claire Zillman, The paid sick leave battle continues, state by state, Fortune, Feb. 11, 2015. For more on local efforts to promote economic equality, *see* Scott L. Cummings & Steven A. Boutcher, Mobilizing Local Government Law for Low-Wage Workers, 2009 U. Chi. Legal Forum 187 (2009).

c.   The Immunity Function (Home Rule as a Shield)

CITY OF LA GRANDE V. PUBLIC EMPLOYEES RETIREMENT BOARD

Oregon Supreme Court
576 P.2d 1204 (1978)

LINDE, JUSTICE.

By a 1971 enactment, the legislative assembly required all police officers and firemen employed by any city, county, or district to be brought within the state's Public Employes Retirement System by July 1, 1973, unless the particular public employer provides them with equal or better retirement benefits. The same statute also required these public employers to pay the premiums on an insurance policy purchased by the state's Department of General Services, providing $10,000 to an officer's or fireman's beneficiaries in case of his or her job-related death, again unless the employer provides equal or better benefits.

The validity of the retirement provisions of the statute was attacked in separate declaratory judgment proceedings brought by the Cities of La Grande and Astoria against various state officials. * * * The cities claim that by requiring them to provide police officers and firemen with retirement and insurance benefits the legislature has invaded a domain reserved to local discretion by the Oregon Constitution.. * * *

I

[The Oregon Constitution provides for home rule in Article XI, Section 2:]

The Legislative Assembly shall not enact, amend or repeal any charter or act of incorporation for any municipality, city or town. The legal voters of every city and town are hereby granted power to enact and amend their municipal charter, subject to the Constitution and criminal laws of the State of Oregon. * * *

The relationship between the authority of the legislature and that of local governments under these provisions during the past 70 years has occupied this court in more than 75 cases. * * * In any given case, it is necessary to distinguish whether it involves (1) the validity of a local act in the absence of a contrary state law; (2) the validity of a state law in the absence of a contrary local act; (3) the validity of a local act said to conflict with a state law; or (4) the validity of a state law said to conflict with a local act. To reduce the effect of the amendments on local authority and their effect on the state's authority to a single formula would only obscure the fact that these are two different questions.

It is useful to recall the role of [home rule] in the state's constitutional arrangements. [Its] central object is to allow the people of the locality to decide upon the organization of their government and the scope of its powers under its charter without having to obtain statutory authorization from the legislature, as was the case before the amendments. Thus the validity of local action depends, first, on whether it is authorized by the local charter or by a statute; . . . second, on whether it contravenes state or federal law. With respect to a state law, or action taken under it, on the other hand, it is elementary that the legislature has plenary authority except for such limits as may be found in the constitution or in federal law. Thus the validity of a state law vis-a-vis local entities does not depend upon a source of authority for the law, nor on whether a locality may have authority to act on the same subject; it depends on the limitations imposed by article XI, section 2, supra.

* * * [B]oth municipalities and the state legislature in many cases have enacted laws in pursuit of substantive objectives, each well within

its respective authority, that were arguably inconsistent with one another. In such cases, the first inquiry must be whether the local rule in truth is incompatible with the legislative policy, either because both cannot operate concurrently or because the legislature meant its law to be exclusive. It is reasonable to interpret local enactments, if possible, to be intended to function consistently with state laws, and equally reasonable to assume that the legislature does not mean to displace local civil or administrative regulation of local conditions by a statewide law unless that intention is apparent. * * * However, when a local enactment is found incompatible with a state law in an area of substantive policy, the state law will displace the local rule. * * *

It is therefore pertinent to the prohibition expressed in article XI, section 2, to determine whether the challenged law is addressed primarily to a concern of the state with the modes of local government or to substantive social, economic, or other regulatory objectives.

II

* * * The provisions of ORS chapters 237 and 243 requiring retirement and insurance benefits for police officers and firemen do not fail the test stated above. The statutes plainly embody a legislative concern with securing the postemployment living standards of persons in these occupations and their families, not with the cities' governmental organization. It is not essential to the legitimacy of this goal whether the legislature singled out police officers and firemen because it deemed these occupations particularly hazardous or the desired benefits difficult and costly to obtain piecemeal, nor whether its assumptions were well founded. In any event, the statutes are addressed to a statewide substantive, social objective rather than any asserted concern with the modes of local government.

* * * [T]he present statutes do not create any agencies of local government, nor do they direct local communities to do so. They oblige local governments to bring their police officers and firemen under the benefits provided respectively by the state's retirement system and a statewide insurance policy, but even that obligation is made contingent upon an option to provide equal or better benefits by other means of the local government's choice. The administrative machinery of these statutes is state administration, not compelled local administration.

III

Though the legislature in these laws has not mandated city administration in the manner that proved fatal in [earlier cases], its pursuit of its statewide social objective undeniably displaces the arrangements (or absence of arrangements) preferred by the local government. This is not uncommon, as many of our cited decisions show. Nor is it generally useful to define a "subject" of legislation and assign it to one or the other level of government. * * * A search for a predominant state or local interest in the "subject matter" of legislation can only substitute for the political process to which we have referred the court's own political judgment whether the state or the local policy should prevail. Moreover, as the foregoing examples show, it misconceives the nature of a "state interest" to focus narrowly on the functions performed by particular groups of employees to the exclusion of a concern with the employees as citizens. The "state" as such has no interest apart from that of its inhabitants, present and future; and the legislature may, if it so chooses, consider the interests of those who perform the job as well as the interests of those dependent on that performance.

The geographic boundaries of local entities are not much more determinative in excluding state concerns. * * * [C]ity police officers and firemen are sometimes assigned duties beyond their cities, but this is hardly needed to demonstrate a state concern. Large complexes of state buildings and state personnel such as college campuses, and indeed the state Capitol, executive offices, and this court, depend on the quality of police and fire protection within city limits, and thousands of persons who frequent city streets and business districts every day are not city residents. The state relies on local governments for many functions deemed important to the state within local boundaries, most recently land use controls. * * *

Finally, as individuals we may differ with legislative policies that mandate substantive standards for programs and activities for which local taxpayers and local officials rather than state legislators will bear the fiscal responsibility. But if there are other constitutional limitations than the "home rule" amendments that preclude the particular financial effect of the statutes involved in these cases, the parties have not brought them to the court's attention. The simple provisions of article XI, section 2, that "(t)he Legislative Assembly shall not enact, amend or repeal any charter or act of incorporation for any municipality, city or town" does not purport to sweep that broadly.

Thus neither the form in which the local policy is cast, nor the "subject" of the state law, nor the existence of local boundaries can by itself determine the validity of a statewide law. Instead, we conclude that the following principles for resolving a conflict between such a law and an inconsistent local provision for the conduct of city government are consistent with our past interpretations of the "home rule" amendments:

When a statute is addressed to a concern of the state with the structure and procedures of local agencies, the statute impinges on the powers reserved by the amendments to the citizens of local communities. Such a state concern must be justified by a need to safeguard the interests of persons or entities affected by the procedures of local government.

Conversely, a general law addressed primarily to substantive social, economic, or other regulatory objectives of the state prevails over contrary policies preferred by some local governments if it is clearly intended to do so, unless the law is shown to be irreconcilable with the local community's freedom to choose its own political form. In that case, such a state law must yield in those particulars necessary to preserve that freedom of local organization.

As we have said, the statutes challenged by the cities in these cases are of the second, substantive kind. The provisions for financial security for police officers and firemen and their dependents in the event of retirement, disability, or death address a social concern with the living standards of these classes of workers, not with local governments as such. Various categories of employees are not placed beyond the reach of the state's social legislation merely because their occupational functions— here police and fire protection, elsewhere perhaps municipal transit or utility or library services—happen to be found in the public sector of local government. While the statewide retirement and insurance plans do displace other plans that local agencies have made, or might make, for these objectives, they are not irreconcilable with the freedom to charter their own governmental structures that are reserved to the citizens of Astoria and La Grande by article XI, section 2. Accordingly, the statutes are constitutional.

FRATERNAL ORDER OF POLICE, COLORADO LODGE #27 V. CITY AND COUNTY OF DENVER

Supreme Court of Colorado
926 P.2d 582 (1996)

JUSTICE SCOTT delivered the Opinion of the Court.

Today, we must decide whether a statutory enactment mandating statewide training and certification of peace officers can impose its requirements upon deputy sheriffs employed by the City and County of Denver, a home rule city, when, under our constitution, Denver is granted the authority to control the qualifications, powers, and duties of its deputy sheriffs. Because we conclude (1) that the Colorado Constitution grants Denver, as a home rule city, authority over the qualifications of its deputy sheriffs and (2) that the state's interest in public safety does not, in light of the limited duties and responsibilities of Denver deputy sheriffs, outweigh the exercise of Denver's authority created by our constitution, we hold that the legislative enactment cannot impose its requirements upon Denver's deputy sheriffs. * * *

I.

In 1992, the Colorado General Assembly enacted the Peace Officers Standards and Training Act (POST Act) to provide uniform training and certification for peace officers entrusted with protecting the safety of the citizens of this state. * * * The POST Act also created the Peace Officers Standards and Training Board (POST Board) to establish certification standards and to certify qualified peace officers. * * *

At all times relevant here, the POST Act required certification for peace officers throughout the state. * * * Under the POST Act, a "peace officer" includes any "deputy sheriff other than one appointed with authority only to receive and serve summons and civil process . . . [who] is employed by the state or a city, city and county, town, judicial district, or county within this state." * * * Despite these statutory provisions, Respondent, the City and County of Denver (Denver), did not require POST certification for its deputy sheriffs.

* * * [T]he petitioners, Fraternal Order of Police of Colorado Lodge #27, Fraternal Order of Police of Colorado State Lodge, and Larry Nead (collectively F.O.P.), filed this civil action seeking a declaratory judgment that, under the 1992 version of the POST Act, Denver deputy sheriffs are entitled to the minimum training prescribed by the POST Board and must receive state certification in accordance with POST Board standards. * * *

II.

A.

Denver is a home rule city existing pursuant to Article XX of the Colorado Constitution. Article XX, Section 6, adopted by the voters in 1912, granted "home rule" powers to municipalities choosing to operate under its provisions and, in doing so, altered the basic relationship of such municipalities to the state. That provision provides in pertinent part:

> Home rule for cities and towns. The people of each city or town of this state . . . are hereby vested with, and they shall always have, power to make, amend, add to or replace the charter of said city or town, which shall be its organic law and extend to all its local and municipal matters.

> Such charter and the ordinances made pursuant thereto in such matters shall supersede within the territorial limits and other jurisdiction of said city or town any law of the state in conflict therewith.

> . . . [S]uch city or town, and the citizens thereof, shall have the powers set out in sections 1, 4 and 5 of this article, and all other powers necessary, requisite or proper for the government and

administration of its local and municipal matters, including power to legislate upon, provide, regulate, conduct and control:

a.   The creation and terms of municipal officers, agencies and employments; *the definition, regulation and alteration of the powers, duties, qualifications and terms or tenure of all municipal officers, agents and employees.*

seem to define same local matters

Colo. Const. art. XX, § 6 (emphasis added).

* * * Although the legislature continues to exercise authority over matters of statewide concern, a home rule city pursuant to Article XX is not necessarily inferior to the General Assembly with respect to local and municipal matters. *Board of County Comm'rs v. City of Thornton*, 629 P.2d 605, 609 (Colo.1981).

B.

Under this constitutional transfer of authority, circumstances may arise, as here, where a home rule provision of the constitution conflicts with a statutory enactment of the General Assembly, and the respective authorities of the state legislature and the home rule municipality must therefore be reconciled. In determining which provision should prevail, we have previously recognized three broad categories of regulatory matters: (1) matters of local concern; (2) matters of statewide concern; and (3) matters of mixed state and local concern. * * * Thus, the determination that a matter is of local concern, statewide concern, or of mixed state and local concern controls the ultimate resolution of such a conflict.

However, we have recognized that no specific legal standard or litmus test exists which can resolve in every case the issue of whether a particular matter is of local, state, or mixed concern. Instead, the determination must be made on an ad hoc basis, taking into consideration the facts of each case. A critical factor in that consideration is the interest of the state in regulating the matter. * * *

III.

* * * [T]here are several general factors to consider in determining whether the state's interest in the matter at hand is sufficient to justify preemption of the inconsistent home rule provisions. These factors include: (1) the need for statewide uniformity of regulation; (2) the extraterritorial impact—i.e., the impact of the municipal regulation or home rule provision on persons living outside the municipal limits; (3) any other state interests; and (4) the asserted local interests in the municipal regulation contemplated by the home rule provision—e.g., does the Colorado Constitution specifically commit a particular matter to state or local regulation.

A.   UNIFORMITY

* * * Here, F.O.P. has failed to demonstrate any pervading state interest, based on the principles of uniformity, for POST Act training and certification of Denver deputy sheriffs. Although statewide uniformity of training for police officers is a legitimate state interest, that interest becomes substantial due to (1) the responsibilities and duties of such officers, which require continuous interaction with citizens on public and private property in the normal course of their daily activities, and (2) the impact of such pervasive encounters upon public safety. Generally, police officers exercise arrest authority and deal with the general public in all matters related to law enforcement. To the contrary, it is undisputed that Denver deputy sheriffs do not have the authority to effect warrantless arrests or to engage in the general patrol and investigative law enforcement duties which are delegated by city charter to the Denver Police Department. Instead, their responsibilities are limited to court related activities, i.e., service of process and duty as bailiffs, or activities related to the Denver detention facilities. In fact, Denver deputy sheriffs do not have the same statewide responsibilities or duties and, hence, impact upon public safety as do police officers. *See Local No. 127*, 185 Colo. at 54, 521 P.2d at 918 (Denver deputy sheriffs not given general police power).

The general duties and responsibilities of Denver deputy sheriffs * * * do not establish any different or additional responsibilities that are intended to or would create a significant impact beyond Denver's boundaries. Thus, we do not perceive a need for statewide uniformity of training that would include Denver deputy sheriffs.

B.   EXTRATERRITORIAL IMPACT

Extraterritorial considerations have been defined as those involving the expectations of state as opposed to local residents. F.O.P. asserts that safety concerns regarding the transportation and incarceration of persons in Denver's detention facilities have an impact beyond Denver's borders so as to create a pervading state interest. We disagree.

* * * Denver's deputy sheriffs are not authorized to make warrantless arrests under the Denver charter, and any contact they have with people outside of the City and County of Denver in the performance of their duties is not pursuant to any prescribed power under the charter and therefore is merely incidental. Thus, we conclude that the extraterritorial impact of Denver deputy sheriffs is, at best, de minimus.

C.   OTHER STATE INTERESTS

F.O.P. asserts that the state has a substantial interest in protecting the public from inadequately trained peace officers, i.e., an interest in "the general public's safety." However, contrary to the conclusion of

F.O.P. and the trial court, the limited authority of Denver deputy sheriffs does not place them on "the front line of law enforcement" either within the City and County of Denver or elsewhere in this state. We have previously determined that, unlike police officers who exercise far greater and more pervasive authority, Denver deputy sheriffs are not engaged in the exercise of general police power and, therefore, do not have any significant impact on the general public.

It is undisputed that the duties of these deputy sheriffs are governed by the Denver charter, that under that charter they do not have the power to make arrests (other than by warrant), and their primary duties involve service within the various Denver courts, as process servers and bailiffs, and as security personnel within Denver's two detention centers. Also, although not determinative under the standard we apply here, Denver has implemented a 10–16 week training program, which includes training in the use of firearms.

In sum, because Denver deputy sheriffs do not have the authority to impact significantly any circumstances outside of the Denver courts or jails, and, as a consequence, will not substantially impact public safety beyond the boundaries of Denver, and because Denver's deputy sheriffs receive extensive training prior to their assignments, we conclude that the state does not have a sufficient interest in their qualifications.

D.   LOCAL INTERESTS

In contrast, Denver's interest in the training and certification of its deputy sheriffs is substantial and has direct textual support in the Colorado Constitution and in case law precedent. First, Article XX, Section 6, gives home rule cities and towns, generally, the power to "legislate upon, provide, regulate, conduct and control . . . the definition, regulation and alteration of the powers, duties, qualifications and terms or tenure of all municipal officers, agents and employees." More specifically as to the City and County of Denver, Article XX, Section 2, provides in pertinent part:

> The officers of the city and county of Denver shall be such as by appointment or election may be provided for by the charter; and the jurisdiction, term of office, duties and *qualifications* of all such officers shall be such as in the charter may be provided; but the charter shall designate the officers who shall, respectively, perform the acts and duties required of county officers to be done by the constitution or by the general law, as far as applicable.

Colo. Const. art. XX, § 2. (emphasis added).

Additionally, we rely upon our own precedent to indicate what constitutes a local concern, as opposed to a statewide concern. In this context, we have previously determined that the duties and responsibilities of Denver deputy sheriffs are limited in scope and that these deputies do not have general police power. We have also stated that the office of sheriff is a county office and not a state office. Thus, Article XX, Sections 2 and 6, along with our case law precedent, provides evidence in text and by context that the qualification and certification of Denver deputy sheriffs is a local concern. Furthermore, Denver has a substantial interest in the qualifications of its own public officers and the recognition of that interest generally in home rule municipalities was affirmed by the voters of the state of Colorado. * * *

V.

We hold that * * * the state of Colorado's interest in the training and certification of Denver deputy sheriffs under the POST Act is insufficient to supersede the authority given to Denver to determine the qualifications of persons serving as its deputy sheriffs in accordance with Article XX, Sections 2 and 6. * * *

JUSTICE LOHR concurring in part and dissenting in part: * * *

The State has a significant interest in setting minimum training and qualification standards applicable to peace officers who serve as Denver deputy sheriffs. Denver's work description for its deputy sheriffs clarifies that Denver deputy sheriffs are in constant contact with prisoners held pursuant to state criminal charges. The deputy sheriffs are responsible for preventing escapes, apprehending escaped prisoners, and other pressing matters of public safety, and the deputy sheriffs act as guardians of the general public in the course of transporting criminal defendants to and from court. In order to perform their other duties, deputy sheriffs must qualify in the use of weapons. * * *

According to Denver's own work description for deputy sheriffs, Denver deputy sheriffs maintain security in Denver detention facilities, and inspect, supervise, observe, instruct, search, and control prisoners in such facilities. The deputy sheriffs "physically subdue[ ] violent prisoners," "chase[ ] inmates on foot to apprehend them," "control or apprehend violent or fleeing prisoners," lift "injured or ill prisoners," execute warrants, serve process, and take individuals into custody. Denver deputy sheriffs testify in court, advise prisoners of court proceedings, and prepare legal documents. Furthermore, Denver deputy sheriffs are responsible for members of the general public during visits to detention facilities and may have to transport prisoners to public medical facilities or protect members of the general public who serve as jurors. Denver even specifically requires Denver deputy sheriffs to transport prisoners to and from "other jurisdictions" if need be. * * * In short, Denver deputy sheriffs are intimately associated with "public safety" and have substantial "extraterritorial impact" in performing their duties as peace officers in Denver, the State capital and center of commerce. * * *

Although Denver deputy sheriffs are not police officers and therefore do not perform the same law enforcement duties as police officers, it does not follow that there is no need for statewide uniformity relating to minimum training and qualification standards for both police officers and Denver deputy sheriffs. * * * Denver requires its deputy sheriffs to act as agents of County or District Courts in executing arrest warrants, and the responsibilities of Denver deputy sheriffs necessarily require the deputy sheriffs to interact with the general public.

* * * Denver detention facilities are not limited to residents of Denver, and any supervising law enforcement officers in the detention facilities have daily interactions with individuals who are not residents of Denver but who have become subject to jurisdiction of the criminal courts in Denver. Furthermore, * * * Denver deputy sheriffs are authorized to execute arrest warrants, a function that can bring them in contact with persons who are not Denver residents.

* * * Denver deputy sheriffs must qualify in the use of weapons, and their prescribed duties involve interaction with both the general public and criminal defendants who face state charges. Additionally, the state has a substantial interest in the welfare and safety of all of its citizens, including residents of Denver.

* * * I conclude that the State has a sufficient interest in outlining minimum training and qualification requirements for Denver deputy sheriffs to support the legislature's imposition of a uniform POST Act certification requirement applicable to Denver deputy sheriffs. * * *

TOWN OF TELLURIDE V. SAN MIGUEL VALLEY CORPORATION

Supreme Court of Colorado
185 P.3d 161 (2008)

JUSTICE RICE delivered the Opinion of the Court.

The Town of Telluride filed an eminent domain action in March 2004 in San Miguel County District Court against San Miguel Valley Corporation * * * to acquire 572 acres of real property located adjacent to Telluride. Telluride sought to condemn this property, commonly known as the Valley Floor, for open space, parks, and recreation. The eminent domain proceeding was set in motion by the citizens of Telluride, who for years have allocated twenty percent of the town's annual revenue to fund the acquisition of the Valley Floor, and who initiated and passed Ordinance 1174 to condemn the land. * * *

While the eminent domain action was pending, the Corporation lobbied the state legislature, which was at the time considering a bill that would limit the ability of municipalities to condemn property and transfer it into private ownership, to attach an amendment that would block Telluride's ability to condemn the Valley Floor. The Corporation's proposed amendment, eventually signed into law as subsection 4b of section 38–1–101, prohibits home rule municipalities such as Telluride from condemning property outside municipal boundaries for parks, recreation, open space, or other similar purposes. After the bill's passage, the Corporation filed a motion to dismiss Telluride's eminent domain action, asserting that pursuant to subsection 4b Telluride had no authority to proceed. * * *

II. Analysis

The threshold question in this appeal is whether the condemnation of property for open space and park purposes falls within the scope of the eminent domain power granted to home rule municipalities in article XX of the Colorado Constitution. Telluride claims that, pursuant to article XX and its home rule charter, it is empowered to condemn the property in the Valley Floor for open space and park purposes. Telluride argues that because subsection 4b prohibits extraterritorial condemnations for open space or similar purposes, the statute represents an unconstitutional abrogation of home rule municipalities' eminent domain power. The Corporation counters that the constitution does not provide home rule municipalities with the authority to condemn extraterritorially for open space and park purposes, and that subsection 4b is carefully tailored not to interfere with powers granted by article XX. As both parties recognize, the General Assembly has no power to enact a law that denies a right specifically granted by the constitution. * * *

Eminent domain is a sovereign power granted to home rule municipalities by article XX of the Colorado Constitution. Section 1 of article XX provides that a home rule municipality:

> shall have the power, within or without its territorial limits, to construct, condemn and purchase, purchase, acquire, lease, add to, maintain, conduct and operate water works, light plants, power plants, transportation systems, heating plants, and any other public utilities or works or ways local in use and extent, in whole or in part, and everything required therefore . . . and . . . the same or any part thereof may be purchased by said city and county which may enforce such purchase by proceedings at law as in taking land for public use by right of eminent domain.

Section 6 of article XX gives each home rule municipality all powers "necessary, requisite or proper for the government and administration of its local and municipal matters." These article XX powers are vested in municipalities through their home rule charters. Telluride's charter gives it the "full right of self-government on local and municipal matters," and further provides that the town has "the right of eminent domain to acquire property both within and without the boundaries of the Town for any purpose deemed by the Town council to be in the Town's best interest." Telluride, Colo., Home Rule Charter, §§ 14.1–14.2 (1997).

The Corporation first argues that the constitution does not provide Telluride authority to condemn extraterritorially for open space and parks because these are not purposes enumerated in article XX, section 1. The Corporation asserts that home rule municipalities can only condemn for purposes that either appear in section 1 or are correlative to the purposes listed in section 1. We disagree.

This court has held on multiple occasions that the purposes specified in section 1 are merely examples of a broader grant of power, namely the power to condemn property for any lawful, public, local, and municipal purpose. For example, in *Fishel v. City & County of Denver,* Denver sought to condemn land outside city limits to be donated to the United States for an air corps technical school and bombing range. We rejected the argument that the condemnation power is limited to the purposes enumerated in section 1, stating:

> In view of the wide scope of such enumerated cases in which the power might be exercised—probably then considered as being all-inclusive—and the circumstance as we have so many times held, that this amendment was designed to give as large a measure of home rule in local municipal affairs as could be granted under a Republican form of government, we have no doubt that the people of Colorado intended to, and, in effect, did thereby delegate to Denver full power to exercise the right of eminent domain in the effectuation of any lawful, public, local, and municipal purpose.

* * * Furthermore, a plain language reading of article XX, taken as a whole, confirms that the purposes enumerated in section 1 do not define the full scope of the eminent domain power. Section 1, which originally applied only to Denver, is made applicable to all home rule municipalities by article XX, section 6. Section 6 grants each home rule city and town "the powers set out in section 1, 4 and 5" of article XX, as well as "all other powers necessary, requisite or proper for the government and administration of its local and municipal matters. . . ." * * *

The Corporation next argues that the condemnation power under article XX is more limited in the context of an extraterritorial condemnation. The Corporation relies on language in section 6 which states that a home rule municipality's charter or local ordinance shall supersede state law within the territorial limits of the municipality. Because this language identifies a distinction between a home rule municipality's powers inside and outside of its jurisdiction, the Corporation asserts that a municipality's eminent domain powers should be construed narrowly when exercised extraterritorially and thus should be restricted to the list of purposes specified in section 1. We have not recognized a distinction between the scope of the extraterritorial and territorial eminent domain powers conferred in article XX, and we do not agree that the language in section 6 regarding supersession supports such a distinction.

* * * We have affirmed extraterritorial condemnations in a number of cases and have not assigned an inferior status to the extraterritorial exercise of the condemnation power. *See, e.g., City of Thornton,* 194 Colo. at 535, 575 P.2d at 389 (holding that Thornton was authorized to condemn extraterritorially for water rights); *Toll,* 139 Colo. at 468, 340 P.2d at 865 (affirming extraterritorial condemnation for flowage easements and channel improvements); *City & County of Denver v. Bd. of Comm'rs,* 113 Colo. 150, 156, 156 P.2d 101, 103 (1945) (holding that Denver could condemn property for construction of airport more than five miles outside of city, despite five-mile limit in conflicting state statute); *Fishel,* 106 Colo. at 584, 108 P.2d at 241 (affirming extraterritorial condemnation for air corps school and bombing range).

* * * [W]e place reliance on the time-honored premise that article XX vests in home rule municipalities every power which the legislature "could have conferred." * * * Applying the same inquiry, we find that the General Assembly has on multiple occasions conferred authority to statutory towns and cities to condemn land for parks, recreation, or open space. *See, e.g.,* § 29–7–104, –107, C.R.S. (2007) (granting municipal corporations the authority to condemn property for "park or recreational purposes or for the preservation or conservation of sites, scenes, open space and vistas"); § 32–1–1005(1)(c), C.R.S. (2007) (granting parks and recreational districts the power to condemn for access to "park and recreational facilities."). Two statutes specify that a condemnation for open space or parks can be extraterritorial. Section 31–25–201(1), C.R.S. (2007), grants cities the authority to condemn extraterritorially "as in the judgment of the governing body of such city may be necessary" for "park or recreational purposes," "parkways," and "open space" within five miles of a city's boundaries. Section 38–6–110, C.R.S. (2007), grants cities the authority to condemn for "park purposes" outside city boundaries, subject to section 31–25–201(1). In sum, the General Assembly's ability to confer upon municipalities the power to condemn for parks and open space is evidenced by the numerous statutes which in fact confer that power, thus confirming that parks and open space are lawful, public, local, and municipal purposes within the scope of article XX.

Second, we recognize that land use policy traditionally has been a local government function in the state, * * * and that Colorado municipalities are active in incorporating open space, parks, and recreation into their land planning. In addition to the statutory towns and cities that have acted to preserve open space pursuant to the statutes described above, many Colorado home rule municipalities of all sizes and geographies manage extensive open space programs. More pertinent to the case at hand, a number of these home rule municipalities have seen fit to acquire open space outside their municipal boundaries. Local planning for open space and park land acquisition and development is a particularly important tool in the state's mountain resort communities, where unprecedented growth places pressure on the environmental qualities and recreational assets upon which these communities depend. We conclude that municipalities, neighboring counties, and the state have traditionally acted on the presumption that land planning for open space and parks is a local government function.

* * * [T]he Corporation argues that, even if article XX grants home rule municipalities extraterritorial authority to condemn property for parks and open space, we must weigh competing state and local concerns implicated by the exercise of this authority to determine whether the authority can be preempted by the legislature. We disagree.

* * * Although we recognize that the analysis of competing state and local concerns is appropriate in evaluating the preemptive effect of a statute on a municipal act, we dispute its relevance in the case at hand, which turns on the conflict between a statute and the state constitution. Our case law dictates that state statutes may preempt home rule municipalities' actions on matters of statewide or mixed state and local concern. In *Town of Telluride,* we held that if a home rule city enacts an ordinance concerning a matter of local concern and that ordinance conflicts with a state statute, the home rule ordinance takes precedence over the state statute. If the matter is one of statewide or mixed state and local concern, we held that the state statute takes precedence over the conflicting home rule ordinance unless the ordinance is authorized by statute or by the constitution. The Corporation urges us to utilize this framework in evaluating the validity of subsection 4b. However, no analysis of competing state and local interests is necessary where a statute purports to take away home rule powers granted by the constitution.

* * * [W]e decline here to evaluate the statewide interests implicated by the extraterritorial condemnation of property by home rule municipalities for open space and parks. The legislature cannot prohibit the exercise of constitutional home rule powers, regardless of the state interests which may be implicated by the exercise of those powers.[8]

---

[8]   Our past cases indicate that, although the legislature may not prohibit the exercise of article XX powers, it may regulate the exercise of those powers in areas of statewide or mixed state and local concern. Therefore, the analysis of competing state and local interests would be appropriate in a case involving a statute which merely regulates home rule municipalities' exercise of their constitutional powers. For example, in City of Commerce City v. State, we held that the General Assembly could impose statewide procedures for the use of photo radar technology in traffic enforcement where there was a significant statewide interest in the uniform

The Corporation next argues that the General Assembly may abrogate home rule powers that are merely implied in the constitution. The Corporation maintains that, although the legislature cannot abrogate or override express provisions of article XX, there is no "express" authority in article XX for extraterritorial condemnation for open space and park purposes. * * * We reject the notion that there are two separate echelons of condemnation powers under article XX—those express and those implied. The Corporation asks us to afford constitutional status only to those condemnation purposes enumerated in section 1 of article XX. However, as stated above, the purposes specified in section 1 are merely examples of a broader grant of power. Article XX grants home rule municipalities the power to condemn property, intra- or extraterritorially, for any lawful, public, local, and municipal purpose. * * * We repeat our holding in *Town of Telluride,* where we stated, "If the matter is one of statewide or mixed state and local concern . . . the state statute takes precedence over the conflicting local action *unless the action is authorized by statute or by the constitution.*" (emphasis added).

Subsection 4b prohibits home rule municipalities from condemning property for parks and open space, thus denying their constitutional power to condemn for any lawful, public, local, and municipal purpose. Subsection 4b provides in part:

> No home rule or statutory municipality shall . . . acquire by condemnation property located outside of its territorial boundaries for the purpose of parks, recreation, open space, conservation, preservation of views or scenic vistas, or for similar purposes . . . except where the municipality has obtained the consent of both the owner of the property to be acquired by condemnation and the governing body of the local government in which territorial boundaries the property is located.

Subsection 4b also provides that the only allowable extraterritorial condemnations are those for "water works, light plants, power plants, transportation systems, heating plants, any other public utilities or public works, or for any purposes necessary for such uses."

Hence, subsection 4b curtails the condemnation power in article XX by limiting it to the enumerated purposes in section 1, and also by removing certain enumerated purposes from the list—namely condemnation for the purpose of "works or ways local in use and extent . . . and everything required therefore." Accordingly, we conclude that

---

regulation of this technology. 40 P.3d 1273, 1284 (Colo.2002). Similarly, in City & County of Denver v. Board of County Commissioners, this court affirmed county regulation of Denver water projects where the development of major new domestic water systems was held to be a matter of statewide concern. 782 P.2d 753, 762 (Colo.1989). However, this line of cases does not compel us to analyze competing state and local concerns in the case at hand, where the legislature purports to abrogate, not regulate, home rule powers granted by the constitution.

subsection 4b is an unconstitutional abrogation of the powers granted to home rule municipalities under article XX. The General Assembly has no power to enact a law that denies a right specifically granted by the constitution. The power of home rule municipalities to condemn for any lawful, public, local, and municipal purpose can only be taken away by constitutional amendment. * * *

JUSTICE COATS, specially concurring.

* * * I agree with the majority that long-standing precedents in this jurisdiction support its conclusion that the creation of open space is a lawful, public, local, and municipal purpose for which Telluride's right to condemn property, even outside its territorial boundaries, is constitutionally guaranteed. None of the parties has asked us to overturn any of those precedents.

I write separately merely to emphasize what I consider to be the import of footnote 8 of the court's opinion. As the court notes, our holding that the legislature cannot *prohibit* the exercise of constitutional home rule powers, regardless of shared state interests, does not suggest that the legislature cannot *regulate* the exercise of those powers. I understand the court's decision today to turn on the fact that section 38–1–101(4)(b), C.R.S. (2007), prohibits home rule cities from condemning property outside their territorial boundaries for open space, without the consent of the property owner. Rather than mere regulation, rationally related to shared state interests, this amounts to a complete abrogation of the right to condemn, the very essence of which is the right to take property without an owner's consent.

Article XX's grant of this power to home rule cities, however, does not purport to designate the exercise of the power to condemn *exclusively* a matter of local interest. As we have noted with regard to the power to legislate generally, certain matters that are of local concern, permitting a municipality to legislate, may also involve legitimate statewide concerns, permitting the state to legislate as well. While we have held it to be within the state's power to preempt a municipality's power to legislate in areas of mixed state and local concern, we have also made clear that the state cannot completely abrogate a municipal power that exists through direct constitutional grant, rather than only indirectly, through the municipality's power to legislate.

The distinction between regulating and actually prohibiting, although difficult to define with precision, is widely accepted. Although the power to regulate invariably entails a certain degree of prohibition, as long as legislative or administrative limitations are reasonably tailored to advance the public welfare and do not absolutely abrogate competing rights, some prohibitory effect is tolerated as both necessary and acceptable, in a host of contexts. * * * I believe the regulation/prohibition dichotomy provides the appropriate basis for challenges to the state's authority to infringe on powers directly granted to home rule cities by the state constitution.

It seems clear to me that the state has a cognizable interest in regulating the acquisition of property, beyond their own boundaries, by so many home rule cities. That interest, however, cannot permit the state legislature to absolutely prohibit the exercise of a constitutionally granted power. Because I believe section 38–1–101(4)(b) does precisely that, I concur in the majority's assessment that it cannot stand.

JUSTICE EID, dissenting.

* * * Because I believe our constitution does not convey to home rule municipalities such exclusive extraterritorial condemnation authority, I would uphold section 38–1–101(4)(b), C.R.S. (2007), against Telluride's constitutional challenge.

* * * Historically * * * we have been quite cautious with regard to condemnations that are extraterritorial in nature. Indeed, the extraterritorial uses we have found to be "local and municipal" in character have hewn closely to the purposes initially enumerated in article XX section 1. *See, e.g., City of Thornton v. Farmers Reservoir & Irrigation Co.,* 194 Colo. 526, 575 P.2d 382 (1978) (water rights for water project); *Toll v. City & County of Denver,* 139 Colo. 462, 340 P.2d 862 (1959) (flowage easements for sewer project); *City & County of Denver v. Bd. of Comm'rs,* 113 Colo. 150, 156 P.2d 101 (1945) (airport); *Fishel,* 106 Colo. 576, 108 P.2d 236 (air corps technical school and bombing field). * * * Unlike the majority, I would continue our cautious stance towards extraterritorial condemnations in the case before us today.

In my view, our caution has been justified by article XX section 6 itself, which draws a distinction between territorial and extraterritorial actions taken by a municipality. It provides that ordinances passed by a home rule municipality's governing body "shall supersede *within the territorial limits . . .* of said city or town any law of the state in conflict therewith." (Emphasis added). Thus, section 6 plainly states that a home rule municipality's ordinance, such as the one giving Telluride the authority to condemn land outside its boundaries for open space, can supersede conflicting state law—here, section 38–1–101(4)(b)—*only* within its own boundaries. By definition, an extraterritorial condemnation implicates land that may be located in a neighboring municipality—precisely the sort of subject matter that has traditionally concerned the General Assembly.

The majority glosses over section 6's clear limitation on extraterritorial actions by stating that we have permitted extraterritorial condemnations in the past.. Yet again, these exterritorial condemnations have been few and far between, and have been closely related to the enumerated purposes in section 1. These narrow precedents hardly compel the conclusion reached by the majority today: that the General Assembly cannot limit a home rule municipality's extraterritorial condemnation authority to those purposes listed in article XX section 1.

NOTES AND QUESTIONS

1. *Categorization and Balancing.* The courts in these cases take very different approaches to how to address conflicting state and local interests. *LaGrande* and *Telluride* determined that the state constitution resolved the issue by clearly handing control of the subject at issue to either the state or the local government. The *Denver* court, on the other hand, finds the subject to be one of mixed state and local concerns and balances two sets of interests. Do you think one approach is better than the other, or is there a place for both?

In *LaGrande*, the Oregon Supreme Court rejected its past practice of "search[ing] for a predominant state or local interest in the 'subject matter' of the legislation." Instead it held that home rule protects from state interference only a narrow core of local interests—"the structural and organizational arrangements" of local governments, and "the manner in which governmental power is granted and exercised, not the concrete uses to which it is put." With respect to everything else—general state laws addressed "primarily to substantive social, economic or other regulatory objectives"—the state's law prevails over a conflicting local ordinance. What is the court's justification for giving up on all efforts to balance state and local interests? Does it follow from the text of the state constitution? The court emphasizes the state legislature's interest in the well-being of all state residents, including those who live in home rule cities, but don't the cities have at least as strong an interest in the well-being of their residents? Given the difficulty of striking a balance, and the concern that in setting the balance the court will be influenced by the substance of the legislation, is this the right approach? Or does this effectively leave home rule at the mercy of the state legislature? The pension and insurance requirements imposed by the state on local governments can be seen as an unfunded mandate of the sort examined earlier in this Chapter. Given the economic impact on local budgets, should the court have given greater weight to the cities' concerns, or is that a matter reserved for the state legislature? For further analysis of the Oregon court's approach to resolving state-local home rule conflicts, *see* Cynthia Cumfer, Original Intent v. Modern Judicial Philosophy: Oregon's Home Rule Case Frames the Dilemma for State Constitutionalism, 76 Ore.L.Rev. 909 (1997).

In *Denver,* the Colorado court began by referring to the traditional categorization of matters as local, statewide, and mixed, but then quickly moved to a balancing approach. Why do you think the court shifted its analysis? What factors were relevant to the Colorado court's balancing test? How do these factors relate to the question of whether or not there was local power to act in the first place? How critical was it that the Denver deputy sheriffs had relatively limited powers? Why is that important? Could Denver have refused to require its full-time police force to obtain POST certification? Why might the balance have come out differently in that instance? What is the state of Colorado's interest in how Denver's law enforcement personnel perform their jobs? Why isn't this an exclusively local matter?

Denver indicated that a significant factor in determining who prevails in a mixed state-local case is the extent that local action has an extraterritorial impact, and the Colorado Supreme Court's decision was predicated in part on a finding that the actions of the Denver deputy sheriffs had little extra-local effect. But in *Telluride* the town's action was totally extraterritorial and this time the Colorado Supreme Court struck down the state's effort to control the locality's extraterritorial action. What accounts for the difference? Given the extraterritorial impact, isn't *Telluride* at least as good a case for balancing as *Denver?* Are you persuaded by the court's finding that the power of extraterritorial eminent domain is "specifically granted" to home rule municipalities by the state constitution? If extraterritorial eminent domain is a constitutionally protected power of home rule municipalities in Colorado, then does it make sense, as the court indicates in footnote 8, also cited by Justice Coats's special concurrence, that the state can still regulate it, for example, by requiring the municipality to comply with certain procedures? Could it be argued that requiring consent of the governing body of the local government within whose territory the land to be condemned is located—one of the provisions of the statute invalidated in *Telluride*—would be valid? The Colorado Supreme Court's *Telluride* decision was the focus of a Symposium in the Denver University Law Review. *See* Symposium: Home Rule, 86 Denv. U. L. Rev. 1239–1473 (2009).

2.   *Imperio and Immunity.* Kenneth Vanlandingham argued that in comparison with other models of home rule, "the imperio theory offers a more substantial guarantee of meaningful home rule power." Kenneth Vanlandingham, Constitutional Municipal Home Rule Since the AMA (NLC) Model, 17 Wm. & Mary L. Rev 1, 26 (1975). Any such guarantee is likely to be limited to the relatively narrow category of matters considered exclusively local. *Cf*, Voss v. Lundvall Bros., 830 P.2d 1061 (Colo.1992) (local ban on drilling of oil wells within city found not to be exclusively local concern); Town of East Greenwich v. O'Neil, 617 A.2d 104 (R.I.1992) (ordinance regulating high voltage electric power transmission lines not purely local). On the other hand, *Telluride* indicates that sometimes the category of "exclusively local" may be significant.

It may also debatable whether local immunity from state displacement is necessarily desirable. With large numbers of relatively small municipalities packed into contemporary metropolitan areas, many local regulations will have impacts that are felt beyond their borders and may affect nonresidents who come into the locality on a regular basis to work or shop or simply while en route to another locality. As increased urbanization and heightened mobility produce greater numbers of contiguous governments and increased travel across multiple government territories, the spillover effects of one government's actions have similarly increased. At the same time, resistance to proposals for increased regionalization, which would require attention to the broader effects of local regulation, has remained strong. *See* Richard Briffault, The Local Government Boundary Problem in Metropolitan Areas, 48 Stanford L.Rev. 1115 (1996) for suggestions about how regional or municipal government units might be better equipped to make certain decisions about "local" issues with substantial extraterritorial impacts. Do these observations provide some justification for those courts that refuse to expand the definition of "exclusively local" for purposes of protection from state law? Certainly, as in *Telluride,* sometimes vindicating the power of one local government can come at the cost to another. *See, e.g.,* Richard Briffault, *Town of Telluride v. San Miguel Valley Corp.:* Extraterritoriality and Local Autonomy, 86 Denv. U. L. Rev. 1311, 1323–28 (2009).

Like Colorado, California is another important *imperio* home rule state. The next case supports the suggestion that courts in *imperio* states may be more protective of local autonomy, while also indicating the difficulties that stance raises.

STATE BUILDING AND CONSTRUCTION TRADES COUNCIL v. CITY OF VISTA

Supreme Court of California
279 P.3d 1022 (2012)

KENNARD, J.

A charter city entered into certain contracts for the construction of public buildings. A federation of labor unions then petitioned the superior court for a peremptory writ of mandate, asserting that the city must comply with California's prevailing wage law notwithstanding local ordinances stating otherwise. The prevailing wage law requires that certain minimum wage levels be paid to contract workers constructing public works.

Under the state Constitution, the ordinances of charter cities supersede state law with respect to "municipal affairs" (Cal.Const., art. XI, § 5), but state law is supreme with respect to matters of "statewide concern" *(California Fed. Savings & Loan Assn. v. City of Los Angeles* (1991) 54 Cal.3d 1, 17, 283 Cal.Rptr. 569, 812 P.2d 916 *(California Fed. Savings)).* Here, petitioner contends that the subject matter of the state's prevailing wage law is a "statewide concern" over which the state has primary legislative authority. The city responds that the matter is a municipal affair and therefore governed by its local ordinances. We agree with the city.

I. FACTS

In 2006, the voters of the City of Vista in San Diego County approved a .5 percent sales tax to fund the construction and renovation of several public buildings. The proposed projects involved the seismic retrofit of an existing fire station and the construction of two new fire stations, a new civic center, a new sports park, and a new stagehouse for the city's Moonlight Amphitheatre. * * * In October 2007, Vista's city council adopted a resolution approving contracts to design and build two fire stations and authorizing the mayor to execute the contracts. The contracts did not require compliance with the state's prevailing wage law. A court action by plaintiff followed. * * *

II. DISCUSSION

A.   California's Prevailing Wage Law

In 1931, the California Legislature enacted the state's prevailing wage law. That law, which was then entitled the Public Wage Rate Act, required contractors on "public works" projects to pay "the general prevailing rate of per diem wages for work of a similar character in the locality in which the work is performed." * * * The law expressly referred to charter cities in a provision requiring such cities to pay prevailing wages in contracts for street or sewer improvement work.

Earlier the same year, Congress had enacted the Davis-Bacon Act (Pub.L. 71–798 (Mar. 3, 1931) 46 Stat. 1494, codified at 40 U.S.C. §§ 3141–3148); the goals of the federal and the state legislation were similar. * * * Simply put, "[p]revailing wage laws are based on the . . . premise that government contractors should not be allowed to circumvent locally prevailing labor market conditions by importing cheap labor from other areas." * * * Many states have adopted some form of a prevailing wage law for public construction projects. *[citing Illinois, New York, Pennsylvania and Texas statutes.]*

When the California Legislature established the Labor Code in 1937, it replaced the 1931 Public Wage Rate Act with a revised, but substantively unchanged, version of the same law. * * * As a result of a 1976 amendment, the prevailing wage law now requires that local wage rates be determined by the Director of California's Department of Industrial Relations rather than by the body awarding the contract but the prevailing wage law's general purpose and scope remain largely unchanged. * * *

B.   California's Home Rule Doctrine

Charter cities are specifically authorized by our state Constitution to govern themselves, free of state legislative intrusion, as to those matters deemed municipal affairs. Article XI, section 5, subdivision (a) of the California Constitution provides: "It shall be competent in any city charter to provide that the city governed thereunder may make and enforce all ordinances and regulations *in respect to municipal affairs,* subject only to restrictions and limitations provided in their several charters and in respect to other matters they shall be subject to general laws. City charters adopted pursuant to this Constitution shall supersede any existing charter, and *with respect to municipal affairs* shall supersede all laws inconsistent therewith." (Italics added.) The roots of this provision trace back more than 100 years. * * * It was originally "enacted upon the principle that the municipality itself knew better what it wanted and needed than the state at large, and to give that municipality the exclusive privilege and right to enact direct legislation which would carry out and satisfy its wants and needs." * * * The provision represents an "affirmative constitutional grant to charter cities of 'all powers appropriate for a municipality to possess . . .' and [includes] the important corollary that 'so far as "municipal affairs" are concerned,' charter cities are 'supreme and beyond the reach of legislative enactment.'"

In California Fed. Savings we set forth an analytical framework for resolving whether or not a matter falls within the home rule authority of charter cities. First, a court must determine whether the city ordinance at issue regulates an activity that can be characterized as a "municipal affair." Second, the court "must satisfy itself that the case presents an actual conflict between [local and state law]." Third, the court must decide whether the state law addresses a matter of "statewide concern." Finally, the court must determine whether the law is "reasonably related to . . . resolution" of that concern, and "narrowly tailored" to avoid unnecessary interference in local governance. "If . . . the court is persuaded that the subject of the state statute is one of statewide concern and that the statute is reasonably related to its resolution [and not unduly broad in its sweep], then the conflicting charter city measure ceases to be a 'municipal affair' pro tanto and the Legislature is not prohibited by article XI, section 5(a), from addressing the statewide dimension by its own tailored enactments."

Here, we reaffirm our view—first expressed 80 years ago (see City of Pasadena v. Charleville (1932)) —that the wage levels of contract workers constructing locally funded public works are a municipal affair (that is, exempt from state regulation), and that these wage levels are not a statewide concern (that is, subject to state legislative control).

C.   Applicability of California's Home Rule Doctrine Is a Question of Law

The Court of Appeal treated the dispute in this case as a factual one, and it characterized its decision against the Union in terms of a failure of proof. * * * Thus, the Court of Appeal here did not hold that the wage levels of contract workers constructing a locally funded public work are categorically a municipal affair and not a statewide concern. Rather, the Court of Appeal held that the legislative record was inadequate to establish a statewide concern and that the Union had failed to prove its case in the trial court.

The Court of Appeal's approach raises the question whether the determination of a statewide concern presents predominantly a legal or a factual question. Fundamentally, the question is one of constitutional interpretation; the controlling inquiry is how the state Constitution allocates governmental authority between charter cities and the state. The answer to that constitutional question does not necessarily depend on whether the municipal activity in question has some regional or statewide effect. For example, we have said that the salaries of charter city employees are a municipal affair and not a statewide concern regardless of any possible economic effect those salaries might have beyond the borders of the city. *(Sonoma County Organization of Public Employees v. County of Sonoma (1979) 23 Cal.3d 296, 316–317, 152 Cal.Rptr. 903, 591 P.2d 1 (Sonoma County).)*

Of course, the inquiry is not wholly removed from historical, and hence factual, realities. In California Fed. Savings, for example, we said: "[C]ourts should avoid the error of 'compartmentalization,' that is, of cordoning off an entire area of governmental activity as either a 'municipal affair' or one of statewide concern. * * * [O]ur cases display a growing recognition that 'home rule' is a means of adjusting the political relationship between state and local governments in discrete areas of conflict. When a court invalidates a charter city measure in favor of a conflicting state statute, the result does not necessarily rest on the conclusion that the subject matter of the former is not appropriate for municipal regulation. It means, rather, that *under the historical circumstances presented,* the state has a more substantial interest in the subject than the charter city."

Nevertheless, the question whether in a particular case the home rule provisions of the California Constitution bar the application of state law to charter cities turns ultimately on the meaning and scope of the state law in question and the relevant state constitutional provisions. Interpreting that law and those provisions presents a legal question, not a factual one. * * * Courts accord great weight to the factual record that the Legislature has compiled * * * and also to any relevant facts established in trial court proceedings. * * * Factual findings by the Legislature or the trial court, however, are not controlling. * * * The decision as to what areas of governance are municipal concerns and what are statewide concerns is ultimately a legal one.

Therefore, the Court of Appeal here gave too much weight to the Union's asserted failure to prove its case, implying that the issue before the court was one of sufficiency of the evidence. The answer to whether the prevailing wage law can be applied constitutionally to charter cities is not conclusively determined solely by the evidentiary record in the trial court or by the legislative record. The question remains one of state constitutional interpretation.

D.   Application of *California Fed. Savings's* Four-Part Test

1.   *Whether the wages of contract workers constructing locally funded public works are a municipal affair*

* * * It is apparent from our analysis in Charleville, that the construction of a *city-operated facility* for the benefit of a *city's inhabitants* is quintessentially a municipal affair, as is the control over *the expenditure of a city's own funds*. Here, the two fire stations in the City of Vista, like the municipal water system in *Charleville* are facilities operated by the city for the benefit of the city's inhabitants, and they are financed from the city's own funds. We conclude therefore that the matter at issue here involves a "municipal affair."

2.   *Existence of an "actual conflict" between state law and charter city law*

* * * Here, no party contends that California's prevailing wage law exempts charter cities from its scope. * * * [W]e conclude that an actual conflict exists between state law and Vista's ordinance.

3.   *Whether the wage levels of contract workers constructing locally funded public works is a statewide concern*

When, as here, state law and the ordinances of a charter city actually conflict and we must decide which controls, "the hinge of the decision is the identification of a convincing basis for legislative action originating in extramunicipal concerns, one justifying legislative supersession based on sensible, pragmatic considerations." * * * In other words, for state law to control there must be something more than an abstract state interest, as it is always possible to articulate some state interest in even the most local of matters. Rather, there must be "a convincing basis" for the state's action—a basis that "justif[ies]" the state's interference in what would otherwise be a merely local affair. * * *

We reached essentially the same conclusion when we addressed the question in our 1932 decision in *Charleville*. We there held that the wage levels of contract workers improving a city-owned reservoir were not a matter of "general state concern." Likewise, the wage levels of contract workers designing and constructing two city-operated fire houses do not appear to be a matter of "general state concern." The Union, however, argues that circumstances have changed since our 1932 *Charleville* decision, and that what was *not* a statewide concern then has since *become* a statewide concern. * * *

The Union points out that as a result of a 1976 amendment to the state's prevailing wage law the wage levels mandated by that law are no longer set by the local body awarding the contract but by the Director of the Department of Industrial Relations, and under the amended law, these mandatory wage levels reflect regional rather than simply local interests. * * * In light of these statutory changes, the Union argues, the wage levels of contract workers constructing locally funded public works have become a matter of statewide concern.

In a related argument, the Union contends that the economy of the state has become more integrated during the 80 years since this court's 1932 decision in Charleville and wage levels in a local area are now more likely to have an effect regionally and statewide. The construction industry in particular, according to the Union, has followed this trend toward economic regionalization, with workers often driving long distances to a job site and multi-employer collective bargaining agreements governing the terms of employment on a regional basis. Because of these economic changes, the Union asserts, the refusal of charter cities to pay prevailing wages has a depressive impact on regional labor standards that was not present in 1932 when *Charleville* was decided. Therefore, the Union argues, the expenditure of city funds on a local public work is no longer a purely local concern; rather, in light of our modern integrated economy, it has become a statewide concern.

The Union further notes that the state's prevailing wage law now requires contractors on public works projects to hire apprentices from state-approved apprenticeship programs, thereby ensuring the proper training of the next generation of skilled construction workers. The Union contends that this requirement of the prevailing wage law is essential to California's long-term economic health. If the prevailing wage law did not include this requirement, the Union argues, then construction contractors bidding competitively on public works projects would refuse to hire apprentices, in an effort to reduce costs; apprentices then might not be able to obtain enough work to support themselves and to complete their on-the-job training requirement. The Union asserts that the training of the next generation of skilled construction workers is a statewide concern, not merely a local concern, and the prevailing wage law has become an integral part of the state's scheme for training these workers.

These arguments by the Union underscore the importance of identifying correctly the question at issue. Certainly regional labor standards and the proper training of construction workers are statewide concerns *when considered in the abstract*. But the question presented here is not whether the state government has an abstract interest in labor conditions and vocational training. Rather, the question presented is whether the state can require a charter city to exercise its purchasing power in the construction market in a way that supports regional wages and subsidizes vocational training, while increasing the charter city's costs. No one would doubt that the state could use *its own* resources to support wages and vocational training in the state's construction industry, but can the state achieve these ends by interfering in the fiscal policies of charter cities? Autonomy with regard to the expenditure of public funds lies at the heart of what it means to be an independent governmental entity.

The Union's arguments also conflict with our previous decisions. In Sonoma County we held that the wages paid by a charter city or county to *its own* employees are a municipal affair and therefore are not subject to regulation by the state Legislature. In that case, the state offered to distribute surplus state funds to local governments to mitigate the impact of Proposition 13.[3] The Legislature, however, then enacted a special provision prohibiting the distribution of surplus state funds to any local agency that granted to its employees a cost-of-living wage or salary increase that exceeded the cost-of-living increase provided to state employees. At issue was whether the latter provision violated the home rule doctrine of the California Constitution. We emphasized in *Sonoma County* that the determination of what constitutes a municipal affair (over which the state has no legislative authority) and what constitutes a statewide concern (as to which state law is controlling) is a matter for the courts, not the Legislature, to decide. Moreover, that the Legislature chose to deal with a problem on a statewide basis, *Sonoma County* said, does not in itself make the problem a statewide concern. Put differently, the concept of statewide concern is not coextensive with the state's police power. Citing numerous cases and an explicit provision of the state Constitution, *Sonoma County* concluded that the salaries of local employees of a charter city are a municipal affair not subject to the state's general laws. * * *

More recently, in *County of Riverside* we * * * concluded that state law could not force a county into binding arbitration over the compensation paid to county employees. Our decision applied two state constitutional provisions: one giving all counties authority to "provide for the . . . compensation . . . of [their] employees" (Cal. Const., art. XI, § 1, subd. (b)), the other prohibiting the Legislature from "delegat[ing] to a private person or body power to . . . interfere with county or municipal corporation . . . money" (*id.*, § 11, subd. (a)). In the course of our analysis, we considered whether the state law at issue might be enforceable because it governed a matter of statewide concern. We rejected the Legislature's assertion that the matter involved a statewide concern. Instead, we concluded that the state law in question impinged too much

---

[3] Proposition 13, an initiative measure that the California electorate passed on June 6, 1978, added article XIII A to the California Constitution, placing significant limits on the taxing power of local and state governments. *[Proposition 13 is considered in Chapter VI.]*

on local rights, *"depriving* the county entirely of its authority to set employee salaries." We also drew an important distinction between state *procedural* laws governing the affairs of local governmental entities (which by their nature impinge less on local affairs) and state laws dictating the *substance* of a public employee labor issue (which impinge much more on local affairs).

Although the * * * cases just cited * * * deal with the wages of *public employees* rather than, as here, the wages of *private employees* constructing local public works projects, the distinction is irrelevant. The Union's arguments here do not depend on whether the workers constructing the public work are public or private employees. If, as the Union contends, the prevailing wage law's shift from a purely local focus to a regional focus has made the wage levels of workers constructing locally funded public works a matter of statewide concern, then that would be true whether the case involved public employees or private employees. Similarly, if, as the Union asserts, the state's economic integration during the 80 years since our 1932 decision in *Charleville, supra,* has made the wages of workers constructing local public works a matter of statewide concern, then that would be true for both public employees and private employees.

Significantly, this case is not like others in which we found a statewide concern to justify the application of a state law to charter cities. For example, our cases have suggested that a state law of broad general application is more likely to address a statewide concern than one that is narrow and particularized in its application. * * * We applied this principle in *People ex rel. Seal Beach Police Officers Assn. v. City of Seal Beach (1984),* and *Professional Fire Fighters, Inc. v. City of Los Angeles (1963),* In the latter two cases, we also noted that the state laws at issue set forth generally applicable *procedural* standards, and consequently impinged less on local autonomy than if they had imposed substantive obligations. In *Seal Beach,* for example, we said: "[T]here is a clear distinction between the *substance* of a public employee labor issue and the *procedure* by which it is resolved. Thus there is no question that 'salaries of local employees of a charter city constitute municipal affairs and are not subject to general laws.' Nevertheless, the process by which salaries are fixed is obviously a matter of statewide concern and none could, at this late stage, argue that a charter city need not meet and confer concerning its salary structure."

Here, the state law at issue is not a minimum wage law of broad general application; rather, the law at issue here has a far narrower application, as it pertains only to the public works projects of public agencies. In addition, it imposes substantive obligations on charter cities, not merely generally applicable procedural standards. These distinctions further undermine the Union's assertion that the matter here presents a statewide concern. * * *

We are aware that the Legislature has recently stated that the wage levels of contract workers constructing locally funded public works are a matter of statewide concern. The Legislature's view is expressed in two amendments to the prevailing wage law, one in 2002 and the other in 2003, each addressing a relatively narrow category of public works. * * *

But as we noted earlier * * * the Legislature's view as to what constitutes a statewide concern is not determinative in resolving the constitutional question before us. * * * [W]e are "especially" hesitant to abdicate to the Legislature's view of the issue "when [as here] the issue involves the division of power between local government and that same Legislature."

In this case, we conclude that no statewide concern has been presented justifying the state's regulation of the wages that charter cities require their contractors to pay to workers hired to construct locally funded public works. In light of our conclusion that there is no statewide concern here, we need not determine whether the state's prevailing wage law is "reasonably related to . . . resolution" of that concern *(California Fed. Savings, supra,* and is "narrowly tailored" to avoid unnecessary interference in local governance.

WERDEGAR, J., dissenting.

* * * The majority asserts that "[t]he wage levels of contract workers constructing locally funded public works are certainly a 'municipal affair.'" No citation to authority is required to conclude that the provision and financing of a proper city infrastructure, whether it be housing, hospitals, libraries or other civic buildings, is the business of a city, chartered or otherwise. Vista has imposed a citywide sales tax increase to pay for the cost of the design, construction and renovation of some of its civic buildings. That these costs are to be borne by Vista alone, and not shared by the state, is a significant factor in favor of finding the public works at issue fall within the municipal affairs doctrine. * * *

The question, however, is not whether the design and physical construction of Vista's civic buildings constitute a municipal affair, as they do, but whether Vista's choice not to require the private construction firms with which it has contracted (or will contract) to pay the state prevailing wage to its construction worker employees is also a matter within the city's municipal affairs. Vista contends a charter city's internal fiscal affairs, including labor and employment issues, necessarily fall within the municipal home rule doctrine. Of relevance is section 5, subdivision (b) of article XI of the California Constitution, which provides a nonexclusive list of the types of matters falling within the municipal home rule doctrine. That section provides: "It shall be competent in all city charters to provide, in addition to those provisions allowable by this Constitution, and by the laws of the State for: (1) the constitution, regulation, and government of the city police force (2) subgovernment in all or part of a city (3) conduct of city elections and (4) plenary authority is hereby granted, subject only to the restrictions of this article, to provide therein or by amendment thereto, the manner in which, the method by which, the times at which, and the terms for which the several municipal officers and employees whose compensation is paid by the city shall be elected or appointed, and for their removal, and for their compensation, and for the number of deputies, clerks and other employees that each shall have, and for the compensation, method of appointment, qualifications, tenure of office and removal of such deputies, clerks and other employees."

In light of this constitutional provision, the salary level of the mayor and city council members clearly falls within a city's municipal affairs, as does the compensation level of the "city police force" as well as those city employees involved in the "subgovernment in all or part of a city" such as "deputies, clerks *and other employees.*" (Cal. Const., art. XI, § 5, subd. (b), * * *

But the more removed workers are from the heart of city government, the less the city's legitimate interest in controlling their compensation. This case, for example, involves no Vista employee. Vista has contracted (or intends to contract) with private design and construction firms, which in turn have hired (or will hire) private construction workers, who will be paid not by Vista but by the construction firms. If a firm underbids the project, it is the firm, not the city, that must still pay the workers. Accordingly, these contract workers cannot fairly be characterized as city employees who are necessary to maintain the "subgovernment in all or part of a city."

To reach its conclusion that Vista's zone of protected municipal affairs nevertheless includes the wages of private construction workers, the majority relies uncritically on City of Pasadena v. Charleville (1932). *Charleville* involved the Public Wage Rate Act of 1931 (PWRA of 1931), a law of significantly less scope and statewide impact than the modern prevailing wage law at issue in this case. More importantly, *Charleville's* reasoning has been overtaken by history. In *Charleville* the court explained that the PWRA of 1931 was a law of limited scope because it did not "purport to fix or provide for the fixation of the wage to be paid *under all employment contracts, public and private* " and suggested that an act purporting to impose a broader, statewide regulation on wages would have encountered "difficulties of constitutional questions" *(ibid.,* citing *Adkins v. Children's Hospital (1923) 261 U.S. 525* [which invalidated a D.C. law imposing a minimum wage for women and minors]). *Adkins* was a notable exemplar of the late *Lochner* period in which the high court extolled the virtues of the freedom to contract over nearly all other freedoms. As is well known, the principles animating that bygone era of constitutional jurisprudence were thereafter repudiated by the United States Supreme Court * * *.

In light of this erosion of the legal assumptions underlying Charleville and because the PWRA of 1931 was markedly less extensive than the modern prevailing wage law, *Charleville* cannot be considered persuasive today. Moreover, given the obvious changes to our state's economy since 1932 when *Charleville* was decided, i.e., its growth and interdependence, the case was long ago eclipsed by more modern economic ideas. Common sense dictates that we abandon *Charleville* as precedent and consign it to the dustbin of history. * * *

Because Vista's interest in controlling the wages of private contract workers is much less than its interest in dictating wage levels of its own employees, and absent the legitimizing effect of *Charleville,* as precedent, the sole remaining consideration supporting Vista's assertion of its municipal autonomy is its desire to save money on its planned public works projects. Every government, state or local, naturally has an interest in conserving public funds. But this general desire is insufficient of itself to invoke the municipal affairs doctrine. Were it otherwise, no state law could ever prevail over local desires, for all conflicting state laws have the potential to increase a city's costs, whether it be to allow a city's firefighters to unionize *(Professional Fire Fighters, Inc. v. City of Los Angeles (1963)),* require cities to meet and confer in good faith with employee representatives regarding wages and hours *(People ex rel. Seal Beach Police Officers Assn. v. City of Seal Beach (1984)),* or give peace officers an administrative appeal before demoting them * * * . Vista must point to more than a ledger sheet to justify its contention that its ordinance falls within the municipal affairs doctrine.

The relative strength of Vista's interest in preserving its public fisc aside, the crux of this case is the majority's conclusion that the prevailing wage law fails to address a matter of statewide concern. In reaching that conclusion, the majority disregards the prevailing wage law's far-reaching economic impact on our state economy. The Legislature has recognized the scope of the prevailing wage law's statewide effect, having explicitly declared its intent in 2002 that "[p]ayment of the prevailing rate of per diem wages to workers employed on public works projects is necessary to attract the most skilled workers for those projects and to ensure that work of the highest quality is performed on those projects" * * * that "[p]ublic works projects should never undermine the wage base in a community, and requiring that workers on public works projects are paid the prevailing rate of per diem wages ensures that wage base is not lowered" and that it is a matter of "statewide concern" that public works undertaken by public agencies pay workers the prevailing wage. A year later, in a 2003 concurrent resolution, the Legislature addressed the prevailing wage law specifically with regard to charter cities, declaring that "the state prevailing wage law [should] apply broadly to all projects subsidized with public funds, *including the projects of chartered cities, as the law addresses important statewide concerns. . . .*" These legislative statements are entitled to great weight. * * *

Even aside from the Legislature's considered views, that the prevailing wage law addresses substantial statewide concerns that would be undermined were charter cities allowed to opt out of the law is not a close question. As a general matter, we have held that the promotion of uniform fair labor standards is an important statewide concern sufficient to override local prerogatives. For example, we held in *People ex rel. Seal Beach Police Officers Assn. v. City of Seal Beach,* that the meet-and-confer provision of the Meyers-Milias-Brown Act (MMBA) (Gov.Code, § 3505) was enforceable against the City of Seal Beach, a charter city, despite its city charter amendment providing, among other things, for the immediate termination of any city employee who participated in a labor strike. We noted that one of the purposes of the MMBA was "to improve personnel management and employer-employee relations within the various public agencies" and that "[t]he meet-and-confer requirement is an essential component of the state's legislative scheme for regulating the city's employment practices." As such, that state interest outweighed the city's admitted power—authorized by the state Constitution under article XI, section 3, subdivision (b)—to amend its city charter.

Similarly, in *Professional Fire Fighters, Inc. v. City of Los Angeles,* the City of Los Angeles, a charter city, argued that application of Labor Code section 1960, which guarantees firefighters the right to join a union, addressed a matter of "purely local concern," and that prior case law had held "that all matters connected with public employment in a chartered city are municipal affairs [citations]." This court rejected the argument, explaining that an examination of the Legislature's intent when enacting section 1960 and several related statutes revealed "the Legislature was attempting to deal with labor relations on a statewide basis." By enacting those state laws, the Legislature "adopted general policies and provided general rights and obligations of labor and management *throughout the state.*" * * * As such, the legislation may impinge upon local control to a limited extent, but it is nonetheless a matter of state concern."

The prevailing wage law is to the same effect. Article XIV of the California Constitution is entitled "Labor Relations." Section 1 of that article provides that "[t]he Legislature may provide for minimum wages and for the general welfare of employees. . . ." The Legislature is thus granted specific constitutional authority to address labor issues on a statewide scale. * * * The evolution of the modern prevailing wage law strongly supports the Legislature's considered view that the wages paid on publicly funded construction projects impacts more than local concerns. * * * [C]onstruction workers travel many miles from their homes to jobsites in the region. To allow Oakland to pay construction workers significantly less than Berkeley, or Anaheim less than Santa Ana, would logically create downward pressure on wages throughout the respective regions, leading to an economic race to the bottom, as contractors—union and nonunion—scramble to underbid competitors for construction contracts. * * *

The prevailing wage law supports the statewide economy in a second way, mentioned but discounted by the majority, requiring contractors on public works projects to participate in a statewide apprenticeship program. This program allows apprentices in the construction trades to learn on the job, ensuring the state will be supplied with a steady stream of skilled and semi-skilled workers in the construction industry. * * * Allowing charter cities to opt out of the prevailing wage law undermines this program by affording them the benefit of it (by using workers trained in state apprenticeship programs) without their paying for the privilege. * * *

Against the considerable weight of the evidence that the prevailing wage law addresses an issue of statewide concern, the majority's answer is not to engage the issue, but to reframe the question. The majority thus asserts that the question is not whether regional labor standards and apprenticeship programs address an issue of statewide concern, but whether "the state can require a charter city to exercise its purchasing power in the construction market in a way that supports regional wages and subsidizes vocational training, while increasing the charter city's costs." What this reframing ignores is that the entire premise of the dispute before us, and the one that has continued to vex courts over the years, is that the state *can* sometimes override a city's local choices—even financial ones—so long as it has sufficient reason (i.e., with a state law addressed to strong statewide concerns). * * *

Thus, while the *effect* of the prevailing wage law, as the majority laments, may be that Vista and other charter cities pay more for their public works projects, the *purpose* of the prevailing wage law, which the majority ignores, is not to make them pay more but to stabilize and support the construction trades. The latter is unquestionably a matter of substantial statewide concern. * * *

LIU, J., dissenting.

I join Justice Werdegar's dissent. I write separately to highlight additional shortcomings in the court's analysis that prevent it from properly resolving this case. * * *

* * * Perhaps the most serious error in the court's analysis is its disregard for the principle that doubts about whether a law is a matter of

statewide concern must be resolved in favor of the legislative authority of the state. Although the present dispute involves a contest between two levels of democratic decisionmaking—local and state—one should not think that democracy (of some kind) will be the winner no matter how we rule. If we were to uphold the prevailing wage law, charter cities could still bring their complaints to the Legislature through the ordinary political process, and it seems at least plausible that state legislators would be attentive to the concerns of local officials on whom they often depend for political support. However, having declared the prevailing wage law unconstitutional as applied to charter cities, the court has placed the issue beyond the ordinary political process. * * *

EMPIRE STATE CHAPTER OF ASSOCIATED BUILDERS AND CONTRACTORS, INC. V. SMITH

Court of Appeals of New York
21 N.Y.3d 309 (2013)

SMITH, J.

The Wicks Law, originally enacted in 1912, requires public entities seeking bids on construction contracts to obtain "separate specifications" for three "subdivisions of the work to be performed"—generally, plumbing, electrical and HVAC (heating, ventilating and air conditioning) work. The law has long been controversial; public entities have complained that it makes contracting more burdensome and expensive. Until 2008, the Wicks Law applied everywhere in the state to contracts whose cost exceeded $50,000.

This case concerns amendments to the Wicks Law enacted in 2008 that raised the $50,000 threshold, imposed so-called "apprenticeship requirements" on some public contracting, and made other changes not relevant here. * * * The new, higher thresholds, unlike the old one, are not uniform throughout the state. They are $3 million in the five counties located in New York City; $1.5 million in Nassau, Suffolk and Westchester Counties; and $500,000 in the other 54 counties.

Plaintiffs' main claim, asserted in their first cause of action, is that the 2008 legislation violates article IX, § 2 of the State Constitution (the Home Rule section) by unjustifiably favoring the eight counties with higher thresholds—i.e., by loosening Wicks Law restrictions to a greater extent for them than for the other counties. * * *

The Home Rule section of the State Constitution says:

"(b) Subject to the bill of rights of local governments and other applicable provisions of this constitution, the legislature: . . .

"(2) Shall have the power to act in relation to the property, affairs or government of any local government only by general law, or by special law only (a) on request of two-thirds of the total membership of its legislative body or on request of its chief executive officer concurred in by a majority of such membership, or (b) except in the case of the city of New York, on certificate of necessity from the governor reciting facts which in the judgment of the governor constitute an emergency requiring enactment of such law and, in such latter case, with the concurrence of two-thirds of the members elected to each house of the legislature." (NY Const, art IX, § 2 [b] [2].)

It is undisputed that neither of the prerequisites described in subdivisions (a) and (b) of section 2 (b) (2)—a so-called "home rule message" or a certificate of necessity from the governor—was met in this case. And we assume, without deciding, that the distinctions drawn between counties in the 2008 legislation make that legislation a "special law," defined in article IX, § 3 (d) (4), as relevant here, to be "[a] law which in terms and in effect applies to one or more, but not all, counties." Nevertheless, we conclude that the legislation was not forbidden by the Home Rule section.

The language of article IX, § 2 (b) (2) seems broadly to prohibit, where the specified prerequisites are not met, the enactment of any special law "in relation to the property, affairs or government of any local government." Another subdivision of the same section, section 2 (c) (i), uses similar language in granting power to local governments:

"every local government shall have power to adopt and amend local laws not inconsistent with the provisions of this constitution or any general law relating to its property, affairs or government."

These two provisions might be read to mean that, in the absence of a home rule message or certificate of necessity, a local government's "property, affairs or government" is an area in which local governments are free to act, but from which the state legislature is excluded unless it legislates by general law. It was long ago recognized, however, that such a reading of the Constitution would not make sense—that there must be an area of overlap, indeed a very sizeable one, in which the state legislature acting by special law and local governments have concurrent powers. As Chief Judge Cardozo put it in his concurring opinion in *Adler v. Deegan* (251 NY 467, 489 [1929]) (interpreting similar language in an earlier Constitution): "The Constitution . . . will not be read as enjoining an impossible dichotomy." He added:

"The test is . . . that if the subject be in a substantial degree a matter of State concern, the Legislature may act, though intermingled with it are concerns of the locality . . . I do not say that an affair must be one of city concern exclusively to bring it within the scope of the powers conferred upon the municipality . . . I assume that if the affair is partly State and partly local, the city is free to act until the State has intervened. As to concerns of this class there is thus concurrent jurisdiction for each in default of action by the other." (*Id.* at 491.)

We have adopted in later cases the test as Chief Judge Cardozo formulated it. * * * And we have found support in the Constitution's text for the view that the permitted spheres of the state legislature and localities overlap. We relied in *Town of Islip* on article IX, § 3 (a) (3) of the Constitution, which says:

"Except as expressly provided, nothing in this article shall restrict or impair any power of the legislature in relation to . . . [m]atters other than the property, affairs or government of a local government." (*See Town of Islip*, 64 NY2d at 55–56.)

This language is not a mere redundancy—a statement that article IX, § 2 (b) (2) does not prohibit what it does not prohibit. A great deal of legislation relates *both* to "the property, affairs or government of a local government" and to "[m]atters other than the property, affairs or government of a local government"—i.e., to matters of substantial state concern. Where that is true, section 3 (a) (3), as we interpreted it in *Town of Islip*, establishes that section 2 (b) (2) does not prevent the State from acting by special law.

This principle controls this case. It can hardly be disputed, and plaintiffs here do not dispute, that the manner of bidding on public construction contracts is a matter of substantial state concern. The existence of the Wicks Law itself for the last century, and of much other legislation governing public contracting (*e.g.* General Municipal Law § 100–a [requiring competitive bidding]) attests to this. The very amendments of which plaintiffs complain, though they do not treat all counties alike, unquestionably affect the state as a whole.

Plaintiffs argue, however, that a finding that the legislation addresses a substantial state concern is not the end of the analysis. Relying on *City of New York v. Patrolmen's Benevolent Assn. of City of N.Y.* (89 NY2d 380 [1996]) (*PBA I*), they say that the Home Rule section also imposes a separate reasonableness test on "special" legislation. Plaintiffs read too much into the *PBA I* decision.

PBA I involved an intervention by the state legislature in a dispute between New York City and one of its employee unions. The City and the PBA had failed to negotiate a collective bargaining agreement, and the City had requested its local Board of Collective Bargaining (BCB) to appoint an impasse arbitration panel. "[A]t that time," the legislature, acting without a home rule message, passed a bill "which purported to give . . . exclusive jurisdiction over negotiation impasses between the City and the New York City police" to the BCB's state counterpart, the Public Employment Relations Board (PERB). The legislature thus sought to create an exception, applicable only to negotiations between New York City and the police, to the statewide rule that local governments could "completely opt out of PERB's jurisdiction over impasse procedures."

We held the legislation invalid under the Home Rule section, finding that it "cannot be upheld under any substantial State interest." To the assertion that the expressed purposes of the legislation—"to create State-wide uniformity with respect to impasse procedures" and to "provide a fairer forum for the New York City police"—were of statewide import, we responded that the legislation "bears no reasonable relationship to those goals." Uniformity could hardly be advanced by legislation applicable to one jurisdiction only, and the "fairness" rationale was shown to be pretextual, because of the "unchallenged substantial equivalency" between PERB's impasse arbitration procedures and those of local bodies.

In short, we found in *PBA I* that the challenged legislation was the sort of state meddling in purely local affairs that the Home Rule section was enacted to prohibit. By contrast, five years later in a second PBA case, *Patrolmen's Benevolent Assn. of City of N.Y. v. City of New York* (97 NY2d 378, 387 [2001]), we upheld legislation providing "that *all* collective bargaining impasses reached between local governments and their police and fire unions are resolved by PERB" (emphasis added). This new statute, we said, "was enacted in furtherance of and bears a reasonable relationship to a substantial State-wide concern."

The legislation here is nothing like the legislation at issue in *PBA I*; its relationship to matters of substantial state concern is obvious and undisputed. Plaintiffs claim that the relationship is not "reasonable" in that nothing in the legislative history, or in the arguments now made by the State, provides a reasonable explanation for the disparity that the 2008 legislation introduced into the Wicks Law thresholds—which are now six times as high in New York City, and three times as high in certain surrounding counties, as in the rest of the state. But *PBA I* did not use "reasonable relationship" in this sense; that case is not an invitation to subject every geographical disparity in statewide legislation to a freestanding reasonableness analysis. The absence of a "reasonable relationship" in *PBA I* established that the challenged legislation was purely parochial, and of no real statewide importance; it could not reasonably be said to advance a substantial state interest. No such claim can be made in this case.

To subject legislation like the 2008 amendments to the Wicks Law to Home Rule analysis would lead us into a wilderness of anomalies. If statewide legislation like this is subject to Home Rule restrictions, how are the restrictions to be implemented? From where must a home rule message come? Plaintiffs' logic leads to the conclusion that there should have been such a message from every one of the 62 counties affected. And if the law was passed in violation of the Home Rule provisions, what is the remedy? Are we to cure the disparity between counties by raising the Wicks Law threshold in 54 counties, or by reducing it in eight counties to the level established elsewhere? Or should we hold the 2008 legislation wholly invalid—so that the Wicks Law threshold remains at $50,000 throughout the state, a result that surely would not please plaintiffs?

We conclude that the Home Rule provisions of the Constitution were never intended to apply to legislation like this. They were intended to prevent unjustifiable state interference in matters of purely local concern. No one contends such interference has occurred here.

NOTES AND QUESTIONS

1.   *Defining Local and State Interests.* In *Vista,* both the majority and the dissents approached the problem of state-local conflict in terms of the framework laid out by the California Supreme Court in California Federal Savings & Loan Ass'n v. City of Los Angeles ("CalFed"), 812 P.2d 916 (1991), which provides that when a state statute conflicts with a local law that addresses a "municipal affair," the state statute will prevail only if it is "reasonably related" to a statewide concern and "narrowly tailored" to advancing that concern. The *Vista* majority, however, concluded that the state prevailing wage law failed even to address a statewide concern so it had no need to determine whether the law was reasonably related to that concern or whether it was narrowly tailored. Are you persuaded that the wages paid workers on municipal construction projects—which was also the focus of the dispute in *Empire State*—raise no issue of statewide concern at all?

The New York court in *Empire State* also avoided balancing; instead, once it concluded there was at least some state concern in the matter, it applied only a relatively weak "reasonable relationship" test to the state law. Unlike California, New York is not an *imperio* state but its home rule amendment does have a quasi-*imperio* procedural rule—the requirement that the state act on matters of local "property, affairs, or government" either by general law or, if by special law, only at the request of the affected local government (the so-called "home rule message"), or, for localities other than New York City, on a message of necessity from the governor and by a super-majority legislative vote. As the court acknowledged, the Wicks Law amendment was a special law unaccompanied by either a home rule message or a message of necessity from the governor. But as the court explained, the New York courts have long departed from the formal text of the constitution and permitted the state to act by special law with respect to local property, affairs or government if there is a state concern. What was the state concern here?

The *Vista* majority was quite insistent that "municipal affair" and "statewide concern" are questions of law and not of fact. The justices took the lower court to task on this point even though the lower court had reached the same result. The court seemed concerned about the potential cost impact of applying the prevailing wage law to city construction projects. Isn't that a question of fact? Would it matter if paying the prevailing wage law has only a modest impact on the cost of public construction projects? The New York court also did not seem interested in examining the factual underpinning for the different Wicks Law thresholds in the different parts of the state.

These opinions also expressed a range of views on the deference, if any, to be given to the legislature's views on the question of the state's interest. What weight, if any, should a court give to a state legislature's declaration that a law affecting local governments is a matter of statewide concern? Does the mere fact of enactment of a state law demonstrate that a matter is of statewide concern? Conversely, given that these cases arise only when there is a state law affecting local government, would giving deference to the legislature's position improperly tip the scales in favor of the state?

2. *Local Public Employment and Contracts.* As these cases—and the earlier *La Grande* and *Denver* decisions—indicate, local public employment and contracting are a key source of state-local conflicts. Personnel costs are a leading local budget expense, and they are crucial to local operations. State-imposed regulation raises the same accountability problems as unfunded state mandates. Local public employees and construction unions may frequently turn to the state to seek legislation requiring cities and counties to provide their employees and contractor employees with new or more generous benefits or work rules. State elected officials can receive political credit—including the votes and campaign contributions of municipal workers and their families—with their decisions to enhance local government working conditions. At the same time, though, it is hard to deny that local public employment issues raise important state concerns. The state has an interest in the well-being of all its residents, including local public employees. There may be uniformity advantages in having one statewide code dealing with issues like pensions, retirement plans, and health benefits. Municipal labor strife involving public safety officers, firefighters, or sanitation workers can have a significant impact on public health and welfare. As a result, such questions as the hiring, promotion, discipline, and termination of public employees; the application of civil service and merit system rules; levels of compensation and entitlement to fringe benefits; collective bargaining; and conflict-of-interest requirements, disclosure requirements, and restrictions on partisan political activity are the frequent subjects of state legislation, and state-local legal and political conflicts. *See* U.S. Advisory Commission on Intergovernmental Relations, Local Government Authority: Need for State Constitutional, Statutory, and Judicial Clarification 14 (1993).

In *Vista,* the majority gave great weight to the municipality's interest in the projects and the potential cost burden of complying with the state law, but given the statewide construction labor market and the apprenticeship program cited by the dissents and acknowledged by the majority, shouldn't the city's costs have been a factor in deciding whether the state law was reasonably related and narrowly tailored to the state's concerns—in effect, in balancing—rather than the basis for a categorical determination that there was no state interest here at all? As the dissenters point out, many state laws have the effect of increasing local costs, but the California Supreme Court has not invalidated all such laws. What role should the financial impact of a state law on local budgets play in determining whether the state law can be applied to a "municipal affair"?

As the discussions in *Vista* and *Empire State* of earlier decisions by those courts indicate, these are difficult issues and the courts have not been models of consistency. The California Supreme Court has struck down some state laws—*see, e.g.,* Sonoma County Organization of Public Employees v. County of Sonoma, 591 P.2d 1 (Cal. 1979) (invalidating state law that prohibited the distribution of certain state funds to local public agencies that granted their employees cost-of-living increases), County of Riverside v. Superior Court, 66 P.3d 718 (Cal. 2003) (invalidating binding arbitration requirement for contracts with law enforcement and firefighter unions)—and upheld others, *see, e.g.,* People ex rel. Seal Beach Police Officers Ass'n v. City of Seal Beach, 685 P.2d 1145 (Cal. 1984) (sustaining law requiring home rule cities to "meet and confer" with public employee union); Baggett v. Gates, 649 P.2d 874 (Cal. 1982) (upholding application to home rule cities of state mandated procedural protections for public safety officers); Professional Fire Fighters Inc. v. City of Los Angeles, 384 P.2d 168 (Cal. 1963) (sustaining law allowing municipal fire fighters to unionize). Similarly, as *Empire State*'s discussion of the different outcomes in the two *Patrolmen's Benevolent Ass'n* cases, 97 N.Y.2d 378 (2001), 89 N.Y.2d 380 (1996), indicates, state intervention in the municipal collective bargaining relationship has been difficult for the New York court, too. *See also* Jett v. City of Tucson, 882 P.2d 426 (Ariz.1994) (upholding a home rule city's procedures for removing a magistrate on grounds of judicial misconduct, notwithstanding different state rule); Ohio Assoc. of Public School Employees v. Twinsburg, 522 N.E.2d 532 (Ohio 1988) (upholding a home rule ordinance excluding local school districts from the jurisdiction of the state civil service commission). United States Elevator Corp. v. City of Tulsa, 610 P.2d 791 (Okla.1980) (state competitive bidding act does not apply to home rule municipality which has its own competitive bidding procedures for public contracts). *But see* City of Roseburg v. Roseburg City Firefighters, 639 P.2d 90 (Or.1981) (applying state Public Employee Collective Bargaining Act to local governments).

A particularly contested area has been the effort by some local governments to require municipal public employees to reside within the city limits. *Compare* City and County of Denver v. State of Colorado, 788 P.2d 764 (Colo.1990) (invalidating state law banning most municipal public employee residency requirements) *and* Ector v. City of Torrance, 514 P.2d 433 (Cal.1973) (municipal home rule provision governing residency supersedes inconsistent state law) *with* Uniformed Firefighters Ass'n v. City of New York, 50 NY2d 85 (N.Y. 1984) (New York City residency requirement preempted by state law) *and* City of Lima v. State, 909 N.E.2d 616 (Ohio

2009) (municipal residency requirements preempted by state law). *See also* Heather Kerrigan, Wisconsin Reignites the Residency Debate, Governing, March 13, 2013 (Wisconsin to preempt municipal public employee residency requirements).

Imperio home rule provides the possibility that local regulations operating in an area that a court finds to be exclusively local or of mixed state-local interests will be sustained notwithstanding a conflicting state law. NML home rule, with its provision that a locality "may exercise all legislative powers not prohibited by law or by charter" (Alaska Const., Art. X, § 11), "not inconsistent with the laws of the General Assembly" (Iowa Const., Art. III, § 38A), or "not expressly denied by general law or charter" (N.M.Const., Art. 10, § 6(D) would appear to invalidate any local ordinance clearly in conflict with state law. *See, e.g.,* Nevitt v. Langfelder, 623 N.E.2d 281 (Ill.1993) (state's Public Employee Disability Act properly divested city of its local authority); Billings Firefighters Local 521 v. Billings, 694 P.2d 1335 (Mont.1985) (state law expressly precluding local regulation of the municipal employment relationship invalidates local attempt to institute hiring procedures that did not conform to state mandates). In People ex rel. Bernardi v. City of Highland Park, 520 N.E.2d 316 (Ill.1988), the Illinois Supreme Court—which has frequently been supportive of home rule— considered an issue very similar to the one addressed in *Vista*, but came out the other way. *Bernardi* addressed whether a home rule municipality must conform to the state Prevailing Wage Act. The court's opinion emphasized the extra-local effect of local wages: One municipality's decision to pay a lower wage, the court noted, "could profoundly depress the prevailing wage in [the surrounding county] and thereby reduce the earnings of workers outside the home rule unit." *Id.* at 322. But the court also emphasized the state's tradition of a longstanding "comprehensive scheme of governmental intervention in the workplace," *id.,* and the distinctive role of state laws in providing for improved working conditions:

> Adopting the defendants' definition of home rule authority in this case would put at risk all of the State's labor laws and invite increasingly localized definition of workers' rights. Consistent with the defendants' arguments, home rule units could condone 12-hour work days, suspend minimum-wage requirements and repeal child-labor laws within their jurisdictions. In those cases, as in many others, superseding local regulation would be justified as affecting only local industries and workers. * * *

> Were home rule authorities allowed to govern their local labor conditions, the Constitution's vision of home rule units exercising their powers to solve local problems would be corrupted and that power used to create a confederation of modern feudal estates which, to placate local economic and political expediencies, would in time destroy the General Assembly's carefully crafted and balanced economic policies. It is precisely for this reason, to avoid a chaotic and ultimately ineffective labor policy, that the State has a far more

vital interest in regulating labor conditions than do local communities. The disintegration of uniform labor rights and standards under State law would certainly follow the breakup of State monopoly in this field, and it is doubtful whether local units of government could agree upon statewide labor policies that would bring to Illinois the benefits of a well-compensated and skilled labor force. * * *

520 N.E.2d at 322–23.

3. *Should There Be a Preference for the State?* Justice Linde in *LaGrande,* Justice Liu dissenting in *Vista,* and the Illinois Supreme Court in *Bernardi* all gave reasons for generally preferring the state over the local. Justice Linde referred to the state's interests in all its inhabitants, including city residents and employees. Justice Liu gave the political argument that "charter cities could still bring their complaints to the Legislature through the ordinary political process, and it seems at least plausible that state legislators would be attentive to the concerns of local officials on whom they often depend for political support." The Bernardi court expressed concern about the impact of "local economic and political expediencies" on labor rights. Are these arguments—or any of them—persuasive for placing a thumb on the scale in close cases in favor of the state?

4. *A Tenth Amendment Parallel.* In National League of Cities v. Usery, 426 U.S. 833 (1976), and Garcia v. San Antonio Metropolitan Transit Authority, 469 U.S. 528 (1985), the United States Supreme Court addressed challenges to the applicability of federal labor laws to state and local government personnel. The Court's difficulty in determining the extent to which Congress should be constrained in enacting legislation in derogation of state autonomy is quite similar to the state courts' attempts to fashion a line between permissible state regulation of the public employees of home rule units and impermissible state interference with municipal control over its own personnel.

JOHNSON V. BRADLEY

Supreme Court of California
841 P.2d 990 (1992)

LUCAS, CHIEF JUSTICE.

In June 1988, State Assemblyman Ross Johnson and State Senator Quentin Kopp (two of the three petitioners in this action) successfully sponsored a statewide initiative, Proposition 73, which added chapter 5 to the Political Reform Act of 1974 (Gov.Code, §§ 81000–91015). Article 3 of chapter 5, entitled "Contribution Limitations," imposed various restrictions on contributions to and by candidates and political committees or parties (§§ 85301–85307), and also provided in section 85300: "No public officer shall expend and no candidate shall accept any public moneys for the purpose of seeking elective office."

Two years later, the voters of the City of Los Angeles amended the city charter by adopting Measure H, a comprehensive campaign, election and ethics reform plan. Measure H provided for: (i) the creation of a city ethics commission to oversee, administer, and enforce the new ethics code; (ii) limitations on campaign contributions; (iii) limitations on the total amount of contributions that a candidate may accept in any election; * * * partial public funding of city political campaigns, and, correspondingly, spending limits on candidates who accept public funds. * * * As codified, this provision is now found in section 313 of the Los Angeles City Charter (hereafter charter section 313).

Subdivision A of charter section 313 sets out "Findings and Purposes." It states: "1. Monetary contributions to political campaigns are a legitimate form of participation in the American political process, but the financial strength of certain individuals or organizations should not permit them to exercise a disproportionate or controlling influence on the election of candidates. [¶] 2. Therefore, this section is enacted to accomplish the following purposes: [¶] (a) To assist serious candidates in raising enough money to communicate their views and positions adequately to the public without excessive expenditures or contributions, thereby promoting public discussion of the important issues involved in political campaigns. [¶] (b) To limit overall expenditures in campaigns, thereby reducing the pressure on candidates to raise large campaign funds for defensive purposes, beyond the amount necessary to communicate reasonably with the voters. [¶] (c) To provide a source of campaign financing in the form of limited public matching funds. [¶] (d) To substantially restrict fund-raising in non-election years. [¶] (e) To increase the value to candidates of smaller contributions. [¶] (f) To reduce the excessive fund-raising advantage of incumbents and thus encourage competition for elective office. [¶] (g) To help restore public trust in governmental and electoral institutions."

Subdivision B of charter section 313 provides for establishment of spending limitations and disbursement of matching funds. It states in relevant part, "The City shall . . . adopt by ordinance limitations on campaign expenditures by candidates for elective City office who qualify for and accept public matching funds. The City shall adopt by ordinance regulations concerning the use of public funds to partially finance campaigns for elective City office through a system of matching public funds for qualifying campaign contributions. . . ." Subdivision C(4) of charter section 313 provides, "[t]he funds used to make payments for matching funds shall come exclusively from City sources of revenues." * * *

Article XI, section 5 of the state Constitution (hereafter article XI, section 5) addresses the "home rule" powers of charter cities in two distinct subdivisions. Subdivision (a) sets out the general principle of local self-governance, and provides: "It shall be competent in any city charter to provide that the city governed thereunder may *make and enforce all ordinances and regulations in respect to municipal affairs,* subject only to the restrictions and limitations provided in their several charters and in respect to other matters they should be subject to general laws. City charters adopted pursuant to this Constitution shall supersede any existing charter, and with respect to municipal affairs shall supersede all laws inconsistent therewith." (Id., subd. (a), italics added.)

Whereas subdivision (a) of article XI, section 5, articulates the general principle of self-governance, subdivision (b) sets out a nonexclusive list of four "core" categories that are, by definition, "municipal affairs." The first three categories of municipal affairs are: (1) regulation, etc., of "the city police force"; (2) "subgovernment in all or part of a city"; and (3) "conduct of city elections." The final category gives charter cities exclusive power to regulate the "manner" of electing "municipal officers." It provides, "(4) *plenary authority* is hereby granted, subject only to the restrictions of this article, to provide [in all city charters for] *the manner in which,* the method by which, the times at which, and the terms for which *the several municipal officers . . . shall be elected. . . .*" (Italics added.)

* * * Respondents and amici curiae on their behalf focus initially on subdivision (b)(4) of article XI, section 5. They assert charter section 313 is a regulation concerning the "manner" by which municipal officers are elected, and thus it is by definition a core municipal affair over which the city may exercise "plenary authority" to the exclusion of all general laws. * * * We are hesitant, however, to embrace the expansive view of article XI, section 5, subdivision (b)(4), advanced by respondents and their amici curiae. They assert, with some force, that partial public financing of municipal election campaigns is "one way to elect municipal officials," although it is "certainly . . . not the only 'manner' in which to do so." They reason that under the plain words of article XI, section 5, subdivision (b)(4), partial public funding of local campaigns, being a "manner" of municipal elections, is a subject within the city's plenary regulatory authority that falls within the core definition of a "municipal affair" under that constitutional provision. Although we believe charter section 313 clearly "implicates" a municipal affair, we need not, and do not, determine whether charter section 313 is by definition a "core" municipal affair under article XI, section 5, subdivision (b)(4), because we conclude that in any event, the charter section is enforceable as a municipal affair under article XI, section 5, subdivision (a). * * *

* * * [T]he voters' intent that a matter be treated on a statewide basis does not make that matter a statewide concern. Furthermore, the bare interest of "uniformity in the manner of electing officials" is no justification for treating public funding of municipal elections as a

statewide concern, because, standing alone, it reveals no "convincing basis for legislative action originating in extramunicipal concerns." In their effort to identify a statewide concern, petitioners advance various arguments relating to fiscal matters. First, they point to ballot arguments advising the voters that "too much money is being spent on political campaigns today." From these and other ballot statements, petitioners conclude the electorate was "clearly informed Proposition 73's aim was reducing the costs of political campaigns through a system of contribution limitations and prohibition on public funding." In other words, they identify as a statewide concern the protection of the public fisc.

We do not doubt that conservation of the *state's* limited funds is a statewide concern. But petitioners, understandably, do not attempt to justify the public funding ban on the ground that it is designed to protect state revenues, because a local public funding law that draws its revenues exclusively from local taxes would obviously not implicate a concern for protecting the state fisc. Instead, petitioners suggest there is a legitimate statewide concern in how local tax proceeds are expended.

On this point, we agree with the Court of Appeal below, which observed, "[W]e can think of nothing that is of greater municipal concern than how a city's tax dollars will be spent; nor anything which could be of less interest to taxpayers of other jurisdictions. [Charter section 313, subdivision (C)4] expressly limit[s] the monies to be utilized for campaign financing to city funds. Thus, payments received by the city from state or federal governmental agencies may not be used. These are the city taxpayers' own dollars and those taxpayers, together with their city council, have voted to utilize those dollars to help finance political campaigns for city elective offices as a central if not critical part of major political campaign and ethics reform. That Proposition 73 expressly dealt with this subject and intended that its prohibition extend to campaigns and candidates for local office does not convert the decision of the City of Los Angeles, to follow a different path with its own money, into a matter of statewide concern."

* * * Finally, petitioners assert: (i) the "integrity of the electoral process" is itself a statewide concern; (ii) section 85300's ban on public funding of election campaigns is reasonably calculated to resolve that statewide concern; and (iii) therefore section 85300 addresses a statewide concern.

We have no reason to doubt petitioners' major premise; the integrity of the electoral process, at both the state and local level, is undoubtedly a statewide concern. The basis for this conclusion was well stated in an Attorney General opinion in 1960, in support of a conclusion that a charter city candidate is obligated to comply with statewide campaign financial disclosure provisions:

"Purity of all elections is a matter of statewide concern, not just a municipal affair. . . . The Legislature . . . has found that it is in the public interest that full and detailed disclosure be made of all contributions and expenditures in election campaigns. It has pointed out that such disclosure had a strong tendency to discourage excessive contributions and corrupt contributions. . . . [¶] So important is the independence and integrity of all elected officials that the reporting of campaign receipts and disbursements is the concern of the entire state as well as of the local communities [citations]. Elected officials of the various municipalities chartered and non-chartered throughout the state of California exercise a substantial amount of executive and legislative power over the people of the state of California, and this legislation aimed at obtaining the election of persons free from domination by self-seeking individuals or pressure groups is a matter of statewide concern." (35 Ops.Cal.Atty.Gen. 230, 231–232 (1960).)

Although we accept petitioners' major premise, we question their minor premise, that section 85300's ban on public financing of election campaigns is reasonably calculated to address the statewide concern regarding the integrity of the electoral process. * * *

Petitioners cite nothing to support the proposition that section 85300's ban on public funding of political campaigns advances in any way the goal of enhancing the integrity of the electoral process. In fact, the opposite appears to be true. As the high court observed in *Buckley v. Valeo, supra,* 424 U.S. 1, 96 S.Ct. 612, 46 L.Ed.2d 659, concerning the federal "matching funds" program for Presidential candidates, "It cannot be gainsaid that public financing as a means of eliminating improper influence of large private contributions furthers a significant governmental interest. S.Rep. No. 93–689, pp. 4–5 (1974) [1974 U.S.Code Cong. & Admin.News, pp. 5590–5591]. In addition, the limits on contributions necessarily increase the burden of fundraising, and Congress properly regarded public financing as an appropriate means of relieving major-party Presidential candidates from the rigors of soliciting private contributions." * * *

The Court of Appeal below agreed: "[T]he use of public funds for campaign financing will not, almost by definition, have a corrupting influence. [Instead] . . . it seems obvious that public money reduces rather than increases the fund raising pressures on public office seekers and thereby reduces the undue influence of special interest groups. . . . [Moreover], the goals of campaign reform and reduction of election costs, including the reduction of the influence of special interest groups and large contributors, is in no way embarrassed by public financing. To the contrary, those goals can only be furthered. . . ."

To these observations we add the following. As explained above, the drafters of the Los Angeles charter amendment sought to create a measure that regulated not only campaign *contributions* (like Proposition 73), but that also imposed limits on *spending* by candidates. The drafters apparently realized that under *Buckley v. Valeo, supra,* 424 U.S. 1, 96 S.Ct. 612, spending limitations may not be imposed unless public financing is offered to and accepted by a candidate. (*Id.,* at pp. 54–59, 96 S.Ct. at pp. 651–54; see especially *id.,* at p. 57, fn. 65, 96 S.Ct. at p. 653, fn. 65.) Accordingly, it appears the drafters provided for partial public financing of campaigns so that they could impose spending limitations consistently with *Buckley v. Valeo, supra.* It follows that, assuming spending limitations may enhance the integrity of the electoral process, a ban on public funding would actually frustrate achievement of that goal.

For all of the above reasons, we conclude section 85300 is not reasonably related to the statewide concern of enhancing the integrity of the electoral process. Having reached this conclusion, we need not address whether the statute is also narrowly tailored to avoid unnecessary incursion into legitimate areas of local concern.

GREATER NEW YORK TAXI ASSOCIATION V. STATE
Court of Appeals of New York
21 N.Y.3d 289 (2013)

PIGOTT, J.

At issue on this appeal is the constitutionality of chapter 602 of the Laws of 2011, as amended by chapter 9 of the Laws of 2012 ("HAIL Act"), which regulates medallion taxicabs (or "yellow cabs") and livery vehicles, vital parts of New York City's transportation system. The Act's stated aim is to address certain mobility deficiencies in the City of New York, namely: the lack of accessible vehicles for residents and nonresidents with disabilities; the dearth of available yellow cabs in the four boroughs outside Manhattan ("outer boroughs"), where residents and nonresidents must instead rely on livery vehicles; and the sparse availability of yellow cab service outside Manhattan's central business district and the two Queens airports, locations where close to 95% of yellow cabs pick up their customers.

I

* * * Yellow cabs operate under a transferable license or medallion, which is a numbered plate issued by the [New York City Taxi & Limousine Commission] TLC that is affixed to the outside of a taxicab as physical evidence that the taxicab has been licensed to operate as a medallion taxicab. These cabs are metered vehicles that must charge uniform rates Y. They possess the exclusive right to pick up passengers pursuant to street "hails" from any location in the City. * * *

In 1956, the New York State Legislature delegated to the City Council the discretionary authority to register, license and limit the number of yellow cabs, and to establish ordinances and regulations regulating parking and passenger pick-up and discharges. Prior to 1996, the City Council had capped the number of medallions that the TLC was permitted to issue at 11,787. Between 1996 and 2008, the City Council approved the issuance of 1,450 additional medallions, resulting in a total of 13,237. Given the limited supply of medallions, their value has increased yearly and the competition for obtaining one is fierce. Moreover, according to the TLC, out of the 13,237 issued medallions, only 231 are cabs that are accessible to people with disabilities.

In contrast to yellow cabs, livery vehicles are prohibited from picking up street hails and may accept passengers only on the basis of telephone contract or other prearrangement. * * * However, this has not prevented some livery vehicles from illegally accepting street hails, where the price of the fare is not regulated. * * *

II

Enacted by the New York State Legislature in the latter part of 2011 and the early part of 2012, the HAIL Act creates, among other things, a "HAIL License Program" that calls for the TLC to issue 18,000 "Hail Accessible Inter-borough Licenses" allowing "for-hire vehicles," i.e., livery vehicles, to accept street hails in the outer boroughs and those areas in Manhattan outside its central business district (HAIL Act §§ 4[b]; 5 [a]). TLC-licensed yellow cabs retain "the exclusive right ... to pick up passengers via street hail in such areas of the city of New York wherein HAIL license holders are prohibited from accepting such passengers." The Act demarcates these areas—Manhattan's central business district and the two Queens airports—as the "HAIL Exclusionary Zone".

* * * The Act calls for HAIL licenses to be distributed in increments of 6,000 over three years, with 20% of the first 6,000 earmarked for accessible vehicles. * * *

III

Plaintiffs, who are medallion owners and their representatives, an association of credit union lenders and credit unions that finance medallion purchases, and a member of the New York City Council, challenge the HAIL Act on the ground that regulation of yellow cab and livery enterprises has always been a matter of local concern. All plaintiffs claim that the Act violates N.Y. Constitution, article IX, § 2(b)(2) ("Municipal Home Rule Clause"). * * *

IV

The Municipal Home Rule Clause grants local governments considerable independence relative to local concerns. Just as there are affairs that are exclusively those of the State, "[t]here are some affairs intimately connected with the exercise by the city of its corporate functions, which are city affairs only" (*Adler v. Deegan,* 251 N.Y. 467, 489, 167 N.E. 705 [1929, Cardozo, Ch. J., concurring]). Nonetheless, " [a] zone . . . exists . . . where State and city concerns overlap and intermingle" (*id.*).

Enacted to protect the autonomy of local governments, the Municipal Home Rule Clause allows the legislature to

> "act in relation to the property, affairs or government of any local government only by general law, or by special law only (a) on request of two-thirds of the total membership of its legislative body or on request of its chief executive officer concurred in by a majority of such membership" (N.Y. Const., art. IX, § 2[b][2]).

Subdivision (a)'s directives are commonly referred to as the "home rule message" requirement because whenever a special law is enacted, it should be at the locality's request.

As plaintiffs point out, the HAIL Act is a special law, i.e., it is a law that "in terms and in effect applies to one or more, but not all . . . cities." Although the Municipal Home Rule Clause could be read to direct that a home rule message was required before the Act's enactment, there is an exception to that requirement where the State possesses a "substantial interest" in the subject matter and "the enactment . . . bear[s] a reasonable relationship to the legitimate, accompanying substantial State concern." * * * The latter requirement serves "as a corollary to the constitutional balancing of overlapping local and state interests requiring that the 'subjects of State concern [be] *directly* and substantially involved' "

Plaintiffs challenge the Act on the ground that the State lacks a substantial interest in the regulation of the yellow cab and livery enterprises in the City, claiming that such regulation has historically been within the province of the City itself. Although the State has delegated certain powers to the City Council concerning the regulation of yellow cabs, that does not mean that it has surrendered its authority to regulate in that area, particularly where the proposed regulation promotes a substantial state interest.

Our review concerning what constitutes a substantial state interest is not dependent on what historically has been the domain of a given locality. Rather, our determination is dependent on the "stated purpose and legislative history of the act in question."

In the cases where we have found a special law to be unconstitutional, we have done so, in part, because the legislation failed to identify a substantial state interest and/or the legislative history did not support the State's reason for enacting it.

We conclude that the HAIL Act addresses a matter of substantial state concern. This is not a purely local issue. Millions of people from within and without the State visit the City annually. Some of these visitors are disabled, and will undoubtably benefit from the increase in accessible vehicles in the Manhattan central business district and in the outer boroughs. The Act is for the benefit of all New Yorkers, and not merely those residing within the City. Efficient transportation service in the State's largest city and international center of commerce is important to the entire State. The Act plainly furthers all of these significant goals.

Section one of the Act explains "that the public health, safety and welfare of the residents of the state of New York *traveling to, from and within* the city of New York is a matter of substantial state concern, including access to safe and reliable mass transportation such as taxicabs" (HAIL Act § 1 [emphasis supplied]). The Act is aimed at accommodating able-bodied and disabled residents and nonresidents of the City who "do not currently have sufficient access to legal, licensed taxicabs available for street hails." Specifically as it relates to residents and nonresidents with disabilities, the legislature concluded that only 1.8% of yellow cabs are accessible, and that an even smaller percentage of the approximately 23,000 livery vehicles are so equipped. The lack of accessible yellow cabs and livery vehicles impacts residents and nonresidents by "inhibit[ing] their basic daily activities" and preventing them "from being able to rely on the street hail system to get to a destination quickly, particularly in an emergency, or to travel to a location not near a subway or bus stop" (*id.*). Thus, it cannot be said that the legislature has offered only "speculative assertions" concerning the "possible State-wide implications of the subject matter."

Plaintiffs find significance in the fact that in the years between 1996 and 2008 when the New York State legislature approved the issuance of 1,450 new medallions, it did so only after the City Council issued a home rule message requesting such an increase. However, the fact that the legislature has previously entertained home rule messages in this field "is not determinative of the issue before us—whether such messages were constitutionally required." Indeed, that the City Council must make a request to the legislature in order to issue and sell new medallions at a market rate only underscores that the State has an interest in the regulation of yellow cab services.

As its sponsor explained, the Act's purpose is to "allow the City to implement a taxi plan that will more effectively service all five boroughs of New York City and greatly increase the availability of accessible taxicabs and for-hire vehicles." The issues the Act addresses are the lack of yellow cabs within the Manhattan central business district that are accessible to the disabled and the general shortage of available yellow cab and livery vehicle transportation in underserved areas of the city, i.e., outside Manhattan's central business district and the two airports.

Plaintiffs next assert that the stated reasons for the Act's enactment must be viewed skeptically because it was not enacted until after negotiations broke down between the Mayor and City Council concerning the increase in taxicab and livery vehicle service in the underserved areas. However, we need not speculate on the legislature's motives "as a judicial construct for statutory analysis" and, instead, must direct our attention to whether the legislature acted within its constitutional purview in passing the legislation. To that end, we conclude that the Act addresses a substantial state interest.

That does not end the inquiry, however, because in order to be upheld as constitutional, the Act must "bear a reasonable relationship" to that state concern. * * * We conclude that a reasonable relationship exists. The Act consists of a series of interlocking provisions to address its stated purposes. The potential issuance of 18,000 HAIL licenses, dispersed in equal amounts over three years, will allow livery vehicles to legally accept street hails from residents and nonresidents in the outer boroughs and in Manhattan outside its central business district. That 20% of the first 6,000 HAIL licenses must be earmarked for accessible vehicles advances the state interest in providing street hail vehicles in those areas for residents and visitors with disabilities. To ensure that the market does not become saturated, the Act gives the TLC the authority to issue an additional 12,000 HAIL licenses once it conducts a market analysis to determine whether the issuance of additional HAIL licenses is necessary. Furthering the legislature's goals, the Act also allows HAIL licensees to apply for grants that will enable them to either purchase accessible vehicles or retrofit existing vehicles to meet the accessibility requirements.

Addressing the legislative finding concerning the lack of accessible yellow cabs in Manhattan's central business district, the Act permits the Mayor to "administratively authorize" the TLC, an executive branch commission, to publicly sell up to 2,000 additional medallions that are restricted to accessible yellow cabs operating within zones where HAIL licensees are prohibited from accepting street hails (HAIL Act § 8). Only 400 of these medallions may be issued initially, with the remainder being issued only after the New York State Department of Transportation approves the Disabled Accessibility Plan as set forth in section 10 of the Act. Construed together, the Act's provisions bear a reasonable relationship to a substantial state interest.

Plaintiffs assert that the Act does not satisfy the "reasonable relationship" prong, claiming that it "eviscerates" the City's separation of powers by transferring to the Mayor the authority to issue up to 2,000 new medallions, and intrudes upon the City's budgeting authority to the extent that it allows the TLC to award $54 million in grants to HAIL licensees without giving the City Council any input as to how much money should be appropriated. * * *

Section 8 of the Act does not "transfer" any of the City Council's powers to the Mayor. Rather, it allows the Mayor to "administratively authorize the TLC" to issue "by public sale" up to 2,000 medallions. This is merely an implementation device and it does not encroach on the City Council's authority under section 2303(b)(4) of the New York City Charter to issue additional taxicab licenses. As the governing body that passed this Act, it was within the state legislature's purview to delegate a portion of the Act's implementation to the Mayor, whose administrative authorization of the sale of the medallions advances a legitimate goal of this law, by securing accessible vehicles where they are needed most. Therefore, section 8 bears a reasonable relationship to the substantial state interest of increasing the supply of accessible yellow cabs.

It also cannot be reasonably argued that section 9's requirement calling for the TLC's establishment of a grant program to distribute up to $54 million in grants for the purchase or retrofitting of accessible HAIL vehicles interferes with the City Council's "power of the purse." First, the requirement furthers the substantial state interest in providing accessible yellow cabs and livery vehicles and bears a reasonable relationship to those goals. Second, the Act does not direct the Mayor to include these grants in the TLC budget, nor does it direct the City Council to appropriate funds to support such grants. Third, the Act purports to raise revenue through the HAIL licensing fees and the potential auctioning off of the medallions, which may presumably offset the up to $54 million in grant money.

Plainly, not only does the Act, including its challenged provisions, address substantial state concerns, but it also "bear[s] a reasonable relationship" to those concerns.

NOTES AND QUESTIONS

1. *Home Rule and the Structure of Local Government.* In *La Grande,* the Oregon Supreme Court said that while it would allow the state to prevail on questions involving substantive social, economic or other regulatory policies, it would engage in more vigorous review of state laws that affect the "structure and procedures of local agencies." Indeed, state courts have on occasion indicated that the structure of local governments and the procedures for staffing them are not simply proper objects of "local" legislation, but are also immune from inconsistent state laws. Some courts have been willing to

give their local governments considerable freedom to depart from state rules governing local government organization. Thus, in City of Tucson v. State, 273 P.2d 624 (Ariz. 2012) the Arizona Supreme Court held that Tucson was not bound by an Arizona statute barring cities from electing their city councils in partisan elections or in ward-based primaries combined with an at-large general election. The court emphasized that "whatever the general difficulties in identifying matters of local concern," it is "absolutely clear that charter city governments"—that is, the cities with populations of 3,500 or more that under the state constitution are authorized to adopt home rule charters—"enjoy autonomy with respect to structuring their own governments." *Id.* at 630. The court acknowledged that the legislature had declared that "the conduct of elections . . . is a matter of statewide concern," but concluded that "whether state law prevails over conflicting charter provisions . . . is a question of constitutional interpretation." The court also assumed that "some aspects of the conduct of local elections may be of statewide concern," such as requiring a uniform date for municipal elections and "other administrative aspects of elections," but found that those are matters "qualitatively different from determining how a city will constitute its governing council." *Id.* Similarly, in Telli v. Broward Co., 94 So.2d 504 (Fla. 2012), the Florida Supreme Court held that Florida counties may adopt term limits for the office of county commissioner. Even though term limits were not clearly authorized by the state constitution and even arguably inconsistent with the otherwise exclusive list in the constitution of disqualifications from holding office, the court concluded that "the ability of counties to govern themselves" under the "broad authority [that] has been granted to them by home rule power through the Florida Constitution" required recognition of the power of counties to adopt term limits for county officers. *Accord*, Kole v. Faultless, 963 N.E.2d 493 (Ind. 2012) (town may reorganize into a city with a council elected entirely at-large and a mayor appointed by the council, even though statute provides that a city is to have an elected mayor and a council elected by districts); Lafourche Parish Council v. Autin, 648 So.2d 343 (La.1994) (home rule unit not covered by state regulation of local boards and commissions); Windham Taxpayers Association v. Board of Selectmen of Windham, 662 A.2d 1281 (Conn.1995) (procedures for local appropriations are of local concern and not subject to general state law); State ex rel. Haynes v. Bonem, 845 P.2d 150 (N.M.1992) (local law concerning size of city commission displaces inconsistent state law); Resnick v. County of Ulster, 376 N.E.2d 1271 (N.Y. 1978) (sustaining county procedure for filling vacancies in county office despite conflict with state law).

2.   *The State Interest and the "Reasonably Related" Requirement.* In *Johnson,* the Court found that the integrity of the political process is a statewide concern. What exactly is the state's interest in the integrity of a *local* political process? Provided that local elections abide by federal and state constitutional norms, why isn't the interest in local political integrity adequately taken care of by the local political process? Why should the state be able to change otherwise constitutional local election rules? Conversely, assuming there is a state interest in local political integrity, why isn't a ban

on public funding reasonably related to that end? The Court assumes that public funding of candidates promotes political integrity, but is it appropriate for the Court to make such a substantive judgment? The state ban on the public funding of candidates was adopted as a result of a voter initiative, so there were no legislative findings justifying the provisions of Proposition 73. But if the restriction had been adopted by the legislature, and if the legislature had determined that public funding was inconsistent with "political integrity" because it gives government a role in deciding which candidates are eligible for public funds, should a court second guess that judgment?

3.   *Law and Politics.* In *Greater New York Taxi Association,* the legislature not only acted with respect to a matter of intense local concern that had traditionally been left to the local government but also intervened in the internal structure of New York City's government with respect to the issuance of new taxi medallions. What was the state's interest, and how were these measures reasonably related to that interest? As the court's brief reference to the breakdown of negotiations between the Mayor and the Council indicates, the state's law grew out of an internal conflict within New York City's government between the Mayor and Council over the regulation of taxis and livery cars. The Mayor lost the battle at the City government level, but was able to outflank the Council and get his measure approved by the state legislature. From a home rule perspective, does this make it easier to accept the state's action as it was essentially an initiative from the City government? Or is it harder, since this was essentially the state intruding directly into an internal City conflict? Or is it irrelevant, if you agree with the court that, given the millions of visitors from the state and elsewhere who visit New York City every year and the City's position as "the State's largest city and international center of commerce," the quality of taxi and livery cab service in New York City is "important to the entire State"?

The political backdrop to *Greater New York Taxi* is a reminder that some state-local legal conflicts are not truly state-local conflicts at all, but may be conflicts among local-level interests, with the local loser going to the state or invoking state law to try to overturn the local decision. In New York City, this happened a number of times during the mayoralty of Michael Bloomberg, a Republican-turned-independent mayor who had to deal with a lopsidedly Democratic council. In addition to turning to the state legislature in the taxi regulation fight that led to *Greater New York Taxi,* the mayor frequently went to court to claim that legislation passed by the city council was preempted by state law. *See, e.g.,* Mayor of the City of New York v. Council of the City of New York, 9 N.Y.3d 23 (N.Y. 2007) (mayor loses claim that law passed over his veto concerning collective bargaining status of certain city employees was preempted by state law); Council of the City of New York v. Mayor of the City of New York, 6 N.Y.3d 380 (2006) (City's Equal Benefits Law, passed over mayoral veto, which would have prohibited city agencies from contracting with firms that failed to provide domestic partners of employees with benefits equal to those provided to employee spouses, held preempted by state law); Mayor of the City of New York v. Council of City of New York, 780 N.Y.S.2d 266 (Sup. Ct. N.Y. Co. 2004) (mayor prevails on claim that law passed over his veto that would prohibit city from doing business with financial firms that engage in predatory lending is preempted). Although it may seem odd for the mayor to go against the home rule authority of his own city, these cases demonstrate that home rule disputes concern not only the principle of local autonomy but the substantive policies pursued by the state and city and the sometimes conflicting political interests of state and city leaders and key interest groups.

4.   *Local Campaign Finance Regulation.* Los Angeles is not the only city to have adopted its own law providing public financing to municipal election candidates. As of 2011, sixteen local governments had adopted programs to provide public financing for candidates in local elections. The largest and oldest of these is New York City's program, which was enacted in 1988, and includes contribution limitations, disclosure requirements, and significant partial public funding (on a matching funds basis) for participating municipal candidates. Other localities that provide public funding for candidates include Austin, Texas; Boulder, Colorado; Long Beach, Oakland, and San Francisco, California; Albuquerque, New Mexico; and Tucson, Arizona. *See* Robert M. Stern, Public Financing in the States and Municipalities, in Costas Panagopoulos, ed., Public Financing in American Elections (Temple Univ. Press 2011). In its 2015 municipal elections, Los Angeles provided eligible candidates with $1.3 million in public funds; candidates raised an additional $6 million in private contributions. In the 2013 elections, which included races for mayor and other city-wide offices, the city provided $9.7 million in public funds, compared with $32.9 million the candidates raised privately. In addition to public financing, more than 130 cities and counties have adopted some form of campaign finance regulation for local elections, such as contribution restrictions or disclosure rules. *See* National Civic League, Local Campaign Finance Reform, www.ncl.org/. *See also* McDonald v. New York City Campaign Finance Bd., 965 N.Y.S.2d 811 (Sup. Ct. N.Y. Co. 2013) (upholding City's contribution limits for candidates for municipal office; even though the City's limits were lower than those provided by state law for municipal elections, the City's limits were not preempted); Nutter v. Dougherty, 938 A.2d 401 (Pa. 2007) (upholding Philadelphia's contribution limits for candidates for municipal office against claim that ordinance was preempted by state law that regulated campaign finances but did not establish contribution limits).

D. PREEMPTION

GOODELL V. HUMBOLDT COUNTY
Supreme Court of Iowa
575 N.W.2d 486 (1998)

TERNUS, JUSTICE.

The regulation of livestock confinement operations is a matter of growing public debate in this state. In the case before us, livestock producers have challenged four ordinances adopted by the Humboldt County Board of Supervisors that regulate large livestock confinement facilities and operations. The plaintiffs claim the ordinances are invalid because they address a matter of statewide concern, and because the county's authority has been preempted by the Iowa legislature. The defendants seek to sustain the validity of the ordinances as a valid exercise of the county's home rule authority. The district court upheld all but one section of one ordinance. * * *

I.   BACKGROUND FACTS AND PROCEEDINGS.

A.   The ordinances. In October of 1996, the Humboldt County Board of Supervisors adopted four ordinances applicable to "large livestock confinement feeding facilities."[1] Each ordinance addresses a different matter of concern to the county: (1) ordinance 22 imposes a permit requirement prior to construction or operation of a regulated facility; (2) ordinance 23 establishes financial security requirements; (3) ordinance 24 implements groundwater protection policies; and (4) ordinance 25 governs toxic air emissions from regulated facilities. * * *

1.   Ordinance 22—permit requirement. Ordinance 22 requires any person who desires to construct a large livestock confinement feeding facility to obtain a "notice of construction or operation" before construction or operation of the facility commences. The owner or operator of the proposed facility must file a completed application with the Humboldt County auditor containing the following information: (1) a blueprint of the facility; (2) a statement of manure management, including a manure disposal plan; (3) the parties who will supervise the construction and initial operation of the facility; (4) a plan for runoff management; (5) identification of agricultural drainage tile lines and the remedial measures to be taken to protect their integrity; and (6)

---

[1]   The term "large livestock confinement feeding facility" is defined identically in all four ordinances . . . [as] a livestock feeding operation in which the animal weight capacity is:

    a) for cattle, more than 500,000 pounds

    b) for swine, more than 300,000 pounds

    c) for chickens, more than 300,000 pounds

    d) for turkeys, more than 500,000 pounds and where the livestock are or can be confined to areas which are totally roofed.

identification of agricultural drainage wells, natural sinkholes, artificial open drainage ditches, ponds, streams, lakes, marshlands, and quarries that may be affected by the new building.

The auditor is required to forward the application to the Humboldt County environmental protection officer. If the application is complete, the environmental protection officer conducts an independent investigation to ensure the proposed facility "complies with all applicable statutes, ordinances, and regulations." Once the environmental protection officer concludes the facility complies, the application is forwarded to the county board of supervisors; at the same time, neighboring property owners are also informed of the pending application. After a thirty-day period for public comment, the board must issue a permit if the requirements of the ordinance have been satisfied. * * *

B.   The lawsuit. This litigation is the consolidation of two actions for declaratory judgment that challenged the county's ordinances. [The trial court granted summary judgment, invalidating Article 1 of Ordinance 25, but upholding the rest of Ordinance 25 and all other ordinances.]* * *

III. HOME RULE AUTHORITY AND PREEMPTION.

* * * Under [Iowa's constitutional grant of home rule authority], counties have the power "to determine their local affairs and government," but only to the extent those determinations are "not inconsistent with the laws of the general assembly." [Iowa Const. art. III, § 39A.] * * *

A.   County home rule authority. The constitutional parameters of county home rule are echoed in chapter 331 of the Iowa Code. Section 331.301 sets forth the general scope of a county's power and its limitations:

> A county may, except as expressly limited by the Constitution, and if not inconsistent with the laws of the general assembly, exercise any power and perform any function it deems appropriate to protect and preserve the rights, privileges, and property of the county or of its residents, and to preserve and improve the peace, safety, health, welfare, comfort, and convenience of its residents.

Iowa Code § 331.301(1). Pursuant to this provision, counties now have the authority to act "unless a particular power has been denied them by statute."

The concept of home rule envisions the possibility that state and local governments will regulate in the same area:

> A county shall not set standards and requirements which are lower or less stringent than those imposed by state law, but may

set standards and requirements which are higher or more stringent than those imposed by state law, unless a state law provides otherwise.

Iowa Code § 331.301(6). * * *

B.   Preemption. Preemption may be express or implied. Both forms of preemption find their source in the constitution's prohibition of the exercise of a home rule power "inconsistent with the laws of the general assembly." Iowa Const. art. III, § 39A . . . Chapter 331 further defines this limitation: "An exercise of a county power is not inconsistent with a state law unless it is irreconcilable with the state law." Iowa Code § 331.301(4).

1.   Express preemption. Express preemption occurs when the general assembly has specifically prohibited local action in an area. * * * Obviously, any local law that regulates in an area the legislature has specifically stated cannot be the subject of local action is irreconcilable with state law.

2.   Implied preemption. Implied preemption occurs in two ways. When an ordinance " 'prohibits an act permitted by a statute, or permits an act prohibited by a statute,' " the ordinance is considered inconsistent with state law and preempted. * * *

Implied preemption may also occur when the legislature has "cover [ed] a subject by statutes in such a manner as to demonstrate a legislative intention that the field is preempted by state law." * * * As we discuss in greater detail below, Iowa law requires some legislative expression of an intent to preempt home rule authority, or some legislative statement of the state's transcendent interest in regulating the area in a uniform manner. This approach is consistent with the legislature's statement in chapter 331 that "[a] county may exercise its general powers subject *only* to limitations *expressly imposed* by a state law." Iowa Code § 331.301(3) (emphasis added); *accord Gruen*, 457 N.W.2d at 343 ("Limitations on a municipality's power over local affairs are not implied; they must be imposed by the legislature.").

We turn now to the specific issues before us in this appeal. * * *

VI.   EXPRESS PREEMPTION—DO THE ORDINANCES CONSTITUTE INVALID
       COUNTY ZONING OF AGRICULTURAL LAND AND STRUCTURES?

A.   County zoning authority. Iowa Code chapter 335 establishes general zoning authority for counties, the scope of such authority, and the procedures for exercising that authority. *See* generally Iowa Code ch. 335. One limitation on the county's zoning power is the express preemption of county zoning of agricultural land and structures:

[N]o ordinance adopted under this chapter applies to land, farm houses, farm barns, farm outbuildings or other buildings or structures which are primarily adapted, by reason of nature and area, for use for agricultural purposes, while so used.

Id. § 335.2. Although the act containing this provision did not state the purpose of the exemption, a predecessor bill having the same exemption asserted that the agricultural exception to county zoning was "intended as a protection for the farmer and his investment in his land." * * *

The parties agree the ordinances enacted by Humboldt County apply to land and structures used for agricultural purposes. * * * The fighting issue is whether any of the ordinances constitute an "ordinance adopted under . . . chapter [335]"; in other words, are the ordinances zoning regulations?* * *

* * * The zoning power of the county regulated by chapter 335 is described in the statute itself. * * * [It] * * * provides that the board "may divide the county . . . into districts . . . and *within such districts* it may regulate and restrict the erection, *construction*, reconstruction, alteration, repair, or *use of buildings, structures or land*." *Id.* § 335.4 (emphasis added). The statute requires that any regulation adopted pursuant to chapter 335 advance certain enumerated objectives, including "to protect health and the general welfare." *Id.* § 335.5.

Based on this statute, the plaintiffs argue any county ordinance that regulates the "use" of buildings or land to protect the public's health or general welfare is zoning. The county responds that the challenged ordinances do not constitute zoning because they do not regulate land usage by district. It points out the challenged ordinances regulate an activity and apply uniformly across the county, irrespective of district classifications. We think the county's understanding of the distinction between a zoning power and a general police power with respect to the regulation of an activity on land is correct.

Historically, zoning regulations took the form of separating geographic areas according to zoning districts and specifying the uses permitted in each district. * * *

Despite expansion in the type of regulation imposed by zoning ordinances, the fundamental attribute of use regulation by district remains. * * *

It is this fundamental attribute that is missing in the challenged ordinances; they regulate an activity irrespective of the location of that activity within the county. Thus, although the ordinances may advance the health and general welfare of the community, they do not do so by regulating the usage of land by district. * * *

* * * [T]hey are not an exercise of the county's zoning power under chapter 335. Therefore, the ordinances are not subject to the agricultural exemption of section 335.2.

VII. IMPLIED PREEMPTION—HAS THE STATE COMPLETELY OCCUPIED THE FIELD OF LIVESTOCK FEEDING OPERATIONS?

The plaintiffs assert the legislature has so fully and extensively regulated livestock feeding operations that any local regulation would be inconsistent with the state regulatory framework. They also argue regulation of animal feeding operations is a matter of statewide concern and should be uniform across the state. Based on the nature of the subject to be regulated, the plaintiffs claim local laws are preempted. In evaluating these arguments, we begin with a review of the guiding legal principles in Iowa on implied preemption.

A. *Applicable analytical framework.* Since the adoption of home rule in Iowa, we have continued to recognize that preemption may occur when the legislature has "cover[ed] a subject by statutes in such a manner as to demonstrate a legislative intention that the field is preempted by state law." * * *

Both parties counsel a broad approach toward ascertaining implied preemption. They suggest that the court consider not only the statutory and regulatory treatment of livestock feeding operations, but also the nature of the issues to be addressed by state and local laws in this area. In essence, they ask the court to make a policy decision as to whether this area *should* be regulated on a statewide basis, rather than to simply decide whether this area *has* been regulated in such a way as to evidence the *legislature's intent* to reserve the area for uniform regulation. * * *

* * * [W]e decline the parties' invitation to engage in a wide-ranging analysis of whether statewide regulation of livestock feeding operations is desirable; our role is merely to ascertain whether the *legislature* has demonstrated *its* intention to handle livestock feeding operations exclusively on a statewide basis, or has demonstrated *its* desire that such operations be subjected to uniform regulation across the state. * * *

A comparison of [prior cases] illustrates the high degree of expression required of the legislature before this court will find subject-wide preemption. These cases show that extensive regulation of an area is not sufficient in the absence of a clear expression of legislative intent to preempt regulation of a field by local authorities, or a clear expression of the legislature's desire to have uniform regulations statewide. Consequently, in this case we look to the statutes and regulations controlling the construction and operation of livestock feeding facilities to determine whether they contain the necessary expression of legislative intent to preclude local regulation.

B.   Application of law to facts. * * *

[T]he plaintiffs cite to three provisions of House File 519, a bill regulating animal feeding operations and recently enacted into law by the general assembly, see 1995 Iowa Acts ch. 195, to support their theory of preemption. These three provisions have been codified as (1) Iowa Code section 657.11, limiting nuisance suits against animal feeding operations, (2) Iowa Code section 455B.201, prohibiting groundwater contamination from manure disposal, and (3) Iowa Code section 455B.173(13), authorizing the Environmental Protection Commission to adopt rules relating to the construction or operation of animal feeding operations. None of these statutes, or the regulations promulgated pursuant to them, however, contain an expression of legislative intent to eliminate local home rule authority in the area of livestock feeding operations. Nor do we find any statement that uniformity or statewide regulation is the goal of the general assembly. * * *

VIII.   IMPLIED PREEMPTION—ARE THE ORDINANCES INCONSISTENT WITH STATE LAW?

A.   General principles. As noted above, a county's exercise of home rule power cannot be "inconsistent with the laws of the general assembly." Iowa Const. art. III, § 39A; *accord* Iowa Code § 331.301. Thus, the constitutional grant of home rule power is "carefully qualified so as to withhold the grant of power where it conflicts with [a] state statute." * * * A local ordinance "is not inconsistent with a state law unless it is *irreconcilable* with the state law." Iowa Code § 331.301(4) (emphasis added). A local law is "irreconcilable" with state law when the local law " 'prohibits an act permitted by statute, or permits an act prohibited by a statute.' " * * *

There is some tension between these general principles and the statutory provision that a local government may "set standards and requirements which are higher or more stringent than those imposed by state law." Iowa Code § 331.301(6). Any distinction between a local ordinance that is inconsistent with state law and one that merely sets a higher standard or requirement is at best subtle. * * *

[T]he Humboldt County ordinances do far more than merely set more stringent standards to regulate confinement operations. These ordinances revise the state regulatory scheme and, by doing so, become irreconcilable with state law. We turn now to an analysis of the Humboldt County ordinances.

B.   Ordinance 22. Ordinance 22 requires a permit from the county before construction or operation of a large livestock confinement facility may commence. The county will not issue a permit unless the applicant has complied "with all applicable statutes, ordinances, and regulations." The plaintiffs claim this ordinance conflicts with Iowa Code section

455B.110 and the permit requirements of the Department of Natural Resources (DNR).

1.   Section 455B.110. This statute prevents the DNR from pursuing an enforcement action against an animal feeding operation without prior approval from the Environmental Protection Commission, unless it seeks to enforce a civil penalty of three thousand dollars or less. *See* Iowa Code § 455B.110. Although chapter 455B allows persons other than the DNR to commence a civil action against any person claimed to be in violation of chapter 455B, this right is restricted. *See id.* § 455B.111. The person commencing the action must be "adversely affected by the alleged violation." *Id.* § 455B.111(3). More importantly, the person seeking to commence suit must give sixty days written notice to the director of the DNR and the alleged violator, specifying the violation and that legal action is contemplated if the violation is not abated. *See id.* § 455B.111(2). No action may be commenced if the DNR or the state is actively prosecuting a civil action against the alleged violator or is actively negotiating an out-of-court settlement. *See id.*

We agree with the plaintiffs that the ordinance is inconsistent with these statutory provisions. Ordinance 22 creates a right in the county to abate a violation of state law by making compliance with state law a condition of obtaining a permit for construction or operation of a confinement facility. If a facility is operated in violation of state law and consequently without the required county permit, the county can bring a civil action to enjoin operation. The ordinance does not require the county to obtain the commission's prior approval nor is the county required to give the DNR and the violator notice of its intent to file an action if the violation is not abated. Thus, the ordinance allows the county to do indirectly what the statute directly forbids. The statute and ordinance are irreconcilable in this respect. Additionally, the ordinance is not faithful to the enforcement scheme established by chapter 455B. Therefore, we conclude the permit requirement of the county ordinance is invalid.

2.   Section 455B.173(13). The legislature has specifically invested the Environmental Protection Commission with the authority to adopt rules "relating to the construction or operation of animal feeding operations," including, but not limited to, "minimum manure control requirements, requirements for obtaining permits, and department evaluations of animal feeding operations." *Id.* § 455B.173(13). The legislature exempted small animal feeding operations from the construction permit requirement. *See id.* Nevertheless, operations not subject to the permit requirement may obtain a permit upon filing an "application meet[ing] standards established by the [DNR]." *Id.* Within these parameters, the DNR has provided by rule that certain animal feeding operations must obtain construction and operation permits. *See* Iowa Admin. Code rr. 567—65.3–.6 (1997). An applicant must submit a

copy of the application to the county board of supervisors in the county where the facility is to be located. *See* Iowa Code § 455B.173(13); Iowa Admin. Code r. 567—65.9(1). The DNR is required to consider the county's comments concerning the applicant's compliance with state statutes and regulations prior to issuing a permit. * * * Because ordinance 22 conditions construction and operation of any large confinement operation upon filing an application and obtaining a permit, we think the ordinance is inconsistent with state law. For example, assume an operation meets state law requirements, but not the county's additional requirements. Under these circumstances, the state rules would allow construction and operation of the facility, but the county ordinance would prohibit it because the operation would not have met the additional requirements of the county's ordinances. The county ordinance would prohibit what the state law would allow. Therefore, ordinance 22 conflicts with the state permit requirement and standards and is invalid.

We think the ordinance also conflicts with the limited role envisioned by the legislature for the county in the permitting process. The county's role is well-defined under chapter 455B; the county may comment on the proposed facility's compliance with state law. Although the DNR considers the county's comments, chapter 455B places the decision-making authority with the DNR. In contrast, ordinance 22 elevates the county's role by allowing the county to determine whether the applicant has complied with state law and making operation or construction of a facility contingent on the *county's* decision to issue a permit. These conflicts are irreconcilable and invalidate ordinance 22. * * *

In summary, ordinance 22 does not merely impose higher standards on livestock confinement operations by adding the county permit requirement to the list of prerequisites for building and operating such a facility. The ordinance actually *changes* the state regulatory system: (1) the county, not the DNR, becomes the decision maker; (2) commission approval is not required for an enforcement action; and (3) notice to the DNR and the violator is not required. * * * Ordinance 22 is irreconcilable with state law.

[The court applied a similar analysis to invalidate the other three ordinances.]

CITY OF NORTHGLENN V. IBARRA

Supreme Court of Colorado
62 P.3d 151 (2003)

JUSTICE BENDER delivered the Opinion of the Court.

For the last fifteen years, Respondent Juliana Ibarra and her husband, Eusebio, have provided foster care services to children in their single family residence in the City of Northglenn. The Ibarras are certified by Lost & Found, Inc., a child placement agency licensed by the State of Colorado. Juliana Ibarra underwent almost ninety hours of specialized training to maintain her certification with Lost & Found, taking classes on various topics including some related to parenting the sexually violated child and/or perpetrator.

In January 2000, Northglenn enacted Ordinance 1248. Section 11–5–2(b)(58) of the ordinance prohibits unrelated, registered sex offenders from living together in a single family home in residential zones in the City of Northglenn. The ordinance also provides that violation of section 11–5–2(b)(58) is a crime and can result in up to one year in jail and/or a fine of $1,000 per day.

At the time that the ordinance became effective, the Ibarras shared their home with four unrelated foster children. Three of those four foster children had been the victims and perpetrators of incest and suffered various mental impairments. Because of adjudications resulting from that incestuous conduct, these three youths were also required to register as sex offenders pursuant to section 18–3–412.5, 6 C.R.S. (2002). The state removed the three children from their parents' homes and placed them with the Ibarras through Lost & Found. In 2000, the oldest of the three children had lived with the Ibarras for three years, the middle child had lived there for one year, and the youngest had been with the Ibarras for approximately four months.

Because the Ibarras continued to share their home with three unrelated adjudicated delinquent children who were also registered sex offenders after the effective date of Ordinance 1248, Northglenn charged Juliana Ibarra with a violation of section 11–5–2(b)(58). Ibarra was convicted of violating Ordinance 1248 and fined $750. * * *

The law that applies to this case is well-established and the parties do not debate its general contours. Article XX, Section 6 of the Colorado Constitution, adopted by Colorado voters in 1912, granted "home-rule" to municipalities opting to adopt home-rule charters. Colo. Const. art. XX, § 6. The effect of this constitutional provision is that certain cities, which have satisfied size requirements and adopted a city charter, may legislate on matters of local concern that preempt any conflicting state legislation. *Id.*

We have recognized that regulated matters fall into one of three broad categories: (1) matters of local concern; (2) matters of statewide concern; and (3) matters of mixed state and local concern. * * * The decision as to whether state or local legislation controls in a given situation often turns on whether a matter is a local, state or mixed concern. * * *

First, in matters of local concern, both home-rule cities and the state may legislate. * * * However, when a home-rule ordinance or charter provision and a state statute conflict with respect to a local matter, the home-rule provision supercedes the conflicting state statute. * * * Second, in matters of statewide concern, the General Assembly may adopt legislation and home-rule municipalities are without power to act unless authorized by the constitution or by state statute. * * * Third, some matters are not exclusively of local or statewide concern, but are properly of concern to both home-rule cities and the state. In these matters of "mixed" concern, local enactments and state statutes may coexist if they do not conflict. * * *

While we have found the terms "local," "state," and "mixed" useful to resolve potential conflicts between local and state legislation, they are not "mutually exclusive or factually perfect descriptions of the relevant interests of the state and local governments." *City and County of Denver v. State,* 788 P.2d 764, 767 (Colo.1990). Oftentimes, matters are not exclusively of local, state, or mixed concern and imperceptibly merge or overlap. *Id.* To determine that a matter is of local, state, or mixed concern is to draw a legal conclusion based on the facts and circumstances of each case. *Id.* At times, we may conclude that a matter is of statewide concern even though there exists a relatively smaller, local interest. Thus, even if the locality may have an interest in regulating a matter to the exclusion of the state under its home-rule powers, such an interest may be insufficient to characterize the matter as being of even "mixed" state and local concern. * * *

We have identified several general factors to be considered when determining whether a matter is of state, local, or mixed concern, including the need for statewide uniformity, whether the municipal legislation has an extraterritorial impact, whether the subject matter is traditionally one governed by state or local government, and whether the Colorado Constitution specifically identifies that the issue should be regulated by state or local legislation. *Id.* at 1280; *Town of Telluride v. Lot Thirty-Four Venture, LLC,* 3 P.3d 30, 37 (Colo.2000); *Denver,* 788 P.2d at 768. This is not an exhaustive list. All of these factors are "directed toward weighing the respective state and local interests implicated by the law," *Telluride,* 3 P.3d at 37, a process that lends itself to flexibility and consideration of numerous criteria. Thus, we have at times considered other factors as relevant to our consideration of whether a subject matter is of state, local, or mixed concern, including any legislative declaration as to whether a matter is of statewide concern and the need for cooperation between state and local government in order to effectuate the local government scheme. * * *

Ultimately, we hold that Ordinance 1248, as it applies to adjudicated delinquent children in foster care homes, regulates a matter of statewide concern. The state's interest in fulfilling its statutory obligations to place and supervise adjudicated delinquent children in foster care homes pursuant to uniform, statewide criteria overrides any home-rule city's interest in controlling land uses within its territorial limits. As a result of this overriding statewide concern, Ordinance 1248 is preempted. To frame these issues and to better understand our reasoning, we review two Colorado statutes: the Colorado Sex Offender Registration Act and the Colorado Children's Code. * * *

[handwritten margin note: wrong analysis for preempt. if mixed state-local means there is no immunity if ordinance is inconsistent w/ state, then preempted.]

The Children's Code defines "foster care" as the placement of a child into the legal custody or authority of a County Department of Social Services for physical placement of the child in a certified or licensed facility. § 19–1–103(51.3). * * * For delinquent children committed to its custody and placed into one of its foster care homes, only the Department can change the initial placement decision and transfer children between its facilities. § 19–2–923(1). * * * In addition to a commitment to the Department of Human Services, the court can order juveniles directly to outside placement. § 19–2–907(1)(g). If the court finds that placement outside of the home is necessary and in the best interests of the juvenile and the community, the court must follow the section 19–2–212 statewide criteria to place the juvenile in the facility or setting that most appropriately meets the needs of the juvenile, the juvenile's family, and the community. § 19–2–907(5)(a). One choice for outside placement is a state supervised and licensed child placement agency. §§ 19–2–907(1)(g), 19–1–103(21). Although the state—through its designee the County Department of Social Services—retains legal custody of the children, the agency determines where and with whom the children shall live, subject to court approval. § 19–1–115(3)(a). In appropriate circumstances, the child placement agency locates foster parents for the physical custody of the child. The agency must find foster parents who can provide treatment that is in the best interests of the juvenile in a state environment where, as the legislature has found, there is an increasing difficulty of attracting foster parents to care for the number of children placed outside of their homes. § 26–5.5–102(c). When potential foster parents are located, the agency ensures that they comply with all statutory requirements, including receiving training through the statewide core curriculum. 12 C.C.R. § 2509–6. Foster parents may also receive specialized training that is designed to provide therapeutic treatment for the psychological or emotional needs of an individual child. These foster parents, as designees of the state, are certified by the child placement agency to provide twenty-four hour family care for the child in their home. * * *

In summary, the Colorado Children's Code mandates that for adjudicated delinquent children in foster care, the state—through either the court or the State Department of Human Services—must consistently follow specific criteria and procedures to protect the best interests of the juvenile and the community.

With Colorado statutes in mind, we must consider and weigh the state and local interests that are implicated by Ordinance 1248. Northglenn argues that Ordinance 1248 is a zoning ordinance and that we have repeatedly held that zoning ordinances are of local concern. Northglenn points out that from the very inception of zoning laws, the regulation of land uses has been a matter for local governments. Thus, Northglenn concludes that Ordinance 1248 must also be of purely local concern and valid pursuant to their home-rule powers. We disagree. Northglenn's argument fails to take into account the very real overlap between Ordinance 1248 and the state's obligations under the Children's Code. * * *

Here, Ordinance 1248 and the Children's Code superficially appear to regulate two different subject matters. Ordinance 1248 regulates the number of registered sex offenders who may live in a single-family residence in Northglenn. The Children's Code regulates the state's placement, movement and supervision of adjudicated delinquent children in foster care homes. On their face, there appears to be no overlap. However, the Colorado Sex Offender Registration Act provides the linking overlap: registered sex offenders are also adjudicated delinquent children, and in this case, living in a foster care home. In other words, Ordinance 1248, as applied, regulates a subset of registered sex offenders who are also covered by the procedures and protections granted to them by the Children's Code. By defining the term "family" in a way that restricts the number of adjudicated delinquent children who may reside with a foster care family, Ordinance 1248 necessarily implicates the state's statutory obligations with respect to those children.

Thus, because Ordinance 1248 was applied to a state-created foster care family, both local and state interests are implicated. The city has an interest in regulating the way that land is used in Northglenn and protecting the welfare of its citizens. The state has an interest in fulfilling its statutory obligation to place and supervise adjudicated delinquent children uniformly pursuant to the procedures and criteria of the Children's Code in a way that protects the best interests of the juvenile and the community. Hence, we must weigh the relative strengths of these interests to determine if Northglenn may regulate the number of adjudicated delinquent foster care children who may reside in one home. We do so by turning to and examining the totality of the circumstances.

* * * Although uniformity in itself is no virtue, we have found statewide uniformity necessary when it achieves and maintains specific state goals. * * *

Here, as evidenced by the comprehensive state statutory scheme, the state must place and supervise adjudicated delinquent children in foster care homes in a manner that is uniform and consistent throughout the state to protect the best interests of the juvenile, the juvenile's family, and the community. Indeed, the General Assembly required the formation of a state working group pursuant to section 19–2–212 to assure uniform and consistent commitment and placement criteria at all stages of a disposition to achieve the goals of the Children's Code for adjudicated delinquent children throughout the state. Those goals mandate that the state guarantee that children removed from their homes are assured their new homes will be where they can feel safe and secure, they will not arbitrarily be removed from those homes, and they can, if appropriate, confidently plan for the future. Ordinance 1248 materially impedes these goals by indiscriminately removing state-placed children from their homes.

Under our uniformity analysis, we have also found uniform access and expectations of consistency important factors to consider in determining whether a matter is of statewide concern.

There is no less need here for the state to ensure that adjudicated delinquent children have uniform access to state-created foster care families and can rely on consistent procedures and practices designed to rehabilitate them.

Ordinance 1248 denies specific adjudicated delinquent children— registered sex offenders living in a foster care home in Northglenn—the uniform access to the treatment that is best suited for their needs. For juvenile offenders such as the Ibarra foster children, the Ordinance denies them access to a setting that is state-created to reduce the rate of recidivism and to assist them in becoming productive members of society.

Ordinance 1248 also denies adjudicated delinquent children residing in a Northglenn foster care home the expectation of consistency that is provided to them by the Children's Code. All children removed from their homes, even those adjudicated as delinquent, must be able to rely on the procedures and protections guaranteed to them in a comprehensive state statutory scheme. Ordinance 1248 prohibits the Ibarra foster children from living together and thus eliminates any expectations of consistent treatment. By doing so, Ordinance 1248 creates a "patchwork approach" to the placement of certain foster care children, * * * focusing on factors such as the locality they live in and their status as registered sex offenders. The state is statutorily required to avoid the patchwork approach and provide uniform treatment to adjudicated delinquent children in a manner that protects their best interests.

* * * We have defined "extraterritorial impact" as a ripple effect that impacts state residents outside the municipality. * * * To find a ripple effect, however, the extraterritorial impact must have serious consequences to residents outside the municipality, and be more than

incidental or *de minimus.* * * * Ordinance 1248 causes such serious consequences.

By limiting the number of registered adolescent sex offenders who may reside in one foster care home, Ordinance 1248 has a significant adverse effect in and outside Northglenn because it decreases the total number of foster care homes available in a statewide system. Ordinance 1248 requires that unrelated children who are also registered sex offenders be placed in separate homes. As the legislature has declared, there is an increasing difficulty attracting foster care parents for the number of children placed outside of their homes. *See* § 26–5.5–102(1)(c). However, Ordinance 1248 forces two of the three children to seek outside placement in a state system that is already in short supply of foster care homes. In Colorado, there were only 3200 homes for the 13,000 foster care children who spent a portion of the year in a foster care home in 2000. * * * By forcing juvenile sex offenders out of foster care homes, Ordinance 1248 has a ripple effect on the availability of homes for all foster care children, particularly those who require the type of treatment that the Ibarras provided to sexually abused victims and perpetrators. This ripple effect is compounded by the fact that other municipalities in Colorado have similar ordinances that limit the number of unrelated sex offender foster care children residing in one home.

* * * Northglenn argues that zoning ordinances regulating land-uses are historically and traditionally matters of local concern. However, * * * Northglenn's categorization of Ordinance 1248 as simply a "zoning ordinance" fails to capture the sweep of this ordinance's impact upon state-placed and state-created foster families involving delinquent juvenile sex offenders.

The facts and circumstances of this case show that Ordinance 1248 regulates state-created foster families in a manner that requires the removal of state-placed delinquent children. The regulation of such state-placed delinquent children implicates the Colorado Children's Code and the state's obligations to those children under the Code. * * * The regulation of such children also implicates the provision of social services through the State Department of Human Services. Colorado statutes have historically and traditionally mandated that the state play the primary role in the provision of social services. The state's social service system is a matter of statewide concern. * * *

Finally, our analysis of the relative provisions of state statutes persuades us that the General Assembly has implied an intent to preempt the regulation of adjudicated delinquent children living in foster care homes. * * * State statutes are so pervasive as to the primary role of the state in the lives of juvenile delinquents removed from their homes and placed in foster care that they imply an intent by the General Assembly to occupy the field. * * *

JUSTICE COATS dissents, and JUSTICE KOURLIS and JUSTICE RICE join in the dissent.

* * * To the extent that both zoning and public safety are legitimate matters of local concern, and the regulation and protection of juveniles, including the designation of foster families, are matters of statewide concern, regulating the number of unrelated sex offenders permitted to live in a single, residential home is a classic example of mixed statewide and local concern. Whether Northglenn's ordinance is a valid exercise of the city's legislative authority should therefore turn on its consistency with state law. * * *

We have indicated that in matters of mixed local and statewide concern, ordinances and state statutes may coexist as long as they are harmonious, * * *, consistent, * * *, or not in conflict, * * *. We have also said that a conflict between state and local legislation exists when a local ordinance authorizes what state legislation forbids, or forbids what state legislation authorizes. * * * With regard to preemption generally, we have delineated three basic ways in which an ordinance or regulation can be preempted by state statute. An ordinance will be considered completely preempted by express statutory language preempting all local authority over the subject matter or by an implicit legislative intent to completely occupy a given field by reason of a dominant state interest, and an ordinance may be partially preempted where its operational effect would conflict with the application of the state statute. * * *

There appears to be no suggestion by the parties (or the majority opinion) that state statutes contain any provision expressly preempting, or for that matter expressly conflicting with, Northglenn's ordinance. As an element of its analysis finding this to be a matter of exclusively statewide concern, however, the majority finds an implied intent of the General Assembly to occupy the entire field, which it describes as "the regulation of adjudicated delinquent children living in foster care homes." * * * Both the majority's extreme narrowing of the "field" of concern and its invalidation of the ordinance only to the extent that it impacts "adjudicated delinquent children in foster care homes," * * * seem more analytically consistent with disapproval of a particular operational effect of the ordinance than finding a legislative intent to occupy an entire field of regulation. Furthermore, if taken at face value, the majority's conclusion that Northglenn's ordinance regulates an area implicitly preempted by the General Assembly would seemingly end the matter, rendering superfluous its analysis of statewide concern. In fact, however, the ordinance does not attempt to compete or interfere in any way with state regulation of adjudicated delinquent children living in foster care homes. It limits the number of unrelated sex offenders who may live in one residential dwelling and, for that reason and that reason alone, operationally affects the ability of state agents to place some children—those who have been adjudicated as sex offenders—in foster care homes that already include one registered sex offender.

We have previously made clear that the Children's Code does not prohibit the prosecution of juveniles for violating municipal ordinances where the municipal ordinance scheme does not "authorize what the Children's Code forbids, or forbid what the Children's Code expressly authorizes." * * * Northglenn's ordinance clearly does not authorize something that the Children's Code, or any other statute, forbids. Neither does it forbid what the Children's Code expressly authorizes. In fact, it can be said to forbid what state statutes authorize only in the sense that the General Assembly has delegated to agents of the Department of Social Services or licensed child placement agencies, within the limits allowed by department regulations, the authority to place children in the department's custody in foster homes. Nowhere has it been suggested that state statutes, or even Social Service regulations, expressly treat the question of multiple registered sex offenders in a single residential dwelling or establish criteria for placement with which the ordinance directly conflicts.

Rather than find that a general grant of discretion to a state agent preempts otherwise valid enactments of home rule cities whenever they, in some way or under some set of circumstances, limit the exercise of that discretion, I think it more reasonable to hold that a general grant of discretion is implicitly limited by otherwise valid law—whether that law is local or statewide. Any other conclusion would be intolerable. Surely it would be unacceptable in the absence of an express delegation of authority to permit even an authorized child placement agency to place a child in violation of health or building code requirements or in areas zoned for other than residential dwellings. In the absence of either an express delegation to do so or a showing of necessity in the fulfillment of a statutory mandate, I consider it unjustified to presume a legislative intent to permit the violation of local law by state agents.

Nothing in our jurisprudence governing legislation in matters of mixed local and statewide concerns unduly limits the General Assembly in overseeing statewide interests. If ordinances like Northglenn's actually have deleterious effects on the placement of registered juvenile sex offenders, the state legislature is in the best position to examine the various local and statewide concerns, evaluate the relevant policy considerations, and if merited, preempt local action. Local action in the interest of public safety, however, should not in my opinion be preempted by the unguided choice of a state agent in a particular case.

WALLACH V. TOWN OF DRYDEN

Court of Appeals of New York
23 N.Y.3d 728 (2014)

GRAFFEO, J.

We are asked in these two appeals whether towns may ban oil and gas production activities, including hydrofracking, within municipal boundaries through the adoption of local zoning laws. We conclude that they may because the supersession clause in the statewide Oil, Gas and Solution Mining Law (OGSML) does not preempt the home rule authority vested in municipalities to regulate land use. * * *

Respondent Town of Dryden is a rural community located in Tompkins County, New York. Land use in Dryden is governed by a comprehensive plan and zoning ordinance. The underlying goal of the comprehensive plan is to "[p]reserve the rural and small town character of the Town of Dryden, and the quality of life its residents enjoy, as the town continues to grow in the coming decades." Despite the fact that oil and gas drilling has not historically been associated with Dryden, its location within the Marcellus Shale region has piqued the interest of the natural gas industry.

The Marcellus Shale formation covers a vast area across sections of a number of states, including New York, Pennsylvania, Ohio and West Virginia. Natural gas—primarily methane—is found in shale deposits buried thousands of feet below the surface and can be extracted through the combined use of horizontal drilling and hydrofracking. To access the natural gas, a well is drilled vertically to a location just above the target depth, at which point the well becomes a horizontal tunnel in order to maximize the number of pathways through which the gas may be removed. The process of hydraulic fracturing—commonly referred to as hydrofracking—can then commence. Hydrofracking involves the injection of large amounts of pressurized fluids (water and chemicals) to stimulate or fracture the shale formations, causing the release of the natural gas. * * *

In 2006, petitioner Norse Energy Corp. USA (Norse), through its predecessors, began acquiring oil and gas leases from landowners in Dryden for the purpose of exploring and developing natural gas resources. * * * After holding a public hearing and reviewing a number of relevant scientific studies, the Town Board unanimously voted to amend the zoning ordinance in August 2011 to specify that all oil and gas exploration, extraction and storage activities were not permitted in Dryden. * * * In adopting the amendment, the Town Board declared that the industrial use of land in the "rural environment of Dryden" for natural gas purposes "would endanger the health, safety and general welfare of the community through the deposit of toxins into the air, soil, water, environment, and in the bodies of residents."

A month later, Norse commenced this * * * proceeding and declaratory judgment action to challenge the validity of the zoning amendment. Norse asserted that Dryden lacked the authority to prohibit natural gas exploration and extraction activities because section 23–0303 (2) of the Environmental Conservation Law (ECL)—the supersession clause in the Oil, Gas and Solution Mining Law—demonstrated that the state legislature intended to preempt local zoning laws that curtailed energy production. [In the companion case, Cooperstown Holstein Corp. (CHC) challenged a very similar ordinance adopted by the Town of Middlefield.] * * *

Norse and CHC * * * assert that the energy policy of New York, as exemplified by the statewide OGSML, requires a uniform approach and cannot be subject to regulation by a melange of the state's 932 towns. They maintain that the OGSML contains a supersession clause that expressly preempts all local zoning laws, like those enacted by the Towns, which restrict or forbid oil and gas operations on real property within a municipality. The Towns, joined by other amici curiae, respond that the courts below correctly concluded that they acted within their home rule authority in adopting the challenged local laws. They urge that the ability of localities to restrict the industrial use of land with the aims of preserving the characteristics of their communities and protecting the health, safety and general welfare of their citizens implicates the very essence of municipal governance. They further contend that, when analyzed under the principles set forth in our precedent, the OGSML and its supersession clause do not extinguish their zoning powers. * * *

Article IX, the "home rule" provision of the New York Constitution, states that "every local government shall have power to adopt and amend local laws not inconsistent with the provisions of this constitution or any general law . . . except to the extent that the legislature shall restrict the adoption of such a local law" (NY Const, art IX, § 2 [c] [ii]). To implement this constitutional mandate, the state legislature enacted the Municipal Home Rule Law, which empowers local governments to pass laws both for the "protection and enhancement of [their] physical and visual environment" (Municipal Home Rule Law § 10 [1] [ii] [a] [11]) and for the "government, protection, order, conduct, safety, health and well-being of persons or property therein" (Municipal Home Rule Law § 10 [1] [ii] [a] [12]). The legislature likewise authorized towns to enact zoning laws for the purpose of fostering "the health, safety, morals, or the general welfare of the community" (Town Law § 261; see also Statute of Local Governments § 10 [6] [granting towns "the power to adopt, amend and repeal zoning regulations"]). As a fundamental precept, the legislature has recognized that the local regulation of land use is "[a]mong the most important powers and duties granted . . . to a town government."

We, too, have designated the regulation of land use through the adoption of zoning ordinances as one of the core powers of local governance. Without question, municipalities may "enact land-use restrictions or controls to enhance the quality of life by preserving the character and desirable aesthetic features of [the community]" * * *.

That being said, as a political subdivision of the State, a town may not enact ordinances that conflict with the State Constitution or any general law (*see* Municipal Home Rule Law § 10 [1] [i], [ii]). Under the preemption doctrine, a local law promulgated under a municipality's home rule authority must yield to an inconsistent state law as a consequence of "the untrammeled primacy of the Legislature to act with respect to matters of State concern." * * * But we do not lightly presume preemption where the preeminent power of a locality to regulate land use is at stake. Rather, we will invalidate a zoning law only where there is a "clear expression of legislative intent to preempt local control over land use."

Aware of these principles, Norse and CHC do not dispute that, absent a state legislative directive to the contrary, municipalities would ordinarily possess the home rule authority to restrict the use of land for oil and gas activities in furtherance of local interests. They claim, however, that the state legislature has clearly expressed its intent to preempt zoning laws of local governments through the OGSML's "supersession clause," which reads:

"The provisions of this article [i.e., the OGSML] shall supersede *all local laws or ordinances relating to the regulation of the oil, gas and solution mining industries*; but shall not supersede local government jurisdiction over local roads or the rights of local governments under the real property tax law" (ECL 23–0303 [2] [emphasis added]).

According to Norse and CHC, this provision should be interpreted broadly to reach zoning laws that restrict, or, as presented here, prohibit oil and gas activities, including hydrofracking, within municipal boundaries.

* * * [T]his question may be answered by considering three factors: (1) the plain language of the supersession clause; (2) the statutory scheme as a whole; and (3) the relevant legislative history. The goal of this three-part inquiry, as with any statutory interpretation analysis, is to discern the legislature's intent. * * *

(1) Plain Language

* * * ECL 23–0303 (2) is most naturally read as preempting only local laws that purport to regulate the actual operations of oil and gas

activities, not zoning ordinances that restrict or prohibit certain land uses within town boundaries. Plainly, the zoning laws in these cases are directed at regulating land use generally and do not attempt to govern the details, procedures or operations of the oil and gas industries. Although the zoning laws will undeniably have an impact on oil and gas enterprises * * * "this incidental control resulting from the municipality's exercise of its right to regulate land use through zoning is not the type of regulatory enactment relating to the [oil, gas and solution mining industries] which the Legislature could have envisioned as being within the prohibition of the statute."

Nevertheless, Norse and CHC, relying on the secondary clause in the OGSML's supersession provision—preserving "local government jurisdiction over local roads or the rights of local governments under the real property tax law" (ECL 23–0303 [2])—contend that the operative text cannot be limited to local laws that purport to regulate the actual operations of oil and gas companies. They submit that the secondary clause's exemption of local jurisdiction over roads and taxes makes sense only if the preemptive span of the operative text is broader than we have allowed because roads and taxes are not associated with "operations." Consequently, they argue that there would have been no need for the legislature to exclude them from the operative language if supersession was limited to local laws aimed at oil and gas operations.

We find this textual argument misplaced because local regulation of roads and taxes can fairly be characterized as touching on the operations of the oil and gas industries and would have been preempted absent the secondary savings clause. The state legislature's decision to preserve "local government jurisdiction over local roads" was appropriate given the heavy truck and equipment traffic typically associated with oil and gas production, including water and wastewater hauling. Local laws dictating the number of daily truck trips or the weight and length of vehicles bear directly on industry operations and would otherwise be preempted absent the secondary clause. Similarly, the preservation of "the rights of local governments under the real property tax law" must be read in conjunction with section 594 of the Real Property Tax Law, which allows municipalities to impose taxes on oil and gas businesses. Because these special taxes are based on the level of production, they can be viewed as affecting the operations of the oil and gas industry, such that it was reasonable for the legislature to carve out an exception from the preemptive scope of the operative text. We are therefore unpersuaded by the claim of Norse and CHC that the plain language of ECL 23–0303 (2) as a whole supports preemption of the Towns' zoning laws.

Indeed, it is instructive to compare the OGSML's supersession clause to other statutes that clearly preempt home rule zoning powers. Unlike ECL 23–0303 (2), such provisions often explicitly include zoning in the preemptive language employed by the legislature (*see e.g.* ECL 27–1107 [prohibiting municipalities from requiring "any approval, consent, permit, certificate or other condition including conformity with local zoning or land use laws and ordinances" for the siting of hazardous waste facilities]; Mental Hygiene Law § 41.34 [f] ["A community residence established pursuant to this section and family care homes shall be deemed a family unit, for the purposes of local laws and ordinances"]; Racing, Pari-Mutuel Wagering and Breeding Law § 1366 ["Notwithstanding any inconsistent provision of law, gaming authorized at a location pursuant to this article shall be deemed an approved activity for such location under the relevant city, county, town, or village land use or zoning ordinances, rules, or regulations"]).

Further, the legislative schemes of which these preemption clauses are a part typically include other statutory safeguards that take into account local considerations that otherwise would have been protected by traditional municipal zoning powers (*see e.g.* ECL 27–1103 [2] [g] [requiring the Department of Environmental Conservation to consider the "impact on the municipality where the facility is to be sited in terms of health, safety, cost and consistency with local planning, zoning or land use laws and ordinances"]; Mental Hygiene Law § 41.34 [c] [allowing municipalities a means of objecting to the placement of community residential facilities]; Racing, Pari-Mutuel Wagering and Breeding Law § 1320 [2] [mandating the consideration of local impacts and community support in the siting of gaming facilities]). Norse and CHC are unable to point to any comparable measures in the OGSML that account for the salient local interests in the context of drilling and hydrofracking activities. * * *

(2) Statutory Scheme

* * * The stated purposes of the OGSML are fourfold: (i) "to regulate the development, production and utilization of natural resources of oil and gas in this state in such a manner as will prevent waste"; (ii) "to authorize and to provide for the operation and development of oil and gas properties in such a manner that a greater ultimate recovery of oil and gas may be had"; (iii) to protect the "correlative rights of all owners and the rights of all persons including landowners and the general public"; and (iv) to regulate "the underground storage of gas, the solution mining of salt and geothermal, stratigraphic and brine disposal wells."

In furtherance of these goals, the OGSML sets forth a detailed regime under which the New York State Department of Environmental Conservation is entrusted to regulate oil, gas and solution mining activities and to promulgate and enforce appropriate rules. In particular, the Department is empowered to "[r]equire the drilling, casing, operation, plugging and replugging of wells and reclamation of surrounding land in accordance with the rules and regulations of the department" (ECL 23–0305 [8] [d]); enter and plug or replug abandoned wells when the owner has violated Department regulations (ECL 23–0305 [8] [e]); compel operators to furnish the Department with a bond to ensure compliance (ECL 23–0305 [8] [k]); order the immediate suspension of drilling operations that are in violation of Department regulations (ECL 23–0305 [8] [g]); require operators to file well logs and samples with the Department (ECL 23–0305 [8] [i]); grant well permits for oil and gas drilling (ECL 23–0501); issue orders governing the appropriate spacing between oil and gas wells to promote efficient drilling and prevent waste (ECL 23–0503); oversee the integration of oil and gas fields to prevent waste (ECL 23–0701, 23–0901); execute leases on behalf of the State for oil and gas exploration and production (ECL 23–1101); and issue permits for underground storage reservoirs (ECL 23–1301).

Based on these provisions, it is readily apparent that the OGSML is concerned with the Department's regulation and authority regarding the safety, technical and operational aspects of oil and gas activities across the State. The supersession clause in ECL 23–0303 (2) fits comfortably within this legislative framework since it invalidates local laws that would intrude on the Department's regulatory oversight of the industry's operations, thereby ensuring uniform exploratory and extraction processes related to oil and gas production. [W]e perceive nothing in the various provisions of the OGSML indicating that the supersession clause was meant to be broader than required to preempt conflicting local laws directed at the technical operations of the industry.

And contrary to the position advanced by Norse and CHC, we see no inconsistency between the preservation of local zoning authority and the OGSML's policies of preventing "waste" and promoting a "greater ultimate recovery of oil and gas" (ECL 23–0301), or the statute's spacing provisions for wells (see ECL 23–0501, 23–0503). Waste is used as a term of art in the OGSML meaning, among other things, the "inefficient, excessive or improper use of, or the unnecessary dissipation of reservoir energy" and the "locating, spacing, drilling, equipping, operating, or producing of any oil or gas well or wells in a manner which causes or tends to cause reduction in the quantity of oil or gas ultimately recoverable" (ECL 23–0101 [20] [b], [c]). The OGSML's overriding concern with preventing waste is limited to inefficient or improper drilling activities that result in the unnecessary waste of natural resources. Nothing in the statute points to the conclusion that a municipality's decision not to permit drilling equates to waste. * * *

(3) Legislative History

* * * As originally enacted, the statute's stated policy was, in part, "to foster, encourage and promote the development, production and

utilization of natural resources of oil and gas in this state in such a manner as will prevent waste." In 1978, the state legislature amended the OGSML to modify its policy by replacing the phrase "*to foster, encourage and promote* the development, production and utilization of natural resources of oil and gas in this state in such a manner as will prevent waste" with "*to regulate* the development, production and utilization of natural resources of oil and gas in this state in such a manner as will prevent waste." * * *

Nothing in the legislative history undermines our view that the supersession clause does not interfere with local zoning laws regulating the permissible and prohibited uses of municipal land. Indeed, the pertinent passages make no mention of zoning at all, much less evince an intent to take away local land use powers. Rather, the history of the OGSML and its predecessor makes clear that the state legislature's primary concern was with preventing wasteful oil and gas practices and ensuring that the Department had the means to regulate the technical operations of the industry. * * *

As a fallback position, Norse and CHC suggest that, even if the OGSML's supersession clause does not preempt all local zoning laws, it should be interpreted as preempting zoning ordinances, like the two here, that completely prohibit hydrofracking. In their view, supported by the dissent, it may be valid to restrict oil and gas operations from certain residential areas of a town * * * but an outright ban goes too far and cannot be seen as anything but a local law that regulates the oil and gas industry, thereby running afoul of the supersession clause. * * *

Manifestly, Dryden and Middlefield engaged in a reasonable exercise of their zoning authority * * * when they adopted local laws clarifying that oil and gas extraction and production were not permissible uses in any zoning districts. The Towns both studied the issue and acted within their home rule powers in determining that gas drilling would permanently alter and adversely affect the deliberately-cultivated, small-town character of their communities. * * * Norse's and CHC's position that the town-wide nature of the hydrofracking bans rendered them unlawful is without merit, as are their remaining contentions.

At the heart of these cases lies the relationship between the State and its local government subdivisions, and their respective exercise of legislative power. These appeals are not about whether hydrofracking is beneficial or detrimental to the economy, environment or energy needs of New York, and we pass no judgment on its merits. These are major policy questions for the coordinate branches of government to resolve. The discrete issue before us, and the only one we resolve today, is whether the state legislature eliminated the home rule capacity of municipalities to pass zoning laws that exclude oil, gas and hydrofracking activities in order to preserve the existing character of their communities. There is no dispute that the state legislature has this right if it chooses to exercise it. But in light of ECL 23–0303 (2)'s plain language, its place within the OGSML's framework and the legislative background, we cannot say that the supersession clause—added long before the current debate over high-volume hydrofracking and horizontal drilling ignited—evinces a clear expression of preemptive intent. The zoning laws of Dryden and Middlefield are therefore valid.

PIGOTT, J. (dissenting).

Environmental Conservation Law § 23–0303 (2) states that "[t]he provisions of this article shall supersede *all* local laws or ordinances *relating* to the regulation of the oil, gas and solution mining industries; but shall not supersede local government jurisdiction over local roads or the rights of local governments under the real property tax law" (emphasis supplied). Municipalities may without a doubt regulate land use through enactment of zoning laws, but, in my view, the particular zoning ordinances in these cases relate to the regulation of the oil, gas and solution mining industries and therefore encroach upon the Department of Environmental Conservation's regulatory authority. For this reason, I respectfully dissent.

The zoning ordinances of Dryden and Middlefield do more than just regulate land use, they regulate oil, gas and solution mining industries under the pretext of zoning. * * * [T]hey purport to regulate the oil, gas and solution mining activities within the respective towns, creating a blanket ban on an entire industry without specifying the zones where such uses are prohibited. In light of the language of the zoning ordinances at issue—which go into great detail concerning the prohibitions against the storage of gas, petroleum exploration and production materials and equipment in the respective towns—it is evident that they go above and beyond zoning and, instead, regulate those industries, which is exclusively within the purview of the Department of Environmental Conservation. In this fashion, prohibition of certain activities is, in effect, regulation.

* * * [T]he ordinances in these appeals do more than just delineate prohibited uses. Where zoning ordinances encroach upon the DEC's regulatory authority and extend beyond the municipality's power to regulate land use generally, the ordinances have run afoul of ECL 23–0303 (2).

CITY OF RIVERSIDE V. INLAND EMPIRE PATIENTS HEALTH AND WELLNESS CENTER, INC.

Supreme Court of California
300 P.3d 494 (Cal. 2013)

BAXTER, J.

The issue in this case is whether California's medical marijuana statutes preempt a local ban on facilities that distribute medical marijuana. We conclude they do not.

Both federal and California laws generally prohibit the use, possession, cultivation, transportation, and furnishing of marijuana. However, California statutes, the Compassionate Use Act of 1996 (CUA; Health & Saf.Code, § 11362.5, added by initiative, Prop. 215, as approved by voters, Gen. Elec. (Nov. 5, 1996)) and the more recent Medical Marijuana Program (MMP; § 11362.7 et seq., added by Stats. 2003, ch. 875, § 2, pp. 6422, 6424), have removed certain state law obstacles from the ability of qualified patients to obtain and use marijuana for legitimate medical purposes. Among other things, these statutes exempt the "collective[ ] or cooperative[ ] cultiva[tion]" of medical marijuana by qualified patients and their designated caregivers from prosecution or abatement under specified state criminal and nuisance laws that would otherwise prohibit those activities.

The California Constitution recognizes the authority of cities and counties to make and enforce, within their borders, "all local, police, sanitary, and other ordinances and regulations not in conflict with general laws." (Cal. Const., art. XI, § 7.) This inherent local police power includes broad authority to determine, for purposes of the public health, safety, and welfare, the appropriate uses of land within a local jurisdiction's borders, and preemption by state law is not lightly presumed.

In the exercise of its inherent land use power, the City of Riverside (City) has declared, by zoning ordinances, that a "[m]edical marijuana dispensary"—"[a] facility where marijuana is made available for medical purposes in accordance with" the CUA (Riverside Municipal Code (RMC), § 19.910.140)—is a prohibited use of land within the city and may be abated as a public nuisance. The City's ordinance also bans, and declares a nuisance, any use that is prohibited by federal or state law. * * * Invoking these provisions, the City brought a nuisance action against a facility operated by defendants. * * * Defendants insist the local ban is in conflict with, and thus preempted by, those state statutes.

As we will explain, we disagree. We have consistently maintained that the CUA and the MMP are but incremental steps toward freer access to medical marijuana, and the scope of these statutes is limited and circumscribed. They merely declare that the conduct they describe cannot lead to arrest or conviction, or be abated as a nuisance, as violations of enumerated provisions of the Health and Safety Code. Nothing in the CUA or the MMP expressly or impliedly limits the inherent authority of a local jurisdiction, by its own ordinances, to regulate the use of its land, including the authority to provide that facilities for the distribution of medical marijuana will not be permitted to operate within its borders. * * *

The federal Controlled Substances Act (CSA; 21 U.S.C. § 801 et seq.) prohibits, except for certain research purposes, the possession, distribution, and manufacture of marijuana. (*Id.,* §§ 812(c) (Schedule I, par. (c)(10)), 841(a), 844(a).)

California statutes similarly specify that, except as authorized by law, the possession (§ 11357), cultivation, harvesting, or processing (§ 11358), possession for sale (§ 11359), and transportation, administration, or furnishing (§ 11360) of marijuana are state criminal violations. State law further punishes one who maintains a place for the purpose of unlawfully selling, using, or furnishing, or who knowingly makes available a place for storing, manufacturing, or distributing, certain controlled substances. (§§ 11366, 11366.5.) The so-called "drug den" abatement law additionally provides that every place used to unlawfully sell, serve, store, keep, manufacture, or give away certain controlled substances is a nuisance that shall be enjoined, abated, and prevented, and for which damages may be recovered. (§ 11570.) In each instance, the controlled substances in question include marijuana.

However, California's voters and legislators have adopted limited exceptions to the sanctions of this state's criminal and nuisance laws in cases where marijuana is possessed, cultivated, distributed, and transported for medical purposes. In 1996, the electorate enacted the CUA. This initiative statute provides that the state law proscriptions against possession and cultivation of marijuana shall not apply to a patient, or the patient's designated primary caregiver, who possesses or cultivates marijuana for the patient's personal medical purposes upon the written or oral recommendation or approval of a physician.

In 2004, the Legislature adopted the MMP. One purpose of this statute was to "[e]nhance the access of patients and caregivers to medical marijuana through collective, cooperative cultivation projects." Accordingly, the MMP provides, among other things, that "[q]ualified patients . . . and the designated primary caregivers of qualified patients . . . , who associate within the State of California in order collectively or cooperatively to cultivate marijuana for medical purposes, shall not solely on the basis of that fact be subject to state criminal sanctions under [s]ection 11357 [possession], 11358 [cultivation, harvesting, and processing], 11359 [possession for sale], 11360 [transportation, sale, furnishing, or administration], 11366 [maintenance of place for purpose of unlawful sale, use, or furnishing], 11366.5 [making place available for purpose of unlawful manufacture, storage, or distribution], or 11570 [place used for unlawful sale, serving, storage, manufacture, or furnishing as statutory nuisance]." * * *

A.   Principles of preemption.

* * * "Land use regulation in California historically has been a function of local government under the grant of police power contained in article XI, section 7. . . . 'We have recognized that a city's or county's power to control its own land use decisions derives from this inherent police power, not from the delegation of authority by the state.' " Consistent with this principle, "when local government regulates in an area over which it traditionally has exercised control, such as the location of particular land uses, California courts will presume, absent a clear indication of preemptive intent from the Legislature, that such regulation is *not* preempted by state statute." [citations omitted]

However, local legislation that conflicts with state law is void. * * * " 'A conflict exists if the local legislation " 'duplicates, contradicts, or enters an area fully occupied by general law, either expressly or by legislative implication.' " [Citations]

"Local legislation is 'duplicative' of general law when it is coextensive therewith. [Citation]

"Similarly, local legislation is 'contradictory' to general law when it is inimical thereto. [Citation]* * * "

The "contradictory and inimical" form of preemption does not apply unless the ordinance directly requires what the state statute forbids or prohibits what the state enactment demands. * * * Thus, no inimical conflict will be found where it is reasonably possible to comply with both the state and local laws.

In addition, "[w]e have been particularly 'reluctant to infer legislative intent to preempt a field covered by municipal regulation when there is a significant local interest to be served that may differ from one locality to another.' " * * * " 'The common thread of the cases is that if there is a significant local interest to be served which may differ from one locality to another then the presumption favors the validity of the local ordinance against an attack of state preemption.' "

B.   The CUA and the MMP do not preempt Riverside's ban.

When they adopted the CUA in 1996, the voters declared their intent "[t]o ensure that seriously ill Californians have the right to obtain and use marijuana for medical purposes" upon a physician's recommendation "[t]o ensure that patients and their primary caregivers who obtain and use marijuana for medical purposes upon the recommendation of a physician are not subject to criminal prosecution or sanction," and "[t]o encourage the federal and state governments to implement a plan to provide for the safe and affordable distribution of marijuana to all patients in medical need" of the substance.

But the operative steps the electorate took toward these goals were modest. In its substantive provisions, the CUA simply declares that (1) no physician may be punished or denied any right or privilege under state law for recommending medical marijuana to a patient (§ 11362.5, subd. I), and (2) two specific state statutes prohibiting the possession and cultivation of marijuana, sections 11357 and 11358 respectively, "shall not apply" to a patient, or the patient's designated primary caregiver, who possesses or cultivates marijuana for the patient's personal medical use upon a physician's recommendation or approval (§ 11362.5, subd. (d)).

When it later adopted the MMP, the Legislature declared this statute was intended, among other things, to "[c]larify the scope of the application of the [CUA] and facilitate the prompt identification of qualified [medical marijuana] patients and their designated primary caregivers" in order to protect them from unnecessary arrest and prosecution for marijuana offenses, to "[p]romote uniform and consistent application of the [CUA] among the counties within the state," and to "[e]nhance the access of patients and caregivers to medical marijuana through collective, cooperative cultivation projects."

Again, however, the steps the MMP took in pursuit of these objectives were limited and specific. The MMP established a program for issuance of medical marijuana identification cards to those qualified patients and designated primary caregivers who wish to carry them. * * * It provided that the holder of an identification card shall not be subject to arrest for possession, transportation, delivery, or cultivation of medical marijuana, within the amounts specified by the statute, except upon reasonable cause to believe the card is false or invalid or the holder is in violation of statute.

The MMP further specified that certain persons, including (1) a qualified patient, or the holder of a valid identification card, who possesses or transports marijuana for personal medical use, or (2) a designated primary caregiver who transports, processes, administers, delivers, or gives away, in amounts no greater than those specified by statute, marijuana for medical purposes to or for a qualified patient or valid cardholder "shall not be subject, on that sole basis, to criminal liability" under section 11357 (possession of marijuana), 11358 (cultivation of marijuana), 11359 (possession of marijuana for sale), 11360 (sale, transportation, importation, or furnishing of marijuana), 11366 (maintaining place for purpose of unlawfully selling, furnishing, or using controlled substance), 11366.5 (knowingly providing place for purpose of unlawfully manufacturing, storing, or distributing controlled substance), or 11570 (place used for unlawful selling, furnishing, storing, or manufacturing of controlled substance as nuisance).

Finally, as indicated above, the MMP declared that "[q]ualified patients, persons with valid identification cards, and the designated primary caregivers of [such persons], who associate within the State of California in order collectively or cooperatively to cultivate marijuana for medical purposes, shall not *solely on the basis of that fact* be subject to *state criminal sanctions* * * *.

1. *No express preemption.*

As indicated above, the plain language of the CUA and the MMP is limited in scope. It grants specified persons and groups, when engaged in specified conduct, immunity from prosecution under specified state criminal and nuisance laws pertaining to marijuana. * * * The CUA makes no mention of medical marijuana cooperatives, collectives, or dispensaries. It merely provides that state laws against the possession and cultivation of marijuana shall not apply to a qualified patient, or the patient's designated primary caregiver, who possesses or cultivates marijuana for the patient's personal medical use upon a physician's recommendation.

Though the CUA broadly states an aim to "ensure" a "right" of seriously ill persons to "obtain and use" medical marijuana as recommended by a physician the initiative statute's actual objectives, as presented to the voters, were "modest" and its substantive provisions created no "broad right to use [medical] marijuana without hindrance or inconvenience" (citations omitted). There is no basis to conclude that the CUA expressly preempts local ordinances prohibiting, as a nuisance, the use of property to cooperatively or collectively cultivate and distribute medical marijuana.

The MMP, unlike the CUA, does address, among other things, the collective or cooperative cultivation and distribution of medical marijuana. But the MMP is framed in similarly narrow and modest terms. As pertinent here, it specifies only that qualified patients, identification card holders, and their designated primary caregivers are exempt from prosecution and conviction under enumerated state antimarijuana laws "solely" on the ground that such persons are engaged in the cooperative or collective cultivation, transportation, and distribution of medical marijuana among themselves.

The MMP's language no more creates a "broad right" of access to medical marijuana "without hindrance or inconvenience" than do the words of the CUA. No provision of the MMP explicitly guarantees the availability of locations where such activities may occur, restricts the broad authority traditionally possessed by local jurisdictions to regulate zoning and land use planning within their borders, or requires local zoning and licensing laws to accommodate the cooperative or collective cultivation and distribution of medical marijuana. Hence, there is no ground to conclude that Riverside's ordinance is expressly preempted by the MMP.

2. *No implied preemption.*

The considerations discussed above also largely preclude any determination that the CUA or the MMP *impliedly* preempts Riverside's effort to "de-zone" facilities that dispense medical marijuana. At the outset, there is no duplication between the state laws, on the one hand, and Riverside's ordinance, on the other * * *. Nor do we find an "inimical" contradiction or conflict between the state and local laws, in the sense that it is impossible simultaneously to comply with both. Neither the CUA nor the MMP *requires* the cooperative or collective cultivation and distribution of medical marijuana that Riverside's ordinance deems a prohibited use of property within the city's boundaries. Conversely, Riverside's ordinance requires no conduct that is forbidden by the state statutes. Persons who refrain from operating medical marijuana facilities in Riverside are in compliance with both the local and state enactments. * * *

The presumption against preemption is additionally supported by the existence of significant local interests that may vary from jurisdiction to jurisdiction. Amici curiae League of California Cities et al. point out that "California's 482 cities and 58 counties are diverse in size, population, and use." As these amici curiae observe, while several California cities and counties allow medical marijuana facilities, it may not be reasonable to expect every community to do so.

For example, these amici curiae point out, "[s]ome communities are predominantly residential and do not have sufficient commercial or industrial space to accommodate" facilities that distribute medical marijuana. Moreover, these facilities deal in a substance which, except for legitimate medical use by a qualified patient under a physician's authorization, is illegal under both federal and state law to possess, use, furnish, or cultivate, yet is widely desired, bought, sold, cultivated, and employed as a recreational drug. Thus, facilities that dispense medical marijuana may pose a danger of increased crime, congestion, blight, and drug abuse, and the extent of this danger may vary widely from community to community.

Thus, while some counties and cities might consider themselves well suited to accommodating medical marijuana dispensaries, conditions in other communities might lead to the reasonable decision that such facilities within their borders, even if carefully sited, well managed, and closely monitored, would present unacceptable local risks and burdens. * * * Under these circumstances, we cannot lightly assume the voters or the Legislature intended to impose a "one size fits all" policy, whereby each and every one of California's diverse counties and cities must allow the use of local land for such purposes.

* * * [A] state law does not "authorize" activities, to the exclusion of local bans, simply by exempting those activities from otherwise applicable state prohibitions. * * * Similarly here, the MMP merely exempts the cooperative or collective cultivation and distribution of medical marijuana by and to qualified patients and their designated caregivers from prohibitions that would otherwise apply under state law. The state statute does not thereby *mandate* that local governments authorize, allow, or accommodate the existence of such facilities.

Defendants emphasize that among the stated purposes of the MMP, as originally enacted, are to "[p]romote uniform and consistent application of the [CUA] among the counties of the state" and to "[e]nhance the access of patients and caregivers to medical marijuana through collective, cooperative cultivation projects" (Stats. 2003, ch. 875, § 1, subd. (b), pp. 6422, 6423). Hence, they insist, the encouragement of medical marijuana dispensaries, under section 11362.775, is a matter of statewide concern, requiring the uniform allowance of such facilities throughout California, and leaving no room for their exclusion by individual local jurisdictions.

We disagree. * * * [T]he MMP's substantive provisions simply remove specified state-law sanctions from certain marijuana activities, including the cooperative or collective cultivation of medical marijuana by qualified patients and their designated caregivers. The MMP has never expressed or implied any actual limitation on local land use or police power regulation of facilities used for the cultivation and distribution of marijuana. We cannot employ the Legislature's expansive declaration of aims to stretch the MMP's effect beyond a reasonable construction of its substantive provisions. * * *

Finally, defendants urge that by exempting the collective or cooperative cultivation of medical marijuana by qualified patients and their designated caregivers from treatment as a nuisance under the *state's* drug abatement laws, the MMP bars local jurisdictions from adopting and enforcing ordinances that treat these very same activities as nuisances subject to abatement. But for the reasons set forth at length above, we disagree. Nuisance law is not defined exclusively by what the *state* makes subject to, or exempt from, its own nuisance statutes. Unless exercised in clear conflict with general law, a city's or county's inherent, constitutionally recognized power to determine the appropriate use of land within its borders (Cal. Const., art. XI, § 7) allows it to define nuisances for local purposes, and to seek abatement of such nuisances.

No such conflict exists here. In section 11362.775, the MMP merely removes *state law* criminal and nuisance sanctions from the conduct described therein. By this means, the MMP has signaled that the *state* declines to regard the described acts as nuisances or criminal violations, and that the *state's* enforcement mechanisms will thus not be available against these acts. Accordingly, localities in California are left free to accommodate such conduct, if they choose, free of state interference. As we have explained, however, the MMP's limited provisions neither expressly nor impliedly restrict or preempt the authority of individual local jurisdictions to choose otherwise for local reasons, and to prohibit collective or cooperative medical marijuana activities within their own borders. A local jurisdiction may do so by declaring such conduct on local land to be a nuisance, and by providing means for its abatement. * * *

Concurring Opinion by LIU, J.

I join the court's opinion and write separately to clarify the proper test for state preemption of local law.

As the court says, "[L]ocal legislation that conflicts with state law is void. [Citation.] ' "A conflict exists if the local legislation ' "duplicates, contradicts, or enters an area fully occupied by general law, either expressly or by legislative implication." ' " * * * The court further states: "The 'contradictory and inimical' form of preemption does not apply unless the ordinance directly requires what the state statute forbids or prohibits what the state enactment demands. [Citations.] Thus, no inimical conflict will be found where it is reasonably possible to comply with both the state and local laws."

The first sentence of the above statement should not be misunderstood to improperly limit the scope of the preemption inquiry. As the court's opinion makes clear elsewhere, state law may preempt local law when local law prohibits not only what a state statute "demands" but also what the statute permits or authorizes.

In a similar vein, the second sentence of the above statement—"no inimical conflict will be found where it is reasonably possible to comply with both the state and local laws"—also should not be misunderstood. If state law authorizes or promotes, but does not require or demand, a certain activity, and if local law prohibits the activity, then an entity or individual can comply with both state and local law by not engaging in the activity. But that obviously does not resolve the preemption question. To take an example from federal law, the Federal Arbitration Act (FAA) promotes arbitration, and a state law prohibiting arbitration of employment disputes would be preempted. (*See AT & T Mobility LLC v. Concepcion* (2011) 563 U.S. 333, 131 S.Ct. 1740, 1747, 179 L.Ed.2d 742.)

Such preemption obtains even though an employer can comply with both the FAA, which does not *require* employers to enter into arbitration agreements, and the state law simply by choosing not to arbitrate employment disputes.

Accordingly, in federal preemption law, we find a more complete statement of conflict preemption: " 'We have found implied conflict pre-emption where it is "impossible for a private party to comply with both state and federal requirements" [citation], *or* where state law "stands as an obstacle to the accomplishment and execution of the full purposes and objectives of Congress." ' " (*Sprietsma v. Mercury Marine* (2002) 537 U.S. 51, 64–65, 123 S.Ct. 518, 154 L.Ed.2d 466, italics added.) This more complete statement no doubt applies to California law. Local law that prohibits an activity that state law intends to promote is preempted, even though it is possible for a private party to comply with both state and local law by refraining from that activity.

I do not understand today's opinion to hold otherwise. In this case, defendants argue that the Medical Marijuana Program (MMP) authorizes and intends to promote what the City of Riverside prohibits: the operation of medical marijuana dispensaries. If such legislative authorization were clear, then the ordinance in question might well be preempted. But I agree with my colleagues that although the MMP provides medical marijuana cooperatives and collectives with a limited exemption from state criminal liability, "state law does not 'authorize' activities, to the exclusion of local plans, simply by exempting those activities from otherwise applicable state prohibitions." * * * Because state law does not clearly authorize or intend to promote the operation of medical marijuana dispensaries, I agree that the City of Riverside's prohibition on such dispensaries is not preempted.

NOTES AND QUESTIONS

1. *Preemption and Home Rule.* The question of local power to act is distinct from the question of whether a local action is displaced by state law. In *Goodell*, the Iowa Supreme Court quickly concluded that local ordinances regulating large livestock confinement facilities were a valid exercise of home rule authority: "Ensuring that livestock operations within a county are conducted in such a manner as to avoid contamination of the environment and interference with others' enjoyment and use of their property is a matter of local concern and therefore, is a 'local affair' within the meaning of the home rule amendment." The Colorado court in *City of Northglenn* also assumed that its cities could adopt the local land use laws in question. Indeed, a court will generally not get to the question of preemption unless it finds some local authority to act.

The question of preemption also overlaps, but can be distinguished from the question of which government—state or local—prevails in case of a conflict. In an NML home rule state, the state will typically prevail in a case of state-local conflict, so the key issue is likely to be whether the state and local laws are actually in conflict. In imperio home rule states, both the issues of whether there is a conflict and who wins if there is one are important. *City of Northglenn* arose in an imperio state, and the Colorado Supreme Court's analysis involved both questions. In *Wallach,* the court clearly assumed that the legislature had the power to preempt local fracking bans. Justice Liu's concurring opinion in *City of Riverside* assumed that the state could preempt local bans on medical marijuana dispensaries if it chose to do so.

2.   *Forms of Preemption.* As the cases indicate, there are several types of preemption arguments: outright conflict; express preemption; and implied preemption.

(a)   *Outright Conflict.* Most state courts abide by the principle codified in Iowa's preemption statute, noted in *Goodell,* which stipulates that a local government "shall not set standards and requirements which are lower or less stringent than those imposed by state law but may set standards and requirements which are higher and more stringent than those imposed by state law, unless a state law provides otherwise." Iowa Code § 331.301(6)(a). In other words, a local government cannot permit something the state forbids, but may forbid something the state allows. If a state adopts a 60 mile per hour highway speed limit, a county could not authorize 65 miles per hour on county roads, but it would be able to lower the speed limit to 55. *Cf.* Miller v. Fabius Township Bd., 114 N.W.2d 205, 210 (Mich.1962) ("Densely populated cities with large numbers of automobiles require more local regulation, even to a greater reduction in speed, than do rural communities. The State prescribes by its statutes the general provisions with respect to problems, and this Court has upheld the right of municipalities to further regulate as long as there is no conflict between the State statute and the municipal ordinance."). In *Miller,* the court held that because a state law limited the time for water skiing on lakes in the state to the period from one hour before sunrise until one hour after sunset, a locality could not authorize midnight water skiing at a local lake, but it could further limit water skiing to the period between 10:00 a.m. and 4:00 p.m. *See id.* at 207–08.

Basic premises of home rule compel the conclusion that local regulation which adds to state regulation must not be deemed automatically in conflict with and preempted by state laws. Otherwise, whenever a state enters a field of regulation, all local requirements, other than those that simply reiterate state law, would add to state law and, thus, would be preempted. What, then, made Humboldt County's requirements inconsistent with, and thus preempted by, state law? Are you persuaded that Humboldt County did "not merely impose higher standards" but "actually change[d] the state regulatory system"?

Outright conflict occurs if the local government purports to do something the state forbids unless there is some specific constitutional protection for the local action or it is a local government acting on a matter of local concern in an imperio state. In Webb v. City of Black Hawk, 295 P.3d 480 (Colo. 2013), the Colorado Supreme Court invalidated an ordinance adopted by a home rule municipality that banned bicycling within the city by cyclists from outside the city who sought to cycle through the city. The local measure conflicted with a state law permitting municipalities to prohibit bicycling on streets and highways only if alternate suitable bike paths were provided, which the Black Hawk measure failed to do. The court ruled that although Black Hawk "has a valid interest in controlling traffic on its local streets," this was not purely a local matter because of the state's interests in the "consistent application of statewide laws to avoid patchwork bicycle regulations that may frustrate residents statewide as well as potentially affecting tourism" and "in improving the state's bicycle transportation infrastructure." *Id.* at 492. As a result, the state prevailed and the local law was preempted. Similarly, a local law is in conflict with state law if it requires something the state forbids. In Town of Telluride v. Lot Thirty-Four Venture, L.L.C., 3 P.3d 30 (Colo. 2000), the Colorado Supreme Court found such an express conflict when it determined that the Town of Telluride's "affordable housing ordinance"—which required property owners in that resort community to create affordable housing for forty percent of the employees generated by any new development—was in conflict with a state law banning local rent control ordinances. The court concluded that by requiring the creation of below-market-rate housing the affordable housing plan "operates to suppress rental values below their market values" and was, thus, rent control within the meaning of the state law, and forbidden. *Id.* at 35–36. Two members of the court disagreed with the court's broad reading of the rent control statute, and dissented. *Id.* at 40, 47.

(b) *Express Preemption and Implied Preemption*. In addition to conflicting state and local laws, preemption will occur when the state expressly prohibits local governments from adopting laws concerning an area subject to state regulation, even if the local law is not in conflict with the state law. Express preemption cases raise two issues: Does the arguably preemptive state law prohibit the local law? Does the state have the power to prohibit the local law? The first question is usually pretty straightforward, although it was more debatable in *Goodell*. Did the state law prohibiting county zoning of agricultural land and structures apply to county regulation of hog factories? Why were the Humboldt County ordinances not considered to be zoning?

Implied preemption results in the displacement of an otherwise valid local law even in the absence of an express state prohibition. Implied preemption is more controversial than express preemption. Implied preemption expands both the amount of preemption and the role of the courts in determining whether local measures are preempted. *Goodell, City of Northglenn, Wallach,* and *City of Riverside* all involved claims of implied preemption.

The Illinois constitution's home rule article disclaims the doctrine of implied preemption. It provides:

Home rule units may exercise and perform concurrently with the State any power or function of a home rule unit to the extent that the General Assembly by law does not specifically limit the concurrent exercise or specifically declare the State's exercise to be exclusive.

Ill. Const.1970, art. VII, § 6(i).

In City of Chicago v. Roman, 705 N.E.2d 81 (Ill.1998), the Illinois Supreme Court rejected the claim that the Illinois Criminal Code preempted Chicago's mandatory minimum sentence of 90 days for a defendant convicted of assault on an elderly person. Under the state criminal code, there was no mandatory minimum for assault. *Roman* rejected the argument that the state law impliedly preempted Chicago's mandatory minimum:

> Some might believe that the courts play an important role in invalidating home rule ordinances that are inconsistent with statutes or that invade a field fully occupied by state legislation. By applying judicial doctrines relating to conflict, inconsistency, and occupation of the field, the courts can, inter alia, promote uniformity of law. However, for several reasons, the 1970 Constitutional Convention was strongly opposed to 'judicial preemption,' and sought a means to reduce its importance. * * * [I]n the present case, the Corrections Code, although quite comprehensive, does not expressly limit the concurrent exercise of the City's home rule power or require such exercise to conform to or be consistent with the Code.

705 N.E.2d at 89–90. Similarly, in Palm v. 2800 Lake Shore Drive Condominium Ass'n, 988 N.E.2d 75 (Ill. 2013), the Illinois Supreme Court rejected a preemption challenge to a Chicago ordinance allowing condominium owners broader access to condominium association books than state law provided. The relevant state statute required unit owners to state a proper purpose for obtaining association books and records; required production of only ten years of records; and gave the association thirty days to respond. Under the Chicago ordinance, by contrast, a unit owner did not have to state a proper purpose for requesting the records, there was no restriction on the age of the documents, and the association had only three business days to produce them. The court held that as the "legislature has not specifically denied the City's exercise of home rule power or required its exercise of that power to be consistent with statutory provisions" the ordinance was not preempted. *Id.* at 85.

The Montana Supreme Court has also held that the doctrine of implied preemption is inconsistent with home rule. *See* Tipco Corp. v. Billings, 642 P.2d 1074 (Mont.1982). *Accord*, Town Pump, Inc. v. Board of Adjustment of the City of Red Lodge, 971 P.2d 349, 357 (Mont.1998) (state liquor regulations did not preempt local regulation of the sale of alcohol as the state had not "specifically denied [municipal] power"). Similarly the dissenters in *City of Northglenn* emphasized that the state had not expressly preempted the local ordinance, contending that if the legislature really thought the local measure interfered with the state program it could expressly so declare. This is also essentially the position that prevailed in *Wallach* and *City of Riverside.*

Most state courts, however, find implied preemption on some occasions. For example, although the New Mexico Constitution's home rule grant provides that municipalities may exercise all legislative powers "not expressly denied" them, the New Mexico Supreme Court has held that state laws may preempt local ones even in the absence of an express statement of preemptive intent. In Casuse v. City of Gallup, 746 P.2d 1103, 1105 (N.M.1987), the court concluded that "any New Mexico law that clearly intends to preempt a governmental area should be sufficient without necessarily stating that affected municipalities must comply and cannot operate to the contrary." *See also* In re Generic Investigation into Cable Television Services, 707 P.2d 1155, 1161 (N.M.1985) ("Although the regulatory authority at issue is not specifically denied to home rule municipalities, . . . the grant of the authority to the [state] Commission makes its exercise by any other governmental body so inconsistent with the Constitution that it is equivalent to an express denial.")

As these cases suggest, implied preemption may involve some weighing of the relative strengths and weaknesses of the arguments for and against state and local regulation of an area. Supporters of the local laws in *City of Northglenn, Wallach,* and *City of Riverside* emphasized the traditional local interest in land use regulation, while the argument for preemption frequently focuses on the effects on people or communities outside the regulating locality, the costs of varying local laws, or the impact on the state's economy or broader social policies. What do you think? Should a strong commitment to local home rule require that all preemption be express or are there circumstances in which courts ought to be able to find that state laws have impliedly preempted local ordinances in the absence of express preemption? For a thoughtful analysis, *see* Paul Diller, Intrastate Preemption, 87 B.U.L. Rev. 1113 (2007).

3. *Municipal Action That Frustrates the Purpose of State Law.* Consider the following Maine law:

> Any municipality . . . may exercise any power or function which the Legislature has power to confer upon it, which is not denied either expressly or by clear implication. . . . The Legislature shall not be held to have implicitly denied any power granted to municipalities under this section unless the municipal ordinance in question would frustrate the purpose of any state law.

30–A Me.R.S.A. § 3001.

In *Goodell,* did the Iowa Supreme Court find, in effect, that the Humboldt County ordinances "frustrated the purpose" of Iowa's laws? What purpose was frustrated? Similarly, did the *Northglenn* ordinance "frustrate the purpose" of the Colorado foster care program? Frustration-of-purpose was also central to the preemption arguments in *Wallach* and *City of Riverside*. Why did the argument succeed in some of these cases and fail in the other? *See also* G.H. v. Township of Galloway, 971 A.2d 401 (N.J. 2009) (finding that municipal ordinances banning convicted sex offenders from living within designated distances of schools, parks, playgrounds and day care centers interfere with the ability of parole officers to carry out their statutorily mandated function of finding appropriate housing for offenders).

4. *Non-Regulation vs. Permission; or Floors and Ceilings.* In determining how much a local government can add to a state regulatory scheme before its action is "inconsistent" with the scheme, characterization of the state's regulation becomes crucial. If the state sets a speed limit, imposes certain health and safety requirements, or mandates certain procedures to assure that a private firm meets environmental standards, is the state merely manifesting indifference to speeds below the limit and behavior that meets the standards and procedures, or is it affirmatively authorizing the private behavior it permits and insulating it from having to comply with additional local rules? If the state is indifferent to matters outside the scope of its regulation, then local action is not inconsistent with state regulation. But if the state has made an affirmative decision that certain matters should not be regulated then local regulations may be inconsistent with that state decision. In other words, is the state law a regulatory ceiling—limiting local initiatives—or a floor on which localities may build?

This is a regularly recurring issue. An excellent example of this problem is Nutter v. Dougherty, 938 A.2d 401 (Pa. 2007). Philadelphia had adopted dollar limits on contributions to candidates for municipal office. Pennsylvania's Election Code prohibited contributions by corporations and banks, and also prohibited anonymous contributions and cash contributions in excess of $100, but did not impose monetary limits on campaign contributions. Challengers to the Philadelphia ordinance contended that the state Election Code "clearly manifests, albeit by omission, the [legislature's] intent not to impose limits on campaign contributions." The state supreme court, however, determined that the legislation's non-action was open to the "counter-interpretation" that it "desire[d] to leave the field open to locally tailored restrictions such as those contained in the Ordinance that are sensitive to peculiarities of the political landscape of a particular municipality." *Id.* at 413–14. Finding that "ambiguities" regarding local authority should be resolved in favor of the municipality, the court rejected the preemption claim and upheld the ordinance.

A similar issue arose in Ohio, when that state's supreme court considered whether a state "predatory lending" law—setting a maximum home mortgage interest rate and caps on points and fees payable by the consumer at closing—preempted tougher local ordinances adopted by the cities of Dayton and Cleveland that imposed more restrictive rules on mortgage rates, points, and fees. Any loan that complied with the local ordinances would comply with the state's restriction, but there would be loans that met the state's requirements but violated the local laws. A divided Ohio Supreme Court held that the local ordinances were preempted. American Financial Services Ass'n v. City of Cleveland, 858 N.E.2d 776 (Ohio 2006). The majority simply stated that "any local ordinances that seek to prohibit conduct that the state has authorized are in conflict with the state statutes and are therefore unconstitutional." *Id.* at 785. The two dissenters found no conflict, noting that

> permission to act without consequence under state law is not equatable to permission to act irrespective of municipal regulation . . . [o]therwise, any form of conduct that could have been but was not expressly prohibited by a state law on the subject would automatically exceed the reach of municipal authority, and there would be little left for municipal regulation.

Id. at 792 (Resnick, J., joined by Pfeifer, J., dissenting). A justice who concurred in the judgment, but did not join the majority opinion, preferred to ground his conclusion on the more functional determination that mortgage regulation and predatory lending are matters of statewide concern that are best dealt with by a uniform statewide law, *id.* at 789 (O'Connor, J., concurring in the judgment only). The dissenters, in turn, responded that "[a] one-size-fits-all rule regarding mortgage rates is ill-suited to a state with the demographic and economic diversity of Ohio." *Id.* at 795. "There is no reason . . . why municipalities afflicted more greatly by the problem of predatory lending cannot create greater protections for their citizens." *Id.* at 797–98 (Pfeifer, J., joined by Resnick, J., dissenting). Which of these analyses and arguments do you find most persuasive? Similarly, in Lawson v. City of Pasco, 230 P.3d 1038 (Wash. 2010), a divided Washington Supreme Court held that the state's Manufactured/Mobile Home Landlord Tenant Act, which by its terms contemplated there would be recreational vehicles (RVs) in the mobile home parks the law regulated, was not in conflict with and did not preempt a local ordinance flatly banning RVs from mobile home parks. In the majority's view, the statute "contains no language creating a right to place RVs in mobile home parks anywhere in the state. . . . The statute simply regulates recreational vehicle tenancies where such tenancies exist." *Id.* at 1042–43. The two dissenters, however, read the state law as "expressly authorizing RVs in mobile home parks" and as "thwart[ing] legislative intent to regulate them." *Id.* at 1044, 1048.

   See also Jancyn Mfg. Corp. v. County of Suffolk, 518 N.E.2d 903, 906 (N.Y.1987) (when state environmental regulations did not prohibit a certain chemical additive but local law did, there was no conflict: "No right or benefit is expressly given to a manufacturer of cesspool additives by the state law which has then been curtailed or taken away by the local law"). *But see* Lansdown Entertainment Corp. v. New York City Dept. of Consumer Affairs, 543 N.E.2d 725, 727 (N.Y.1989) (state law prohibiting the sale of alcoholic beverages after 4:00 a.m. but explicitly permitting bar patrons to continue to consume their drinks until 4:30 a.m. preempts New York City ordinance imposing a 4:00 a.m. closing time for those establishments: "[T]he State law specifically allows patrons to remain on the premises consuming alcohol until 4:30 a.m., while the local law does not. This is not a tiny overlap, but a direct conflict.")

5. *State Licenses.* Affirmative state permission of certain activity— and, thus, some protection from local regulation—is more likely to be found when the state issues a license to the person or firm engaging in the activity sought to be regulated by the local government. The license represents the state's determination that the licensee is qualified to undertake the activity for which she has been licensed. That may preclude additional local qualifications to undertake the activity. But should the state licensing scheme invalidate all additional local regulation of the activity? Suppose the locality is not concerned with qualifications for the activity but wants to ban the activity outright.

This issue has arisen with respect to local efforts to prohibit or curtail the use of personal watercraft (PWC), also known as jet skis. Where jet ski aficionados have received state licenses or fulfilled state-imposed registration requirements, they have argued that their state permits preempt local regulation. The Supreme Court of Washington rejected that argument: "Registration of a vessel is nothing more than a precondition to operating a boat. No unconditional right is granted by obtaining such registration. Statutes often impose preconditions which do not grant unrestricted permission to participate in an activity. Purchasing a hunting license is a precondition to hunting, but the license certainly does not allow hunting of endangered species, . . . or hunting inside the Seattle city limits." Weden v. San Juan County, 958 P.2d 273, 281 (Wash. 1998). A dissenting judge, however, argued that the county ordinance "defeats the state license by completely banning all PWCs from the marine waters of the very county most appropriate for the very activity the State has seen fit to license, [and] the state license is robbed of its only purpose (to allow use of the craft) as the county ordinance now renders the state permit a license to do nothing at all." *Id.* at 295. *See also* Barnhill v. North Myrtle Beach, 511 S.E.2d 361 (S.C.1999) (court upholds ordinance restricting the launching and beaching of jet skis between 9:00 a.m. and 5:00 p.m.). *Contra* Village of Wauconda v. Hutton, 684 N.E.2d 1364 (Ill.App.1997) (court invalidates village ordinance requiring operators of personal watercraft to use a personal flotation device as inconsistent with state Boat Registration and Safety Act).

6. *Fracking.* In the past decade, hydraulic fracturing, or "fracking," has become a new flashpoint of state-local conflict. As *Wallach* explained, fracking technology involves the injection of water and chemicals at high pressure into rock formations to unlock and release natural gas. It has been hailed by proponents as a crucial means of reducing American dependence on imported oil; of reducing greenhouse-gas emissions by shifting American energy use from oil and coal to "cleaner" natural gas; as a source of employment; and, by cutting energy costs, as a boost to the economy. Critics, however, have expressed grave reservations about gas or fracking fluid contaminating groundwater; toxic air emissions from gas leaks; chemical

spills; and the improper disposal of toxic substances in fracking fluid. From a state and local government perspective, perhaps the key point is that the benefits are largely national and state (including tax payments to state governments) but the costs are largely local, including, in addition to those mentioned, noise and vibrations from drilling and increased truck traffic, impacts on the natural environment, and the social disruption resulting from intensive industrial activity in previously agricultural or residential areas. As a result, communities from New York to North Carolina to Texas to California have sought to restrict fracking within their borders. These measures typically raise preemption issues as many states have laws regulating oil and gas drilling.

State courts have reached a wide range of results. In *Wallach*, as we have seen, New York's highest court held that the state's pre-existing oil and gas law did not preempt local power to ban fracking through zoning, but indicated that the legislature had the power to amend its law to preempt such local ordinances. In Robinson Township v. Commonwealth, 83 A.3d 901 (Pa. 2013), the Pennsylvania Supreme Court went much further, in effect holding that at least some aspects of fracking regulation must occur at the local level. *Robinson Township* invalidated a 2012 amendment to the state's oil and gas law—Act 13—that specifically prohibited any local regulation of oil and gas operations, including environmental protections; and imposed statewide uniformity on all local zoning ordinances with respect to the development of oil and gas resources, effectively permitting drilling in all zoning districts. Three justices, of the six participating, determined that by requiring municipalities to disregard all environmental issues raised by fracking, Act 13 violated Pennsylvania's Environmental Rights Amendment, Pa Const. Art. I, § 27, which establishes a "right to clean air, pure water, and to the preservation of the natural, scenic, historic, and esthetic values of the environment;" makes the state "trustee of these resources;" and directs it to "conserve and maintain them for the benefit of all the people." In addition, the court ruled that Act 13's wholesale preemption of local zoning was inconsistent with the constitution's command to protect the state's environmental resources:

> "In Pennsylvania, terrain and natural conditions frequently differ throughout a municipality, and from municipality to municipality. As a result, the impact on the quality, quantity, and well-being of our natural resources cannot reasonably be assessed on the basis of a statewide average. Protection of environmental values, in this respect, is a quintessential local issue that must be tailored to local conditions."

83 A.3d at 979. A fourth justice concurred in striking down Act 13 but declined to rely on the Environmental Rights Amendment. Instead, he wrote that the legislature "unconstitutionally, as a matter of substantive due process, usurped local municipalities' duty to impose and enforce community planning, and the concomitant reliance of property owners, citizens, and the like on that community planning." *Id.* at 1001. Justice Baer observed that

while it might be "possible" for the legislature, "through a law applicable statewide, [to] remove *en toto* from local municipalities the apparatus it provided to vindicate the individual substantive due process rights of Pennsylvanian landowners" he was "skeptical that the legislature could devise a scheme of statewide scope that sufficiently protects substantive due process." *Id.* at 1002–03. Two justices dissented, finding that Act 13 fell easily within the state's power to control its municipalities. *Id.* at 1010.

Other courts have struck down local anti-fracking measures. In State ex rel. Morrison v. Beck Energy Corp., 317 N.E.3d 128 (Ohio 2015), a closely divided Ohio Supreme Court held that a set of ordinances adopted by the City of Munroe Falls to regulate oil and gas drilling within its borders were preempted by state law. The city sought to prohibit any construction or excavation activity without a "zoning certificate" issued by the zoning inspector. It also imposed a one-year delay on drilling even after a municipal zoning certificate is granted, payment of a performance bond, and a public hearing at least three weeks prior to the start of drilling. A plurality of three justices found that the city permit requirement, when applied to a company that had obtained a permit from the Ohio Department of Natural Resources (ODNR) to drill within the city, created "a classic licensing conflict under our home-rule precedent. We have consistently held that a municipal-licensing ordinance conflicts with a state-licensing scheme if the 'local ordinance restricts an activity which the state license permits.'" *Id.* at 136. More broadly, the plurality concluded that the state law giving the ODNR exclusive authority to regulate the permitting, location, and spacing of oil and gas wells and production operations within Ohio also prohibited municipal efforts, like the Munroe Falls ordinances that "unfairly impede[ ] or obstruct[ ]" the activities and operations covered by state law. *Id.* at 137. The concurring opinion of two justices, including one who also signed the majority opinion, agreed that the Munroe Falls ordinances were invalid but sought to emphasize that the court's ruling did not address whether the state's oil and gas drilling statute preempted local land use ordinances that "address only the traditional concerns of zoning laws, such as ensuring compatibility with local neighborhoods, preserving property values, or effectuating a municipality's long-term plan for development, by limiting oil and gas wells to certain zoning districts without imposing a separate permitting regime applicable only to oil and gas drilling." *Id.* at 138. Three justices dissented, finding that state law did not specifically prohibit local zoning regulation of oil and gas drilling, and that municipalities could supplement state law with their own nonconflicting regulation. In the words of the principal dissent's rather colorful conclusion, "[t]here is no need for the state to act as the thousand-pound gorilla, gobbling up exclusive authority over the oil and gas industry, leaving not even a banana peel of home rule for municipalities." *Id.* at 146.

Two other court decisions invalidating local fracking restrictions on preemption grounds are Northeast Natural Energy LLC v. City of Morgantown, 2011 WL 3584376 (W.Va.Cir.Ct. 2011) and Colorado Oil & Gas

Ass'n v. City of Longmont, 2014 WL 3690665 (Colo. D. Ct., Boulder Co. 2014) (enjoining municipal ban but staying injunction pending appeal). There is also an extensive and growing law review literature on the subject. *See, e.g.,* John Abendroth, Fracking in Illinois: Implementation of the Hydraulic Fracturing Regulatory Act and Local Government Regulatory Authority, 35 No. Ill. U.L. Rev. 575 (2015); Jamal Knight & Bethany Gullman, The Power of State Interest: Preemption of Local Fracking Ordinances in Home-Rule Cities, 28 Tul. Env. L.J. 297 (2015); James K. Pickle, Fracking Preemption Litigation, Wash. & Lee J. Energy, Climate & Env. 293 (2014); Alex Ritchie, On Local Fracking Bans: Policy and Preemption in New Mexico, 54 Nat. Resources J. 255 (2014); Joel Minor, Local Government Fracking Regulations: A Colorado Case Study, 33 Stan. Env. L.J. 61 (2014); John R. Nolon & Victoria Polidoro, Hydrofracking: Disturbances Both Geological and Political: Who Decides?, 44 Urb. Law. 507 (2012).

7. *Medical Marijuana.* The medical marijuana ordinance at issue in *City of Riverside* implicated all three levels of government. As the California Supreme Court indicated, the federal Comprehensive Drug Abuse Prevention and Control Act of 1970 (commonly referred to as the Controlled Substance Act), 21 U.S.C. §801 et seq. criminalizes the manufacture, distribution, or possession of marijuana. Along with heroin and LSD, marijuana is classified as a Schedule I drug, with no accepted medical use. 21 U.S.C. § 812(b)(1). The United States Supreme Court has held that applying the CSA to purely intrastate growers and users of marijuana for medical purposes does not violate the Commerce Clause of the United States Constitution, Gonzales v. Raich, 545 U.S. 1 (2005), and has held that regardless of state law there is no medical necessity defense to the CSA's ban on manufacturing and distributing marijuana, United States v. Oakland Cannabis Buyers' Cooperative, 532 U.S. 483 (2001). In 1996, however, California voters approved Proposition 215, which led to the Compassionate Use Act referred to in the *City of Riverside* opinion, and over the next two decades, 23 states and the District of Columbia adopted measures authorizing the medical use of marijuana. A number of those states—Alaska, Colorado, Oregon, and Washington—now also authorize the recreational use of marijuana. *See* J. Herbert DiFonzo & Ruth C. Stern, Divided We Stand: Medical Marijuana and Federalism, 27 no. 5 Health Law 17 (2015). The resulting tension between continuing federal criminalization and extensive state-level decriminalization has become another federalism sore spot. Federal law provides no exemption for medical marijuana use in states which have decriminalized it, but the Department of Justice has "signaled its willingness to dilute enforcement of the CSA" by advising selected United States Attorneys that federal drug enforcement efforts should not target individuals who are "in clear and unambiguous compliance" with state medical marijuana laws. *Id.* at 19. Nonetheless, federal law still shadows state practices, providing support, for example, for employers who, pursuant to drug-free workplace policies, discharge medical marijuana users. *See id.* at 20–21. Given the possibility that state decriminalization laws could be deemed preempted by the federal CSA a law review case note on the *City of Riverside* decision praised the

California Supreme Court's narrow reading of the state law as the "safest approach" to avoiding federal preemption. Recent Case, 127 Harv. L. Rev. 1204 (2014). *See also* Symposium: Medical Marijuana Legalization, A Growing Trend: Social, Economic, and Legal Implications, 35 No. Ill. U.L. Rev. (Issue 3, Summer 2015).

ALLIED VENDING, INC. V. CITY OF BOWIE
Court of Appeals of Maryland
631 A.2d 77 (1993)

KARWACKI, J.

We issued a writ of certiorari in this case to determine the validity of ordinances * * * which restrict the placement of state-licensed cigarette vending machines to locations which are not generally accessible to minors. The Circuit Court for Prince George's County determined that the ordinances were valid. We shall hold that the municipal ordinances are pre-empted by state law, more specifically, the cigarette licensing scheme provided by Maryland Code (1957, 1991 Cum.Supp.), Article 56, §§ 607 through 631, and therefore, shall reverse.

I.

On July 23, 1990, the City of Takoma Park enacted Ordinance No. 1990–39, which repealed and reenacted with amendments, Chapter 10B of the Takoma Park Code ("Takoma Park ordinance"). As enacted, § 10B–15(a) provides that "[n]o person shall sell tobacco products through a vending machine without first obtaining a permit for the placement of a cigarette vending machine in compliance with the provisions of [this ordinance]." Section 10B–16 provides:

"(a) No permit shall be issued for placement of a cigarette vending machine except in locations which are not generally accessible to or frequented by minors, such as bars, cocktail lounges, liquor stores, and private clubhouses for members of fraternal or civic organizations not operated as public businesses or open to the general public.

"(b) Notwithstanding the foregoing, no permit shall be issued for a cigarette vending machine which is:

(1) Located in a coat room, restroom, unmonitored hallway, outer waiting area, or similar unattended or unmonitored area of a bar, cocktail lounge, liquor store, private clubhouse or other place to which minors are not generally permitted access; or

(2) Accessible to the public when the establishment is closed.

* * * The purposes for the enactment of these provisions were set forth in the ordinance's preamble as follows:

"WHEREAS, the Council wishes to discourage minors from experimenting with smoking and to make tobacco products less accessible to minors by restricting where cigarette vending machines are placed . . . and . . .

"WHEREAS, smoking by minors is detrimental to the public health and contrary to public policy; and . . .

"WHEREAS, smoking has been linked to lung cancer, respiratory disease and heart disease; and . . .

"WHEREAS, the Surgeon General has determined that smoking is the leading cause of preventable death; and . . .

"WHEREAS, nicotine in tobacco has been found by the Surgeon General to be a powerfully addictive drug and it is therefore important to prevent minors from using nicotine until they are mature and capable of making an informed and rational decision; and

"WHEREAS, everyday more than 3,000 minors begin smoking; and

"WHEREAS, one-half of all smokers began smoking before the age of 18; and

"WHEREAS, Article 27, Section 404 of the Annotated Code of Maryland prohibits the sale of tobacco products to minors; and

"WHEREAS, despite the Maryland state law, access by minors to tobacco products is a major problem; and

"WHEREAS, cigarette vending machines are often located in unattended or unmonitored areas where minors can readily purchase tobacco products; and

"WHEREAS, a City permit requirement which would allow the placement of cigarette vending machines only in establishments which are not generally accessible to or frequented by minors or are not open to the general public would help restrict the access of minors to tobacco products; and

"WHEREAS, a City cigarette vending machine permit is necessary for regulatory purposes to more effectively restrict the access of minors to tobacco products in the interest of public health." * * *

II.

* * *

B.

Prior to the enactment of the ordinances, the licensing of cigarette vending machines was accomplished exclusively in accordance with Md.Code (1957, 1991 Cum.Supp.), Article 56, §§ 607 through 631. Sections 607 through 631 are comprehensive provisions governing the appropriate licenses necessary to sell cigarettes in Maryland at wholesale, retail, over-the-counter, and through cigarette vending machines. In order to operate a cigarette vending machine within this State, a vendor must obtain two licenses for each machine.

* * * Section 617(3) is a recent addition to the section, added by Chapter 301 of the Acts of 1989. Chapter 301 raised the minimum age of a person, from 16 years to 18 years of age, to whom it is lawful to sell cigarettes or other tobacco products. *See* Md.Code (1957, 1992 Repl.Vol.), Art. 27, § 404. * * *

C.

The powers of incorporated municipalities are provided in Article XI–E of the Maryland Constitution and Article 23A of the Maryland Code. *Mayor of Forest Heights v. Frank*, 291 Md. 331, 342, 435 A.2d 425, 431 (1981). Under Article XI–E, § 3 of the Maryland Constitution, each municipal corporation in Maryland is vested with "the power and authority * * * to amend or repeal an existing charter or local laws relating to the incorporation, organization, government, or affairs of said municipal corporation heretofore enacted by the General Assembly of Maryland, * * * and to amend or repeal any charter adopted under the provisions of this Article." This authority is qualified by Article XI–E, § 6, of the Maryland Constitution which provides that "[a]ll charter provisions, or amendments thereto, adopted under the provisions of this Article, shall be subject to all applicable laws enacted by the General Assembly." Likewise, Maryland Code (1957, 1990 Repl.Vol.), Article 23A, § 2 provides:

> "(a) The legislative body of every incorporated municipality in this State, except Baltimore City, by whatever name known, shall have general power to pass such ordinances not contrary to the Constitution of Maryland, public general law, or, except as provided in § 2B of this article, public local law as they may deem necessary in order to assure the good government of the municipality, to protect and preserve the municipality's rights, property, and privileges, to preserve peace and good order, to secure persons and property from danger and destruction, and to

protect the health, comfort and convenience of the citizens of the municipality. . . ."

Following this delegation of general power, Article 23A, § 2(b) grants certain express powers to municipal corporations and provides in relevant part:

> "(b) In addition to, but not in substitution of, the powers which have been, or may hereafter be, granted to it, such legislative body also shall have the following express ordinance-making powers: . . .

Express authorization →

> (32) To exercise the licensing authority granted in Article 56 and other provisions of the law.

> (33) Subject to the limitations imposed under Article 24 of the Code, the Tax-General Article, and the Tax-Property Article, to establish and collect reasonable fees and charges:

> (i) For the franchises, licenses, or permits authorized by law to be granted by a municipal corporation. . . ."

The ability of a municipal corporation to regulate businesses through licensing and permitting processes is circumscribed in part by Article 56, § 12. Section 12 provides in relevant part:

> "Except as otherwise expressly provided in this article, no county, city or other political subdivision of this State shall require any person, firm or corporation to obtain a permit or license to transact in such county, city or other political subdivision any business or occupation for which it or he is required to obtain a State license under the provisions of this article, nor shall any county, city or other political subdivision of this State levy an occupational tax or fee upon such person, firm or corporation for transacting any such business or engaging in any such occupation for which such State license is required. Notwithstanding the provisions of this section, any county, city or other political subdivision of this State may require permits or licenses to be obtained where necessary for regulatory purposes in the interest of the public health, safety or morals."

Although municipalities may require permits or licenses for regulatory purposes in the interest of the public health, safety or morals, this authority is "subject to all applicable laws enacted by the General Assembly." Md. Const. Art. XI–E, § 6. Moreover, ordinances passed pursuant to such authority are permissible as long as they are "not contrary to the Constitution of Maryland [or] public general law. . . ." Art. 23A, § 2(a). In short, if the General Assembly has pre-empted a certain field, such as the sale of cigarettes through cigarette vending machines, it is irrefutable that municipalities have no authority to legislate in that field.

III.

* * * As we recently explained in *Talbot County v. Skipper*, 329 Md. 481, 487–88, 620 A.2d 880, 883 (1993), state law may pre-empt local law in one of three ways: 1) pre-emption by conflict, 2) express pre-emption, or 3) implied pre-emption. Over the last twenty-five years, we have frequently examined the concept of implied pre-emption. * * *

Although there is no particular formula for determining whether the General Assembly intended to pre-empt by implication an entire area, and though our decisions have considered several factors, we have stated repeatedly that " '[t]he primary indicia of a legislative purpose to pre-empt an entire field of law is the comprehensiveness with which the General Assembly has legislated the field.' " *Skipper*, 329 Md. at 488, 620 A.2d at 883. * * *

Among the secondary factors we have considered in determining whether pre-emption by implication exists are the following: 1) whether local laws existed prior to the enactment of the state laws governing the same subject matter, 2) whether the state laws provide for pervasive administrative regulation, 3) whether the local ordinance regulates an area in which some local control has traditionally been allowed, 4) whether the state law expressly provides concurrent legislative authority to local jurisdictions or requires compliance with local ordinances, 5) whether a state agency responsible for administering and enforcing the state law has recognized local authority to act in the field, 6) whether the particular aspect of the field sought to be regulated by the local government has been addressed by the state legislation, and 7) whether a two-tiered regulatory process existing if local laws were not pre-empted would engender chaos and confusion. [citations omitted]

A.

In light of the comprehensive state-licensing scheme for cigarette vending machines provided by Article 56, §§ 607 through 631, we conclude that the sale of cigarettes through cigarette vending machines is one of those "areas[s] in which the Legislature has acted with such force that an intent by the State to occupy the entire field must be implied. . . ." *Montgomery Ass'n*, 274 Md. at 59, 333 A.2d at 600.

* * * [T]he state law governing the sale of cigarettes through vending machines requires a permit, §§ 611, 631, specifies the contents of the application, § 612, requires the issuance of the license by the Comptroller or clerk of the proper circuit court if the application requirements are satisfied, §§ 613, 631, authorizes the licensee to engage in the licensed business, §§ 614, 631, establishes provisions for the term and renewal of the licenses, §§ 615 and 631, establishes additional requirements in order to keep the license, including the proper labeling of the cigarette vending machine with an identification label and a warning label, § 617, COMAR 03.02.03.04D, provides for inspection of the cigarette vending machines, Md.Code (1990 Repl.Vol.), § 11–507 of the Commercial Law Article and Md.Code (1988), § 2–107 of the Tax-General Article, establishes grounds for denial of a license and specifies the circumstances under which a license can be suspended or revoked, §§ 618–622, and provides numerous criminal offenses punishable by jail or fines for failure to comply with the state laws. §§ 622, 630, 631. *See Skipper*, 329 Md. at 489–91, 620 A.2d at 884–85.

We conclude that "[t]hese statutory provisions manifest the general legislative purposes to create an all-encompassing state scheme," *Skipper*, 329 Md. at 491, 620 A.2d at 885, to regulate the sale of cigarettes through cigarette vending machines. Moreover, other factors support our conclusion that the state has pre-empted the field of regulation of the sale of cigarettes through vending machines.

For many years the General Assembly has exercised exclusive control over the sale of cigarettes. Since 1890, a county license to make retail sales of cigarettes has been required, Ch. 91 of the Acts of 1890, and since 1956, the cigarette vending machine operator's license and cigarette retailer's license have been required, Ch. 90 of the Acts of 1956. Further, the General Assembly recently addressed the sale of cigarettes to minors through vending machines, the stated purpose for enactment of the municipal ordinances in this case. In Chapter 301 of the Acts of 1989, the General Assembly sought to curb the purchase of cigarettes by minors through vending machines by requiring that each vending machine display a conspicuous label stating the minimum age required for the lawful sale of cigarettes and the penalty for such a violation.

* * * What we stated in *Montgomery Ass'n* can be adapted to the instant case:

"In view of the General Assembly's long and exclusive control of [the sale of cigarettes] in this State, the Legislature's failure to foresee and take action expressly to prevent future local government trespass in this area of exclusive state legislative authority is no support for the validity of the . . . ordinances."

274 Md. at 60 n. 5, 333 A.2d at 600 n. 5.

These ordinances attempt to regulate an area in which no local control has traditionally been allowed. * * *

Although the particular aspect of the field sought to be regulated by the [local ordinances] is not addressed by §§ 607 through 631, i.e., the physical location of the cigarette vending machines on the premises, * * * a two-tiered, or multi-tiered regulatory process depending on the number of jurisdictions that enact similar ordinances, would invite chaos and confusion, * * * engendering, as it may be in this case, a requirement tantamount to a ban. The trial court determined that all of the cigarette vending machines in this case were generally accessible to minors. If we were to uphold these municipal ordinances and the vendors could not comply with these ordinances, the ordinances would be tantamount to a ban on cigarette vending machines in locations in which the State has granted the vendors a license to operate those vending machines.

Since the enactment of Ch. 301 in 1989, the General Assembly has experienced a spate of legislative activity concerning the sale of cigarettes from vending machines. House Bill No. 1384 of the 1990 General Assembly session, House Bill No. 663 of the 1991 session, and House Bill No. 172 of the 1992 session would have banned cigarette vending machines on a state-wide basis, but each of those bills died in the House Committee on Ways and Means. House Bill No. 1383 of the 1990 General Assembly session, House Bill Nos. 39 and 662 of the 1991 session, Senate Bill No. 625 of the 1991 session, Senate Bill No. 187 of the 1992 session, and House Bill Nos. 555 and 554 of the 1992 session would have prohibited cigarette vending machines in places where minors had access to them, but each of those bills also died in committee. If the General Assembly intended to change existing law governing the sale of cigarettes through vending machines, it certainly has had the opportunities to do so. The failure to enact such measures "strongly suggests that there was no intent to allow local governments to enact different . . . requirements." *Skipper*, 329 Md. at 493, 620 A.2d at 886.

* * * In short, through the enactment of Article 56, §§ 607 through 631, the General Assembly has manifested an intent for the State to completely occupy the field of the sale of cigarettes through vending machines rendering any local or municipal ordinances in this area constitutionally invalid.

NOTES AND QUESTIONS

1. *Occupation of the Field.* Occupation of the field does not require a finding that the local ordinance is inconsistent or in conflict with state law. Instead the theory of "field preemption" is that the extensive scope of state regulation reflects a state intent to preempt all local regulation. Why have such a doctrine? Given the state's authority to preempt and given the state legislature's extensive regulation of the field in question, why not simply require the state legislature to formally preempt local action? With respect to cigarette vending machine regulation, is this an area where local regulation is particularly problematic? Does local regulation have extra-local effects? Are there special reasons to require uniform statewide regulation of cigarette vending machines?

2. *Defining the "Field."* Maryland state law regulates various aspects of cigarette vending machines by requiring a license, specifying the procedures for obtaining a license, establishing the term and renewal of the license, and providing for inspection of licensed machines. But there is no state law with respect to the location of licensed vending machines. Assuming the state had fully occupied the field of the rules and procedures for licensing cigarette vending machines, and that the cigarette vendors' interest in reducing their costs of compliance creates a state interest in uniform state rules, should the location of cigarette vending machines be treated as a separate field where there isn't as strong an interest in statewide uniformity? Or, instead of imposing distinctive rules and potentially costly interlocal variation on vendors, could the county simply ban cigarette vending machines within its borders?

Does the court tell us how it decided what the relevant field is? Are there principles for defining a "field" and marking it off from other fields?

Compare *Allied Vending* with the decision of the New York Court of Appeals in DJL Restaurant Corp. v. City of New York, 749 N.E.2d 186 (N.Y. 2001). *DJL* involved the claim that New York's City's "adult establishment" zoning ordinance ("AZR")—which requires that "adult establishments" that feature topless dancing be confined to the City's manufacturing and high density commercial districts—was preempted by New York State's comprehensive regulation, under the Alcohol Beverage Control ("ABC") Law, of establishments licensed to dispense alcoholic beverages.

> Plaintiffs argue that the City's AZR makes impermissible inroads in a preempted field. They contend that the AZR conflicts with the ABC Law in several important respects. They note, for example, that the ABC Law has its own provisions governing nudity in licensed premises * * *. They also point out that the AZR requires a minimum of 500 feet between an adult establishment and a school or place of worship, while the ABC Law requires only 200 feet * * *. Thus, plaintiffs argue, owing to these and similar points of conflict, the AZR is unenforceable against them. * * *

> The City, on the other hand, contends that the AZR is a local law of general application. Because its thrust is zoning and not the regulation of alcohol, the AZR applies across the board to all adult establishments whether they sell alcoholic beverages or not. The City also emphasizes that the AZR is directed at alleviating the secondary effects of adult establishments, and any impact on those that happen to sell alcoholic beverages is merely incidental to the City's land use scheme. We agree with the City.

> The Legislature enacted the ABC Law to promote temperance in the consumption of alcoholic beverages * * *. In carrying out its objectives, the ABC Law preempts its field by comprehensively regulating virtually all aspects of the sale and distribution of liquor.

* * * Alcohol, however, is not land. Indeed, the ABC Law and the AZR are directed at completely distinct activities. * * *

To be sure, by regulating land use a zoning ordinance "inevitably exerts an incidental control over any of the particular uses or businesses which * * * may be allowed in some districts but not in others" * * * Nevertheless, as we have observed, "separate levels of regulatory oversight can coexist" * * *. State statutes do not necessarily preempt local laws having only "tangential" impact on the State's interests. * * * Local laws of general application—which are aimed at legitimate concerns of a local government—will not be preempted if their enforcement only incidentally infringes on a preempted field.

* * * The AZR * * * applies not to the regulation of alcohol, but to the locales of adult establishments irrespective of whether they dispense alcoholic beverages. In short, plaintiffs come under both regulatory schemes because they simultaneously engage in two distinct activities, each involving an independent realm of governance. * * * A liquor licensee wishing to provide adult entertainment must do so in a location authorized by the AZR—not because it is selling liquor, but because it is providing adult entertainment. Conversely, if an adult establishment wishes to sell liquor, it must obtain a liquor license and comply with the ABC Law. That the ABC Law and the AZR have some overlapping requirements is merely peripheral * * *.

Id. at 190–92. Do *Allied Vending* and *DJL* take different approaches to the questions of "field" definition, or was the New York City ordinance less an intrusion into the area regulated by the state than the ordinances at issue in *Allied Vending*?

3. *State Law and the Local Role in Regulating Smoking.* The Maryland Court of Appeals reaffirmed its commitment to the *Allied Vending* decision in Altadis USA, Inc. v. Prince George's County, 65 A.3d 118 (Md. 2013), which held that state statutes preempted two Prince George's County ordinances that sought to bar the distribution or sale of loose or "unpackaged" cigars, defined as cigars not sold in sealed packages containing at least five cigars. The county acted in response to the apparent practice of cocaine and marijuana users of buying cheap cigars, removing some of the tobacco, and replacing it with those illegal substances. *See id.* at 119. Reviewing *Allied Vending*, the court concluded that the state had fully occupied the field of the packaging, distribution, and sale of tobacco products to the exclusion of the county's action. The court noted and gave weight to the fact that the state legislature had considered bills to ban the sale of individual cigars, but had failed to act: "The General Assembly's rejection of bills imposing the same requirements as the local legislation is significant in a preemption analysis." *Id.* at 125, *citing Allied Vending*. However, not all state courts have found that state laws regulating tobacco products preclude further local regulation.

State courts have concluded that none of these statutes preempted local laws regulating or prohibiting cigarette vending machines. *See, e.g.,* Vatore v. Commissioner of Consumer Affairs, 634 N.E.2d 958 (N.Y. 1994) (upholding local regulation restricting cigarette vending machines to taverns); Bravo Vending v. City of Rancho Mirage, 20 Cal.Rptr.2d 164 (Cal. App. 1993) (upholding local law that totally bans cigarette vending machines); Take Five Vending v. Town of Provincetown, 615 N.E.2d 576 (Mass.1993) (upholding total prohibition of vending machines). *But see* Automatic Refreshment Service, Inc. v. City of Cincinnati, 634 N.E.2d 1053 (Ohio App.1993) (state laws occupy the field and thus preempt local cigarette regulation).

Among the state court decisions considering and affirming the local power to go beyond state law in addressing smoking and the sale of cigarettes are Amico's Inc. v. Mattos, 789 A.2d 899 (R.I. 2002), Modern Cigarette, Inc. v. Town of Orange, 774 A.2d 969 (Conn. 2001), and Steffes v. City of Lawrence, 160 P.3d 843 (Kan. 2007). In *Amico's* the Rhode Island Supreme Court held that the state law requiring larger eating facilities to maintain separate smoking and nonsmoking sections did not preempt a local ordinance requiring restaurants of any size either to be smoke-free or to provide an enclosed, self-ventilated smoking section. The court found the ordinance was "not inconsistent" with state law; rather, the "more stringent smoking regulations imposed by the town advance" the public health purposes of the state law. In the absence of evidence that the legislature intended to set a maximum standard, the court ruled the statute "sets a floor rather than a ceiling in regulating smoking in restaurants." 789 A.2d at 907. The court also rejected the argument that the state had occupied the field of the regulation of smoking in restaurants, concluding that the state's delegation to cities and towns of the power to license restaurants and bars included the authority to "defin[e] the context in which those activities would take place." *Id.* at 908. In *Modern Cigarette*, the Connecticut Supreme Court found that a town ordinance completely banning cigarette vending machines within its borders was not preempted by a state law restricting the placement of cigarette vending machines to areas accessible only to adults. Both measures were aimed at curtailing youth smoking:

> "We recognize that the state has a significant interest in monitoring youth access to tobacco, as it should. Simply because the legislature has chosen to legislate on the subject does not mean, however, that the municipalities are without the power to regulate activities with local effects. * * * The issue of youth access to tobacco also is very much a local matter. * * * Because the ordinance does not frustrate the state's objective in limiting youth access to tobacco products, and indeed, is fully consistent with that purpose, it is valid."

774 A.2d at 984. In *Steffes*, the Kansas Supreme Court rejected the argument that a state law authorizing cities to regulate smoking in public places preempted a local ordinance banning smoking in enclosed public places (such as the plaintiff's bar). Although the plaintiff argued that complete prohibition is inconsistent with regulation, the court found that the "the legislature has

set a floor, but not a ceiling, for how much a city should regulate smoking." 160 P.3d at 849.

Is the area of smoking and cigarette regulation one in which uniform state regulation is necessary? Is it an area in which—due to the lack of extraterritorial effects, and the differences in local preferences and concerns—courts should be willing to assume local power to act? How should that affect the preemption decision?

4. *The Search for Legislative Intent.* Most courts treat the issue of preemption as one of legislative intent, with extensive state regulation signifying the state legislature's intent to occupy the field. *See, e.g.*, People v. Diack, 24 N.Y.3d 674 (N.Y. 2015) ("comprehensive and detailed" regulatory scheme "with respect to identification and monitoring of registered sex offenders" occupies the field of sex offender residency restrictions and so preempts local ordinances regulating sex offender residency); Midcoast Disposal, Inc. v. Town of Union, 537 A.2d 1149, 1151 (Me.1988) (local ban of privately owned facilities for the deposit of out-of-town solid waste held preempted by state law; extensive state regulation constituted a comprehensive and exclusive regulatory scheme that impliedly denied local power by revealing a "clear legislative intention to remove any authority a municipality may [otherwise] have had. . . ."). On the other hand, even a fairly comprehensive state law does not always fully occupy a field. In Mendenhall v. City of Akron, 881 N.E.2d 255, 263–64 (2008), the Ohio Supreme Court found that although the state legislature "has enacted a detailed statute governing criminal enforcement of speeding regulations" that did not prevent a city from imposing a civil fine, enforceable through a city administrative process, for speeding in school zones.

Sometimes, state legislation declares its intent. In State v. Kirwin, 203 P.3d 1044 (Wash. 2009), the Washington Supreme Court held that a state law making littering a civic infraction punishable by a maximum $50 penalty did not occupy the field of littering regulation and so preempt a local ordinance making littering a misdemeanor with the possibility of jail time or a fine because the law stated that the legislature's "intent . . . is to add to and to coordinate existing recycling and litter control and removal efforts and not to terminate or supplant such efforts." *Id.* at 1048. *Accord*, Lawson v. City of Pasco, 230 P.3d 1038, 1041 (Wash. 2010) (state's Manufactured/Mobile Home Landlord-Tenant Act does not occupy the field of mobile home tenancies as "certain provisions" of the state law "expressly contemplate some local regulation" and "expressly reference local ordinances to which landlords and tenants may be subject in the context of mobile home parks").

The state's intent may also be gleaned from the subjects on which the state law focuses. In Sherwin-Williams Co. v. City of Los Angeles, 844 P.2d 534 (Cal.1993), the California Supreme Court determined that a state statute prohibiting the sale of aerosol paint to minors did not preempt a local law prohibiting commercial displays of aerosol paint products. Although both laws were "graffiti-prevention measures," the state law was concerned with regulating the purchasers and the places of purchase of aerosol products, whereas the local ordinance was intended to establish rules for the display of these goods in order to reduce theft. The argument that the laws were intended to combat different evils saved the local ordinance from judicial invalidation. Similarly, in C.I.C. Corporation v. East Brunswick, 628 A.2d 753 (N.J. A.D. 1993), the court rejected the argument that the state cigarette legislation preempted a municipal ordinance banning the sale of cigarettes to minors. "[T]he legislative intent of the two [state] Cigarette Acts was to raise revenues and control abuses arising from non-licensed sale of cigarettes, such as smuggling. The purpose of [the local ordinance] is to prevent the sale of cigarettes to minors; the focus is on the purchasers, not the sellers, of cigarettes. Thus, the purposes of the laws are quite different." 628 A.2d at 758. Courts may also rely on canons of statutory interpretation like *expressio unius est exclusio alterius*—the axiom that the express inclusion of one subject implies the exclusion of other subjects from similar treatment. *See, e.g.,* Vatore v. Comm'r of Consumer Affairs, *supra* (state law regulating minors' access to tobacco products did not preempt city ordinance that banned cigarette vending machines in all public places except taverns; as the legislature had expressly declared that one provision of the state's law—prohibiting free distribution of tobacco products—preempted all local laws the court concluded the legislature had not intended to preempt any other local measures). *But see* Franklin County v. Fieldale Farms Corp., 507 S.E.2d 460 (Ga.1998), a state law that expressly authorized local imposition of fees for monitoring industrial, hazardous, and biomedical waste in landfills was treated as evidence that the state intended to preempt all other local regulation of such waste disposal.

Occupation of the field is also more likely to be found where the detailed state law addresses a subject that has traditionally been a matter of state, not local, concern. *See, e.g.*, Easthampton Savings Bank v. City of Springfield, 21 N.E.3d 922 (Mass. 2014) (mortgage foreclosure process).

5. *Federal Preemption Law.* Preemption is not just a state-local issue; federal law may also preempt state and local measures. And, as Justice Liu's concurring opinion in *City of Riverside, supra,* indicates, federal preemption principles may also be invoked in state-local disputes. The United States Supreme Court applies a "presumption against the pre-emption of state police power regulations." Cipollone v. Liggett Group, 505 U.S. 504, 518 (1992). *See also* Rice v. Santa Fe Elevator Corp., 331 U.S. 218, 230 (1947) ("we start with the presumption that the historic powers of the States were not to be superseded by the Federal Act unless that was the clear and manifest purpose of Congress"); Florida Lime & Avocado Growers, Inc. v. Paul, 373 U.S. 132, 142 (1963) ("federal regulation of a field of commerce should not be deemed preemptive of state regulatory power in the absence of persuasive reasons—either that the nature of the regulated subject matter permits no other conclusion, or that the Congress has unmistakably so ordained").

Like many state courts, however, the Supreme Court also applies doctrines of implied preemption and occupation of the field to find that Congress intended federal laws to preempt state or local measures even in the absence of express preemption. *See, e.g.,* Geier v. American Honda Motor Co., Inc., 529 U.S. 861 (2000) (federal law requiring some but not all cars to have airbags held to preempt state tort law determination that a car without an airbag is negligently designed, notwithstanding federal provision that compliance with federal standards did not exempt anyone from state tort liability); United States v. Locke, 529 U.S. 89 (2000) (due to "history of significant federal presence" in the area, state law regulating the design and operation of oil tankers is preempted by federal tanker regulation notwithstanding lack of express Congressional preemption of state law).

CINCINNATI BELL TELEPHONE CO. V.
CITY OF CINCINNATI

Supreme Court of Ohio
693 N.E.2d 212 (1998)

MOYER, CHIEF JUSTICE.

The question presented is whether a municipality is preempted by R.C. 5727.30 et seq. from enacting a net profits tax. Our analysis of the law causes us to conclude that a tax enacted by a municipality pursuant to its taxing power is valid in the absence of an express statutory prohibition of the exercise of such power by the General Assembly. Accordingly, we reverse the judgment of the court of appeals.

I

Municipal taxing power in Ohio is derived from the Ohio Constitution. Section 3, Article XVIII of the Constitution, the Home Rule Amendment, confers sovereignty upon municipalities to "exercise all powers of local self-government." As this court stated in *State ex rel. Zielonka v. Carrel* (1919), 99 Ohio St. 220, 227, 124 N.E. 134, 136, "[t]here can be no doubt that the grant of authority to exercise all powers of local government includes the power of taxation."

However, the Constitution also gives to the General Assembly the power to limit municipal taxing authority. Section 6, Article XIII provides that "[t]he General Assembly shall provide for the organization of cities, and incorporated villages, by general laws, and restrict their power of taxation * * * so as to prevent the abuse of such power." Section 13, Article XVIII provides that "[l]aws may be passed to limit the power of municipalities to levy taxes and incur debts for local purposes * * *." *See Franklin v. Harrison* (1960), 171 Ohio St. 329, 14 O.O.2d 4, 170 N.E.2d 739.

Appellants assert that their local net profits taxes are valid because the General Assembly has not, pursuant to these constitutional powers, expressly preempted such a tax from local imposition. Appellants Blue Ash and Fairfax and amicus suggest that the doctrine of implied preemption, upon which appellees rely, be abrogated. Implied preemption of taxation, these appellants and amicus argue, is an anachronistic doctrine, which is rooted in public policy considerations and derives no support from the Constitution. For the reasons that follow, we agree.

II

In *State ex rel. Zielonka v. Carrel*, this court concluded that the exercise of the taxing power is granted to municipalities pursuant to Section 3, Article XVIII of the Ohio Constitution. 99 Ohio St. at 227, 124 N.E. at 136. In arriving at that conclusion, this court raised, in dicta, the question of whether the General Assembly could impliedly preempt municipal taxing power. * * *

This court then considered that question and established the doctrine of implied preemption in *Cincinnati v. Am. Tel. & Tel. Co.* (1925), 112 Ohio St. 493, 147 N.E. 806. There, the city of Cincinnati attempted to levy an excise tax, at an annual flat rate, on all railroads, telegraph companies, and telephone companies operating or doing business within the city limits. At the same time, the state levied excise taxes, on income measured by gross receipts, upon the same companies. Former G.C. 5483, 5484, and 5486. This court concluded that the municipal taxes were preempted by the state excise taxes, reasoning that "[t]he power granted to the municipality by Section 3, Article XVIII, of the Constitution * * * does not extend to fields within such municipality which have already been occupied by the state." *Id.* at paragraph two of the syllabus. * * *

That the court has struggled to apply the doctrine it created in *Cincinnati v. AT & T* is reflected by subsequent attempts to define what it meant in its holding that municipal taxing power "does not extend to *fields* within such municipality which have already been occupied by the state." (Emphasis added.) *Cincinnati v. AT & T*, paragraph two of the syllabus. In one case, we implied that "field" might be defined by the types of taxes involved, i.e., excise as opposed to income taxes. *Angell v. Toledo* (1950), 153 Ohio St. 179, 41 O.O. 217, 91 N.E.2d 250. In *Angell*, we stated that "[i]n the interpretation of the Ohio Constitution an income tax is not to be treated as an excise tax." *Id.* at 183. We added that "Ohio municipalities have the power to levy and collect income taxes in the absence of pre-emption by the General Assembly of the field of *income taxation* * * *." (Emphasis added.) *Id.* at paragraph one of the syllabus. Justice Taft, concurring in *Angell*, wrote that "the occupation by the state of a small portion of a particular field of taxation does not necessarily indicate the intention of the General Assembly to exclude municipalities from the portion of such field not so occupied." *Id.* at 186.

In contrast, this court has at other times taken a broader view of what constitutes the "field" of taxation. In *Haefner*, the court premised its application of implied preemption on an analysis of the entire taxing scheme imposed upon utilities by the General Assembly. Similarly, Chief Justice O'Neill, concurring in *Cleveland*, stated that "if the General Assembly has levied a tax on a particular *subject matter*, it will be presumed that the General Assembly has impliedly exercised its power to prohibit a local tax on the same subject matter." (Emphasis added.)

III

The difficulty encountered by this court in applying the doctrine of implied preemption is perhaps best illustrated by our statement in *East Ohio Gas* that "[a] reading of the cases cited above will demonstrate that the language of this court, in asserting or denying the doctrine of preemption by implication, has sometimes been obscure, ambiguous, inconsistent and on occasion, almost contradictory to previous cases in stating the grounds upon which the court's judgment was based." Today we end that confusion by analyzing municipal taxing power within the context of the source of that power—the Ohio Constitution. * * *

Pursuant to Section 13, Article XVIII, and Section 6, Article XIII, the Constitution confers power upon the General Assembly to limit the exercise of taxing power by a municipality. These provisions should be interpreted coextensively with the general grant of local governing authority to municipalities under Article XVIII. By the grant of this authority, the intention of the Home Rule Amendment was to eliminate statutory control over municipalities by the General Assembly. *See Perrysburg* at 255, 140 N.E. at 598. Its passage granted " 'municipalities sovereignty in matters of local self-government, *limited only by other constitutional provisions.*' " * * * Given this general, broad grant of power that municipalities enjoy under Article XVIII, the Constitution requires that the provisions allowing the General Assembly to limit municipal taxing power be interpreted in a manner consistent with the purpose of home rule.

The clauses from which the General Assembly derives power to limit the exercise of municipal taxing power indicate that "[l]aws may be passed to limit the power of municipalities to levy taxes and incur debts * * *," Section 13, Article XVIII, and that "[t]he General Assembly shall provide for the organization of cities, and incorporated villages, by general laws, and *restrict their power of taxation* * * *." (Emphasis added.) Section 6, Article XIII. These provisions clearly delegate power to the General Assembly to limit exercise of the municipal taxing power. When these provisions are interpreted in relation to the purpose and scope of the Home Rule Amendment, it is evident that a proper exercise of this limiting power requires an express act of restriction by the General

Assembly. The mere enactment of state legislation that results in an occupation of a field of taxation is not sufficient to constitute an exercise of the General Assembly's constitutional power to limit municipal taxation. To construe the enactment of such legislation to impliedly preempt municipal taxing powers would contravene the principle underlying Article XVIII—that municipal powers are derived from the Constitution and not from the General Assembly. * * * The adoption of Section 3, Article XVIII meant that municipalities were entitled to exercise, fully and completely, "all powers of local self-government." Among those powers is the power of taxation. Accordingly, given the delegation, by the people of the state, of power to levy taxes for municipal purposes, the exercise of that power is to be considered in all respects valid, unless the General Assembly has acted affirmatively by exercising its constitutional prerogative. In the absence of an express statutory limitation demonstrating the exercise, by the General Assembly, of its constitutional power, acts of municipal taxation are valid.

* * * Very clearly, there is no provision in the Ohio Constitution that contains words preventing a municipality from exercising its taxing power simply because the General Assembly has enacted tax legislation of its own. Rather, the foregoing analysis indicates a balanced delegation of power, by the people, to municipalities and the General Assembly with respect to municipal taxing power. This balance is best maintained by interpreting the specific limiting power of the General Assembly so that it does not engulf the general power of taxation delegated to municipalities.

IV

The remaining cornerstone of the doctrine of implied preemption is this court's stated "antipathy to 'double taxation.'" *East Ohio Gas* at 77, 36 O.O.2d at 58, 218 N.E.2d at 610. In East Ohio Gas, this court stated that the primary basis undergirding the doctrine was a desire to prevent double taxation. *Id.*

While there may be a desire to avoid double taxation as a matter of public policy, there is no constitutional prohibition against double taxation. This court stated in *Sandusky Gas & Elec. Co. v. State* (1926), 114 Ohio St. 479, 490, 151 N.E. 685, 688, that double taxation "does not render the statute invalid or the order of the tax commission violative of any provision of either the federal or the state Constitution." Plainly, multiple taxation of the same subject matter exists in the form of taxation imposed by municipal, state, and federal governments against net income.

Additionally, we have not always adhered to our position regarding double taxation. This court had no "antipathy to double taxation" in *Thompson v. Cincinnati* (1965), 2 Ohio St.2d 292, 31 O.O.2d 563, 208 N.E.2d 747, where we held that both the city of Cincinnati and the city of

Loveland could legally tax the same income of a person who lived in Loveland but was employed in Cincinnati. In paragraph four of the syllabus, we held that "[a] resident of one municipal corporation who receives wages as a result of work and labor performed within another municipal corporation may be lawfully taxed on such wages by both municipal corporations."

V

There is no constitutional provision that directly prohibits both the state and municipalities from occupying the same area of taxation at the same time. Rather, the Constitution presumes that both the state and municipalities may exercise full taxing powers, unless the General Assembly has acted expressly to preempt municipal taxation, pursuant to its constitutional authority to do so. Our interpretation of that authority today is consistent with the constitutional powers granted to municipalities under Article XVIII, and our law that Article XVIII powers may be limited only by other constitutional provisions.

Having determined that there is no constitutional basis that supports the continued application of the doctrine of implied preemption, we are compelled, by virtue of the foregoing analysis, to overrule *Cincinnati v. Am. Tel. & Tel. Co., East Ohio Gas v. Akron*, and paragraph four and the portion of paragraph three of the syllabus in *Haefner v. Youngstown* that is inconsistent with our holding today. The power to restrict municipal taxing power as granted by Section 13, Article XVIII and Section 6, Article XIII of the Ohio Constitution requires the General Assembly to preempt municipal taxing power by express statutory provision.

Accordingly, we hold that the taxing authority of a municipality may be preempted or otherwise prohibited only by an express act of the General Assembly.

NOTES AND QUESTIONS

1. *Taxation and Home Rule.* Fiscal autonomy is probably the least developed aspect of self-government for most American localities. Whereas most states give home rule localities some authority over the structure of local government, local personnel, and the adoption of local laws regulating people, land, or activity within the locality, "[o]nly a handful of states have [constitutional] provisions that directly address the question of fiscal initiative." U.S. Advisory Commission on Intergovernmental Relations, Local Government Authority: Need for State Constitutional, Statutory, and Judicial Clarification 14 (1993). An academic study conducted just a few years later put the number of states that give localities any fiscal home rule at twelve, with five granting only limited fiscal authority. *See* Dale Krane, Platon N. Riggs, and Melvin B. Hill, Jr., eds., Home Rule in America: A Fifty-State Handbook (CQ Press 2001). Ohio's grant of taxing power to its municipalities as part of home rule is, thus, quite unusual. More common are

provisions like the New York Constitution's declaration that the state legislature's control over "the power of taxation shall never be surrendered," N.Y. Const. Art. XVI, § 1, or the Washington constitution's statement that the legislature "may . . . vest" in local governments "the power to assess and collect taxes" for local purposes, Wash. Const. Art XI, § 12. To be sure, many states do grant local governments taxing powers, particularly the power to tax real property, and local governments may raise money through means other than taxation, such as the collection of user fees and service charges. But it is rare for home rule to include the power to tax. Even where local governments are granted taxing authority, that power is typically subject to other constraints, such as state constitutional tax and expenditure limitations. This is more fully addressed in Chapter VI.

Some observers have called for greater fiscal home rule, arguing that "constraints on the fiscal tools available to a locality interfere with the ability of local governments to realize the benefits of decentralization." Clayton P. Gillette, Fiscal Home Rule, 86 Denv. U. L. Rev. 1241, 1243 (2009). Lack of fiscal autonomy can limit local revenues and, thus, constrain the number and quality of local government services. So, too, the lack of fiscal home rule can affect local tax policy, including the mix of taxes—on property, sales, or incomes—and, thus, local choices concerning who should bear the burdens of local revenue-raising. See id. at 1243–44. And lack of taxing authority also limits local regulatory options as taxes can play an important role in effective regulatory regimes. See Erin Adele Scharff, Taxes as Regulatory Tools: An Argument for Expanding New York City's Taxing Authority, 86 N.Y.U. L. Rev, 1556 (2011). On the other hand, some kinds of local tax initiatives, such as a definition of the tax base for sales or income taxes that differs from those used by the state or other localities could impose undesirable costs on people or firms who do business in multiple localities. Cf. Darien Shanske, Local Fiscal Autonomy Requires Constraints: The Case for Fiscal Menus, 25 Stan. L. & Pol. Rev. 9, 27–29 (2014).

Should a state constitutional provision giving local governments home rule with respect to "local affairs" or "municipal matters" be interpreted to include the power to impose taxes, such as a tax on sales transactions within the locality, on gross receipts in the locality, or on incomes earned in the locality? What are the arguments in favor of including the power to adopt new taxes in the local power to act? What are the arguments against? Should it matter whether the locality is in an imperio or an NML/NLC state?

Where the state constitution does provide for local fiscal initiative, how strongly should local measures be protected from state preemption? Could you argue that local taxation is a "municipal affair" not subject to state preemption? Compare Weekes v. City of Oakland, 579 P.2d 449, 456–63 (Cal.1978) (concurring opinion of Richardson, J., contending that a municipal income tax is a "municipal affair" under California home rule amendment and, thus, protected from state preemption) with City of Chicago v. StubHub, Inc., 979 N.E.2d 844, 855–57 (Ill. 2011) (finding City's ordinance requiring online ticket auctioneers like StubHub to collect and remit the City's amusement tax on admission to entertainment events in the City to be in conflict with and preempted by state law giving online auctioneers the option of either collecting those taxes or notifying ticket resellers of their own liabilities for such taxes; the court noted StubHub's objection that if other municipalities followed Chicago's lead, "there could potentially be a patchwork of local regulations. The legislature considered such burdens, and decided not to impose them, preferring instead a more comprehensive and uniform approach"); City of New York v. State, 730 N.E.2d 920, 924–27 (N.Y.2000) (even assuming state law repealing city's authorization to tax the incomes of commuters affects the "property, affairs, and government" of New York City, the law is "supported by substantial State interest" and thus not subject to state constitutional provision limiting state's ability to adopt measures that impinge on local home rule). *See also* Hildebrand v. City of New Orleans, 549 So.2d 1218 (La.1989) (upholding local inheritance tax on property within the locality as lawful exercise of home rule powers, and rejecting the arguments that tax is preempted by state laws regulating the descent and distribution of property and that the local tax would have a negative impact on state revenue raising powers).

2.   *State Limitations on Local Taxation Authority*. Even states that recognize local power to initiate taxation usually have some state statutory or constitutional limit or condition on local taxation powers. Ohio law, for example, prohibits local taxation of "intangible income." Ohio Rev. Code Ann. § 718.01. A taxpayer unsuccessfully argued that Akron's tax on lottery winnings fell afoul of that prohibition. Fisher v. Neusser, 660 N.E.2d 435 (Ohio 1996). *See also* Hopkins v. City of Kansas City, 894 S.W.2d 156 (Mo. 1995) (employee contributions to deferred compensation plans are "earned income" for, and thus fall within, state statutory authorization of municipal taxation on earned income).

States may bar municipal imposition of broad-based taxes like an income tax or a sales tax while authorizing localities to tax firms for the privilege of doing business within local borders. If the amount of tax reflects the amount or value of activity engaged in by the business, the community may be open to the claim that its charge is actually one of the types of taxes the locality is not authorized to impose. In Town of Eagle v. Scheibe, 10 P.3d 648 (Colo. 2000), the Colorado Supreme Court considered the claim that a local hotel occupancy tax of $2 per day per occupied room was not a permitted occupation tax but a forbidden income tax. Recognizing that under Colorado law the income tax is reserved to the state, the court determined that the occupation tax is intended "to compensate a municipality for the use of its services and facilities. * * * An occupation tax is a means to require a business located within a municipality to pay its fair share of the expenses incurred by the municipality of providing those services and facilities." 10 P.3d at 651. Thus, the court concluded it is permissible for the amount of occupation tax paid by hotels to fluctuate with the degree of hotel occupancy since that was a reasonable "approximation of the degree of municipal services utilized." *Id.* at 654. *But cf.* Cox Cable New Orleans v. City of New

Orleans, 624 So.2d 890 (La.1993) (holding that a local tax on cable subscription fees was not authorized by a state law permitting municipal amusement taxes but, instead, fell within the prohibition of sales taxes).

E. CONCLUSION

A STUDY AID TO QUESTIONS OF LOCAL POWER AND STATE-LOCAL CONFLICTS

As we have seen, the issues of when a local government has power to act and whether a local action is preempted by a conflicting state law are complex. This Section distills the multiple principles that mark this area of the law into a sequence of questions. Its four steps provide a linear guide through an area that is often fraught with circular reasoning. As you read through these steps, see if you can find at least one main case or note case from Sections C or D of this Chapter that illustrates the question discussed or principle asserted.

First, what is the source of the local power at issue?

(A) Is the local power one expressly delegated by a state enabling law?

(B) Is the local government acting pursuant to home rule authority? Home rule may be granted by

- state constitutional amendment

- state statute

- broad judicial interpretation of a state enabling law granting general welfare or police powers, as in *State v. Hutchinson.*

Second, does the local enactment fall within the scope of the power granted by the State?

(A) If the locality has not been granted home rule, does **Dillon's Rule** apply?

- If so, then in order to be valid the local power must have been expressly granted by the state or necessarily implied in the powers expressly granted by the state or essential to the accomplishment of the powers granted

- If Dillon's Rule has been modified or rejected by the state, the replacement rule of construction is likely to take a more generous view of the scope of delegated power.

(B) If the locality is acting pursuant to home rule authority, does the local action affect a "local" or "municipal" matter? If so, then the local government is likely to have power to act unless the local measure is preempted by a valid state law.

- Home rule may take **imperio, NML/NLC** or **hybrid** forms. A court may be more likely to find that a matter is "local" or "municipal" in a state that uses NML/NLC language in granting localities home rule powers, but the distinction between imperio and NML/NLC home rule in the scope of authority to initiate local laws is not sharp or consistent across the states.

- Is the local ordinance a private or local law governing civil relationships? Even if so, can it be characterized as incident to the exercise of an independent municipal power?

Third, is the local law in conflict with a state law?

(A) Is the local law expressly prohibited by state law?

(B) Even if not prohibited by state law, is the local law inconsistent with state law? (**implied preemption**)

(C) Even if the local law is not inconsistent with a specific state law, has the state occupied the field in which the locality is acting? (**occupation of the field**)

In some **NML home rule** states, the state constitution may preclude implied preemption and field preemption and may instead require that a state statute expressly conflict with a local law or expressly deny a local power in order to preclude an otherwise valid local measure. Courts in these states, however, vary in their interpretation of these constitutional provisions.

Fourth, if state and local laws conflict, is the state law valid and does the state have the power to preempt local action?

(A) The state law may be invalid under a state constitutional provision dealing with local governments, such as the restrictions on special acts, special commissions, or unfunded mandates, or as a result of some other constraint on state legislative action.

(B) In an **NML home rule** state, the state legislature always has the power to preempt local laws. There are no subject matter areas immunized from state regulation by home rule. So, if the state law is valid, the state law will preempt the local law.

(C) In an **imperio home rule** state, consider whether the matter is of **exclusively local** concern or whether it is of **mixed state and local** concern.

- If the matter is **exclusively local**, the locality can prevail despite the conflict.

- If it is a **mixed state/local matter**, the answer will depend on such factors as the nature of the local interest, the nature of the state interest, whether the subject is specifically addressed in the state constitution, the presence and extent of extraterritorial effects, the importance of a uniform state rule, and whether the matter is one traditionally regulated by states or localities. State law usually prevails in cases where the subject is a mixed state/local matter, but not always.

In most, albeit not all, preemption disputes the critical issue is whether there is a conflict. In NML states, a valid state law will ordinarily preempt a local law. In imperio states, the state will usually, albeit not always, prevail if the matter is not exclusively local—and most disputes involve mixed state/local matters rather than exclusively local ones.

CHAPTER V

INTERLOCAL RELATIONS AND METROPOLITAN AREA PROBLEMS

■ ■ ■

A. INTRODUCTION

NEAL R. PEIRCE
CITISTATES: HOW AMERICA CAN PROSPER
IN A COMPETITIVE WORLD
(Seven Locks Press 1993)

What would a visitor from another planet, approaching the dark side of planet Earth, first discern? Obviously, it would be the clusters of light where humans congregate in great numbers. And approaching any one of them, the visitor would see, as soon as dawn came, a fully integrated organism: a concentration of human development, of roads and rivers and bridges and masses of buildings, all arrayed together, people and vehicles, air, water, and energy, information and commerce, interacting in seemingly infinite ways. This is, of course, the citistate, the *true city* of our time, the closely interrelated, geographic, economic, environmental entity that chiefly defines late 20th-century civilization.

Some of the features one *can't* see from the air are as significant as those one can. Consider nation-state boundaries. Unless they fall along river lines or abut oceans, they are not to be seen from "up there." The same phenomenon applies within metropolitan areas. All those dividing lines between center cities, suburbs, counties, townships, and urban villages—the dividing lines politicians tell us are so utterly significant— are not to be seen from above. Indeed, between work and home, for errand and entertainment and shopping, the Earth's people cross such municipal lines billions of times each day.

The inescapable oneness of each citistate covers a breathtaking range. Environmental protection, economic promotion, work force preparedness, health care, social services, advanced scientific research and development, philanthropy—success or failure on any one of those fronts ricochets among *all* the communities of a metropolitan region. No man, woman, family, or neighborhood is an island.

. . . In the new international economy, . . . only markets with scale and diversity are likely to succeed. A citistate divided against itself will prove weak and ineffectual. Political boundaries do *not* seal off problems of pollution, solid waste disposal, transportation, schools, inadequate infrastructure. Advertise a suburb by itself and you may be able to offer an above-average labor force and housing stock, but probably fewer educational centers and no really significant concentrations of financial and legal services. Advertise a center city alone and you may talk of great centralized facilities but end up exposing to your potential catch conditions of severe poverty and lack of a skilled labor force. But mix the two together and there is at least a possibility that the strengths will prove complementary and the citistate will be in the ballpark of competition for trade and sophisticated new industries.

RICHARD BRIFFAULT
THE LOCAL GOVERNMENT BOUNDARY PROBLEM IN METROPOLITAN AREAS
48 Stanford L. Rev. 1115 (1996)

The governance of metropolitan areas is the central problem for local government law today. Local government law has traditionally been associated with the organization and powers of discrete localities. Such localities, typically, are relatively small in both population and area, with densely populated cores bounded by lightly populated fringes that set them off from other, similar localities. Residents of particular discrete localities have relatively high levels of interaction with each other and much less intense interactions with residents of other localities. Local government law enables the people who live within these discrete areas to organize themselves into distinct political units and gives those units power to make decisions with respect to a range of public policies and services. Although the extent of power granted to localities varies considerably from state to state—and often from locality to locality within a particular state—the essence of local autonomy is the ability of people within distinct small areas to decide for themselves by democratic means the matters that fall within the competence of local authority.

As the twentieth century draws to a close, however, most Americans live not in discrete, compact localities, but rather in sprawling metropolitan areas. In 1990, 193 million people, or 78 percent of the total population of the United States, lived in metropolitan areas, as defined by the Census Bureau. The twenty-one most populous metropolitan areas (those with two million people or more) included 101 million people, or 40 percent of the population. Slightly more than half of all Americans lived in the thirty-nine major metropolitan areas that contain one million people or more.

Major metropolitan areas are far larger in population and territory than the localities that have traditionally been the subject of local government law. The San Francisco Bay Area contains six million people—a population greater than that of forty states—and seven thousand square miles—almost the size of Massachusetts. Metropolitan Houston consists of 3.7 million people spread over an even more capacious 7151 square miles. Nearly 2.6 million people live in the almost six thousand square miles that make up greater Seattle. Metropolitanization has also transformed the localities within metropolitan areas. The defining features of traditional localities—intensity of interaction within the locality and separation of that locality from others—are increasingly absent in the metropolitan setting. Metropolitan area residents do not concentrate their activities within their home locality, nor do metropolitan area businesses typically draw most of their workers or customers from their home localities. Metropolitan localities frequently lack internal focal points, such as a downtown, village commons, park, community facility, or other place for casual socializing. Such localities remain the physical settings for residences, enterprises, and other organizations within their borders, but they are certainly not "communities" in the traditional warm and fuzzy sense of the term.

How are metropolitan areas to be governed? Not one major metropolitan area is governed by a single all-encompassing general purpose local government. Some metropolitan areas have special-purpose regional governmental entities. These bodies, however, are sometimes limited in territorial scope to just a portion of the metropolitan area. They are typically governed by appointed rather than elected officials. Most importantly, they nearly always lack the plenary taxing, regulatory, and service-delivery authority characteristic of general purpose municipal governments. . . .

Although there are few local governments of metropolitan scope, the major metropolitan areas are hardly without local governments. In 1987, the typical metropolitan area had 113 local governments, including forty-seven general purpose governments, such as a county or a municipality. The profusion of governments is even greater in larger metropolitan areas. There are over 1250 local governments in the Chicago area, including six counties and 261 municipalities; nearly 300 local governments in the Pittsburgh area, including more than 100 municipalities; more than 300 governments in greater Seattle, including three counties and sixty-five cities and towns; and approximately 350 governments, including 168 cities and towns, in metropolitan Baltimore. Even in the Sunbelt, which tends to have fewer localities per metropolitan area, greater Phoenix has 138 governments, including twenty-one municipalities, while Hampton Roads, Virginia, the nation's twenty-seventh largest metropolitan area, has at least seventy-five units of government.

The lack of an overarching government for a metropolitan area, and the existence instead of a multiplicity of small, abutting, and sometimes overlapping local governments is not necessarily a problem. Indeed, the public choice school celebrates this governance structure, claiming it creates a metropolitan "market place" that expands the range of public policy choices available to residents, increases their satisfaction with local government services and decisions, and improves the responsiveness of local government to citizen preferences. Public choice scholars oppose the creation of general purpose regional governments. They contend that the public benefits from the current mix of interlocal competition and voluntary interlocal agreements, supplemented by special purpose regional bodies to take advantage of regional economies of scale in provision of capital-intensive physical infrastructure, are significant. . . .

The traditional metropolitan reform strategy assumes that only a government of regional scope can efficiently and democratically handle regional problems. Public choice and political decentralizationists, however, argue that by taking power out of local hands regional governments threaten the core value of local autonomy. . . .

RICHARD F. WAGNER AND WARREN E. WEBER
COMPETITION, MONOPOLY, AND THE
ORGANIZATION OF GOVERNMENT
IN METROPOLITAN AREAS
18 J. L. & Econ. 661 (1975)

There are two primary structural features of the organization of government in metropolitan areas. One is the *fragmentation* of governments, and the other is the *overlapping* of governments. The fragmentation of governments refers to the provision of the same service or services by a multitude of governments. Fragmentation means that such services as police, fire, and recreation will normally be provided by a large number of mutually exclusive municipal corporations. . . . Governmental fragmentation would seem to be substantial. For instance, over one-half of the metropolitan areas with population exceeding 250,000 according to the 1967 Census of Governments contained more than 100 units of government.

The overlapping of governments refers to the independent supply of separate components of public output by different units of government. Hence, as confronted by an individual citizen, these governments "overlap" one another. For instance, such services as fire, police, and recreation could be provided by a municipal corporation, while education was being provided by an independent school district, with the boundaries of the school district often being noncoterminous with the boundaries of the municipal corporation. Moreover, such services as flood control, sanitation, and hospital facilities could be provided by single-function governments created specifically for the provision of those particular services. Once again, the boundaries of these special districts are often noncoterminous with those of the other units of government. When overlapping is combined with fragmentation, an individual not only will be able to choose among a number of mutually exclusive governments providing the same service, but also will typically find that his bundle of public services is supplied by a multitude of governments.

. . . [T]he fragmentation and the overlapping of governments has been greeted with considerable hostility. Fragmentation, the critics claim, increases the cost of obtaining coordination among units of government, while overlapping, the same critics claim, results in the creation of an unnecessary duplication of administrative apparatus. As a remedy it is suggested not only that the number of competing governments be slashed, but also that the overlapping of governments be curtailed. Such proposals . . . treat governments as if they automatically would act as competitive suppliers of public output, presumably by virtue of their being "democratic."

. . . [T]here would seem to be conceptual reasons, supported by empirical evidence, for generally opposing governmental reorganizations or "reforms" that reduce fragmentation and overlapping. At least this would be so if it were felt that it was preferable to have governments act more like competitive suppliers of public output than like monopolistic suppliers. . . . [A]n increase in the number of competing and overlapping governments will lead the public economy more closely to perform as a competitive industry.

NOTES AND QUESTIONS

1. *Framing the Regionalism Debate: Efficiency.* Proponents of metropolitan or regional government have long contended that services and regulation will be more efficiently provided when local government is coterminous with the region it serves. They see the metropolitan area as a whole, rather than the dozens, if not hundreds, of individual localities within it as constituting an economic and social unit. Advocates of regional government claim that regional entities would reduce waste, duplication, and the negative external impacts of multiple local governments, while creating economies of scale in the provision of services. Wagner and Weber—and other writers building on the work of Charles Tiebout, discussed in Chapter I—sharply question that premise. They argue, instead, that fragmentation generates competition among governments, offers residents more choices, and enhances government accountability to local people. Moreover, they assert, economies of scale are unlikely in large metropolitan areas. Instead, they

claim that the diseconomies associated with large-scale bureaucracies are a more likely result. In their view, any efficiencies from a regional approach could be obtained by voluntary agreements between local governments.

Peirce refocuses the efficiency debate in terms of the interconnectedness of localities within a region and of the ability of regions to compete with other regions. A study by the National League of Cities found that in the 25 metropolitan areas with the most rapid income growth, central city incomes also increased. Conversely, in the 18 metropolitan areas that experienced income decline, central city income declined in all but four instances. The report implies that metropolitan area suburbs have a stake in the economic well-being of their central cities. *See* National Leagu of Cities, All in It Together: Cities, Suburbs and Local Economic Regions (1993). According to Peirce, the following factors contribute to what he calls "the interdependence imperative:" (1) central city image is crucial to regional welfare; (2) new employers will need to tap city markets to fill their work force; (3) failure to address inner-city social problems will affect all taxpayers in the form of higher costs for prisons and welfare; (4) inner-city crime affects the image of the entire region; (5) environmental issues can only be addressed on a region-wide basis; and (6) regional cooperation will bring enhanced political clout. Neal R. Peirce, Citistates, *supra,* at 131–32.

Professors Nestor Davidson and Sheila Foster have made a Tieboutian argument for regionalism. In *The Mobility Case for Regionalism*, 47 U.C.Davis L. Rev. 63 (2013), they argue that Tiebout's insights about competition for consumer voters actually applies with more force at the regional level, as different metropolitan areas compete for human capital, skilled workers, and wealthy taxpayers. If citizens make choices between regions rather than between municipalities, the "mobility case for regionalism" suggests that local governments have strong incentives to join forces to at the regional level, and that regional governance may be crucial.

2. *Framing the Regionalism Debate: Equity.* Regional and metropolitan efforts also have the potential to promote equity and social justice in regions marked by racial segregation and sharp disparities in local wealth, tax bases, and quality of services. The creation of a regional tax base would permit the redistribution of the funds supporting local services from wealthier to poorer communities within a region, and would facilitate sharing of the costs of social services by more evenly distributing resources and spreading the burdens and negative impacts associated with high levels of urbanization and concentrated poverty. *See, e.g.*, Georgette Poindexter, Towards a Legal Framework for Regional Redistribution of Poverty-Related Expenses, 47 Wash. U. J. Urb. & Contemp. L. 3 (1995). Regional land use regulation could also reduce exclusionary local zoning and promote racial integration. *See* David Rusk, Cities Without Suburbs (Woodrow Wilson Center Press 2d ed. 1995). *But see* Edward Zelinsky, Metropolitanism, Progressivism, and Race, 98 Colum.L.Rev. 665, 667–68 (1998) (arguing "it is unlikely that any structural innovation, like the establishment of metropolitan government" can change the attitudes that led to segregated

suburbs; the need is not "to recast the structure of municipal government, but . . . to revise the preferences of the American people; in this area, organizational reform cannot substitute for the alteration of popular predilections").

3. *Framing the Regionalism Debate: Democracy.* In a metropolitan area, local decisions frequently have regional effects. As a result, proponents of metropolitan governance argue that in order for all those affected by a government's action to participate and be heard in local decision-making, those local powers that generate externalities, such as land use regulation, should be exercised at the regional level: "In metropolitan areas, democracy requires giving the regional electorate a voice in local decisions that have regional consequences. Only by widening the scale of participation to include all those affected by local actions can local decision-making in metropolitan regions be made truly democratic." Richard Briffault, Localism and Regionalism, 48 Buff.L.Rev. 1, 21–22 (2000) ("Regionalism is . . . localism for metropolitan areas."). Critics of regionalism, however, argue that metropolitan governments would be less responsive and less conducive to active citizen participation and input. *See, e.g.,* Zelinsky, *supra,* 98 Colum.L.Rev. at 667. Indeed, as we noted in Chapter I, the belief that smaller local government units are better able to promote democratic participation in governance has long been central to the case for local autonomy. Governments in smaller units are easier to communicate with and more accessible; as a result, the potential strength of an individual voice is greater. In fact, according to this perspective, effective local democracy requires *more,* and not *less,* autonomy for small local units. *See* Gerald E. Frug, The City as a Legal Concept, 93 Harv.L.Rev. 1057, 1067–70 (1980). Professor Frug and Professor Richard Thompson Ford would reconcile decentralized decision-making with protection of regional interests by allowing nonresidents to vote in local elections, and by creating institutions that would require local governments to deliberate more with each other concerning the scope of local powers and the effects of local policies. *See* Richard Thompson Ford, Beyond Borders: A Partial Response to Richard Briffault, 48 Stan.L.Rev. 1173, 1188–89 (1996). For criticisms of these approaches, *see* Richard Briffault, The Local Government Boundary Problem in Metropolitan Areas, *supra,* 48 Stan. L. Rev. at 1151–64; Sheryll D. Cashin, Building Community in the Twenty-first Century: A Post-Integrationist Vision for the American Metropolis, 98 Mich. L. Rev. 1704 (2000).

Regionalism is a pervasive issue for local government law. Regional questions include the spillover effects of local actions, interlocal conflicts, interlocal inequalities, the provision of some services on a regional basis, regional coordination of policies and programs, interlocal cooperative activities, and regional institutions. Although there are few metropolitan area regional *governments,* there are a host of regional *governance* mechanisms. As you read the materials in this Chapter, consider how these mechanisms seek to meet regional needs and concerns while preserving the economic and participatory benefits of local autonomy. See if you think we need stronger regional institutions or whether, instead, the benefits of more decentralized decisionmaking counsel against more regionalism.

B. INTERLOCAL CONFLICTS AND REGIONAL PROBLEMS

1. INTERLOCAL CONFLICTS OVER LAND USE REGULATION

AUSTIN INDEPENDENT SCHOOL DISTRICT V. CITY OF SUNSET VALLEY

Supreme Court of Texas
502 S.W.2d 670 (1973)

SAM D. JOHNSON, JUSTICE.

This suit was filed by the Austin Independent School District against the City of Sunset Valley * * * In issue is the authority of the City * * * to wholly prohibit the location of school facilities within its boundaries.

The City of Sunset Valley is served by, is a part of, and is entirely within the boundaries of the Austin Independent School District. Though it enjoys all the grade levels and supporting facilities of the School District for its children, the City has only one facility, an elementary school, within its boundaries. Pursuant to Art. 1011a, Vernon's Tex.Rev.Civ.Stat.Ann., the City enacted a zoning ordinance whereby the entire City would be residential. The ordinance contemplates only residential construction for all the City. Sunset Valley was incorporated as a general law city and at the time of trial had a population of about 250 persons.

The duly elected trustees of the Austin Independent School District, after extensive study, research and deliberation, determined to construct the centralized auxiliary facilities supportive of school purposes in issue here. Taking into consideration all relevant factors and acting for and in the interest of the entire School District, the trustees determined to locate the auxiliary facilities within the corporate limits of the City of Sunset Valley. The proposed improvements consist of about 62 acres and include a football stadium, a field house, an athletic field and a bus garaging center with repair and maintenance facilities. The proposed facilities would not be auxiliary to the existing elementary school or any proposed classroom building; they were rather designed and located to serve a substantial part of the multiple schools of the district which are located throughout its boundaries.

The School District's attorney called upon the City to issue it a building permit, amend its zoning ordinances or de-annex the acreage.

The City refused these proposals and threatened to enforce the penal provisions of its ordinances if construction began.

It was under these circumstances that the School District filed the instant suit for declaratory judgment and injunctive relief against the City. The School District sought a declaration that the zoning ordinances of the City were ineffective to prevent the School District from erecting the proposed facilities. * * *

At the outset two significant factors which permeate this opinion must be recognized fully. First, that the reasonableness of the School District's action is not before this court. The trial court judge filed findings of fact and conclusions of law, stating explicitly that the School District did not act unreasonably in selecting this particular site. These findings were not attacked on appeal and are not before this court. Second, and equally clear, that there is no issue of nuisance before the court. It is apparent from the record and was conceded by both counsel in oral argument that there is no theory of nuisance to be considered.

The issue is therefore presented whether, under this record, the City may utilize its zoning powers to wholly exclude from within its boundaries school facilities reasonably located. We conclude that it may not. Section 1, Article VII of the Constitution of Texas, Vernon's Ann.St., directs the Legislature to 'establish . . . an efficient system of public free schools.' The Legislature has delegated this duty, in part, to independent school districts; it has conferred necessary powers of eminent domain upon such districts, Tex.Ed.Code § 23.31 (1972), V.T.C.A., and it has conferred upon trustees of such districts 'exclusive power to manage and govern the public free schools of the district.' Tex.Ed.Code § 23.26(b) (1972).

All parties as well as the court below agree that, as a general rule, cities cannot exclude schools from areas zoned residential. 3 Yokley, Zoning Law and Practice § 28–58 (3d ed. 1967). The City contends, however, that the School District is subject to the zoning regulations of the City * * *

The City must rely on Tex.Rev.Civ.Stat.Ann. art. 1011a, the statute granting cities the right to zone, for proof of legislative intent to subject school districts to the zoning authority of cities. The Missouri zoning statute, chapter 89, § 89.020, in language *identical* to that in the Texas statute, provides that the city is empowered to 'regulate and restrict . . . the location and use of buildings, structures and land for trade, industry, residence or other purposes.' The court in State v. Ferriss, [304 S.W.2d 896 (Mo.1957)], discussing this statute, said, '(c)learly, it contains no express grant of power to cities to regulate or restrict the location of schools. . . .' 304 S.W.2d at 900.

* * * here the question is whether a school district, with no question as to the reasonableness of its action and no question of public nuisance involved, may locate school facilities in an area which a city has zoned for residential use.

* * * The determination flowing from the foregoing is not that the School District can act with impunity, however. Bearing in mind that the reasonableness of the School District's action is not before the court, it may be profitable to examine a solution obtained in two jurisdictions in cases where this was not so, in cases involving conflicts between city zoning laws and the location of educational facilities. In New Jersey and Delaware immunity from city zoning laws is tempered by an inquiry into the reasonableness of the school authorities' actions. City of Newark v. University of Delaware, 304 A.2d 347 (Del.Ch.1973); Rutgers, State University v. Piluso, 60 N.J. 142, 286 A.2d 697 (1972); Washington Twp. v. Ridgewood Village, 26 N.J. 578, 141 A.2d 308 (1958). The most recent Delaware case on this issue says, 'it is clear that the University in its growth and development should not be subject to restriction or control by local land use regulations. This immunity is absolute unless the City in a given instance can show that its exercise is unreasonable or arbitrary.' City of Newark v. University of Delaware, supra, 304 A.2d at 349. Even though the reasonableness of the School District's action is not before the court, the City in the instant case would have the court go one step beyond these cases and hold here that a school district is subject to the zoning power of a city. This additional step is without support in the law of this state or any other jurisdiction. In effect, the City would shift the burden of proof entirely and require the School District to prove that the zoning ordinance of the City is unreasonable. The court is of the opinion that the broadest weight of authority and the better reasoned position in this type instance is that expressed in *City of Newark*. * * *

POPE, JUSTICE (concurring).

I concur in the result, not by reason of the School District's immunity from the police regulations embodied in the municipal ordinances, but by reason of the unassailed findings and conclusions of the trial court that the School District acted reasonably.

It is the duty of cities, not school districts, to enact ordinances in the exercise of their police powers. Neither schools nor any other person or entity should be free from such regulations in the usual situation. * * *

A school's immunity from reasonable police regulations should be limited by a rule of reasonableness. * * * An important consideration, among others, in determining the reasonableness of an ordinance which excludes a school from a particular site is whether the ordinance permits schools at other alternative locations and the suitability of alternate sites. * * * In such cases the burden of proof should be on the party who seeks to avoid the zoning regulation and would require that party to prove the reasonableness of the claimed immunity. * * *

NOTES AND QUESTIONS

1. *Conflicts Between Regional and Local Interests.* Note that the school district encompasses Sunset Valley as well as other municipalities, including Austin, Texas. Does the court's resolution of the dispute guarantee that the local concerns have been heard and dealt with? Is it likely that the interests of the town of 250 will be protected by the decisionmaking process of the large school district? The appellate court had upheld the application of the city ordinance to prohibit construction of the proposed facilities. The court also provided a fuller description of the 62-acre construction project: "a football stadium to seat 15,000 persons; a field house with a seating capacity of 5,000 to 7,000 persons; and an athletic field with at least one baseball diamond; and a school bus facility to serve as a repair, maintenance, and garaging center." 488 S.W.2d 519, 520. Do these facts reflect on the reasonableness of the proposal? Is it relevant that the dispute is between a regional special district, which is limited to the performance of a single function, and a general purpose local government? Should it be relevant whether the local government seeks to prohibit or merely condition the use proposed by the other government? *See also* Blanch v. Suburban Hennepin Regional Park District, 449 N.W.2d 150 (Minn.1989) (park district can acquire property for regional park without approval of any affected municipality or other government unit). Should the analysis be different when a regional entity seeks to locate a facility outside its own territory? *See* City of Bells v. Greater Texoma Utility Authority, 790 S.W.2d 6 (Tex.App.1990) (municipal zoning applies to regional district in proposed construction of a solid waste disposal facility outside its borders). In Texas Midstream Gas Servs. v. City of Grand Prairie, 608 F.3d 200 (5th Cir. 2010), a federal court narrowly interpreted the main case, holding that although an entity with eminent domain power can choose to locate a facility at a preferred location in conflict with local zoning authority, other local regulatory restrictions, such as setback restrictions, would apply. Is that consistent with the way you read the *Austin School District* case?

2. *Resolving Intergovernmental Conflicts.* Conflicting assertions of regulatory power frequently arise between many different types of governmental units. The fact patterns are quite varied: Should a local zoning code apply to the siting of regional railroad systems? Should city regulations apply to buildings owned and operated by the state? Should a county be able to deny zoning permission for the establishment of a municipal landfill? Should a city be able to operate a swimming pool in another city when the host city's regulations do not allow that use? State courts have adopted various approaches to this type of intergovernmental conflict:

(a) *The Eminent Domain Test.* Under this approach, if a governmental entity has condemnation powers, it is immune from the regulatory control of the government in whose territory it operates. In City of Washington v. Warren County, 899 S.W.2d 863 (Mo. 1995), for instance, the court applied that rule to hold that a municipal airport authority was not subject to county zoning regulations. *See also* Seward County Bd. of Commissioners v. City of Seward, 242 N.W.2d 849 (Neb.1976).

(b) *The Superior Sovereign Test.* Courts applying this test rank the competing governmental units within the hierarchy of state sovereignty. Immunity from governmental regulation will be granted to the governmental agency deemed the "higher" sovereign. Under that theory, for instance, state agencies automatically receive exemption from all local regulation. The New Mexico Supreme Court applied the rule in City of Santa Fe v. Armijo, 634 P.2d 685 (N.M.1981), when it held that the city could not apply its historical district zoning ordinances to state land so as to stop the operation of oil field pumping rigs on the premises of a state office building.

(c) *The Governmental Function Test.* This rule turns on whether the governmental agency seeking immunity from zoning and other regulatory controls is deemed to be exercising a governmental rather than a proprietary function. Prisons, courthouse facilities, and firehouses have all been found to constitute immune governmental functions, while governmentally-owned waterworks and waste disposal facilities, deemed proprietary functions, have been subjected to the regulations of the governments in whose territory they are located. *E.g.*, Mass. Bay Transp. Auth. v. City of Somerville, 883 N.E.2d 922 (Mass. 2008) (advertising on state agency's property immune from local zoning regulation); City of Selma v. Dallas County, 964 So.2d 12 (Ala. 2007) (county construction of communications tower on courthouse premises immune from city historic preservation ordinance and ordinance regulating wireless telecommunications facilities); Lane v. Zoning Board of Adjustment of City of Talladega, 669 So.2d 958 (Ala.App.1995) (county jail immune from municipal zoning ordinance).

(d) *The Preeminent Power Test.* Some courts determine which local government must yield to the other's regulations by analyzing the conflicting powers themselves. They look to enabling legislation and underlying statutory purposes and conclude that one of the disputed powers is preeminent. *See, e.g.*, Borough of Tunkhannock v. County of Wyoming, 507 A.2d 438 (Pa.Cmwlth.1986) (because county is required by law to provide prison, municipal zoning inapplicable to prohibit new construction).

(e) *The Legislative Intent Test.* Incorporating bits of all of the tests described above, some courts apply a so-called "legislative intent" test. This test explicitly recognizes that the answer is ultimately up to the legislature's discretion and that, in the absence of specific statutory reference to the problem, the court must glean legislative intent from the relevant language and the overall statutory scheme. The Michigan Supreme Court has endorsed this test for many years, *see* Dearden v. Detroit, 269 N.W.2d 139 (Mich. 1978), yet it has recognized that though the test is "relatively straightforward in concept," it has been "difficult to apply." *See* Burt Tp. v. Dept. of Natural

Resources, 593 N.W.2d 534, 536 n.3 (Mich. 1999) (holding that state's Department of Natural Resources is subject to township's zoning ordinance in construction of a boat launch). The court applied the test in at least three subsequent cases. *See* Byrne v. State, 624 N.W.2d 906 (Mich. 2001) (state police immune from local zoning in construction of communications tower); and Pittsfield Charter Township v. Washtenaw County, 664 N.W.2d 193 (Mich. 2003) (county's construction of homeless shelter is immune from township zoning ordinance); Charter Tp. of Northville v. Northville Public Schools, 666 N.W.2d 213 (Mich. 2003) (school building and site plans, which had been approved by state superintendent, immune from local zoning restrictions). Surveying its own difficulty applying the test in previous cases, and restating its earlier admonition that there are no particular "talismanic" words to indicate legislative intent, the court "came full circle" in the *Northville* case. It concluded that the statute's grant of "sole and exclusive jurisdiction" to the state superintendent indicated unequivocal legislative intent that the decisions be immune from other governments' regulations. The court noted that "[t]he fact that the Legislature does not have to use talismanic words does not mean that, if it does, they are to be disregarded." *Id.* at 217. The court indicated that the comprehensive analysis becomes unnecessary if there is an explicit statutory directive. *See also* Herman v. Berrien County, 750 W.2d 570 (2008) (concluding that county's outdoor shooting range was not indispensable to its firearms training function, and thus not entitled to blanket immunity from township noise regulations).

(f)   *The Balancing Test.* Many states have eschewed the categorical approaches described above and adopted a broader, ad hoc balancing test. The New Jersey Supreme Court, for instance, in Rutgers, The State University v. Piluso, 286 A.2d 697 (N.J.1972), rejected the traditional immunity tests as "absolute," "ritualistic," and "simplistic." *Id.* at 701. Instead, it adopted a balancing test that requires judicial evaluation of five factors: "the nature and scope of the instrumentality seeking immunity, the kind of function or land use involved, the extent of the public interest to be served thereby, the effect local land use regulation would have upon the enterprise concerned, and the impact upon legitimate local interests." *Id.* at 702. *See also* City of Ames v. Story County, 392 N.W.2d 145 (Iowa 1986) (adopting balancing and remanding case to determine whether county zoning ordinance applied city's proposed waste disposal plant); Independent School District v. Oklahoma City, 722 P.2d 1212 (Okla.1986) (applying balancing text to immunize school district from zoning ordinance). In a case of first impression, the Alaska Supreme Court adopted the balancing of interests test as the "most enlightened," *see* Native Village of Eklutna v. Alaska Railroad Corp., 87 P.3d 41(Ak. 2004), but it insisted that the railroad seeking immunity from a native community's zoning laws make a good faith effort to comply with local regulation. The court made clear that it will not engage in balancing until the entity seeking immunity from local laws can show it tried and failed to reach an accommodation with the local government.

For a critical appraisal of the various judicial approaches to interlocal conflicts in the land use context, *see* Laurie Reynolds, The Judicial Role in Intergovernmental Land Use Disputes: The Case Against Balancing, 71 Minn.L.Rev. 611 (1987).

3. *Application of the Tests.* Which of the tests described in Note 2 better accommodate the legitimate competing interests that are likely to be involved in an intergovernmental conflict? Apply those tests to the following hypothetical situations:

(a) The county has announced plans to build a jail within the borders of a large municipality in the county. Under the city's building codes, sprinkler systems are required. Jail officials, however, strongly object to placing sprinkler heads in individual cells, fearing that the metal protrusions will be used either as weapons or as a means for suicidal inmates to hang themselves. If the dispute winds up in court, how should a court resolve the issue?

(b) A large state university in a home rule municipality wants to erect a changing electronic message sign at a busy corner where its indoor arena is located. The city zoning ordinance, which flatly prohibits these signs, is supported by mounting evidence about increased traffic accidents caused by motorists who read such signs instead of paying attention to the road. The university's request for local approval is denied, but it then proceeds to put up the sign without a permit. If the city sues, how should a court resolve this dispute?

4. *A Cautionary Tale.* In *Gurba v. Community High School Dist. No. 155,* 40 N.E.3d 1 (Ill. 2015), a school district located in a residential area of the City of Crystal Lake erected new fifty-foot-high bleachers on its football field that were higher, larger, and closer to the property line of adjacent residences than the old bleachers had been. The district did so without seeking zoning approval or stormwater management approval from the city, and in violation of a city stop-work order. Three neighbors, claiming that the bleachers failed to comply with local zoning and negatively affected their property values, sued. In a case that elicited dueling amicus briefs from the Illinois Association of School Boards, the Illinois Municipal League, and other groups, the Illinois Supreme Court ultimately concluded that the legislature had not exempted school property from municipal or home rule zoning authority, and that the application of local zoning laws to school district property did not unduly interfere with the state's plenary power over public education. The cost to the school district of tearing down the challenged bleachers and replacing them with seating that complied with local zoning exceeded $1.2 million. The school district also had to pay legal fees—its own and those of the prevailing plaintiffs—in excess of $500,000, as well as significant fines that accrued while the noncompliant bleachers were standing. In retrospect, the advantages to the school district of seeking to work with the city at the start of the construction project seem obvious.

VILLAGE OF BARRINGTON HILLS V. VILLAGE OF HOFFMAN ESTATES

Supreme Court of Illinois
410 N.E.2d 37 (1980)

UNDERWOOD, JUSTICE:

Plaintiffs, the village of Barrington Hills (Barrington Hills) and the village of South Barrington (South Barrington), filed a complaint challenging the adoption of particular zoning ordinances and the construction of an open-air theater against * * * the village of Hoffman Estates. The circuit court of Cook County dismissed their complaint on the ground that plaintiffs lacked standing to maintain their action, and the appellate court affirmed. (75 Ill.App.3d 461, 31 Ill.Dec. 397, 394 N.E.2d 599.) We granted leave to appeal.

* * * The subject property consists of approximately 212 acres located in Barrington Township, Cook County. The corporate limits of Barrington Hills * * * and South Barrington * * * "are adjacent or in close proximity to the property".

It is alleged in the complaint * * * that the Nederlander Group plans to develop this real estate for an open-air music theater, to be known as the Poplar Creek Music Theater, which would contain approximately 6,000 seats in an auditorium structure and space in the open for an additional 14,000 persons. The project would also require parking spaces for 6,000 to 7,500 automobiles and would involve commercial and concession activities ancillary to the operation of the theater programs. Among the performances contemplated by the developers are rock concerts, jazz festivals, and country-and-western musical programs, all of which would be electronically amplified.

Following a public hearing pertaining to the annexation of the subject property, Hoffman Estates on August 22, 1979, adopted three ordinances: Ordinance No. 1039–1978 authorized the execution of an annexation agreement between the defendants; Ordinance 1040–1978 authorized annexation of the real estate; and Ordinance No. 1041–1978 rezoned a portion of the property to B-2 central business district and the remainder to F farming district to permit the construction and operation of the theater. Prior to the passage of these ordinances, the real estate was located in an unincorporated area of Cook County and was classified in the R-1 single-family residence district under the Cook County zoning ordinance.

The subject property is located at a substantial distance from the residentially developed area of Hoffman Estates but is in close proximity to residentially developed areas within the corporate limits of Barrington Hills and South Barrington. Pursuant to zoning ordinances, both plaintiffs had adopted comprehensive plans which would restrict the use of the land in the vicinity of the subject property to low-density single-family residences and to agricultural uses.

Plaintiffs further alleged that the annexation and zoning of the subject property for use and development of the contemplated project would occasion special injury and damage to them in their corporate capacities because of safety hazards on roads and highways within their corporate limits due to traffic congestion; the need to provide additional traffic police at an estimated annual cost to Barrington Hills of at least $42,000 and to South Barrington of not less than $24,000; the diversion of their existing police manpower from their ordinary duties to control theater crowds and to protect their residences from the disorderly activity that might result from persons attending the performances; the cost of purchasing additional squad cars for use only during the period when the proposed music theater would be in operation and of adding additional permanent police officers to their payroll; the expense of clearing from the roads and highways within their corporate limits the litter and debris which would result from crowds arriving or leaving the theater; the exhaust emissions from increased vehicular traffic which would degrade ambient air quality; the substantial increase in sound levels in the vicinity of the subject property resulting from music amplification and traffic; the adverse effects upon property values and hence tax revenues within the corporate limits of both villages; and the general impairment of the health, safety and welfare of residents of both municipalities. * * *

Defendants argue that according plaintiffs standing to sue will invite chaos in the relationships between municipalities and flood the courts with zoning litigation. Our holding, however, is not so broad, since it conditions a municipality's standing to challenge the zoning decisions of other governmental units upon a clear demonstration that it would be substantially, directly and adversely affected in its corporate capacity.

* * * [I]t is admitted for purposes of the motion to dismiss that the development of the proposed project under the challenged zoning ordinances will cause Barrington Hills and South Barrington to suffer special damages in their corporate capacities in the form of a loss of municipal revenues due to a diminution in property values, an increase in municipal expenditures for the hiring of additional police manpower and squad cars to monitor vehicular congestion, the additional expense of clearing litter and debris on their roads and highways that would result from theater crowds, the degradation of ambient air quality due to vehicular exhaust and the increase in sound levels resulting from the electronic amplification of music and traffic flows. * * * [T]hese effects of the rezoning * * * portend direct, substantial and adverse effects upon the plaintiff municipalities in the performance of their corporate obligations, thus giving them a real interest in the subject matter of the controversy. Their complaint was therefore improperly dismissed.

NOTES AND QUESTIONS

1. *Municipal Standing in Regional Disputes.* State courts are increasingly willing to grant standing to one local government to challenge the action of another. In City of Brentwood v. Metropolitan Board of Zoning Appeals, 149 S.W.3d 49 (Tenn. App. 2004), the court allowed the city of Brentwood to challenge Nashville's decision to authorize placement of a billboard at its border. It concluded that Brentwood's claim that the billboard would "do great damage to the otherwise aesthetically appealing entrance to Brentwood, thereby hurting the image of the City and its attractiveness to future residents, businesses, tourists and other visitors," *id.* at 59, was within the scope of interests sought to be protected by Nashville's zoning ordinance. In Village of Chestnut Ridge v. Town of Ramapo, 841 N.Y.S.2d 321 (N.Y. A.D. 2007), Ramapo had changed its zoning law to allow the construction of adult student living facilities in areas close to four other villages. The court held that, although the villages had no standing to assert the unconstitutionality of the law, they did have standing to challenge the legality of the town's action under the home rule statute.

2. *Substantive Challenges to Municipal Action by Another Unit of Local Government.* Assuming that a local government is found to have standing to challenge another local government's actions, what substantive arguments could the neighboring locality raise? In her analysis of intergovernmental disputes over commercial development, Professor Shelley Ross Saxer suggests theories of nuisance, breach of duty to legislate for the regional welfare, due process violations, and, perhaps, the inadequacy of any environmental impact statement that has been prepared. Shelley Ross Saxer, Local Autonomy or Regionalism?: Sharing the Benefits and Burdens of Suburban Commercial Development, 30 Ind.L.Rev. 659 (1997). In Quinton v. Edison Park Development Corp., 285 A.2d 5 (N.J.1971) the court emphasized that municipalities have a duty to "look beyond municipal lines in the discharge of their zoning responsibilities," and ordered the city to provide a buffer zone, similar to the one provided under the zoning ordinance to residents, that would protect non-residents whose land abutted a shopping center site. A federal court recognized the justiciability of a city's claim that a neighbor city's zoning ordinance arbitrarily and capriciously violated due process standards in Township of River Vale v. Town of Orangetown, 403 F.2d 684 (2d Cir.1968). Professor Saxer also describes a municipal challenge to an adjacent city's approval of a new shopping mall based on the argument that the environmental review process had been deficient. *See* 30 Ind.L.Rev. at 670. The small number of these cases, though, certainly suggests that a municipality will face considerable difficulty in mounting a successful legal challenge to the land use decision of a neighboring unit of local government.

3. *Alternatives to Litigation.* Professor Saxer's article cited in Note 2 concludes that litigation is an unproductive and costly method for protecting a municipality's legitimate interests in the activities of its neighbors. Under her proposal, all municipalities would have a right "not to be substantially impacted by land use decisions made by adjacent communities." Saxer, 30

Ind.L.Rev., *supra*, at 683–92. She suggests mediation and binding arbitration as the preferable way to resolve interlocal conflicts over the negative extraterritorial impact of local land use decisions. *Id.* at 685. What type of procedures would you suggest? Would it involve participation in the existing local land use regulatory framework?

4.   *Statutory Barriers to Municipal Standing in Regional Governance.* Several states, while mandating regional review of local land use decisions, explicitly limit standing to challenge those decisions. In Florida, for example, the Florida Land and Water Commission is the administrative agency charged with reviewing challenges to local zoning or development decisions. Under the law establishing the agency and its powers, standing is granted only to "the owner, the developer, an appropriate regional planning agency . . . or the state land planning agency." Fla. Stat. Ch. 380 § 380.07(2). Even without explicit statutory guidance on standing, a court may deny municipal standing on the ground that it is inconsistent with a comprehensive regulatory scheme. In City of Elgin v. County of Cook, 660 N.E.2d 875 (Ill.1995), the court denied municipal standing in a city's challenge to a county ordinance that granted final zoning approval for the establishment of a landfill. To satisfy *Barrington Hills'* requirement that the city establish a direct injury in its corporate capacity, the city of Elgin had alleged that the landfill would cause economic injury to the municipality because it "will lead to more traffic, which will cause increased road maintenance and traffic control expenditures and . . . will diminish or impair property values such that there will be a decrease in property tax revenues." *Id.* at 882. The court denied standing, finding that the extensive permitting procedures established by the Illinois Environmental Protection Act preempted individual municipal challenges:

> Given the pressing need for pollution control facilities, the Act encourages the development of environmentally sound facilities through the establishment of a uniform, statewide environmental policy dealing with such facilities. With this goal in mind, it would be anomalous to allow third parties such as the instant plaintiff municipalities to challenge local zoning ordinances authorizing the siting of regional pollution control facilities. This is particularly so where the applicant is a municipal joint-action agency established pursuant to the Intergovernmental Cooperation Act and with the express purpose of developing a waste management plan for northern Cook County. . . . Indeed, if extraterritorial challenges by third-party municipalities are allowed in the courts of this State, it is unlikely that any significant landfill, regardless of how necessary and environmentally sound, will ever again be developed in Illinois. As evidenced in the instant case, no matter where a landfill is sited, neighboring units of local government not participating in the landfill's development will typically employ their considerable legal arsenals to prevent indefinitely the development of such facilities. Thus, where the appropriate unit of local government approves the

siting of a pollution control facility pursuant to section 39(c), and that facility is contained solely within that unit's own geographic boundaries, we hold that extraterritorial third-party challenges to these siting decisions to the courts of this State are incompatible with the purposes of the Act.

Id. at 884.

Is limiting municipal standing the best way to ensure wise implementation of this complex permitting process? A different approach would be to impose extraterritorial obligations on local governments themselves, that is, to require that local governments consider whether their actions further the region's health, safety, and welfare. This goal could be achieved through judicial decision or legislative action. The following cases and notes illustrate both approaches.

ASSOCIATED HOME BUILDERS OF THE GREATER EASTBAY, INC. v. LIVERMORE

Supreme Court of California
557 P.2d 473 (1976)

TOBRINER, JUSTICE.

We face today the question of the validity of an initiative ordinance enacted by the voters of the City of Livermore which prohibits issuance of further residential building permits until local educational, sewage disposal, and water supply facilities comply with specified standards. Plaintiff, an association of contractors, subdividers, and other persons interested in residential construction in Livermore, brought this suit to enjoin enforcement of the ordinance. The superior court issued a permanent injunction, and the city appealed.

* * * Finding that excessive issuance of residential building permits has caused school overcrowding, sewage pollution, and water rationing, the ordinance prohibits issuance of further permits until three standards are met: "1. EDUCATIONAL FACILITIES—No double sessions in the schools nor overcrowded classrooms as determined by the California Education Code. 2. SEWAGE—The sewage treatment facilities and capacities meet the standards set by the Regional Water Quality Control Board. 3. WATER SUPPLY—No rationing of water with respect to human consumption or irrigation and adequate water reserves for fire protection exist."

* * * Plaintiff urges that we affirm the trial court's injunction on a ground which it raised below, but upon which the trial court did not rely. Plaintiff contends that the ordinance proposes, and will cause, the prevention of nonresidents from migrating to Livermore, and that the ordinance therefore attempts an unconstitutional exercise of the police power, both because no compelling state interest justifies its infringement upon the migrant's constitutionally protected right to travel, and because it exceeds the police power of the municipality.

The ordinance on its face imposes no absolute prohibition or limitation upon population growth or residential construction. It does provide that no building permits will issue unless standards for educational facilities, water supply and sewage disposal have been met, but plaintiff presented no evidence to show that the ordinance's standards were unreasonable or unrelated to their apparent objectives of protecting the public health and welfare. Thus, we do not here confront the question of the constitutionality of an ordinance which limits or bars population growth either directly in express language or indirectly by the imposition of prohibitory standards; we adjudicate only the validity of an ordinance limiting building permits in accord with standards that reasonably measure the adequacy of public services.

As we shall explain, the limited record here prevents us from resolving that constitutional issue. We deal here with a case in which a land use ordinance is challenged solely on the ground that it assertedly exceeds the municipality's authority under the police power; the challenger eschews any claim that the ordinance discriminates on a basis of race or wealth. Under such circumstances, we view the past decisions of this court and the federal courts as establishing the following standard: the land use restriction withstands constitutional attack if it is fairly debatable that the restriction in fact bears a reasonable relation to the general welfare. For the guidance of the trial court we point out that if a restriction significantly affects residents of surrounding communities, the constitutionality of the restriction must be measured by its impact not only upon the welfare of the enacting community, but upon the welfare of the surrounding region. We explain the process by which the court can determine whether or not such a restriction reasonably relates to the regional welfare. * * *

Most zoning and land use ordinances affect population growth and density. (*See Construction Ind. Ass'n, Sonoma Cty. v. City of Petaluma*, [(9th Cir.1975)], 522 F.2d 897, 906; Note, Op. cit., supra, 26 Stan.L.Rev. 585, 606–607, fn. 91.) As commentators have observed, to insist that such zoning laws are invalid unless the interests supporting the exclusion are compelling in character, and cannot be achieved by an alternative method, would result in wholesale invalidation of land use controls and endanger the validity of city and regional planning. * * *

We conclude that the indirect burden upon the right to travel imposed by the Livermore ordinance does not call for strict judicial scrutiny. The validity of the challenged ordinance must be measured by the more liberal standards that have traditionally tested the validity of land use restrictions enacted under the municipal police power.

This conclusion brings us to plaintiff's final contention: that the Livermore ordinance exceeds the authority conferred upon the city under the police power. * * *

We * * * reaffirm the established constitutional principle that a local land use ordinance falls within the authority of the police power if it is reasonably related to the public welfare. Most previous decisions applying this test, however, have involved ordinances without substantial effect beyond the municipal boundaries. The present ordinance, in contrast, significantly affects the interests of nonresidents who are not represented in the city legislative body and cannot vote on a city initiative. We therefore believe it desirable for the guidance of the trial court to clarify the application of the traditional police power test to an ordinance which significantly affects nonresidents of the municipality.

When we inquire whether an ordinance reasonably relates to the public welfare, inquiry should begin by asking Whose welfare must the ordinance serve. In past cases, when discussing ordinances without significant effect beyond the municipal boundaries, we have been content to assume that the ordinance need only reasonably relate to the welfare of the enacting municipality and its residents. But municipalities are not isolated islands remote from the needs and problems of the area in which they are located; thus an ordinance, superficially reasonable from the limited viewpoint of the municipality, may be disclosed as unreasonable when viewed from a larger perspective.

These considerations impel us to the conclusion that the proper constitutional test is one which inquires whether the ordinance reasonably relates to the welfare of those whom it significantly affects. If its impact is limited to the city boundaries, the inquiry may be limited accordingly; if, as alleged here, the ordinance may strongly influence the supply and distribution of housing for an entire metropolitan region, judicial inquiry must consider the welfare of that region. * * *

We explain the process by which a trial court may determine whether a challenged restriction reasonably relates to the regional welfare. The first step in that analysis is to forecast the probable effect and duration of the restriction. In the instant case the Livermore ordinance posits a total ban on residential construction, but one which terminates as soon as public facilities reach specified standards. Thus to evaluate the impact of the restriction, the court must ascertain the extent to which public facilities currently fall short of the specified standards, must inquire whether the city or appropriate regional agencies have undertaken to construct needed improvements, and must determine when the improvements are likely to be completed.

The second step is to identify the competing interests affected by the restriction. We touch in this area deep social antagonisms. We allude to the conflict between the environmental protectionists and the egalitarian humanists; a collision between the forces that would save the benefits of nature and those that would preserve the opportunity of people in general to settle. Suburban residents who seek to overcome problems of inadequate schools and public facilities to secure 'the blessing of quiet seclusion and clean air' and to 'make the area a sanctuary for people' (*Village of Belle Terre v. Boraas, supra*, 416 U.S. 1, 9, 94 S.Ct. 1536, 1541, 39 L.Ed.2d 797) may assert a vital interest in limiting immigration to their community. Outsiders searching for a place to live in the face of a growing shortage of adequate housing, and hoping to share in the perceived benefits of suburban life, may present a countervailing interest opposing barriers to immigration.

Having identified and weighed the competing interests, the final step is to determine whether the ordinance, in light of its probable impact, represents a reasonable accommodation of the competing interests. We do not hold that a court in inquiring whether an ordinance reasonably relates to the regional welfare, cannot defer to the judgment of the municipality's legislative body. But judicial deference is not judicial abdication. The ordinance must have a *real and substantial* relation to the public welfare. * * * There must be a reasonable basis in fact, not in fancy, to support the legislative determination. * * * Although in many cases it will be 'fairly debatable' (*Euclid v. Ambler Co., supra*, 272 U.S. 365, 388, 47 S.Ct. 114, 71 L.Ed. 303) that the ordinance reasonably relates to the regional welfare, it cannot be assumed that a land use ordinance can *never* be invalidated as an enactment in excess of the police power.

The burden rests with the party challenging the constitutionality of an ordinance to present the evidence and documentation which the court will require in undertaking this constitutional analysis. Plaintiff in the present case has not yet attempted to shoulder that burden. Although plaintiff obtained a stipulation that as of the date of trial the ordinance's goals had not been fulfilled, it presented no evidence to show the likely duration or effect of the ordinance's restriction upon building permits. We must presume that the City of Livermore and appropriate regional agencies will attempt in good faith to provide that community with adequate schools, sewage disposal facilities, and a sufficient water supply; plaintiff, however, has not presented evidence to show whether the city and such agencies have undertaken to construct the needed improvements or when such improvements will be completed. Consequently we cannot determine the impact upon either Livermore or the surrounding region of the ordinance's restriction on the issuance of building permits pending achievement of its goals.

With respect to the competing interests, plaintiff asserts the existence of an acute housing shortage in the San Francisco Bay Area, but presents no evidence to document that shortage or to relate it to the probable effect of the Livermore ordinance. Defendants maintain that Livermore has severe problems of air pollution and inadequate public facilities which make it reasonable to divert new housing, at least temporarily, to other communities but offer no evidence to support that claim. Without an evidentiary record to demonstrate the validity and significance of the asserted interests, we cannot determine whether the instant ordinance attempts a reasonable accommodation of those interests.

In short, we cannot determine on the pleadings and stipulations alone whether this ordinance reasonably relates to the general welfare of the region it affects. The ordinance carries the presumption of constitutionality; plaintiff cannot overcome that presumption on the limited record before us. Thus the judgment rendered on this limited record cannot be sustained on the ground that the initiative ordinance falls beyond the proper scope of the police power. * * *

The judgment of the superior court is reversed, and the cause remanded for further proceedings consistent with the views expressed herein.

WRIGHT, C.J., and McCOMB, SULLIVAN and RICHARDSON, JJ., concur.

MOSK, JUSTICE (dissenting).

I dissent.

Limitations on growth may be justified in resort communities, beach and lake and mountain sites, and other rural and recreational areas; such restrictions are generally designed to preserve nature's environment for the benefit of all mankind. They fulfill our fiduciary obligation to posterity. As Thomas Jefferson wrote, the earth belongs to the living, but in usufruct.

But there is a vast qualitative difference when a suburban community invokes an elitist concept to construct a mythical moat around its perimeter, not for the benefit of mankind but to exclude all but its fortunate current residents.

* * *

The majority, somewhat desultorily, deny that the ordinance imposes an absolute prohibition upon population growth or residential construction. It is true that the measure prohibits the issuance of building permits for single-family residential, multiple residential and trailer residential units until designated public services meet specified standards. But to see such restriction in practicality as something short of total prohibition is to employ ostrich vision.

First of all, the ordinance provides no timetable or dates by which the public services are to be made adequate. Thus the moratorium on permits is likely to continue for decades, or at least until attrition ultimately reduces the present population. Second, it is obvious that no inducement exists for present residents to expend their resources to render facilities adequate for the purpose of accommodating future residents. It would seem more rational, if improved services are really contemplated for any time in the foreseeable future, to admit the new residents and compel them to make their proportionate contribution to the cost of the educational, sewage and water services. Thus it cannot seriously be argued that Livermore maintains anything other than total exclusion.

* * * [M]ay Livermore build a Chinese Wall to insulate itself from growth problems today? And if Livermore may do so, why not every municipality in Alameda County and in all other counties in Northern California? With a patchwork of enclaves the inevitable result will be creation of an aristocracy housed in exclusive suburbs while modest wage earners will be confined to declining neighborhoods, crowded into sterile, monotonous, multifamily projects, or assigned to pockets of marginal housing on the urban fringe. The overriding objective should be to minimize rather than exacerbate social and economic disparities, to lower barriers rather than raise them, to emphasize heterogeneity rather than homogeneity, to increase choice rather than limit it. * * *

NOTES AND QUESTIONS

1. *Moratoria and Other Growth Controls.* Courts have considered a variety of land use techniques that, like the one upheld in *Livermore*, limit residential development because of the municipality's inability to provide adequate services. *See e.g.,* Construction Industry Association v. City of Petaluma, 522 F.2d 897 (9th Cir.1975) (upholding town plan that restricted development to 500 units per year); Droste v. Board of County Comm'rs, 159 P.3d 601 (Colo. 2007) (upholding county's temporary development moratorium notwithstanding fact that county had no general zoning powers); Golden v. Planning Bd. of Town of Ramapo, 285 N.E.2d 291 (N.Y.1972) (upholding town development plan that conditioned issuance of building permits on adequacy of a number of public services). In contrast, the Massachusetts Supreme Judicial Court invalidated a municipality's restriction on development because although "a town may allow itself breathing room to plan for the channeling of normal growth, it may not turn that breathing room into a choke hold against further growth." Zuckerman v. Town of Hadley, 813 N.E.2d 843, 850 (Mass. 2004). In the same year, however, the court upheld a different town's designation of its entire territory as a "district of critical planning concern," which severely restricted the number of available building permits. The court determined that evidence in the record supported the town's finding that the designation would preserve

the town's natural, coastal and recreational resources. *See* Home Builders Assoc. of Cape Cod v. Cape Cod Comm., 808 N.E.2d 315 (Mass. 2004).

Local power to adopt development moratoria may be constrained by other state constitutional or statutory measures. In Biggers v. City of Bainbridge Island,169 P.3d 14 (Wash. 2007), a closely divided court held that a city was barred from imposing a moratorium on certain shoreline developments. In the majority's view, the state's constitutional authority over navigable waters and their shorelines meant that regulatory control over the shoreline rested exclusively with the state. In addition, the court found that the state's shoreline management act preempted the local measure. Lack of service capacity may act as effectively as a moratorium to prevent growth, however. In Skagit D06, LLC v. Growth Mgmt. Hearings Bd., 170 Wash.App. 1035 (Wash. Ct. App. 2012), the court rejected a challenge to local limits on growth adopted because of lack of public services. The plaintiffs had argued that the limits constituted a de facto moratorium. The line between government action that overtly stops growth and government action (or inaction) that makes growth impossible is not easy to define.

How can courts distinguish those ordinances that properly plan for orderly growth and development from those that impermissibly neglect the regional welfare? In *Petaluma*, for instance, the plaintiff's experts claimed that if all municipalities in the area adopted similar growth restrictions, a 25% shortfall of needed housing units would result. Similarly, a dissenting judge in *Ramapo* criticized the ordinance for its "parochial stance without regard to its impact on the region or the State," 285 N.E.2d at 305 (Breitel, J., dissenting). Can you articulate principles that would strike the proper balance between those competing interests? Or should the court ignore the regional impact of local actions?

2.   *Post-Livermore Legislation.* In 1979, three years after the court's decision in *Livermore*, the California legislature adopted the following statute:

Limitation on construction of housing units; consideration; findings.

In carrying out the provisions of this chapter, each county and city shall consider the effect of ordinances adopted pursuant to this chapter on the housing needs of the region in which the local jurisdiction is situated and balance these needs against the public service needs of its residents and available fiscal and environmental resources. Any ordinance adopted pursuant to this chapter which, by its terms, limits the number of housing units which may be constructed on an annual basis shall contain findings as to the public health, safety, and welfare of the city or county to be promoted by the adoption of the ordinance which justify reducing the housing opportunities of the region.

Cal.Gov. Code § 65863.6.

For one year, between 1980 and 1981, the above section of the California statutes was replaced by this provision:

> In carrying out the provisions of this chapter, any ordinance which operates to limit the number of housing units which may be constructed on an annual basis shall contain findings which justify reducing the housing opportunities of the region. The findings shall include all of the following:
>
> (a) A description of the city's or county's appropriate share of the regional need for housing.
>
> (b) A description of the specific housing programs and activities being undertaken by the local jurisdiction. . .
>
> (c) A description of how the public health, safety, and welfare would be promoted by such adoption or amendment.
>
> (d) The fiscal and environmental resources available to the local jurisdiction. With respect to a charter city, this section shall apply to any zoning ordinance adopted by such charter city.

In 1981, the legislature returned to the original version. As between the two approaches to growth limitations, which statutory directive is more likely to address the problem Justice Mosk expressed in his *Livermore* dissent? Does either section do a good job of balancing local, regional, and statewide concerns? Does either section provide a substantive basis for judicial review? In *Building Industry Ass'n of Southern California, Inc. v. City of Camarillo*, 718 P.2d 68 (Ca.1986), the California Supreme Court held that the law did not apply to growth control ordinances adopted directly by the voters through the initiative process, thus removing cases like *Livermore* from the statute's purview.

3. *Allocation of the Burden.* Both the majority and the dissent in *Livermore* agreed that municipal laws with broader regional impacts can be challenged as impermissibly neglecting the more general public welfare. They differed sharply, however, on the allocation of the burden of proof on this issue. The California legislature resolved that dispute:

> *Ordinances limiting building permits or development of buildable lots for residential purposes; impact on supply of residential units; actions challenging validity.*
>
> (a) Any ordinance enacted by the governing body of a city, county, or city and county which (1) directly limits, by number, the building permits that may be issued for residential construction or the buildable lots which may be developed for residential purposes, or (2) changes the standards of residential development on vacant land so that the governing body's zoning is rendered in violation of Section 65913.1 of the Government Code [which requires cities to zone vacant land to meet regional needs] is presumed to have an impact on the supply of residential units available in an area which

includes territory outside the jurisdiction of the city, county, or city and county.

(b) With respect to any action which challenges the validity of an ordinance specified in subdivision (a) the city, county, or city and county enacting the ordinance shall bear the burden of proof that the ordinance is necessary for the protection of the public health, safety, or welfare of the population of the city, county, or city and county.

Cal.Evid.Code § 669.5.

As the next case shows, a local land use decision may have a significant impact on the regional supply of affordable housing even without imposing an explicit limit on housing starts.

BRITTON v. TOWN OF CHESTER

Supreme Court of New Hampshire
595 A.2d 492 (1991)

BATCHELDER, JUSTICE.

In this appeal, the defendant, the Town of Chester (the town), challenges a ruling by the Master (R. Peter Shapiro, Esq.), approved by the Superior Court (Gray, J.), that the Chester Zoning Ordinance is invalid and unconstitutional. * * *

The plaintiffs brought a petition in 1985, for declaratory and injunctive relief, challenging the validity of the multi-family housing provisions of the Chester Zoning Ordinance. * * * The town of Chester lies in the west-central portion of Rockingham County, thirteen miles east of the city of Manchester. * * * The available housing stock is principally single-family homes. There is no municipal sewer or water service, and other municipal services remain modest. The town has not encouraged industrial or commercial development; it is a "bedroom community," with the majority of its labor force commuting to Manchester. Because of its close proximity to job centers and the ready availability of vacant land, the town is projected to have among the highest growth rates in New Hampshire over the next two decades. * * *

The plaintiffs in this case are a group of low-and moderate-income people who have been unsuccessful in finding affordable, adequate housing in the town, and a builder who, the master found, is committed to the construction of such housing. At trial, two plaintiffs testified as representative members of the group of low-and moderate-income people. Plaintiff George Edwards is a woodcutter who grew up in the town. He lives in Chester with his wife and three minor children in a one-bedroom, thirty-foot by eight-foot camper trailer with no running water. Their annual income is $14,040, which places them in the low-income category.

Roger McFarland grew up and works in the town. He lives in Derry with his wife and three teenage children in a two-bedroom apartment which is too small to meet their needs. He and his wife both work, and their combined annual income is $24,000. Under the area standards, the McFarlands are a moderate-income family. Raymond Remillard is the plaintiff home builder. A long-time resident of the town, he owns an undeveloped twenty-three-acre parcel of land on Route 102 in the town's eastern section. Since 1979, he has attempted to obtain permission from the town to build a moderate-sized multi-family housing development on his land.

The zoning ordinance in effect at the beginning of this action in 1985 provided for a single-family home on a two-acre lot or a duplex on a three-acre lot, and it excluded multi-family housing from all five zoning districts in the town. In July, 1986, the town amended its zoning ordinance to allow multi-family housing. Article six of the amended ordinance now permits multi-family housing as part of a "planned residential development" (PRD), a form of multi-family housing required to include a variety of housing types, such as single-family homes, duplexes, and multi-family structures.

We first turn to the ordinance itself, because it does, on its face, permit the type of development that the plaintiffs argue is being prohibited. The master found, however, that the ordinance placed an unreasonable barrier to the development of affordable housing for low- and moderate-income families. Under the ordinance, PRDs are allowed on tracts of not less than twenty acres in two designated "R-2" (medium-density residential) zoning districts. Due to existing home construction and environmental considerations, such as wetlands and steep slopes, only slightly more than half of all the land in the two R-2 districts could reasonably be used for multi-family development. This constitutes only 1.73% of the land in the town. This fact standing alone does not, in the confines of this case, give rise to an entitlement to a legal remedy for those who seek to provide multi-family housing. However, it does serve to point out that the two R-2 districts are, in reality, less likely to be developed than would appear from a reading of the ordinance.

Article six of the ordinance also imposes several subjective requirements and restrictions on the developer of a PRD. Any project must first receive the approval of the town planning board as to "whether in its judgment the proposal meets the objectives and purposes set forth [in the ordinance] in which event the Administrator [i.e., the planning board] may grant approval to [the] proposal subject to reasonable conditions and limitations." Consequently, the ordinance allows the planning board to control various aspects of a PRD without reference to any objective criteria. One potentially onerous section permits the planning board to "retain, at the applicant's expense, a registered professional engineer, hydrologist, and any other applicable professional to represent the [planning board] and assist the [planning board] in determining compliance with [the] ordinance and other applicable regulations." The master found such subjective review for developing multi-family housing to be a substantial disincentive to the creation of such units, because it would escalate the economic risks of developing affordable housing to the point where these projects would not be realistically feasible. In addition, we question the availability of bank financing for such projects, where the developer is required to submit a "blank check" to the planning board along with his proposal, and where to do so could halt, change the character of, or even bankrupt the project.

* * *

RSA 674:16 authorizes the local legislative body of any city or town to adopt or amend a zoning ordinance "[f]or the purpose of promoting the health, safety, or *the general welfare of the community*." (Emphasis added.) The defendant asserts that the term "community" as used in the statute refers only to the municipality itself and not to some broader region in which the municipality is situated. We disagree.

* * *

We have previously addressed the issue of whether municipalities are required to consider regional needs when enacting zoning ordinances which control growth. In *Beck v. Town of Raymond*, 118 N.H. 793, 394 A.2d 847 (1978), we held that "[growth] controls must not be imposed simply to exclude outsiders, *see Steel Hill Dev. v. Town of Sanbornton*, [469 F.2d 956 (1st Cir.1972)]; *Nat'l Land and Inv. Co. v. Kohn*, 419 Pa. 504, 215 A.2d 597 (1965), especially outsiders of any disadvantaged social or economic group, *see S. Burlington County N.A.A.C.P. v. Township of Mount Laurel*, 67 N.J. 151, 336 A.2d 713, *appeal dismissed*, 423 U.S. 808 [96 S.Ct. 18, 46 L.Ed.2d 28] (1975)." *Beck*, 118 N.H. at 801, 394 A.2d at 852. We reasoned that "each municipality [should] bear its fair share of the burden of increased growth." *Id.* Today, we pursue the logical extension of the reasoning in *Beck* and apply its rationale and high purpose to zoning regulations which wrongfully exclude persons of low-or moderate-income from the zoning municipality.

In *Beck*, this court sent a message to zoning bodies that "[t]owns may not refuse to confront the future by building a moat around themselves and pulling up the drawbridge." *Id.* The town of Chester appears willing to lower that bridge only for people who can afford a single-family home on a two-acre lot or a duplex on a three-acre lot. Others are realistically prohibited from crossing.

Municipalities are not isolated enclaves, far removed from the concerns of the area in which they are situated. As subdivisions of the

State, they do not exist solely to serve their own residents, and their regulations should promote the general welfare, both within and without their boundaries. Therefore, we interpret the general welfare provision of the zoning enabling statute, RSA 674:16, to include the welfare of the "community", as defined in this case, in which a municipality is located and of which it forms a part.

A municipality's power to zone property to promote the health, safety, and general welfare of the community is delegated to it by the State, and the municipality must, therefore, exercise this power in conformance with the enabling legislation. *Durant v. Town of Dunbarton*, 121 N.H. 352, 354, 430 A.2d 140, 142 (1981). Because the Chester Zoning Ordinance does not provide for the lawful needs of the community, in that it flies in the face of the general welfare provision of RSA 674:16 and is, therefore, at odds with the statute upon which it is grounded, we hold that, as applied to the facts of this case, the ordinance is an invalid exercise of the power delegated to the town pursuant to RSA 674:16–30. We so hold because of the master's finding that "there are no substantial and compelling reasons that would warrant the Town of Chester, through its land use ordinances, from fulfilling its obligation to provide low[-] and moderate[-]income families within the community and a proportionate share of same within its region from a realistic opportunity to obtain affordable housing."

* * * The zoning ordinance evolved as an innovative means to counter the problems of uncontrolled growth. It was never conceived to be a device to facilitate the use of governmental power to prevent access to a municipality by "outsiders of any disadvantaged social or economic group." *Beck*, 118 N.H. at 801, 394 A.2d at 852. The town of Chester has adopted a zoning ordinance which is blatantly exclusionary. This court will not condone the town's conduct. * * *

NOTES AND QUESTIONS

1. *Exclusionary Impact of Zoning Ordinances*. All local zoning regulations affect the supply and cost of housing. Although some, like the ordinance challenged in *Livermore*, are more obvious and explicit in their impact, any regulation of lot size or square footage, design standards, or types of permitted housing, will have an effect on price. The term "exclusionary zoning" has come to be applied to local zoning measures that appear to impose unnecessary or unjustifiable costs. The implication is that the purpose of the zoning requirement is to exclude low- or moderate-income families who cannot afford the costlier housing mandated by the locality.

In the middle decades of the twentieth century many state courts upheld local zoning that would subsequently be considered exclusionary on the theory that these measures reflected simply a local effort to maintain or improve local living conditions, promote the community's general character, preserve open space, protect property values, or enhance community aesthetics. Assuming that such zoning affected only the property rights of landowners rather than the interest in housing or the selection of a place in which to live, the standard of review of an arguably exclusionary measure was whether it was "reasonably calculated to advance the community as a social, economic, and political unit." Vickers v. Township Comm., 181 A.2d 129, 137 (N.J.1962). *See* Richard Briffault, Our Localism, Part I: The Structure of Local Government Law, 90 Colum. L. Rev. 1, 39–41 (1990). Many of these measures also reflected local fiscal self-interest. With the provision of local services heavily dependent on local property tax revenues, exclusionary zoning had the effect of driving up taxable property values within the community. In addition, by tending to reduce local densities, exclusionary zoning reduced demand for costly locally-financed services, like elementary and secondary education.

Starting in the mid-1960s, courts in some states, most notably Pennsylvania, New Jersey, New York, California, and Connecticut, as well as New Hampshire, began to focus on the exclusionary impact of local measures like large minimum lot sizes, large floor area requirements, the exclusion of apartments, and the exclusion of mobile homes. Turning from the local interest to the regional impact on housing, these courts held exclusionary zoning unlawful under state zoning doctrines. *See, e.g.*, Builders Service Corp. v. Planning & Zoning Com'n of East Hampton, 545 A.2d 530 (Conn.1988) (minimum floor area requirement invalidated because of its discriminatory impact on low income families), Geiger v. Zoning Hearing Board of Township of North Whitehall, 507 A.2d 361 (Pa.1986) (invalidating local exclusion of mobile homes from township), National Land & Investment Co. v. Kohn, 215 A.2d 597 (Pa.1965) (four acre minimum lot size invalidated). Several state legislatures have limited local discretion to exclude mobile homes. *See, e.g.*, Mich. Stat. Ann. § 19.855(107)(3) (prohibiting exclusion of mobile homes); Ind. Code § 36–7–4–1106 (requiring local governments to treat mobile homes like all other single family residences). Many state courts, however, continued to uphold local ordinances that have exclusionary effects. *See* Julian Conrad Juergensmeyer and Thomas E. Roberts, Land Use Planning and Control Law 268–79 (1998).

2. *Expanding the Scope of the Exclusionary Zoning Claim.* Although the claim in *Britton* was specifically limited to the need for affordable housing, the court's language was broad, stressing the interconnectedness of municipalities in a region and the requirement that all municipalities address the regional welfare. It is perhaps not surprising that this focus has been the basis for lawsuits alleging regional impacts of other local zoning actions. In Community Resources for Justice, Inc. v. Manchester, 917 A.2d 707 (N.H. 2007), the court held that the city's decision to ban correctional facilities was subject to *Britton*-like scrutiny, stressing that the plaintiff's proposed halfway house implicates the general welfare. It also noted that the effect of upholding the ban would be to encourage other local governments to follow suit, effectively pushing the use out of New Hampshire. The court

remanded the case for resolution of this issue, which had not been addressed below. Should *Britton*'s rationale be extended to apply to other municipal zoning decisions? Does it make suspect a total exclusion of any use reasonably to be expected in the region?

3. *Exclusionary Zoning in Federal Courts.* The combined effect of a number of Supreme Court decisions in the 1970s limited the availability of federal remedies for exclusionary zoning challenges. The Court held that there is no constitutionally protected right to housing, *see* Lindsey v. Normet, 405 U.S. 56 (1972); that wealth is not a suspect classification for equal protection purposes, *see* San Antonio Independent School Dist. v. Rodriguez, 411 U.S. 1 (1973); and that constitutional claims of racial discrimination in zoning required proof of discriminatory intent, rather than the lesser standard of discriminatory impact, *see* Arlington Heights v. Metropolitan Housing Development Corp., 429 U.S. 252 (1977). Village of Belle Terre v. Boraas, 416 U.S. 1 (1974), rejected right to travel and freedom of association challenges to a zoning ordinance that excluded individuals on the basis of family status. In addition, Warth v. Seldin, 422 U.S. 490 (1975), found that non-residents lacked standing to challenge a suburban municipality's allegedly exclusionary ordinance.

Federal claims asserting that local zoning has a racially discriminatory impact may be brought under the federal Fair Housing Act, 42 U.S.C. § 3601 et seq. *See, e.g.,* Huntington Branch, NAACP v. Huntington, 844 F.2d 926 (2d Cir.), *aff'd,* 488 U.S. 15 (1988) (invalidating as racial discrimination under the Fair Housing Act municipality's refusal to rezone property to allow construction of low income housing project; discriminatory impact standard applied). *See also* Texas Dep't of Housing & Community Affairs v. Inclusive Communities Project, Inc., 135 S.Ct. 2507 (2015) (racially disparate impact claims cognizable under the federal Fair Housing Act).But there is no federal statutory ban on local zoning that has economically exclusionary effects.

4. *The Builder's Remedy.* In addition to invalidating Chester's zoning ordinance, *Britton* ordered the town to issue a building permit to the plaintiff developer. Similarly, Massachusetts' "Anti-Snob Zoning Law" provides recourse to a builder or developer who seeks to build affordable housing and is stymied by local regulators. Appeal of a local zoning denial to a state housing appeals committee may result in a builder's remedy unless the local government can establish that health and safety concerns are more pressing than the regional need for affordable housing. *See* Mass.Gen.Laws. Ch. 40B, §§ 20–23. Builder's remedy permits in Massachusetts produced over 20,000 housing units in the 1980s and 1990s. *See* Scott A. Bollens, Concentrated Poverty and Metropolitan Equity Strategies, 8 Stan.L. & Policy Rev. 11, 16 n.63 (1997). The builder's remedy may be likened to the attorneys fees awarded to a successful civil rights plaintiff. It provides an incentive to challenge exclusionary local ordinances, and, with the builder's remedy limited to plaintiffs who will build some affordable housing, it contributes to the regional stock of affordable housing. On the other hand, the remedy takes control of local development out of the hands of the community and can

enable developers to disregard legitimate community decisions regarding the siting of new development.

The linchpin of cases like *Britton* is the judicial insistence that municipalities consider the regional, and not simply their own municipal, welfare when they adopt land use regulations. So long as the political decision is made at the local level, by individuals elected by the residents of a municipality, though, is it realistic to expect that a city will incorporate a regional perspective in its deliberations? Does the builder's remedy create an impetus for municipal action that the political process alone would not produce?

5.   *Land Regulation and the Cost of Housing.* Although a survey of land use techniques is beyond the scope of this text, the connection between regulation and price is worth noting. Though many civic-minded citizens regard zoning and other land use regulations as an important, indeed essential, tool for the preservation of residential quality of life, many critics have argued that local regulation merely keeps the costs of housing artificially high. President George H.W. Bush's Advisory Commission on Regulatory Barriers to Affordable Housing issued a report concluding that local land regulations unnecessarily drive the cost of decent housing out of reach of many low and moderate income citizens. The commission urged judicial invalidation of zoning unless a local government can show that the challenged regulation is necessary for advancement of "a vital and pressing governmental interest." *See* Not in My Backyard: Removing Barriers to Affordable Housing (1991).

6.   *From Exclusionary Zoning to Inclusionary Zoning.* Though judicial invalidation of impermissibly exclusionary zoning ordinances will remove barriers to affordable housing, it does not guarantee that such housing will be built. As a result, some communities have taken an additional step to modify their zoning laws to provide for the actual construction of low and moderate income housing. Several techniques are available, and can be adopted either as incentives (such as providing bonuses to developers who agree to build) or as mandates (such as requiring developers to devote a certain percentage of new units to affordable housing). Though voluntary programs appear to satisfy most legal requirements, at least one court invalidated a local ordinance that required the developer to include low- and moderate-income housing in a residential development, *see* Board of Supervisors v. DeGroff Enterprises, 198 S.E.2d 600 (Va.1973) (mandatory set-asides constitute an unconstitutional taking of private property without compensation). The New Jersey Supreme Court, as described in the following Note, has taken the judicial lead in seeking to insure that all communities provide for their fair share of the regional demand for affordable housing, by requiring them not only to remove exclusionary barriers but also to adopt affirmative measures that will result in the actual construction of affordable housing units.

NOTE: MOUNT LAUREL *AND INCLUSIONARY ZONING*

The *Mount Laurel* cases referred to by the court in *Britton* undoubtedly constitute the most dramatic and significant exclusionary zoning litigation in the country. At one time, the New Jersey Supreme Court had upheld local exclusionary zoning measures. *See, e.g.,* Fanale v. Borough of Hasbrouck Heights, 139 A.2d 749 (N.J.1958) (sustaining local prohibition of multi-family dwellings); Fischer v. Township of Bedminster, 93 A.2d 378 (N.J.1952) (upholding five-acre minimum lot requirement); Lionshead Lake, Inc. v. Township of Wayne, 89 A.2d 693 (N.J.1952) (large minimum floor space requirement). In 1975, however, the court recanted and held exclusionary zoning unlawful. The court emphasized that local zoning must serve the "general welfare" of the state as a whole and not just the self-interest of the zoning locality: "[I]t is fundamental and not to be forgotten that the zoning power is a police power of the state and the local authority is acting only as a delegate of that power. . . . [T]he welfare of the state's citizens beyond the borders of the particular municipality cannot be disregarded and must be recognized and served." Southern Burlington County N.A.A.C.P. v. Township of Mt. Laurel, 336 A.2d 713, 726–27 (N.J.1975) (*Mount Laurel I*). Moreover, the court's concern about the growing interlocal separation of rich and poor and the implications of economic segregation for the quality of local public services and access to housing and employment opportunities led it to require more than the elimination of exclusionary devices. Instead, the court articulated a vision of a state composed of integrated, mixed-income communities, and held that local zoning ordinances must further that goal. The court required each zoning locality "affirmatively to plan and provide, by its land use regulations, the reasonable opportunity for an appropriate variety and choice of housing, including, of course, low and moderate cost housing, to meet the needs, desires and resources of all categories of people who may desire to live within its boundaries." *Id.* at 728.

The court initially indicated that it would leave primary responsibility for the satisfaction of the *Mount Laurel* requirement to local governments. Little low- and moderate-income housing was built in the New Jersey suburbs—including in Mount Laurel itself—and eight years later the case was back before the court. Its decision in *Mount Laurel II* stressed its frustration with local resistance to the implementation of its earlier opinion and announced a fundamental shift in focus, establishing wide-ranging affirmative obligations for municipal officials in the exercise of their zoning powers. *See* Southern Burlington County N.A.A.C.P. v. Township of Mt. Laurel, 456 A.2d 390 (N.J.1983) (*Mount Laurel II*). Professor J. Peter Byrne describes the background, the holdings, and the legislative response to these bold judicial decisions.

J. PETER BYRNE, BOOK REVIEW,
ARE SUBURBS UNCONSTITUTIONAL?
85 Geo. L. J. 2265 (1997)

The original Mount Laurel case began under dramatic circumstances. Mount Laurel itself, seven miles west of Philadelphia, was a nondescript expanse of truck farms rapidly converting to pricey subdivisions. Although most of the land was undeveloped, nearly all of it was zoned for single-family homes on large lots or for industrial use. Nowhere could anyone construct multifamily homes or place mobile homes. The original plaintiffs included several low-income black residents of the town, who had been denied a zoning change to construct subsidized housing (for which they had secured a commitment for public financing). Some of these residents descended from freed slaves whose families had lived in the town since the Revolution, but could not afford new housing. . . . [T]he mayor advised this group at a sweltering meeting at the black church in Mount Laurel, Jacob's Chapel, "If you people can't afford to live in our town, then you'll just have to leave."

. . . The [Mount Laurel] court rested its holding solely on the state constitution, avoiding review by an increasingly conservative United States Supreme Court. The court did not deny that exclusionary zoning might be in the rational interests of a majority of a suburb's residents, but insisted that the "general welfare" which zoning long had been constitutionally required to advance was that of the state as a whole. Given that, local ordinances that did not provide a realistic opportunity for a fair share of the region's low income housing needs were unconstitutional. . . .

The court's provision for a remedy was mild and conciliatory, remanding to allow Mount Laurel time to consider how it would meet its new constitutional obligations. An extended period of shilly-shallying ensued both for Mount Laurel and for other suburbs engaged in similar litigation. . . .

Doubts about the court's resolve were settled in Mount Laurel II, in 1983. The Court strongly reaffirmed the principle of what now was called Mount Laurel I, but mandated a host of specific remedies that every municipality in the state had to embrace. The court seized upon a state plan adopted (for quite limited purposes) to designate "growth areas," and towns within those areas had to provide not just for their own resident poor but also for a fair share of projected regional needs for low and moderate income housing. Litigation over fair share requirements would result in mandates for specific numbers of units. Removing regulatory barriers alone would no longer suffice to satisfy the principle; suburbs would need to adopt a variety of "affirmative" or "inclusionary" devices such as mandatory set-asides. The court sought to make its remedial regime effective by assigning all exclusionary zoning cases to three hand-picked trial judges who would develop expertise in administering such cases. Finally, the court changed the dynamics of Mount Laurel litigation entirely by approving a builder's remedy: developers proposing to include an appropriate percentage of low and moderate income housing in their project could challenge the constitutionality of a town's ordinance and—if they prevailed—be awarded the right to construct their projects. A substantial controversy surrounds the remedial regime enforced by the three trial judges in the wake of Mount Laurel II. Developers, rather than poor people or public interest organizations representing their interests, brought nearly all of the suits, seeking to build projects prohibited by challenged ordinances, and many prevailed. The judges found innovative means to resolve tricky questions—such as setting the methodology for determining fair shares by locking planners in a room without lawyers—and creatively employed special masters to help towns develop acceptable plans. Houses got built, but political opposition gained strength. * * *

The court in Mount Laurel II lamented that legislative inaction had made judicial action necessary to redress a complex social wrong. Intense resentment and apprehension by local governments, particularly toward the builder's remedy, stimulated political initiative. [The state adopted a Fair Housing Act, which established the Council on Affordable Housing to implement the state's *Mount Laurel* obligation]. * * * [T]he statute represents the first political commitment in the United States to statewide planning to expand the number and locations of affordable housing units for low and moderate income people. The court promptly sustained the constitutionality of the FHA, and most pending cases were transferred from the courts to COAH.

One of the most interesting and controversial elements of the FHA is the Regional Contribution Agreement (RCA), which permits a suburb to transfer up to half of its fair share obligation to another community in its region in exchange for cash. The suburb avoids dedicating land to residences for poor people, while the transferee—usually a city—gains funds to renovate or construct housing for the poor already within it. In effect, affluent suburbs subsidize housing in beleaguered cities. While both the suburb and the city may view such exchanges as optimal, RCAs certainly represent a retreat from Mount Laurel I's commitment to integrate the suburbs economically and racially.

How much has been accomplished in fact? Here is the proverbial half-full, half-empty glass: * * * by 1993, 14,000 units of low and moderate income housing had been or were being built in the New Jersey suburbs. * * * 14,000 units equal 9% of total New Jersey housing permits during the period; moreover, another 11,000 units had been rehabilitated and land for another 30,000 had been appropriately zoned. * * * [C]onstruction has been hampered by a depressed housing market and shrinking federal subsidies; [moreover, the state law emphasizes] * * * owner-occupied moderate income developments, as opposed to low income rentals. Only in April 1997 did Mount Laurel itself finally approved a 140-unit rental development for low income residents, organized by the lawyer in the original suit and the daughter of the lead plaintiff, Ethel R. Lawrence, for whom the complex will be named.

2. INTERLOCAL FISCAL INEQUALITY

a. School Finance Reform

Whether measured in terms of local budgets, the local government workforce, the impact on local communities, or the broader implications for the economy and society, public elementary and secondary education is the most important service provided by local governments. Current estimates of total annual government spending on education place the figure at $536 billion. This huge amount of funding is also marked by extensive interlocal inequalities. In most states, local governments are responsible for financing a significant fraction of education expenses. The principal source of local revenues for education is the property tax. Nationally, local revenues account for 44% of total public school expenditures; state revenues have increased somewhat, bringing the total percentage of state funding also up to 44%. The range among the states, however, is quite large. Illinois has the highest percentage of local funding for schools, nearly 60%. The states with the lowest percentage of local funding are Hawaii (3.5%) and New Mexico (15%). National Center for Education Statistics, Digest of Education Statistics (2013).

There are enormous differences in the amount of taxable property per school-age child among different localities. These differences are the direct result of the uneven geographical distribution of tax-generating properties, such as industrial facilities, commercial centers, and expensive residences. The property tax is considered more fully in Chapter VI, but, for present purposes, it is important to recognize that the revenue generated by property taxes is largely a function of two variables—the total assessed valuation of the property subject to the tax, and the tax rate. In the Texas decision, *Edgewood Independent School District v. Kirby*, examined below, the state supreme court noted that while the wealthiest Texas community boasted $14,000,000 of assessed property value per student, the poorest had a meager $20,000 for each student. Consider the implications of that differential for the property tax system. For the richest district to generate a modest $2,000 per student, it would levy a tax rate of less than .015%. The poorest district, in contrast, would require a very high property tax rate of 10% to collect the same amount. So long as the local property tax remains a substantial component of school funding formulas, these disparities are inevitable.

Over the past four decades, parents and poorer school districts across the country have filed lawsuits challenging the constitutionality of state school funding statutes. As of 2008, legal challenges had been filed and decided in 46 states, in all but Mississippi, Nevada, Utah, and Iowa. One effect of these cases has been to modestly reduce the local—and increase the state—share of school funding. Before 1970, local revenues actually accounted for a majority of the money spent on public schools. A second effect has been to force state courts to come to grips with the meaning of state constitutional equal protection clauses and education requirements, the role of the states in addressing interlocal inequalities, the relationship between localities and states in financing public education, and the courts' proper role in addressing these highly charged and politically, financially and socially significant questions.

School finance litigation began with lawsuits in federal courts based on the Constitution's Equal Protection Clause. In San Antonio Independent School District v. Rodriguez, 411 U.S. 1 (1973), the United States Supreme Court considered and rejected a federal equal protection challenge to Texas' local property tax-based system of funding public schools. The Court determined that the appropriate standard of review was the rational basis test and not strict judicial scrutiny. The Court chose rational basis review because school district wealth is not a suspect classification, and education is not a fundamental constitutional right. District wealth was not a suspect class in part because district wealth was not identical to the wealth of district residents. Due to the effect of commercial and industrial property on school district tax bases, the Court found that many poor people lived in relatively wealthy school districts. Moreover, the absence of "traditional indicia of suspectness," and the lack of a "history of purposeful unequal treatment," *id.* at 28, led the Court to conclude that the majoritarian political process adequately protected the interests of poorer districts. As for education, although the Court proclaimed its "abiding respect for the vital role of education in a free society," *id.* at 32, it stressed that the Constitution makes no mention of education. Thus, the Court concluded that reliance on the local property tax to fund education rationally furthered a legitimate state objective: "While assuring a basic education for every child in the State, it permits and encourages a large measure of participation in and control of each district's schools at the local level." *Id.* at 49.

With the federal courthouse door effectively closed by *Rodriguez,* school finance reformers turned to state constitutions and state courts. They have relied on state equal protection clauses, state constitutional provisions requiring public education systems, and the interplay of these equal protection and education provisions. Thus, turning *Rodriguez* around, they argued that the presence in nearly all state constitutions of education articles meant that education was a fundamental right for state equal protection purposes. The courts of California, Serrano v. Priest, 557 P.2d 929 (Cal.1976); Connecticut, Horton v. Meskill, 376 A.2d 359 (Conn.1977); New Jersey, Robinson v. Cahill, 303 A.2d 273 (N.J.1973); Washington, Seattle School Dist. No. 1 v. State, 585 P.2d 71 (Wash.1978); West Virginia, Pauley v. Kelly, 255 S.E.2d 859 (W.Va.1979); Wyoming, Washakie County School District No. 1 v. Herschler, 606 P.2d 310 (Wyo.1980); and Arkansas, DuPree v. Alma School District, 615 S.W.2d 90 (Ark.1983), found that the traditional property tax-based school finance system violated state equal protection clauses. Only in *DuPree*, however, did a state supreme court find that the local property tax system of funding public education violated the rational basis test. For all of these courts, however, the fundamental flaw in school funding formulas was the inequality that inevitably arises when school districts must rely on the wealth of their jurisdiction's property to fund school operations.

Many state courts rejected the equal protection argument. *See, e.g.*, Shofstall v. Hollins, 515 P.2d 590 (Ariz.1973); Lujan v. Colorado State Board of Education, 649 P.2d 1005 (Colo.1982); McDaniel v. Thomas, 285 S.E.2d 156 (Ga.1981); Thompson v. Engelking, 537 P.2d 635 (Idaho 1975); Hornbeck v. Somerset County Board of Education, 458 A.2d 758 (Md.1983); Board of Educ., Levittown Union Free School Dist. v. Nyquist, 439 N.E.2d 359 (N.Y.1982); Fair School Finance Council of Oklahoma, Inc. v. State, 746 P.2d 1135 (Okla.1987); Danson v. Casey, 399 A.2d 360 (Pa.1979); Kukor v. Grover, 436 N.W.2d 568 (Wis.1989), *endorsed in* Vincent v. Voight, 614 N.W.2d 388 (Wis. 2000). These courts relied on concerns similar to those invoked by the United States Supreme Court in *Rodriguez*.

Standing alone, the equality claim may not currently have much traction, but wealth-based discrepancies in funding continue to form the basis of successful school finance challenges, as the next case illustrates.

GANNON V. STATE

Supreme Court of Kansas
319 P.3d 1196 (2014)

PER CURIAM:

This is a "school finance" case that concerns Article 6 of the Kansas Constitution as well as various Kansas educational statutes. They include K.S.A. 72–6405 *et seq.*(School District Finance and Quality Performance Act or SDFQPA) and K.S.A. 72–8801 *et seq.* (capital outlay levy).

* * * We * * * hold that the [trial court] correctly ruled that the State created unconstitutional, wealth-based disparities by prorating the supplemental general state aid payments to which certain districts were entitled under K.S.A.2012 Supp. 72–6434 for their local option budgets.

FACTS AND PROCEDURAL HISTORY

Because of the nature of this case, a short overview of funding for K–12 public education in Kansas is helpful in understanding the case's history, the arguments made by the parties to the panel, and the panel's holdings.

SDFQPA Summary

The SDFQPA establishes the formula and mechanism through which most funds for K–12 public education are obtained by Kansas school districts. The formula provides a fixed amount of funding for each student through "base state aid per pupil," also known as BSAPP. A district's full-time equivalent enrollment is adjusted by adding various weightings based on the recognition that the needs of some students require more resources for their education than others. Once a school district's enrollment is adjusted per the weightings, that figure is multiplied by the BSAPP. The resulting product is the amount of state financial aid to which the school district is entitled.

Funding for the BSAPP is derived from two sources: local effort and state financial aid. The majority of school districts' local effort consists of property tax funds, as each district is statutorily required to impose a mill levy upon taxable tangible property in its territory. Because property values vary widely throughout the state, the amount of money each district can raise by the required mill levy also varies widely. So the State provides additional funds to less wealthy districts through "general state aid."

If a district's local effort funds equal its state financial aid entitlements, it receives no additional money from the State, *i.e.*, general state aid. And if a district's local effort funds exceed its state financial aid entitlement, the excess is remitted to the State. For those districts qualifying for general state aid, their amount is what remains after subtracting their local effort funds from their state financial aid entitlement.

Although local effort and state financial aid comprise most of the funds available for K–12 education, school districts can access additional funds in several ways, two of which are at issue in this case.

First, a local school board can impose an additional mill levy on property in its district to fund a local option budget (LOB) to augment the funds that are distributed through the BSAPP. After application of a statutory formula, in order to account for differences in property wealth among the districts, the less wealthy ones may also qualify for, and receive from the state, "supplemental general state aid."

Second, a local board can also impose an additional mill levy on property in its district to fund capital outlay expenses such as purchasing certain equipment. Although not part of the SDFQPA, the capital outlay mechanism, like the LOB's, also accounts for differences in districts' property wealth. After application of a statutory formula, the less wealthy districts may also qualify for, and receive from the state, "school district capital outlay state aid."

[The court first described previous school finance litigation in Kansas, known as the *Montoy* litigation, a series of four supreme court holdings. In the first *Montoy* case, the court held that the state school funding formula violated the state constitutional requirement that school funding "make suitable provision for finance of the educational interests of the state." The second gave the legislature guidance on how to modify its funding formula to meet the constitutional standard. In the third case, the court invalidated the legislative response to its earlier holding. In the fourth *Montoy* opinion, issued in 2006, the court concluded that the legislative decision to increase school funding by a total of $755 million satisfied its constitutional obligation, and the court dismissed the litigation.]

Post Montoy

In the wake of a national economic recession, the 2009 legislature began reducing education funding. The BSAPP appropriation was reduced from the 2006 legislature's statutorily specified amount of $4,433 to $4,400 in fiscal year 2009. And although the 2009 legislature had initially established BSAPP at $4,492 for fiscal year 2010 and beyond, the appropriation for fiscal year 2010 was reduced to $4,012. Additionally, the legislature began to withhold qualifying districts' funding entitlements to capital outlay aid and began to prorate, *i.e.,* reduce, the qualifying districts' funding entitlements to supplemental general state aid. * * *

Legislative reductions in K–12 education funding continued. By fiscal year 2012, the legislature essentially had reduced BSAPP to $3,780, while cuts to BSAPP in fiscal years 2009 to 2012 totaled more than $511 million. And the legislature continued to withhold capital outlay aid and to prorate supplemental general state aid to otherwise-entitled districts. * * *

The plaintiffs [four school districts] raised eight counts, alleging a variety of constitutional and statutory violations related to school finance. Specifically, they alleged that the State violated the requirements of Article 6, Section 6(b) by failing to provide a suitable education to all Kansas students, consider the actual costs of education, and distribute education funds equitably. In support, the plaintiffs alleged that the State had (1) decreased overall education funding; (2) decreased the BSAPP; (3) required the use of LOB funds to pay for basic educational expenses; (4) prorated supplemental general state aid; (5) withheld capital outlay state aid; and (6) underfunded special education.

The plaintiffs also alleged in a separate count that the State's failure to distribute capital outlay aid payments beginning in fiscal year 2010 created an inequitable, unconstitutional distribution of funds.

* * * As for the merits, the State argued that it had complied with its constitutional duty to make suitable provision for finance of the educational interests of the state. It contended that Kansas schools are receiving funds at record levels when all sources of state, local, and federal funds are taken into account. It also highlighted the districts' holding of millions of dollars in unspent, available cash reserves. The State further argued no scientific evidence proved that additional funding for education would appreciably improve student performance or the quality of education provided. It also contended that students are generally performing well on assessments and that most schools have been able to meet accreditation requirements. Finally, it denied that education is a fundamental right under the Kansas Constitution.

* * * The panel generally held that the State had violated Article 6, Section 6(b) by failing to provide suitable funding for education. More specifically, for plaintiffs' capital outlay claims the panel held that via K.S.A.2012 Supp. 72–8814(c) the legislature's elimination of capital outlay state aid payments beginning in fiscal year 2010 created unconstitutional, wealth-based disparities among districts. And because the State failed to provide any such aid to districts with lower property wealth, the panel further held that K.S.A. 72–8801 *et seq.*—the act authorizing all districts to assess capital outlay mill levies—was unconstitutional and therefore inoperable. * * *

ANALYSIS

* * * We have recognized that Article 6 contains at least two components: equity and adequacy. *See Montoy II,* 278 Kan. at 775, 120 P.3d 306. For example, there we held that "[t]he equity with which the funds are distributed" is a critical factor "for the legislature to consider in achieving a suitable formula for financing education." 278 Kan. at 775, 120 P.3d 306. We also emphasized that "[i]ncreased funding may not in and of itself make the [education] financing formula constitutionally suitable." 278 Kan. at 775, 120 P.3d 306; see also *U.S.D. No. 229 v. State,* 256 Kan. 232, 256–57, 885 P.2d 1170 (1994) (quoting with approval the district court) ("'The standard most comparable to the Kansas constitutional requirement of "suitable" funding is a requirement of adequacy found in several state constitutions.'"). Here, the plaintiffs make both adequacy and equity-based challenges.

[Under the adequacy theory, the court found that the trial court had applied the improper legal standard, and remanded for the court to decide whether the school funding system is "reasonably calculated to have all public school students meet or exceed standards set by the Board of Education."]

EQUITY

The equity test

This court has frequently spoken of the equity requirement in Kansas education litigation. *See, e.g., Montoy v. State,* 279 Kan. 817, 840, 112 P.3d 923 (2005) (*Montoy III*) ("extraordinary declining enrollment provisions cannot be allowed to exacerbate inequities"); *Montoy II,* 278 Kan. at 775, 120 P.3d 306 ("equity with which the funds are distributed . . . [is] critical factor [ ]for legislature to consider in achieving a suitable formula for financing education"); *U.S.D. No. 229,* 256 Kan. at 258, 885 P.2d 1170 (" 'inequitable distribution of finances' "); *cf. Provance v. Shawnee Mission U.S.D. No. 512,* 231 Kan. 636, 643, 648 P.2d 710 (1982) ("The ultimate State purpose in offering a system of public schools is to provide an environment where quality education can be afforded equally to all.").

And as this court held more than 40 years ago when discussing the purposes of the Unified School District Act of 1963:

"Some school districts increased rapidly in taxable wealth while others remained relatively static. It appeared desirable therefore to make changes in our educational system to secure equal educational opportunities for the children in different districts. *Changes seemed necessary to equalize the tax burdens brought on by population shifts.*" (Emphasis added.) *Hand v. Board of Education,* 198 Kan. 460, 464, 426 P.2d 124 (1967). * * *

While this court has often spoken of the requirement of equity in this area, it has not clearly defined the term. Perhaps our clearest guidance came in *Montoy IV,* where we held equity was not necessarily the equivalent of equality: "Equity does not require the legislature to provide equal funding for each student or school district. In *Montoy II,* we rejected the plaintiffs' claim that the school finance act violated the Equal Protection Clause of the United States and Kansas Constitutions." *Montoy v. State,* 282 Kan. 9, 22, 138 P.3d 755 (2006) (*Montoy IV*); *cf. U.S.D. No. 229,* 256 Kan. at 259–68, 885 P.2d 1170 (rejecting Blue Valley plaintiffs' claim that the SDFQPA violated the right of equal protection contained in Section 1 of the Kansas Constitution Bill of Rights).

And in the *Montoy* litigation, we spoke repeatedly of increasing and exacerbating inequities. For example, in *Montoy III,* when discussing the local option budget (LOB) we held:

"We also agree with the plaintiffs and the Board that, in fact, *the legislation's increase in the LOB cap exacerbates the wealth-based disparities between districts.* Districts with high assessed property values can reach the maximum LOB revenues of the 'district prescribed percentage of the amount of state financial aid determined for the district in the school year' (K.S.A. 72–6433[a][1], amended by S.B. 43, sec. 17) with far less tax effort than those districts with lower assessed property values and lower median family incomes. Thus, the wealthier districts will be able to generate more funds for elements of a constitutionally adequate education that the State has failed to fund." (Emphasis added.) *Montoy III,* 279 Kan. at 834, 112 P.3d 923.

Accordingly, we concluded that "the inequity-producing local property tax measures mean that the school financing formula . . . still falls short of the standard set by Article 6, § 6 of the Kansas Constitution." 279 Kan. at 840, 112 P.3d 923. * * *

Our test for equity in K–12 public education finance is clarified and succinctly stated as follows: School districts must have reasonably equal access to substantially similar educational opportunity through similar tax effort. Simply put, equity need not meet precise equality standards. As the Vermont Supreme Court has held, "[m]oney is clearly not the only variable affecting educational opportunity, but it is one that government can effectively equalize." *Brigham v. State,* 166 Vt. 246, 256, 692 A.2d 384 (1997).

With this test established, we now turn to the major equity holdings of the panel in its 250-page memorandum opinion and entry of judgment.

*The panel correctly held the State created unconstitutional, wealth-based disparities by eliminating all capital outlay state aid payments to which certain school districts were otherwise entitled under K.S.A.2012 Supp. 72–8814(c). * * *

Discussion

As noted, boards of education may adopt a resolution to impose additional mill levies on taxable tangible property in their school districts to exclusively pay for capital improvements such as construction and maintenance of new buildings, as well as for purchase of certain equipment and authorized investments. K.S.A.2013 Supp. 72–8801; K.S.A. 72–8804. According to the Kansas Department of Education, purchases could include items as varied as science and laboratory equipment, computers, and buses. The resolution is subject to protest petition, and the levy is currently capped at 8 mills. K.S.A.2013 Supp. 72–8801(a), (b).

In addition to direct revenues from their capital outlay mill levies, the levying districts with lower property wealth qualify for extra monies from the "school district capital outlay state aid fund." *See* K.S.A.2013 Supp. 72–8814. Each fiscal year, a district that levies taxes for capital outlay may be entitled to aid equal to the amount levied by the district multiplied by that district's state aid percentage factor. A district's state aid percentage factor is calculated by first determining the median assessed valuation per pupil (AVPP) of all school districts rounded to the nearest $1,000. For every $1,000 a district's AVPP is above the median AVPP, its state aid percentage factor is decreased by 1%. For every $1,000 a district's AVPP is below the median AVPP, its state aid percentage factor is increased by 1%. The state aid computation percentage is 25%. K.S.A.2013 Supp. 72–8814(b)(4). So, a hypothetical district in which the AVPP is $10,000 below the median AVPP would have a state aid percentage factor of 35%, which would entitle it to capital outlay payments in an amount equal to its capital outlay levy revenues multiplied by 35%. A district's state aid percentage factor may not exceed 100%. *See* K.S.A.2013 Supp. 72–8814(b).

The legislature authorized capital outlay state aid payments during the 2006, 2007, and 2008 legislative sessions for fiscal years 2007, 2008, and 2009, respectively. But during the 2009 legislative session it did not authorize those payments for fiscal year 2010 and has failed to do so since.

* * * Using plaintiff U.S.D. No. 259 as an example, the panel found that the Wichita district would have been entitled to approximately $4.3 million in capital outlay state aid payments during fiscal year 2012. It further found there was no evidence indicating that the district no longer needed those funds, *i.e.,* there was no factual basis for eliminating the payments.

The panel determined that the funds normally used for districts' capital outlay expenditures would instead probably have had to come from other funds, *e.g.,* LOB funds or BSAPP-generated funds that logically would have to be diverted from their own particular intended uses. The panel therefore concluded that the lack of capital outlay state aid funding distorted and exacerbated wealth-based disparities, *i.e.,* inequities among districts.

* * * The State specifically argues that there is no evidence—and the panel made no finding—that less than full funding of capital outlay state aid has created unequal educational opportunities. The plaintiffs respond with purported examples in the record.

We address these arguments by first observing what is unquestioned: The legislature itself has acknowledged inequity in its school financing structure. More specifically, the legislature originally enacted K.S.A.2005 Supp. 72–8814 in an attempt to address the differences in property wealth among school districts and their resultant ability to raise revenue. While per K.S.A.2013 Supp. 72–8801 each board of education may assess a capital outlay tax levy of 8 mills upon taxable tangible property in its district, disparity results because property values subject to those levies vary among districts. As an example of such disparity, the panel observed the extreme differences between the school districts in Galena, U.S.D. No. 499, and Burlington, U.S.D. No. 244. Both are similar in size—about 800 students—but at opposite ends of the spectrum for assessed property value. The panel found that one mill raises approximately $18,000 to $19,000 in Galena and approximately $350,000 to $400,000 in Burlington.

Not surprisingly, the "school district capital outlay state aid" described and computed in K.S.A.2013 Supp. 72–8814 is commonly known in Kansas education circles—and repeatedly referred to by the parties and the panel—as capital outlay *equalization* payments. If there was no equalization to be performed, *i.e.,* no inequality or inequity to be solved, the legislature's passage of K.S.A.2005 Supp. 72–8814 would have been meaningless—a result we assume the legislature did not intend. *See Hawley v. Kansas Dept. of Agriculture,* 281 Kan. 603, 631, 132 P.3d 870 (2006).

According to a Kansas Department of Education spreadsheet in the record, qualifying districts had received equalization payments in fiscal year 2009 of approximately $22 million. Then beginning in fiscal year 2010 the legislature decided to eliminate its solution to this inequality by stopping all equalization payments. While the payments stopped, the panel found the needs they had been designed to address had not: "We have no evidence that the needs intended by these character of payments [capital outlay state aid] abated suddenly in [fiscal year] 2010 and thereafter. Common sense says they would be ongoing."

Addressing the State's specific argument, we conclude the panel drew a reasonable inference of ongoing need from these facts in evidence: Millions of dollars of equalization payments historically made to address need abruptly stopped for all qualifying districts. * * * Once payments have stopped, it logically follows that the inequity the equalization aid was originally designed to cure remains present—when, as here, there is no evidence of record demonstrating that the inequity or inequality disappeared on its own. And the State points us to nothing in the record to demonstrate the problem was cured by other means.

Second, impliedly contained in the panel's finding of past, and ongoing, capital outlay aid need, and its repeated identification of the past and future problem-solving payments as "equalization payments," is a finding of past, and ongoing, unequal educational opportunity. * * * This is borne out by the panel's acknowledgment of the vast disparities in assessed property values between the similarly sized Galena and Burlington school districts—and of the loss of $4.3 million to plaintiff Wichita school district in fiscal year 2012 alone for possible purchase of computers and other equipment.

In short, we find the panel findings are supported by substantial competent evidence. *See Unruh,* 289 Kan. at 1195, 221 P.3d 1130 (in determining whether substantial competent evidence supports the district court findings, appellate court disregards any conflicting evidence or other inferences that might be drawn from the evidence).

In addressing equity, the panel had strongly denounced wealth-based disparities in education funding, remarking that "[t]hroughout the litigation history concerning school finance in Kansas, wealth based disparities have been seen as an anathema, one to be condemned and disapproved. . . ." Its language choice suggested a "zero tolerance" for any wealth-based disparity, *i.e.,* perhaps requiring the same or higher standard under equal protection law that we rejected in prior school finance decisions. *See Montoy IV,* 282 Kan. at 22, 138 P.3d 755 ("In *Montoy II,* we rejected the plaintiffs' claim that the school finance act violated the Equal Protection Clause of the United States and Kansas Constitutions.").

But wealth-based disparities should not be measured against such mathematically precise standards. *Cf. Montoy IV,* 282 Kan. at 22, 138 P.3d 755 ("Equity does not require the legislature to provide equal funding for each student or school district."). To violate Article 6, the disparities instead must be unreasonable when measured by our test: School districts must have reasonably equal access to substantially similar educational opportunity through similar tax effort.

Nevertheless, we readily conclude the inequity resulting from the withholding of all the capital outlay equalization funding fails our test, *i.e.,* nonpayment creates—or perhaps returns the qualifying districts to—an unreasonable, wealth-based inequity. We would reach the same conclusion applying the principles of equity underlying our decision in *Montoy II. See, e.g., Montoy III,* 279 Kan. at 838, 112 P.3d 923 (Because the capital outlay provision "is based on local property tax authority, the amount of revenue a district can raise is tied to property value and median family income; thus the failure to provide any equalization to those districts unable to access this funding perpetuates the inequities produced by this component.").

Simply put, we agree with the panel's conclusion. . . .

We agree that the infirmity can be cured in a variety of ways—at the choice of the legislature. And the legislature should have an opportunity to promptly cure. Any cure will be measured by determining whether it sufficiently reduces the unreasonable, wealth-based disparity so the disparity then becomes constitutionally acceptable, not whether the cure necessarily restores funding to the prior levels.

[The court similarly concluded that state withdrawal of funding to supplement the LOB generated by extra tax levies in low wealth districts similarly created unconstitutional inequality.]

NOTES AND QUESTIONS

1. *Legislative Responses in Times of Fiscal Stress.* The *Gannon* court emphasized that the legislature had a number of options, and a fair amount of discretion, in shaping its response. Though that may be true, the swift legislative response, HB 2506, perhaps predictably, appropriated $134 million and restored the funding to the previous levels. Can you suggest other responses that would have met the court's standard? Although the court noted several times that its standard of "equity" was different from, and did not require, "equality," how could the legislature have removed the inequity without adopting equalizing spending reforms?

2. *Natural Consequence of Decentralization or Purposeful Governmental Action?* For many courts the question framing school finance reform litigation is whether interlocal inequalities are simply a natural consequence of the decentralization of public education to the local level or are, instead, attributable to actions of the state. In rejecting an equal protection challenge, the court in McInnis v. Shapiro, 293 F.Supp. 327 (N.D.Ill.1968), *aff'd*, 394 U.S. 322 (1969) assumed that interdistrict wealth inequalities are simply an "inevitable consequence of decentralization." *Id.* at 333. The California Supreme Court painted quite a different picture when it stressed "the extent to which governmental action is the cause of wealth classifications.... Governmental action drew the school district boundary lines, thus determining how much local wealth each district would contain...." Serrano v. Priest, 487 P.2d 1241, 1254 (Cal.1971). Consider these perspectives in light of the discussion of boundaries in Chapter III. Consider also the debate within the Supreme Court over the propriety of interdistrict busing in dealing with school segregation in Milliken v. Bradley, 418 U.S. 717 (1974), discussed in Chapter II.

3. *Local Control, Real or Imagined—And for Whom?* The main argument advanced by defenders of the local tax-based system of financing schools is that it promotes local control which, in turn, protects parents' rights, promotes choice and diversity in education, increases accountability, and facilitates public participation in education decision-making. *See* Richard Briffault, The Role of Local Control in School Finance Reform, 24 Conn. L. Rev. 773 (1992). This view was advanced in the following frequently cited passage from the Supreme Court's *Rodriguez* opinion:

> The persistence of attachment to government at the lowest level where education is concerned reflects the depth of commitment of its supporters. In part, local control means . . . the freedom to devote more money to the education of one's children. Equally important, however, is the opportunity it offers for participation in the decisionmaking process that determines how those local tax

dollars will be spent. Each locality is free to tailor local programs to local needs. Pluralism also affords some opportunity for experimentation, innovation, and a healthy competition for educational excellence. An analogy to the Nation-State relationship in our federal system seems uniquely appropriate. Mr. Justice Brandeis identified as one of the peculiar strengths of our form of government each State's freedom to 'serve as a laboratory; and try novel social and economic experiments.' No area of social concern stands to profit more from a multiplicity of viewpoints and from a diversity of approaches than does public education.

San Antonio Independent School District v. Rodriguez, 411 U.S. 1, 49–50 (1973).

Critiques of this rationale have tended to rely on three arguments. First, some have argued that due to extensive state and federal regulation of education, true local control is illusory. Between 1982 and 1986, for instance, eleven states passed extensive school reform packages, and 45 states imposed new requirements for high school graduation. By 1989, 45 states had established teacher competency exams, and many states now have legislation on the books that authorize the state to seize control of failing school districts. In addition, the federal role in education imposes significant limitations on local control. Large sums of money frequently come with conditions attached for the recipient school districts. Prior to 2001, federal involvement focused primarily on special education, but that changed dramatically with passage of the No Child Left Behind Act, 20 U.S.C. §§ 6301–6578, which conditions federal funds on schools' ability to demonstrate "adequate yearly progress" in improving student achievement.

The second argument is that local control has meaning only for those districts able to generate sufficient property tax revenue; for the poor districts with low levels of assessed property valuation within their borders, local control is an empty term. Without funds, a local government's exercise of formal legal power over schools does not translate into real power and control. Finally, the third line of argument asserts that it may be possible to have local policy control even though funding is provided by the states. For a critique of the local control argument, see Laurie Reynolds, Uniformity of Taxation and the Preservation of Local Control in School Finance Reform, 40 U.C. Davis L. Rev. 1835, 1886–88 (2007).

4. *Equalization Reform in School Finance.* Although a number of courts invalidated school finance systems under state equal protection clauses, state courts have not adopted a single clear definition of what equal protection requires. One possibility is that equal protection requires that children in every school district throughout the state benefit from exactly the same level of funding. Such perfect equality is, however, difficult to achieve. If the state system relies on local property taxation, with state aid utilized to raise up the poorer districts to the same level of spending enjoyed by the affluent districts then, given the local tax base disparities within a state, the

state legislature may have to appropriate an enormous amount of money in equalizing school aid—or engage in the politically difficult action of forcing more affluent districts to limit their spending. Although a few states, such as Colorado, Washington, and Texas, have imposed caps on school districts' ability to raise revenues, those caps have not accomplished much equalization. *See* Laurie Reynolds, Skybox Schools: Public Education as Private Luxury, 82 Wash.U.L.Q. 755, 779–797 (2004).

A second approach is to find that equality is satisfied when all schools receive a guaranteed minimum amount deemed adequate to meet basic educational needs while leaving local districts free to supplement above and beyond that minimum. *See, e.g.,* Tennessee Small School Systems v. McWherter, 894 S.W.2d 734 (Tenn.1995); Helena Elementary School District v. State, 769 P.2d 684 (Mont.1989); Seattle Sch. Dist. No. 1 of King County, Washington v. State, 585 P.2d 71 (Wash. 1978). Determining the difference between necessities and luxuries, in order to set the basic floor to which all districts are entitled, however, has proven difficult.

A third type of equalization, known as district power equalization, guarantees that identical local property tax rates will generate equal per capita revenues, regardless of the differences in local wealth. The state guarantees that a poor district that undertakes a certain level of local effort will receive the same revenues as an affluent district that makes the same effort. *See* Gail F. Levine, Note, Meeting the Third Wave: Legislative Approaches to Recent Judicial School Finance Rulings, 28 Harv.J. on Legis. 507 (1991). District power equalization respects local autonomy in that it lets each locality continue to decide its local commitment to education. But it can be criticized for making the level of local spending depend on the wishes of the district's taxpayers, rather than focusing on the amount of money needed to properly educate its children.

5. *Do Equalization Orders Produce Equality?* After decades of school funding litigation, substantial inequality remains. Several studies published by the U.S. General Accounting Office—now the Government Accountability Office—conclude that, on average, wealthy districts continue to spend more per student than poor districts; that federal funds, rather than state funds, account for most of the equalization; and that equalization would require enormous state funding increases along with stringent limits on local taxing discretion. One study showed how, notwithstanding state funding increases in response to judicial equalization orders, local district increases in tax efforts preserved the pre-equalization gaps. *See* U.S. G.A.O., School Finance. State Efforts to Equalize Funding Between Wealthy and Poor School Districts (1998); U.S. G.A.O., School Finance. State Efforts to Reduce Funding Gaps Between Poor and Wealthy Districts (1997); U.S. G.A.O., School Finance. Three States' Experiences With Equity in School Funding (1995). Other studies have been slightly more positive. One found that over twenty years states that responded to court orders declaring their funding schemes unconstitutional and requiring them to adopt reforms had larger increases in state spending and greater equality than other states. *See*

William N. Evans, Sheila Murray, and Robert Schwab, Schoolhouses, Courthouses, and Statehouses after Serrano, 16 J. Pol'y Analysis and Management 10 (1997). Another concluded that though overall intrastate funding equality improved slightly, the relative rankings for most states changed little. *See* Michele Moser and Ross Rubenstein, The Equality of Public School District Funding in the United States: A National Status Report, 62 Pub. Admin. Rev. 63 (2002). A study by The Tax Foundation concluded that states subject to judicial mandates spent less per pupil than revenue growth trends before the court mandate would have predicted. *See* Chris Atkins, *Appropriation by Litigation: Estimating the Cost of Judicial Mandates for State and Local Education Spending* (Tax Foundation 2007). Does the disputed efficacy of judicial mandates, when coupled with the apparent lack of equalization typically achieved, influence your assessment of the use of equal protection challenges in school funding cases? Does it have a bearing on the argument over whether judicial or legislative intervention is preferable?

Jeffrey Metzler, *Inequitable Equilibrium: School Finance in the United States*, 36 Ind. L. Rev. 561 (2003), found that equality of educational opportunity was completely unrelated to the formulas adopted by a state's school funding statutes. That is, none of the approaches described above was better or worse at achieving equalization. [A]lthough legislative response to judicial invalidation might temporarily achieve greater equalization, Metzler found a predictable push back towards the "inequitable equilibrium" that existed prior to the litigation: "In many states, the distribution of education resources is primarily a function of the distribution of political power in the state. This distribution is the 'equilibrium point,' and in many states it is an inequitable equilibrium insofar as it permits wealthy districts, even at lower tax rates, to spend more per student than poor districts." *Id.* at 564.

6. *Beyond Equality.* The Connecticut Supreme Court, in its 1977 decision in Horton v. Meskill, 376 A.2d 359 (Conn.1977), ordered substantial equalization of school funding. Nearly twenty years later, in another protracted series of cases, plaintiffs relied on Connecticut's unusual constitutional provision guaranteeing protection from segregation to challenge the way in which school district boundaries had been drawn in the Hartford area. The parties on both sides stipulated that school funding met the *Horton* court's equalization directive: in fact, the average Hartford per pupil expenditure was $8126, while the average in the surrounding suburbs was $7331. Nevertheless Hartford student achievement levels continued to lag behind their suburban counterparts. *See* Sheff v. O'Neill, 678 A.2d 1267 (Conn.1996). Similarly, the New Jersey court's decision in Abbott v. Burke, 643 A.2d 575, 579 (N.J.1994), found that equalization in per pupil spending would not satisfy the state's constitutional obligation because many at-risk children in poor districts may actually require more resources than other children.

EDGEWOOD INDEPENDENT SCHOOL DISTRICT
V. KIRBY

Supreme Court of Texas
777 S.W.2d 391 (1989)

MAUZY, JUSTICE.

* * *

The basic facts of this cause are not in dispute. The only question is whether those facts describe a public school financing system that meets the requirements of the Constitution. As summarized and excerpted, the facts are as follows.

There are approximately three million public school children in Texas. The legislature finances the education of these children through a combination of revenues supplied by the state itself and revenues supplied by local school districts which are governmental subdivisions of the state. Of total education costs, the state provides about forty-two percent, school districts provide about fifty percent, and the remainder comes from various other sources including federal funds. School districts derive revenues from local ad valorem property taxes, and the state raises funds from a variety of sources including the sales tax and various severance and excise taxes.

There are glaring disparities in the abilities of the various school districts to raise revenues from property taxes because taxable property wealth varies greatly from district to district. The wealthiest district has over $14,000,000 of property wealth per student, while the poorest has approximately $20,000; this disparity reflects a 700 to 1 ratio. The 300,000 students in the lowest-wealth schools have less than 3% of the state's property wealth to support their education while the 300,000 students in the highest-wealth schools have over 25% of the state's property wealth; thus the 300,000 students in the wealthiest districts have more than eight times the property value to support their education as the 300,000 students in the poorest districts. The average property wealth in the 100 wealthiest districts is more than twenty times greater than the average property wealth in the 100 poorest districts. Edgewood I.S.D. has $38,854 in property wealth per student; Alamo Heights I.S.D., in the same county, has $570,109 in property wealth per student. * * *

Property-poor districts are trapped in a cycle of poverty from which there is no opportunity to free themselves. Because of their inadequate tax base, they must tax at significantly higher rates in order to meet minimum requirements for accreditation; yet their educational programs are typically inferior. The location of new industry and development is strongly influenced by tax rates and the quality of local schools. Thus, the property-poor districts with their high tax rates and inferior schools are unable to attract new industry or development and so have little opportunity to improve their tax base.

The amount of money spent on a student's education has a real and meaningful impact on the educational opportunity offered that student. High-wealth districts are able to provide for their students broader educational experiences including more extensive curricula, more up-to-date technological equipment, better libraries and library personnel, teacher aides, counseling services, lower student-teacher ratios, better facilities, parental involvement programs, and drop-out prevention programs. They are also better able to attract and retain experienced teachers and administrators. * * *

Based on these facts, the trial court concluded that the school financing system violates the Texas Constitution's equal rights guarantee of article I, section 3, the due course of law guarantee of article I, section 19, and the "efficiency" mandate of article VII, section 1. The court of appeals reversed. We reverse the judgment of the court of appeals and, with modification, affirm the judgment of the trial court.

Article VII, section 1 of the Texas Constitution provides:

A general diffusion of knowledge being essential to the preservation of the liberties and rights of the people, it shall be the duty of the Legislature of the State to establish and make suitable provision for the support and maintenance of an efficient system of public free schools.

* * *

The State argues that, as used in article VII, section 1, the word "efficient" was intended to suggest a simple and inexpensive system. Under the Reconstruction Constitution of 1869, the people had been subjected to a militaristic school system with the state exercising absolute authority over the training of children. *See* Tex. Const. art. VII, § 1, interp. commentary (Vernon 1955). Thus, the State contends that delegates to the 1875 Constitutional Convention deliberately inserted into this provision the word "efficient" in order to prevent the establishment of another Reconstruction-style, highly centralized school system.

While there is some evidence that many delegates wanted an economical school system, there is no persuasive evidence that the delegates used the term "efficient" to achieve that end. *See* Journal of the Constitutional Convention of the State of Texas 136 (Oct. 8, 1875); S. McKay, Debates in the Texas Constitutional Convention of 1875 107, 217, 350–351 (1930). It must be recognized that the Constitution requires an "efficient," not an "economical," "inexpensive," or "cheap" system. The language of the Constitution must be presumed to have been carefully selected. * * * The framers used the term "economical" elsewhere and could have done so here had they so intended.

There is no reason to think that "efficient" meant anything different in 1875 from what it now means. "Efficient" conveys the meaning of effective or productive of results and connotes the use of resources so as to produce results with little waste; this meaning does not appear to have changed over time. * * *

Considering "the general spirit of the times and the prevailing sentiments of the people," it is apparent from the historical record that those who drafted and ratified article VII, section 1 never contemplated the possibility that such gross inequalities could exist within an "efficient" system. *See Mumme v. Marrs*, 120 Tex. 383, 40 S.W.2d 31, 35 (1931). At the Constitutional Convention of 1875, delegates spoke at length on the importance of education for all the people of this state, rich and poor alike. * * * Other delegates recognized the importance of a diffusion of knowledge among the masses not only for the preservation of democracy, but for the prevention of crime and for the growth of the economy.

In addition to specific comments in the constitutional debates, the structure of school finance at the time indicates that such gross disparities were not contemplated. Apart from cities, there was no district structure for schools nor any authority to tax locally for school purposes under the Constitution of 1876. B. Walker and W. Kirby, The Basics of Texas Public School Finance 5, 86 (1986). The 1876 Constitution provided a structure whereby the burdens of school taxation fell equally and uniformly across the state, and each student in the state was entitled to exactly the same distribution of funds. *See* Tex. Const. art. VII, § 5 (1876). The state's school fund was initially apportioned strictly on a per capita basis. B. Walker and W. Kirby at 21. Also, a poll tax of one dollar per voter was levied across the state for school purposes. *Id.* These per capita methods of taxation and of revenue distribution seem simplistic compared to today's system; however they do indicate that the people were contemplating that the tax burden would be shared uniformly and that the state's resources would be distributed on an even, equitable basis.

If our state's population had grown at the same rate in each district and if the taxable wealth in each district had also grown at the same rate, efficiency could probably have been maintained within the structure of the present system. That did not happen. Wealth, in its many forms, has not appeared with geographic symmetry. The economic development of the state has not been uniform. Some cities have grown dramatically, while their sister communities have remained static or have shrunk. Formulas that once fit have been knocked askew. Although local conditions vary, the constitutionally imposed state responsibility for an efficient education system is the same for all citizens regardless of where they live.

We conclude that, in mandating "efficiency," the constitutional framers and ratifiers did not intend a system with such vast disparities as now exist. Instead, they stated clearly that the purpose of an efficient system was to provide for a "general diffusion of knowledge." The present system, by contrast, provides not for a diffusion that is general, but for one that is limited and unbalanced. The resultant inequalities are thus directly contrary to the constitutional vision of efficiency. * * *

By statutory directives, the legislature has attempted through the years to reduce disparities and improve the system. There have been good faith efforts on the part of many public officials, and some progress has been made. However, as the undisputed facts of this case make painfully clear, the reality is that the constitutional mandate has not been met.

The legislature's recent efforts have focused primarily on increasing the state's contributions. More money allocated under the present system would reduce some of the existing disparities between districts but would at best only postpone the reform that is necessary to make the system efficient. A band-aid will not suffice; the system itself must be changed.

We hold that the state's school financing system is neither financially efficient nor efficient in the sense of providing for a "general diffusion of knowledge" statewide, and therefore that it violates article VII, section 1 of the Texas Constitution. Efficiency does not require a per capita distribution, but it also does not allow concentrations of resources in property-rich school districts that are taxing low when property-poor districts that are taxing high cannot generate sufficient revenues to meet even minimum standards. There must be a direct and close correlation between a district's tax effort and the educational resources available to it; in other words, districts must have substantially equal access to similar revenues per pupil at similar levels of tax effort. Children who live in poor districts and children who live in rich districts must be afforded a substantially equal opportunity to have access to educational funds. Certainly, this much is required if the state is to educate its populace efficiently and provide for a general diffusion of knowledge statewide.

Under article VII, section 1, the obligation is the legislature's to provide for an efficient system. In setting appropriations, the legislature must establish priorities according to constitutional mandate; equalizing educational opportunity cannot be relegated to an "if funds are left over" basis. We recognize that there are and always will be strong public interests competing for available state funds. However, the legislature's responsibility to support public education is different because it is constitutionally imposed. Whether the legislature acts directly or enlists local government to help meet its obligation, the end product must still be what the constitution commands—*i.e.* an efficient system of public free schools throughout the state. *See Lee v. Leonard Indep. School Dist.*, 24 S.W.2d 449, 450 (Tex.Civ.App.—Texarkana 1930, writ ref'd). This does not mean that the state may not recognize differences in area costs or in costs associated with providing an equalized educational opportunity to atypical students or disadvantaged students. Nor does it mean that local communities would be precluded from supplementing an efficient system established by the legislature; however any local enrichment must derive solely from local tax effort. * * *

Although we have ruled the school financing system to be unconstitutional, we do not now instruct the legislature as to the specifics of the legislation it should enact; nor do we order it to raise taxes. The legislature has primary responsibility to decide how best to achieve an efficient system. We decide only the nature of the constitutional mandate and whether that mandate has been met. Because we hold that the mandate of efficiency has not been met, we reverse the judgment of the court of appeals. The legislature is duty-bound to provide for an efficient system of education, and only if the legislature fulfills that duty can we launch this great state into a strong economic future with educational opportunity for all.

Because of the enormity of the task now facing the legislature and because we want to avoid any sudden disruption in the educational processes, we modify the trial court's judgment so as to stay the effect of its injunction until May 1, 1990. However, let there be no misunderstanding. A remedy is long overdue. The legislature must take immediate action. We reverse the judgment of the court of appeals and affirm the trial court's judgment as modified.

ROSE v. COUNCIL FOR BETTER EDUCATION

Supreme Court of Kentucky
790 S.W.2d 186 (1989)

STEPHENS, CHIEF JUSTICE.

The issue we decide on this appeal is whether the Kentucky General Assembly has complied with its constitutional mandate to "provide an efficient system of common schools throughout the state."

In deciding that it has not, we intend no criticism of the substantial efforts made by the present General Assembly and by its predecessors, nor do we intend to substitute our judicial authority for the authority and discretion of the General Assembly. We are, rather, exercising our constitutional duty in declaring that, when we consider the evidence in the record, and when we apply the constitutional requirement of Section 183 to that evidence, it is crystal clear that the General Assembly has fallen short of its duty to enact legislation to provide for an efficient system of common schools throughout the state. In a word, the present system of common schools in Kentucky is not an "efficient" one in our view of the clear mandate of Section 183. The common school system in Kentucky is constitutionally deficient.

* * *

DEFINITION OF "EFFICIENT"

We now hone in on the heart of this litigation. In defining "efficient," we use all the tools that are made available to us. In spite of any protestations to the contrary, we do not engage in judicial legislating. We do not make policy. We do not substitute our judgment for that of the General Assembly. We simply take the plain directive of the Constitution, and, armed with its purpose, we decide what our General Assembly must achieve in complying with its solemn constitutional duty. * * *

The sole responsibility for providing the system of common schools is that of our General Assembly. It is a duty—it is a constitutional mandate placed by the people on the 138 members of that body who represent those selfsame people.

The General Assembly must not only establish the system, but it must monitor it on a continuing basis so that it will always be maintained in a constitutional manner. The General Assembly must carefully supervise it, so that there is no waste, no duplication, no mismanagement, at any level.

* * *

A child's right to an adequate education is a fundamental one under our Constitution. The General Assembly must protect and advance that right. We concur with the trial court that an efficient system of education must have as its goal to provide each and every child with at least the seven following capacities: (i) sufficient oral and written communication skills to enable students to function in a complex and rapidly changing civilization; (ii) sufficient knowledge of economic, social, and political systems to enable the student to make informed choices; (iii) sufficient understanding of governmental processes to enable the student to understand the issues that affect his or her community, state, and nation; (iv) sufficient self-knowledge and knowledge of his or her mental and physical wellness; (v) sufficient grounding in the arts to enable each student to appreciate his or her cultural and historical heritage; (vi) sufficient training or preparation for advanced training in either academic or vocational fields so as to enable each child to choose and pursue life work intelligently; and (vii) sufficient levels of academic or vocational skills to enable public school students to compete favorably with their counterparts in surrounding states, in academics or in the job market.

* * *

Lest there be any doubt, the result of our decision is that Kentucky's entire system of common schools is unconstitutional. There is no allegation that only part of the common school system is invalid, and we find no such circumstance. This decision applies to the entire sweep of the system—all its parts and parcels. This decision applies to the statutes creating, implementing and financing the system and to all regulations, etc., pertaining thereto. This decision covers the creation of local school districts, school boards, and the Kentucky Department of Education to the Minimum Foundation Program and Power Equalization Program. It covers school construction and maintenance, teacher certification—the whole gamut of the common school system in Kentucky.

While individual statutes are not herein addressed specifically or considered and declared to be facially unconstitutional, the statutory system as a whole and the interrelationship of the parts therein are hereby declared to be in violation of Section 183 of the Kentucky Constitution. Just as the bricks and mortar used in the construction of a schoolhouse, while contributing to the building's facade, do not ensure the overall structural adequacy of the schoolhouse, particular statutes drafted by the legislature in crafting and designing the current school system are not unconstitutional in and of themselves. Like the crumbling schoolhouse which must be redesigned and revitalized for more efficient use, with some component parts found to be adequate, some found to be less than adequate, statutes relating to education may be reenacted as components of a constitutional system if they combine with other component statutes to form an efficient and thereby constitutional system. * * *

NOTES AND QUESTIONS

1. *From Equality to Adequacy. Edgewood* and *Rose* reflected a dramatic turn in the legal doctrinal basis of school finance litigation, with litigants and courts shifting their primary focus from state equal protection clauses to state constitutional requirements concerning public education. Instead of arguing that existing systems were unconstitutional because of interdistrict inequalities, plaintiffs argued, and many courts agreed, that the states were failing even in their obligations to provide adequate education in many poorer school districts. Due to the conceptual difficulties in defining equality and the political resistance to legal requirements that would require either "leveling up" the poorest districts to the resources of the richest ones, or "leveling down" the spending of the richer districts, many plaintiffs and courts found that adequacy constituted a more feasible goal for enhancing the resources available to poorer districts. *See* Peter Enrich, Leaving Equality

Behind: New Directions in School Finance Reform, 48 Vand.L.Rev. 101, 143–59 (1995). Indeed, with the state in *Edgewood* arguing that equalizing Texas school funding at the level of the wealthiest school districts would cost more than four times the total annual state budget, *see* Gail F. Levine, Note, Meeting the Third Wave: Legislative Approaches to Recent Judicial School Finance Rulings, 28 Harv.J.Legis. 507, 511 (1991), equalization without lowering wealthy district spending might be a political impossibility, while limiting spending by wealthy districts would certainly draw intense opposition and would seem to create a conflict between equality and school quality.

To be sure, the differences between the adequacy and equality norms are not as sharp as the doctrinal labels might suggest. Assuming that more affluent districts spend more money to provide quality education, interlocal inequalities suggest the inadequacy of spending in poorer districts. By the same token, achieving adequacy in poorer districts promotes equality. The *Edgewood* court, though it based its holding on the adequacy principle, insisted that Texas children are entitled to "substantially equal access" and "substantially equal opportunity." 777 S.W.2d at 397. *See also* Joshua E. Weishart, Transcending Equality vs. Adequacy, 66 Stan.L.Rev. 477 (2014) (equality and adequacy are "reciprocal" concepts).

Adequacy theories have been endorsed by courts in a significant number of states in addition to Texas and Kentucky. *See, e.g.*, Connecticut Coalition for Justice in Education Funding, Inc. v. Rell, 990 A.2d 206 (Conn. 2010); Claremont Sch. Dist. v. Governor, 794 A.2d 744 (N.H. 2002); Abbeville County Sch. Dist. v. State, 515 S.E.2d 535 (S.C. 1999); Leandro v. State, 488 S.E.2d 249 (N.C.1997); DeRolph v. State, 677 N.E.2d 733 (Ohio 1997); Reform Educational Financing Inequities Today v. Cuomo, 655 N.E.2d 647 (N.Y.1995); Roosevelt Elementary School Dist. No. 66 v. Bishop, 877 P.2d 806 (Ariz.1994); McDuffy v. Secretary of Exec. Office of Ed., 615 N.E.2d 516 (Mass.1993); Helena Elem. Sch. Dist. No. 1 v. State, 769 P.2d 684 (Mont.1989). Other courts have rejected adequacy claims. *See* Lobato v. State, 304 P.3d 1132 (Colo. 2013); Ex parte James, 836 So.2d 813 (Ala. 2002); Comm. for Educational Rights v. Edgar, 672 N.E.2d 1178 (Ill. 1996); Coalition for Adequacy and Fairness in School Funding, Inc. v. Chiles, 680 So.2d 400 (Fla.1996); Pawtucket v. Sundlun, 662 A.2d 40 (R.I.1995); Unified Sch. Dist. No. 229 v. State, 885 P.2d 1170 (Kan.1994); Skeen v. State, 505 N.W.2d 299, 319–20 (Minn.1993); Gould v. Orr, 506 N.W.2d 349 (Neb.1993). *See generally* William Thro, The Third Wave: The Impact of Montana, Kentucky, and Texas Decisions on the Future of Public School Finance Reform Litigation, 19 J.L. & Educ. 219 (1990); Kevin Randall McMillan, Note, The Turning Tide: The Emerging Fourth Wave of School Finance Reform Litigation and the Courts' Lingering Institutional Concerns, 58 Ohio St. L.J. 1867 (1998). In at least one instance, a judicial rejection of adequacy claims produced a constitutional amendment. In Florida, Article IX, Section 1 of the state constitution was amended in response to the court's holding to describe education as a "fundamental value" and a "paramount duty of the state."

2. *Postscript to Edgewood.* The Texas legislature's first response to Edgewood, known as Senate Bill 1, eliminated much of the interdistrict inequality by raising new taxes, but the state supreme court declared the act unconstitutional in Edgewood Indep. School Dist. v. Kirby (*Edgewood* II), 804 S.W.2d 491 (1991). The court noted that while the law did establish a guaranteed amount of revenue per student, it failed to address the underlying causes of the funding disparity that allowed the 132 richest districts to spend significantly more than the remaining districts. Soon after, Senate Bill 351 completely revamped the school district governance structure by creating 188 county education districts that would levy school taxes. That law was invalidated in Carrollton-Farmers Branch Independent School Dist. v. Edgewood Indep. School Dist. (*Edgewood* III), 826 S.W.2d 489 (1992), because it violated the state constitutional prohibition of state property taxes and because it impermissibly imposed a property tax without voter approval. Finally, in Edgewood Indep. School Dist. v. Meno (*Edgewood* IV), 917 S.W.2d 717 (1995), the supreme court upheld the legislature's third attempt, Senate Bill 7. That law preserved much of Texas' pre-existing two-tiered school funding system, which focused on equalizing revenues for districts that impose equal tax rates. Tier 1 guarantees a basic state allotment of $2300 per student to all districts, so long as a school district levies the required minimum tax rate on all district property. If that tax rate does not generate the $2300, the state will make up the difference. Tier 2 operates in a similar manner to equalize revenues for districts that choose to tax beyond the minimum rate. By guaranteeing it will make up the shortfalls attributable to low assessed valuation in any given district, the state has in essence ensures that equal tax rates will generate equal revenues. Most controversial of the funding reforms was the "recapture" provision, which imposed a $320,000 per student maximum taxable property value cap. Any district whose property wealth exceeds this amount must choose one or more of the following statutory options: (1) to consolidate with another district; (2) to detach property from its district; (3) to contribute money to the state that corresponds to the amount of excess funding generated by the property; (4) to pay for the education of non-resident students; and (5) to consolidate its tax base with another district. Tex. Educ. Code §§ 36.003, 36.004. Although the court upheld the statute as constitutional, it emphasized its disappointment with the legislative scheme: "For too long, the legislature's response to its constitutional duty to provide for an efficient system has been little more than crisis management. The rationality behind such a complex and unwieldy system [as Senate Bill 7] is not obvious. We conclude that the system becomes minimally acceptable only when viewed through the prism of history. Surely, Texas can and must do better." 917 S.W.2d at 726.

After *Edgewood* IV, funding levels were equalized for 90% of Texas students. Todd Smith, My Education on Education, Fort Worth Star-Telegram, July 10, 1999, at 15. Attorneys for the *Edgewood* plaintiffs recommended that their clients end their legal battle against the state. Phillips Brooks, Attorney Urging an End to School Finance Lawsuit, Austin American-Statesman, June 5, 1999 at B3. Two articles offer positive assessments of the Texas school finance reform. *See* Eleanor Dougherty, Getting Beyond Policy: School Reform in Practice, 6 Va. Soc. Pol'y & L.127 (1998); Joseph F. Johnson, The Influence of a State Accountability System on Student Achievement in Texas, 6 Va.J.Soc.Pol'y & L.127 (1998). For a detailed account of the *Edgewood* litigation, *see* J. Steven Farr and Mark Trachtenberg, The Edgewood Drama: An Epic Quest for Education Equity, 17 Yale L. & Policy Rev. 607 (1999).

Not all school districts are happy with the Texas school funding reforms. Shortly after the supreme court issued its opinion in *Edgewood* IV, four wealthy school districts filed suit to invalidate the property tax recapture system, derisively labeled as "Robin Hood" provisions. By capping the rates at which districts can tax, and by redistributing locally raised property tax revenues, the plaintiffs alleged the state violated the constitutional prohibition of state-level property taxes. In 2003, the Texas Supreme Court reversed the lower courts' dismissal of the lawsuit and remanded the case for trial. *See* West Orange-Cove Consolidated I.S.D. v. Alanis, 107 S.W.3d 558, 562 (Tex. 2003). After a bench trial, the lower court found in favor of the school districts, and the state supreme court affirmed. *See* Neeley v. West Orange-Cove Consolid. Indep. Sch. Dist., 176 S.W.3d 746 (Tex. 2005). The court concluded that school districts retain no meaningful discretion over their property tax levy, and are essentially forced to tax at maximum rates. As a result, the court found that the local property tax was the constitutional equivalent of a state property tax, which is prohibited under Texas' constitution. The court refused, however, to enter the adequacy debate, and declined to find that the current statewide average of $10,000 per student was inadequate, opining that "more money does not guarantee better schools or more educated students." *Id.* at 788. The Texas legislature shifted the source of school funding somewhat in response to the decision, reducing local property taxes and increasing taxes on businesses. After another lawsuit was filed to challenge the legislature's decision to cut more than $5 billion from public school funding, in August, 2014, the trial judge in *Texas Taxpayer and Student Fairness Coalition v. Williams* invalidated the entire system on adequacy grounds. The holding has been appealed directly to the Texas Supreme Court. News reports suggest that legislative action will await the court's decision in the case.

3. *The Aftermath of Rose.* By specifically enumerating the types of basic skills it expected all public school students to acquire, *Rose* went well beyond the more typical and more limited judicial order invalidating school funding on adequacy grounds. As the full opinion describes in great detail, the *Rose* court relied extensively on the brief filed by an education advocacy group and on the findings of a committee appointed by the trial judge. That committee, established after the trial court's invalidation of the Kentucky school system but before issuance of the final remedial order, held hearings around the state and identified specific student outcomes that would constitute an adequate education. Those findings were included in the supreme court's opinion.

The Kentucky Education Reform Act, Ky.Rev.Stat.Ann. §§ 156.005–.990, unusual if not unique for the speed with which it was passed and the breadth of its reform, has been described as perhaps "the most comprehensive . . . statewide education reforms in the nation." *See* Molly A. Hunter, All Eyes Forward: Public Engagement and Educational Reform in Kentucky, 28 J.L. & Educ. 485 (1999). On the financial side, the state adopted a district power equalization formula and increased state funding dramatically by raising state sales and income taxes. The reforms extended well beyond funding, however; the law required extensive revamping of educational curricula and school governance standards. Hunter's article provides a detailed description and analysis of the *Rose* litigation and Kentucky's statutory response.

4.   *Standards and School Finance Litigation.* The adequacy doctrine appeals to those who seek clear expectations for school performance and assessment mechanisms for evaluating achievement. This "marriage of standards and school finance litigation," James E. Ryan, Standards, Testing, and School Finance Litigation, 86 Tex. L. Rev. 1223 (2008), can be seen in the federal No Child Left Behind Act (NCLB), 20 U.S.C. §§ 6301–6578. Adopted as an amendment to and reauthorization of the Elementary and Secondary Education Act, NCLB conditions receipt of federal funds for schools on the states' establishment of an accountability system to evaluate their children's annual academic progress and a framework for raising overall student achievement. Under NCLB, the state must set clear timelines for improving student academic performance on standardized tests in language and math. The states themselves, however, set the standards of proficiency deemed appropriate for their constituency. Annual state reports of academic achievement and progress towards those goals must disaggregate data to track the progress of students along the lines of race, ethnicity, gender, disability status, migrant status, English proficiency, and economic disadvantage. 20 U.S.C. § 6311(h) (1). Failure to make "adequate yearly progress" toward the statute's ultimate goal of 100 percent proficiency for almost all students by 2014 triggers a number of sanctions, ranging from requirements that schools "needing improvement" establish a two-year plan to improve student achievement, to more serious "corrective actions," to the ultimate sanction of school restructuring.

NCLB put the spotlight on objective standards and test scores as a measure of school adequacy. How might this increased reliance on achievement levels influence the shape of a school finance claim? For Professor James Ryan, shifting adequacy's focus to outcomes and achievements is "wrongheaded as a matter of prescription." *See* Ryan, *supra*, at 1224. In his view, courts are generally ill-equipped to evaluate the adequacy of outputs. He argues that comparability of resource inputs is a better measure and one that is more within the judicial competence. *See id.* at 1239–61. Professor Ryan questions the appropriateness of using standards as the focal point of the adequacy lawsuit. For a discussion of the way in which objective measures of student failure and achievement may allow adequacy plaintiffs to use "failure in the classroom . . . [to achieve] success in the courtroom," *see* Michael Heise, *The Courts, Educational Policy, and Unintended Consequences*, 11 Cornell J.L. & Pub. Pol'y 633, 634 (2002).

Standards arguments are working their way into legal challenges to state educational systems. In King v. State, 818 N.W.2d 1 (Iowa 2012), the plaintiffs argued that the state's failure "to establish statewide public school educational standards, assessments, and teacher training, recruitment, and retention programs" constituted a violation of its constitutional duty under the education clause. Though the court carefully refused to resolve the question whether these claims were nonjusticiable, as the State argued, it did hold that the allegations did not state a claim under the state constitution.

5. *Money and Educational Quality*. Underlying all the school finance reform litigation is the assumption that money is a crucial determinant of educational quality. Some commentators, however, have asserted that the amount of school funding is not significantly correlated with levels of student achievement. The argument originated in the 1966 Coleman Report which concluded that "[s]chools bring little influence to bear on a child's achievement that is independent of his background and general social context." J. Coleman, Equality of Educational Opportunity 325 (1966). *Accord,* Eric A. Hanushek, The Impact of Differential Expenditures on School Performance, 18 Educ.Res. 45, 50 (1989) ("expenditures are not systematically related to student achievement"). Others vigorously dispute this. One study of the entire Texas public school system, for instance, concluded that teacher quality, as gauged by literacy levels, years of experience, and extent of formal education, is an important predictor of student test scores. Ronald F. Ferguson, Paying for Public Education: New Evidence on How and Why Money Matters, 28 Harv.J.Legis. 465, 488 (1991). Though the scholarly debate is unresolved, evidence does suggest that equalization of revenues will not eliminate disparities in educational achievement, or at least that a longer time period is needed before results can be seen. Money alone may not be sufficient to eliminate interlocal disparities in school quality, but money appears to be necessary to improve quality in poorer districts.

The "throwing money at school" argument is usually used to challenge proposals for increasing government spending in poor and underachieving schools. Should the question be asked with regard to all school districts? If the research is correct, and if family background and peer group are the most important determinants of educational achievement, aren't wealthy communities also incurring needless expenses? Which theory, adequacy or equality, is better able to respond to the relationship between wealth and educational achievement?

6. *The Meaning of Adequacy*. It is worth remembering that many of this country's schools display shockingly decrepit conditions. The Ohio Supreme Court provided a graphic, lengthy description of some of its poorer schools. *See* DeRolph v. State, 677 N.E.2d 733, 743–44 (Ohio 1997) (*DeRolph I*). Some of the most jarring conditions included carbon monoxide leakage,

coal dust emissions, falling chunks of plaster, cockroaches, band practice in a coal bin, special education classes in a closet, raw sewage on the baseball field, arsenic in the drinking water, and classrooms without textbooks. The court's fact-finding suggests that many state schools would be deemed inadequate by any measure.

The first *DeRolph* opinion held that Ohio's school funding formula violated that state's education clause, which mandates a "thorough and efficient system of common schools throughout the state." In subsequent years, the Ohio Supreme Court issued four more opinions in the ongoing litigation. In *DeRolph* IV (DeRolph v. State, 780 N.E.2d 529 (Ohio 2002)), the court ordered the state legislature to enact a "complete systematic overhaul" of the state's system, describing the legislative response to date as "nibbling at the edges." *See id.* at 530. Finally, in State ex rel. State v. Lewis, 789 N.E.2d 195 (Ohio 2003), the supreme court abruptly ended state judicial involvement in the dispute, issuing a writ of prohibition forbidding the lower courts from exercising jurisdiction over the *DeRolph* case. Unwilling to continue to spar with a recalcitrant legislature over the contours of a constitutional finance plan, the court concluded that "The duty now lies with the General Assembly to remedy an educational system that has been found . . . to still be unconstitutional." *Id.* at 202.

Consider the broader question of judicial and legislative roles in the next case.

COMMITTEE FOR EDUCATIONAL RIGHTS V. EDGAR

Supreme Court of Illinois
672 N.E.2d 1178 (1996)

JUSTICE NICKELS delivered the opinion of the court:

This appeal draws us into the sensitive and controversial area of public school finance. The plaintiffs in this action are the Committee for Educational Rights (which consists of more than 60 school districts associated pursuant to an intergovernmental agreement), the boards of education of 37 school districts named individually, and a number of students and their parents.

* * * In their five-count complaint, plaintiffs allege that under the present financing scheme, vast differences in educational resources and opportunities exist among the State's school districts as a result of differences in local taxable property wealth. During the 1989–90 school year, the average tax base in the wealthiest 10% of elementary schools was over 13 times the average tax base in the poorest 10%. For high school and unit school districts, the ratios of the average tax bases in the wealthiest and poorest districts were 8.1 to 1 and 7 to 1, respectively, during the 1989–90 school year.

Plaintiffs allege in their complaint that the general state aid formula does not effectively equalize funding among wealthy and poor districts. While the general state aid formula ensures minimum funding at the foundation level, the wealthiest districts are able to raise funds through property taxes considerably in excess of the foundation level. Moreover, the provision of a minimum grant—equal to 7% of the foundation level— to even the wealthiest school districts is counterequalizing.

Plaintiffs allege that disparities among wealthy and poor districts are reflected in various measures of educational funding; in several "key indicators" of educational quality (such as the percentage of teachers with master's degrees, teacher experience, teacher salaries, administrator salaries and pupil/administrator ratios); and in a comparison of the facilities, resources and course offerings in two neighboring school districts with dramatically disparate tax bases. According to the complaint, these disparities are attributable to variations in property wealth rather than tax effort; on average, the poorest school districts tax at higher rates than the wealthiest. * * *

ANALYSIS

I

* * * Section 1 of article X of the Illinois Constitution of 1970 provides:

"A fundamental goal of the People of the State is the educational development of all persons to the limits of their capacities.

The State shall provide for an efficient system of high quality public educational institutions and services. Education in public schools through the secondary level shall be free. There may be such other free education as the General Assembly provides by law.

The State has the primary responsibility for financing the system of public education." (Emphasis added.) Ill. Const.1970, art. X, § 1.

[The court first held that the state constitutional requirement of an "efficient system" had been satisfied.]

* * *

B

The remaining question under section 1 of the education article pertains to its guarantee of a system of "high quality" educational institutions and services. There is no dispute as to the nature of this guarantee in the abstract. Instead, the central issue is whether the quality of education is capable of or properly subject to measurement by the courts. Plaintiffs maintain that it is the courts' duty to construe the constitution and determine whether school funding legislation conforms with its requirements and cite a number of decisions from other jurisdictions in which courts have concluded that similar constitutional challenges are capable of judicial resolution. As explained below, however, we conclude that questions relating to the quality of education are solely for the legislative branch to answer.

Historically, this court has assumed only an exceedingly limited role in matters relating to public education, recognizing that educational policy is almost exclusively within the province of the legislative branch. * * *

Plaintiffs insist that our present constitution accommodates a more active judicial role in implementing the constitutional guarantee of an efficient system of high quality educational institutions and services. In this regard, plaintiffs stress that while the 1870 Constitution specified that the General Assembly shall provide a system of public schools, the 1970 Constitution expressly places that duty on the State. In plaintiffs' view, the change in language signifies that section 1 of the education article is no longer merely a mandate to the General Assembly, but is a mandate to all three branches of the State government: the executive branch, the legislative branch and the judicial branch. Surely, however, this provision does not alter the roles or expand the powers assigned to the different branches of government by the constitution. Courts may not legislate in the field of public education any more than they may legislate in any other area. In reviewing legislation, the role of the courts is now, as before, to ensure that the enactment does not exceed whatever judicially enforceable limitations the constitution places on the General Assembly's power. Courts are no more capable of defining "high quality educational institutions and services" under our present constitution than they were able to define a "good common school education" under the 1870 Constitution. * * *

To hold that the question of educational quality is subject to judicial determination would largely deprive the members of the general public of a voice in a matter which is close to the hearts of all individuals in Illinois. Judicial determination of the type of education children should receive and how it can best be provided would depend on the opinions of whatever expert witnesses the litigants might call to testify and whatever other evidence they might choose to present. Members of the general public, however, would be obliged to listen in respectful silence. We certainly do not mean to trivialize the views of educators, school administrators and others who have studied the problems which public schools confront. But nonexperts—students, parents, employers and others—also have important views and experiences to contribute which are not easily reckoned through formal judicial factfinding. In contrast, an open and robust public debate is the lifeblood of the political process in our system of representative democracy. Solutions to problems of educational quality should emerge from a spirited dialogue between the people of the State and their elected representatives. * * *

We are well aware that courts in other jurisdictions have seen fit to define the contours of a constitutionally guaranteed education and to establish judicial standards of educational quality reflecting varying degrees of specificity and deference to the other branches of government. * * * By and large these courts have viewed the process of formulating educational standards as merely an exercise in constitutional interpretation or construction. For the reasons already stated, we disagree; we will not "under the guise of constitutional interpretation, presume to lay down guidelines or ultimatums for [the legislature]." Seattle School District, 90 Wash.2d at 579, 585 P.2d at 128 (Rosellini, J., dissenting, joined by Hamilton & Hicks, JJ.).

Rather, we agree with the views of the dissenters in several of the cases cited above. In Seattle School District, Justice Rosellini lamented the court's usurpation of the legislative prerogative in the area of educational policy:

"I would be surprised to learn that the people of this state are willing to turn over to a tribunal against which they have little if any recourse, a matter of such grave concern to them and upon which they hold so many strong, though conflicting views. If their legislators pass laws with which they disagree or refuse to act when the people think they should, they can make their dissatisfaction known at the polls. They can write to their representatives or appear before them and let their protests be heard. The court, however, is not so easy to reach[citation] nor is it so easy to persuade that its judgment ought to be revised. A legislature may be a hard horse to harness, but it is not quite the stubborn mule that a court can be. Most importantly, the court is not designed or equipped to make public policy decisions, as this case so forcibly demonstrates." Seattle School District, 90 Wash.2d at 563–64, 585 P.2d at 120 (Rosellini, J., dissenting, joined by Hamilton & Hicks, JJ.).

* * *

We conclude that the question of whether the educational institutions and services in Illinois are "high quality" is outside the sphere of the judicial function. To the extent plaintiffs' claim that the system for financing public schools is unconstitutional rests on perceived deficiencies in the quality of education in public schools, the claim was properly dismissed. * * *

NOTES AND QUESTIONS

1. *Judicial Involvement in Legislative Responses*. As the main cases in this section indicate, school funding challenges usually result in multiple rounds of litigation, judicial opinion, and statutory responses. The judiciary, of course, lacks the power to legislate or to tax and the authority to establish social policy. Thus, the *Edgewood* court's deference to legislative discretion is typical: "[W]e do not now instruct the legislature as to the specifics of the legislation it should enact . . . . The legislature has primary responsibility to decide how best to achieve an efficient system. We decide only the nature of the constitutional mandate and whether that mandate has been met." 777 S.W.2d at 399.

In contrast, *Rose* is frequently cited as an example of heightened judicial involvement in the specifics of school reform. Other courts, building on *Rose*, have delved even more into the specifics of educational policy. Wyoming's highest court, for instance, went so far as to define adequacy as necessarily including, among other things: "small schools, small class size, low student/teacher ratios," Campbell County School District v. State, 907 P.2d 1238, 1279 (1995).

Professor Neal Katyal, while recognizing the importance of judicial enforcement of constitutional norms, supports broad deference to legislative discretion in these cases. He used the decision in Sheff v. O'Neill, 678 A.2d 1267 (Conn.1996), to illustrate:

> The court provided strong judicial advice—that the school financing scheme was unconstitutional—and coupled that advice with a short fuse—that the legislature must remedy the matter or the court would do so on its own. The beauty of the decision is that, by separating out the advice and fuse issues, the court was able to avoid the problem many other state courts have faced in similar litigation: Declaring a school financing statute unconstitutional requires judicial remedies that smell of legislative usurpation. That problem has led many state courts to manipulate text and history to simply affirm their financing schemes as constitutional rather than to confront the thorny issues surrounding remedies. *Sheff* teaches that courts, by creatively deciding when not to decide a matter, may hew to both a constitution-protecting and legislature-respecting line.

Neal Kumar Katyal, Judges as Advicegivers, 50 Stan.L.Rev. 1709, 1790 n.389 (1998).

Does your analysis of the cases and their aftermath suggest that Professor Katyal is correct? Or does judicial deference to legislative prerogative result in excessive legislative delay and incomplete responses to judicial mandates? Do the actual results in the cases increase your skepticism about the power of the courts to effectuate social change, or do they harden your resolve that the courts must continue to prod unwilling legislatures into action?

2.   *School Finance and State-Local Relations.* The school financing cases have significant implications for our thinking about the state-local relationship. By placing responsibility for school failures and inadequacy squarely on the state, the courts hearken back to the foundational principle of complete state control over the local government system. Thus, the cases tend to result in more state oversight in the areas of curriculum, student achievement, and fiscal solvency. In the New York City school funding litigation, the state argued that the city bore some of the responsibility for inadequate educational achievement. It noted, for instance, that while the state had increased its funding to the city, the city's school spending had declined. The court's response was categorical: "[T]he State Constitution reposes responsibility to provide a sound basic education with the State, and if the State's subdivisions act to impede the delivery of a sound basic education it is the State's responsibility under the constitution to remove such impediments." Campaign for Fiscal Equity v. State, 719 N.Y.S.2d 475, 527–28 (N.Y.Sup.2001). The New York Court of Appeals issued an opinion agreeing with most of the trial court's conclusions. The court ordered the state to determine the "actual cost of providing a sound basic education in New York City," to reform the current funding scheme to ensure "that every school in New York City would have the resources necessary" to provide that education, and to "ensure a system of accountability to measure whether the reforms actually provide the opportunity for a sound basic education." *See* Campaign for Fiscal Equity v. State, 801 N.E.2d 326 (N.Y. 2003).

3.   *Justiciability and Judicial Exhaustion.* Due to concerns about judicial intrusion into a traditionally legislative domain, some state courts refused to rule on the merits of the school funding challenge and relied instead on separation of powers concerns to deny judicial involvement. Judicial opinions in Illinois (the *Edgar* opinion), Rhode Island (City of Pawtucket v. Sundlun, 662 A.2d 40 (R.I. 1995)), Florida (Coalition for Adequacy and Fairness in School Funding, Inc. v. Chiles, 680 A.2d 400 (Fla. 1996)), and Pennsylvania (Marrero v. Commonwealth, 709 A.2d 956 (Pa. Cmwlth. 1998)), were the initial standardbearers of this line of argumentation, while the vast majority of state courts jumped headlong into the merits of the school funding challenge. After 2002, however, courts in many more states either refused to rule on the merits of school funding challenges or simply decided to end the litigation after years of back and forth with the legislature. *See* Ex Parte James, 836 So.2d 813 (Ala. 2002) (noting the "obvious impracticalities of judicial oversight," court concludes that merits of challenge are nonjusticiable); Bonner ex rel. Bonner v. Daniels, 907 N.E.2d 516 (Ind. 2009) (state constitution's education clause does not impose an affirmative duty on the state but rather vests total discretion in legislature); Hancock v. Commissioner of Educ., 822 N.E.2d 1134 (Mass. 2005) (terminating judicial involvement in the ongoing litigation); Stroebe v. State, 127 P.3d 1051 (Mont. 2006) (challenge to school funding system

currently nonjusticiable); Nebraska Coalition for Educ. Equity and Adequacy v. Heineman, 731 N.W.2d 164 (Neb. 2007) (citing the lack of "judicially discoverable or manageable standards" and concluding that school funding decisions are legislative); State ex rel. State v. Lewis, 789 N.E.2d 195 (Ohio 2003) (terminating judicial involvement notwithstanding legislative failure to respond to earlier judicial mandates); Oklahoma Educ. Ass'n v. State, 158 P.3d 1058 (Ok. 2007) (concluding that lawsuit would impermissibly require the court to "invade the Legislature's power to determine policy"). Similarly, in 2007, trial judges in Indiana and Kentucky dismissed lawsuits challenging school funding laws, relying on separation of powers and the political question doctrine. Two other state supreme courts, however, have weighed in on the side of justiciability. *See* Gannon v. State, 319 P.3d 1196 (Kan. 2014); Davis v. State, 804 N.W.2d 618 (S.D. 2011). The National Access Network provides online summaries of these and other recent and ongoing school finance litigation. *See* http://www.schoolfunding.info/. What might account for the number of state courts that have refused to get involved in judicial involvement in school funding disputes?

4. *Focusing on the Remedy.* Undoubtedly, one of the causes of judicial reluctance to become embroiled in school finance litigation is the seemingly unending cycle of litigation that judicial involvement produces. The Nebraska court said it more colorfully than most: "The landscape is littered with courts that have been bogged down in the legal quicksand of continuous litigation and challenges to their states' school funding systems. Unlike those courts, we refuse to wade into that Stygian swamp." Nebraska Coalition for Educ. Equity and Adequacy v. Heineman, 731 N.W.2d 164, 183 (Neb. 2007). The New Jersey Supreme Court issued no fewer than 23 opinions after it first invalidated the state's school finance statute in Robinson v. Cahill, 303 A.2d 273 (1973), issuing *Robinson* I–VI, followed by 18 opinions in the follow-up litigation in Abbott v. Burke, 495 A.2d 376 (N.J. 1985). In 2011, the court once again ordered the State to fully fund the education finance reform it had adopted in response to these many lawsuits. Abbott ex rel. Abbott v. Burke, 20 A.3d 1018 (N.J. 2011).

What accounts for this? It may have to do with legislative resistance to the spirit, if not the letter, of the court's decree, and it may also reflect the enormous cost that compliance would impose on state coffers. It may also have something to do with the way the plaintiffs structure their complaints. Most frequently, they seek broad judicial condemnation of inequality or inadequacy, without explicit focus on the remedy. The next case suggests a narrowly focused doctrinal argument, based squarely on fundamental principles of state and local government law, which might give courts a middle ground for decisionmaking—that is, invalidating a funding source without interfering with the essential legislative function of crafting school funding legislation.

CLAREMONT SCHOOL DISTRICT V. GOVERNOR

Supreme Court of New Hampshire
703 A.2d 1353 (1997)

BROCK, CHIEF JUSTICE.

In this appeal we hold that the present system of financing elementary and secondary public education in New Hampshire is unconstitutional. To hold otherwise would be to effectively conclude that it is reasonable, in discharging a State obligation, to tax property owners in one town or city as much as four times the amount taxed to others similarly situated in other towns or cities. This is precisely the kind of taxation and fiscal mischief from which the framers of our State Constitution took strong steps to protect our citizens. * * * We hold that the property tax levied to fund education is, by virtue of the State's duty to provide a constitutionally adequate public education, a State tax and as such is disproportionate and unreasonable in violation of part II, article 5 of the New Hampshire Constitution. * * *

I

Funding for public education in New Hampshire comes from three sources. First, school districts are authorized to raise funds through real estate taxation. Locally raised real property taxes are the principal source of revenue for public schools, providing on average from seventy-four to eighty-nine percent of total school revenue. Second, funds are provided through direct legislative appropriations, primarily in the form of Foundation Aid, Building Aid, and Catastrophic Aid. Direct legislative appropriations account for an average of eight percent of the total dollars spent on public elementary and secondary education, ranking New Hampshire last in the United States in percentage of direct support to public education. Third, approximately three percent of support for the public schools is in the form of federal aid.

At the present time, the State places the responsibility for providing elementary and secondary public education on local school districts. State statutes, rules, and regulations delineate the requirements to be followed by school districts. * * * For example, school districts are required to provide standard schools for 180 days per year, RSA 189:1,:24 (1989); provide transportation, RSA 189:6 (Supp.1996); provide meals to students, RSA 189:11–a (1989); purchase and provide textbooks, RSA 189:16 (1989); meet minimum standards for school approval, RSA 186:8 (1989); provide special education services, RSA 186:6 (1989); and participate in the school improvement and assessment program, RSA ch. 193–C (Supp.1996).

To comply with the State's requirements, school districts must raise money for their schools with revenue collected from real estate taxes. RSA 194:34 (1989); RSA 198:1–:7 (1989 & Supp.1996). Every year, the selectmen of each town are required to assess an annual tax of $3.50 on each $1,000 of assessed value for the support of that district's schools. RSA 198:1. Each school district then details the sums of money needed to support its public schools and produces a budget that specifies the additional funds required to meet the State's minimum standards. A sum sufficient to meet the approved school budget must be assessed on the taxable real property in the district. RSA 197:1 (1989); RSA 198:5. The commissioner of revenue administration computes a property tax rate for school purposes in each district. Using the determined rate, city and town officials levy property taxes to provide the further sum necessary to meet the obligations of the school budget. * * *

The plaintiffs argue that the school tax is a unique form of the property tax mandated by the State to pay for its duty to provide an adequate education and that the State controls the process and mechanism of taxation. Because of the purpose of the tax and the control exerted by the State, the plaintiffs contend that the school tax is a State tax that should be imposed at a uniform rate throughout the State. The State argues that "[b]ecause the school tax is a local tax determined by budgeting decisions made by the district's legislative body and spent only in the district, it meets the constitutional requirement of proportionality." According to the State, "property taxation is a stable and expan[dable] source of revenue which allows the citizens of New Hampshire to decide how to organize and operate their schools in a manner which best meets the needs of their children." The question of whether property taxes for schools are local or State taxes is an issue of first impression.

Part II, article 5 of the State Constitution provides that the legislature may "impose and levy proportional and reasonable assessments, rates, and taxes, upon all the inhabitants of, and residents within, the said state." This article requires that "all taxes be proportionate and reasonable—that is, equal in valuation and uniform in rate." * * * "[T]he test to determine whether a tax is equal and proportional is to inquire whether the taxpayers' property was valued at the same per cent of its true value as all the taxable property in the taxing district." *Bow v. Farrand*, 77 N.H. 451, 451–52, 92 A. 926, 926 (1915). "[T]he property shall be valued within a reasonable time before the tax is assessed." *Id.* at 452, 92 A. at 926.

In defining the taxing district, the trial court reasoned that whether a tax is a State tax or a local tax depends on "the entity that controls the mechanics of assessment and collection" and "the disposition of the tax revenues after their collection." The court found that each municipality controls the mechanics of assessment and collection of local property taxes, including the budgeting function and the determination of the local assessed value of property within each municipality. In addition, the court found that the property tax, once collected, is managed and expended by each municipality in accordance with its budget and thus does not become a part of the State treasury. The court concluded, therefore, that the school tax is a local tax and not a State tax. Because the trial court found there was no evidence that the school tax operated disproportionately within any local taxing district, it concluded that there was no violation of part II, article 5.

Determining the character of a tax as local or State requires an initial inquiry into its purpose.

> In order . . . that the tax should be proportional . . . it is required that the rate shall be the same throughout the taxing district;—that is, *if the tax is for the general purposes of the state, the rate should be the same throughout the state*; if for the county, it should be uniform throughout the county;—and the requisite of proportion, or equality and justice, can be answered in no other way.

State v. U.S. & C. Express Co., 60 N.H. 219, 243 (1880) (Stanley, J.) (emphasis added).

We find the purpose of the school tax to be overwhelmingly a State purpose and dispositive of the issue of the character of the tax.

"[T]he local school district, an entity created by the legislature almost two centuries ago, exists for the public's benefit, to carry out the mandates of the State's education laws." *Opinion of the Attorney General*, No. 82–100–I (Sept. 8, 1982) (citation omitted). "Indeed, school district monies, a public trust, can only be spent in furtherance of these educational mandates, and to promote the values set forth in the 'Encouragement of Literature' clause, N.H. CONST., pt. 2, Art. 83." *Id.* As we held in *Claremont I,* "part II, article 83 imposes a duty on the State to provide a constitutionally adequate education to every educable child in the public schools in New Hampshire and to guarantee adequate funding." *Claremont I,* 138 N.H. at 184, 635 A.2d at 1376.

Providing an adequate education is thus a duty of State government expressly created by the State's highest governing document, the State Constitution. In addition, public education differs from all other services of the State. No other governmental service plays such a seminal role in developing and maintaining a citizenry capable of furthering the economic, political, and social viability of the State. * * * That the State, through a complex statutory framework, has shifted most of the responsibility for supporting public schools to local school districts does not diminish the State purpose of the school tax. Although the taxes levied by local school districts are local in the sense that they are levied upon property within the district, the taxes are in fact State taxes that have been authorized by the legislature to fulfill the requirements of the

New Hampshire Constitution. * * * For purposes of analysis under part II, article 5, therefore, the taxing district is the State.

The question then is whether the school tax as presently structured is proportional and reasonable throughout the State in accordance with the requirements of part II, article 5. Evidence introduced at trial established that the equalized tax rate for the 1994–1995 school year in Pittsfield was $25.26 per thousand while the rate in Moultonborough was $5.56 per thousand. The tax rate in Pittsfield, therefore, was more than four times, or over 400 percent, higher than in Moultonborough. Likewise, the equalized tax rate for the 1994–1995 school year in Allenstown was $26.47 per thousand while the rate in Rye was $6.86 per thousand—a difference in tax rates of almost 400 percent. We need look no further to hold that the school tax is disproportionate in violation of our State Constitution. * * *

Because the diffusion of knowledge and learning is regarded by the State Constitution as "essential to the preservation of a free government," N.H. CONST. pt. II, art. 83, it is only just that those who enjoy such government should equally assist in contributing to its preservation. The residents of one municipality should not be compelled to bear greater burdens than are borne by others. In mandating that knowledge and learning be "generally diffused" and that the "opportunities and advantages of education" be spread through the various parts of the State, N.H. CONST. pt. II, art. 83, the framers of the New Hampshire Constitution could not have intended the current funding system with its wide disparities. This is likely the very reason that the people assigned the duty to support the schools to the State and not to the towns.

There is nothing fair or just about taxing a home or other real estate in one town at four times the rate that similar property is taxed in another town to fulfill the same purpose of meeting the State's educational duty. Compelling taxpayers from property-poor districts to pay higher tax rates and thereby contribute disproportionate sums to fund education is unreasonable. Children who live in poor and rich districts have the same right to a constitutionally adequate public education. Regardless of whether existing State educational standards meet the test for constitutional adequacy, the record demonstrates that a number of plaintiff communities are unable to meet existing standards despite assessing disproportionate and unreasonable taxes. "If modern conditions make ancient divisions or plans for distributing the tax burden inequitable, it would seem to be a plain legislative duty to enact such constitutional laws as will remedy the defect." *Opinion of the Justices*, 84 N.H. at 581, 149 A. at 332–33; *see State v. Express Co.*, 60 N.H. at 247 (Doe, C.J.) ("methods of dividing the public expense, equitable enough for practical purposes in the last century, would now be good cause of complaint"). We hold, therefore, that the varying property tax rates across the State violate part II, article 5 of the State Constitution in that such taxes, which support the public purpose of education, are unreasonable and disproportionate. To the extent that the property tax is used in the future to fund the provision of an adequate education, the tax must be administered in a manner that is equal in valuation and uniform in rate throughout the State.

NOTES AND QUESTIONS

1. *The Importance of State Control.* For the *Claremont* court, the education clause was key to the uniformity argument. Because the education clause makes education a state duty, the court reasoned that all taxes for education are levied in fulfillment of a state purpose and thus subject to the uniformity clause at the state level. Under New Hampshire's school finance statute, the state was directly involved in local taxation, because it required all local districts to levy an identical minimum property tax. Is state control of local tax efforts crucial to the holding in *Claremont*? Suppose all local property taxes for schools were, as they are in many states, left solely to local discretion? How would the absence of actual state control affect the argument that because the duty to provide education is a state duty, lack of local uniformity is fatal to the school funding system? In other words, is the presence of the state duty enough to make the uniformity argument?

2. *Uniformity of Taxation and State and Local Government Law.* Though the *Claremont* court does not mention it, the "limit not grant" principle provides an important doctrinal justification for the court's holding that locally levied school taxes are actually state, and not local, taxes for purposes of the uniformity clause. As we saw in Chapter I, state constitutions, in contrast to their federal counterpart, are limits and not grants of state power. Thus, in the absence of a state duty to provide education, the current landscape, with its mix of state and local revenue sources and its wide range of local property tax rates, would be an unremarkable implementation of state discretionary sovereignty. In every state constitution, however, an education clause explicitly puts the duty to provide education on the state. *See* Yohance C. Edwards and Jennifer Ahern, Note, Unequal Treatment in State Supreme Courts: Minority and City Schools in Education Finance Reform Litigation, 79 N.Y.U. L. Rev. 326, 327 n.2 (2004). From that point forward, the state's previously unlimited discretion over funding public schools is subject to the textual limit that has created a state duty. As a result, the argument can be made that all statutory transfers of power to local school districts should be evaluated as implementations of state, and not local, power. For elaboration of that argument, *see* Laurie Reynolds, Uniformity of Taxation and the Preservation of Local Control in School Finance Reform, 40 U.C. Davis L. Rev. 1835 (2007).

3. *The Vermont Experiment.* One of the few states that has gone far to detach property wealth from education spending is Vermont. Under state law, all non-residential property is subject to a uniform state property tax,

whose revenues go to the state for redistribution to local schools. "Non-residential" is defined broadly to include all property that does not serve as the owner's primary residence, in essence extracting from the local property tax base all of Vermont's second homes. Their presence had previously created the phenomenon of "gold towns"—those with extremely high property value that could tax at very low rates yet generate high per student revenues.

With respect to local residential property, each Vermont school district must select its own property tax rate for schools. Taxing at the minimum rate designated by state law guarantees that the district will receive the state determined per capita revenues. Any school district that wishes to spend more is free to do so with voter approval and must raise its tax rate by the percentage it wishes to increase its tax revenues. Thus, all local school taxes in Vermont are subject to a district power equalizer system, meaning that tax rate and not property value is the sole determinant of revenues. This of course means that the state in essence takes revenue from rich towns whose property tax rate generates more than the spending target, and transfers it to poor towns, whose target rate levied on its local residential property will not produce the revenue goal. In addition, all towns that want to spend more than 125% of the state-guaranteed amount must pay an additional tax or penalty. This means that extremely high spending comes at a stiff price, somewhat similar to a luxury tax. *See* Laurie Reynolds, Skybox Schools: Public Education as Private Luxury, 82 Wash. U. L. Q. 755 (2005). For an extensive description of Vermont's law, *see* Vermont Department of Education, Overview of Vermont's Education Funding System Under Act 60 (2003). Does the Vermont system strike an appropriate balance between local control and the need for providing equal educational opportunity for all children, irrespective of the wealth of the child's community?

4. *Moving to Full State Funding?* In 1978, the Washington Supreme Court held that the entire burden of funding a constitutionally sound education falls directly on the state. In Seattle School District No. 1 of King County v. State, 585 P.2d 71 (1978), the court concluded that the state's constitutional mandate requires it to find "regular and dependable tax sources" to make "ample provision for basic education." Local property tax revenues, the court concluded, did not meet that standard. In the Washington court's view, then, whatever the legitimacy of local supplemental revenues, the state was constitutionally compelled to fund its constitutional mandate completely with state funds. The legislative response, and the nominal adoption of a "full state funding approach," limited local supplemental spending to 8% of total school budgets. Thirty years later, with some local levies reaching 30%, another round of litigation began. The supreme court once again invalidated the state's school finance scheme, holding that the legislature had not met its clearly articulated obligation to "fully fund [the constitutionally required level of education] through regular and dependable tax sources." McCleary v. State, 269 P.3d 227, 261 (Wash. 2012). Somewhat surprisingly, the state argued once again that local levies, as well as federal grants, could constitute "regular and dependable" funding sources for

purposes of evaluating its constitutional compliance. Repeating its earlier pronouncements, however, the court stressed that only funding from the state itself could qualify. Two years later, in the face of no legislative progress towards the court-imposed standard, the supreme court held the legislature in contempt for noncompliance with an earlier order in the *McCleary* litigation. Sanctions were held in abeyance, giving the legislature until the end of the 2015 legislative session to comply. *See* McCleary v. State, Supreme Court No. 84362–7 (Sept. 11, 2014).

Other state supreme courts appear to have drawn on the Washington court's line of reasoning. *See* Opinion of the Justices, 765 A.2d 673, 677 (N.H. 2000); Brigham v. State, 692 A.2d 384, 392 (Vt. 1997); Montoy v. State, 112 P.3d 923, 937 (Kan. 2005); Campbell County Sch. Dist. v. State, 907 P.2d 1238, 1274 (Wyo. 1995). The holdings impose the absolute requirement that the state fulfill its constitutional mandate to provide education with state, and not local, revenues. Just like the Washington court, however, these courts have accepted the possibility that the state might be able to authorize the use of a local property tax to provide educational opportunities that go above and beyond the state's constitutional mandate. The sentiment of the Kansas court is typical: "We fully acknowledge that once the legislature has provided suitable funding for the state school system, there may be nothing in the constitution that prevents the legislature from allowing school districts to raise additional funds for enhancements to the constitutionally adequate education already provided." *Montoy*, 112 P.3d. at 923. Only the Wyoming Supreme Court injected a note of caution about local supplementation:

> Once the legislature achieves the constitutional mandate of a cost-based, state-financed proper education, then assuming the legislature has a compelling reason for providing a mechanism by which local districts may tax themselves in order to enhance their programs in an equitable manner, that appears to be constitutionally permissible. However, we inject two notes of caution. First, in [another state court case] the two dissenting state supreme court justices did not believe strict scrutiny permits a local enhancement mechanism. * * * Second, local enhancement may also result in substantive innovations which should be available to all school districts as part of a proper education. The definition of a proper education is not static and necessarily will change. Should that change occur as a result of local innovation, all students are entitled to the benefit of that change as part of a cost-based, state-financed proper education.

Campbell County, 907 P.2d at 1274.

If these "full state funding" states ultimately allow the preservation of local property taxing discretion to supplement state funding, the history of school finance reform in Washington suggests that it is likely to undo the equalizing their courts have decreed. Does this suggest that equality is an unrealistic goal in school finance? Or should courts continue to seek compliance with *Brown v. Board of Education*'s definition of education as "a right which must be made available to all on equal terms," 347 U.S. 483, 493 (1954)?

5. *Preserving Education Dollars in State Budgets.* One of the disappointing results of increased proportional state responsibility for education funding is that the total revenues spent on education frequently decrease. *See* Jeffrey Metzler, Inequitable Equilibrium: School Finance in the United States, 36 Ind. L. Rev. 561, 580 (2003). Education must compete with the state's other spending priorities. One way to protect education dollars from the give and take of the state budget process would be to guarantee an untouchable stream of revenues for education. A state-level property tax would be one possible source. Levying the tax at the state level would equalize property tax rates across the state. For further analysis of the practical effects of property taxation, *see* Edward A. Zelinsky, The Once and Future Property Tax: A Dialogue with my Younger Self, 23 Cardozo L. Rev. 2199, 2201–02 (2002). Are the property tax's disadvantages offset by the benefits of statewide equal funding of education?

6. *A National Responsibility?* Professor—and now California Supreme Court Justice—Goodwin Liu has suggested that the U.S. Constitution should be interpreted as guaranteeing an adequate education for all children. In Interstate Inequality in Educational Opportunity, 81 N.Y.U. L. Rev. 2004 (2007), he based his claim on the broader argument that the Fourteenth Amendment's guarantee of national citizenship is the source of substantive individual rights. In the context of education, he argued that this federal right should be implemented by Congress in three different ways: first, in the establishment of national education standards to be adopted voluntarily by the states; second, by amending Title I of the Elementary and Secondary Education Act of 1965 to equalize distribution of federal funding for the education of poor children; and third, in the enactment of a national funding strategy to guarantee an appropriate revenue floor for education spending in all states. This program would not equalize resources nationwide, but would rather establish a high national minimum. Similar arguments are appearing in other outlets. Can you identify the legal and political strengths and weaknesses of reducing the local and increasing the federal role in primary and secondary public education?

b. A Regional Response to Interlocal Fiscal Inequality

BURNSVILLE V. ONISCHUK

Supreme Court of Minnesota
222 N.W.2d 523 (1974)

OTIS, JUSTICE.

The issue raised by this appeal is the constitutionality of Ex.Sess.L.1971, c. 24, Minn.St. 473F, commonly referred to as the

'Metropolitan Fiscal Disparities Act.' The trial court held the statute to be in violation of Minn.Const. art. 9, § 1, and we reverse.

* * *

The purposes of c. 24 are set forth in the act as follows:

Minn.St. 473F.01. 'The legislature finds it desirable to improve the revenue raising and distribution system in the seven county Twin Cities area to accomplish the following objectives:

(1) To provide a way for local governments to share in the resources generated by the growth of the area, without removing any resources which local governments already have;

(2) To increase the likelihood of orderly urban development by reducing the impact of fiscal considerations on the location of business and residential growth and of highways, transit facilities and airports;

(3) To establish incentives for all parts of the area to work for the growth of the area as a whole;

(4) To provide a way whereby the area's resources can be made available within and through the existing system of local governments and local decision making;

(5) To help communities in different stages of development by making resources increasingly available to communities at those early stages of development and redevelopment when financial pressures on them are the greatest;

(6) To encourage protection of the environment by reducing the impact of fiscal considerations so that flood plains can be protected and land for parks and open space can be preserved; and

(7) To provide for the distribution to municipalities of additional revenues generated within the area or from outside sources pursuant to other legislation.'

Under Minn.St. 473F.02, the area affected by the act * * * includes Minneapolis and St. Paul and the suburban metropolitan municipalities immediately adjacent to them, numbering some 250 local units of government in all. Although the formulas for achieving the purposes of the act are complex in the extreme, the stated objectives are relatively simple. In order to prevent an ill-advised competitive scramble by individual units of government within the 7-county area for commercial-industrial development to improve their tax base, the act contemplates pooling 40 percent of the increase throughout the area of all commercial-industrial valuation subsequent to January 2, 1971. For the revenue needs of each unit of government, the county auditor will thereupon impose two separate levies, one on 60 percent of the increment in its commercial-industrial valuation, if it has contributed to the pool, plus all other taxable property in that particular unit of government, and a separate levy on the metropolitan pool, representing the 40-percent increment in commercial-industrial valuation. Under this scheme, all units of government receive some distribution of the area-wide tax base although from year to year, as conditions change, some units will contribute more to the pool than will be distributed to them.

The effect of the system is to reallocate the area-wide tax base thus pooled to all municipalities in direct relation to need and inverse relation to fiscal capacity. Need is measured by population, and fiscal capacity is measured by the market value of taxable property per capita. Consequently, the units of government with large population and low fiscal capacity are favored in reallocation over those with small population and high fiscal capacity.

The local levy of each unit of government is divided by the local tax base to determine the local mill rate which is then applied to all commercial-industrial property which has not been pooled and to all other taxable property. The area-wide levies of all units of government are combined into a total levy against the area-wide tax base. The area-wide levy divided by area-wide tax base establishes an area-wide tax rate which is then applied to the value of each item of industrial-commercial property which has not been subjected to local tax rates. As previously noted, the value of commercial-industrial property to which the area-wide rate is applied varies from year to year, depending on its rate of growth in each municipality.

Since the amount a particular municipality will realize from the area-wide levy is always in direct proportion to the amount it will realize from its local tax levy, the opportunity for 'raiding' the area-wide tax base is minimal or nonexistent.

When the area-wide tax levies have been collected, they are channeled through the county to the state treasurer and distributed to local units of government on the basis of the fiscal capacity of each. The area-wide tax base distribution index which determines the amount of the area-wide levy to which each unit of government is entitled is computed by multiplying the population of the municipality by a fraction, the numerator of which is the average fiscal capacity of all the municipalities in the area for the preceding year, and the denominator of which is the fiscal capacity of that particular municipality, and multiplying the product by two. * * *

THE CONSTITUTIONALITY OF C. 24.

The trial court held that c. 24 violated Minn.Const. art. 9, § 1, the pertinent provisions of which are as follows:

> * * * Taxes shall be uniform upon the same class of subjects, and shall be levied and collected for public purposes * * *.

[The trial court concluded that:]

> In general the law fails to pass the test not only of practical and common sense equality but totally fails to pass the test of constitutional uniformity requiring that the burden of a tax must fall equally and impartially upon all persons and properties subject to it.

* * *

In essence, the issue then is whether those units of government within the metropolitan area which in a given year contribute more of their tax base to the pool than is redistributed to them are sufficiently benefitted to meet the constitutional requirement of uniformity. * * *

Plaintiffs argue with considerable force that [prior cases] preclude the metropolitan area from disbursing area-wide tax revenues to individual municipalities. We agree that a literal reading of our prior opinions supports plaintiffs' position. Our decision to reverse therefore hinges on what we deem to be a developing concept of the meaning of the word 'benefit.' It seems to us that the phrase 'special benefit' no longer adequately serves the constitutional requirement of uniformity. In a seven-county area which is heavily populated, we are of the opinion that it is no longer necessary for units of government providing tax revenue to receive the kind of tangible and specific benefits to which our court has previously referred in order to satisfy the uniformity clause.

* * * Under existing tax practices, in order to improve their fiscal capacity, local units of government vie for commerce and industry to improve the fiscal capacity of its residents without considering the resulting impact on long-range planning and the utilization of their resources. The seven-county metropolitan area, it is pointed out, has a high degree of mobility and political, social, and economic interdependence. There is an increasing use of facilities in one municipality by those who reside or work in a different municipality. The payment of taxes in a metropolitan area may have only slight relationship to the use and enjoyment which residents make of other areas in the district. Defendants argue effectively that the indiscriminate encouragement of commerce and industry in a particular municipality may detrimentally and irretrievably affect policies and plans for the development of parks and open spaces and frustrate well-considered housing policies for both low-income and moderate-income residences.

The Fiscal Disparities Act recognizes that to some extent the location of commercial-industrial development may be irrelevant to the question of the cost of services which are added to a municipality's budget occasioned by the location of such a development within its boundaries. It should be borne in mind that all commercial-industrial property except 40 percent of its increment since January 1971 remains in the tax base for the municipality where it is located.

In other words, in terms of traditional balancing of benefits and burdens, the benefits conferred on residents of a particular municipality because of the location of commercial-industrial development within its boundaries may far exceed the burdens imposed on that municipality by virtue of the additional cost of servicing and policing the particular development which has located there. It is the theory of the Fiscal Disparities Act that the residents of highly developed commercial-industrial areas do enjoy direct benefits from the existence of adjacent municipalities which provide open spaces, lakes, parks, golf courses, zoos, fairgrounds, low-density housing areas, churches, schools, and hospitals.

We have concluded that the statutory scheme for revenue sharing embodied in c. 24 reaches a constitutional accommodation between the tax burdens imposed and the benefits derived therefrom to a degree which satisfies the requirements of the uniformity provisions of Minn.Const. art. 9, § 1. * * * The legislature enjoys a familiarity with the problems of fiscal disparities which is denied the courts. The presumption of constitutionality which the statute enjoys has not been overcome by any explicit demonstration that its application results in a 'hostile and oppressive discrimination' against the residents of particular units of government. Accordingly, the judgment of the district court is reversed.

NOTES AND QUESTIONS

1. *Justifying Redistribution.* The Minnesota Supreme Court suggests two justifications for redistributing some of the benefits of commercial property growth across the region. First, tax base redistribution may mute some of the intense interlocal competition for business and industry, a competition which, the court suggests, may have negative consequences even for the communities that succeed in attracting industry. Second, the court points out that the communities in which new businesses are located benefit from the services and amenities available in other communities. Indeed, as Neal Peirce suggested at the outset of this chapter, those services and amenities in the communities outside the locality that has enjoyed commercial property growth may directly affect the ability of that locality to attract new business investment. In effect, the court found the Fiscal Disparities Act less a redistributive measure and more a reflection of the fact that the region as a whole functions as a unit for the attraction of economic growth. Are you persuaded?

Minnesota created a second tax-base sharing region with the passage of the Range Fiscal Disparities Act, Minn. St. Ch. 276A (1998). This act applies to allocate revenues generated by mineral production in a rural part of the state. The state supreme court upheld the Act against the same kinds of legal challenges it rejected in the main case. *See* Walker v. Zuehlke, 642 N.W.2d 745 (Mn. 2002). Is the rationale for urban, metropolitan area tax sharing compelling in a rural setting?

2.   *Political Coalitions and Regional Sharing.* Professor Myron Orfield, formerly a Minnesota legislator, is a key proponent of regional governance, and especially the redistribution of the benefits of regional growth to poorer areas within the region. His book, Metropolitics: A Regional Agenda for Community and Stability (Brookings Inst. Press 1997), describes the formation of a political coalition that has continued to promote region-wide solutions in the Twin Cities area. A subsequent article details the legislative obstacles to passage of the Fiscal Disparities Act and makes the regionalist case for tax-base sharing. *See* Myron Orfield and Nicholas Wallace, The Minnesota Fiscal Disparities Act of 1971: The Twin Cities' Struggle and Blueprint for Regional Cooperation, 33 Wm. Mitchell L. Rev. 591 (2007). According to Orfield, in most metropolitan areas, the population breakdown is: 20–40% in central cities; 25–30% in older declining suburbs; 10–15% in low tax-base developing suburbs; remainder in high tax base wealthy suburbs—what Orfield calls the "favored quarter." Myron Orfield, Conflict or Consensus? Forty Years of Minnesota Metropolitan Politics, Vol. 16, No. 4 Brookings Review 31 (1998). In his view, there is a natural alliance in the interests of central cities and older suburbs, many of which face common problems of aging infrastructure, high social service needs, and declining tax bases. In practice, however, central city-older suburb coalitions have proven difficult to create and sustain. For a review of the barriers to and possibilities for such local self-interest-based regional coalitions, *see* Sheryll D. Cashin, Localism, Self-Interest, and the Tyranny of the Favored Quarter: Addressing the Barriers to New Regionalism, 88 Geo. L.J. 1985 (2000).

3.   *Other Forms of Regional Tax-Base Sharing.* The Fiscal Disparities Act provides for a transfer from high-growth to low-growth localities within the Twin Cities area. Other approaches look to region-wide taxes to support specific programs or services. *See, e.g.,* Georgette C. Poindexter, Towards a Legal Framework for Regional Redistribution of Poverty-Related Expenses, 47 Wash.U.J.Urb. & Contemp.L. 3 (1995) (calling for regional taxation to finance social services for the poor, who, in most metropolitan areas, are concentrated in the central cities). Other areas use regional taxes to fund regional services, like mass transit, or cultural facilities that may be located in the central city but draw visitors from around the region. *See* Allan D. Wallis, The Third Wave: Current Trends in Regional Governance, 83 Nat'l Civ. Rev. 290, 305–06 (1994) (describing regional taxes in Denver metropolitan area that support museums, the zoo, botanical gardens, a performing arts center and a baseball stadium). In two metropolitan areas, Louisville-Jefferson County, Kentucky, and Dayton-Montgomery County,

Ohio, localities engaged in voluntary tax-base sharing to fund new economic development programs. *See id.* at 297–98; H.V. Savitch, et al, The Regional City and Public Partnerships 65, 73 *in* In The National Interest: The 1990 Urban Summit (Century Foundation Press 1991).

Could regional financing mechanisms be used to address the fiscal inequalities among school districts? What obstacles, political and legal, would you anticipate? *See* Kirk J. Stark, Note, Rethinking Statewide Taxation of Nonresidential Property for Public Schools, 102 Yale L.J. 805 (1992) for an evaluation of a proposed statewide property tax for schools similar to the Minneapolis scheme. *See also* Myron Orfield, The Region and Taxation: School Finance, Cities, and the Hope for Regional Reform, 55 Buff. L. Rev. 91 (2007). The Supreme Court of Wisconsin, in Buse v. Smith, 247 N.W.2d 141 (1976), invalidated a state law that required wealthy school districts to pay a portion of their property tax revenues into a state fund for redistribution to less affluent districts. The court concluded that the "negative aid" provisions violated state requirements of uniform taxation. Similarly, the Texas Supreme Court, in one of the *Edgewood* cases described in the previous section, invalidated a state law that created county education districts ("CEDs") for purposes of property tax levy and distribution. Because both the tax rate and the distribution of the proceeds were set by the state legislature, the Texas Supreme Court determined that the CEDs were "purely ministerial" and, thus, that the tax, although nominally imposed by the CEDs, was actually a state tax and therefore a violation of a state constitutional provision forbidding a state property tax. Carrollton-Farmers Branch Ind. School Dist. v. Edgewood Ind. School Dist., 826 S.W.2d 489, 500–03 (Tex.1992). Had the CEDs been given greater autonomy, the regional property tax, intended to equalize the fiscal disparities of local school districts, might have been sustained.

4. *Preventing the Race to the Bottom?* California has taken a different approach to regional competition for tax revenues. It seeks to stop the intermunicipal competition to lure vehicle dealerships and big box retailers by prohibiting governmental financial incentives for retailer relocation within the same market area. *See* Cal.Gov.Code § 53084 (2007). A state appellate court applied the law to invalidate a sales tax rebate offered by a city to attract a large office supply company from a nearby municipality. The city had offered a total financial assistance package estimated at $18 million over five years. *See* City of Carson v. City of La Mirada, 125 Cal.App.4th 532 (Cal. App. 2004). In 2014, the issue was in the courts again, as the California appellate court held that the statute does not bar local financial assistance to a company more than two years after it relocated. City of Palmdale v. City of Lancaster, 223 Cal.App. 4th 978 (Cal. App. 2014).

5. *Voluntary Burden Sharing in Interlocal Relationships.* Professor Clayton Gillette has argued that local governments in metropolitan regions have good reason to engage in intermunicipal "burden sharing," which he defined as "interlocal agreements to alleviate socio-economic disparities within a region." *See* Clayton P. Gillette, Regionalization and Interlocal

Bargains, 76 N.Y.U. L. Rev. 190, 194 (2001). Pointing to the growing evidence that suburban prosperity is closely linked to central city health, Gillette stressed that affluent suburbs have a selfish reason to be concerned about the economic well-being of the poorer segments of the metropolitan area. If that is the case, he suggested, the relative scarcity of those burden-sharing agreements must be due to legal principles, organizational structures, and the costs of monitoring compliance. His proposal prefers voluntary redistributional regional efforts over formalized and mandatory alternatives. For criticism of Gillette's proposal, *see* Laurie Reynolds, Intergovernmental Cooperation, Metropolitan Equity, and the New Regionalism, 78 Wash. L. Rev. 93, 149–153 (2003). As you read the next section, ask yourself whether any of the cooperative structures described in the cases could be used to accomplish burden-sharing and whether, in your estimation, they are likely to be used.

C. INTERLOCAL COOPERATION

Local government units engage in intergovernmental cooperative ventures for a number of reasons. Most commonly, a government will determine that a particular service can be offered more efficiently and more cheaply if the service territory is enlarged to encompass the land base of one or more other local government jurisdictions. Public transportation, sewage, and waste disposal are a few of the services for which economies of scale can frequently be achieved if local governments combine forces. Other important incentives for intergovernmental cooperation include a lack of qualified personnel or the unavailability of adequate facilities within a small local government's territory. For many local governments, the ability to provide better and cheaper services without a loss of governmental autonomy makes intergovernmental cooperation an attractive alternative to formal government consolidation and other regionalization initiatives (which are discussed in Section C of this Chapter). Intergovernmental cooperation is widespread: a survey conducted in the early 1980s estimated that more than half of the country's local government units participate in some sort of intergovernmental effort. More than 40 states specifically authorize intergovernmental cooperation, either by constitutional provision, statutory enabling acts, or both. In fact, many states actively encourage intergovernmental efforts, primarily through outright incentive grants, financial planning assistance, or technical support. *See* Advisory Commission on Intergovernmental Relations, State Laws Governing Local Government Structure and Administration 9 (1993). As the next case illustrates, threshold questions about the scope of local government power to cooperate can derail intergovernmental agreements.

CITY OF DECATUR V. DEKALB COUNTY

Supreme Court of Georgia
713 S.E.2d 846 (2011)

HINES, JUSTICE.

This is an appeal by plaintiffs City of Decatur, City of Chamblee, City of Doraville, and City of Stone Mountain ("Cities") from an order of the Superior Court of DeKalb County granting summary judgment to defendant DeKalb County ("County") in this litigation for alleged breach of an intergovernmental agreement ("IGA") entered into by the County and the Cities for the distribution of funds generated by a special sales tax instituted pursuant to the Homestead Option Sales and Use Tax Act ("HOST"), OCGA § 48–8–100 et seq. The superior court found that the IGA is unconstitutional as violative of the Intergovernmental Contracts Clause of the Georgia Constitution, 1983 Ga. Const., Art. IX, Sec. III, Par. I(a). For the reasons that follow, we affirm.

* * * In January 1998, the County and the Cities, which are municipalities located within the county, entered into a 49-year agreement for the expenditure of tax revenue generated by a HOST, which had been approved by the County's electorate in 1997. The County and the Cities disagreed about the calculation of the funds to be distributed to the Cities, and in 2000, the Cities filed suit against the County initially seeking damages for breach of the IGA, conversion, and attorney fees. * * *

The analysis begins and ends with our State Constitution. It sets debt limits for counties, municipalities, and other political subdivisions, and provides that new debt cannot be incurred without the assent of a majority of its qualified voters. 1983 Ga. Const., Art. IX, Sec. V, Par. I(a). Furthermore, the general rule is that a local government "may not enter into a contract that lasts longer than that government's term of office." Greene County School Dist. v. Greene County, 278 Ga. 849, 850, 607 S.E.2d 881 (2005); OCGA § 36–30–3(a). However, the Intergovernmental Contracts Clause found in Art. IX, Sec. III, Par. I(a) of the 1983 Georgia Constitution "provides an exception to that rule, and allows political subdivisions of the State to contract with one another or with other public agencies, so long as the term of the contract does not exceed 50 years." Greene County School Dist. v. Greene County, supra at 850, 607 S.E.2d 881. This exception does not give the State and its institutions and subdivisions the authority " 'to enter into any and every contract which they might in their discretion deem advisable.' " Id. The agreement must satisfy certain requirements. It must involve "the provision of services, or . . . the joint or separate use of facilities or equipment" and "deal with activities, services, or facilities which the contracting parties are authorized by law to undertake or provide." (Punctuation omitted.) Id. at

851, 607 S.E.2d 881; Nations v. Downtown Dev. Auth., 255 Ga. 324, 328, 338 S.E.2d 240 (1986).

Thus, the validity of the IGA at issue in this case hinges on whether, in substance, it is for the provision of "services" or "the joint or separate use of facilities or equipment" authorized by law. If the language of the contract is plain, unambiguous, and capable of only one reasonable interpretation, that interpretation must control, and no construction of the contract is required or even permissible. Unified Govt. of Athens-Clarke County v. McCrary, 280 Ga. 901, 903, 635 S.E.2d 150 (2006). The language of the present IGA is plain and unambiguous; it is an agreement about how to divide and distribute HOST revenues between DeKalb County and the Cities, with the Cities agreeing "to expend the monies disbursed . . . solely for capital outlay projects to be located within the geographical boundaries of DeKalb County and to be owned, operated or both either by the County, one of more Municipalities or any combination thereof." The focus and clear purpose of the agreement is to provide a formula for the distribution of the HOST revenues; simply, it is a revenue-sharing agreement. * * *

This IGA does not involve "the joint or separate use of facilities." Compare Reed v. State of Ga., 265 Ga. 458(1), 458 S.E.2d 113 (1995) (construction and operation of water projects); Clayton County Airport Auth. v. State of Ga., 265 Ga. 24, 24–25(1), 453 S.E.2d 8 (1995) (expansion and use of airport); Berry v. City of East Point, 277 Ga.App. 649, 652–653(6)(a), 627 S.E.2d 391 (2006) (sewer project arrangement); Hay v. Newton County, 246 Ga.App. 44, 47(3), 538 S.E.2d 181 (2000) (acquisition and development of industrial park). Nor can it credibly be deemed an agreement for the provision of authorized "services." "Services" in the context of a "contract for services" has been defined as "[a]n intangible commodity in the form of human effort, such as labor, skill, or advice." Black's Law Dictionary, p. 1372 (7th ed. 1999). Such a definition comports with this Court's decisions addressing intergovernmental agreements that are agreements for authorized services. See and compare Ambac Indem. Corp. v. Akridge, 262 Ga. 773, 425 S.E.2d 637 (1993) (contract for garbage and solid waste disposal services); Youngblood v. State of Ga., 259 Ga. 864, 866–867(4), 388 S.E.2d 671 (1990) (contract for services involving construction of a recreational facility); Frazer v. City of Albany, 245 Ga. 399, 400(2), 265 S.E.2d 581 (1980) (contract to finance construction of a civic center and for the services of the hiring of a manager to advise and consult regarding its construction). The fact that the present IGA requires the Cities to expend the tax proceeds in accordance with the mandates of the Homestead Option Sales and Use Tax Act, OCGA § 48–8–102, does not transform it into either a contract for services or one for the use of facilities. Indeed, the true nature of the IGA as a revenue-sharing contract is well-demonstrated by the very pleadings in this litigation filed by the Cities. The complaint unequivocally stated, inter alia, that the Cities objected to the lack of an equalization provision in the then proposed HOST legislation; that in order to secure the Cities' support for the legislation, the County promised the Cities that it would "enter into an intergovernmental agreement with them under which each municipality would receive an annual 'equalization payment'" from the capital improvement portion of the HOST proceeds; that such promise was memorialized by a "Tax Allocation Agreement," the express purpose and intent of which was to "equalize the HOST tax reduction benefits to all DeKalb County citizens"; and accordingly, the prepared IGA "followed the tax equalization intent and effect of the Tax Allocation Agreement."

Consequently, it must be concluded that the agreement between DeKalb County and the Cities is not a valid intergovernmental contract under the 1983 Georgia Constitution, Art. IX, Sec. III, Par. I(a), and therefore, that summary judgment was properly granted to DeKalb County.

NOTES AND QUESTIONS

1. *Sales Tax as Property Tax Relief.* DeKalb County's HOST was approved by voters in 1996. When implemented, the HOST increased the sales tax county-wide by one penny on the dollar. The idea behind HOST is that it provides property tax relief (80% of the revenues are essentially rebated to homeowners through an increase in their property tax homestead exemption), while some of the revenues (20%) are used by the governments in the county for infrastructure improvements. Because HOST revenues can only be used to offset taxes levied by the county, city residents (who pay both city and county property taxes) received less tax relief overall than county residents. The purpose of the intergovernmental agreement was to equalize the tax benefit for all residents of DeKalb County by distributing to city governments revenues to reflect the savings city residents would have received if they had lived in the unincorporated part of DeKalb County. The legal battles began as a fight over the formula that should be used for equalization purposes, but later the county argued that the entire agreement was impermissible.

2. *Scope of Cooperative Power.* Is the court's strict construction of the intergovernmental cooperation act consistent with the law's clear policy of fostering cohesive, supra-municipal solutions to challenges and problems facing local governments? Does tax-sharing present any particular evil or accountability problem that other types of cooperative ventures might not? If not, what could explain the court's unwillingness to authorize this type of cooperation?

3. *Types of Intergovernmental Cooperation.* Intergovernmental agreements usually take one of three forms: (1) contract for services, whereby

one government pays another to provide a service; (2) joint services agreement, in which two or more governments provide a service jointly; and (3) collaborative establishment of a new governmental unit, in which a separate entity is formed to provide the desired service. *See* Advisory Commission on Intergovernmental Relations, State and Local Roles in the Federal System 327 (1982). Although the categorization is by no means a rigid one, and the lines of distinction among the different types of governmental cooperation may blur as local governments experiment with new ways of collaboration, the framework is a helpful starting point. As you examine the legal issues presented in the next few cases, consider whether the formal structure of the legal relationship between or among local governments affects its enforceability, the accountability it provides its citizens, the transparency of its operations, and the political and financial costs it will create.

1. CONTRACT FOR SERVICES

DURANGO TRANSPORTATION, INC. V. CITY OF DURANGO
Colorado Court of Appeals
824 P.2d 48 (1991)

Opinion by JUDGE DAVIDSON.

This case comes before us on remand from the Colorado Supreme Court for consideration of whether the intergovernmental agreement between the City of Durango and the County of La Plata is valid. * * *

This action arose out of an intergovernmental agreement between the City of Durango (City) and La Plata County (County) which provided that the City would operate a mass transit system between areas in the City and the County. Pursuant to this agreement, the City establishes fares with advice and recommendation from the Transit Advisory Board which is made up of both City and County appointees.

Durango Transportation, Inc., (DTI) a private corporation which has authority from the Public Utilities Commission (PUC) to operate a mass transit system within the County, brought this action alleging that the defendants, the City, the County, and the Advisory Board, were infringing upon this authority. Among other things, DTI argued that the City could not operate beyond its jurisdiction without PUC authority and, thus, that the agreement which purports to allow such an operation is invalid.

* * *

On remand the sole remaining issue to be addressed is whether the intergovernmental agreement between the City and the County is valid.

I.

DTI first contends that the agreement is unlawful under the Colorado Constitution and statutory law. We disagree.

The constitutional provision governing intergovernmental agreements, Colo. Const. art. XIV, § 18(2)(a), provides as follows:

"Nothing in this constitution shall be construed to prohibit the state or any of its political subdivisions from cooperating or contracting with one another or with the government of the United States to provide any function, service, or facility lawfully authorized to each of the cooperating or contracting units, including the sharing of costs, the imposition of taxes, or the incurring of debt."

Similarly, the enabling statutory provision regarding such agreements states:

"Governments may cooperate or contract with one another to provide any function, service, or facility lawfully authorized to each of the cooperating or contracting units, including the sharing of costs, the imposition of taxes, or the incurring of debt, only if such cooperation or contracts are authorized by each party thereto with the approval of its legislative body or other authority having the power to so approve." Section 29–1–203(1), C.R.S. (1986 Repl.Vol. 12A)

DTI argues that the constitutional and statutory phrase "lawfully authorized to each" means that each contracting entity must be fully authorized to perform the subject activity. Essentially, DTI is arguing that this phrase means that the City can only contract with the County to perform those functions which the City could lawfully perform alone. Thus, according to DTI, although the City can operate a transit system within its own boundaries without PUC authority, pursuant to *City & County of Denver v. Public Utilities Commission*, 181 Colo. 38, 507 P.2d 871 (1973), it cannot operate beyond these boundaries and into the County without PUC authority. Therefore, it asserts that any agreement between the City and County which allows the City to operate in such a manner is invalid.

Defendants, however, contend that this phrase means only that each contracting entity must be lawfully authorized to perform the subject activity within its respective jurisdiction. Thus, according to defendants, since both the City and County are authorized to operate mass transit systems within their respective boundaries, the activity is "lawfully authorized to each" and the agreement is valid.

In our view, the phrase "lawfully authorized to each" is susceptible to either interpretation and, thus, is ambiguous. Therefore, to determine the meaning of this phrase, we must look to the statute as a whole and construe it in light of the legislative purpose it was designed to accomplish. * * *

The legislative declaration to the enabling intergovernmental agreements statute provides that the purpose of this statute is:

"[To permit and encourage] governments to make the most efficient and effective use of their powers and responsibilities by cooperating and contracting with other governments, and to this end this [statute] shall be liberally construed." Section 29–1–201, C.R.S. (1986 Repl.Vol. 12A)

In addition, counties have not only the powers which are expressly conferred on them, but also such incidental implied powers "as are reasonably necessary to carry out powers expressly conferred." *Adams County Golf, Inc. v. Colorado Department of Revenue*, 199 Colo. 423, 610 P.2d 97 (1980); *Farnik v. Board of County Commissioners*, 139 Colo. 481, 341 P.2d 467 (1959).

Similarly, cities also have "such implied and incidental powers, authority, and privileges as may be reasonably necessary, proper, convenient, or useful" to carry out the powers and authority granted to them. Section 31–15–101(2), C.R.S. (1986 Repl.Vol. 12B); see also Colo. Const. art. XX, § 6.

* * *

If the interpretation urged by DTI were adopted, then intergovernmental agreements could be made only when both entities had pre-existing functional and territorial authority to engage in the subject activity. Such an interpretation would place significant limits on the type of allowable intergovernmental agreements because at least one of the contracting entities would have to have pre-existing authority to operate outside its jurisdictional boundaries. In addition, if this interpretation were accepted, it would appear there would be no need for the constitutional or statutory provisions authorizing intergovernmental cooperation since at least one of the entities could perform the subject activity without the cooperation of the other.

In our view, to adopt this interpretation would not encourage governments to make the most efficient and effective use of their powers by cooperating and contracting with other governments as intended by the General Assembly. *See* § 29–1–201. Rather, we conclude it is more in accord with the statutory scheme to construe the phrase "lawfully authorized to each" to mean only that each entity must have the authority to perform the subject activity within its jurisdictional boundaries.

* * * [H]ere there are two governmental entities which control the terms of the service provided to the citizens. And, just like the citizens in the City, the citizens of the County here do "have the power to effect change in the governing board responsible for the quality of service provided by a county owned mass transit system operating within county boundaries." *City of Durango v. Durango Transportation, Inc., supra.*

Thus, since each respective group of citizenry in the City and County can effect change through the electoral process, it follows that if they are dissatisfied with an intergovernmental contract entered into by their responsible governing boards, they can also exercise their rights by recalling the elected officers who approved the contracts.

Thus, there is no need for PUC oversight here since the contracting boards are directly responsible to their respective electorate. Recognition of the intent that these agreements be subject to the control of the citizenry is also evinced by the intergovernmental agreement statute which provides that such agreements may be entered into "only if [they] are authorized by each party thereto with the approval of its legislative body or other authority having the power to so approve." Section 29–1–203(1), C.R.S. (1986 Repl.Vol. 12A). * * *

II.

DTI also contends that the intergovernmental agreement is invalid because there is not equal participation between the City and County in operating the transit system. Specifically, DTI argues that the City is solely responsible for the management and operation of the transit system whereas the County has no role in its operation, nor does it assume any liability with respect to the system. Thus, DTI argues, "all the County did was give the City the authority to operate a bus system in the county without PUC authority," and such an attempt to circumvent the PUC's authority should not be validated as a "true" intergovernmental agreement. We disagree.

* * *

There is absolutely nothing in this statute which indicates that financial or management participation is required of each of the contracting entities. In addition, DTI has not cited any authority for its position that an arrangement, such as the one here, invalidates an intergovernmental agreement. Therefore, the fact that the County, by its own admission, was not in a financial position to contribute to the operation of the system or to incur any potential liability from its operation does not in any way impair or erode the contractual arrangement.

To the contrary, the "lead agency" concept in intergovernmental agreements, whereby one of the contracting entities is empowered to perform a function for the other contracting parties, has been endorsed by other jurisdictions which also have considered this issue. * * *

UTAH COUNTY V. IVIE
Utah Supreme Court
137 P.3d 797 (2006)

DURRANT, JUSTICE:

This is the second case in which Appellants (collectively "Spring Canyon") have appeared before us to challenge local governments' attempts to condemn Spring Canyon property for the construction of a road. The road would connect two Provo City streets over an island of unincorporated Utah County. In the first case, Provo City v. Ivie, we held that Provo City did not have the statutory or constitutional power necessary to condemn Spring Canyon's property because the property is located in unincorporated Utah County.

BACKGROUND

In 1970, Utah County and Provo City first planned to, at some point, build a collector street between Provo Canyon Road at 4525 North and University Avenue at 4800 North. In June of 2002, traffic congestion in the area was such that Provo City instituted a condemnation action to acquire the property needed to build the road. Although the proposed road would connect two Provo City streets, it would cross over an island of unincorporated Utah County land owned by Appellants Kay J. Ivie, Devon R. Ivie, Kristine J. Lee, Edward R. Lee, Spring Canyon Limited Partnership, and Canyon Acres Limited Partnership (collectively "Spring Canyon"). The district court in that case originally granted an order of immediate occupancy, but, following an interlocutory appeal, we reversed the order and held that Provo City did not have the power to condemn land outside its corporate boundaries because (1) Provo is not a charter city and could therefore not avail itself of the extraterritorial condemnation power granted in article XI, section 5(b) of the Utah Constitution, and (2) no other then-existing statute granted them the power to do so. Provo City v. Ivie, 2004 UT 30, ¶ 18, 94 P.3d 206.

In May of 2003, during the pendency of its appeal, Provo City entered into an agreement with Utah County purportedly under the Interlocal Cooperation Act, Utah Code Ann. §§ 11–13–101 to –314 (2003 & Supp.2005) (the "ICA"). The Agreement provided that Utah County would condemn the necessary property, and Provo City would pay all expenses required to do so. In May of 2004, following the Court's decision in Provo City v. Ivie, Utah County filed the condemnation complaint and motion for order of immediate occupancy that are at issue in this case. Spring Canyon subsequently filed a motion to dismiss based on the theory that

Utah County was unlawfully "lend[ing] its condemning powers to Provo City." * * *

[Spring Canyon's motion to dismiss was denied, and the supreme court granted its interlocutory appeal of that ruling.]

ANALYSIS

I. UTAH COUNTY'S AGREEMENT WITH PROVO CITY DOES NOT LIMIT ITS POWER TO CONDEMN SPRING CANYON'S PROPERTY

Spring Canyon's appeal of the district court's denial of its motion to dismiss depends entirely on the effect, if any, that the Agreement between Utah County and Provo City has on Utah County's condemnation power. We will first discuss the validity of the Agreement and whether it limits Utah County's condemnation power. * * *

A. *Utah County and Provo City Were Authorized to Enter into the Agreement Pursuant to Their General Contracting Power*

Spring Canyon argues that because Provo City lacks the power to condemn the subject property, both the Agreement and the exercise by Utah County of its eminent domain power pursuant to the Agreement were unlawful and invalid under the ICA. Spring Canyon's primary argument is that the ICA requires that all parties to an agreement have the power to do everything contemplated by the agreement. We conclude that local governments have authority to enter into agreements pursuant to their general contracting powers so long as each entity does not exceed its individual power, and, although the ICA provides for contracting only where all parties to an interlocal agreement have the power to do all acts under the agreement, the ICA does not abrogate local governments' general contracting power.

We first examine the limits of local governments' general contracting power. Before the Legislature passed the ICA in 1965, local governments had the power to contract with one another under general powers granted by the state constitution and various statutes. * * * The limit on these general contracting powers was presumably that no governmental party to a contract could exceed its individual powers in fulfilling its obligation under the contract. Thus, two governmental entities of unequal power could contract in their areas of inequality so long as neither exceeded its own powers in performing the contract.

The Agreement in this case does not require any performance by either Utah County or Provo City that is beyond the individual authority of that entity. The terms of the Agreement material to this appeal require Utah County to condemn the property for the road and Provo City to pay the expenses of condemnation, installation, and maintenance of the road. Utah County has authority to condemn property under Utah Code section 17–50–302(2)(a)(ii). Provo City has authority "to appropriate money for any purpose that, in the judgment of the municipal legislative body, provides for the safety, health, prosperity, moral well-being, peace, order, comfort, or convenience of the inhabitants of the municipality." *Id.* § 10–8–2(3) (Supp.2005). Paying for the construction and for the maintenance of a public road certainly falls within Provo City's authority under this provision. Thus, absent the ICA, the Agreement is a valid exercise of both Utah County's and Provo City's general contracting powers. We are called upon to determine, however, whether the ICA operates to limit these general contracting powers.

Spring Canyon argues that because the ICA, specifically Utah Code section 11–13–212(1)(a), allows for interlocal agreements only where each party has the power to do all acts contemplated in the agreement, it must also preclude all other agreements between local governmental entities. Utah County counters that Spring Canyon's proposed interpretation would lead to logically inconsistent results because a local government could condemn property for a street if a private party paid the expenses, see 7 Patrick J. Rohan & Melvin A. Reskin, Nichols on Eminent Domain, § 5.02[3] (3d ed.2006), but could not do the same where another local government pays the expenses. We conclude that although the ICA does not provide a source of power for cooperative action between local governments of unequal power in their area of inequality, it also does not preclude local governments from contracting with each other in these areas under their general contracting power.

It is true that Utah Code section 11–13–212 only allows agencies to contract with one another "to perform any service, activity, or undertaking which each public agency . . . is authorized by law to perform." Utah Code Ann. § 11–13–212(1)(a) (2003). We further stated in *CP National Corp. v. Public Service Commission* that "the intent of the [ICA] appears to be to allow the municipalities collectively to exercise powers which they already possess individually." 638 P.2d 519, 521 (Utah 1981). But while these sources support Spring Canyon's argument that the ICA only authorizes contracting among local governments of equal power, they do not support the argument that the ICA precludes all other contracts between local governments. Spring Canyon offers no evidence that the Legislature intended the ICA to have that effect.

Indeed, the ICA's stated purpose is "to permit local governmental units to make the most efficient use of their powers by enabling them to cooperate with other localities on a basis of mutual advantage" and also "to provide the benefit of economy of scale." Utah Code Ann. § 11–13–102 (2003). This purpose statement demonstrates that the Legislature intended the ICA to expand rather than limit local governments' ability to cooperate. Additionally, we can find no provision of the ICA that removes existing powers from local governments. Where the Legislature has not clearly limited the general contracting powers of local governments, we construe those powers broadly. State v. Hutchinson, 624 P.2d 1116, 1126–27 (Utah 1980). Thus, the ICA does not abrogate local governments' power to contract among themselves under their general contracting power.

In sum, although the ICA did not empower Utah County and Provo City to enter into the Agreement, the Agreement is nevertheless valid under their general contracting powers. * * *

ENGLISH V. BOARD OF EDUCATION OF TOWN OF BOONTON

United States Court of Appeals
301 F.3d 69 (3d Cir.2002)

BECKER, CHIEF JUDGE.

* * * Under New Jersey law, Lincoln Park has an obligation to educate, at its own expense, all persons, between the ages of five and twenty who are domiciled within the district. N.J.S.A. § 18A:38–1. New Jersey law, however, does not require that Lincoln Park construct and maintain its own schools in order to fulfill this obligation. Rather, Lincoln Park, like any New Jersey school district, may enter into a send-receive relationship with another district whereby it sends its pupils to the receiving district's schools for one grade or more, N.J.S.A. § 18A:38–8, in return for a tuition payment that does not exceed the "actual cost" of the students enrolled, N.J.S.A. § 18A:38–19, with "actual cost" defined in detail by the New Jersey Administrative Code. See N.J.Admin.Code § 6A:23–3.1.

Over fifty years ago, rather than build its own high school, Lincoln Park elected to enter into a send-receive relationship with neighboring Boonton for the education of its high school students, and that relationship has continued to the present day. Although the Lincoln Park-Boonton relationship has persisted for more than half a century, it has not been without its share of acrimony, as there have been at least four major lawsuits between the districts on topics ranging from the Lincoln Park representative's right to receive information to overcharging of tuition to Lincoln Park. See English I, 135 F.Supp.2d at 591.

According to New Jersey law, when a sending district's students "comprise less than 10 percent of the total enrollment of the pupils in the grades of the receiving district in which the pupils of the sending district will be enrolled, the sending district shall have no representation on the receiving board of education." N.J.S.A. § 18A:38–8.2(a)(1). When, however, the sending district's pupils "comprise at least 10 percent of the total enrollment of the pupils in the grades of the receiving district in which the pupils of the sending district will be enrolled," the sending district's board of education is entitled to appoint one member to serve on the receiving district's board. N.J.S.A. § 18A:38–8.2(a)(2). The level of representation of the sending district remains fixed at one representative regardless of whether students from the sending district constitute 10% or 90% of the relevant population of the receiving district's schools.

* * * [F]or the 2001–02 school year, Lincoln Park provided 52% of the high school's combined student population. Additionally, according to the most recent census data, Lincoln Park's total population amounts to 56% of the combined population of the two towns but, despite its larger population, Lincoln Park, as per N.J.S.A. § 18A:38–8.2, is entitled to only one representative on the Boonton Board. Moreover, state law limits the vote of the Lincoln Park representative on the Boonton Board to the following issues:

> a. Tuition to be charged the sending district by the receiving district and the bill lists or contracts for the purchase, operation or maintenance of facilities, equipment and instructional materials to be used in the education of the pupils of the sending district;

> b. New capital construction to be utilized by sending district pupils;

> c. Appointment, transfer or removal of teaching staff members providing services to pupils of the sending district, including any teaching staff member who is a member of the receiving district's central administrative staff; and

> d. Addition or deletion of curricular and extracurricular programs involving pupils of the sending district.

N.J.S.A. § 18A:38–8.1.

State law mandates that neither the sending nor the receiving district may sever its send-receive relationship without the approval of the State's Commissioner of Education ("Commissioner"). N.J.S.A. § 18A:38–13. To obtain approval, the district seeking to withdraw from the relationship must submit a feasibility study addressing the educational and financial implications of severance and the effect on the racial composition of the student population of each of the districts. *Id.* If the Commissioner concludes that "no substantial negative impact" will result from the severance, he or she "shall grant" the severance. *Id.* Despite the grievances of some of its residents, Lincoln Park has apparently never officially sought to withdraw from its send-receive relationship with Boonton.

* * * The plaintiffs alleged that N.J.S.A. § 18A:38–8.2's allocation of one representative to a sending district on the receiving district's board was unconstitutional as applied because it deprived English and other residents of Lincoln Park of their right to proportional representation. Upon cross-motions for summary judgment, the District Court granted

summary judgment for the plaintiffs, concluding that the constitutional principle of "one person, one vote" had been violated by N.J.S.A. § 18A:38–8.2 as applied to Lincoln Park. * * *

In *Holt Civic Club v. City of Tuscaloosa*, 439 U.S. 60, 69, 99 S.Ct. 383, 58 L.Ed.2d 292 (1978), the Supreme Court expressly recognized geographical limits on the "one person, one vote" principle. There the Court addressed the constitutionality of an Alabama statute that subjected Holt, an unincorporated community on the outskirts of the city of Tuscaloosa, to the city's "police jurisdiction," which meant that Holt was subject to Tuscaloosa's police and sanitary regulations and the criminal jurisdiction of Tuscaloosa's courts, as well as the city's power to license businesses, trades, and professions. Despite Tuscaloosa's exercise of "police jurisdiction" over Holt, the statute did not entitle Holt residents to vote in Tuscaloosa elections, an exclusion which was challenged as a violation of "one person, one vote."

In concluding that the scheme was constitutional, the Court distinguished prior cases in which a violation of the "one person, one vote" principle had been found as those where the franchise had been denied "to individuals who were physically resident within the geographic boundaries of the governmental entity concerned." *Id.* at 68. The court held that, because Holt residents lived outside the boundaries of Tuscaloosa, the governmental unit at issue, "one person, one vote" was not implicated and the scheme needed to survive only rational basis review to be upheld. Applying rational basis review, the Court concluded that the scheme bore "some rational relationship to a legitimate state purpose," *id.* at 70, and upheld Tuscaloosa's extraterritorial exercise of municipal powers over Holt. *Id.* at 74–75.

* * * We read *Holt* as meaning that strict scrutiny will be applied to the exclusion of non-residents from the elections of a particular governmental entity only when that unit of government exercises a level of control over the non-residents' lives close to or equal to that which it exercises over those who actually reside within its borders. However, the mere fact that a municipality's actions may have an impact—even a substantial impact—on non-residents does not entitle those non-residents to vote in the municipality's elections. *See Holt*, 439 U.S. at 69–70 (noting that despite the fact that a city's decisions may have "dramatic extraterritorial effects" on non-residents, those non-residents are not entitled to vote in the city's elections).

Applying this tempered view of *Holt*, we are constrained to hold that the residents of Lincoln Park have no right to vote in the election of Boonton's School Board. This is not a case in which the Boonton Board "exercis[es] precisely the same governmental powers over residents of [Lincoln Park] as it does over those residing within its [district's] limits."

Id. at 72 n. 8. Lincoln Park residents are subject to the extraterritorial powers of the Boonton Board only with respect to their high school-aged children. For matters concerning K–8 education, the residents of Lincoln Park exercise exclusive control through their own school board elected solely by Lincoln Park residents. Moreover, the Boonton Board's control over high school education is only one of its many responsibilities affecting the residents of Boonton. The Board is also responsible for the district's K–8 educational program, as well as matters that affect the district as a whole, such as school facilities and the district's central administrative staff.

* * * New Jersey has legitimate reasons for limiting the representation of Lincoln Park in the Boonton Board's decisions. As noted above, under New Jersey law there is always the possibility that Lincoln Park, as a sending district, might sever its relationship with Boonton. *See* N.J.S.A. § 18A:38–13. As a result, it can fairly be said that Lincoln Park residents do not have the same vested interest in the long-term affairs of the Boonton school district—such as capital improvements, employee pension plans, and other long-term commitments—as do Boonton residents. Moreover, as discussed earlier, some of the items on which a sending district's representative is entitled to vote affect more than just the school that the district's students attend. *See, e.g.,* N.J.S.A. § 18A:38–8.1(d) (selection "of the receiving district's central administrative staff"). It makes sense, therefore, for New Jersey to limit the power of the sending district's representative so as to preserve the receiving district's control over matters that affect the school district as a whole.

Perhaps in an ideal system of government, the residents of Lincoln Park would be entitled to a level of representation on the Boonton Board that is exactly proportional to their level of "interest" in the Board's functions, if such a figure could be calculated. Indeed, the District Court, through its remedy's mathematical formula for determining different levels of representation for Lincoln Park as to different issues addressed by the Boonton Board, appears to have attempted to achieve such precision. The Constitution, however, does not require that a system of government be "the soundest or most practical form of internal government possible" from "a political science standpoint." *Holt,* 439 U.S. at 73–74. Rather, imprecision in democratic representation is tolerated, so long as the basic principles of "one person, one vote," described above, are not offended.

* * * For all of these reasons, we are satisfied that N.J.S.A. § 18A:38–8.2 as applied to Lincoln Park does not violate the principle of "one person, one vote."

* * * In allocating one representative to sending districts that provide more than 10% of a receiving school's population, New Jersey seeks to allow a sending district some voice—but only a modest voice—in the receiving district's affairs. * * * [W]e do not consider it irrational for New Jersey to limit the power of the sending district's representative so as to preserve the receiving district's control over matters that affect the school district as a whole.

We recognize that under N.J.S.A. § 18A:38–8.2, a sending district that provides 90% of the students in particular grades of a receiving district will be entitled to the same number of representatives on the receiving district's school board—one—as a sending district that provides only 10% of the students at particular levels. However, the mere fact that N.J.S.A. § 18A:38–8.2's representation scheme might have been crafted with more precision "[f]rom a political science standpoint" does not mean that the current system is irrational, for "this Court does not sit to determine whether [New Jersey] has chosen the soundest or most practical form of internal government possible." 439 U.S. at 73–74. Rather, because we conclude that the New Jersey send-receive representation scheme "bear[s] some rational relationship to a legitimate state purpose," we will uphold it as applied to Lincoln Park. *Id.* at 70; *accord Hawkins v. Johanns*, 88 F.Supp.2d 1027 (D.Neb.2000) (upholding similar send-receive scheme under rational basis review despite fact that sending district received no representation on the receiving district's school board). * * *

NOTES AND QUESTIONS

1. *Scope of Authority to Cooperate.* The states tend to take two different approaches in determining whether one local government has the power to enter into a cooperative agreement with another. Under the "mutuality of powers" approach, each participating unit of government must be authorized to exercise the power or provide the service dealt with in the cooperative agreement. New York's constitution, for example, authorizes state and local governments "to provide cooperatively, jointly, or by contract any facility, service, activity or undertaking which each participating local government has the power to provide separately." N.Y. Const. Art. IX, § 1(c).

By contrast, under the "power of one unit" approach only one cooperating unit of government must have independent authorization to engage in the particular activity that is the topic of the agreement. As a result, the other governmental participants are able to undertake a task jointly that they were powerless to accomplish individually. Illinois appears to adopt the "power of one unit" approach. Its Intergovernmental Cooperation Act provides:

> § 3. Intergovernmental agreements. Any power or powers, privileges or authority exercised or which may be exercised by a public agency of this State may be exercised and enjoyed jointly with any other public agency of this State and jointly with any public agency of any other state or of the United States to the extent

that laws of such other state or of the United States do not prohibit joint exercise or enjoyment.

5 ILCS 220/3.

In a challenge to an intergovernmental agreement which, in essence, authorized a county to condemn property on behalf of a city, the appellate court rejected the argument that the agreement was invalid because only the county possessed the necessary powers: "Respondents vehemently urge that the intergovernmental agreement . . . is a subterfuge and that the city should not be allowed to do indirectly through the county what it cannot do on its own. The very purpose of [the intergovernmental cooperation section of the Illinois Constitution and the Intergovernmental Cooperation Act] is to allow a local government to do indirectly that which it cannot do directly as long as it is otherwise lawful." County of Wabash v. Partee, 608 N.E.2d 674, 679 (Ill.App.1993). In essence, the court concluded that the legislature intended to allow a substantive enhancement or enlargement of local government power by use of cooperative agreements.

Although the Utah court in *Ivie* recites the standard version of the "mutuality of powers" approach to interlocal cooperation, does its holding in effect read that limit out of the law in Utah? What kind of intergovernmental contract would be invalidated under the approach taken by the court?

2. *Till Death Do Us Part?* New Jersey law establishes three methods for terminating a send-receive relationship. First, pursuant to a petition filed with the State Commissioner of Education, a declaration of severance may issue if the Commissioner concludes that "no substantial negative impact will result" from the severance. N.J.Stat.Ann. § 18 A:38–13. Second, the two districts may petition to form an "all purpose" regional school district, essentially consolidating both districts' schools into one system. And third, state law allows the creation of a "limited purpose" regional school district, which would consolidate only a portion of the districts' schools, for instance, their high school system. N.J.Stat.Ann. § 18 A:13–2. The latter two alternatives also require administrative approval, however. In a case decided after *Boonton*, plaintiffs sought to terminate a similar send-receive relationship. *See* Board of Educ. of Branchburg v. Livingston, 312 F.3d 614 (3d Cir. 2002). The parties in *Livingston* agreed that withdrawal under the three statutory options was impossible, at least for the "foreseeable future." *See id.* at 620. The Commissioner had disallowed a severance, citing a negative financial impact on both districts and the fact that Branchburg's school system would be virtually all-white. Creation of either type of regional school district was also disallowed. Nevertheless, the court found that the impossibility of severance did not warrant a different result from *Boonton*, again relying on the Supreme Court's opinion in *Holt Civic Club v. City of Tuscaloosa*.

3. *Political Representation and Intergovernmental Agreements.* *Boonton* may be an unusual case, but concerns about political representation and accountability may arise in many contracts for services. In *Durango,* for

instance, although representational challenges were not raised, the court observed that the existing formal government structures will amply protect the interests of both county and city residents. That is, both city and county residents elected their respective representatives, who in turn negotiated the agreement and appointed the members of the transit board. Do you agree that the ultimate electoral check is sufficient? As between city residents, whose elected representatives directly control the city transit agency, and county residents, whose elected representatives have contracted with the city, which group has more meaningful access and a greater likelihood that the transit agency will address their concerns? Would a provision reserving the county's ability to withdraw from the agreement adequately protect the county's interest?

4. *Financial Inequities.* The private carrier that challenged the intergovernmental agreement in *Durango* argued that the county's participation was in essence a sham, noting that the county was not required, and indeed not able, to contribute financially to the transportation system. Does the court's approval of the "lead agency" arrangement satisfy you that the formal agreement adequately protects the financial integrity of both governmental units? Should the court engage in more searching review? Are there structural safeguards that could be incorporated into state law to address these concerns? The ACIR found that apprehension about inequitable apportionment of costs was rated as a substantial adverse factor in interlocal agreements by more than one-third of the local governments it surveyed. *See* Advisory Commission on Intergovernmental Relations, State Laws Governing Local Government Structure and Administration 9 (1993).

5. *Effect of Statutory Obligations on Intergovernmental Cooperative Agreements.* The authority of a local government to enter intergovernmental service contracts may be affected by a wide range of legal constraints. In Western Washington University v. Washington Federation of State Employees, 793 P.2d 989 (Wash.App.1990), a state university proposed to abolish its campus police force and contract for city police services on campus. Opponents successfully argued that the university's statutory authority to enter the intergovernmental agreement was limited by its responsibilities under higher education laws that regulated layoffs. Similarly, in City of Hamilton v. Public Water Supply District #2, 849 S.W.2d 96 (Mo.App.1993), the court held that state law requiring that municipal water rates reflect capitalization costs invalidated an intergovernmental contract that expressly exempted the water district from paying those costs. *See also* Elk Grove Township Rural Fire Protection District v. Mount Prospect, 592 N.E.2d 549 (Ill.App.1992) (invalidating intergovernmental contract for fire protection because it violated statute prohibiting adoption of blanket tax levies over a multi-year period). If the intergovernmental cooperative power has a constitutional source, however, a court may conclude that statutory limitations are inapplicable. *See* City of Decatur v. DeKalb County, 589 S.E.2d 561 (Ga. 2003). A different issue is whether an intergovernmental contract operates to deprive a governmental unit of powers expressly

delegated to it by law. *See* Cibolo Creek Municipal Authority v. City of Universal City, 568 S.W.2d 699 (Tex.App.1978) (contract between city and special district could not prohibit district from exercising its statutory right to collect fee from city residents).

6. *Intergovernmental Cooperation and Dillon's Rule.* Refresh your memory of Dillon's Rule, discussed in Chapter IV. Consider its impact on the "mutuality of powers" and "power of one unit" approaches to intergovernmental cooperation. Can Dillon's Rule co-exist with one, both, or neither of the two? Two lower courts have concluded that Illinois' "power of one unit" approach has implicitly abrogated Dillon's Rule of strict construction for purposes of evaluating intergovernmental agreements. Wabash County v. Partee, 608 N.E.2d 674 (Ill.App.1993) (Dillon's Rule not applicable to city-county agreement that county will condemn property even though prior case had held that city had no authority to condemn subject property); Buffalo, Dawson, Mechanicsburg Sewer Commission v. Boggs, 470 N.E.2d 649 (Ill.App.1984) (intergovernmental commission has both powers expressly granted to it by statute and any other power validly transferred by any participating governmental unit). Is that the proper result? Can you articulate a possible analysis for the less deferential "mutuality of powers" approach?

7. *Intergovernmental Cooperation in the Absence of State Intergovernmental Cooperation Act.* Local governments located in states without broad cooperative enabling authority are more likely to face challenges to their power to contract with other government units. In Gade v. Chittenden Solid Waste Dist., 989 A.2d 491 (Vt. 2009), for instance, the plaintiffs raised legal challenges to a town's contract with a solid waste district for provision of solid waste facilities and services, arguing that the agreement was an impermissible delegation of police powers, as well as raising more general ultra vires challenges. Although the governmental agreement was ultimately upheld by the court, a state intergovernmental cooperation act would have eliminated the years of legal uncertainty.

2. JOINT SERVICES AGREEMENT

STATE V. PLAGGEMEIER
Washington Court of Appeals
969 P.2d 519 (1999)

SEINFELD, P.J.

The State appeals the dismissal of a driving citation issued by a Poulsbo police officer who arrested the driver outside Poulsbo city limits. The officer was acting pursuant to the consent provision of a Mutual Aid Agreement among five jurisdictions. The trial court dismissed the charge, finding the agreement invalid because it failed to comply with the Interlocal Cooperation Act, RCW 39.34. We conclude that the consent section of the agreement, which allows the police officers of each jurisdiction to exercise their police powers within the other four jurisdictions, is independently enforceable under the Washington Mutual Aid Peace Officers Powers Act of 1985, RCW 10.93.070. Consequently, we reverse.

FACTS

The Kitsap County Sheriff and the police chiefs of Bainbridge Island, Bremerton, Port Orchard, and Poulsbo signed a Mutual Aid Agreement (Agreement) that was to commence on December 15, 1995. The preamble of the Agreement states:

> Whereas, an entity known as the Bremerton-Kitsap County DWI Task Force has been created for the purpose of targeting, apprehending and successfully prosecuting individuals guilty of traffic infractions and offenses in general and DWI's in particular; and

> Whereas, it is the desire of various law enforcement agencies within Kitsap County to participate in such Task Force; and

> Whereas, multi-agency participation in such a Task Force is possible by virtue of the Washington Mutual Aid Peace Officer Powers Act set forth in Chapter 10.93 RCW and/or by the Interlocal Cooperation Act set forth in Chapter 39.34 RCW;

Sections 1 through 10 of the Agreement provide for the creation of the task force and contain provisions related to the one year length of the agreement; the financial responsibility of each agency; the creation of a "joint board" to administer the agreement; the designation of a task force coordinator and a description of the coordinator's responsibilities; and the liability of the coordinator's employer. Sections 11 and 12 of the Agreement deal with the consent of the signatories "to the full exercise of peace officer power within their respective jurisdictions" by officers engaged in Task Force operations and provide that the consent "shall be valid" during the signatories' tenure.

None of the five law enforcement agencies submitted the Agreement to their governing legislative bodies for ratification. Nor did any of them file the Agreement with their county auditor.

In April 1996, a Poulsbo police officer, acting pursuant to the agreement, arrested Thomas Plaggemeier outside the city limits and cited him for driving while under the influence of intoxicants. Plaggemeier moved for dismissal of the charge, claiming that the arresting officer was acting outside his geographic jurisdiction and, thus, the arrest was unlawful. The Kitsap County District Court agreed and dismissed the charge. * * *

On appeal, the State argues that RCW 10.93 does not require that a law enforcement mutual aid agreement comply with RCW 39.34.

DISCUSSION

I. THE MUTUAL AID AGREEMENT AND THE INTERLOCAL COOPERATION ACT

The following provision of the Mutual Aid Act is at issue here and states in pertinent part:

> Under the interlocal cooperation act, chapter 39.34 RCW, any law enforcement agency referred to by this chapter may contract with any other such agency and may also contract with any law enforcement agency of another state, or such state's political subdivision, to provide mutual law enforcement assistance.

RCW 10.93.130.

Plaggemeier contends that a plain reading of the statute indicates that compliance with RCW 39.34 is necessary to validate any law enforcement mutual aid agreement. The State, in turn, asks us to liberally construe RCW 10.93 to allow law enforcement agencies to enter into contracts or agreements on their own initiative. It contends that requiring all mutual aid agreements to comply with RCW 39.34 would render RCW 10.93 surplusage.

* * *

The Legislature enacted the Mutual Aid Act to modify common law restrictions on law enforcement authority. To give effect to that intent, RCW 10.93 sets forth circumstances under which a law enforcement officer may enforce criminal and traffic laws outside the officer's jurisdiction. * * *

We find no case law discussing RCW 10.93.130, and the legislative history provides no insight into the Legislature's intent regarding this provision. But a plain reading of the statute, in context with the remaining provisions of RCW 10.93 and with RCW 39.34, shows that its function is to inform law enforcement agencies that they have authority under the Interlocal Cooperation Act, RCW 39.34, to enter agreements for mutual law enforcement assistance. A corollary of RCW 10.93.130 is that mutual law enforcement assistance agreements must comply with RCW 39.34 and obtain legislative ratification. Legislative ratification of mutual aid agreements is necessary because such agreements involve the allocation of fiscal resources that properly fall under the function of local legislative bodies. *See In re Juvenile Director,* 87 Wash.2d 232, 248, 552 P.2d 163 (1976).

This reading of RCW 10.93.130 does not render RCW 10.93 surplusage. RCW 10.93.130, a provision of very limited scope, merely gives notice of an agency's authority under RCW 39.34 to enter a mutual law enforcement assistance agreement. It does not independently grant authority to enter such agreements; RCW 39.34 does.

* * *

II. THE SIGNIFICANCE OF RCW 10.93.070(1) AND SEVERABILITY

The State also argues that RCW 10.93.070(1) authorizes the Agreement without the local legislative body ratification required by RCW 39.34. We disagree that it supports the entire agreement but, as we discuss below, it does support the consent provisions of the agreement.

RCW 10.93.070(1) allows a peace officer to enforce traffic and criminal laws outside the officer's jurisdiction "[u]pon the prior written consent of the sheriff or chief of police" of the jurisdiction in question.
* * *

The three-page Agreement here is much broader than the limited scope of enforcement actions contemplated by RCW 10.93.070(1). The Agreement establishes a set of administrative procedures and cites to RCW 39.34 along with RCW 10.93. And the language of the Agreement follows closely the requirements of RCW 39.34.030. It clearly fits under RCW 10.93.070(3), which authorizes action "[i]n response to a request for assistance pursuant to a mutual law enforcement assistance agreement with the agency of primary territorial jurisdiction." Thus, it must comply with the ratification and filing requirements. RCW 39.34.030(2); RCW 39.34.040.

Here, as the State concedes, there was neither ratification nor filing of the Agreement. Consequently, the Agreement as a whole is invalid under the Interlocal Cooperation Act, RCW 39.34.

We do agree with the State, however, that RCW 10.93.070(1) supports the consent provisions of the Agreement. The Agreement contains within it two separate agreements: one that establishes an administrative body and policies among the different agencies, and another that grants consent for extrajurisdictional law enforcement. Although the Agreement as a whole is invalid under the Interlocal Cooperation Act, contract law allows the enforcement of only the consent portion, pursuant to RCW 10.93.070.

* * *

In essence, the Agreement is a composite of two independent agreements, an agreement to create and work together in the task force and a consent to extrajurisdictional law enforcement. Upon the deletion of the administrative agreement (Sections 1 through 10), the remaining sections provide valid consent notice under RCW 10.93.070(1). *See*

Rasmussen, 70 Wash.App. at 857–58, 855 P.2d 1206; *Ghaffari,* 62 Wash.App. at 876, 816 P.2d 66. * * *

NOTES AND QUESTIONS

1. *Source of Cooperative Powers.* Note that the *Plaggemeier* court states that the Mutual Aid Act gives no independent authority to the cities. Is that consistent with its holding? By upholding the consent provisions without the legislative ratification required by the more general Interlocal Cooperation Act, doesn't the court necessarily find that the Mutual Aid Act authorized a municipal action that would otherwise be beyond the scope of its cooperative powers under the Interlocal Cooperation Act? After this case, could the city council of either of the two cities invalidate the consent agreement? Or does the Mutual Aid Act give the chief of police and the sheriff the power to act without municipal consent? Could the state possibly have intended to insulate from city legislative control the decision to authorize another police force to act within a city's jurisdiction? Is that the essence of this holding? Compare the joint services agreement at issue in *Plaggemeier* with the contract for services described in *Durango.* Do they raise different concerns about the scope of authority of governmental units or the extent to which intergovernmental cooperative ventures either promote or frustrate general governmental accountability to its citizens?

2. *Relationships with Other Statutes. Plaggemeier* suggests a more general problem of statutory interpretation in states whose legislatures supplement general intergovernmental cooperation statutes or constitutional provisions with enabling acts that deal specifically with a particular type of cooperative venture. In those states, is the more general statute an independent source of power for the local government, or must the government point to an enabling act authorizing the type of agreement it is considering? Does the specific enabling act limit what would otherwise be broader discretion and flexibility under the general constitutional or statutory provisions dealing with interlocal cooperation? *See, e.g.,* Jefferson v. Missouri Department of Natural Resources, 863 S.W.2d 844 (Mo.1993) (local government must follow statute authorizing creation of intergovernmental solid waste management districts and cannot rely on state constitutional protection of intergovernmental cooperation); Ferraro v. Zoning Board of Adjustment of Township of Holmdel, 574 A.2d 38 (N.J.1990) (statute authorizing municipality to confer "sole supervision" over land to adjacent municipality did not authorize transfer of zoning power to that municipality); 1000 Friends of Florida, Inc. v. State, 824 So.2d 989 (Fla. App. 2002) (intergovernmental planning and annexation agreements upheld against challenge that they circumvented state mandates for public participation in connection with amendment to comprehensive plan). A similar issue involves the extent to which home rule units can execute agreements without following statutory limitations. The Missouri Supreme Court has held that home rule authority includes independent, inherent power to formulate

intergovernmental agreements without adherence to statutory guidelines. Cape Motor Lodge, Inc. v. Cape Girardeau, 706 S.W.2d 208 (Mo.1986).

3. *Blurring the Distinctions.* Many states, through the adoption of broadly worded intergovernmental cooperation acts, leave it to the local governments themselves to determine the form and the extent of their joint cooperative efforts. Texas' Interlocal Cooperation Act, for instance, provides that its purpose is to "increase the efficiency and effectiveness of local governments by authorizing them to contract, to the greatest possible extent, with one another and with agencies of the state." Tex. Gov't Code Ann. § 791.001. As described in the introduction to this Section, in this casebook we have used the ACIR's three-part categorization. We recognize, however, that the labels may not fully capture the scope of all possible cooperative efforts. Consider whether you would categorize the following intergovernmental agreement as a contract for services, joint services agreement, or as a hybrid combining elements of the two: State law authorizes Texas municipalities to prohibit nuisances within 5,000 feet of municipal boundaries. Pursuant to that law, Texas City passed an ordinance prohibiting the sale of fireworks within 5,000 feet of city limits. League City, a home rule entity, passed the identical ordinance. Subsequently, pursuant to an intergovernmental agreement, League City ceded to Texas City the power to enforce the law in the 5,000-foot area outside of League City. Disgruntled sellers sought to invalidate the ordinance, but the court upheld the agreement. *See* PPC Enterprises, Inc. v. Texas City, 76 F.Supp. 2d 750 (S.D. Tex. 1999). Irrespective of its compliance with statutory and constitutional requirements, do you think that this type of cooperation is a good idea?

3. CREATING A NEW GOVERNMENTAL ENTITY PURSUANT TO INTERGOVERNMENTAL AGREEMENT

GOREHAM v. DES MOINES METROPOLITAN AREA SOLID WASTE AGENCY

Supreme Court of Iowa
179 N.W.2d 449 (1970)

LARSON, JUSTICE.

Plaintiffs, who are residents, property owners, and taxpayers of the cities of Des Moines and West Des Moines, Iowa, brought this action at law against the Des Moines Metropolitan Area Solid Waste Agency (hereafter called the Agency) and its members asking an interpretation of chapter 28E, Code of Iowa 1966, and chapter 236, Acts of the Sixty-third General Assembly, First Session, with reference to the power and authority of the Agency under those laws. * * *

Fairly summarized, the Stipulation of Facts filed herein on March 30, 1970, states as follows:

On August 8, 1966, the City Manager of the defendant City of Des Moines, by memorandum to the City Council, informed it that the city was confronted with a serious problem relating to the collection and disposal of solid waste, in that the solid waste facility operated by the City of Des Moines was fast filling up. The impact of the report was heightened by the fact that the local units of government in the near metropolitan Des Moines area were using the Des Moines dump to a greater extent for the disposition of some or all of their solid waste and were using local dumps in the area surrounding Des Moines to a lesser extent for the disposition of a portion of their solid waste. The memorandum proposed a study and demonstration project for the metropolitan area which contained approximately 430 square miles. The manager recommended that the communities in the metropolitan area engage in a cooperative effort in disposing of their solid waste.

* * *

On November 28, 1966, the City Council of the City of Des Moines, by resolution, authorized the execution of a contract, * * * between the City of Des Moines and the other thirteen governmental units in the metropolitan area. * * *

Subsequent thereto the defendant municipalities entered into an * * * intergovernmental agreement [which] created the Metropolitan Area Solid Waste Agency.

Pursuant to said agreement the Agency was duly organized, officers were elected and a director was hired to manage the affairs of the Agency under the direction of the Agency board which was composed of one representative from the governing body of each member of the Agency, each having one vote for every 50,000 or fraction thereof population in his area of representation.

* * *

Chapter 28E entitled 'Joint Exercise of Governmental Powers' purports to authorize any political subdivision of the State of Iowa and certain agencies of the state or federal government to join together to perform certain public services and by agreement create a separate legal or administrative entity to render that service. Its worthy purpose is clearly expressed in section 28E.1. Section 28E.2 provides definitions, and section 28E.3 purports to define the limitations upon the participants as follows:

'28E.3. *Joint exercise of powers.* Any power or powers, privileges or authority exercised or capable of exercise by a public agency of this state may be exercised and enjoyed jointly with any other public agency of this state having such power or powers, privilege or authority, and jointly with any public agency of any other state or of the United States to the extent that laws of such other state or of the United States permit such joint exercise or enjoyment. Any agency of the state government when acting jointly with any public agency may exercise and enjoy all of the powers, privileges and authority conferred by this chapter upon a public agency.'

Sections 28E.4 and 28E.5 provide for the agreement and its contents as follows:

'28E.4. *Agreement with other agencies.* Any public agency of this state may enter into an agreement with one or more public or private agencies for joint or co-operative action pursuant to the provisions of this chapter, *including* the creation of a separate entity to carry out the purpose of the agreement. Appropriate action by ordinance, resolution or otherwise pursuant to law of the governing bodies involved shall be necessary before any such agreement may enter into force. (Emphasis supplied.)

'28E.5. Specifications. Any such agreement shall specify the following:

'1. Its duration.

'2. The precise organization, composition and nature of any separate legal or administrative entity created thereby together with the powers delegated thereto, provided such entity may be legally created.

'3. Its purpose or purposes.

'4. The manner of financing the joint or co-operative undertaking and of establishing and maintaining a budget therefor.

'5. The permissible method or methods to be employed in accomplishing the partial or complete termination of the agreement and for disposing of property upon such partial or complete termination.

'6. Any other necessary and proper matters.'

* * * Although appellants contend the creation of a separate legal entity or public body is solely a function of the legislature, we find no unconstitutional delegation of legislative power involved in this law providing for the creation of the Des Moines Metropolitan Area Solid Waste Agency. It is not the mere establishment or creation of such an agency or entity that causes trouble, but the functions to be performed by that agency in the legislative field which must be examined closely to

determine whether there has been an unlawful delegation of legislative authority. * * *

In this connection it must also be noted that administrative agencies may be delegated certain legislative functions by the legislature when properly guidelined, and that when this is done, the distinction between such agencies and public bodies, corporate and politic, which have been delegated proper legislative functions, has largely disappeared. Ordinarily the latter body is created by an act of the legislature and the former by an already-established public body with legislative authority. However, the power and authority of each must be measured by the legality of the delegation thereof. If such power is derived from the State Legislature, is adequately guidelined, and does not violate the separation-of-powers provision of the State Constitution set forth in Article III, Section 1, the exercise thereof should be sustained.

Thus, our primary problem here is whether the authority provided in chapter 28E of the 1966 Code and chapter 236, Acts of the Sixty-third General Assembly, constitutes a lawful delegation of legislative power.

* * *

Generally, when the legislature has adequately stated the object and purpose of the legislation and laid down reasonably-clear guidelines in its application, it may then delegate to a properly-created entity the authority to exercise such legislative power as is necessary to carry into effect that general legislative purpose.

The purpose of this legislation, as recognized in chapter 28E, is to provide a solution to the growing problems of local government including the problem of collection and disposal of solid wastes by public bodies and to cooperate with the Office of Solid Waste of the United States Department of Health, Education and Welfare to accomplish that purpose by joint efforts. We further observe that this purpose may soon be made a legal requirement for all communities throughout the entire land under federal law. We are satisfied that this is health and general welfare legislation and that the legislative policy and purpose for chapter 28E is sufficiently stated. It amounts to this, that public agencies or governmental units may cooperate together to do anything jointly that they could do individually.

True, if chapter 28E is examined without reference to the powers granted the various governmental units by other legislation, the factors constituting sufficient guidelines might well be said to be insufficient. But this legislation must be interpreted with reference to the power or powers which the contracting governmental units already have. The pre-existing powers contain their own guidelines. The legal creation of a new body corporate and politic to jointly exercise and perform the powers and responsibilities of the cooperating governmental unit would not be unconstitutional so long as the new body politic is doing only what its cooperating members already have the power to do. * * *

Chapter 28E does not attempt to delineate the various governmental or proprietary functions which the individual governmental units may be implementing. While such a broad approach may be unwise, as appellants argue, it is not unconstitutional so long as the cooperating units are not exercising powers they do not already have.

With this in mind, it appears that chapter 28E supplies sufficient guidelines for the purposes necessary to the chapter. That is, the units are authorized to handle what might be called the mechanical details of implementing the joint project either by the creation of a separate entity or by using a joint administrator or board for the purpose of implementing the agreement reached. The agreement itself, of whatever nature, must have its specific contents delineated in section 28E.5 and specifically prohibits governmental units being involved in the new entity, except insofar as the new entity is in fact performing the same responsibilities as the units involved.

Thus, when the entire chapter is examined, it would appear that the delegations of power to the governmental units made by the legislature in chapter 28E are constitutional.

NOTES AND QUESTIONS

1. *Delegation of Power.* To what does the *Goreham* court apply its delegation analysis? The state can transfer legislative power to local legislatures? Does the delegation doctrine affect the permissible scope of that transfer? Or is the court more concerned with the transfer of power from the municipalities to the regional entity? How do the court's concerns about accountability and loss of democratic control apply to the transfers of power that are present in this case? Does it matter whether the members of the regional authority are elected or appointed? Is the problem that even though a locality's representative on a regional body may be directly accountable to the local government, that representative may be outvoted by other representatives on the regional body so that the locality may be bound to actions it opposed? That problem could be addressed by a requirement of unanimous consent of the participating local governments before the regional government could act. However, a unanimous consent rule could make regional action more difficult. Does some combination of voluntary local decision to participate in a regional joint venture plus local representation— but not a veto—on the regional body's governing board provide sufficient protection for the interest in local self-determination? Is your answer to that question affected by how easy or difficult it is for a local government to withdraw from a regional body? (If the regional body has issued bonds to

finance regional infrastructure, a participating locality may be unable to shed its share of the regional debt obligation).

Though the *Goreham* court rejected the delegation argument, a few years later the Iowa Supreme Court expressed greater concern about the loss of local political control that can result from an intergovernmental agreement. In Barnes v. Department of Housing and Urban Development, 341 N.W.2d 766 (Iowa 1983), the court invalidated an intergovernmental agreement that purported to transfer ultimate decisionmaking power about housing projects from a local government to a regional housing authority created under the same act applied in *Goreham*. The court concluded that the intergovernmental cooperation act did not allow a municipality to create a regional entity that would be able to decide whether to undertake a low-income housing project. Note that the intergovernmental cooperation statute authorizes the joint exercise of "any power or powers, privileges or authority exercised or capable of exercise by a public agency of this state . . . " Iowa Stat. § 28E.3. How can the statute be interpreted to support the line drawn by the court? Should it be relevant that the city council in *Goreham* engaged in extensive deliberation, study and policy formulation before embarking on the intergovernmental venture? In contrast, might the *Barnes* court have thought that the city was simply trying to pass the buck for a difficult policy decision to an unelected entity?

The creation of a new unit of government may insulate some municipal functions from the political check. In Kubicek v. City of Lincoln, 658 N.W.2d 291 (Neb. 2003), for instance, individuals challenged the city's creation of the Joint Antelope Valley Authority, which had been formed with two other units of local government to implement a multi-year revitalization, transportation and flood control project. The city's charter stipulated that no "board, commission or authority . . . shall be established until such action has been approved by a majority vote of the electors." The court held that the provision applied only to those entities created pursuant to local ordinance, not, as in this case, pursuant to city council resolution. Because the city charter had previously been amended by the local electorate to permit intergovernmental cooperative endeavors, the court held that the creation of the Authority was an administrative decision (and thus properly taken pursuant to council resolution rather than ordinance) that was immune from the local election requirement.

2. *Intergovernmental Conflicts in Intergovernmental Cooperation.* When several municipal governments create an intergovernmental entity, they should consider the possibility of future discord. Depending on the terms of the agreement, a municipality may have ceded its governmental power to a new entity over which it no longer exercises control. In Barling v. Fort Chaffee Redevelopment Authority, 60 S.W.3d 443 (Ark. 2001), several local governments formed a redevelopment authority to deal with land that had once been a federal military base. One of the municipalities objected to the authority's land use plans for the property and sued to have those plans declared invalid because of their conflict with city zoning ordinances. The

court held that the municipality had irrevocably ceded its land use and zoning powers over the property when it signed the intergovernmental agreement. It rejected the municipality's claims that the agreement was an impermissible delegation of power to an administrative body and that it constituted an invalid contracting away of its legislative power. The case should serve as a cautionary note for local governments that are contemplating the creation of an intergovernmental entity.

3. *Status of Intergovernmental Entity.* Disputes surrounding the legal status of an entity created pursuant to intergovernmental cooperative authority are wide-ranging. Questions will arise over the applicability of statutory, common law, and constitutional limitations on local government powers. In Johnson v. Piedmont Municipal Power Agency, 287 S.E.2d 476 (S.C.1982), for instance, a number of municipalities, acting pursuant to state enabling legislation, created an intergovernmental agency for the purpose of issuing bonds to finance the purchase of an ownership interest in a privately-owned nuclear power plant. Municipal residents sued, claiming that the arrangement violated the provision of the state constitution requiring local voter approval before a local government may issue debt. The court held that the election requirement did not apply since the debt was issued by the intergovernmental agency, not the individual municipalities. A dissenting justice, noting that the project entailed hundreds of millions of dollars of debt, characterized the intergovernmental entity as "a sort of alter ego created for the purpose of doing indirectly that which the Constitution forbids municipalities to do directly." *Id.* at 484 (Littleton, J., dissenting).

4. *Liability of Intergovernmental Entities.* In Allis-Chalmers v. Emmet County Council of Governments, 355 N.W.2d 586 (Iowa 1984) the defendant contracted with Allis-Chalmers for purchase of a trash shredder system. Subsequent disputes led to nonperformance of the contract. When the seller corporation sued, the court held that the intergovernmental council of governments was not a separate legal entity amenable to suit. In addition, by analogy to the law defining liability of shareholders of private corporations, the court found that the individual component governments of that intergovernmental entity were not liable. Is this an instance of local governments using an intergovernmental body to shield itself from liability for actions in which it had participated? *See also* White v. Liberty Eylau Independent School District, 920 S.W.2d 809 (Tex.App.1996) (school district contracted for transportation services with county agency; district not liable for school bus accident); Ross v. United States, 910 F.2d 1422 (7th Cir.1990) (city contracted with county for shoreline patrols for land within the city's territory; county was sole government liable in connection with a drowning; court stressed that the agreement was not "merely a method for the city to escape legal liability"); Huntington Beach v. Westminster, 66 Cal.Rptr.2d 826 (Cal.App.1997) (apportioning liability between two municipalities for injuries sustained in an incident involving two police forces pursuant to mutual aid agreement).

5. *Interlocal Agreements and Regionalization.* Interlocal cooperation may involve not just arrangements between two or more local governments at the same level, such as two municipalities or townships, but also agreements between local governments and regional bodies. A Colorado statute, for instance, authorizes local governments to transfer numerous functions to a regional entity:

Designation of services.

(1) Subject to local authorization as provided in section 32–7–112, local governing bodies, by resolution, or the people, by petition, . . . may, by resolution, initiate one or more of the following services or combinations thereof:

(a) Domestic water collection, treatment, and distribution;

(b) Urban drainage and flood control;

(c) Sewage collection, treatment, and disposal;

(d) Public surface transportation;

(e) Collection of solid waste;

(f) Disposal of solid waste;

(g) Parks and recreation;

(h) Libraries;

(i) Fire protection;

(j) Hospitals, including convalescent nursing homes, ambulance services, and any other health and medical care facilities or services;

(k) Museums, zoos, art galleries, theaters, and other cultural facilities or services;

(l) Housing;

(m) Weed and pest control;

(n) Central purchasing, computer services, equipment pool, and any other management services for local governments, including procurement of supplies; acquisition, management, maintenance, and disposal of property and equipment; legal services; special communication systems; or any other similar services to local governments which are directly related to improving the efficiency or operation of local governments;

(o) Local gas or electric services or heating and cooling services from geothermal resources, solar or wind energy, hydroelectric or renewable biomass resources, including waste and cogenerated heat . . . ;

(p)   Jails and rehabilitation; and

(q)   Land and soil preservation.

Colo. Rev. Stat. § 32–7–111.

6.   *The Regional Effect of Intergovernmental Cooperation.* Interlocal cooperation may enable local governments to deal with regional problems without creating a regional government. Interlocal cooperation may also allow small, outlying areas to receive more extensive urban services without having to agree to annexation to a central city. *See* County of Rockingham v. City of Harrisonburg, 294 S.E.2d 825, 830 (Va.1982) (noting that cooperation among local governments was encouraged by legislature as "alternative to territorial expansion of cities"); *see also* Village of Sherman v. Village of Williamsville, 435 N.E.2d 548, 551 (Ill.App.1982) (quoting proceedings of constitutional convention: "We think, in the long run, that vigorous intergovernmental cooperation will reduce the need for special districts").

The most famous instance of interlocal contracting as an alternative to annexation is the Lakewood Plan. In the 1950s, Lakewood was a rapidly growing area in Southern California adjacent to the city of Long Beach. To avoid annexation by Long Beach, an attorney for a local developer, together with county officials, devised a plan whereby the community could incorporate as a city but contract with the county to receive all the county services it had received as an unincorporated area plus additional services necessitated by population growth. Lakewood became the first municipality founded on the basis of purchasing all its basic services from another unit of local government. The plan assured Lakewood it would receive municipal services while protecting it from annexation and allowing it to govern itself and exercise its own taxing and police powers. The Lakewood Plan provoked an explosion of incorporation activity in Southern California, with twenty-five new suburban municipalities incorporated in a seven-year period. It continues to provide a model for suburbs seeking a fiscally feasible method of sustaining political independence. *See* Robert L. Bish & Vincent Ostrom, Understanding Urban Government: Metropolitan Reform Reconsidered 59–69 (AEI Press 1973). For a more critical evaluation, suggesting that the Lakewood Plan contributed to greater interlocal wealth and service inequalities in Southern California, *see* Gary Miller, Cities by Contract: The Politics of Municipal Incorporation 103 (MIT Press 1981). The role of the Lakewood Plan in facilitating incorporation is also considered in Chapter II.

D. REGIONAL GOVERNANCE STRUCTURES

1. REGIONAL SPECIAL DISTRICTS

MARSHALL V. NORTHERN VIRGINIA TRANSPORTATION AUTHORITY

Supreme Court of Virginia
657 S.E.2d 71 (2008)

Opinion by S. BERNARD GOODWYN.

In this appeal, we are asked to consider * * * whether the Constitution prohibits the General Assembly from delegating its power of taxation to a political subdivision charged with the responsibility of addressing regional transportation issues affecting certain localities of the Commonwealth, when that political subdivision is not a county, city, town, or regional government, and is not an elected body. * * *

In 2002, the General Assembly created NVTA [Northern Virginia Transportation Authority] as a political subdivision of the Commonwealth. * * * NVTA encompasses the Counties of Arlington, Fairfax, Loudoun, and Prince William, and the Cities of Alexandria, Fairfax, Falls Church, Manassas and Manassas Park ("the Northern Virginia localities"). * * * The governing board of NVTA consists of 14 voting members and two non-voting members.

The voting members of NVTA's governing board are the chief elected officers of the governing body for each named county and city, two members of the House of Delegates appointed by the Speaker of the House, one member of the Senate appointed by the Senate Committee on Rules, and two citizens appointed by the Governor, all of whom reside in the nine localities embraced by NVTA. See Code § 15.2–4832. Any chief elected officer of a governing body of a member city or county may name a designee, but each such designee must be "a current elected officer" of the applicable governing body. Id. Decisions of NVTA must be approved by a "super-majority" of the voting members. See Code § 15.2–4834.

NVTA's powers are limited by its enabling legislation to activities pertaining to regional transportation. See Code §§ 15.2–4830, –4838, and –4840. NVTA is empowered, among other things, to prepare a regional transportation plan for the Northern Virginia localities and to construct or acquire transportation facilities that are either specified in the plan or constitute a regional priority. Id. NVTA may issue bonds to finance such projects. See Code §§ 15.2–4839, –4519.

In 2007, both houses of the General Assembly passed and the Governor signed the legislation that became Chapter 896. * * * Under various provisions contained in Chapter 896, NVTA has the authority, in its sole discretion, to impose seven regional taxes and fees ("the regional taxes and fees").

The regional taxes and fees NVTA is authorized to impose within the Northern Virginia localities are: an additional annual vehicle license fee; an additional initial vehicle registration fee; an additional vehicle inspection fee; a local sales and use tax on vehicle repairs; a regional congestion relief fee; a local rental car transportation fee; and an additional transient occupancy tax. For each such tax and fee, the General Assembly specified the subject of taxation and fixed the amount or rate.

The General Assembly designated the revenue raised from imposition of the regional taxes and fees for the sole purpose of financing bonds and providing revenue for transportation projects and purposes in the nine localities embraced by NVTA. * * *

After conducting a public hearing, NVTA's governing body voted to impose the regional taxes and fees authorized by Chapter 896, effective January 1, 2008. The governing body also adopted a resolution authorizing the issuance of bonds of NVTA in a principal amount not to exceed $130 million, to be paid from the pledgeable NVTA revenues, which include revenues from the regional taxes and fees. * * *

[NVTA instituted a bond validation proceeding as required by state law, asking the circuit court to determine the validity of bonds it proposed to issue. Some citizens and local governments in the area filed responsive pleadings as defendants in opposition. The lower court upheld the bonds; this appeal followed.]

We have long recognized the principle that the power of a government to tax its people and their property is essential to government's very existence. * * * This power to tax, which is inherent in every sovereign state government, is a legislative power that the Constitution vests in the General Assembly.

* * * Defendants and Loudoun County contend that by authorizing NVTA to impose the regional taxes and fees, Chapter 896 effects a constitutionally prohibited delegation of the General Assembly's taxing authority to a political subdivision whose governing board is not elected by the citizens to serve in that capacity.

NVTA and the Commonwealth respond that NVTA's power to impose the regional taxes and fees, as authorized by Chapter 896, does not constitute a "true" delegation of legislative authority because the General Assembly specified the subject of the regional taxes and fees, dictated the amount or rate of the taxes and fees, and mandated that the revenue derived be spent in a certain manner. NVTA and the Commonwealth contend that the General Assembly retains authority and control over the regional taxes and fees, and remains free to amend, repeal, or restrict NVTA's power to impose them. Thus, NVTA and the Commonwealth maintain that the Constitution does not prohibit the General Assembly from authorizing NVTA to impose the regional taxes and fees within the restrictions prescribed in Chapter 896. We disagree with the arguments advanced by NVTA and the Commonwealth.

Initially, we observe that neither NVTA nor the Commonwealth disputes that the main purpose of the regional taxes and fees, authorized in Chapter 896, is to raise revenue. We consistently have held that when the primary purpose of an enactment is to raise revenue, the enactment will be considered a tax, regardless of the name attached to the act. * * * In accordance with this authority, we conclude that each of the regional taxes and fees provided in Chapter 896 constitutes a tax, because they all are designed to produce revenue to be used for the purpose of financing bonds and supplying revenue for transportation purposes in the Northern Virginia localities. Code §§ 15.2–4838.1(C)(3), –4840(12). Thus, we must consider whether by those provisions of Chapter 896, the General Assembly has delegated a portion of its taxing authority to NVTA.

The General Assembly has delegated its authority when it enacts a law authorizing another entity to determine whether the law will be imposed. * * * Here, although the General Assembly specified in Chapter 896 the form, substance, and use of the regional taxes and fees, the General Assembly retained no authority to decide whether the regional taxes and fees would be imposed, leaving that decision solely to NVTA. *See* Code § 15.2–4840(12). Although the General Assembly can later pass a law to amend or repeal NVTA's authority to impose taxes, this does not negate the fact that the sole discretion to impose the regional taxes and fees presently rests with NVTA. Therefore, we hold that because the regional taxes and fees specified in Chapter 896 may be imposed in the sole discretion of NVTA, the General Assembly has delegated its taxing authority to NVTA with regard to the imposition of those taxes and fees.

We must now determine whether the General Assembly's delegation of this taxing authority to NVTA violates the Constitution. The Constitution of Virginia "is not a grant of legislative powers to the General Assembly, but is a restraining instrument only, and, except as to matters ceded to the federal government, the legislative powers of the General Assembly are without limit. * * * As we have stated, the General Assembly may enact any law or take any action "not prohibited by express terms, or by necessary implications by the State Constitution or the Constitution of the United States." * * *

In determining the constitutionality of the General Assembly's delegation of taxing authority to NVTA, we consider the explicit language of the Constitution. That explicit language demonstrates the special status that the legislative taxing power occupies in the Constitution, and reflects the greater restrictions that the Constitution places on the General Assembly's exercise of the taxing power. The following provisions of the Constitution guide our analysis in this case.

Article I, Section 6 of the Constitution states, in relevant part

> that all men . . . cannot be taxed . . . without their own consent, or that of their representatives duly elected. . . .

Article IV, Section 1 of the Constitution provides that:

> The legislative power of the Commonwealth shall be vested in a General Assembly, which shall consist of a Senate and House of Delegates.

Article IV, Section 11 of the Constitution states, in relevant part, that:

> No bill which . . . imposes, continues, or revives a tax, shall be passed except by the affirmative vote of a majority of all the members elected to each house.

> * * * [T]he people of Virginia approved a Constitution that places restrictions on the General Assembly's exercise of the taxing power. In fact, greater restrictions are placed on the taxing power than are placed on the exercise of most other types of legislative power. For example, under Article IV, Section 11, the General Assembly is prohibited from enacting legislation imposing a tax without an affirmative vote of a majority of all members elected to each house * * *

Upon review of the constitutional provisions set forth above, we conclude that the Constitution, in keeping with rights enumerated in Article I, Section 6 of the Constitution's Bill of Rights, clearly contemplates that taxes must be imposed only by a majority of the elected representatives of a legislative body, with the votes cast by the elected representatives being duly recorded. The constraints that the citizens of Virginia have placed upon the General Assembly regarding the imposition of taxes would be rendered meaningless if the General Assembly were permitted to avoid compliance with these constraints by delegating to NVTA the decisional authority whether to impose taxes. * * *

The General Assembly also may not accomplish through Chapter 896, indirectly, that which it is not empowered to do directly, namely, impose taxes on the citizenry in the absence of an affirmative, recorded vote of a majority of all members elected to each body of the General Assembly. Thus, by enacting Chapter 896, the General Assembly has failed to adhere to the mandates of accountability and transparency that the Constitution requires when the General Assembly exercises the legislative taxing authority permitted by the Constitution.

If payment of the regional taxes and fees is to be required by a general law, it is the prerogative and the function of the General Assembly, as provided by Article IV, Section 1 of the Constitution, to make that decision, in a manner which complies with the requirements of Article IV, Section 11 of the Constitution. Accordingly, we hold that the provisions of Chapter 896 permitting NVTA to impose the regional taxes and fees are invalid because they violate the Constitution. Therefore, such taxes and fees that NVTA has already imposed are null and void.
* * *

NOTES AND QUESTIONS

1. *Establishing the Constitutionality of Regional Special Districts.* When regional special districts became widespread in the 1970s, many were subject to state constitutional challenges. State supreme courts routinely upheld the districts against a host of legal arguments. *See, e.g.,* Hoogasian v. Regional Transportation Authority, 317 N.E.2d 534 (Ill. 1974) (rejecting argument state had impermissibly delegated legislative power when it created the Regional Transportation Authority); Camp v. Metropolitan Atlanta Rapid Transit Authority, 189 S.E.2d 56 (Ga.1972) (rejecting claims of deficiency in process of legislative ratification, and upholding district's taxation powers against claims of unequal treatment and improper delegation); Rye v. Metropolitan Transportation Authority, 249 N.E.2d 429 (N.Y.1969) (rejecting claim that creation of district violated special act ban). These cases are representative of the general judicial unwillingness to second guess the legislative choice of how best to build and pay for public services that require massive infrastructure. *See also* Pierce County v. State, 148 P.3d 1002, 1017 (Wash. 2006) (rejecting challenge that state had no authority to allow elected officials to decide to establish a regional transit authority without a public vote).

2. *Revenue-Raising Techniques.* Regional special districts exercise a wide range of revenue-raising techniques, and generalizations are difficult. Some are limited to recouping their operating costs through charging user fees, *e.g.,* Beatty v. Metropolitan St. Louis Sewer District, 867 S.W.2d 217 (Mo.1993) (describing district's power to collect user charges and per unit charges for capital improvements, but holding that district must get voter approval to raise the rates). Some are allowed to levy property taxes, *e.g.,* Brookfield v. Milwaukee Metropolitan Sewerage District, 491 N.W.2d 484 (Wis.1992) (authorizing district to charge for capital costs on the basis of property value); Wash.Rev.Code § 70.44.060(6) (authorizing hospital district to levy a property tax "not to exceed fifty cents per thousand dollars of assessed value, and an additional annual tax on all taxable property within such public hospital district not to exceed twenty-five cents per thousand dollars of assessed value"). Some can impose general charges on property and activity within the district, *e.g.,* Anema v. Transit Construction Authority, 788 P.2d 1261 (Colo.1990) (affirming district's ability to finance planning of a transit system by imposing charge on all commercial property and levying an

"employment assessment" on each employer). Others can impose sales taxes, *e.g.*, Camp v. Metropolitan Atlanta Rapid Transit Authority, 189 S.E.2d 56 (Ga.1972) (upholding legislative delegation of sales tax power to regional special district to fund rapid transit system); Sheehan v. Central Puget Sound Reg. Transp. Auth., 123 P.3d 88 (Wash. 2005) (motor vehicle excise taxes upheld against challenge that they were prohibited property taxes). According to a highly regarded study of special districts, approximately 63% have powers of property taxation. *See* Kathryn A. Foster, The Political Economy of Special-Purpose Government 14 (Georgetown Univ. Press 1997).

The Virginia supreme court's opinion breaks with the prevailing judicial acceptance of legislative discretion in the allocation of revenue-raising powers to special districts. Other courts have upheld special district taxation powers against challenges of unconstitutional delegation of legislative powers. *See, e.g.,* International Paper Co. v. Hilton, 966 So.2d 545 (La. 2007); Larson v. Seattle Popular Monorail Authority, 131 P.3d 892 (Wash. 2006). In Campbell v. Hilton Head No. 1 Pub. Serv. Dist., 580 S.E.2d 137 (S.C. 2003), the court rejected the argument that the grant of taxation power to the district violated the Republican Guarantee Clause of the U.S. Constitution, U.S. Const., art. IV, § 4.

The revenue-raising powers of regional special districts are discussed in depth in Chapter VI. At this point, though, it is worth considering whether your comfort with the amount of discretionary power exercised by these single purpose units of government, whose directors are frequently appointed rather than elected, depends on the checks imposed on the unit's ability to raise revenue from its citizens. The more the special district's powers resemble general taxation, the more similar it seems to a general purpose city or county government. In contrast, so long as its powers are narrowly circumscribed to recoupment of carefully calculated costs by imposing charges for usage of the service, the less it resembles a general purpose local government. Does that distinction suggest differences in terms of accountability and responsiveness to citizen input, which might in turn have implications for the appropriate level of judicial review?

3. *The Powers of Special Districts.* Special districts undertake other legislative-like functions, such as adopting ordinances. Although those ordinances are frequently directly related to the implementation of their revenue-raising powers, *see, e.g.,* Mann v. Granite Reeder Water and Sewer Dist., 141 P.3d 1117 (Idaho 2006) (upholding ordinance passed by district to establish a local improvement district), they may also establish regulatory standards. *See, e.g.,* Hunters, Anglers and Trappers Assoc. of Vermont v. Winooski Valley Park Dist., 913 A.2d 391 (Vt. 2006) (upholding park district's ability to prohibit hunting and trapping on district land, notwithstanding state law prohibiting municipalities from regulating those activities. *See also* Wauconda Fire Pro. Dist. v. Stonewall Orchards, LLP, 828 N.E.2d 216 (Ill. 2005) (fire district has authority to enact and enforce fire prevention regulations); Green v. Cleary Water, Sewer & Fire Dist., 910 So.2d 1022 (Miss. 2005) (district may enact ordinance to regulate disposal of wastewater

of residents who were not connected to district's sewer system). Could the Virginia court's rationale apply to invalidate this type of special district activity?

4. *Where Will the Money Come From?* What will the NVTA do now? Without the power of taxation, how will it generate the revenue necessary for its continued provision of service? The court's opinion applies broadly to invalidate both the taxes and fees the legislature had allowed NVTA to levy. The distinction between taxes and non-taxes is explored in Chapter VI. Narrowly targeted user fees, assessments and other charges that correlate benefit received to service provided are used by nearly all special districts for revenue-raising purposes. For an examination of the trend away from general taxation toward non-tax revenue devices, *see* Laurie Reynolds, Taxes, Fees, Assessments, Dues, and the "Get What You Pay For" Model of Local Government, 56 Fla. L. Rev. 373 (2004). If the NVTA cannot adopt any revenue-raising devices itself, can the state legislature do it on NVTA's behalf? If so, is there any real benefit to the court's holding in terms of government accountability? Would you support a proposal to have the NVTA's commissioners elected by the voters in its territory?

SETO V. TRI-COUNTY METROPOLITAN TRANSPORTATION DISTRICT OF OREGON

Supreme Court of Oregon
814 P.2d 1060 (1991)

GRABER, JUSTICE.

This case concerns the siting by the Tri-County Metropolitan Transportation District of Oregon (Tri-Met) of the Westside Corridor Project (the Project), the Portland metropolitan region's light rail extension. The 1991 Legislative Assembly enacted Senate Bill 573 (Or.Laws 1991, ch. 3) (the Act), which establishes an exclusive, speedy siting process for the Project. SB 573, §§ 1, 3. The Act places review of the Tri-Met Final Order with the Land Use Board of Appeals (LUBA) and directs that any judicial review of LUBA's decision be heard in this court, which is charged with deciding the case as expeditiously as possible. SB 573, §§ 8, 9(3). LUBA's Final Opinion and Recommendation, issued pursuant to the Act, recommended that the Tri-Met Final Order be affirmed.

The Act establishes an alternative to the usual land use siting and judicial review process, which is governed by ORS chapter 197. SB 573, §§ 1, 3. The extensive legislative preamble to the operative provisions of the Act states, among other things: The Project, at a total estimated cost of nearly $1 billion, is the largest public works project in Oregon's history. Various regional and state governmental bodies have identified the Project as the region's and the state's highest transportation priority and a high air-quality priority. The Project is important to help implement significant parts of the comprehensive plans of Multnomah and Washington counties, as well as those of the cities of Portland, Hillsboro, and Beaverton. A full funding agreement with the federal Urban Mass Transportation Administration (UMTA) must be signed by September 30, 1991, in order to assure that the federal government supplies 75 percent of the funding, rather than 50 percent or less, a difference of about $227 million. The usual process for local land use decisions and for administrative and judicial review would extend well beyond September 30, 1991. Final resolution of the land use issues must be accomplished by July 31, 1991, if the agreement with UMTA is to be signed by September 30, 1991. * * *

A brief description of the process established by the Act will provide necessary background for understanding the legal issues that petitioners raise. The first step in the siting process was for the Land Conservation and Development Commission (LCDC) to establish criteria for Tri-Met to use in making decisions on the light rail route, associated facilities, and highway improvements. SB 573, § 4. LCDC issued an order establishing criteria. Its order was subject to direct review in this court, SB 573, § 5, but no petition for review was filed. Tri-Met then went through a process to apply LCDC's criteria, resulting in a Final Order adopted April 12, 1991. *See* SB 573, § 6 (describing Tri-Met's process).

All affected governmental entities must amend their land use plans and regulations to make them consistent with the Tri-Met Final Order and must issue necessary and consistent construction permits. SB 573, § 7(1) and (2). Those conforming acts "shall not be reviewable by any court or agency." SB 573, § 7(3).

LUBA reviewed the Tri-Met Final Order. That review was exclusive and superseded, for the purposes of the Project, other laws relating to review of land use or other Tri-Met decisions. SB 573, § 8(1). * * *

With respect to Home Rule, petitioners note that the construction of the Project directly affects a geographic area containing five local governments. Petitioners assert that matters originally committed to those local governments under ORS chapter 197, i.e., adoption of comprehensive land use plan amendments, have been effectively reallocated to Tri-Met by SB 573 for purposes of the Project. That assertion is true, of course, but the exercise of state authority, even if it were on a subject of local interest and activity, does not necessarily violate constitutional Home Rule provisions.

* * * SB 573 plainly is addressed to * * * legitimate state objectives. * * * Land use regulation is addressed primarily to substantive social, economic, or other regulatory objectives of the state. *See, e.g.,* ORS 197.005 (need for statewide land-use planning program); ORS 197.835 (requiring local comprehensive plans and land-use regulations to comply

with LCDC's statewide goals and rules). Moreover, this particular transportation project has significant regional and statewide economic and social consequences. The non-federal funding for the Project is both regional and statewide: The voters in the Tri-Met district have approved a $125 million bond measure (increasing local property taxes) to fund the Project, and the state legislature has passed a law authorizing a revenue bond issue of up to $115 million to be financed and repaid by statewide lottery funds. SB 573 (preamble); HB 2128.

The state Department of Transportation has identified the Project as its highest transportation priority; the state Department of Environmental Quality has identified the Project as a high regional air-quality priority; and the state Department of Energy has identified the Project as one of its emission-reduction strategies for the Portland area. SB 573 (preamble). In House Bill 2128, which the 1991 Legislative Assembly just enacted, the legislature finds that the development, acquisition, and construction of light rail systems—including the Project:

"will accomplish the purpose of creating jobs and furthering economic development in Oregon, by, among other advantages:

"(a) Providing an important element of the public infrastructure that provides the basic framework for continuing and expanding economic activity in this state[.]" HB 2128, § 1(1).

Portland is the largest city in the state and a center of state economic activity. Its metropolitan area is geographically and strategically important with respect to the economic development and resources of the state. * * *

Petitioners, for their part, have pointed to no circumstance that would suggest that the Project is not geared primarily to accomplishing legitimate state economic, social, and regulatory objectives. We conclude that SB 573 is a general law addressed primarily to those objectives. Even if there were contrary policies preferred by the affected local governments, SB 573 is intended to prevail over them. *See* SB 573, §§ 1, 3 (establishing an exclusive siting process); § 7(1) and (2) (affected local government entities must amend their land use plans and regulations to make them consistent with the Tri-Met Final Order and must issue construction permits). * * *

The Final Opinion and Recommendation of the Land Use Board of Appeals is affirmed. The Final Order of the Tri-County Metropolitan Transportation District of Oregon is affirmed.

NOTES AND QUESTIONS

1. *Home Rule, Local Autonomy, and Regional Special Districts.* Most regional special districts encompass the territory of one or more multi-

purpose local government units, such as a municipality, town or village. Since many of these districts are located in metropolitan areas, they are likely to overlap with the jurisdiction of at least one home rule unit. Regional special districts themselves, though, are universally ineligible for home rule status. *See* Evins v. Richland County Historic Preservation Comm., 532 S.E.2d 876 (S.C. 2000). Although state courts, as in *Seto,* generally find that regional service needs trump the argument that home rule prevents the creation of regional service districts, at least one court found such a district inconsistent with the state constitutional provision for home rule. *See* Four-County Metropolitan Capital Improvement District v. Board of County Commissioners of County of Adams, 369 P.2d 67 (Colo.1962). In that case, the challengers claimed that the district would improperly interfere with home rule powers in several ways. Although an absolute majority of voters in the Denver area had approved formation of the district, that majority was due to lopsided support for the district within the city of Denver. Majorities of voters from each of the surrounding counties in the district had voted against it. In addition, the district's governing board was to be chosen by the legislative bodies of the participating counties and municipalities, rather than elected directly. The enabling statute gave the district broad and very general powers to finance (via sales tax) and construct capital improvements. The district would have become responsible for the widening of city streets in Denver. Which of these factors should be relevant to the court's decision on the district's legality in light of the home rule claim? One justice dissented, emphasizing the need for metropolitan solutions to the Denver area's infrastructure needs. *Id.* at 74–76 (McWilliams, J., dissenting). A concurring justice, while giving rhetorical support to "joint planning, joint effort, and mutual consideration and respect to arrive at proper solutions," found that the statute impermissibly established an "enveloping district . . . to perform local duties already delegated elsewhere by our constitution." *See id.* at 74 (Sutton, J., specially concurring).

In a dispute between a home rule city and a regional water and sewer district, the Indiana Supreme Court upheld the city's power to provide services to a school located outside its borders but within its extraterritorial jurisdiction, notwithstanding the regional special district's express authority to provide sewer services to land within ten miles of the city's corporate borders. In City of North Vernon v. Jennings Northwest Regional Utilities, 829 N.E.2d 1 (Ind. 2005), the court held that the state's Home Rule Act (with its grant of expansive powers) trumped the district's narrower authorization.

Did the siting process reviews in *Seto* provide for adequate consideration of local interests? What weight should the state give to local concerns about, for instance, the location of the rail lines, rail stations, and road crossings? How about more narrow interests such as the design of the station and the amenities it will provide? Is it possible to assure meaningful local input even in the absence of local control?

2.   *Categorization of Regional Special Districts*. The somewhat uncertain legal status of regional special districts creates opportunity for

wide-ranging litigation on a variety of issues. If, for instance, a regional special district is deemed to be a municipal corporation, it will not be entitled to assert the state's sovereign immunity; if, in contrast, it constitutes an instrumentality of the state, sovereign immunity may attach. *See, e.g.,* Beentjes v. Placer County Air Pollution Control Dist., 397 F.3d 775 (9th Cir. 2005) (regional special district not entitled to state's sovereign immunity and thus subject to Americans with Disabilities Act); Calvert Investments v. Louisville & Jefferson County Metropolitan Sewer District, 805 S.W.2d 133 (Ky.1991) (regional special district, as a municipal corporation, is liable under state tort law). In a related issue, a Texas court concluded that a regional transit authority performed essential public functions, and thus was protected by a statutory damages cap available to governmental, but not proprietary, activities undertaken by local governments. Salvatierra v. Via Metropolitan Transit Authority, 974 S.W.2d 179 (Tex.App.1998). *See also* Scott v. Shapiro, 339 A.2d 597 (Pa.Cmwlth.1975) (regional transportation authority not a state instrumentality and thus immune from state sunshine laws requiring disclosure and transparency in state proceedings); Fisher v. Southeastern Pennsylvania Transportation Authority, 431 A.2d 394 (Pa.Cmwlth.1981) (authority not subject to state law that provides full pay to state employees while they are on active duty with any reserve unit of the armed services). For exploration of issues surrounding state and local governmental tort liability and immunity, *see* Chapter VII.

The classification problem may extend to the regional district's operations as well. In Anema v. Transit Construction Authority, 788 P.2d 1261 (Colo.1990), the court concluded that the regional transit authority did not constitute a "service authority" for purposes of Colorado's statutory requirements of voter approval for fee assessments. Although classification is always difficult in local government law, regional special districts tend to display an unusually broad range of powers, methods of creation, means of selecting directors, and permitted financing capabilities, thus making categorization a particularly challenging undertaking.

3.   *The Accountability Problem.* The Illinois Regional Transportation Authority is run by a board of directors, composed of thirteen appointed members: four by the mayor of Chicago; four by those members of the county board of Cook County who do not represent the city of Chicago; three by the chairs of the county boards of other suburban counties; the Chair of the Chicago Transit Authority ex officio; and a Chairman appointed by a vote of three-fourths of the other directors. 70 ILCSS 3615/301. The Illinois Supreme Court rejected a one person, one vote challenge to the RTA's appointment procedure, concluding that the system was rationally related to the "legitimate state interest of providing safe, efficient, and affordable public transportation." *See* Stroger v. Regional Transp. Auth., 778 N.E.2d 683, 692 (Ill. 2002). Many regional special districts have similarly appointed governing boards, *e.g.*, Wash. Rev. Code § 70.44.040 (hospital district commissioners); Tex. Transp. Code Ann. § 451.502 (board of directors of regional transit authority). The Central Puget Regional Transit Authority is a regional

special district whose board members are appointed, but all of whom are themselves elected officials. Does this respond to the accountability concern? *See* Laurie Reynolds, Local Governments and Regional Governance, 39 Urb. L. 483 (2007). Even when special district boards are selected through popular election, voter participation is typically low, rarely exceeding 2–5%. *See* Nancy Burns, The Formation of American Local Governments: Private Values in Public Institutions 12–13 (Oxford Univ. Press 1994). Thus, the democratic accountability of regional special districts remains a serious issue.

STATE EX REL. ANGEL FIRE HOME AND LAND OWNERS ASSOCIATION, INC. v. SOUTH CENTRAL COLFAX COUNTY SPECIAL HOSPITAL DISTRICT

New Mexico Court of Appeals
797 P.2d 285 (1990)

HARTZ, JUDGE.

The South Central Colfax County Special Hospital District (the "hospital district") and other appellants seek reversal of the district court's ruling that the New Mexico Special Hospital District Act, NMSA 1978, Sections 4–48A–1 to –18 (Repl.Pamp.1984 & Cum.Supp.1989) (the "SHDA") is unconstitutional.

* * *

The SHDA authorizes creation of special hospital districts for "constructing, acquiring, operating and maintaining one or more public hospital facilities for the benefit of the inhabitants of the district." § 4–48A–3(A). If the district is composed of portions of more than one county, the portion in each county is called a "subdistrict." § 4–48A–2(E). When a petition for creation of a district is signed by enough registered voters in each subdistrict (ten percent of the votes cast for governor in the subdistrict at the last general election, § 4–48A–4(B)), the issue is submitted to a vote of the registered voters residing in the proposed district. § 4–48A–5. The district must be approved by a majority vote in each subdistrict. § 4–48A–5(F). The governing body of the district is a board of trustees consisting of at least five members—one elected by each subdistrict and the remainder elected at large. § 4–48A–6. To supplement income from hospital facilities, the district may raise money through assessment of ad valorem taxes to finance general obligation bonds, § 4–48A–14, or to pay for the operation and maintenance of hospitals and the operational costs of the district. § 4–48A–16. General obligation bonds (which are for such purposes as the purchase, construction or renovation of a hospital facility, § 4–48A–12) may be issued only after approval in a district-wide election. § 4–48A–12. Ad valorem taxes for operational and maintenance expenses can be imposed only with the approval of the voters in each subdistrict within the district. § 4–48A–16.

The territorial area to be included in the district must be designated in the petition seeking creation of the district. § 4–48A–4(A). The boundaries must satisfy the requirements of Section 4–48A–2(C), which reads:

"[S]pecial hospital district" means a district wherein a public hospital is located or is proposed to be created, and which:

(1)   is composed of contiguous and compact territory lying wholly within a single county; or

(2)   is composed of contiguous and compact territory which includes all or a portion of two or more counties or any combination thereof; and

(3)   contains within its boundaries one or more incorporated municipalities; or whose boundaries coincide and are concurrent with the territorial areas of one or more political subdivisions within such county or counties[.]

A special hospital district cannot include territory already included within another special hospital district. § 4–48A–3(B).

The core of the Land Owners' arguments is that the SHDA does not preclude proponents of a special hospital district from drawing the boundaries of a district so as to impose a substantial portion of the tax burden upon areas that do not materially benefit from the district. They cite their own situation as an example of such impropriety. The area of the hospital district coincides with the area of three contiguous school districts within Colfax County. The Land Owners assert that the Moreno Valley (where the Land Owners reside) contains only one-fourth of the electorate but one-half of the property tax base for the hospital district. They contend that the Moreno Valley will not benefit from the district, because the only hospital presently within the boundaries of the district is significantly farther away from the valley than the hospital in Taos, which is thirty miles from Angel Fire, within an adjacent county. Thus, in their view, they will not receive any benefit from the district but were included within the district only because its proponents, who reside in other portions of the district, wanted the Moreno Valley residents to pay half the costs of the district.

* * *

Challenges to local governmental boundaries by those who contend that the tax burdens arising from inclusion far exceed the benefits are usually answered by pointing to promotion of the general welfare. In *Ruberoid Co. v. North Pecos Water & Sanitation District*, 158 Colo. 498, 408 P.2d 436 (1965) (En Banc), the court rejected a claim that land not specially benefitted by the district should be excluded. The court said that water and sanitation districts are not created to improve property, but for the public health and welfare.

In *State ex rel. Pan American Production Co. v. Texas City*, 157 Tex. 450, 303 S.W.2d 780 (1957), *appeal dismissed*, 355 U.S. 603, 78 S.Ct. 533, 2 L.Ed.2d 523 (1958), a city annexation included uninhabitable land which allegedly could not benefit from municipal services. The court said, "Benefits may be intangible and incapable of exact ascertainment, but it is constitutionally sufficient if taxes are uniform and are for public purposes in which the City has an interest." *Id.* at 455, 303 S.W.2d at 783. *Cf. Carter v. Hamlin Hosp. Dist.*, 538 S.W.2d 671 (Tex.Ct.App.1976) (no denial of equal protection in legislature's including within hospital district an area whose owners will pay 40% of the taxes but will not use the hospital), *cert. denied*, 430 U.S. 984, 97 S.Ct. 1680, 52 L.Ed.2d 378 (1977).

* * *

To be sure, on occasion legislatures provide for the assessment of property taxes in direct proportion to benefits received, as when improvement districts are established. * * * Yet, failure of the legislature to provide for such a method of assessment is not necessarily an oversight. In some circumstances, special assessments are inappropriate because the governmental activity does not so much improve or benefit property as it promotes general welfare. *See Heavens v. King County Rural Library Dist.*, 66 Wash.2d 558, 404 P.2d 453 (1965) (En Banc) (invalidating legislation permitting special assessments to pay for library, because library is for general welfare of the community at large, not to enhance value of specific property). Special hospital districts have the latter function; they are designed to promote public health rather than to provide a specific benefit to real estate. Moreover, the legislature may properly have the *purpose* of imposing a tax that is disproportionate to benefits in order to redistribute income. * * *

In short, there appears to be no constitutional prohibition against including property within a special hospital district even though the property and its inhabitants will not benefit from inclusion. We need not, however, rely on that proposition in its extreme form. As we will explain later in this opinion, we fail to see how one could establish a total absence of benefit from inclusion in a special hospital district of relatively limited boundaries. Thus we will not hold the SHDA unconstitutional on its face solely because the tax/benefit ratio for certain property owners may differ from that for others within a special hospital district.

The Land Owners point out, however, that the disproportion between burdens and benefits is not the consequence of direct action by a legislative body; rather, the disparity is the consequence of the drawing of district boundary lines by the private persons who petition for creation of the district and benefit from the alleged unfairness. In other words, although creation of a district in which benefits and burdens are distributed disproportionately is not per se violative of substantive due process, the method of creation of a district may be constitutionally suspect if it improperly encourages such a result. * * *

Before evaluating whether the potential for abuse under the SHDA is excessive, we put the issue in perspective. First, Article IV, Section 24 of the New Mexico Constitution encourages, if it does not mandate, some delegation of legislative authority in setting boundaries for local governments. That section expressly prohibits the state legislature from incorporating cities, towns, or villages. Although it does not specifically forbid legislative formation of other local governmental bodies, it states that "where a general law can be made applicable, no special law shall be enacted." Thus, the legislature should, if possible, set guidelines for the creation of special hospital districts, without itself specifying the boundaries.

Second, in funding a special hospital district, there is no way to avoid the imposition of tax burdens greatly disproportionate to benefits. Health-conscious residents may use hospital facilities less often than heavy smokers; small families, less than large ones. If the tax is an ad valorem tax, a non-resident land owner could pay substantial taxes with only a minimal, if any, direct benefit, while a resident who owns no property (as well as non-resident tourists who need medical attention) may receive substantial benefits without paying any taxes. The practical impossibility of drawing the boundaries of a district created to benefit the public welfare in such a way that a uniform tax rate will result in equivalent cost/benefit ratios for all inhabitants or all property within the district is surely one reason why courts have rejected contentions that particular legislatively created districts impose disproportionate burdens upon specific taxpayers.

It follows from the above two observations that the legislature cannot provide for special hospital districts without delegating authority to create districts within which tax burdens will be disproportionate to the benefits arising from the district. The question of whether it is "fair" to include property within a district is necessarily one of degree. We know of no method of quantifying the calculation of fairness. All one can expect of the legislature is that it set outer limits that prevent gross inequities. We believe that the SHDA is adequate in that regard.

For example, the SHDA prohibits incorporation of an area into two different hospital districts. Subjecting one area to taxation by two districts contravenes legislative policy. Similarly, by requiring each subdistrict separately to approve a special hospital district, the SHDA prohibits voters in one county from compelling residents of another county to belong to the same district. The statutory requirements that districts be contiguous and compact prevent voters in one portion of a county from expanding the tax base of a district by reaching out to include any territory they wish. In addition, and perhaps most importantly, the SHDA states that the activities of the district are to be conducted "for the benefit of the inhabitants of the district," § 4–48A–3(A), thereby requiring that the district provide benefits to all areas within it. Even if this language is merely directory, an issue we need not reach here, we must presume, when a statute is challenged on its face, that sworn public officials—the board of trustees of the district—will act in accordance with their statutory duties. * * * One method by which the district can serve its inhabitants is, of course, to provide new hospital facilities for portions of the district that had no facilities when the district was created. Thus, the balance between benefits and burdens for those residing in a particular portion of the district cannot necessarily be determined by what benefits are available at the outset of the district's existence.

* * *

We see no reason to doubt that the legislature made a considered judgment that districts created in accordance with the SHDA would not impose unfair burdens on taxpayers within such districts. Indeed, we presume that the legislature made that judgment, because "every presumption is to be indulged in favor of the validity and regularity of legislative enactments." *In re Estate of Welch*, 80 N.M. 448, 449, 457 P.2d 380, 381 (1969). The legislature properly could have decided that the SHDA adequately prevents unfairness by requiring that districts (1) be compact and contiguous, (2) be separately approved in each subdistrict, and (3) be governed "for the benefit of the inhabitants of the district." Given the limitations imposed on districts by the statute, we conclude that the statute withstands the constitutional challenge. * * *

NOTES AND QUESTIONS

1.   *The Relationship Between Charges and Benefits.* The landowners in this case argued that they should be excluded from the hospital district because they will receive no benefit in exchange for the property taxes assessed by the district. The court considers two possible responses to the argument—that these landowners may in fact receive a benefit; and, in the alternative, that the legitimacy of the tax can be sustained even if there is no benefit. The court implies that it would require a closer nexus between benefit and charge if the district were funded by a special assessment rather than by a property tax. In contrast to the more familiar general taxation techniques, special assessments are levied against property within the governmental unit's territory to pay for improvements that are deemed to

provide a special benefit to the property itself. *See* Chapter VI for a detailed comparison of the two devices.

The use of a special assessment tends to reinforce the conception of the special district as primarily a service provider. Conversely, the use of general taxation is more consistent with a governmental unit formed to promote the general welfare. Other cases confirm this distinction. In Kendall v. Douglas, Grant, Lincoln & Okanogan Counties Public Hospital District No. 6, 820 P.2d 497 (Wash.1991), the court concluded that a hospital district tax was "levied for the benefit of the entire Hospital District and not a tax assessed for local improvements inuring to the benefit of specific land." *Id.* at 503. On that basis, and because of the "practical impossibility of drawing the boundaries of a district . . . in such a way that a uniform tax rate will result in equivalent cost/benefit ratios for all inhabitants or all property," *id.* at 503, the court refused to analyze the relationship between the district's financial charge and benefit to the landowner. *See also* Andrews v. County of Madison, 369 N.E.2d 532 (Ill.App.1977) (sewer district charge more similar to general tax than special assessment); Ruberoid Co. v. North Pecos Water & Sanitation District, 408 P.2d 436 (Colo.1965) (water and sanitation district can include land not specially benefitted because district's mission is for general public health and welfare rather than to improve property). Thus, the analytical line appears to be between, on the one hand, those districts whose improvements and projects are intended to improve property and, on the other hand, those whose mandate encompasses the general welfare of the region. As you can imagine, that is often a very fine distinction.

2. *Regional Special Districts and Boundaries—Who Draws the Lines?* Should the court have been more concerned about the role of private petitioners in crafting the district's boundaries? The *Angel Fire* court relied on an earlier case that had also rejected claims that a regional district failed to provide a benefit, Albuquerque Metropolitan Arroyo Flood Control Authority v. Swinburne, 394 P.2d 998 (N.M.1964). That case, however, involved a challenge to a regional special district that had been created directly by state legislation, rather than by landowner petition. Should the difference in how the districts are created influence a court's assessment of a property owner's objection to inclusion in the district? Should private individuals be able to corral wealthy landowners within a larger group in order to force them to subsidize a service they don't want? Recall the discussion of local government formation and boundary change in Chapter III. Is the procedure in *Angel Fire* comparable to the way in which most incorporation and annexation laws allow landowners to select the territory proposed for annexation or incorporation so as to ensure majority approval while at the same time providing an adequate tax base?

3. *Intergovernmental Disputes.* Our earlier discussion of interlocal conflicts considered the ways in which courts and legislatures might deal with intergovernmental disputes, primarily involving conflicting plans for the use of real property within the territory of one governmental unit. Which of the possible analytical approaches mentioned there is most suitable when one

of the entities is a regional special district? Consider the facts of Evanston v. Regional Transportation Authority, 559 N.E.2d 899 (Ill.App.1990). In that case, the city sought to apply its zoning ordinance to prevent the RTA from constructing a bus storage and maintenance facility. In the litigation arising out of the city's denial of the required permit, the court held that the RTA's proposal was exempt from the municipality's zoning ordinance. Evanston is a home rule municipality; nevertheless, the court concluded that "to permit a regional district to be regulated by a part of that region was incompatible with the [district]'s purpose." *Id*. at 904. Does that conclusion adequately reflect the likelihood that the RTA's decisionmaking process would incorporate local concerns about the siting of the bus barn? Is a single purpose regional district as well-suited as a general purpose municipality to protect the local general welfare? Should our decision about immunity from local police power be sensitive to the nature of the decisionmaker that seeks to assert immunity? Is it relevant that Evanston apparently did not want to lose the property tax revenues that would result from governmental use of the site? *See also* Blanch v. Suburban Hennepin Regional Park District, 449 N.W.2d 150 (Minn.1989) (park district can acquire property for regional park without approval of any affected municipality or other government unit).

4.   *Regional Special Districts as Metropolitan Governance Structures.* Most metropolitan areas have at least one regional special district similar to those described in these cases. In most instances, these government units exist for one reason only—to provide a single regional service. Although they may exercise significant powers with respect to their service, they may have limited political visibility. Consider the following description of the Los Angeles area:

> The South Coast Air Quality Management District exercises such immense powers over vehicle use, traffic congestion, land use, and job growth that many people call it a *de facto* regional government— albeit unelected and essentially unaccountable. The L.A. region also has multihundred-million or billion-dollar-a-year special districts in charge of transportation, water supply, waste disposal. Each agency's professionals do what seems logical from their own narrow point of view—building roads or transit lines, cleaning up L.A.'s putrid air, dealing with toxic wastes, for example. But *not one of them* is entrusted with the whole—seeing whether and how the pieces fit together. Cumulatively, for example, they spend $71 million a year on planning activities, virtually none of it coordinated.

Neal R. Peirce, Citistates, *supra*, at 318.

Even if regional special districts may raise concerns about voter accountability and limited vision, consider whether they are nevertheless a necessary part of metropolitan areas. How else could a metropolitan area plan and build an efficient public transit system? Having a specialized, single purpose focus, moreover, enables the directors of the district to maintain a high level of expertise, knowledge, and enthusiasm about their mandate. Possible regional legislative structures that might avoid some of the pitfalls while capturing the benefits are explored in Richard Briffault, The Local Government Boundary Problem in Metropolitan Areas, 48 Stan.L.Rev. 1115, 1164–70 (1996); Jerry Frug, Decentering Decentralization, 60 U.Chi.L.Rev. 253 (1993).

2.   CREATING A MULTI-PURPOSE REGIONAL STRUCTURE

Although multi-purpose regional governments are rare, examples can be seen in the Municipality of Metropolitan Seattle, the Portland Metropolitan Services District, and the Twin Cities Metropolitan Council in Minnesota. As their histories reveal, the origins of these regional government entities were relatively modest. Each was initially created to address a specific problem that was indisputably regional in scope. In the case of Seattle, it was water pollution; for Portland and Minneapolis, it was urban sprawl. Starting out as something akin to a single-purpose regional special district, these entities gradually acquired new regulatory responsibilities, such as transit, waste collection, or airport planning. As they became more visible and more powerful, heightened public scrutiny was inevitable. In the case of Seattle, those growing pains led to significant restructuring, while the Minneapolis response was to strengthen the existing regional government structure. The case and notes that follow illustrate the wide range of possible innovations for regional governmental efforts and anticipate some of the legal challenges faced by those who advocate federative solutions to metropolitan fragmentation.

CUNNINGHAM V. MUNICIPALITY OF METROPOLITAN SEATTLE

United States District Court
751 F.Supp. 885 (W.D.Wash.1990)

[Editors' Note: This case challenges the constitutionality of Seattle's "metropolitan municipal corporation," known as Metro, which had been created in 1958 to administer sewer services and to address the urgent environmental problems of Lake Washington and the Puget Sound. Pursuant to state law, Metro's governing Council was appointed by the elected legislative bodies of cities, the county, and smaller special districts throughout the area. Appointees consisted of both a number of elected officials and citizen representatives from each of the participating governmental units. In 1960, the Supreme Court of Washington upheld the constitutionality of Metro against challenges that Metro violated prohibitions of special legislation, delegation of legislative powers, and taxation without representation. Municipality of Metropolitan Seattle v.

Seattle, 357 P.2d 863 (Wash.1960). By the late 1980s, the Metro Council had grown to 44 members, and its functions had expanded to include the provision of mass transit services and development of regional land planning policies.]

DWYER, DISTRICT JUDGE.

The plaintiffs, registered voters in King County, Washington, challenge the constitutionality of the method by which the governing council of the Municipality of Metropolitan Seattle ("Metro") is selected. Metro is the entity in charge of water pollution abatement and public transportation throughout the county. The defendants are Metro and its current chairperson. Both sides have moved for summary judgment. * * *

The plaintiffs' primary challenge to the selection of the Metro Council is brought under the one person, one vote principle of the Equal Protection Clause of the Fourteenth Amendment. * * *

It does not matter whether the governmental powers possessed be deemed "legislative" or "administrative"; if the body possessing them is elected, the one person, one vote principle applies. *Hadley*, 397 U.S. at 55–56, 90 S.Ct. at 794–95. The one person, one vote principle does not forbid the states to use appointed, as distinguished from elected, bodies to carry out governmental functions, nor does it preclude experiments in new forms of local government. *Sailors v. Board of Education*, 387 U.S. 105, 110–111, 87 S.Ct. 1549, 1553, 18 L.Ed.2d 650 (1967). It also does not apply to an elected body whose functions are so narrow as to be not "governmental." *Salyer Land Co. v. Tulare Lake Basin Water Storage Dist.*, 410 U.S. 719, 727–30, 93 S.Ct. 1224, 1229–31, 35 L.Ed.2d 659 (1973); *see also Ball v. James*, 451 U.S. 355, 364, 101 S.Ct. 1811, 68 L.Ed.2d 150 (1981).

* * *

The arguments in Metro's behalf have emphasized its successes and have warned that a change in its structure may jeopardize its future. There is no doubt that Metro has been a great historic achievement. It was formed in 1958, before the Supreme Court's decisions applying the one person, one vote rule to state and local governments. Its original aim was to bring local governments together in a federation to clean up pollution in Lake Washington. In this Metro succeeded, and it has gone on to implement a water pollution abatement and sewage disposal program and a major public transportation system. The voters of King County have rejected a proposal to turn Metro's functions over to the county government.

The difficulty with these arguments is that efficiency and acceptance cannot justify a denial of equal protection of the laws. The citizens who criticize Metro's operations, and who seek to make it more democratic and responsive (as they see it), may be a minority, but the constitutional issue cannot be decided by a show of hands. That the buses run on time cannot justify a dilution of any citizen's right to vote.

* * *

There are always risks in change, but often worse ones in rigidity. There is no reason to believe that the vigorous governments and citizens of this region will fail to make Metro a continuing success if a change in the method of selecting its council is required to meet constitutional standards.

Metro is the only municipal corporation ever to exist under its authorizing statute, RCW Ch. 35.58.

The statute grants to the Metro Council legislative, financial, and other decision-making powers to carry out its functions of water pollution abatement and public transportation throughout King County. The broad purpose of Metro, according to the statute, is to "provide for the people . . . the means of obtaining essential services not adequately provided by existing agencies of local government." RCW § 35.58.010.

* * * The act grants to Metro "all powers which are necessary to carry out the purposes of the metropolitan municipal corporation and to perform authorized metropolitan functions." RCW § 35.58.180.

The statute recognizes that Metro is empowered to perform governmental functions, stating: "All functions of local government which are not authorized as provided in this chapter to be performed by a metropolitan municipal corporation, shall continue to be performed by the counties, cities and special districts. . . ." RCW § 35.58.180.

Metro is authorized to operate a mass transit system and water pollution abatement facilities. RCW §§ 35.58.050(3),–.200(2). It sets minimum standards for water pollution abatement facilities connected to its systems. Local governments with connected systems may not construct abatement facilities "without first securing [Metro's] approval." RCW 35.58.200(5). Metro is empowered to "take all actions necessary" to secure the benefits, and meet the requirements, of federal and state water pollution programs developed under the federal water pollution control act, 33 U.S.C. § 1251 et seq. It can compel its component agencies to comply with the requirements of national discharge elimination system permits issued to Metro or to the component agencies. RCW § 35.58.200(7).

Several powers are authorized for Metro's use in financing its operations: fixing rates and charges for local agencies' use of Metro water pollution abatement facilities; imposing charges directly on sewage system users who connect to Metro sewage facilities or establish new sewer service; appropriating general funds; levying sales taxes (with voter approval); levying excise or business and occupation taxes; issuing general obligation bonds for transit or water pollution abatement activities (some bonds require voter approval); and appropriating funds from its budget.

* * *

Metro also possesses certain police powers. It can adopt rules and regulations "as shall be necessary or proper to enable it to carry out authorized metropolitan functions" and can provide penalties for their violation, enforceable in King County Superior Court. RCW § 35.58.360. It can require certain King County political subdivisions to discharge sewage into Metro facilities, if it first declares that such action is necessary for public safety, health, and welfare. RCW § 35.58.200(3).

Metro currently exercises, or has exercised, many of these powers. It operates, in a county with more than 1.4 million residents, a county-wide mass transit system and a sewage system. Metro has contracted for the construction of facilities for its systems, sometimes amid public controversy. It charges connected local government entities for sewage services, and imposes a direct charge on new users of its sewage system. It has levied sales taxes (with voter approval) and a motor vehicle excise tax, and has issued millions of dollars worth of bonds. Its current annual budget is more than half a billion dollars. It has condemned property to support its activities. It has adopted and amended a comprehensive water pollution abatement plan, and is planning future mass transit systems to accommodate population growth. It has established programs to combat drug-abuse problems related to its transit operations.

* * *

Metro's reliance on *Salyer Land Co. v. Tulare Lake Basin Water Storage District*, 410 U.S. 719, 727–30, 93 S.Ct. 1224, 1229–31, 35 L.Ed.2d 659 (1973), is misplaced. The Court there carved out an exception to the one person, one vote principle for official bodies that do not exercise "governmental" functions. * * *

Metro, with its broad governmental powers and important impact on the lives of all residents of King County, cannot qualify for the *Salyer* exception. The Supreme Court has found governmental bodies with far more limited functions to be within the scope of the one person, one vote principle. * * *

Equal protection of the laws requires that the one person, one vote principle be honored if a governmental body is elected, not if it is appointed. * * * Plaintiffs contend that the Metro Council is elected. Defendants argue that it is appointed. The two sides agree that the question turns on whether a majority of the board members are deemed elected or appointed. *Cf. Oliver v. Board of Educ.*, 306 F.Supp. 1286, 1289

(S.D.N.Y.1969) (applying one person-one vote doctrine to board with five elected and two appointed members).

The Metro Council has forty-two members. * * *

It is uncontested that the King County Executive is an elected member of the Council. The statute provides that one member "shall be the elected county executive of the central county." RCW § 35.58.120(1). Thus, while a candidate for executive is not listed on the ballot as a candidate for the Metro Council, he is in fact running for both offices. The result is exactly the same as if the ballot title read "County Executive/Member of Metro Council."

[The court described similar provisions that made other mayors and King County Council members ex officio members of the Metro Council.] * * *

The foregoing categories—the county executive, mayors, King County Council members, and Seattle City Council members—add up to twenty-four members who are elected to the Metro Council because they take office automatically upon election to their county or city positions. They are chosen by the voters at the polls. There is no step in their designation, no act of selection, beyond the voters' decision to place them in office. These Metro Council members come within the Supreme Court's holding twenty years ago in *Hadley*, restated last year in Board of Estimate: "Whenever a state or local government decides to select persons by popular election to perform governmental functions. . . ." *Hadley*, 397 U.S. at 56, 90 S.Ct. at 795, quoted in *Board of Estimate*, 109 S.Ct. at 1437. These twenty-four are "selected by popular election."

* * *

Since a majority of its members are elected, the Council must be held to be an elected body. Because it exercises governmental powers, the method of selecting it must comply with the one person, one vote principle. * * *

There are various ways to cure the constitutional defect in the current method of selecting the Metro Council. The state and Metro should be given a reasonable time and opportunity to arrive at a legislative solution. While they are doing so the operations of Metro should not be disrupted and the November 1990 election of officials who will serve on the Metro Council should go forward without change. * * *

NOTES AND QUESTIONS

1. *The Aftermath.* Suburban and Seattle city officials predicted that regional cooperation would suffer with proportionate representation based on population. For those officials, the key to Metro's success had been its roughly equal sharing of power among central city, county, and suburbs. Though

those factions were widely divergent in population, Metro supporters contended that the arrangement appropriately gave equal force to each of three important perspectives of regional development. Can this interpretation of equal representation be used to counter or to modify the applicability of one person, one vote principles for regional governments? After a proposed merger between Metro and King County failed in a 1991 election, the voters approved a transfer of Metro's powers to King County in 1992. While basically preserving the structure of the preexisting countywide legislative body, the King County Council, the voters approved an increase in districts from nine to thirteen and required the creation of three special regional committees: transit, water quality and regional land use policy. These committees, whose membership was patterned after the Metro system declared unconstitutional in the main case, were to be comprised of county council members, Seattle City Council members, and elected suburban officials. Can you think of other ways to achieve proportional allocation of power among county, central city, and suburbs? *See* Bob Lane, Ballot Issues—Saying We Do: Metro, County Will Tie the Knot, Seattle Times, Nov. 4, 1992, at C8.

2.   *The County as Regional Government.* The merger of Metro with King County created a body with two very different responsibilities. Although the county assumed Metro's regional responsibilities, it also retained its function as the primary local government and service provider to the 400,000 King County residents who do not live in incorporated municipalities. When King County assumed Metro's functions the regional focus and purpose of the county government became more pronounced. In 1997, a Charter Review Commission called for creation of an "Unincorporated King County Council" as the analogue to the municipal governments in King County that have always dealt with local problems and services. In addition to giving the unincorporated areas an exclusively local legislative body, this allows the King County Council to focus on the broader regional issues formerly handled by Metro. *See* Phyllis Lamphere, Gene Colin, and Robert George, County Free of Local Responsibility Will Strengthen Regional Role, Seattle Post-Intelligencer, July 25, 1997, at A13.

Do you agree that the current allocation of power is an impediment to the articulation of broad regional policies? Would the creation of yet another local government be a wise or viable decision, especially in an area whose territory is constantly changing due to incorporations of new governments and annexations by existing governments? Should this new local government have taxing powers to finance local services to residents in the unincorporated areas? Because counties frequently impose only one uniform tax levy on all property within county borders, and because some proportion of county revenues pays for services that only the unincorporated areas use, city residents may pay for local county services that they do not receive. The creation of an unincorporated county council might eliminate some of that subsidization of county services by city residents. The potential for using the county as a metropolitan governance unit is significant. David Rusk's analysis of major metropolitan areas in the early 1990s, in fact, concluded that the county encompasses most of the metro area in a significant percentage of cases, accounting for more than 40% of the national population. *See* David Rusk, Cities Without Suburbs 95–96 (1993).

3. *Electing a Regional Government: The Portland Experiment.* Portland's Metropolitan Service District (also known as "Metro") was created in 1979 to provide comprehensive land use planning for the Portland area and to design its transportation system. It covers four counties, including Portland and twenty-three other municipalities. Pursuant to a constitutional amendment adopted in a 1993 statewide vote, Metro was authorized to adopt a home rule charter, under which it became the only elected regional government in the country. Over the years, Metro acquired other regional functions, including the provision of solid waste disposal services, operating the zoo, and managing the Oregon Convention Center.

Perhaps the most important, and certainly the most controversial, power entrusted to Metro has been the establishment of the Portland area's urban growth boundary (UGB). Under state law, municipalities must create a line of demarcation between urban land, which is either already developed or deemed developable, and rural land, where densities and types of development are heavily restricted. Proponents of the UGB assert that this growth control technique maximizes the public interest and minimizes the unnecessary conversion of rural land, while avoiding the negative consequences and public costs associated with uncontrolled urban sprawl. Critics, however, contend that the UGB has increased real estate prices, thus decreasing the availability of affordable housing for low- and moderate-income residents, shifted development to farther outlying areas not within Metro's jurisdiction that are receptive to growth, and facilitated the development of "ranchettes" or "martini farms" that meet the rural density requirements while breaking up agricultural land into large plots for weekend or vacation use. Metro's Region 2040 Growth Concept asserts that new development can be contained within current growth boundaries so long as the regional rapid transit system is completed. The subsequent voter approval of bond issues for the construction of the next segment of the light rail system and for government purchase of open space indicates that the public supports the plan. Jonathan Barnett and Ruth Knack, Shaping Our Cities: It's Your Call, 61 Planning 10 (1995). In 1997, the Oregon Supreme Court resolved several minor disputes surrounding a proposed statewide initiative to abolish Metro. Sizemore v. Myers, 953 P.2d 360 (Or.1997). Supporters dropped the initiative drive before election day, perhaps because public opinion polls consistently showed that two-thirds or more of the area population supports Metro.

4. *One Person, One Vote and Regional Governance.* As the *Cunningham* decision indicates, courts have generally been hostile to the argument that local units *per se* are entitled to representation in an elected regional government if that would cause substantial deviation from the rule of population equality. *See, e.g.,* Board of Estimate v. Morris, 489 U.S. 688

(1989). Alternatives to election by local subunits which would permit greater representation for smaller subunits than would be possible on a one person, one vote basis include (i) region-wide election but with a requirement that candidates be residents of different subunits; (ii) election by subunits with representatives given votes weighted according to subunit population; (iii) appointment by elected local officials, with number of seats allocated to a subunit based on criteria other than population.

Should the courts be willing to recognize a "regionalism" exception to a strict application of the one person, one vote requirement, comparable to the exception for special districts? *See* Richard Briffault, Who Rules at Home? One Person/One Vote and Local Government, 60 U.Chi. L. Rev. 339, 401–19 (1993). Or do the history of regional governance efforts in Seattle in the aftermath of *Cunningham*, as well as the developments in greater Portland, suggest that one person, one vote is not a serious barrier to regional governance?

5. *Addressing Fragmentation and Overlap: The Twin Cities Experiment.* The Metropolitan Council, a regional "overlay" governmental unit in the Minneapolis-St. Paul area, was created by state law in 1967. Composed of seventeen members appointed by the governor, its original mandate was to coordinate long range plans for the region and to recommend land use policies to local governments within its territories. Specifically, the Met Council was directed to prepare and adopt a Metropolitan Development Guide for the seven-county area. That initial project consumed seven years of hearings, studies, and reports. In 1976, the legislature adopted an incremental increase in Council powers, authorizing it to approve or deny local comprehensive plans on the basis of their consistency with the Metropolitan Development Guide. For a detailed history of the Met Council and its evolving responsibilities, *see* Judith A. Martin, In Fits and Starts: The Twin Cities Metropolitan Framework, *in* Donald N. Rothblatt and Andrew Sancton eds., Metropolitan Governance: American/Canadian Intergovernmental Perspectives 205–241 (Inst. Govt'l Studies Press 1993).

Until 1994, the Met Council acted in a loose supervisory capacity, coordinating policies with various other metropolitan agencies, such as the Metropolitan Waste Control Commission and the Metropolitan Airport Commission. Though regionalization of some policy formulation had been accomplished, the existence of multiple, relatively independent agencies continued to impede the formulation of a truly coordinated regional approach to problems such as land use, housing, transit, and the environment. The passage of the Metropolitan Reorganization Act of 1994 transformed the Met Council "from a $40-million-a-year regional planning agency, with loose supervisory control over regional agencies, to a $600-million-a-year regional government directly operating regional sewers and transit systems." Myron Orfield, Metropolitics, *supra,* at 129. A companion piece of legislation, which would have changed the Met Council from an appointed to an elected body, failed by one vote. Consider whether the evolution of Seattle's Metro Council and the resulting *Cunningham* decision might suggest a similar fate for a Met Council that continues to be staffed with appointed members.

    6. *Proposals for More Extensive Regionalization of Local Governments.* Paul Boudreaux's E Pluribus Unum Urbs: An Exploration of the Potential Benefits of Metropolitan Government on Efforts to Assist Poor Persons, 5 Va.J.Soc.Pol'y & L. 471 (1998) argues that a regional government structure is necessary to combat poverty. Peter Salsich, in Thinking Regionally About Affordable Housing and Neighborhood Development, 28 Stetson L.Rev. 577 (1999) asserts that low- and moderate-income housing policy cannot be effective without a metropolitan governmental entity in control of land use and taxation decisions. David Rusk, the former mayor of Albuquerque, is a leading proponent of metropolitan governance. He urges state governments to consider four different approaches: (1) unifying local governments, either by empowering urban counties, by consolidating county and municipal governments, or by creating a regional government for the metropolitan area; (2) authorizing municipal annexation without approval of property owners; (3) limiting the creation of new municipalities; and (4) promoting public partnerships for joint action among local governments. David Rusk, Cities Without Suburbs, *supra.*

    Regionalization also has its critics. Some oppose consolidation on the grounds that it deprives citizens of their choice of service providers and removes the incentives for improvement and efficiency that results from interlocal competition. Others argue that bigger government brings a reduced sense of community empowerment and decreases government responsiveness. Moreover, the political hurdles are enormous. Entrenched local government bureaucracies and the apparent public preference for continued suburbanization are but two of the major obstacles to metropolitan governance.

    Myron Orfield's strategy in Metropolitics for successful regionalization efforts can be summed up in one piece of advice for the central city: "It's the Older Suburbs, Stupid." That phrase captures much of the current political reality of many major metropolitan areas. As the first ring of suburbs age, he argues, they have begun to show the same signs of decline and decay as the central city. Influx of the poor, aging infrastructure, and exodus of the mobile middle class to more distant suburbs affect both central city and older suburbs alike. To capitalize on what he sees as a natural alliance, Orfield recommends joint legislative efforts to seek the imposition of regional fair housing obligations, property tax sharing, and a redirection of government infrastructure spending from urban fringe to central city and inner suburban ring.

3. MOVING TOWARD CONSOLIDATION?

    If consolidation is defined as the total merger of pre-existing local governments into one new unit, the most recent major consolidation in the United States occurred in 1898. In that year, after more than ten years of planning, deliberation, and referenda, the New York legislature combined all the territory on the New York side of the New York harbor into what is now known as New York City. For a history of that process, *see* Richard Briffault, Voting Rights, Home Rule and Metropolitan Governance: The Secession of Staten Island as a Case Study in the Dilemmas of Local Self-Determination, 92 Colum.L.Rev. 775, 780–82 (1992). More recently, a few metropolitan areas have implemented so-called "two tier" or "federative" forms of metropolitan government. Under that approach, pre-existing local governments are generally preserved while a region-wide entity acquires more area-wide powers. The case and notes that follow describe some of the two-tier consolidations.

STATE EX REL. TOMASIC V. UNIFIED GOVERNMENT OF WYANDOTTE COUNTY/KANSAS CITY, KANSAS

Supreme Court of Kansas
955 P.2d 1136 (1998)

ABBOTT, JUSTICE:

This is an original action in quo warranto. The action was filed by Wyandotte County District Attorney Nick Tomasic seeking a ruling on the constitutionality of the Consolidation Act, K.S.A.1997 Supp. 12–340 et seq., which authorized a procedure whereby the voters of Wyandotte County (County) could adopt a consolidated government for County and Kansas City, Kansas (City).

The parties filed a stipulation of facts. By way of background, we include a portion of the stipulation of facts.

"The County is comprised of 155.7 square miles and has a 1996 estimated population of 153,427. The County is the smallest county in Kansas. The County has the fourth largest population in the State of Kansas among Kansas counties.

"The County includes four (4) incorporated municipalities and a small unincorporated area of 2.7 square miles, the Loring area, which is south of Bonner Springs. The four incorporated municipalities are the City, Edwardsville, Bonner Springs and Lake Quivira.

"The City is a city of the first class. It is comprised of 127.85 [square] miles, and has a 1996 estimated population of 142,654. The City is the second largest city in Kansas in terms of population and the largest city in Kansas in land area.

"Approximately 82.1% of the County is within the geographic boundaries of the City.

"The City is the county seat of the County. The County Courthouse and most of the county officials are located in the City.

[The other three incorporated municipalities in the county are much smaller. Their population ranges between 1,000 and 6,500, and their territorial base covers from slightly over one square mile to approximately 16 square miles.]

"The unincorporated Loring area of the County covers 2.7 square miles. Its 1996 estimated population is 95. * * *

"Pursuant to the Consolidation Act, on or about May 15, 1996, Governor William Graves appointed five (5) private citizens to form the Consolidation Study Commission of Kansas City, Kansas and Wyandotte County (the 'Commission'). * * * The members were not elected officials or employees of any of the governmental entities in the County.

"The Consolidation Act charged the Commission with the responsibility to study the consolidation of the City and the County governments, or the consolidation of certain offices, functions, services and operations thereof, and to prepare and adopt a plan addressing such consolidation of governments or offices, functions, services and operations, as deemed appropriate.

"From May through October, 1996, the Commission held public hearings and meetings for the purposes of providing and receiving information about the consolidation of governmental services. * * *

"In November of 1996, pursuant to the Act, the Commission adopted a preliminary plan for the consolidation of the City and County governments. * * *

"Following adoption of the preliminary plan, the Commission held three (3) public hearings to solicit public opinion about the preliminary plan.

"The Commission modified certain provisions of the preliminary plan following receipt of comments at the hearings.

"A Consolidation Study Report (the 'Plan') dated January 13, 1997, was prepared and adopted by the Commission. The Plan was submitted to the Kansas Governor and Legislature on January 13, 1997 * * *

"The Plan provides for a new consolidated form of government, to be known as the Unified Government of Wyandotte County/Kansas City, Kansas (the 'Unified Government'). The existing governments of the City and the County are replaced by a governing body composed of a Mayor/Chief Executive and a ten member Unified Board of Commissioners. Eight Commission members are nominated and elected in eight newly created districts. Two County-wide Commission members are nominated from two newly created districts comprised of the four northern-most and four southern-most districts; these Commission members are elected at large. The Mayor/Chief Executive has veto power which can be overridden by a two-thirds majority of the Unified Board of Commissioners.

"The Plan provides for the appointment of a County Administrator by the Mayor/Chief Executive with the consent of the Unified Board of Commissioners. The County Administrator is directly responsible for the daily functions of the Unified Government. * * *

"The Kansas Legislature did not adopt a concurrent resolution on or before February 12, 1997, rejecting the Plan. Neither the Governor nor the Kansas Legislature acted in any manner on the Plan. * * *

"Pursuant to the Consolidation Act, the Plan was submitted to the qualified electors of the County (which included City residents) at the April 1, 1997 election. Fifty-nine and six-tenths percent (59.6%) of the electors voting on the Plan voted in favor thereof. * * *

"The Consolidation Act provides that the Unified Government is a county with all the powers, functions and duties afforded to counties under the Constitution and laws of the State, and is also a city of the first class with all the powers, functions and duties afforded to cities of the first class under the Constitution and laws of the State. The Consolidation Act provides that upon the effective date of consolidation of the City and County governments, the territory of the Unified Government includes all of the territory of the County for purposes of exercising powers, duties and functions of a county, and all of the territory of the County, except the territory of Bonner Springs, Edwardsville, Lake Quivira and the unincorporated areas of the County for purposes of exercising the powers, duties and functions of the City. * * *

"The Unified Government has operated as a consolidated city/county since the effective date of consolidation. * * *

"Pursuant to the Plan, the elected offices of County Clerk, County Treasurer, County Surveyor and Public Administrator became appointed positions. All functions performed by these officials will be retained in the newly appointed positions. * * *

"The Plan provides that several offices have been retained for county-wide elections: Sheriff, District Attorney and the Register of Deeds. * * *

"As of the date hereof, the Unified Government has merged some City and County departments, including the parks departments, clerks departments, legal departments and personnel departments, and merged functions of many other departments. [Approximately] 2,000 employees of the Unified Government have signed up under new health care plans under which they [became] covered as of January 1, 1998. The Unified Government has issued industrial revenue bonds. It has sent tax bills and is collecting taxes. It has carried out all aspects of consolidated city-county government, has taken official actions, has entered into contracts and has prosecuted persons for violations of municipal ordinance and state law. The Unified Government is proceeding with its capital improvements program and with economic development projects and tax increment financing projects that will require the use of the powers of eminent domain and the issuance of general obligation bonds."

* * *

II.   DELEGATION OF LEGISLATIVE POWER

* * * [A] legislature may delegate an administrative power to a different branch of government. Administrative power is the power to administer or enforce a law, as opposed to the legislative power to make a law. The legislature does not need constitutional authority to delegate administrative power because it is not delegating a power reserved for its branch of government under art. 2, § 1.

* * *

A delegated power constitutes administrative power if the delegation contains sufficient policies and standards to guide the nonlegislative body in exercising the delegated power. * * * In other words, the legislature may enact general provisions and delegate to an administrative body the discretion to " 'fill in the details' " if the legislature establishes " 'reasonable and definite standards to govern the exercise of such authority.' " *State v. Ponce*, 258 Kan. 708, 712, 907 P.2d 876 (1995) (quoting *Kaufman v. Kansas Dept. of SRS*, 248 Kan. 951, 956, 811 P.2d 876 [1991]) * * *.

The relator argues that the Act contained only two stated factors to guide the Commission in the exercise of its delegated power. These factors were found in K.S.A.1997 Supp. 12–343 and require the Commission to consider, in making a consolidation recommendation:

> "(1) . . .   the   efficiency   and   effectiveness   of   the administrative operations of the city and county [and]

> "(2) . . .   the costs and benefits of consolidating the city and county or certain city and county offices, functions, services and operations."

* * *

Clearly, we are dealing with a complex area of law involving social and economic issues. The legislature provided for an independent public body (the Commission) to study the issue of consolidation, provided funds for a Commission staff, and gave sufficient power to the Commission to study, draft, and redraft a plan. K.S.A.1997 Supp. 12–344 sets forth specific items the Commission, as an administrative body, was required to provide for in the Plan, should it recommend consolidation. It provides:

"(a) Any plan submitted by the commission shall provide for the exercise of powers of local legislation and administration not inconsistent with the constitution or other laws of this state.

"(b) If the commission submits a plan providing for the consolidation of certain city and county offices, functions, services and operations, the plan shall:

"(1) Include a description of the form, structure, functions, powers and officers and the duties of such officers recommended in the plan.

"(2) Provide for the method of amendment of the plan.

"(3) Authorize the appointment of, or elimination of elective officials and offices.

"(4) Specify the effective date of the consolidation.

"(5) Include other provisions determined necessary by the commission.

"(c) If the plan provides for the consolidation of the city and county, in addition to the requirements of subsection (b) the plan shall:

"(1) Fix the boundaries of the governing body's election districts, provide a method for changing the boundaries from time-to-time, any at-large positions on the governing body, fix the number, term and initial compensation of the governing body of the consolidated city-county and the method of election.

"(2) Determine whether elections of the governing body of the consolidated city-county shall be partisan or nonpartisan elections and the time at which such elections shall be held.

"(3) Determine the distribution of legislative and administrative duties of the consolidated city-county officials, provide for consolidation or expansion of services as necessary, authorize the appointment of a consolidated city-county administrator or a city-county manager, if deemed advisable, and prescribe the general structure of the consolidated city-county government.

"(4) Provide for the official name of the consolidated city-county.

"(5) Provide for the transfer or other disposition of property and other rights, claims and asserts of the county and city."

We are convinced that the legislature only delegated to the Commission the administrative power to draft a plan which was to be submitted to the voters of Wyandotte County for their approval or rejection. Most of our existing statutory law has been drafted by committees, and the statute books contain many laws that allow options to the voters to decide matters of public concern. Nothing can be more basic than to allow voters of a given area to decide the form of government they desire.

* * * [T]he standards which the legislature provided in the Act herein were definite and sufficient so to guide the Commission in determining if consolidation should occur and, if so, how much information should be included in the Plan. Such standards defined the parameters of the Commission's discretion. It would have been both impractical and unnecessary for the legislature to have provided more detail in the Act when it delegated the power at issue to the Commission. Instead, the legislature directed the Commission, as an administrative agency, to utilize administrative power and "fill in the details" within the definite outline set forth in the Act. The Act is not an unconstitutional delegation of legislative power to an administrative agency. This issue fails.

III. ART. 2, § 20 OF THE KANSAS CONSTITUTION

Art. 2, § 20 of the Kansas Constitution provides:

"Enacting clause of bills; laws enacted only by bill. The enacting clause of all bills shall be 'Be it enacted by the Legislature of the State of Kansas:' *No law shall be enacted except by bill.*" (Emphasis added.)

* * * [O]nce the Plan was approved by voters, it converted the Wyandotte County elective offices of county clerk, county treasurer, public administrator, and county surveyor to appointive positions in the Unified Government. This was done without formal amendment to the [statutes providing for these positions]. The relator takes issue with this change because the legislature had previously determined that these positions in Wyandotte County must be elective, not appointive, positions.

* * * [T]he relator asserts that the Act violates art. 2, § 20, which prohibits any law from being enacted except by bill, because the Plan attempts to amend statutes, by exempting the Unified Government from their application, without submitting such amendments in the form of a bill to the legislature.

* * *

The voters of Wyandotte County did not enact new law by adopting the Plan. Rather, they exercised the express authority given to them by the legislature and adopted a local option—the Plan. The legislature properly delegated the job of filling in the details of the Plan to the Commission. It provided the Commission with certain guidelines or factors that must be included in the Plan, should the Commission recommend consolidation. * * *

However, neither the Plan nor the voters of Wyandotte County implicitly amended these statutes. Rather, the voters simply exercised the authority specifically granted to them by the legislature, in the Act, to adopt a local option (the Plan), which authorized the elimination of several elective offices, as the Act specifically authorized the Plan to do. The legislature was fully aware that these changes might occur and approved of these changes by passing the Act, which authorized such changes.

The Plan did not first need to be submitted to the legislature in the form of a bill to be proper. The Act does not violate art. 2, § 20 of the Kansas Constitution for the failure to include such a provision. * * *

The Act does not specifically repeal or amend any prior law. Thus, all prior laws still apply to the Unified Government, unless the prior laws conflict with the Act or the Plan. If such conflict occurs, then the Plan's provisions, as authorized in the Act, prevail because the Act is the more specific, more recent statute. * * *

NOTES AND QUESTIONS

1. *Too Much or Too Little Legislative Involvement?* The Kansas court considered and rejected a number of other legal challenges, including arguments involving the allegedly unconstitutional delegation of legislative power to a private entity, the uniformity provision of the state constitution, the constitutional guarantee of home rule, Kansas City's charter, and the single subject rule. Most of the legal challenges involved the allocation of decisionmaking power in two different directions: horizontally, among the branches of state government; and vertically, from the legislature to the commission and to the voters. In some cases, the relator questioned the legislature's decision to give up power; in other cases, the claim was that the legislature had improperly tried to retain power. Can you articulate the possible justifications for the way in which the legislature attempted to allocate power among itself, the governor, the commission, the voters, and the existing local government units subject to the consolidation? How might the well-established tradition of local self-determination in the formation and change of governmental boundaries (*see* Chapter III) have affected the court's approach to the way in which the legislature chose to structure the consolidation process? Should the legislature adopt general consolidation enabling legislation, akin to general incorporation and annexation statutes, or should the legislature tailor the rules and procedures to particular cases? Do the legal principles used by the court to analyze each individual challenge suggest a coherent vision of how a consolidation proposal can best protect the affected interests while ensuring orderly and efficient procedures? Can you

suggest a better way to structure the consolidation process? Would unilateral legislative action or some other system have been preferable?

2.   *Elements of a Successful Consolidation Campaign.* Consolidations such as the one in Kansas City have been extremely rare in the United States. Between 1805 and 1977, only twenty-seven city-county consolidations occurred, most typically in areas with populations under 100,000. One commentator identified four major obstacles to consolidation: (1) the longstanding American tradition of small and medium sized communities; (2) widespread distrust of, and even hostility towards, cities; (3) suburbanization and its promise of country living and upward mobility; and (4) strong patterns of housing segregation along the lines of social class, race, ethnicity, and religion. John Kincaid, Regulatory Regionalism in Metropolitan Areas: Voter Resistance and Reform Persistence, 13 Pace L.Rev. 449, 453–55 (1993). Despite these obstacles, Kansas City organizers were successful in their campaign. The leaders of the movement attributed their success to six important ingredients: (1) endorsement by influential government officials; (2) allegations of corruption in city government; (3) citizen dissatisfaction with government services; (4) participation in consolidation efforts by members of minority groups; (5) extensive face-to-face canvassing and media exposure; and (6) fear of future annexation by the city. Robert P. Stigman, Consolidation Crusaders Reap Rewards of Success, Kansas City Star, Oct. 24, 1997, at C5.

3.   *State Consolidation Laws.* Consolidation between or among cities is allowed by statute in 42 states; in 34 of them, a referendum is required to obtain majorities of citizens voting in each city. In the remaining states, some require that voters of only one city approve the consolidation, and a few authorize consolidation without voter involvement. Consolidation of cities and counties is allowed in only 14 states; most of these states require a referendum at either the county or city level. *See* U.S. Advisory Commission on Intergovernmental Relations, State Laws Governing Local Government Structure and Administration 9 (1993).

One study of Minnesota's fairly typical law concluded that the statutory procedures actually favor anti-consolidation interests in several ways. The author argued that the statute improperly gives existing city councils, with their strong instinct for self-preservation, important roles in the consolidation process. In addition, she criticized the way in which the law makes state funds available for city council consolidation studies but not for citizen-led studies, and creates financial disincentives to consolidate by requiring that the unconsolidated cities transfer all assets to the consolidated city while retaining liability for all existing debts. Her proposed statutory modifications would enhance the independence of local consolidation commissions, provide for consolidation of existing debts, and correct the resource imbalance that allows city councils unlimited freedom to spend to defeat consolidation campaigns. *See* Beth Walter Honadle, The Barriers to Citizen-Led Municipal Consolidations: An Analysis of Minnesota's Municipal Boundary Adjustment Law, 17 Hamline J.Pub.L. & Pol'y 63 (1995).

4. *Vertical and Horizontal Consolidations.* Reread the *Tomasic* court's description of the pre-consolidation territorial boundaries of city and county. Can you see why the Kansas City consolidation can be described as primarily a vertical, rather than horizontal, consolidation? Can you suggest why such a consolidation faces fewer political obstacles than what might be termed a horizontal consolidation? Might that explain why the Commission excluded the municipalities of Edwardsville, Bonner Springs, and Lake Quivira from the consolidation proposal? In fact, all recent consolidation efforts have been vertical rather than horizontal. That is, none have merged autonomous municipalities into one new regional government, but, rather, have combined the previously overlapping territories of county and city. To the extent that the county's boundaries include an entire metropolitan region, though, city-county consolidation will produce a regional governance structure. In fact, one study concluded that vertical consolidation of central city with surrounding county would bring metropolitan governance to 256 metropolitan areas, accounting for 42% of the national population. For another 60 metropolitan areas, which contain more than one county, more extensive horizontal consolidations would be necessary. David Rusk, Cities Without Suburbs, *supra,* at 95–96.

5. *The Nashville Experience.* The Metropolitan Government of Nashville and Davidson County resembles the consolidation described in *Tomasic.* Created in 1963, the steps toward consolidation followed the sequence of state enabling legislation, creation of charter commission, and acceptance of charter by majorities of city and county governments. Nashville's Metro Government, however, preserved two "service districts," drawn along prior city-county boundaries, which established a two-tier taxation scheme. The urban services district, encompassing the former city, pays a higher tax rate than the county's general service district. The supreme court of Tennessee upheld this allocation of tax burden in Frazer v. Carr, 360 S.W.2d 449, 454–456 (Tenn.1962), noting that a single, uniform tax rate would be "unjust and unequal," *id.* at 456, because of the different level of services required by the taxpayers in those two areas. Two other features of Metro have been described as hindrances to metropolitan efficiency. First, yielding to the resistance of entrenched politicians, Metro's legislative Council simply combined the pre-existing county and city legislatures, resulting in a rather large forty-member body. Second, because reformers were unable to abolish constitutional protection for a number of elected county officers, including the sheriff, trustee, and register of deeds, departmental consolidations have been rocky at times. Ellen Dahnke, The 'Metro Experiment'; Nashville Blazed a Trail in '63 with its Consolidation, The Tennessean, Sept. 9, 1999, at 1D.

Nor has consolidation completely stopped the creation of smaller units of government within Metro. Tennessee law provides that "no municipality and no public service district, including, but not limited to, a utility district, sanitary district or school district, shall thereafter be created [in a consolidated county]" Tenn. Code Ann. § 7–1–104 (1992). When Metro proposed to build a landfill within its borders, residents near the site formed a watershed district. Under state law, landfill permits require the approval of watershed districts. The state supreme court held that the watershed district did not constitute a prohibited "public service district," rejecting Metro's arguments about increased fragmentation, duplication, and inefficiency. State ex rel. Metropolitan Government of Nashville and Davidson County v. Spicewood Creek Watershed District, 848 S.W.2d 60 (Tenn.1993).

Notwithstanding the consolidation, Metro has not been immune from the suburbanization exodus that has plagued other central city areas. Between 1994 and 1995, for example, 7,600 people moved from Metro to outlying suburban areas, while 7,000 people moved into Metro. Those moving into Metro had incomes that were lower than the incomes of those moving out. The resulting decrease in the average Metro income, though not drastic, has implications for the demand for social services and for Metro's local revenue-raising capacity. Renee Elder, Population Swap Costs Metro; Nashville's Average Income Keeps Falling as Higher-Income Families Migrate to Suburbs, The Tennessean, Aug. 19, 1997, at 1A.

6.   *Variations on a Theme: Consolidation Efforts in Miami and Indianapolis.* One of the initial, and most basic, decisions to be made by regional reformers is how to deal with the cities that already exist within the area. In their consolidation efforts, Miami and Indianapolis dealt with that issue in fundamentally different ways. As you read the following descriptions, compare the resulting regional structures and try to identify the political interests protected by each decision, what kinds of facts are likely to influence the choice, as well as the relative benefits and disadvantages of each approach.

With the adoption of its home rule charter in 1957, Metropolitan Dade County, which encompasses the city of Miami, became the first major metropolitan area to embrace a regional approach to local governmental structure. Under the terms of the Florida Constitution, "the Metropolitan Government of Dade County may exercise all the powers conferred now or hereafter by general law upon municipalities." Fla.Const. art. VIII, § 6(f). While the constitutional enhancement of the county's power was clear, the language did not clarify the division of functions and powers between the county and the existing cities. The reform, however, left in place all existing municipal government entities. As interpreted in an early decision by the Florida Supreme Court, Metropolitan Dade County had the power to regulate only "those municipal functions and services that are susceptible to, and could be most effectively carried on under, a uniform plan of regulation applicable to the county as a whole." Miami Shores Village v. Cowart, 108 So.2d 468, 471 (Fla.1958). As a corollary, the court stressed, "municipal autonomy as to the purely local function or powers of the municipalities in Dade County," *id.*, was protected from infringement by the metropolitan county. With this operating principle established at the start, the allocation of power between existing municipal government and metropolitan county was left to be sorted out by application of a local versus regional dichotomy.

For a good description and analysis of the early history of Metropolitan Dade County, *see* Note, The Urban County: A Study of New Approaches to Local Government in Metropolitan Areas, 73 Harv.L.Rev. 526 (1960).

The relationship between Metropolitan Dade County and the residents of the unincorporated parts of the county has not been harmonious. Those residents look to the county for their municipal services, yet the county also provides countywide services to all county residents. The county commission is elected by residents of both incorporated and unincorporated areas. In Levy v. Miami-Dade County, 254 F.Supp.2d 1269 (S.D.Fla. 2003), residents in the unincorporated areas alleged an unconstitutional dilution of their vote by the residents of incorporated cities. The court rejected the claim of overinclusive voting rights and malapportionment. So long as the county serves both constituencies (the unincorporated area and the cities), is there any way to solve the problem? Should the county be severed into two distinct governmental entities, one for each type of services?

The 1970 creation of Unigov in Indianapolis was accomplished by state statutory mandate. It resulted in an outright merger between the county and city legislative bodies, and their respective administrative offices and departments, into a new legislative council. The mayor of Indianapolis became Unigov's first chief executive, and the legislative council was created to consist of 25 members elected from newly drawn single-member districts, along with four at-large members. The consolidation, however, was not total: three municipalities, sixteen townships, a hospital authority, airport authority, and twenty-two separate school districts remained outside the purview of Unigov. Notwithstanding the preservation of some independent local government units, Unigov was able to achieve a substantial consolidation of much of the area's local property tax base. *See* David J. Bodenhamer and Robert G. Barrows, eds., The Encyclopedia of Indianapolis 62–63 (Indiana U. Press 1994). The state's supreme court upheld Unigov's constitutionality in Dortch v. Lugar, 266 N.E.2d 25 (Ind.1971), rejecting the challenges of invalid delegation of power, special legislation, impairment of contract, and equal protection violations.

In comparing the two approaches to the fate of a region's major city, ask yourself which is likely to produce a more unified regional response to the area's needs. The strength of Metropolitan Dade County lies in the extent to which it is able to preempt municipal regulation. Unigov, in contrast, while it faces no competition from Indianapolis, is left to deal with a few small pockets of unconsolidated municipalities and a number of independent special districts. Another distinction lies in the relevant demographics. When Metropolitan Dade County was created, Miami comprised only one-third of the county's population; Indianapolis was the home of nearly 70% of Marion County's population. And finally, compare the methods with which each entity was created. Metropolitan Dade County was formed by local adoption of a county charter; Unigov, in contrast, was the handiwork of the state legislature.

4. INTERSTATE COMPACTS

The incentives for interstate cooperation are similar to those that emerge within a single state. The presence of large, densely populated urban areas in multistate regions frequently creates efficiency rationales for interstate cooperative attempts in the provision of services. In 2012, there were fifteen metropolitan areas with populations one million or area that spanned state lines. These included New York, Philadelphia, Washington, Cicago, and Boston. (Three major metropolitan areas—Detroit, San Diego, and El Paso—cross an international border; that presents distinctive problems that are beyond the scope of this book.) Moreover, just as economic forces are insensitive to state borders, natural ecological boundaries do not respect political line-drawing either. Many of the nation's important natural sites (the Chesapeake Bay, Lake Tahoe, and the Columbia River Gorge, to name a few) straddle state lines and are thus likely subjects for multistate environmental cooperation. The Supreme Court has recognized the potential that interstate agencies could respond to " 'interests and problems that do not coincide nicely either with the national boundaries or with State lines' [or] . . . interests that 'may be badly served or not served at all by the ordinary channels of National or State political action.' " Hess v. Port Authority Trans-Hudson Corporation, 513 U.S. 30, 40 (1994) (citation omitted).

Though the economic and ecological impetuses for cooperation may be the same irrespective of state boundaries, interstate cooperative agreements entail an additional legal consideration—the Compact Clause of the federal Constitution, which provides: "No State shall, without the Consent of Congress, . . . enter into any Agreement or Compact with another State . . . " U.S.Const. art. I, § 10, cl. 3.

EASTERN PARALYZED VETERANS ASSOCIATION, INC. v. CITY OF CAMDEN

Supreme Court of New Jersey
545 A.2d 127 (1988)

O'HERN, J.

This case presents a troublesome dilemma for resolution. It involves a cooperative undertaking by a bi-state agency and a New Jersey municipal agency to create in New Jersey a downtown mass transportation center, [the Camden Transportation Center (CTC)]. * * *

Both the Camden Housing Authority and the Delaware River Port Authority (DRPA), a bi-state agency of New Jersey and Pennsylvania, had the best of intentions. Under their cooperative plan, the Camden Housing Authority was to erect and construct a mass transit terminal in which DRPA's subsidiary Port Authority Transportation Corporation (PATCO) train service would operate.

The issue in this appeal has been presented as whether New Jersey's barrier-free design requirements in aid of the handicapped may be applied to the DRPA's operations or facilities. * * *

The controversy concerns the provision of an elevator for handicapped access to PATCO's underground train system. * * *

The Delaware River Port Authority was created with the approval of Congress by an interstate compact between the State of New Jersey and the Commonwealth of Pennsylvania. N.J.S.A. 32:3–2. The primary purpose of the DRPA is the development and maintenance of bridges and port facilities between the two states. In addition, the Authority is authorized to provide a rail transportation service (PATCO service) between the City of Philadelphia and various communities within the port district in New Jersey. N.J.S.A. 32:3–2(b). * * *

The DRPA, then, is not the agency of a single state, but rather a public corporate instrumentality of both New Jersey and Pennsylvania. *Yancoskie v. Delaware River Port Auth.*, 155 N.J.Super. 1, 4, 382 A.2d 77 (1977), *aff'd*, 78 N.J. 321, 395 A.2d 192 (1978); *see also Yancoskie v. Delaware River Port Auth.*, 478 Pa. 396, 387 A.2d 41 (Pa.1978) (Pennsylvania's immunity does not extend to this agency). "It follows that neither creator state can unilaterally impose additional duties, powers or responsibilities upon the Authority." *Nardi v. Delaware River Port Auth.*, 88 Pa. Commw. 558, 560, 490 A.2d 949, 950 (1985) (citing *C.T. Hellmuth & Assocs., Inc. v. Washington Metropolitan Area Transit Auth.*, 414 F.Supp. 408 (D.Md.1976), and *Bell v. Bell*, 83 N.J. 417, 416 A.2d 829 (1980)).

* * * [T]o hold that the DRPA is subject to the New Jersey Uniform Construction Code would result in the imposition, unauthorized by the bi-state compact, of substantial duties or responsibilities on that Authority. Both New Jersey and Pennsylvania have consistently required complementary state legislation for single-state jurisdiction to be exercised over the Authority. * * *

Only when the compact itself recognizes the jurisdiction of the compact states may it be subject to single-state jurisdiction. For example, in *People v. City of South Lake Tahoe*, 466 F.Supp. 527, 537 (E.D.Cal.1978), California was held to have the right to impose environmental quality regulations on the regional authority only because that agency's own charter provided that the ordinance, rules, and regulations adopted by the bi-state agency merely " 'establish[ed] a minimum standard applicable throughout the basin, and any political subdivision may adopt and enforce an equal or higher standard applicable to the same subject of regulation in its territory.' " 466 F.Supp. at 537 (citation omitted). Similarly, the DRPA's charter provides, for example, that land acquisition in each state be governed by that state's law of eminent domain. However, the DRPA's compact does not contemplate single-state jurisdiction in general. Hence, we conclude that the trial court erred in ruling that the DCA [(New Jersey Department of Community Affairs)] could unilaterally impose on the DRPA the obligations set forth in the New Jersey Uniform Construction Code and the New Jersey Law Against Discrimination.

* * *

The corollary of the proposition that neither state may individually impose its will on the bi-state agency is that the agency may be made subject to complementary or parallel state legislation. *Cf. Delaware River Joint Toll Bridge Comm'n v. Colburn*, supra, 310 U.S. 419, 60 S.Ct. 1039, 84 L.Ed. 1287 (where compact prescribed procedures for land acquisition in each state, no unilateral departure could be made by agency). The DRPA does not dispute this principle; indeed, it distinguishes from the present case the example that Pennsylvania DRPA employees must observe stop-lights in New Jersey, by replying that Pennsylvania and New Jersey have similar legislation in this regard. *See Nardi v. Delaware River Port Auth.*, supra, 88 Pa. Commw. at 564 n. 10, 490 A.2d at 952 n. 10 (if disability pay enactments of New Jersey and Pennsylvania were substantially similar, court could find agreement by the states concerning extent of disability pay). The trial court's approach to the present case did not consider whether the New Jersey regulation could be sustained on the basis that there were substantially similar legislative acts in both New Jersey and Pennsylvania. The DRPA has not had occasion to attempt to construct a major facility in Pennsylvania, and the record is silent on whether in such a case DRPA would have to provide handicapped access under Pennsylvania law.

We invited supplemental briefs from the parties with respect to this issue, but find that the parties are in substantial disagreement on this point. The EPVA argues that "[i]f construction of the CTC were deemed a 'renovation' of the PATCO station, it would be required to be accessible [to the handicapped] under 49 C.F.R. § 27, 67(b)"; that provision, part of the Department of Transportation's 1979 regulations governing handicap accessibility to programs receiving federal funds, mandates accessibility of such renovated facilities "to the maximum extent feasible." Hence, since the burdens, although of federal origin, would be the same in either state, there is no point in objecting to the elevator. However, the DRPA insists that the CTC, as a replacement for the Broadway PATCO station, is not a "renovation." The DRPA contends that unlike New Jersey's Uniform Construction Code and Barrier-Free Design Code, Pennsylvania's statutes governing handicap accessibility would not require elevators in a Pennsylvania counterpart of the CTC; however, if elevators were provided, they would have to be made accessible to and operable by the physically handicapped.

DCA argued before us that this feature of the matter was irrelevant. In DCA's view, the DRPA is independently subject to the requirements of the Uniform Construction Code whenever the DRPA undertakes a construction activity in New Jersey: the Code states that it applies to all bistate agencies. N.J.S.A. 52:27D–129 b. However, when Pennsylvania and New Jersey intended that local law would govern an area relevant to their compact, such as acquisitions by eminent domain, N.J.S.A. 32:3–13.51, or consent for highway connections to the bi-state toll bridge, N.J.S.A. 32:3–13.55, they so specified. Thus " '[w]e fail to see how either state could enact laws involving and regulating the bi-state agency unless both states agree thereto.' " *Bell*, supra, 83 N.J. at 424, 416 A.2d 829 (citation omitted). Some showing of agreement by both states to the enforcement of the Uniform Construction Code at DRPA's New Jersey facilities will be required to sustain this theory.

We have no hesitancy to decide the question of law but believe that it is fact-sensitive. In fairness to the parties, we should give them an opportunity to present any relevant data concerning the specifics of the construction. Suffice it to observe that there are sufficient disputed facts that we should hesitate to decide an important question of law without a developed record.

* * *

If a facility were being built by anyone else in New Jersey, the handicapped could not be excluded. Based on the record before us, we are uncertain whether Pennsylvania would require the same result.

* * *

This State lacks the sovereign authority to direct the DRPA to cede jurisdiction to New Jersey. Just as "[a] State cannot be its own ultimate judge in a controversy with a sister State," *West Virginia ex rel. Dyer v. Sims*, 341 U.S. 22, 28, 71 S.Ct. 557, 560, 95 L.Ed. 713, 722 (1951), so too a single state cannot dictate the policy of a bi-state agency. We hold that the State of New Jersey cannot exercise unilateral jurisdiction over the DRPA; to the extent that the judgment of the trial court involves a mandatory injunction to compel the DRPA to comply with the directives of the Department of Community Affairs, that judgment must be vacated.

We vacate the judgment and remand the case to the trial court for further proceedings. In view of our conclusion that the DRPA, by virtue of its agreement with Camden, consented to the jurisdiction of the appropriate New Jersey governmental agency for approval of the construction plans, supra at 134, the trial court shall receive evidence concerning the DRPA's contention that the installation of the elevator would unduly disrupt or interfere with its rail operations. Unless the DRPA can sustain its burden of proving such disruption or interference, the trial court shall be authorized to enter judgment requiring the Agency to comply with the directives of the Department of Community Affairs. In the alternative, the trial court may consider whether there is complementary legislation in New Jersey and Pennsylvania that would make equivalent the DRPA's obligation in each state to provide barrier-free access to handicapped persons. * * *

NOTES AND QUESTIONS

1.   *Applicability of State Law to Interstate Compacts.* The New Jersey courts have had several occasions to apply the principles articulated in the main case. In International Union of Operating Engineers v. Delaware River and Bay Auth., 688 A.2d 569 (N.J. 1997), the court concluded that New Jersey labor laws applied to DRBA's collective bargaining agreements, and in Ballinger v. Delaware River Port Auth., 800 A.2d 97 (N.J. 2002), it held that state common law principles of retaliatory discharge applied to DRPA employees. The analytical principle in the main case, distinguishing between the imposition of parallel, as opposed to unilateral, statutory burdens, has widespread acceptance. Its application requires a particularized factual inquiry. *See, e.g.,* HIP Heightened Independence and Progress, Inc. v. Port Auth. of New York and New Jersey, 693 F.3d 345 (3rd Cir. 2012) (state disability protection law not applicable to train station renovations undertaken pursuant to interstate compact); Delaware River Port Auth. v. Fraternal Order of Police, 290 F.3d 567 (3d Cir.2002) (DRPA has a duty under state common law to bargain collectively with its employees); Kansas City Area Transportation Authority v. Missouri, 640 F.2d 173 (8th Cir.1981) (transportation authority required to sell advertising on its vehicles); King v. Port Authority of New York, 909 F.Supp. 938 (D.N.J.1995) (New Jersey anti-discrimination laws not applicable to interstate Port Authority); Bunk v. Port Authority of New York and New Jersey, 676 A.2d 118 (N.J.1996) (state disability laws apply to Port Authority employees); Ampro Fisheries v. Yaskin, 606 A.2d 1099 (N.J.1992) (state fishing regulations apply to compact territory); Redbird Engineering Sales Inc. v. Bi-State Development Agency of Missouri-Illinois Metropolitan District, 806 S.W.2d 695 (Mo.App.1991) (applying state bond requirements for public work projects to interstate compact authorizing construction of a public transportation facility).

New York takes a slightly different, though equally fact-specific, approach. In Agesen v. Catherwood, 260 N.E.2d 525, 526–27 (N.Y.1970), the court distinguished between the compact agency's "internal operations," which are immune from state law, and "conduct affecting external relations," which are subject to state law. Using that two-part categorization, the court held that New York's prevailing wage requirements could not apply to the compact agency's operations. Which of these approaches better protects the state interests at stake in interstate compacts?

2.   *Effects of Permanency on State Sovereignty and Participatory Democracy.* Interstate compacts require legislative relinquishment of

discretionary police powers, binding the compacting state to the terms, superseding inconsistent state law, and severely limiting what would otherwise be state flexibility to revoke or amend action taken in response to subsequent developments. Professor Jill Hasday argues that the permanency of interstate compacts, while facilitating planning and financing, adversely affects both the sovereign prerogatives of the compacting states as well as the democratic participatory interests of the general citizenry. Her critique agrees with two prevalent, and seemingly inconsistent, criticisms of interstate compacts: that the agencies are unresponsive and unaccountable to public concerns; and that they are also "disappointingly toothless in practice." Jill Elaine Hasday, Interstate Compacts in a Democratic Society: The Problem of Permanency, 49 Fla.L.Rev. 1, 22 (1997). Professor Hasday explains the first problem as a natural consequence of the agency's broad immunity from political checks, both in terms of the compact's amendment and its termination. The second she attributes to the states' natural hesitancy to endow an unaccountable deliberative agency with broad powers. She concludes that in the case of interstate compacts whose purpose is to establish an ongoing administrative agency to provide regional services or manage regional resources, the scope should be as narrow as possible, and the state should reserve the most liberal amendment and termination provisions possible. Do you agree with her assessment of the negative features of interstate compacts? Other commentators are more positive in their evaluation of the Compact Clause as offering a regional solution to interstate problems, *e.g.*, Dale D. Goble, The Compact Clause and Transboundary Problems: 'A Federal Remedy for the Disease Most Incident to a Federal Government,' 17 Envtl.L. 785 (1987); Charles J. Meyers, The Colorado River, 19 Stan.L.Rev. 1 (1966).

3. *Interstate Compacts and Congressional Consent.* Not all joint action taken by two or more states falls within the Compact Clause's requirement of congressional consent. In Northeast Bancorp, Inc. v. Board of Governors of the Federal Reserve System, 472 U.S. 159 (1985), the Supreme Court concluded that parallel state statutes designed to establish reciprocity for out-of-state bank holding companies did not constitute a compact within the meaning of the constitutional clause: ". . . [S]everal of the classic indicia of a compact are missing. No joint organization or body has been established . . . . Neither statute is conditioned on action by the other State, and each State is free to modify or repeal its law unilaterally. Most importantly, neither statute requires a reciprocation [by other states]." *Id.* at 175. Even if interstate action meets the threshold definition of compact for purposes of the Compact Clause, congressional consent is not always required. Since the Court's decision in Virginia v. Tennessee, 148 U.S. 503 (1893), application of the Compact Clause has been limited to those agreements "tending to the increase of political power in the States, which may encroach upon or interfere with the just supremacy of the United States." *Id.* at 519.

Once an interstate agreement is deemed a compact that triggers the Constitution's requirement of congressional consent, the issue becomes whether Congress has in fact consented. In this regard, congressional discretion is wide ranging: "Congress may consent to an interstate compact by authorizing joint state action in advance or by giving express or implied approval to an agreement the States have already joined." Cuyler v. Adams, 449 U.S. 433, 441 (1981). Congressional discretion may be even broader than the *Cuyler* Court suggested. Consider the following comment from an early 19th century case: "[T]he constitution makes no provision respecting the mode or form in which the consent of Congress is to be signified, very properly leaving that matter to the wisdom of that body, to be decided upon according to the ordinary rules of law, and of right reason." Green v. Biddle, 21 U.S. (8 Wheat.) 1, 85–86 (1823). On that basis, one modern court has upheld congressional delegation of consent to the Secretary of Agriculture to authorize an interstate compact to raise prices for dairy farmers. Milk Industry Foundation v. Glickman, 132 F.3d 1467 (D.C.Cir.1998).

4. *Sovereign Immunity.* As interpreted by the Supreme Court, the Eleventh Amendment of the Constitution extends sovereign immunity to the states, unless properly waived or abrogated. Supreme Court cases suggest that sovereign immunity will rarely be available to protect interstate compacting agencies from suit. In Lake Country Estates, Inc. v. Tahoe Regional Planning Agency, 440 U.S. 391 (1979), the Court used the following reasoning to conclude that sovereign immunity should not extend to a regional planning agency established pursuant to a congressionally approved interstate compact:

> If an interstate compact discloses that the compacting States created an agency comparable to a county or municipality, which has no Eleventh Amendment immunity, the Amendment should not be construed to immunize such an entity. Unless there is good reason to believe that the States structured the new agency to enable it to enjoy the special constitutional protection of the States themselves, and that Congress concurred in that purpose, there would appear to be no justification for reading additional meaning into the limited language of the Amendment.

Id. at 401.

Subsequently, in Hess v. Port Authority Trans-Hudson Corp., 513 U.S. 30 (1994), the Port Authority justified its asserted entitlement to state sovereign immunity on the basis of the following facts: (1) all commissioners are appointed by the compacting states; (2) state court decisions had consistently treated the authority as a state agency; and (3) the functions of the agency were state, rather than local, in their scope. Applying what appears to be a presumption against sovereign immunity for agencies created by interstate compacts, the Court concluded that neither the compacting states' solvency nor dignity would be implicated by subjecting the agency to suit. Crucial to that two-part conclusion were the facts that: ". . . [T]he Port Authority is financially self-sufficient; it generates its own revenues, and it pays its own debts." *Id.* at 52.

5. REGIONALISM OR BALKANIZATION?

The limited appeal of consolidation efforts and the typical patterns of suburbanization have left many metropolitan areas in a similar situation with regard to growth, demographics, and economic factors—a growing gap between, on the one hand, central cities and their inner ring suburbs, and on the other, the more distant, more affluent suburbs. Redistribution of wealth and redefinition of the scope of government power are frequently the source of conflict between those two broadly defined segments of metropolitan areas. The following examples of efforts to rearrange the regional landscape come from reports in the popular press. As you consider them, you should: (1) suggest how and why the distinct interest groups have emerged; (2) identify how the arrangement can be expected to affect the region in terms of the three criteria we used to introduce the regionalism debate (that is, efficiency, equity, and democracy); (3) consider who should be the decisionmaker for the type of proposals contemplated or adopted; and (4) suggest alternative ways to deal with the problem.

a. Atlanta and Fulton County: Shifting to an All-City County?

Fulton County, Georgia covers 529 square miles and includes the City of Atlanta. Its current population of just under one million reflects a fifty percent increase since 1990. Fulton County is racially and economically split, with the north primarily white and affluent, and the south predominantly African American and poor. It is governed by six elected County Commissioners. The County provides municipal services, such as planning, parks, public works and public safety, for the unincorporated territory. It also is responsible for general countywide services, such as the court system, the public health district, and public housing, for all land within the borders of the County. Since 2004, the amount of unincorporated area within Fulton County has decreased steadily. In that year, the Georgia legislature changed the law regulating municipal incorporation, making it easier for unincorporated areas to incorporate as municipalities. Between 2004 and 2007 four new municipalities incorporated, leaving Fulton County with one sprawl, unincorporated enclave with a population of about 45,000. In November, 2007, 85% of the voters there rejected a proposal to incorporate that land as the City of South Fulton.

Sandy Springs is one of the newly incorporated cities. It is an affluent suburban community north of Atlanta. For years it had complained that its taxes subsidized poor communities to the south. Eva Galambos, the mayor of Sandy Springs, commented in an interview that since incorporation, her city has three times as many police officers, and the streets are cleaner. "The most stunning thing," she added, "is that we're not paying more taxes." In addition, Sandy Springs and the other newly incorporated cities in Fulton County have all outsourced at least some city services to a Denver-based company. In Sandy Springs' case, there is a city staff of five (for its 87,000 residents), and the private company provides tax and revenue collections, planning and zoning, and parks and recreation. Allocation of service responsibility is similar for the other new Fulton County cities.

Under state law, with municipal incorporation comes the right to a dedicated portion of the county's sales tax revenues. Because of the incorporations, Fulton County's share of those revenues has been cut almost in half. The Georgia Assembly has considered cutting that share further by giving the communities in the unincorporated South Fulton area the sales tax revenues they would have gotten had the voters approved incorporation. Fulton County may soon be left with little sales tax revenue and no unincorporated territory that relies on it for general municipal services. That means that many of the County's current functions could no longer be funded and would no longer be needed. As a result, Fulton County now faces the prospect of a radical restructuring and even more severe budget cuts.

b. Houston and The Woodlands: Regional Participation Agreements

Under Texas law, cities can annex land within their extraterritorial jurisdiction. For decades, Houston's aggressive annexation policy served its goal of growing without becoming surrounded by other incorporated municipalities. These forced annexations frequently produced bitter resentments, and in fact the Texas legislature responded to some particularly nasty annexation battles by making it more difficult for cities to annex. Under current law, cities have to announce their annexation plans years in advance, with requirements for negotiation and arbitration in contested situations. When Houston began to consider annexation of The Woodlands, a planned community located about twenty-five miles away from downtown, the community opposition was solid.

Residents in The Woodlands voted overwhelmingly in November 2007 to create the Town Center Improvement District, a special district governed by an elected board and with authority to levy property taxes. It replaces two resident associations and a commercial owners association as the new governing entity. Under the terms of a voluntary agreement, Houston has agreed to drop its plans to annex. In return, The Woodlands will pay $16 million to help fund regional projects, such as improvements to nearby lakes, parks, and roads. It will also make quarterly sales tax payments to Houston, currently expected to be around $45 million annually. Those payments will cease after 99 years. Failure to make the payments would enable Houston to resort to annexation proceedings. For its part, Houston will not have to provide services to a growing population of more than 80,000, all of whom expect trash pickup, police and fire, water, and sewer services.

The Woodlands' Town Center Improvement District has also entered into a similar, but smaller, regional participation agreement with the nearby municipality of Conroe to terminate that city's announced annexation plans of Harper's Landing, a part of The Woodlands. Under that agreement, the special district will pay $320,000 for a year's worth of fire protection services, and it will also pay Conroe one-sixteenth of one percent of The Woodland's sales tax revenue generated in Harper's Landing.

CHAPTER VI

STATE AND LOCAL FINANCE

■ ■ ■

As we have seen, states and local governments play a vital role in providing a wide range of public services and engaging in extensive regulatory programs. In order to carry out these functions, they must be able to raise and spend substantial sums of money. State and local finance is subject to legal constraints, and, in turn, has been shaped by state and local efforts to avoid those constraints, many of which grow out of state constitutions. To a degree unparalleled by our federal constitution, state constitutions contain many detailed provisions concerning the power of state and local governments to spend and lend money, to levy taxes, and to borrow. State constitutions have attempted to limit the purposes of state spending, control the level of taxation, borrowing and spending, and have imposed a range of substantive and procedural restrictions on the ability of states and localities to raise money. Federal constitutional doctrines have also played an important role in shaping state and local finances.

This chapter considers some of the legal issues that affect state and local finance. Section A briefly considers state constitutional limits on government spending. Beginning in the early nineteenth century, state constitutional law sought to limit the goals of state and local spending, and the ability of states and localities to use state or local funds to aid the private sector. The resulting "public purpose doctrine" was relaxed over the course of the twentieth century, as courts came to accept a greater state role in supporting private sector projects, and a greater state interest in the health of the private sector. As you read these materials, consider whether a coherent distinction between public and private purposes can be drawn, and whether courts can or should be the institution that defines and enforces public purpose requirements.

Section B turns to the very large topic of revenues, focusing particularly on local revenue. The first subsection deals with the property tax, which has been both the most important and the most controversial source of support for local governments. It is the revenue source that has received the most attention in state constitutions, and, with the onset of the "tax revolt" in the late 1970s, it has probably been the principal flashpoint of state and local political controversy as well.

The second subsection deals with what we call "the rise of nontax taxes," such as special assessments, regulatory fees, user charges, and development impact fees. Although the legal roots of these revenue sources can be traced back to the nineteenth century, they became critically important to states and local governments in the last quarter of the twentieth century in response to the increased legal and political constraints on new general taxes, especially the property tax. The rise of these new revenue sources, thus, provides a fascinating illustration of the ability of legal restrictions to spawn new devices that abide by the letter of the law but challenge its spirit. A central aspect of these nontax taxes is that they shift the burden of paying for some public goods or services from the community as a whole to discrete subgroups within the community, such as particular neighborhoods, service users, or newcomers. Some of these devices may also make it possible for some subgroups to pay for and thus provide themselves with higher levels of services than are made available for the community as a whole. The nontax taxes, thus, have important implications for the nature, as well as the financing, of local governments.

The third subsection briefly considers two other major sources of state and local revenues—sales taxes and income taxes. These taxes are of particular importance to state governments. Although we will spend little time on the legal issues they generate, it is important to appreciate the central role of these taxes in financing state governments.

Section C explores the issues raised by state and local borrowing. It first considers the binding nature of state and local debt obligations under both the federal and state constitutions. It then examines a central consequence of the state and local duty to repay debts—the widespread existence of state constitutional limitations on debt. Paralleling the rise of nontax taxes studied in Section B, the final subsection then looks at the emergence of "nondebt debts" and "nongovernment governments"—state- or locally-created agencies whose obligations are not considered debts of their parent governments. A central question for this Section is whether the widespread evasion of state constitutional debt limits should lead to a reconsideration of the need for such limitations, or whether, instead, states should focus on ways of making these limits more effective.

Finally, section D examines the increasingly pressing problem of state and local fiscal distress. In 2013, Detroit, Michigan became the largest local government in American history to file for bankruptcy. Although Detroit's case is particularly striking, many states and local governments have had to deal with significant fiscal pressures. States have adopted new measures for monitoring local fiscal performance and have enacted laws providing for oversight boards and, on occasion, the imposition of receivers or appointed fiscal managers for troubled localities. Nor was Detroit the only significant local government that turned to federal bankruptcy law to restructure its debts. States have also grappled with serious fiscal problems; some of their efforts to address those problems—particularly the cost of public employee pensions and retiree benefits—have triggered litigation. This section considers some of the legal issues raised by state and local efforts to deal with fiscal distress.

A.   PUBLIC PURPOSE REQUIREMENTS

MAREADY V. CITY OF WINSTON-SALEM

Supreme Court of North Carolina
467 S.E.2d 615 (1996)

WHICHARD, JUSTICE:

* * * This action challenges twenty-four economic development incentive projects entered into by the City or County pursuant to N.C.G.S. § 158–7.1. The projected investment by the City and County in these projects totals approximately $13,200,000. The primary source of these funds has been taxes levied by the City and County on property owners in Winston-Salem and Forsyth County. City and County officials estimate an increase in the local tax base of $238,593,000 and a projected creation of over 5,500 new jobs as a result of these economic development incentive programs. They expect to recoup the full amount of their investment within three to seven years. The source of the return will be revenues generated by the additional property taxes paid by participating corporations. To date, all but one project has met or exceeded its goal. * * *

Article V, Section 2(1) of the North Carolina Constitution provides that "the power of taxation shall be exercised in a just and equitable manner, for public purposes only." In *Mitchell v. North Carolina Indus. Dev. Fin. Auth.*, 273 N.C. 137, 159 S.E.2d 745 (1968), Justice (later Chief Justice) Sharp, writing for a majority of this Court, stated:

> The power to appropriate money from the public treasury is no greater than the power to levy the tax which put the money in the treasury. Both powers are subject to the constitutional proscription that tax revenues may not be used for private individuals or corporations, no matter how benevolent.

Id. at 143, 159 S.E.2d at 749–50.

* * * The enactment of N.C.G.S. § 158–7.1 leaves no doubt that the General Assembly considers expenditures of public funds for the promotion of local economic development to serve a public purpose. Under this statute,

[e]ach county and city in this State is authorized to make appropriations for the purposes of aiding and encouraging the location of manufacturing enterprises, making industrial surveys and locating industrial and commercial plants in or near such city or in the county; encouraging the building of railroads or other purposes which, in the discretion of the governing body of the city or of the county commissioners of the county, *will increase the population, taxable property, agricultural industries and business prospects of any city or county.* These appropriations may be funded by the levy of property taxes pursuant to G.S. 153A–149 and 160A–209 and by the allocation of other revenues whose use is not otherwise restricted by law.

N.C.G.S. § 158–7.1(a) (1994) (emphasis added). * * *

This Court has addressed what constitutes a public purpose on numerous occasions. It has not specifically defined "public purpose," however; rather, it has expressly declined to "confine public purpose by judicial definition[, leaving] 'each case to be determined by its own peculiar circumstances as from time to time it arises.'" *Stanley v. Department of Conservation & Dev.*, 284 N.C. 15, 33, 199 S.E.2d 641, 653 (1973) (quoting *Keeter v. Town of Lake Lure*, 264 N.C. 252, 264, 141 S.E.2d 634, 643 (1965)). As summarized by Justice Sharp in *Mitchell:*

A slide-rule definition to determine public purpose for all time cannot be formulated; the concept expands with the population, economy, scientific knowledge, and changing conditions. As people are brought closer together in congested areas, the public welfare requires governmental operation of facilities which were once considered exclusively private enterprises, and necessitates the expenditure of tax funds for purposes which, in an earlier day, were not classified as public. Often public and private interests are so co-mingled that it is difficult to determine which predominates. It is clear, however, that for a use to be public its benefits must be in common and not for particular persons, interests, or estates; the ultimate net gain or advantage must be the public's as contradistinguished from that of an individual or private entity.

Mitchell, 273 N.C. at 144, 159 S.E.2d at 750 (citations omitted).

* * * *Mitchell v. North Carolina Industrial Development Financing Authority* * * * held unconstitutional the Industrial Facilities Financing Act, a statute that authorized issuance of industrial revenue bonds to finance the construction and equipping of facilities for private corporations. * * * We find *Mitchell* distinguishable.

* * * [T]he holding in *Mitchell* clearly indicates that the Court considered private industry to be the primary benefactor of the legislation

and considered any benefit to the public purely incidental. Notwithstanding its recognition that any lawful business in a community promotes the public good, the Court held that the "Authority's primary function, to acquire sites and to construct and equip facilities for private industry, is not for a public use or purpose." *Id.* at 159, 159 S.E.2d at 761. The Court rightly concluded that direct state aid to a private enterprise, with only limited benefit accruing to the public, contravenes fundamental constitutional precepts. In reiterating that it is not the function of the government to engage in private business, the opinion quoted with approval the following language from the Supreme Court of Idaho:

> "An exemption which arbitrarily prefers one private enterprise operating by means of facilities provided by a municipality, over another engaged, or desiring to engage, in the same business in the same locality, is neither necessary nor just. . . . It is obvious that private enterprise, not so favored, could not compete with industries operating thereunder. If the state-favored industries were successfully managed, private enterprise would of necessity be forced out, and the state, through its municipalities, would increasingly become involved in promoting, sponsoring, regulating and controlling private business, and our free private enterprise economy would be replaced by socialism. The constitutions of both state and nation were founded upon a capitalistic private enterprise economy and were designed to protect and foster private property and private initiative."

Id. at 153, 159 S.E.2d at 756 (quoting *Village of Moyie Springs v. Aurora Mfg. Co.*, 82 Idaho 337, 349–50, 353 P.2d 767, 775 (1960)). Thus, the Court implicitly rejected the act because its primary object was private gain and its nature and purpose did not tend to yield public benefit.

These concerns also influenced the Court in *Stanley v. Department of Conservation & Dev.*, 284 N.C. 15, 199 S.E.2d 641, which plaintiff also contends is binding precedent. In Stanley this Court was asked to determine the constitutionality of the Pollution Abatement and Industrial Facilities Financing Act, which allowed the creation of county authorities to finance pollution control or industrial facilities for private industry by the issuance of tax-exempt revenue bonds. The Court held the Act unconstitutional. The result in *Stanley* turned on the fact that the Act in question was "patently . . . designed to enable industrial polluters to finance, at the lowest interest rate obtainable, the pollution abatement and control facilities which the law is belatedly requiring of them." *Id.* at 32, 199 S.E.2d at 653. * * * The Court concluded that "pollution control facilities are single-purpose facilities, useful only to the industry for which they would be acquired." *Id.* at 39, 199 S.E.2d at 657. Therefore, "the conclusion is inescapable that [the private corporation] is the only direct beneficiary of the tax-exempt revenue bonds which the . . .

Authorities propose to issue and that the benefit to the public is only incidental or secondary." *Id.* at 38, 199 S.E.2d at 656.

Thus, as in *Mitchell*, the outcome flowed inexorably from the fundamental concept underlying the public purpose doctrine, viz, that the ultimate gain must be the public's, not that of an individual or private entity. Significantly, the direct holdings of these cases—that industrial revenue bond financing is unconstitutional—were overturned by a specific constitutional amendment. In 1973 the North Carolina Constitution was amended to add Article V, Section 9, which allows counties to create authorities to issue revenue bonds for industrial and pollution control facilities. While this amendment was narrowly tailored to address a specific situation, it nonetheless diminishes the significance of *Mitchell* and *Stanley* in the context presented here.

* * * In 1973 Article V, Section 2(7) was added to the North Carolina Constitution, specifically allowing direct appropriation to private entities for public purposes. This section provides:

> The General Assembly may enact laws whereby the State, any county, city or town, and any other public corporation may contract with and appropriate money to any person, association, or corporation for the accomplishment of public purposes only.

N.C. Const. art. V, § 2(7). "Under subsection (7) *direct disbursement* of public funds to private entities is a constitutionally permissible *means* of accomplishing a public purpose provided there is statutory authority to make such appropriation." *Hughey v. Cloninger*, 297 N.C. 86, 95, 253 S.E.2d 898, 904 (1979). Hence, the constitutional problem under the public purpose doctrine that the Court perceived in *Mitchell* and *Stanley* no longer exists.

While *Mitchell* and its progeny remain pivotal in the development of the doctrine, they do not purport to establish a permanent test for determining the existence of a public purpose. The majority in *Mitchell* posed the question: "Is it *today* a proper function of government for the State to provide a site and equip a plant for private industrial enterprise?" *Mitchell*, 273 N.C. at 145, 159 S.E.2d at 751 (emphasis added). This explicit recognition of the importance of contemporary circumstances in assessing the public purpose of governmental endeavors highlights the essential fluidity of the concept. While the *Mitchell* majority answered the question in the negative, the passage of time and accompanying societal changes now suggest a positive response.

This Court is no stranger to the question of what activities are and are not for a public purpose. The following cases demonstrate the great variety of facilities, authorities, and activities which have been deemed to be public purposes. [The court cited more than 25 of its earlier holdings, going back as far as 1887, to demonstrate the wide range of activities deemed to constitute a public purpose. Among the publicly funded activities found within the definition of public purpose were aid to education, housing assistance, funds to build transportation facilities, professional training courses, construction of parks and playgrounds, and purchase of an electric generator]. * * * While these cases * * * may not have involved industrial development as the challenged project, they reflect a trend toward broadening the scope of what constitutes a valid public purpose that permits the expenditure of public revenues. The General Assembly may provide for, inter alia, roads, schools, housing, health care, transportation, and occupational training. It would be anomalous to now hold that a government which expends large sums to alleviate the problems of its citizens through multiple humanitarian and social programs is proscribed from promoting the provision of jobs for the unemployed, an increase in the tax base, and the prevention of economic stagnation.

This Court most recently addressed the public purpose question in *Madison Cablevision v. City of Morganton*, 325 N.C. 634, 386 S.E.2d 200 (1989), where it unanimously held that N.C.G.S. § 160A, art. 16, part 1, which authorizes cities to finance, acquire, construct, own, and operate cablevision systems, does not violate the public purpose clause of Article V, Section 2(1). The Court stated that "two guiding principles have been established for determining that a particular undertaking by a municipality is for a public purpose: (1) it involves a reasonable connection with the convenience and necessity of the particular municipality; and (2) the activity benefits the public generally, as opposed to special interests or persons." *Madison Cablevision*, 325 N.C. at 646, 386 S.E.2d at 207 (citations omitted). Application of these principles here mandates the conclusion that N.C.G.S. § 158–7.1 furthers a public purpose and hence is constitutional.

As to the first prong, whether an activity is within the appropriate scope of governmental involvement and is reasonably related to communal needs may be evaluated by determining how similar the activity is to others which this Court has held to be within the permissible realm of governmental action. We conclude that the activities N.C.G.S. § 158–7.1 authorizes are in keeping with those accepted as within the scope of permissible governmental action.

Economic development has long been recognized as a proper governmental function. In *Wood v. Town of Oxford*, 97 N.C. 227, 2 S.E. 653, this Court upheld the statutory, voter-approved borrowing of money for the purchase of railroad capital stock and donations by towns located along a privately owned, for-profit railroad. The Court stated:

It may not always be easy to apply the rule of law to determine what is a legitimate object of such expenditures. It is clear, however, that they may be made for such public improvements and advantages as tend directly to provide for and promote the general good, convenience and safety of the county or town making them, as an organized community, although the advantage derived may not reach every individual citizen or taxpayer residing there.

* * * Urban redevelopment commissions have power to acquire property, clear slums, and sell the property to private developers. In that instance, as here, a private party ultimately acquires the property and conducts activities which, while providing incidental private benefit, serve a primary public goal.

As to the second prong of the *Madison Cablevision* inquiry, under the expanded understanding of public purpose, even the most innovative activities N.C.G.S. § 158–7.1 permits are constitutional so long as they primarily benefit the public and not a private party. "It is not necessary, in order that a use may be regarded as public, that it should be for the use and benefit of every citizen in the community." *Briggs v. City of Raleigh*, 195 N.C. 223, 226, 141 S.E. 597, 599–600. Moreover, an expenditure does not lose its public purpose merely because it involves a private actor. Generally, if an act will promote the welfare of a state or a local government and its citizens, it is for a public purpose.

Viewed in this light, section 158–7.1 clearly serves a public purpose. Its self-proclaimed end is to "increase the population, taxable property, agricultural industries and business prospects of any city or county." However, it is the natural consequences flowing therefrom that ensure a net public benefit. The expenditures this statute authorizes should create a more stable local economy by providing displaced workers with continuing employment opportunities, attracting better paying and more highly skilled jobs, enlarging the tax base, and diversifying the economy. * * *

The public advantages are not indirect, remote, or incidental; rather, they are directly aimed at furthering the general economic welfare of the people of the communities affected. While private actors will necessarily benefit from the expenditures authorized, such benefit is merely incidental. It results from the local government's efforts to better serve the interests of its people. Each community has a distinct ambience, unique assets, and special needs best ascertained at the local level. Section 158–7.1 enables each to formulate its own definition of economic success and to draft a developmental plan leading to that goal. This aim is no less legitimate and no less for a public purpose than projects this Court has approved in the past.

Finally, while this Court does not pass upon the wisdom or propriety of legislation in determining the primary motivation behind a statute, it may consider the circumstances surrounding its enactment. In that regard, a Legislative Research Commission committee made a report to the 1989 General Assembly, warning that:

> The traditional foundations of North Carolina's economy— agriculture and manufacturing—are in decline. And, the traditional economic development tool—industrial recruitment— has proven inadequate for many of North Carolina's communities. Low wages and low taxes are no longer sufficient incentives to entice new industry to our State, especially to our most remote, most distressed areas.

N.C. Legislative Research Commission, Committee on Economic Development and Recruiting, Report to the 1989 N.C. General Assembly, at 15. In the economic climate thus depicted, the pressure to induce responsible corporate citizens to relocate to or expand in North Carolina is not internal only, but results from the actions of other states as well. To date, courts in forty-six states have upheld the constitutionality of governmental expenditures and related assistance for economic development incentives. * * * Considered in this light, it would be unrealistic to assume that the State will not suffer economically in the future if the incentive programs created pursuant to N.C.G.S. § 158–7.1 are discontinued. As Chief Justice Parker noted in his dissent in *Mitchell*:

> North Carolina is no longer a predominantly agricultural community. We are developing from an agrarian economy to an agrarian and industrial economy. North Carolina is having to compete with the complex industrial, technical, and scientific communities that are more and more representative of a nation- wide trend. All men know that in our efforts to attract new industry we are competing with inducements to industry offered through legislative enactments in other jurisdictions as stated in the legislative findings and purposes of this challenged Act. It is manifest that the establishment of new industry in North Carolina will enrich a whole class of citizens who work for it, will increase the per capita income of our citizens, will mean more money for the public treasury, more money for our schools and for payment of our school teachers, more money for the operation of our hospitals like the John Umstead Hospital at Butner, and for other necessary expenses of government. This to my mind is clearly the business of government in the jet age in which we are living. Among factors to be considered in determining the effect of the challenged legislation here is the aggregate income it will make available for community distribution, the resulting security of their [sic] income, and the opportunities for more lucrative employment for those who desire to work for it.

* * * The General Assembly thus could determine that legislation such as N.C.G.S. § 158–7.1, which is intended to alleviate conditions of unemployment and fiscal distress and to increase the local tax base, serves the public interest. New and expanded industries in communities within North Carolina provide work and economic opportunity for those who otherwise might not have it. This, in turn, creates a broader tax base from which the State and its local governments can draw funding for other programs that benefit the general health, safety, and welfare of their citizens. The potential impetus to economic development, which might otherwise be lost to other states, likewise serves the public interest. We therefore hold that N.C.G.S. § 158–7.1, which permits the expenditure of public moneys for economic development incentive programs, does not violate the public purpose clause of the North Carolina Constitution.

JUSTICE ORR, dissenting:

* * * Although there is undoubtedly some benefit to the general public, as noted with approval in the majority opinion, "direct state aid to a private enterprise, with only limited benefit accruing to the public, contravenes fundamental constitutional precepts."

* * * In examining the stated purposes of the grants, it is obvious that the $13.2 million was authorized for the specific benefit of the companies in question. The money expended was directly for the use of these private companies to pay for such activities as on-the-job training for employees, road construction, site improvements, financing of land purchases, upfitting of the facilities, and even spousal relocation assistance. In weighing these direct "private benefits" paid for by the taxpayers against the limited "public benefits," only one conclusion can be reached—that the trial court correctly held that the expenditures in question were not for a public purpose. The opposite conclusion reached by the majority can be reached only by ignoring the weight of the private benefits and relying instead on the assumption that simply creating new jobs and increasing the tax base is a public purpose that justifies the payment of tax dollars to the private sector. As previously noted, there is simply no evidence to support such a conclusion, and the majority's position must fail.

* * * Article V, Section 2(7), allows the government to "contract with and appropriate money to any person, association, or corporation for the accomplishment of public purposes only." N.C. Const. art V, § 2(7). I find the majority's reliance on Article V, Section 2(7) to be of no significance in that a straightforward reading of the amendment simply permits the payment of tax dollars to private enterprise "for the accomplishment of [a] public purpose[ ]." As previously noted, unless one is willing to conclude that any expenditure that creates jobs and increases the tax base is "a public purpose," that amendment has no substantive effect on the

holdings in *Mitchell* and *Stanley*, and thus not on this case. In fact, the amendment merely allows government to perform a public purpose by contracting with the private sector to actually accomplish the public purpose.

The majority also relies on a "changing times" theory to ignore the law as set forth in *Mitchell* and *Stanley*. While economic times have changed and will continue to change, the philosophy that constitutional interpretation and application are subject to the whims of "everybody's doing it" cannot be sustained.

Finally, the majority chooses to ignore the principles set forth in the *Stanley* case for determining what is a public purpose. Justice Sharp, writing for a unanimous Court, stated:

> * * * (1) An activity cannot be for a public purpose unless it is properly the "business of government," and it is not a function of government either to engage in private business itself or to aid particular business ventures. . . . It is only when private enterprise has demonstrated its inability or unwillingness to meet a public necessity that government is permitted to invade the private sector. In *Martin v. Housing Corp.*, [277 N.C. 29, 175 S.E.2d 665], and *Wells v. Housing Authority*, [213 N.C. 744, 197 S.E. 693 (1938)], revenue bonds issued by two public housing agencies for the purpose of providing housing for low-income tenants were held to be for a public purpose. Governmental activity in that field was not an intrusion upon private enterprise, which had eschewed the field. Further, the primary benefits passed directly from the public agency to the public and not to a private intermediary.
>
> (2) Aid to a private concern by the use of public money or by tax-exempt revenue-bond financing is not justified by the incidental advantage to the public which results from the promotion and prosperity of private enterprises.
>
> (3) In determining what is a public purpose the courts look not only to the end sought to be attained but also "to the means to be used." . . . Direct assistance to a private entity may not be the means used to effect a public purpose. "It is the essential character of the direct object of the expenditure which must determine its validity, and not the . . . degree to which the general advantage of the community, and thus the public welfare, may be ultimately benefitted by their promotion." 63 Am. Jur. 2d Public Funds § 59 (1972).

Stanley, 284 N.C. at 33–34, 199 S.E.2d at 653–54 (alteration in original).

* * * Finally, many of the arguments presented to this Court rest on public policy. Advocates for these business incentives contend that without them, North Carolina will be at a significant competitive disadvantage in keeping and recruiting private industry. They further contend that the economic well-being of our state and its citizens is dependent on the continued utilization of this practice. These arguments are compelling, and even plaintiff admits that a public purpose is served by general economic development and recruitment of industry. However, plaintiff and those supporting his point of view argue that direct grants to specific, selected businesses go beyond the acceptable bounds of public purpose expenditures for economic development. Instead, they say that this is selected corporate welfare to some of the largest and most prosperous companies in our State and in the country. Moreover, these opponents contend that the grants are not equitably applied because they generally favor the larger companies and projects and, in this case, under the County's Economic Incentives Program Guidelines, completely eliminate retail operations from being considered. In challenging the actual public benefit, a question also is raised about the economic loss and devastation to smaller North Carolina communities that lose valued industry to larger, wealthier areas. For example, the move of Southern National Bank headquarters from Lumberton to Winston-Salem undoubtedly adversely affected Lumberton.

Also troubling is the question of limits under the majority's theory. If it is an acceptable public purpose to spend tax dollars specifically for relocation expenses to benefit the spouses of corporate executives moving to the community in finding new jobs or for parking decks that benefit only the employees of the favored company, then what can a government not do if the end result will entice a company to produce new jobs and raise the tax base? If a potential corporate entity is considering a move to Winston-Salem but will only come if country club memberships are provided for its executives, do we sanction the use of tax revenue to facilitate the move? I would hope not, but under the holding of the majority opinion, I see no grounds for challenging such an expenditure provided that, as a result of such a grant, the company promises to create new jobs, and an increased tax base is projected. * * *

UTAH TECHNOLOGY FINANCE CORP. V. WILKINSON

Supreme Court of Utah
723 P.2d 406 (1986)

HOWE, J.:

The Attorney General and the State Treasurer, and Utah Technology Finance Corporation filed suits against each other in district court to determine the constitutionality of the Utah Technology and Innovation Act (the Act). * * *

The Act was passed by the legislature in 1983 and bestowed upon UTFC the power "to take all action necessary or desirable to encourage and assist in the research, development, promotion and growth of emerging and developing technological and innovative small businesses throughout Utah." The Act specifically authorized UTFC to provide capital for equity investment or to make direct loans to assist and encourage emerging and developing small businesses.

In 1985, section 63–60–3 of the Act was amended to include the following legislative findings: The development of high technology was necessary to insure progress. Small emerging businesses have a substantially greater rate of innovation and development in high technology and create new employment at a greater rate than mature businesses. Fostering the development of high technology in this state "is necessary to assure the welfare of its citizens, the growth of its economy, adequate employment for its citizens and progress." This was to be accomplished by UTFC through "assisting and participating in the organization, capital formation, management, growth, development, and disposition of small and emerging businesses. . . ."

UTFC, in endeavoring to aid developing small high-tech businesses, agreed to commit $1 million of public funds appropriated to it to secure a limited partnership interest in Venture Fund I, a private, for-profit limited partnership. Venture Fund I proposes to use that amount, as well as private capital, to subscribe to stock providing selected small high-tech businesses with startup capital. * * *

[At] issue is whether the Act violates the provisions of article VI, section 29 of the Utah Constitution, which provides:

> The Legislature shall not authorize the State, or any county, city, town, township district or other political subdivision of the State to lend its credit or subscribe to stock or bonds in aid of any railroad, telegraph or other private individual or corporate enterprise or undertaking.

A.   LENDING OF CREDIT

In the ninety years which have passed since the adoption of the Utah Constitution, thirteen cases have been appealed to this Court in which it was contended that section 29 had been violated. In all of them, the specific assertion was made that there was a lending of credit in aid of private enterprise. In the first seven cases decided, this Court, with little or no mention of what actually constitutes the lending of credit, concluded that there was no direct aid to private enterprise; instead, a public purpose was served, and hence there was no unconstitutional lending of credit. * * *

Only in the last six cases did we hold that there was no actual lending of credit. * * * These cases all involved the issuance of revenue bonds, and we reasoned that because they were payable only out of the revenues of the project and the bonds were not an indebtedness of the state or one of its subdivisions, there was in fact no lending of its credit. In the first of these six cases, *Allen v. Tooele County,* [21 Utah 2d 383, 445 P.2d 994 (1968)] we, for the first time, made a partial definitive statement of what constitutes the lending of credit. There, we said that Tooele County could be deemed to "lend its credit" to the private enterprise only if "the county might in some eventuality be required to pay the obligation [of the private enterprise]." * * *

Many other state constitutions contain a prohibition against the lending of credit. Some also interdict the "giving" of credit and various other means of assistance. [The court reviewed judicial opinions from Maryland, New York, Iowa, Illinois, Kentucky, and Florida] * * *

Iowa, like Maryland, had taken its credit clause from the New York Constitution. The Iowa court, in construing that clause in a veteran's bonus case, said:

> What is meant herein by a loan of credit? When one signs an accommodation note and delivers it to his neighbor, he loans his credit to his neighbor. He has not created a debt to him. The neighbor is authorized to use the credit with third parties; but he is also under obligation to the maker to protect him against liability and ultimately to return the note. When one becomes surety for his neighbor and signs his promissory notes to third parties, he loans his credit. . . . The liability of the surety is always secondary, and not primary. It is a liability for the debt of another, which such other is bound to pay. And herein is the delusion of suretyship. The surety assumes a secondary liability in the optimistic assurance and belief always that the primary debtor will pay, and that he will never be required to perform the obligation. . . . It was to remove this delusion of suretyship, with its snare of temptation, that this section of the Constitution was adopted. It withheld from constituted authorities of the state all power or function of suretyship. It forbade the incurring of obligations by the indirect method of secondary liability. This is the field and the full scope of this section. It does not purport to deal with the creation of a primary indebtedness for any purpose whatever.

* * * [W]e find nothing in the Act which would authorize a lending of credit as we defined it in *Allen v. Tooele County, supra,* and as defined by other courts in the cases which we have just discussed, viz., the state is not empowered to become a surety or guarantor of another's debts. The

Act authorizes UTFC to provide capital for equity investment or to make direct loans to assist and encourage emerging and developing small businesses. In addition, research grants are authorized. These powers are to be exercised with private funds and with funds appropriated to UTFC by the legislature. The Act does not empower UTFC to become a surety or guarantor of the debts of the fledgling businesses it assists. Indeed, the Act does not even permit UTFC to incur any debt of its own. Thus, UTFC cannot become a debtor and in fact would become a creditor if it made a direct loan to an emerging business as provided for in the Act. However, as we have seen, the lending of state funds is not a lending of credit. We hold that the Act does not violate article VI, section 29 of the Utah Constitution insofar as it forbids the lending of the state's credit in aid of a private undertaking.

Closely related to the prohibition against the lending of the state's credit, although technically not a part of it due to the narrow and specific wording of section 29, is the principle of law that public funds cannot be expended for private purposes. * * * We find no violation of that principle here. The legislature in rather lengthy findings has determined that the aiding of emerging high-tech businesses will foster the growth of the state's economy and assist in creating employment for the citizens of the state. These findings are entitled to respect and weight by the judiciary and should not be overturned unless palpably erroneous. * * *

What is public purpose varies and changes with the times. In 1890, it was held that the purchasing and operating of an electrical distribution system to supply electricity to homes was not a public purpose. *Mauldin v. City Council of Greenville*, 33 S.C. 1, 11 S.E. 434 (1890). In contrast, in the past twelve years we have found public purpose in industrial development by a county * * *; eradication of urban blight by a quasi-municipal corporation * * *; and the providing of funds for low-and moderate-income housing by a state agency. * * * We cannot say in the face of those precedents that the stimulation of Utah's economy and the creation of employment is not a legitimate public purpose. It is closely related to industrial development and not different in kind. Whatever our private views on the matter might be, we must concede that the legislature's determination that a public benefit would result was within its latitude. The Supreme Court of Connecticut in *Wilson v. Connecticut Product Development Corp.*, 167 Conn. 111, 355 A.2d 72 (1974), upheld legislation similar to the Utah Technology and Innovation Act. The Connecticut Act provided venture capital to create new products and industry, resulting in increased employment and public revenue. It was there contended that the success of any enterprises which might be assisted is speculative and that any ultimate benefits to be realized by the State are remote. The court, however, dismissed those claims, stating that in disputing the business judgment of the legislature the claimants have not demonstrated that the Act does not serve a public purpose. Said the court: "The strong presumption of the act's constitutionality will not be overcome simply because the plaintiff's economic forecasts differ from those of the legislature."

B.   SUBSCRIPTION TO STOCK

In none of the thirteen cases which have been appealed to this Court involving section 29 has there been a subscription by the state or its political subdivisions to stocks or bonds in aid of any private enterprise. In *Utah State Land Board v. Utah State Finance Commission*, 12 Utah 2d 265, 365 P.2d 213 (1961), the question was presented whether the Utah State Land Board could constitutionally purchase corporate securities in its investment of the public funds which it manages. We held that the Land Board could do so since it would not be in aid of any railroad, telegraph, or other private enterprise. The underlying purpose of the investment program was to invest for the benefit of the state, and therefore there was no lending of credit in aid of private enterprise. The prohibition contained in section 29 against subscribing to stock was not specifically mentioned in the Court's opinion. It is clear, however, that there was no subscription of stock since the Land Board was simply purchasing outstanding shares owned by stockholders who desired to sell them on the open market. Clearly, this did not constitute the subscription to stock which section 29 interdicts.

In contrast, the Act before us authorizes UTFC to use funds appropriated to it by the legislature as matching sources of capital for equity investment in emerging and developing technological and innovative small businesses. Accordingly, UTFC has committed $1 million of public funds to purchase a limited partnership interest in Venture Fund I, which proposes to use that amount, together with private funds, to subscribe to stock in selected small high-tech businesses. This is clearly the subscription to stock in aid of private enterprise which section 29 prohibits. UTFC seeks judicial approbation on the ground that the subscription to stock in fledgling businesses has been found by the legislature to be in the public interest. However, the legislature's findings of a public interest is of no avail in this instance. The constitutional convention in promulgating section 29 and its subsequent adoption by the electorate of this state have foreclosed any speculation or further debate on that issue. Clearly, the subscription to stock in emerging businesses is to aid them. Whether the public benefits thereby is of no consequence. This means of assistance is forbidden by section 29. . . . The state is foreclosed from subscribing, even though the legislature may determine that public benefits will flow therefrom. The part of the Act which authorizes UTFC to subscribe to stock is unconstitutional and must fail.

NOTES AND QUESTIONS

1. *Public Purpose Requirements: Their Rise and Fall.* According to one study, the constitutions of forty-six of the fifty states "contain provisions that expressly bar the use of state financial resources" from aiding private enterprise. Dale F. Rubin, Constitutional Aid Limitation Provisions and the Public Purpose Doctrine, 12 St. Louis U. Pub. L. Rev. 143, 143 n.1 (1993). The remaining states employ judicial doctrines that require that taxpayer funds be spent only for public purposes. These restrictions date back to the middle decades of the nineteenth century. Before that, American state governments were actively involved in providing financial assistance to private firms, particularly banks and transportation companies. The enormous success of the Erie Canal, which opened in 1825, in energizing New York's economy inspired a massive state investment in turnpikes, canals, and railroads over the next two decades.

States built transportation systems themselves, went into partnership with private firms, or lent or gave funds to, or solicited investment for, the firms that would build and own the new roads, canals, and railways. States bought railroad and canal company stock, gave or loaned state bonds to transportation firms, or provided loan guarantees. To cover the costs of assisting these firms, the states engaged in massive borrowing. With relatively limited investment capital available in the United States, most of the money came from Europe. Foreign investors felt more secure lending to state governments than to often unknown private firms engaged in relatively speculative projects. Aggregate state debt rose from $12.8 million in 1820 to $231 million in 1843, with most of the money attributable to the financing of transportation systems. With transportation improvements likely to influence the course of economic development, states aggressively competed with each other for canals and railroads, and private entrepreneurs used whatever influence they could to get state legislators to back their projects. Waste, mismanagement, and overbuilding often resulted. *See* Alberta M. Sbragia, Debt Wish: Entrepreneurial Cities, U.S. Federalism, and Economic Development 19–43 (U. Pittsburgh Press 1996).

The Panic of 1837 led to a contraction in economy activity, and by 1839 most of the states were in the grip of a severe economic crisis. Due to the drop in trade, many of the canals and railways were unable to raise revenues sufficient to pay their debts. Many others were unfinished and could not raise the funds necessary to complete construction and thereby collect the revenues necessary to pay for the costs already incurred. Although many states sought to cover their debts, and raised taxes to do so, nine states defaulted on their interest payments, including four—Arkansas, Florida, Michigan, and Mississippi—which repudiated all or part of their debts.

In reaction to this financial fiasco, the states in the 1840s and 1850s engaged in a wave of constitutional revision. One aspect of that revision—which is the focus of Section C of this Chapter—sought to make it more difficult for the states to incur debts. Typically, this involved the adoption of new procedural hurdles like the requirement of voter approval of new state bonds. The other aspect sought to limit the purposes and techniques of state spending through the ratification of public purpose requirements, prohibitions on the gift or loan of state credit, or bans on direct state investment in business corporation obligations. Initially, these provisions applied only to activities of state governments. Soon state legislatures were working to circumvent these restrictions by authorizing local governments to provide assistance to private firms, particularly railroads, akin to the aid the states had been providing in the 1820s and 1830s. Another round of waste, overbuilding, speculation, and economic crisis in the 1860s and 1870s led many states to amend their constitutions and impose public purpose and aid limitation provisions on local governments as well.

Even in the absence of an express public purpose restriction in the state constitutional text, some state courts began to hold that all spending of taxpayer dollars must be for a public purpose. In the leading case of Sharpless v. Mayor of Philadelphia, 21 Pa. 147, 167 (1853), Chief Justice Black of the Pennsylvania Supreme Court concluded that it would be "palpably unconstitutional" to use tax dollars for a private purpose. The United States Supreme Court subsequently indicated that the use of tax dollars for a private purpose would violate the Due Process Clause, *see* Citizens' Savings & Loan Association v. Topeka, 87 U.S. (20 Wall.) 655 (1874).

These public purpose requirements did not necessarily bar all government financial assistance to the private sector. *Sharpless* held that municipal aid to a privately owned railroad could serve a public purpose. "The public has an interest in such a road," the court asserted, even if privately owned, because a railroad provides "comfort, convenience, increase of trade, opening of markets, and other means of rewarding labor and promoting wealth." 21 Pa. at 169. Other state courts, however, concluded that the public purpose requirement limited state aid to the private sector, including railroads. *See* Rubin, *supra*, at 156–62. Certainly, during the heyday of the public purpose requirement, from the 1870s through the 1930s, courts invalidated a wide variety of programs intended to assist private firms and individuals. *See, e.g.*, Allen v. Inhabitants of Jay, 60 Me. 124 (1872) (invalidating government aid to factories); Lowell v. Boston, 111 Mass. 454 (1873) (financial assistance to private residential housing development violated public purpose requirement); Opinion of the Justices, 291 Mass. 567 (1935) (use of tax revenues to insure banks against loss on home mortgages held not within "public purpose" limitation).

Starting in the late 1930s, the tide began to turn. In 1936, Mississippi, a poor agricultural state in the grip of the Great Depression, adopted a program of attracting new industry by allowing municipalities to issue bonds to finance the construction of factories and the acquisition of machinery and equipment for long-term lease to private firms willing to relocate to the state. The Mississippi Supreme Court upheld the program against a public purpose challenge, *see* Albritton v. City of Winona, 178 So. 799, *app. dis.*, 303 U.S. 627

(1938). The use of public funds for industrial development began to spread, first to other poor Southern states, and then, as industry began to move South, to the industrial states of the North. Eventually, state programs began to go beyond the support of manufacturing to include assistance to commercial, retail, service, and tourism firms. Today, virtually all the states and many localities are engaged in programs to attract and retain a wide range of private economic activity.

As state and municipal economic development initiatives spread, courts came to broaden the notion of public purpose to include increased employment and tax base growth, and to approve programs that involved assistance to individual firms. Initially, many of these programs were funded by revenue bonds, that is, bonds backed solely by new revenues to be generated by the industry receiving assistance. (Revenue bonds are discussed more fully in Section C.) With state liability limited to the project financed by the state assistance, courts could find that taxpayer dollars were not at risk. *See, e.g.,* Basehore v. Hampden Industrial Development Auth., 248 A.2d 212 (Pa.1968). Other courts did not distinguish between programs financed by revenue bonds and programs backed by treasury funds generally. *See, e.g.,* State ex rel. Beck v. City of York, 82 N.W.2d 269 (Neb.1957). Some courts resisted the general trend and continued to invalidate public financial assistance to private businesses. *See, e.g.,* Village of Moyie Springs v. Aurora Mfg. Co., 353 P.2d 767 (Idaho 1960); Mitchell v. North Carolina Indus. Dev. Fin. Auth., 159 S.E.2d 745 (N.C.1968). (Note that the *Maready* court discussed and purported to distinguish *Mitchell*. Has *Mitchell* really been overruled?) Where courts were initially reluctant to permit direct state assistance to private firms, states, like North Carolina, often amended their constitutions to permit at least some forms of industrial development assistance.

By the end of the twentieth century, as *Maready* notes, virtually every state court had upheld at least some economic development programs that involved cash grants, loans, tax breaks, or other forms of state assistance to individual firms. Landmark decisions include Common Cause v. Maine, 455 A.2d 1 (Me.1983), in which the Maine Supreme Court upheld the state's plan to commit $15 million in taxpayer funds to improve the facilities of the Bath Iron Works in order to persuade the company to remain in Portland, Maine and not move to Boston, Massachusetts, and Hayes v. State Property & Bldgs. Comm'n of Kentucky, 731 S.W.2d 797 (Ky.1987), in which a sharply divided Kentucky Supreme Court upheld a package of inducements—with direct costs estimated at between $125 and $268 million—to persuade Toyota Motor Corporation to open a plant in the state. *But cf.* Holding's Little America v. Board of County Comm'rs, 712 P.2d 331 (Wyo.1985) (no public purpose in providing aid to a hotel and restaurant); Purvis v. City of Little Rock, 667 S.W.2d 936 (Ark.1984) (no public purpose in financing a hotel). *Compare* Hucks v. Riley, 357 S.E.2d 458 (S.C.1987) (public interest in tourism development provides public purpose justifying use of state funds to finance privately owned and operated lodging and restaurant facilities). *See also* Bordeleau v. State of New York, 18 N.Y.3d 305, 318 (N.Y. 2011) (upholding provision of state funds to non-profit organizations promoting agricultural products grown or produced within the state as "for the overall benefit of the public and the State's competitiveness"). As a result of these developments, "[t]oday, state constitutional 'public purpose' requirements are largely rhetorical. State legislatures define what public purposes are and receive great deference when they determine that a particular program promotes the public purpose." Richard Briffault, The Disfavored Constitution: State Fiscal Limits and State Constitutional Law, 34 Rutgers L.J. 907, 914 (2003).

2.   *Public Purpose: The Judicial Role.* The public purpose requirement, to some extent, states a constitutional truism that government action must be for the benefit of the public as a whole, rather than for the benefit of private interests. Certainly, as *Sharpless* suggests, that must be the case when government uses tax dollars, which, are, after all, compulsory payments from the taxpayers. There can be no constitutional justification in compelling a taxpayer to make a payment to someone else unless there is a public interest in that transfer. The public purpose requirements also grow out of the particular economic and political circumstances of the 1830s and later eras, when significant government investment in and financial support for private firms resulted in huge debts and unanticipated burdens on the taxpayers. Public purpose litigation arises most commonly when the government proposes to make payments to private firms or individuals. Yet, as courts have regularly acknowledged, private firms, such as railroads, can provide public benefits. Moreover, there are few public programs that benefit *all* members of the public equally. Even classic public purpose programs, such as education, can provide some members of the public—children and their parents, and teachers and school system employees—more benefits than others.

How, then, should "public purpose" be defined, and what should the role of the courts be in enforcing the constitutional public purpose requirements? Is the issue of whether a particular spending program serves a public purpose largely a matter for an elected state or local legislature to decide? Should courts defer to legislative determination of public ends, checking only to make sure that the legislature has made appropriate findings and that the program satisfies some minimal rationality standard? Or should the courts impose their own public purpose criteria? Assuming broad deference to the legislature to determine public goals, should the courts assess whether a particular program is likely to achieve its ends, or whether the public benefits are worth the public costs?

For the most part, courts, as in the *Maready* and *Wilkinson* cases, defer to legislative determinations of both what constitutes a public purpose and whether the program in question is likely to serve that purpose. *See, e.g.,* Delogu v. State, 720 A.2d 1153, 1155 (Me. 1998) (legislative determinations that a spending, loan, or tax incentive program will promote a public purpose are to be accepted if "not . . . irrational"); Libertarian Party of Wisconsin v.

State, 546 N.W.2d 424, 433–34 (Wis.1996) ("Although this court is not bound by the declaration of public purpose contained in any legislation, what constitutes a public purpose is, in the first instance, a question for the legislature to determine and its opinion must be given great weight by this court.") (stadium financing); State ex rel. Brown v. City of Warr Acres, 946 P.2d 1140, 1145 (Okla.1997) ("It is not for the courts to second guess the wisdom of the City Council in agreeing to the details of the plan."). *See also* Friends of the Parks v. Chicago Park Dist., 786 N.E.2d 161, 166–67 (Ill. 2003) (courts must defer to legislative findings "unless the plaintiffs make a threshold showing that the findings are evasive and that the purpose of the legislation is principally to benefit private interests"; upholding public financing of renovations to stadium owned and operated by city park district but used by privately owned professional football team). *Cf.* Turken v. Gordon, 224 P.3d 158, 165–66 (Ariz. 2010) ("the primary determination of whether a specific purpose constitutes a 'public purpose' is assigned to the political branches of government, which are directly accountable to the public;" however, the state constitutional ban on gifts to the private sector is violated when a governmental payment "is grossly disproportionate to what is received in return").

Should judicial review be more stringent when a spending program provides a considerable benefit to one or a small number of particular firms or individuals, especially powerful present or prospective local employers, like in the Bath Iron Works or Toyota cases? There may be a public benefit in the jobs these employers provide and the contribution they make to the local tax base, but there may also be a danger that the legislature's judgment about the public benefit was unduly swayed by the political clout of a powerful private firm. On the other hand, the economic impact of a major employer's departure may suggest there is a public purpose in inducing that employer to remain in the locality. *Cf.* Poletown Neighborhood Council v. City of Detroit, 304 N.W.2d 455 (Mich.1981) (finding that Detroit's condemnation of a residential neighborhood in order to obtain and transfer land to General Motors, a major local employer, so the company could construct a new plant in Detroit and not leave the city, satisfies eminent domain's "public use" requirement), *overruled by* County of Wayne v. Hathcock, 684 N.W.2d 765 (Mich. 2004).

Given that many economic development programs provide a mix of general public and targeted private benefits, should a court try to assess the relative proportion of public and private benefits? Does a program that provides a small public benefit but a very large private benefit run afoul of the public purpose requirement? Or should such a program be upheld so long as there is some net public benefit? Can a court measure and compare the relative public and private benefits of a public spending program? *Compare* Baycol, Inc. v. Downtown Development Auth., 315 So.2d 451 (Fla.1975) (public financing of garage connected to private shopping mall provided only an "incidental" public purpose and was primarily intended to benefit the mall) *and* Brown v. Longiotti, 420 So.2d 71 (Ala.1982) (construction of a retail establishment did not serve a "significant public purpose") *with* State v. City of Miami, 379 So.2d 651 (Fla.1980) (private benefits from public financing of a garage "incidental" to primary public benefit of downtown redevelopment). Are there some kinds of benefits—like the country club memberships raised by the dissenting judge in *Maready*—that are so private that even if they aided the relocation of a firm to the state or locality providing the benefit they ought to be deemed beyond the scope of the public purpose doctrine?

Even after *Maready*, economic development programs continued to remain controversial in North Carolina and to be a focus of litigation. *See, e.g.,* Haugh v. County of Durham, 702 S.E.2d 814 (N.C. App. 2010); Blinson v. State, 651 S.E.2d 268 (N.C. App. 2007), *app. dis.* 661 S.E.2d 240 (2008); Peacock v. Shinn, 533 S.E.2d 842 (N.C. App.), *app. dis,* 546 S.E.2d 110 (2000). The measure that drew the most attention was a package of tax breaks and incentives worth approximately $260 million that the North Carolina Legislature enacted in 2005 to induce Dell, Inc. to locate a computer assembly plant in the state. The Dell incentives were challenged in the *Blinson* litigation and upheld. Academic commentary on the Dell package and the *Blinson* decision was highly critical. *See, e.g.,* Anne C. Choe, Blinson v. State and the Continued Erosion of the Public Purpose Doctrine in North Carolina, 87 N.C.L. Rev. 644 (2009). In 2009, Dell announced it was closing its facility in Winston-Salem, laying off more than nine hundred employees. *See* Randle B. Pollard, "Was the Deal Worth It"? The Dilemma of States With Ineffective Economic Incentives Programs, 11 Hastings Bus. L.J. 1, 20 (2015). *See also* C. Tyler Mulligan, Economic Development Incentives and North Carolina Local Governments: A Framework for Analysis, 91 N.C. L. Rev. 2021 (2013).

3.   *The Commerce Clause Question.* In addition to direct financial assistance like that at issue in *Maready*, many states and local governments offer a wide range of tax incentives—such as reduction or deferral of, exemption from, or credits for property, sales, corporate income, or other business taxes—for new investment in the state or locality. *See* Pollard, *supra* Note 2, 11 Hastings Bus. L. J. at 8–10. The Supreme Court has held that discriminatory taxation of out-of-state business can fall afoul of the so-called Dormant Commerce Clause, although direct subsidies for new investment does not normally raise a Commerce Clause problem. *See, e.g.,* New Energy Co. of Indiana v. Limbach, 486 U.S. 269, 278 (1988). Professor Peter Enrich has argued that many state tax incentive economic development programs are vulnerable to Dormant Commerce Clause challenge. *See* Peter D. Enrich, Saving the States from Themselves: Commerce Clause Constraints on State Tax Incentives for Business, 110 Harv. L. Rev. 277 (1996). In a case litigated by Professor Enrich, a panel of the United States Court of Appeals for the Sixth Circuit agreed that an investment tax credit offered by Toledo, Ohio to induce DaimlerChrysler to open a new vehicle assembly plant near an existing facility violated the Dormant Commerce Clause (although the court also sustained a personal property tax exemption that was part of the same incentive package). *See* Cuno v. DaimlerChrysler,

Inc., 386 F.3d 738 (6th Cir. 2004). The Supreme Court reversed, finding that the plaintiff state and local taxpayers lacked standing to bring the Commerce Clause challenge. DaimlerChrysler Corp. v. Cuno, 547 U.S. 332 (2006). Standing has continued to be an issue in the litigation of Commerce Clause challenges to tax incentive programs. *See, e.g.,* Morgan L. Holcomb and Nicholas Allen Smith, The Post-Cuno Litigation Landscape, 58 Case W. Res. L. Rev, 1157 (2008); Jeannette K. Doran, The People Versus Corporate Welfare: North Carolina's Opportunity to Reverse Perversion of the Commerce Clause and to Reinvigorate the Public Purpose Doctrine, 33 Camp. L. Rev, 381 (2011). On the merits of whether the Dormant Commerce Clause applies to tax incentive programs, *see, e.g.,* Dan T. Coenan, Business Subsidies and the Dormant Commerce Clause, 107 Yale L.J. 965 (1998): Note, Location Incentives and the Negative Commerce Clause: A Farewell to Arms?, 89 Marq. L. Rev. 583 (2006).

   4.   *Lending of Credit.* The constitutional lending of credit prohibition raises its own set of issues. In some states the restriction on lending of credit is limited to assistance to private enterprise. *See, e.g.,* Hawaii Const., art. VII, § 4; Iowa Const., art VIII § 1; City of Charlottesville v. DeHaan, 323 S.E.2d 131 (Va.1984); *cf.* Brower v. State of Washington, 969 P.2d 42 (Wash.1998) (lending of credit restriction does not apply if loan advances a "fundamental purpose" of government). In other states, however, the lending of credit ban is more restrictive. A government program might serve a public purpose, but the technique—the gift or loan of the state's or locality's credit—may still be proscribed. *See* Port of Longview v. Taxpayers of Longview, 527 P.2d 263 (Wash.1974); Note, State Constitutional Provisions Prohibiting the Loaning of Credit to Private Enterprise—A Suggested Analysis, 41 U. Colo. L. Rev. 135, 140 (1969).

   What, then, does lending of credit mean? The courts tend to fall into two camps. Most courts, as reflected in *Wilkinson,* find a lending of credit only when the state serves as a surety or guarantees a loan made by another lender to a borrower. *See, e.g.,* Barnhart v. City of Fayetteville, 900 S.W.2d 539 (Ark.1995) (unconditional guarantee of bonds is unconstitutional lending of credit). Under that definition, a state does not lend credit when it provides direct financial assistance to a private party even when the state had to borrow money to provide that assistance. Some courts, however, have found that a state lends its credit within the meaning of the prohibition when it borrows money and provides the proceeds to another entity. In effect, the state has obligated its taxpayers into the future for the benefit of a private actor. *See* Washington Higher Educ. Facilities v. Gardner, 699 P.2d 1240 (Wash.1985); Wein v. Comptroller of State of New York, 386 N.E.2d 242 (N.Y.1979). *Cf.* State of Florida v. Inland Protection Financing Corporation, 699 So.2d 1352 (Fla.1997) (no lending of credit in issuance of revenue bonds to obtain funds to aid private firms as revenue bonds do not pledge public credit).

   Which approach makes more sense? On the one hand, it seems odd that a state barred from acting as a surety for a loan to a private entity is permitted to make a gift or loan directly to that entity. In the latter case, the state has certainly placed its funds at risk, whereas in the former the state may never have to spend a dime if the borrower repays the loan. On the other hand, as the *Wilkinson* court suggested, it may be that state legislators and the public will more closely scrutinize, and more carefully assess, the costs and benefits of a direct commitment of state funds than a merely contingent liability which may never come due. As in the railroad and canal era of the 1820s and 1830s, unduly optimistic legislators not forced to appropriate funds or required to estimate the likelihood that the state will have to honor its commitment may too easily succumb to the delusion of suretyship and provide a guarantee in the absence of some restriction.

5. *Limits on Stock Subscriptions.* Responding to one of the most popular techniques of providing state support to canals and railroads in the 1820s and 1830s, a number of state constitutions prohibit not just aid to, but also investments in, business corporations. *See, e.g.,* Mich. Const., art. IX, § 19; Ohio Const., art. VIII, § 4. Unlike the vague notion of "public purpose," these restrictions impose specific limits on governments. In *Wilkinson*, for example, the Utah Supreme Court agreed that the program of assistance to high tech companies served a public purpose and did not involve a gift or loan of the state's credit, but ruled that state purchase of stock of fledgling high tech companies violated the state constitution despite the public benefits that would result. *See also* West Virginia Trust Fund, Inc. v. Bailey, 485 S.E.2d 407 (W.Va.1997) (West Virginia law authorizing the investment of state employee pension funds in corporate stock violates the state constitutional provision prohibiting the state from becoming "a joint owner or stockholder in any company or association"). Again, as when a state constitution bans a state or local government from acting as a surety for a private enterprise while permitting public gifts or loans to private firms, there may be something odd about permitting a state to give or lend money to private firms while prohibiting them from taking an equity position which would also enable them to share in any appreciation in the firm's value. States may apparently undertake a risk of loss but not a chance for gain. These provisions reflect mid-and late-nineteenth century concerns about the entanglement of government and the private sector, and seek to draw a line between the two. Do you think the line they draw is a wise one or that it should be reconsidered?

6. *Public Purpose and Public Use.* The debate over, and decline in enforcement of, state constitutional public purpose requirements to some extent resembles the issues raised concerning the "public use" language in the eminent domain provision of the Fifth Amendment to the United States Constitution—"nor shall private property be taken for public use without just compensation." In Kelo v. City of New London, 545 U.S. 469 (2005), the United States Supreme Court embraced a relatively capacious definition of "public use"—treating it as essentially synonymous with "public purpose," *see id.* at 479–80—and indicated that it would be relatively deferential to state and local government determinations that a particular taking served a public

purpose. *See id.* at 480–81. Specifically, the Court held that a state or local government taking for transfer to private ownership as part of a local economic development program could satisfy the public use requirement. *Kelo* generated a storm of controversy and many calls for a more restrictive approach to eminent domain that would limit the ability to take private property for economic development purposes. *Kelo* noted that "nothing in our opinion precludes any State from placing further restrictions on its exercise of the takings power." *Id.* at 489. Indeed, several state courts have adopted a narrower definition of "public use" and have determined that private property cannot be taken for retransfer to other private owners as part of an economic development program. *See, e.g.,* County of Wayne v. Hathcock, 684 N.W.2d 765 (Mich. 2004) (overruling the *Poletown* decision cited in Note 2, *supra*), City of Norwood v. Horney, 853 N.E.2d 1115, 1123 (Ohio 2006) ("although economic factors may be considered in determining whether private property may be appropriated, the fact that the appropriation would provide an economic benefit to the government and community, standing alone, does not satisfy the public-use requirement"). Are the questions for the courts posed by the public purpose requirement for the spending of government funds and the public use requirement for eminent domain similar, or is there a case for differential treatment and different degrees of deference to state and local governments' use of these tools for economic development purposes?

7.   *The Uncertain Public Benefits of State and Local Economic Incentive Programs.* State and local governments devote considerable effort and resources to economic incentive programs. These include: financial incentives, such as grants, or direct or subsidized loans; infrastructure improvements; free or reduced-cost land; reduced public utility charges; technical assistance and other free services; tax exemptions and abatements; and the investment of public funds directly into privately-owned businesses. *See* Pollard, *supra* Note 2, 11 Hastings Bus. L.J. at 8–12. Although there is no comprehensive tabulation of such programs, one study undertaken in 2012 determined that they cost states and local governments at least $80 billion a year, primarily in tax breaks. *See* Louise Story, As Companies Seek Tax Deals, Governments Pay High Price, N.Y. Times, Dec. 1, 2012. Many of those programs provide very large benefits for a handful of companies. GoodJobsFirst, a public interest organization critical of these programs, identified seven deals in which individual companies received $100 million or more in targeted benefits, and an additional eleven deals with benefits to individual firms ranging between $40 million and $93 million *See* GoodJobsFirst, The Job-Creation Shell Game (January 2013). Despite their widespread use, it is unclear whether or how much such targeted incentive programs actually promote economic development. Most studies, acknowledging the uncertainty of data and the difficulty in determining what factors actually drive corporate actions, have found that government financial assistance and tax breaks have a minimal effect on firms' locational decisions. *See, e.g.,* Dan Gorin, Economic Development Incentives: Research Approaches and Current Views, 93 Fed. Res. Bull. 69 (2009); Alan Peters & Peter Fisher, The Failures of Economic Development Incentives, 70 J. Am. Plan. Ass'n 27 (2004). Access to markets,

raw materials, and transportation; the quality and cost of labor; and the cost of land and materials are the major factors affecting firms' production costs and hence are generally much more important factors in determining whether a firm will move to or remain in a particular site. Government grants, loans, and tax breaks generally do not have a big enough impact on corporate costs to affect location decisions. They are often not even as important as such factors as climate and living conditions for corporate officers and employees. *See, e.g.*, Peter K. Eisinger, The Rise of the Entrepreneurial State: State and Local Economic Development Policy in the United States 200–24 (U. Wisc. Press 1988); Rachel Weber, Why Local Economic Development Incentives Don't Create Jobs: The Role of Corporate Governance, 32 Urb. Law. 97 (2000). Economic development programs may have the unfortunate consequence of "giving money to firms for doing what they would have done anyway." Stephen Ellis, Grant Hayden, and Cynthia Rogers, A Game Changer for the Political Economy of Economic Development Incentives, 56 Ariz. L. Rev. 953, 949 (2014). Government assistance, however, may have an impact in determining where within a metropolitan area a corporation will invest. As the same market access and labor force conditions may prevail throughout the area, the company has greater discretion in choosing between one locality and another in the same area. Indeed, many of the biggest economic development incentive packages involve competitions between neighboring states—Kansas and Missouri, New Jersey and New York, Tennessee and Mississippi, Massachusetts and Rhode Island—that may result in the movement of jobs a few miles across a state line in the same metropolitan area. *See* The Job-Creation Shell Game, *supra*. *See also* Charles Chieppo, Rhode Island and Massachusetts Chase Private Jobs with Public Money, Governing, June 25, 2013. Firms are often skillful at playing off competing states or localities against each other and in extracting government payments or tax exemptions, which, although not critical to corporate location decisions, are beneficial nonetheless. *See, e.g.*, Bryan D. Jones & Lynn W. Bachelor, Local Policy Discretion and the Corporate Surplus, 245, *in* Richard B. Bingham & John P. Blair, eds, Urban Economic Development (Sage Pub., Inc. 1984). Communities caught up in the psychology of "bidding wars" for specific firms may wind up offering more in incentives than makes economic sense. *See* Ellis, Hayden, and Rogers, *supra*, 56 Ariz. L. Rev. at 961.

States and local governments have difficulty in calculating the benefits of their incentive programs, both before an incentive is offered and after the business relocation or expansion has occurred. *See, e.g.*, NC Justice Center, Getting Our Money's Worth? An Evaluation of the Economic Model Used for Awarding State Business Subsidies (March 2007) (sharply criticizing the economic model used by the North Carolina Department of Commerce to justify the offer of substantial incentives to Dell, Inc.); Pollard, *supra* Note 2, 11 Hastings Bus. L.J. at 15–23 (reviewing different methodologies for assessing the effectiveness of incentive programs); Mike Maciag, How Local Governments Are (or Aren't) Examining Economic Development Dollars, Governing, Nov. 5, 2014. Moreover, even when an incentive program affects corporate investment the effect may not be long-lasting. Typically, corporations make few specific commitments with respect to the number of jobs they will create or how long they will remain at their new site in exchange for the benefits they receive. In the absence of specific contractual terms, localities have generally been unsuccessful in arguing that companies that receive loans, land, or tax abatements are required to remain within the community. *See, e.g.*, Charter Township of Ypsilanti v. General Motors Corp., 506 N.W.2d 556 (Mich.Ct.App.1993) (company's receipt of a long-term tax abatement for a new plant does not estop the company from closing the plant during the abatement period); City of Yonkers v. Otis Elevator Co., 649 F.Supp. 716 (S.D.N.Y.1986) (dismissing breach of contract and equitable estoppel claims). *See also* Pollard, *supra*, at 21–22.

Due to the intensive interstate and interlocal competition for economic development and tax base, states and localities remain committed to economic development programs. Although taxes and government assistance may be lesser factors in corporate decision-making, they are factors that governments can control—although some critics argue that investments in education or transportation infrastructure would pay off better in the long run. Other critics have sought to improve economic development programs by requiring better recordkeeping to determine what impacts the programs actually have; tying incentives to the production of higher-quality jobs, as by requiring employers that receive incentives to pay a "living" wage that is in excess of the minimum wage; and by including clawback contractual provisions that would rescind incentives or even require repayment if recipients fail to provide a specified number of jobs for a specified time period. *See, e.g.*, Weber, *supra*; Michael LaFave, Taking Back the Giveaways: Minnesota's Corporate Welfare Legislation and the Search for Accountability, 80 Minn.L.Rev. 1579 (1996); Kary L. Moss, The Privatizing of Public Wealth, 23 Fordham Urb. L.J. 101 (1995). At the very least states and local governments ought to collect and maintain data on the cost and effectiveness of their economic development programs, and make that data accessible online for public inspection, assessment, and evaluation. An important step in the direction of greater transparency for economic incentive programs was the decision of the Governmental Accounting Standards Board (GASB), effective as of the end of 2015, to require that governments include in their financial statements information concerning their tax abatement programs, including the tax abated, the legal authority for the abatement, eligibility criteria, the abatement mechanism, provisions for recapturing abated taxes, the commitments made by abatement recipients, the gross dollar amount abated, and any commitments made by the government in addition to the abatement as part of the tax abatement agreement. *See* Government Accounting Standards Series, Statement No. 77 of the Governmental Accounting Standards Board: Tax Abatement Disclosures (Aug. 2015).

B. REVENUES

In 2013, states and local governments raised approximately $3.42 trillion in revenues. Of that amount, just $585 billion came from the federal government, so that more than $2.8 trillion came from state and local sources. U.S. Census Bureau, State and Local Government Finance: 2013. Local governments raised more than $1.7 trillion, with $71 billion coming directly from the federal government, $469 billion coming from the states, and roughly $1.17 trillion coming from local sources.

State constitutions and statutes extensively regulate state and local revenues. Two central themes in the state law of state and local finance have been the regulation of the property tax—historically, the single most important state or local tax—and the emergence of other revenue-raising devices that circumvent state constitutional limitations on the property tax. Consequently, these two themes will be the principal focal points of this Section, with the final subsection giving brief attention to state and local sales and income taxes.

1. THE GENERAL AD VALOREM TAX ON PROPERTY

Historically, the property tax has been the single greatest source of revenue for local government. At the start of the twentieth century, the property tax accounted for 51% of the tax dollars collected by all levels of American government—federal, state, and local; for 82% of total state and local tax collections; and for 89% of all local government tax collections. At that time, the property tax funded both states and local governments. Indeed, in 1902, the property tax accounted for 53% of all state tax dollars. Over the next several decades, the states effectively turned the property tax over to their local governments and came to rely on other revenue sources, particularly sales, excise and income taxes. Today, the property tax accounts for less than two percent of state tax revenues nationwide, and in many states the state government receives no property tax dollars at all.

The property tax, however, is a financial mainstay of local government. Localities rely on three broad categories of funds: local taxes, nontax local sources, and intergovernmental assistance. "Own-source" revenue is particularly valuable as it provides localities some protection against the variability of federal and state aid. The property tax accounts for roughly half of all local own-source revenue, and nearly three-quarters of local tax revenue. The remaining locally-generated funds come from fees, user charges, and sales and income taxes. Even taking intergovernmental aid into account, the property tax accounts for more than a quarter of all local revenue. It is the single largest source of local funds, and the key local government revenue source under local government control. It is also the local revenue source which has been most subject to legal regulation.

What Is the Property Tax? As the caption to this section of the text suggests, it is a (i) general, (ii) ad valorem, (iii) tax on (iv) property.

General: The property tax is for the general support of local government, rather than targeted at financing particular programs intended to benefit particular members of the community. Local taxpayers presumably benefit from local tax-funded expenditures on such programs as public safety, fire protection, sanitation, etc., but there is no requirement that they do so. Nor is there any requirement that the benefits they receive match the taxes they pay. This is important because, as we will see below, there are "benefits taxes" or "assessments" which are justified in terms of the benefits the tax-funded expenditures provide the taxpayer, so that there must be a nexus between the tax or assessment paid and the benefit received.

Ad Valorem: The property tax obligation of a particular taxpayer is measured by the value of the property subject to tax. In other words it is not a "head" tax imposed on each member or household in the community, or a flat tax that everyone pays equally. Nor is it like a user charge, where the amount of the charge depends on how much the payer uses the service. As we will see, a central difficulty of the property tax, and one cause of its longstanding unpopularity, is determining the value of the property subject to tax.

Tax: A tax is a compulsory payment. By contrast, user fees or charges are voluntary in the sense that one can avoid the fee by forgoing the service subject to the fee or charge. An individual can avoid paying a bridge toll or the admissions fee for the municipal golf course by simply not driving over the bridge or not using the golf course. But the property tax, like other taxes, is an obligation imposed on the owners of property within the jurisdiction of the taxing unit.

Property: Most importantly, the property tax is a tax on property or wealth, not a tax on income or consumption. Wealth is an important measure of ability to pay, so the property tax to some extent reflects ability to pay. Many of the services provided by local governments—public safety, fire prevention and control, water supply and the removal of wastes, street maintenance— benefit property so the value of property taxed may also be a rough proxy for the benefits funded by the tax. *See, e.g.*, Darien Shanske, Revitalizing Local Political Economy Through Modernizing the Property Tax, 68 Tax.L. Rev. 143, 144 (2014) ("[a] *local* property tax that pays for *local* public goods . . . operates according to the benefit principle, at least roughly").

In the nineteenth century, states sought to apply the tax to all forms of property—real property, that is, land and structures attached to the land; personal property, such as jewelry, household effects, farm implements, business equipment and inventory; and intangibles, like commercial paper, stocks and bonds, licenses, franchises, accounts receivable and other legally protected interests that were a source of wealth. Intangibles, however, may be difficult to detect and to value. Intangibles and many forms of personal property can easily be moved out of the jurisdiction when property is assessed for tax purposes. As the property tax became an increasingly local tax, its scope was narrowed by law to focus primarily on real property. Although in many states some forms of personal property, particularly motor vehicles and business equipment and inventory are subject to the property tax, ninety percent of the value of property subject to tax is real property.

Now largely focused on land and improvements to land, the property tax is a good tax for local governments. Land is immobile and inelastic. The supply of land is fixed and does not respond to changes in the local tax rate. Of course, a significant part of the tax represents a tax on buildings and other improvements, and these can be affected by tax rates, and, especially, by the differences in tax rates among local governments. Still, given the multiplicity of local governments and the ease of movement among them, the property tax is probably the tax least vulnerable to interlocal mobility; it is certainly less vulnerable than the income tax or the sales tax.

Although the property tax is better suited to local governments than taxes that target more mobile revenue sources, like incomes or sales, it suffers from two major, and interrelated, problems. The first is the question of *assessment*. The property tax applies to the value of a given property, but how is that value determined? The income tax applies to incomes, and for most people the size of one's income is determined by adding up wages or salaries, other payments for services, bank interest, stock dividends, or gains on the sales of assets. Sales and other excise taxes apply to the purchases of goods or services, with the purchase price clearly determining the tax. The property tax applies to the value of property, but unless that property has changed hands recently in an arm's-length open-market transaction, the value of that property is inherently uncertain. It is difficult to determine if a particular property is accurately assessed, or if it is assessed fairly relative to other properties in the jurisdiction. Assessment—that is, the determination of the value of property for property tax purposes—is central to the administration of the tax. Popular beliefs about the fairness or unfairness of assessment practices have had a major impact on the law governing the property tax. There is also evidence that the assessment system tends "systematically to favor privileged groups who are more likely to appeal their assessments." Shanske, *supra,* 68 Tax. L. Rev. at 148.

The second problem grows out of the uncertain *relationship between wealth and income.* Property is a tax on wealth but is paid out of current income. Over the long run, wealth and income are likely to be related, as people purchase properties that their incomes enable them to afford or as their property serves as a source of income. But there are periods when the two diverge. During the Great Depression, incomes dropped sharply, but property values remained stable or declined only modestly. People were unable to pay their taxes, tax delinquencies soared, and several states adopted property tax limits. In the late 1970s, during a period of rapid inflation in housing prices in many areas, property values—and taxes—rose much more rapidly than incomes. This led to a second wave of tax revolts, and the adoption of more limits on taxes. The divergence between wealth and income may also relate to different stages in the life-cycle. Retirees who bought their homes many years ago when they were employed but who currently live on fixed incomes may feel particularly pressed by the property tax if rising property values drive up their assessments.

HELLERSTEIN V. ASSESSOR OF THE TOWN OF ISLIP

Court of Appeals of New York
332 N.E.2d 279 (1975)

WACHTLER, J.

Petitioner, an owner of real property located on Fire Island, claims that the entire assessment roll for the Town of Islip is void. * * * She argues * * * that the assessments are illegal because they were not made in accordance with section 306 of the Real Property Tax Law which states: "All real property in each assessing unit shall be assessed at the full value thereof." This, we have held, means market value, unless that cannot be established "and then other tests of full value must be used." Here it is conceded that all assessments throughout the township are based on a *percentage* of market value.

* * * Section 306 of the Real Property Tax Law has an ancient lineage. In 1788 the New York Legislature directed "the assessors of each respective city, town and place in every county of this State [to] make out a true and exact list of the names of all the freeholders and inhabitants and opposite the name of every such person shall set down the real value of all his or her whole estate real and personal as near as they can discover the same". * * * The term "full value" first appeared in a draft revision of 1826–1828 providing that

> "All real and personal estate liable to taxation, the value of which shall not have been specified by affidavit of the person taxed, shall be estimated by the assessor at its full value, as they

would themselves be willing to receive the same in payment of a just debt due from a solvent debtor; * * *"

(Report of the Commissioners to Revise the Statute Laws of 1826–1828, ch XIII, tit II, art 2, § 16, "Of the manner in which assessments are to be made".) * * *

* * * [D]espite the fact that the custom of fractional assessments appears to be at least as old as the statute (see Kilmer, Legal Requirements for Equality in Tax Assessments, 25 Albany L. Rev., 203, 210), it has prompted very little litigation. In several of the older cases the problem can be seen lurking in the background; but it is only during the last 10 years that we find the practice being directly challenged in the courts.

It appears the first case touching this point surfaced in our court in 1852 (*Van Rensselaer v. Witbeck*, 7 NY 517, 522). At issue there was the validity of an assessment certificate which differed from the statutory form in certain respects which we found to be material.

> "The assessors have taken the precaution to negative all presumption that they had done their duty, by certifying that they had estimated the real estate, not according to its value, 'but as they deemed proper,' and the personal, not 'according to their best information and belief, of its value,' but 'according to the usual way of assessing.' We are informed by the learned judge who delivered the opinion of the supreme court, that the usual method is to estimate property at less than half its value, under the obligation of an official oath, which requires its full value to be stated; If this be so, the practice should be corrected. . . ."

In *People ex rel. Board of Supervisors v. Fowler* (55 NY 252, 254) the supervisors of Westchester County sought a writ of mandamus, compelling the assessors of the Town of Rye to file a proper certificate of assessment. Once again, the problem arose because of fractional assessments and, although 21 years had elapsed since the *Witbeck* decision, our attitude toward the custom had not changed. * * *

In the case now before us, the lower courts made no reference to these early decisions. They relied instead on *C. H. O. B. Assoc. v. Board of Assessors of County of Nassau* (45 Misc 2d 184, affd 22 A D 2d 1015, affd 16 NY2d 779) and its progeny * * * In *C. H. O. B.*, the trial court stated (p 192):

> "Section 306 provides that all real property shall be assessed at full value thereof. Although full value has been held to be synonymous with market value . . . the courts have uniformly held that this section does not mandate assessments at 100% of

full or market value. It requires merely that the assessments be at a uniform rate or percentage of full or market value for every type of property in the assessing unit. (*Matter of Mid-Island Shopping Plaza v. Podeyn, supra; Matter of Hartley Holding Corp. v. Gabel*, 13 NY2d 306; People ex rel. *Yaras v. Kinnaw*, 303 NY 224). The Legislature through subdivision 3 of section 720 of the Real Property Tax Law has acknowledged and apparently sanctioned this State-wide practice."

When the case reached our court in 1965, we affirmed without opinion (16 NY2d 779). * * *

Thus the custom of fractional assessments, once roundly condemned as a flagrant violation of the statute, has endured and acquired a new life through a kind of legislation by violation.

The *C.H.O.B.* decision assumes that fractional assessment is an ancient custom, never before challenged, which has, over the years, acquired recognition and, by implication, legal status from the courts and the Legislature. As the township notes, it involves two basic arguments: (1) By holding in "numerous cases" that "assessments [must] be at a uniform rate or percentage of full or market value for all property in the assessing unit" we have decided, sub silentio, "that section 306 does not mandate assessments at 100% of full or market value" and thus fractional assessments are legal; (2) by establishing the State Board of Equalization the Legislature has indicated that section 306 of the Real Property Tax Law does not require assessment at 100% of market or full value but only that assessments be made at a uniform percentage of full value for every type of property within the assessing unit. Neither argument bears up under close analysis.

Regarding the first point we note that historically an assessment which was at or below full value, but above the average rate, presented a dilemma to the courts. On the one hand there was a rather obvious violation of equal protection. But on the other hand the requirements of the statute had been met and if the court ordered a reduction from full value, it would be compelling the assessors to "do an unlawful act". * * * Thus many courts "held themselves precluded by the letter of the law from doing more than advise the complainant that he had the theoretically satisfactory privilege of suing out a writ of mandamus to compel the assessors to revalue every other piece of property in the jurisdiction" (1 Bonbright, Valuation of Property, p 501).

The Supreme Court felt that this approach denied the taxpayer an effective remedy. They put an end to the practice and resolved the dilemma, by holding that "where it is impossible to secure both the standard of the true value, and the uniformity and equality required by law, the latter requirement is to be preferred" (*Sioux City Bridge Co. v.*

Dakota County, 260 U.S. 441, 446). Now that the courts have been forced to choose equality over the full value standard—when it appears that one or the other must be violated—the respondent draws the type of conclusion the courts originally sought to avoid.

Viewed against this background it is obvious that these inequality decisions, reducing assessments to the uniform rate, are not premised on the legality of fractional assessments (*see, e.g., Russman v. Luckett*, 391 SW2d 694, 697, 698 [Ky]) and it is ironic that the township has inferred that they are.

Similarly we find no merit to the argument that by establishing the State Equalization Board the Legislature has indicated that the requirements of section 306 are satisfied if assessments are simply made at a uniform percentage of full value throughout the taxing unit. As the petitioner noted the State Equalization Board is only concerned with maintaining equality among taxing units. It " 'does not purport to measure the ratio of assessed valuation to full value of any individual property' " * * * nor is it designed to insure that assessments are made at a uniform percentage of full value within the taxing unit. The only significance the board has in relation to this problem is found in section 720 of the Real Property Tax Law which permits a taxpayer in an inequality proceeding to rely on the ratio established by the board in proving his claim. But this provision was merely designed to ease the taxpayers' burden of proof in inequality cases * * * which, as indicated earlier, is not premised on the legality of fractional assessments.

The creation of the board however, does reflect the Legislature's awareness of the fact that the local officials charged with making assessments pursuant to section 306 are using a percentage of full value, and we recognize that "Where the practical construction of a statute is well known, the Legislature is charged with knowledge and its failure to interfere indicates acquiescence". * * * But the application of this principle presupposes first, that the statute is capable of more than one interpretation, and secondly, that our court has not previously resolved the ambiguity. If there is any ambiguity in section 306 it is found solely in the term "value". But once that is resolved—and, as indicated we have determined that market value is the standard—it is quite evident that the "full" measure, and not a percentage must be used. * * * Thus, in this case, the "practical construction" is nothing more than a violation, which, no matter how persistent, widespread and uncorrected, cannot alter the meaning of the statute. * * *

One of the most peculiar aspects of the township's case is the narrowness of their defense of the practice of fractional assessments. They are satisfied to rest on the theory "thus it has been, thus it always must be", without making any effort to explain how the custom began, whether it serves any useful purpose, and what would happen if the assessors complied, or were made to comply, with the strict letter of the law. * * *

The vast majority of States require assessors, either by statute or constitutional prescription, to assess at full value, true value, market value or some equivalent standard. (*See* Note, 68 Yale L J 335–387). Two States have expressly provided by statute that this requires assessment at 100% of value (see 13 Ariz Rev Stat Ann., § 42–227; California Revenue & Taxation Code, §§ 401, 408). Several States have specifically authorized fractional assessments, and this seems to be the modern trend. In 1917 there were four States in this latter category (see *Greene v. Louisville Interurban R. R. Co.*, 244 U.S. 499, 516); by 1958 there were eight (see Note, 68 Yale LJ 335, 387); and, as of 1962 15 States had enacted legislation providing for fractional assessments, either at a fixed percentage or according to local option (Note, 75 Harvard L Rev, 1374, 1377, n 28).

Where full value is required, the standard has been almost universally disregarded. A 1957 study by the United States Census Bureau placed the average assessment ratio in the country at 30% of actual value (see Bird, The General Property Tax: Findings of the 1957 Census of Governments 40).

No one seems to know exactly how the practice of fractional assessment began. In an early case the Supreme Court suggested that: "If we look for the reason for this common consent to substitute a custom for the positive rule of the statute, it will probably be found in the difficulty of subjecting personal property, and especially invested capital, to the inspection of the assessor and the grasp of the collector. The effort of the land-owner, whose property lies open to view, which can be subjected to the lien of a tax not to be escaped by removal, or hiding, to produce something like actual equality of burden by an underevaluation of his land, has led to this result" (*Cummings v. National Bank*, 101 U.S. 153, 163).

This may well explain the origin of the rule, but it does not account for its remarkable powers of endurance, especially in a State like New York, which has removed personal property from the tax rolls (Real Property Tax Law, § 300). Its survival depends on other factors none of which are particularly commendable.

Bonbright, in his treatise (op. cit.), lists (p 498)

"several reasons for the persistence of partial valuation. Gullible taxpayers associate a larger valuation with a larger tax, or at any rate are less contentious about a relatively excessive assessment if it does not exceed their estimate of true value. The ability to maintain a stable rate and to increase revenue by tampering with the tax base—a change which calls for less publicity and less opposition—is naturally desired by the party in power. Occasionally, partial valuation is intended as a substitute for a varied system of rates; i.e., different forms of property, while nominally taxed at the same rate, are in fact taxed at differing rates by being assessed at different proportions of full values. * * *

"Another inducement to undervaluation has been that, since the state relies on the property tax for part of its revenue, the county assessors seek to lighten their constituents' burden at the expense of the rest of the state by assessing the local property at a lower percentage than is applied elsewhere. This process has often resulted in a competition between counties as to which could most nearly approach the limit of nominal valuation." * * *

Most of these considerations have probably served to perpetuate the custom in New York; but there may be other factors at work.

This State, of course, does not depend on real property taxes as a source of State revenue. However the State does supply financial aid to communities based primarily on assessed valuation (State Finance Law, § 54, subd 1, par c; § 54, subd 2, pars a, c) and this undoubtedly furnishes "another inducement to undervaluation." The activities of the State Equalization Board are meant to correct this problem but as one commentator observes "possibly local tax officials believe that there is no harm in trying" (Johnson, Fractional Ratios and Their Effect on Achievement of Uniform Assessment, the Property Tax: Problems and Potentials, Tax Institute of America, p 210).

Since the State Constitution provides that "[assessments] shall in no case exceed full value" (NY State Const, art XVI, § 2) assessing at a percentage of value discourages claims of unconstitutional overvaluation. Then the taxpayer is left with the far more difficult task of proving comparative inequality.

Obviously these reasons are all good reasons for abolishing the custom (see, e.g., Note, 68 Yale LJ 335, op. cit.; Note, 75 Harvard L Rev 1374; Kilmer, Legal Requirements for Equality in Tax Assessments, 25 Albany L Rev 203, op. cit.). As Bonbright observes (op. cit., pp 497–498): "Theoretically the taxpayer's pocket is not in the least affected by uniform undervaluation or overvaluation. Systematic undervaluation diminishes the tax base and the tax rate must therefore rise in order to supply the required government revenue. * * * The objections to the practice of undervaluation are patent. In the first place, except where sanctioned by statute, it involves a generally known and sanctioned disregard by officials of the law requiring them to assess property at its full and fair value. The other great vice is that the percentage of undervaluation is rarely a matter of common knowledge, so that it is extremely difficult to ascertain whether there is uniformity in the proportion or whether, through incompetence, favoritism, or corruption of the assessors, some portions of the taxpaying body are bearing the others' burdens, as between either individuals or local groups."

In recent years the high courts in several States, noting the mounting criticism, have held that full value means what it says and that the practice of fractional assessments is illegal (*see, e.g., Switz v. Township of Middletown*, 23 NJ 580; *Ingraham v. Town & City of Bristol*, 144 Conn 374; *Russman v. Luckett*, 391 SW2d 694 [Ky]; *Bettigole v. Assessors of Springfield*, 343 Mass 223; *Walter v. Schuler*, 176 So 2d 81 [Fla]; *Southern Ry. Co. v. Clement*, 415 SW2d 146 [Tenn]).

In sum, for nearly 200 years our statutes have required assessments to be made at full value and for nearly 200 years assessments have been made on a percentage basis throughout the State. The practice has time on its side and nothing else. It has been tolerated by the Legislature, criticized by the commentators and found by our own court to involve a flagrant violation of the statute. Nevertheless the practice has become so widespread and been so consistently followed that it has acquired an aura of assumed legality. The assessors in Islip inherited the custom and it is conceded that they have continued it. Throughout the years taxes have been levied and paid, or upon default, tax liens have arisen, followed by foreclosure and ultimate transfer of title, all on reliance on the apparent legality of fractional assessments. * * *

The petitioner recognizes that if we invalidate the assessment roll this could bring "fiscal chaos to the Town of Islip". * * * [W]e will not, in this action, on the equity side, disturb the settled assessment rolls. The taxes levied and paid, the tax liens, matured or pending, and completed transfers of foreclosed properties made in reliance on the assessment rolls are matters not now before the court and on which therefore it should not pass. We assume however that should these questions arise, the courts will exercise the sound discretion with which they are vested. To this extent we agree with the courts below that the petitioner was not entitled to have the past assessment rolls declared a nullity.

This does not mean however that we must indorse the practice or withhold relief insofar as future assessments are concerned. Future compliance with the full value requirement will undoubtedly cause some disruption of existing procedures, but time should cure the problem. The difficulty of transition is sufficient reason to defer relief, but not to deny it. The petitioner thus is entitled to an order directing the township to make future assessments at full value as required by section 306 of the Real Property Tax Law. * * *

JONES, J. (dissenting).

As is stated in the majority opinion, the literally explicit provision of section 306 which it is now sought for the first time in our court to enforce has an ancient lineage. As the majority also recognizes, however, paralleling the long history of statutory address to "full value" has been the equally venerable practice of fractional assessment. With but a few, desultory exceptions, the custom of fractional assessment has been followed without challenge until recently. * * *

From a different point of view we note that notwithstanding what we must assume has been the awareness of fractional assessment practice on the part of individual legislators (on few issues are voter pleas more continuous or persistent than those in search of tax relief!) no legislation has been adopted over the years to require abandonment of the uniform, State-wide practice. * * *

Not only has there been a failure on the part of the Legislature to interfere with fractional assessments; legislation has been enacted which was clearly predicated on the practice of fractional assessments. New York State began establishing equalization rates in 1859. From then until 1912 State equalization rates, set only for whole counties, were used to equalize assessed valuations of the various counties in order to apportion State property taxes among the counties during the period when the State was levying direct taxes on property. In 1912 the State began to establish equalization rates for individual cities, towns and villages. In 1958, in the same chapter in which it enacted present *section 306* of the Real Property Tax Law, the Legislature also adopted article 12 of the Real Property Tax Law which provides for the establishment of State equalization rates. The critical significance of this continuing pattern of legislative activity, of course, is that it was all premised on the assumption that there was an existing practice of fractional assessments and the implicit expectation that the practice would continue. Had the Legislature intended to insist on State-wide full value assessment there would, of course, have been no occasion for equalization machinery or procedures.

It must be evident that the local boards of assessors, the agencies of government charged with responsibility for implementation of the statutory scheme for assessment of real property, construe the statutory provisions to authorize fractional assessments. In other contexts we have repeatedly held that if not irrational or unreasonable the construction given a statute by the agency charged with responsibility for its administration should be upheld * * *.

* * * [I]n the light of the history of both enactment and failure to enact on the part of our State Legislature, of the construction uniformly placed on the statutory assessment procedures by those charged with

direct responsibility thereunder, and of what I can only characterize as the general acceptance by taxpayers and municipal authorities alike of fractional assessments, I conclude that it ill becomes the judiciary, in what I conceive to be an exaggerated emphasis on the literal but long-ignored terminology of the statute, to overturn a practice of such venerable and broadly accepted status.

BELAS V. KIGA

Supreme Court of Washington
959 P.2d 1037 (1998)

GUY, J.

This is an original action brought by 10 elected county assessors challenging the constitutionality of a portion of a 1997 referendum which changed the method of assessing real property for the purpose of levying property taxes. The county assessors argue the new scheme violates the uniformity requirement of the Washington Constitution and unfairly shifts the tax burden from owners of rapidly appreciating property to owners of property which is staying more stable in value or which is depreciating in value. We agree with the assessors that the challenged provisions violate article VII of our state constitution. The apparent intent of value averaging was to accommodate taxpayers experiencing large increases in real property market values. To accomplish this, however, value averaging shifts the tax obligation to other taxpayers not experiencing large value increases. While the goal of alleviating rapid increases in taxes is laudable, the method used is unfair and unconstitutional.

* * *

"Value averaging" is a value limitation mechanism which is designed to limit large increases in real property assessments for individual parcels of property. Real property assessed values will be recalculated each year and annual increases will be limited to the lesser of market value or a calculated limited value. The calculated limited value imposes an increase limit of either 15 percent over the prior year's assessed value or 25 percent of the market change of value if the change exceeds 60 percent, whichever is greater. * * *

The effect of this limit is that: (1) for property with a market increase of less than 15 percent, the assessed value of a parcel will be its full market value; (2) for property with a market increase of between 15 percent and 60 percent, the assessed value will increase only by 15 percent from the previous year's assessed value; and (3) for properties with a market increase of greater than 60 percent, the assessed value will increase only by 25 percent of the actual market increase. For example,* * * if a $100,000 property increased in value by 10 percent, the new *appraised* value would be \$110,000 and the new *assessed* value (upon which the tax rate would be applied to determine tax liability) would also be \$110,000. If a \$100,000 property increased in value by 50 percent, the new appraised value would be \$150,000 but the new assessed value (upon which the tax rate would be applied) would only be \$115,000. If a \$100,000 property increased by 80 percent, the new appraised value would be \$180,000, but the new assessed value (upon which the tax rate would be applied) would be \$120,000.

* * * Article VII of the state Constitution deals with revenue and taxation. The limitations on the assessment of property are contained in Const. art VII, secs. 1 and 2. Article VII, sec. 1 provides in relevant part:

> All taxes shall be uniform upon the same class of property within the territorial limits of the authority levying the tax. . . . The word "property" as used herein shall mean and include everything, whether tangible or intangible, subject to ownership. All real estate shall constitute one class: Provided, That the legislature may tax mines and mineral resources and lands devoted to reforestation by either a yield tax or an ad valorem tax. . . . Such property as the legislature may by general laws provide shall be exempt from taxation.

Const. art. VII, sec. 2 provides in relevant part:

> Except as hereinafter provided and notwithstanding any other provision of this Constitution, the aggregate of all tax levies upon real and personal property by the state and all taxing districts now existing or hereafter created, shall not in any year exceed one per centum of the true and fair value of such property in money[.]

* * * The principle underlying the property tax system is that it is an ad valorem tax, meaning the tax is based on property value. * * * Where taxes are levied on a valuation (or ad valorem) basis, an assessment is indispensable. It is the first step in taxation and the foundation of what follows. * * * Under Const. art. VII, sec. 2 (amend. 55) there is no requirement that property be assessed at 100 percent of true and fair value. The validity of a particular tax levy is measured by whether aggregate levies exceed one percent of true and fair value and whether the taxpayer is being treated in accord with the uniformity requirement of Const. art. VII, sec. 1 (amend. 14). Taxpayers must be treated uniformly with other taxpayers in their class. * * *

Tax uniformity requires both an equal tax rate and equality in valuing the property taxed. * * * An "assessment ratio" is the fractional relationship an assessed value bears to the market value of the property in question. * * * Referendum 47 intentionally creates a different assessment ratio for property which is appreciating at a rate in excess of

15 percent than it does for property which is not appreciating as rapidly. This difference in assessment ratio causes a lack of uniformity in the tax burden.

The Assessors correctly contend that under article VII, sec. 1, unless specifically exempted from taxation, all real estate constitutes one class which must be taxed uniformly. Delaying the full valuation assessment for property experiencing large value increases gives advantage to some taxpayers and penalizes others within the same class. Prior to Referendum 47, all owners of nonexempt real property shared the burden of taxation equally by paying a uniform rate per dollar of value. As a result of the new law, certain property owners will pay a lower amount of tax per dollar of actual value than others in their class, even if the properties are identical in all physical respects and the owners are identical in terms of income and personal characteristics. Those who will pay less are taxpayers who have experienced a value increase greater than 15 percent within a year.

The Assessors point out that value averaging does not change taxing district budgets; the total amount of the tax levy that must be collected remains the same. To compensate for the reduced collections from the rapidly appreciating properties, value averaging shifts the distribution of tax collection to taxpayers owning properties with smaller value increases, no value increases, or even value decreases. Therefore, the Assessors conclude that taxpayers experiencing sluggish or no property value growth, or even declining values, will be penalized by a disproportionate tax burden. We agree.

The result of value averaging will be that overall levy rates would have to increase to avoid the revenue loss which would be caused by the nonrecognition of the increase in market value of those properties which are rapidly appreciating. The effects in a number of counties would be that the owners of more modest property would experience increases in their taxes to offset the decreases of those owners who would benefit by the application of value averaging. Several examples contained in the Agreed Facts illustrate this effect:

• In Jefferson County, the properties experiencing the largest increases in value have been waterfront and water view property along the Hood Canal and the Quimper Peninsula, some doubling in value in four years. Other communities have experienced only slight property value increase, if any. These are the mostly timber-dependent communities that have experienced an economic downturn or lower income retirement areas. Under Referendum 47, such communities will be taxed at higher levy rates due to a lower overall tax base for county-wide taxing districts and the state levy. * * *

• In Lewis County, the Assessor projects that Referendum 47's value averaging would have a serious impact on 70 percent of the parcels which are not experiencing an increase that would have limited their assessed value. The Assessor has explained that these are the properties which are typically owned by lower income families and senior citizens with limited incomes and resources. The other 30 percent of real property parcels will have their assessed values limited by value averaging; these are generally the higher priced properties. In Lewis County, the owners of the more desirable homes will pay less tax. Levy rates will increase for all owners in each levy area and some owners will be taxed on a lower assessed value (a portion of market value) than others. * * *

The International Association of Assessing Officers has produced a "Standard on Property Tax Policy," which includes the following standard on valuation increase limits:

> Limits that constrain changes in assessed or appraised value of property may appear to provide control, but actually distort the distribution of the property tax, destroying property tax equity and increasing public confusion and administrative complexity. Owners whose properties are increasing in value more rapidly than the permitted rate of increase . . . receive a windfall at the expense of those whose properties are decreasing in value or are increasing at lower rates. In effect, valuation increase limits result in lower effective property tax rates for owners of desirable property and higher effective property tax rates for owners of undesirable property. Legislators and the public should be made aware of these inequities and be actively discouraged from pursuing such limitations. * * *

We conclude the Assessors have shown beyond a reasonable doubt that the value averaging formula created by Referendum 47 violates the uniformity clause of article VII, sec. 1 of our state Constitution.

The Department of Revenue * * * argues that value averaging is valid under the constitutional power to grant tax "exemptions," and that the Legislature has broad authorization to exempt property or "property value" from taxation. * * *

In Washington, there are many exemptions from property taxes. While article VII, sec. 1 requires taxes on real property to be uniform, there are exceptions to this in the state Constitution. Article VII, sec. 1 exempts public property, including federal, state, county and municipal, from real estate taxes. Article VII, sec. 10 (amend. 47) provides that notwithstanding the provisions of article VII, secs. 1 and 2, the Legislature shall have the power to grant to retired property owners relief from the property tax on real property occupied as a residence and the Legislature may limit such relief to those owners below a specific level of income. Article VII, sec. 11 (amend. 53) permits special valuation of farms, agricultural lands, timberlands, and certain other open space lands.

The statutory exemptions, most of which are codified in RCW 84.36, include such property as: churches and parsonages; certain nonprofit organizations for veterans, blood banks, public meetings, daycare, homes for the sick, libraries, hospitals, care for the aging, housing for the homeless, training of medical staff, rebroadcasting of signals by government agencies; schools; art, scientific or historical exhibits; humane societies; distribution of water; conservation of ecological systems or open space; and sheltered workshops for the handicapped. * * * By statute (and by specific constitutional grant of authority to the Legislature), disabled or retired persons with low income have some exemptions from taxation for their residences, and timberlands may be taxed on use rather than on an ad valorem basis. Qualifying multi-unit housing in urban centers with insufficient housing can obtain a 10-year exemption for the value of construction, conversion or rehabilitation. Historical properties may obtain an exemption for 10 years for the cost of rehabilitation. * * *

These exemptions fall in basically three classes: where the exemption is defined by some characteristic of the property owner (i.e., low-income, retired or disabled); use of the property creates the exemption (i.e., homes for the sick, aging or homeless); or the use to which the property is put meets some public need or encourages a publicly-desired use (i.e., historical landmark or timber preservation). * * *

While the Legislature, or the people in their legislative role, may exempt property from taxation, the question before us is whether an exemption was created in Referendum 47. This Court has long held that exemptions from taxation must be clear. * * *

It is widely recognized that tax exemptions create inequities in the distribution of the tax burden, even where the exempted property is being used for some function which it would be the duty of the state to perform if it were not performed by private individuals or organizations. This is so because rarely are the benefits of an exempted property conferred only upon those who must bear the increased tax burden. * * * Not only does the granting of exemptions result in an unequal distribution of the tax burden, but it also reduces the amount of revenue available to the governing body through reduction of the tax base.

* * * Nothing in Referendum 47 or in the 1997 Voters Pamphlet labels or describes this method of assessing value as an exemption from taxation. * * *

We conclude value averaging was not explained to the voters as an exemption from taxation. Exemptions may not be created by implication.

We conclude value averaging is an assessment formula and not a tax exemption.

Since the value averaging formula was not enacted as an exemption from taxation, if the formula results in nonuniform taxes within the class of real estate, it will violate article VII.

* * * [T]he Department of Revenue argues that this Court has not required strict uniformity in the taxation of real estate. The Department relies on cases that hold that cyclical assessment is constitutionally acceptable. * * * [S]ome counties revalue individual parcels of real property in cycles rather than yearly. In *Carkonen v. Williams*, 458 P.2d 280 (1969), we held that cyclical revaluation of property is compatible with the constitutional uniformity provision, "provided [such programs] be carried out systematically and without intentional discrimination." We recognized that the assessors' staffing levels were completely inadequate to permit annual inspection and revaluation of all parcels of real property in the county. We concluded that the sheer physical problem of annually inspecting property, coupled with the staff and budgetary allocations, allows the cyclical approach. * * *

Value averaging pursuant to Referendum 47 is essentially different than systematic cyclical reappraisal of property. In a four-year cycle county, each and every parcel of property must be reappraised every fourth year and then every parcel enjoys three years of being frozen at that appraised value. All property is treated the same and enjoys the same advantages. However, in the value averaging formula, only a subclass of property enjoys a nonrecognition of value and this advantage can continue indefinitely if the property continues to appreciate. Value averaging does not defer tax in one year and recoup it later or allow it to be spread over several years; rather, it shifts tax to other property owners. Because each year's tax liability is a separate debt, the tax preference granted to rapidly appreciating property is shifted to other owners in that given year. This tax shift is not remedied in future years and the favored property never pays back the nonrecognized taxes that were not billed.

* * *

The effect of value averaging is that owners of property with rapidly increasing value need not pay taxes at the same assessment ratio as owners with less rapidly appreciating property. Owners of less rapidly appreciating property would have to pay taxes on 100 percent of the fair market value of their property, while the owners of rapidly appreciating property would pay taxes on a lesser percentage of their property's value. Since in any given tax year the total tax burden stays the same, taxes are effectively shifted to owners of property with less rapidly increasing or with depreciating values. This violates the uniformity requirement of

Const. art. VII, sec. 1 (amend. 14). * * * The value averaging formula intentionally applies different assessment ratios to different parcels of real property. Since proportionate taxation cannot exist without uniformity of assessment, the value averaging scheme violates the constitutional uniformity requirement.

NOTES AND QUESTIONS

1. *Full Value and Fractional Assessment.* As the New York Court of Appeals noted in the *Hellerstein* case, the states traditionally required that property be assessed at "full value." In most states, the principle was enshrined in the state constitution; in New York, the full value requirement was in a statute, albeit one that dated back to the eighteenth century. The full value principle had two purposes. First, it capped assessments. Property could not be assessed at more than its full value. Second, it attempted to assure equal treatment among property taxpayers. If all property was assessed at full value, then each taxpayer would be assessed at the same percentage of value—100%. No taxpayer would be assessed at a higher—or lower—percentage of value than any other taxpayer.

As *Hellerstein* also points out, although full value was the general principle of assessment, it was frequently ignored in practice. In most local jurisdictions, de facto fractional assessment was the rule. That is, most property was assessed at a fraction of its full value. That fraction, however, was usually determined not by local legislation or even by administrative regulation, which would have made the fraction uniform for all property within the jurisdiction. Instead, the fraction was, typically, a decision made by assessors, often on a parcel-by-parcel basis.

Hellerstein indicates why de facto fractional assessment might be appealing to local officials. The system makes it difficult for taxpayers to challenge their assessments. Initially, as the court noted, there might be no legal basis for challenging an assessment, even for a taxpayer overassessed relative to her neighbors, since her assessment was still below full value and any reassessment would put her further below the formal legal standard. Eventually, assessment below full value became grounds for legal complaint if a taxpayer was assessed at a higher fraction of value than other taxpayers in the community. But in a system of de facto fractional assessment, overassessment is difficult for a taxpayer to detect and prove. The taxpayer has to determine not only her assessment and the assessments of other property owners in the jurisdiction, but also the real market values of those properties.

De facto fractional assessment also provides a means for quietly raising taxes without formal local legislative action. The tax paid by any individual taxpayer is calculated by multiplying the property's assessed valuation by the local tax rate. Thus, local governments could increase tax revenues without adopting a formal increase in the tax rate by administrative manipulation of the informal assessment rate.

With state aid to local governments often inversely proportional to local property wealth, fractional assessment also became a means of holding down the measure of local property wealth and, thus, increasing state aid. As *Hellerstein* explains, New York sought to cope with this ploy by calculating the different average percentages of value property was assessed at in different counties and municipalities and then "equalizing" those interlocal differences in order to determine a consistent measure of local property wealth. The *Hellerstein* majority rejected the argument that New York's practice of "equalizing" local fractional assessments constituted tacit legislative ratification of such local fractional assessments.

A factor not mentioned by the court is that de facto fractional assessment provided a means of reducing the property tax burden on homeowners relative to other property owners, particularly businesses. Full value assessment, combined with a uniformity provision like the one in *Belas,* means that all owners of property of a certain value will pay the same tax. For businesses, however, the property tax may be treated as part of the cost of doing business and may be factored into their charges to consumers. Homeowners lack that opportunity, and, consequently, may find the same tax rate to be more burdensome. In many localities, homeowners are the dominant voting bloc. De facto fractional assessment, with homeowners typically assessed at a much lower fraction of value than businesses, provides a covert way of holding down the tax burdens of homeowners relative to business owners. It became the norm in many local jurisdictions.

There may be a policy justification, as well as a political explanation, for this preference for homeowners, but de facto fractional assessment also often led to discrimination within the class of homeowners. Long-term residents and residents of more established neighborhoods often enjoyed lower assessment ratios than newcomers and residents of newer neighborhoods. Lower fractional assessments could be used to reward political supporters of local incumbents, and they could be used to discriminate against ethnic and racial minorities. *Cf.* Coleman v. Seldin, 687 N.Y.S.2d 240 (N.Y.Sup.Ct.1999) (claim of disparate racial impact in local assessment practice).

2. *Uniformity and Classification. Belas* illustrates the common state constitutional requirement of uniformity. The uniformity standard applies both to the rate of taxation and to the rate of assessment. In some states, uniformity has replaced full value as the rule of assessment. The equal protection aspect of full value can be captured as well by a requirement that all property be assessed at the same percentage of value, even if less than 100%, as by full value itself.

In many states, uniformity is accompanied by classification, that is, variation in the rate of assessment and/or the rate of taxation according to the "classification" of the property. The most common classifications of property are based on use. Thus, property may be classified as "business"— with some jurisdictions separately treating commercial, industrial, and public utility uses—"agricultural," and "residential," with some jurisdictions distinguishing further among owner-occupied single-family homes; multi-family rental apartment buildings; and condominiums. *See, e.g.,* Krupp Place 1 Co-op, Inc. v. Board of Review of Jasper Co., 801 N.W.2d 9 (Iowa 2011) (two multi-unit apartment buildings to be treated as residential cooperatives subject to residential, not commercial, assessment rate); Hartford/Windsor Healthcare Properties, LLC v. City of Hartford, 3 A.3d 56 (Conn. 2010) (nursing homes commercial, not residential, property for assessment purposes); Board of Supervisors of Harrison Cty. v. Duplantier, 583 So.2d 1275 (Miss.1991) (upholding classification of second-home condominiums as not residential); Castlewood, Inc. v. Anderson County, 969 S.W.2d 908 (Tenn.1998) (upholding classification of residential condominium units as commercial). Homeowner property is nearly always assessed at the lowest percentage of value, and business property at the highest. These classifications and assessment ratios for each class may be spelled out in the state constitution, or the constitution may simply authorize the legislature to classify property for purposes of assessment.

Uniformity plus classification is intended to produce consistent treatment within a class, while permitting differences among classes. Thus, it formalizes and rationalizes the tradition of de facto fractional assessments. Indeed, many states adopted classification systems in response to court orders requiring compliance with long-dormant full value requirements. Classification makes transparent the actual assessment ratios and can eliminate the hidden intra-class inequities that marked de facto fractional assessment. However, it also moves the property tax away from the concept of a pure revenue-raising mechanism, with tax liability based simply on property value, to a system that incorporates policy goals, such as the protection of homeowners or farmers.

Belas' description of value-averaging and tax exemptions as shifting the burden of taxation from one group of property owners to another could also be applied to classification accompanied by differential assessment. Is this necessarily unfair, or could it be an appropriate use of the assessment system to advance policy goals? Does the danger that classification can be manipulated to advantage certain interests outweigh the potential policy benefits?

If the state constitution simply authorizes the legislature to classify property, should a court impose limits on that legislative discretion? In *Belas*, the Washington Constitution simply stated that "[a]ll taxes shall be uniform upon the same class of property." 959 P.2d at 1041. Could the Department of Revenue have argued that Referendum 47's value averaging provision simply constituted a classification according to the rate of change in property value, with property characterized by stable values in one class, and property marked by rapidly appreciating value in a different class? Would cushioning the blow of rapid property appreciation be a sound basis for property classification?

3.   *Fair Market Value and True Tax Value.* Typically, "value" for tax purposes means fair market value, or the price the property would command in an arm's-length open-market transaction. Calculating that value may be difficult. For property that has not been the subject of a transaction recently, fair market value is necessarily uncertain, although recent sales of similar property may provide a benchmark. Where similar sales are lacking, the process of property valuation becomes more difficult, but other techniques of assessment can be used.

As the Montana Supreme Court has explained, state and local governments utilize three general techniques for valuing property:

(1) the cost approach, (2) the market data approach, and (3) the income approach.

The cost approach involves estimating the depreciated cost of reproducing or replacing the building and site improvements. . . . To this depreciated cost is added the estimated value of the land. The widest application of the cost approach is in the appraisal of properties where the lack of adequate market and income data preclude the reasonable application of other traditional approaches.

The market data approach involves the compilation of sales and offerings of properties which are comparable to the property being appraised. The sales and offerings are then adjusted for any dissimilarities and a value range obtained by comparison of those properties. . . . Its application is contingent upon the availability of comparable sales, and therefore finds its widest range in the appraisal of vacant land and residential properties.

The income approach measures the present worth of the future benefits of the property by the capitalization of the net income stream over the remaining economic life of the property. This approach involves making an estimate of the "effective gross income" of a property, derived by deducting the appropriate vacancy and collection losses from its estimated economic rent, as evidenced by the yield of comparable properties. From this figure, applicable operating expenses, including insurance and reserve allowances for replacements, are deducted, resulting in an estimate of net income which may then be capitalized into an indication of value.

Albright v. State of Montana, 933 P.2d 815, 817–18 (Mont.1997).

As *Albright* indicates, the market, or comparable sales, approach is the primary means of valuing residential property. The replacement cost and income capitalization methods are used in valuing commercial, industrial, and other business properties that change hands infrequently and, thus, produce few comparable sales but generate income. *See, e.g.,* Nestle USA, Inc. v. Wisconsin Dep't of Revenue, 795 N.W.2d 46 (Wisc. 2011) (sustaining use of replacement cost method to assess value of infant formula production facility when no sales data was available); Board of Managers of French Oaks

Condominium v. Town of Amherst, 23 N.Y.3d 168 (N.Y. 2014) (applying income capitalization assessment to income-producing property); Canyon Villas Apartments Corp. v. State, 192 P.3d 746 (Nev. 2008). The income approach requires determination of the net income stream generated by the property, which is then discounted (or capitalized) at an appropriate rate to determine the value of the property. The selection of the discount rate, in effect, determines the rate of return on the property, and is, thus, critical to the determination of its value.

4. *Use Value.* In State Board of Tax Commissioners v. Town of St. John, 702 N.E.2d 1034 (Ind. 1998), the Indiana Supreme Court found that the state constitution's requirement of a "just valuation for taxation for all property" "does not require an assessment to be based upon the highest and best use of the property" but, instead, could be based on actual use of land and improvements. This represents a departure from market value assessment since the market value of a property ordinarily reflects not just its current use, but also potential future uses. Many states permit at least some categories of property to be assessed according to "use value." The most common application of use value assessment is for agricultural property. Agricultural property on the outskirts of a metropolitan area may have the potential for conversion to industrial or residential uses within the near future. These potential uses can drive up property values—and property taxes—even while the property is still being used for less lucrative agricultural purposes. To prevent the increased tax burden attributable to potential future nonagricultural uses from accelerating the conversion of agricultural land to nonagricultural purposes, states may provide that agricultural property—and often forest property and open space—shall be assessed at its current use value. In several states, in order for the landowner to benefit from this provision, she must commit to keeping the property in agricultural use for a minimum period of time, such as ten years. If the property is converted to nonagricultural use before that time has expired, the owner may be required to pay additional taxes for the period the use value assessment was employed plus a penalty. *See, e.g.,* Nunes v. Marino, 707 A.2d 1239 (R.I.1998) (sustaining application of land use change tax to farmland withdrawn from state's Farm, Forest, and Open Space Program after just three years); Opinion of the Justices, 627 A.2d 92 (N.H.1993) (finding constitutional proposed legislation that would impose both a penalty and a land use change tax on property withdrawn from current use open space assessment program in less than ten years). The question of whether property assessed on an agricultural current use base is actually being used for agricultural purposes is often controversial.

5. *Market Value, Equity, and Stability in Assessments.* As *Belas* indicates, there can be some tension between assessing according to fair market value and providing for stability in assessments. The same question dogged New York's efforts to comply with the *Hellerstein* ruling. The state legislature struggled with the matter for six years; in 1981, it repealed the full value statute, and adopted legislation authorizing classification and

permitting local taxing jurisdictions to hold constant the share of the local tax burden borne by each of the classes. Recognizing the particularly complex assessment structure that had emerged in suburban Nassau County, the legislature specifically provided that although the County should promote greater equality of assessment within specific classes of property (such as one- and two-family homes, apartments, and commercial property) no property could have its assessments increased by more than six percent in one year or twenty percent over five years. This led to a civil rights lawsuit fifteen years later, on the theory that "because market values for houses in affluent areas had increased sharply while market values had remained stagnant or declined in low-income areas, poor and minority homeowners were shouldering a disproportionate and discriminatory share of the countywide property tax burden." O'Shea v. Board of Assessors of Nassau County, 8 N.Y.3d 249, 256 (N.Y. 2007). The county ultimately settled the suit by agreeing to a comprehensive reassessment of over 400,000 parcels over a three-year period, at a cost of $35 million. While the overall assessment for residential properties declined, the assessments for some properties rose substantially. The New York Court of Appeals upheld the reassessment, finding that the County could "bring assessed values in line with market values . . . in order to reduce accumulated and significant tax disparities between poorer and more affluent residential areas, without changing the tax burden of the residential class as a whole." *See id.* at 261.

6.   *The Judicial Role in Property Assessment.* A central strand running through these cases concerns the role of the courts in reviewing the rules governing property assessment. The *Hellerstein* majority and the Washington Supreme Court in *Belas* emphasized the importance of principle and compliance with constitutional or statutory norms over political decision-making. Was the *Hellerstein* court correct to ignore what appeared to be decades, if not centuries, of state legislative acquiescence in fractional assessment? Was *Belas* right in rejecting what appears to be a rational means of dealing with a central problem of the property tax—rapid appreciation of land values without necessarily an accompanying appreciation in incomes? The Washington court was certainly correct in finding that value averaging necessarily increased the burden on other taxpayers. But should the principle of equality necessarily trump concerns about predictability and stability of tax obligations? Should the relative weighting of the two interests be left to the political process? As we will see shortly, the burden of rapidly appreciating property values was central to the tax revolt of the late 1970s and early 1980s that, in turn, left a permanent mark on the property tax systems of many states.

7.   *Value Averaging and Declining Property Values.* Note that the tension between equality and stability of tax obligations may also be relevant in a market where property values are falling. Localities may want to limit the impact of rapidly declining property values on their assessment rolls in order to protect the stability of local revenues and expenditures. A sharply divided Montana Supreme Court held that state's assessment law requiring

that property value changes be phased in at no more than 2% a year was unconstitutional when applied to a landowner whose property value had dropped sharply from one year to the next, so that the state law limiting the reduction in his appraised value meant that he was being assessed at 124% of his market value. *See* Roosevelt v. Montana Dep't of Revenue, 975 P.2d 295 (Mont.1999). However, the same court subsequently concluded that the state could adhere to its statutory provision of assessing property just once every six years, notwithstanding a landowner's claim that his property's value had dropped since the last assessment and thus was overassessed relative to comparable, more recently assessed properties. Covenant Investments, Inc. v. State Dep't of Revenue, 308 P.3d 54 (Mont. 2013).

NORDLINGER V. HAHN
Supreme Court of the United States
505 U.S. 1 (1992)

BLACKMUN, J.

In 1978, California voters staged what has been described as a property tax revolt by approving a statewide ballot initiative known as Proposition 13. * * *

Proposition 13 followed many years of rapidly rising real property taxes in California. From fiscal years 1967–1968 to 1971–1972, revenues from these taxes increased on an average of 11.5 percent per year. *See* Report of the Senate Commission on Property Tax Equity and Revenue to the California State Senate 23 (1991). In response, the California Legislature enacted several property tax relief measures, including a cap on tax rates in 1972. *Id.*, at 23–24. The boom in the State's real estate market persevered, however, and the median price of an existing home doubled from $31,530 in 1973 to $62,430 in 1977. As a result, tax levies continued to rise because of sharply increasing assessment values. *Id.*, at 23. Some homeowners saw their tax bills double or triple during this period, well outpacing any growth in their income and ability to pay. *Id.*, at 25. *See also* Oakland, Proposition 13—Genesis and Consequences, 32 Nat. Tax J. 387, 392 (Supp. June 1979).

By 1978, property tax relief had emerged as a major political issue in California. In only one month's time, tax relief advocates collected over 1.2 million signatures to qualify Proposition 13 for the June 1978 ballot. * * * On election day, Proposition 13 received a favorable vote of 64.8 percent and carried 55 of the State's 58 counties. * * * California thus had a novel constitutional amendment that led to a property tax cut of approximately $7 billion in the first year. Senate Commission Report, at 28. A California homeowner with a $50,000 home enjoyed an immediate reduction of about $750 per year in property taxes. *Id.*, at 26.

As enacted by Proposition 13, Article XIIIA of the California Constitution caps real property taxes at 1% of a property's "full cash value." § 1(a). "Full cash value" is defined as the assessed valuation as of the 1975–1976 tax year or, "thereafter, the appraised value of real property when purchased, newly constructed, or a change in ownership has occurred after the 1975 assessment." § 2(a). The assessment "may reflect from year to year the inflationary rate not to exceed 2 percent for any given year." § 2(b).

Article XIIIA also contains several exemptions from this reassessment provision. One exemption authorizes the legislature to allow homeowners over the age of 55 who sell their principal residences to carry their previous base-year assessments with them to replacement residences of equal or lesser value. § 2(a). A second exemption applies to transfers of a principal residence (and up to $1 million of other real property) between parents and children. § 2(h).

In short, Article XIIIA combines a 1% ceiling on the property tax rate with a 2% cap on annual increases in assessed valuations. The assessment limitation, however, is subject to the exception that new construction or a change of ownership triggers a reassessment up to current appraised value. Thus, the assessment provisions of Article XIIIA essentially embody an "acquisition value" system of taxation rather than the more commonplace "current value" taxation. Real property is assessed at values related to the value of the property at the time it is acquired by the taxpayer rather than to the value it has in the current real estate market.

Over time, this acquisition-value system has created dramatic disparities in the taxes paid by persons owning similar pieces of property. Property values in California have inflated far in excess of the allowed 2% cap on increases in assessments for property that is not newly constructed or that has not changed hands. *See* Senate Commission Report, at 31–32. As a result, longer-term property owners pay lower property taxes reflecting historic property values, while newer owners pay higher property taxes reflecting more recent values. For that reason, Proposition 13 has been labeled by some as a "welcome stranger" system—the newcomer to an established community is "welcome" in anticipation that he will contribute a larger percentage of support for local government than his settled neighbor who owns a comparable home. Indeed, in dollar terms, the differences in tax burdens are staggering. By 1989, the 44% of California home owners who have owned their homes since enactment of Proposition 13 in 1978 shouldered only 25% of the more than $4 billion in residential property taxes paid by homeowners statewide. *Id.*, at 33. If property values continue to rise more than the annual 2% inflationary cap, this disparity will continue to grow.

According to her amended complaint, petitioner Stephanie Nordlinger in November 1988 purchased a house in the Baldwin Hills neighborhood of Los Angeles County for $170,000. The prior owners bought the home just two years before for $121,500. Before her purchase, petitioner had lived in a rented apartment in Los Angeles and had not owned any real property in California. * * *

In early 1989, petitioner received a notice from the Los Angeles County Tax Assessor, who is a respondent here, informing her that her home had been reassessed upward to $170,100 on account of its change in ownership. She learned that the reassessment resulted in a property tax increase of $453.60, up 36% to $1,701, for the 1988–1989 fiscal year.

Petitioner later discovered she was paying about five times more in taxes than some of her neighbors who owned comparable homes since 1975 within the same residential development. For example, one block away, a house of identical size on a lot slightly larger than petitioner's was subject to a general tax levy of only $358.20 (based on an assessed valuation of $35,820, which reflected the home's value in 1975 plus the up-to-2% per year inflation factor). According to petitioner, her total property taxes over the first 10 years in her home will approach $19,000, while any neighbor who bought a comparable home in 1975 stands to pay just $4,100. The general tax levied against her modest home is only a few dollars short of that paid by a pre-1976 owner of a $2.1 million Malibu beachfront home.

After exhausting administrative remedies, petitioner brought suit against respondents in Los Angeles County Superior Court. She sought a tax refund and a declaration that her tax was unconstitutional. * * * [The trial court dismissed her complaint and the Court of Appeal affirmed the dismissal.] It noted that the Supreme Court of California already had rejected a constitutional challenge to the disparities in taxation resulting from Article XIIIA. *See Amador Valley Joint Union High School Dist. v. State Bd. of Equalization*, 22 Cal. 3d 208, 583 P.2d 1281, 149 Cal. Rptr. 239 (1978). Characterizing Article XIIIA as an "acquisition value" system, the Court of Appeal found it survived equal protection review, because it was supported by at least two rational bases: first, it prevented property taxes from reflecting unduly inflated and unforeseen current values, and, second, it allowed property owners to estimate future liability with substantial certainty.

The Court of Appeal also concluded that this Court's more recent decision in *Allegheny Pittsburgh Coal Co. v. Webster County*, 488 U.S. 336 (1989), did not warrant a different result. At issue in Allegheny Pittsburgh was the practice of a West Virginia county tax assessor of assessing recently purchased property on the basis of its purchase price, while making only minor modifications in the assessments of property that had not recently been sold. Properties that had been sold recently were reassessed and taxed at values between 8 and 35 times that of properties that had not been sold. This Court determined that the unequal assessment practice violated the Equal Protection Clause.

The Court of Appeal distinguished Allegheny Pittsburgh on grounds that "California has opted for an assessment method based on each individual owner's *acquisition* cost," while, "in marked contrast, the West Virginia Constitution requires property to be taxed at a uniform rate statewide according to its estimated *current* market value" (emphasis in original). 225 Cal. App. 3d at 1277–1278, 275 Cal. Rptr. at 695. Thus, the Court of Appeal found: "Allegheny does not prohibit the states from adopting an acquisition value assessment method. That decision merely prohibits the arbitrary enforcement of a current value assessment method" (emphasis omitted). *Id.*, at 1265, 275 Cal. Rptr. at 686. * * * The Supreme Court of California denied review. * * *

The Equal Protection Clause of the Fourteenth Amendment, § 1, commands that no State shall "deny to any person within its jurisdiction the equal protection of the laws." Of course, most laws differentiate in some fashion between classes of persons. The Equal Protection Clause does not forbid classifications. It simply keeps governmental decisionmakers from treating differently persons who are in all relevant respects alike.

* * *

The appropriate standard of review is whether the difference in treatment between newer and older owners rationally furthers a legitimate state interest. In general, the Equal Protection Clause is satisfied so long as there is a plausible policy reason for the classification, * * * the legislative facts on which the classification is apparently based rationally may have been considered to be true by the governmental decisionmaker, * * * and the relationship of the classification to its goal is not so attenuated as to render the distinction arbitrary or irrational. * * * This standard is especially deferential in the context of classifications made by complex tax laws. * * *

As between newer and older owners, Article XIIIA does not discriminate with respect to either the tax rate or the annual rate of adjustment in assessments. Newer and older owners alike benefit in both the short and long run from the protections of a 1% tax rate ceiling and no more than a 2% increase in assessment value per year. New owners and old owners are treated differently with respect to one factor only—the basis on which their property is initially assessed. Petitioner's true complaint is that the State has denied her—a new owner—the benefit of the same assessment value that her neighbors—older owners—enjoy.

We have no difficulty in ascertaining at least two rational or reasonable considerations of difference or policy that justify denying petitioner the benefits of her neighbors' lower assessments. First, the State has a legitimate interest in local neighborhood preservation, continuity, and stability. * * * The State therefore legitimately can decide to structure its tax system to discourage rapid turnover in ownership of homes and businesses, for example, in order to inhibit displacement of lower income families by the forces of gentrification or of established, "mom-and-pop" businesses by newer chain operations. By permitting older owners to pay progressively less in taxes than new owners of comparable property, the Article XIIIA assessment scheme rationally furthers this interest.

Second, the State legitimately can conclude that a new owner at the time of acquiring his property does not have the same reliance interest warranting protection against higher taxes as does an existing owner. The State may deny a new owner at the point of purchase the right to "lock in" to the same assessed value as is enjoyed by an existing owner of comparable property, because an existing owner rationally may be thought to have vested expectations in his property or home that are more deserving of protection than the anticipatory expectations of a new owner at the point of purchase. A new owner has full information about the scope of future tax liability before acquiring the property, and if he thinks the future tax burden is too demanding, he can decide not to complete the purchase at all. By contrast, the existing owner, already saddled with his purchase, does not have the option of deciding not to buy his home if taxes become prohibitively high. To meet his tax obligations, he might be forced to sell his home or to divert his income away from the purchase of food, clothing, and other necessities. In short, the State may decide that it is worse to have owned and lost, than never to have owned at all.

* * *

Petitioner argues that Article XIIIA cannot be distinguished from the tax assessment practice found to violate the Equal Protection Clause in *Allegheny Pittsburgh*. Like Article XIIIA, the practice at issue in *Allegheny Pittsburgh* resulted in dramatic disparities in taxation of properties of comparable value. But an obvious and critical factual difference between this case and *Allegheny Pittsburgh* is the absence of any indication in *Allegheny Pittsburgh* that the policies underlying an acquisition-value taxation scheme could conceivably have been the purpose for the Webster County tax assessor's unequal assessment scheme. In the first place, Webster County argued that "its assessment scheme is rationally related to its purpose of assessing properties *at true current value*" (emphasis added).... Moreover, the West Virginia "Constitution and laws provide that all property of the kind held by petitioners shall be taxed at a rate uniform throughout the State according to its estimated market value," and the Court found "no suggestion" that "the State may have adopted a different system in practice from that specified by statute." * * *

By contrast, Article XIIIA was enacted precisely to achieve the benefits of an acquisition-value system. *Allegheny Pittsburgh* is not controlling here.

Finally, petitioner contends that the unfairness of Article XIIIA is made worse by its exemptions from reassessment for two special classes of new owners: persons aged 55 and older, who exchange principal residences, and children who acquire property from their parents. * * * The two exemptions at issue here rationally further legitimate purposes. The people of California reasonably could have concluded that older persons in general should not be discouraged from moving to a residence more suitable to their changing family size or income. Similarly, the people of California reasonably could have concluded that the interests of family and neighborhood continuity and stability are furthered by and warrant an exemption for transfers between parents and children. Petitioner has not demonstrated that no rational bases lie for either of these exemptions.

* * *

Time and again, however, this Court has made clear in the rational-basis context that the "Constitution presumes that, absent some reason to infer antipathy, even improvident decisions will eventually be rectified by the democratic process and that judicial intervention is generally unwarranted no matter how unwisely we may think a political branch has acted" (footnote omitted). *Vance v. Bradley*, 440 U.S. 93, 97 (1979). Certainly, California's grand experiment appears to vest benefits in a broad, powerful, and entrenched segment of society, and, as the Court of Appeal surmised, ordinary democratic processes may be unlikely to prompt its reconsideration or repeal. *See* 225 Cal. App. 3d at 1282, n. 11, 275 Cal. Rptr. at 698, n. 11. Yet many wise and well-intentioned laws suffer from the same malady. Article XIIIA is not palpably arbitrary, and we must decline petitioner's request to upset the will of the people of California.

JUSTICE STEVENS, dissenting.

* * * Simply put, those who invested in California real estate in the 1970's are among the most fortunate capitalists in the world. * * *

Proposition 13 has provided these successful investors with a tremendous windfall and, in doing so, has created severe inequities in California's property tax scheme. These property owners (hereinafter "the Squires") are guaranteed that, so long as they retain their property and do not improve it, their taxes will not increase more than 2% in any given year. As a direct result of this windfall for the Squires, later purchasers must pay far more than their fair share of property taxes. * * *

As a result of Proposition 13, the Squires, who own 44% of the owner-occupied residences, paid only 25% of the total taxes collected from homeowners in 1989. Report of Senate Commission on Property Tax Equity and Revenue to the California State Senate 33 (1991) (Commission Report). These disparities are aggravated by § 2 of Proposition 13, which exempts from reappraisal a property owner's home and up to $1 million of other real property when that property is transferred to a child of the owner. This exemption can be invoked repeatedly and indefinitely, allowing the Proposition 13 windfall to be passed from generation to generation. * * * Such a law establishes a privilege of a medieval character: Two families with equal needs and equal resources are treated differently solely because of their different heritage. * * *

Just three Terms ago, this Court unanimously invalidated Webster County, West Virginia's assessment scheme under rational-basis scrutiny. Webster County employed a de facto Proposition 13 assessment system: The County assessed recently purchased property on the basis of its purchase price but made only occasional adjustments (averaging 3–4% per year) to the assessments of other properties. Just as in this case, "this approach systematically produced dramatic differences in valuation between . . . recently transferred property and otherwise comparable surrounding land." *Allegheny Pittsburgh*, 488 U.S. at 341.

The " 'intentional systematic undervaluation,' " *id.*, at 345, found constitutionally infirm in *Allegheny Pittsburgh* has been codified in California by Proposition 13. That the discrimination in *Allegheny Pittsburgh* was de facto and the discrimination in this case de jure makes little difference. * * * If anything, the inequality created by Proposition 13 is constitutionally more problematic because it is the product of a state-wide policy rather than the result of an individual assessor's mal-administration.

Nor can *Allegheny Pittsburgh* be distinguished because West Virginia law established a market-value assessment regime. Webster County's scheme was constitutionally invalid not because it was a departure from *state law*, but because it involved the relative " 'systematic undervaluation . . . [of] property *in the same class*' " (as that class was defined by state law). *Allegheny Pittsburgh*, 488 U.S. at 345 (emphasis added). Our decisions have established that the Equal Protection Clause is offended as much by the arbitrary delineation of classes of property (as in this case) as by the arbitrary treatment of properties within the same class (as in *Allegheny Pittsburgh*). * * * Thus, if our unanimous holding in

Allegheny Pittsburgh was sound—and I remain convinced that it was—it follows inexorably that Proposition 13, like Webster County's assessment scheme, violates the Equal Protection Clause. Indeed, in my opinion, state-wide discrimination is far more invidious than a local aberration that creates a tax disparity.

The States, of course, have broad power to classify property in their taxing schemes and if the "classification is neither capricious nor arbitrary, and rests upon some reasonable consideration of difference or policy, there is no denial of the equal protection of the law." *Brown-Forman Co. v. Kentucky*, 217 U.S. at 573. * * *

Consistent with this standard, the Court has long upheld tax classes based on the taxpayer's ability to pay, *see, e.g., Fox v. Standard Oil Co. of New Jersey*, 294 U.S. 87, 101 (1935); the nature (tangible or intangible) of the property, *see, e.g., Klein v. Jefferson County Board of Tax Supervisors*, 282 U.S. 19, 23–24 (1930); the use of the property, *see, e.g., Clark v. Kansas City*, 176 U.S. 114 (1900); and the status (corporate or individual) of the property owner, *see, e.g., Lehnhausen v. Lake Shore Auto Parts Co.*, 410 U.S. 356 (1973). Proposition 13 employs none of these familiar classifications. Instead it classifies property based on its nominal purchase price: All property purchased for the same price is taxed the same amount (leaving aside the 2% annual adjustment). That this scheme can be named (an "acquisition value" system) does not render it any less arbitrary or unreasonable. Under Proposition 13, a majestic estate purchased for $150,000 in 1975 (and now worth more than $2 million) is placed in the same tax class as a humble cottage purchased today for $150,000. The only feature those two properties have in common is that somewhere, sometime a sale contract for each was executed that contained the price "$150,000." Particularly in an environment of phenomenal real property appreciation, to classify property based on its purchase price is "palpably arbitrary." *Allied Stores of Ohio, Inc. v. Bowers*, 358 U.S. 522, 530 (1959). * * *

A *legitimate* state interest must encompass the interests of members of the disadvantaged class and the community at large as well as the direct interests of the members of the favored class. * * * In my opinion, Proposition 13 sweeps too broadly and operates too indiscriminately to "rationally further" the State's interest in neighborhood preservation. No doubt there are some early purchasers living on fixed or limited incomes who could not afford to pay higher taxes and still maintain their homes. California has enacted special legislation to respond to their plight. Those concerns cannot provide an adequate justification for Proposition 13. A state-wide, across-the-board tax windfall for all property owners and their descendants is no more a "rational" means for protecting this small subgroup than a blanket tax exemption for all taxpayers named Smith would be a rational means to protect a particular taxpayer named Smith who demonstrated difficulty paying her tax bill.

Even within densely populated Los Angeles County, residential property comprises less than half of the market value of the property tax roll. App. 45. It cannot be said that the legitimate state interest in preserving neighborhood character is "rationally furthered" by tax benefits for owners of commercial, industrial, vacant, and other nonresidential properties. It is just short of absurd to conclude that the legitimate state interest in protecting a relatively small number of economically vulnerable families is "rationally furthered" by a tax windfall for all 9,787,887 property owners in California.

* * *

The second state interest identified by the Court is the "reliance interests" of the earlier purchasers. * * * In this case, those who purchased property before Proposition 13 was enacted received no assurances that assessments would only increase at a limited rate; indeed, to the contrary, many purchased property in the hope that property values (and assessments) would appreciate substantially and quickly. It cannot be said, therefore, that the earlier purchasers of property somehow have a reliance interest in limited tax increases.

Perhaps what the Court means is that post-Proposition 13 purchasers have less reliance interests than pre-Proposition 13 purchasers. The Court reasons that the State may tax earlier and later purchasers differently because

> "an existing owner rationally may be thought to have vested expectations in his property or home that are more deserving of protection than the anticipatory expectations of a new owner at the point of purchase. A new owner has full information about the scope of future tax liability before acquiring the property, and if he thinks the future tax burden is too demanding, he can decide not to complete the purchase at all. By contrast, the existing owner, already saddled with his purchase, does not have the option of deciding not to buy his home if taxes become prohibitively high."

This simply restates the effects of Proposition 13. A pre-Proposition 13 owner has "vested expectations" in reduced taxes *only* because Proposition 13 gave her such expectations; a later purchaser has no such expectations because Proposition 13 does not provide her such expectations. But the same can be said of any arbitrary protection for an existing class of taxpayers. Consider a law that establishes that homes with even street numbers would be taxed at twice the rate of homes with odd street numbers. It is certainly true that the even-numbered homeowners could not decide to "unpurchase" their homes and that those considering buying an even-numbered home would know that it came with an extra tax burden, but certainly that would not justify the arbitrary imposition of disparate tax burdens based on house numbers. So it is in this case. Proposition 13 provides a benefit for earlier purchasers and imposes a burden on later purchasers. To say that the later purchasers know what they are getting into does not answer the critical question: Is it reasonable and constitutional to tax early purchasers less than late purchasers when at the time of taxation their properties are comparable? * * *

In my opinion, it is irrational to treat similarly situated persons differently on the basis of the date they joined the class of property owners. * * * Similarly situated neighbors have an equal right to share in the benefits of local government. It would obviously be unconstitutional to provide one with more or better fire or police protection than the other; it is just as plainly unconstitutional to require one to pay five times as much in property taxes as the other for the same government services. In my opinion, the severe inequalities created by Proposition 13 are arbitrary and unreasonable and do not rationally further a legitimate state interest.

NOTES AND QUESTIONS

1.   *The Federal Equal Protection Clause and State and Local Taxation.* As *Nordlinger* indicates, the Supreme Court has interpreted the federal equal protection clause to give states and local governments considerable discretion in designing their tax systems. As the Court explained in Lehnhausen v. Lake Shore Auto Parts Co., 410 U.S. 356, 359 (1973), "[w]here taxation is concerned and no specific federal right, apart from equal protection, is imperiled, the States have large leeway in making classifications and drawing lines which in their judgment produce reasonable systems of taxation." *See also* Armour v. City of Indianapolis, 132 S.Ct. 2073, 2080 (2012) ("we have repeatedly pointed out that '[l]egislatures have especially broad latitude in creating classifications and distinctions in tax statutes,'" *quoting and citing* Regan v. Taxation with Representation, 461 U.S. 540, 547 (1983); Allied Stores of Ohio v. Bowers, 358 U.S. 522, 527 (1959) ("the Equal Protection Clause of the Fourteenth Amendment . . . imposes no iron rule of equality, prohibiting the flexibility and variety that are appropriate to reasonable schemes of state taxation. The State may impose different specific taxes upon different trades and professions and may vary the rate of excise upon various products."). Thus, in *Lehnhausen,* the Court unanimously upheld an Illinois constitutional provision prohibiting the imposition of an ad valorem personal property tax on individuals but permitting the imposition of such a tax on corporations and other non-individuals. Previously, the Court had expressly found that the Equal Protection Clause permitted the classification and differential taxation of different types of property. *See*

Charleston Federal Savings & Loan Ass'n v. Alderson, 324 U.S. 182 (1945); Nashville, C. & St. L. Ry. v. Browning, 310 U.S. 362, 369 (1940). *See also* Kottel v. State, 60 P.3d 403 (Mont. 2002) (under state equal protection and tax uniformity constitutional provisions, state tax classifications are subject only to rational basis review).

In Allegheny Pittsburgh Coal Co. v. County Com'n of Webster County, 488 U.S. 336 (1989), however, the Court held unconstitutional Webster County's practice of reassessing property only upon a change in ownership. This led to large disparities in assessment of properties within the same assessment class. *Allegheny Pittsburgh* immediately raised questions about the constitutionality of Proposition 13, since Proposition 13 enshrined the practice of reassessment on resale in the California Constitution. *Nordlinger* dispelled the shadow over Proposition 13 raised by *Allegheny Pittsburgh*.

Taken together, *Allegheny Pittsburgh* and *Nordlinger* appear to mean that the gross disparities in property taxation that result when property of similar current fair market value is assessed according to acquisition value are unconstitutional when they result from the unauthorized actions of a local assessor but constitutional when required by state law. Why is de facto acquisition value assessment so much worse than de jure acquisition value assessment? Why is there a greater *federal* constitutional concern about the former than about the latter?

2.   *Acquisition Value Assessment.* As Justice Blackmun explained, Proposition 13 was a response to rapidly escalating property values, particularly home values, in California in the mid-1970s. With the legislature failing to reduce tax rates, property taxes soared much faster than incomes. The tax became, in effect, a tax on unrealized capital gains. Ironically, assessment reform adopted in the late 1960s to assure greater uniformity and consistency in assessment practices led to the more rapid reflection of rising property values in homeowner assessments. *See* Jack Citrin, Proposition 13 and the Transformation of California Government, 1 Cal. J. Pol. & Pol'y 1, 1– 3 (2009). Proposition 13 sought to narrow the widening gap between incomes and property values by introducing acquisition value assessment. Under an acquisition value system, the assessed valuation of a particular parcel reflects not its market value, or even its current use value, but the value of the parcel when it was purchased, which could have been many years—or decades—earlier. A study of Proposition 13 undertaken in the early 1990s found that between 1975 (the baseline year for property assessment under Proposition 13) and 1991, 43% of the homeowner properties in Los Angeles County had not changed hands. These properties were assessed at their 1975 values, plus a two percent per year increase. A home that last changed hands in 1975 was assessed at less than twenty percent of the value of a home with the same market value that had been purchased by its current owner in 1991. *See* Arthur O'Sullivan, Terri A. Sexton, Steven M. Sheffrin, Property Taxes and Tax Revolts: The Legacy of Proposition 13, at 59 (Cambridge U. Press 1995). Is this unfair? Are you persuaded by the Supreme Court's

conclusion that acquisition value assessment can be justified as a means of protecting neighborhood stability and tax burden reliability?

O'Sullivan, et al. found that within the class of homeowners, the principal beneficiaries of Proposition 13 were the elderly and low-income households. Because these groups were less mobile than the younger or more affluent, they were concentrated in homes that were assessed at the earlier base years. *See id.* at 138. As a result, the effect of Proposition 13's discrimination against newcomers and the mobile was, surprisingly, mildly progressive. This complicates the question of whether Proposition 13 is equitable: "With its disparate assessments of identical property, Proposition 13 clearly violates the principle of horizontal equity that equally situated individuals should be treated equally. On the other hand, Proposition 13 fares better under the principle of vertical equity, which dictates progressive taxation." *See id.*

O'Sullivan, et al. also found that by triggering large increases in tax liability when property changes hands, Proposition 13 discourages mobility. But they found the effect to be relatively modest. A different provision of Proposition 13 imposed a 1 percent cap on the property tax rate in California. As a result, the property tax is comparatively small relative to the cost of the acquisition of a home. *See id.*

On the other hand, although Proposition 13 was driven by the anxieties of homeowners, much of the benefit accrued to businesses since the measure applied the acquisition value standard to all property, business as well as residential. According to O'Sullivan, et al., the acquisition value assessment burdens new businesses while, in effect, subsidizing older, existing businesses. "Taxing new activity at a higher rate than existing activity is not sound policy and has no policy rationale." *Id.* at 142. Even for residential property, although the elderly and low-income homeowners may benefit as a class because they tend to be less mobile, the benefits of Proposition 13 are not keyed to income. A low-income household that changes its home will have to pay property tax in its new home at its higher current value; a wealthy household that remains in the home that it has owned since 1975 pays at the low acquisition value rate. And for two households that both acquired their homes in 1975, the dollar benefit of Proposition 13 is directly tied to the dollar value of the home. Owners of more expensive homes enjoy a greater tax saving than the owners of less expensive homes.

California is not the only state that seeks to limit the effect of rising property values on property tax liability. *See, e.g.,* Mark Haveman & Terri A, Sexton, Property Tax Assessment Limits: Lessons from Thirty Years of Experience 14 (Lincoln Inst. of Land Policy 2008) (examining the experience of eighteen states that imposed limits on increases in individual assessments). These reflect the concern that property value increases can be unrelated to changes in the owner's income. Assessment increase limits are intended to protect long-term homeowners on fixed incomes. However, there is evidence that much of the benefit goes to homeowners with higher incomes who own more valuable properties, often in affluent neighborhoods with rapidly appreciating property values. Although income need not rise with property values, often the two go together. *See, e.g.,* Andrew T. Hayashi, Property Taxes and Their Limits: Evidence from New York City, 25 Stan. L. & Pol'y Rev. 33 (2014).

3. *Other Forms of Property Tax Relief.* Acquisition value assessment is one method of buffering the effect of unrealized property appreciation on tax burdens. Other techniques may be used to provide benefits more narrowly to groups with low or fixed incomes. One common method is the *residential circuit breaker*, which provides property tax relief in the form of a rebate or tax credit in state income taxes when a household's property tax bill exceeds a specified percentage of its income. Typically, the program's availability is limited to households whose income falls below a statutory ceiling. Circuit-breaker "advocates compare it to its electrical namesake—when there is an overload relative to income, the circuit breaker shuts off the property tax system." Steven D. Gold, Property Tax Relief 55 (Lexington Books 1979). About two-thirds of the states with circuit-breaker programs restrict relief to the elderly and/or disabled, but the others make it available to all income-eligible homeowners. Some states also open their circuit-breaker programs to renters, calculating that a percentage of their rent is attributable to the landlord's property tax. Circuit-breakers are more clearly progressive than acquisition value assessment, as the benefits are directly tied to income and to the burden of the property tax relative to income. For local governments, they have the additional appeal of placing the cost of tax relief on the state since the circuit-breaker works through the state income tax. In contrast, acquisition value assessment operates by reducing assessable property value within the locality and, thus, places the cost of tax relief on the local government.

In addition to circuit-breakers, most states have homestead exemptions or credits. Under the exemption, a portion of the value of a home is subtracted from its assessed valuation when the property tax is applied.

4. *Proposition 13 in the California Courts.* Proposition 13 did not simply revamp property tax assessments. It also imposed new limits on state and local taxes generally. Section 3 of the initiative provided that any new increases in state tax rates would require approval by at least two-thirds of the members of the state legislature, and barred any new state ad valorem taxes on real property. Section 4 stipulated that "cities, counties, and special districts" may adopt "special taxes" only with the approval of two-thirds of the local electorate, and completely prohibited any new local ad valorem property taxes or transactions or sales taxes on the sale of real property. Like most state constitutional provisions authorizing the initiative, the California constitution provides that voter-initiated amendments may address only a "single subject," and may amend, but not revise, the state constitution. Cal. Const. Art. II, § 8(d) ("single subject"). Art. XVIII, § 3 (constitutional amendment and revision). In Amador Valley Joint Union High School District v. State Board of Equalization, 583 P.2d 1281 (Cal. 1978), the

California Supreme Court rejected claims that Proposition 13 violated these constitutional provisions, finding that all the elements of Proposition 13 related to tax relief (thus satisfying the single subject rule), and that it was not so broad as to amount to a revision.

The broadly-phrased limits imposed on new local taxes by Section 4 of Proposition 13 have been a continuing source of litigation, compounded by California's complex local government and tax structure. Some of the court decisions limiting the scope of the tax limitations triggered the enactment of new voter-initiated fiscal limits. In Los Angeles Cty. Transp. Comm'n v. Richmond, 643 P.2d 941 (Cal. 1982), the California Supreme Court, citing Proposition 13's predominant concern with property tax relief, held that a "special district" in section 4 meant only a district with the power to levy a property tax. The Court candidly admitted its preference for a narrow interpretation of the ambiguous portions of Proposition 13, describing the two-thirds vote requirement as "fundamentally undemocratic," even if constitutional, because it interfered with local majority rule. *Id.* at 945. Similarly, in City and County of San Francisco v. Farrell, 648 P.2d 935 (Cal.1982), the Court took a narrow approach to "special tax" and held that it applied only to taxes earmarked for special purposes. As a result, the court concluded that San Francisco's new payroll and gross receipts tax, which produced revenues for the city's general fund, was not a "special tax" subject to the two-thirds voter approval requirement.

In 1986, California voters responded by passing Proposition 62, a statutory initiative that provides that all local taxes are either "general" or "special." General taxes could be approved by a simple majority of all local voters, while special taxes require approval by two-thirds of local voters. The Proposition's definition of "district" encompassed all districts, including those without property-taxing power. "The manifest purpose of Proposition 62 as a whole was to increase the control of the citizenry over local taxation by requiring voter approval of all new local taxes imposed by all local governmental entities." Santa Clara Co. Local Transp. Auth. v. Guardino, 902 P.2d 225, 235 (Cal. 1995). In Rider v. County of San Diego, 820 P.2d 1000 (Cal.1991), the California Supreme Court again considered the meanings of special taxes and special districts. The state legislature had created, and authorized counties to create, numerous special agencies with the power to raise revenues to finance or administer certain county facilities. Though these agencies were nominally independent, they were subject to close county oversight. Agency taxes were subject to voter approval, but were arguably general taxes for the general support of the agency, and so could be approved by a simple majority vote. *Rider*, for example, involved the San Diego County Regional Justice Facility Financing Agency, which was authorized to finance the construction and operation of criminal detention and courthouse facilities and, with the approval of a simple majority of local voters, to impose a one-half of one percent sales tax to fund its operations. The Agency was territorially coterminous with the county; two of the Agency's seven directors were members of the county board of supervisors; and the county "retained substantial control over operations and expenditures." *Id.* at 1005. The California Supreme Court determined that the term "special district" in Proposition 13 would henceforth be interpreted to include "any local taxing agency created to raise funds for city or county purposes to replace revenues lost by reason of the restrictions of Proposition 13," *id.* at 1006, and, relying on lower court findings that the creation of the agency was "purposeful circumvention" of Proposition 13, held that the district was a "special district" and its taxes "special taxes" subject to the two-thirds voter approval requirement. *See also* Coleman v. County of Santa Clara, 75 Cal.Rptr.2d 516 (Cal. Ct. App. 1998) (measure approving increase in sales tax for "general county purposes" is a general tax, not a special tax, and thus requires the approval of only a majority of local voters even though at the same election voters passed an "advisory" measure expressing intent that any new sales tax funds be spent on specified transportation improvements); Neecke v. City of Mill Valley, 46 Cal.Rptr.2d 266 (Cal.Ct.App.1995) ("municipal services tax" whose proceeds go into the general fund of the city requires approval of only a simple majority of local voters).

The meaning of "special tax" has been repeatedly tested in cases involving special assessments and local fees. In Knox v. City of Orland, 841 P.2d 144 (Cal. 1992), the California Supreme Court held that a special assessment imposed on real property for the purpose of funding a special benefit to the assessed property is not a special tax within Proposition 13 and so not subject to the two-thirds voter approval requirement. In response to the growing use of special assessments to raise revenue outside the scope of the tax limitations, California voters in 1996 passed Proposition 218, which added new substantive and procedural restrictions on special assessments. *See* Cal. Const. Art. XIIID; Silicon Valley Taxpayers Ass'n, Inc. v. Santa Clara Co. Open Space Auth., 187 P.3d 37 (Cal. 2008). The growing use of user fees and other charges that the courts defined as not "taxes" led to the passage in 2010 of Proposition 26 which amended sections 3 and 4 of Proposition 13 to expand the definition of tax to include many fees and charges. The tax/fee line continues to be contested. *See, e.g.,* Schmeer v. County of Los Angeles, 213 Cal.App.4th 1310 (Cal. App. 2013) (paper bag carryout charge not a "tax" which requires voter approval). The legal issues posed by special assessments and user fees and charges, and the distinction between assessments, fees, and charges on the one hand and taxes on the other, are discussed later in this chapter.

5. *Federal Constitutional Limits on State and Local Taxation.* Although many state constitutions cap local property tax rates and/or property tax assessments, and some states limit total state revenues, there is no comparable federal constitutional limitation on the level of taxation. This point is well-illustrated by the Supreme Court's decision in City of Pittsburgh v. Alco Parking Corp., 417 U.S. 369 (1974), which involved a due process challenge to a twenty-percent city tax on the gross receipts of nonresidential parking garages. The parking garage owners asserted that the tax was

invalid because it was so high as to make their businesses unprofitable. The Supreme Court rejected the argument:

> The claim that a particular tax is so unreasonably high and unduly burdensome as to deny due process is both familiar and recurring, but the Court has consistently refused either to undertake the task of passing on the 'reasonableness' of a tax that otherwise is within the power of Congress or of state legislative authorities, or to hold that a tax is unconstitutional because it renders a business unprofitable.

417 U.S. at 373.

The Pittsburgh parking tax did not apply to parking facilities operated by the public Parking Authority. The plaintiffs argued that even if the 20% rate was not unconstitutionally excessive on its own, the combination of the high rate and the untaxed public competition amounted to an uncompensated taking. The Supreme Court was not persuaded:

> Nor are we convinced that the ordinance loses its character as a tax and may be stricken down as too burdensome under the Due Process Clause if the taxing authority, directly or through an instrumentality enjoying various forms of tax exemption, competes with the taxpayer in a manner thought to be unfair by the judiciary. This approach would demand not only that the judiciary undertake to separate those taxes that are too burdensome from those that are not, but also would require judicial oversight of the terms and circumstances under which the government or its tax-exempt instrumentalities may undertake to compete with the private sector. The clear teaching of prior cases is that this is not a task that the Due Process Clause demands of or permits to the judiciary. We are not now inclined to chart a different course.

Id. at 376.

The Court indicated that judicial deference to the rate of taxation would apply even though the tax had a regulatory as well as a revenue-raising purpose:

> Insofar as this record reveals, for the 20% tax to have a destructive effect on private operators as compared with the situation immediately preceding its enactment, the damage would have to flow chiefly, not from those who preferred the cheaper public parking lots, but from those who could no longer afford an increased price for downtown parking at all. If this is the case, we simply have another instance where the government enacts a tax at a 'discouraging rate as the alternative to giving up a business,' a policy to which there is no constitutional objection.

> The parking tax ordinance recited that '(n)on-residential parking places for motor vehicles, by reason of the frequency rate of their use, the changing intensity of their use at various hours of the day,

their location, their relationship to traffic congestion and other characteristics, present problems requiring municipal services and affect the public interest, differently from parking places accessory to the use and occupancy of residences.' By enacting the tax, the city insisted that those providing and utilizing nonresidential parking facilities should pay more taxes to compensate the city for the problems incident to offstreet parking. The city was constitutionally entitled to put the automobile parker to the choice of using other transportation or paying the increased tax.

Id. at 377–79.

GUINN V. LEGISLATURE OF THE STATE OF NEVADA
Supreme Court of Nevada
71 P.3d 1269 (2003)

AGOSTI, C.J.

The Governor of Nevada has petitioned this court for a writ of mandamus declaring the Legislature to be in violation of the Nevada Constitution, and compelling the Legislature to fulfill its constitutional duty to approve a balanced budget—including an annual tax to defray the state's estimated expenses for the biennium beginning July 1, 2003, and appropriations to fund public education during that fiscal period—by a time certain. We agree that our intervention is appropriate in this extraordinary circumstance.

The Legislature failed to fund education in the 72nd Regular Session and in two special sessions and is evidently in a deadlock over the means of raising the necessary revenues. As a result, Nevada's public educational institutions are in crisis because they are unable to proceed with the preparations and functions necessary for the 2003–2004 school year.

It is apparent that the Legislature has failed to fulfill its constitutional mandate because of the conflict among several provisions of the Nevada Constitution. Therefore, we, in our judicial role as interpreters of the Nevada Constitution, must reconcile the provisions which cause the present crisis.

* * * We order the Legislature to fulfill its obligations under the Constitution of Nevada by raising sufficient revenues to fund education while maintaining a balanced budget. Due to the impasse that has resulted from the procedural and general constitutional requirement of passing revenue measures by a two-thirds majority, we conclude that this procedural requirement must give way to the substantive and specific constitutional mandate to fund public education. Therefore, we grant the petition in part and order the clerk of this court to issue a writ of

mandamus directing the Legislature of the State of Nevada to proceed expeditiously with the 20th Special Session under simple majority rule.

The Governor filed this writ petition after the Legislature failed to approve a balanced budget before the start of fiscal year 2004, which started on July 1, 2003. The Governor is responsible for the faithful execution of the state's laws and is also responsible for proposing a state budget and submitting it to the Legislature. Pursuant to Article 9, Section 2 of our Constitution, the Legislature is responsible for approving a balanced budget. Also, Article 11, Section 6 of our Constitution compels the Legislature to support and maintain the public school system.

The Legislature must appropriate the money needed for all state government expenditures and provide for an annual tax to defray the state's estimated expenses for the two fiscal years following its regular biennial session. Fiscal year 2004 began on July 1, yet the Legislature has thus far failed in its obligation to support and maintain the public school system. No money has been appropriated to fund this constitutionally mandated obligation. Our Constitution's Article 4, Section 19 provides that the State Treasurer cannot release general funds from the state treasury without specific legislative appropriation.

The Governor began the 2003 legislative session with a request for $980 million in new revenues to balance his proposed budget for the 2003–2005 biennium. The Legislature did not fund education in its 72nd Regular Session, which ended on June 3, 2003, but, after making substantial cuts in the Governor's budget, appropriated $3,264,269,361 for various government functions. The Governor signed these appropriations into law. Existing revenues are expected to meet these appropriations.

Since the conclusion of the Legislature's general session, two special sessions have been convened. On June 3, 2003, the Governor convened the Legislature in the 19th Special Session to appropriate funds for the K–12 school system and to provide an adequate tax plan to provide for funding. The Legislature failed to reach an agreement on a tax plan. The Governor adjourned the 19th Special Session at the request of the Senate Majority Leader and the Speaker of the Assembly on June 12, 2003. That same day, the Governor convened the Legislature for a second special session to begin on June 25, 2003. The Legislature convened, but had not passed a bill to raise the required revenues for the educational system by the start of the new fiscal year, July 1, 2003. The Senate and Assembly recessed by mutual consent, because of their inability to pass a revenue measure by a two-thirds majority.

Since its enactment in 1864, the Nevada Constitution has required a simple majority of each house to pass a bill or joint resolution. Article 4, Section 18(1) provides that "a majority of all the members elected to each house is necessary to pass every bill or joint resolution." In 1993, the Legislature rejected a resolution that proposed to amend the Constitution to create an exception to the simple majority rule and require a two-thirds majority of each house to increase existing taxes or impose new taxes. Ultimately, by initiative, the citizens accepted an identical proposal as a constitutional amendment. The constitutionally required second vote on the initiative occurred in 1996, at a time when the state enjoyed a budget surplus and public sentiment strongly favored restricted tax increases. Article 4, Section 18(2) of our Constitution now requires a two-thirds vote of each house "to pass a bill or joint resolution which creates, generates, or increases any public revenue in any form, including but not limited to taxes, fees, assessments and rates, or changes in the computation bases for taxes, fees, assessments and rates."

In 1997, 1999 and 2001, the Legislature was able to work within these new constraints without major difficulties because the state operated under a budget surplus and no major tax increases required a vote in the Legislature. By 2003, however, the state's economic picture had changed drastically. The Legislature, faced with a rapidly increasing population, a substantial budget deficit and record-high needs, was unable to reach a two-thirds majority and left its constitutional obligations unfulfilled.

The Legislature's failure to fulfill its constitutional duties by the beginning of the new fiscal year has precipitated an imminent fiscal emergency. Nevada now faces an unprecedented budget crisis. Schools have not been funded for the upcoming school year. Teachers have not been hired. Educational programs have been eliminated. Planning for the academic year is not possible, and the state's bond rating may be jeopardized. This court has been petitioned to resolve the crisis. In light of the above circumstances, it appears there is no plain, speedy and adequate remedy in the ordinary course of law, and this court's intervention is warranted.

At the heart of this case is the two-thirds supermajority requirement for revenue-raising legislation. The Legislature is unable to fulfill its constitutional duties to fund the public schools and to adopt a balanced budget because it has not met the two-thirds vote requirement. The Legislature's failure to provide funds for public education, to pass the concomitant revenue generating package and to balance the state's budget after having had the opportunities of one general session and two special sessions to do so, leads us to the inevitable conclusion that it is futile to order the Legislature to debate further within the parameters of Article 4, Section 18(2). As constitutional construction is purely a province of the judiciary, we undertake to resolve the tension between the legislature's constitutional obligation to fund public education and the constitutional provisions requiring a simple majority to enact appropriations bills but a two-thirds majority to generate or increase public revenue to fund those appropriations.

Clearly, this court has no authority to levy taxes or make appropriations. Only our Legislature has been given the constitutional mandate to make appropriations, levy taxes, and to balance the state's budget. However, when constitutional provisions are incompatible with one another or are unworkable, or when the enforcement of one prevents the fulfillment of another, this court must exercise its judicial function of interpreting the Constitution and attempt to resolve the problem.

When construing constitutional provisions, we apply the same rules of construction used to interpret statutes. Our task is to ascertain the intent of those who enacted the provisions at issue, and "to adopt an interpretation that best captures their objective. We must give words their plain meaning unless doing so would violate the spirit of the provision." Whenever possible, we construe provisions so that they are in harmony with each other. Specific provisions take precedence over general provisions. Finally, constitutional provisions should be interpreted so as to avoid absurd consequences and not produce public mischief.

Nevada's Constitution clearly expresses the vital role that education plays in our state in Article 11. Of particular importance are Sections 1, 2, and 6. Section 1 mandates:

> The legislature shall encourage by all suitable means the promotion of intellectual, literary, scientific, mining, mechanical, agricultural, and moral improvements, and also provide for a superintendent of public instruction and by law prescribe the manner of appointment, term of office and the duties thereof.

Section 2 mandates:

> The legislature shall provide for a uniform system of common schools, by which a school shall be established and maintained in each school district at least six months in every year . . . and the legislature may pass such laws as will tend to secure a general attendance of the children in each school district upon said public schools.

And Section 6 requires the Legislature to provide for the support and maintenance of the public schools.

Our Constitution's framers strongly believed that each child should have the opportunity to receive a basic education. Their views resulted in a Constitution that places great importance on education. Its provisions demonstrate that education is a basic constitutional right in Nevada.

When a procedural requirement that is general in nature prevents funding for a basic, substantive right, the procedure must yield. Here, the application of the general procedural requirement for a two-thirds majority has prevented the Legislature as a body from performing its obligation to give life to the specific substantive educational rights enunciated in our Constitution. * * * It is paramount that we give Section 18(2) a construction that will preserve the basic right of education. Other states with constitutional provisions similar to ours have also given significant import to the educational clauses of their constitutions.

Our Legislature has failed to accomplish its constitutionally mandated tasks of funding Nevada's public education system and balancing the budget. In order to allow the Legislature to fulfill its constitutional mandate in this regard, the general language of Section 18(2) must give way to the simple majority requirement of Article 4, Section 18(1) in order that the specific provisions concerning education are not defeated.

Based upon the Legislature's failure over the last several weeks to fund the constitutionally mandated arena of education, we observe that its adherence to the Constitution's two-thirds majority provision defeats the Constitution's public education funding requirements. We conclude that an irreconcilable conflict exists with respect to the relevant constitutional provisions. Because the Governor has seen fit to petition this court in mandamus, and because evidently further legislative discussions are futile, it becomes the responsibility of this court to order the Legislature to fund public education and to balance the budget. It is a waste of public resources to simply tell the Legislature to forge on and deliberate and negotiate further, since that body has failed to perform its constitutionally required function. As a result, this court is faced with the onerous task of weighing the various constitutional provisions and, in effect, prioritizing them.

The two-thirds majority requirement is a procedural requirement. It is a process requirement by which legislative action is accomplished and decisions that weigh the public interests are accounted for. In the area of taxation this means that the Legislature must agree by a two-thirds majority as to which mechanisms will be employed to generate revenue. Without a two-thirds majority, revenue measures may not be enacted. This general constitutional provision does not purport to say what the substance of the revenue measures ought to be, only that whatever they be, they are acceptable to two-thirds of the elected members of each house of the Legislature.

In contrast, the Constitution requires specifically, as a matter of substantive constitutional law, that public education be funded. The framers have elevated the public education of the youth of Nevada to a position of constitutional primacy. Public education is a right that the people, and the youth, of Nevada are entitled, through the Constitution, to access. If the procedural two-thirds revenue vote requirement in effect denies the public its expectation of access to public education, then the two-thirds requirement must yield to the specific substantive educational right.

The Legislature must resume its work of funding education and selecting appropriate methods of revenue generation to balance the state's budget. Therefore, we grant the petition as to the Legislature of the State of Nevada and direct this court's clerk to issue a writ of mandamus directing the Legislature to proceed expeditiously with the 20th Special Session under simple majority rule. The relief prayed for in the petition as to the Lieutenant Governor and the individual legislators and in the counter-petition is denied.

GUINN V. LEGISLATURE OF THE STATE OF NEVADA

Supreme Court of Nevada
76 P.3d 22 (2003)

PER CURIAM:

On July 10, 2003, we entered an opinion in this matter partially granting the Governor's petition for a writ of mandamus and denying the counter-petition filed by twenty Legislators. * * * On July 21, 2003, the counter-petitioners filed a rehearing petition, asking us to recall our writ of mandamus, reconsider our opinion, and grant one of the remedies suggested in the counter-petition. Later that same day, the Legislature fulfilled its constitutional duties to fund the public school system and balance the budget, and it adopted the revenue-raising legislation required to balance the budget by a two-thirds supermajority. According to the Legislature,

> The Court's ruling in this case facilitated a shift from the tension that was caused by an externally-imposed requirement to achieve a 2/3 consensus, to a situation where the legislators were internally motivated to achieve a 2/3 consensus voluntarily. This shift in perception allowed reevaluation of fixed positions which led expeditiously to the passage of Senate Bill No. 8. . . .

The counter-petitioners then supplemented their rehearing petition and moved this court to withdraw its opinion. * * *

* * * In 1993, a member of the Legislature sponsored a resolution that proposed amending the Constitution to require a two-thirds majority of each house to increase certain existing taxes or impose new taxes.

At a hearing on the proposed resolution, legislators asked one of the main proponents if the other states with similar provisions required a supermajority to approve the state budget as well as new taxes, or if these states retained a simple majority for budget approval and a supermajority for funding. Legislative members pointed out to the proponent that the proposed amendment did not address the budget, only changes in revenue. Thus the Constitution, if amended, would require a two-thirds majority to change the existing revenue structure, but only a simple majority to approve the budget.

The members noted that once the budget is approved, the Nevada Constitution requires that revenue be increased to balance the budget where the cost of services exceeds projected revenue. Finally, the legislators expressed their concerns that the proposed language would create the potential for a constitutional crisis because a minority of legislators might disagree with the majority's lawfully approved budget and therefore refuse to consider any revenue increases until their budgetary concerns were met, thus creating a deadlock. The amendment, according to one legislator, "was actually empowering a smaller group of people not to fund the budget." The legislators were concerned that the process would allow a minority of the Legislature, representing a minority of this State's citizens, to control public services, contrary to the wishes of a majority of the Legislature, representing a majority of the citizens.

The proponent did not answer the questions posed by other legislators, but indicated that the issues would be researched and additional information would be provided to committee members. The record does not reflect whether additional information was provided, and the Legislature declined to approve the proposal. The proponents then took the proposal directly to Nevada's voters through the initiative process.

Unfortunately, the initiative petition and proposed amendment did not resolve the conflict discussed in the legislative hearings. Although the initiative's proponents were aware of the potential conflict that could result from requiring a simple majority for appropriations and a supermajority for new or increased public revenue, they did not specifically address this problem in the initiative's language. Nor did the arguments for and against passage, presented in the voter information and sample ballot pamphlet, discuss the issue or the effect the proposal could have on other constitutional rights or the state's overall fiscal integrity.

* * *

In construing the Constitution, our primary objective is to discern the intent of those who enacted the provisions at issue, and to fashion an interpretation consistent with that objective. However, when the enactors' intent cannot be determined, rules of constitutional construction require us to attempt to harmonize differing provisions so as to give as much effect as possible to each provision. We look beyond the plain language of constitutional provisions to ascertain intent "when a construction is urged which would result in an absurd situation" or when provisions are subject to conflicting interpretations.

The language of Article 4, Section 18(1) and Article 4, Section 18(2) is clear on its face. But in operation, the two provisions resulted in legislative paralysis in one general and two special sessions. The parties advanced conflicting interpretations of the provisions' requirements. We thus looked to extrinsic evidence surrounding the supermajority provision's enactment to determine its intended effect.

As mentioned earlier, Article 4, Section 18(2) originated as Ballot Question 11 during the 1994 and 1996 general elections. The supermajority requirement was intended to make it more difficult for the Legislature to pass new taxes, hopefully encouraging efficiency and effectiveness in government. Its proponents argued that the tax restriction might also encourage state government to prioritize its spending and economize rather than explore new sources of revenue. But neither the ballot question nor its explanation in the voter pamphlet informed voters of the likelihood of legislative paralysis and its effect on the state's fiscal and educational integrity. Indeed, even the initiative's prime sponsor was unsure of the consequences of reposing within a small group of legislators the power to block majority-approved appropriations. And, in 1993, he represented to the Assembly that the supermajority requirement "would not hamstring state government or prevent state government from responding to legitimate fiscal emergencies."

The voters were not privy to the Assembly's concerns that culminated in the requirement's legislative rejection, and the requirement's proponents failed to address those concerns when presenting the initiative. Because the voters were not informed of the problems the amendment would cause if a minority of legislators disagreed with the majority over the level of services to be provided to Nevada citizens, we could not determine how the voters intended to resolve such a conflict. * * *

When a court is faced with conflicting policies arising out of multiple constitutional provisions in a specific factual situation, it must, if it can, strike a balance between the provisions. * * *

In reconciling the competing provisions of Nevada's constitutional requirements to fund education and balance the budget with the supermajority requirements for changing the tax structure, we believed that the appropriate analysis required weighing the interests protected by each provision, under the specific facts of this case, to determine whether the net benefit that accrued to one of those interests exceeded the net harm done to the other. The essential issue was whether the supermajority requirement could be improperly used by a few to challenge the majority's budget decisions, thereby preventing the Legislature from performing its other constitutional duties.

The primary interest supported by permitting the Legislature to suspend the supermajority requirement in this case was nothing less than the constitutional mandate to fund public education. . * * * Our State Constitution's framers explicitly and extensively addressed education, believing strongly that each child should have the opportunity to receive a basic education.

In addition, we were necessarily concerned with the interest of preserving the democratic process. A majority of legislators, representing a majority of the citizens of this state, make decisions on the services to be provided and the future of the state. These include what programs to provide for children, the disabled and senior citizens; the construction and repair of roads and streets; funding of agencies to protect our citizens from telemarketing schemes or fraudulent transactions; costs associated with law enforcement activities; and staffing and location of state offices to avoid delays or long distance travel to obtain necessary documents such as drivers' licenses, vehicle or corporate registrations. Where these matters have been discussed and duly voted upon, the Constitution requires that the decision of the majority be respected.

Against public education, the democratic process and fiscal interests, we balanced the interests fostered by the supermajority requirement. The two-thirds requirement was intended, according to the information supplied to the voters in the 1994 and 1996 elections, to limit the influence of special interest groups, ensuring that one group would not control changes in the tax structure. The voter pamphlet also indicated that the amendment might promote more efficiency in government. These interests are legitimate and important, but they do not outweigh the need to fund education or abide by the majority rule mandated by Article 4, Section 18(1). To avoid an impasse harmful to public education, we determined that the supermajority provision could not be improperly used to avoid majority rule on budget appropriations. Accordingly, we held that the Legislature could suspend the supermajority rule in favor of a vote by a legislative majority, in this very narrow circumstance, in order to fulfill its obligations to fund education and balance the budget.

Resolution of the impasse was entirely in the hands of the Legislature. If the minority abided by the Constitution and recognized that majority rule controlled budget appropriations issues and thus the need to generate an amount of revenue, the impasse would end and the only issue remaining, what changes to make in the revenue structure to achieve a balanced budget, would proceed by the two-thirds supermajority. This is, in fact, what happened. After our decision, the majority made concessions on the budget. Although some legislators would still have preferred additional cuts, they recognized that the Constitution required them to abide by the majority's decision and move on to determine how to balance the budget. Two-thirds of the members of both houses of the Legislature then approved the tax changes necessary to balance the budget. Our opinion did not eliminate the two-thirds requirement, but it did indicate that the supermajority provision could not be used to avoid other constitutional duties.

* * *

The two-thirds supermajority provision, as passed, created the potential for an absolute budgetary stalemate in the Legislature; that potential was realized this year and has done significant damage to public education. A judicial resolution of the constitutional conflict was necessary, so that the Legislature could perform its constitutionally mandated duties. Our prior opinion did just that. We dismiss the rehearing petition.

MAUPIN, J., dissenting:

The rehearing petition in this matter should be granted, the writ of mandamus dissolved and the prior majority opinion vacated. First the Nevada State Legislature completed its work without resort to the remedy afforded by this court in the writ. It ultimately complied with the Nevada Constitution as written by appropriating funds for the state educational system and creating the new revenue sources to pay for the appropriations by a two-thirds vote. Second, the perceived crisis the majority sought to address in the writ was averted by the legislative action just mentioned. Third, the majority now indicates that the original decision had discrete application to the limited circumstances of the 2003 legislative sessions; thus a need for precedent for future sessions does not exist. Accordingly, the entire matter is moot.

I most strongly take issue with the court's comments on rehearing that the supermajority initiative was flawed from its inception and that the Nevada electorate twice approved it without an understanding that a stalemate between appropriations and taxes could eventuate. The initiative was vetted through two elections and we should not from this vantage point presume to say what the voters of this state knew or did not know. In any case, the potential for such a conflict was inherent in the proposal and the people of this state had every right to make it more onerous for the Legislature to create new revenue streams for the operation of government. Nothing in this constitutional construct prevents the Legislature from crafting a balanced budget and, as noted, the Legislature ultimately complied with the super-majority requirement.

This court did not invalidate the tax initiative as somehow being unconstitutional. Having thus affirmed its basic validity, we must recognize that such initiatives, however inconvenient to the operatives of government they may be at times, represent the ultimate form of citizen consent to government. Accordingly, it is not for us, the supreme court of this state, to criticize the wisdom of a valid initiative embraced by an overwhelming majority of Nevadans.

I am therefore of the belief that we should, in response to the petition for rehearing, vacate the writ of mandamus and the prior opinion issued in aid of it.

NOTES AND QUESTIONS

1. *A Simple Question of Construction?* In its first *Guinn* opinion, the Nevada Supreme Court suggested that it was engaged in a relatively mechanical question of constitutional construction that could be resolved by the application of general, objective legal principles, such as the priority of substance over process, and of a specific rule over the general. But is this persuasive? Even assuming that substance trumps procedure, is the two-thirds voting rule merely procedural? Surely, it had the substantive intent and effect of making it more difficult to increase taxes. So, too, even assuming that the specific prevails over the general, is it so clear which provision—the tax-voting requirement or education funding—is specific and which is general? Nor did the court even mention a standard rule of construction—that a subsequent law prevails over an inconsistent earlier one. Assuming that educational funding and the two-thirds vote on taxes are inconsistent constitutional provisions, does the approach taken by the court in *Guinn I* provide a satisfactory resolution of the problem?

2. *An Undemocratic Rule?* The second *Guinn* opinion makes a more frontal assault on the two-thirds rule. The court points out that the two-thirds vote is inconsistent with majority rule, and it undermines the significance of voter approval of the requirement by noting that the voters were not informed about the potential impact on state operations and state fiscal integrity. Note that *Guinn II* does not give as much weight to the conflict between the two-thirds rule and the constitutional education-finance obligation. Instead it presents the case as involving a conflict between the two-thirds vote for taxes and majority rule in budget-making across the board. Are you persuaded by the court's concerns about the two-thirds rule? Do they outweigh concerns about judicial intervention here? Did the *Guinn* decision advance or undermine democratic governance? In that connection, how important is it that the tax measure the legislature ultimately enacted had had the support of the Governor—who brought the lawsuit—and a two-thirds majority of the upper house of the legislature, and was just one vote shy of two-thirds (the vote was 27–15) in the lower house? For some commentary on *Guinn, see* William D. Popkin, Interpreting Conflicting Provisions of the Nevada State Constitution, 5 Nev. L.J. 308 (2004); Jeffrey

W. Stempel, The Most Rational Branch: *Guinn v. Legislature* and the Judiciary's Role as Helpful Arbiter of Conflict, 4 Nev L.J. 518 (2004); Steven R. Johnson, Supermajority Provisions, *Guinn v. Legislature,* and a Flawed Constitutional Structure, 4 Nev. L.J. 491 (2004).

Guinn is the rare, if not unique, case of a court disregarding a state constitutional amendment that neither violated the federal constitution nor was adopted in violation of the procedures for amending the state constitution. The court's concern about the anti-democratic implications of a supermajority requirement for legislation increasing taxes, however, was echoed in a Washington state supreme court decision invalidating a voter-initiated statute that required a two-thirds legislative vote to pass any bill containing a tax increase. The court concluded that the measure violated the constitutional provision conditioning the passage of bills on the approval of "a majority of the members elected to each house." The court determined that a simple majority vote was the maximum as well as the minimum requirement for passing a bill. League of Educ. Voters v. State, 295 P.3d 743, 749–52 (Wash. 2013) (en banc). The court also emphasized that a supermajority requirement for ordinary legislation "alters our system of government" and "would allow special interests to control resulting legislation." *Id.* at 751. Setting the voting requirement high enough for certain types of bills "essentially ensur[es] that those types of bills would never pass. Such a result is antithetical to the notion of a functioning government." *Id.* Nearly all the states that have adopted a supermajority vote requirement for the approval of new taxes or tax increases have done so by constitutional amendment. *See id.* at 752; Alaskans for Efficient Gov't Inc. v. State, 153 P.3d 296, 299–300 (Alaska 2007).

NOTE ON TAX AND EXPENDITURE LIMITATIONS

California's adoption of Proposition 13 sparked a nationwide wave of state constitutional and statutory changes to limit state and local taxation and spending. Within six months of Proposition 13's passage, tax limitation measures were on the ballots in 17 states, with all but five measures approved. Forty-three states adopted new property tax limitations or relief plans between 1978 and 1980. *See* Terry Schwadron & Paul Richter, California and the American Tax Revolt 6 (U. Cal. Press 1984). The tax revolt continued into the early 1980s, but ebbed later in that decade, surged again in the early 1990s, and continued to generate constitutional amendments and statutory programs aimed at reducing state and local taxation and spending into the twenty-first century

The tax revolt had many elements. The principal focus was the property tax, but the limits on the property tax took many forms. Idaho, for example, passed a measure virtually identical to Proposition 13, limiting property taxes to one percent of assessed value and restricting increases in assessments to two percent per year. Massachusetts took a somewhat different approach, requiring each city and town to reduce its effective property tax yield to 2.5% of total assessed valuation and limiting the increase in total revenue raised by the property tax in each locality to 2.5% per year. Not surprisingly, the Massachusetts measure, adopted in 1980, is known as Proposition 2½. Unlike Proposition 13, Proposition 2½ does not limit the tax rate or the rate of increase in taxes for individual properties. Proposition 2½ also permits cities, by local referendum, to "override" the 2.5% limit on the rate of revenue increase (but not the 2.5% levy cap) to fund specified programs.

By one count, forty-six states have some form of constitutional or statutory limitation on local taxation or expenditures ("TELs"). While some of these limits date back to the late nineteenth century, most were adopted or strengthened in the aftermath of Proposition 13. *See* Daniel R. Mullins & Bruce A. Wallin, Tax and Expenditure Limitations: Introduction and Overview, 24 Pub. Budgeting & Fin. 2, 3–10 (2004). These provisions tend to focus on the property tax and may include tax rate ceilings; limits on the amount of revenue that may be generated from the property tax, independent of the tax rate; or limits on assessment increases. *Id.* A number of states limit expenditure growth or general revenue increases, which may go beyond the property tax. Some, like Colorado's Taxpayer Bill of Rights (TABOR), Colo. Const., Art. X, § 20, and Michigan's Headlee Amendment, Mich. Const. Art. IX, § 31, require voter approval of all new taxes or tax rate increases. Missouri's Hancock Amendment, Mo. Const., Art. X, § 22, requires voter approval of fee increases as well. As we will see later in this chapter, the determination of what constitutes a "fee" subject to the voter approval requirement has been the subject of dispute.

As *Guinn* indicates, TELs have also been imposed on state governments. Twenty-eight states have adopted TELs, either by constitutional amendment or by statute. These seek to limit state spending or revenue growth by tying it to growth in state population, personal income, or inflation. Many of these were adopted by voter initiative. *See* Nat'l Ass'n of State Budget Officers, Budget Processes in the States 40, 61–64 (2015). As in *Guinn*, some of these restrictions are procedural. The constitutions of sixteen states require a legislative supermajority (ranging from 60% to 75%) to approve some or all new taxes or tax increases, and eight states (including seven with legislative supermajority requirements) require voter approval for some or all new or increased state taxes. National Conference of State Legislatures, Majority and Supermajority Requirements in Legislative Powers over Revenue Increases (March 2006). For an argument that state measures conditioning new taxes or tax increases on voter approval can promote local democracy, *see* Kirk J. Stark, The Right to Vote on Taxes, 96 Nw. U. L. Rev. 121 (2001). For a criticism of that position, *see* Richard Briffault, The Disfavored Constitution: State Fiscal Limits and State Constitutional Law, 34 Rutgers L.J. 907, 952–55 (2003). *See also* Mathew D. McCubbins, Putting the State Back into State Government: The Constitution and the Budget, *in* Constitutional Reform in California: Making State Government More Effective and Responsive 366 (Bruce E. Cain & Roger Noll eds., IGS Press 1995) (finding that the California constitution's requirement of a two-thirds vote in each legislative house to pass a new tax increase has contributed to "gridlock and irresponsibility . . . much more frequently . . . than mature compromise").

Empirical research on TELs has found four broad effects, although the effects vary considerably from state to state according to the terms of the specific restrictions. First, TELs have contributed to a reduction in the role of the property tax in funding local government. In California, which adopted one of the most stringent property tax limits in the country, the share of county revenue from the property tax dropped from 33.2% in 1977–78 to 11.6% in 1995–96. *See* Terri A. Sexton, Steven M. Sheffrin, Arthur O'Sullivan, Proposition 13: Unintended Effects and Feasible Reforms, 52 Nat'l Tax J. 99, 107 (1999). For California cities, the share of general revenue from the property tax declined from 24% in 1977 to 15% in 1982, rising to 17% in 2002. *See* Christopher Hoene, Fiscal Structure and the Post-Proposition 13 Fiscal Regime in California's Cities, 34 Pub. Budgeting & Fin. 51, 62 (2004). Nationally, including the states that did not adopt property tax limits, property tax revenues as a share of total state and local general revenues dropped from 22% in 1977 to just 16% in 2001, rebounding slightly to 18% in 2010. *See* Tax Policy Center, Tax Policy Briefing Book (2013).

Second, TELs appear to have contributed to an increase in the role of sales taxes, assessments, fees, and service charges in funding local governments. *See, e.g.,* Colin H. McCubbins & Mathew D. McCubbins, Proposition 13 and the California Fiscal Shell Game, 2 Cal. J. Pol. & Pol'y 1, 22 (2010) ("legislators have come up with creative alternatives for government financing, substituting away from the traditional *ad valorem* property taxes towards fees, assessments, and income and sales taxes"). For California cities, for example, the percentage of general revenue from other taxes and charges rose from 27% in 1977 to 43% in 2002. Hoene, *supra. See also* Gary M. Galles & Robert L. Sexton, A Tale of Two Tax Jurisdictions: The Surprising Effects of California's Proposition 13 and Massachusetts' Proposition 2½, 57 Am. J. Econ. & Soc. 123 (1998) (finding that local governments made up lost property tax revenue through increases in non-tax fees and charges). Local tax limits also provide incentives to local governments to promote and compete for commercial development and for the sales tax revenue such development may generate. *See* Jonathan Schwartz, Prisoners of Proposition 13: Sales Taxes, Property Taxes, and the Fiscalization of Municipal Land Use Decisions, 71 So. Cal. L. Rev. 183 (1997).

Third, TELs appear to have contributed to a shift in power from local governments to the states. *See* Hoene, *supra,* at 70 ("[p]ossessing less control over their own fiscal fortunes, cities became more dependent upon the largesse and goodwill of state government and the California voters—sources that have proven neither reliable nor friendly to cities"); Mark Skidmore, Tax and Expenditure Limitations and the Fiscal Relationships Between State and Local Governments, 99 Pub. Choice 77, 95–98 (1999); Alvin D. Sokolow, The Changing Property Tax and State-Local Relations, 28 Publius J. Fed. 165 (1998). The limits on local governments are typically more stringent than those imposed on the states, and the cap on the local property tax made local governments more dependent on state aid. For California counties, for example, the share of revenue from intergovernmental transfers rose from 50.6% in 1977–78 to 64.1% in 1995–96. In addition, TELs can give state governments a greater role with respect to local revenues. In California, prior to the enactment of Proposition 13, a city, a county, a school district and multiple special districts with territorial jurisdiction over the same land were each capable of imposing a property tax on the same parcel. Under Proposition 13, the total tax levied on a particular parcel is limited to 1% of assessed value with the proceeds "apportioned according to law." As a result, the state now decides the share each type of local government gets from the local property tax.

Fourth, although TELs may affect the use of a particular tax, like the property tax, or affect spending levels immediately after enactment, recent studies have found that the vast majority have been ineffective at their stated goals of reducing state and local taxes, spending, or budgets over time. *See, e.g.,* Colin H. McCubbins & Mathew D. McCubbins, Cheating on Their Taxes: When Are Tax Limitations Effective at Limiting State Taxes, Expenditures, and Budgets?, 67 Tax. L. Rev. 507 (2014); Benjamin Zycher, State and Local Spending: Do Tax and Expenditure Limits Work? (Amer. Enterp. Inst. 2013); David Gamage and Darien Shanske, The Trouble with Tax Increase Limitations, 6 Alb. Gov't L. Rev. 50 (2013). This may be due, in part, to the willingness of local voters to approve tax increases or waivers of tax or spending caps, which, if one goal of TELs is to assure voter approval of tax increases, may be counted as a success for the TELs. But TELs have also been circumvented by the development and increased use of other revenue sources, which has led to a more complex and less transparent state and local financing system. Moreover, due to the increased utilization of special revenue-raising districts, the local government structure in many states has become even more fragmented and byzantine. The adoption of TELs may also increase local fiscal stress, particularly for smaller localities, and affect local spending priorities even when they do not change levels of spending. *See, e.g.,* Judith I. Stallman, Impacts of Tax & Expenditure Limits on Local Governments: Lessons from Colorado and Missouri, 37 J. Reg. Analysis & Pol'y 62 (2007). TELs may also increase state borrowing and indebtedness. *See, e.g.,* Myungsoon Hur, Fiscal Limits and State Fiscal Structure: An Analysis of State Revenue Structure and Indebtedness, 28 Mun. Fin. J. 19 (2007).

What is the case for constitutionalizing tax and expenditure limitations? "New taxes and tax increases trigger an immediate burden on current voters, and anti-tax forces are well-represented in the political process. Politicians who enact high taxes may be punished by the voters in the next election, and few politicians are likely to doubt the political significance of anti-tax sentiment." Richard Briffault, The Disfavored Constitution: State Fiscal Limits and State Constitutional Law, 34 Rutgers L.J. 907, 950 (2003). Why is a legal, as well as a political, check on taxation necessary? Is state constitutional limitation of local taxation particularly problematic, given the existence of vigorous interlocal competition for mobile taxpayers—that is, an exit option—as well as the possibility of local political opposition? Does a uniform state-wide restriction on all localities fail to acknowledge the interlocal variations in needs, circumstances and preferences recognized by home rule? Does the existence of these restrictions reflect popular doubt about the effectiveness of ordinary political controls over government, especially local government? Does their evasion reflect the ongoing difficulty of holding together the public's hostility to taxes with its desire for a certain level of state and local services that requires some form of public financing?

2.   THE RISE OF NON-TAX TAXES

a.   Special Assessments and Special Benefits Taxation

McNALLY v. TOWNSHIP OF TEANECK

Supreme Court of New Jersey
379 A.2d 446 (1977)

SCHREIBER, J.

The Township of Teaneck, pursuant to N.J.S.A. 40:56–1, which authorizes a municipality to assess lands benefitted by a local improvement, levied special assessments against 313 residential properties for reimbursement of the costs of paving streets and installing curbs. Owners of 74 properties appealed asserting that the criteria used in determining the amounts of the assessments were improper. * * *

In March 1971 the Township adopted an ordinance providing that new paving and new curbs would be installed on parts of eleven streets located in three residential areas. These were designated as local improvements, the cost to be assessed upon the lands in the vicinity of the improvement in accordance with N.J.S.A. 40:56–1 et seq. The ordinance also stated that the assessments "shall in each case be as nearly as may be in proportion to and not in excess of the peculiar benefit, advantage or increase in value which the respective lots and parcels of real estate shall be deemed to receive by reason of such improvement. The total amount of the assessments so levied shall not exceed the cost of said improvement. The portion of such cost which shall not be so assessed shall be paid by the Township as in the case of a general improvement which is to be paid for by general taxation."

Upon completion of the project the Township appointed three residents of the municipality as commissioners to assess property owners for such improvement. N.J.S.A. 40:56–22. * * *

The total project costs consisted of $331,280 for the street paving, $12,105 for the curbing, and 7% overhead. These costs were itemized by streets and were furnished to the commissioners by the Township

Engineer, Milton Robbins. The respective street costs varied depending upon such factors as the soil condition and size of the street. The accuracy and reasonableness of these figures are not in dispute.

Proposed assessments were calculated on a front-foot basis, that is, the total cost on a particular street was divided by the total foot frontage and the resultant figure multiplied by the foot frontage of each property. Thereafter, each commissioner visually inspected the improvements and the properties. After having satisfied themselves that the improvements were properly installed, checking the layout of each property on the municipal tax map and considering whether any special circumstances existed, the commissioners compared the allocated cost per property with the increased value in the land. The commissioners met on numerous occasions and held two public meetings with the property owners, some of whom appeared and voiced their objections to the proposed assessments. The commissioners concluded that in each instance the cost of the improvement did not exceed the enhanced value of the property.

* * *

In their complaint the landowners asserted that the assessments were improper because "there was no attempt made to assess for the peculiar benefits" to each property as a result of the improvement. They sought the return of any monies which had been paid and a restraint to enjoin the Township from assessing the plaintiffs on any basis other than the peculiar benefits or increased value received. * * *

Municipalities are authorized to undertake the paving or repaving of a street and the curbing of a sidewalk along a street as local improvements. By definition a local improvement is one the cost of which in whole or in part "may be assessed upon the lands in the vicinity thereof benefitted thereby." The governing body may in the ordinance authorizing a local improvement provide that a part of the costs be paid by the municipality. * * *

The commissioners are charged with examining the improvement and viewing all lands and real estate "upon the line and in the vicinity thereof benefitted thereby. . . ." They must also hold a public hearing, after notifying the affected property owners by mail and by publication in a newspaper. *Id.* Witnesses may be examined under oath and the commissioners may "make a just and equitable assessment of the benefits conferred upon any real estate by reason of such improvements having due regard to the rights and interests of all persons concerned, as well as to the value of the real estate benefitted."

Certain guidelines are statutorily mandated. The total amount of the assessment levied cannot exceed the total project cost less any municipal contribution. Further, all assessments are to be "as nearly as may be in proportion to and not in excess of the peculiar benefit, advantage or increase in value which the respective lots and parcels of real estate shall be deemed to receive by reason of such improvement." If the total cost exceeds the assessments, the municipality must pay the difference. * * *

The key issue in this case is whether utilization of cost per front-foot basis, when employed in conjunction with the judgment of commissioners based upon their visual observations and examinations of each property and their individual experiences, is appropriate in fixing assessments for paving streets and installing curbs in a residential neighborhood.

Use of the cost per foot frontage formula has been constitutionally sustained. *Webster v. Fargo*, 181 U.S. 394 (1901). It has long been embedded in our history as an appropriate tool for commissioners to use. * * * It has likewise been sanctioned in many other jurisdictions.

Whether the property subject to assessment has been benefitted and, if so, the extent thereof are factual issues. The ultimate test is, of course, the difference between the market value of the land before and after the improvement. * * *

The cost of the new pavement and curb is evidence of its value to the abutting property owner. In the absence of any proof to the contrary the enhancement in value presumably would be equated with that cost. That is comparable to the use of cost to ascertain increased market value for general tax assessments when an improvement is made to an existing structure. In that case, in the absence of other evidence, the value increase would usually be presumptively equivalent to the cost. * * *

Exaction of more than the special benefit to the property owner would constitute a taking of private property for public use without compensation. *Norwood v. Baker*, 172 U.S. 269 (1898); *The Tide-water Company v. Coster*, 18 N.J.Eq. 518, 526–531 (E. & A. 1866). So, if it is shown that the market value enhancement is less than cost, then the assessment must be reduced accordingly. * * *

The two statutory ceilings that the total assessments may not exceed the total costs and that the individual assessment must not be in excess of the enhanced value assure property owners that they will not be charged more than a fair share of the improvement cost. *State, Agens, pros., v. Mayor, etc., of Newark*, 37 N.J.L. 415, 422–423 (E. & A. 1874). In this manner the assessments will not be in excess of the peculiar benefit to a particular property, even though as a result property owners may pay, inter se, varying amounts. The statute refers to the relationship of the betterment to each owner's property and not to the relationship among property owners.

The special assessment is not a tax which comes within the constitutional provision requiring that property be assessed for taxation under general laws and by uniform rules. The purpose of a special assessment is to reimburse the municipality in whole or in part for a particular expenditure. The scheme of the local improvement law makes it abundantly clear that its function is not to raise funds for revenue purposes. * * * The ordinance, authorized by statute promulgated under the State's police power, simply created a method of levying assessments on those who have received a special benefit from the expenditure. * * *

The commissioners here were well qualified to perform their functions. Their collective experiences included service on prior commissions, operation of a business, practice as an attorney and accountant, ownership and operation of realty holdings, and instruction in courses on real estate appraisal and taxation. * * * These commissioners complied with all the statutory requisites. They viewed the properties affected to determine whether there were any circumstances which would warrant a different treatment of any particular property or whether they were all substantially the same. They afforded the property owners an opportunity to be heard and to present evidence, expert or otherwise, to demonstrate the lack of uniformity or unusual nature of their property as well as proof that the assessment exceeded the difference between the market value before and after completion of the project. The property owners adduced no such evidence, expert or otherwise. * * *

As indicated above, use of the cost per front-foot formula for pavement and curbs by the commissioners who viewed the improvements and each of the properties and applied their own judgment and expertise adequately established the incremental values, there being no indication in the record that the parcels on a per street basis lacked substantial uniformity. Those findings are buttressed by the expert's testimony that the increased values and benefits to each of these properties were equal to or exceeded the assigned costs of the pavement and curbs.

The trial court invalidated these assessments (even though the benefits exceeded those assessments) because of the widely differing percentages among the 73 properties of the ratios of their respective assessments to incremental value and assessments to value of the real estate before the improvement. This rationale raised sua sponte by the trial court rests upon some underlying misconceptions. First, imposition of the special assessment is not a general tax which constitutionally requires uniformity. N.J.Const. (1947), Art. VIII, § 1, par. 1. The special assessment is a means of reimbursing a municipality for a capital expenditure which was specially advantageous to certain properties. Second, the statute does not call for a comparison of benefits among property owners. Third, the costs of the improvement allocable to each property do not necessarily result in the same percentage of increased value of each parcel. For example, assume pavement costs of $2500 each for a $25,000 and a $50,000 home on comparable adjoining lots. Though the value increase of both properties may be the same, the percentage increase in value of one would be 10% as compared to 5% for the other. So long as neither owner is required to pay more than the benefit received and the method of determining the amount of that benefit is reasonable and applied uniformly to all property owners, the statutory mandate has been satisfied.

Contrary to the trial court's expectation the ratios of the assessment to the realty value before betterment and of the assessment to the incremental value may vary widely. Elimination of the divergence among plaintiffs in their assessment to before improvement value ratios, as suggested by the trial court, would require application of the lowest ratio of assessment to before improvement value to each of the 313 properties. This would effectively thwart the municipality's efforts to obtain reimbursement, result in a bonanza to many property owners who would be paying a lower percentage of the pro rata costs, and thrust the additional burden on all the municipality's taxpayers. Neither the statute nor the constitution calls for this.

Attempts to equalize the varying ratios of assessment to enhancement among plaintiffs might also produce anomalous effects. If one were to apply the lowest ratio to each property the same results as described above would occur. Or, if one were to assess at full benefit, certain property owners would be called upon to pay more than their allocable cost of the improvement whereas others would pay less than their proportionate share. The commissioners applied the same front-foot formula to all properties, with due regard to any special circumstances affecting any particular parcel. There is no evidence that different ratios of allocated costs were applied. The same standards and criteria were applied to every property and the resulting special assessments arrived at did not violate any rights in an equal protection sense. Thus the method results in a balancing of costs and is a practical workable device for assessment commissioners.

2ND ROC-JERSEY ASSOCIATES V. TOWN OF MORRISTOWN

Supreme Court of New Jersey
731 A.2d 1 (1999)

HANDLER, J.

The principal issue raised in this appeal is whether assessments imposed on real property in a municipal Special Improvement District are unconstitutional because residential properties are excluded from the assessments. * * *

In 1993, the Town of Morristown enacted Ordinance 0–42–93, entitled "An Ordinance Creating A Special Improvement District Within

The Town Of Morristown And Designating A District Management Corporation." The ordinance was passed pursuant to N.J.S.A. 40:56–65 to –89, which authorized municipalities to establish Special Improvement Districts (SIDs). The statute provided for the creation of a District Management Corporation empowered to fund, manage, acquire, and oversee the rehabilitation of properties in SID districts, and to attract new businesses. N.J.S.A. 40:56–83(b). The SID was created due to declining economic conditions in Morristown. The stated purposes of the ordinance were to:

> (a) promote economic growth and employment within the Business District;

> (b) foster and encourage self-help programs to enhance the local business climate;

> (c) create a self-financing Special Improvement District to assist in meeting community needs, goals and objectives;

> (d) designate a District Management Corporation to assist in managing self-help programs and in carrying out local needs, goals and objectives.

Many New Jersey municipalities have created SIDs pursuant to the enabling statute. The overwhelming majority of these SIDs, like the Morristown SID, use real property value as the basis for determining SID special assessments. The Morristown ordinance specifically exempted residential property from the SID special assessment, viz:

> (c) All properties within the [SID] that are used for residential purposes, and those portions of mixed use properties that are residential are deemed excluded from the assessing or taxing provisions of this ordinance and are expressly exempt from any tax or assessment made for Special Improvement District purposes.

> * * *

The annual budget for the SID in 1994 was $500,000. A special assessment was made on all subject property within the SID on the basis of 105% of the property's assessed value for local real property tax purposes. * * *

Plaintiffs focus their constitutional challenge on the 1995 amendment to N.J.S.A. 40:56–66(b), which allows municipalities to exclude residential properties from the SID assessment. That exclusion, according to plaintiffs, violates several constitutional principles. They contend foremost that the exclusion of residential property is unconstitutional because the SID special assessment is a tax, rather than a special assessment, and therefore violates the Uniformity Clause of the

New Jersey Constitution, which requires real property taxes to be applied uniformly to all classes of real property. N.J. Const. art. VIII, § 1, ¶ 1(a). * * *

The Uniformity Clause of the New Jersey Constitution applies to the taxation of real property. It requires that all property be assessed for taxation "under general laws and by uniform rules" and according to the "same standard of value." N.J. Const. art. VIII, § 1, ¶ 1(a). * * * The Legislature may exempt certain property from the Uniformity Clause either by general laws or for the specified purposes enumerated in the exemption clause. N.J. Const. art. VIII, § 1, ¶ 2, viz:

> Exemption from taxation may be granted only by general laws. Until otherwise provided by law all exemptions from taxation validly granted and now in existence shall be continued. Exemptions from taxation may be altered or repealed, except those exempting real and personal property used exclusively for religious, educational, charitable or cemetery purposes, as defined by law, and owned by any corporation or association organized and conducted exclusively for one or more of such purposes and not operating for profit.

* * * If the assessments authorized by the SID statute and imposed by the implementing ordinance are deemed to be real property taxes, then the exclusion of residential properties could constitute preferential tax treatment in violation of the uniformity and exemption clauses of the Constitution. Therefore, the important issue is whether, as a matter of constitutional interpretation, the SID impositions constitute real property taxes or special assessments.

It is well recognized that the Uniformity Clause of the Constitution is inapplicable to special assessments. * * *

Traditionally, the differences between an assessment and a tax include: an assessment supports local improvements, while a tax finances general operations; an assessment is a one-time charge, while a tax is annual; and an assessment requires that the benefit be direct, while a tax requires no such direct benefit. The improvement must benefit the assessed property, and that benefit must be special and local, that is, the benefit to the specific property must be substantially greater than to the public in general. The benefit can be measured by increased market value or by the overall economic effect of the improvement. *Ibid.* Lastly, the benefit must be certain rather than speculative, although it may arise in the future. *Ibid.* These salient features of the special assessment are codified by statute. N.J.S.A. 40:56–1 authorizes municipalities to impose special assessments for local improvements such as sewage, paving, and water. * * *

The traditional definition of special assessments was predicated on a physical improvement or "public work," such as the installation of sidewalks, paving, or water and sewage systems, that produced a tangible benefit for the property subject to the assessment. The definition of special assessments, however, has not been rigidly interpreted. It has been generally recognized that "[t]he construction of a public improvement is not a necessary requisite for the levy of a special assessment since an 'improvement' may simply be the furnishing of or making available a vital service, such as fire protection or garbage disposal." *Charlotte County v. Fiske*, 350 So.2d 578, 580 (Fla.App.2d 1977); see *South Trail Fire Control District v. Town Hall*, 273 So.2d 380 (Fla.1973) (upholding special assessment levied solely on commercial properties to support fire protection service); Further, the improvement need not be "local" in the sense of being specifically affixed or adherent to the assessed property. For example, the creation of parking lots and parking spaces has been upheld in several states as a proper object for special assessments. *E.g., Trivalent Realty Co. v. Town of Westport*, 2 Conn. App. 213, 477 A.2d 140 (1984) (upholding assessment for off-street parking lot as a qualified "municipal improvement"); *City of Whittier v. Dixon*, 24 Cal.2d 664, 151 P.2d 5 (1944) (upholding special assessment for creation of public parking spaces).

This Court has similarly upheld assessments for improvements that result only in a general or indirect benefit and enhanced economic effect on property. *E.g., Ridgewood, supra*, 55 N.J. 62, 259 A.2d 218 (noting that golf course may not see rise in value from sewage system but nevertheless must pay for special improvement). A property owner may benefit from an improvement even though the benefit is not presently apparent. "The fact that a landowner has no present, immediate use for the improvement is [ ] immaterial, so long as the use of the improvement is accessible and available to the land sought to be assessed for any use to which the property may legitimately be put." *Id.* at 68–69, 259 A.2d 218.

The SID special assessment does not conform to the prototypical special assessment. Unlike N.J.S.A. 40:56–21, which authorizes special assessments for local improvements that are essentially identified with specific properties, the SID statute, N.J.S.A. 40:56–73, permits special assessments that bestow general benefits consisting of services and improvements on a class of properties within the SID. The underlying improvements that are funded by the SID assessments are not necessarily physical, concrete, or permanent, nor are they directly adherent to the specific commercial properties that are assessed. Further, the benefits to the commercial properties are derived from improvements that are generalized and relatively intangible; the benefits consist of the results of the provision of ongoing public activities and services, such as advertising campaigns, meter bagging, street sweeping, the encouragement of tourism, hospitality guides, and business recruitment, as well as physical improvements, such as streetscape enhancement, supplemental lighting, and other aesthetic measures. N.J.S.A. 40:56–83(b). These kinds of services supplement traditional municipal services, but they are specifically intended and designed to better commercial properties and promote economic growth in the business community. *See Fanelli v. City of Trenton*, 135 N.J. 582, 590, 641 A.2d 541 (1994). Further, while traditional special assessments are one-time payments for a specific improvement, the SID assessments are levied annually for continuing services and recurrent improvements and are collected to finance the SID's ongoing operations.

* * *

We conclude that the core of the definition of a special assessment that makes the imposition a special assessment rather than a general tax is not that the benefit necessarily or primarily consists of physical improvements that are permanent in nature and are local in that they are adherent to or identified with specific individual properties that are directly and tangibly benefitted thereby. Rather, the special assessment is used to provide a combination of services and improvements that are intended and designed to benefit particular properties and demonstrably enhance the value and/or the use or function of the properties that are subject to the special assessment.

Plaintiffs argue that even if the assessments are upheld as special assessments that confer benefits to the commercial properties, the method of assessment was overly broad and not sufficiently tailored to the benefit received by individual properties. For that reason, plaintiffs contend, the assessments are invalid.

A valid special assessment must be "as nearly as may be in proportion" to the benefit received. *McNally, supra*, 75 N.J. at 33, 379 A.2d 446. It must not be in "substantial excess" of the special benefits to the land. *See Village of Norwood v. Baker*, 172 U.S. 269, 279 (1898). Special assessments, however, need not be measured with mathematical precision.

Plaintiffs concede that the benefit produced by the SIDs is greater for the commercial properties in Morristown. According to plaintiffs, however, not all commercial properties benefit equally from the activities of the SID. Plaintiffs further contend that the SID provides benefits to the Town as a whole, and that all properties, residential, mixed use, and commercial, ought to be similarly assessed for its funding. Therefore, a method based on property taxation that uniformly assesses only commercial properties does not justly distribute the burden of the SID in proportion to the benefit.

None of the benefits provided by the SID are aimed directly at residences and none of its budget is spent directly on residential properties. Although a portion of the SID budget is spent on beautification and street cleaning, services from which residents also benefit, a larger portion is spent on hospitality guards (who assist visitors to Morristown, not residents), business and retail recruitment, advertising campaigns and facade loans and grants to commercial and retail properties. In addition, the SID is responsible for aesthetic or cosmetic physical improvements that serve as part of a larger effort aimed exclusively at benefitting commercial properties.

This Court set forth the limitations on the levying of special assessments for conventional local improvements in *McNally, supra*, sustaining the assessment to each property so long as it was "as nearly as may be in proportion to and not in excess of the peculiar benefit" received by the property. 75 N.J. at 40, 379 A.2d 446. Such assessments are "presumptively correct and the taxpayers [have] the burden of overcoming that presumption by clear and convincing evidence." *Id*. at 44–55, 379 A.2d 446.

Plaintiffs contend that real property tax assessments should never be the basis for determining special assessments. They assert that the various properties should be assessed differently based on the type of land-use. Office/hotel space, for example, should be assessed differently from retail store space, because retail stores receive greater benefits from the SID. In a report submitted to the trial court, plaintiffs compared the method of assessment in the Morristown SID to other SIDs. The Buffalo Place SID in Buffalo, New York, imposes charges based on three considerations: location, basis, and use. A Seattle SID, the object of litigation in City of Seattle, supra, differentiates the assignment of costs by type of land use, with retail paying a higher percentage than office properties. 787 P.2d at 42–43. The New Brunswick, New Jersey SID uses a similar method. The majority of SIDs in New Jersey, however, use the property value method of assessment, as does the Center City SID in Philadelphia. * * *

The Appellate Division was aware of the classical method to determine assessments strongly urged by plaintiffs, that is, "the difference between the market value of the land before and after the improvement." *McNally, supra*, 75 N.J. at 42, 379 A.2d 446. The Court found, however, that this method would be "overwhelming" to the SID, and would divert its existing resources to expert valuation of increased market value rather than to the services and improvements the SID was meant to provide.

The Appellate Division identified several other methods of apportioning the special assessment burden among the properties benefitting from SID improvements, which the court acknowledged might yield a fairer result. The court noted, however, that apportionment based on property size, front footage, and the "block by block" rule, as well as other factors relevant to benefit, are included in the tax assessment structure, and concluded that it was not unreasonable for Morristown to use the existing tax assessment structure to determine the SID assessment. The trial court also took this approach, noting in its final order upholding the special assessment formula applied in the SID, that it "does not exclude the possibility that a municipality might act more fairly and in a qualitatively better way if it were to use the more complex procedure suggested by the [plaintiffs' report]." The Appellate Division identified several aspects of the SID assessment that supported its fairness and reliability: (1) "the assessments will be adjusted" annually; (2) the ordinance will be amended "so that the commercial portion of all mixed-use properties within the SID would be assessed"; (3) "the assessor and MPI will closely evaluate the nature of the programs and the benefits conferred every year to assure continuing fairness in the assessment process."

It is not unreasonable for Morristown to select one of the simpler methods of valuing benefits during the initial phase of the SID. The tax system offers several advantages in that it is updated periodically and provides property owners with a basis to challenge erroneous tax assessments and the derivative SID assessments. Although a more complex method might yield a fairer apportionment, it would be substantially more expensive and difficult to employ in the early stages of the SID. * * *

Plaintiffs also raise the closely-related contention that because "the methodology used by Morristown results in an assessment that is not proportional with the benefit conferred," the special assessment violates the Takings Clause of the New Jersey Constitution and the Fifth Amendment to the United States Constitution. N.J. Const. art. I, ¶ 20; U.S. Const. amend. V. The analysis of whether the measure of an assessment on property is constitutional under due process and takings principles in the context of this case is essentially the same as that applicable under the tax clauses of our Constitution. * * *

In this constitutional context, plaintiffs seek strict compliance with this Court's definition of benefit as " 'the difference between the market value of the lands before the improvement and the market value of the land immediately after the improvement.' " *McQueen v. Town of West New York*, 56 N.J. 18, 23, 264 A.2d 210 (1970) (quoting *In re Public Service Electric & Gas Co.*, 18 N.J.Super. 357, 363–65, 87 A.2d 344 (App.Div.1952)). However, while noting that "the classical and perfect method is to obtain an expert appraisal of the dollar value of each individual parcel of land ante-and post improvement," the Court in

McQueen pointed out that other methods would also be acceptable as long as they are just and equitable. *Id.* at 24, 264 A.2d 210.

The classical method of apportionment is not applicable in this case because of the difficulty of determining the immediate increase in value attributed to the creation of the SID. The method of assessment must necessarily be adapted to the benefit conferred. Where, as here, the nature of the benefit is general and intangible, and the quantum of the benefit is imprecise, the method of valuing that benefit based on property values is rational and appropriate. Plaintiffs, as already demonstrated, have not offered any evidence to satisfy their burden of proving that the assessment does not match the benefit.

In determining whether the SID assessments are valid special assessments as a matter of constitutional construction, considerations of legislative purpose and intent and public policy are highly relevant.

Public policy and legislative will strongly impel the Court to exercise latitude when reviewing SID ordinances. The legislative findings expressed in the statute provide:

> (1) that district management corporations may assist municipalities in promoting economic growth and employment within business districts; (2) that municipalities should be encouraged to create self-financing special improvement districts and designated district management corporations to execute self-help programs to enhance their local business climates; and (3) that municipalities should be given the *broadest possible discretion* in establishing by local ordinance the self-help programs most consistent with their local needs, goals and objectives.

[N.J.S.A. 40:56–65 (emphasis added).]

It is clear that the Legislature intended that SID assessments be considered special assessments. The framework of the enabling legislation provides that the SID would be financed by the properties especially benefitted by the improvements. The legislative scheme also ensures that SID assessments do not take on the characteristics of general taxes. The statute provides that funds generated by the SID assessment will be segregated into a special account and will be used only for SID purposes.

In weighing considerations of policy, the Court is enjoined to view the issue in a broader context. Forty states, including New Jersey, have adopted legislation enabling the creation of SIDs, which various states also term Business Improvement Districts, Community Development Districts, Municipal Improvement Districts, and Economic Development Districts. * * * Of these states, the vast majority have constitutional provisions requiring uniformity of taxation similar to New Jersey's, but they have yet to strike down SID legislation as unconstitutional. As of 1995, at least twenty-five other municipalities in New Jersey had established SIDs.

The urban setting in which SIDs are created is central to understanding the benefit offered by the Morristown SID. Urban sprawl, that is, a landscape dotted by planned office developments and malls connected by highways and thoroughfares, has resulted in the diminishing vitality of traditional city centers, such as Morristown's Green. Increasingly, office developments and shopping malls provide services associated with town centers, such as dry cleaning, pharmacies and food courts, while town centers, which already have such services as a result of being integrated communities, languish.

SIDs provide a quasi-public solution to this problem. SIDs are an attempt to achieve privately what municipal government has struggled unsuccessfully to do. . . . SIDs are organized and financed by property owners and merchants, operate on the basis of state and local laws, and use revenues garnered from self-taxation to finance various services and capital improvements not provided by the municipality. * * *

These considerations are germane in determining the validity of the Morristown SID. The SID, as earlier noted, was formed as a response to declining economic conditions in Morristown and specifically to the closing of Macy's in the Town center. The reports of both parties indicated that the SID's activities were necessary to keep Morristown and its businesses competitive in a market increasingly dominated by suburban malls and office parks. These reports furnish an evidentiary basis for the conclusion that SIDs offer a benefit to commercial property.

NOTES AND QUESTIONS

1. *The Theory of the Special Assessment.* The theory of the special assessment is that it is not a tax. As a result, unless state law specifically provides otherwise, the assessment is not subject to the state constitutional constraints that apply to taxes, such as uniformity, caps on tax rates or tax levies, or voter approval requirements for new taxes or tax increases. *See, e.g.,* County of Fresno v. Malmstrom, 156 Cal.Rptr. 777 (Cal.App.1979) (special assessment not tax subject to Proposition 13's 1% property tax cap); Zahner v. City of Perryville, 813 S.W.2d 855 (Mo.1991) (Missouri's Hancock Amendment requirement of voter approval of tax increases does not apply to special assessments). Other rules applying to taxes may not apply to assessments either. Charitable property is ordinarily exempt from property taxation, but may be subject to a special assessment. Crittenton v. Reed, 932 S.W.2d 403 (Mo. 1996). Similarly, constitutional provisions that preclude an elected legislature from delegating the power to tax to an appointed body may not apply when the legislature delegates power to impose an assessment. *See*

Hagley Homeowners Ass'n, Inc. v. Hagley Water, Sewer and Fire Auth., 485 S.E.2d 92 (S.C.1997).

If the special assessment is not a tax, then what is it? *McNally* states that the special assessment is an exercise of the police power to require landowners "who have received a special benefit" from a local government expenditure to reimburse the local government. How does this differ from a tax?

2. *Distinguishing a Special Assessment from the Property Tax.* The special assessment is not a tax but it looks a lot like the property tax. It is coercive, like a tax. Although it seeks reimbursement for a benefit, the benefit is one that a local government has chosen to provide landowners, but not necessarily one that landowners have requested. Although state laws often require local governments to seek neighborhood property owner approval for—or permit property owner protests to block—an assessment, unanimous consent is rarely required. As a result, a landowner who has affirmatively protested a local decision to authorize an assessment-funded improvement may still be subject to the assessment. The assessment, thus, more closely resembles a tax than a service fee, in which, as discussed below, fee payers choose individually to accept a service and pay a fee. The assessment is also enforced like a tax. The New Jersey court in *McNally* reported that an unpaid assessment operated as a lien on property. Sometimes, as in *2nd Roc-Jersey Associates*, individual assessments are calculated on the same basis as the property tax, that is, on the assessed valuation of the property. *Accord*, City of Boca Raton v. State of Florida, 595 So.2d 25 (Fla.1992); Bellevue Assocs. v. City of Bellevue, 741 P.2d 993 (Wash.1987).

If assessments and property taxes are so similar, yet have such different legal consequences, it becomes vital to be able to tell them apart. What distinguishes the assessment from a tax? Central to the special assessment is the idea of a special or local benefit. The special assessment must provide some general or public benefit, otherwise there would be no justification for public action. However, in order to be financed by a special assessment, there must be a distinct, special benefit to the subset of the general public that is subject to the assessment. The classic example is the street paving and curb installation in *McNally*. The general public benefits from the improved circulation of traffic throughout the community that street and curb improvements provide. But the landowners whose properties front directly on the streets so improved realize the additional benefit of improved access to their properties.

Traditionally, special assessments have been used to finance physical improvements—streets, sidewalks, street lighting, and utility hook-ups—abutting, adjacent to, or connecting with the land of the property owners subject to the assessment. *See, e.g.*, Property Owners Ass'n v. City of Ketchikan, 781 P.2d 567 (Alaska 1989) (special assessment used to finance roads, water, sewers, and telephone and power lines); Rinker Materials Corp. v. Town of Lake Park, 494 So.2d 1123 (Fla.1986) (roadway, drainage, water and sewer improvements). In the nineteenth century, the special assessment was a common way for paying for these improvements. *See* Stephen Diamond, The Death and Transfiguration of Benefit Taxation: Special Assessments in Nineteenth Century America, 12 J. Leg. Stud. 201 (1983). Conversely, if an improvement benefits the community as a whole, courts have held that it may not be financed by a special assessment. *See, e.g.,* Heavens v. King County Rural Library Dist., 404 P.2d 453 (Wash.1965) (special assessment could not be used to finance a public library); Ruel v. Rapid City, 167 N.W.2d 541 (S.D.1969) (special assessment could not be used to finance a convention center); Lipscomb v. Lenon, 276 S.W. 367 (Ark.1925) (assessment could not be used to fund a public auditorium).

2nd Roc-Jersey Associates expands the concept of "special benefit" in two ways. First, the assessment funded the on-going provision of public services rather than the one-shot financing of capital improvements. Assessments have been used to fund special services, but their principal use has been to finance new physical infrastructure. Second, the advertising campaigns, street sweeping, tourism promotion, and business recruitment programs funded by the assessments did not have any direct, physical connections to particular parcels. Again, assessments have been used to fund infrastructure that serves a geographic district rather than distinct parcels. *See, e.g.,* Wing v. City of Eugene, 437 P.2d 836 (Ore. 1968) (off-site parking facility). But the Morristown SID's use of the special assessment to pay for public services that provide "generalized and relatively intangible" benefits to a geographically large area represents a significant expansion in the use of the assessment. Do you agree with the court that a property tax charge used to fund area-wide services ought to be treated as an assessment and not a tax? (Remember: If this had been a property tax, the exemption of residential property from taxation would have been subject to a Uniformity Clause challenge. In other jurisdictions, the surcharge might have been subject to a tax cap or a voter approval requirement). For the court, what distinguished the SID assessment from a tax?

Business improvement districts are a local government innovation that emerged after 1975 and became widespread in the late 1980s and early 1990s. They commonly rely on the special assessment to furnish services in downtown areas. These services involve a mix of traditional municipal services—such as security, street maintenance and street cleaning—as well as business-oriented services like marketing, promotions, and business services. They generally rely on special assessments, imposed and collected by local governments, to fund their programs. *See* Richard Briffault, A Government for Our Time? Business Improvement Districts and Urban Governance, 99 Colum.L.Rev. 365, 446–454 (1999). Courts have generally upheld the use of assessments to fund BID services. *See, e.g.,* Dahms v. Downtown Pomona Property, 96 Cal. Rptr.3d 10 (Cal. App. 2009); Zimmerman v. City of Memphis, 67 S.W.2d 798 (Tenn. App. 2001); McGowan v. Capital Center, Inc., 19 F.Supp.2d 642 (S.D. Miss. 1998); Williams v. Anne Arundel Cty., 638 A.2d 74 (Md.1994) (assessment funded maintenance of and "special security for" community property); City of Seattle v. Rogers Clothing for Men, Inc., 787 P.2d 39 (Wash.1990) (assessment funded a "marketing program" aimed at decorating and beautifying public places, maintaining signs, and advertising, and a "maintenance program" providing graffiti removal, street cleaning, and security); Evans v. City of San Jose, 4 Cal.Rptr.2d 601 (Cal. App. 1992) (assessment used to fund downtown promotion services not a "special tax" within Proposition 13 and therefore not subject to voter approval).

The growing use of assessments to fund area-wide programs is not limited to BIDs. *See, e.g.*, City of Boca Raton v. State, 595 So.2d 25 (Fla.1992) (upholding use of special assessment to fund downtown improvements); Knox v. City of Orland, 841 P.2d 144 (Cal. 1992) (assessment to maintain parks); Grais v. City of Chicago, 601 N.E.2d 745 (Ill.1992) (upholding levy on commercial property in downtown "special services area" to fund design and construction of a new public transportation system for central Chicago). *See also* R. Lisle Baker, Using Special Assessments as a Tool for Smart Growth: Louisville's New Metro Government as a Potential Example, 45 Brandeis L.J. 1 (2006) (discussing use of special assessment to fund new parks, open space, transit stations, and arenas).

3.   *Determining Individual Assessments.* Assuming that a program provides a special benefit rather than a general benefit, so that the special assessment may be used to finance it, the special assessment presents two further questions: (a) Who may be subject to the assessment? (b) How is the assessment an individual landowner pays determined?

(a)   *Who May Be Required to Pay an Assessment?* In theory, only landowners whose lands benefit from the improvement or services funded by the assessment may be required to pay the assessment. Traditionally, these landowners are defined territorially. A state or local government creates a geographic district in which it has determined that all the landowners would benefit from the improvement. Sometimes when an assessment is intended to fund an improvement that serves a large area, the district may be divided into zones, with landowners in the zones closer to the improvement assessed at a higher rate than those more physically distant from the improvement. Sometimes, as in *2nd Roc-Jersey Associates*, the territorial definition may be combined with a land use definition, so that assessments are imposed, for instance, only on commercial users in a district. These definitions may be challenged as underinclusive, which is similar to the argument that a benefit is general, and therefore ought not to be financed by an assessment at all. *See, e.g.*, Grais v. City of Chicago, 601 N.E.2d 745 (Ill.1992) (downtown commercial landowners contended unsuccessfully that "owners of property outside the perimeter and residential property inside the perimeter should share in the cost" of downtown transit system "because providing public transportation is a general function of government, and because all the property will benefit from the special service."). Courts may uphold the definition of the assessment district when all property subject to assessment benefits even if property outside the district also benefits.

Conversely, a landowner may claim that the assessment district is overinclusive, and that her property should not be assessed because it does not benefit from the improvement. A landowner whose property would not benefit from an improvement has a constitutional right to be excluded from the assessment district. *See, e.g.*, Myles Salt Co. v. Board of Commissioners, 239 U.S. 478 (1916). Courts, however, tend to be relatively deferential to legislative determinations that a property would benefit from an improvement. *See, e.g.*, Duncan Development Corp. v. Crestview Sanitary Dist., 125 N.W.2d 617 (Wis.1964). Thus, in a case involving owners of land at a high elevation who opposed their inclusion in a flood control district, the California Supreme Court found:

> To say . . . that any given possible tract of land is not directly subject to overflow is not to say that it cannot be benefitted. . . . [C]ourts have regarded an incidental or indirect benefit as sufficient to justify the imposition of a part of the burden of the improvement. Such indirect benefit may result from the improvement of the neighboring and surrounding land, and the consequent increase in the value of all land within the district. . . . At least, it is impossible to say that the Legislature could not fairly so determine. . . . Apart from any other consideration, the protection of the roads in any one of the water sheds, and the maintenance of communications with others might be a matter of very direct concern to all of the land embraced within the district.

Los Angeles County Flood Control Dist. v. Hamilton, 169 P. 1028, 1031 (Cal.1917). *Accord*, Albuquerque Metro. Arroyo Flood Control Auth. v. Swinburne, 394 P.2d 998 (N.M.1964). *But see* Douglass v. Spokane Co., 64 P.3d 71 (Wash. App. 2003) (properties not connected to sewer improvement project did not benefit from it and so could not be subject to special assessment to pay for it); Harrison v. Board of Supervisors, 118 Cal.Rptr. 828 (Ct.App.1975) (property may not be subject to a storm sewer special assessment when neither the property itself nor private properties and streets in the immediate vicinity had experienced flooding problems).

In Evans v. City of San Jose, 4 Cal.Rptr.2d 601 (Ct.App.1992), the owner of an apartment house challenged the imposition of a BID assessment. She contended that her apartment building would not benefit from downtown promotional activities the assessment would fund. The California court, however, deferred to the determination of the city council "that downtown promotion inures to the benefit of businesses and landlords within the BID." *Id.* at 608.

In *2nd Roc-Jersey Associates*, the Morristown SID excluded residential properties from the assessment, an action subsequently ratified by the New Jersey legislature. Suppose, however, that New Jersey law permitted a SID to assess residential property, and the Morristown SID had done so. In light of the services performed by the SID, should a court affirm that determination?

In determining whether a property benefits from an assessment, courts generally hold that potential future use, not just present use, must be taken into account. An improvement may be funded by an assessment even if it does not benefit the owner's current use. *See, e.g.*, Gray v. City of Indianola, 797 N.W.2d 112 (Ia. 2011); Horak Prairie Farm, L.P. v. City of Cedar Rapids, 748 N.W.2d 504 (Ia. 2008). *But cf.* D'Antuono v. City of Springfield, 180 N.E.2d 607, 610 (Ohio App.1960) ("It is well established that assessments may be based on potential and prospective benefits to land, but an assessment that completely ignores the difference in value between an immediate opportunity of use and a use that is prospective only is generally regarded as arbitrary and unreasonable. Here the prospective benefits appear too speculative and remote to justify the assessment.").

(b) *How Much May a Landowner Be Required to Pay?* There are two limits on the size of an assessment. First, total assessments imposed for a project may not exceed the cost of the project even if the sum of the individual benefits are well in excess of total costs. This prevents the government from using the assessment to realize a net revenue gain. Second, with respect to each individual landowner, the payment required may not exceed the benefit, defined as increase in market value, provided by the improvement. If the sum of the individual benefits is less than the total cost, the municipality or district must make up the difference from general revenues.

How was individual benefit determined in *McNally*? The process in New Jersey combined three factors—allocating the project cost among landowners according to a formula; use of assessment commissioners to review the preliminary allocation; and opportunity for landowners to demonstrate that their assessments exceeded their benefits. The initial allocations relied on front-footage, that is, the amount of linear feet attributable to each parcel's street frontage. Front-footage is a common method of calculating the benefit to an individual parcel. It reflects the widespread use of the special assessment to fund linear facilities like streets, sidewalks, and sewers. Does this strike you as an acceptable method for determining individual benefit? How important was the role of the assessment commissioners? How important was the presumption in favor of the accuracy of the assessment? What did it take for a landowner to overcome that presumption?

In *2nd Roc*, the court agreed with the legislature and the Morristown SID that the benefit to an individual parcel could be based on its assessed valuation. How well do you think this mechanism captures individual benefits? How does it differ from a non-uniform increase in the property tax? The court emphasized the difficulty of calculating individual benefits from area-wide services not tied to specific parcels. Does that justify greater deference to the assessment methodology of the SID or greater skepticism about whether an assessment should be used at all?

Does the court's public policy argument for the SID justify the use of the assessment device? Historically, the special assessment was often a one-shot device to fund basic facilities for new areas. As Professor Stephen Diamond has suggested, the special assessment operated as a kind of admission charge for residents of newly developed city districts. Residents in older parts of the city, who had already paid for their own streets, sidewalks, and sewers, resented being taxed to finance improvements for newer parts of town. The newcomers were forced to shoulder the costs of their infrastructure through assessments, but then "[o]nce that entrance fee into the municipal general tax pool had been paid," public financing of general services would follow. *See* Diamond, *supra*, 12 J. Leg. Stud. at 238. BIDs, however, serve older commercial areas, rather than newer residential ones. Nor does the BID cease operation once the new infrastructure is in place. BIDs are, potentially, long-term structures. Do you think the problems of downtown urban areas, as outlined by the court, justify this contemporary adaptation of the assessment?

A central issue in both *McNally* and *2nd Roc* was equity among the class of assessment-payers. Even assuming no landowner's assessment is greater than his benefit, should it be a matter of concern if one landowner's assessment represents a higher fraction of his benefit than does his neighbor's? As noted, the Uniformity Clause is generally not directly applicable to assessments. Should uniformity concerns apply even if the clause itself is inapplicable?

4. *State Constitutional Limits on the Special Assessment.* The spread of TELs has led to the growing use of special assessments which are often exempt from tax limitations. In California, the leading case was Knox v. City of Orland, 841 P.2d 144 (Cal. 1992), in which the California Supreme Court upheld a city's levy on real property to fund park maintenance as a special assessment, and so not subject to Proposition 13's requirement of voter approval for new taxes. In response, California voters in 1996 approved Proposition 218, which added Articles XIII C and XIII D to the state constitution, and extended Proposition 13's limitations on ad valorem taxes and special taxes to assessments and property-related fees and charges, including the two-thirds vote requirement. The amendment narrowed the definition of "special benefit" necessary to justify an assessment by providing that "general enhancement of property value does not constitute 'special benefit.'" Art. XIII D, § 2(i). A government proposing an assessment must calculate the "proportionate special benefit derived by each identified parcel" subject to the assessment, with proportionate special benefit "determined in relationship to . . . the capital cost of a public improvement, the maintenance and operation expenses of a public improvement, or the cost of the property related service being provided." Art. XIII D, § 4(a). Moreover, the assessment must be submitted to the vote of the landowners subject to assessment, with their ballots weighted according to the amount they are to be assessed. For an analysis of the voting rights issues raised by this procedure, *see* Derek P. Cole, Special Assessment Law Under California's Proposition 218 and the Open Person-One Vote Doctrine, 29 McGeorge L. Rev. 845 (1998). Silicon Valley Taxpayers Ass'n v. Santa Clara Co. Open Space Auth., 187 P.3d 37 (Cal. 2008), illustrates the impact of the

amendment. In that case, the California Supreme Court determined that the Santa Clara County Open Space Authority failed to carry its burden of proof that the proposed assessment of 314,000 property owners for the funding of the purchase of open space in an eight hundred square mile district would provide a special benefit to the landowners subject to assessment. The authority claimed that the increased open space would result in increased economic activity, expanded employment opportunity, and improved public health; in reduced crime; and in the enhancement of the overall quality of life of people living and working in the proposed assessment district. But the court found that the authority had failed to link specific benefits to specific properties. The assessment had been narrowly approved by a majority of the votes cast by landowners (with votes weighted according to the amount each parcel was to be assessed), but the court emphasized that under Proposition 218 an assessment must also meet the substantive requirement that individual benefits be proportional to individual assessments.

5. *Benefits Taxes*. Special assessments are assessments against landowners. But the benefit principle underlying the special assessment has a wider scope. Notwithstanding the general requirement of uniformity, states and localities may target a special tax on a narrowly defined subset of the community when the revenues from the tax are used to fund a program that benefits the taxpayers. A pair of Illinois cases involving the renovation of Chicago's McCormick Place exhibition hall illustrate this technique.

In Geja's Café v. Metropolitan Pier & Exposition Authority, 606 N.E.2d 1212 (Ill.1992), the Illinois Supreme Court sustained the imposition of a 1% retailers' occupation tax on sales of food and beverages in three narrowly drawn districts. In addition to its limited territorial scope, the tax applied only to the sales of food or beverage consumed (i) on the premises where sold or (ii) off the premises when sold by a restaurant or full service bar. The revenues generated by the taxes were to be used to fund construction of a convention center and renovation of an existing exhibition hall. Restaurant owners in the taxing districts argued that the territorial lines, and the distinctions between food and beverage sellers and other retailers and between sale of carry-out food purchased at restaurants and carry-out food from grocery stores, violated the Uniformity Clause of the state constitution. Rejecting their challenge, the Court held that the tax could be limited to "the class of persons . . . likely to benefit directly from a particular project while exempting those who will benefit only indirectly." *Id.* at 1218. Recognizing that although residents and retailers throughout the Chicago area might benefit to some degree from the convention center project, the court asserted:

> Where taxes are imposed based on the benefits realized by a particular group, the taxing body is not required to tax everyone who may receive a benefit, no matter how indirect. Instead the taxing body may decide to tax only those who are likely to benefit in a direct and immediate way.

Id. The Court held that the Authority had met "minimum standards of reasonableness and fairness" in justifying the territorial and commercial distinctions drawn by the tax. *Id.* In particular, the court agreed that as conventioneers from out of town were far more likely to take out prepared foods from restaurants rather than buy groceries in order to prepare meals in their hotel rooms, the tax's distinction between restaurants and grocery stores was reasonable.

In Allegro Services Ltd. v. Metropolitan Pier & Exposition Auth., 665 N.E.2d 1246 (Ill.1996), the Court reaffirmed its determination that taxation according to benefit satisfied the Illinois Uniformity Clause, while indicating a willingness to defer to governmental determinations of benefit. *Allegro Services* involved challenges to the imposition of an airport departure tax on providers of ground transportation services from Chicago's airports. Again, the revenues would be used to defray the cost of improvements to Chicago's McCormick Place. Among those taxed were not simply those companies that brought passengers to Chicago, but also bus, van and limousine services that transported arriving passengers to the Chicago suburbs. These companies, which were not licensed to operate in the City of Chicago, complained that they would not benefit from the improvements financed by the tax and, thus, could not be subject to the tax.

The Illinois Supreme Court rejected the argument, finding that non-Chicago service providers would benefit in at least two ways. First, as the Chicago-licensed service providers could also operate outside the city, "the generally increased demand for transportation from the airports into the city owing to the McCormick Place expansion project" will reduce competition from city-licensed operators for the suburban market. Second, the demand for downtown hotel rooms during major McCormick Place events "is likely to divert other visitors to hotels in the suburbs thereby increasing the demand for transportation from the airports to those hotels." *Id.* at 1254. Although plaintiffs protested "that these benefits are too indirect in comparison with the benefits to city-licensed operators, . . . the benefits identified are nonetheless tangible and would appear to represent reasonable conclusions about the dynamics of related market forces in the local economy." *Id.* at 1255. Do you agree that the benefits to the suburban airport transportation service operators from the McCormick Place renovations are sufficiently greater than the benefits to Chicago area firms and residents generally to justify subjecting those operators to the McCormick Place benefits tax?

Special taxes may also be imposed on firms to pay for the costs of programs attributable to the firms' activities. *See, e.g.,* Arangold Corp. v. Zehnder, 787 N.E.2d 786 (Ill. 2003) (sustaining tax imposed on wholesale distributors of noncigarette tobacco products to fund program for long-term care for the indigent, noting evidence of the connection between use of tobacco products and diseases that could require long-term care for the indigent). *But cf.* U.S.G. Italian Marketplace, L.L.C. v. City of Chicago, 775 N.E.2d 47, 54 (Ill. App. 2002) (striking down litter tax ordinance imposed on retail sale of carry-out food; the tax applied to businesses that sold food for both eat-in and carry-out consumption but not to businesses that sold only carry-out food; that distinction was "not reasonably related" to the "legislative purpose of raising revenue in order to remove and dispose of litter caused by patrons of places for eating which sell carry-out food, nor is it reasonably related to the City's stated purpose of reducing the amount of litter generated").

6. *Equity Considerations in Benefits Taxation.* In *2nd Roc*, the special assessment was challenged by some downtown businesses on the theory that it was unfair to subject them to an assessment that financed a community-wide benefit. In other cases, however, people outside an assessment district argue that relying on the special assessment device to fund a service or improvement is unfair because it means that those districts with more resources will get better public services while poorer districts may get inferior services and fewer physical improvements.

Thus, in Prattville, Alabama, the city's practice was to pave local streets only when 51% of the property owners on the street indicated to the city that they would be willing to pay a street paving assessment. As a result, the streets were paved in front of the homes of 97% of white residents but only 65% of black residents "due to the difference in the respective landowners' ability and willingness to pay for the property improvements." Hadnott v. City of Prattville, 309 F.Supp. 967, 970 (M.D.Ala.1970). *Hadnott* determined that reliance on the assessment, and hence ability to pay, did not violate the Equal Protection Clause. Later courts have found that although use of the special assessment is not per se unconstitutional, discriminatory use will constitute an equal protection violation. *See, e.g.,* Williams v. City of Dothan, 818 F.2d 755 (11th Cir.1987) (city's action in contributing 14.8% of cost of a water and sewer improvement project in predominantly black area compared with an average of 31.43% of cost contribution in predominantly white areas held to have a racially discriminatory effect); Ammons v. Dade City, 783 F.2d 982 (11th Cir.1986) (assessment policy to fund street paving applied in a racially discriminatory manner when city required residents of black area, but not of white areas, to pay for assessment in advance of receiving improvement, city paved some streets without requiring assessments, and city frequently forgave assessment liens). The issues surrounding equality claims in the provision of public services are discussed in Chapter VII.

b. Regulatory Fees and User Charges

Regulatory fees and user charges are a significant source of local revenues. In 2013, fees and charges, including fees for utility services, accounted for approximately 18% of all of state and local government revenue and 28% of own-source revenues. U.S. Census Bureau, State and Local Government Finance: 2013 State and Local Government. The spread of TELs since the adoption of Proposition 13 has contributed significantly to the increased use of fees and charges.

The cases in this section illustrate three broad categories of fees and charges. One type grows out of the public regulatory side of state and local governments. When an activity imposes costs on the community that justify governmental regulation, the community can require a license, inspection, or permit as a precondition for that activity. Moreover, the licensing governmental unit may charge the regulated entity for the costs associated with the implementation of the licensing scheme. *See, e.g.,* Trent Meredith, Inc. v. City of Oxnard, 170 Cal.Rptr. 685 (Cal.App.1981) (fees charged for building permit); Mills v. County of Trinity, 166 Cal.Rptr. 674 (Cal.App.1980) (fees for processing subdivision, zoning, and land use applications). *Sinclair Paint Co. v. State Board of Equalization,* the first case in this section, raises questions about the scope of governmental discretion to define the regulatory costs to be recouped by a fee.

A second set of charges grows out of the proprietary side of state and local governments. Local governments have traditionally been able to charge for commercial uses of public lands, such as the refreshment concession in a city park, or access to a public right of way to string telephone wire or lay cables. *City of Gary v. Indiana Bell,* the next case in this section, reflects an effort to leverage municipal control over what the Indiana Supreme Court called "public grounds" into new revenue from telecommunications companies as they rewire or upgrade preexisting telephone services or install new facilities to meet the demands of the information age.

The third, and perhaps the most common, type of user charge is the utility fee, that is, a charge for publicly provided water, electric power, sewage services, etc. *City of Huntington v. Bacon* illustrates local efforts to extend the fee-for-service principle from the utility setting to core public services.

Like the special assessment, fees and charges are, legally, not taxes. They are, therefore, usually not subject to state constitutional constraints on taxation. Like the special assessment, the power to impose a fee grows out of the police power. User charges are, thus, appealing to state and local governments for legal reasons. But there are equity, efficiency, and fiscal rationales for user charges, too.

When a service is financed by a user charge, only the users of the service pay for it. Given that public services involve costs, it may be fair for payment to come from the people who benefit from the service. Certainly, it seems fairer to charge the costs of the municipal golf course to golfers than to force everyone in the city to pay for it. Similarly, the costs of regulating and overseeing bars, taverns and other places that sell alcohol may fairly be placed on the regulated businesses (and passed along by them to their customers) since they benefit from being allowed to do business.

Fees can promote efficiency by requiring the user of a municipal service to internalize the costs of her use. If the charge is set appropriately, consumers will use the service only when the benefit to them is greater than its cost. This discourages wasteful overuse, which is more likely when the costs of the service are spread across the entire community rather than just service users. Fees also send signals to governments about how much of a good or service to provide. Low demand ought to discourage overinvestment, while heavy demand would cause either increased supply or higher charges to reflect the higher value of the service. Moreover, if there are private alternatives to the municipally provided service, implementation of a user charge will make the municipality sensitive to revenue losses if consumers turn from the municipal to private providers and, thus, may provide the municipality with an incentive to be an efficient and responsive competitor.

Fiscally, user charges, which are restricted to funding the service for which the charge was imposed, tend to provide a more certain source of revenue than is the case for programs funded out of general revenue. Because user fees are exempted from redistribution to other programs, they provide a guaranteed funding base.

User charges may also raise equity, efficiency, and fiscal concerns. Although from one perspective, it may be fair to require people to pay for what they use, allocation of services on the basis of ability to pay can have the effect of reducing consumption by low-income people. If there is a broad social interest in universal availability of a particular service, the fee might have to be set below the cost of providing the service—or dropped altogether—to avoid excluding people who cannot otherwise afford to pay. Further, both the equity and the efficiency of the user charge turns on the extent to which the full benefits of the service are realized by the person subject to the charge. Some services may provide broad social benefits to the community at large, as well as to the immediate user. In that case, financing the service solely from a user charge would be unfair and unwise, since many indirect beneficiaries of the service would not contribute to its operation and the user charge would not reflect the full social benefit of the service. Thus, for instance, the benefits of mass transit systems extend beyond the mass transit riders who use the system and pay the fares. Motorists, who enjoy reduced traffic congestion, and local residents generally, who enjoy reduced air pollution, also benefit. Consequently, it would be ill-advised to place the full cost of the mass transit system on riders. If riders were charged the full cost of the system, the number of riders would decrease, and motorists and residents generally would be worse off. In practice, most transit systems rely on both fares and general tax dollars for financing.

Even the fiscal benefits of user charge financing may be debated. Fees and charges are most usable for goods and services whose consumption may be limited to those who pay the charge. This may mean that those services will be well-funded. However, services that cannot use fees or charges, or for which fees and charges are inappropriate because the service is intended to be redistributive, may be inadequately funded. Moreover, when user fees are earmarked for the service funded by the charge, there may be no possibility of transfer to services funded out of general revenues. For a critical assessment of the impact of the growing use of special assessments and fees in local finance, *see* Laurie Reynolds, Taxes, Fees, Assessments, Dues, and the "Get What You Pay For" Model of Local Government, 56 Fla. L. Rev. 373 (2004).

SINCLAIR PAINT CO. V. STATE BOARD OF EQUALIZATION
Supreme Court of California
937 P.2d 1350 (1997)

CHIN, J.

In 1991, by simple majority vote, the Legislature enacted the Childhood Lead Poisoning Prevention Act of 1991 (the Act). The Act provided evaluation, screening, and medically necessary follow-up services for children who were deemed potential victims of lead poisoning. The Act's program was entirely supported by "fees" assessed on manufacturers or other persons contributing to environmental lead contamination. The question arises whether these fees were in legal effect "taxes" required to be enacted by a two-thirds vote of the Legislature. (*See* Cal. Const., art. XIII A, § 3.)

Contrary to the trial court and Court of Appeal, we conclude that the Act imposed bona fide regulatory fees, not taxes, because the Legislature imposed the fees to mitigate the actual or anticipated adverse effects of the fee payers' operations, and under the Act the amount of the fees must bear a reasonable relationship to those adverse effects. * * *

When the Legislature enacted the Act in 1991, it explained the Act's background and purpose in findings that described the numerous health hazards children face when exposed to lead toxicity and declared four state "goals," namely, (1) evaluating, screening, and providing case management for children at risk of lead poisoning, (2) identifying sources of lead contamination responsible for this poisoning, (3) identifying and utilizing programs providing adequate case management for children found to have lead poisoning, and (4) providing education on lead-poisoning detection and case management to state health care providers.

The Act directs the Department to adopt regulations establishing a standard of care for evaluation, screening (i.e., measuring lead concentration in blood), and medically necessary follow-up services for children determined to be at risk of lead poisoning. If a child is identified as being at risk of lead poisoning, the Department must ensure "appropriate case management," i.e., "health care referrals, environmental assessments, and educational activities" needed to reduce the child's exposure to lead and its consequences. Additionally, the Act requires the Department to collect data and report on the effectiveness of case management efforts. * * *

The Act states that its program of evaluation, screening, and follow-up is supported *entirely* by fees * * * impose[d] * * * on manufacturers and other persons formerly and/or presently engaged in the stream of commerce of lead or products containing lead, or who are otherwise responsible for identifiable sources of lead, which have significantly contributed and/or currently contribute to environmental lead contamination. The Department must determine fees based on the manufacturer's or other person's past and present responsibility for environmental lead contamination, or its "market share" responsibility for this contamination.

Those persons able to show that their industry did not contribute to environmental lead contamination, or that their lead-containing product does not and did not "result in quantifiably persistent environmental lead contamination," are exempt from paying the fees.

* * * Section 3 of article XIII A [Proposition 13] restricts the enactment of changes in state taxes, as follows:

"From and after the effective date of this article, any changes in State taxes enacted for the purpose of increasing revenues collected pursuant thereto whether by increased taxes or changes in methods of computation must be imposed by an Act passed by not less than two-thirds of all members . . . of the Legislature, except that no new ad valorem taxes on real property, or sales or transaction taxes on the sales of real property may be imposed."

* * * Are the "fees" section 105310 imposes in legal effect "taxes enacted for the purpose of increasing revenues" under article XIII A, section 3, and therefore subject to a two-thirds majority vote? * * *

We first consider certain general guidelines used in determining whether "taxes" are involved in particular situations. * * * The cases recognize that "tax" has no fixed meaning, and that the distinction between taxes and fees is frequently "blurred," taking on different meanings in different contexts. * * * In general, taxes are imposed for revenue purposes, rather than in return for a specific benefit conferred or privilege granted. * * * Most taxes are compulsory rather than imposed in response to a voluntary decision to develop or to seek other government benefits or privileges. * * * But compulsory fees may be deemed legitimate fees rather than taxes.

* * *

The cases uniformly hold that *special assessments* on property or similar business charges, in amounts reasonably reflecting the value of the benefits conferred by improvements, are not "special taxes" under article XIII A, section 4. * * *

Similarly, *development fees* exacted in return for building permits or other governmental privileges are not special taxes if the amount of the fees bears a reasonable relation to the development's probable costs to the community and benefits to the developer. * * *

According to Sinclair, because the present fees have been imposed solely to defray the cost of the state's program of evaluation, screening, and follow-up services for children determined to be at risk for lead poisoning, they are not analogous to either special assessments or development fees, for they neither reimburse the state for special benefits conferred on manufacturers of lead-based products nor compensate the state for governmental privileges granted to those manufacturers. As the Court of Appeal observed, the fees challenged here "do not constitute payment for a government benefit or service. The program described in the Act bears no resemblance to regulatory schemes involving special assessments, developer fees, or efforts to recoup the cost of processing land use applications where the benefit analysis is typically applied. The face of the Act makes clear the funds collected are used to benefit children exposed to lead, not Sinclair or other manufacturers in the stream of commerce for products containing lead."

Appellants argue, however, that the challenged fees fall squarely within a third recognized category not dependent on government-conferred benefits or privileges, namely, *regulatory fees* imposed under the police power, rather than the taxing power. We agree.

We have acknowledged that the term "special taxes" in article XIII A, section 4, " 'does not embrace fees charged in connection with regulatory activities which fees do not exceed the reasonable cost of providing services necessary to the activity for which the fee is charged and which are not levied for unrelated revenue purposes.' [Citations.]" (*Pennell v. City of San Jose* (1986) 42 Cal.3d 365, 375 (*Pennell*), affd. on other grounds *sub nom. Pennell v. San Jose* (1988) 485 U.S. 1 * * *.

Pennell upheld rental unit fees that a city imposed under its rent control ordinance to assure it recovered the actual costs of providing and administering a rental dispute hearing process. We explained in *Pennell* that regulatory fees in amounts necessary to carry out the regulation's purpose are valid despite the absence of any perceived "benefit" accruing to the fee payers. * * *

We observe that Sinclair, in moving for summary judgment, did not contend that the fees exceed in amount the reasonable cost of providing the protective services for which the fees are charged, or that the fees were levied for any unrelated revenue purposes. Moreover, Sinclair has not yet sought to establish that the amount of the fees bears no reasonable relationship to the social or economic "burdens" that Sinclair's operations generated. * * * Sinclair does contend, however, that the Act is not regulatory in nature, being primarily aimed at producing revenue.

According to Sinclair, the challenged fees were in effect "taxes" because the compulsory revenue measure that imposed them was not part of a regulatory effort. The Court of Appeal agreed, relying on prior cases indicating that where payments are exacted solely for revenue purposes and give the right to carry on the business with no further conditions, they are taxes. The Court of Appeal held that "Placing the factors distinguishing taxes and fees along a continuum, we conclude the monies paid by Sinclair pursuant to the Act are more like taxes than fees. *There is nothing on the face of the Act to show the fees collected are used to regulate Sinclair.* Apart from mere calculation of the payment, the Department's regulatory authority involves implementation of the program to evaluate, screen, and provide followup services to children at risk for lead poisoning. The Act does not require Sinclair to comply with any other conditions; it merely requires Sinclair to pay what the Department determines to be its share of the program cost."

Contrary to the Court of Appeal, we believe [the Act] imposes bona fide regulatory fees. It requires manufacturers and other persons whose products have exposed children to lead contamination to bear a fair share of the cost of mitigating the adverse health effects their products created in the community. Viewed as a "mitigating effects" measure, it is comparable in character to similar police power measures imposing fees to defray the actual or anticipated adverse effects of various business operations.

From the viewpoint of general police power authority, we see no reason why statutes or ordinances calling on polluters or producers of contaminating products to help in mitigation or cleanup efforts should be deemed less "regulatory" in nature than the initial permit or licensing programs that allowed them to operate. Moreover, imposition of "mitigating effects" fees in a substantial amount (Sinclair allegedly paid $97,825.26 in 1991) also "regulates" future conduct by deterring further manufacture, distribution, or sale of dangerous products, and by stimulating research and development efforts to produce safer or alternative products. * * *

SDG&E [*San Diego Gas & Elec. Co. v. San Diego Co. Pollution Control Dist.* (Cal. App. 1988)] involved regulatory fees comparable in some respects to the fees challenged here. There, 1982 legislation empowered local air pollution control districts to apportion the costs of their permit programs among all monitored polluters according to a formula based on the amount of emissions they discharged. * * * The *SDG&E* court observed that "to show a fee is a regulatory fee and not a special tax, the government should prove (1) the estimated costs of the service or regulatory activity, and (2) the basis for determining the manner in which the costs are apportioned, so that charges allocated to a payor bear a fair or reasonable relationship to the payor's burdens on or benefits from the regulatory activity." * * *

In SDG&E, the amount of the regulatory fees was limited to the reasonable costs of each district's program, and the allocation of costs based on emissions "fairly relates to the permit holder's burden on the district's programs." Accordingly, the court concluded that the fees were not "special taxes" under article XIII A, section 4. (*SDG&E, supra*, 203 Cal.App.3d at p. 1148.)

As the court observed in *SDG&E*, "Proposition 13's goal of providing effective property tax relief is not subverted by the increase in fees or the emissions-based apportionment formula. A reasonable way to achieve Proposition 13's goal of tax relief is to shift the costs of controlling stationary sources of pollution from the tax-paying public to the pollution-causing industries themselves. . . ." (*SDG&E, supra*, 203 Cal.App.3d at p. 1148.) In our view, the shifting of costs of providing evaluation, screening, and medically necessary follow-up services for potential child victims of lead poisoning from the public to those persons deemed responsible for that poisoning is likewise a reasonable police power decision. * * *

The fact that the challenged fees were charged after, rather than before, the product's adverse effects were realized is immaterial to the question whether the measure imposes valid regulatory fees rather than taxes. *City of Oakland v. Superior Court* seems close on point. There, the court upheld city fees imposed on retailers of alcoholic beverages to defray the cost of providing and administering hearings into nuisance problems associated with the prior sale of those beverages. The court first observed that "If a business imposes an unusual burden on city services, a municipality may properly impose fees pursuant to its police powers" to assure that the persons responsible "pay their fair share of the cost of government." (*City of Oakland v. Superior Court, supra*, 45 Cal.App.4th at p. 761.) The court concluded that "The ordinance's primary purpose is regulatory—to create an environment in which nuisance and criminal activities associated with alcoholic beverage retail establishments may be reduced or eliminated. Thus, the fee imposed . . . is not a tax imposed to pay general revenue to the local governmental entity, but is a regulatory fee intended to defray the cost of providing and administering the hearing process set out in the ordinance." (*Id.* at p. 762.)

The court in *United Business* [*United Business Com. v. City of San Diego* (Cal. App. 1979)] applied the "regulation/revenue" distinction to conclude that sign inventory fees adopted to recover the city's cost of inventorying signs and bringing them into conformance with law were regulatory fees, not revenue-raising taxes. The court observed that, under the police power, municipalities may impose fees for the purpose of legitimate regulation, and not mere revenue-raising, if the fees do not exceed the reasonably necessary expense of the regulatory effort.) Quoting with approval from an earlier decision, the court noted that, if revenue is the primary purpose, and regulation is merely incidental, the imposition is a tax, but if regulation is the primary purpose, the mere fact that revenue is also obtained does not make the imposition a tax. Moreover, according to *United Business*, if a fee is exacted for revenue purposes, and its payment gives the right to carry on business without any further conditions, it is a tax. * * *

The Court of Appeal, citing *United Business*, stressed that the challenged fees were exacted solely for revenue purposes, and their payment gave Sinclair and others the right to carry on the business without any further conditions. We see two flaws in that analysis. First, all regulatory fees are necessarily aimed at raising "revenue" to defray the cost of the regulatory program in question, but that fact does not automatically render those fees "taxes." As stated in *United Business*, if regulation is the primary purpose of the fee measure, the mere fact that the measure also generates revenue does not make the imposition a tax. * * *

Second, we find inconclusive the fact that the Act permits Sinclair and other producers to carry on their operations without any further conditions specified in the Act itself. As we have indicated, fees can "regulate" business entities without directly licensing them by mitigating their operations' adverse effects. * * *

Accordingly, we conclude the trial court erred in granting Sinclair summary judgment on the constitutional issues. Of course, Sinclair should be permitted to attempt to prove at trial that the amount of fees assessed and paid exceeded the reasonable cost of providing the protective services for which the fees were charged, or that the fees were levied for unrelated revenue purposes. Additionally, Sinclair will have the opportunity to try to show that no clear nexus exists between its products and childhood lead poisoning, or that the amount of the fees bore no

772   STATE AND LOCAL FINANCE   CH. VI

reasonable relationship to the social or economic "burdens" its operations generated.

CITY OF GARY, INDIANA V. INDIANA BELL TELEPHONE CO.

Supreme Court of Indiana
732 N.E.2d 149 (2000)

SULLIVAN, J:

Ameritech Indiana sought declaratory and injunctive relief to prevent the City of Gary from imposing a "requirements-based fee" on telecommunications providers using City rights-of-way. The trial court declared the fee void as an improper tax issued beyond the City's powers. We reverse in part, finding that the City was initially entitled to charge compensation for the private, commercial use of its real estate, until the legislature affirmatively said otherwise.

On January 6, 1998, the City of Gary enacted Ordinance Nos. 6970 & 6971, which were signed by the Mayor two days later. Ordinance No. 6970 establishes a telecommunications policy for the City and creates the Gary Access, Information, and Telecommunications Trust ("GAITT") to, inter alia, "[e]nsure that telecommunications is available as a community resource for individuals, organizations, and businesses on an affordable basis." The GAITT is charged with several responsibilities under Ordinance No. 6970, including the development, implementation, and collection of fees comprising fair and reasonable compensation for the commercial use of public rights-of-way.

Ordinance No. 6971 is a companion ordinance that imposes a "requirements-based fee" on all telecommunications providers using the City's rights-of-way. The total "requirements-based fee" for 1998 was to be $20,000,000. This initial aggregate fee represented "approximately fifteen percent of the telecommunications providers' local revenues, based on the national average revenue per capita reported by the U.S. census," with credits for public, educational, and government access, as well as institutional access. Ameritech Indiana's share of this total initial fee was $3.2 million* * *. Ordinance No. 6971 contemplates telecommunications providers discharging some or all of their "requirements-based fee" by furnishing in-kind telecommunications services. In future years, the total "requirements-based fee" would be calculated in one of three ways: (1) based upon an assessment of the City's "requirements," (2) based upon a percentage not to exceed 15% of the providers' gross revenues, or (3) based upon a "growth factor" calculated from the providers' telecommunications revenues multiplied by the previous year's "requirements-based fee."

* * *

We begin our analysis by looking to Indiana's Home Rule Act. Pub.L. No. 211, 1980 Ind. Acts 1657 (codified as amended at Ind.Code §§ 36–1–3–1 to –9 (1993)). The Home Rule Act abrogated the traditional rule that local governments possessed only those powers expressly authorized by statute and declared that a local government possesses "[a]ll other powers necessary or desirable in the conduct of its affairs." Ind.Code § 36–1–3–4(b)(2). * * *

Among the various powers "need[ed] for the effective operation of government as to [its] local affairs," Ind.Code § 36–1–3–2, are those labeled *proprietary* whereby local governments "act[ ] in a private or proprietary capacity" for the "peculiar and special advantage of its inhabitants, rather than for the good of the State at large," *Taylor v. State*, 663 N.E.2d 213, 216–17 (Ind.Ct.App.1996).

A local government's specified power to manage the "public grounds" falling within its borders, *see* Ind.Code § 36–1–3–9(a), includes the unspecified power to operate in a proprietary capacity to charge fair and reasonable compensation for the private, commercial use of these public grounds, irrespective of the label placed on the compensation. * * *

In determining that the fee was an improper tax, the trial court found it significant that "Gary has offered no authority for the proposition that a municipality may charge rent for use of public rights of way by public utilities operating under certificates of territorial authority issued by the IURC." As we just explained, however, the Home Rule Act abrogated the traditional rule that local governments possessed only those powers expressly authorized by statute. * * *

Simply put, the City of Gary need not have the specific statutory authorization to charge companies compensation for commercial use of its real estate to generate private profit. * * *

In *Ace Rent-A-Car* [*v. Indianapolis Airport Authority*, 612 N.E.2d 1104 (Ind.App.1993)], the governing entity was the Indianapolis Airport Authority ("IAA"), a municipal corporation empowered with the *specific* authority to " 'adopt a schedule of reasonable charges and to collect them from all users of facilities and services within the district.' " *Id.* at 1106 (quoting Ind.Code § 8–22–3–1 (1993)). As such, the IAA imposed "a fee upon all off-airport car rental companies, along with all off-site hotels, motels and parking lots for the privilege of using airport roadways to operate their shuttle services." *Id.* As the fee pertained to off-airport car rental companies, they "would be assessed a fee of 7% of all sales for the rental of automobiles to customers originating at the airport." *Id.* (internal quotations omitted). * * *

Ultimately, the court concluded that "the airport's very existence provides a marketplace from which Ace Rent-A-Car derives an economic benefit," so that a user fee "based on a percent of the rental sales of automobiles made to customers originating at the airport represents at least one fair, although imperfect, method of measuring 'use'." *Id.* at 1107–08 (relying in part on *Alamo Rent-a-Car v. Sarasota-Manatee Airport Auth.*, 906 F.2d 516, 519, 521–22 (11th Cir.1990), *cert. denied*, 498 U.S. 1120 (1991) (deeming a broad construction of the term "use" as appropriate where the benefit derived by the user depended on the existence of the entire airport facility)).

Here, Gary rights-of-way provide a marketplace from which Ameritech derives an economic benefit, so that Gary's fee, based in part on a percentage of the company's gross revenues, is at least one fair, if imperfect, method of measuring Ameritech's use of Gary rights-of-way. The revenue-based aspect of the fee does not ipso facto transform it into a tax.

Furthermore, as the Court of Appeals in *Ace Rent-A-Car* noted,

> A tax is compulsory and not optional; it entitles the taxpayer to receive nothing in return, other than the rights of government which are enjoyed by all citizens. *Ennis v. State Highway Commission* (1952), 231 Ind. 311, 108 N.E.2d 687, 693. On the other hand, a user fee is optional and represents a specific charge for the use of publicly-owned or publicly-provided facilities or services. *Commonwealth Edison Co. v. Montana* (1981), 453 U.S. 609, 621–22.

Id. * * *

Ameritech receives considerably more "than the rights of government which are enjoyed by all citizens," *Ace Rent-A-Car*, 612 N.E.2d at 1108, when it conducts business in Gary rights-of-way. The requirements-based fee is not a tax but instead is compensation, representing a specific charge assessed against Ameritech for its commercial use of Gary-owned rights-of-way to generate private profit.

Next, the Court of Appeals invalidated Gary's requirements-based fee as an improper tax based on the City's avowed purpose to use the fee revenues "to finance improvements to communications networks in the City's schools and government buildings—the type of improvements normally funded by tax revenues." *City of Gary*, 711 N.E.2d at 83 (relying on *City of Portage v. Harrington*, 598 N.E.2d 634 (Ind.Ct.App.1992)).

Having found that the requirements-based fee is not an impermissible tax but is instead valid compensation charged by Gary for the private, commercial use of its real estate, we find it unnecessary to consider the purpose for which the fee revenues will be used. * * *

These determinations notwithstanding, we nevertheless agree with the Court of Appeals that Gary was without authority to charge the fee as of March 13, 1998. On this date, the Indiana Legislature amended

Indiana Code § 8–1–2–101(P.L. 127–1998) by adding new subsection (b) to prohibit municipalities from receiving any form of "payment" other than the "direct, actual, and reasonably incurred management costs" for a utility's occupation of a public right-of-way. *See City of Gary*, 711 N.E.2d at 84–85 ("A municipality cannot continue to enforce an ordinance that has been superseded by subsequent legislation of the General Assembly.").

The City of Gary emphatically argued both in its briefs and at oral argument that the 1998 amendment to Indiana Code § 8–1–2–101, adding subsection (b), only addressed "occupancy" of rights-of-way by utilities, thereby not preempting Gary's Home Rule powers to collect compensation for the "use" of rights-of-way.

However, in looking to the plain language of the statute—always our first line of inquiry—we cannot ignore the legislature's clear mandate that "direct, actual, and reasonably incurred *management costs* do not include rents, franchise fees, *or any other payment by a public utility. . . .*" Ind.Code § 8–1–2–101(b) (emphasis added). * * *

NOTES AND QUESTIONS

1. *Regulation or Revenue?* In *Sinclair*, the California Supreme Court placed a great deal of weight on the regulatory/revenue distinction. In theory, a fee is adopted to regulate the fee payer, whereas a tax is imposed to raise revenue. Yet, all fees raise revenue, and many taxes have the potential to regulate by discouraging the activity taxed. The court of appeals was influenced by the fact that the fee in question was not used to "regulate" Sinclair in the sense of covering the government's costs of determining whether the company abided by applicable rules or should be licensed to continue its operations. In what sense did the fee regulate Sinclair?

For a similar case, *see* Nuclear Metals, Inc. v. Low-Level Radioactive Waste Management Board, 656 N.E.2d 563 (Mass.1995), in which the Supreme Judicial Court of Massachusetts upheld the imposition of an assessment on the generators of low-level radioactive waste in the state to cover the operating costs of the state board charged with planning how the state would meet its obligations under federal law to dispose of the waste safely. The fee payers argued that "the board functions as a planning agency and provides no service for which it may legitimately exact a fee." The Court, however, found it "appropriate that the entities which generate low-level radioactive waste (and not the taxpayers of the Commonwealth) should shoulder costs associated with protecting the public from the hazards posed by the waste." *Id.* at 569. *See also* Apartment Ass'n of Los Angeles Co. v. City of Los Angeles, 14 P.3d 930 (Cal. 2001) (city ordinance imposing an inspection fee on private landlords not a tax on property within California's constitutional tax restrictions but is instead a regulatory fee on the business of renting or leasing apartments).

Charges may be treated as regulatory fees, not taxes, even when the activity regulated has broad public benefits. In *Silva v. City of Attleboro*, 892 N.E.2d 792 (Mass. App. 2008), a Massachusetts appeals court ruled that a charge imposed on funeral directors for the issuance of a burial permit was a tax, not a fee "because the payer of the fee derives no benefit that is not shared by the general public [as] proper interment is mandatory." *Id.* at 794. The Supreme Judicial Court reversed, emphasizing that the burial permit charge benefits the payers as well as the general public: "In exchange for payment of the burial permit charges, funeral directors and their clients (on whose behalf the former act) receive particularized benefits in the form of a well-regulated industry for the disposal of human remains. The administration of the burial permit process by municipal boards of health provides assurances that the decedent's body is disposed of properly. The process also helps to police the industry by allowing the board of health to ensure that funeral directors have complied with applicable regulations governing the disposition of human remains and to take action against those who do not." Silva v. City of Attleboro, 908 N.E.2d 722, 727 (Mass. 2009). The court also upheld the burial permit charges as fees because they were "reasonably proportional" to the expenses of the boards of health in administering the regulatory process even though the charges were deposited in the general fund and not in a fund dedicated to the specific regulatory program. *Id.* at 728–29. If the proceeds of a regulatory fee do greatly exceed the administrative costs of regulating the fee payer, the fee may be considered a revenue-raising device and, therefore, a tax. *See, e.g.*, President Riverboat Casino-Missouri, Inc. v. Missouri Gaming Commission, 13 S.W.3d 635 (Mo.2000) (admission fee on riverboat casinos held a tax where the receipts exceeded the Gaming Commission's administrative costs by a ratio of three-to-one for three consecutive fiscal years).

As taxes are typically more heavily regulated than fees, governments usually want a charge to be classified as a fee, not a tax, but sometimes the legal rules cut the other way. In Morning Star Co. v. Board of Equalization, 135 Cal.Rptr.3d 457 (Cal. App. 2011), the court found that an annual charge imposed on most businesses with at least fifty employees which use, generate, store or conduct activities in California related to hazardous materials was a tax and not a regulatory fee because "it does not seek to regulate the Company's use, generation or storage of hazardous material but to raise money for the control of hazardous material generally." *Id.* at 469. The court rejected arguments that the charge—imposed pursuant to a statute passed by two-thirds of the legislature, as required by the California constitution for new taxes—violated federal constitutional limits on taxes, noting "the deferential standard of review" and "rational basis test" used when state taxes are challenged on federal constitutional grounds. *Id.* at 470.

2. *After Sinclair.* In 2010, California voters approved Proposition 26, which amended articles XIII A and XIII C of the California Constitution to expand the definition of "tax" subject to the state legislative supermajority

and local voter approval requirements to include "any levy, charge or exaction of any kind," with certain specific exceptions, including:

- a "charge imposed for a specific benefit conferred or privilege granted [or specific government service or product provided] directly to the payor that is not provided to those not charged, and which does not exceed the reasonable costs ... of conferring the benefit or granting the privilege [or providing the service or product] to the payor;"

- a "charge imposed for reasonable regulatory costs ... incident to issuing licenses and permits, performing investigations, inspections, and audits ... and the administrative enforcement and adjudication thereof;"

- charges for entrance to or use, rental or lease of state or local government property;

- a "charge imposed as a condition of property development;" and

- fines and penalties imposed for violating the law.

The amendment placed on the charging government "the burden of proving by a preponderance of the evidence that a levy, charge, or other exaction is not a tax, that the amount is no more than necessary to cover the reasonable costs of the government activity, and that the manner in which those costs are allocated to a payor bears a fair or reasonable relationship to the payor's burdens on, or benefits received from, the governmental activity." Proposition 26 "was largely a response to *Sinclair Paint.*" Schmeer v. Co. of Los Angeles, 153 Cal.Rptr.3d 352, 361 (Cal. App. 2013). Had Proposition 26 been on the books when the charge at issue in *Sinclair Paint* was enacted, should the outcome of that case have been different? *See* Darien Shanske, Going Forward by Going Backward to Benefit Taxes, 3 Cal. J. Pol. & Pol'y 1, 5–9 (2011) (discussing likely impact of Proposition 26 and its relationship to *Sinclair*). *Cf. Schmeer, supra* (Proposition 26 inapplicable to Los Angeles county ordinance prohibiting retail stores from providing plastic carryout bags and requiring them to charge customers ten cents for each paper carryout bag provided; as the ten cent charge is paid to the stores and not remitted to the county it is not a "tax" without the meaning of Proposition 26).

3. *Local Rights-of-Way and Telecommunications Regulation.* The *City of Gary* court assumed that the city controlled its public rights of way in a proprietary capacity, that is, like a private landowner, rather than in a regulatory capacity. A regulatory fee would be limited to defraying the "direct, actual, and reasonably incurred management costs" of regulating Indiana Bell's use of the rights-of-way whereas a proprietary charge could be seen as the cost of renting the city's property and calculated as a percentage of the company's revenue attributable to use of the rights-of-way. The question of whether a city controls its rights-of-way as a proprietor or as a regulator is a contested one. *See* Gardner F. Gillespie, Rights-of-Way Redux:

Municipal Fees on Telecommunications Companies and Cable Operators, 107 Dick. L. Rev. 209 (2002) (arguing that a municipality is a regulator not proprietary owner of city rights-of-way). *See also* American Telephone & Telegraph Co. v. Village of Arlington Heights, 620 N.E.2d 1040, 1045 (Ill.1993) ("municipalities only have regulatory power over public streets and cannot charge tolls for their use"). Of course, even as a regulator a municipality may in some situations be able to contract with a utility for a payment based on a percentage of the utility's revenue. *See also* Burns v. City of Seattle, 164 P.3d 475 (Wash. 2007) (city could contract with a utility for payment based on percentage of utility's revenues in exchange for city's promise to forbear from establishing its own municipal utility). The municipal ability to use control over local rights-of-way to obtain payments from firms engaged in telecommunications activity is also affected by federal law. *See, e.g.*, Thomas W. Snyder and William Fitzsimmons, Putting a Price on Dirt: The Need for Better Defined Limits on Government Fees for Use of the Public Right-of-Way Under Section 253 of the Telecommunications Act of 1996, 64 Fed. Comm. L.J. 137 (2011).

4. *Home Rule and Preemption. City of Gary* turned on questions of home rule and preemption. Another case in which state-local conflict affected local authority to impose a fee is Boston Gas Co. v. City of Newton, 682 N.E.2d 1336 (Mass.1997), in which the city required public utility companies seeking to excavate a public right-of-way to pay an application fee of $25 and additional inspection and maintenance fees. The fee level depended on the extent of excavation and was set to cover the cost of city inspections and to take into account the city's projection of a 25% reduction in the useful life of streets and sidewalks due to the excavations. The Supreme Judicial Court held that the fees based on the reduction in useful life were preempted by a state law requiring utility companies that undertake excavations to restore all streets and highways to their condition prior to the excavation. The city's assumption that excavations would reduce the useful life of public ways was held to be inconsistent with the legislature's assumption that a street could be restored to its former condition; thus, the local fee was preempted. The court also concluded that the city's inspection fee was preempted by a provision of the state statute that "can be fairly read as placing the burden of fulfilling such statutory duties squarely on the shoulders of the public utility," *id.* at 1340, as well as by state laws providing for the regulation of public utilities by the state. The court, however, concluded that the city could impose the $25 application fee to cover its costs in processing applications for excavation permits. *Id.* at 1343.

BEATTY V. METROPOLITAN ST. LOUIS SEWER DISTRICT

Supreme Court of Missouri
867 S.W.2d 217 (1993)

ROBERTSON, JUDGE.

In this case we return to our continuing struggle to define the perimeters of the Hancock Amendment and particularly of Article X, Section 22(a) of the Missouri Constitution. The specific issue is whether the respondent may raise its sewer charges without approval of district voters. The trial court held that respondent could raise its charges without a vote, relying principally on this Court's recent decision in Keller v. Marion County Ambulance District, 820 S.W.2d 301 (Mo. banc 1991). A divided panel of the court of appeals reversed the judgment of the trial court and ordered respondent to submit its charges to the voters for approval. The court of appeals, en banc, ordered transfer of the case to this Court. We have jurisdiction, Mo. Const. art. V, § 10, and now reverse the judgment of the trial court and remand the case with directions to enter an order declaring respondent's charges subject to Article X, Section 22(a) of the Missouri Constitution.

Prior to 1954, various private and governmental entities provided sewer service to the residents of the City of St. Louis and St. Louis County. On February 9 of that year, the voters of the region adopted a plan to create the Metropolitan St. Louis Sewer District ("MSD") to provide an integrated sewer system for the City of St. Louis and a majority of St. Louis County. The plan required the mayor of the City of St. Louis and the county executive of St. Louis County to appoint a six-member board of trustees to operate MSD. The plan also gave that board authority to impose ad valorem taxes and establish charges for sewer services. Under the plan, MSD took title to most of the existing sanitary and storm water sewer systems within the boundaries of the district. Today, MSD serves approximately 420,000 accounts, including single and multifamily dwellings and commercial and industrial customers, and owns and operates an extensive system of collector and interceptor sewers and treatment plants, all of which are subject to state and federal regulation. The continued ability of MSD to maintain and improve its sewer collection and treatment facilities and meet increasingly demanding state and federal regulations depends on MSD's ability to provide a revenue stream sufficient for those purposes.

For residential property, the board imposes a flat fee for sewer service. The amount of the fee remains the same no matter how much waste a residential customer sends into the system. Nonresidential customers pay a base charge plus a charge measured by the volume of waste the property adds to the system. Nearly all of the property owners within MSD receive MSD sewer charges. Failure to pay a sewer charge results in a lien against real property by operation of law. MSD is quick to point out, however, that approximately 9,000 parcels of property do not use the system and pay no service charge. These parcels escape the charge because they have an alternate means of sewage disposal or are unimproved.

* * * On December 17, 1991, this Court issued its decision in Keller. A deeply divided Court held that a local ambulance district's increased charges for ambulance service were not fees within the meaning of Article X, Section 22(a). MSD read Keller in light of its financial needs and increased its wastewater charges by $4.00 per month without voter approval. * * *

Article X, Section 22(a), prohibits a political subdivision of this state "from increasing the current levy of an existing tax, license or fees [sic], above that current levy authorized by law or charter when this section is adopted without the approval of the required majority of the qualified voters of that * * * political subdivision voting thereon." MSD is a political subdivision of the state. Thus, the question before the Court is whether the sewer charge imposed by MSD is a "tax, license or fees" [sic] within the meaning of Article X, Section 22(a). If so, such charges cannot be increased without prior voter approval. * * *

Keller overruled Roberts v. McNary, 636 S.W.2d 332 (Mo. banc 1982). In doing so, Keller rejected "the contention that all fees—whether user fees or tax-fees—are subject to the Hancock Amendment." 820 S.W.2d at 304. To assist in determining whether a governmental charge is a tax within the meaning of Article X, Section 22(a), or user fee not subject to constitutional controls, Keller suggested a five-pronged analysis. Keller, 820 S.W.2d at 304–5, n. 10. * * *

1.   WHEN IS THE FEE PAID?

Keller informs that fees subject to Article X, Section 22(a), are "likely due to be paid on a periodic basis while fees not subject to [Article X, Section 22(a)] are likely due to be paid only on or after provision of a good or service to the individual paying the fee." Id. at 304. Mr. Beatty argues that the sewer charge is paid on a periodic basis and thus falls within Keller's first test for inclusion within Article X, Section 22(a). MSD counters that sewer charges are payments for services rendered by MSD to the sewer customer and are thus goods or services under Keller's initial test.

MSD misunderstands the first Keller test. The question posed there is not whether the political subdivision provides a service but the regularity with which the fee is paid. In this case, the fee is imposed and paid on a periodic—quarterly—basis. Because the first Keller test concerns itself only with timing, we resolve the first issue in favor of Mr. Beatty's position.

2. WHO PAYS THE FEE?

Keller says that a fee subject to Article X, Section 22(a) is "likely to be blanket-billed to all or almost all of the residents of the political subdivision while a fee not subject to [Article X, Section 22(a)] is likely to be charged only to those who actually use the good or service for which the fee is charged." *Id.* at 304. The record in this case reveals that only 9,000 of the approximately 420,000 parcels of real estate in the district are not subject to MSD charges. Mr. Beatty argues that this is "almost all;" MSD argues that only those persons receiving its sewer service pay the fee. While it is true that almost all residents of the district pay the charge, it is also true that only those persons who actually use MSD's services pay the charge. On application of the second prong of the *Keller* test, MSD has the better side of the argument.

3. IS THE AMOUNT OF THE FEE TO BE PAID AFFECTED BY THE LEVEL OF GOODS OR SERVICES PROVIDED TO THE FEE PAYER?

The third *Keller* test suggests that fees subject to Article X, Section 22(a) are "less likely to be dependent on the level of goods or services provided to the fee payer while fees not subject to [Article X, Section 22(a)] are likely to be dependent on the level of goods or services provided to the fee payer." *Id.* at 304. Mr. Beatty argues that the charge imposed by MSD bears no relation to the amount of the services MSD provides its customers; MSD argues that its charges, though admittedly uniform, reflect the estimated, average use a residential customer makes of MSD's services and, as to nonresidential customers, bears a direct relationship to the amount of service received.

Keller's third test focuses on the individual paying the fee. In order for a governmental charge to appear to be a user fee under *Keller*'s third criteria, the charge imposed must bear a *direct* relationship to the level of services a "fee payer" actually receives from the political subdivision. If MSD's argument as to residential customers were correct, every tax, license, or fee would appear more like a user fee than an Article X, Section 22(a) tax. An economist could easily construct a model to show that any fee government collects is based on the "estimated, annual" use of governmental services by a taxpayer. Because the vast majority of MSD fee payers are residential, we conclude that Mr. Beatty has the better argument here.

4. IS THE GOVERNMENT PROVIDING A SERVICE OR GOOD?

The fourth *Keller* factor asks whether the charge paid by the "fee payer" is directly related to a service provided by a political subdivision. This factor distinguishes non-Article X, Section 22(a) fees from taxes generally, the latter being paid without relation to any specific service provided by government. On this fourth factor, MSD prevails; it clearly provides a service in return for a direct payment.

5.   HAS THE ACTIVITY BEEN HISTORICALLY AND EXCLUSIVELY PROVIDED
BY THE GOVERNMENT?

Each of the parties in this case points to a plethora of historical examples of the private or public provision of sewer services to assist their position. Application of the fifth factor is inconclusive, given the mix of public and private entities that have supplied sewer service historically.

In sum, application of the *Keller* test to the facts of this case provides no clear answer as to the nature of MSD's charges.

Reduced to its essence, the Hancock Amendment reveals the voters' basic distrust of the ability of representative government to keep its taxing and spending requirements in check. As an additional bulwark against local government abuse of its power to tax, the voters amended the constitution to guarantee themselves the right to approve increases in taxes proposed by political subdivisions of the state. Whether a governmental charge is a tax is the issue with which *Keller* struggled. And as *Keller* shows, the language employed in Article X, Section 22(a), is ambiguous.

In the face of ambiguous language in the organic document of the state, this Court is required to attempt to ascertain the intent of the voters from the language they adopted and to resolve doubts as to meaning in favor of that intent. Where, as here, genuine doubt exists as to the nature of the charge imposed by local government, we resolve our uncertainty in favor of the voter's right to exercise the guarantees they provided for themselves in the constitution.

As we have previously said, the facts of this case do not clearly define the nature of MSD's charges. Only fee payers who use its services pay for MSD's services. The charge imposed, however, is not directly related to the amount of services an individual, residential fee payer uses. In the end, our uncertainty as to the nature of the charge MSD imposes is heightened by the fact that unpaid sewer charges trigger a lien against real property by operation of law. Thus, we resolve our doubts in favor of the taxpayers and hold that MSD's charges are subject to Article X, Section 22(a), and may not be increased without prior voter approval.

HOLSTEIN, JUDGE, concurring in result.

I concur in result with the majority opinion. I add these comments only by way of pointing out that I do not join in the majority's application of the five-part test taken from the footnote of *Keller v. Marion Co. Ambulance Dist.*, 820 S.W.2d 301 (Mo. banc 1991).

I concede that I lacked enthusiasm when this Court adopted the proposition that a "fee," as used in article X, § 22(a) of the Constitution, only means those fees which are, in reality, a tax. But that is now the law.

* * * I do not here suggest abandonment of the fundamental holding in *Keller*. At the same time, I believe that the five criteria noted in footnote 10 of the *Keller* opinion are so vague and subject to manipulation that they will necessarily result in repetitive litigation and are unworkable. Careful consideration of the facts of this case according to the five criteria demonstrate how the factors may be manipulated by both government and taxpayer litigants to support their conclusions.

1.   When is the fee paid?

The first criterion posits two questions regarding when the fee is paid: 1) are the fees paid on a periodic basis, and 2) are the fees paid only on or after the provision of a good or service to the individual paying the fee? If the answer to the first question is "yes" and the second is "no," then the fee is less likely to require voter approval. With regard to the first question, I agree with the majority that the answer is yes. As with all routinely recurring services, fees come due periodically. But the answer to the second question is also yes. The fees are calculated on the *previous year's cost* of operating the sewer system. Thus, under the first criterion, it is unclear whether the charge of MSD is subject to Hancock. In any event, this element may be manipulated so that charges may only occur after the rendering of services.

2.   Who pays the fee?

The second criterion also is a two-pronged question. The first is, is this blanket billed to all or most all of the residents of the political subdivision? If the answer is "yes," then the fee is more like a tax. I suggest the answer is "yes" because assessing a fee against *all* tracts which have sewer service and in excess of 97% of all parcels, including those not having sewer service, is a blanket billing of "all or almost all" residents in the district. The second question posed under the second criterion is whether the charge is made only to those "who actually use the good or service for which the fee is charged." This question, if answered affirmatively, means the charge is more like a fee. Here again, the answer is a resounding yes. Virtually every property owner uses sewers. In other words, this criterion also is indecisive in determining whether this is a tax or a fee. Again, by simply narrowing the class of persons subject to the fee, this element can be manipulated.

3.   Is the amount of the fee to be paid affected by the level of goods or services provided to the fee payer?

Under the third *Keller* test, charges dependent upon the level of goods or services provided are not as likely to be subject to article X, § 22(a). The majority suggests that if MSD based its charges on some method of measuring the quantity of sewage, such as the amount of water usage, rather than based on the type of usage, whether residential or nonresidential, MSD's charges are more likely to qualify as fees not subject to Hancock. In other words, through the mere expedient of manipulating the method by which the fees are assessed, a charge which is unconstitutional will become constitutional. Here again, I find that neither MSD nor the taxpayer has the better of the argument on this point.

4.   Is the government providing a service or good?

I agree wholeheartedly with the majority on this point. MSD is providing a service. However, I do not believe that proof that a service is being provided is a valid basis for distinguishing between taxes and fees. Assessing a "public safety" fee to each citizen who calls for police or fire protection or a "cross walk" fee to parents who have children of school age does not make those charges any less like a tax. The fourth factor is, I believe, bogus. A governmental agency may always identify some service that it performs for its fee and thereby justify any charge it makes to its citizens.

5.   Has the activity been historically and exclusively provided by the government?

Here again, the fifth factor is inconclusive given the mix of public and private entities that supply sewer services. In *Keller* I noted that in much of rural Missouri, ambulance services are exclusively provided by the government. In urban Missouri, sewer services are often provided by local government, and that has been true for many years. This factor will almost always be inconclusive, as it is here, where the charge is deemed a tax, and was in *Keller*, where the charge was deemed not a tax.

This brief analysis demonstrates that the five factors of footnote 10 from *Keller* are unworkable. Four of the five factors are highly subject to manipulation so that fees charged for a service in one community must have voter approval, but a fee for the same service in another community need not have voter approval. The fifth factor is almost always inconclusive. We should find objective standards by which to distinguish fees from taxes. Only if we are wholly unable to articulate workable standards should overruling *Keller* be considered. I again predict that we have not seen the last of this type of litigation.

We have now taken the five factors from a footnote and elevated them to the basis for analysis of this case. By promoting the factors to ratio decidendi, we have given force to what was heretofore not fully part of the reasoning in *Keller*. I cannot join in an opinion which enlarges the status of the five factors from the footnote. Nevertheless, the Court reaches a correct result under the law. The majority opinion makes substantial headway by stating that any uncertainty is to be resolved in favor of the voter's rights guaranteed by the Constitution. The burden is placed squarely on a governmental subdivision to show its charges are permissible without a vote. On that principle alone, this case should be reversed. I concur in that result.

NOTE

The Hancock Amendment is the rare tax and expenditure limitation measure that explicitly restricts fees as well as taxes. In Roberts v. McNary, 636 S.W.2d 332 (Mo.1982), the Missouri Supreme Court found that it applied to all local fees. In Keller v. Marion County Ambulance Dist., 820 S.W.2d 301 (Mo.1991), the Court changed its position and found that the Amendment applied only to fees that were tantamount to taxes, and that it did not apply to user fees. *Keller* concluded with a footnote that lays out the five factors that are the focus of the *Beatty* case. Do these questions help distinguish between a fee and a tax? Why is the timing of the payment of the fee relevant? Why is historical practice relevant? Is the concurrence right that there will be many cases in which the answers to each of the *Keller* questions will support the case for both tax and fee? As one commentator has noted, "litigation surrounding the Hancock Amendment has been plentiful and expensive." Note, There Must Be a Better Way: The Unintended Consequences of Missouri's Hancock Amendment, 80 Mo. L. Rev, 275, 292 (2015). The Missouri courts have repeatedly had to grapple with the question of when is a fee really a fee and when is it really a tax in disguise. Two cases from the current decade indicate the difficulty of the issue.

In Arbor Investment LLC v. City of Hermann, 341 S.W.3d 673 (Mo. 2011) (en banc), the Missouri Supreme Court held that a city's charges for electricity, natural gas, water, sewer, and refuse services were true fees, so that increases were not subject to the Hancock Amendment's voter approval requirement. Although, as in *Beatty,* the fees were billed on a monthly basis, the bills in *Arbor* "are sent out only for service that already has been provided at the time the bill is sent," thereby indicating a fee. *Id.* at 684. Similarly, as in *Beatty,* residents receiving a service were not charged for it, again supporting the finding of a fee. With the exception of a small flat "communications fee" surcharge to finance 911 service added quarterly to some utility bills, the size of an individual customer's fee reflected the extent of utility service usage. Thus, the third factor supported a finding of a fee. So did the fourth *Keller* factor, as all parties agreed that payers were receiving a service. The fifth factor went the other way. The city was the sole provider of utility services in Hermann, and had passed an ordinance barring competition from private providers: "The exclusivity of service at the current time," the court said, "tilts in favor" of treatment as a tax. *Id.* at 685–86. The overall "weighing of factors" led to a ruling of fee, not tax. What do you see as the principal differences supporting the different results in *Beatty* and *Arbor*? An additional argument raised by the challengers to the utility charge increases in *Arbor* was that the city was raising more money through the utility charges than it needed to finance the utilities and was transferring the excess revenues to its general fund, thus making the fees, in practice, taxes. The court disagreed, holding that charges greater than system costs are not for that reason fees. But the court also noted that "if a charge were so excessive as to be effectively unrelated to the service being provided . . . would be relevant to the fourth *Keller* factor of whether a service is being provided for the fee." *Id.* at 687. The city's fees were not so exorbitant. Should the court have given greater weight to this factor? *Cf. Apodaca v. Wilson*, 525 P.2d 876 (N.M.1974) (upholding power of Albuquerque City Commission to impose sewer and water service charges in excess of system costs and to transfer surplus revenues to the municipal general fund; comparing city utility service to the operations of a private utility, the court determined a municipality could earn a "reasonable" profit).

Two years after *Arbor* the Missouri Supreme Court in *Zweig v. Metropolitan St. Louis Sewer District*, 412 S.W.3d 223 (Mo. 2013) (en banc) struck down the MSD's effort to treat its "stormwater user charge" as a fee and not a tax for Hancock Amendment purposes. The charge was to be used to operate, maintain and improve the stormwater drainage system, and to support stormwater planning, permitting, and public education. Although the MSD could already draw on property tax surcharges on sewer system customers, the district claimed that was not enough in light of the increased obligations imposed by federal and state environmental laws. The new charge was to be imposed on landowners based on the square footage of "impervious area (e.g., roofs, patios, parking lots, streets, sidewalks, etc.) on each owner's property" on the theory that stormwater run-off from impervious property—unlike water that could be absorbed by open land—contributes to the burden on the drainage system. *Id.* at 230. The problem with treating the charge as a fee is that unlike a wastewater sewer system—which can be used only by landowners connected to the system—storm waters flow into the system through a mix of natural and artificial waterways and there is no way to tell "where the water [entering the system] originates or how much storm water discharges into the system during a particular storm or over any period of time." *Id.* at 228. So, too, storm water usage by individual landowners cannot be directly measured. "MSD has no way of knowing how much storm water any particular landowner is discharging into that system at any particular time. . . . Accordingly, the storm water charge is not . . . a user fee for a landowner's actual use of MSD's drainage system." *Id.* at 235. Landowners were being charged as landowners (albeit according to the amount of their impervious land) not as system users. Although it might be "fair" to require owners of impervious land collectively to pay for improvements to the system, the charge failed the *Keller* test because the MSD could not link a particular landowner's charge to his fee "in individualized transactions." *Id.* at 236. Does this mean that charges for stormwater drainage systems must be treated as taxes even if the charge is tied to the amount of impervious land, which does relate to the burden the landowner places on the system? *But see Storedahl Properties, LLC v. Clark County*, 178 P.3d 377 (Wash. App. 2008) (finding charge to finance improvements to storm water system is a fee not a tax, where individual landowner charges were based on land use and impervious surface; although there needs to be a relationship between the fee charged and the service received "so long as the rate is reasonably based on the amount of the property owner's contributing to the problem, the fee is directly related to the service provided"). Twietmeyer v. City of Hampton, 497 S.E.2d 858 (Va.1998) (upholding monthly storm water management fee of $12.50 for nonresidential properties and $2.50 for residential properties).

A student note on the *Zweig* case concluded that the Hancock Amendment has achieved "exactly what its namesake [Mel Hancock, the leader of a group called the Taxpayers Survival Association] wanted: a limitation on Missouri revenue" but at the cost of "inadequate public services." Note, *supra*, 80 Mo. L. Rev. at 293. The author proposes that the tax limitation amendment be revised so that it is limited to income, sales, and property taxes, or, in the alternative, that the legislature to disregard voter rejection of a tax increase if both houses of the legislature approve the new levy by a two-thirds vote. "This option would give the voters a say, but would also allow the legislature to determine if some revenue must be raised regardless of voters' opinions." *Id.* at 296. What do you think of these alternatives?

CITY OF HUNTINGTON V. BACON

Supreme Court of Appeals of West Virginia
473 S.E. 2d 743 (1996)

McHUGH, CHIEF JUSTICE:

The two cases before us were consolidated for argument and opinion. In the first case, the appellants, John Bacon, Carole Bacon, and other owners of buildings in the City of Huntington (hereinafter "the Bacons") appeal the April 25, 1995 order of the Circuit Court of Cabell County which granted summary judgment for the City of Huntington. In the second case, the Circuit Court of Cabell County certified a question to this Court from a declaratory judgment action in which the City of Huntington (hereinafter "City") and the Cabell County Board of Education (hereinafter "Board of Education") are parties.

Both cases involve the resolution of the following issue: Whether the City's municipal service fee imposed upon owners of buildings at an annual rate plus a percentage based upon the square footage of space contained in each structure on the lot in order to defray the cost of fire and flood protection services is a fee or tax. For reasons explained below, we find the municipal service fee to be a fee and not a tax.

* * * In 1990 the City passed an ordinance imposing a municipal service fee in order to defray the cost of providing fire and flood protection services:

> On or after July 1, 1990, there is hereby imposed upon all users of Municipal services a municipal service fee for each lot or parcel of land containing any building or structure owned by each user. The fee shall be imposed at an annual rate of seventy

dollars ($70.00) per lot plus $0.0375 per square foot of floor space contained in each building or structure existing on each such lot.

Ordinance § 773.03 * * *. The term "user" in the above ordinance is defined in the following manner:

> For purposes of this article, 'user of municipal services' and 'user' refers to any person, firm, corporation or governmental entity of any kind owning any building or structure, whether residential, commercial, governmental or otherwise, within the limits of the City which benefits from fire and/or flood protection services provided by the City.

Ordinance § 773.02.

In 1991 the City amended ordinance § 773.03 by increasing the rate to $80.00 per lot and $0.0575 per square foot. Additionally, that amendment allocated $250,000.00 of the municipal service fee collected between 1991 and 1994 to the improvement of streets and municipal infrastructure. According to the City, since 1994, the municipal service fee is no longer being used to improve streets and municipal infrastructure.

The City filed suit against the Bacons in order to collect the municipal service fee assessed against them. The Bacons maintained they were not required to pay the municipal service fee because the fee was a tax which violated the Tax Limitation Amendment found in W. Va. Const. Art. X, § 1. * * *

On February 16, 1989, the City brought a declaratory judgment action to seek a declaration of its rights to recover certain municipal fees assessed against the Board of Education. * * * The Board of Education, in the action now before us, maintains that the municipal service fee is a tax * * * which it is exempt from paying pursuant to W. Va.Code, 11–3–9 [1990]. * * *

The City derives all of its power as well as its existence from the legislature. * * * Therefore, the City only has the authority to impose the fees or taxes which are authorized by the legislature. * * * The legislature specifically authorized municipalities "to impose by ordinance upon the users of ['essential or special municipal service, including, but not limited to, police and fire protection * * * and any other similar matter'] *reasonable rates, fees and charges* to be collected in the manner specified in the ordinance[.]" W. Va.Code, 8–13–13 [1971]. * * *

[I]n recognition of the legislature's constitutional power to determine this State's fiscal policy, this Court has accorded it and municipalities wide latitude in how they choose to fund municipal services, such as those for fire and flood protection. *See* W. Va. Const. Art. VI, § 51; Art. X, § 3;

and Art. X, § 5. The legislature's power to determine this State's fiscal policy is limited only by the Constitution. * * *

Though our case law reveals a somewhat convoluted history in the area of taxes and fees, this Court has generally operated on the premise that charges for services rendered by a municipality are user fees and not taxes. *See City of Charleston v. Board of Education,* 158 W.Va. 141, 145, 209 S.E.2d 55, 57 (1974) (the charge for fire protection is a fee and not a tax); *City of Moundsville v. Steele,* 152 W.Va. 465, 164 S.E.2d 430 (1968) (charge of $0.25 per front foot for street improvement is a fee and not a tax); and *Duling Bros. Co. v. City of Huntington,* 120 W.Va. 85, 89–90, 196 S.E. 552, 554–55 (1938) (charges for a flood control program are not subject to ordinary taxing regulations). This premise is based on the following definitions of tax and fee: "[T]he primary purpose of a tax is to obtain revenue for the government, while *the primary purpose of a fee is to cover the expense of providing a service* or of regulation and supervision of certain activities." *River Falls v. St. Bridget's Catholic Church,* 182 Wis.2d 436, 513 N.W.2d 673, 675 (App.1994) (citing *State v. Jackman,* 60 Wis.2d 700, 211 N.W.2d 480, 485 (1973) and emphasis added).

On the other hand, where the "operation and effect" of a service charge appears to impose a tax, then this Court examines the service charge more closely. For example, in *City of Fairmont v. Pitrolo Pontiac-Cadillac,* 172 W.Va. 505, 308 S.E.2d 527 (1983) this Court found the police service charge imposed by the City of Fairmont to be an ad valorem tax which violated the Tax Limitation Amendment found in W. Va. Const. Art. X, § 1 rather than a user fee. We determined that the "operation and effect" of the police service charge was the same as the "operation and effect" of an ad valorem tax because the police service fee, like an ad valorem tax, was imposed according to the value of the property. * * *

Conversely, if the "operation and effect" of the service charge imposed by a municipality does not give the appearance of being a tax, and if an ordinance enacted pursuant to W. Va.Code, 8–13–13 [1971] "reasonably serves the purpose for which it was enacted," then this Court will defer to the municipality's wisdom in imposing the service charge.

In the case before us, the Bacons and the Board of Education maintain the City's municipal service fee is, in fact, an ad valorem tax because the rate of the fee is based upon the square footage of space contained in each structure. * * * Although the City's municipal service fee is assessed on a regular basis, it is not based upon the value of the property. Under the language of the municipal service fee ordinance, a building worth several million dollars which has the same square footage as a building worth a fraction of that would be assessed identical municipal service fees. By imposing a charge based upon a structure's square footage, the City creatively avoided the results in *City of*

Fairmont. However, the square footage assessment does not make the municipal service fee, in fact, an ad valorem tax.

The Bacons and the Board of Education also argue that the municipal service fee falls within the traditional definition of a property tax: " 'The consensus of opinion appears to be that a property tax is a charge on the owner of property by reason of his ownership alone without regard to any use that might be made of it, *Bromley v. McCaughn*, 280 U.S. 124, 136,' " *City of Fairmont*, 172 W.Va. at 509, 308 S.E.2d at 531. The Bacons and Board of Education focus on the above definition in isolation which can often be misleading. For example, in this case the City imposed its municipal service fee on the primary users of its flood and fire protection services. These primary users happen to be property owners. Thus, the City did not impose the municipal service fee on the owners of property by reason of their ownership alone. Instead, the fee is imposed upon property owners by reason of their use of fire and flood protection services. Therefore, the municipal service fee is not a property tax in this instance.

Lastly, the Bacons and the Board of Education argue that because the proceeds from the collection of the municipal service fee are not used exclusively to pay for fire and flood protection services, the municipal service fee is a tax. We agree that the proceeds from the collection of the municipal service fee must be used exclusively to pay for fire and flood protection services. As previously noted, in the past, the City earmarked proceeds from the collection of the municipal service fee to improve streets and municipal infrastructure. *See* Ordinance § 773.03(c) (1991) ("Of the amount collected under this fee, the amount of $250,000.00 shall be allocated to improve streets and municipal infrastructure each year for the fiscal years 1991–1992, 1992–1993 and 1993–1994.") The "operation and effect" of using the proceeds to improve streets and municipal infrastructure makes the municipal service fee a tax. Currently, however, the municipal service fee is not being used in this manner. Therefore, as long as the proceeds generated from the collection of the municipal service fee are not earmarked for use other than to defray the cost of providing fire and flood protection services and as long as the proceeds do not exceed the costs of providing fire and flood protection services, we find that the "operation and effect" of the municipal service fee to be that of a fee.

Accordingly, we hold that an ordinance which imposes a municipal service fee pursuant to W. Va.Code, 8–13–13 [1971] upon the owners of buildings at an annual rate plus a percentage based upon the square footage of space contained in each structure on the lot for the sole purpose of defraying the cost of fire and flood protection services is a user fee rather than a tax and therefore, is not in violation of the Tax Limitation Amendment found in W. Va. Const. Art. X, § 1.

* * * The Bacons and the Board of Education * * * [contend] that the ordinance which imposes the municipal service fee for fire and flood protection services is unreasonable as applied to them. First, they maintain that the fee is unreasonable because it is not imposed upon all users of the fire and flood protection services. For instance, fire departments respond to automobile accidents, hazardous materials spills, tenant's fires, and vacant lots which might catch fire, yet the ordinance does not impose the municipal service fee on any of these potential users. Thus, the Bacons and the Board of Education conclude that the municipal service fee for fire and flood protection does not reasonably burden the users of the services.

We disagree. * * * This Court has * * * recognized that charges for services provided by municipalities cannot always be equally achieved upon all users. This Court will uphold the fee if it is sufficiently related to the use of the special service for which the fee is imposed.

In the case before us, although the municipal service fee is not imposed upon all users of the City's fire and flood protection services, common sense dictates that owners of property benefit most by these services. Thus, the ordinance reasonably imposes a service fee which is sufficiently related to the use of the City's fire and flood protection services.

Second, the Bacons assert that the municipal service fee for flood protection services is unreasonably imposed upon them because their buildings are located at an elevation substantially above the flood wall. Thus, they argue they should not be required to pay fees for services from which they will never benefit.

In *City of Princeton v. Stamper*, 195 W.Va. 685, 466 S.E.2d 536 (1995), we addressed a similar issue. In that case, the City of Princeton enacted an ordinance which imposed a mandatory service fee on its residents for the collection and removal of refuse. The appellants argued that they should not be required to pay the mandatory service fee because they chose to use the services of a private hauler rather than the City of Princeton. We rejected this argument and held that "a mandatory service fee on the collection and removal of residential refuse regardless of actual use, in order to prevent a health menace from imperiling an entire community, is a reasonable and valid exercise of police powers granted to the City of Princeton under W. Va.Code 8–13–13 (1971)." * * * In arriving at our conclusion we stated that "[a]ll residents, regardless of how they personally choose to dispose of their refuse, receive a benefit in the collection and disposal of refuse from other premises in the community." *Id*. at 688, 466 S.E.2d at 539.

Similarly, in this case, all property owners benefit from the flood wall protection services. * * *

[W]hile the Bacons may not immediately or directly benefit from the flood protection service fee, the City has determined that all property owners benefit from flood protections services, which gives the ordinance "a presumptive validity." * * * We do not find that the ordinance is unreasonable.

NOTES AND QUESTIONS

1. *Fire and Flood Protection Fee.* The West Virginia court's principal arguments that the Huntington charge is a fee and not a tax appear to be: (a) a liberal reading of local government power, (b) the fact that the fee is based on square footage and not ad valorem, and (c) the earmarking of the proceeds for fire and flood protection services. After *Huntington*, is there any limitation on the level of local taxation so long as the locality is able to base liability on something other than property values, and the local government is able to earmark the revenue generated for a specific municipal purpose rather than the general fund? Maybe not in West Virginia. The state's highest court upheld as a "user fee" the City of Charleston's "city service fee," which consisted of a one dollar a week charge on each individual who works within the city limits, and collected by employers within the city limits. The revenues were earmarked for "police protection and street maintenance" and were not placed in the city's general fund. The court concluded that the plaintiffs failed to show that the fee payers were not receiving the services funded by the fee. The only restriction on the city's ability to fund city services through fees, in addition to the requirement that the fee revenues be earmarked for those services, was that the amount of the fee "bear a direct and reasonable relationship to the actual services provided in exchange for the fee." Cooper v. City of Charleston, 624 S.E.2d 716 (W. Va. 2005). *See also* City of Clarksburg v. Grandeotto, Inc., 513 S.E.2d 177 (W.Va.1998) (Roman Catholic Diocese of Wheeling-Charleston may be required to pay Huntington's fire and flood protection fee notwithstanding state constitutional exemption of religious property from taxation); *but cf.,* United States v. City of Huntington, 999 F.2d 71, 74 (4th Cir.1993), *cert. denied,* 510 U.S. 1109 (1994) (barring city from collecting fire and flood protection fee from the federal government with respect to federal property in the city because the fee "is a thinly disguised tax"). In what sense is the Huntington or Charleston fee a user charge? How is service usage tied to payment of the fee? The question of when and to whom a fire department provides services that can be financed by a fee—and not require a tax—sharply divided the Mississippi Supreme Court in Alfonso v. Diamondhead Fire Protection Dist., 122 So.3d 54 (Miss. 2013). The fire protection district was funded partly by ad valorem taxes and partly by a monthly "fire protection services" fee on property owners. Contending that they "receive a service from the fire department only if the department responds to an emergency call," the property owners contended that the fee was unlawful as state law authorized fire districts to impose fees only "for services rendered." The majority agreed with the fire district that "many day-to-day actions are required for it to have

the ability to put out fires," including equipment maintenance and repairs, firefighter training, planning, fire hydrant inspection, and public education programs, and that property values benefited from these activities, so that "the substance of the charge was consistent with a fee, not a tax." *Id.* at 57. The dissenters rejected this reasoning, noting that "services rendered" language in the statute refers to only "those specific services delivered to a specific customer." *Id.* at 65. They reasoned that the fire department's activities, other than emergency response, while beneficial to property owners, did not constitute a "direct service" from the department and ought to be financed by ad valorem taxes.

2. *Fees for Traditional Municipal Services.* Courts in other jurisdictions have been less receptive to municipal efforts to extend the user charge concept from the utility setting to core municipal services. In Covell v. City of Seattle, 905 P.2d 324 (Wash.1995), the Washington Supreme Court invalidated Seattle's "residential street utility charge," which imposed a charge of $2 per month per housing unit (and an additional $1.35 per unit in multi-family housing), and a charge on business properties determined by the number of people employed at the business. The revenues generated were spent on maintaining, repairing, and improving the city's streets. Even though the revenues were earmarked for street purposes, the court found that the charge was not voluntary and that its purpose was to raise revenue, not to regulate: "The revenue to be collected bears no relationship to the regulation of street traffic, but is to generate funds for the nonregulatory function of repairing streets. It is clear that the primary purpose of the charge is to raise revenue." *Id.* at 331. *See also* Heartland Apartment Ass'n, Inc. v. City of Mission, 352 P.3d 1073 (Kans. App. 2015) ("transportation user fee" imposed on all improved real estate to support street maintenance is a tax, not a fee; charge is mandatory for all landowners; it is not used to provide any special service or benefit to any specific landowner or landowners; and finances a "core governmental service"); Collier County v. State, 733 So.2d 1012 (Fla. 1999) (fee imposed on property owners cannot be used to fund "general police-power services" such sheriff services, libraries, parks, election services, public health services, and public works that provide "no direct special benefit" to the properties charged).

Emerson College v. City of Boston, 462 N.E.2d 1098 (Mass.1984), was arguably a closer case. The state legislature authorized the city to impose a charge for fire protection against the owners of certain buildings that, "by reason of their size, type of construction, use and other relevant factors" required the city to employ additional firefighters or special equipment. The so-called augmented fire services availability (AFSA) charge applied to approximately two percent of the buildings in Boston, and funded thirteen percent of the fire department's expenses. The Massachusetts Supreme Judicial Court agreed that the AFSA charge "bears some similarity to the user fee" but ultimately concluded it was a tax, and hence could not be applied to Emerson College, a tax-exempt educational institution:

Fees are legitimate to the extent that the services for which they are imposed are sufficiently particularized as to justify distribution of the costs among a limited group (the "users," or beneficiaries, of the services) rather than the general public. The benefits of "augmented" fire protection are not limited to the owners of AFSA buildings. The capacity to extinguish a fire in any particular building safeguards not only the private property interests of the owner, but also the safety of the building's occupants as well as that of surrounding buildings and their occupants.

Id. at 1105–06. The court also relied on the fact that payment of the fee was compelled, not voluntary, and that the AFSA payments were not earmarked for AFSA services but were combined with other funds for police and fire services.

Did the Massachusetts court go too far in finding that the presence of a public benefit meant that the city could not impose an extra assessment on buildings that, in the event of fire, imposed special costs? Is there a viable middle position between the *City of Huntington* assumption that anything goes so long as ad valorem taxation is avoided and proceeds are earmarked, and *Emerson College's* assumption that in dealing with services that benefit the public as a whole, funding ought to come from general taxes?

3.   *Other Constitutional Constraints on Fees.* The principal state constitutional issue concerning fees appears to be whether a specific fee is a tax—subject to tax limitations, uniformity, or exemptions for religious and educational institutions—or a fee. However, some constitutional constraints apply to fees, too. Equal protection concerns may apply to fee structures and to rules determining who pays a fee and who does not. *See, e.g.,* Skyscraper Corp. v. County of Newberry, 475 S.E.2d 764 (S.C.1996) (upholding solid waste disposal fee against challenge that ordinance's classifications violated equal protection). Some state constitutional rules may bar the imposition of certain fees. Thus, a state constitutional guarantee of a "thorough and efficient system of free schools" was held to bar a county school board from charging for textbooks and materials necessary for completion of the required school curriculum. *See* Randolph County Board of Educ. v. Adams, 467 S.E.2d 150 (W.Va.1995). *See also* Hartzell v. Connell, 679 P.2d 35 (Cal. 1984) (imposition of fees for extracurricular music and sports activities violates constitutional commitment to free public school system).

c.   Development Impact Fees: Making Growth Pay for Itself

Development impact fees are one-time charges on new development to pay for public facilities required to serve that development. Impact fees grew out of the local government practice of requiring developers to provide critical on-site infrastructure as a condition of local approval of a new subdivision. Originally, these exactions were limited to requiring that the developer provide basic infrastructure, such as paved streets, gutters, curbs, and lighting; they soon expanded to require developer provision of utility connections and stormwater detention. Over time, "the range of exaction objectives broadened, with large subdividers increasingly required to donate sites for public buildings and parks in addition to providing local streets and utility connections." Alan A. Altshuler & Jose Gomez-Ibañez, Regulation for Revenue: The Political Economy of Land Use Exactions 16 (Brookings Inst. Press 1993). With the expansion of such development conditions to include facilities not directly connected to the new development, localities began to first permit and then require developers to make monetary payments in lieu of the dedication of land or in-kind exactions.

In the late 1970s, local requirements concerning monetary payments—now known as "development impact fees"—surged. This was due partly to the tax revolt, which made tax dollars less available for new public facilities. To a significant degree, the rise of development impact fees is yet another manifestation of the search for non-tax revenue sources which has been the hallmark of the post-Proposition 13 era. At the same time, the federal government substantially curtailed its subsidization of local government public facilities. From 1955 through 1978, federal aid to states and localities for infrastructure expanded from 0.8% of gross national product to 3.6%, but from 1978 to 1991, federal aid shrank to 2.8% of GNP. *See* Arthur C. Nelson, Development Impact Fees: The Next Generation, 26 Urb. Law. 541, 542 (1994). Yet due to federal and state environmental mandates, the costs of the public infrastructure dealing with water supply, waste water treatment, and solid waste disposal have risen.

Most importantly, though, the rise of development impact fees represents a new ambivalence about growth. A driving force behind the enormous expansion in development impact fees is not simply the circumvention of tax limitations but making growth pay for itself.

> Throughout American history the most consistent theme in local governance has been the pursuit of growth: more people, more jobs, more real estate development. . . . The predominant pattern of inter-local relations has been of jurisdictions competing vigorously—with subsidies, tax abatements, zoning variances, and other regulatory adjustments—for investment dollars. . . .

> Intense competition to attract and hold major employers still abounds. But critical shifts occurred in the 1970s and 1980s. Public attitudes toward development became far more ambivalent. With the diffusion of environmental values, the number of localities determined to restrain growth for quality of life reasons increased dramatically. With rising awareness of the impact of growth on public service demand, the number of

localities seeking to ensure that new development 'paid its own way' likewise increased.

Altshuler & Gomez-Ibanez, *supra*, at 8–9.

Traditionally, local governments assumed that the cost of providing public services to new residents and businesses could be covered by the revenues generated by the increase in the tax base produced by growth. This has changed, not only because of the changing circumstances in public finance, but also because of an increased sophistication in calculating the costs of growth. The tax revolt limited the ability of local governments to take advantage of tax base growth, and its effects have been exacerbated by reductions in intergovernmental aid and increases in the cost of infrastructure improvements. Moreover, because analyses of the fiscal impact of growth typically focused on operating expenses and relied on historical data concerning capital costs, they tended to underestimate the cost of new physical infrastructure. A more careful accounting of capital costs led many local governments to conclude that new growth would not pay for itself. *See id.* at 77–96. *See generally* Ronald H. Rosenberg, The Changing Culture of American Land Use Regulation: Paying for Growth with Impact Fees, 59 SMU L. Rev. 177 (2006).

The most common uses for impact fees are to fund roads; water, sewer and storm water systems; parks; and fire protection services. Less common, but authorized in some states, are impact fees for policing, libraries, solid waste facilities, and schools. *See* National Impact Fee Survey: 2012, www.impactfees.com. Among the states in which impact fees are most heavily used are Florida, California, Arizona, Colorado, Washington, Oregon, Georgia, and Utah. Fees are generally calculated according to land uses—such as single-family and multi-family residential, and retail, office, and industrial. In 2012, a survey of impact fees in 271 jurisdictions found that nationally the average fee for a single-family home was $11,583, albeit with considerable variation from state to state. Fees in California were considerably more than double the national average. *Id.*

Legally, the development impact fee combines features of the special assessment and the user charge. Like the traditional special assessment, the impact fee is intended to be a one-time charge to fund new infrastructure. Like the user charge, it attempts to measure the cost of serving new consumers. It differs from both the assessment and the charge, however, in that it is imposed in advance, before the new service users have actually arrived in the community. Moreover, it is increasingly used to fund expansions in services and infrastructure that serve the community as a whole (old-timers and newcomers together) to take into account the incremental burden posed by the newcomers, rather than just to pay for new facilities provided solely to the newcomers. As a result, assuring that the development fees cover only the costs of growth and do not constitute a means of taxing developers to pay for services to the community as whole becomes a more important issue. As you read the cases in this section, consider how effective state legislation and judicial oversight are in assuring impact fees charge only for costs attributable to growth.

HOME BUILDERS ASS'N OF CENTRAL ARIZONA V. CITY OF SCOTTSDALE

Supreme Court of Arizona
930 P.2d 993 (1997)

CHARLES E. ARES, JUDGE PRO TEM.

Driven by the Groundwater Management Act of 1980 to drastically reduce its dependence on underground water, the City of Scottsdale imposed a water resources development fee on all new realty developments. The Home Builders Association of Central Arizona (HBA), some of whose members paid the fee under protest, challenged in superior court the fee's validity under Arizona's enabling act, A.R.S. § 9–463.05. * * *

Before adopting the development fee at issue here, the city undertook a detailed study of the water resources needed to comply with the Groundwater Management Act. The study, "Water Resources Plan 1985," concluded that Scottsdale clearly lacks sufficient water for the future. It also found that Scottsdale would need to raise capital to acquire new supplies of surface water and to construct a system to transport that water.

Anticipating the need for more water, Scottsdale had already purchased Planet Ranch and its surface water rights in the Bill Williams River in La Paz and Mohave Counties. City planners proposed that water from Planet Ranch be brought to the city through a canal system tied to the [Central Arizona Project (CAP)]. Planet Ranch cost more than $11 million, and the cost of carrying the water to the CAP aqueduct was estimated at $18 million more. In addition, the water resources plan proposed the city increase its recharge capacity by constructing Water Factory 21, an advanced effluent treatment plant that would produce potable water. Other sources of surface water such as the purchase or lease of water rights from various native American tribes were also outlined in the plan.

To assist in accumulating capital, the plan proposed the adoption of a development fee for all new real estate developments. The city council adopted Ordinance No.1940, imposing a fee of $1,000 per single family residence, $600 per apartment unit, and $2,000 per acre foot of estimated water consumption for other new uses. The fees are imposed as a condition on the approval of new developments.

HBA challenged the Scottsdale fee for failing to meet the requirements of the enabling statute:

A.R.S. § 9–463.05. Development fees; imposition by cities and towns

A. A municipality may assess development fees to offset costs to the municipality associated with providing necessary public services to a development.

B. Development fees assessed by a municipality under this section are subject to the following requirements:

1. *Development fees shall result in a beneficial use to the development.*

2. Monies received from development fees assessed pursuant to this section shall be *placed in a separate fund and accounted for separately and may only be used for the purposes authorized by this section.* Interest earned on monies in the separate fund shall be credited to the fund.

3. The schedule for payment of fees shall be provided by the municipality. The municipality shall provide a credit toward the payment of a development fee for the required dedication of public sites and improvements provided by the developer for which that development fee is assessed. The developer of residential dwelling units shall be required to pay development fees when construction permits for the dwelling units are issued.

4. *The amount of any development fees assessed pursuant to this section must bear a reasonable relationship to the burden imposed upon the municipality to provide additional necessary public services to the development.* The municipality, in determining the extent of the burden imposed by the development, shall consider, among other things, the contribution made or to be made in the future in cash by taxes, fees or assessments by the property owner towards the capital costs of the necessary public service covered by the development fee.

5. If development fees are assessed by a municipality, such fees shall be assessed in a non-discriminatory manner.

(emphasis added).

* * * Taken as a whole, the evidence overwhelmingly supported the city's decision that it needed more water. The trial court found HBA failed to prove Scottsdale had an adequate water supply for the foreseeable future. The court also found the city reasonably could have concluded that it needed to acquire new water resources. * * * Despite that conclusion, the court held any benefit to the developers who were assessed the fee was too remote in time and speculative in nature to satisfy the benefit criterion of § 9–463.05(B)(1).The record discloses that the trial judge's conclusion in this respect was based on * * * testimony that it was possible Planet Ranch water might never be brought to Scottsdale if an alternative source of water were developed. * * *

We agree with the court of appeals that the trial judge committed error. The adoption of Ordinance No.1940 was a legislative act that came to the court cloaked with a presumption of validity. * * * Land use regulations of general application will be overturned by the courts only if a challenger shows the restrictions to be arbitrary and without a rational relation to a legitimate state interest. * * * Development or impact fees are presumed valid as exercises by legislative bodies of the power to regulate land use.

It is important to recognize just what the presumption means. It means, first, that the factual underpinning for the city council's decision, i.e., that the city needed more water, must stand unless shown to be without factual support. Clearly, HBA failed to make that showing. Second, the presumption also means that the wisdom of Scottsdale's choice of methods of meeting its water needs is a legislative, not a judicial, question. The purchase of Planet Ranch may not have been, as HBA has asserted, a wise one, but that question is not for this or any other court. * * * The only issue finally before the trial court, aside possibly from the reasonableness of the fee, was whether the fee conferred a benefit as required by the statute.

We have difficulty understanding this question to be an open one of fact. Scottsdale needs more water. If it does not get it before the deadline for reaching safe yield, it must stop approving new development. Both state zoning laws and the Groundwater Code prohibit the approval of a subdivision plat unless it is supported by a certificate of an assured water supply. The fee will be used to acquire new water supplies, and the city will be able to move toward its goal of demonstrating an assured 100-year water supply. Developers who pay the fee and thus contribute to the capital needed for water surely will receive a benefit from the city's ability to approve new developments. Without the assurance of a water supply, developers would be unable to develop and market their land.

The real fault with Scottsdale's fee, as found by the trial court, was not its failure to confer a benefit in fact but that the means chosen by the city were not sufficiently concrete and immediate to satisfy the requirement of § 9–463.05.

This was error in two respects. First, it led the court into the realm of legislative choices. When the court required assurance that whatever plans Scottsdale had developed at the time of adopting the fee would actually be followed, it undertook to test the wisdom and practicability of the city's legislative decisions. There was no evidence that the plans were a sham or inherently improbable, just that they might, in a search for economy, be changed. Scottsdale was dealing with a complex, ever-changing problem in predicting future growth and water needs. The city's decision to impose a development fee to be used to acquire the water needed to meet future needs was based on substantial evidence. Once plausible plans for acquiring that water had been adopted, whether to persist in those plans over the several years the project would require is surely a legislative, not judicial, decision. Courts must accord municipalities considerable deference and upset their legislative decisions only if they are shown to be arbitrary and without factual justification.

Second, the trial court's finding that the Scottsdale plan was too amorphous and speculative rested on an unarticulated but erroneous construction of § 9–463.05. The trial court implied that the statute requires plans more mature and "locked in" than Scottsdale's were. Such a reading of the statute was incorrect.

Where the language of a statute is clear and unambiguous, courts are not warranted in reading into the law words the legislature did not choose to include. * * * The plain language of § 9–463.05 contains no such requirement as the trial judge imposed here. It simply requires that the fee confer a beneficial use on the developer.

A development or impact fee is not a special assessment levied on a landowner whose property is immediately benefitted by access to such public improvements as sidewalks, sewers, and water works. In those cases, the legislature has required "preliminary plans that show the location and the type and character of the proposed improvements and estimates of the cost and expenses," as a basis for calculating the precise amount of the assessment. * * * With this more restrictive legislation already in place, the legislature adopted the development fee statute without such limiting language. The omission seems to us significant. Interestingly, when the proposal to authorize development fees was first introduced in the Arizona Senate as Senate Bill 1197, it required a development fee to confer a *direct benefit* on the developer. That term was dropped from the bill before final passage. Quite clearly, the legislature did not intend to require development fees to rest on such concrete plans as are mandated for special assessments.

We also believe that a requirement such as the one the trial judge read into the statute would be incompatible with the nature of the development fee and would thwart the apparent purpose of the legislature. Development or impact fees are designed to assist in raising the capital necessary to meet needs that surely will arise in the foreseeable future but whose precise details may not at the outset be quite clear. To require more fixed and certain plans would make it difficult, if not impossible, to prepare in advance for the consequences of continued growth.

Nevertheless, § 9–463.05 requires that the fee result in a benefit to the developer, and because the term is not self-defining, courts must necessarily pour content into it. That content must be derived, however, from the legislature's intent, as faithfully as the courts can determine it. * * * State courts had developed a fairly large body of law regarding the validity of development or impact fees by the time § 9–463.05 was adopted. *See* generally Brian W. Blaesser & Christine M. Kutopp, Impact Fees: The "Second Generation," 38 Wash. U.J. Urb. & Contemp. L. 55 (1990); Julian C. Juergensmeyer & Robert M. Blake, Impact Fees: An Answer to Local Governments' Capital Funding Dilemma, 9 Fla. St. U.L. Rev. 415 (1981). Read together, the state cases have produced a widely accepted standard for assessing the validity of these fees. *See, e.g., Collis v. City of Bloomington*, 310 Minn. 5, 246 N.W.2d 19 (1976); *College Station v. Turtle Rock Corp.*, 680 S.W.2d 802 (Tex.1984); *Jordan v. Village of Menomonee Falls*, 28 Wis.2d 608, 137 N.W.2d 442 (1965). That standard requires first that the exaction imposed on the developer be factually related to the need for public services created by the proposed development. Second, the nature and extent of the exaction must bear a reasonable relationship to that portion of the public burden created by the proposed development. *Jordan*, 137 N.W.2d at 447–49. * * *

Under the Arizona statute, a development fee can only be imposed to help pay the costs of providing public services to a proposed development. The fees are rationally related to a need created by the development; when they are spent to provide the needed services, the developer benefits. * * * The benefit criterion of § 9–463.05 is explicit and requires the fee to bear a reasonable relationship "to the community burden."

An examination of cases applying what is sometimes called the dual nexus test reveals that development fees have been upheld where they are imposed to finance public improvements the need for which will arise in the foreseeable, though not immediate, future. * * *

There is nothing in the history of development fees in state courts to suggest that our legislature intended, by its use of the term "beneficial use," to require the benefit to be based on "locked in" or unchangeable plans. Scottsdale is faced with a long term, complex series of projects designed to meet the requirements of the Groundwater Management Act. We would be reluctant to deprive the city of the flexibility needed to deal with these projects unless the legislature made it clear that it intended no such flexibility. Given the plain language of § 9–463.05, we hold it has not done so.

The trial judge may have been concerned that a broad reading of the benefit criterion might tempt a city to use the development fee as an unequal tax for the benefit of its general treasury. The very terms of the statute guard against that possibility. They require the fees to be segregated and used only for the purpose for which they were imposed. We are sensitive to the need to ensure that development fees are not used to impose on developers a burden all the taxpayers of a city should bear equally. The value of land a developer seeks to develop will be enhanced by the acquisition of water that is essential to new development. The developer thus receives a special benefit in new public services, and § 9–463.05 ensures that he will pay his fair share of its capital cost. * * *

We hold that § 9–463.05 requires that when a municipality, in its legislative discretion, decides that new developments will require additional public services, it need only develop such plans as will indicate a good faith intent to use development fees to provide those services within a reasonable time. It is clear that Scottsdale's fee meets this standard.

COUNTRY JOE, INC. v. CITY OF EAGAN

Supreme Court of Minnesota
560 N.W.2d 681 (1997)

KEITH, CHIEF JUSTICE

* * * On February 14, 1978, the Eagan city council adopted a resolution imposing a road unit connection charge payable as a condition to issuance of all building permits within the city. The resolution stated that its purpose was to provide "an equitable source of funding for major county and city street construction * * * in order to accommodate new development and traffic generated from future anticipated residential, commercial and industrial construction * * *."

The charge was prompted by a study conducted by the city's consulting engineers in 1977, which projected a shortfall of $1.11 million in funds available to finance major street construction in the city through the year 2000. The consulting engineers proposed that the city make up this shortfall by imposing a road unit connection charge, patterned after the water and sewer connection charges already imposed by the city pursuant to state law. See Minn.Stat. § 444.075, subd. 3 (1996).

The city deposits road unit connection charges collected into a Major Street Fund account, along with other sources of road funds. Funds are not earmarked for any particular project and the city does not attempt to link expenditures to any particular funding source. In addition to major street construction costs, miscellaneous charges such as sealcoating and the purchase of signal lights are occasionally paid out of the account.

The original plan recommended that the charge "be reviewed annually and totally revised every 5 years in order to adjust for any significant changes in construction costs, revenue projections or changes in the development pattern within the City of Eagan." In December 1979, the city revised its estimated costs of construction upward to include the addition of pedestrian walkways to the city's street design. As a consequence, the city increased the road unit connection charge for a single family residence from $75 to $185. Except for annual increases based on an inflationary index, the plan has not been updated since this initial revision of 1979. The inflation-adjusted charge for a single family residence had increased from the initial $75 to $410 at the time this lawsuit was filed in 1994.

On appeal, the city contends that the imposition of a road unit connection charge is a lawful exercise of its implied powers under Minnesota law. The city suggests that the authority to finance road improvements can be implied from several sources, including the city's municipal planning authority under Minn.Stat. ch. 462; the implied power to impose an "impact fee" to fund infrastructure improvements, as currently recognized in numerous other states; and the city's power to collect regulatory and license fees pursuant to its general welfare powers under Minn.Stat. § 412.221, subd. 32.

The city of Eagan is a "statutory city," meaning it is a municipal corporation that has not adopted a home rule charter as provided for under Minnesota law. As a limited statutory creation, the city has no inherent powers beyond those "expressly conferred by statute or implied as necessary in aid of those powers which have been expressly conferred." *Mangold Midwest Co. v. Village of Richfield*, 274 Minn. 347, 357, 143 N.W.2d 813, 820 (1966). We first consider the city's contention that the road unit connection charge is a valid exercise of its implied municipal planning authority under Minn.Stat. ch. 462, the Municipal Planning Act. The policy statement introducing the act clearly expresses the legislature's intent to confer broad planning authority on cities: "It is the purpose of sections 462.351 to 462.364 to provide municipalities, in a single body of law, with the necessary powers and a uniform procedure for adequately conducting and implementing municipal planning." Minn.Stat. § 462.351. The city asserts that the road unit connection charge is merely an example of its lawful exercise of the broad planning authority conferred upon it under the act.

* * * That the Municipal Planning Act expressly confers broad municipal *planning* powers on cities does not necessarily imply that the legislature similarly intended to confer broad *financing* powers under the act. In fact, the legislature's actions support the opposite conclusion. Although the legislature expressly provided for the sewer and water charges after which the city patterned its road unit connection charge, it failed to provide such authorization for a road charge. That this lack of express statutory authorization was not the result of legislative oversight is evidenced by statutory provisions expressly establishing special assessments as the mechanism by which cities are empowered to finance road improvements.

* * * [T]he Minnesota legislature has *specifically provided* a funding mechanism for road improvements; therefore, no funding mechanism need be implied to effectuate the legislative grant of authority to undertake road improvements. * * * Accordingly, we conclude that the authority to impose a road unit connection charge cannot be implied from the city's municipal planning authority.

The city next contends that the court of appeals erred in rejecting case law from other jurisdictions approving of similar charges as "impact fees." Impact fees have been lauded by local governments in recent years as a welcome means to "shift a portion of the cost of providing capital facilities to serve new growth from the general tax base to the new development generating the demand for the facilities." Martin L. Leitner & Susan P. Schoettle, A Survey of State Impact Fee Enabling Legislation, in Exactions, Impact Fees and Dedications: Shaping Land-Use Development and Funding Infrastructure in the Dolan Era 60 (Robert H. Freilich & David W. Bushek eds., 1995).

An impact fee has been defined as a form of development exaction that is:

- in the form of a predetermined money payment;

- assessed as a condition to the issuance of a building permit, an occupancy permit or plat approval;

- pursuant to local government powers to regulate new growth and development and provide for adequate public facilities and services;

- levied to fund large-scale, off-site public facilities and services necessary to serve new development;

- in an amount which is proportionate to the need for the public facilities generated by new development.

Brian W. Blaesser & Christine M. Kentopp, Impact Fees: The "Second Generation," in 1991 Zoning and Planning Handbook 255, 264 (Kenneth H. Young ed., 1991).

Commentators suggest that an impact fee differs from a tax in that an impact fee is levied as "compensation for the services rendered." *Id.* at

266 (citation omitted). Thus, key to the concept of a true impact fee is that the amount assessed a developer must reflect the cost of infrastructure improvements necessitated by the development itself. Conversely, "a charge having no relation to the services rendered, assessed to provide general revenue rather than compensation, is a tax." *Id.* Impact fees have also been distinguished from special assessments: "The primary difference is that special assessments represent a measure of the *benefit* of public improvements on new or existing development, whereas impact fees typically measure the *cost* of the demand or need for public facilities as a result of new development only." *Id.* at 267 (emphasis added).

The contractors argue that impact fees are lawful only if such fees are authorized, or appropriately limited, by state enabling legislation. * * *

We conclude, however, that we need not reach the issue of whether impact fees are authorized in Minnesota in order to pass on the validity of the road unit connection charge imposed by the city. By definition, an impact fee must be "in an amount which is proportionate to the need for the public facilities generated by new development." Blaesser & Kentopp at 264. In this case, however, the city essentially ignored its own consulting engineers' recommendation that the road unit connection charge be periodically updated to account for changes in costs, revenue projections, or patterns of development. Thus, for the period in question, there is insufficient evidence that the charge was proportionate to the need created by the development upon which the burden of payment fell. Accordingly, we reserve the issue of whether impact fees are authorized under Minnesota law, but reject the city's contention that the road unit connection charge draws its authorization as such a fee.

* * * We conclude that the charge is a revenue measure, benefitting the public in general, and is not an authorized exercise of the city's police powers. In reaching this conclusion, we find it significant that revenues collected from the road unit connection charge are not earmarked in any way to fund projects necessitated by new development, but instead fund all major street construction, as well as repairs of existing streets. Because it is not a purely regulatory or license fee but instead a revenue measure, the road unit connection charge is a tax which must draw its authorization, if at all, from the city's powers of taxation. * * *

The taxing authority afforded municipalities under state law is delineated in Minn.Stat. § 412.251. * * * [T]here is nothing in the statute suggesting the authority to impose anything similar to a road unit connection charge. . . . Accordingly, we conclude that the road unit connection charge cannot find validity under the city's power of taxation.

VOLUSIA COUNTY V. ABERDEEN AT ORMOND BEACH, L.P.

Supreme Court of Florida
760 So.2d 126 (2000)

QUINCE, J.

Aberdeen at Ormond Beach, L.P., owns Aberdeen at Ormond Beach Manufactured Housing Community (Aberdeen), a mobile home park in Ormond Beach that provides housing for persons at least 55 years of age or older. Aberdeen brought suit against Volusia County and the Volusia County School Board (Volusia County) to challenge the constitutionality of public school impact fees assessed on new homes constructed at Aberdeen.

As a mobile home park, Aberdeen is regulated by Chapter 723, Florida Statutes. Its minimum age requirements comply with the "housing for older persons" exemption of the Federal Fair Housing Act. Aberdeen's Supplemental Declaration of Covenants, Conditions and Restrictions (Supplemental Declaration) contains the following provisions:

> exceptions to the minimum age requirement are permitted under limited circumstances; persons under eighteen are prohibited from permanently residing in any dwelling unit; the developer reserves the absolute right to modify or revoke all other covenants; and restrictions are binding upon owners for thirty years from the date of recordation.

* * * As of July 1998, Aberdeen housed 142 people, 119 of whom were over 60. No children have ever lived in Aberdeen, and the youngest resident ever was 42.

Effective October 1, 1992, Volusia County enacted Ordinance No. 92–9, imposing countywide public school impact fees on new dwelling units constructed in Volusia County. The ordinance's definition of "dwelling unit" ("living quarters for one family only") included single and multi-family housing, but excluded nursing homes, adult congregate living facilities and group homes. Volusia County, Fla., Ordinance 92–9, art. 1, § 4 (July 2, 1992). In addition, the ordinance furthered the County's policy of ensuring "that new development should bear a proportionate share of the cost of facility expansion necessitated by such new development." *Id.* art. 1, § 2(l).

[The fee structure was subsequently modified by Ordinance No. 97–7.] * * * Ordinance 97–7 lowered the impact fee and permitted adjustments "to reflect any inflation or deflation in school construction costs." *Id.* § VII, (enacting code § 70–175(d)). In calculating the fee, the County utilized the student generation rate, which is the average number of public school students per dwelling unit. Pursuant to the Volusia

County impact fee ordinances, Aberdeen has paid $86,984.07 under protest for 84 homes as of July 31, 1998.

Aberdeen filed suit against Volusia County, claiming, inter alia, that public school impact fees were unconstitutional as applied to Aberdeen because of the deed restrictions prohibiting minors from living on the property. In response, the County argued that exempting Aberdeen would convert the impact fee into a "user fee," thereby violating the state constitutional guarantee of a free public school system. * * *

In *St. Johns County* [*v. Northeast Florida Builders Ass'n, Inc.*, 583 So.2d 635 (Fla.1991)] the plaintiffs attacked the impact fee ordinance as unconstitutional on its face. * * * The ordinance allocated the cost of new schools to each new unit of residential development. * * * In addition, the ordinance permitted households to adjust the fee in individual cases. *See id.* at 640. The Court rejected the argument that dwelling units without children did not have an impact on the school system, noting that occupants would change and children would "come and go." *Id.* at 638. The Court likewise rejected the argument that the "benefits" prong of the dual rational nexus test requires that "every new unit of development benefit from the impact fee in the sense that there must be a child residing in that unit who will attend public school." *Id.* at 639. However, the Court ultimately found that the ordinance was defective because fee funds could be spent within municipalities whose residents were not subject to the fee. * * *

* * * In *St. Johns County*, the Court expressly adopted the dual rational nexus test for determining the constitutionality of impact fees: the local government must demonstrate reasonable connections between (1) "the need for additional capital facilities and the growth in population generated by the subdivision" and (2) "the expenditures of the funds collected and the benefits accruing to the subdivision." *St. Johns County*, 583 So. 2d at 637 (quoting *Hollywood, Inc. v. Broward County*, 431 So. 2d 606, 611–12 (Fla. 4th DCA 1983)). Volusia County argues that the test requires needs and benefits to be assessed based on countywide growth, and that the specific-need/special-benefit analysis is limited to the water and sewer line context. This argument, however, is without merit.

The language of the test itself belies the assertion that a countywide standard should be employed. The first prong of the test explicitly requires a nexus between the County's need and the "growth in population generated by the subdivision." 583 So. 2d at 637. Similarly, the test's second prong ensures that "benefits accrue to the subdivision." *Id.* Thus, the explicit references to subdivisions indicate that the standard is not tailored to countywide growth, but to growth of a particular subdivision.

Furthermore, this Court in *St. Johns County* adopted the dual rational nexus test exactly as it was enunciated in *Hollywood, Inc. v. Broward County*, 431 So. 2d 606 (Fla. 4th DCA 1983), which applied the test to parks. The test ensures that the Broward County requirements—the fee must "offset needs sufficiently attributable to the subdivision" and the fee revenue must be "sufficiently earmarked for the substantial benefit of the subdivision residents"—are satisfied. *Id.* at 611. Moreover, this Court in *St. Johns County* reaffirmed the Dunedin requirement that the fees must "be spent to benefit those who have paid the fees." *St. Johns County*, 583 So. 2d at 639. Thus, the Court's use of the dual rational nexus test has not been limited to the water and sewer line context.

Additionally, in *Collier County v. State*, 733 So. 2d 1012 (Fla.1999), we reaffirmed the specific-need/special-benefit standard. Construing *St. Johns County*, we said, "The fee in St. Johns County was invalid because it did not provide a unique benefit to those paying the fee." *Id.* at 1019. We further explained that the fee at issue in *Collier County* was an invalid tax because "the services to be funded by the fee are the same general police-power services provided to all County residents." *Id.* Thus, we expressly repudiated a countywide standard for determining the constitutionality of impact fees. * * *

[I]mposing a countywide standard would eviscerate the substantial nexus requirement. This nexus is significant because of the distinction between taxes and fees. As this Court noted in *Collier County*, "There is no requirement that taxes provide any specific benefit to the property; instead, they may be levied throughout the particular taxing unit for the general benefit of residents and property." *Collier County*, 733 So. 2d at 1016 (quoting *City of Boca Raton v. State*, 595 So. 2d 25, 29 (Fla.1992)). Fees, by contrast, must confer a special benefit on feepayers "in a manner not shared by those not paying the fee." 733 So. 2d at 1019. We likewise noted in *State v. City of Port Orange*, 650 So. 2d 1, 3 (Fla.1994), that "the power of a municipality to tax should not be broadened by semantics which would be the effect of labeling what the City is here collecting a fee rather than a tax." Thus, a liberal reading of the dual rational nexus test would obliterate the distinction between an unconstitutional tax and a valid fee.

* * * Volusia County contends that the "need" prong of the test is satisfied because Aberdeen's growth directly affects the student generation rate used in calculating the fee, that is, the average number of public school students per dwelling unit. Volusia County notes that all residential dwellings, including adult communities, are considered when determining the student generation rate. Consequently, the County contends Aberdeen affects the student generation rate and amount of the fee because if the number of households without children increases, the rate decreases, and therefore the fee decreases.

The issue, however, is not whether Aberdeen influences the student generation rate or the amount of the impact fee, but whether Aberdeen increases the need for new schools. Indeed, Ordinance 97–7 defines "land development activity" as "any change in land use or any construction or installation of a dwelling unit, or any change in the use of any structure that will result in *additional* students in the public schools of the District." Volusia County, Fla., Ordinance 97–7, § III (May 15, 1997) (adopting County Code § 70–171(aa) (emphasis added). In addition, the test itself clearly frames the issue: whether there is a "need for *additional* capital facilities." *St. Johns County*, 583 So. 2d at 637 (emphasis added). * * * Aberdeen does not generate any students. That all residential units were included in the initial student generation rate is insufficient to establish a substantial nexus between Aberdeen's growth and the need for new schools. Thus, Aberdeen's purported effect on the student generation rate does not satisfy the dual rational nexus test.

       * * *

Volusia County is also unable to satisfy the "benefits" prong of the dual rational nexus test. Because no children can live at Aberdeen, impact fees collected at Aberdeen will not be spent for Aberdeen's benefit, but for the benefit of children living in other developments. Volusia County contends that Aberdeen benefits from the construction of new schools because they also serve as emergency shelters and sites for adult education classes. However, the connection between the expenditure of impact fee funds for the construction of new schools and the tangential benefit of having places of refuge in natural disasters is too attenuated to demonstrate a substantial nexus. Put another way, the schools are built primarily for the educational benefit of school-age children and, to the extent that Aberdeen derives any incidental benefit from their construction, it is insufficient to satisfy the dual rational nexus test.

In sum, Aberdeen neither contributes to the need for additional schools nor benefits from their construction. Accordingly, the imposition of impact fees as applied to Aberdeen does not satisfy the dual rational nexus test.

Volusia County also argues that requiring an exemption for age-restricted communities converts the impact fees into user fees, thereby violating the constitutional guarantee of free public schools. In *City of Port Orange*, we defined user fees as fees that are "charged in exchange for a particular governmental service which benefits the party paying the fee in a manner not shared by other members of society." *City of Port Orange*, 650 So. 2d at 3. We further explained that "the party paying the fee has the option of not utilizing the governmental service and thereby avoiding the charge." *Id.* In *St. Johns County*, we held that article IX, section 1 of the Florida Constitution prohibits counties from imposing school user fees on new development.[6] *See St. Johns County*, 583 So. 2d at 640. Specifically, we said that exempting households simply because they did not contain students constituted an unconstitutional user fee. *St. Johns County*, 583 So. 2d at 640. We further indicated that a school impact fee will not be deemed a prohibited user fee simply because adult-only facilities are exempt: "We would not find objectionable a provision that exempted from the payment of an impact fee permits to build adult facilities in which, because of land use restrictions, minors could not reside." *Id.* at 640 n.6.

* * * [E]xempting deed-restricted adult communities cannot be equated to exempting households that do not have children. As previously mentioned, the reasoning underlying *St. Johns County*'s holding was that some units had the potential to generate students. *See St. Johns County*, 583 So. 2d at 638 ("During the useful life of the new dwelling units, school-age children will come and go."). Thus, where there is no potential to generate students, there is no impact warranting the imposition of fees. Furthermore, this interpretation is wholly consistent with our Court's statement that deed-restricted housing could be exempt. Therefore, the lower court's construction of *St. Johns County* does not convert the impact fee into an unconstitutional user fee.

DREES COMPANY V. HAMILTON TOWNSHIP

Supreme Court of Ohio
970 N.E.2d 916 (2012)

PFEIFFER, J.

In this case we consider whether Hamilton Township, a limited-home-rule township, was authorized under Ohio law to impose its system of impact fees upon applicants for zoning certificates for new construction or redevelopment within its unincorporated areas. We hold that the impact fees operated as taxes; thus, Hamilton Township was not authorized to impose them pursuant to R.C. 504.04(A)(1).

Appellee Hamilton Township is a township that has adopted a limited-home-rule government, as defined by R.C. Chapter 504, and is located in Warren County. It has seen significant growth in recent years; the population grew from 5,900 in 1990, to 9,630 in 2000, to 23,556 in 2010. * * *

On May 2, 2007, the board of trustees passed Amended Resolution No. 2007–0418, descriptively titled "Amended Resolution Implementing Impact Fees Within the Unincorporated Areas of Hamilton Township,

---

[6] Prior to 1998, article IX, section 1 provided for a "uniform system of free public schools." Art. IX, § 1, Fla. Const. (1968). As amended in 1998, the section provides that "adequate provision shall be made by law for a uniform, efficient, safe, secure, and high quality system of free public schools." Art. IX, § 1, Fla. Const.

Ohio for Roads, Fire and Police, and Parks." The resolution adopted a schedule of fees to be charged to applicants for zoning certificates for new construction or redevelopment. The resolution included four categories of fees: a road-impact fee, a fire-protection-impact fee, a police-protection-impact fee, and a park-impact fee. The parties in this case made the following stipulation regarding the purpose of the resolution:

> The purpose of the impact fee is to benefit the property by providing the Township with adequate funds to provide the same level of service to that property that the Township currently affords previously developed properties.

> The Resolution assesses an impact fee to previously undeveloped property, and property undergoing redevelopment, to offset increased services and improvements needed because of the development.

The amount of the fees varies based upon the land use. Owners of property to be used for single-family detached dwellings, multifamily units, and hotel/motel rooms are assessed fees on a per-unit basis. Owners of property to be used for retail/commercial, office/institutional, industrial, warehouse, church, school, nursing-home, and hospital purposes are assessed fees on a per-1,000-square-feet basis. Only owners of property to be used for single-family detached and multifamily units are assessed the park component of the impact fees.

For example, the fees for the owner of property to be used as a single-family detached dwelling, broken down by category, are $3,964 for roads, $335 for fire, $206 for police, and $1,648 for parks, for a total assessment of $6,153. The fees, per 1,000 square feet, for the owner of property to be used for retail/commercial purposes are $7,265 for roads, $432 for fire, and $265 for police, for a total assessment of $7,962. * * *

All impact fees collected by the township are deposited into impact-fee accounts, not into a general fund. The resolution created accounts for each of the four types of impact fees. Money in each discrete account may be used only for the purpose of the account. The accounts do not contain geographic subaccounts. * * * Funds must be spent on projects initiated within three years of the fees' collection; any money not spent within seven years of its collection is refunded to the current owner of the property.

The resolution permits the township to give credits to offset against the impact fees for certain improvements. A land owner or developer can receive partial or full credit for contributions toward the cost of major roadway-system improvements, provided the roadway is on the township's thoroughfare plan. However, no credit will be given for dedication of right-of-ways or for improvements to the major roadway system that primarily serve traffic generated by the improved property, such as acceleration/deceleration lanes into and out of the property.

* * * The township will not issue a zoning certificate until the applicant has paid the applicable impact fee. * * * Appellants * * * brought this action against appellees, the township and its trustees, seeking a declaratory judgment, injunctive relief, and damages, alleging that the impact fees are contrary to Ohio law and are unconstitutional. * * * The trial court granted the township's motion, holding as follows:

> Hamilton Township, pursuant to its statutory limited police powers, may make and fund improvements to benefit new development by use of its system of impact fees, because the resolution is not in conflict with any other Ohio statute, and because it is sufficiently narrowly tailored to provide services to the class of fee payers in exchange for the fees.

The Twelfth District Court of Appeals affirmed. * * *

In Ohio, "townships are creatures of the law and have only such authority as is conferred on them by law." * * * Hamilton Township is a limited-home-rule township created under R.C. Chapter 504. R.C. 504.04(A)(1) states that limited-home-rule townships may, by resolution,

> [e]xercise all powers of local self-government within the unincorporated area of the township, other than powers that are in conflict with general laws, except that the township shall comply with the requirements and prohibitions of this chapter, and *shall enact no taxes other than those authorized by general law* * * *.

(Emphasis added.)

This opinion focuses on whether the impact fees imposed by the township are taxes "other than those authorized by general law." Ohio law already empowers townships to employ specified methods of taxation to raise money to pay for police and fire service, parks, and roads. There is no dispute in this case that the impact fees at issue do not meet the requirements of those methods of taxation, so if the impact fees are actually taxes, they violate R.C. 504.04.

* * * First, the township's assessment lacks [a] regulatory aspect * * * [T]he assessment at issue is not imposed in furtherance of statutes designed to protect the public from harms associated with a specific industry. Rather, it is a revenue generator with the stated purpose of guaranteeing a consistent level of services to all members of the community. It does not encourage the assessed parties' compliance with certain statutory obligations or protect the public from specific threats.

Second, * * * the revenue generated by the assessment in this case is spent on typical township expenses inuring to the benefit of the entire community. It is true that the Hamilton Township assessments are not placed into the general fund; rather, the revenue goes into separate funds for roads, fire, police, and parks. However, * * * although the funds are segregated, the *use* of the money from the funds is general in nature. The money is not earmarked so that it is spent to improve the area around the particular property upon which the assessments are imposed; in other words, there are no geographic subaccounts among the accounts. For instance, there is no requirement that money placed into the police fund goes to create a police substation near a new neighborhood. Instead, the funds can be spent on any police expenditure throughout the community. Within the specific fund, money is spent in a general way, all toward the normal expenditures of government.

Third, * * * assessed parties get no particular service above that provided to any other taxpayer for the fee that they pay. As taxpayers and residents of Hamilton Township, they are entitled to police and fire protection and to use township parks and roadways. They already pay taxes for those services; in fact, when they improve their property, they pay higher taxes than they did when the property was undeveloped. But targets of the assessment receive no greater benefit than any other taxpayer despite the payment of the additional assessment.

* * * [T]he entities paying the assessment are not part of a single industry or group. The assessment applies to a fairly large swath of people—anyone who wants to engage in any type of development in the township. However, it also is not imposed on every township resident. That pushes the needle further from a classic tax, but not into the realm of a classic fee. The * * * ultimate use of the revenue, places the assessment solidly in the realm of taxation. The fact that the funds from the assessments are segregated into separate accounts is irrelevant; the fact that the revenue is earmarked for police protection, fire protection, road improvement, and parks that benefit the entire community is the key factor. The assessments raise revenue for the public's benefit. All members of the community will benefit from improved roadways and parks, as well as from consistent levels of police and fire protection.

* * * [T]he potential public benefit appears to be the main reason for the assessment. But in addressing the tax-versus-fee question, the court of appeals put great stock in one of the stipulations that the parties agreed to in this case, using it as proof that the assessments were made for the benefit of the targeted property:

[Appellants'] claim flies in the face of the parties stipulated facts, which state, in pertinent part:

"The purpose of the impact fee is to benefit *the property* by providing the Township with adequate funds to provide the same level of service to *that property* that the Township currently affords previously developed properties." (Emphasis added.)

To quote [appellants], "[i]n order to be classified as a fee, a charge must specially benefit the property that pays the fee." Based on the parties stipulated facts, that is exactly what occurs here; namely, a payment to the Township to obtain a zoning certificate in order to build on property within its unincorporated areas so that "*that property*" can receive the same level of service provided to previously developed properties. By stipulating to these facts, [appellants] are now bound by their agreement.

(Emphasis sic.)

It is unlikely that appellants would stipulate to a fact that dooms their claim. More importantly, the stipulation implicitly recognizes that the goal is for the township to have the necessary funds to allow *all* properties in the township to maintain their same level of service despite recent, rapid growth. The parties also stipulated that the impact fees were imposed "to offset increased services and improvements needed because of the development." The impact fees are intended to prevent any diminishment of services to *anyone* in the township.

Lest there be any doubt as to whether the impact-fee resolution was designed to affect the whole community, the factual findings in the resolution itself contain statements indicating that maintaining the general welfare of the community is the aim of the resolution. The resolution states that the impact-fee system "assures the continuation of capital services *to benefit one of the fastest growing townships in the State of Ohio and the United States of America,* utilizing a system which is widely accepted as a valid exercise of the police power to protect health, safety and the wellbeing of the community." (Emphasis added.) The board states in the resolution that "*the protection of the health, safety, and general welfare of the citizens and property owners of the Township*" requires that the major roadway facilities, fire-protection and police-protection facilities, and the park facilities of the township "be improved to maintain them at their current levels of service in order to meet the demands of new development." (Emphasis added.)

* * * [T]he assessment results in no direct service to the landowner, other than the issuance of a zoning certificate, for which there is already a separate $200 fee. When the amount of the fee exceeds the cost and expense of the service, the fee constitutes a tax. The impact fees are a revenue-generating measure designed to support infrastructure improvements benefiting the entire township. "Taxation refers to those general burdens imposed for the purpose of supporting the government, and more especially the method of providing the revenues which are expended for the equal benefit of all the people."

Having analyzed the substance of the assessments, and not merely their form, we conclude that the impact fees charged by Hamilton Township in this case constitute taxes. Since those taxes were not authorized by general law, Hamilton Township was not authorized to impose them pursuant to 504.04(A)(1). Accordingly, we reverse the judgment of the court of appeals and remand the matter to the trial court.

NOTES AND QUESTIONS

1. *The "Double Nexus" Test*. As the cases indicate, impact fees must satisfy two requirements: first, that the fee be used to satisfy a public need created by the development subject to the fee; and second, that the amount of the fee be proportionate to the burden created by the development. These two requirements are needed to assure that the fee is really a fee and not a tax as a matter of state law, and that the fee satisfies the due process clause of the federal constitution. How do the state statutes in these cases satisfy these requirements? How closely do the courts assess the evidence presented by localities that their fees meet the double nexus test? In general, courts require only that localities demonstrate a reasonable basis for concluding that a development will generate certain costs, and that the fee will correspond to those costs. Thus, in Home Builders Ass'n of Dayton & the Miami Valley v. City of Beavercreek, 729 N.E.2d 349 (Ohio 2000), the Ohio Supreme Court held that to justify its roadway impact fee a town need only show that its "methodology" for calculating the fee reflected the need for improvements caused by the development, and that the methodology would be acceptable if "based on generally accepted traffic engineering practices." The court also indicated that it would defer to the local government's determination concerning the methodology for calculating the fee:

> The role of a court in reviewing the constitutionality of an impact fee ordinance is not to decide which methodology provides the best results. Given that impact fee ordinances are not subject to precise mathematical formulation, choosing the best methodology is a difficult task that the legislature, not the courts, is better able to accomplish. Rather, a court must only determine whether the methodology used is reasonable based on the evidence presented.

Id. at 357.

Courts may be more assertive in requiring that fees be segregated into special accounts for development-related projects, and not commingled with general public funds. *See, e.g.*, Raintree Homes, Inc. v. Village of Long Grove, 906 N.E.2d 751 (Ill. App. 2009) (invalidating "open space impact fee" because it would finance maintenance and preservation of existing open space and not just acquisition of new open space, and thus was not "specifically and uniquely attributable" to developer activity); Idaho Building Contractors Ass'n v. City of Coeur d'Alene, 890 P.2d 326 (Idaho 1995). *Cf.* Russ Building Partnership v. City & County of San Francisco, 234 Cal.Rptr. 1 (Ct.App.1987), *aff'd in part, rev'd in part on other grounds*, 750 P.2d 324 (Cal.), *app. dismissed*, 488 U.S. 881 (1988) (upholding transit impact development fee imposed on new office space to fund improvements to mass transit system intended to cope with increased ridership due to downtown office development; funds were not earmarked for general revenue purposes).

2.   *Local Power to Impose Impact Fees.* Both *Country Joe* and *Drees* involved fees imposed by non-home-rule localities in the absence of an express grant of authority from the state legislature to do so. In an earlier decision, *Home Builders Ass'n of Dayton*, discussed in Note 1, *supra,* the Ohio Supreme Court upheld a fee imposed by a home rule city notwithstanding the lack of express statutory authority to do so. As one commentator has pointed out, the Ohio court in *Drees* made no mention of *Beavercreek,* not even to distinguish it. Alan C. Weinstein, The Ohio Supreme Court's Perverse Stance on Development Impact Fees and What to Do About It, 60 Cleve. St. L. Rev. 655, 673 (2012). After *Drees*, "Ohio now has different tests for judging the legality of a development impact fee depending on whether the challenged fee was enacted by a municipality or a township." *Id.* at 675. Professor Weinstein contends this is "perverse" as there is relatively little new development in municipalities whereas "rapid development" in suburban townships "creates the most pressing need for impact fees." *Id.* at 676. It is unclear how much the analysis in *Drees* was driven by the municipality/township distinction or whether instead it reflected a change in the court's standard for distinguishing a fee from a tax.

Twenty-eight states have adopted impact fee enabling legislation. *Id.* at 678. Many state courts appear to require some explicit statutory delegation, although the issue is complicated by the preemption question that arises when a state authorizes impact fees for some purposes but not others. *See, e.g.,* Board of County Commissioners v. Bainbridge, Inc., 929 P.2d 691 (Colo.1996) (because state had specifically authorized counties to impose a limited requirement on developers concerning dedication of land or payment of fee for school facilities, counties were precluded from adopting their own school impact fees); Southern Nevada Homebuilders Ass'n, Inc. v. City of North Las Vegas, 913 P.2d 1276 (Nev.1996) (state law authorized impact fees for drainage, sanitary sewers, storm sewers, streets, and water; as a result, impact fee to expand fire and emergency medical services is unauthorized); State of Florida v. City of Port Orange, 650 So.2d 1 (Fla.1994) (transportation utility fee unauthorized by statute and invalid). *See also* New Jersey Builders Ass'n v. Mayor & Township Committee of Bernards Township, 528 A.2d 555 (N.J.1987) (development fee to finance community road improvement plan held invalid where state law authorized fees for only those reasonable and necessary street improvements required within the new subdivision or development). *But cf.* Grupe Devel. Co. v. Superior Court, 844 P.2d 545 (Cal.

1993) (local school impact fees, previously held to be permissible even without specific state authorization now held preempted by state law barring them).

Even in the absence of express enabling legislation some state courts have found authority for local adoption of impact fees either in the grant of home rule powers or in statutory authority to local governments to operate and maintain physical infrastructure to provide certain services. *See, e.g.,* St. Clair Co. Home Builders Ass'n v. City of Pell, 61 So.3d 992 (Ala. 2010) (city's statutory authority to establish and maintain water and sewer systems provides authority to impose an impact fee on developers to support improvements to the system; these fees are distinguishable from the development impact fee to fund "governmental infrastructure" specifically authorized by statute for another county).

Where the power to impose impact fees has been granted, it can be interpreted quite broadly. In Home Builders Ass'n of Central Arizona v. City of Mesa, 243 P.3d 610 (Ariz. App. 2010), the court concluded that the statutory authority to charge impact fees for "necessary public services" included the power to levy a "cultural facilities development fee." The statute did not define "necessary" but the court determined the term ought to be read broadly and would be limited only "to existing services that are already provided by the municipality, or those identified in a properly promulgated general place or infrastructure improvement plan." *Id.* at 615. The court upheld the Mesa fee because the city traditionally provided cultural services and was able to show its cultural facilities, like other public facilities, would be burdened by population growth. As in the *Scottsdale* case, the city was not required to provide a specific cultural facilities development plan or prove that residents of a particular development subject to the fee would use those facilities. The court was satisfied by evidence that demand for cultural facilities would likely be proportional to population growth.

3. *School Impact Fees and Free Public Schools.* New schools are one of the costliest consequences of residential growth, so local governments have a strong interest in impact fees that would help them finance new schools. Virtually all state constitutions, however, require that public education be free. If local governments cannot charge user fees—that is, tuition—to attend public schools, how can they impose school impact fees?

A Massachusetts court held a school impact fee to be invalid because "it failed to benefit fee payers in a manner not shared by other members of the community." Greater Franklin Developers Ass'n, Inc. v. Town of Franklin, 730 N.E.2d 900, 902 (Mass. App.), *rev. den.* 738 N.E.2d 750 (Mass. 2000). Although part of the problem was that the fee could be used to fund capital improvements to existing schools which would benefit both students coming from homes subject to the fee and students from older homes, the court assumed that education inherently benefits the town as a whole: "First and foremost, expanded school capacity benefits the entire community. We hardly need state that society as a whole gains with the education of its children and suffers at the lack." *Accord,* Daniels v. Point Pleasant, 129 A.2d 265 (N.J.

1957) (invalidating ordinance raising the cost of building permits to cover the increased school costs incurred by growth). Other state courts have agreed with Florida that impact fees may be used to finance new school facilities required by growth. *See, e.g.,* Candid Enterps., Inc. v. Grossmont Union H.S. Dist., 705 P.2d 876 (Cal. 1985). *But cf.* Raintree Homes, Inc. v. Village of Long Grove, 906 N.E.2d 751 (Ill. App. 2009) (local school impact fee to support general school operations invalid where state law authorized impact fees for acquisition of land for schools but not to pay for school operations); Grupe Devel. Co. v. Superior Court, 844 P.2d 545 (Cal. 1993) (local school impact fee preempted by state law).

In *Volusia County*, the Florida Supreme Court held that a valid school impact fee cannot apply to age-restricted residential units but must apply to unrestricted residential units that house no school age children in fact. Is the difference between the two types of households that significant?

4. *Who Pays the Development Impact Fee?* Development impact fees are formally imposed on developers, but, depending on such factors as the extent of competition in the housing market, the differences (or lack of differences) in the fees across comparable communities in the same metropolitan area, and other factors, some portion of the impact fee may be passed along to the purchaser who buys a home or commercial unit subject to the fee, or may be passed back to the owners of developable land in the community that adopts the fee. According to Altshuler and Gomez-Ibanez, "[m]ost economists agree that developers will pass on most of the cost of exactions to buyers and renters if exactions are applied over a long period of time and the level of exactions does not vary much within the relevant property market." Regulating for Revenue, *supra,* at 98. However, in the short run, in communities with unusually high exactions, in very hot real estate markets, or in communities that are trying to limit the number of building permits below the level the market would otherwise demand, the exaction is likely to come out of the developer's income or out of the prices landowners would otherwise be able to get for developable land. *See id.* at 100–05. *See also* Arthur C. Nelson, Development Impact Fees: The Next Generation, 26 Urb. Law. 541, 549–51 (1994) (the costs of impact fees are likely to be shared by landowners, land developers, builders, and home buyers; "in competitive markers and after a transition period, impact fees will be passed backward to the owners of vacant land").

Empirical studies have come up with divergent findings concerning the impact fee burden borne by new residents. Dresch and Sheffrin, in their study of the effects of impact fees in Contra Costa County, California (in the Bay Area), found that in the eastern part of the county only 25% of the fees was passed along in housing prices, but this may have been due to a slump in the housing market during the period studied. By contrast, in the western and more affluent part of the county, fee prices were fully passed along (fees constituted 6–7% of the sales price). *See* Marla Dresch & Steven M. Sheffrin, *The Role of Development Fees and Exactions in Local Public Finance,* 13 State Tax Notes 1411 (Dec. 1, 1997). A study of the effect of impact fees on single family homes in eight Chicago suburbs from 1995 to 1997 found that fees were fully passed along to home buyers. *See* Brett M. Baden & Don L. Coursey, "An Examination of the Effects of Impact Fees on Chicago's Suburbs," https://www.researchgate.net/publication/46460761_An_Examination _of_the_Effects_of_Impact_Fees_on_Chicago's_Suburbs.

A related question concerns the differential effects of impact fees on more and less affluent families. Impact fees are more regressive than property taxes. The amount of a fee is usually based on the cost imposed on the community by a new home of average size, but often the same fee is imposed on all homes. A flat fee of $2,000 is a much higher percentage of a $100,000 home than of a $400,000 home. Thus, an impact fee is likely to have a greater impact on moderate-income buyers than on more affluent ones. Moreover, to the extent that buyers of more expensive homes are less sensitive to marginal increases in the purchase price than are buyers of more moderately priced homes, "then developers have an incentive to build higher-priced houses. This, too, has the consequence of pricing low-income people out of suburban neighborhoods." Baden & Coursey, *supra*.

Nelson, however, points to several countervailing considerations. To the extent that impact fees, by providing a means of paying for new infrastructure, lower the price of developable land, they lower the cost of housing. In addition, the availability of impact fees may make local governments more inclined to permit the construction of more housing, thus also reducing housing prices. Nelson, *supra,* at 551. Moreover, Nelson contends that "next generation impact fee programs will be more precise in relating proportionality to house size, and, by implication, income." *Id.* at 554. Such a fee would be based on the number of square feet per person in the housing unit, which would be more closely related to income. Nelson also suggests waiving impact fees for low- and moderate-income housing. *See id.* at 556–57.

5.   *Fees and Fairness*. To the extent developers can pass along impact fees, the fees enable communities to require newcomers to pay for new facilities or for the expansion of existing facilities that are used by the community as a whole. Newcomers also contribute their property tax dollars to the ongoing support of local services. Is it fair to charge them extra, through the development fee, for community services? Is it fair to say that their movement into the community—"growth"—is the cause of the need for new facilities, and that therefore they should be required to contribute something in addition to their taxes? Is protecting old-time residents from the costs of growth an appropriate local policy goal? Is your answer to these questions affected by whether, in the absence of development impact fees, communities would be able to limit growth altogether?

6.   *Impact Fees for Social Purposes*. In Holmdel Builders Ass'n v. Township of Holmdel, 583 A.2d 277 (N.J.1990), the New Jersey Supreme Court upheld local development impact fees imposed on commercial and residential development that were used to fund affordable low- and

moderate-income housing. In so doing, the court indicated it would take a more relaxed approach to the question of whether new development was a cause of the need for new affordable housing. Relying on the *Mount Laurel* doctrine, discussed in Chapter V, and the centrality of affordable housing under New Jersey land use regulation, the court held: "Inclusionary zoning through the imposition of development fees is permissible because such fees are conducive to the creation of a realistic opportunity for the development of affordable housing; . . . it is fair and reasonable to impose such fee requirements on private developers when they possess, enjoy, and consume land which constitutes the primary resource for housing." *Id.* at 288. In California Bldg Indus. Ass'n v. City of San Jose, 351 P.3d 974 (Cal. 2015), *cert. den.* 2016 WL 763863 (2016), the California Supreme Court upheld an "inclusionary zoning" ordinance that requires all new residential development projects of twenty or more units to sell at least fifteen percent of the for-sale units at prices affordable to low- or moderate-income households, or, as one of several alternatives, to pay an "in lieu fee based on the median sales prices of a housing unit to a moderate income family." The court rejected the argument that an inclusionary zoning requirement could be sustained only if shown to be necessary to mitigate any negative impacts the development would have on the availability of affordable housing. The court found, instead, that the requirement was justified by the city's interests in increasing the amount of affordable housing and in distributing affordable housing throughout the city in economically diverse developments. *But see* San Telmo Assocs. v. City of Seattle, 735 P.2d 673 (Wash.1987) (holding requirement that developers who demolish low-income housing and replace it with commercial facilities either provide replacement housing or contribute to a housing fund is an attempt to shift the social cost of providing low-income housing from the public to developers and, thus, an unauthorized tax rather than a form of land use regulation).

There is also some evidence that by varying the level of impact fees in different zones based on the difference between the lower costs of serving new developments in areas that are already developed versus the higher costs of adding services in more remote locations, a city may be able to use the fees to promote in-fill development and discourage sprawl. *See* Gregory S. Burge, et al, Can Development Impact Fees Help Mitigate Urban Sprawl?, 79 J. Am. Plan'g Ass'n 235 (2013).

7.   *Development Impact Fees and the Takings Clause.* In Koontz v. St. Johns River Water Management Dist., 133 S.Ct. 2586 (2013), the Supreme Court held for the first time that monetary exactions imposed as a condition for a land use permit are subject to challenge under the Takings Clause. *Koontz* has important but as yet uncertain implications for development impact fees.

Since the Court's earlier decisions in Nollan v. California Coastal Commission, 483 U.S. 825 (1987), and Dolan v. City of Tigard, 512 U.S. 374 (1994), requirements that landowners provide a government with an interest in land as a condition for obtaining approval of a new land use have been subject to challenge under the Takings Clause. The Court required that there be some "nexus" between the condition on development and the government's interest in restricting development, and that there be some "rough proportionality" between the condition imposed and the problems caused by the development. Both *Nollan* and *Dolan* involved regulatory schemes under which the local government had required the dedication of real property by the owner as a condition for issuing the necessary development permit. By contrast, the development impact fee requires the payment of money.

For two decades the lower courts struggled with the question of whether the Takings Clause and the *Nollan/Dolan* test apply to monetary fees that are a condition for permission to develop land. *Koontz* resolved the issue, holding that the Takings Clause applies "when the government commands the relinquishment of funds linked to a specific, identifiable property interest such as a . . . parcel of real property." 133 S.Ct. at 2600.

Koontz, however, said little about how to apply the *Nollan/Dolan* test to specific fees. Some of the leading pre-*Koontz* lower court decisions applying a Takings Clause analysis to fees had done so only for ad hoc, individualized impositions, not for broadly applicable, legislatively adopted fee programs. In the leading case of Ehrlich v. City of Culver City, 911 P.2d 429 (Cal. 1996), the California Supreme Court applied a Takings analysis to an impact fee but limited the application of *Nollan/Dolan* to situations in which "a local government imposes special, discretionary permit conditions on development by individual property owners." *Id.* at 447. The case involved a rezoning request by the owner of a private tennis club to authorize the construction of a condominium complex. Because the land use change would result in the loss of recreational opportunities, the city council had conditioned its approval on the plaintiff's willingness to pay a $280,000 fee to fund additional recreational facilities. The court held that such an individualized fee determination triggered review under *Nollan/Dolan*, adding the qualification that "it is not at all clear that the rationale (and the heightened standard of scrutiny) of *Nollan* and *Dolan* applies to cases in which the exaction takes the form of a *generally* applicable development fee or assessment." *Id.* The court held the Culver City fee met *Nollan*'s essential nexus requirement, but that the city had failed to show that the fee satisfied *Dolan*'s "rough proportionality" rule. Similarly, in *City of Scottsdale,* the first case reproduced in this section, the Arizona Supreme Court cited *Ehrlich* to support its determination that *Dolan*, if applicable to monetary exactions at all, applied only to a "city's adjudicative decision to impose a condition tailored to the particular circumstances of an individual case." 930 P.2d at 1000. *Accord,* Krupp v. Breckenridge Sanitation Dist., 19 P.3d 687 (Colo. 2001). A number of commentators have embraced the ad hoc or adjudicative versus legislative distinction, and would limit *Koontz*'s Takings Clause analysis to the former situation. *See, e.g.,* John M. Newman, Koontz v. St. Johns River Water Management District: The Constitutionality of Monetary Exactions in Land Use Planning, 76 Mont. L. Rev. 359, 375 (2015); Lee Anne Fennell and Eduardo Peñalver, Exactions Creep, 2013 Sup. Ct. Rev. 287,

340–41 (2013). *See also* San Remo Hotel v. City & Co. of San Francisco, 27 Cal.4th 643, 671 (2002) ("[a] council that charged extortionate fees for all property development, unjustified by mitigation needs, would likely face widespread and well-financed opposition in the next election. Ad hoc, individual monetary exactions deserve special judicial scrutiny mainly because, affecting fewer citizens and evading systematic assessment, they are more likely to escape such political controls").

Koontz, however, did not draw the ad hoc/legislative distinction. Instead, the Court cited three cases in which state supreme courts declined to make that distinction and applied *Nollan/Dolan* to legislative impact fee requirements. 133 S. Ct. at 2602. In one of those state court decisions, Town of Flower Mound v. Stafford Estates Ltd P'ship, 135 S.W.3d 620, 641 (Tex. 2004), the Texas Supreme Court expressed doubt that "a workable distinction can always be drawn between actions denominated adjudicative and legislative."

Applying the Takings Clause to a development impact fee need not be fatal to the fee. Many of the state court assessments of whether an impact fee is a true fee and not an invalid tax for state legal purposes closely resemble the *Nollan/Dolan* essential nexus and rough proportionality requirements. In Home Builders Ass'n of Dayton, *supra,* a case cited in Koontz, 133 S.Ct. at 2602, the Ohio Supreme Court applied the *Nollan/Dolan* test in upholding a roadway impact fee. The court readily concluded there was a "reasonable relationship between the city's interest in constructing new roadways and the increase in traffic generated by new developments," *id.* at 356, thus satisfying *Nollan*. Turning to the question of rough proportionality, the court held that *Dolan*'s concern would be satisfied if the town could show that its "methodology" for calculating the roadway impact fee reflected the need for improvements caused by the development, and that the methodology would be acceptable if "based on generally accepted traffic engineering practices." The court also indicated that it would defer to the local government's determination concerning the methodology for calculating the fee. Although, as discussed in Note 2, *Beavercreek*'s approach to Ohio law is in some tension with *Drees,* the basic point remains that the factors necessary for an impact fee to pass muster under state law would tend to support the fee's constitutionality under *Nollan* and *Dolan*.

3. OTHER REVENUE SOURCES

a. Local Governments

In 2013, property taxes, special assessments, and user fees and charges in the aggregate accounted for 75% of local government own-source revenue. *See* U.S. Census Bureau, State and Local Government Finance 2013. Most of the remaining local own-source revenues are generated by sales and income taxes. Sales taxes—including general, broad-based sales taxes on a wide range of retail transactions, as well as selective sales taxes targeted at particular categories of transactions—accounted for 11% of local own-source revenues and personal and corporate income taxes for another 4% of local source revenues. *Id.* Miscellaneous other sources accounted for the rest. Different types of local governments derive differing percentages of their revenues from different sources. School districts, for example, are particularly dependent on the property tax while sales and income taxes play a larger role in financing cities and counties.

Local sales taxes are widespread. Currently, thirty-eight states authorize local sales taxes. Three of those states—California, Utah, and Virginia—also impose a mandatory statewide local add-on to state sales taxes. In the states that authorize local sales taxes, tax rates vary from locality to locality, with the lowest average in Idaho (0.01%) and the highest in Alabama and Louisiana (4.91% each). Tax Foundation, State and Local Sales Tax Rates in 2015. A 2007 study found that all nine of the nation's largest cities relied on general sales tax revenue; in four of the nine cities the sales tax was collected by both the city and the county. *See* New York City Independent Budget Office, Comparing State and Local Taxes in Large U.S. Cities (Feb. 2007). Generally, local sales taxes closely copy state sales taxes—applying to the same tax base and containing the same exclusions and exemptions. Most states collect local and state sales taxes together and then remit the local share to local governments.

Local income taxes are less common. In 2011, the Tax Foundation found that local income taxes were levied in just seventeen states, affecting 4,943 local jurisdictions. *See* Joseph Henchman and Jason Sapia, Local Income Taxes: City- and County-Level Income and Wage Taxes Continue to Wane (Tax Foundation, Aug. 31, 2011). The local income tax is most common in Pennsylvania, with more than 2,960 municipalities and school districts imposing it; half of all the localities in the United States that levy an income tax are in Pennsylvania. It is also widespread in Ohio, where it may be found in over 770 localities, and in Kansas and Iowa. The number of localities using the tax is smaller in Indiana and Maryland, but as the tax is imposed by all the counties in those states, the local income tax is effectively state-wide. Most local income tax rates range from one to two percent, with some less than one percent and the highest a little over four percent. The highest average rate, 1.55%, was in Maryland. (The income tax in the District of Columbia, which performs many of the functions of both a city and a state, is much higher.) Local income taxes are usually a flat rate or only slightly graduated according to income. *Id.*

Local income taxes were first imposed during the Depression, when declining property values forced local governments to look to other sources of revenue. The first local income tax was in Philadelphia;

thereafter the income tax was adopted by selected cities in Ohio, Kentucky, Missouri, and Michigan. *Id.* The tax is imposed in many major cities in the East and Midwest, including New York City; Philadelphia; Baltimore; Birmingham, Alabama; Cleveland; Cincinnati; Columbus; Detroit; Kansas City, Missouri; Louisville, Kentucky; Pittsburgh; St. Louis; Wilmington, Delaware; and Washington, D.C. In the West, three Colorado cities, including Denver, impose flat taxes on employee compensation, and San Francisco imposes a payroll tax on larger firms. Most city income taxes apply only to the earnings of local residents, although some cities tax local residents' incomes from property and investments as well as wages. Some cities in some states are also authorized to tax the in-city earnings of nonresidents, such as commuters. Often the commuter tax rate is lower than the rate applicable to residents. In their study of the finances of large cities, Helen F. Ladd and John Yinger argue that greater availability of a commuter earnings tax and the concomitant spreading of the costs of financing services needed to meet the social burdens of the central cities across metropolitan areas would alleviate the serious fiscal problems facing many central cities. A commuter tax also "recognizes the city's connections with its suburbs. Placing some of the tax burden on suburbanites accounts for the benefits they receive from city services, and it lowers the regressiveness of the metropolitan tax system, to which both city and suburbs belong." Helen F. Ladd & John Yinger, America's Ailing Cities: Fiscal Health and the Design of Urban Policy 300 (Johns Hopkins Univ. Press 1989).

Generally, both local sales and income taxes require specific state authorization, *see, e.g.*, Carter Carburetor Corp. v. City of St. Louis, 203 S.W.2d 438 (Mo.1947), City & County of Denver v. Sweet, 329 P.2d 441 (Colo.1958), although the Michigan Supreme Court held that the general grant of home rule power "for laying and collecting rents, tolls, and excises" provided sufficient statutory basis for Detroit's income tax, *see* Dooley v. City of Detroit, 121 N.W.2d 724 (Mich.1963). The Ohio Supreme Court similarly found that the constitutional grant of home rule included the power to impose a municipal payroll tax, *see* Angell v. City of Toledo, 91 N.E.2d 250 (Ohio 1950). States also generally have power to preempt local sales and income taxes. *See, e.g.*, California Federal Savings & Loan Ass'n v. City of Los Angeles, 812 P.2d 916 (Cal.1991) (state income tax on financial corporations preempts city license tax on financial corporations); *but cf.* Weekes v. City of Oakland, 579 P.2d 449, 456–63 (Cal.1978) (concurring opinion of Richardson, J., contending that a municipal income tax is a "municipal affair" under California home rule amendment and, thus, protected from state preemption).

In 1999, New York State repealed New York City's authority to tax the incomes of its commuters. The decision nicely illustrates the power of state governments with respect to the local power to tax incomes. Under the New York constitution, a "home rule" message—that is, a request from the affected municipality—is required when the legislature passes a special law relating to the "property, affairs or government" of a city. The New York Court of Appeals, however, held that, given the impact of the commuter tax on non-residents of New York City, the tax was a matter of state concern so that a home rule message was not required. *See* City of New York v. State, 730 N.E.2d 920 (N.Y.2000).

b. States

State finances rely heavily on a combination of sales taxes, personal and corporate income taxes, fees and charges, and intergovernmental assistance. In 2013 federal aid was the single largest source of state funds and accounted for 30% of total state general revenues. Sales taxes (including general retail sales taxes, selective taxes, such as the tax on motor fuels, and gross receipts taxes) came next, accounting for 23% of total state revenue, 34% of state own-source revenues, and 47% of state tax revenues. Individual and corporate income taxes provided 21% of total state revenues, 31% of state own-source funds, and 42% of state tax revenues. Fees, charges, and miscellaneous taxes provided the rest of state revenues. U.S. Census Bureau, State and Local Government Finances 2013. These percentages vary considerably from state to state. Nearly all states—45 out of 50—impose a sales tax, at rates ranging from 2.9% to 7.5%, with 35 states taxing sales at rates ranging from 4% to 6%. *See* Tax Foundation, State and Local Sales Tax Rates, *supra*. When state and local sales taxes are added together, the top combined rate exceeds nine percent, with Tennessee at 9.45% and Arkansas at 9.26%. The base for the sales tax also varies from state to state. Most apply to all retail purchases of tangible personal property, except for goods that are expressly exempted. Most states exempt grocery food purchases, and some exempt low-priced clothing and nonprescription drugs and medicines. Sales taxes are considered to be regressive, since the tax paid is based on the amount and price of the goods bought, not the income of the purchaser. Although more affluent people spend more money on the consumption of goods, low income people devote a higher proportion of their incomes to the purchase of goods. As a result, low income people usually pay a higher percentage of their incomes in sales taxes than do upper income people. *See* Michael P. Ettlinger, et al., Who Pays? A Distributional Analysis of the Tax System in All 50 States, 11 State Tax Notes 311 (July 29, 1996) (seven of the ten most regressive state tax systems rely heavily on sales taxes). Some states have made their sales taxes less regressive by exempting items—such as food, medicine or clothing below a certain price—that constitute a significant portion of the spending of low income people.

State sales taxes traditionally focused on the purchase of goods, rather than the purchase of services. With the dramatic growth in the service economy, sales tax revenues began to lag behind growth in the economy as a whole. As a result, states are increasingly taxing services. Currently, thirty-seven states tax selective personal and professional services, and four states tax most services other than those specifically exempted. The services most commonly subject to the sales tax are telephone, cable and direct satellite television, and utility services, auto repairs and servicing; admissions to amusement parks, professional sports, and cultural events; health club services; and services to businesses, such as advertising, printing, and graphic design. *See* John L. Mikesell, Considering Sales Taxation of Services in Indiana: A Report Prepared for the Indiana Fiscal Policy Institute 6–8 (March 2015). *See also* Kirk J. Stark, The Uneasy Case for Extending the Sales Tax to Services, 30 Fla. St. U. L. Rev. 435 (2003).

State personal income taxes are nearly as widespread as the sales tax. Forty-three states levy individual income taxes. Forty-one tax wage and salary income, while two—New Hampshire and Tennessee—tax only interest and dividends, and not earned income. Most state personal income taxes rely on the federal Internal Revenue Code and apply state rates to a federally defined tax base (usually either federal taxable income or federal adjusted gross income). However, state personal income taxes vary considerably according to their rates, the degree of graduation in their rate structures, and the use of credits and exemptions. Eight states have single-rate tax structures, with one rate applying to all taxable income, while thirty-three levy graduated-rate income taxes. *See* Tax Foundation, State Individual Income Tax Rates and Brackets for 2015. State personal income taxes contribute an element of progressivity to state tax systems, and the income tax is also more elastic—that is, responsive to changes in income—than other sources of revenue.

C. BORROWING AND DEBT LIMITATIONS

Borrowing plays a central role in state and local finance. State and local governments borrow literally billions of dollars every year. In 2013, the total amount of state debt outstanding was approximately $1,137 billion, which reflected a $270 billion increase in seven years. *See* Council of State Governments, The Book of the States (2014). Local governments accounted for an additional $1,817 billion in outstanding debt, bringing total state and local debt outstanding to $2,955 billion. *See* U.S. Census Bureau, State and Local Government Finances: 2013. When spread across the total U.S. population, that amounts to a little more than $9,330 per person.

State and local borrowing is subject to extensive legal regulation—by state constitutional provisions that impose substantive and procedural constraints on the issuance of new debt; by state statutes that regulate the content of state obligations and the procedures for their issuance; by the federal tax code and federal securities laws; and by the Contracts Clause of the United States Constitution. After a brief review of the different ways of classifying state and local debt, this section will focus, in subsection (1), on the state and federal constitutional provisions that protect the interests of those who buy state and local debt obligations; in subsection (2), on the state constitutional provisions that limit the ability of states and local governments to issue debt; and, in subsection (3), on the many legal techniques state and local governments have developed to avoid those limitations.

Classifying State and Local Debt. State and local debt can be classified in a number of ways—according to the duration of the debt; according to the nature of the government pledge backing the debt; and according to the treatment of the debt under the United States Internal Revenue Code.

Duration. State and local debt may be either *short-term* or *long-term*. *Short-term debt* consists of obligations that mature, and therefore must be repaid, within a relatively short period of time. Typically referred to as *notes*, short-term debt usually comes due within a year of its issuance. Notes are often issued to deal with short-term cash flow problems. If, for example, as the fiscal year draws to a close, expenditures are running ahead of revenues, a state or local government may issue notes to borrow money so it may finish the fiscal year with a balanced budget. The state will pledge to pay the interest and repay the principal on the notes with taxes or other revenues that it expects to receive in the next fiscal year. As a result, these notes are often referred to as tax anticipation notes ("TANs"), revenue anticipation notes ("RANs"), or tax and revenue anticipation notes ("TRANs"). Notes may also be issued to expedite construction of a new capital project. Although capital construction is typically financed by long-term debt, or bonds, the state or locality may wish to start construction before it has actually sold the bonds and received the proceeds. To do that, it may issue bond anticipation notes ("BANs") which are backed by the proceeds from the sale of the bonds.

Short-term debt is a relatively minor factor in state and local borrowing. Only $32 billion—or a little more than one percent—out of the total $2,954 billion in state and local debt outstanding in 2013 consisted of short-term debt. Short-term debt is typically exempted from many of the state constitutional restrictions on borrowing. However, this may be contingent on the notes actually being repaid out of regular revenue rather than being carried over with a new issuance of short-term debt. Thus, in Wein v. State of New York, 347 N.E.2d 586, 592 (N.Y.1976), the New York Court of Appeals held that it would violate the state constitution for the state to issue notes "if it cannot be reasonably anticipated at the time the notes are issued that the State will have sufficient committed taxes and revenues, based on authentic estimates, to pay the obligations within one year of the date of issue."

It may, however, be difficult for a court to determine whether, when a state issues short-term notes, the issuer will be able to repay the notes without additional borrowing. In a case decided the year after *Wein*, the New York Court of Appeals rejected the argument that when the state of New York had sustained deficits two years in a row, a planned issuance of short-term debt was unconstitutional because the state would probably have to borrow again in the next year to pay off the new notes. In effect, the plaintiff contended that through a succession of short-term notes the state was annually rolling over a long-term deficit. The court, however, held that despite the past deficits it would accept the state's budget estimates, which showed a balanced budget for the coming fiscal year, and it placed the burden on the challenger to prove that a deficit was likely to occur. Wein v. Carey, 362 N.E.2d 587 (N.Y.1977).

Long-term debt is, of course, the opposite of short-term debt. When a state or locality issues long-term debt, typically referred to as bonds, it does not have to repay the principal for at least ten, and often as many as thirty or forty, years. The issuer will, however, pay bondholders interest over the life of the bonds.

The vast preponderance of state and local debt is long-term. States and local governments incur long-term debt in order to finance capital facilities, which can include schools, prisons, other government buildings, bridges, tunnels, highways, mass transit systems, power plants, water supply systems, and solid waste and waste water treatment systems. Indeed, bonds finance roughly two-thirds of the capital expenditures of state and local governments. *See* Department of Revenue of Kentucky v. Davis, 553 U.S. 328, 333 (2008). States and localities rely on long-term debt to finance these projects for two reasons. First, it expedites the construction and completion of the projects. New capital infrastructure can be very costly. It might not be possible to finance a big project out of ordinary tax revenues without either a massive tax increase or severe cuts in expenditures for ordinary and necessary services. A government could attempt to rely on ordinary revenues by stretching out construction of the facility over many years. But such "pay-as-you-go" financing could delay the completion and efficient operation of the project until many years into the future. By borrowing, the government can secure early completion of the project and receipt of its benefits—much as a family takes out a mortgage to finance the acquisition of a home, begins living in it immediately, and repays the mortgage lender over time.

Second, borrowing is a means of achieving intergenerational equity. Whereas people benefit from expenditures for government services—policing, garbage pick-ups, park maintenance—during the year the expenditures are incurred, the benefits from a new capital project may be received in the future. A capital project has—or should have—a long "useful life." It would be unfair to require current taxpayers to fully pay for a new sewer, bridge, or school through a hefty tax increase or cuts in services when the benefits of the project will be received by taxpayers over many decades. Long-term bonds enable a government to spread the cost of the project over time, so that future beneficiaries participate in financing it. As the Supreme Court explained, "[b]onds place the cost of a project on the citizens who benefit from it over the years . . . and they allow for public work beyond what current revenues can support." Kentucky v. Davis, *supra*, 553 U.S. at 342.

Nature of the Obligation. State and local debts fall into two broad categories: *general obligation* debt and *nonguaranteed* debt. *General obligation* bonds, or "full faith and credit" debt, are guaranteed by the full revenue-raising capacity of the issuer. By contrast, *nonguaranteed* debt—also known as limited obligation debt or revenue bonds—is backed only by specified revenue sources. In a revenue bond, the government issuer borrows money to pay for a specific project. In contrast to a general obligation bond, the bondholder, or lender, does not receive the government's unconditional promise to repay the debt. Rather, under the terms of repayment, the government promises only that the revenues generated by the funded project, once it is completed, will be used to repay the bondholders. Thus, if the project fails or does not live up to revenue expectations, the bondholders are left without repayment of their original loan to the government. As revenue bonds entail a higher degree of risk, they typically pay a higher rate of return than full faith and credit bonds.

Historically, most state and local debt consisted of general obligation bonds. In recent decades, however, nonguaranteed debt has become the principal form of state and local borrowing. Between 1992 and 2013, the nonguaranteed debt share of total state and local debt ranged between 61% and 72%. *See* Steven Maguire and Jeffrey M. Stupak, Tax-Exempt Bonds: A Description of State and Local Government Debt 7 (Congressional Research Service, Jan. 9, 2015).

Federal Tax Status. The Internal Revenue Code applies different tax treatment to state and local debt issued to finance *public purpose* projects versus state and local debts that finance *private activity* projects. Section 103(a) of the Internal Revenue Code provides that, subject to certain exceptions, "gross income" for federal income tax purposes does not include the interest on any state or local bond. In other words, a taxpayer who buys a state or local bond does not have to pay federal income tax on the interest she receives from the bond. As a result, a state or local bond issuer can pay a much lower interest rate than a corporate bond issuer. Historically interest rates on tax-exempt state and local bonds have been about thirty percent lower than on comparable taxable investments although in recent years the interest differential has diminished. *See* Tax-Exempt Bonds, *supra*, at 2. This constitutes a substantial federal subsidy—in terms of foregone federal income tax payments—for state and local governments. In 2013, the forgone tax revenue from the exclusion of interest income on tax-exempt bonds came to $28.4 billion. *Id.* at 3. Until the Supreme Court's decision in South Carolina v. Baker, 485 U.S. 505 (1988), many commentators assumed this tax exemption was constitutionally mandatory. *South Carolina* involved a provision of the federal Tax Equity and Fiscal Responsibility Act ("TEFRA") of 1982 which limited the availability of the tax exemption for state and local bond interest to only those bonds issued in "registered" form, that is, where the identity of the purchaser is recorded in a central registry. Historically, many state and bonds had been issued in "bearer" form, with no record of the owners maintained. TEFRA denied the availability of the tax exemption to state and local bearer bonds. The Supreme Court upheld Congress's power to do so.

Most state governments that tax personal incomes also exempt from taxation the interest on municipal bonds issued by the taxing state and its political subdivisions, while still taxing interest on bonds issued by other states and localities. This differential tax exemption was upheld by the Supreme Court against a challenge based on the Commerce Clause in *Department of Revenue of Kentucky v. Davis, supra.* In so doing, the Court gave weight to the role of municipal bonds in "[f]unding the work of government." 553 U.S. at 334. The Court noted that "the issuance of debt securities to pay for public projects is a quintessentially public function." *Id.* at 342. Due to the "public character of the enterprise supported by the tax preference," *id.*, the usual presumption against discriminatory taxation did not apply.

As noted in Section A of this Chapter, state and local governments have long engaged in programs to aid private industry. Section A explored the application of state constitutional "public purpose" requirements to these programs. Many states and localities financed their private sector assistance programs through the issuance of tax-exempt debt, taking advantage of the federal tax exemption to subsidize their economic development programs. By 1981, such private activity bonds accounted for an estimated 48% of all new state and local bond issues and were contributing to a growing federal revenue loss.

In the 1980s, Congress enacted a series of measures that effectively distinguished between *public purpose* bonds (a term not actually used in the Internal Revenue Code) and *private activity* bonds (a term defined in section 141 of the Internal Revenue Code). The specific definition of and restrictions on private activity bonds are subject to legislative and regulatory change, but the basic concept is that when a bond's proceeds are used primarily by private sector actors, or when the bond is primarily secured by private funds, it is a private activity bond, whose interest is subject to federal income taxation unless it falls into one of the specified categories deemed "qualified" for tax-exempt treatment. Over time, Congress has expanded the types of private activities eligible for tax-exempt financing and has increased the permitted volume of private activity bonds for selected activities and issuers. Tax-Exempt Bonds, *supra*, at 9–13. In addition, Congress has periodically since 1997 authorized "tax credit bonds"—temporary tax provisions that offer an investor a federal tax credit or the issuer a direct payment instead of exempting bond interest from federal income tax. One of the most well-known of these was the Build America Bond ("BAB") program authorized by the American Recovery and Reinvestment Act of 2009 to stimulate recovery from the recession. Under the BAB program, which ran from 2009 through 2010, the U.S. Treasury either paid states and local governments issuing bonds a subsidy of 35% of the interest they owed investors or provided bond investors with tax credits to reduce their tax liability. With the exception of the BABs, each tax credit bond program was designated for a specific purpose, location, or project, such as public school construction and renovation; clean renewable energy projects; refinancing of existing government debt in regions affected by natural disasters; conservation of forest land; energy conservation; or economic development. *See* Tax-Exempt Bonds, *supra,* at 14–15.

1. THE ENFORCEMENT OF STATE AND LOCAL DEBT OBLIGATIONS

FLUSHING NATIONAL BANK V. MUNICIPAL ASSISTANCE CORPORATION FOR THE CITY OF NEW YORK

Court of Appeals of New York
40 N.Y. 2d 731 (N.Y. 1976)

CHIEF JUDGE BREITEL.

* * * On November 13, 1975, because of the city's desperate fiscal paralysis, the Legislature, in Extraordinary Session, passed, and the next day the Governor approved, the New York City Emergency Moratorium Act (L 1975, ch 874, as amd by ch 875). The act imposes a three-year moratorium on actions to enforce the city's outstanding short-term obligations, namely, tax anticipation notes (TANS), bond anticipation notes (BANS), revenue anticipation notes (RANS), budget notes, and urban renewal notes (URNS). The act provides that the moratorium will be effective only with respect to those noteholders who have been offered, and have declined, an opportunity "voluntarily" to exchange their notes for an equal principal amount of long-term bonds issued by the Municipal Assistance Corporation for the City of New York (MAC). The act also provides that during the moratorium the noteholders who have declined to exchange their notes for MAC bonds are to be paid interest at an annual rate of at least 6%. * * *

MAC is an intermediate finance agency created to assist the city in its financial stringency (L 1975, ch 169). Neither the faith and credit of the State nor of the city is pledged to the obligations of MAC, but only certain revenues which the city may raise or receive from the State * * *.

After defining the moratorium period as three years from the effective date of the act (§ 2, subd 3), the core moratorium provisions read as follows:

"§ 3. Enforcement of judgments and liens on account of short-term obligations suspended.

"During the moratorium period, and notwithstanding any inconsistent provisions of any law, general, special or local, or of any agreement or short-term obligation, no act shall be done, and no action or special proceeding shall be commenced or continued in any court in any jurisdiction, seeking to apply or enforce against the city, or any political subdivision, agency, instrumentality or officer thereof, or their funds, property, receivables or revenues, any order, judgment, lien, set-off or counterclaim on account of any short-term obligation, or the indebtedness or liability evidenced thereby . . . although the payment of such short-term obligation may be due by the terms thereof or any general or special or local law or agreement.

"§ 4. Actions upon short-term obligations suspended.

"During the moratorium period, and notwithstanding any inconsistent provisions of any law, general, special or local, or of any agreement or short-term obligation, no action or special proceeding shall be commenced or continued upon any short-term obligation, or the indebtedness or liability evidenced thereby, although the payment of such short-term obligation may be due by the terms thereof or any general or special or local law or agreement."

On November 14, 1975, the effective date of the Moratorium Act, approximately $5 billion in city notes were outstanding and were scheduled to mature within the following 12 months. Of the $5 billion in notes, about $2.1 billion were held by MAC, $250 million were held by the State, and $1.049 billion were held by 11 New York clearing house banks and various city employees' pension and bond sinking funds. At about the same time, the clearing house banks and the city funds agreed to extend their notes to July 1, 1986. After two MAC exchange offers, about $1 billion in notes remain with the public, including plaintiff Flushing National Bank. * * *

The State Constitution regulates closely the debt-incurring power of local governments. Key to this case is that a city may not contract indebtedness unless it has "pledged its faith and credit for the payment of the principal thereof and the interest thereon" (NY Const, art VIII, § 2). * * *

A pledge of the city's faith and credit is both a commitment to pay and a commitment of the city's revenue generating powers to produce the funds to pay. Hence, an obligation containing a pledge of the city's "faith and credit" is secured by a promise both to pay and to use in good faith the city's general revenue powers to produce sufficient funds to pay the principal and interest of the obligation as it becomes due. That is why both words, "faith" and "credit", are used and they are not tautological. * * *

A "faith and credit" obligation is, therefore, entirely different from a "revenue" obligation, which is limited to a pledge of revenues from a designated source or fund. * * * It is also in contrast to a "moral" obligation, which is backed not by a legally enforceable promise to pay but only by a "moral" commitment.

The constitutional requirement of a pledge of the city's faith and credit is not satisfied merely by engraving a statement of the pledge in the text of the obligation. The last is a strange argument made by respondents. It is difficult to understand the financial value of such a commitment as contrasted with a "moral" obligation, wisely prohibited by the Constitution for municipalities (NY Const, art VIII, § 2). Instead, by any test, whether based on realism or sensibility, the city is constitutionally obliged to pay and to use in good faith its revenue powers to produce funds to pay the principal of the notes when due. The effect of the Moratorium Act is, however, to permit the city, having given it, to ignore its pledge of faith and credit to "pay" and to "pay punctually" the notes when due. Thus, the act would enable the city to proceed as if the pledge of faith and credit had never been.

It is argued that the city has insufficient funds to pay the notes and cannot in good faith use its revenue powers to pay the notes. The city has an enormous debt and one that in its entirety, if honored as portions become due, undoubtedly exceeds the city's present capacity to maintain an effective cash flow. But it is not true that any particular indebtedness of the city, let alone the outstanding temporary notes, is responsible for any allocable insufficiency. In short, what has happened is those responsible have made an expedient selection of the temporary noteholders to bear an extraordinary burden. The invidious consequence may not be justified by fugitive recourse to the police power of the State or to any other constitutional power to displace inconvenient but intentionally protective constitutional limitations.

The constitutional prescription of a pledge of faith and credit is designed, among other things, to protect rights vulnerable in the event of difficult economic circumstances. Thus, it is destructive of the constitutional purpose for the Legislature to enact a measure aimed at denying that very protection on the ground that government confronts the difficulties which, in the first instance, were envisioned. * * *

* * * [The state Constitution expresses] a constitutional imperative: debt obligations must be paid, even if tax limits be exceeded. A Constitution is no less violated because one would undermine only its prevailing spirit, and, arguably, not its letter. * * * However, in this case there is no split; spirit and letter speak in unison.

Thus, it is disingenuous to contend that, since the constitutional language allowing the city to exceed tax limits to pay its indebtedness is in form permissive, it may be disregarded. Similarly disingenuous is the argument that the Legislature has not unconstitutionally restricted the power of the city to levy taxes to pay its indebtedness because the city is "free" under the Moratorium Act to pay the notes if it wishes. The problem is not that, but that the city is free under the questioned legislation not to pay them.

* * * [T]he Moratorium Act, if it were valid, would bar all remedies for a period of three years. For this there is no warrant. And the city's position on the appeal and the discussions publicized in connection with the exchange offers of MAC bonds for the temporary notes make quite clear that the noteholders would have to have a life expectancy of longer than three years if they expect the city voluntarily to redeem the notes. In short, if a three-year moratorium be valid, then one for a longer period should be valid, and perhaps too, one so long until all the noteholders take MAC bonds "voluntarily" in exchange for their notes.

* * *

In sum, to hold, as respondents would have the court do, that the operative effect of the faith and credit clause is exhausted when the indebtedness has been incurred would result in an economic and legal chimera. The only practical significance of a pledge of faith and credit with respect to an indebtedness must be in relation to its payment here on earth and on its due day. To interpret the constitutional provision otherwise would be to honor it as a form of window-dressing but to deny it substantive significance. * * *

The dissenting opinion in impressive eloquence portrays the dire straits of the city. The portrait is a correct one, but the duty of this court is to determine constitutional issues which sometimes accommodate and sometimes prohibit the facile and sometimes too facile solution of difficult problems. But it is a Constitution that is being interpreted and as a Constitution it would serve little of its purpose if all that it promised, like the elegantly phrased Constitutions of some totalitarian or dictatorial Nations, was an ideal to be worshipped when not needed and debased when crucial. * * *

Emergencies and the police power, although they may modify their applications, do not suspend constitutional principles. * * * The notes in suit provided that the city pledged its faith and credit to pay the notes and to pay them punctually when due. The clause and the constitutional mandate have no office except when their enforcement is inconvenient. A neutral court worthy of its status cannot do less than hold what is so evident.

The city and State, and to some extent the National Government, for almost two years have been engaged in a most difficult struggle to resolve the city's grave fiscal and economic problems. For well over a year many financial transactions have occurred on the assumption, however strained, that the moratorium would be constitutionally acceptable. In order to minimize market and governmental disruptions which might ensue it would be injudicious at this time to allow the extraordinary remedies in the nature of injunction and peremptory mandamus sought by plaintiff. Plaintiff and other noteholders of the city are entitled to some judicial relief free of throttling by the moratorium statute, but they are not entitled immediately to extraordinary or any particular judicial measures unnecessarily disruptive of the city's delicate financial and economic balance. * * * It would serve neither plaintiff nor the people of the City of New York precipitately to invoke instant judicial remedies which might give the city no choice except to proceed into bankruptcy. The strenuous and valiant efforts by the city and State administrations, with the aid of the National Government, should be given as much leeway as constitutional decency permits. Yet none of this means that remedy can be denied to plaintiff or to noteholders beyond the short period necessary to prepare for the consequences of the determination to be made in this case.

COOKE, J, dissenting.

* * * [I]n November of 1975, * * * in Extraordinary Session, the Legislature enacted the New York State Emergency Moratorium Act for the City of New York. * * * [T]he Legislature found "that the grave public emergency found and declared to exist by the legislature in adopting the New York State Financial Emergency Act for the City of New York has

dramatically worsened in the last two months. * * * There is * * * an imminent danger that the city of New York will be unable to pay its outstanding short-term indebtedness and even to provide those basic services essential to the health, safety and welfare of its inhabitants and the continuation of orderly government in the city." * * * The Legislature's express purpose in enacting the Emergency Moratorium Act was "to ameliorate the disastrous consequences, to taxpayers, to holders of short-term obligations and to city residents, of an inability by the city to meet its financial and governmental responsibilities in full * * * [and] to avoid undue disruption of the process of financial recovery already underway, so as to facilitate restoration of the city's financial integrity and the payment of all its obligations."

* * *

A faith and credit pledge simply means that the issuing government *agrees* to be generally obligated to pay the indebtedness out of all the government's revenues, rather than restrictively obligated only from specific revenues; it expresses an *undertaking* by the government to be irrevocably obligated in good faith to use such of its resources and taxing power as may be authorized or required by law for the full and prompt payment of the obligation according to its terms. * * *

The faith and credit pledge, as the words imply, requires no more than that the city make a good faith effort to use its resources, credit and powers to pay its indebtedness. This effort must be measured in the light of the city's over-all financial condition and its over-all obligations to its citizens and others. * * * An intensive and sustained effort has been made by those managing the city's affairs to restore its financial credit. Every step exhibits the city's good faith.

Some items are worthy of mention. In December, 1974, the Mayor directed a hiring freeze (Executive Order No. 24) so that between December 31, 1974 and July 31, 1975 there was a net reduction of about 18,500 full-time city employees, through layoffs or attrition, reducing the city's annual expenditure by an estimated $265 million. A "crisis budget" was adopted for the fiscal year commencing July 1, 1975. The real estate tax for fiscal 1975–1976 was increased 11% over the prior year. In July, 1975 additional taxes, expected to yield about $325 million, were imposed. On June 10, 1975, the Legislature enacted the New York State Municipal Assistance Corporation Act (L 1975, ch 168) and created the Municipal Assistance Corporation for the City of New York (L 1975, ch 169), which corporation, by the sale of bonds to the public, underwriters, the 11 New York clearing house banks and the city and State pension funds, provided the city with a total of about $1.9 billion through September 5, 1975. In August, 1975, the city enacted Local Law No. 43 providing for a wage freeze effective for the first pay period ending on or subsequent to

September 1, 1975. In September, 1975, the Legislature enacted the New York State Financial Emergency Act for the City of New York (L 1975, chs 868–870). Pursuant thereto, the city, with the approval of the Emergency Financial Control Board, adopted a three-year financial plan to balance the budget in fiscal 1977–1978 reducing the annual expenditure rate by an additional $724 million. To effect a reduction of $200 million in fiscal 1975–1976, the Mayor directed all city agencies to reduce their expenditure rates by an additional 8% during the remainder of said year, except for police, fire, correction and sanitation departments for which an additional 3% was directed and the New York City Health and Hospitals Corporation, the Board of Education and the Board of Higher Education for which an additional 4 ½% was ordered. As of October 31, 1975, the city's full-time employees had been reduced by 35,887 persons, resulting in annual personnel cost savings of approximately $510 million. The hiring freeze continued, it having been estimated that an additional 13,000 would leave the city's employ by June 30, 1976. The city halted all new construction and suspended work on 46 city-funded construction projects then underway. Eight fire companies were disbanded and seven schools and a municipal hospital were closed. Extensive efforts were made to obtain Federal assistance.

* * * The police power of the State, difficult of exact definition and demarcation, is but another name for the basic authority inherent in every sovereignty to pass all laws for the internal regulation and government of the State, necessary for the public safety and welfare. * * * It is one of the necessary attributes of civilized government. * * *

Of course, the police power is to be exercised within constitutional limitations. * * *

It is readily conceded that the constitutional prescription of a pledge of faith and credit is operative in the event of mere "difficult economic circumstances", as suggested by the majority. * * * The situation here, however, far transcends such a rather common municipal predicament. * * *

Since there properly was found a "grave public emergency" and "an imminent danger that the city of New York will be unable * * * even to provide those basic services essential to the health, safety and welfare of its inhabitants and the continuation of orderly government in the city," the Legislature had not only the "power" but the "immediate duty" to adopt the questioned measure. A city of eight million, deprived of even the most basic of services, would be a terrible tragedy, nothing short of a disaster, and an emergency, dire and critical in nature. * * *

NOTES AND QUESTIONS

1. *The New York City Fiscal Crisis.* The New York City fiscal crisis broke in early 1975, when the City was unable to market its short-term notes. New York's Mayor, Abraham Beame, had included plans to issue $8.3 billion in short-term notes as part of his budget plan for fiscal 1974–75. Not only was that the largest issue in the City's history, but it was an extraordinary amount of short-term notes by any standard. By comparison, more than twenty years later, in 1996, the total amount of short-term notes issued by the fifty states in the aggregate was just $6.1 billion. New York City had become increasingly dependent on short-term notes during the early 1970s. In the 1960s, the City undertook relatively generous social programs and increased the wages and benefits of its public employees. Initially those programs were financed by local revenues, including increased federal and state aid. In the 1970s, the combination of a recession, a weakened local economy, increased social service needs and reduced intergovernmental assistance undermined the city's ability to finance its programs out of revenues. Instead of cutting spending, the City began running operating deficits which it covered by issuing short-term notes. With each passing year its short-term debt grew, as new notes were issued to cover both operating deficits and the principal and interest on the prior year's notes. Initially, lenders were eager to buy the City's offerings as the City was offering relatively high interest rates. By the winter of 1974–75, as short-term debt levels mushroomed to historic levels and the City failed to reduce its operating deficit, investors became increasingly concerned about the City's ability to meet its obligations. By early 1975, the City was unable to sell its notes.

In June 1975, the State created the Municipal Assistance Corporation ("MAC"), which consisted of appointees of the governor. Since the City was unable to market its bonds and notes, MAC was given the authority to issue long-term debt which the City could use to repay its short-term obligations. The state committed the revenue from a stock transfer tax and the City's sales tax to secure MAC's bonds. MAC was also given the power to review the City's budget, approve short-term borrowing, and revamp the City's accounting rules. MAC, however, failed to restore the bond market's confidence in the City's ability to pay its debts, and MAC had difficulties selling long-term bonds. Faced with a mountain of maturing short-term note obligations, and with both MAC and the City unable to issue the new debt necessary for the City to refinance its notes, the nation's largest city was on the verge of default.

In September 1975, the State adopted the Financial Emergency Act, which created the Emergency Financial Control Board ("EFCB") composed of the Governor, the Mayor, the State and City controllers and three prominent businessmen. The EFCB

> was given authority to develop and approve a financial plan for the city, approve all city borrowing, administer a freeze on city wages,

and set up the EFCB fund as a repository for all city revenue. The Financial Emergency Act also appropriated $750 million of state revenue to the city, with the stipulation that other forms of financial assistance would be made available to the city from its pension funds and the banks; authorized direct purchase of MAC bonds by state employee pension funds . . . and froze city wages. . . .

By making the EFCB trustee of all city revenue, with authority to control all investment and spending decisions in the city, and by ensuring minority representation of city politicians on the board, the governor effectively removed control of the city's fiscal process from its elected officials.

Ester R. Fuchs, Mayors and Money: Fiscal Policy in New York and Chicago 89–90 (U. Chi. Press 1992).

Ultimately, even these measures proved inadequate to solve the fiscal crisis. Potential investors in City debt sought a federal guarantee of MAC securities. Initially President Ford refused, but the New York City crisis soon had a broad financial impact:

Cities across the country were already confronting increased interest rates on their securities. October 17 [1975] provided a preview of what a New York City default could do to the international financial markets. On that day, with the prospect of actual default quite real, prices declined sharply in the stock market and trading in bonds virtually stopped, currency trading in Europe almost stopped, and world gold prices rose.

. . . [Ultimately, President] Ford agreed to support the New York Seasonal Financing Act after the state agreed to pass a new city tax package and issue a moratorium on city notes, offering investors the opportunity to trade them for MAC bonds at higher interest rates. This bill provided for federal short-term loans to the city of up to $2.3 billion bearing interest at a rate 1 percent higher than the Treasury borrowing rate. . . . [T]he federal government ma[d]e money on New York's fiscal crisis.

Id. at 90–91.

With federal guarantees in place, MAC was able to market its obligations. The City, however, was unable to sell its own debt until 1979. The statutory authorization for the EFCB expired in 1978, but the state replaced it with a less powerful monitoring and advisory Financial Control Board ("FCB"), although the FCB was also authorized to assume the stronger powers of the EFCB if the City concluded a fiscal year with an operating deficit of more than $100 million.

The *Flushing National Bank* decision had little direct effect on the City's fiscal recovery. Although held unconstitutional, the moratorium had bought the City nearly a year and a half to improve its financial condition—fully a year elapsed between the enactment of the moratorium law and the Court of

Appeals decision, and another four months passed before the City actually had to begin paying off the notes. New York City was able to pay off the short-term notes that became due as a result of the *Flushing National Bank* decision without having to turn to the credit markets. *See* Martin Shefter, Political Crisis/Fiscal Crisis: The Collapse and Revival of New York City 155, 164 (Basic Books, Inc. 1985).

2.   *Shared Sacrifice or Preferred Position?* The resolution of the New York City fiscal crisis involved sacrifices by a variety of stakeholders. Public employees submitted to a wage freeze, and agreed to invest their pension funds in municipal securities. Some City employees lost their jobs. City taxpayers paid higher taxes, and state taxpayers paid for assistance to the City. City residents absorbed steep reductions in municipal services. Many financial institutions also agreed to invest in MAC and City securities. Was the Court of Appeals correct in concluding that noteholders could not be required to share in these sacrifices by foregoing for a time repayment of their investment in the City's short-term notes? Does the City's pledge of its faith and credit to notebuyers—and not to taxpayers, employees, or residents—place noteholders in a preferred position when a financial emergency occurs?

How far does the "faith and credit" obligation run? If the crisis had continued, would the City have been required to fire additional employees or raise taxes further? What if the City were to argue that additional service cuts or tax increases would drive away taxpaying residents and tax-generating activity and, thus, endanger the economic health of the City?

Should there be an "emergency" exception to the faith and credit obligation? Who should determine whether an emergency exists, the legislature or the courts?

Professor Gillette has suggested that the decision was less than a complete victory for the City's creditors: "What the Court of Appeals gave with one hand . . . it withdrew with the other. The court ostensibly did not want to authorize creditors to bankrupt the city in order to obtain payment. Once it articulated a clear entitlement in favor of creditors, the court expressed an unwillingness to enforce it. Instead, the court implicitly authorized creditors to use their entitlement to negotiate an appropriate settlement with the state and city. . . . [T[he right to payment that the court had endorsed up to the penultimate paragraph of its opinion appeared much less secure in the face of 'the city's grave fiscal and economic problems.'" Clayton P. Gillette, Bondholders and Financially Distressed Municipalities, 39 Fordham Urb. L.J. 639, 648–49 (2012). Reviewing the long history of conflicts between the claims of bondholders and those of residents in financially distressed municipalities, Professor Gillette determined that courts have not consistently favored one side or the other, although a few states have enacted statutory regimes that give priority to bondholders. *Id.* at 639–54. One factor that has led some states to favor bondholders over residents is "fear of contagion," that is, that "local defaults would impose additional costs on other localities or the state itself." *Id.* at 654. He argues that because bond underwriters may be in the best position to assess and price the risks posed by a particular bond issuance it would make sense to give priority to residents—"[b]ondholders who have been compensated ex ante to take risks have little basis to complain when those risks materialize." *Id.* at 677.

3. *Short-Term vs. Long-Term City Interests.* On its face, *Flushing National Bank* was a sharp rebuff to New York City's interests and threatened to plunge the City into default. On the other hand, the decision may have been beneficial to the long-term interests of the City and other local governments. By signaling an emphatic commitment to the enforcement of the City's faith and credit obligation, the court may have given investors greater confidence in the credit of the City and of other localities. This may have facilitated the City's ability to begin borrowing again once it had balanced its operating budget. By reducing the riskiness of local obligations, the decision may have also lowered the interest rate the City had to pay in order to persuade investors to buy its bonds and notes.

UNITED STATES TRUST COMPANY OF NEW YORK v. STATE OF NEW JERSEY

Supreme Court of the United States
431 U.S. 1 (1977)

MR. JUSTICE BLACKMUN delivered the opinion of the Court.

This case presents a challenge to a New Jersey statute * * * as violative of the Contract Clause[1] of the United States Constitution. That statute, together with a concurrent and parallel New York statute repealed a statutory covenant made by the two States in 1962 that had limited the ability of The Port Authority of New York and New Jersey to subsidize rail passenger transportation from revenues and reserves. * * *

The Port Authority was conceived as a financially independent entity, with funds primarily derived from private investors. The preamble to the compact speaks of the "encouragement of the investment of capital," and the Port Authority was given power to mortgage its facilities and to pledge its revenues to secure the payment of bonds issued to private investors. * * *

In 1958, Assembly Bill No. 16 was introduced in the New Jersey Legislature. This would have had the Port Authority take over, improve, and operate interstate rail mass transit between New Jersey and New York. The bill was opposed vigorously by the Port Authority on legal and financial grounds. The Port Authority also retaliated, in a sense, by including a new safeguard in its contracts with bondholders. This prohibited the issuance of any bonds, secured by the general reserve fund,

---

[1] "No State shall ... pass any ... Law impairing the Obligation of Contracts. ..." U.S.Const., Art. I, § 10, cl. 1.

for a new facility unless the Port Authority first certified that the issuance of the bonds would not "materially impair the sound credit standing" of the Port Authority. * * * Bill No. 16 was not passed. * * *

In 1960 the takeover of the Hudson & Manhattan Railroad by the Port Authority was proposed. This was a privately owned interstate electric commuter system then linking Manhattan, Newark, and Hoboken through the Hudson tubes. It had been in reorganization for many years, and in 1959 the Bankruptcy Court and the United States District Court had approved a plan that left it with cash sufficient to continue operations for two years but with no funds for capital expenditures. * * * A special committee of the New Jersey Senate was formed to determine whether the Port Authority was "fulfilling its statutory duties and obligations," * * * The committee concluded that the solution to bondholder concern was "(l)imiting by a constitutionally protected statutory covenant with Port Authority bondholders the extent to which the Port Authority revenues and reserves pledged to such bondholders can in the future be applied to the deficits of possible future Port Authority passenger railroad facilities beyond the original Hudson & Manhattan Railroad system." * * *

The statutory covenant of 1962 was the result. The covenant itself was part of the bistate legislation authorizing the Port Authority to acquire, construct, and operate the Hudson & Manhattan Railroad and the World Trade Center. The statute in relevant part read:

> "The 2 States covenant and agree with each other and with the holders of any affected bonds, as hereinafter defined, that so long as any of such bonds remain outstanding and unpaid and the holders thereof shall not have given their consent as provided in their contract with the port authority, (a) . . . and (b) neither the States nor the port authority nor any subsidiary corporation incorporated for any of the purposes of this act will apply any of the rentals, tolls, fares, fees, charges, revenues or reserves, which have been or shall be pledged in whole or in part as security for such bonds, for any railroad purposes whatsoever other than permitted purposes hereinafter set forth." * * *

The "permitted purposes" were defined to include (I) the Hudson & Manhattan as then existing, (ii) railroad freight facilities, (iii) tracks and related facilities on Port Authority vehicular bridges, and (iv) a passenger railroad facility if the Port Authority certified that it was "self-supporting" or, if not, that at the end of the preceding calendar year the general reserve fund contained the prescribed statutory amount, and that all the Port Authority's passenger revenues, including the Hudson & Manhattan, would not produce deficits in excess of "permitted deficits."

* * * With the legislation embracing the covenant thus effective, the Port Authority on September 1, 1962, assumed the ownership and operating responsibilities of the Hudson & Manhattan through a wholly owned subsidiary, Port Authority Trans-Hudson Corporation (PATH). * * *

The PATH fare in 1962 was 30 cents and has remained at that figure despite recommendations for increase. * * * As a result of the continuation of the low fare, PATH deficits have far exceeded the initial projection. Thus, although the general reserve fund had grown to $173 million by 1973, substantially increasing the level of permitted deficits to about $17 million, the PATH deficit had grown to $24.9 million. * * *

[In 1973] the 1962 covenant was * * * repealed with respect to bonds issued subsequent to the effective date of the new legislation. * * *

New Jersey had previously prevented outright repeal of the 1962 covenant, but its attitude changed with the election of a new Governor in 1973. In early 1974, when bills were pending in the two States' legislatures to repeal the covenant retroactively, a national energy crisis was developing. * * * This time, proposals for retroactive repeal of the 1962 covenant were passed by the legislature and signed by the Governor of each State. 1974 N.J.Laws, c. 25; 1974 N.Y.Laws, c. 993.

Home Building & Loan Assn. v. Blaisdell, 290 U.S. 398 (1934), is regarded as the leading case in the modern era of Contract Clause interpretation. At issue was the Minnesota Mortgage Moratorium Law, enacted in 1933, during the depth of the Depression and when that state was under severe economic stress, and appeared to have no effective alternative. The statute was a temporary measure that allowed judicial extension of the time for redemption; a mortgagor who remained in possession during the extension period was required to pay a reasonable income or rental value to the mortgagee. A closely divided Court, in an opinion by Mr. Chief Justice Hughes, observed that "emergency may furnish the occasion for the exercise of power" and that the "constitutional question presented in the light of an emergency is whether the power possessed embraces the particular exercise of it in response to particular conditions." * * * [T]he general purpose of the Clause was clear: to encourage trade and credit by promoting confidence in the stability of contractual obligations. * * * Nevertheless, a State "continues to possess authority to safeguard the vital interests of its people. * * * This principle of harmonizing the constitutional prohibition with the necessary residuum of state power has had progressive recognition in the decisions of this Court." * * *

[T]he Contract Clause does not prohibit the States from repealing or amending statutes generally, or from enacting legislation with retroactive effects. Thus, as a preliminary matter, appellant's claim requires a determination that the repeal has the effect of impairing a contractual obligation.

In this case the obligation was itself created by a statute, the 1962 legislative covenant. It is unnecessary, however, to dwell on the criteria for determining whether state legislation gives rise to a contractual obligation. The trial court * * * and appellees do not deny, that the 1962 covenant constituted a contract between the two States and the holders of the Consolidated Bonds issued between 1962 and the 1973 prospective repeal. * * *

The parties sharply disagree about the value of the 1962 covenant to the bondholders. Appellant claims that after repeal the secondary market for affected bonds became "thin" and the price fell in relation to other formerly comparable bonds. This claim is supported by the trial court's finding that "immediately following repeal and for a number of months thereafter the market price for Port Authority bonds was adversely affected." * * * Appellees respond that the bonds nevertheless retained an "A" rating from the leading evaluating services and that after an initial adverse effect they regained a comparable price position in the market. Findings of the trial court support these claims as well. * * * The fact is that no one can be sure precisely how much financial loss the bondholders suffered. Factors unrelated to repeal may have influenced price. In addition, the market may not have reacted fully, even as yet, to the covenant's repeal, because of the pending litigation and the possibility that the repeal would be nullified by the courts.

In any event, the question of valuation need not be resolved in the instant case because the State has made no effort to compensate the bondholders for any loss sustained by the repeal. As a security provision, the covenant was not superfluous; it limited the Port Authority's deficits and thus protected the general reserve fund from depletion. Nor was the covenant merely modified or replaced by an arguably comparable security provision. Its outright repeal totally eliminated an important security provision and thus impaired the obligation of the States' contract. * * *

* * * Although the Contract Clause appears literally to proscribe "any" impairment, this Court observed in *Blaisdell* that "the prohibition is not an absolute one and is not to be read with literal exactness like a mathematical formula." 290 U.S., at 428. Thus, a finding that there has been a technical impairment is merely a preliminary step in resolving the more difficult question whether that impairment is permitted under the Constitution. * * *

The trial court concluded that repeal of the 1962 covenant was a valid exercise of New Jersey's police power because repeal served important public interests in mass transportation, energy conservation, and environmental protection. * * * Yet the Contract Clause limits otherwise legitimate exercises of state legislative authority, and the existence of an important public interest is not always sufficient to overcome that limitation. * * *

The States must possess broad power to adopt general regulatory measures without being concerned that private contracts will be impaired, or even destroyed, as a result. Otherwise, one would be able to obtain immunity from the state regulation by making private contractual arrangements. This principle is summarized in Mr. Justice Holmes' well-known dictum: "One whose rights, such as they are, are subject to state restriction, cannot remove them from the power of the State by making a contract about them." *Hudson Water Co. v. McCarter*, 209 U.S. 349, 357 (1908).

Yet private contracts are not subject to unlimited modification under the police power. The Court in *Blaisdell* recognized that laws intended to regulate existing contractual relationships must serve a legitimate public purpose. 290 U.S., at 444–445. A State could not "adopt as its policy the repudiation of debts or the destruction of contracts or the denial of means to enforce them." *Id.*, at 439. Legislation adjusting the rights and responsibilities of contracting parties must be upon reasonable conditions and of a character appropriate to the public purpose justifying its adoption. *Id.*, at 445–447. As is customary in reviewing economic and social regulation, however, courts properly defer to legislative judgment as to the necessity and reasonableness of a particular measure. * * *

When a State impairs the obligation of its own contract, the reserved-powers doctrine has a different basis. The initial inquiry concerns the ability of the State to enter into an agreement that limits its power to act in the future. As early as *Fletcher v. Peck*, the Court considered the argument that "one legislature cannot abridge the powers of a succeeding legislature." 6 Cranch, at 135. It is often stated that "the legislature cannot bargain away the police power of a State." *Stone v. Mississippi*, 101 U.S. 814 (1880). This doctrine requires a determination of the State's power to create irrevocable contract rights in the first place, rather than an inquiry into the purpose or reasonableness of the subsequent impairment. In short, the Contract Clause does not require a State to adhere to a contract that surrenders an essential attribute of its sovereignty.

In deciding whether a State's contract was invalid ab initio under the reserved-powers doctrine, earlier decisions relied on distinctions among the various powers of the State. Thus, the police power and the power of eminent domain were among those that could not be "contracted away," but the State could bind itself in the future exercise of the taxing and spending powers. Such formalistic distinctions perhaps cannot be dispositive, but they contain an important element of truth. Whatever the propriety of a State's binding itself to a future course of conduct in other contexts, the power to enter into effective financial contracts cannot be questioned. Any financial obligation could be regarded in theory as a relinquishment of the State's spending power, since money spent to repay debts is not available for other purposes. Similarly, the taxing power may have to be exercised if debts are to be repaid. Notwithstanding these effects, the Court has regularly held that the States are bound by their debt contracts.

The instant case involves a financial obligation and thus as a threshold matter may not be said automatically to fall within the reserved powers that cannot be contracted away. Not every security provision, however, is necessarily financial. For example, a revenue bond might be secured by the State's promise to continue operating the facility in question; yet such a promise surely could not validly be construed to bind the State never to close the facility for health or safety reasons. The security provision at issue here, however, is different: The States promised that revenues and reserves securing the bonds would not be depleted by the Port Authority's operation of deficit-producing passenger railroads beyond the level of "permitted deficits." Such a promise is purely financial and thus not necessarily a compromise of the State's reserved powers.

Of course, to say that the financial restrictions of the 1962 covenant were valid when adopted does not finally resolve this case. The Contract Clause is not an absolute bar to subsequent modification of a State's own financial obligations. As with laws impairing the obligations of private contracts, an impairment may be constitutional if it is reasonable and necessary to serve an important public purpose. In applying this standard, however, complete deference to a legislative assessment of reasonableness and necessity is not appropriate because the State's self-interest is at stake. A governmental entity can always find a use for extra money, especially when taxes do not have to be raised. If a State could reduce its financial obligations whenever it wanted to spend the money for what it regarded as an important public purpose, the Contract Clause would provide no protection at all. * * *

The only time in this century that alteration of a municipal bond contract has been sustained by this Court was in *Faitoute Iron & Steel Co. v. City of Asbury Park*, 316 U.S. 502 (1942). That case involved the New Jersey Municipal Finance Act, which provided that a bankrupt local government could be placed in receivership by a state agency. A plan for the composition of creditors' claims was required to be approved by the agency, the municipality, and 85% in amount of the creditors. The plan would be binding on nonconsenting creditors after a state court conducted a hearing and found that the municipality could not otherwise pay off its creditors and that the plan was in the best interest of all creditors. *Id.*, at 504.

Under the specific composition plan at issue in *Faitoute*, the holders of revenue bonds received new securities bearing lower interest rates and later maturity dates. This Court, however, rejected the dissenting bondholders' Contract Clause objections. The reason was that the old bonds represented only theoretical rights; as a practical matter the city could not raise its taxes enough to pay off its creditors under the old contract terms. The composition plan enabled the city to meet its financial obligations more effectively. "The necessity compelled by unexpected financial conditions to modify an original arrangement for discharging a city's debt is implied in every such obligation for the very reason that thereby the obligation is discharged, not impaired." *Id.*, at 511. Thus, the Court found that the composition plan was adopted with the purpose and effect of protecting the creditors, as evidenced by their more than 85% approval. Indeed, the market value of the bonds increased sharply as a result of the plan's adoption. *Id.*, at 513.

It is clear that the instant case involves a much more serious impairment than occurred in *Faitoute*. No one has suggested here that the States acted for the purpose of benefitting the bondholders, and there is no serious contention that the value of the bonds was enhanced by repeal of the 1962 covenant. Appellees recognized that it would have been impracticable to obtain consent of the bondholders for such a change in the 1962 covenant. * * *

Mass transportation, energy conservation, and environmental protection are goals that are important and of legitimate public concern. Appellees contend that these goals are so important that any harm to bondholders from repeal of the 1962 covenant is greatly outweighed by the public benefit. We do not accept this invitation to engage in a utilitarian comparison of public benefit and private loss. * * * [A] State cannot refuse to meet its legitimate financial obligations simply because it would prefer to spend the money to promote the public good rather than the private welfare of its creditors. We can only sustain the repeal of the 1962 covenant if that impairment was both reasonable and necessary to serve the admittedly important purposes claimed by the State.

The more specific justification offered for the repeal of the 1962 covenant was the States' plan for encouraging users of private automobiles to shift to public transportation. The States intended to discourage private automobile use by raising bridge and tunnel tolls and to use the extra revenue from those tolls to subsidize improved commuter railroad service. Appellees contend that repeal of the 1962 covenant was necessary to implement this plan because the new mass transit facilities could not possibly be self-supporting and the covenant's "permitted deficits" level had already been exceeded. We reject this justification because the repeal was neither necessary to achievement of the plan nor reasonable in light of the circumstances.

The determination of necessity can be considered on two levels. First, it cannot be said that total repeal of the covenant was essential; a less drastic modification would have permitted the contemplated plan without entirely removing the covenant's limitations on the use of Port Authority revenues and reserves to subsidize commuter railroads. Second, without modifying the covenant at all, the States could have adopted alternative means of achieving their twin goals of discouraging automobile use and improving mass transit. Appellees contend, however, that choosing among these alternatives is a matter for legislative discretion. But a State is not completely free to consider impairing the obligations of its own contracts on a par with other policy alternatives. Similarly, a State is not free to impose a drastic impairment when an evident and more moderate course would serve its purposes equally well. * * *

We also cannot conclude that repeal of the covenant was reasonable in light of the surrounding circumstances. * * * [T]he need for mass transportation in the New York metropolitan area was not a new development, and the likelihood that publicly owned commuter railroads would produce substantial deficits was well known. * * * It was with full knowledge of these concerns that the 1962 covenant was adopted. Indeed, the covenant was specifically intended to protect the pledged revenues and reserves against the possibility that such concerns would lead the Port Authority into greater involvement in deficit mass transit.

During the 12-year period between adoption of the covenant and its repeal, public perception of the importance of mass transit undoubtedly grew because of increased general concern with environmental protection and energy conservation. But these concerns were not unknown in 1962, and the subsequent changes were of degree and not of kind. We cannot say that these changes caused the covenant to have a substantially different impact in 1974 than when it was adopted in 1962. And we cannot conclude that the repeal was reasonable in the light of changed circumstances.

We therefore hold that the Contract Clause of the United States Constitution prohibits the retroactive repeal of the 1962 covenant.

MR. JUSTICE BRENNAN, with whom MR. JUSTICE WHITE and MR. JUSTICE MARSHALL join, dissenting.

* * * In an era when problems of municipal planning increasingly demand regional rather than local solutions, the Port Authority provides the New York-New Jersey community with a readymade, efficient regional entity encompassing some 1,500 square miles surrounding the Statue of Liberty. As the Court notes, from the outset public officials of

both New York and New Jersey were well aware of the Authority's heavy dependence on public financing. Consequently, beginning in the decade prior to the enactment of the 1962 covenant, the Authority's general reserve bonds, its primary vehicle of public finance, have featured two rigid security devices designed to safeguard the investment of bondholders. First, pursuant to a so-called "1.3 test," the Authority has been disabled from issuing new consolidated bonds unless the best one-year net revenues derived from all of the Authority's facilities at least equal 130% of the prospective debt service for the calendar year during which the debt service for all outstanding and proposed bonds would be at a maximum. Second, according to a procedure known as a "section 7 certification," the Authority may not issue bonds to finance additional facilities unless it "shall certify" that the issue "will not, during the ensuing ten years or during the longest term of any such bonds proposed to be issued . . . , whichever shall be longer, . . . materially impair the sound credit standing of the Authority. . . ." * * *

The 1962 covenant existed alongside these security provisions. Viewed in simplest terms, the covenant served to preclude Authority investment and participation in transportation programs by shifting the financial focal point from the creditworthiness of the Authority's activities as a whole to the solvency of each proposed new transit project. Whereas the 1.3 and section 7 tests permit expanded involvement in mass transportation provided that the enormous revenue-generating potential of the Authority's bridges and tunnels aggregately suffice to secure the investments of creditors, the covenant effectively foreclosed participation in any new project that was not individually "self-supporting." Both parties to this litigation are in apparent agreement that few functional mass transit systems are capable of satisfying this requirement.

Whether the 1962 New Jersey Legislature acted wisely in accepting this new restriction is, for me, quite irrelevant. What is important is that the passage of the years conclusively demonstrated that this effective barrier to the development of rapid transit in the port region squarely conflicts with the legitimate needs of the New York metropolitan community, and will persist in doing so into the next century. * * *

[T]he Court apparently holds that a mere "technical impairment" of contract suffices to subject New Jersey's repealer to serious judicial scrutiny and invalidation under the Contract Clause. * * *

Obviously, the heart of the obligation to the bondholders and the interests ostensibly safeguarded by the 1962 covenant is the periodic payment of interest and the repayment of principal when due. The Court does not, and indeed cannot, contend that either New Jersey or the Authority has called into question the validity of these underlying obligations. No creditor complains that public authorities have defaulted on a coupon payment or failed to redeem a bond that has matured. In fact, the Court does not even offer any reason whatever for fearing that, as a result of the covenant's repeal, the securities in appellant's portfolio are jeopardized. * * *

* * * One of the fundamental premises of our popular democracy is that each generation of representatives can and will remain responsive to the needs and desires of those whom they represent. Crucial to this end is the assurance that new legislators will not automatically be bound by the policies and undertakings of earlier days. In accordance with this philosophy, the Framers of our Constitution conceived of the Contract Clause primarily as protection for economic transactions entered into by purely private parties, rather than obligations involving the State itself. * * * The Framers fully recognized that nothing would so jeopardize the legitimacy of a system of government that relies upon the ebbs and flows of politics to "clean out the rascals" than the possibility that those same rascals might perpetuate their policies simply by locking them into binding contracts. * * *

This theme of judicial self-restraint and its underlying premise that a State always retains the sovereign authority to legislate in behalf of its people was commonly expressed by the doctrine that the Contract Clause will not even recognize efforts of a State to enter into contracts limiting the authority of succeeding legislators to enact laws in behalf of the health, safety, and similar collective interests of the polity in short, that State's police power is inalienable by contract. * * *

In the present case, the trial court * * * properly found appellant's claim to be wanting in all material respects: In a detailed and persuasive discussion, the court concluded that neither New Jersey nor New York repealed the covenant with the intention of damaging their creditors' financial position. Rather, the States acted out of "vital interest(s)," for "(t)he passage of time and events between 1962 and 1974 satisfied the Legislatures of the two states that the public interest which the Port Authority was intended to serve could not be met within the terms of the covenant." 134 N.J.Super., at 194, 338 A.2d, at 873. * * * Not only have Authority bonds remained "an 'acceptable investment,' " but "(t)he claim that bondholder security has been materially impaired or destroyed by the repeal is simply not supported by the record." *Id.*, at 196, 338 A.2d, at 874. * * *

I would not want to be read as suggesting that the States should blithely proceed down the path of repudiating their obligations, financial or otherwise. Their credibility in the credit market obviously is highly dependent on exercising their vast lawmaking powers with self-restraint and discipline. * * * But in the final analysis, there is no reason to doubt that appellant's financial welfare is being adequately policed by the political processes and the bond marketplace itself. The role to be played by the Constitution is at most a limited one. * * *

JUSTICES STEWART and POWELL took no part in the decision of this case.

NOTES AND QUESTIONS

1.   *The Contracts Clause and the Police Power. U.S. Trust* was the first Supreme Court decision in nearly four decades to invalidate state legislation under the Contracts Clause. As you can see, the seven participating Justices struggled to come up with a standard that protects bondbuyers who have made a contract with a government agency but also prevents a state legislature from contracting away its police power and thereby disabling a later legislature from taking effective action to meet the needs and concerns of its current residents. Do you understand what the police power problem is and how it would be implicated by a state's statutory commitment to bondholders?

2.   *The Meaning of "Impairment." Although U.S. Trust* brought new life to the Contracts Clause, the Court refrained from finding that all alterations of a contractual obligation constitute an "impairment." What was the basis for the Court's finding that the 1974 legislation retroactively repealing the Port Authority bond covenants constituted an impairment of the bonds? The repealer did not repudiate or reduce the obligation to pay interest and repay principal (the interest and principal payments are collectively known as debt service). Nor, unlike the New York City moratorium law, did the repealer purport to defer the Port Authority's duty to repay. In what sense was the repealer a "much more serious impairment" than the composition plan— which reduced interest rates and provided for later maturity dates—in *Faitoute Iron & Steel Co. v. City of Asbury Park?*

Justice Brennan's dissent focuses on the various protections Port Authority bondholders enjoyed. The "1.3" covenant in the Port Authority bonds constituted a pledge not to issue new bonds unless the annual net revenues derived from all of the Authority's facilities were equal to at least 130% of the Authority's annual debt service needs for all outstanding and proposed bonds. Another bond covenant required the Port Authority to certify that any new bond issue would not "materially impair the sound credit standing of the Authority." Given these protections for bondholders, how did the repealer injure their interests?

3.   *Justifications for an "Impairment."* The Court also held that not all contract impairments are unconstitutional. The Court was willing to consider whether an impairment was reasonable and necessary to attain an important public goal. Given that "mass transportation, energy, conservation and environmental protection are goals that are important and of legitimate public concern" and that the repealer would have made it easier for New Jersey to advance those goals, why was the repealer "neither necessary to achievement of the plan nor reasonable in light of the circumstances"? How

"reasonable and necessary" does a government measure have to be before it can justify an impairment of a contractual obligation? Is the dissent right in arguing that the "reasonable and necessary" test improperly involves the courts in assessing the appropriateness of governmental techniques to attain legitimate ends? The ambiguity built into the "reasonable and necessary" phrase has led to some disagreement among the circuit courts as to how to apply *U.S. Trust*'s standard, with some courts highly deferential to state measures and others much less so. *See* Michael Cataldo, Revival or Revolution: U.S. Trust's Role in the Contracts Clause Circuit Split, 87 St. John's L. Rev. 1145 (2013).

4. *The Contracts Clause and the Marketplace.* Does the *U.S. Trust* Court, in a way similar to the New York Court of Appeals in *Flushing National Bank,* seem to express a constitutional bias in favor of the interests of bondholders, as opposed to taxpayers, public employees, government service recipients, or the community as a whole? Does such a bias seem appropriate to you? Is it relevant that many—but not all—bondholders are not residents of the jurisdiction whose bonds they hold? Is it relevant that many—but again not all—bondholders are more affluent than state or local residents on average? Does the Contracts Clause itself compel such a bias?

Or would you agree with Justice Brennan that the protection of bondholders should be left to the political process and the bond marketplace? Justice Brennan suggests that state and local governments will be reluctant to impair bond obligations out of concern that such efforts will be punished by the reluctance of investors to buy the bonds of governments that fail to adhere to their commitments. Do you think that provides the appropriate level of security for the holders of state and local debt obligations? Do you think that by strengthening the Contracts Clause's protection for state and local bonds, the *U.S. Trust* decision ultimately made it easier for governments to borrow at lower interest rates? If so, how?

5. *State and Private Contracts.* Justice Blackmun suggests that courts should be more inclined to find that state legislation unconstitutionally impairs contracts undertaken by government agencies than contracts involving just private parties. In his view, governments are too easily tempted to avoid their own obligations. Justice Brennan's dissent, by contrast, would make it particularly difficult for a court to invalidate a law that impaired a contract resulting from a state law since that would be a more serious interference with the ability of the state to govern. Which argument do you find more persuasive? *See also* Revival or Revolution, *supra,* 87 St. John's L. Rev. at 1171–75 (arguing that precedent called for a single approach to impairments of both public and private contracts, albeit with special protection for the reserved powers of the states).

6. *The Contracts Clause and New York's Faith and Credit Clause.* *Flushing National Bank* was decided one year before *U.S. Trust.* The plaintiffs in the New York case had also made a Contracts Clause argument, but the New York Court of Appeals relied entirely on New York's faith and

credit clause. (In a portion of *Flushing National Bank* not excerpted here, the dissenting judge had relied heavily on pre-*U.S. Trust* Contracts Clause cases in finding that the state's full faith and credit clause was not violated.) After *U.S. Trust* how would the New York moratorium law fare under the Contracts Clause? Was there an impairment? Was the moratorium reasonable and necessary to achieve legitimate state goals?

7. *The Port Authority.* The Port Authority of New York and New Jersey was established in 1921 by a bistate compact to effectuate "a better co-ordination of the terminal, transportation and other facilities of commerce in, about and through the port of New York." The compact, as the U.S. Constitution requires, Art. I, § 10, cl. 3, received congressional consent. Nominally a creature of the states of New York and New Jersey, the Port Authority exercised considerable independence in determining what projects it would finance. The Authority inserted the bond covenants concerning rail-related deficits and successfully pushed the states to enact legislative guarantees of the covenants in order to protect itself from having to participate in the financing of mass transit projects in the New York metropolitan area. A big winner in the *U.S. Trust* litigation, then, was the Port Authority. Because Port Authority bonds issued before 1974 contained the covenant limiting participation in rail projects, and because those bonds were intended to mature over thirty or more years, those covenants limited the ability of the Port Authority to participate in mass transit projects into the twenty-first century.

For a critical evaluation of the Port Authority and other public authorities and their use of bond covenants to evade control by parent state governments, *see* Annmarie Hauck Walsh, The Public's Business: The Politics and Practices of Government Corporations (MIT Press 1980).

2. STATE CONSTITUTIONAL LIMITATIONS ON STATE AND LOCAL DEBT

The vast majority of state constitutions impose some limitation on the ability of their states and local governments to incur debt. These constitutional limitations take a variety of forms. Some bar state debt outright. *See, e.g.,* Ind. Const., Art. X, § 5 (prohibiting state debt except "to meet casual deficits in the revenue," pay state debts, repel invasion, suppress insurrection or provide for state defense); W.Va. Const., Art. X, § 4 (same). Others impose very low dollar limits on the amount of debt a state may incur. *See, e.g.,* Ariz. Const., Art. IX, § 5 (total state debt limited to $350,000); R.I. Const., Art. VI, § 16 (total state debt limited to $50,000, except in time of war, insurrection, or invasion).

Some state constitutions cap debt or debt service at a fraction of taxable wealth or revenues. *See, e.g.,* Haw. Const., Art. VII, § 13 (debt service on state debt limited to eighteen and one-half percent of the average of State general fund revenues of the State in the three fiscal years immediately preceding such issuance; local government debts limited to 15% of total assessed value of real property in each political subdivision); Nev. Const., Art. IX, § 3 (aggregate state debt limited to 2% of assessed valuation of property in state); Wash. Const., Art. VIII, § 1 (debt service on aggregate state debt limited to 8.5% of the average of state revenues over the six prior fiscal years; that cap to drop to 8.25% after July 1, 2016, and to 8% in 2034). Tying the debt limit to a fraction of property wealth or revenues is a particularly widespread way of limiting local government debt. *See, e.g.,* Ky. Const., § 158 (permissible local government debt set at between 2% and 10% of local assessed valuation, according to type and population of locality). This approach suggests an attempt to limit debt to the "carrying capacity" of the state or locality, so that new borrowing does not result in burdensome taxation or cuts in existing services.

Most commonly, state constitutions rely on a procedural restriction: debt may not be incurred without the approval of a majority (or supermajority) of voters in a referendum, *see, e.g.,* Okla. Const., Art. X, § 25; a supermajority vote in the state legislature, *see, e.g.,* Del. Const., Art. VIII, § 3 (no state debt may be incurred without the approval of three-fourths of the members of each house of the state legislature); or some combination of state legislative supermajority and state voters, *see, e.g.,* Mich. Const., Art. IX, § 15 (state long-term debt requires approval of two-thirds of members of each house of legislature and a majority of state voters in a referendum).

For state governments in particular the procedural requirements are the real restrictions on debt. Since state constitutions can be amended, an absolute prohibition of debt or a low dollar cap on the amount of debt can be circumvented by a constitutional amendment authorizing a specific bond issue. As a result, the legal requirements for a constitutional amendment—typically a combination of a legislative supermajority and voter approval—also become the requirements for the issuance of debt. For example, the Alabama Constitution flatly bars state debt, but it has at least forty-one provisions authorizing specific bond issues for specific purposes. For localities, however, unless state voters are willing to approve a state constitutional amendment, the local referendum requirement and/or local debt limit tied to local wealth restricts local debt.

The state constitutional limitations on public debt date back to the middle decades of the nineteenth century. They grew out of the same events that led to the adoption of the Public Purpose requirements studied in Section A of this Chapter—the extensive state borrowing to finance canals, railroads and other improvements in the 1830s, the economic depression that began in 1837, and the resulting financial crisis in which many states were unable to pay off the debts they had so readily assumed. In 1841 and 1842 nine states defaulted on their debts, and others struggled to pay them off. The state taxpayers who were burdened by these obligations led a successful movement to make it more difficult for states to assume new debts. Rhode Island was the first state to act, adopting a provision in 1842 that barred all new debt in excess of $50,000 "without the express consent of the people." New Jersey followed in 1844 with a constitutional amendment barring any debt in excess of $100,000 unless approved by a vote of the people. By 1860, a total of nineteen states had adopted debt limitations, and most of the Reconstructed southern states and western states admitted to the Union after the Civil War included debt limitations in their constitutions. *See* A. James Heins, Constitutional Restrictions Against State Debt 3–12 (U. Wisc. Press 1963). In most states, these constitutional restrictions on state debt were subsequently supplemented by restrictions on the ability of local governments to incur debt.

Apart from the specific historical background that led to the adoption of the first wave of debt limitations, constitutional restrictions on state and local debt may be justified as a means of reconciling the conflict between short-term and long-term interests that debt creates. Earlier in this section, we discussed why, as a matter of intergenerational equity, states and localities ought to be able to incur debt to finance projects that have long useful lives. Spreading those costs over a period of decades is appropriate since the benefits will be received over a period of decades as well. But the ability to shift the costs of debt into the future may also induce elected officials to incur debt too easily. While the costs of new debt may not be fully realized until the future, the benefits of the project financed by the debt may be received immediately during their terms of office. Thus, current elected officials may be tempted to approve projects that are not fully cost justified. After all, they can get the credit for the new project, but the blame for the additional taxes needed to finance these projects or for the diversion of tax dollars away from other future needs will be borne by their successors.

Moreover, certain groups, such as construction companies and unions, bond underwriters, or users of a specific facility, may be especially benefitted by a new bond issue whose cost is spread over the entire jurisdiction and into the future. These groups may use their campaign contributions or votes to give elected officials an additional incentive to approve a bond issue.

A central goal of the constitutional limits on debt, then, is to offset the temptations that cause elected officials to incur debt too easily. On the other hand, the wisdom of many of the specific limitations can be challenged. The principal substantive limitations attempt to tie the amount of debt or debt service to some fraction of state or local wealth or revenues. Many of these restrictions, however, are anachronistic. They define state or local wealth in terms of assessed property valuation when many jurisdictions derive a significant portion of their revenues from other sources. Thus, property-based limits may understate the ability of states and local governments to carry new debt. Conversely, many states set different debt limitations for different, albeit overlapping, local governments, so that cities, counties and special districts may each be allowed to incur debt up to some specific fraction of the local tax base. The total tax-backed debt burden for taxpayers is, however, cumulative. Moreover, even if the debt limits were more effectively keyed to local ability to pay, the enormous variation between states and among local governments within states concerning the fraction of taxable resources that may be used to back new debt "belies the notion that there is some consensus about the optimal level of debt." Robert S. Amdursky & Clayton P. Gillette, Municipal Debt Finance Law: Theory and Practice 171 (Aspen Pub. 1992). Nor is it clear that ability to pay is the best test of whether a bond issue ought to go forward. Debt can play an important role in meeting local needs, and in providing infrastructure vital to the future economic health of the community. But there is no obvious metric for determining future needs.

The wisdom of requiring a referendum has also been challenged. If politicians may be too tempted to approve new debt, voters may not be sufficiently attentive to the potential long-term benefits of the program the debt would finance. Low voter participation in bond issue elections may reflect a lack of interest in or understanding of the cost and benefit questions that bond issues pose, and the voters who do participate may not be fully representative of the electorate as a whole. The voters may be unprepared to make the policy judgments ordinarily delegated to representatives, and voter majorities may be reluctant to approve the financing of projects that benefit minorities.

Nonetheless, given the potentially binding long-term nature of state and local debt, state and local bond issues do have the quasi-constitutional effect of a constitutional amendment committing future generations to certain courses of action. As we have noted, state constitutional amendments typically require state legislative supermajorities and/or voter approval. Thus, the analogy to the special procedural requirements for adopting a constitutional amendment provides some support for a special procedure involving a legislative supermajority and/or approval by the voters as a prerequisite to the approval of long-term debt.

Most debt limits apply only to debt backed by the full faith and credit of the issuing government. As noted previously, most state and local debt is nonguaranteed debt that is supported not by the faith and credit of the issuing state or locality but by specified revenue sources. In classic point-counterpoint fashion, much as the binding nature of the commitment of full faith and credit led states to adopt constitutional provisions making it difficult to incur debts, state and local legislatures, chafing under those restrictions and seeking to fund popular programs, developed new financial instruments that enable them to borrow without pledging their faith and credit. Like state and local taxation, where constitutional restrictions on taxation have led states and localities to rely increasingly on non-tax taxes, state and local debt restrictions have led states and localities to initiate new forms of borrowing that are non-debt debts. These devices, and their treatment in state courts, are the focus of the next subsection.

3.   THE RISE OF NON-DEBT DEBTS

a.   The Special Fund Doctrine

State evasion of constitutional debt limits began with the so-called special fund doctrine in the late nineteenth century. That doctrine focused on borrowing to finance the construction of physical infrastructure—projects that, once in operation, could generate revenue sufficient to pay off the debt incurred. To build a bridge, the state would borrow money, promise bondbuyers to impose a toll on use of the facility, and pledge the proceeds for repayment of the bonds. State courts soon agreed that so long as the state limited its obligation to the "special fund" of moneys generated by the project and disclaimed any duty to come up with additional funds even if the revenue produced by the project was insufficient to pay the interest and principal on the bond, a revenue bond was not "debt" within the meaning of state constitutional restrictions.

Over time, the special fund concept spread beyond debts backed solely by service charges imposed on the facility financed by the borrowing. As the cases below indicate, state courts have increasingly had to deal with claims that debt financed by a specified revenue source that is not attributable exclusively to the new facility and is not backed by the full faith and credit of the state is outside the scope of state constitutional debt restrictions.

CONVENTION CENTER AUTHORITY V. ANZAI
Supreme Court of Hawaii
890 P.2d 1197 (1995)

MOON, C.J.

The plaintiff Convention Center Authority, State of Hawai'i (the Authority) seeks to obtain a determination as to whether the bonds authorized by the 1993 Legislature to build and operate a convention center would be exempt from the constitutional debt limit. * * *

The Authority was established by the legislature in 1988, after much discussion regarding the development and construction of a convention center in Hawai'i. The Authority is a corporate body consisting of seven members who are appointed by the governor. * * *

The [transient accommodation tax or "TAT"] was adopted by the legislature in 1986 and is a tax imposed on operators of transient accommodations, which include hotels, apartments, condominiums, and the like, that are customarily occupied for less than 180 days. * * * Prior to its adoption, the proponents of the TAT had proposed that the proceeds of the TAT be dedicated to the funding of activities designed to enhance the tourist industry, including a convention center. * * * [But] no portion of the TAT was earmarked for either the tourist industry, the [Hawaii Visitors Bureau], or the convention center. The proceeds from the five percent tax went directly into the state's general fund.

* * * [T]he 1988 act [establishing the Convention Center Authority] did not provide any specific mechanism for financing the convention center.

In 1993, the legislature revisited the convention center issue. * * * As part of comprehensive amendments to the 1988 act, the 1993 legislature authorized the issuance of * * * $350,000,000 in revenue bonds to finance the development and construction of a convention center. * * * The legislature further increased the TAT by one percent, from five percent to six percent, and specifically earmarked the one percent increase for deposit into the Convention Center Capital and Operations Special Fund, to be dedicated to the payment of expenses associated with the development, construction, and operation of the convention center.

* * * After the 1993 legislation had been enacted, the Authority sought to have the Director issue the bonds authorized by the legislature. The Director refused, asserting that it was unclear whether the bonds authorized by the legislature were exempt from the calculation of the state debt subject to the constitutional debt limitation. * * *

Article VII, section 13 of the Hawai'i Constitution defines the debt limit of the State:

> A sum equal to fifteen percent of the total of the assessed values for tax rate purposes of real property in each political subdivision, as determined by the last tax assessment rolls pursuant to law, is established as the limit of the funded debt of such political subdivision that is outstanding and unpaid at any time.

Section 13 also sets out specific exceptions to the debt limit:

In determining the power of the State to issue general obligation bonds or the funded debt of any political subdivision under section 12, the following shall be excluded:

. . . 2. Revenue bonds,[9] if the issuer thereof is obligated by law to impose rates, rentals and charges for the use and services of the public undertaking, improvement or system or the benefits of a loan program or a loan thereunder or to impose a user tax, or to impose a combination of rates, rentals and charges and user tax, as the case may be, sufficient to pay the cost of operation, maintenance and repair, if any, of the public undertaking, improvement or system or the cost of maintaining a loan program or a loan thereunder and the required payments of the principal of and interest on all revenue bonds issued for the public undertaking, improvement or system or loan program, and if the issuer is obligated to deposit such revenues or tax or a combination of both into a special fund and to apply the same to such payments in the amount necessary therefor.

* * * The Convention Center Capital and Operations Special Fund, which would directly secure the bonds in the case of revenue bonds or reimburse the general fund in the case of reimbursable general obligation bonds, has two sources: (1) the revenue from the convention center,[12] once completed; and (2) the one percent increase in the TAT earmarked by the legislature for the convention center. The outcome-dispositive issue, therefore, is whether the one percent increase in the TAT earmarked for the development and construction of the convention center qualifies as a "user tax," or more specifically, whether such tax is "substantially derived" from the convention center as those terms are used in the definition of "user tax" in article VII, section 12(9) of the Hawai'i Constitution.

* * * [I]n order to qualify as a "user tax" under article VII, section 12(9) of the Hawai'i Constitution, the tax in question must be "substantially derived" from the "consumption, use or sale of goods and services in the utilization of the functions or services furnished by a public undertaking, improvement or system." When authorizing the issuance of the bonds in question and earmarking the one percent increase in the TAT for the convention center, the 1993 legislature made the following findings:

---

[9] Article VII, section 12(7) of the Hawai'i Constitution defines "revenue bonds" as "all bonds payable from the revenues, or user taxes, or any combination of both, of a public undertaking, improvement, system or loan program and any loan made thereunder and secured as may be provided by law."

[12] There is no dispute that revenue from the convention center is a proper means of financing the bonds, or that revenue bonds secured by such revenue would be exempt from the constitutional debt limit.

The revenue bonds issued by the authority to finance the convention center are to be repaid entirely from the convention center capital and operations special fund. This special fund is funded by revenues from the transient accommodations tax and operations of the convention center. *The [TAT] is substantially derived from a function of the convention center to increase and maintain sales of hotel rooms and other transient accommodations.*

Act 7, § 11 (emphasis added).

The Authority asserts that the last finding that the TAT as a whole, and necessarily the earmarked one percent thereof, is "substantially derived" from a "function of the convention center" that increases and maintains sales of hotel rooms, was based upon substantial testimony and other legislative evidence and is entitled to deference by this court. The Director agrees that the findings are entitled to substantial deference by this court, but asserts that the findings are not dispositive of whether the revenues meet the "substantially derived" test under article VII, section 12(9) of the Hawai'i Constitution.

We agree that the legislature's findings are entitled to substantial deference; however, "American legislatures must adhere to the provisions of a written constitution. * * * Our ultimate authority is the Constitution; and the courts, not the legislature, are the ultimate interpreters of the Constitution." * * * We therefore turn to an analysis of the nature of the relationship between a purported "user tax" and a public project, as required by the term "substantially derived" set out in article VII, section 12(9) of the Hawai'i Constitution.

* * * The Director acknowledges that the constitutional language demonstrates that the requisite nexus need not be precise and concedes that a logical nexus between the TAT revenue and the proposed convention center exists. The Director further maintains, and we agree, that the nature of this nexus is composed of at least two parts: (1) a "temporal" element, which raises the primary issue whether the convention center must be in existence before the earmarked portion of the TAT can qualify as a "user tax"; and (2) a "causal" element, which raises the issue of the logical relationship between TAT revenue and the convention center. We first address the temporal element.

* * * Hawai'i's Constitution has had some form of debt limitation in place essentially from its inception. Under the Organic Act, the debt limit was set at ten percent of the assessed value of real property. The limit was subsequently increased to fifteen percent at the 1950 Constitutional Convention. * * * Even in Hawai'i's original 1959 constitution, not all debt was included in applying the debt limitations. Specifically, certain revenue bonds and improvement district bonds were exempted. However,

the exemption for revenue bonds in the 1959 Constitution was very narrow. In order for the underlying debt to be exempt from the constitutional debt limit, the revenue from the public undertaking was required to be the "only security for such indebtedness." *Employees' Retirement Sys. v. Ho*, 44 Haw. 154, 168, 352 P.2d 861, 872 (1960) (citing Haw. Const. art. VI, § 3, ¶ 7 (1959)).

In *Ho*, this court had occasion to consider the excludability of certain highway and airport bonds in light of the revenue bond exclusion of the 1959 Constitution. * * * The highway revenue bonds were secured by a special fund financed solely by the proceeds from highway vehicle fuel taxes. The aviation revenue bonds were also secured by a special fund financed by the proceeds from aviation fuel taxes and the revenues of the Hawai'i Aeronautics Commission. Both the highway vehicle fuel taxes and the aviation fuel taxes were in existence and were generating revenue before their respective projects were initiated. Holding that both types of bonds were not excludable from the constitutional debt limit, this court noted that * * * a revenue bond must be secured only by the revenues from the public project being financed by the revenue bonds. Further, because both the highway and airport revenue bonds financed projects that did not yet exist and were secured by highway and aviation fuel taxes, respectively, they were not secured solely by revenues of their respective projects and were therefore not excludable from the debt limit.

Specifically in response to the *Ho* decision, the delegates to the 1968 Constitution Convention amended the revenue bond exclusion to allow revenue bonds to be excludable from the debt limit even if they were secured by "user taxes," and not solely by the revenues of the projects. * * * The amendments are instructive to the present case in two ways. First, as evinced by the delegates' use of the term "user taxes" in the amendments to the language of the revenue bond exclusion, and the constitutional history's indication that the delegates expressly intended to address *Ho*, the delegates considered the taxes at issue in *Ho* to be "user taxes."

Second, from the language of the statutes authorizing bond issuance, it is clear that the highway and aviation revenue bonds addressed in *Ho* financed projects which were not yet in existence. * * *

In light of the foregoing, we conclude that it is not necessary for a public project to have been constructed in order for the taxes involved in the financing of the public project to qualify as "user taxes" as that term is defined in article VII, section 12(9) of the Hawai'i Constitution. * * *

* * * As noted above, the Director concedes that there is a logical relationship between TAT revenues and the proposed convention center and further does not deny that the convention center will generate additional hotel and motel occupancy, thereby resulting in increased TAT

revenues. The Director does contend, however, that a question remains as to whether the quantum of occupancy associated with the convention center bears a sufficient relationship to the earmarked portion of the TAT. * * *

The Authority argues that a direct correlation between the percentage of the TAT earmarked for financing the convention center and the projected percentage increase in room sales attributable to the proposed convention center is not constitutionally required in this context. We agree for three principal reasons.

First * * * the presence of the modifier "substantially" in the term "substantially derived" demonstrates that the requisite nexus need not be precise. We believe that to interpret the language of section 12(9) as requiring "perfect congruence," as the Authority phrases it, between the percentage of the TAT earmarked for the convention center and the percentage increase in occupancy that could realistically be expected from the convention center, would run counter to the intent of the delegates, as clearly demonstrated by their use of the term "substantially" in the definition. The definition requires *some* causal relationship between the tax and the project, but that relationship does not require the precision suggested by the Director.

Second, insofar as the legislature is better equipped than this court to examine the relationship between a proposed convention center and TAT revenues, we accord substantial deference to the legislature's findings regarding that relationship. * * *

Finally, we believe that perceiving a relationship between a proposed convention center and TAT revenues comports with common sense. Prospective conventioneers invariably would need places to stay while attending functions conducted at the convention center. * * *

We therefore hold that the proposed convention center bears a rational causal relationship to TAT revenues. In combination with our earlier conclusion that construction of the proposed convention center need not be completed in order for the earmarked portion of the TAT involved in the financing of the convention center to qualify as a "user tax," we hold that the TAT qualifies as "user tax" as defined in article VII, section 12(9) of the Hawai'i Constitution. Accordingly, the revenue bonds authorized by the 1993 legislature to finance the proposed convention center are excludable from the debt limit pursuant to article VII, section 13(2) of the Hawai'i Constitution.

* * * Much of the impetus behind the instant litigation stemmed from the state Bond Counsel's reluctance to certify that the bonds involved in the present case were not subject to the debt limit in light of an Indiana Supreme Court decision purportedly holding that the TAT is not a "user tax" * * *.

The Indiana case referred to * * * is *Eakin v. State ex rel. Capital Improvement Board of Marion County*, 474 N.E.2d 62 (Ind.1985). In *Eakin*, the Indiana General Assembly had enacted a series of statutes that provided a mechanism for the financing of the proposed expansion of the Indianapolis Convention Center. The revenue scheme authorized by the statutes consisted of three separate excise taxes: (1) a one percent tax on the sale of food and beverages sold for immediate consumption on or near the convention center at retail establishments in Marion County; (2) a five percent tax on admissions to professional sporting events held in the convention center; and (3) a hotel/motel tax. The revenues collected under these taxes were placed in a trust fund, which, together with the operating revenues of the convention center, were the only funds pledged to the retirement of the construction bonds. * * * After approval by the mayor, the County Auditor, *Eakin*, refused to affix his signature to the bonds * * *.

First noting that article 13, section 1 of the Indiana Constitution limited the indebtedness of any political or municipal corporation in the State to two percent of the value of the taxable property within the corporation, the *Eakin* court noted that there were a number of financial liabilities in the public domain that were not included within the term "indebtedness" contained in article 13 of the Indiana Constitution. One such category was debts within the "special taxing district" exception, which in turn has been subdivided into two exceptions, the "Special Funds" doctrine and the revenue bond exception. The revenue bond exception provided that bonds that were to be paid solely from a fund created by revenues from the project for which the bonds were sold were exempt from the constitutional debt limit. The *Eakin* court agreed with the CIB's [Capital Improvement Board's] argument for inclusion of taxes on revenues, in essence user taxes, in the definition of "revenue" for purposes of exclusion of debt from the debt limit, "as long as there exists a nexus between the revenue taxed and the project for which the bonds were issued." *Id.* at 66. The court, however, did not agree with the CIB's second argument for expansion of the revenue bond exception because the revenue from the second two types of taxes—the tax on the retail food service industry and the hotel/motel tax—could not properly be attributed as income of the Indianapolis Convention Center. * * *

Eakin is distinguishable from the present case in two important ways. First, the holding in *Eakin* was premised largely on the fact that the entirety of the taxes involved went toward financing the improvement of the Indianapolis Convention Center. * * * [T]he *Eakin* court held that the tax on the revenue of the hotel/motel and retail food businesses in the Marion County area did not have a sufficient nexus to the convention center because "to argue all retail food and lodging income in Marion County is directly or indirectly related to the existence of an expansion of a preexisting facility is untenable." *Id.* at 66. In the present case, however, only one-sixth of the TAT revenue is dedicated toward the financing of the convention center.

Second, unlike Hawai'i's Constitution, which contains several express provisions for various types of debts excludable from the debt limit, the entirety of the Indiana Constitution's provisions regarding municipal debt consisted of a single broadly worded section:

> § 1. Limitation on indebtedness—Excess void.—No political or municipal corporation in this State shall ever become indebted in any manner or for any purpose to an amount in the aggregate exceeding two per centum on the value of the taxable properly within such corporation, to be ascertained by the last assessment for State and county taxes, previous to the incurring of such indebtedness; and all bonds or obligations, in excess of such amount, given by such corporations, shall be void: Provided, That in time of war, foreign invasion, or other great public calamity, on petition of a majority of the property owners, in number and value, within the limits of such corporation, the public authorities, in their discretion, may incur obligations necessary for the public protection and defense to such amount as may be requested in such petition.

Ind. Const. art. XIII, § 1. As a result, all of the "exceptions" to the debt limit contained in the Indiana Constitution were products of judicial interpretation of the term "indebtedness," insofar as the types of debt judicially determined to be outside the definition of "indebtedness" were not subject to the debt limitation. *See Eakin*, 474 N.E.2d at 65. The generality of the terms of the Indiana Constitution, therefore, inherently accorded wider discretion upon the Indiana courts in their interpretations. The Hawai'i Constitution's provisions regarding exclusions from the debt limit, on the other hand, are specific enumerated exceptions, precisely crafted to cover particular circumstances, and are supported by a correspondingly specific constitutional intent to which we must fastidiously adhere. *Eakin*, therefore, is inapposite to the issue at hand and does not control our interpretation of the Hawai'i Constitution.

NOTES AND QUESTIONS

1. *Special Fund and "User Taxes".* The earliest special fund cases involved user charges—that is, fees or tolls for use of the facility constructed with funds obtained by bonds backed by the charges. Arguably, there is no impact on state revenues since none of the tolls would have been received if the facility had not been built. Can the same be said about bonds backed by so-called "user taxes"? No doubt some increase in user tax revenues is attributable to the new facility. The question for the court is often posed in terms of the "nexus" between the new facility and the user tax proceeds

pledged to finance the bonds. The Hawaii Supreme Court applied a moderate "substantial nexus" test, and, through a combination of deference to the legislature and application of judicial notice that the Convention Center was likely to generate TAT revenues, was willing to assume that the additional one percent of the TAT would be attributable to the Convention Center.

The Indiana Supreme Court, in the *Eakin* case discussed and distinguished by the Hawaii Supreme Court, required a much tighter nexus. However, *Eakin* involved the pledge of all of the revenues from a tax while *Convention Center Authority* relied on the commitment of an additional percentage of a tax.

The Oklahoma Supreme Court seems to have adopted an even looser definition of nexus than Hawaii. The Oklahoma case involved the issuance of $300 million of bonds to finance new construction and improvements to the state's highway system; the bonds were backed, in part, by pre-existing taxes on motor fuels, diesel fuels, gasoline, aircraft fuels, and vehicle license fees and registration fees. A majority of the Oklahoma court concluded that "[t]he combination of taxes and fees creates a revenue stream which is directly related to the construction and maintenance of highways in the self-evident sense that the creation, maintenance—indeed the very existence—of the State's highway system is the prerequisite for the generation of the revenue stream." The court stressed that "the bonds will be retired by pre-paid direct taxes on the ultimate consumers who purchase petroleum products through funds earmarked for improvement of Oklahoma's roads." In re Oklahoma Capitol Improvement Authority, 958 P.2d 759, 764 (Okla.1998). Improvements to the Oklahoma state highway system could increase driving in the state and, thus, arguably increase the revenues produced by motor fuel taxes and driver and automobile registration fees—although it is hard to see how highway improvements would increase revenues produced by the aviation fuel tax. The court did not, however, suggest that revenues earmarked for the bond issue were comparable to increases in the auto-and gas-related revenue that the highway improvements funded by the bonds might produce. Four justices of the Oklahoma Supreme Court dissented. For a sharp critique of this Oklahoma decision, *see* Note, Oklahoma Constitutional Law: Highway Robbery: In re Oklahoma Capitol Improvement Authority: The Eulogy for Oklahoma Constitutional Debt Limitations, 53 Okla L. Rev. 319 (2000). In view of the policies underlying debt restrictions, as discussed at the beginning of this section, which of these varied judicial approaches makes the most sense to you?

2.   *Bond Validation Proceedings. Convention Center Authority* was a conflict between two state agencies, the Convention Center Authority and the State Director of Budget and Finance, who is required to prepare financial statements that certify, inter alia, that the total indebtedness of the state is within constitutional limits. In this case, the Director expressed concern that the Authority's debt would be counted against the state debt ceiling. Many states have adopted procedures under which the agency issuing a bond, or some state official with fiscal responsibilities, may seek judicial validation of

a proposed bond issue before the bonds are offered for sale. Such proceedings provide potential investors with an extra level of security concerning the bonds.

3. *Old Revenues and New.* Is the key aspect of a special fund that the state's liability is limited or that the special fund involves the commitment of only new revenues? In State of West Virginia ex rel. Marockie v. Wagoner, 438 S.E.2d 810 (W.Va. 1993) (*"Marockie I"*), the West Virginia Supreme Court of Appeals invalidated a scheme to finance school improvements through revenue bonds that would be backed by a dedicated portion of the proceeds of the state sales tax. The court held that "a special fund to retire bonds cannot come from existing taxes that are deposited in the general revenue fund. . . . If this practice were permitted, then a debt would be created that would burden the existing general revenue fund in violation" of the debt limitation provision of the state constitution. *Id.* at 814–15. Even though the state had not pledged its full faith and credit and had clearly limited its duty to repay to a specified revenue stream, the bonds were considered debt because they involved the commitment of old revenues that had previously gone into the general fund. *See also* Opinion of the Justices, 665 So.2d 1357 (Ala.1995) (bond issue—to fund incentives to persuade Mercedes-Benz to locate in the state—backed by annual interest earned on investments of the Alabama Trust Fund is debt because state constitution requires that interest earnings on Trust Fund investments be paid into the state's general fund upon receipt).

The West Virginia court, however, subsequently modified its position. In State ex rel. Marockie v. Wagoner, 446 S.E.2d 680 (W. Va. 1994) (*"Marockie II"*), it held that school improvement bonds issued by a state authority would be considered revenue bonds where they were backed by a special fund, created by the legislature, that consisted of net profits from the state lottery even though the lottery had been created years before the school improvement bonds had been authorized. The law creating the lottery had provided that lottery funds are not to be treated as part of the general fund of the state. "Since the legislature specifically provided . . . that the net profits from the West Virginia Lottery are not to be treated as part of the general revenue of the State," the legislature could treat bonds backed by lottery profits as revenue bonds exempt from the constitutional debt restriction. *Id.* at 688. In State ex rel. West Virginia Regional Jail and Correctional Facility Auth. v. West Virginia Investment Mgt. Bd., 508 S.E.2d 130 (W. Va. 1998), the court went further, upholding a mechanism that would use the proceeds of preexisting state insurance taxes to finance bonds for the construction and renovation of jails and correctional facilities. "In the present case, the Legislature designated a specific source of revenue as a funding mechanism and limited the amount dedicated and transferred annually from that fund to the Jail Authority. This is in accord with its authority . . . to establish guidelines and procedures for the prudent investment of State or public funds. Considering the great importance of constructing, renovating, and repairing jails and correctional centers so as to meet constitutional requirements for the housing of prisoners, we believe the built-in limitations contained in [the legislation] are in sufficient conformity with the requirements of [the state constitutional debt limitation] and override the narrow strictures of the special fund doctrine as articulated in *Marockie*." *Id.* at 138. *Accord*, State ex rel. West Virginia Citizens Action Group v. West Virginia Economic Devel. Grant Comm., 580 S.E.2d 869, 887–89 (W.Va. 2003) (economic development bonds backed by lottery proceeds deposited into a special fund not subject to constitutional debt limitation).

CITY OF HARTFORD V. KIRLEY

Supreme Court of Wisconsin
493 N.W.2d 45 (1992)

ABRAHAMSON, JUSTICE.

* * * The City of Hartford (City) seeks a declaratory judgment that the tax incremental bonds (TIF bonds) it plans to issue for Tax Incremental District No. 4 (TID No. 4) pursuant to sec. 66.46 do not constitute debt within the meaning of art. XI, sec. 3, of the Wisconsin Constitution.

* * * The controversy arises from the City's creation on June 13, 1988, of Tax Incremental District No. 4. TID No. 4 consists of approximately 1,120 acres sited for an industrial project. To pay a portion of the project costs associated with TID No. 4, the City issued $4,155,000 of general obligation anticipation notes. As of May 14, 1991, as a result of this borrowing, the City was left with less than $2,000,000 in general obligation borrowing capacity within its constitutional debt limit. On that date, the Common Council of the City of Hartford authorized the issuance of $2,300,000 in TIF bonds for TID No. 4. The City had not previously issued TIF bonds. * * *

Section 66.46 of the Wisconsin statutes, adopted in 1975, authorizes cities and villages to create tax incremental districts to assist them in financing public improvement projects in areas which are "blighted", * * * in need of "rehabilitation or conservation work" * * * or suitable for "industrial sites." * * *

Financing through TIF bonds is premised on the assumptions that increased tax revenue will be generated by development in the tax incremental district and that this increased tax revenue will be sufficient to pay the holders of TIF bonds in full. The process by which a municipality levies and collects property taxes is not altered by the creation of a tax incremental district. The municipality remains free to adjust the annual rate of taxation and all property owners pay the same tax rate without regard to whether they are located inside or outside of the TIF district. * * *

When a municipality creates a tax incremental district, the Wisconsin department of revenue determines the aggregate equalized value of all taxable property within the district. This beginning value is termed the "tax incremental base." Annually thereafter, the department recalculates the aggregate equalized value of all taxable property in the district. This latter figure less the tax incremental base is termed the "value increment." The value increment represents the increase (or decrease) of the aggregate equalized property value that has occurred in the tax incremental district since its creation.

The value increment is then used to calculate the incremental tax revenues (the tax increment) which, at least in theory, are attributable to development in the tax incremental district. To calculate incremental tax revenues, the total local general property taxes levied on all taxable property within the district in a year are multiplied by a fraction having as its numerator the value increment for that year in that district and as its denominator that year's aggregate equalized value of all taxable property in the district. * * *

In the years following the creation of a tax incremental district, all incremental tax revenues collected in the tax incremental district must be deposited into a special fund for that district. * * *

No monies may be paid out of the special fund except to pay project costs of the district, to reimburse the municipality for the payment of project costs, or to satisfy the claims of holders of bonds issued with respect to the district. * * * The TIF bonds are payable only out of the special fund Each TIF bond shall contain the statements necessary to show that it is only payable out of the special fund and that it does not constitute an indebtedness of the municipality or a charge against its general taxing power. Under the statute the local legislative body shall irrevocably pledge all or a part of such special fund to the payment of such bonds or notes.

Several other passages of section 66.46 are relevant to an understanding of the nature of the TIF bonds. Section 66.46(7), entitled "Termination of Tax Incremental Districts," provides that the tax incremental district shall terminate when the earliest of three events occurs. One such event is dissolution of the district by the local legislative body. Upon dissolution of the district the municipality becomes liable for all unpaid project costs actually incurred which are not paid from the special fund. The statute expressly provides that the municipality's termination of the district does not make the municipality liable for any TIF bonds issued.

Also relevant is the legislature's apparent recognition that, given the uncertain nature of a TIF bondholder's claim against the municipality, the municipality may need to make additional pledges of security in order to attract bond purchasers. Thus, "to increase the security and marketability of tax incremental bonds," the legislature explicitly authorizes a municipality to take actions, "not inconsistent with the Wisconsin constitution," to make the bonds more secure or otherwise to increase their marketability. The City apparently exercised this statutory option when it promised in the amended bond resolution that the City would "take no action . . . to terminate the District prior to discharge and satisfaction of the Bonds." By making this promise, the City's obligation to deposit monies into the special fund may thus be absolute for 23 years if the City does not repay the bonds before that time.

Finally, and central to this controversy, is sec. 66.46(9)(b)1 which states that TIF bonds "shall not be included in the computation of the constitutional debt limitation of the city." * * *

Article XI, sec. 3(2), of the Wisconsin Constitution limits the power of cities to become indebted, stating:

> (2) No county, city, town, village, school district, sewerage district or other municipal corporation may become indebted in an amount that exceeds an allowable percentage of the taxable property located therein equalized for state purposes as provided by the legislature. In all cases the allowable percentage shall be 5 percent * * *

The history of the Wisconsin constitutional provisions concerning municipal debt manifests both an abhorrence of public debt and a willingness to increase the debt, especially for school purposes. * * * This constitutional debt limitation seeks to ensure that a political subdivision does not become overburdened by obligations. * * *

Our cases have identified several indicia of debt in the constitutional sense. The City asserts that two of these indicia demonstrate that no debt has been created in this case: 1) the City may avoid its obligation and 2) the obligation is not enforceable against the City or its assets.

We agree with the City that it may avoid any further obligation under the TIF bonds if, when the district terminates, the special fund is not sufficient to pay the bondholders in full. We also agree with the City that the bondholders' right to payment cannot be enforced against the City or any of its assets other than the special fund. Nevertheless, during a period possibly as long as 23 years from the creation of the district, the City has a financial obligation it does not have the power to avoid. The City must pay over part of its general property tax revenues to the TIF bondholders by allocating any tax increments from the district to the special fund. * * *

The City compares its TIF bonds to obligations secured by special assessments. Debts secured by special assessments (as authorized by statute) are incurred for special improvements and are financed by a special tax on the properties they benefit. The obligations do not burden any property of the municipality other than the revenues from the special assessment tax pledged as repayment. * * * This kind of obligation does not constitute debt under art. XI, sec. 3(2). We agree with the City that there are similarities between its TIF bonds and obligations payable from special assessments. Like a special assessment, tax incremental financing holds a designated district responsible for paying the costs of localized improvements.

However, * * * [u]nlike special assessments, which are generated in addition to general property taxes, tax increments are not independent sources of revenue. Nor does tax incremental financing involve a special tax; the tax incremental district has no taxing power, and the municipality does not impose any special taxes to pay off TIF bonds. Rather, the City will collect tax increments as a part of its general property taxes; the general property tax is the source of the revenue in the special fund. In contrast, no part of the funds raised through special assessments is part of the general property tax revenue. * * *

In addition, funds derived from special assessments cannot be used to pay the general expenses of a municipality. When the municipality repays its obligation from monies collected by special assessments on the properties benefitting from the improvements, its general property tax revenues are not affected. In contrast, the special fund created to repay TIF bonds is derived from general property taxes and could be used to meet other expenses, were the use of the special fund not expressly limited by statute.

The City next analogizes TIF bonds to revenue obligations in which the project (which is acquired or constructed with proceeds from the sale of the obligations), as well as the revenues generated by the project, are the sole security for the obligations. In both revenue obligations and TIF bonds, the municipality has an absolute obligation to pay, but its obligation is limited to payment from specified sources. Our court has held that obligations payable solely out of the property acquired or constructed, or out of revenue generated from the project, are not debt. * * *

The City argues that under the tax increment statute, the tax incremental district itself is analogous to the revenue producing enterprise under revenue obligations. We view the two types of obligations as dissimilar because of the nature of the funds from which they are paid. The infrastructure constructed with the funds raised through the City's TIF bonds does not generate revenue directly. This dissimilarity is critical.

* * * According to the City, its TIF bonds are not debt in the constitutional sense because the City can pay its bondholders and be no worse off for having entered into the transaction. The City argues that its TIF bonds are not debt because, absent the creation of the tax incremental district, the tax increments deposited to secure the TIF bonds would not exist. The City asserts that the TIF bonds are thus comparable to revenue obligations because both are paid from revenues that would not be available to the City *but for* the improvements funded by the liability incurred. The crux of the City's position is that regardless of the source of the monies pledged to secure the TIF bonds, the monies would not exist absent the creation of the TIF district. The City's argument does not consider that an increase in land value may occur without the development project because of inflation or because of improvements unrelated to the project.

Even assuming, arguendo, that the tax increments would not have existed but for the district's creation, we conclude that the City's TIF bonds for TID No. 4 constitute debt because they are payable solely from general property tax revenue. This court has in the past recognized a distinction between the pledging of general tax revenues and the pledging of project revenues. * * *

If the City's TIF bonds for TID No. 4 were payable directly from the general property tax revenues of the City, they clearly would constitute debt under art. XI, sec. 3. The result should not be different because the tax increment statute and the TIF bond declare that TIF bonds for TID No. 4 shall be paid from only part of the general tax revenues. Tax increments are collected as general property tax revenues. The tax increment statute merely allows a municipality to carve out a portion of its general property tax revenues for payment of the debt service on its TIF bonds for TID No. 4.

The issuance of the TIF bonds for TID No. 4 obligates the City to pay the holders of the bonds from funds collected through the exercise of the general taxing power of the City. Thus, the City's general taxing power is the real security for the TIF bonds. The City's obligation to deposit monies in the special fund is the source of credit supporting the decision of investors to purchase the TIF bonds. The City's credit is its power to levy general property taxes. Accordingly, when the City issues its TIF bonds for TID No. 4 and pledges a part of its power to levy general property taxes, it pledges its credit.

The very fact that the constitutional debt limit is calculated as a percentage of the taxable property located within a municipality's boundaries shows that the drafters of the constitutional provision were concerned about a municipality's incurring excessive obligations to be paid out of general property tax revenues. To hold that TIF bonds payable from the general property tax revenues are not debt would permit the City to commit large portions of its general property tax revenues to special funds without regard to the constitutional debt limitation in art. XI, sec. 3. Such a holding would virtually nullify the constitutional debt limitation. Accordingly, we conclude that by pledging all or a part of its power to levy general property taxes to pay the TIF bonds for TID No. 4, the City is incurring debt in the constitutional sense.

We conclude that the proposed tax incremental financing for TID No. 4 based on general property taxes represents a "carving out" from the City's general property tax revenues of a discrete source of revenue that is "absolutely obligated" for a significant period of time to the retirement of the TIF bonds for TID No. 4. The resulting impairment of the City's general property tax revenues to pay TIF bond obligations for TID No. 4 for this period creates debt within the meaning of art. XI, sec. 3, of the Wisconsin constitution.

NOTES AND QUESTIONS

1. *Tax Increment Financing.* Authorized in forty-nine states and the District of Columbia, Tax Increment Financing ("TIF") "is the most widely used local government program for financing economic development in the United States." Richard Briffault, The Most Popular Tool: Tax Increment Financing and the Political Economy of Local Government, 77 U.Chi.L.Rev. 65, 65 (2010). "The theory of TIF is that the revenue growth generated within a territorially defined district is earmarked, for a period of years, to pay for physical infrastructure and other expenditures designed to spur economic growth within that district. By generating new growth, those improvements and expenditures produce the incremental revenues that are used to pay for the program that sparked the growth. TIF is typically presented as self-financing, with its expenditures paid for by the increased revenues resulting from TIF-financed growth, without a tax increase." *Id.* at 66. TIF is popular with local governments because it is "highly decentralized, with the decisions concerning whether to adopt TIF, where to place the district, and what type of development to promote determined locally." Moreover, "TIF enables local governments to pursue what is often the principal local development goal—increased tax base—while avoiding the political and legal limits on increased local taxation." *Id.* at 66–67.

2. *Tax Increment as Special Fund.* Why are bonds backed solely by the incremental property taxes in the Tax Increment District not considered special fund bonds? Although the *City of Hartford* court suggests that diversion of incremental tax revenues to the TIF bonds represents a loss of revenue for the city, the theory of the tax increment finance legislation is that new infrastructure investment (financed by the bonds) is necessary to spur economic growth in the district. Isn't the nexus between the bond-financed improvements and the incremental tax revenue comparable to the nexus between the convention center and the added one percent of Transient

Accommodation Tax in *Convention Center Authority v. Anzai*? Should the case have come out differently if the City had not also made a commitment not to interfere with the TID for the next 23 years?

State courts have divided over whether TIF debt is a pledge of property tax revenues subject to state constitutional debt restrictions or is, instead, a limited commitment of a special fund composed of incremental revenues. *Compare* Oklahoma City Urban Renewal Auth. v. Medical Technology & Research Auth., 4 P.3d 677 (Okla. 2000) (city's unconditional obligation to apportion ad valorem taxes in excess of base assessed value for retirement of long-term technology bonds issued by authority constitutes "debt" subject to constitutional voter approval requirement); State ex rel. County Comm. of Boone Cty. v. Cooke, 475 S.E.2d 483 (W.Va. 1996) (TIF plan created debt within meaning of constitutional provision); In re Request for Advisory Opinion on Constitutionality of 1986 PA 281, 422 N.W.2d 186 (Mich.1988) (tax increment bonds bring into play the general taxing power of a municipality); Miller v. Covington Development Authority, 539 S.W.2d 1 (Ky.1976) (obligation payable from general property tax is debt under state constitution); Richards v. City of Muscatine, 237 N.W.2d 48 (Iowa 1975) *with* Strand v. Escambia County, 992 So.2d 150 (Fla. 2008) (TIF debt exempt from voter approval requirement because it does not commit local full faith and credit); Fults v. City of Coralville, 666 N.W.2d 548 (Iowa 2003); Tax Increment Financing Comm. of Kansas City v. J.E. Dunn Constr. Co., Inc., 781 S.W.2d 70 (Mo. 1989) (TIF debt not municipal debt and therefore not subject to municipal debt limitations); South Bend Pub. Transp. Corp. v. City of South Bend, 428 N.E.2d 217 (Ind. 1981) (as TIF bonds apply to only incremental tax revenues, the original taxing power of the municipality is not changed); Denver Urb. Ren. Auth. v. Byrne, 618 P.2d 1374 (Colo. 1980) (TIF does not deprive a city of any preexisting revenue). *See generally* Philip J.F. Geheb, Tax Increment Financing Bonds as "Debt" Under State Constitutional Debt Limitations, 41 Urb. Law. 725 (2009).

3. *TIFs and Tax Uniformity.* Property owners in a TIF district are assessed on the same basis as other property owners in the jurisdiction, but the revenues produced by any increment in the assessment are returned to the district, and to the benefit of those property owners, rather than contributed to the general revenues of the city. Should this be treated as inconsistent with the requirement of tax uniformity? Most state courts that have considered the question have rejected the uniformity attack, finding that TIF departs from uniformity only with respect to spending, whereas state constitutional uniformity requirements apply only to tax assessments or tax rates. *See, e.g.,* Delogu v. State, 720 A.2d 1153 (Me.1998); Meierhenry v. City of Huron, 354 N.W.2d 171 (S.D.1984); Denver Urban Renewal Authority v. Byrne, 618 P.2d 1374 (Colo.1980); Tribe v. Salt Lake City Corp., 540 P.2d 499 (Utah 1975); Richards v. City of Muscatine, 237 N.W.2d 48 (Iowa 1975).

4. *TIFs and Interlocal Conflict.* TIFs can also be a source of interlocal conflict. This can occur in two ways. First, property in a TIF district may be within several taxing units—such as a city and a school district—but many

TIF statutes authorize the municipality to "capture" all tax increments, and not merely those that correspond to the city's pro rata share of the total tax levy. This results in a loss of property tax revenues for other taxing districts, most frequently the school district. *Cf.* City of Parker v. State, 992 So.2d 171 (Fla. 2008) (upholding authority of city to create a TIF district and divert property tax revenues to it even though the city itself did not levy an ad valorem property tax). Proponents, of course, argue that the school district is losing nothing because the growth would not have occurred except for the TIF. Indeed, they argue that the school district will ultimately reap the rewards of increased property tax revenues. Most TIF districts, however, last for 20 years; the promise of increased funds at the end of a 20-year cycle rarely satisfies the current financial needs of many school districts. Some state courts have exempted school district revenues from diversion to the TIF. *See* Leonard v. City of Spokane, 897 P.2d 358 (Wash.1995) (relying in part on state constitutional provision that ". . . the state tax for common schools shall be exclusively applied to the support of the common schools"). *But see* In re Request for Advisory Opinion on Constitutionality of 1986 PA 281, 422 N.W.2d 186 (Mich.1988) (upholding TIF against challenge that it impermissibly diverted school tax funds). Many of the challenges to TIF formation have been brought by school districts and other overlapping governments, and some states have imposed constraints on municipal diversion of school district revenues to TIFs. *See* Briffault, The Most Popular Tool, *supra*, 77 U. Chi. L. Rev. at 88–89. California, which pioneered the development of TIFs, moved to wind up and dissolve TIF-funded community redevelopment agencies to deal with a school funding crisis partly attributable to the diversion of property tax revenues from school districts to the redevelopment agencies. *See* California Redevelopment Ass'n v. Matosantos, 267 P.32d 580 (Cal. 2011); George Lefcoe, Redevelopment in California: Its Abrupt Termination and a Texas-Inspired Proposal for a Fresh Start, 44 Urb. Law. 767, 801 (2012) (noting that the redevelopment agency share of property tax revenues statewide had reached twelve percent and was as high as twenty-five percent in some counties).

Second, TIF plays a role in the interlocal competition for new business investment. "TIF adoption is frequently a copycat phenomenon, with a municipality more likely to implement a TIF program when other municipalities in the vicinity have done so." Briffault, *supra*, 77 U. Chi. L. Rev. at 90. Although TIF was originally developed to support the renewal of blighted urban areas and industrial redevelopment, it is increasingly used for greenfields projects on undeveloped land in the suburbs and the urban fringe and to support large commercial developments that can draw shoppers (and sales tax dollars) from a broad area. With many local governments within a metropolitan area using TIFs in competition with each other, "there is often little or no regional gain in fiscal health or jobs." *Id.* at 90–91. *Accord,* Joe Wilson, Given a Hammer: Tax Increment Financing Abuse in the St. Louis Region, 34 St. Louis U. Pub. L. Rev. 83, 84 (2014) (discussing the heavy use of TIF by municipalities in St. Louis region "as a weapon of economic development against neighboring municipalities in the region" leading to the diversion of "two billion public dollars" to developers for projects including "a variety of big-box stores and other retail options in a region that is rife with such options already").

b.   Service Purchase Agreements

A second important technique for the avoidance of state debt limitations grows out of the longstanding state and local practice of entering into long-term contracts for the purchase of basic operating goods and services, such as electricity, water, solid waste disposal, or space for government offices. There may be benefits to the government—such as a lower price or greater assurance that its service requirements will be met—from a long-term purchase agreement. But such an arrangement raises some of the same dangers, in terms of binding future taxpayers, as a bond issue. Courts generally hold that such long-term contracts are not "debt" in the constitutional sense so long as the government's duty to pay is tied to the continuing receipt of service when the payment is made.

> Long term contracts for the purchase of necessary services, such as electricity and water, have long been held not to violate constitutional and statutory provisions prohibiting municipal incorporations from incurring indebtedness, when the agreements specify that periodic installments will be paid as service is furnished. Those contracts do not create a present indebtedness for the aggregate of all installments for the terms of the contracts contrary to the municipal debt limitations of [the state constitution] but are obligations that mature periodically as each installment comes due.

State of West Virginia ex rel. Council of the City of Charleston v. Hall, 441 S.E.2d 386, 389 (1994) (citations omitted).

As the next several cases illustrate, the principle that long-term contracts tied to the regularly recurring receipt of services are not "debt" has been extended to allow states and local governments to finance construction of the facilities that produce the services.

BOARD OF SUPERVISORS OF FAIRFAX COUNTY V. MASSEY

Supreme Court of Virginia
169 S.E.2d 556 (1969)

I'ANSON, Justice.

* * * The [Washington Metropolitan Area Transit] Authority was created as a body corporate and politic by the Washington Metropolitan Area Transit Authority Compact (Compact), an interstate agreement between Virginia, Maryland, and the District of Columbia * * * to plan, develop, finance, and provide improved transit facilities and service for

the Washington Metropolitan Area Transit Zone (Zone). The Zone encompasses the District of Columbia; the counties of Arlington and Fairfax, and the cities of Alexandria, Falls Church and Fairfax in Virginia; and Montgomery and Prince George's counties in Maryland. * * *

The Authority has adopted a mass transit plan for the Zone. It proposes to construct a combination subway and surface rapid rail system, 97.7 miles in length, with stations to serve the most densely populated areas of the Zone.

The estimated cost of constructing the transit system is $2,494,600,000. Funds are to be obtained from the following sources: The Authority will issue tax-exempt gross revenue bonds in the amount of $835,000,000; the federal government will contribute $1,147,044,000; and political subdivisions in the Zone will contribute the sum of $573,522,000. Of this amount, $149,900,000 will come from political subdivisions in Virginia. The shares of [Fairfax] County and [the City of Falls Church] are $61,900,000 and $800,000, respectively. The County and City have authorized the issuance of general obligation bonds in these amounts, and have entered into a capital contributions agreement with the Authority for the payment of these sums during the estimated ten-year construction period. * * *

Article VII, § 18(a), of the Compact, and Code § 15.1–1357(b)(3) of the [Virginia Transportation District Act of 1964] authorize the County and City to enter into contracts with the Authority to contribute to the capital for construction and/or acquisition of facilities, and for meeting expenses and obligations *in the operation of such facilities.* * * *

Under the [Transit Service] Agreement, the County and City will underwrite their proportionate shares of any deficits incurred in the operating expenses of the transit system by making monthly service payments in advance to the Authority, beginning with the first day of the fiscal year next succeeding the initial operation date and ending June 30, 2040. * * *

Each year the Authority is required to make a complete review of its financial condition, rate and fare structure, and the procedures, schedules and standards of transit service. On the basis of such data the Authority shall determine the transit service to be provided and the rate and fare structure for the ensuing year. The Authority is also required to determine whether the estimated revenues of the transit system, after making provision for debt service and reserve requirements for that year on the Authority's transit revenue bonds, will be sufficient to cover the cost of operation and maintenance incurred. The extent to which the revenues are insufficient for this purpose is the "operating deficiency requirement" for the ensuing year. There is then added to or subtracted from the estimated "operating deficiency requirement" such amounts as are required to adjust for the difference between results of operations for the preceding year. The "operating deficiency requirement" as thus adjusted constitutes the aggregate service payment.

The aggregate service payment is allocated among the political subdivisions in the Zone in accordance with a prescribed formula. The amounts thus allocated constitute the service payment to be made by each political subdivision. * * * After the end of each year an adjustment is made to reflect the obligation of each political subdivision on the basis of the actual operating deficiency. If there is no operating deficiency for a particular year, the service payments are returned.

The obligation of each political subdivision to make its service payment is conditioned upon transit service being rendered to it. If no transit service is rendered in any particular year, no service payment is required for that year. And if the Authority furnishes any political subdivision less than 85 percent of the service, measured in train miles or number of trains, previously determined by the Authority for a particular year, the amount of the service payment is reduced in accordance with the service actually furnished for that year. Service payments shall be applied by the Authority only to the payment of its operating expenses and temporary borrowings to meet operating expenses, and shall not be applied to any other purposes.

Under the financial plan of the Authority, gross revenue derived from the operation of the transit system will be pledged to secure the payment of the principal and interest to the holders of transit bonds in accordance with the terms of the bond indenture. * * *

Sections 115(a) and 127 of the Constitution of Virginia are designed to control indebtedness of localities, but each approaches the problem in a different way. Section 115(a) limits county debt by requiring a referendum approved by the qualified voters. * * * Section 127 limits the indebtedness of cities and towns to eighteen percent of local taxable real estate values. * * *

[T]he paramount inquiry here is whether by executing the contract designated "Transit Service Agreement" the County and City will incur debts in violation of the constitutional limitations.

Petitioners say that to constitute a debt within the meaning of constitutional limitations, there must be a present obligation; and that since the Agreement requires the County and City to make the service payments when, as, and if transit service is rendered, and then only if available revenues of the transit system are inadequate, this creates nothing more than a contingent liability and not a present indebtedness.

Petitioners rely on the principle that a local government may lawfully contract for necessary services such as water, electricity, or sewerage, over a period of years and agree to pay therefor in periodic installments as the services are furnished. In such cases the amounts to be paid as the services are rendered under such contracts do not give rise to a present indebtedness of such local governments, and such contracts are not rendered invalid by the fact that the aggregate of the installments exceeds the debt limitation. * * *

We do not think, however, that the principle relied on is applicable in the present cases. Our examination of the authorities cited by the petitioners did not reveal a single case in which the local governments underwrote or guaranteed the deficit incurred in the operation of the facilities furnishing the services under their contracts. * * *

Although the County's and City's contract is designated a "Transit Service Agreement," the label placed upon it does not necessarily make it such. The obligations of the County and City under the Agreement are for more than just payments for transit service. They agree to pay that amount by which the "operating expenses" exceed the revenues from the transit system after provision is first made for debt service and reserve requirements for the revenue bonds issued by the Authority. The "operating expenses" include all the expenses of operation, maintenance, renewals and replacement of the facilities of the system, interest on temporary borrowings to meet expenses of operation, and payments to reserves for such expenses as may be required by the terms of any contract of the Authority with or for the benefit of the transit bond holders. The payments to be made by the County and City guarantee the continued operation of the transit system during the life of the contract, which expires June 30, 2040, since the operating revenues are pledged to the payment of the transit bonds. While it is true that the payments required of the County and City do not go directly to the payment of debt service, their obligations to pay the "operating expense" deficit in effect amount to making payments on the Authority's bonds. The obligations of the County and City to underwrite and guarantee an unknown "operating expense" deficit of the transit system are fixed and absolute and constitute a present debt within the meaning of the constitutional limitations on County and City debt or indebtedness. * * *

Thus we hold that the obligations of the County and City under the Agreement constitute debt or indebtedness within the meaning of the constitutional prohibitions. * * *

BOARD OF SUPERVISORS OF FAIRFAX COUNTY V. MASSEY

Supreme Court of Virginia
173 S.E.2d 869 (1970)

I'ANSON, Justice.

* * * [T]he Washington Metropolitan Transit Authority * * * has made basic changes in its plans for financing the transit system and has submitted new agreements which the Board of Supervisors of the County and the Council of the City have adopted.

The new agreements provide that the County and City will make transit service payments to the Authority based on the number of train miles operated within the County and the City and the number of their residents using the system. * * *

The Authority's new financial plan eliminates the requirements of the original plan that the County and City underwrite their proportionate shares of the deficits incurred in operating the transit system. The new agreements provide that in consideration of the transit service to be provided by the Authority, the County and City shall pay to the Authority annually, beginning in the first year of full operation of the transit system (estimated to be 1980) the sum of:

"(I) an amount equal to 1 1/4 cents for each Transit Trip by a resident of the County [or City] during such Fiscal Year, as determined by the Authority in accordance with Section 3.2, plus

"(ii) an amount equal to twenty cents for each Train Mile within the County [or City] during such Fiscal Year, as determined by the Authority in accordance with Section 3.3."

The number of transit trips is based on surveys of the ridership of the system which are required to be made annually in accordance with certain designated procedures approved by the Authority. * * * The number of train miles is based on the Authority's records. Train miles are defined as the total number of miles traveled in revenue service by all trains of the system during a fiscal year within the boundaries of a political subdivision. Thus the obligations of the County and City are dependent upon the furnishing of transit service.

The estimated cost of construction of the transit system and the amounts to be obtained by grants or contributions are the same as under the Authority's original financial plan. The Authority, however, will issue net revenue bonds in the amount of $880,000,000, an increase of $45,000,000, to fund the initial part of a bond reserve, the balance of which is to be funded from transit service revenues.

The sole inquiry here is whether the County and the City will incur a debt or indebtedness in violation of §§ 115(a) and 127 of the Constitution of Virginia by executing the new agreements. * * *

[T]he rule that arises out of the peculiar nature of service contracts * * * recognizes that a commitment for services to be paid for only after the services are rendered is *not* a commitment for debt or indebtedness within the meaning of constitutional limitations or prohibitions. Rather this commitment is to honor each year the account payable incurred for services rendered that year. * * *

The service contract doctrine had its genesis many years ago in contracts of municipalities with private companies to furnish water and electricity. With the growth of population, the need of urban areas for increased services, and the broadened concept of responsibility of local governments to provide community services, the service contract doctrine has been applied to a variety of municipal services other than to water and electricity [citing cases involving long-term contracts with private entities for the provision of hospital care for the indigent, ambulance service for the indigent, garbage removal, and the lease of space]. * * *

The record in the present case shows that the agreements of the County and City with the Authority are for an essential public service for the benefit of their residents; that the obligations of the County and City to pay for the transit service are conditioned upon the service being rendered; and that their obligations are to pay over a period of years in periodic annual installments as service is rendered. * * *

The agreements of the County and City to pay in yearly installments for the transit service rendered their residents during those years do not create a debt or indebtedness within the meaning of §§ 115(a) and 127 of the Constitution of Virginia.

BULMAN V. MCCRANE
Supreme Court of New Jersey
312 A.2d 857 (1973)

CONFORD, P.J.A.D. (Temporarily Assigned)

The Chancery Division struck down as offensive to our constitutional debt limitation provision, Const. of 1947, Art. VIII, Sec. II, Par. 3, a proposed arrangement by the State to take a 25 year lease on a building to be erected by a developer on state-owned land and to be used by the State as a records storage center and printing facility. * * *

The State was to have the option to purchase at fixed, progressively declining figures during the 10th, 15th and 20th years of the lease, failing which, title to the building would revert to the State at the end of the term. * * *

[The Chancery Court] concluded "that the arrangement in this case is an installment contract of purchase and not a lease" and therefore violates the debt clause. * * * Found influential were the circumstances

(a) that the State retained ownership of the land, with the "incongruous result if, at the expiration or earlier termination of the lease, the builder-developer should own a building on land title to which was in the State" * * *; (b) the fact that the proposed building would have value at the end of the term, of which the State would get the benefit without further cost * * *; (c) the builder-developer would be recapturing during the period of the lease his total cost of construction, profit and financing expense. * * *

We begin with the fact that the agreement here is in form a lease and with the normal assumption that those who challenge the validity of actions of public officials apparently within their statutory powers must carry the burden of demonstrating such invalidity. If the concept of a lease here is defensible theoretically, then * * * there is no present debt, and no constitutional violation. In such event, it should surely make no difference * * * that the parties could have formulated this transaction as an installment purchase had they wished to do so.

Putting to one side, for the moment, the terminal reversion of title to the lessee, the lease terms generally are harmonious with the theory of a lease as opposed to a sale. The lessor pays the taxes (not exceeding those levied in the third lease year). * * * As customary, the lessor repairs and maintains the exterior, the lessee the interior. And most significantly, damage to the building impairing usability for the lessee's purposes suspends the rent, and if repairs are not completed within six months the lessee has the option to terminate the lease. * * * While the trial judge adverted to the fact that there is no reserved right of termination and entry by the lessor in event of a default by lessee, this is at best a neutral factor, since, contemplating the alternative position that the transaction is an installment sale, there would ordinarily be a provision for acceleration and forfeiture for nonpayment of installments—a stipulation absent here. * * * Realism suggests that the lessor's failure to demand a reentry clause is attributable to total confidence that the State will pay the rents as due.

The heart of the Chancery Division decision lies in the circumstances that the developer-builder recaptures his whole investment, costs and profit during the term of the lease, and, inferentially, at any option stage, and that a building inferably still usable at the end of the term goes to the State at that time without additional consideration if a purchase option is not exercised earlier by the State as lessee.

* * * [I]n the present case * * * the State owns the land. At the end of the 25 year term, absent a clause for reversion of the structure to the lessee, the lessor would own a building of no value to him without title to the land. He would be economically compelled to leave the building on site since the cost of removal and relocation would be prohibitive even if otherwise economically practicable. * * *

[T]here is nothing anomalous in the present builder-developer being permitted to collect as rental sufficient to recover his total investment including the depreciation inherent in his reversion as a wasting asset destined to become devoid of economic value at the end of the term. The fact that the State may be advantaged by ultimately acquiring title to a potentially useful building as the residue of a transaction otherwise faithful to the theory of a lease (certainly so from the viewpoint of the lessor) represents no good reason for judicial assiduity in laying hold of that circumstance to destroy the transaction as an unconstitutional debt. The sole obligation of the State here is for future installments of rent. They will presumably be paid out of current revenues as annually appropriated for the purpose. Under settled principles, there is no present debt in the constitutional sense.

NOTES AND QUESTIONS

1.   *The Service Contract Payment and the Definition of Debt.* In *Massey I*, the local governments' annual payments were to be determined by applying an allocation formula to the operating deficit (which included the cost of debt service). In *Massey II*, the local governments' payments were based on the number of transit trips and the number of train miles within the jurisdictions. There was, however, no evidence in the court's opinion that the formula for calculating the county and city charges in *Massey II* actually reflected either the cost of delivering transit services or the value of those services to the county. If the service charges in *Massey II* reflected an effort to estimate future operating deficits and to allocate the costs according the extent of service in the local jurisdiction, should the *Massey II* agreement have been treated the same as the agreement in *Massey I*?

2.   *Lease or Installment Purchase?* In *Bulman*, the Chancery Court attempted to determine whether the transaction was more akin to an installment purchase or lease. Why is that relevant to the question of whether or not the agreement created a "debt" in the constitutional sense? The Chancery Court was also concerned that the builder-developer would be recapturing during the period of the lease "his total cost of construction, profit and financing expense." Why would that be a problem? Should it matter whether the state is purchasing a service—leaseable space—or the facility that provides the service? What was the basis for the New Jersey Supreme Court's conclusion that the agreement did not create a "debt"? For a very different treatment of a similar lease-finance contract *see* Montano v. Gabaldon, 766 P.2d 1328, 1330 (N.M.1989) (county financed construction of county jail through contract with private firm; under terms of contract, county would acquire ownership of jail, which was located on county-owned land, at end of lease period; "[t]he arrangement is in essence an installment-purchase agreement for the acquisition of a public building, with outside financing and payments spread over twenty years, and as such it requires voter approval").

3. *Public Purpose and Private Activity. Bulman* places a different spin on the relationship between public and private actors than we have seen elsewhere in this chapter. In other settings, states and localities have taken advantage of the tax subsidy for state and local debt to borrow money to provide subsidies to private firms as part of an economic development program. Such arrangements may be challenged as violating public purpose constraints intended to limit government aid to private actors. In *Bulman,* however, a government turned to the private sector to help the government evade state constitutional debt restraints. If the state had sought to borrow to obtain the funds to build the records storage and printing facility, the bond issue would have required voter approval. Through the lease arrangement, a private company undertook the construction and financing of the new building, with the backing of the state's contract to make annual lease payments sufficient to cover the private entity's costs and expected profit.

4. *"Hell or High Water" Arrangements.* In both *Massey II* and *Bulman,* the contracts made the government obligations to pay contingent on the actual delivery of the service. This was critical to their evasion of their state debt restrictions. *Cf.* Dieck v. Unified Sch. Dist. of Antigo, 477 N.W.2d613 (Wis. 1991) (lease-purchase agreement to finance construction of a school not debt because school district has option each year to terminate by not appropriating funds for the following year's rental payment); St. Charles City-Co. Library Dist. v. St. Charles Library Bldg Corp., 627 S.W.2d 64 (Mo. App. 1981) (lease-purchase agreement to finance new library structured as an annual lease with twenty-four successive options to renew for one year not debt because it does not create a binding long-term obligation). An illustration of the critical importance of that contingency is provided by the cases that grew out of a multi-billion dollar conflict involving the Washington Public Power Supply System ("WPPSS") (pronounced "Whoops") and dozens of small cities and public utility districts in the Pacific Northwest. In 1976, a time of growing concern about a prospective energy shortage in the region, WPPSS proposed to issue bonds to finance the construction of two nuclear-powered generating plants. WPPSS entered into agreements with local governments in Washington, Oregon, and Idaho—the "participants" in the arrangement—in which it agreed to sell them power produced by the two plants in exchange for their commitment to make payments to WPPSS. The payment obligation of each locality was based on its percentage share of the "project capability" purchased. The local payments would cover the projects' operating expenses and debt service. The local payment obligations were expressly limited to revenues derived from the operation of their utility systems, which would receive the power generated by the projects. Each participant committed to establish, maintain and collect electrical charges adequate to cover its payment obligations.

Most importantly, each participant contracted to:

> make the payments to be made to ... [WPPSS] under this Agreement whether or not any of the Projects are completed, operable or operating and notwithstanding the suspension,

interruption, interference, reduction or curtailment of the output of either Project for any reason whatsoever in whole or in part. Such payments shall not be conditioned upon performance or nonperformance by [WPPSS] or by any other Participant or entity under this or any other agreement. . . .

This provision was known as the "hell or high water" clause. Do you see why?

In 1982, WPPSS terminated the two projects because it was unable to get sufficient financing. However, it had already issued $2.25 billion in bonds. As a result, many small communities were faced with substantial financial obligations, but would receive no power. For example, Bonners Ferry, Idaho, with a population of 1,906, was committed to paying $10.7 million, or $29,752 a month for the thirty-year life of the WPPSS bonds. The local governments sought to escape liability by asserting that their commitments to WPPSS constituted debt, which had not satisfied the requirements of the appropriate state constitutions. The representatives of the bondholders countered that the obligations were authorized by various exceptions to the debt limitations, particularly the service contract doctrine.

Two state supreme courts, citing the "hell or high water clause," found that the agreement was not a service contract but unconstitutional debt. According to the Idaho Supreme Court, the local governments were "neither acquiring, owning, maintaining, or operating a plant, nor purchasing electrical power." They were "underwriting another entity's indebtedness in return for merely the possibility of electricity." Asson v. City of Burley, 670 P.2d 839, 850 (Idaho 1983). Similarly, the Washington Supreme Court found that the "purchase of 'project capability' under this agreement is essentially an unconditional guaranty of payments on the revenue bonds, secured by a pledge of the participants' utility revenues, in exchange for a share of any power generated by these projects. * * * The unconditional obligation to pay for no electricity is hardly the purchase of electricity." Chemical Bank v. Washington Public Power Supply System, 666 P.2d 329, 335 (Wash.1983), aff'd on reconsideration, 691 P.2d 524 (Wash. 1984). See also Vermont Dep't of Pub. Serv. v. Massachusetts Mun. Wholesale Elec. Co., 558 A.2d 215 (Vt. 1988) (on similar reasoning finding that statutory authority for Vermont municipal electric utilities to purchase electric power did not authorize "hell or high water" purchase of project capability).

The Oregon Supreme Court, however, disagreed. It concluded that the state's constitutional debt limit applied only to obligations backed by tax revenues and not, as in the WPPSS situation, the commitment of utility charges. DeFazio v. Washington Public Power Supply System, 679 P.2d 1316, 1329–33 (Ore. 1984). The Court also rejected the argument that the Oregon cities had exceeded their authority to enter into long-term service purchase agreements when they agreed to the "hell or high water" clause. Emphasizing that the question implicated the home rule autonomy of Oregon municipalities, the Court concluded that the right of local self-government included the right to make mistakes and the responsibility to be bound by agreements:

> If a city may commit itself to purchase at cost whatever a supplier using its best efforts can produce from facilities which will be financed in reliance on the city's contract, however small the production and however expensive the product turns out to be then we see no reason why this authority stops at contracting to pay the costs if small and costly deliveries should turn out to be none at all.

> These agreements proved unwise in retrospect, and with the benefit of hindsight they appear to have been unwise when made. But that is no reason to find them unauthorized. When a city has authority to provide electric power or other public services, that authority cannot well be construed to permit wise but to exclude unwise contracts.

Id. at 1337.

c. Non-Appropriation Clauses, Moral Obligation Debt, and Borrowing by Public Authorities

DYKES V. NORTHERN VIRGINIA TRANSPORTATION DISTRICT COMM'N

Supreme Court of Virginia
411 S.E.2d 1 (1991)

WHITING, JUSTICE.

* * * In order to finance a part of the cost of completing the Fairfax County Parkway, the Fairfax County Board of Supervisors (the county) approved a proposed contract (the contract) with the Northern Virginia Transportation District Commission (the commission). The contract would obligate the commission to issue its "Transportation Contract Revenue Bonds" (the bonds) in an aggregate amount not to exceed $330,000,000. In return, the county would agree to fund the annual principal and interest payments and other listed expenses of the bond issue, to be disbursed by a trustee. These funds would come from the county's "general revenues" and from "the Business, Professional and Occupational License Tax . . . or any other revenue appropriated . . . in substitution for or in addition thereto by" the county.

However, Section 4.05 of the contract would provide that

> [t]he obligation of the County to make any payments . . . is contingent upon the appropriation for each fiscal year by the Board of Supervisors of the County of funds from which such payments can be made. The County shall not be liable for any amounts that may be payable pursuant to this Contract unless and until such funds have been so appropriated for payment and

then only to the extent thereof. It is understood and agreed by the parties hereto that nothing in this Contract shall be deemed to obligate the Board of Supervisors of the County to appropriate any sums on account of any payments to be made by the County hereunder. This Contract shall not constitute a pledge of the full faith and credit of Fairfax County or a bond or debt of Fairfax County. . . .

As security for the payment of the bonds, the commission would transfer its interest in the contract by a proposed trust agreement (the trust agreement). The trust agreement, and the bonds themselves, would provide that "[t]he Bonds are limited obligations of the Commission payable solely from" the moneys provided to the Trustee by the County. The trust agreement further would provide that "[t]he obligation of the County . . . to make such payments . . . is subject to and contingent upon the annual appropriation by the County of moneys for such purpose."

On May 4, 1990, * * * the commission and the county, as a "Plaintiff/Intervenor" (the plaintiffs), filed this bond validation proceeding against the "[t]axpayers, property owners and citizens" of Fairfax County and other localities serviced by the commission. Osgood Tower, Marcia P. Dykes, and "John Doe and Jane Doe numbers 1–25," Fairfax County citizens and taxpayers (the taxpayers), opposed the bond validation.

* * *

The taxpayers argue that because the indebtedness represented by the bond issue would extend for a period beyond the fiscal year of its proposed year of issue, it would be a long-term debt contracted by the county without voter approval. Therefore, the taxpayers contend that the bond issue would violate * * * Article VII, § 10(b) [of the Virginia Constitution].

The plaintiffs respond that the financing plan would not violate Article VII, § 10(b) because they say that contracts subject to appropriation and bonds payable solely from payments pursuant to such contracts are not "debts" as prohibited by the Virginia Constitution. * * *

The plaintiffs rely upon three cases in which an analogous constitutional limitation was considered in connection with long-term indebtednesses proposed for the state's benefit. In those cases, we held that those indebtednesses would not be within the constitutional limitations because they were to be paid solely from special funds derived from the revenues of the financed projects. * * * Here, there is no special fund because *no* income will be derived from the use of the Parkway; the *only* source of revenue for bond payments will be the county's annual appropriations from its occupational license receipts and other state revenues.

The plaintiffs contend that this would make no difference because we said in *Baliles* [*v. Mazur*, 297 S.E.2d 695 (1982)] that "[t]he overriding consideration, therefore, is whether the legislative body is obligated to appropriate the funds, not the source or composition of the special fund." [id.] at 700. That statement, however, was made in response to a contention that the "special fund" doctrine could not be applicable in *Baliles* because the rent to be paid by the Commonwealth for its use of the buildings was a "fund consist[ing] entirely of money appropriated by the legislature." As noted above, however, *Baliles* concerned a revenue-generating project and is therefore inapposite. Thus, this is the first case in which we have considered the implications of Article VII, § 10(b) in circumstances where the facility financed will not be a revenue-generating project.

In *Terry v. Mazur*, 362 S.E.2d 904 (1987), we considered a statutory scheme purporting to authorize the Commonwealth Transportation Board to issue revenue bonds to finance highway improvements. The bonds were to be secured by a "pledge" of future excise and other taxes, as well as fees relating to motor vehicles. The Attorney General contended that the bond issue met the requirements of the "special fund" doctrine, and was therefore constitutionally permissible without submission to a vote of the people. We disagreed, refusing to extend the "special fund" doctrine to projects other than those which generate their own revenues. We adhere to that view.

The plaintiffs also contend that the bonds would not be a "debt" of the county because the bonds would be issued by the commission, not by the county. That, in our view, is a mere subterfuge. Because the trust agreement and the bonds themselves look to annual appropriations of the county's funds as the sole source for repayment of the bonds, it is of no consequence that bonds would be issued by the county's alter ego. * * *

Although the contract permits the county to discontinue its promised appropriations, we must also consider the practical effect of such a calamitous event in deciding whether the county in fact would be bound to continue to service the bond issue and, therefore, has incurred a "debt" proscribed by Article VII, § 10(b). The county recognizes the importance of its fiscal integrity. It has been advised that the bond issue would not affect its triple A bond rating. In fact, the contract would prohibit the county from changing its designation of the proceeds of its annual business, professional, and occupational tax as the primary source of appropriations for its annual bond payments without obtaining "confirmation from those rating agencies that shall have . . . rated and maintained ratings on the Bonds, that the then current ratings on the Bonds will not be reduced as a result of such change."

The county also recognizes the disastrous effect that would follow any failure by the board of supervisors to make an annual appropriation and the county argues that such a disaster would never be permitted to occur. That argument implicitly acknowledges that the bond issue would have the practical effect of a long-term debt binding the county. * * *

It is obviously contemplated that the issuance of the bonds in accordance with the contract would bind future boards of supervisors to make annual appropriations of sufficient funds to finance the bonds. Manifestly, the animating purpose of the bond contract arrangement is to create a long-term debt, without submitting the debt to a vote of the qualified voters of Fairfax County.

We hold, therefore, that the obligation thus incurred would be a "debt contracted by the county" in violation of Article VII, § 10(b) and, hence, that the bond issue would be invalid.

CARRICO, CHIEF JUSTICE, dissenting.

* * * It might be obvious to the majority that the county would be bound to make annual appropriations of sufficient funds to finance the bonds, but it is not obvious to me. This is what the majority is saying: The practical effect of the county's exercise of its contractual right to discontinue the promised appropriations is to make it legally obligated to continue the promised appropriations.

I thought I knew what the term "practical effect" meant. I also thought I knew what the term "legally obligated" meant. And, to me, the two terms meant quite different things. Much to my surprise and dismay, however, the majority says the two terms mean the same thing, and I daresay the business and financial communities in this state will be equally surprised and dismayed at the majority's revelation.

It appears, therefore, that "practical effect" is the basis of the majority's invalidation of the bonds in question. If that is the basis, I consider it far too slender a reed to support such drastic action.

Rather, in my opinion, the bonds should be invalidated only if the county has undertaken an unconditional express obligation to continue making appropriations to pay the full amount of the bonds. I do not believe the county has undertaken such an obligation, and I would say this whether or not a special fund exists in this case. * * *

UPON REHEARING

LACY, JUSTICE.

* * * The threshold issue for consideration is whether Art. VII, § 10(b) is applicable to the debt in issue. That section states in pertinent part:

> No debt shall be contracted by or on behalf of any county or district thereof . . . except by authority conferred by the General Assembly by general law. The General Assembly shall not authorize any such debt . . . unless . . . provision be made for submission to the qualified voters of the county or district thereof . . . for approval or rejection by a majority vote of the qualified voters voting in an election on the question of contracting such debt. Such approval shall be a prerequisite to contracting such debt.

1. COMMISSION DEBT

Dykes argues that this section is applicable to bonds issued by the Commission because the Commission is a *"district* 'created' by one or more cities and counties . . . proposing to issue bonds 'by or on behalf of' the County." This argument is unpersuasive. The use of the word "district" in the name of the Commission is insufficient to extend application of the section to it. Furthermore, the Constitution speaks in terms of a "district thereof." The Commission was authorized and created by statute, and is comprised of the Cities of Alexandria, Fairfax, and Falls Church, and the Counties of Arlington and Loudoun, in addition to Fairfax. The Commission clearly was not "created" by Fairfax County, and is not a "district thereof."

The Commission is an independent political subdivision in the same manner as are housing authorities, water and sewer authorities, and industrial development authorities. The enabling legislation, like that of these other authorities vested with the power to incur bonded indebtedness, affirms that debt so incurred is that of the entity, not of the Commonwealth or of any other political subdivision. * * * This statement is repeated in the bonds themselves, as well as in other documents constituting the financing proposal. We have repeatedly held that the debt incurred by legislatively created, independent political subdivisions, whatever their title, is not the debt of the Commonwealth or of any other governmental unit, and we affirm that holding here. * * * Therefore, the debt which will be incurred by the Commission in issuing the bonds is not subject to the provisions of Art. VII, § 10(b) of the Virginia Constitution.

2. COUNTY DEBT

The contract provides that the Commission will issue the bonds and that the County in turn will fund the annual principal and interest payments and other listed expenses of the bond issue. The repayment funds will come from the County's general revenues, including the Business, Professional, and Occupational License Tax "or any other revenue appropriated" by the County. Under the terms of the contract, however, the County's obligation to make the payments to the Commission "is subject to and contingent upon the annual appropriation by the County of moneys for such purpose."

Neither Tower nor Dykes seriously argues that the terms of the financing documents impose a *legally* enforceable obligation on the County to appropriate the funds or to repay the bonds. Indeed, the contract, the trust agreement, and the bonds * * * each specifically states that the County is not obligated to appropriate funds or levy taxes for the payment of the bonds and that the financing proposals do not constitute a pledge of the full faith and credit of the County.

Rather, Dykes and Tower invite us to define "debt" as used in Art. VII, § 10(b) as something other than a legally enforceable obligation to pay. Dykes says constitutional debt exists because the financing proposal creates obligations which the "County cannot avoid." Tower argues that "subject to appropriation" financing constitutes a pledge of the County's full faith and credit, thereby establishing constitutional debt. Both rely on factors such as the understandings and expectations of bondholders, county officials, and bond rating agencies as creating obligations on the County. While these indicia may be significant in other contexts, such as whether the financing scheme is good or wise policy, or in determination of the investment grade or credit worthiness of the bonds, here we are only concerned with the limited question whether these indicia, or any other, establish a "debt" of the County subject to Art. VII, § 10(b).

* * * No debt is created for constitutional purposes if the state or county "incurred no legal liability to underwrite the project." * * * The debt created must involve a "binding and direct commitment," * * * a commitment which can be enforced against the maker. There must be a *legal* obligation.

"Subject to appropriation" financing does not create constitutionally cognizable debt because it does not impose any enforceable duty or liability on the County. * * *

Under the financing proposal at issue, neither the County nor its general revenues is liable for repayment of the debt incurred by the bond issue. In the absence of a legal obligation, the County has not incurred a debt cognizable under Art. VII, § 10(b).

STEPHENSON, JUSTICE, with whom WHITING, JUSTICE, and POFF, SENIOR JUSTICE join, dissenting.

* * * Never before has this Court validated a bond issue like the one in question. I find the scheme employed by the County to be a shocking, patent attempt to circumvent and nullify the requirement of voter approval contained in § 10(b).

By the proposed contract with the Commission, the County would agree to make annual payments sufficient to pay the debt service on the bonds. The funds for these payments are derived solely from, and are contingent upon, annual appropriations from the County's general revenues.

* * * Is anyone so naive that they truly believe that the County, in reality, is not compelled to make annual appropriations until the bonds are retired? What are some of the consequences if the County ceases to make the appropriations? Obviously, the bondholders would have no recourse, and their bonds would be worthless. Quite obviously, also, the County's credit would be seriously impaired, if not destroyed.

The § 10(b) requirement of voter approval of long-term county debt has existed for more than six decades. The requirement was not deleted when our Constitution was revised in 1971.

More recently, the General Assembly proposed an amendment to § 10 that would have allowed counties to issue bonds, without voter approval, "for transportation purposes, the principal and interest on which [would have been] payable exclusively from the pledge of the revenues and receipts of any local taxes. * * *" Acts 1989, c. 670; Acts 1990, cc. 736, 881. On November 6, 1990, however, this proposal was rejected overwhelmingly by the Commonwealth's voters.

Today, the majority, in effect, has sanctioned what the voters rejected. Consequently, by employing the approved scheme, counties now are at liberty to create bond indebtedness, payable from their general revenues, without submitting the matter to their voters. For all practical purposes, the § 10(b) debt proscription has been nullified by judicial fiat.

SCHULZ V. STATE OF NEW YORK

Court of Appeals of New York
639 N.E.2d 1140 (1994)

KAYE, CHIEF JUDGE.

This challenge to a 1993 statute authorizing a multibillion dollar bond issue for State and local transportation improvements continues a debate on financing public works projects that has engaged our State throughout its history. The instant litigation attacks the statute both as imprudent fiscal policy and as violative of debt-limiting provisions of the

State Constitution. The wisdom of legislation, of course, is not a matter for the courts. As to legality, we conclude—as did both the trial court and Appellate Division—that the statute before us does not violate the State Constitution. * * *

The plan provides $10.47 billion for the Dedicated Highway and Bridge Trust Fund (Highway Fund) operated by the State Thruway Authority, and $9.56 billion for the Dedicated Mass Transportation Trust Fund (Mass Transportation Fund), operated by the Metropolitan Transportation Authority (MTA). Both Funds, created in 1991, would under the 1993 statute receive revenues—subject to annual appropriation by the Legislature—from taxes and fees derived from use of the Authorities' facilities: vehicle registration fees, the motor fuel tax, the petroleum and aviation fuel business tax, and miscellaneous highway use taxes. * * *

The Act authorizes the Thruway Authority to issue up to $4 billion in 30-year bonds for highway and bridge construction. * * *

The Act sets forth several provisos relating to Thruway Authority bonds. Any bonds issued pursuant to authorizations contained in the Act do not constitute a debt of the State. In the words of the Act:

> "The notes, bonds or other obligations of the authority authorized by this section shall not be a debt of the state and the state shall not be liable thereon, nor shall they be payable out of any funds other than those of the authority pledged therefor; and such bonds and notes shall contain on the face thereof a statement to such effect." * * *

Moreover, the statute in the same section declares that the State has "no continuing legal or moral obligation to appropriate money for payments due" under any agreements entered into to effect the implementation of the goals of the Act.

Restrictions on State liability must be included in any cooperative agreements flowing from the Act. * * * Further, Thruway Authority bonds issued pursuant to the Act are payable only by legislative appropriations from the Highway Fund and no other source. * * *

With regard to the MTA, the Act sets up a $9.56 billion capital funding program for the five-year period ending December 31, 1996. The existing—but not previously funded—Mass Transportation Trust Fund and the Metropolitan Mass Transportation Operating Assistance Fund would receive appropriations from user-derived taxes and fees and, in turn, would pay into a newly created MTA Dedicated Tax Fund. * * *

The Act does not require the MTA to issue bonds, but if it chooses to do so, it may use the Tax Fund for security and debt service. Any bonds issued by the MTA are subject to the same statutory provisos on State liability as the Thruway Authority bonds. * * *

Plaintiffs contend first that debt contracted by the public authorities is indistinguishable from debt contracted by the State and thus within the [state constitution's] referendum requirement. Alternatively, they argue that the Act—by pledging appropriation of public revenues— compromises the legal independence of the public authorities involved, subjecting them to the debt-limiting provisions imposed on the State. They urge moreover, that as a practical matter the Legislature always will appropriate money for the Funds rather than risk damaging the State's credit rating. The effect of long-term appropriation-risk bonds, they say, is to "contract debt" within the meaning of article VII, § 11, and the failure to submit the proposed law to a public referendum renders the enactment unconstitutional.

* * * [W]e begin analysis with a history of the referendum requirement and the origin of public authorities.

The State Constitution of 1777, our first, provided that the legislative power of this State is to be vested in the Senate and Assembly (art II). The unlimited grant of legislative authority—when exercised in the arena of borrowing and spending—led to abuses and prompted a movement for reform of State borrowing practices. * * * Following the onset of economic depression in 1837, private railroad corporations defaulted on obligations that had been assumed on the strength of liberally granted State credit. The State assumed the liabilities, with no hope of reimbursement, and by 1845 more than three fifths of the entire State debt was the result of such loans. Public works were suspended in response to the debt crisis. * * *

The precursor to the referendum requirement of article VII, § 11 * * * was adopted under the Constitution of 1846 (former art VII, § 12) as part of a sweeping reform of public borrowing practices, in an effort to protect the State from the uncertain and possibly disastrous consequences of incurring future liabilities—"liabilities easy for a current generation to project but a burden on future generations". * * * Known as "the people's resolution," the amendment reserved to voters the power to determine, by referendum, whether a proposed law creating debt would take effect * * *. State debt that extends beyond one year, therefore, is subject to the referendum requirement of article VII, § 11. * * *

The referendum requirement is not simply a limit on discretion. * * * [I]t [i]s legally impossible for the Legislature to contract debt in the absence of approval by the people through referendum: such approval is a condition precedent to the creation of debt. Any purported long-term debt created in the absence of a public referendum is simply not legally binding on the State.

Following adoption of the referendum requirement, the Legislature sought ways to provide long-term funding for public works projects that would not require public referendum. In 1851, without public referendum, the Legislature authorized issuance of canal certificates, to be paid from canal revenues, which by their terms were not to be deemed to create a debt against the State. While we struck down the statute because it failed to comply with a constitutional mandate as to application of canal revenues (*see, Newell v. People*, 7 NY 9, 92), we noted in passing that even though purchasers of the canal certificates may have no legal remedy against the State if canal revenues proved insufficient to pay the certificates, the State would no doubt make good on them by reason of moral obligation. Moreover, canal revenues paid out to certificate holders represented money that would be diverted from public coffers. The declaration that the certificates were not to be deemed debt was therefore "an evasion, if not a direct violation, of the constitution."

The Legislature then passed a series of town bonding acts that authorized—and later compelled—cities to borrow money to invest in railroad company stock. The question whether the State could authorize one of its instrumentalities to undertake commitments the Constitution prohibited the State itself from undertaking reached this Court in *Bank of Rome v. Village of Rome* (18 NY 38). We upheld the scheme, leading to ratification of constitutional restrictions on municipal debt in 1874, 1884 and 1894.

Shortly after the turn of the century, the Legislature devised a new vehicle for funding public works projects that appeared to insulate the State from the burden of long-term debt: legislative creation of legally separate public benefit corporations, known as public authorities, to discharge particular functions. The first such entity was the Port of New York Authority, created in 1921. * * * In theory, a public authority would be self-supporting, able to meet debt obligations through revenues obtained from its own valuable assets, such as fares and user fees. Such public benefit corporations would separate their administrative and fiscal functions from those of the State * * * to " 'protect the State from liability and enable public projects to be carried on free from restrictions otherwise applicable' " * * *.

We rejected an early challenge to the effectiveness of language disclaiming the State's liability for public authority debts, where bonds were secured solely by the revenues of the issuing authority. * * * Although public authority debt was not legally binding on the State, we nevertheless recognized * * * that the State might choose to honor a liability as a moral obligation. We stated, however, that whether to recognize a moral obligation is within the discretion of the State:

"[I]t rests solely with the State through its Legislature to determine whether it will recognize a claim even though founded upon equity and justice and allow it to be developed into a legal demand and . . . the exercise of this choice cannot be delegated to any one else[.] . . ."

([*Williamsburgh Savings Bank v. State of New York*, 243 N.Y. 231] at 244–245 . . .) * * *

To prevent the State from assuming public authority debt as a moral obligation—and to overrule constitutionally the effect of *Williamsburgh*—the 1938 Constitution (our present Constitution) explicitly empowered public authorities to issue bonds and incur debt but prevented the State from assuming that liability:

"Neither the state nor any political subdivision thereof shall at any time be liable for the payment of any obligations issued by such a public corporation heretofore or hereafter created, nor may the legislature accept, authorize acceptance of or impose such liability upon the state or any political subdivision thereof; but the state or a political subdivision thereof may, if authorized by the legislature, acquire the properties of any such corporation and pay the indebtedness thereof" (NY Const, art X, § 5).

* * * Debate at the Constitutional Convention included discussion of whether the State would be liable in the event an authority were unable to meet its obligations, and the language of the amendment was tailored to make clear that it would not. The Chair of the Committee on the Legislature and its Powers, George Fearon, supported the new provision, stating, " 'I believe that when people buy [authority] bonds they should know definitely and certainly that the credit of the State of New York and that the credit of the municipality is not behind those bonds. There should not be any question about it' " * * *.

By article VII, § 8 and article VIII, § 1 of the 1938 Constitution, the prohibition against gifts or loans of State credit was made applicable to public corporations. * * * While the provision bars the State from lending its "credit" to a public corporation, the State is nonetheless free to give money to a public authority and to commit itself to giving future gifts. * * * The distinction is rooted in the fact that the granting of State money—while depleting current State coffers and making those funds unavailable for other purposes—nevertheless does not bind future generations or create the same dangers of collapse, insolvency and crisis associated with the abuse of credit. * * *

The Constitution was adopted by the people on November 8, 1938 at a general election, giving full recognition to the existence of public benefit corporations, their independent capacity to contract debt, and the continued power of the State to make gifts of money to those authorities.

Thus, contrary to plaintiffs' contention, there can be no question that—for the purpose of contracting their own legally binding obligations—the Thruway Authority and the MTA are public benefit corporations existing independently of the State. * * *

That the 1938 Constitution expressly empowered public authorities to contract debt independently of the State lends further support to the conclusion that the Act, by authorizing the Thruway Authority and the MTA to issue bonds, does not contract legally binding debt upon the State. * * *

Though the debt of the Thruway Authority and MTA are not a legal obligation of the State, plaintiffs also contend that the Act contracts debt of the State by imposing a moral obligation on the Legislature to continue appropriating revenue to the special Funds. A moral obligation, however, is not in and of itself "debt". * * * Debt, within the contemplation of the State constitutional debt-limiting provisions, has a settled meaning * * *, and we are not persuaded that plaintiffs' argument for an expanded definition has merit.

* * * [P]laintiffs characterize the Act as creating "moral obligation" debt—a term apparently coined in the 1960's to describe appropriation-risk bonds that could not legally bind the Legislature beyond a session but would create a "moral obligation" to appropriate money should a public authority be unable to redeem its bonds. * * * The existence of such a moral obligation would provide some assurance (though not an enforceable legal obligation) to bondholders that the bonds would retain their value.

The bonds authorized by the Act were not labelled "moral obligation bonds" by the Legislature, and entirely apart from nomenclature the Act does not create such an obligation. The Act requires a statement on the face of the bonds that they are not a debt of the State and are payable only out of the Authorities' funds. Moreover, the Act disavows existence of a moral obligation on the part of the State to appropriate revenues in the future. These disclaimers—particularly when read in light of the constitutional prohibition against State assumption of authority debt (NY Const, art X, § 5)—are sufficient to remove any reasonable expectation on the part of bondholders that the State will guarantee return in the event of default on the part of the Authority or that the bonds place them in privity with the State. * * * Plaintiffs' heavy reliance on *Williamsburgh* (243 NY 231, supra) as establishing the possibility that the State could be held liable on a moral obligation is unavailing. First—unlike the Act—the statute at issue in *Williamsburgh* expressly recognized the possibility of a moral obligation. Second, article X, § 5 was adopted after *Williamsburgh* precisely to overrule constitutionally the possibility of the State assuming a moral obligation as to debt of a public authority.

Most critically, a moral obligation cannot be judicially imposed upon the State in the absence of its consent to be so bound. * * * Even where a moral obligation exists, that circumstance creates no enforceable right on behalf of the aggrieved party. Rather, where circumstances support a determination that the State has a valid moral obligation to honor a private claim, we will permit the State to waive immunity from liability. But that is a unilateral right * * * and the effect is simply to permit adjudication of a claim.

In short, a moral obligation does not create "debt," since it creates no enforceable right on the part of the one to whom the obligation is owed. Moreover, the Act could not make plainer that the State recognizes no moral obligation on its part to continue appropriations. Plaintiffs' claim that the Act creates a moral obligation to pay which falls within the constitutional definition of "debt" therefore also must fail.

Plaintiffs point as well to the State's need to protect our economy as binding future Legislatures to continue with annual appropriations to the Funds for the life of the bonds. They claim that, in reality, the bonds are backed by the State's full faith and credit because the consequences of default would be ruinous, assuring that appropriations will be made. Indeed, plaintiffs document instances where State officials appear to have characterized the future appropriations as legal obligations of the State, despite the Act's disclaimers. Thus, in plaintiffs' view, the Act obligates the State to continue appropriations for the life of the bonds—some 30 years—creating long-term State "debt."

We have previously held that a proposal to fund in a subsequent year, subject to legislative appropriation and explicit disclaimer, does not create legally binding debt. * * * [W]hile the Legislature might endeavor to incur future liabilities, to be appropriated on a year-to-year basis without submitting the spending plan to the people, "[n]o harm or loss has or can come from this practice." Such spending plans are effectual only to the extent subsequent Legislatures indeed do "give effect to them by providing the means and directing their payment, but the discretion and responsibility is with them as if no former appropriations had been made. No duty or obligation is devolved upon them by the acts of their predecessors". * * * If unaffected by future Legislatures, the laws will simply "remain upon the statute books, but * * * only * * * as monuments of the extravagance, recklessness or folly of those by whom they were enacted," creating no legally binding debt or liability upon the State. * * *

While the Legislature might make the appropriations to the Funds, to be used in turn to service the Authorities' debt, it is not bound to do so. Should it fail to do so, and the Authority default, the State is not liable to the bondholders under the provisions of the Act. Because the State does not become indebted, the financing subject to appropriation does not constitute the lending of credit or assumption of the liability of a public corporation, or indebtedness of the State for purposes of the constitutional limits on such debt. * * * Instead, the funds—if appropriated—constitute a permissible gift of money to a public corporation out of existing revenues, creating no debt. * * * Laws making annual appropriations from a special fund do not and cannot create debts within the meaning of the referendum requirement. * * *

If (as plaintiffs urge) modern ingenuity, even gimmickry, have in fact stretched the words of the Constitution beyond the point of prudence, that plea for reform in State borrowing practices and policy is appropriately directed to the public arena. * * *

LONEGAN V. STATE OF NEW JERSEY

Supreme Court of New Jersey
819 A.2d 395 (2003)

PORITZ, C.J.

Today we reject a broad challenge to the validity of fourteen New Jersey statutes authorizing contract or appropriations-backed debt. By our holding, we reaffirm over fifty years of precedent from this Court and align the Court, as before, with the decisions from a majority of our sister states. Our decision is based in the unambiguous and clear language of Article VIII, Section II, paragraph 3, of the New Jersey Constitution (the Debt Limitation Clause or Clause), and in the State's reliance on the Court's precedents when crafting complex financing mechanisms responsive to changing market conditions. We are well aware of the need to maintain stability in respect of the variety of financial instruments authorized by the Legislature, and of the litigation that would result if we attempt to establish classes of debt that are governed by the Clause and classes that are not. To reject, at this late date, traditional legal rules relating to debt could have unintended consequences not anticipated by the Court. We leave to the legislative and executive branches, where it properly resides, the policy decision whether to propose a constitutional amendment redefining or otherwise altering the scope of the Debt Limitation Clause, or whether to restrain the creation of appropriations-backed debt by other means should the other branches deem such measures appropriate.

Lonegan I was decided on August 21, 2002. In its initial opinion, the Court held that the issuance of appropriations-backed debt authorized by the Educational Facilities Construction and Financing Act (EFCFA) was not violative of the Debt Limitation Clause. Our holding recognized that the Legislature had enacted EFCFA to fulfill its constitutional obligation to fund new school construction mandated by this Court in Abbott v. Burke, 153 N.J. 480, 710 A.2d 450 (1998) (*Abbott V*). We observed that "the debt authorized by EFCFA is *sui generis*" because of its constitutional underpinnings in the Education Provision of our Constitution, as reinforced by Article VIII, Section IV, paragraph 2 (the School Fund Provision), which "separately authorizes state-backed school bonds without reference to the Debt Limitation Clause." In light of the State's reliance on the Court's general approval of a similar financing scheme in *Abbott V,* and on "our long line of precedents validating similar debt issued by an independent authority," we sustained the state's school construction financing scheme.

Although the EFCFA challenge was at the core of *Lonegan I*, the plaintiffs attempted a broad attack on all legislative programs financed through appropriations-backed debt. Nonetheless, the Court chose to limit its holding to EFCFA because plaintiffs failed to provide argument sufficiently anchored in the specific financing schemes authorized by the statutes they found objectionable. Unwilling to resolve issues of constitutional import without legal and factual context, we sought a more focused discussion from the parties and "direct[ed] the Clerk of the Court to establish a schedule for additional briefing and reargument." * * *

To place the Court's inquiry in context, we recount in condensed form the substantive background provided in *Lonegan I*. We begin, as we must, with the language of the Clause:

> The Legislature shall not, in any manner, create in any fiscal year a debt or debts, . . . which together with any previous debts or liabilities shall exceed at any time one per centum of the total amount appropriated by the general appropriation law for that fiscal year, unless the same shall be authorized by a law for some single object or work distinctly specified therein. . . . [S]uch law shall provide the ways and means, exclusive of loans, to pay the interest of such debt or liability as it falls due, and also to pay and discharge the principal thereof within thirty-five years from the time it is contracted; and the law shall not be repealed until such debt or liability and the interest thereon are fully paid and discharged. No such law shall take effect until it shall have been submitted to the people at a general election and approved by a majority of the legally qualified voters of the State voting thereon.

N.J. Const. art. VIII, § 2,¶ 3.

In *Lonegan I* we explained that "[t]he scope and meaning of the restrictions imposed on the legislative branch by the [Debt Limitation] Clause have been discussed at length in an extensive body of case law spanning more than fifty years and covering a wide variety of bonding mechanisms adopted by the Legislature to meet the capital funding needs of the State." We observed:

"In those cases the Court has almost universally sustained statutes authorizing the issuance of debt that is not backed by the full faith and credit of the State, generally when the debt is undertaken by an independent authority, most often when that authority has a revenue source available to service the principal and interest on the debt. The Court has reasoned that the Debt Limitation Clause is not implicated when the State is not legally obligated on debt issued subject to future annual appropriations."

Those conclusions directly followed from our review of that case law under the framework found in In re Loans of the Property Liability Insurance Guaranty Association, 124 N.J. 69, 75–76, 590 A.2d 210 (1991). There, Justice Handler analyzed the two dominant strains in the Court's Debt Limitation Clause jurisprudence: " 'decisions hold[ing] that the constitutional provision does not apply to the creation of debt by independent public corporate entities, . . . [and] decisions generally find[ing] that legislative expressions of intent to provide future funding do not create present debts of the State subject to the . . . [C]lause.' " We observed that decisions in the first category "rely on the legal autonomy of the issuing authority[,] . . . on specific language disclaiming any enforceable obligation on the part of the State," and, in some instances, on the availability of a special revenue source, whereas decisions in the second category "hold[ ] . . . that the Legislature's expression of intent to provide future funding does not create debt subject to the Debt Limitation Clause." *Ibid. See* Enourato v. N.J. Bldg. Auth., 90 N.J. 396, 448A.2d 449 (1982) (holding that bonds issued by New Jersey Building Authority for construction of facilities to be leased by State did not violate the Clause because payments were "subject to legislative appropriations" and State did not pledge full faith and credit to guarantee bonds); N.J. Sports and Exposition Auth. v. McCrane, 61N.J. 1, 292 A.2d 545 (explaining that "the debt clause applies only to obligations which are legally enforceable against the State" and that debts of corporate agency created by Legislature neither bind State nor fall under Debt Limitation Clause). * * * Most important, despite the differences among the individual bonding mechanisms under consideration, we found that a unifying thread linked both groups of cases, to wit, that "the Debt Limitation Clause applies only when the State is legally obligated to make payments authorized by the Legislature."

[T]he plaintiffs have presented argument regarding specific state statutes authorizing the issuance of appropriations-backed debt through independent state agencies and designed to fund diverse programs serving various short-and long-term objectives. *See, e.g.,* New Jersey Economic Development Authority Act (funding initiatives to promote economy of New Jersey, increase employment opportunities, assist in development or redevelopment of political subdivisions of State, reduce industrial and commercial environmental pollution and promote commercial enterprise within State); New Jersey Transportation Trust Fund Authority Act of 1984(authorizing initiatives to further State's transportation infrastructure, including public highways, public transportation projects and mass transit passenger service); New Jersey Sports and Exposition Authority Law, (providing stadiums and other buildings and facilities in the Hackensack meadowlands for athletic contests and other expositions); New Jersey Educational Facilities Authority Law, (financing construction of dormitories and educational facilities for public and private institutions of higher education); County College Capital Projects Fund Act, (authorizing financing of county college capital projects); Tobacco Settlement Financing Corporation Act, (providing for acquisition and management of State's national tobacco settlement receipts). Plaintiffs assert that the financing mechanisms employed by those statutes generally have "common features" that, together, render them unconstitutional: a state authority that is authorized to "issue bonds for a [s]tate purpose;" language permitting the State Treasurer to enter into an agreement with the authority to pay the debt service on the authority's bonds; and language requiring "payments under the [s]tate contract [to be] 'subject to annual appropriations.'" In plaintiffs' view, the subject to appropriation qualification is meaningless because, as a practical matter, the State cannot default on such bonds without substantial negative impact on its credit rating and, therefore, on its access to financial markets. As a result, "subject to appropriation bonds" are effectively "full faith and credit bonds." Because both types of debt are supported by the State's general taxing power, both require voter approval under the Debt Limitation Clause.

* * * [T]he plaintiffs have narrowed the scope of their challenge by redefining contract or appropriations debt. They now describe this type of debt as a

> liability of the State, or any independent authority created by the State, which is unsupported by an adequate and independent revenue source, and which is to be amortized exclusively or primarily by funds derived from annual appropriations, or by tax-based revenue that is properly payable into the State's General Fund, absent a constitutional dedication of revenue.

So circumscribed, plaintiffs' challenge now distinguishes certain revenue bonds from most other contract debt. Debt that finances a toll road or bridge, a college, or a sports and entertainment facility, and that is retired from a "special fund" comprised of revenues generated by the financed facility or project (*e.g.*, from toll collections, tuition payments, or ticket sales), is exempt from the requirements of the Clause because general tax revenues are not tapped for repayment.

Further, although plaintiffs' definition of contract debt does not on its face exempt bonds issued to finance the construction of facilities that are subsequently leased back to the State, a practice sustained by this Court in *Enourato, supra,* plaintiffs do not challenge this type of contract debt. In such cases, the lease proceeds used to retire the bonds, like contract or appropriations-backed debt, are paid from general appropriations pursuant to contractual arrangements; however, plaintiffs consider those transactions distinct legal obligations that do not offend the Debt Limitation Clause so long as they are *"bona fide* leases" reflecting the fair market rental of the facility and containing terms typically found in commercial leases.

In its response to our inquiries, the State argues that the new rule advanced by plaintiffs is unsupported by the language of the Clause, and if adopted by this Court, would severely unsettle the State's financial operations. In the State's view, fifty years of this Court's jurisprudence have provided the Legislature with an objective and workable legal benchmark around which to craft fiscal policy without having to guess whether a particular borrowing scheme will offend the Debt Limitation Clause. To break with our past decisions and extend the Debt Limitation Clause to those debts that the State has no legal obligation to repay would inject uncertainty into State borrowing practices by "mir[ing] the Court in[to] drawing arbitrary and artificial distinctions among legally indistinguishable funding arrangements in complex commercial transactions[.]"

The State also claims that a number of state financing mechanisms that are "far removed from bond financing," such as "multi-year contract[s] subject to appropriation[s]," would be rendered constitutionally suspect, causing additional disruption to the state's finances. * * * In its supplemental brief, the State sets forth in detail the number and types of programs financed through appropriations-backed debt, ranging from the authority bonds specifically challenged by plaintiffs to lease-purchase agreements for real property, equipment, and services, and tax and revenue anticipation notes. In reliance on our past decisions, the State has made repayment subject to future appropriations and expressly disclaimed any enforceable legal obligation, thereby structuring those programs to comport with the bright line rule previously enunciated by this Court.

In response to plaintiffs' charge that there is no substantive difference between appropriations-backed debt and general obligation debt, * * * The State argues that there are constitutionally significant differences between the Legislature being "highly likely," rather than being "legally bound," to repay its debts. The prevailing rule, grounded in the plain language of the Clause and in those differences, provides the Legislature with the legal certainty it needs to develop fiscal policy.

We agree with the State. Under our case law, only debt that is legally enforceable against the State is subject to the Debt Limitation Clause. In reliance on that rule, the State has responded to changes in the financial markets that reflect modern economic realities. The variety of financing mechanisms employed in both the private and the public sectors today were unheard of when the Debt Limitation Clause was made a part of our Constitution in 1844. Had the framers been prescient, they might have written the Clause differently. By its terms, however, the Clause as written requires voter approval only when the State is legally required to make payment on the debt it has incurred.

The Debt Limitation Clause was adopted in 1844 because of concerns about binding obligations imposed on future generations of taxpayers and because of unchecked speculation by the state. In *Lonegan I,* we observed that New Jersey's constitutional debt restriction was enacted originally to "protect against the type of financial debacle experienced" by other states that had borrowed without restraint during the 1830s. Those states financed public projects and speculated in western lands or banking schemes only to default on their obligations during the economic downturn that followed. Today, states are routinely involved in activities such as road and railway construction and expansion, as well as other public works projects, that in the past were considered speculative but now are seen as essential and appropriate governmental functions. * * * When contract or appropriations-backed debt is issued, however, the State does not pledge its full faith and credit and is not legally bound to make payment on that debt

In sum, the variety of functions assumed by the government since the 1800s, and the sophisticated means now used to finance those functions, make it difficult if not impossible to differentiate among acceptable and unacceptable types of twenty-first century appropriations-backed debt under a nineteenth-century paradigm. * * * Even the plaintiffs concede that the Clause does not require the State to obtain voter approval each time appropriations-backed bonds are issued. They fail, however, to draw principled distinctions between structured lease payments and revenue bonds, and the types of appropriations-backed debt they find objectionable.

In *Lonegan I* * * * we discussed those cases that treated appropriations-backed debt "as legislative decisions to circumvent debt limitation restrictions." *Id.* at 453–54 (citing Montano v. Gabaldon, 766 P.2d 1328, 1330 (N.M. 1989); State ex rel. Ohio Funds Mgt. Bd. v. Walker, 561 N.E.2d 927, 932 (Ohio 1990)). Those cases "rely . . . on practical considerations relating to the source of debt payments or the category of expenses funded by the debt." Thus, in Winkler v. State of West Virginia School Building Authority, 434 S.E.2d 420 (W. Va. 1993), the court invalidated a system of contract bond financing for school construction

similar to the program we upheld in Lonegan I. Although the state had
expressly disclaimed liability for the bonds issued by the School Building
Authority, the court held that they constituted debts of the state because
the only source of repayment for the bonds was general appropriations.
Notably, the court distinguished appropriations-backed bonds from self-
liquidating bonds and from lease financing. Subsequently, in Marockie v.
Wagoner, 438 S.E.2d 810 (W. Va. 1993), decided five months after
Winkler, supra, the court invalidated a statute which authorized the use
of existing sales tax revenues to repay bonds issued by the School
Building Authority. The court declared that "a special fund to retire
bonds cannot come from existing taxes that are deposited in the general
revenue fund," but added: "[I]f the Legislature creates a new tax source or
increases the amount to be paid on an existing tax account, the new or
increased amount may be used to liquidate revenue bonds" so long as the
monies do not first pass through the general fund. Then, in McGraw v.
Caperton, 446 S.E 2d 921 (W. Va. 1994), a case involving computer
equipment contracts, the court declared that "one year contracts with
multiple renewals and non-binding cancellation clauses do not create the
type of debt prohibited" by the West Virginia Debt Limitation Clause. In
those cases, the West Virginia Supreme Court of Appeals reaffirmed and
expanded the exceptions to its holding in *Winkler.* Indeed, the court
appears to have indicated in *Marockie* that *any* increase in taxes set apart
as a special fund could be used to support revenue bonds. Both cases
suggest that the scope of exceptions to a broad rule of invalidity is a
shifting concept that leads to uncertainty and generates litigation.

In respect of lease arrangements, whether or not the State takes title
to the facilities on termination of the lease, those arrangements are,
generally, a subspecies of appropriations-backed debt. The Legislature
appropriates the rental payments from general revenues pursuant to a
lease agreement, which payments then are used to retire bonds issued to
finance the construction of the leased facilities. As with other types of
appropriations-backed debt, the State is not legally bound to make the
rental payments and can opt not to do so. And, most likely, non-payment
would adversely affect the State's credit rating. Yet, a variety of theories
have been advanced to sustain such lease arrangements, *i.e.,* that the
State must, in the normal course, lease facilities to carry out the
operations of government; that a *bona fide* lease does not expend tax
dollars over and above the amount required for those operations; and
that, under the common-law, lease payments are not debts until they fall
due each year.

We do not discern constitutionally significant differences among
these types of debt. We are therefore wary of taking the path followed by
the minority of courts that have adopted the plaintiffs' approach. The
dissent's "view [that] the phrase 'in any manner' constitutes a broad

umbrella . . . cover [ing] any legislative enactment that binds the state, either by design or by indirect result, to the payment of incurred debt out of general revenues," clearly goes too far. Even our dissenting colleagues draw back from that extreme approach by excluding debt supported by "adequate" and "independent" revenues, despite the difficulty in determining both adequacy and independence. They also would exclude "labor agreements, leases, and any other arrangement or transaction that does not require the State's contractual borrowing of funds," even though, in certain of those transactions debt costs are included and the State is bound for a period of years. Under the reasoning of the dissent, the "in any manner" language of the Clause would appear to cover those arrangements. We are therefore unable to discover a principled basis for the exemptions accepted by the dissent.

In *Lonegan I,* Justice Stein focused on Standard and Poors' statement that " 'a significant credit deterioration for all types of debt issued by [a] defaulting government' " will occur if the State declines to appropriate contract debt payments. (Stein, J., concurring in part and dissenting in part) (quoting Standard & Poors, Revised Lease and Appropriation Backed Debt Rating Criteria (June 13, 2001)). Justice Stein further asserted that "[n]o one disagrees that the State, as a practical matter, must repay its appropriations debt in order to maintain the stability of its credit in the bond market." For him, the Court's longstanding interpretation of the Clause has led to a "legal artifice that permits the State to issue [appropriations] debt . . . without voter approval," with the result that the State "increasingly has relied on [such] debt in recent years."

The State acknowledges that payments on appropriations debt are "highly likely." It is certainly the case that in recent years appropriations debt has increased substantially, and that the financial markets anticipate the likelihood of legislative appropriations when they set interest rates on the different types of state debt. We, too, acknowledge the realities of the marketplace. Yet, as Justice Stein also pointed out,

> the Debt Limitation Clause may no longer be the most relevant contemporary standard for determining whether the issuance of additional State debt is economically sound.

He observed "that the bond rating agencies consider the ratio of debt service to annual revenues to be a more accurate gauge of a State's capacity to carry additional debt." However that determination is made, in our view, judgments about the issuance of debt when the State's full faith and credit is not implicated are best left to the other branches of government.

The concerns expressed by a minority of jurisdictions, and echoed by the dissents in *Lonegan,* can be addressed only by the Legislature in our tri-partite system of government. We are unwilling to disrupt the State's financing mechanisms in the circumstances presented to us, and agree with the majority of state courts interpreting their own constitutions that the restrictions of the Debt Limitation Clause do not apply to appropriations-backed debt.

LONG, VERNIERO, and ZAZZALI, JJ., dissenting.

Today's decision construes the Debt Limitation Clause so narrowly that the Clause no longer applies, except in those increasingly rare instances when the State seeks to incur general-obligation indebtedness. * * *

The aim of the Debt Limitation Clause is to place a constraint on government. It is one of the few clauses intended to empower the people by giving them a direct voice in managing the State. The framers recognized that some transactions might provide immediate funding to fuel governmental projects but disperse the true financial costs to future generations. They enacted the Debt Limitation Clause to reserve to the people the right to decide whether a particular level of debt is essential to satisfy an important public purpose.

* * * The sheer volume of contract or appropriations debt ($10.8 billion or seventy-five percent of the State's June 30, 2002, debt of $14.3 billion) makes it virtually impossible for the State to default on such obligations without severe and unacceptable harm to New Jersey's credit rating. Thus, for all practical purposes, the State ultimately is responsible for that indebtedness within the meaning of the Debt Limitation Clause.

We would hold that the Debt Limitation Clause is violated when the Legislature, without voter approval, enacts legislation authorizing an authority or other State entity to borrow money or otherwise incur indebtedness, in excess of the threshold set forth in the Clause, that is (1) unsupported by adequate revenues that are independent of taxpayer funds, and (2) amortized primarily or completely by annual legislative appropriations. Excluded from that holding would be labor agreements, leases, and any other arrangement or transaction that does not require the State's contractual borrowing of funds.

To rule otherwise is to trespass on the right of voters to approve or disapprove the State's ever-increasing contract indebtedness. We acknowledge that our intended holding would require the legislative and executive branches to alter significantly the manner in which they approach that form of indebtedness. Accordingly, we would stay our disposition for an appropriate period to afford the other branches the opportunity to address the mandate of the Debt Limitation Clause by the least disruptive methods. We also would grandfather all existing transactions that otherwise might be constitutionally infirm, leaving them undisturbed.

Lastly, we reject the notion that we should steer clear of our intended remedy because it simply is too difficult to implement or too burdensome to the State. This Court must never avoid its duty on that basis.

NOTES AND QUESTIONS

1.   *The Non-Appropriation Clause.* Both service-purchase and lease-financing arrangements generally include clauses that condition the government's obligation to pay on the receipt of services. The effect is to make the government's commitment less than fully binding and, thus, not debt. Nonetheless, it is generally assumed that as long as the governmental entity receives the goods or services contracted for it will make the appropriations provided for under the contract. In *Dykes* and *Schulz*, however, the contracting governments did not tie their obligation to pay to the receipt of services. Indeed, it is not clear that they were actually receiving services at all. The government's "commitment" to make payments—which would function as debt service—to the entity that had actually issued the debt was made contingent not on the future receipt of services but simply on the government's future willingness to continue to abide by that commitment. Where a contract contains such a "subject to appropriation" clause, the government has truly incurred a non-debt debt.

Most courts have held that such "subject to appropriation clause" arrangements are not "debt" in the state constitutional sense on the theory that since the government is not legally bound to make future payments the concerns that gave rise to the debt limitation provisions are not triggered. In a footnote to the *Lonegan* opinion not reprinted here, the New Jersey Supreme Court cited to decisions in thirty-two states upholding some form of subject-to-appropriation debt. *See* 819 A.2d at 404 n.2. Like the dissenters in *Dykes* and *Lonegan*, however, a handful of courts have emphasized the practical reality that subsequent state or local legislatures will feel obligated to continue to make appropriations under the contract in order to protect their credit ratings, and, thus, their ability to issue general obligation debt at reasonable rates of interest. *See, e.g.,* Winkler v. State School Building Authority, 434 S.E.2d 420, 432–33 (W.Va.1993) ("If the bonds are not paid, it is obvious that the State's credit will be impaired. . . . We simply cannot ignore . . . the practical reality that will be visited upon a state's credit if there is a default in the bonds."). The courts taking the majority view have denied that the economic or political pressures to abide by the nonbinding promise to make future payments have any legal significance. *See, e.g.,* State ex rel. Kane v. Goldschmidt, 783 P.2d 988, 997 (Ore. 1989) ("The State's promise of repayment is conditioned upon the willingness of future legislative assemblies to appropriate funds. The State does not promise that future legislatures will appropriate any funds. . . . Nor does the fact that the legislature may feel compelled to make payments in a future biennium out of fiscal concern to protect its credit rating convert the state's obligation into a legal one.").

Who do you think has the better argument—the judges who say that the debt limitations apply to legally binding debt only, or those who argue that "practical reality" will effectively compel states and localities to appropriate debt service payments?

2.   *New Jersey's Lonegan Litigation.* The *Lonegan* litigation grew out of a challenge to $8.6 billion in bonds for repairing and constructing new public schools—the "largest, most comprehensive school construction program in the nation." Lonegan v. State, 809 A.2d 91, 104 (N.J. 2002) ("*Lonegan I*"). The program was a consequence of New Jersey's longstanding school finance reform litigation. The bonds were to be issued by a state authority, and backed by a contract pursuant to which the state committed, subject to annual appropriation, to pay the authority an amount each year that would cover the costs of debt service. As the state's obligation was subject-to-appropriation, the voter approval the New Jersey constitution requires for new state debt was neither sought nor obtained. The state supreme court found that as the school construction program involved the "provision of constitutionally required" educational facilities and was a direct response to the court's own orders the financing plan did not violate the debt limitation provision. The court, however, intimated that subject-to-appropriation debts outside the shelter of the education finance requirements might be subject to challenge. The court noted that New Jersey's growing use of subject-to-appropriation debt raised the "troubling question" of whether the state's debt limitation "retains its purpose and vitality" and warned that "[a] literal interpretation of the Debt Limitation Clause that eviscerates the strictures the Clause expressly contains cannot serve the constitutional mandate," *id.* at 93. As you can see, however, the court ultimately sustained the general exemption of subject-to-appropriation debt from the state's constitutional debt restriction. The court appeared to have been strongly influenced by a concern that treating appropriation-backed debt as debt subject to constitutional limitations would "disrupt the State's financing mechanisms" as well as by the difficulty of drawing lines that would distinguish inappropriate uses of appropriation-backed debt from uses, like lease-financing, that the dissenters were willing to accept. Do you agree with the majority that whether or not the debt is formally binding is the line most appropriate for a court to draw, and that, in any event, it is too late in the day for the court to change the rules for the state's financial practices? Does this makes the Debt Limitation Clause meaningless?

In the November 2008 general election, New Jersey voters approved an amendment to the Debt Limitation Clause which provides that the legislature shall no longer "create[ ] or authorize[ ] the creation of a debt or liability of an autonomous public corporate entity . . . which debt or liability has a pledge of an annual appropriation as the ways and means to pay the interest of such debt or liability as it falls due and pay and discharge the principal of such debt" without voter approval. N.J. Const., Art. VIII, Sec. 2, ¶3.b. Voter approval is not required for authority bonds that are paid off either from "an independent non-State source of revenue paid by third persons for the use of" the object or work financed by the bonds, or "from a source of State revenue otherwise required to be appropriated" by another provision of the state constitution. *Id.* How does this provision respond to the *Lonegan* decision?

3.   *Moral Obligation Debt.* Non-appropriation clause debt may be seen as a new incarnation of a borrowing device, referred to by the New York Court of Appeals in *Schulz*, that was very popular in the 1960s and 1970s—the moral obligation bond. As explained by a special New York State investigative commission created in 1976 following the financial failure of one of the state's public authorities:

> The moral obligation bond was first introduced to New York State in 1960 with the establishment of the New York State [Housing Finance Agency ("HFA")]. It was then becoming difficult if not impossible to secure voter approval in statewide referenda to permit the issuance of full faith and credit bonds for housing development. It was also difficult to market revenue bonds that were based on housing revenues. The moral obligation thus was designed to facilitate the marketing of housing revenue bonds and to provide an interest rate on those bonds approximating that of the State's full faith and credit obligations. . . .

> The State itself issues no moral obligation bonds. They are issued by State public authorities under statutory authorization that provides for the creation out of funds raised by the bonds of a reserve fund equal to one year's debt service on the bonds. If a public authority, because it does not have sufficient revenues, is obliged to draw on the reserve fund to meet debt service, the Governor must so certify to the Legislature which is then obligated to consider whether it will or will not appropriate the amount needed to make up the deficiency in the reserve. The arrangement places no legal obligation on the Legislature or on the State. It merely insures that a deficiency in a reserve will be brought to the attention of the Legislature. . . .

> The language of the statute could well mislead one not trained in governmental "words of art." For it states that upon receipt of the certification from the Governor "the Legislature shall apportion" the amount necessary to make up such a deficiency. Technically, "apportion" does not mean "appropriate," and though it appeared to mandate that the Legislature replenish the reserve, it does not do so as a matter of law.

Restoring Credit and Confidence: A Report to the Governor by the New York State Moreland Act Commission on the Urban Development Corporation and Other State Financing Authorities 3–4 (1976).

As the Commission's report indicates, the moral obligation bond was a device through which states sought to extend the use of the special fund revenue bond to projects, such as low- and moderate-income housing, that could not clearly generate the funds to pay off the bonds used to finance them. Investors were wary of buying bonds offered by housing finance agencies that were backed simply by tenant rentals and federal housing assistance. The nonbinding provision for state funds in the event that the revenues of bond-financed projects were unable to cover debt service provided investors with the extra comfort necessary to market the bonds at reasonable interest rates. Despite its nonbinding nature, the device proved extremely successful in the short term, resulting in the "explosive financing of the HFA role beyond housing to hospitals, universities and mental institutions." *Id.* Other states soon followed, providing nonbinding state safety nets for public authority revenue bonds issued to finance the construction of new housing and other social goals. Most state courts concluded that a legislature's mere "moral" obligation to appropriate debt service when authority revenues fell short was not enough to trigger the state's debt restrictions. *See, e.g.*, Steup v. Indiana Housing Finance Authority, 402 N.E.2d 1215 (Ind.1980); Utah Housing Finance Agency v. Smart, 561 P.2d 1052 (Utah 1977); State ex rel. Warren v. Nusbaum, 208 N.W.2d 780 (Wis.1973); Massachusetts Housing Finance Agency v. New England Merchants Nat'l Bank, 249 N.E.2d 599 (Mass.1969). *But see* Witzenburger v. State ex rel. Wyoming Community Development Authority, 575 P.2d 1100 (Wyo.1978).

The moral obligation bond came under a cloud as a result of the experience of New York's Urban Development Corporation ("UDC"). Created in 1968 to finance both residential construction and industrial redevelopment in depressed urban areas, "UDC . . . embarked on projects inherently more risky than those undertaken by HFA and financed these by moral obligation bonds. These projects, incidentally, were thought by private enterprise to be too risky to be undertaken by operating subsidies." Restoring Credit and Confidence, *supra*, at 4. Following cutbacks in federal housing subsidies in 1973, UDC ran into financial difficulties and in 1975 it defaulted on an issue of short-term notes. Ultimately, the state appropriated the funds necessary to bail the agency out. Following the UDC experience, the moral obligation device went into a period of decline. But the more recent rise of non-appropriation clause debt suggests the continuing appeal of non-binding obligations as a means of circumventing state debt limitations.

In one sense, the non-appropriation clause debt is less troubling than the 1960s-style moral obligation bond. In the old moral obligation bond, the state did not make any initial appropriation to the authority issuing the debt. The issuing authority was primarily responsible for debt service on the bonds, with the state's "commitment" only a safety net. "The assumption was, as publicly stated by [New York's] Governor Rockefeller, that these projects would not cost the state a penny." *Id.* at 4. Contemporary non-appropriation clause obligations dispense with the illusion that they involve no cost to the state. Rather, from the beginning, the state spends public funds to pay for public authority bond costs. As a result, they can be factored into budget projections and counted as part of regularly recurring government costs. Yet, by treating non-appropriation clause obligations as part of baseline expenses, the device only heightens the tension with the spirit of state constitutional debt restrictions—which is either to limit the amount of such ongoing obligations or to require voter approval before they are assumed. Whereas moral obligation debt assumed that the government would never have to pay, non-appropriation clause debt relies on the government's legal freedom to choose not to pay at some point in the future—even though that freedom may never be exercised.

NOTE ON PUBLIC AUTHORITIES AND DEBT LIMITATIONS

As *Dykes*, *Schulz* and *Lonegan* indicate, public authorities play a critical role in non-appropriation clause debt and in the rise of nonguaranteed debt generally. Public authorities—along with variously named commissions, public benefit corporations and special districts—are a distinctive feature of state and local governance. They are usually created by a general purpose government to provide one or a limited number of services within their jurisdiction. Typically, they are governed by appointees rather than elected representatives, with the appointees named by the state or local government that created the authority. They are also designed to be quasi-autonomous from their parent governments. Once in office the members of the governing boards of public authorities are protected from removal and may serve longer terms than the elected officials who appointed them. Typically, public authorities lack the power to tax, and rely for funds instead on fees generated by their own facilities, appropriations from other governments, or taxes imposed and earmarked by elected general purpose governments for their benefit.

Public authorities have multiple functions. They are a mechanism to construct and operate infrastructure and related services—bridges, tunnels, mass transit, highways, water supply and flood control, port development, electricity—over large regions without having to amalgamate all the localities in the region into a single regional government. They can provide a means of insulating from direct political control such infrastructure and other services that are often seen as raising primarily engineering or other technical questions rather than political issues. Most importantly, they have come to provide a means of issuing public debt outside the strictures of state debt limits.

Indeed, to a considerable extent the spread of public authorities is connected to state debt limits; in the states that employ more restrictive debt limits, a higher percentage of debt is issued by public authorities than in less restrictive states. *See* Beverly S. Bunch, The Effect of Constitutional Debt Limits on State Governments' Use of Public Authorities, 68 Public Choice 57 (No. 1, Jan., 1991). Many authorities were created to facilitate the issuance of special fund revenue bonds. It may have been easier for courts to accept that revenue bond debt was not state or local debt when the entity issuing the bond—and financing and operating the facility that would generate the funds to pay off the resulting debt—was a quasi-autonomous government that lacked taxing power or the legal authority to pledge the faith and credit of the parent state or locality. Early on, public authority debt was held not to be the debt of its parent government, and was, thus, not subject to the parent government's debt restrictions. *See, e.g.,* Robertson v. Zimmermann, 196 N.E. 740 (N.Y.1935); Comereski v. City of Elmira, 125 N.E.2d 241 (N.Y.1955). Most states continue to treat public authority debt as exempt from state constitutional restrictions on state or general purpose local government debt even when the public authority is not financing the debt out of revenues produced by authority facilities. Unless the state constitution contains a specific provision applying debt limitations to public authorities, public authority debts are likely to be exempt from state constitutional restriction.

Public authorities have been criticized for promoting the fragmentation of state and local government. With independent authorities controlling valuable revenue-producing infrastructure and responsible for providing many important services, elected governments may find it more difficult to pursue coherent policy programs. Public authorities may treat the investment community rather than local residents or elected governments as their primary constituency. Indeed, as *U.S. Trust v. New Jersey* indicates, public authorities may use their borrowing powers to bolster their independence and make it more difficult for elected governments to use public authority resources for public programs.

Conversely, elected governments may use public authorities to get around debt limits in order to finance capital projects. Building authorities are a classic instance of this. Patterned after the lease-financing arrangement upheld in *Bulman v. McCrane*, states have authorized the creation of nominally independent public building authorities which can issue revenue bonds—but cannot pledge the faith and credit of the state—to finance the construction of facilities that will be leased to the state. State rental payments for use of the building authority-financed facilities are then used to finance the bonds; once the lease is completed, and the facility fully paid off, it typically becomes the property of the state. As the lease payments are "subject to appropriation," there is no state debt, and the building authority's debt is not subject to the constitutional debt limit. These arrangements are usually upheld by state courts. *But see* In the Matter of Constitutionality of Chapter 280, Oregon Laws 1975, 554 P.2d 126, 131 (Ore. 1976) (use of building authority device to avoid the state constitution's debt limit was "a scheme which would fool only a lawyer").

More generally, a public authority may be legally independent of the state or locality and have an independent mission, but the authority and the general purpose government may develop a cozy relationship so that the government can use the authority to avoid state debt limits. This arrangement is sufficiently common that it has a name—"conduit" or "backdoor" financing.

New York state has used public authorities to cover operating deficits in the state budget. In 1990, the state authorized the sale and lease-back of two state-owned assets, the Attica Correctional Facility and a portion of a highway, to a re-born Urban Development Corporation. The sales were financed by UDC bonds, which in turn were secured by the pledge of "rents" paid by the state to lease back Attica and the highway. UDC did not seek voter approval for its bond issue, and the state did not seek voter approval for its "subject to appropriation" lease. The authority device provided a handy way for the state to incur long-term debt to balance its budget without a referendum. *See* Schulz v. State of New York, 615 N.E.2d 953 (N.Y. 1993). *See also* Board of Directors of the Louisiana Recovery District v. All Taxpayers, 529 So.2d 384 (La.1988) (state facing fiscal emergency created "recovery district" with boundaries coterminous with the state, and authorized it to impose a one cent sales tax to finance nonguaranteed bonds to be used to assist the state in dealing with its deficit; constitutional requirement of voter approval for general obligation bonds inapplicable since recovery district bonds are not general obligation bonds).

NOTE ON THE COSTS AND CONSEQUENCES OF AVOIDING DEBT LIMITATIONS

The principal impact of the debt restrictions appear to be on the form, not the amount, of state debt: Most state debt today is nonguaranteed—73 percent, up from 14 percent in 1940, and 50 percent in 1962. Nine states have no long-term general obligation debt, but every state has some nonguaranteed debt. Although some state courts define "debt" broadly to require some revenue bonds and lease-payment financing to obtain voter approval, and some states have amended their constitutions to impose some constraints on nonguaranteed debt, in many states nonguaranteed debt is still not "debt" strictly by the state constitution. As needs for borrowed funds have grown, many states have evaded debt proscriptions by shifting to nonguaranteed debt.

Richard Briffault, Balancing Acts: The Reality Behind State Balanced Budget Requirements 46 (Twentieth Century Fund Press 1996).

The rise of nonguaranteed debt does not simply evade debt limits; it imposes costs of its own:

First, it increases the costs of borrowing. Nonguaranteed debt is by definition less secure than debt that carries a pledge of the full faith and credit of the state. As a result, interest rates on nonguaranteed debt are higher than on general obligation bonds. Moreover, nonguaranteed debt is usually more complicated in form than full-faith-and-credit debt. The issuer has to make pledges to lenders concerning the operation of the facility financed by the borrowing, the depositing of revenues in funds dedicated to debt service, reserve funds, carrying charges during the period of construction, and so on. Nonguaranteed bonds therefore carry higher legal, administrative, underwriting, and insurance costs.

See id. at 46–47.

Second, as we have already seen, by stimulating the creation of public authorities, special commissions, and other quasi-autonomous limited purpose governments, debt restrictions have contributed to the "baroque structure of state and local government, and to the major role played by un-elected authorities and similar agencies that are technically independent of the state or of general purpose local governments." Richard Briffault, Foreword: The Disfavored Constitution: State Fiscal Limits and State Constitutional Law, 34 Rutgers L.J. 907, 926 (2003). Indeed, some public authorities, such as state building authorities, exist only to evade debt restrictions since their sole revenues are lease payments appropriated by state or local governments.

Third, it may be argued that the widespread judicial acceptance of the evasion of debt limits has undermined whatever moral force those limits once had. In some states, debt limitations are truly disfavored constitutional provisions, enforced only for the letter, and not the spirit, of the restrictions. *Id.* at 939–44. *Bulman v. McCrane, supra,* spoke candidly of the court's unwillingness "to find constitutional evasion" and its preference for a judicial approach of "broad tolerance to permit public financing devices of needed facilities not constituting on their face present, interest-bearing obligations of the State itself." 312 A.2d at 861. The Wisconsin Supreme Court recognized the tension between the state constitution's "abhorrence of public debt" and the court's endorsement of a lease-payment scheme to finance a new public high school when it held that: "It is not an illegal evasion of the constitution to accomplish a desired result, lawful in itself, by finding a legal way to do it." Dieck v. Unified School District of Antigo, 477 N.W.2d 613, 619 (Wis.1991). These state judges "like other state elected officials, appear to believe that debt limits are more likely to get in the way of good government than to promote it." *See* Briffault, The Disfavored Constitution, *supra*, 34 Rutgers L.J. at 948.

Even where courts have taken a less deferential approach to debt arrangements, they have failed to develop clear and consistent rules. Kentucky courts "have developed doctrinal rules flexible enough to permit judicial re-evaluation of the legislature's original intention" to borrow. As a result, Kentucky's debt limits "do not operate to prohibit state debt; instead they operate to assure a [judicial] second look at the decision to incur debt." Stewart E. Sterk & Elizabeth S. Goldman, Controlling Legislative Shortsightedness: The Effectiveness of Constitutional Debt Limitations, 1991 Wisc.L.Rev. 1301, 1344–45 (1991). Similarly, the Illinois Supreme Court "has demonstrated a capacity to reach any conclusion it wants about the constitutionality of any particular financing scheme." *Id.* at 1347–48. Virginia's highest court has adopted doctrines that "effectively [allow it] . . . to substitute its judgment for that of the state legislature." *Id.* at 1348. Overall, judges on many state courts "behave as if they can separate good debt from bad," *id.* at 1360, with politics "almost certainly play[ing] an important—although unquantifiable—role in constitutional debt decisions." *Id.* at 1359.

In short, whatever the wisdom of the concept of constitutional limitations on debt in principle, in practice in many states we have the worst of both worlds: stiff limits written into the constitution on general obligation debt combined with heavy use of creative financing devices that tend to drive up the cost of borrowing, encourage the fragmentation of state and local governance, and give the courts a major role in fiscal decision-making.

Given both the competing values involved in imposing constitutional limitations on borrowing, and the extensive record of judicially validated evasions of those limits, consider two possible approaches to state constitutional limitations on state and local debt: (i) redefining the limits to apply to many of the avoidance techniques, such as special fund bonds, lease-financing, and non-appropriation debt (this could be accompanied by raising limit levels or permitting the commitment of a greater fraction of state or local revenues to debt service); or (ii) abandoning the project of constitutional debt limitation, and leaving the matter to politics and the fiscal marketplace. Many debt limits are out-of-date and inconsistent with effective financing of the projects and services people have come to want from their states and local governments. "Debt limitations might be more defensible, and might receive more effective judicial enforcement, if they were increased to levels consistent with current capital needs." Briffault, *supra*, 34 Rutgers L.J. at 948. On the other hand, it is likely to be difficult to come up with a debt limit formula that properly balances protection for future taxpayers with attention to the long-term capital investment needs of states and local governments.

D. DEALING WITH FISCAL DISTRESS

There is nothing new about states and local governments having to deal with fiscal distress. As Professor David Skeel has written, "[i]n the early days of the Republic, the prospect of an American state defaulting on its obligations was a real and present threat. After the Panic of 1837, states did just that. So notorious were the states that they were lampooned in faction and verse. To Scrooge, the tightfisted hero of Charles Dickens's A Christmas Carol, bills of exchange for which the payment has been delayed were like 'a mere United States security.'" David A. Skeel, Jr., States of Bankruptcy, 79 U. Chi. L. Rev. 677, 678 (2012). In the late nineteenth century, local governments frequently sought to avoid making payments on their debts. *See, e.g.,* Clayton P. Gillette, Bondholders and Financially Stressed Municipalities, 39 Fordham Urb. L. J. 639 (2012). Thousands of municipalities defaulted on their debt obligations during the Great Depression; in 1933, about seven percent of the municipal debt outstanding was in default. Juliet M. Moringiello, Goals and Governance in Municipal Bankruptcy, 71 Wash. & Lee L. Rev. 403, 440 (2014). *See also* John E. Petersen, Municipal Defaults: Eighty Years Make a Big Difference, 33 Mun. Fin. J. 27, 30–37 (2013). Between the mid-1970s and 1990s, New York City, Cleveland, Bridgeport, and Philadelphia all had to address serious fiscal issues. In the 1990s, a misguided investment strategy caused prosperous Orange County, California to enter into bankruptcy. *See* Mark Baldassare, When Government Fails: The Orange County (U. Cal. Press 1998).

The extent of municipal fiscal distress, however, rose sharply with the onset of the Great Recession in 2007–09. Professor Michelle Wilde Anderson found that twenty-eight cities with at least 15,000 residents declared bankruptcy or entered a formal state receivership during the five years following September 2008. *See* Michelle Wilde Anderson, The New Minimal Cities, 123 Yale L.J. 1118, 1124–25 (2014). Her list included Detroit, Michigan; Harrisburg and Pittsburgh, Pennsylvania; and Stockton and San Bernardino, California. As she noted, her count omitted smaller fiscally troubled cities, as well as special districts and counties, although in this period Jefferson County, Alabama, home to that state's biggest city, also filed for bankruptcy. *Id.* at 1131–32. And fiscal problems did not end with the economic recovery after the recession. At a conference on state oversight, bankruptcies, and recovery held in May 2014, one of the speakers reviewed the events of the preceding month:

> " . . . in . . . New York State, we see that last Friday, the state comptroller, who monitors local governments, put out a report saying that he had now been able to monitor 2,300 local governments and had found 142 that are in some kind of distress. In Pennsylvania, the city of Shamokin has $800,000 of unpaid bills—the gas company cut off the gas to City Hall at one point—and the city council, since April 1 had voted to ask the state to put the city in Pennsylvania's Act 47 intervention program, which would make Shamokin the 28th city in that program. . . . Moving over to Michigan, the governor declared the city of Lincoln Park in distress; they will now decide whether there will be an emergency manager there. . . . Going down to Missouri, the state legislature is bailing out a school district outside of St. Louis because it cannot pay its bills. And going west, to North Las Vegas, we see where the governor of Nevada met with union leaders in that community to try to get them to make some concessions to help Las Vegas stay afloat."

Gregory Lipitz, Stephen Fehr, Thomas Neff, and William Kannel, State Oversight, Bankruptcies, and Recovery, 35 Mun. Fin. J. 55, 56–57 (2015).

The causes of fiscal distress are varied, interactive, and debated. Professor Omer Kimhi has grouped them into two major categories— socio-economic decline, and local (mis)management. *See* Omer Kimhi, Reviving Cities: Legal Remedies to Municipal Fiscal Crises, 88 Bos. U. L. Rev. 633, 637–47 (2008). Socio-economic decline includes the long-term effects of late twentieth century and early twenty-first century economic restructuring and deindustrialization on older manufacturing centers and mill towns; the departure of middle-class residents for the suburbs; and increasing poverty and crime, blighted neighborhoods, and declining property values, with the attendant impact on the local tax base. Professor Anderson noted that nearly all the cities in her study had declining populations, high and rising poverty rates, and unemployment and mortgage foreclosure rates that were well above national averages. 123 Yale L.J. at 1130–45. These socio-economic factors were often compounded by highly fragmented metropolitan area governance structures and state-imposed constraints on local revenues. Many declining cities are in economically stable or growing regions yet the cities are unable to tap into the region's tax base, while even cities that continue to remain employment centers for their regions may find it difficult to effectively tax commuters. *See, e.g.,* Melissa Maynard, Michigan and Detroit: A Troubled Relationship (Pew Charitable Trusts, Stateline, July 31, 2013) (noting that state law makes it difficult for the city to enforce its income tax on local employers and that a state law repealing a local residency requirement for municipal employees contributed to the flight of middle-class residents).

Local fiscal management—or mismanagement—has also contributed to fiscal distress. Many localities have highly fragmented internal governance structures, which enable local interest groups to obtain higher levels of spending while making it difficult for political leaders to maintain fiscal discipline. *See* Kimhi, *supra,* 88 Bos. U. L. Rev. at 643–47; Clayton P. Gillette, Dictatorships for Democracy: Takeovers of Financially Failed Cities, 114 Colum. L. Rev. 1373, 1421–1433 (2014). Elected officials may be short-sighted, providing their employees with generous pension plans or commitments to pay for retiree health costs, which may seem to be a cheap way of buying labor peace when entered into, but become very costly for future administrations. Pensions and retiree benefits have emerged as a major cause of municipal fiscal stress. *See, e.g.,* Cities Squeezed by Pension and Retiree Health Care Shortfalls (Pew Charitable Trusts Issue Brief, March 2013).

Local officials may be financially unsophisticated. A number of cities have gotten into trouble when they entered into complex financial arrangements—to maintain service or spending levels while avoiding tax increases—that turned sour and saddled the cities with significant additional costs. As Professor Gillette notes, "some of the more notorious recent examples of fiscal distress involve sophisticated investments that were arguably inappropriate for municipal officials with limited comprehension of the transactional risks to which they were exposed." 114 Colum. L. Rev. at 1388 & n. 79 *See also,* Liz Farmer, Cities Paying Millions to Get Out of Bad Bank Deals, Governing (March 6, 2015); Eric Schulzke, The Great Gamble: One Fiscal Gimmick Has Already Caused

Multiple Cities to Declare Bankruptcy. So Why Do So Many Places Keep Betting On It?, Governing (Jan. 2013).

And sometimes municipal fiscal decisions may have been tainted by corruption. The bankruptcy of Jefferson County, Alabama was affected in significant part by undisclosed payments of more than $8.2 million by J.P. Morgan Securities, Inc. and two of its managing directors to local broker-dealers who were also close friends of members of the Jefferson County Commission to assure that the commissioners would vote to award $5 billion in county sewer bond and swap deals to J.P. Morgan. After the U.S. Securities and Exchange Commission brought charges J.P. Morgan settled by agreeing to pay $75 million in penalties eventually turned over to Jefferson County, and to forfeit more than $647 million of claimed swap termination fees. Jefferson County filed for bankruptcy in November 2011 after failing to restructure $3.2 billion in sewer bond-related obligations. *See* Shelly Sigo, SEC Says Settlement Reached in Jefferson County Sewer Case, The Bond Buyer, Oct. 5, 2015. *See also* Steven Yaccino, Kwame Kilpatrick, Former Detroit Mayor, Sentenced to 28 Years in Public Corruption Case, N.Y. Times, Oct. 10, 2013; Pew Charitable Trusts, The State Role in Local Government Financial Distress (July 2013) at 37 (noting that economically-challenged Camden, New Jersey also suffered from corruption, with three mayors going to prison).

These different causes may interact. Declining cities often incurred significant pension and retiree health care obligations dating back to when they were larger cities with larger work forces, so that the "legacy" costs of former employees may be greater than the costs of current employees. To pay these costs, older cities may have to raise taxes or cut services, thereby making their cities even less attractive places to work or do business and accelerating decline. To cover their expenses without raising taxes, they may turn to risky investment options, which may backfire and deepen their fiscal problems. *See, e.g.,* Christine Sgarlata Chung, Government Budgets as the Hunger Games: The Brutal Competition for State and Local Government Resources Given Municipal Securities Debt, Pension and OBEP Obligations, and Taxpayer Needs, 33 Rev. Banking & Fin. L. 663, 724–35 (2014). Aging communities are also often saddled with aging and inadequate infrastructure, such as water supply and waste water and solid waste disposal systems, which may be in need of significant repair as well as upgrades to meet current environmental standards. Decaying infrastructure contributes to urban decline while paying for improvements results in new debts. Financially stressed localities may be able to muddle through during relatively prosperous times but an exogenous shock—like the sharp decline in housing prices that began in 2007 and the subsequent recession—can cut deeper into property values and revenues and increase costs. *See, e.g.,*

Omer Kimhi, Chapter Nine of the Bankruptcy Code: A Solution in Search of a Problem, 27 Yale J. Reg. 351, 360 (2010) ("[a]lthough urban crises are usually characterized by slow and gradual economic deterioration, municipal bankruptcy filings were often caused by a one-time sudden exogenous event"); James E. Spiotto, The Role of the State in Supervising and Assisting Municipalities, Especially in Times of Financial Distress, 34 Mun. Fin. J. 1, 5–6 (2013) (noting that natural or manmade disasters and "lingering legal issues and surprise court decisions" contribute to municipal fiscal distress). State governments are also subject to rising pension and retiree health costs and to the revenue hit resulting from economic shocks like a recession and they may try to balance their budgets by cutting back on aid to local governments, thereby pushing the most fiscally fragile cities, counties and special districts to cut services further and approach insolvency.

The materials in this section consider two legal mechanisms for enabling fiscally distressed local governments to deal with their problems. The first subsection considers various forms of state intervention in local fiscal affairs. These range from doing almost nothing, to active monitoring, to providing technical assistance and fiscal support, to the appointment of financial control boards, receivers, or emergency managers that in varying degrees take local fiscal affairs out of the hands of local elected officials. As you shall see, although these mechanisms can involve some state fiscal assistance, they primarily reflect the local fiscal mismanagement perspective on local fiscal distress. The second subsection turns to the principal mode of federal intervention—municipal bankruptcy. Although a federal municipal bankruptcy law has been on the books since the 1930s, until the mid-2000s it was used primarily by special districts and only very rarely by cities and counties. Since 2008, that changed with high profile bankruptcies involving Vallejo, Stockton, and San Bernardino, California; Jefferson County, Alabama; and Detroit, Michigan. The goal of municipal bankruptcy is to allow local governments to restructure—and possibly reduce—their debts so that they can get a "fresh start" on addressing current problems. But like state oversight boards and receivers, it is debatable whether bankruptcy can address the deeper structural problems of small, poor, declining communities in fragmented metropolitan areas. Although the primary focus of these materials is local fiscal distress, this section concludes with a brief discussion of contemporary state fiscal problems.

1. STATE OVERSIGHT AND INTERVENTION

MOREAU V. FLANDERS

Supreme Court of Rhode Island
15 A.3d 565 (2011)

JUSTICE FLAHERTY, for the Court.

We are called upon to determine the constitutionality of G.L.1956 chapter 9 of title 45, in the face of a challenge by the Mayor and City Council of the City of Central Falls. * * *

The City of Central Falls long has enjoyed the reputation of being one of America's most densely populated cities. Packed within 1.2 square miles live 19,000 people. The General Assembly created the city in 1895, partitioning it from the neighboring Town of Lincoln. Over the years, Central Falls became a bustling industrial center and the home to a variety of proud immigrant and ethnic groups. Over time, however, the city experienced financial distress, and by 1991, it no longer had the financial resources to operate its schools, resulting in a takeover by the state. In more recent years, Central Falls, like other communities, has continued to struggle financially. With the closure of several manufacturing facilities, the city's tax base dwindled, causing its fiscal woes to become exacerbated. With its largest taxpayers gone, no land to develop, and confronted with the crushing realities of a devastating local and national economy, there is no surprise that the city's leaders felt that their backs were up against the wall. And thus, believing there was no other viable solution to the city's dire financial plight, the mayor and city council in May 2010, petitioned the Superior Court for the appointment of a receiver, a petition that was granted by the court. * * *

The circumstances preceding this verified petition, which named the City of Central Falls as defendant, included a June 30, 2009, independent audit, which revealed: (1) that the city had total net assets of negative $16,866,819; (2) an annual operating budget for 2010 and a proposed operating budget for 2011 just under $18 million, with anticipated shortfalls of $3 million for 2010 and $5 million for 2011; (3) municipal bond indebtedness of over $10 million; (4) the city's sale of much of its chief pension fund to satisfy current pension obligations; (5) accrued pension fund liability exceeding $35 million, supported by assets of only $4 million; (6) the city's failure to make any contributions to the pension fund in 2009, despite a requirement that it make a contribution in excess of $2.7 million for that year; (7) the fact that increasing the property tax rate by the maximum allowed under the state cap of 4.5 percent would yield additional revenues of less than $500,000; and (8) a request by Central Falls to the General Assembly to grant it the authority to file for

Chapter 9 bankruptcy pursuant to Title 11 of the United States Code, providing for the adjustment of debts of a municipality. * * *

As a result of the petition for judicial receivership, the already precarious credit rating of Central Falls was reduced to "junk-bond" status. Even more ominously, state officials were informed by financial rating agencies that, as a result of Central Falls' receivership, capital markets would view debt financing to Rhode Island cities and towns as extremely risky, and that as a consequence such financing would become more expensive for Rhode Island municipalities. Faced with that scenario, the General Assembly determined that judicial receiverships, initiated solely at the discretion of a municipality, were not in the best interest of the citizens of Central Falls or the state, and that municipally initiated judicial receiverships threatened the financial well-being of all the state's cities and towns, and of the state itself. The General Assembly moved with alacrity * * *. On June 11, 2010, a major revision was signed into law. Significantly, § 45–9–1, as amended by P.L.2010, ch. 27, § 1, set forth:

> "**Declaration of policy and legal standard.** It shall be the policy of the state to provide a mechanism for the state to work with cities and towns undergoing financial distress that threatens the fiscal well-being, public safety and welfare of such cities and towns, or other cities and towns or the state, with the state providing varying levels of support and control depending on the circumstances. The powers delegated by the General Assembly in this chapter shall be carried out having due regard for the needs of the citizens of the state and of the city or town, and in such a manner as will best preserve the safety and welfare of citizens of the state and their property, and the access of the state and its municipalities to capital markets, all to the public benefit and good."

Of great significance, this revision foreclosed the right of municipalities to petition the courts for the appointment of a judicial receivership, as had been done by Central Falls. This was of particular relevance to Central Falls because § 4 of the act (P.L.2010, ch. 27) made the revision retroactive to May 15, 2010—four days before the order of the Superior Court that granted the mayor and city council's request for a judicial receiver.

* * * In a letter on July 16, 2010, the director of the Department of Revenue appointed Pfeiffer as receiver for the city. In turn, by letter dated July 19, 2010, Pfeiffer informed Mayor Moreau that he had been appointed receiver of Central Falls and that he had assumed the duties and functions of the office of mayor. The receiver wrote:

"R.I. Gen. Laws § 45–9–7 provides the receiver with 'the right to exercise the powers of the elected officials' of a municipality and that the 'powers of the receiver shall be superior to and supersede the powers of the elected officials'. That statute further provides that the elected officials of the city or town 'shall serve in an advisory capacity to the receiver'.

"Effective immediately, I have assumed the duties and functions of the Office of Mayor. As a result of my role, your responsibility will be limited to serving in an advisory capacity, on such occasions as my office may seek input from you. Accordingly, pursuant to R.I. Gen. Laws § 45–9–6(d)(g) your compensation will be reduced to $1,000.00 bi-weekly effective today."

In a resolution passed on August 4, 2010, the city council authorized the hiring of independent legal counsel "for guidance and/or litigation concerning the numerous matters that currently affect the City, the Central Falls Community as a whole and the discharge of [the] City Council's obligations * * *." The very next day, citing relevant provisions of the act, the receiver informed the city council by letter of his decision to rescind the resolution. Specifically, the receiver cited §§ 45–9–7(b)(1) and 45–9–6(d)(17). Section 45–9–6(d)(17) grants the receiver the power to "[a]lter or rescind any action or decision of any municipal officer, employee, board, authority or commission within fourteen (14) days after receipt of notice of such action or decision." The receiver's letter concluded, "I will review the organization of the Office of Solicitor to [e]nsure that the Council receives legal advi[c]e it may require from time to time to perform its duties."

Obviously unhappy with that turn of events, on September 20, 2010, the city council passed a four-page resolution entitled, "In Support of the Mayor and the City Council contend [sic] it is necessary to determine the constitutionality of R.I. General Laws 45–9–3, 45–9–5, 45–9–6 and 45–9–7." That resolution authorized the engagement of independent legal counsel to file a legal action to challenge the constitutionality of the act. However, on September 22, 2010, the receiver, by letter to the council president, rescinded the resolution of September 20, 2010 as well. That letter said that "with respect to the issue of whether the Act or any sections thereunder should be subject to constitutional challenge, under R.I. Gen. Laws Section 45–9–7(c), the City Council is hereby directed to serve solely in an 'advisory' capacity." * * *

The appellants, the mayor and city council, contend that the act treads upon the city's right to self-governance as guaranteed by article 13 of Rhode Island's Constitution. Section 1 of article 13, generally referred to as the home-rule charter amendment, provides that "[i]t is the intention of this article to grant and confirm to the people of every city and town in this state the right to self government in all local matters." Specifically, the mayor and city council argue that the act offends article 13, section 4, which says in pertinent part:

> "The general assembly shall have the power to act in relation to the property, affairs and government of any city or town by general laws which shall apply alike to all cities and towns, *but which shall not affect the form of government of any city or town.*" (Emphasis added.)

In their brief, the mayor and city council argue that, in a manner "completely counter to the democratic principle of checks and balances," the broad powers vested in the receiver pursuant to the act impermissibly "affect the form of government" of Central Falls.

* * * [T]he challenged act applies on its face to all cities and towns. In our opinion, it is beyond question an enactment of general application. The act does not refer to the City of Central Falls or to any municipality by name. Indeed, the "Declaration of policy and legal standard" of § 45–9–1 asseverates that "[i]t shall be the policy of the state to provide a mechanism for the state to work with cities and towns undergoing financial distress" and "shall be carried out having due regard for the needs of the citizens of the state and of the city or town * * * all to the public benefit and good." Therefore, we are satisfied that the challenged act is an act of general application that indeed "applies alike" to all municipalities.

The second, and perhaps thornier, issue necessary to determine whether a challenged enactment violates protections afforded to municipalities under the home-rule charter amendment is whether the act affects the form of government of any city or town.

The mayor and city council specifically posit that "§ 45–9–7 alters a municipality's form of government as it operates to anoint an appointed receiver with the powers of both the legislative branch and the executive branch of government[,] forming a new government * * *." Section 45–9–7(b) provides that "[t]he receiver shall have the following powers:

> "(1) All powers of the fiscal overseer and budget commission under §§ 45–9–2 and 45–9–6. Such powers shall remain through the period of any receivership;

> "(2) The power to exercise any function or power of any municipal officer or employee, board, authority or commission, whether elected or otherwise relating to or impacting the fiscal stability of the city or town including, without limitation, school and zoning matters; and

"(3) The power to file a petition in the name of the city or town under Chapter 9 of Title 11 of the United States Code, and to act on the city's or town's behalf in any such proceeding."

Section 45–9–7(c) further provides that:

"Upon the appointment of a receiver, the receiver shall have the right to exercise the powers of the elected officials under the general laws, special laws and the city or town charter and ordinances relating to or impacting the fiscal stability of the city or town including, without limitation, school and zoning matters; provided, further, that the powers of the receiver shall be superior to and supersede the powers of the elected officials * * *."

As all parties involved in this action readily acknowledge, and as is rationally inescapable, the powers granted to the receiver under the act are broad and encompassing; however, this fact alone does not lead us to conclude that the form of government of a city or town has been altered. * * *

The mayor and city council argue that the powers of the receiver are "dictatorial" in nature. We do not agree. Although the powers of the receiver are broad and sweeping, they nonetheless are contained and channeled in at least three significant ways: (1) the standards imposed by several sections of the act set forth a deliberate and progressive mechanism by which the state provides the town or city with "varying levels of support and control depending on the circumstances," § 45–9–1; (2) under oversight powers at § 45–9–7, "[t]he director of revenue may, at any time, and without cause, remove the receiver and appoint a successor, or terminate the receivership"; and (3), the receiver—having been appointed under express provisions of the act—is subject to administering any and all powers delegated in accordance with the stated policy purpose of the act as set forth within § 45–9–1. The powers delegated to the receiver are properly cabined because they are to be carried out with "due regard for the needs of the citizens of the state and of the city or town, * * * as will best preserve the safety and welfare of citizens of the state and their property, and the access of the state and its municipalities to capital markets, all to the public benefit and good." Section 45–9–1.

* * * [A]ppellants point out that under the current version of the act, the director of the Department of Revenue, § 45–9–7, "shall appoint a receiver for the city or town for a period as the director of revenue may determine." For this reason, they argue, "it cannot be definitely determined that a receivership initiated pursuant to *R.I. Gen. Laws § 45–9–1 et seq.* is not permanent," and thus, it constitutes an alteration of the local form of governance. We do not totally discount the underlying

concerns of appellants, but we nonetheless conclude that the act does not violate the constitution.

In our opinion, the absence of an explicit sunset provision in the statutory framework is indeed a flaw, but we are keenly appreciative of the awesome responsibility of the General Assembly in situations such as this, where the municipality's financial viability is imperiled. Despite the presence of the blemish that the absence of a sunset provision constitutes, we are satisfied that there are sufficient standards that can serve as an objective measure of when the receiver's oversight should terminate and that, accordingly, the statute passes constitutional muster. The oversight by the director of the Department of Revenue must end within a reasonable time after the municipality regains financial stability in accordance with the guidelines set forth in the statute. Moreover, judicial relief, by means of an action seeking a declaratory judgment and/or injunctive relief, would be available to municipalities that contend that a receiver has overstayed his statutory authority. Further, although the receivership is not limited to a specified durational term, that fact alone does not lead to the legal conclusion that the authority of the receiver is either unlimited or never-ending. Provisions of the act not only anticipate but also provide for the termination of any of the state-appointed agents—be it an overseer, a budget commission, or a receiver—when the municipality's fiscal health has improved. *See, e.g.,* § 45–9–10(a) (providing that an administration and finance officer reporting to the executive official of the municipality will be appointed "upon a determination, in writing, by the director of revenue that the financial condition of the city or town has improved to a level such that a fiscal overseer, a budget commission or a receiver is no longer needed"). Finally, and perhaps most significant to a temporal consideration, § 45–9–7(c) provides that, even when a receiver has assumed the powers of elected officials, these same elected officials "shall continue to be elected in accordance with the city or town charter, and shall serve in an advisory capacity to the receiver." The express preservation of elected offices and the incumbents who hold those offices, even those serving under onerous impositions of state authority, leads us to conclude that the impact of the act on a town or city's form of government remains temporary.

Therefore, we are of the opinion that although there has been a temporary impact on the form of government in this instance, because the director of the Department of Revenue and receiver have invoked their statutory powers, that impact is channeled, incidental, and temporary. Under these circumstances, we hold that the legislation does not alter the form of government of any city or town generally, or of Central Falls in particular * * *.

Although it is true that the home-rule amendment altered the traditional view that a municipality, as a creature of the state, has no inherent right to self-government except those powers granted to it by the state legislature, the right to self-government granted under our state constitution is limited strictly to local matters, and in no way affects the sovereignty of the state. * * *

It is undisputed that "[t]he fiscal collapse of a [city or town] can affect the entire state's financial interests * * *."

> "The General Assembly has consistently recognized the importance of sound fiscal practices in cities and towns by enacting statutes ensuring financial stability notwithstanding the provisions of home-rule charters.

> "[The provision] clearly affects a matter of statewide concern because (1) the state has consistently exercised oversight over municipal budgets and debt obligations; (2) the insolvency of even a single city or town sufficiently threatens the credit of those outside a home-rule city or town; and (3) the uniform regulations provided * * * are desirable and necessary to ensure the state's objectives of fiscal stability essential to good government."

Here, the mayor and city council simply cannot meet the high burden of establishing that the act is clearly arbitrary and unreasonable, having " 'no substantial relation to the public health, safety, morals, or general welfare.' " * * *

As to the contention that the act is unconstitutionally vague, appellants specifically point to provisions in the act that permit a receiver to be appointed after a finding by the director of the Department of Revenue that a "fiscal emergency" exists. * * * The mayor and city council highlight (1) the fact that the act does not provide a definition for the term "Fiscal Emergency" and (2), that because § 45–9–8 empowers the director of the Department of Revenue to appoint a receiver after determining that a fiscal emergency exists, "without having first appointed a fiscal overseer or a budget commission," constitutionally impermissible vagueness results. Although it is true that the term "fiscal emergency" is undefined by the statute, this single factor does not determine constitutional vagueness, nor does the absence of definition nullify the enactment's "supposed mandated application."

First, in its entirety, § 45–9–8 requires that the director of the Department of Revenue must make a determination that a city or town is facing a fiscal emergency "in consultation with the auditor general." Section 45–9–8 simply does not authorize the director of the Department of Revenue to determine at her sole discretion that a fiscal emergency exists. Second, such a standard is consistent with how we have interpreted the limits of permissible delegation, recognizing that modern problems of ever-increasing complexity require administrative expertise. * * * *

Here, we are satisfied that the delegation of power to the director of the Department of Revenue to determine and declare, after consultation with the auditor general of the state, that a "fiscal emergency" exists in a particular municipality is not unconstitutionally vague. * * * This is all the more apparent when one reads the act in its entirety, and particularly the crafted language of § 45–9–3(b), which sets forth five distinct factors that are relevant to a finding that the fiscal well-being of a city or town may be threatened. These enumerated factors include projected deficits, missed audit filings, downgrading by a recognized rating agency, inability to access credit markets on reasonable terms, and a municipality's failure to respond timely to state requests for financial information. * * *

We are of the opinion that the grant of authority to the director of the Department of Revenue is amply confined and guided by intelligible standards and principles. As previously discussed, § 45–9–1 effectively specifies the policy by which the receiver, or any official tasked by the director of the Department of Revenue with administering the act, are directed and constrained. Moreover, we are satisfied that the deliberate triggering mechanisms of the act that provide for "varying levels of support and control depending on the circumstance" are intelligible and demonstrate an architecture of staged delegations of power constructed to respond to the requisite degree of fiscal crisis. See § 45–9–1. * * *

[A]ppellants point with particularity to § 45–9–7(c), which grants the receiver all powers "relating to or impacting the fiscal stability of the city or town including, without limitation, school and zoning matters * * *." This, they argue, is but one illustration of the excessive power given to the receiver, and in the case of zoning, would allow him to be, in essence, a one-person zoning board, with the unlawful flexibility to brush aside all the statutory protections set forth in the Rhode Island Zoning Enabling Act of 1991, and the municipal zoning ordinances, including notice to the abutters of proposed changes and public notice of hearings. We consider these arguments to be speculative, and we are not persuaded by them.

First, on its face, there is no inconsistency between the statute and the notice provisions of the zoning law. * * * [B]ecause the act provides only that the receiver may exercise the powers of an authority or office to the limits of that authority or office, and no further, we see no inconsistency between the temporary power vested in the receiver and the notice and hearing requirements in zoning matters.

Second, there is simply no record of any person complaining of wrongful or abusive conduct by the receiver in the area of zoning or any of the other possibly compelling but fictive examples presented by appellants. We do not hesitate to say that judicial relief would be available to any person who could demonstrate excessive conduct by the receiver in the area of zoning, or, for that matter, a failure of the director of the Department of Revenue to enforce and administer her duties under the act—including, but not limited to, for instance, her duty to terminate a receivership once the fiscal conditions of a municipality are sufficiently improved. But, since the record is devoid of any such contention or conduct, appellants' complaints about outcomes that are absurd or shocking to the conscience, particularly resulting from the receiver's zoning power, are completely speculative in nature. In the face of a broadside attack on the constitutionality of the statute as a whole, we need not address a contention that never may ripen.

NOTES AND QUESTIONS

1.   *The State Role in Addressing Local Fiscal Distress: An Overview.* Through state constitutional provisions and laws dealing with local government boundaries and powers generally and local taxation and debt in particular, the states inevitably shape local government finances. Some states have gone further and have adopted programs specifically intended to address local fiscal distress. A 2013 study by the Pew Charitable Trusts identified nineteen states that have enacted laws providing for state intervention in local fiscal affairs. *See* The State Role in Local Government Financial Distress (Pew Charitable Trusts, July 2013). *Cf.* James E. Spiotto, The Role of the State in Supervising and Assisting Municipalities, Especially in Times of Financial Distress, 34 Mun. Fin. J. 1, 11 (2013) (counting twenty-three states that have implemented municipal debt supervision or debt restructuring mechanisms to aid municipalities). Other states have adopted ad hoc intervention measures, responding to specific crises in particular places rather than more general programs. *See id.* at 17–18 (discussing ad hoc establishments of financial control boards or appointments of receivers by Massachusetts for communities including Chelsea, Lawrence, and Springfield). Even for states with legislation on the subject, the nature of state intervention varies considerably from state to state.

North Carolina takes an unusually proactive approach. In 1931 in response to a wave of municipal bond defaults during the Great Depression, the state created the Local Government Commission which "constantly monitors both the financial management and the debt management of local governments." Omer Kimhi, Reviving Cities: Legal Remedies to Municipal Financial Crises, 88 Bos. U. L. Rev. 633, 679 (2008). All local governments in the state must submit regular financial statements to the commission, which assesses the financial condition of each locality. Any local government that wishes to issue new debt must receive the commission's approval, which it will provide only if it concludes that the locality is financially able to meet the expected debt obligation. The commission monitors a set of seven financial indicators "that provide warning signs for potential financial crises" and it requires local governments to maintain a general fund balance of at least eight percent of their annual expenditures. "[F]ailure to meet this threshold [is] a sign of economic deterioration warranting state attention." *Id.* at 680. If a locality gets into fiscal difficulty, the commission provides technical assistance. If fiscal problems worsen, the commission can take over a locality's finances—with the power to take corrective actions to increase revenues—until the problem is resolved. *Id; see also* Pew Charitable Trusts, The State Role, *supra*, at 33–35. The commission's oversight is credited with the strong credit ratings of North Carolina's localities. *Id.*

Most state programs are more reactive, responding to a range of factors, including local budget deficits, inability to meet payroll or pay bondholders, losses from imprudent investments, or failure to keep up with public pension payments. *Id.* at 8. Some respond to requests for assistance from the affected local government, while in others the state may take the lead. State intervention can take the form of information gathering, technical advice, regular and detailed reporting requirements, and substantive but non-binding recommendations; financial oversight coupled with the power to withhold state aid from localities that ignore the oversight board's recommendations; or in more extreme cases the temporary takeover of local finances by a state agency, a financial control board (that may include a mix of state and local members, or consist just of state appointees), or a state-appointed receiver or emergency financial manager. *See* Omer Kimhi, A Tale of Four Cities: Models of State Intervention in Distressed Localities Fiscal Affairs, 80 U. Cinn. L. Rev. 882, 892–910 (2012) (discussing the varied experiences of the state advisory board for Miami, Florida; oversight board for Philadelphia, Pennsylvania; financial control board for New York City; and state-appointed receiver for Chelsea, Massachusetts.).

Some state interventions are accompanied by financial assistance, including direct grants, low-interest loans or loan guarantees, or the creation of new state entities to help troubled localities sell bonds, but in recent years "few offer these options to municipalities in practice because of dwindling state revenue and the risk that the state will have to dole money out to every city or county that asks for help." The State Role, *supra,* at 19. A small number of states also give receivers, state agencies, or control boards power to renegotiate existing labor contracts, reduce services, or raise revenues by increasing existing taxes or fees or imposing new ones. In Central Falls, Rhode Island, the receiver raised property taxes four percent in five successive years. *Id.*

State intervention programs have had a mixed record of success. Many observers credit New York State's actions in addressing New York City's fiscal crisis of the mid-1970s—including the creation of a Municipal Assistance Corporation to enable the City to borrow and an Emergency Financial Control Board composed of state and local appointees and empowered to constrain the City's expenditures, labor contracts, and debt level—with enabling the City to resolve its problems and transform its financial management and budgeting processes going forward. *See, e.g.,* Kimhi, A Tale of Four Cities, *supra,* at 905–10; David A. Skeel, Jr., States of

Bankruptcy, 79 U. Chi. L. Rev. 677, 726–29 (2012); Spiotto, The Role of the State, *supra*, 34 Mun. Fin. J. at 14–15. The Pennsylvania Intergovernmental Cooperation Authority ("PICA"), created by that state in 1991 helped Philadelphia emerge from an acute fiscal crisis by monitoring and making recommendations concerning the city's finances, and requiring it to develop, report in detail on, and adhere to a five-year financial recovery plan. PICA did not have the formal power to impose its views, but it could withhold state funds if it determined that the city was not adhering to the financial plan. "Although the board did not implement the recovery plans itself, . . . [its] existence forced Philadelphia politicians to be financially disciplined" and it "gave local officials the political cover required to initiate financial reforms." Kimhi, *supra*, 80 U. Cinn. L. Rev. at 904.

Other programs have been less successful. Pennsylvania's Act 47, enacted in 1987, is intended "to help financially troubled municipalities 'help themselves' by adopting a fiscal recovery plan without relying on bailouts from the state. The law establishes a process to identify municipalities in fiscal distress, then hire a state-appointed coordinator who drafts and implements a recovery plan in cooperation with the distressed municipality's governing body." Michelle Wilde Anderson, Who Needs Local Government Anyway? Dissolution in Pennsylvania's Distressed Cities, 24 Widener L.J. 149, 161–62 (2015). Over nearly three decades, twenty-eight cities and towns were found to be sufficiently financially distressed to enter the program, but only nine obtained a clean financial bill of health. Some municipalities have been in the program for more than twenty-five years. *Id.* Some observers suggest that the program's lack of success is attributable at least in part to state laws that protect public employee and retiree benefits and that limit local taxation, as well as to the limited powers of the state coordinator, who can prepare a recovery plan for a locality but cannot force the locality to implement it. *See* Pew Charitable Trusts, The State Role, *supra*, at 30–32. It may also be the case that given the combination of economic decline and regions fragmented into large numbers of small localities, many local governments may lack the tax base to be economically viable. *See id.*; Anderson, *supra*.

New Jersey actively oversees local government finances through the state's Division of Local Government Services, which has the power to review local budgets before they are adopted to make sure localities can pay their debts. The state has intervened with grants, loans, and, on occasion, the appointment of a control board or an emergency manager. *See* Pew Charitable Trusts, *supra,* at 36–38; Stephen C. Fehr, Atlantic City Takeover Shows New Jersey's Resolve to Help Its Troubled Cities, Pew Trusts Stateline, Jan. 28, 2015. Although New Jersey municipalities have met their debt obligations, poor cities with constrained tax bases like Camden remain fiscally troubled and the state has been cutting back on its "transitional aid" to stressed communities. *See* Pew Charitable Trusts, *supra,* at 36–38. Other states, like Alabama and California, have traditionally avoided efforts to aid financially troubled localities. *See* Pew Charitable Trusts, *supra*, at 27–29, 42–44.

2.   *State Intervention and Local Democracy.* In response to the local fiscal problems triggered, or exacerbated, by the 2007–09 recession, two states—Michigan and Rhode Island—enacted intervention programs that were far more intrusive into local decision-making than most prior state measures. Both states had previously adopted mechanisms of state oversight and intervention in the event of local fiscal distress but in 2010–11 they passed new laws that "significantly ratcheted up" state powers over local finances. Michelle Wilde Anderson, Democratic Dissolution: Radical Experiments in State Takeovers of Local Governments, 39 Fordham Urb. L.J. 577, 593 (2012). Rhode Island had previously provided for the creation of budget commissions with a mix of state and local appointees, and dominated by local stakeholders. The new law provided for the appointment of a state receiver, who would assume the powers of all local officials, reducing the mayor and council to an advisory role. Triggered by a financial crisis in Central Falls—the subject of the *Moreau v. Flanders* dispute—the law made the receiver "the sole government of Central Falls." Receivers "raised taxes, renegotiated union contracts, closed the library and community center, . . . laid off employees," cut pensions, and ultimately filed for municipal bankruptcy. *Id.* at 595–97. The *Moreau* court rejected the arguments that the broad powers of the receiver and the vague standards for determining the existence or resolution of a fiscal emergency were inconsistent with local home rule. Do you agree?

Michigan had enacted legislation authorizing the appointment of emergency fiscal managers for local governments as far back as 1990. In 2011, the state strengthened the law to give the emergency manager full local governing authority, displacing the elected local leadership, as well as powers to adopt a budget; modify, reject, or terminate contracts; suspend collective bargaining; and consolidate or eliminate city departments. *See id.* at 587–88. A voter referendum repealed that law in November 2012, but the legislature immediately passed a new and very similar measure in December 2012. As of 2014, local financial emergencies had been declared and emergency managers appointed in the cities of Allen Park, Benton Harbor, Detroit, Ecorse, Hamtramck, Flint, Pontiac, the Detroit Public School District and other public school districts. *See* John Philo, Under Pressure: Democracy in Local Governments During Times of Financial Distress, 50 Willamette L. Rev. 549, 560–62 (2014).

These measures have been controversial. The broad powers given to the state-appointed receiver and the complete displacement of elected local officials have been criticized as deeply inconsistent with the long-standing and widely-held commitment to local self-government. *See, e.g.*, Anderson, Democratic Dissolution, *supra*; Philo, *supra*. The concerns about the impact on local democracy are compounded when there are racial or partisan differences between the taken-over city and the government of the taking-over state. *See, e.g.*, Melissa Maynard, Michigan and Detroit: A Troubled

Relationship, Pew Charitable Trusts Stateline, July 31, 2013 (Detroit's elected leadership is black and Democratic, while [Michigan Governor] Snyder is a white Republican backed by a GOP-controlled legislature"). Professor Gillette, however, has sharply challenged the anti-democratic critique narrative, pointing out that takeover boards or receivers are typically appointed only when local governments have failed to provide their residents the goods and services they expect. He argues that the population decline associated with local fiscal distress is actually a reflection of the failure of local governance, as residents, unhappy with local government performance, vote with their feet and leave town. Clayton P. Gillette, Dictatorships for Democracy: Takeovers of Financially Failed Cities, 114 Colum. L. Rev. 1373, 1402–05 (2014). Professor Gillette contends that the financial management reforms a control board or receiver may impose can provide local residents with improved decision-making structures going forward as well as better models for the organization of local government, *id.* at 1419–45, so that in the long run aggressive state intervention may improve local democracy. Professor Gillette also notes that local residents are not the only people affected by local fiscal distress. The failure of local government to meet its obligations can affect the credit ratings and access to capital markets of other localities in the state, and the ability of the state itself to borrow. *Id.* at 1416–18. The Rhode Island Supreme Court in its opinion in Moreau invoked this fear of "contagion" when it observed that the "insolvency of even a single city or town sufficiently threatens the credit of those outside a home-rule city or town." In addition to credit ratings, local fiscal problems that affect local public health and safety can have an impact on neighboring communities and the economic health of the region or state. *See, e.g.,* The State Role, *supra,* at 16–17.

To some extent the debate over the implications of state intervention for local democracy turns on the details of state law, such as the triggers for intervention, the rules for terminating a receivership, the extent of the receiver's powers and the role for local leaders or appointees during the period of greater state control. They also reflect an underlying disagreement over the causes of local fiscal distress and especially the degree to which inadequate local financial decision-making structures and mismanagement by local officials—as opposed to broader socio-economic factors and fragmented regions—is responsible. What do you think? Are state control boards and state-appointed receivers a threat to the value of local self-government? Even if so, are there situations in which they may be necessary?

The debate over emergency manager laws took on a new intensity in 2016 when national attention turned to the water crisis in Flint, Michigan. In April 2014, Flint's state-appointed financial manager sought to save money by switching Flint's water supply from treated Lake Huron water —Flint's traditional water source—to the "polluted and corrosive Flint River." Paul Egan, Flint Water Crisis Clouds Rick Snyder's Upcoming State Address, Governing, Jan. 18, 2016. The Flint River water caused lead from Flint's aging pipes to leach into the water supply, causing extremely elevated levels of the heavy metal. The water source change might also have been a possible cause of an outbreak of Legionnaires' disease in the area. The health effects from the corroded pipes may continue even after Flint's return to using Lake Huron water. Residents complained about the taste, smell and appearance of Flint's drinking water immediately afte the switch, but their concerns were ignored until late 2015. "The fact the contamination happened while Flint was under a state emergency manager also vaults the scandal beyond contaminated water . . . calling into question" Michigan's tough emergency manager law. *Id.* To be sure, as another commentator pointed out, the cost-saving decision "was ultimately motivated by the city's overall dire situation" which is sadly representative of "the broader, ongoing failure of basic services in America's most troubled cities." David Z. Morris, Did Michigan's Emergency Manager Law Cause the Flint Water Crisis?, Fortune, Feb. 18, 2016. But it is possible that the extended failure of government to respond to the well-founded health concerns raised by residents following the water supply switch was related to the lack of a democratically accountable local government.

3. *State Intervention and Federal Bankruptcy.* State intervention can be a means of avoiding bankruptcy. "States that intervene often want to avoid the stigma that would come from their cities filing for bankruptcy protection. Bankruptcy is usually an act of desperation that damages a city's prospects for economic growth and its ability to borrow money for improvements to roads, sewers, schools and other capital projects. Its image can be damaged for years." Pew Charitable Trusts, The State Role, *supra*, at 14. Indeed, the government of Connecticut actively opposed Bridgeport's efforts to file for bankruptcy, much as Pennsylvania blocked Harrisburg's bankruptcy filing and instead appointed a receiver for its capital city. With state intervention and assistance, New York City, Philadelphia, and Cleveland were all able to address their problems without filing for bankruptcy. However, state intervention may come too late to address local fiscal problems, or local debts may be impossible to manage without the restructuring that bankruptcy can provide. Although the Rhode Island legislature enacted the law at issue in *Moreau* in order to forestall unilateral action by Central Falls to file for bankruptcy, the receiver ultimately did file for bankruptcy—although the receiver's actions before and during the bankruptcy may have enabled that city to move through bankruptcy relatively quickly. *See id.* at 40–41. So, too, as we shall see in the next case, the appointment of an emergency manager for Detroit was simply a step, albeit a crucial one, on the road to that city's bankruptcy filing. State intervention and federal bankruptcy may not simply be alternatives but also complementary, with the one providing a basis for reforming the city's financial decision-making structure and the other enabling the city to reduce its debt overhang going forward. *See, e.g.*, Juliet M. Moringiello, Goals and Governance in Municipal Bankruptcy, 71 Wash. & Lee L. Rev. 403, 425–29 (2014).

2.   MUNICIPAL BANKRUPTCY

IN RE CITY OF DETROIT, MICHIGAN, DEBTOR

United States Bankruptcy Court
504 B.R. 97 (E.D. Mich. 2013)

STEVEN RHODES, BANKRUPTCY JUDGE.

* * * The City of Detroit was once a hardworking, diverse, vital city, the home of the automobile industry, proud of its nickname—the "Motor City." It was rightfully known as the birthplace of the American automobile industry. In 1952, at the height of its prosperity and prestige, it had a population of approximately 1,850,000 residents. In 1950, Detroit was building half of the world's cars.

The evidence before the Court establishes that for decades, however, the City of Detroit has experienced dwindling population, employment, and revenues. This has led to decaying infrastructure, excessive borrowing, mounting crime rates, spreading blight, and a deteriorating quality of life. The City no longer has the resources to provide its residents with the basic police, fire and emergency medical services that its residents need for their basic health and safety. Moreover, the City's governmental operations are wasteful and inefficient. Its equipment, especially its streetlights and its technology, and much of its fire and police equipment, is obsolete. To reverse this decline in basic services, to attract new residents and businesses, and to revitalize and reinvigorate itself, the City needs help. * * *

Introduction to the Facts Leading Up to the Bankruptcy Filing

A. The City's Financial Distress

1. The City's Debt

The City estimates its debt to be $18,000,000,000. This consists of $11,900,000,000 in unsecured debt and $6,400,000,000 in secured debt. It has more than 100,000 creditors.

According to the City, the unsecured debt includes:

$5,700,000,000 for "OPEB" through June 2011, which is the most recent actuarial data available. "OPEB" is "other post-employment benefits," and refers to the Health and Life Insurance Benefit Plan and the Supplemental Death Benefit Plan for retirees;

$3,500,000,000 in unfunded pension obligations;

$651,000,000 in general obligation bonds;

$1,430,000,000 for certificates of participation ("COPs") related to pensions; $346,600,000 for swap contract liabilities related to the COPs; and $300,000,000 of other liabilities, including $101,200,000 in accrued compensated absences, including unpaid, accumulated vacation and sick leave balances; $86,500,000 in accrued workers' compensation for which the City is self-insured; $63,900,000 in claims and judgments, including lawsuits and claims other than workers' compensation claims; and $13,000,000 in capital leases and accrued pollution remediation. * * *

2. Pension Liabilities

The City's General Retirement System ("GRS") administers the pension plan for its nonuniformed personnel. The average annual benefit received by retired pensioners or their beneficiaries is about $18,000. * * * Generally these retirees are eligible for Social Security retirement or disability benefits.

The City's Police and Fire Retirement System ("PFRS") administers the pension plan for its uniformed personnel. The average annual benefit received by retired pensioners or their beneficiaries is about $30,000. Generally, these retirees are not eligible for Social Security retirement or disability benefits. * * *

The Pension Benefit Guaranty Corporation does not insure pension benefits under either plan. * * *

Using current actuarial assumptions, the City's required pension contributions, as a percentage of eligible payroll expenses, are projected to grow from 25% for GRS and 30% for PFRS in 2012 to 30% for GRS and 60% for PFRS by 2017. Changes in actuarial assumptions would result in further increases to the City's required pension contributions.

3. OPEB Liabilities

The OPEB plans consist of the Health and Life Insurance Benefit Plan and the Supplemental Death Benefit Plan. The City's OPEB obligations arise under 22 different plans, including 15 different plans alone for medical and prescription drugs. These plans have varying structures and terms. The plan is a defined benefit plan providing hospitalization, dental care, vision care and life insurance to current employees and substantially all retirees. The City generally pays for 80% to 100% of health care coverage for eligible retirees. The Health and Life Insurance Plan is totally unfunded; it is financed entirely on a current basis.

As of June 30, 2011, 19,389 retirees were eligible to receive benefits under the City's OPEB plans. The number of retirees receiving benefits

from the City is expected to increase over time. * * * Of the City's
$5,700,000,000 OPEB liability, 99.6% is unfunded.

4. Legacy Expenditures—Pensions and OPEB

During 2012, 38.6% of the City's revenue was consumed servicing
legacy liabilities. The forecasts for subsequent years, assuming no
restructuring, are 42.5% for 2013, 54.3% for 2014, 59.5% for 2015, 63% for
2016, and 64.5% for 2017.

5. The Certificates of Participation

The transactions described here are complex and confusing. * * * In
2005 and 2006, the City set out to raise $1.4 billion for its underfunded
pension funds, the GRS and PFRS. The City created a non-profit Service
Corporation for each of the two pension funds, to act as an intermediary
in the financing. The City then entered into Service Contracts with each
of the Service Corporations. The City would make payments to the
Service Corporations, which had created Funding Trusts and assigned
their rights to those Funding Trusts. The Funding Trusts issued debt
obligations to investors called "Pension Obligation Certificates of
Participation. ("COPs"). Each COP represented an undivided
proportionate interest in the payments that the City would make to the
Service Corporations under the Service Contracts.

The City arranged for the purchase of insurance from two monoline
insurers to protect against defaults by the funding trusts that would
result if the City failed to make payments to the Service Corporations
under the Service Contracts. This was intended to make the investments
more attractive to potential investors. One insurer was XL Capital
Assurance, Inc., now known as Syncora. The other was the Financial
Guaranty Insurance Company.

Some of the COPs paid a floating interest rate. To protect the Service
Corporations from the risk of increasing interest rates, they entered into
hedge arrangements with UBS A.G. and SBS Financial (the "Swap
Counterparties"). Under the hedges, also known as "swaps" (bets, really),
the Service Corporations and the Swap Counterparties agreed to convert
the floating interest rates into a fixed payment. Under the swaps, if the
floating interest rates exceeded a certain rate, the Swap Counterparties
would make payments to the Service Corporations. But if the floating
interest rates sank below a certain rate, the Service Corporations would
make payments to the Swap Counterparties. Specifically, there were
eight pay-fixed, receive-variable interest rate swap contracts, effective as
of June 12, 2006, with a total amount of $800,000,000.

Under the swaps, the City was also at risk if there was an "event of
default" or a "termination event." In such an event, the Swap

Counterparties could terminate the swaps and demand a potentially enormous termination payment. * * *

In 2008, interest rates dropped dramatically. As a result, the City lost on the swaps bet. Actually, it lost catastrophically on the swaps bet. The bet could cost the City hundreds of millions of dollars. The City estimates that the damage will be approximately $45,000,000 per year for the next ten years.

[That led to new negotiations among the City, the Service Corporations, and the Swaps Counterparties to restructure the swap contracts. In March 2012, the COPs were downgraded. On June 14, 2013, the City failed to make a required payment of approximately $40,000,000 on the COPs. This default triggered Syncora's liability as insurer on the COPs. Syncora made a payment and then claimed $15 million from a specific City account dedicated to financing the COPs. That led to litigations between the City and Syncora, and between Syncora and the Swaps Counterparties as well as to new negotiations between the City and the Swaps Counterparties over the City's interest in buying out the swaps.]

* * * Returning, finally, to the underlying obligations—the COPS, the City estimates that as of June 30, 2013, the following amounts were outstanding:

$480,300,000 in outstanding principal amount of $640,000,000 Certificates of Participation Series 2005 A maturing June 15, 2013 through 2025; and

$948,540,000 in outstanding principal amount of $948,540,000 Certificates of Participation Series 2006 A and B maturing June 15, 2019 through 2035.

6. Debt Service

Debt service from the City's general fund related to limited tax and unlimited tax GO debt and the COPs was $225,300,000 for 2012, and is projected to exceed $247,000,000 in 2013. The City estimates that 38% of its tax revenue goes to debt service rather than to city services. It further estimates that without changes, this will increase to 65% within 5 years.

7. Revenues

Income tax revenues have decreased by $91,000,000 since 2002(30%) and by $44,000,000 (15%) since 2008. Municipal income tax revenue was $276,500,000 in 2008 and $233,000,000 in 2012. Property tax revenues for 2013 were $135,000,000. This is a reduction of $13,000,000 (10%) from 2012. Revenues from the City's utility users' tax have declined from approximately $55,300,000 in 2003 to approximately $39,800,000 in 2012(28%). Wagering taxes receipts are about $170–$180,000,000 annually. However, the City projects that these receipts will decrease through 2015 due to the expected loss of gaming revenue to casinos opening in nearby Toledo, Ohio.

State revenue sharing has decreased by $161,000,000 since 2002(48%) and by $76,000,000 (30.6%) since 2008, due to the City's declining population and significant reductions in statutory revenue sharing by the State.

8. Operating Deficits

The City has experienced operating deficits for each of the past seven years. Through 2013, it has had an accumulated general fund deficit of $237,000,000. However, this includes the effect of recent debt issuances— $75,000,000 in 2008; $250,000,000 in 2010; and $129,500,000 in 2013. If these debt issuances are excluded, the City's accumulated general fund deficit would have been $700,000,000 through 2013.

In 2012, the City had a negative cash flow of $115,500,000, excluding the impact of proceeds from short-term borrowings. In March 2012, to avoid running out of cash, the City borrowed $80,000,000 on a secured basis. The City spent $50,000,000 of that borrowing in 2012. In 2013, the City deferred payments on certain of its obligations, totaling approximately $120,000,000. * * * [T]hese deferrals were for current and prior year pension contributions and other payments. With those deferrals, the City projects a positive cash flow of $4,000,000 for 2013. If the City had not deferred these payments, it would have run out of cash by June 30, 2013. Absent restructuring, the City projects that it will have negative cash flows of $190,500,000 for 2014; $260,400,000 for 2015; $314,100,000 for 2016; and $346,000,000 for 2017. The City further estimates that by 2017, its accumulated deficit could grow to approximately $1,350,000,000.

9. Payment Deferrals

The City is not making its pension contributions as they come due. It has deferred payment of its year-end Police and Fire Retirement System contributions. As of May 2013, the City had deferred approximately $54,000,000 in pension contributions related to current and prior periods and approximately $50,000,000 on June 30, 2013 for current year PFRS pension contributions. Therefore, the City will have deferred $104,000,000 of pension contributions. Also, the City did not make the scheduled $39,700,000 payments on its COPs that were due on June 14, 2013.

B. The Causes and Consequences of the City's Financial Distress

* * * 1. Population Losses

Detroit's population declined to just over 1,000,000 as of June 1990. In December 2012, the population was 684,799. This is a 63% decline in population from its peak in 1950.

2. Employment Losses

From 1972 to 2007, the City lost approximately 80% of its manufacturing establishments and 78% of its retail establishments. The number of jobs in Detroit declined from 735,104 in 1970 to 346,545 in 2012. Detroit's unemployment rate was 6.3% in June 2000; 23.4% in June 2010; and 18.3% in June 2012. The number of employed Detroit residents fell from approximately 353,000 in 2000 to 279,960 in 2012.

3. Credit Rating

The City's credit ratings are below investment grade. As of June 17, 2013, S & P and Moody's had lowered Detroit's credit ratings to CC and Caa3, respectively. * * *

5. The Crime Rate

During calendar year 2011, 136,000 crimes were reported in the City. Of these, 15,245 were violent crimes. In 2012, the City's violent crime rate was five times the national average and the highest of any city with a population in excess of 200,000. The City's case clearance rate for violent crimes is 18.6%. The clearance rate for all crimes is 8.7%. These rates are substantially below those of comparable municipalities nationally and surrounding local municipalities.

6. Streetlights

As of April 2013, about 40% of the approximately 88,000 streetlights operated and maintained by the City's Public Lighting Department were not working.

7. Blight

There are approximately 78,000 abandoned and blighted structures in the City. Of these, 38,000 are considered dangerous buildings. The City has experienced 11,000—12,000 fires each year for the past decade. Approximately 60% of these occur in blighted or unoccupied buildings. The average cost to demolish a residential structure is approximately $8,500. The City also has 66,000 blighted vacant lots.

8. The Police Department

In 2012, the average priority one response time for the police department was 30 minutes. In 2013, it was 58 minutes. The national average is 11 minutes. The department's manpower has been reduced by approximately 40% over the last 10 years. * * *

9. The Fire Department

The average age of the City's 35 fire stations is 80 years, and maintenance costs often exceed $1,000,000 annually. The fire department's fleet has many mechanical issues, contains no reserve vehicles and lacks equipment ordinarily considered standard. * * * In February 2013, Detroit Fire Commissioner Donald Austin ordered firefighters not to use hydraulic ladders on ladder trucks except in cases involving an "immediate threat to life" because the ladders had not received safety inspections "for years." During the first quarter of 2013, frequently only 10 to 14 of the City's 36 ambulances were in service. * * *

10. Parks and Recreation

The City closed 210 parks during fiscal year 2009, reducing its total from 317 to 107(66%). It has also announced that 50 of its remaining 107 parks would be closed and that another 38 would be provided with limited maintenance. * * *

C. The City's Efforts to Address Its Financial Distress

The City has reduced the number of its employees by about 2,700 since 2011. As of May 31, 2013, it had approximately 9,560 employees. The City's unionized employees are represented by 47 discrete bargaining units. The collective bargaining agreements covering all of those bargaining units expired before this case was filed. The City has implemented revised employment terms, called "City Employment Terms" ("CET"), for nonunionized employees and for unionized employees under expired collective bargaining agreements. It has also increased revenues and reduced expenses in other ways. It estimates that these measures have resulted in annual savings of $200,000,000.

The City cannot legally increase its tax revenues. Nor can it reduce its employee expenses without further endangering public health and safety. * * *

E. The Events Leading to the Appointment of the City's Emergency Manager

* * * On December 21, 2011, Andy Dillon, the state treasurer, reported to the governor that "probable financial stress" existed in Detroit and recommended the appointment of a "financial review team" pursuant to [Public Act] 4 [the Local Government and School District Fiscal Accountability Act of 2011]. In making this finding, Dillon's report cited:

> the inability of the City to avoid fund deficits, recurrent accumulated deficit spending, severe projected cash flow shortages resulting in an improper reliance on inter-fund and

external borrowing, the lack of funding of the City's other post-retirement benefits, and the increasing debt of the City[.]

* * * On December 27, 2011, the governor announced the appointment of a ten member Financial Review Team. * * * On March 26, 2012, the Financial Review Team submitted its report * * * [which] found that "the City of Detroit is in a condition of severe financial stress[.]"

In early 2012, the City and the State of Michigan negotiated a 47 page "Financial Stability Agreement," more commonly called the "Consent Agreement." * * * The Consent Agreement created a "Financial Advisory Board" ("FAB") of nine members selected by the governor, the treasurer, the mayor and the city council. The Consent Agreement granted the FAB an oversight role and limited powers over certain City reform and budget activities. The FAB has held, and continues to hold, regular public meetings and to exercise its oversight functions set forth in the Consent Agreement.

* * * On December 14, 2012, * * * Treasurer Dillon reported to the governor that * * * a "serious financial problem" existed within the City. * * * Upon receipt of Treasurer Dillon's report, the governor appointed another Financial Review Team * * *. On February 19, 2013, the Financial Review Team submitted its report to the governor, concluding, "* * * that a local government financial emergency exists within the City of Detroit because no satisfactory plan exists to resolve a serious financial problem." * * * On March 1, 2013 * * * the governor announced his determination under [Public Act] 72 [the Local Government Fiscal Responsibility Act of 1990] that a "financial emergency" existed within the City. * * * On March 12, 2013, the governor conducted a public hearing to consider the city council's appeal of his determination. On March 14, 2013, the governor confirmed his determination of a "financial emergency" within the City and requested that the Local Emergency Financial Assistance Loan Board ("LEFALB") appoint an emergency financial manager under P.A. 72. On March 15, 2013, the LEFALB appointed Kevyn Orr as the emergency financial manager for the City of Detroit. * * * On March 28, 2013, the effective date of P.A. 436 [the Local Financial Stability and Choice Act of 12012] P.A. 72 was repealed, and Mr. Orr became the emergency manager of the City under §§ 2(e) and 31 of P.A. 436.

The emergency manager acts "for and in the place and stead of the governing body and the office of chief administrative officer of the local government." He has "broad powers in receivership to rectify the financial emergency and to assure the fiscal accountability of the local government and the local government's capacity to provide or cause to be provided necessary governmental services essential to the public health, safety, and welfare."

The Emergency Manager's Activities

On June 14, 2013, Mr. Orr organized a meeting with approximately 150 representatives of the City's creditors, including representatives of: (a) the City's debt holders; (b) the insurers of this debt; (c) the City's unions; (d) certain retiree associations; (e) the Pension Systems; and (f) many individual bondholders. At the meeting, Mr. Orr presented the June 14 Creditor Proposal, and answered questions. At the conclusion of the meeting, Mr. Orr invited creditor representatives to meet and engage in a dialogue with City representatives regarding the proposal.

This proposal described the economic circumstances that resulted in Detroit's financial condition. It also offered a thorough overhaul and restructuring of the City's operations, finances and capital structure, as well as proposed recoveries for each creditor group. * * * On June 20, 2013, Mr. Orr's advisors met with representatives of the City's unions and four retiree associations. In the morning they met with representatives of "non-uniformed" employees and retirees. In the afternoon they met with "uniformed" employees and retirees. In these meetings, his advisors discussed retiree health and pension obligations. Approximately 100 union and retiree representatives attended the two-hour morning session. It included time for questions and answers. Approximately 35 union and retiree representatives attended the afternoon session, which lasted approximately 90 minutes.

On June 25, 2013, Mr. Orr's advisors and his senior advisor staff members held meetings in New York for representatives and advisors with all six of the insurers of the City's funded bond debt; the pension systems; and U.S. Bank, the trustee or paying agent on all of the City's bond issuances. Approximately 70 individuals attended this meeting. At this five-hour meeting, the City's advisors discussed the 10-year financial projections and cash flows presented in the June 14 Creditor Proposal, together with the assumptions and detail underlying those projections and cash flows; the City's contemplated reinvestment initiatives and related costs; and the retiree benefit and pension information and proposals that had been presented to the City's unions and pension representatives on June 20, 2013. * * * On June 26 and 27, 2013, Mr. Orr's advisors held individual follow-up meetings with each of several bond insurers. * * *

On July 10, 2013, the City and certain of its advisors held meetings with representatives and advisors of the GRS, as well as representatives and counsel for certain non-uniformed unions and retiree associations and representatives and advisors of the PFRS, as well as representatives and counsel for certain uniformed unions and retiree associations. * * * The purposes of each meeting were to provide additional information on the City's pension restructuring proposal and to discuss a process for reaching a consensual agreement on pension underfunding issues and the treatment of any related claims.

On July 11, 2013, the City and its advisors held separate follow-up meetings with representatives and advisors for select non-uniform unions and retiree associations, the GRS, certain uniformed unions and retiree associations, and the PFRS to discuss retiree health issues. * * *

On July 16, 2013, Mr. Orr recommended to the governor and the treasurer in writing that the City file for chapter 9 [federal bankruptcy] relief. An emergency manager may recommend a chapter 9 filing if, in his judgment, "no reasonable alternative to rectifying the financial emergency of the local government which is in receivership exists." On July 18, 2013, Governor Snyder authorized the City of Detroit to file a chapter 9 bankruptcy case. M.C.L. § 141.1558(1) permits the governor to "place contingencies on a local government in order to proceed under chapter 9." However, the governor's authorization letter stated, "I am choosing not to impose any such contingencies today. Federal law already contains the most important contingency—a requirement that the plan be legally executable, 11 USC 943(b)(4)." Accordingly, his authorization did not include a condition prohibiting the City from seeking to impair pensions in a plan.

At 4:06 p.m. on July 18, 2013, the City filed this chapter 9 bankruptcy case. * * *

[Constitutional Challenges]

* * *

Article I, Section 8 of the United States Constitution provides: "The Congress shall have Power To ... establish ... uniform Laws on the subject of Bankruptcies throughout the United States." * * *

[Contracts Clause]

The Contracts Clause of the United States Constitution, which is Article I, Section 10, provides, "No State shall ... pass any ... Law impairing the Obligation of Contracts, ... " AFSCME [the American Federation of State, County, and Municipal Employees—the union representing many Detroit public employees] argues that chapter 9 violates the Contracts Clause. This argument is frivolous. * * * "The Bankruptcy Clause necessarily authorizes Congress to make laws that would impair contracts. It long has been understood that bankruptcy law entails impairment of contracts." * * *

[Tenth Amendment]

The question of whether a federal municipal bankruptcy act can be administered consistent with the principles of federalism reflected in the Tenth Amendment has already been decided. In *United States v. Bekins,*

304 U.S. 27, 58 S.Ct. 811, 82 L.Ed. 1137 (1938), the United States Supreme Court specifically upheld the Municipal Corporation Bankruptcy Act, 50 Stat. 653 (1937), over objections that the statute violated the Tenth Amendment. In upholding the 1937 Act, the *Bekins* court found:

> The statute is carefully drawn so as not to impinge upon the sovereignty of the State. The State retains control of its fiscal affairs. The bankruptcy power is exercised in relation to a matter normally within its province and only in a case where the action of the taxing agency in carrying out a plan of composition approved by the bankruptcy court is authorized by state law. It is of the essence of sovereignty to be able to make contracts and give consents bearing upon the exertion of governmental power. . . . The reservation to the States by the Tenth Amendment protected, and did not destroy, their right to make contracts and give consents where that action would not contravene the provisions of the Federal Constitution.

* * * The Court quoted approvingly, and at length, from a House of Representatives Committee report on the 1937 Act:

> There is no hope for relief through statutes enacted by the States, because the Constitution forbids the passing of State laws impairing the obligations of existing contracts. Therefore, relief must come from Congress, if at all. The committee are not prepared to admit that the situation presents a legislative no-man's land. It is the opinion of the committee that the present bill removes the objections to the unconstitutional statute, and gives a forum to enable those distressed taxing agencies which desire to adjust their obligations and which are capable of reorganization, to meet their creditors under necessary judicial control and guidance and free from coercion, and to affect such adjustment on a plan determined to be mutually advantageous.

Id. at 51, 58 S.Ct. 811 (quotation marks omitted).

* * * The cases now firmly establish that the Contracts Clause of the United States Constitution bars a state from enacting municipal bankruptcy legislation. * * * In *In re Jefferson Cnty., Ala.,* 474 B.R. 228, 279 (Bankr.N.D.Ala.2012), *aff'd sub nom. Mosley v. Jefferson Cnty. (In re Jefferson Cnty.),* 2012 WL 3775758 (N.D.Ala. Aug. 28, 2012), the court stated, "A financially prostrate municipal government has one viable option to resolve debts in a non-consensual manner. It is a bankruptcy case. Outside of bankruptcy, nonconsensual alteration of contracted debt is, at the very least, severely restricted, if not impossible." * * *

Chapter 9 Is Constitutional As Applied in This Case.

Several of the objecting parties also raise "as-applied" challenges to the constitutionality of chapter 9 under the Tenth Amendment to United States Constitution. Although variously cast, the primary thrust of these arguments is that if chapter 9 permits the State of Michigan to authorize a city to file a petition for chapter 9 relief without explicitly providing for the protection of accrued pension benefits, the Tenth Amendment is violated. The Court concludes that these arguments must be rejected.

a. When the State Consents to a Chapter 9 Bankruptcy, the Tenth Amendment Does Not Prohibit the Impairment of Contract Rights That Are Otherwise Protected by the State Constitution.

* * * The state constitutional provisions prohibiting the impairment of contracts and pensions impose no constraint on the bankruptcy process. The Bankruptcy Clause of the United States Constitution, and the bankruptcy code enacted pursuant thereto, explicitly empower the bankruptcy court to impair contracts and to impair contractual rights relating to accrued vested pension benefits. Impairing contracts is what the bankruptcy process does. * * *

For Tenth Amendment and state sovereignty purposes, nothing distinguishes pension debt in a municipal bankruptcy case from any other debt. If the Tenth Amendment prohibits the impairment of pension benefits in this case, then it would also prohibit the adjustment any other debt in this case. *Bekins* makes it clear, however, that with state consent, the adjustment of municipal debts does not impermissibly intrude on state sovereignty. * * *

b. Under the Michigan Constitution, Pension Rights Are Contractual Rights.

The Plans seek escape from this result by asserting that under the Michigan Constitution, pension debt has greater protection than ordinary contract debt. The argument is premised on the slim reed that in the Michigan Constitution, pension rights may not be "impaired or diminished," whereas only laws "impairing" contract rights are prohibited. * * *

At common law, before the adoption of the Michigan Constitution in 1963, public pensions in Michigan were viewed as gratuitous allowances that could be revoked at will, because a retiree lacked any vested right in their continuation. * * *

In the 1963 Constitution, this provision enhancing the protection for pensions was included: "The accrued financial benefits of each pension plan and retirement system of the state and its political subdivisions shall be a contractual obligation thereof which shall not be diminished or impaired thereby." Mich. Const. art. IX, § 24.

* * * [I]n *In re Constitutionality of 2011 Pa. 38,* 490 Mich. 295, 806 N.W.2d 683 (2011), the Michigan Supreme Court unequivocally stated, "The obvious intent of § 24 * * * was to ensure that public pensions be treated as *contractual obligations* that, once earned, could not be diminished." * * *

[T]he slight difference in the language that protects contracts and the language that protects pensions does not suggest that pensions were given any extraordinary protection. * * * Because under the Michigan Constitution, pension rights are contractual rights, they are subject to impairment in a federal bankruptcy proceeding. Moreover, when, as here, the state consents, that impairment does not violate the Tenth Amendment. Therefore, as applied in this case, chapter 9 is not unconstitutional.

Nevertheless, the Court is compelled to comment. No one should interpret this holding that pension rights are subject to impairment in this bankruptcy case to mean that the Court will necessarily confirm any plan of adjustment that impairs pensions. * * *

Public Act 436 Does Not Violate the Michigan Constitution.

Section 109(c)(2) of the bankruptcy code requires that a municipality be "specifically authorized, in its capacity as a municipality or by name, to be a debtor under such chapter by State law, or by a governmental officer or organization empowered by State law to authorize such entity to be a debtor under such chapter." 11 U.S.C. § 109(c)(2). The evidence establishes that the City was authorized to file this case. The issue is whether that authorization was proper under the Michigan Constitution.

Section 18 of P.A. 436, M.C.L. § 141.1558, establishes the process for authorizing a municipality to file a case under chapter 9 of the bankruptcy code:

> (1) If, in the judgment of the emergency manager, no reasonable alternative to rectifying the financial emergency of the local government which is in receivership exists, then the emergency manager may recommend to the governor and the state treasurer that the local government be authorized to proceed under chapter 9. If the governor approves of the recommendation, the governor shall inform the state treasurer and the emergency manager in writing of the decision. . . . The governor may place contingencies on a local government in order to proceed under chapter 9. Upon receipt of written approval, the emergency manager is authorized to proceed under chapter 9.

> This section * * * empowers the emergency manager to act exclusively on the local government's behalf in any such case under chapter 9.

* * * Certain objectors argue that P.A. 436 violates Article VII, Section 22 of the Michigan Constitution, which states:

> Under general laws the electors of each city and village shall have the power and authority to frame, adopt and amend its charter, and to amend an existing charter of the city or village heretofore granted or enacted by the legislature for the government of the city or village. Each such city and village shall have power to adopt resolutions and ordinances relating to its municipal concerns, property and government, subject to the constitution and law. No enumeration of powers granted to cities and villages in this constitution shall limit or restrict the general grant of authority conferred by this section.

The argument is that the appointment of an emergency manager for a municipality under P.A. 436 is inconsistent with the right of the electors to adopt and amend the City charter and the city's right to adopt ordinances. AFSCME asserts that "Michigan is strongly committed to the concept of home rule [.]" "This 'strong home rule' regime reflects a bedrock principle of state law, . . . all officers of cities are to 'be elected by the electors thereof, or appointed by such authorities thereof' not by the central State Government." * * * AFSCME further asserts that in authorizing the appointment of an emergency manager with broad powers that usurp the powers of elected officials, "P.A. 436 offends the 'strong home rule' of Detroit and that the Emergency Manager is not lawfully authorized to file for bankruptcy on behalf of the City or to act as its representative during chapter 9 proceedings."

AFSCME's argument fails for the simple reason that the broad authority the Michigan Constitution grants to municipalities is subject to constitutional and statutory limits. This constitutional provision itself embodies that principle. It states, "Each such city and village shall have power to adopt resolutions and ordinances relating to its municipal concerns, property and government, *subject to the constitution and law.*" Mich. Const. art. VII, § 22 (emphasis added). State law recognizes the same limitation on local government authority. * * *

* * * The Michigan case law establishes that the powers granted to municipalities by the "home rule" sections of the Michigan Constitution are subject to the limits of the power and authority of the State to create laws of general concern. * * *

P.A. 436 permits the governor to "place contingencies on a local government in order to proceed under chapter 9." M.C.L. § 141.1558(1). The governor did not place any contingencies on the bankruptcy filing in this case. * * * Several of the objectors argue that the pension clause of the Michigan Constitution, article IX, section 24, obligated the governor to include a condition in his authorization that would prohibit the City from impairing pension benefits in this bankruptcy case. * * * [A]ny such contingency in the law itself would be ineffective and potentially invalid. For the same reason, any such contingency in the governor's authorization letter would have been invalid, and may have rendered the authorization itself invalid under 11 U.S.C. § 109(c). Accordingly, this objection is overruled.

* * *

To be eligible for relief under chapter 9, the City must establish that it is "insolvent." 11 U.SC. § 109(c)(3). Several individual objectors and AFSCME challenge the City's assertion that it is insolvent.

For a municipality, the bankruptcy code defines "insolvent" as a "financial condition such that the municipality is—(i) generally not paying its debts as they become due unless such debts are the subject of a bona fide dispute; or (ii) is unable to pay its debts as they become due." 11 U.S.C. § 101(32)(C).

The test under the first prong "looks to current, general non-payment." * * * When considering the second prong, courts take into account broader concerns, such as longer term budget imbalances and whether the City has sufficient resources to maintain services for the health, safety, and welfare of the community. * * * The Court finds that the City of Detroit was, and is, insolvent under both definitions in 11 U.S.C. § 101(32)(C). * * *

Specifically, in May 2013, the City deferred payment on approximately $54,000,000 in pension contributions. On June 30, 2013, it deferred an additional $5,000,000 fiscal year-end payment. The City also did not make a scheduled $39,700,000 payment on its COPs on June 14, 2013. Ex. 43 at 8. It was also spending much more money than it was receiving, and only making up the difference through expensive and even catastrophic borrowings. * * *

The evidence was overwhelming that the City is unable to pay its debts as they become due. The evidence established that there are many, many services in the City which do not function properly as a result of the City's financial state. * * * Most powerfully, however, the testimony of Chief Craig established that the City was in a state of "service delivery insolvency" as of July 18, 2013, and will continue to be for the foreseeable future.

* * * [W]hile the City's tumbling credit rating, its utter lack of liquidity, and the disastrous COPs and swaps deal might more neatly establish the City's "insolvency" under 11 U.S.C. § 101(32)(C), it is the City's service

delivery insolvency that the Court finds most strikingly disturbing in this case.

* * * For these reasons, the Court finds that the City has established that it is insolvent as 11 U.S.C. § 109(c)(3) requires and as 11 U.S.C. § 101(32)(C) defines that term.

To establish its eligibility for relief under chapter 9, the City must establish that it desires to effect a plan to adjust its debts. 11 U.S.C. § 109(c)(4). The Court concludes that the evidence overwhelmingly established that the City does desire to effectuate a plan in this case. Mr. Orr so testified. More importantly, before filing this case, Mr. Orr did submit to creditors a plan to adjust the City's debts. Plainly, that plan was not acceptable to any of the City's creditors. It may not have been confirmable under 11 U.S.C. § 943, although it is not necessary to resolve that question at this time. Still, it was evidence of the City's desire and intent to effect a plan. There is simply no evidence that the City has an ulterior motive in pursuing chapter 9, such as to buy time or to evade creditors.

Indeed, the objecting creditors do not contend that there was any such ulterior motive. They assert no desire on the part of the City or its emergency manager to buy time or evade creditors. Rather, their argument is that the plan that the emergency manager has stated he intends to propose in this case is not a confirmable plan. It is not confirmable, they argue, because it will impair pensions in violation of the Michigan Constitution.

Certainly the evidence does establish that the emergency manager intends to propose a plan that impairs pensions. The Court has already so found. * * * Nevertheless, the objectors' argument must be rejected. * * * [A] chapter 9 plan may impair pension rights. The emergency manager's stated intent to propose a plan that impairs pensions is therefore not inconsistent with a desire to effect a plan.

The fifth requirement for eligibility is found in § 109(c)(5).

An entity may be a debtor under chapter 9 of this title if and only if such entity—. . .

> (5)(A)has obtained the agreement of creditors holding at least a majority in amount of the claims of each class that such entity intends to impair under a plan in a case under such chapter;
>
> (B) has negotiated in good faith with creditors and has failed to obtain the agreement of creditors holding at least a majority in amount of the claims of each class that such entity intends to impair under a plan in a case under such chapter;

(C) is unable to negotiate with creditors because such negotiation is impracticable; or

(D) reasonably believes that a creditor may attempt to obtain a transfer that is avoidable under section 547 of this title.

This section was enacted because Congress recognized that municipal bankruptcy is a drastic step and should only be taken as a last resort. * * * Therefore, it added a requirement for pre-bankruptcy negotiation to attempt to resolve disputes.

* * * [T]he Court finds that negotiations were in fact, impracticable * * *. Congress adopted § 109(c)(5)(C) specifically "to cover situations in which a very large body of creditors would render prefiling negotiations impracticable." * * * The list of creditors for the City of Detroit is over 3500 pages. Ex. 64 (Dkt. # 1059) It lists over 100,000 creditors. It is divided into fifteen schedules including the following classifications: Long-Term Debt; Trade Debt, Employee Benefits; Pension Obligations, Non-Pension Retiree Obligations; Active Employee Obligations; Workers' Compensation; Litigation and Similar Claims; Real Estate Lease Obligations; Deposits; Grants; Pass-Through Obligations, Obligations to Component Units of the City; Property Tax-Related Obligations; Income Tax-Related Obligations. * * *

Long term debt, including bonds, notes and loans, capital lease, and obligations arising under the COPs and swaps, is listed at over $8,700,000,000 or approximately 48.52% of the City's total debt. Within this category are several series of bonds where individual bondholders are not identified. Many of these bondholders are not represented by any organization.

As noted above, pension obligations are estimated at almost $3,500,000,000 or 19.33% of the City's total debt. The City estimates over 20,000 individual retirees are owed pension funds. * * *

The Court is satisfied that when Congress enacted the impracticability section, it foresaw precisely the situation facing the City of Detroit. It has been widely reported that Detroit is the largest municipality ever to file bankruptcy. * * * The sheer size of the debt and number of individual creditors made pre-bankruptcy negotiation impracticable—impossible, really. * * *

The last requirement for eligibility is set forth in 11 U.S.C. § 921(c), which provides, "After any objection to the petition, the court, after notice and a hearing, may dismiss the petition if the debtor did not file the petition in good faith or if the petition does not meet the requirements of this title." * * *

The City's alleged bad faith in filing its chapter 9 petition was a central issue in the eligibility trial. Indeed, in one form or another, all of the objecting parties have taken the position that the City did not file its chapter 9 petition in good faith and that this Court should exercise its discretion under 11 U.S.C. § 921(c) to dismiss the case. * * *

1. The Objectors' Theory of Bad Faith

* * * It must be recognized that the narrative that the Court describes here is a composite of the objecting parties' positions and presentations on this issue. No single objecting party neatly laid out this precise version with all of the features described here. Moreover, it includes the perceptions of the objecting parties whose objections were filed by attorneys, as well as the many objecting parties who filed their objections without counsel. Naturally, these views on this subject were numerous, diverse, and at times inconsistent.

The Court will use an italics font for its description of this narrative, not to give it emphasis, but as a reminder that these are **not** the Court's findings. As noted, this is only the Court's perception of a composite narrative that appears to ground the objectors' various bad faith arguments:

According to this composite narrative of the lead-up to the City of Detroit's bankruptcy filing on July 18, 2013, the bankruptcy was the intended consequence of a years-long, strategic plan.

*The goal of this plan was the impairment of pension rights through a bankruptcy filing by the City. * * ***

*The plan was executed by the top officials of the State of Michigan, including Governor Snyder and others in his administration, assisted by the state's legal and financial consultants * * *. The goals of the plan also included lining the professionals' pockets while extending the power of state government at the expense of the people of Detroit.*

Always conscious of the hard-fought and continuing struggle to obtain equal voting rights in this country and an equal opportunity to partake of the country's abundance, some who hold to this narrative also suspect a racial element to the plan.

*** * Another important part of the plan was for the state government to starve the City of cash by reducing its revenue sharing, by refusing to pay the City millions of promised dollars, and by imposing on the City the heavy financial burden of expensive professionals.*

The plan also included suppressing information about the value of the City's assets and refusing to investigate the value of its assets—the art at the Detroit Institute of the Arts; Belle Isle; City Airport; the Detroit Zoo; the Department of Water and Sewerage; the Detroit Windsor Tunnel; parking operations; Joe Louis Arena, and City-owned land.

The narrative continues that this plan also required active concealment and even deception, despite both the great public importance of resolving the City's problems and the democratic mandate of transparency and honesty in government. The purposes of this concealment and deception were to provide political cover for the governor and his administration when the City would ultimately file for bankruptcy and to advance their further political aspirations. Another purpose was to deny creditors, especially those whose retirement benefits would be at risk from such a filing, from effectively acting to protect those interests.

This concealment and deception were accomplished through a public relations campaign that deliberately misstated the ultimate objective of P.A. 436—the filing of this case. It also downplayed the likelihood of bankruptcy, asserted an unfunded pension liability amount that was based on misleading and incomplete data and analysis, understated the City's ability to meet that liability, and obscured the vulnerability of pensions in bankruptcy. It also included imposing an improper requirement to sign a confidentiality and release agreement as a condition of accessing the City's financial information in the "data room."

As the bankruptcy filing approached, a necessary part of the plan became to engage with the creditors only the minimum necessary so that the City could later assert in bankruptcy court that it attempted to negotiate in good faith. The plan, however, was not to engage in meaningful pre-petition negotiations with the creditors because successful negotiations might thwart the plan to file bankruptcy. * * *

Another oft-repeated phrase that was important to the objectors' theory of the City's bad faith was "foregone conclusion." This was used in the assertion that Detroit's bankruptcy case was a "foregone conclusion," as early as January 2013, perhaps even earlier.

* * * The Court acknowledges that many people in Detroit hold to this narrative, or at least to substantial parts of it. The Court further recognizes, on the other hand, that State and City officials vehemently deny any such improper motives or tactics as this theory attributed to them. They contend that the case was filed for the proper desired and necessary purpose of restructuring the City's debt, including its pension debt, through a plan of adjustment. * * *

The Court finds, however, that in some particulars, the record does support the objectors' view of the reality that led to this bankruptcy filing. It is, however, not nearly supported in enough particulars for the Court to find that the filing was in bad faith.

* * * The issue that this evidence presents is how to evaluate it in the context of the good faith requirement. For example, during the orchestrated lead-up to the filing, was the City of Detroit's bankruptcy filing a "foregone conclusion" as the objecting parties assert? Of course it was, and for a long time.

Even if it was a foregone conclusion, however, experience with both individuals and businesses in financial distress establishes that they often wait longer to file bankruptcy than is in their interests. Detroit was no exception. Its financial crisis has been worsening for decades and it could have, and probably should have, filed for bankruptcy relief long before it did, perhaps even years before. * * *

Then the issue becomes what impact does it have on the good faith analysis that Detroit probably waited too long. Perhaps it would have been more consistent with our democratic ideals and with the economic and social needs of the City if its officials and State officials had openly and forthrightly recognized the need for filing bankruptcy when that need first arose. It is, after all, not bad faith to file bankruptcy when it is needed.

City officials also could have avoided the appearance of pretext negotiations, and the resulting mistrust, by simply announcing honestly that because negotiating with so many diverse creditors was impracticable, negotiations would not even be attempted. The law clearly permits that, and for good reason. It avoids the very delay, and, worse, the very suspicion that resulted here.

* * * The objectors also argue that the City filed the petition so that its pension obligations could be impaired and that this is inconsistent with the remedial purpose of bankruptcy. Again, discharging debt is the primary motive behind the filing of most bankruptcy petitions. That motivation does not suggest any bad faith. * * *

* * * [T]he City did make some efforts to improve its financial condition before filing its chapter 9 petition. * * * Those efforts include reducing the number of City employees, reducing labor costs through implementation of the City Employment Terms, increasing the City's corporate tax rate, working to improve the City's ability to collect taxes, increasing lighting rates, deferring capital expenditures, reducing vendor costs, and reducing

subsidies to the Detroit Department of Transportation. Despite those efforts, the City remains insolvent.

The fact that the City did not seriously consider any alternatives to chapter 9 in the period leading up to the filing of the petition does not indicate bad faith. By this time, all of the measures described in Mr. Orr's declaration had largely failed to resolve the problem of the City's cash flow insolvency. * * *

Over 38% of the City's revenues were consumed by servicing debt in 2012, and that figure is projected to increase to nearly 65% of the budget by 2017 if the debt is not restructured. Without revitalization, revenues will continue to plummet as residents leave Detroit for municipalities with lower tax rates and acceptable services.

Without the protection of chapter 9, the City will be forced to continue on the path that it was on until it filed this case. In order to free up cash for day-to-day operations, the City would continue to borrow money, defer capital investments, and shrink its workforce. This solution has proven unworkable. It is also dangerous for its residents.

If the City were to continue to default on its financial obligations, as it would outside of bankruptcy, creditor lawsuits would further deplete the City's resources. On the other hand, in seeking chapter 9 relief, the City not only reorganizes its debt and enhances City services, but it also creates an opportunity for investments in its revitalization efforts for the good of the residents of Detroit. * * *

The Court concludes that under 11 U.S.C. § 109(c), the City of Detroit may be a debtor under chapter 9 of the bankruptcy code.

NOTES AND QUESTIONS

1.   *Introduction to Municipal Bankruptcy.* Congress enacted the first municipal bankruptcy law in 1934. The Great Depression had hit many municipalities hard. Property values dropped and nonpayment of taxes soared. Cities were compelled to raise their tax rates, which worsened the nonpayment problem. The debt burden as a percentage of assessed valuation rose sharply as well, and some localities defaulted on their debts. Although debt obligations are protected by the Contracts Clause, bondholders had limited recourse. Many of the remedies traditionally used by creditors to compel borrowers to pay their debts were unavailable in the municipal bond context. Courts were unwilling to order the seizure of municipal assets, place liens on taxes or other revenues, or direct cities to cut spending on government operations. *See* Michael W. McConnell & Randal C. Picker, When Cities Go Broke: A Conceptual Introduction to Municipal Bankruptcy, 60 U. Chi. L. Rev. 425, 428–450 (1993). A court could issue a writ of mandamus to compel a city to use available revenues to pay debts or to raise taxes, but given the economic crisis such action might very well backfire and

"precipitate a financial meltdown that would leave creditors worse off than before." *Id.* at 449. "Creditors thus had an incentive to negotiate debt relief." But a restructuring which would result in a creditor accepting less than the amount to which it was entitled would only bind those creditors willing to participate, and there was no legal means to prevent holdouts from refusing to accept such a deal. "State law could not remedy this problem, because forcing an unwilling creditor to compromise his claim would be an unconstitutional impairment of contract." *Id.* at 450.

Enter municipal bankruptcy. As originally enacted, municipalities that had negotiated the settlement of their debts with most of their creditors could submit the settlement to a federal bankruptcy court. If the requisite percentage of creditors—initially seventy-five percent—approved the settlement, and if the court concluded that the settlement was "fair, equitable and for the best interests of the creditors," the holdouts would also be bound. *Id.* at 451. Although the law made a municipality's authority to file for bankruptcy contingent on state approval, the Supreme Court, by a 5–4 vote, determined that the measure was inconsistent with federalism and the power of states to control their municipalities. *See* Ashton v. Cameron Co. Water Imp. Dist., 298 U.S. 513 (1936). State sovereignty, the Court asserted, could not be "surrendered" even with the consent of the state. The problems resulting from municipal fiscal distress remained acute, however, and Congress tried again in 1937. The 1937 Act, which became chapter 9 of the federal bankruptcy code, differed only slightly from the 1934 Act, but the Court upheld it, as the *Detroit* court explained. *See* United States v. Bekins, 304 U.S. 27 (1938). The Court concluded that the requirement of state authorization solved the federalism problem; the law was consistent with the traditional state-city relationship as it allowed a state to "invite[ ] the intervention of the bankruptcy power to save the agency which the State alone is powerless to rescue." *Id.* at 54.

Chapter 9 has been amended several times since the 1930s, most importantly in 1976 when, during the New York City fiscal crisis, Congress revised the conditions for filing for bankruptcy. The original model of municipal bankruptcy was intended to aid the locality that had reached an arrangement with most of its creditors and wanted to bind the holdouts. But that would not easily work for a large, complex city with many creditors, including bondholders who held their bonds in bearer form "and were therefore difficult to identify." Juliet M. Moringiello, Goals and Governance in Municipal Bankruptcy, 71 Wash. & Lee L. Rev. 403, 453–54 (2014). "The 1976 Act simplified the entry requirement" to permit a municipality to file, inter alia, on a showing that negotiating with its creditors was impracticable. *Id.* at 454. The 1976 law added some features from the corporate bankruptcy context including provision of an automatic stay of all suits against the municipal debtor, power to avoid prepetition fraudulent or preferential transfers, and power of a debtor in bankruptcy to reject executory contracts. *Id.* at 454–55.

The 1976 law also reinforced the principle of state control of local government, providing that nothing in the Act "shall be construed to limit or impair the power of any State to control by legislation or otherwise, any municipality or any political subdivision of or in such State in the exercise of its political or governmental powers." Further amendments were adopted in 1988 and 1994, including the requirement that a municipality be specifically authorized by its state to file for bankruptcy. Previously, some municipalities had argued and some courts had found that general state grants to sue and be sued or to exercise home rule powers provided the necessary authority in the absence of a state prohibition. Now a state must have expressly authorized a bankruptcy filing—although this can be done by general legislation and need not be for a specific municipality—and the state may impose its own conditions on access to bankruptcy. *Id.* at 461. Currently, twelve states specifically authorize local governments to file for bankruptcy, another twelve states provide conditional authorization, and three states provide a limited authorization. Twenty-one states provide no authorization, while two states specifically bar a bankruptcy filing. *See* Pew Charitable Trusts, The State Role in Local Government Financial Distress (July 2013) at 9–11. California conditions eligibility to file on pre-filing participation in a "neutral evaluation process" with an outside mediator to see if the municipality's problems can be resolved short of bankruptcy. *See*, e.g., In re City of Stockton, 493 B.R. 772, 784–87 (E.D. Cal. 2013) (discussing pre-filing negotiation process in Stockton bankruptcy). However, the process can be bypassed in the event of an immediate financial emergency. The State Role, *supra*, at 43. Although a state as "gatekeeper" can impose conditions on a municipality's filing for bankruptcy, or bar a filing altogether, "once a chapter 9 case has been filed in the circumstances authorized by the state, the federal Bankruptcy Code controls all proceedings in the case. . . . The specialized relief in the form of the ability to cause municipal contracts to be impaired under the exclusive federal authority to impair contracts implemented by the Bankruptcy Code is available to a state on an all-or-nothing, take-it-or-leave-it basis." In re City of Stockton, 526 B.R. 35, 51, 55 (E.D. Cal. 2015). The limited power of the state to affect the rights of different creditors once the municipality is in bankruptcy is underscored by 11 U.S.C. 903(1), which provides that "a State law prescribing a method of composition of indebtedness of such municipality may not bind any creditor that does not consent to such composition." This provision, adopted in 1978, effectively overturned Faitoute Iron & Steel Co. v. City of Asbury Park, 316 U.S. 502 (1942), which had upheld a New Jersey law, enacted during the Depression before the federal municipal bankruptcy law, which permitted a plan of adjustment over the objection of creditors if the city and 85% of the creditors agreed. The Court reasoned that the measure did not violate the Contracts Clause because as a practical matter given the city's financial condition the plan of adjustment was "the only proven way for assuring payment of unsecured municipal obligations." *Id.* at 512. Today, even if such a plan would be consistent with the Contracts Clause it is barred by chapter 9.

Municipal bankruptcy differs from corporate bankruptcy. "Underlying corporate bankruptcy is the theory that a corporation can be reorganized to maximize its going-concern value for the benefit of its creditors and if such a reorganization is impossible the corporate assets can be liquidated and distributed to the entity's creditors." Moringiello, *supra*, at 433. But a municipal bankruptcy court lacks the power to liquidate a municipality or to reorganize it. Insolvent or not, the municipality will continue in the organizational form directed by state law and the locality's charter. This follows from the federalist command of 11 U.S.C. § 904 which provides that a bankruptcy court has no power to "interfere with any of the political or governmental powers of the debtor; any of the property revenues of the debtor; or the debtor's use and enjoyment of any income-producing property." As a federal bankruptcy court recently put it, "a federal court can use no tool in its toolkit—no inherent authority power, no implied equitable power . . . no writ, no stay, no order—to interfere with a municipality regarding political or governmental powers, property or revenues, or use or enjoyment of income-producing property." In re City of Stockton, 478 B.R. 8, 20 (E.D. Cal. 2012). The court's role is limited to protecting the municipality from the claims of its creditors during the bankruptcy proceeding and to approving a plan of adjustment proposed by the municipality. More like an individual bankruptcy than a corporate bankruptcy, the aim of municipal bankruptcy is to give the municipality debt relief and a "fresh start."

2. *The Eligibility Question.* The issue for the court in the *Detroit* case was whether the City of Detroit was eligible to file for bankruptcy. Among the ways in which municipal bankruptcy differs from other forms of bankruptcy is in the entry into the bankruptcy process. On the one hand, municipal bankruptcy must be voluntary. An involuntary petition, filed by creditors rather than by the debtor, is not available against a municipality. On the other hand, "[c]hapter 9 is unique among voluntary Bankruptcy Code cases in that a municipality must litigate its way to the order for relief before restructuring its debt" by satisfying five statutory requirements that make it eligible to file. In re City of Stockton, 493 B.R. 772, 776 (E.D. Cal. 2013). Eligibility is not automatic, especially when challenged by the state or creditors. *See, e.g.,* In re City of Bridgeport, 129 B.R. 332 (D. Conn. 1991); In re Boise County, 465 B.R. 156 (D. Idaho 2011); In re Harrisburg, 465 B.R. 744 (M.D. Pa. 2011). The five statutory requirements are that the debtor (i) is a municipality; (ii) has been specifically authorized by its state to file; (iii) is insolvent; (iv) "desires to effect a plan" to adjust its debts; and (v) has either obtained an agreement from creditors holding a majority of its debts, negotiated in good faith in an unsuccessful attempt to do so or "is unable to negotiate with creditors because such negotiation is impracticable." 11 U.S.C. § 109(c). Even if the debtor satisfies these requirements, the court may still dismiss the petition "if the debtor did not file the petition in good faith." 11 U.S.C. § 921(c). Which of these eligibility requirements was at issue in the *Detroit* case?

The treatment of Detroit's pension plan obligations came up several times in the court's assessment of Detroit's eligibility to file for bankruptcy. What was the objectors' argument that the state constitution's pension provision affected Detroit's authority to file? How did the pension question shape the discussion of the City's having a plan of adjustment and its good faith in filing? How did this and other state law questions—such as Michigan's home rule provision—affect the federal law question of eligibility to file for bankruptcy? What did the court conclude about the extent to which pension obligations would be protected in bankruptcy?

Consider also how the court addressed the question of municipal insolvency. In the *Stockton* bankruptcy case, the court discussed three types of insolvency: cash insolvency, that is, "inability to generate and maintain cash balances to pay expenditures as they come due;" " 'budget insolvency,' which is the inability to create a balanced budget that provides sufficient revenues to pay expenses occurring within the budgeted period;" and " 'service delivery insolvency,' which is a municipality's inability to pay for all the costs of providing services at the level and quality required for the health, safety, and welfare of the community." 493 B.R. at 781. How did the *Detroit* court approach these issues?

3.   *The Grand Bargain: Detroit Emerges from Bankruptcy.* As the *Stockton* court put it, being allowed to file is "like a qualifying round in a competition; success leads only to the main event—the process of achieving a viable plan of adjustment." *Id.* at 776. The Detroit bankruptcy was by far the largest municipal bankruptcy—whether measured by the number of people affected or the dollar value of the debts at stake—in United States history. Given the very large number of competing interests, as well the political conflicts and public suspicions referred to by the court in its discussion of the "good faith" issue, most observers expected that Detroit's bankruptcy would be a long and difficult process. Instead, Detroit emerged from bankruptcy in less than eighteen months with new financial support from the state, foundations, and private sources, and a plan that enabled Detroit to settle with every major creditor group, shed $7 billion in debt and commit to $1.7 billion in reinvestment and restructuring initiatives over a ten-year period to improve the City government's infrastructure and its municipal public services. *See* In re City of Detroit, 524 B.R. 147 (E.D. Mich. 2014).

The heart of the Detroit plan of adjustment is what the court called "The Grand Bargain," *id.* at 169–82, which grew out of and drew together two major issues: the rights of Detroit's public employee pensioners and the status of the extremely valuable art collection in the Detroit Institute of Art ("DIA"). In his eligibility decision, Judge Rhodes indicated that pension plan obligations were no more protected in bankruptcy than commitments to other unsecured creditors, such as general obligation bondholders, but he also "emphasize[d] that the court would "not lightly or casually exercise the power under federal bankruptcy law to impair pensions." *Cf.* In re City of Stockton, 526 B.R. 35, 59 (E.D. Cal. 2015) ("[n]one of this means that public pensions can be rejected or unilaterally modified willy-nilly"). Although Detroit may have been insolvent, arguably it could be required to sell its assets—such as the art collection—to pay its creditors, particularly retirees entitled to receive pensions. In the media, this was treated as a conflict between the value of the fine arts and the needs of the City's middle- and moderate-income pensioners. Legally, it was uncertain who owned the art and whether it could be sold. As the court noted, "several parties, including at times the City itself, have taken the position that the City holds title to several significant pieces of art in the DIA and has the right to sell them outright to pay its obligations to its creditors." On the other hand, the Michigan Attorney General and the DIA took the position that all the art at the DIA is held in charitable trust for the benefit of the people of the State as a whole and so could not be sold to pay the City's debts. 524 B.R, at 176–77.

Ultimately, through the Grand Bargain that included financial contributions from the state and from local wealthy individuals, businesses, and local and national foundations, the DIA art collection was saved and the pensions significantly protected. The principal elements of the Grand Bargain are:

- $195 million for the pension funds from the State, conditioned on the funds establishing investment committees.

- An annual payment by the DIA of $100 million for twenty years to the pension funds from contributions from individuals, local foundations and the business community.

- An additional $366 million in contributions to the pension funds over twenty years from various other local and national foundations. The foundations participating in the Grand Bargain included the Ford Foundation, the Kresge Foundation, the W.K. Kellogg Foundation, the Knight Foundation, and eight others.

- The transfer of all the City's right, title and interest in the DIA's art to the DIA to be held in perpetual charitable trust for the people of the City and State, with the DIA committing to "provide an array of art programs at no cost or discounted cost to the residents of the state."

- The City's adoption of certain pension governance mechanisms, including the creation of a review board and the production of annual reports to ensure acceptable fiscal practices and procedures for the management and investment of pension funds.

- Pension plan cuts including a reduction to 45% of the annual cost-of-living-adjustment amount provided by the pre-bankruptcy collective bargaining agreement for the police and firefighters plan; a reduction of 4.5% of the accrued pension amount and complete elimination of cost-of-living-adjustments for other pensioners; and new less generous pensions for City employees starting July 1, 2014. These cuts were approved as part of the overall plan by 82% of those in the police and firefighter pension plan and 73% of those in the general pension plan.

- The pension cuts to be partially offset for low-income pensioners, and limited restoration of some of the cuts if after 2023 funding levels exceed certain targets.

- Additional sources of funding for the pension plans starting in 2023.

- Adoption of new pension plan governance structures, funding level commitments, and more conservative assumptions concerning the return on investments.

As Judge Rhodes observed, "the treatment of pension claims . . . has been a significant issue in this case." 524 B.R. at 180.

> "It is therefore a vast understatement to say that the pension settlement is reasonable. It borders on the miraculous. No one could have foreseen this result for the pension creditors when the City filed this case. Without the outside funding from the Grand Bargain, the City anticipated having to reduce pensions by as much as 27%. . . . The pension reductions . . . are minor compared to any reasonably foreseeable outcome for these creditors without the pension settlement and the Grand Bargain. At the same time, the Court recognizes that even these relatively minor pension reductions will cause real and, in some cases, severe hardships. However, this bankruptcy, like most, requires shared sacrifice because the City is insolvent. . . ."

Id. at 181–82. Indeed, the pensioners did better than most creditor groups other than the holders of secured debt and certain general obligation bonds. The court defended the higher rate of recovery for pensioners in terms of the City's nature as a "municipal service enterprise" with

> a "mission . . . to provide municipal services to its residents and visitors to promote their health, welfare, and safety. Its employees and retirees are and were the backbone of the structures by which the City fulfills its mission, The City, therefore, has a strong interest in preserving its relationships with its employees, in enhancing their motivation, and in attracting skilled new employees, consistent with its financial resources The City has reasonably and properly concluded that the discrimination in favor of the pension claims is necessary to its mission."

Id. at 257.

Although significant, the Grand Bargain was just one component of a very complex multi-part plan of adjustment. Some other key elements included:

- Creating a new governance structure for other post-employment benefits, with some reduction in benefits; after initial funding from City and private donor contributions, the City would be relieved from having to fund these benefits.

- Settlements with various bondholder groups, and swaps participants for less than their full claims.

- Creative settlements with the bond insurers involving the transfer of certain City properties, development rights, and a parking garage concession to entities controlled by the insurers. One settlement involved a development agreement in which the creditors would have the option to acquire and develop the land on which Joe Louis Arena and its garages sit. The City would demolish the structures and undertake any necessary environmental remediation, and cover the developer's eligible project costs and provide tax increment financing incentives. The court described this deal as a win-win for both the creditor and the City: "[T]he City has presented credible evidence that the Joe Louis Arena is currently considered a liability. . . . Because of this agreement, land that might have stood vacant and unused will become a shining demonstration of Detroit's recovery." 524 B.R. at 197.

- An agreement between the City and Wayne, Oakland, and Macomb Counties to create the Great Lakes Water Authority. These counties and their customers obtained their water and sewer services from the Detroit Water and Sewerage Department ("DWSD"). Under this deal, DWSD's assets would be transferred to the new authority, which would pay $428.5 million as DWSD's share of the public employee pension plan and other expenses.

- A commitment by the City to undertake $1.7 billion in restructuring and reinvestment initiatives focused on the remediation of residential blight; public safety; organizational efficiencies, including reforms in its finance and human resources department; and improvements to residential and business services.

- The City to be subject to oversight by a Financial Review Commission and committed to maintaining a cash balance equal to at least five percent of its annual projected expenditures.

Applying the statutory criteria that the plan of adjustment be proposed in good faith, feasible, not inconsistent with state law, in the best interest of the creditors, not unfairly discriminatory against dissenting creditors and fair and equitable to them, the court confirmed the plan of adjustment.

4.   *Municipal Bankruptcy After Detroit*. Municipal bankruptcies are rare. Between 1954 and the end of 2012 only 62 cities, towns, villages and counties filed for bankruptcy, and 29 of those petitions (46%) were dismissed without a plan of adjustment being filed. *See* James E. Spiotto, The Role of the State in Supervising and Assisting Municipalities, Especially in Times of Financial Distress, 34 Mun. Fin. J. 1, 28 (2013). Even the spike in filings during the Great Recession—with filings by Harrisburg, Jefferson County, Stockton, San Bernardino, and Detroit—was limited given the overall scope of municipal fiscal distress. Many filings involved unusual situations such as mismanaged large infrastructure projects or inability to pay multi-million dollar legal judgments. *See* Pew Charitable Trusts, After Municipal Bankruptcy 2 (August 2015). The first municipality to file for bankruptcy after Detroit was tiny Hillview, Kentucky, population 8,000, which was hit by a $11.4 million damages judgment in a contract dispute with a local company. *See* Elizabeth Campbell, Kentucky Town is First to File for Bankruptcy After Detroit, Aug. 20, 2015, Bloomberg Business. The scale of the Detroit bankruptcy was so different from any other municipal filing that it is uncertain what lessons ought to be drawn from the Detroit experience. But certain points are worth noting.

First, although the bankruptcy law assumes a relatively passive court whose only role is to evaluate a plan of adjustment proposed by the municipal debtor and no ability to alter municipal governance or state-city relations, the Detroit bankruptcy court was extremely active and effectively brokered many changes in governance structures and political relationships. As Professor Melissa Jacoby explains, the Detroit case involved "active case management, deal-making and heavy settlement promotion, building teams of court adjuncts who interacted extensively with city officials and other parties," intensive use of mediators, and a " 'court of the people' " process in which Judge Rhodes gathered information and policy recommendations from a wide range of participants including individual retirees and even residents who technically lacked creditor status. *See* Melissa B. Jacoby, Federalism Form and Function in the Detroit Bankruptcy, 33 Yale J. Reg. ___ (Winter 2016). She refers to this as the "Detroit Blueprint," which, although formally respectful of the federalism constraints built into the bankruptcy law, enabled the court to use its ultimate power to approve or reject a plan of adjustment to become "a significant institutional actor throughout Detroit's restructuring, via official court proceedings as well as behind the scenes." *Id.*

Second, the case indicates that when handled effectively by a judge who is able to obtain the cooperation of the governor, emergency manager, mayor and council, and leading stakeholders, bankruptcy can be a potentially positive experience for a city, involving not only the clearing of debts, but structural reforms, a new level of civic engagement, and a new commitment to investments in public services. On the other hand, not all bankruptcy experiences are as swift or as positive. Vallejo, California, for example, remained financially troubled even after emerging from bankruptcy. *See* After Municipal Bankruptcy, *supra*, at 7. And bankruptcy can be costly, with significant legal, mediator, and expert fees. *Id.* at 4. Should the Detroit experience make the residents of fiscally distressed cities less apprehensive about filing for bankruptcy?

Third, *Detroit* indicates that contractual pension benefits can be reduced in bankruptcy but that pensioners may still be treated more favorably than other creditors, including bondholders. However, preferential treatment of pensioners will not always be the case and states may do more to protect bondholders. Although the *Detroit* court concluded that the Michigan constitution's pension protection provision did not give pensioners a protected legal interest that a bankruptcy court must respect, bankruptcy courts will prioritize claims that are specially protected by the state. When Central Falls, Rhode Island was in fiscal distress and on the verge of bankruptcy, the state passed a law securing municipal general obligation bonds with a statutory lien on property taxes and general fund revenues. R.I. Gen. L. § 45–12–1. That enabled general obligation bondholders to receive full and uninterrupted payment of debt service and may have contributed to Central Falls's relatively short stay in bankruptcy. Following the Detroit bankruptcy, California passed a similar law and other states are considering such a measure. *See* Liz Farmer, In Post-Detroit Bankruptcy Era, California Protects Investors Before Pensioners. Governing, July 30, 2015. A bankruptcy proceeding in a state that gives a security lien, and thus payment priority, to bondholders, could result in a plan of adjustment quite different from Detroit's. Such laws can be "credit positive" for local governments, *id.* But how do they square with what Judge Rhodes referred to as the municipal services "mission" of a city?

3.   STATE FISCAL CONCERNS

The 2007–09 recession also subjected many states to fiscal distress. State government tax revenues were hit much harder than the overall economy, plunging twelve percent nationwide between 2008 and 2010, with even steeper drops in certain large states like California (14.9%), Texas (15.4%) and Illinois (18.7%). *See* Report of the State Budget Crisis Task Force 8 (July 2012). Even as the states struggled to balance their budgets by cutting expenditures, the recession led to increased demands for social safety net spending. States turned to a host of gimmicks— including sales of assets, raids on dedicated funds, and stalling on payments to vendors—to close budget gaps. Some resorted to "securitizing" future revenue streams, that is, issuing bonds backed by a revenue source that otherwise would have provided annual revenue for the state, effectively borrowing from the future to pay current costs. *See id.* at 58, 60. Some simply issued bonds to raise the money to cover their operating expenditures. The "wall of debt" used to fund California's 2012–13 operating budget was estimated at $28 billion. *Id.* at 59. During the period of greatest state fiscal stress, there was serious consideration, at least within the scholarly community, of the possibility of permitting

STATE AND LOCAL FINANCE

states to file for bankruptcy or, in the alternative, of providing for emergency federal intervention in state finances comparable to state emergency intervention in local finances. *See, e.g.,* Peter Conti-Brown & David A. Skeel, Jr., eds., When States Go Broke: The Origins, Context, and Solutions for the American States in Fiscal Crisis (Cambridge Univ. Press 2012); Peter Conti-Brown, 7 Duke J. Const. L. & Pub. Pol. 43 (2012); David A. Skeel, Jr., States of Bankruptcy, 79 U. Chi. L. Rev. 677 (2012). State bankruptcy raises a host of constitutional and operational issues, and the issue faded as the post-recession economic recovery strengthened. But the recession surely "exposed fiscal problems that states were able to avoid or defer" during periods of prosperity. *See* Budget Crisis Task Force, *supra,* at 13. A full analysis of state fiscal concerns is beyond the scope of this casebook, but three points relevant to both the recent fiscal crisis and state finances going forward are worthy of note.

First, state tax systems are increasingly subject to economic shocks and are becoming inadequate to meeting state spending needs. *See id.* at 46–53; Josh Barro, Structural Challenges in State Budgeting, in When States Go Broke, *supra,* at 77–86. The share of state revenues from sales taxes and personal and corporate income taxes has grown over time, but these taxes are particularly vulnerable during economic downturns. The sales tax is a tax on consumption, but consumer spending drops during a recession and some of the mainstays of the sales tax, like the sale of durable goods, are likely to be particularly hard hit. Income tax revenues are even more threatened when a recession increases unemployment and leads to reduced working hours even for those who are employed. If a state has a progressive income tax, with higher levels of income taxed at higher rates, then when an individual loses income not only will there be less income to tax but it may be taxed at a lower rate. "High-income taxpayers tend to have especially volatile incomes," in part because a relatively large share of their income consists of capital gains, which may be especially hard hit during a recession. *See id.* at 81. Even in prosperous times, the sales tax base has been eroded by the shift of the economy from goods to services, which are often exempt from taxation, and to Internet sales. Although online sales are subject to tax, as a practical matter states have limited capacity to get online-only retailers to collect and remit the tax. *See id* at 83.

Second, the recession revealed problems with state budget practices. The constitutions or statutes of forty-nine states—the exception is Vermont—require balanced budgets, but they frequently fail to define the budget subject to the requirement or such basic fiscal concepts as "revenue." *See, e.g.,* The Volcker Alliance, Truth and Integrity in State Budgeting 3 (2015). *See also* Isabel Rodriguez-Tejedo and John Joseph Wallis, Fiscal Institutions and Fiscal Crises in When States Go Broke, *supra*, at 15–19. With rare exceptions, courts have been extremely reluctant to enforce balanced budget requirements. *See, e.g.,* Wein v. Carey, 41 N.Y.2d 498 (N.Y. 1977); Bishop v. Government of Maryland, 380 A.2d 220 (Md. 1977). *See generally* Richard Briffault, Courts, Constitutions and Public Finance in Elizabeth Garrett, Elizabeth A. Graddy & Howell E. Jackson, eds., Fiscal Challenges: An Interdisciplinary Approach to Budget Policy 428–30 (Cambridge Univ. Press 2008). For the rare exception, *see* Lance v. McGreevey, 853 A.2d 856 (N.J. 2005). Consequently, many states resort to "short-term budget sleight of hand to make it appear that spending does not exceed revenue. The techniques include shifting the timing of receipts and expenditures across fiscal years; borrowing long term to fund current expenditures; employing nonrecurring revenue sources to cover recurring costs; and delaying funding of public worker pension obligations and other postemployment benefits (OPEB), principally retiree health care." Volcker Alliance, *supra*, at 3. While these actions may enable a state to get through a fiscal crisis without disrupting services or raising taxes, they add to the bills that future taxpayers have to pay and "the long-term consequences require a continued search for plugs to fill gaps in future budget cycles." *Id.* This may lead to fiscal vulnerability in future downturns. More generally, these maneuvers undermine fiscal transparency, making it more difficult for the public and even some lawmakers to grasp the true status of the state's finances.

As the recession demonstrated, state budgeting suffers from a short-term focus. In thirty states, the budget is a one-year document; in the remaining states it covers two years, although some provide for the possibility of revision after one year. Volcker Alliance, *supra*, at 7. Short-term cash-based budgeting leads a state to structure its budgetary decision-making just to get through the current fiscal year. This can lead to the failure to maintain reserve—or "rainy day"—funds needed for economic downturns, the sale of assets for less than their value, failure to fund long-term needs like maintenance and replacement of public infrastructure, and, similarly, failure to maintain actuarially sound public employee pension systems. *Id.* at 16–17.

Third, the funding of pension plans has been a particularly contentious issue. Many state and local employee pension plans are chronically underfunded, and the underfunding problem was exacerbated by the recession. Pension plans are supported by the investment of government-contributed (and some employee-contributed) funds in income-producing assets. When, during the recession, market values dropped sharply, governments had to contribute more, even as government revenues also fell and other expenses rose. *See, e.g.,* Amy B. Monahan, State Fiscal Constitutions and the Law and Politics of Public Pensions, 2015 U. Ill. L. Rev. 117, 120, 130. *Accord*, Olivia S, Mitchell,

Public Pension Pressures in the United States, in When States Go Broke, *supra*, at 60. In the 2007–2011 period, states and local governments underpaid their annually required contributions to their public employee pension plans by $50 billion. *See* Budget Crisis Task Force, *supra*, at 36–38.

Elected officials may be tempted to underfund pension plans—sometimes by relying on unduly rosy projections of the likely market returns on the funds already in the plans, and sometimes by simply failing to make the contributions that even their own calculations of pension plan finances would require them to make. Governments in California, Illinois, and New Jersey underpaid their pension contributions before the recession, during the recession, and after the recession. Due to prior contributions to the funds, there was usually enough money in the pension plans to pay current-year pension obligations—which were earned by current retirees in the past when they were active public employees. But such a "pay-as-you-go" approach shifts the costs of paying pension compensation for this year's workers on to future taxpayers and makes the availability of adequate funding in the future uncertain, especially in jurisdictions that are trimming their workforces. Over time, as in Detroit, a growing share of taxpayer dollars goes to paying the "legacy" costs of pensions—and other benefits, like health insurance—attributable to retired employees, rather than for the public employees providing current services. Indeed, in 2011 more than 20% of all revenues received by the state of Illinois were required to pay for public employee pensions. *See* Mitchell, *supra*, at 66. Under current actuarial assumptions, state and local pensions are underfunded by nearly $1 trillion. Some economists have argued that this number actually reflects unduly optimistic assumptions about future market returns on invested funds, so that the underfunded amount is even bigger. Budget Crisis Task Force, *supra,* at 35.

Critics note that public sector pension plans are often more generous than private sector plans. Public plans are primarily "defined benefit" plans in which employees are guaranteed a stream of benefits in retirement, with the amounts based on the retiree's salary and years of services. By contrast, most private sector employees have defined contribution plans, in which contributions to the plan are made as a specified percentage of compensation but no particular payment is specified. *See* Mitchell, *supra*, at 58. As a result, public sector pensions often replace a higher percentage of pay for employees than do private sector pensions. *Id.* at 57. Moreover, when, during periods of prosperity, a pension system appears to be well-funded, governments face pressure from employees and retirees to enhance their benefits by, for example, lowering eligibility ages, providing more generous cost-of-living adjustments (COLAs), or defining the salary base for the retirement benefit in terms of the employee's most-highly-paid salary periods. *See* Budget Crisis Task Force, *supra*, at 41–42. On the other hand, it is worth noting that a number of states and local governments do not participate in the Social Security system and so their employees are more dependent on their pensions than their private sector counterparts, Mitchell, *supra*, at 59, and that public pensions are not protected by the Pension Benefit Guaranty Corp.

In response to the recession many states made major changes in their pension plans and retiree benefits. "Between 2009 and 2011, 43 states either increased employee contributions or cut benefits or both." *Id.* at 42. Some of these changes triggered legal disputes. Pension plans are often parts of collective bargaining agreements or other contracts protected by the Contracts Clause and state constitutional equivalents, and many state constitutions—such as Arizona, Hawaii, Illinois, Michigan, and Oregon—include provisions specifically providing that state pensions or retirement systems constitute "an enforceable contractual relationship, the benefits of which shall not be diminished or impaired." States may generally be able to provide for lower benefits for—or greater employee contributions from—new hires without constitutional difficulty. *But cf.* Retired State Employees Ass'n v. State of Louisiana, 119 So.32d 568 (La. 2013) (state constitutional requirement that changes to any pension plan "benefit provisions having an actuarial cost" be approved by two-thirds of each house of the legislature to be effective applies even to changes that affect only new hires). But that does little to reduce current pension fund contribution requirements, so some states have sought to increase contributions from and reduce future cost-of-living adjustments for current employees.

In 2013–15, several state supreme courts considered challenges to state laws cutting retirement benefits or increasing employee costs. These cases often involved analysis of state constitutional provisions protecting contracts or pension benefits specifically. As befits the difficult issues raised by these cases, there was no clear pattern to the decisions. But the cases, and the laws they considered, illustrate the nature of the pension plan problem for state finances.

Sometimes the state prevailed. The Florida Supreme Court, for example, reasoned that changes that did not diminish the benefits available to persons already retired as of the 2011 effective date of the law could be applied to current employees—even though "the changes diminish the total expected retirement benefits that could have accrued over the entire projected life" of the employee's state employment—without violating the Contracts Clause or the state constitution's protection of collective bargaining. Scott v. Williams, 107 So.3d 379, 386 (Fla. 2013). The changes did not impair "any benefits tied to service performed prior to the amendment date" and so were considered "prospective changes within the authority of the legislature to make." *Id.* at 389. Similarly, the Michigan Supreme Court upheld a 2012 statute that increased the contributions required of current public school employees to pay for retiree health care and for their pension plans. The court noted that the employees could opt out of the increases. If so, they would receive smaller pension benefit increases than the employees who chose to pay the higher contributions. With respect to the health benefit, they could opt entirely out of the retiree health care program and instead make an employer-matched contribution into a special account—or make no contribution at all. The court determined that by providing the opt-outs the state avoided any impairment of contract as the employees were not compelled to make the additional payments. AFT Michigan v. State of Michigan, 866 N.W.2d 782 (Mich. 2015). The court also determined that employees had no contractual right to the pre-existing higher pension increase level that the 2012 law conditioned on payment of an additional contribution. The court emphasized its sympathy with the state's need to adjust to "changing fiscal conditions," *id.* at 792, in "balancing and limiting a strained public budget," *id.* at 810.

The Supreme Court of Oregon was more sympathetic to that state's public employees. Although it agreed that the state could reduce the COLA for benefits earned on or after the effective date of the 2013 law cutting benefits, it held that the state could not reduce the future COLAs of current employees with respect to benefits earned before the effective date of the law. Moro v. State of Oregon, 351 P.3d 1 (Ore, 2015). Applying the Contracts Clause analysis of *United States Trust Co. v. New Jersey*, 431 U.S. 1 (1977)—discussed in Section C of this chapter—to the Oregon Constitution's Contracts Clause, the court concluded that the state pension plan was a contract between the state and its public employees, that the pre-2013 COLA provisions were part of that contract, and that the COLA reduction was an impairment. 351 P.3d at 18–38. The court then rejected the state's claim that the changes were "reasonable and necessary to an important public purpose." The court noted the state's argument that the changes would reduce the amount the state had to contribute to the pension system, thereby freeing up more money for other public services, like public safety and education, without having to increase taxes. *Id.* at 38–39. But it concluded that the state had failed to show either that current public service funding levels were inadequate or that the state was unable to raise taxes to cover any additional spending. *Id.*

The Illinois Supreme Court was even more protective of public employees and critical of the state. In Kanerva v. Weems, 13 N.E.3d 1228 (Ill. 2014), the court held that provisions of the state's retirement program that obligated the state to contribute to the costs of the retiree insurance health plan and survivor benefits were part of the pension system benefits protected by the state constitution's prohibition of the impairment or diminishment of pension benefits. *Id.* at 1240. *Accord,* Everson v. State of Hawaii, 228 P.3d 282 (Hawaii 2010). As a result, the court struck down a 2012 law providing for an increase in the contribution to the plan required of retired public employees. 13 N.E.3d at 1244.

Kanerva protected the interests of current retirees. The next year, in In re Pension Reform Litigation, 32 N.E.3d 1 (Ill. 2015), the court went further and invalidated much of a 2014 law that reduced retirement benefits of pre-existing employees by delaying for up to five years the eligibility of younger employees for retirement benefits; capping the maximum salary that could be considered in calculating the monthly retirement payment; limiting the rate of annual increases and eliminating some increases; and making other changes that would result in smaller base pensions for some employees. *Id.* at 11. The court noted that the changes were driven by the fact that the state-funded retirement systems were underfunded, containing only 41% of the funding necessary to meet their accrued liabilities based on the market value of their assets. *Id.* at 9. Even in 2013, after the worst of the recession had passed, the state was "experiencing significant difficulties in meeting its other obligations" and had "implemented a variety of measures, including delaying payments to creditors and vendors who do business with the State, reducing or eliminating a variety of governmental programs, enacting a temporary income tax increase," and reducing pension benefits for new hires. *Id.* at 10. Yet, as the court also caustically noted, Illinois's history of underfunded pension plans long predated the recession. The funding rate had been just 41.8% in 1970—which had led to the inclusion of the Pension Protection Clause when the state adopted a new constitution that year. *Id.* at 6, 10. In its analysis, the Illinois Supreme Court quickly concluded that the various pension provisions amended by the 2014 law were part of the contract-based pension benefits protected by the Pension Protection Clause, even though they affected only future benefits. *Id.* at 18. *Accord,* Fields v. Elected Officials' Retirement Plan, 320 P.3d 1160 (Ariz. 2014). The Court then turned to—and quickly dismissed—the state's principal argument that given the state's dire fiscal situation its " 'reserved sovereign powers,' i.e., its police powers" authorized it to disregard the Pension Protection Clause. Invoking *U.S. Trust v. New Jersey, supra,* the court noted the United States Supreme Court's concern "that particular scrutiny of legislative action is warranted when, as here, a state seeks to impair a contract to which it is itself a party and its interest in avoiding the contract or changing its terms is financial." 32 N.E.3d at 21. The Illinois court found that Illinois's pension funding problems were not a surprise but "entirely forseeable" so that the amendments could not be justified as a "reasonable and necessary" response to an unanticipated emergency. "[A]ccepting the State's position that reducing retirement benefits is justified by economic circumstances would require that we allow the legislature to do the very thing the pension protection clause was designed to prevent it from doing." *Id.* at 25.

The last of the major 2015 pension funding decisions involved New Jersey, another state with a severe underfunding problem. In 1997, the state by statute granted to members of the public pension funds a " 'non-forfeitable right to receive benefits,' a right defined to mean that benefits could not be reduced once the right to them attached." Burgos v. State, 118 A.3d 270 (N.J. 2015) (quoting N.J.S.A. 43:3C–9.5(a)-(b)). Between 1997 and 2012, the state repeatedly failed to make its annual required contribution to the plans; indeed, it had paid less than ten percent of its statutorily required contribution into the pension system. *Id.* at 301 (Albin, J., dissenting). "Successive legislatures and administrations balanced yearly budgets while shortchanging the fund necessary to make good the deferred compensation owed to public workers." *Id.* In 2011, in a "historic compromise," the state finally began to tackle the problem. Public employees agreed to accept greater pension deductions from their paychecks in exchange for a commitment by the state to close the underfunding gap by making a payment to the pension funds equal to one-seventh of the actuarially-determined funding gap each year for seven years, so that the plans would be fully funded by the end of fiscal year 2018. To assure the employees that the state would live up to its end of the bargain, the 2011 law provided that the annual required contribution would be included as a line item in the annual appropriation act, that each member of the state's pension system would have "a contractual right to the annual required contribution amount being made," and that the state's failure to make the required annual contribution "shall be deemed to be an impairment of the contractual right of each employee." N.J.S.A. 43:3C–9.5(c). The state made its required contributions for the first two fiscal years, but in 2014 Governor Chris Christie announced that due to a "severe and unanticipated revenue shortfall" the state would make less than half its required 2014 contribution. Subsequently the Governor item-vetoed the legislature's appropriation of the full pension contribution required by the 2011 law for the next fiscal year, cutting the state's payment to about 43% of the amount due. 118 A.3d at 278–79.

When members of the pension funds sued, a divided New Jersey Supreme Court held that the "contractual right" language in the statute did not actuallycreate a legally binding commitment because of the state's Debt Limitation Clause—which had previously received the court's sustained attention in the *Lonegan* litigation considered in Section C of this chapter. The majority reasoned that such a contractual commitment was like bonded debt. Under the Debt Limitation Clause, "the State cannot by contract or statute create a binding and legally enforceable financial obligation above a certain amount that applies year to year without voter approval," *id,* at 284–85, and the 2011 pension deal had not been approved by the voters. Consequently, despite the "contractual" language, the state's pension funding commitment was no more binding than the subject-to-appropriation commitments upheld in *Lonegan.* The state was free to make the commitment and to live up to it through annual appropriations, but it was also free not to appropriate to the pension plan the annual contributions called for by statute.

Despite stronger investment returns since the end of the recession and many legislative reforms adopted by the states during and after the recession, pensions, along with unfunded retiree health care costs, remain significant long-term obligations for most states. The shortfall in pension funding is expected to continue in the $800–$900 billion range in the near future. Pew Charitable Trusts, The State Pensions Funding Gap: Challenges Persist (July 14, 2015). Indeed, in most states, pensions and other employee-retirement-related expenses were a greater long-term obligation than public debt. *See* Pew Charitable Trusts, Size of Long-term Obligations Varies Across States (August 19, 2014). Some states continue to turn to risky investment strategies to cover the pension funding gap while minimizing the impact on state budgets. *See* Pew Charitable Trusts Stateline, Despite Risks, State and Local Governments Turn to Pension Obligation Bonds (Aug, 12, 2015). As one pension scholar put it, "[a]t the end of the day, the size of the public pension shortfall remains dauntingly large and discouragingly expensive to fix." Mitchell, *supra, at 70.*

CHAPTER VII

THE BUSINESS OF GOVERNMENT

∎ ∎ ∎

A. LOCAL SERVICE DELIVERY

Local governments provide a wide array of services, including such basic activities as police and fire protection, primary and secondary education, water supply and waste removal, and the maintenance of streets and highways. Three factors typically affect the range of services offered by general purpose governments: the degree of urbanization; the strength of the local tax base; and the preferences of the residents as reflected in the local political process. This section considers the role of the courts and legal requirements in shaping and constraining local government service delivery decisions.

1. DUTY TO PROVIDE SERVICES

ADAMS V. BRADSHAW
Supreme Court of New Hampshire
599 A.2d 481 (1991)

THAYER, JUSTICE.

* * *

Most of the relevant facts of this case are not in dispute. The Town[1] built a sewer system in 1932 to service properties in its village area. In its present state, this system collects raw sewage from approximately fifty properties and spews it, untreated, into the Connecticut River. In 1971, the Town voted to establish a capital reserve fund for the purpose of constructing a sewage disposal unit, and voted several times thereafter to transfer tax revenue into this fund. Twice the Town hired engineers to study the feasibility of various sewage disposal options, but made no move to build a disposal unit. These engineers did not discuss construction of individual septic systems on the affected properties as an alternative to a type of wastewater treatment facility.

---

[1] [Editors' note: The New England "town" is similar to what is called a township in other parts of the country. However, towns frequently exercise broad powers similar to general purpose local governments. Their territory may, as in this case, include villages and other incorporated forms of local government.]

973

Meanwhile, the Town learned that its State and federal permits to pollute the Connecticut River would expire on July 1, 1988, and would not be renewed. In May 1987, the Town asked the State Water Supply and Pollution Control Division (the WSPCD) to determine the feasibility of individual septic systems in lieu of the Town's sewer. The WSPCD completed its study in August 1987, and informed the Town in mid-September that a wastewater treatment facility for the sewer could not be designed and constructed in time to meet the State and federal July 1, 1988, deadline.

Thus, the defendants turned to subsurface disposal options. At a special town meeting[2] in November 1987, the Town voted to hire engineers "to design individual on-site subsurface disposal systems for the present users of the Monroe Town Sewer System," and to pay for their services out of the Town's capital reserve fund, which at that time totalled approximately $200,000. * * *

The July 1, 1988, deadline arrived, but the Town continued to operate its sewer in violation of State and federal law. As a result, the State sued the Town. The plaintiffs also sued the Town, and the selectmen individually. * * *

In February 1989, before the trial court took any action on the petition, the Town held a special meeting to determine the fate of the Town sewer, and to decide what, if anything, it should do to help the village property owners dispose of their sewage. A majority of the Town citizens voted to completely abandon the Town sewer and leave the village property owners to their own devices. The townspeople also passed Article 5, allowing the Town to construct individual subsurface disposal systems for Town-owned buildings located in the village area. The plaintiffs * * * requested the trial court to:

"order the Defendants not to expend money for the purposes set forth in Article 5 as voted on February 10, 1989 for the lack of a valid appropriation and valid vote to withdraw funds from the capital reserve fund . . . [;]

enter an order preventing the abandonment of the village sewer system . . . [; and]

enter an order compelling the Town to construct a wastewater treatment plant in compliance with State and federal requirements and that the cost of the plant be paid by the Town and the users charged for operation and maintenance."

---

    [2]   [Editors' note: Another unusual feature of New Hampshire local government structure is the town meeting, where citizens participate directly in local government by casting their votes on pending legislation.]

In April 1989, the Town and the State entered into a consent decree in the State's lawsuit against the Town. The decree gave the Town a new deadline of October 15, 1989, for ending its discharge of raw sewage into the river. Several property owners in the village area constructed septic systems during the ensuing months and ceased utilization of the Town sewer. But by the time of the superior court's order in this case, the sewer was still in operation, and was still pumping untreated sewage into the river.

The superior court, by order dated March 13, 1990, ruled that both the expenditure of money from the capital reserve fund and the vote to discontinue the Town sewer were legal. * * * The court went on, however, to rule that discontinuance of the sewer constitutes inverse condemnation, requiring just compensation by the Town, and enjoined discontinuance of the sewer pending any appeal or suit by the individual property owners for just compensation. * * *

We first address the plaintiffs' argument that the Town had no authority to discontinue its sewer service to the residents of the village area. The plaintiffs state in their brief that * * * "[o]nce a town has chosen to provide a town sewer system, the town cannot withdraw that essential service because of water pollution but, rather, . . . must take the necessary steps to abate the water pollution."

We disagree. RSA 149–I:1 grants municipalities the authority to "construct and maintain" sewers and declares that a sewer constructed by a municipality "shall be the property of the [municipality]." Thus, "[a] sewerage system constructed by a municipal corporation is its property and its right to regulate and control the use of it is a necessary incident of its ownership." *Mitchel v. Dover*, 98 N.H. 285, 289, 99 A.2d 409, 412 (1953).

Concomitant with the right to regulate and control one's property is the right to dispose of it as one sees fit, and no statutory language is needed to support this self-evident principle. "Courts generally regard public sewers and drains as the property of the municipal corporations in which they are built, and they may be protected and controlled as any other property of the municipality, and no private person has the right to interfere with them." E. McQuillin, The Law of Municipal Corporations § 31.29, at 259 (3d ed.1991). Under most circumstances, a municipality may discontinue its sewer, leaving those previously served by it to dispose of their sewage by other means. * * *

The defendants had ample cause to revoke the plaintiffs' license to use the Town sewer; it became a nuisance, as evidenced by the State's suit against the Town for polluting the Connecticut River without a permit. Although the trial court found that three affected properties are incapable of supporting on-site septic systems (a finding which the defendants contest), the defendants aver that the Town will work creatively with these property owners to ensure that no one is forced to vacate his or her property solely because of a sewer shutdown. The defendants' apparent willingness to accommodate the village property owners as much as possible in their search for new means to dispose of their sewage, where such accommodation was not necessarily required, strengthens our conclusion that the defendants had cause to discontinue the Town sewer.

The plaintiffs' second argument is that the Town's decision to choose discontinuance of the sewer over construction of a wastewater treatment facility violates part I, article 12 of the New Hampshire Constitution. This argument actually consists of two assertions. First, the Town should have voted to construct a wastewater treatment facility. We cannot, however, second-guess a Town's decision to spare its taxpayers the cost of a treatment facility. * * * "A municipality's decision not to make major capital improvements to an existing drainage system is immune as a discretionary decision." E. McQuillin § 31.17, at 230. * * *

The second part of the plaintiffs' argument is that the Town's decision to discontinue the sewer constituted a taking without just compensation, in violation of part I, article 12; in other words, inverse condemnation. The trial court agreed with the plaintiffs on this issue and the defendants appeal that ruling, arguing that the plaintiffs have no vested property right in the Town sewer. * * *

Eugene McQuillin's treatise is a respected authority on the subject of municipal corporations. He states that "the right given to a property owner to connect with a municipal sewer . . . does not become a vested right merely because the user was put to considerable expense in constructing a drain from the premises and connecting it with the sewer." E. McQuillin § 31.31, at 289. A municipality may, he asserts, disconnect a property owner's drain from a sewer for cause "without being liable to the owner of the drain in damages." *Id.*

This view apparently has been accepted by all states confronted with the issue. * * *

In view of this weight of authority and sound reasoning, we also hold that a property owner has no vested right in a sewer connection. The plaintiffs' attempt to distinguish the above-cited cases because each involved one sewer line and not an entire municipal sewer system requires little comment. A property owner does not gain a vested right in a sewer system simply because the neighbors are similarly situated. In the absence of a property right, no taking for purposes of part I, article 12 of the State Constitution has occurred, * * * and we therefore reverse the trial court's finding of inverse condemnation. * * *

FIRST PEOPLES BANK OF NEW JERSEY V. TOWNSHIP OF MEDFORD

Supreme Court of New Jersey
599 A.2d 1248 (1991)

POLLOCK, J.

First Peoples Bank of New Jersey (the Bank) challenges both facially and as applied the sewer ordinance of Medford Township (Medford or the Township). In unreported opinions, the Law Division and the Appellate Division sustained the ordinance. We granted the Bank's petition for certification and now affirm.

I

In the mid-1970s Medford experienced rapid land use development that overburdened the municipal sewer system. Consequently, the New Jersey Department of Environmental Protection (DEP) imposed a sewer connection ban. Medford's initial response was to adopt a "Flow Equalization Plan," which involved the use of holding tanks to store effluent during peak periods. By 1983, the sewer plant was again at its limit. DEP imposed a second sewer ban ordering the Township to increase the capacity of its pumping station. Land use development came to a halt. The Township's need to construct additional sewer capacity, combined with the problems of financing the construction, led to the enactment of ordinances 1983–10 and –11.

Not challenged on this appeal is ordinance 1983–10, which appropriates $4.6 million to increase the capacity of the Township's sewage treatment plant from 1.3 to 1.75 million gallons a day. Instead, the Bank challenges ordinance 1983–11, which provides for the administration of the increased sewer capacity.

The intent of the ordinance, according to section 1, is "to establish the rules and regulations for connections to the Sewage Treatment Plant upon expansion, and to establish appropriate fees for the repayment of such notes and bonds as may be issued in order to finance and pay for the expansion to said plant." In that section, the governing body found that

it is in the best interest of the Township to establish a priority list such that proposed users of the system desiring to connect to the system can pay for said connections and receive priority in and to the additional capacity to be generated by virtue of said expansion, subject, however, to the rights and interests of the Township to control the allocation of said capacity in the best interests of the Township and its residents in order that said reservation of capacity is not irrevocably committed to a proposed user who may not construct and/or build a project using part of the expanded capacity.

Thus, the ordinance contemplated the receipt of connection fees to pay for the additional capacity. It also contemplated that Medford would control the issuance of connection permits "in the best interests of the Township."

The central feature of the ordinance provides property owners with the option to purchase connection permits before obtaining municipal land use approvals. * * *

The purpose of the provision allowing a developer to purchase sewer permits before obtaining final approval is to finance the cost of sewer plant improvements and to retire the debt incurred for those improvements. Consistent with this purpose, the cost of permit fees escalated annually until 1987. In effect, the ordinance granted a "discount" for the early purchase of permits.

The Township retains control over sold, but unused, permits in section 4H(1)(h), which provides:

> At such time as the committed capacity of the sewage treatment plant equals seventy-five per cent (75%) of the total permitted treatment or design capacity of the sewage treatment plant, and at any time thereafter, the Township may elect, at Township's sole option, to repurchase said permit. This repurchase shall be accomplished by giving written notice to the record owner of any said permit, stating the Township's intention to repurchase six (6) months from the date of said notice.

So essential to the project was the sale of permits that the Township attorney in December 1983 sent a letter to the owners of property who had received land use approvals or who would "require the use of public sewer when the property is developed." The letter warned that "unless there is financial cooperation from those landowners who will benefit from the additional capacity, the project cannot be completed." * * *

The Bank received the letter, but did not purchase any permits.

The plant's increased capacity of 450,000 gallons per day enabled Medford to make available 1,800 additional permits for sewer connections. * * *

In total, the Township issued 1,770 of 1,800 permits, reserving 30 permits for emergency purposes. It then temporarily suspended the further issuance of sewer permits. Two days later the Bank unsuccessfully sought several sewer permit applications. * * * [O]n May 3, 1988, [the Township] imposed a sewer moratorium. The Bank thereupon challenged the validity of the ordinance and requested a court order directing Medford to accommodate the development of the Bank's property by expanding the capacity of the sewage plant or by repurchasing unused permits.

II

A

* * * Expansion of a sewage treatment plant to serve future development is both costly and uncertain. In the early stages, the number of users may not suffice to bear the capital cost of construction. Borrowed capital may not be available without assurance of the success of the development to be served by the plant. * * *

Confronted with a lack of sewage capacity and concerned about its ability to finance construction, the Township devised a system to raise the funds to finance the expansion of plant capacity. The Township's concern about raising revenue is reflected in the fee schedule, which provides that sewer permits purchased in 1983 would cost only $2,000, and that the fee would gradually escalate until 1987 and thereafter, when a permit would cost $4,000. Furthermore, the maximum number of permits a landowner could purchase is tied to the number of units that can be built on the owner's land. In sum, the plan is rationally related to a legitimate governmental purpose, the financing and allocation of sewage capacity.

Furthermore, the system allowed equal access to all developers. Any property owner, including the Bank, could have purchased the permits. All potential owners received the notice of sewer capacity expansion, and all knew of the limited supply of existing permits. In effect, the ordinance required developers to decide whether to purchase permits. The Bank decided not to make any such purchase. * * * Neither the ordinance nor its implementation disadvantaged any developer in deciding whether to purchase permits. The playing field was level.

B

In this Court, the dispute about the reasonableness of the ordinance centers on section 4H(1)(h), which governs the repurchase by the Township of unused permits. The Bank contends that the ordinance does not contain adequate standards to guide the municipality in determining whether to exercise its option to repurchase. * * *

The Bank argues that by selling all remaining permits * * *, the Township has effectively prevented the Bank from developing its land. The Township acknowledges that it may not use the absence of adequate sewer capacity as a means of preventing otherwise-permissible land use development. All parties agree that the Township must retain sufficient control to assure that sewer permits are either used or repurchased so that others may use them. Without an adequate repurchase provision, the ordinance could result in the improper delegation of access to the sewer system to private landowners who, by purchasing permits, could prevent other owners from developing their land.

The inquiry thus becomes a search for adequate standards to guide the exercise of municipal discretion when considering the repurchase of permits. * * *

We * * * find that the challenged ordinance, although not exquisitely drafted, contains sufficient standards to withstand the Bank's challenge. * * *

Section 1 of the challenged ordinance provides that the allocation system is subject to the rights and interests of the Township to control the allocation of said capacity in the best interests of the Township and its residents in order that said reservation of capacity is not irrevocably committed to a proposed user who may not construct and/or build a project using part of the expanded capacity. Additionally, the preamble of ordinance 1983–10, the companion ordinance to 1983–11, indicates the general policy goals governing the municipality's right of repurchase. The relevant provisions state:

> * * *
>
> WHEREAS, the Township Council desires to renovate the existing Sewage Treatment Plant which will increase the design capacity of the plant and enable the conversion to a tertiary treatment process in order to provide for the highest quality treatment possible for the protection of Township residents, downstream owners and adjoining municipalities; and
>
> * * *
>
> WHEREAS, the Township Council remains concerned that there are sufficient customers of the water and sewer utility to equitably spread the cost of maintaining and operating the utility in order to keep annual usage rates as reasonable as possible; and
>
> WHEREAS, the utilization of public sewer will allow moderate growth within the designated growth areas, particularly commercial and light industrial development that will insure a sufficient mix and variety of tax ratables to promote a stable tax base in the municipality.

From those clauses we glean that Medford, when exercising its right of repurchase, must consider the public health, safety, and welfare, a reasonable and equitable allocation of costs, and the allowance of moderate growth.

Nothing indicates that the Township has acted arbitrarily in deciding whether to exercise its repurchase option. If the Township were to so act, a court might direct it to exercise its option to repurchase. * * * At oral argument, the Township's attorney informed us that the Township had repurchased approximately fifteen permits and that it was considering the repurchase of others. * * *

III

The final question is whether this Court should order the Township to expand the sewer plant to provide sufficient capacity for the Bank's development. The lower courts refused to issue such an order, characterizing the matter as a nonjusticiable political question. We need not go so far as to say that courts may never order an expansion of sewer capacity. It suffices to hold that the facts of this case do not justify such an intrusion in municipal affairs.

* * *

Here, Medford has not been arbitrary or unreasonable in implementing the ordinance. All developers enjoyed equal access to the limited supply of sewer permits. The challenged ordinance is a reasonable, if homespun, attempt to meet the sewage treatment needs of a developing community.

This is not a case in which a municipality has rigidly refused to construct needed sewer capacity. The record does not support an inference that Medford's refusal "is the result of a determination not to discharge a plain duty. . . ." * * * Because of a municipality's greater familiarity with local conditions and expertise in constructing sewer capacity, a court should supplant the exercise of municipal discretion only in a compelling case. This is not such a case.

The judgment of the Appellate Division is affirmed.

NOTES AND QUESTIONS

1. *The Extent of Municipal Discretion.* The *Adams* court echoed the general rule that, in the absence of a statutory mandate, municipalities have broad discretion to deny services. Yet it also noted that the town was willing to help the village property owners find new sources of sewage treatment, and that the current sewer system violated state and federal law. The court stressed that the town had "ample cause" to shut down the sewer. What if those facts were not present? Do you think the court would still uphold the town's decision? *See also* Sunset Cay, LLC v. City of Folly Beach, 593 S.E.2d 462 (S.C. 2004) (refusing to force city to extend sewer system outside central commercial district); Chicago Association of Commerce and Industry v. Regional Transportation Authority, 427 N.E.2d 153 (Ill.1981) (refusing to order restoration of discontinued transportation services); Commonwealth v. Carroll County Fiscal Court, 633 S.W.2d 720 (Ky.App.1982) (refusing to order county to build its own jail; upholding decision to pay to house prisoners in other jurisdictions).

Citizen reliance on municipal services does not appear to constrain local discretion to end a service. In City of Prattville v. Joyner, 698 So.2d 122 (Ala.1997), the court reversed an earlier application of estoppel to prevent a municipality from terminating services. It concluded that the plaintiffs' reliance to their detriment on the provision of services should not interfere with a local government's flexibility in making service allocation decisions.

2.   *Duty to Provide Services?* What role should the courts play in determining whether a locality has a duty to provide services? Do the opportunities for political participation in local decision-making and to exit to another locality adequately protect local residents and make judicial intervention inappropriate? Is there a greater case for judicial intervention when a locality refuses to provide a generally available service to a particular resident as opposed to the locality's decision not to provide the service at all?

3.   *Reasonable Refusal to Provide Services.* By adopting the general standard that municipal refusals to extend existing services to residents must be reasonable, do the courts unwisely assume the power to second guess complex and multi-faceted decisions about timing, sequence, and funding of what are frequently quite substantial capital investments? *Compare* the New Jersey court's holding in *Medford* with its 1952 decision in Reid Development Corp. v. Parsippany-Troy Hills Township, 89 A.2d 667 (N.J.1952). In *Reid,* the court ordered the township to extend its water mains to the plaintiff's land. The township had refused to offer water service to the landowner unless he agreed to reconfigure his subdivision to ensure that no lot had less than 100 feet of lake frontage. Chiding the town for injecting "wholly alien considerations related to planning and zoning," *id.* at 670, and noting the absence of economic justifications for the denial, the court concluded that the township could not use the provision of water service as a "means of coercing the landowner into acceptance of the minimum lot-size restriction upon his lands, however serviceable to the common good." *Id.* at 671. Where is the line between Medford's effort to absorb growth while providing for services and Parsippany-Troy Hills Township's apparently impermissible attempt to shape growth by conditioning the provision of sewers on the developer's willingness to conform to the city's norms about acceptable development?

4.   *Land Use Planning Disguised as Service Provision.* Consider the court's analysis in Associated Home Builders v. Livermore in Chapter V. Undoubtedly, a municipality's control of the infrastructure required for development, such as sewers and water, gives it a powerful, though indirect, tool for limiting and sometimes stopping development it finds objectionable. That seems to be the basis of the *Parsippany-Troy Hills Township* case described in Note 3. Other courts are less sensitive to those underlying tensions. *E.g.,* Spring v. Bradley, 733 A.2d 1038 (Md.1999) (landowner seeking to build affordable housing unable to compel town to provide water and sewer services); Mogan v. Harlem, 775 P.2d 686 (Mont.1989) (denial of water and sewer permits for proposed low-income housing held to be within scope of city's discretion). The supreme court of Vermont has approved of a municipality's use of a sewer allocation ordinance as a general growth control

device. *See* Brennan Woods Ltd. Partnership v. Town of Williston, 782 A.2d 1230 (Vt. 2001). How should a court balance the landowner's assertion of the broader public interest in the provision of low-income or affordable housing against the city's claim to the exercise of discretion in the provision of public services?

5.   *Extension of Services and Affordable Housing.* In New Jersey, the supreme court's famous *Mount Laurel* opinions imposed on developing municipalities a legal obligation to provide their "fair share" of the region's need for low and moderate income housing. *See* Southern Burlington County N.A.A.C.P. v. Township of Mt. Laurel, 336 A.2d 713 (N.J. 1975); Southern Burlington County N.A.A.C.P. v. Township of Mt. Laurel, 456 A.2d 390 (N.J. 1983). These cases are discussed in Chapter V. A municipality's service extension policy could have a substantial impact on the availability of affordable housing. In several cases, the New Jersey courts had to reconcile the tension between municipal discretion to refuse to extend services extraterritorially and the municipality's obligation to facilitate the development of affordable housing. In Dynasty Building Corp. v. Borough of Upper Saddle River, 632 A.2d 544 (N.J. Ct. App. 1993) and Samaritan Center, Inc. v. Borough of Englishtown, 683 A.2d 611 (N.J. Law Div. 1996), the courts required local governments to provide extraterritorial sewer services to affordable housing developments, concluding that the municipalities' discretion in service provision issues was trumped by their duty to contribute to the provision of affordable housing. Subsequently, the state supreme court refused to extend the scope of those cases, holding that a developer who contributes to a municipality's affordable housing fund is not automatically entitled to extraterritorial sewer connections. *See* Bi-County Development of Clinton v. Borough of High Bridge, 805 A.2d 433 (N.J. 2002). If the municipality has a *Mt. Laurel* obligation to provide the extraterritorial service, how should the cost of access to the municipal system be allocated between the developer and the municipality?

6.   *Municipally Owned Utilities.* With the necessary statutory authorization, or pursuant to its home rule authority, a municipality may own and operate its own utility. Power and water are the services most frequently offered by a municipally owned utility company. These entities are frequently exempt from the state regulatory framework applicable to other utility companies if the city provides its service solely within its territorial jurisdiction. Once a municipality goes beyond its own jurisdiction to provide service to nonresidents, however, state regulation will often apply.

Municipalities may earn profits from the rates charged to their users. The rates are generally upheld if they are deemed by a court to constitute a fair return on the municipality's investment. If clearly unreasonable or discriminatory, however, the rate may be invalidated. Though a few state courts have held otherwise, the majority view is that the municipality's profits may be dedicated to any valid municipal purpose and need not be reinvested in the utility.

2. MUNICIPAL SERVICE PROVISION TO NONRESIDENTS

CITY OF TEXARKANA V. WIGGINS

Supreme Court of Texas
246 S.W.2d 622 (1952)

SMITH, J.

Respondents, all nonresidents of the City of Texarkana, Texas, filed this suit against Petitioner, the City, seeking to enjoin it in the operation of its municipally-owned water and sewer systems from charging nonresidents higher water and sewer rates than those paid by persons residing within the corporate limits of the city. * * *

Prior to August, 1948, the City of Texarkana, Texas, and surrounding territory, was served by the American Water Works, Inc., a privately-owned utility corporation. At that time the Petitioner purchased from this utility corporation all its property serving the city and surrounding territory, payment being made with proceeds derived from the sale of revenue bonds previously authorized by vote of the citizens of the city. An ordinance of the city, enacted on August 27, 1948, adopted for the municipally owned utility the schedule of rates theretofore charged by the American Water Works; this schedule of rates remained in effect until August 8, 1950. The system of rates charged by the American Water Works was, of course, nondiscriminatory in that both residents and nonresidents were charged the same rate for service.

On August 8, 1950, Petitioner passed an ordinance providing that water service to nonresident consumers would be furnished at one and one-half times the rate which applied within the corporate limits of the city. The ordinance further provided that sewer service to nonresident users would be furnished "at a rate double the rate applying within the city limits." A water tapping charge for all connections to the water system for residential use outside the city was fixed at $50.00; the water tapping charge for users within the city was set at $10.00 on unpaved streets, and $15.00 on paved streets.

Respondents are all residents of the City of North Texarkana, Texas, which adjoins the Petitioner on the north. The east-west streets in the City of Texarkana, Texas, are numbered consecutively, beginning with 1st Street in the business district of the City of Texarkana, Texas, and continuing to 36th Street in the City of North Texarkana. The line marking the corporate limits of the City of Texarkana, Texas, lies in the center of 29th Street. The north-south streets, which continue through both cities, bear the same names throughout their entire lengths. In short, the geographical line upon which the rate differentiation is based is an arbitrary line marking the limits of a political subdivision.

Petitioner contends that it is under no legal duty to furnish water and sewage disposal service to the Respondents; that if it does furnish such service to Respondents it is under no legal duty to charge the Respondents the same rate as is charged residents, but that it may make such charge as appears to be for the best interest of the City of Texarkana. This latter contention is based upon the provisions of Article 1108, section 3, R.C.S. of Texas, which provides:

> "Any town or city in this State which has or may be chartered or organized under the general laws of Texas, or by special Act or charter, and which owns or operates waterworks, sewers, gas or electric lights, shall have the power and right:

>> "3. To extend the lines of such systems outside of the limits of such towns or cities and to sell water, sewer, gas and electric light and power privileges or service to any person or corporation outside of the limits of such towns or cities, or permit them to connect therewith under contract with such town or city under such terms and conditions as may appear to be for the best interest of such town or city; provided that no electric lines shall, for the purposes stated in this section, be extended into the corporate limits of another incorporated town or city."

Respondents contend that the city in operating its water and sewer systems is acting in its proprietary capacity, that it is subject to the same rules and regulations as privately-owned utility corporations engaged in the same or similar business, and that the rates established by the ordinance of August 8, 1950, being discriminatory, are void and their collection should be enjoined.

We cannot agree with Petitioner's contention that this statute is sufficient to authorize it to charge a discriminatory rate for utilities furnished to nonresidents than to its residents. Under the facts in this case, the city has dealt with the residents and nonresidents as one class or unit. * * * Since 1948 the same rates have been charged consumers living within and without the city. No other utility exists within the area to furnish water and sewer service.

The common-law rule that one engaged in rendering a service affected with a public interest or, more strictly, what has come to be known as a utility service, may not discriminate in charges or service as between persons similarly situated is of such long standing and is so well recognized that it needs no citation of authority to support it. The economic nature of the enterprise which renders this type service is such that the courts have imposed upon it the duty to treat all alike unless there is some reasonable basis for a differentiation. Statutes have been enacted in almost every state making this common-law rule a statutory one. * * *

It is settled in this state that the Petitioner, upon the purchase by it of the property of the privately-owned utility was subject to this same rule prohibiting unreasonable or unjustified discrimination in rates and service. * * * [I]n the absence of (1) a showing that the discrimination has a reasonable basis or (2) a statute to the contrary, a municipality may not discriminate in charges or service as between those similarly situated. Many decisions have transported the concept of proprietary capacity, as distinguished from a governmental capacity, from the cases involving the liability of a governmental unit for the torts of its agents to these decisions involving the duty of a municipality to offer its utility service at nondiscriminatory rates and have found in this concept a basis for the rule set out above. The concept of proprietary capacity is, however, hardly helpful in this situation. The real reason for the rule that, in so far as treatment of consumers is concerned, the municipally-owned utility is no different from the privately-owned utility is that the economic nature of the business has not changed; it remains a monopoly in spite of the change in ownership.

The change from private to public ownership may, in theory at least, eliminate or lessen the profit motive, but the consumer of utility services still cannot pick and choose his supplier of water as he does his grocer. The utility consumer is thus at the mercy of the monopoly and, for this reason, utilities, regardless of the character of their ownership, should be, and have been, subjected to control under the common-law rule forbidding unreasonable discrimination.

We do not pass upon the question whether the Petitioner is under a legal duty to serve Respondents with water and sewage disposal, nor do we pass on the question whether the rates charged by Petitioner, whether within or without its corporate limits, are required to be "reasonable" as that term is understood in public utility parlance (i.e., a "reasonable" rate yields "a fair return on fair value"). But assuming that Petitioner has no duty to serve, it does not follow, under the common-law rule at least, that having elected to serve it may do so on such terms as it chooses to impose. The contention that the Petitioner, being under no legal obligation to serve, may do so on such terms as it chooses to impose brings before us a familiar argument in a new guise. It is the old, and logically appealing, argument that the greater includes the lesser power, that a governmental unit having the greater power of granting or withholding a privilege of service it perforce must have the lesser power of offering the privilege or service on whatever terms it may impose. * * * [But] the greater does not always include the lesser power and we think it important that this be understood for it has been the source of what we conceive to be error in the decision, in other jurisdictions, of the question before us.

The Petitioner being subject to the rule prohibiting unjustified discrimination between consumers of utility service, the question presents itself whether there is in fact any justification for treating the Respondents differently than the residents of the Petitioner city. * * * The Petitioner does not contend that the costs of supplying the service to Respondents vary so as to justify the difference in charges and the record is devoid of any evidence upon which to base such a contention. As was pointed out by the Court of Civil Appeals in its opinion below, the discrimination cannot be justified on the ground that the residents of the City of Texarkana, Texas, are liable to taxation to pay for acquisition of the water system. We are brought again, then, to what is apparent from the record of this case: the only difference between consumers who pay more and those who pay less for Petitioner's utility service lies in the fact that the former reside north of 29th Street while the latter reside South of 29th Street. The limits of a municipal corporation, of themselves, do not furnish a reasonable basis for rate differentiation. * * *

Under the common-law rules, then, the ordinance is void. But the petitioner contends that all this has been changed by the statute referred to above. * * * We find nothing in this [statute] which would authorize the city to discriminate, at its pleasure, between its patrons. The first part of the section merely gives the city the right to extend its service to persons residing beyond the corporate limits of the city. This the city has done. The language "or permit them to connect therewith under contract with such town or city under such terms and conditions as may appear to be for the best interest of such town or city," if construed to accord with Petitioner's view, would return us to the primitive state of development in utility control when rates were determined by friendship and political power or pressure. * * * This we cannot believe to have been the intent and purpose of the statute nor is its language such as to compel such a conclusion. * * * [A]ssuming that this provision of Section 3 gives the power to fix rates, the granting of such power, without express authority to fix unreasonably discriminatory rates, implies that the rate fixed pursuant thereto shall be, if not reasonable, at least not discriminatory.

* * * [W]e think it clear that the legislature did not intend to create a class of consumers against which the city could discriminate for any reason or without reason.

* * * [T]he effect of the statute is that when a city decides to exercise this power to provide its utility service to customers outside the city limits it may then fix such service charges as it decides the situation requires; if it requires a higher charge than is fixed against residents of the city for the same service, the city may exact the higher rate. But

whatever it fixes, a rate status between the city and its outside customers is thereby established and the city cannot thereafter arbitrarily change the rate so as to discriminate, or further discriminate, between them and customers residing in the city. This conclusion is certainly in line with well-established principles of public utility law.

CALVERT, J., joined by Justices SMEDLEY, GARWOOD, and GRIFFIN, dissenting.

The conclusion reached by the majority is contrary to the overwhelming weight of authority as evidenced by the decisions in those states in which the question has been decided under applicable common law rules. * * *

The citizens of North Texarkana do not occupy the same relationship toward the City of Texarkana as do its own citizens. "The primary purpose of a municipal corporation is to contribute towards the welfare, health, happiness and public interest of the inhabitants of such city, and not to further the interest of those residing outside of its limits." *City of Sweetwater v. Hamner*, Tex. Civ. App., 259 S.W. 191, 195. The City of Texarkana owes to its own citizens a duty to see that their health and welfare are protected through the continuing availability of water and sewer lines and facilities. It owes no such duty to the citizens of North Texarkana. It may furnish water and sewer services and facilities to residents of North Texarkana so long and only so long as the residents of that municipality contract for such services and the authorities of that municipality permit; but being under no duty to furnish in the first instance it may discontinue such services, on reasonable notice, with or without cause. Being entitled to discontinue the services according to its want, it follows that the City can continue them on its own terms and conditions. This was its common law right. It is now its statutory right.

SLOAN V. CITY OF CONWAY

Supreme Court of South Carolina
555 S.E.2d 684 (2001)

JUSTICE MOORE.

Appellants are water customers located within the service area of respondent Grand Strand Water and Sewer Authority (Grand Strand). They receive their water service as nonresident customers of respondent City of Conway (City). Appellants' action challenges City's 1996 ordinance raising water rates for all nonresident customers. The trial judge granted summary judgment to City and Grand Strand. We affirm.

FACTS

Grand Strand was created as a special purpose district in 1971 to distribute water and provide sewer systems in Horry County between the

Inland Waterway and the Atlantic Ocean except in designated areas including incorporated municipalities. Grand Strand's authority includes the ability to construct and maintain facilities and to sell water to municipalities. * * *

By agreements signed in 1982, 1985, and 1989, Grand Strand and City divided the provision of services in certain areas within Grand Strand's territory. Where appellants are located, Grand Strand provides sewer service and City provides water service. All of City's water is purchased wholesale from Grand Strand's Bull Creek plant.

In 1996, Grand Strand raised the rates it charges City for sewer treatment, a charge unrelated to City's cost of providing water service in the disputed area. After studying other municipalities' water rates for out-of-city customers, City decided it could raise revenue to offset this increased cost by increasing its water rates to out-of-city customers. City raised the rate 33%. This rate hike resulted in an increase from the previous rate of 1½ times the in-city rate to double the in-city rate. Grand Strand charges its own customers at cost, a lower rate than appellants must pay.

* * *

Appellants contend City has a duty to charge them reasonable rates and the double rate for out-of-city customers is unreasonable because it is unrelated to the cost of providing the service. They claim there is at least a factual issue regarding reasonableness and summary judgment should not have been granted.

Our decision in *Childs v. City of Columbia,* 87 S.C. 566, 70 S.E. 296 (1911), is dispositive here. In *Childs,* we held a municipality has "no public duty to furnish water to [a nonresident] at reasonable rates or to furnish it at all." 70 S.E. at 298. Any right a nonresident has arises only by contract. Further, a city actually has "an obligation to sell its surplus water *for the sole benefit of the city at the highest price obtainable." Id.* (emphasis added). We concluded the nonresident plaintiff had no basis to challenge the out-of-city rate which, in that case, was four times the in-city rate. *See also Calcaterra v. City of Columbia,* 315 S.C. 196, 432 S.E.2d 498 (Ct.App.1993) (following *Childs* and holding higher rates for out-of-city water customers cannot be challenged under the S.C. Unfair Trade Practices Act).

Appellants attempt to avoid the holding of *Childs* by relying on S.C.Code Ann. § 5–31–670 (1976) which post-dates that decision. This section provides:

> Any city or town or special service district may, after acquiring a waterworks or sewer system, *furnish water to persons for reasonable compensation* and charge a minimum and reasonable

sewerage charge for maintenance or construction of such sewerage system within such city or town or special service district.

(emphasis added). Appellants contend this statute modified *Childs* by imposing a reasonableness standard on water rates for nonresident customers.

We find this statute does not affect our holding in *Childs*. We reached our decision in *Childs* even while considering a constitutional provision that required "reasonable compensation" for municipal water service. Such a provision, whether constitutional or statutory, does not apply for the benefit of nonresidents unless expressly provided. *Childs,* 70 S.E. at 298. Here, § 5–31–670 does not expressly apply to nonresident municipal water customers. Absent a specific legislative directive, there is no reasonable rate requirement for water service to nonresidents.

Further, under *Childs,* City's duty to appellants arises only from contract. In this case, the 1982 agreement between City and Grand Strand provides that City's water rates to the area must be reasonable in that they may be no more than the rates charged all other out-of-city customers. Under the 1989 agreement, City may also determine reasonable rates by "taking into account the capital, administrative, and other applicable costs of the City." Read together, these agreements provide City's rates to the area are reasonable if they are the same as the rates charged all other out-of-city customers or, if rates to the area are higher than those for other out-of-city customers, they are reasonable if based upon increased costs in serving the area in question. Here, appellants are charged the same rates as all other out-of-city customers and City has therefore met its contractual obligation to charge reasonable rates.[10]

Because City has no duty to charge reasonable rates other than by agreement, and its rates comply with this agreement, summary judgment was properly granted. * * *

AFFIRMED.

---

[10] To the extent appellants argue the disparity in treatment between in-city customers and out-of-city customers is unconstitutional, we find their argument without merit. A legislative classification does not violate equal protection if there is any reasonable hypothesis to support it. *Lee v. S.C. Dep't of Natural Resources,* 339 S.C. 463, 530 S.E.2d 112 (2000). Here, out-of-city customers pay no taxes to City and this is a reasonable basis for disparate treatment. To violate due process, the ordinance must have no reasonable relationship to any legitimate governmental interest. *R.L. Jordan Co. v. Boardman Petroleum, Inc.,* 338 S.C. 475, 527 S.E.2d 763 (2000). Raising revenue to meet increasing municipal needs is a legitimate governmental goal and selling water at higher rates to customers who do not pay taxes is rationally related to this goal.

NOTES AND QUESTIONS

1. *Scope of Allowable Discretion.* Do the courts in the two main cases have irreconcilably different ideas about municipal duties to nonresidents? Do statutory differences satisfactorily explain the different results? The Utah Supreme Court in Platt v. Town of Torrey, 949 P.2d 325 (Utah 1997), adopted a standard similar to the one articulated in *City of Texarkana*. The Utah court stressed that although discriminatory treatment of nonresidents need not "be justified dollar for dollar," courts should make sure that the treatment is "reasonable." The determination of reasonableness is broad enough to include an assessment of overall risk allocation as between residents and nonresidents, a consideration of outstanding financial indebtedness on the part of the municipality, and municipal contributions to the functioning of the system that may not be included in the rate structure. *Id.* at 333–34. A dissenting justice objected that the holding placed district courts in the position of "profit referees in water sale contracts between municipalities and nonresidents," *id.* at 335. Taking the line of analysis offered in *Sloan,* the Virginia Supreme Court upheld a municipality's 100% surcharge on non-residents for water and sewer services. The dissenting opinion argued that it was improper to leave nonresidents at "the mercies of an unregulated monopoly against which they have no redress either at the polls or in the courts." Leesburg v. Giordano, 701 S.E.2d 783 (Va. 2010). *Accord,* Skallerup v. City of Hot Springs, 309 S.W.3d 196 (Ark. 2009). Is judicial intervention in these disputes justified? Is "reasonableness" a workable criterion? Should the level of judicial review depend on whether the plaintiffs are residents or nonresidents of the government from which they seek services?

Though it is generally true that nonresidents have no enforceable right to municipal services, if a municipality decides to provide services to some nonresidents, its discretion may thereafter be limited. Courts will invalidate municipal refusals to extend services, or unequal treatment in the provision of those services, under a standard of unreasonable discrimination. In some jurisdictions, the standard is termed the "holding out" exception; that is, once the municipality establishes itself as a general service provider to nonresidents, it assumes that obligation to similarly situated nonresidents. Spring v. Bradley, 733 A.2d 1038 (Md.1999). Determining whether any particular differential treatment of nonresidents is legitimate requires judicial scrutiny of the facts and of the proffered municipal justification.

2. *Extraterritorial Services and the Proprietary Model.* When a local government—even a "democratic" local government like a city—provides services beyond its borders, the courts typically consider this to be a form of local proprietary activity. The locality is seen as a "business enterprise," Bleick v. City of Papillion, 365 N.W.2d 405, 407 (Neb.1985), providing a service to customers for a fee, rather than a city responding to—and politically accountable to—its citizens.

As *City of Texarkana* indicates, however, the use of the proprietary model does not necessarily determine whether a locality can charge nonresidents more for comparable services. A court may view the city-nonresident relationship as akin to a private contractual relationship and presume that the city can propose whatever contract terms it deems fit. Nonresidents lack the political controls over a city that residents enjoy—that is, they cannot vote city officials out of office—but they presumably have the power that purchasers of services generally enjoy: they can decline to buy a service if they find the terms unattractive, and they can take their business elsewhere. However, where, due to the nature of the service or to the lack of alternative public or private sector service providers, the municipality effectively has a monopoly, a court may impose limitations on a local government similar to the restrictions ordinarily applicable to privately-owned public utilities. Instead of being able to distinguish between residents and nonresidents, the locality, like other regulated utilities, would then be required to treat all service recipients equally, and would be prohibited from discriminating against nonresidents due to the mere fact that they live outside the city line. The only permissible price differentials would be those resulting from the higher cost of serving nonresidents. This is the approach taken by the *City of Texarkana* majority. Can you articulate an alternative interpretation that would justify the South Carolina court's approach to the same issue?

3. *Services as Leverage.* Refer back to the opinion of the Ohio Supreme Court in Bakies v. City of Perrysburg in Chapter III. In that case, the court upheld the city's policy of terminating services to nonresidents unless the property owners agreed to municipal annexation. *Accord*, Brown v. City of Huntsville, 891 So.2d 295 (Ala. 2004); Allen's Creek Properties, Inc. v. City of Clearwater, 679 So.2d 1172 (Fla.1996); Yakima County (West Valley) Fire Pro. Dist. No. 12 v. City of Yakima, 858 P.2d 245 (Wash. 1993). *See also* Mitchell v. Wichita, 12 P.3d 402, 410 (Kan.2000) (upholding 55% surcharge on nonresident recipients of city water and sewer services; differential was justified in part by the city's policy of setting rates at a high level to encourage annexation). *But see* Verry v. City of Belle Fourche, 598 N.W.2d 544 (S.D.1999) (state law required the provision of municipal services to all buildings within a certain distance of city boundaries; city powerless to impose additional conditions). Why would a city want to force nonresidents to accept annexation in exchange for services? Does this suggest that the city has set the rates too low for nonresidents? After all, if the city recoups all its costs in providing the service, what difference does it make whether the property is within or without the city's borders? What other benefits does the city obtain from annexation?

Disputes over conditions imposed by municipalities on nonresidents' ability to receive services typically involve government attempts to induce annexation. In MT Dev., LLC v. City of Renton, 165 P.3d 427 (Wash. App. 2007), however, the municipality sought to condition sewer service on the nonresident property owners' compliance with its comprehensive plan.

Although the Washington Supreme Court, in the *Yakima* case cited in the last paragraph, upheld municipal power to condition extraterritorial service delivery on consent to annexation, the Washington appellate court held that Renton's effort to link service to acceptance of the city's land use regulation amounted to impermissible zoning. Is requiring consent to zoning distinguishable from—and more impermissible than—requiring consent to annexation?

4. *Municipal Purchase of Existing Utility Corporation.* In *City of Texarkana*, the court noted the important fact that the city purchased a public utility that had been providing service to nonresidents. In essence, the court declined to penalize the nonresident customers of the utility, who had no voice in the change of ownership and for whom the essential nature of the business remained unchanged. When a local government decides to purchase an ongoing utility whose territorial base will frequently be larger than the territory of the purchasing government, difficult questions will often arise about the rights of the utility's former customers who are now "nonresidents" for purposes of the municipality's service territory. *See, e.g.,* Albee v. Judy, 31 P.3d 248 (Idaho 2001) (court interprets purchase agreement as requiring extension of water service to nonresident property owners).

5. *State Regulation of Public Utilities.* Even if the state court does not impose limits on municipal discretion in its provision of services to nonresidents, state constitutional or statutory provisions may apply. In some states, municipal utilities are subject to the jurisdiction of the same utility commission that regulates the rates and conditions of service of private utility service providers. In those states, extraterritorial service delibery would, thus, be subject to state regulatory oversight. *See, e.g.,* Board of County Comm'rs of Arapahoe v. Denver Bd. of Water Comm'rs, 718 P.2d 235 (Colo.1986). Is the regulatory administrative approach preferable to the more wide ranging judicial supervision illustrated by the main cases?

6. *Discrimination Against Nonresidents Within the City.* May a city discriminate against nonresidents who utilize city services within the city's territorial borders? In County Board of Arlington County v. Richards, 434 U.S. 5 (1977), the United States Supreme Court considered a challenge under the federal Equal Protection Clause to a local ordinance that prohibited nonresident parking while providing special permits for residents. The Court applied the minimal scrutiny standard and upheld the ordinance:

> To reduce air pollution and other environmental effects of automobile commuting, a community reasonably may restrict on-street parking available to commuters, thus encouraging reliance on car pools and mass transit. The same goal is served by assuring convenient parking to residents who leave their cars at home during the day. A community may also decide that restrictions on the flow of outside traffic into particular residential areas would enhance the quality of life there by reducing noise, traffic hazards, and litter. By

definition, discrimination against nonresidents would inhere in such restrictions.

The Constitution does not outlaw these social and environmental objectives, nor does it presume distinctions between residents and nonresidents of a local neighborhood to be invidious. The Equal Protection Clause requires only that the distinction drawn by an ordinance like Arlington's rationally promote the regulation's objectives.

Id. at 7. *See also* Zaroogian v. Town of Narragansett, 701 F.Supp. 302 (D.R.I.1988) (rejecting federal equal protection challenge to local ordinance restricting lockers, shower and a changing room at a popular and crowded beach to local residents).

State courts often uphold local ordinances that charge nonresidents higher fees for using certain city facilities, provided the nonresidential fee is "reasonable." *See, e.g.*, Broeckl v. Chicago Park District, 544 N.E.2d 792 (Ill.1989) (moorage fee); McFall v. Shawnee, 559 P.2d 433 (Okla.1976) (lakeside lot rentals). Differentials are particularly likely to be sustained where a part of the cost of the facility is paid for by general local taxes. If, however, the facility or service provided concerns a matter considered to be a fundamental aspect of state citizenship, local discrimination against nonresidents may violate state law. *See, e.g.*, Borough of Neptune City v. Borough of Avon-by-the-Sea, 294 A.2d 47 (N.J.1972) (ownership of ocean beaches is vested in the State in trust for the people of the state as a whole; consequently, a municipality may not charge nonresidents more than residents for use of a municipal public beach).

In a striking decision, the Connecticut Supreme Court held that the town of Greenwich's exclusion of nonresidents from Greenwich Point Park, a town park with a beachfront on Long Island Sound, violated the First Amendment of the United States Constitution and the free speech provisions of the Connecticut Constitution. Leydon v. Town of Greenwich, 777 A.2d 552 (Conn. 2001). The court noted that the First Amendment sharply constrains the ability of government to restrict expression on public property, like streets or parks, that has traditionally been used for public meetings and the discussion of public questions. The court concluded that Greenwich Point Park is such "a traditional public forum because it has the characteristics of a public park." *Id.* at 569. As a result, the town could exclude a speaker from the park only if the exclusion was narrowly drawn to achieve a compelling state interest. *Id.* at 571. As the exclusion of nonresidents operated to prevent nonresidents from speaking and engaging in expressive activities within the park, the exclusion was subject to strict judicial scrutiny. And since the town failed to offer any compelling reason for excluding nonresidents from the park, *see id.* at 572, the nonresident exclusion violated the First Amendment. Greenwich responded to the court's decision by opening its beaches—but at a price: Nonresidents have to pay $10 each for day beach passes, with parking an additional $20. Thus, a day at the beach for a family of four could run as much as $60. Moreover, passes cannot be purchased at the beach, but only at the civic center or town hall, and with cash only. *See* Greenwich Beach Open to All, But Bring Money and Patience, N.Y. Times, May 28, 2002, at B5. Madison, another Connecticut beach community, does not even sell beach passes on weekends; other Connecticut shore towns have been more welcoming. *See* Sudhin S. Thanawala, Town Beaches Still Not So Open, Hartford Courant, Sept. 26, 2002, at B1. A federal district court dismissed plaintiffs' First Amendment claim for injunctive relief. *See* Kempner v. Greenwich, 562 F.Supp. 2d 242 (D. Conn. 2008).

    7.   *Local Services and Ability to Pay.* Should municipalities be able to charge wealthier residents higher rates for the same services? What kind of legal challenges would the wealthier residents be able to use in a dispute over such a fee schedule? *See* Tom I. Romero, The Color of Water, 15 U. Denv. L. Rev. 329 (2012).

3.   INEQUALITY IN SERVICE DELIVERY

MOUNT PROSPECT STATE BANK V. VILLAGE OF KIRKLAND

Appellate Court of Illinois
467 N.E.2d 1142 (1984)

REINHARD, JUSTICE:

Plaintiff, Mount Prospect State Bank, as trustee under a land trust, appeals from an order of the trial court granting the motion to dismiss of defendant, the village of Kirkland. Plaintiff raises the following issues on appeal: (1) whether it was a denial of equal protection to deny plaintiff refuse collection service where the service was provided to other village residents and paid from general tax revenues * * *.

* * * Plaintiff owns a parcel of property in the village of Kirkland known as Congress Lake Estates, which contains 70 to 77 mobile homes. This is the only mobile home park in the village and only plaintiff, not the individual mobile homeowners, is a party to this suit. Defendant, pursuant to a contract, commencing May 1, 1982, and terminating April 30, 1985, with Saturn Disposal Systems, Inc. (Saturn), provides refuse collection service to residences within the village. Defendant pays for these services with general village tax receipts. The contract provides, in pertinent part, that Saturn "shall make one weekly unlimited pick-up of garbage * * * from each residence in the VILLAGE." The contract defines "residence" as including "each occupied single family dwelling and each occupied unit or apartment situated in a multiple family apartment building or separate apartments in single family dwellings converted to multiple family use." "Residence" expressly does not include "mobile homes located in Congress Lake Estates." The contract specifies that there are 317 residences in the village as of the date of the contract.

In its three-count amended complaint plaintiff sought an order of mandamus directing defendant to provide plaintiff with the "same refuse collection that it affords other taxpaying residential property owners," compensatory damages for denying plaintiff this service for 19 years, and punitive damages under "Title 42, Section 1983, U.S.Code." Essentially, this complaint alleged that plaintiff was the owner of real estate containing "70–77 residential homes;" that defendant supplies refuse service in the village which it pays for from general village tax receipts; that the contract for refuse service indicates a "residence" for which this service is provided does not include mobile homes located in "Congress Lake Estates;" that such a contract violates plaintiff's right to equal protection as it arbitrarily classifies types of property and excludes plaintiff from a governmental service provided to others in the village; and that plaintiff has been discriminated against for 19 years during which time it paid for its own refuse collection.

In its order granting defendant's motion to dismiss, the trial court noted that the parties had agreed that plaintiff's facility was the only mobile home park in the village. The court concluded that while naming and excluding the mobile home park specifically in the contract might raise an equal protection argument, the agreed fact was that this was the only mobile home park in the village and plaintiff was not being discriminated against with respect to any other such mobile home parks in the village. The court further found, inter alia, that it did not violate equal protection to exclude plaintiff's property from refuse collection services.

Plaintiff argues on appeal that it has been unconstitutionally denied equal protection of the laws because the defendant's refuse collection policy arbitrarily discriminates against mobile home parks. It maintains that the exclusion of its mobile home park from refuse collection unfairly classifies it with "second class status." Plaintiff claims no rational basis exists for treating it differently than other residential taxpayers and that this different treatment, which requires it to pay for refuse collection service through its payment of general property taxes without receiving the collection service provided to other village residents, is therefore a denial of equal protection. Plaintiff argues it is entitled to mandamus ordering the village to provide plaintiff with this service.

A government may "differentiate between persons similarly situated as long as the classification bears a reasonable relationship to a legitimate legislative purpose." * * * There is a presumption of validity of these legislative classifications and the burden is on the party challenging the classification to establish its invalidity. * * * Where no fundamental right or suspect class is involved, the classification "need have only a rational relationship to a legitimate State purpose to be upheld." *People v. Gurell* (1983), 98 Ill.2d 194, 204, 74 Ill.Dec. 516, 456 N.E.2d 18;

Harrington v. City of Chicago (1983), 116 Ill.App.3d 137, 139, 72 Ill.Dec. 94, 452 N.E.2d 26.

No fundamental right to garbage collection exists (*Goldstein v. City of Chicago* (7th Cir.1974), 504 F.2d 989, 991), and mobile home park owners are not among the "suspect" classes recognized by the courts. (*Illinois Housing Development Authority v. Van Meter* (1980), 82 Ill.2d 116, 119–20, 45 Ill.Dec. 18, 412 N.E.2d 151; *San Antonio Independent School District v. Rodriguez* (1973), 411 U.S. 1, 61, 93 S.Ct. 1278, 1311, 36 L.Ed.2d 16, 59 (Stewart, J., concurring).) Thus, the classification challenged here will be upheld if it bears a rational relationship to a legitimate governmental purpose. (*People v. Gurell* (1983), 98 Ill.2d 194, 204, 74 Ill.Dec. 516, 456 N.E.2d 18.) If the court can discern any reasonable basis for the classification, it will be upheld. (*Harrington v. City of Chicago* (1983), 116 Ill.App.3d 137, 139, 72 Ill.Dec. 94, 452 N.E.2d 26.) This test for constitutional validity is often referred to as the "rational basis" test. * * *

It has been held that a distinction between multiple-family structures and single-family residences may be made with a municipality providing garbage service to single-family residences while excluding multiple-family structures. (*Szczurek v. City of Park Ridge* (1981), 97 Ill.App.3d 649, 659, 52 Ill.Dec. 698, 422 N.E.2d 907.) The reasons given in *Szczurek* included the "more demanding needs" of multiple-family structures and "the greater amount of refuse generated by them." (97 Ill.App.3d 649, 657–59, 52 Ill.Dec. 698, 422 N.E.2d 907.) Similar reasons can be conceived here. Plaintiff's property contains between 70 and 77 mobile homes. With such a large number of mobile homes existing on plaintiff's property, it is reasonable to conclude that the refuse collection needs of this property would vary significantly from the needs of other residents of the village. In fact, as of the date of the contract, there were only 317 residences in the village that would receive refuse pickup service. Including plaintiff's property with some 70 to 77 mobile homes in the refuse pickup contract would substantially increase the amount of refuse to be picked up resulting in a significant expense to the village. Also, greater flexibility and frequency of refuse pickup than the village could provide may be necessary to meet the needs of the residents of this mobile home park. (*See Szczurek v. City of Park Ridge* (1981), 97 Ill.App.3d 649, 656, 52 Ill.Dec. 698, 422 N.E.2d 907.) Additionally, a mobile home park may provide greater problems of access for refuse trucks than residences located on city streets.

We further note that the contract, by its inclusion of only residences, excludes commercial enterprises within the village from refuse collection service. Plaintiff's property, with its 70 to 77 mobile homes, has more the character of commercial property than it does residential, which we believe is a rational basis for a classification in view of greater refuse generally generated by a commercial enterprise.

Plaintiff's complaint only generally alleges an arbitrary classification and does not allege facts which would indicate that no rational basis for the distinction between it and residences in the village exist. It does not allege specific facts, for example, that apartment buildings with comparable numbers of units exist in the village and receive refuse collection service, or that other mobile homes similarly situated in the village receive the service. For the foregoing reasons, the presumption of validity of the village's actions has not been overcome, and a rational basis for the classification has been shown.

* * * Because we conceive facts that justify the exclusion of plaintiff's mobile home park from refuse collection, we hold that plaintiff's complaint only generally alleging an equal protection violation was properly dismissed.

AFFIRMED.

WHS REALTY CO. v. TOWN OF MORRISTOWN
Superior Court of New Jersey
733 A.2d 1206 (1999)

HAVEY, P.J.A.D.

This appeal presents a challenge to Morristown's garbage collection ordinance which provides free collection service to all residential dwellings of three or less units as well as condominium developments where no more than 50% of the units are owned by one person or entity. Excluded from the ordinance are all multi-family dwellings of four or more units. Therefore, plaintiff's garden apartment complex, consisting of 140 units, does not receive collection service.

Plaintiff filed a complaint in the Law Division claiming that the ordinance violates its right to due process and equal protection of the laws guaranteed by the United States and New Jersey Constitutions. * * *

The Town defendants now appeal from the judgment invalidating the ordinance. * * *

I

If a legislative classification " 'neither burdens a fundamental right nor targets a suspect class,' " we must uphold the constitutionality of legislation " 'so long as it bears a rational relation to some legitimate end.' " *Vacco v. Quill*, 521 U.S. 793, 799, 117 S.Ct. 2293, 2297, 138 L.Ed.2d 834, 841 (1997) (quoting *Romer v. Evans*, 517 U.S. 620, 631, 116 S.Ct. 1620, 1627, 134 L.Ed.2d 855, 865 (1996)); *see also 515 Assocs. v. Newark*, 132 N.J. 180, 197, 623 A.2d 1366 (1993). Under the federal rational basis test, a classification made by legislation is presumed to be valid and will be sustained if it is "rationally related to a legitimate state interest." *Cleburne v. Cleburne Living Ctr.*, 473 U.S. 432, 440, 105 S.Ct. 3249, 3254, 87 L.Ed.2d 313, 320 (1985); *Drew Assocs. of N.J. v. Travisano*, 122 N.J. 249, 264, 584 A.2d 807 (1991). Essentially the same type of analysis has been adopted respecting evaluation of equal protection claims under Article I, paragraph 1 of the New Jersey Constitution. *Property Owners & Manager Ass'n v. Parsippany-Troy Hills*, 264 N.J.Super. 538, 544, 624 A.2d 1381 (App.Div.), *certif. denied*, 134 N.J. 561, 636 A.2d 519 (1993).

A municipal ordinance is accorded the same presumption of constitutionality as all legislation. *Strauss v. Township of Holmdel*, 312 N.J.Super. 610, 619, 711 A.2d 1385 (Law Div.1997) (citing *Pleasure Bay Apartments v. Long Branch*, 66 N.J. 79, 93–94, 328 A.2d 593 (1974)). The challenger of the ordinance must "refute all possible rational bases for the differing treatment, whether or not the Legislature cited those bases as reasons for the enactment." *League of Municipalities v. State*, 257 N.J.Super. 509, 518, 608 A.2d 965 (App.Div.1992), *certif. dismissed*, 133 N.J. 423, 627 A.2d 1132 (1993).

The parties agree that, since the Town's ordinance does not implicate a suspect class or fundamental right, the rational basis test applies. Therefore, plaintiff has the burden of demonstrating that classification by the ordinance lacks a rational basis. A municipality's exercise of its police power in classifying by ordinance, must be sustained if it can be justified on any reasonably conceivable state of facts. *Taxpayer Ass'n of Weymouth Township, Inc. v. Weymouth Township*, 80 N.J. 6, 40, 364 A.2d 1016 (1976). However, a governmental agency " 'may not rely on a classification whose relationship to an asserted goal is so attenuated as to render the distinction arbitrary or irrational.' " *Doe v. Poritz*, 142 N.J. 1, 92, 662 A.2d 367 (1995) (quoting *Cleburne, supra,* 473 U.S. at 446–47, 105 S.Ct. at 3258, 87 L.Ed.2d at 324). "Furthermore, some objectives . . . are not legitimate state interests." *Ibid.*

II

A municipality is not mandated to provide for municipal garbage removal. A municipality "*may* provide for the . . . collection or disposal of solid waste, and *may* establish and operate a system therefor. . . ." N.J.S.A. 40:66–1a (*emphasis added*). Also, when a municipality chooses to provide the service, it may, pursuant to its police power, impose reasonable restrictions by ordinance. *Pleasure Bay, supra,* 66 N.J. at 85, 328 A.2d 593. In *Pleasure Bay*, for example, the Court upheld municipal regulations limiting municipal service to curbside collection. *Id.* at 95, 328 A.2d 593. * * *

However, once the service is provided by a municipality, "there can be no invidious discrimination" in limiting the service to certain classifications. *Boulevard Apartments, Inc. v. Mayor of Lodi*, 110 N.J.Super. 406, 411, 265 A.2d 838 (App.Div.), *certif. denied*, 57 N.J. 124, 270 A.2d 27 (1970). There is a violation of equal protection of the laws "unless the service is available to all persons in like circumstances upon the same terms and conditions. Persons situated alike shall be treated alike." *Ibid.* (citing *Reid Dev. Corp. v. Parsippany-Troy Hills Township*, 10 N.J. 229, 233, 89 A.2d 667 (1952)).

* * * [T]he proofs adduced during the plenary hearing made clear that there is nothing about the mechanics or costs of solid waste collection that justifies differentiating between apartment complexes and other residents within the community. As the trial court observed during an early stage of the proceedings, "people are people," and the type and quality of solid waste generated by all types of residential dwellings is the same. In fact, the evidence demonstrated that because there are fewer residents living in individual apartment units than single-family or condominium units, apartment units generate less solid waste. Moreover, the Town's Director of Public Works conceded that it would be more cost-effective to pick up solid waste from four dumpsters serving 140 apartment units than picking up solid waste from 140 separate single-family residential units at curbside. He also acknowledged that the mechanics for collection from dumpsters is the same for apartment units and condominiums.

There is also no rational basis for differentiating between apartment units and other residential dwellings on the basis that apartment owners may realize a profit from their investment. *Boulevard*, *supra*, 110 N.J.Super. at 411, 265 A.2d 838. We observed in *Boulevard*:

> The resolution in question makes no distinction between owner-occupied dwellings and those rented for income. The evidence reveals that there are numerous rented multi-family dwellings containing from two to eight family units which are not precluded from receiving municipal garbage collection service. Moreover, the resolution on its face provides for collection from public housing projects and various places of business.

[*Ibid.*]

Here, the trial court accepted the reports of both parties' planners indicating that only 58% of the one, two and three-unit family dwellings which are provided garbage collection service are owner-occupied. Conversely, 42% of the units receiving the service are occupied by renters. The trial court found significant the more telling fact that only 27% and 11.7% of two and three-family structures respectively, are owner-occupied. The implication is that these nonoccupying owners are no less motivated by profit than owners of apartment complexes, and thus should not be treated differently. * * *

III

The Town defendants nevertheless argue that the proofs adduced during the plenary hearing support their claim that the Town's garbage collection ordinance is rationally related to fostering home ownership. They rely for the most part on our court's holding in *League of Municipalities, supra,* that the goal of fostering home ownership is a legitimate governmental objective. 257 N.J.Super. at 521, 608 A.2d 965. * * *

During the plenary hearing in the present case, the Town's Mayor testified that Morristown has a policy of fostering home ownership. It was his view that "[s]trong residential neighborhoods [are] the fabric of the community." He testified that residents living in their own home have a "pride in their community," maintain their residences and have a long-term commitment to their neighborhood and the Town, whereas neighborhoods consisting of apartment dwellings tend to be in a declining condition, and house a highly "transient" population. It was his belief that the garbage collection ordinance "promote[s] the concept of ownership" because it provides a financial incentive to purchase a home within the community. He also cited the "psychological aspect" of free garbage collection. According to the Mayor, when a resident owns his or her own home, he or she "expect[s] garbage pickup," thereby providing "uniformity" which promotes "cleanliness for the neighborhood."

* * *

Plaintiff's planner testified that he found no document or study submitted by the Town or available in the planning field at large supporting the notion that free garbage collection fosters home ownership. The planner knew of no study demonstrating that people make a decision on purchasing a home based on whether or not the municipality provides free garbage collection. He also rejected the Town defendants' claim that the Master Plan supports home ownership over the creation of a rental-unit inventory, noting that the Master Plan calls for the construction of a variety of housing types for all income levels.

The trial court found that the facts did not support the Town's claim that the ordinance fostered home ownership. The court observed that as a "conceptual matter," once a municipality provides garbage collection to residential dwellings, there is no rational basis to distinguish one resident from another. * * *

We agree with the trial court that the plenary hearing demonstrated no basis in fact for the Town's claim that the garbage collection ordinance fosters home ownership. * * *

Moreover, we find no meaningful support in the Town's Master Plan for the proposition that a distinction, for garbage collection service purposes, should be made between homeowners and apartment dwellers. While the Master Plan recommends encouraging and maintaining residential neighborhoods, it also recommends that the Town "provide for a greater diversity of housing types to meet . . . [the] needs of a wide range of incomes and age levels." The plan in fact predicts that "[m]ulti-family housing, particularly moderate density development, will constitute the major portion of new housing units in the Town." Notably, plaintiff's planner stated in his report that, from a sound planning viewpoint,

> a more accurate planner's view of a varied housing stock is that it services households at different stages of the life cycle as well as different income groups. Young married couples often choose rental units as an affordable [entry] to the community. As family incomes rise and children appear, detached single-family homes become the shelter of choice. Toward the end of the cycle, senior citizens often return to rental units for reduced maintenance responsibilities and lower costs.

This trend underscores a clear countervailing policy to fostering home ownership: the provision of affordable housing to young married couples, senior citizens and other low and medium-income residents. * * *

In short, encouraging home ownership may be a permissible and even laudable legislative objective. However, based on the evidence adduced during the plenary hearing, we conclude that the garbage collection ordinance is an example of legislation "whose relationship to an asserted goal is so attenuated as to render the distinction arbitrary or irrational." *Cleburne, supra,* 473 U.S. at 446, 105 S.Ct. at 3258, 87 L.Ed.2d at 324. Simply put, fostering home ownership is not a rational basis for defendants' classification scheme.

* * *

VI

The Town defendants also contend that the trial court erred by failing to consider the fiscal impact to Morristown as a factor justifying its refusal to extend garbage collection service to the plaintiff and other apartment complexes.[3] We recognize that "[municipalities] have considerable latitude in allocating their . . . resources." *King v. Smith,* 392 U.S. 309, 318–19, 88 S.Ct. 2128, 2134, 20 L.Ed.2d 1118, 1126 (1968). However, "[a]lthough preservation of fiscal integrity is a valid state

---

[3] The Town's Director of Public Works testified that it would cost the Town at least $412,000 to provide garbage collection service to apartments in the municipality. In his report to the court, the Director indicated that a new garbage truck, new recycling truck and several roll-off containers for recyclables would have to be purchased.

interest, a [municipality] may not accomplish that goal by establishing 'invidious' distinctions between citizens." *Sanchez v. Department of Human Servs.*, 314 N.J.Super. 11, 27, 713 A.2d 1056 (App.Div.1998) (citing *Shapiro v. Thompson*, 394 U.S. 618, 633, 89 S.Ct. 1322, 1330, 22 L.Ed.2d 600, 614 (1969)).

A statutory classification which is "invidious" is one in which the challenged discrimination has failed to meet either the strict scrutiny or rational relationship test, and is therefore unconstitutional. 314 N.J.Super. at 29–30, 713 A.2d 1056. In the present case, the trial court determined that the Town's garbage collection scheme bore no rational relationship to any legitimate state interest. Therefore, it implicitly found that the classification created "invidious" distinctions. *Ibid.* An invidious classification cannot be sustained solely because it saves money. *Shapiro*, 394 U.S. at 633, 89 S.Ct. at 1330, 22 L.Ed.2d at 614. "The saving of [municipal] costs cannot justify an otherwise invidious classification." *Ibid.* Thus, the trial court correctly declined to sustain the ordinance based on the fiscal impact providing garbage collection service to apartment complexes will have.

NOTES AND QUESTIONS

1. *Writs of Mandamus.* The plaintiffs in *Kirkland* sought a writ of mandamus against the municipal government. This common law writ is used to order a government official to perform some required action. The function of mandamus is to enforce a clearly existing legal right—not to establish the existence of legal rights. Subject to the routine standing requirement, mandamus may be used to enforce performance of official duties owed to individuals or to the public generally.

The essential requirements for mandamus are: (1) The law must impose on the public official an official duty to perform some act; (2) The official must have failed to perform that act; (3) The act must be ministerial, involving no discretion and not requiring the exercise of judgment; (4) The party seeking the writ of mandamus must have a clear legal right to compel performance of the act; (5) The party seeking the writ must have no other adequate remedy.

Most commonly, mandamus cases involve a duty imposed by a statute. The key issue is most often whether the duty imposed by the statute is ministerial or discretionary. *See, e.g.,* DelGobbo v. Town of Watertown, 69 A.3d 1000 (Conn. App. 2013) (denying writ of mandamus to order town to enforce its own zoning regulations); Kusky v. Town of Islip, 699 N.Y.S.2d 69 (App.Div.1999) (refusing to issue writ of mandamus to compel town to construct "adequate" public beach toilet facilities, because determination of whether toilet facilities are "adequate" within the meaning of the state's sanitary code is an exercise of judgment); Gwinnett County v. Ehler Enterprises, Inc., 512 S.E.2d 239 (Ga.1999) (holding that county board of commissioner's decision to deny application for a special use permit was discretionary because zoning ordinance's list of guidelines were expressly not exhaustive); Willoughby v. Grim, 581 N.W.2d 165 (S.D.1998) (issuing writ of mandamus and holding that the words "shall" and "all" in a statute imposed a ministerial duty on township supervisors to arrange for construction, repair and maintenance of all secondary roads within the township).

Is mandamus an appropriate remedy if a plaintiff establishes municipal negligence for failure to treat the water supply for bacteria and seeks to require municipal treatment? *See* AlliedSignal, Inc. v. City of Phoenix, 182 F.3d 692 (9th Cir.1999) (mandamus improper under Arizona law, even though municipal action might constitute actionable negligence; the plaintiff had not alleged that the city had violated statutory or regulatory standards). What if a plaintiff seeks a judicial order to compel the submission of a voter initiative to the electorate pursuant to state constitutional or statutory directive? *Compare* Board of County Commissioners of the County of Archuleta v. County Road Users Ass'n, 11 P.3d 432 (Colo.2000) (mandamus not available because county's statutory duty to submit a voter initiative to the electorate was not ministerial; county had discretion to review proposed initiative for compliance with statutory requirements) *with* Dean v. Williams, 6 S.W.3d 89 (Ark.1999) (county's duty to call election in response to initiative petition purely ministerial and enforceable by mandamus).

2. *Rational Basis Review in Service Provision.* Note that the courts in the two preceding principal cases apply the same standard to the challenged municipal practice. Are the differences in result justified by the facts, or do the two courts have a different understanding of the meaning of "rational"? The *WHS* court discussed evidence arguing against the city's decision to foster home ownership; for instance, the court recounts testimony urging municipalities to foster affordable housing for low and moderate income residents. How is that relevant to whether the garbage ordinance violates the Equal Protection Clause? Does the fact that the plaintiffs in both cases are residents of the local government they sue argue for or against judicial deference to municipal discretion? Is the political check an appropriate remedy for these complaints?

3. *Equality in Fee Structures.* Municipal fee structures are also subject to challenge on equality grounds. The case of *City of Texarkana v. Wiggins* earlier in this Chapter raised the issue in the context of discrimination against nonresidents. Should the same rules apply to discriminations among residents of the same locality? Consider, for instance, a city's decision to distinguish "new" from "old" users in setting water and sewer rates. In Loomis v. City of Hailey, 807 P.2d 1272 (Idaho 1991), the court upheld the classification on reasonableness grounds, even though only the new users' fee included a charge for replacement of existing facilities and equipment. *See also* City of New Smyrna Beach v. Fish, 384 So.2d 1272 (Fla.1980) (upholding city garbage fees that charged multifamily dwellings approximately five times the rate paid by single family homes). How would the *Kirkland* and *WHS* courts analyze these classifications?

4.   *Olech's "Class of One."* In Village of Willowbrook v. Olech, 528 U.S. 562 (2000), the Supreme Court held that the petitioner's status as an individual, or a so-called "class of one," did not disqualify her from pursuing an equal protection challenge. The Village conditioned her connection to the municipal water supply on granting the Village a 33-ft. easement across her property. Other similar property owners were only required to give a 15-ft. easement. Noting that "the number of individuals in a class is immaterial for equal protection analysis," *id.* at 564 n.1, the Court held that Ms. Olech had stated a claim "under traditional equal protection analysis" and evaluated that claim under the rational basis test. In his concurrence, Justice Breyer cautioned against transforming "many ordinary violations of city or state law into violations of the Constitution," and said he would require that claimants show some "ill will" or "illegitimate animus" on the part of the government. Hundreds of lower court cases have cited *Olech*, and the role of animus in a "class-of-one" analysis varies among the courts of appeals. The landscape became more complicated after the Supreme Court's decision in Enquist v. Oregon Dept. of Agriculture, 553 U.S. 591(2008). In that case, the court held that the class of one claim under equal protection is not available in the public employment context. An in-depth description of the lower court struggles and confusion can be found in William D. Araiza, *Flunking the Class of One, Failing Equal Protection*, 55 Wm. & Mary L. Rev, 435 (2013).

Should animus be required in a class-of-one claim, even in the absence of a rational basis? Some Seventh Circuit judges, including Judge Posner, believes that the answer is yes. *See* Swanson v. City of Chetek, 719 F.3d 780 (7th Cir. 2013); Geinosky v. City of Chicago, 675 F.3d 743 (7th Cir. 2012); Del Marcelle v. Brown County Corp., 680 F.3d 887 (7th Cir. 2012). Or should plaintiffs be allowed to prove *either* a lack of rational basis *or* ill will? *See* Scarbrough v. Morgan County Board of Education, 470 F.3d 250 (6th Cir. 2006); Nevel v. Village of Schaumburg, 297 F.3d 673 (7th Cir. 2002). May animus be used to demonstrate that a rational basis is mere pretext, or will a rational basis vindicate state action even where ill will can be demonstrated? *Compare* Squaw Valley Development Co. v. Goldberg, 375 F.3d 936 (9th Cir. 2004), *with Nevel, supra.* Do any of these approaches strike the right balance between preventing a large volume of litigation while allowing truly injured plaintiffs a remedy? One commentator argues that in light of the confusion plaintiffs should always be prepared to plead and prove facts indicating animus. *See* Michael S. Giaimo, Challenging Improper Land Use Decision-Making Under the Equal Protection Clause, 15 Fordham Envtl. L. Rev. 335 (2004). Another has suggested that due process, not equal protection, is the proper approach. *See* William D. Araiza, Irrationality and Animus in Class-of-One Equal Protection Cases, 34 Ecology L.Q. 493 (2007). How would a "class of one" equal protection argument differ from an arbitrary and capricious challenge under the due process clause?

DOWDELL V. CITY OF APOPKA

United States Court of Appeals
698 F.2d 1181 (11th Cir.1983)

VANCE, CIRCUIT JUDGE:

The situs of this case is the small city of Apopka, Florida located in the fern and foliage growing region north of Orlando. More specifically, it is the poor, geographically separate, black community of that city. The plaintiffs * * * are a * * * class comprising the black residents of Apopka "who are, or have been, subjected to the discriminatory provision of municipal services." * * *

Plaintiffs charged the City of Apopka, its mayor, and four council members with discrimination in the provision of seven municipal services: street paving and maintenance, storm water drainage, street lighting, fire protection, water distribution, sewerage facilities, and park and recreation facilities. After a preliminary finding by the Office of Revenue Sharing that the City was discriminatory in the provision of several of these services, an agreement was reached on improvements in street lighting and fire protection, and the district court filed an order settling these claims. The case went to trial on the remaining five issues.

The district court found intentional discrimination in the provision of street paving, the water distribution system, and storm drainage facilities in violation of the fourteenth amendment; * * * The court issued an order enjoining Apopka from initiating or constructing any new municipal services or improvements in the white community until such time as the disparities in the black community facilities were eliminated and impounding all of the city's federal revenue sharing funds with the stipulation that they be used only to pay for capital improvements in the municipal services provided to the residents of the black community. * * *

To trigger strict scrutiny analysis under the fourteenth amendment, preliminary findings of both disparate impact and discriminatory intent are required. *Washington v. Davis*, 426 U.S. 229, 96 S.Ct. 2040, 48 L.Ed.2d 597 (1976). Appellants contend that the facts adduced in evidence do not support a finding of discriminatory intent. * * *

We can reach no such conclusion. Substantial evidence, including video tapes, photographs, charts, and the testimony of community residents and of qualified experts who made on-site surveys revealed a disparity in the provision of street paving, water distribution, and storm water drainage.[3] Appellants do not question the accuracy of these

---

[3] The district court found that 42% of the street footage in the black community was unpaved as compared to 9% in the white community and that 33% of the black community residences fronted on such unpaved streets while only 7% of the residences in the white community did so. As regards storm drainage, the court found that while 60% of the residential streets in the white community had curbs and gutters, no streets in the black community had curbs and gutters. Additionally, it found that water service in many homes in the black

statistical findings. Rather, they assert an absence of responsibility for them, claiming them, variously, to be beyond municipal jurisdiction or the result of historical and environmental forces. Their arguments are insubstantial and were properly rejected by the trial court.[4]

Refutation of Apopka's attempt to deny municipal responsibility for these services one by one does not conclude our inquiry into discriminatory intent. The gravamen of plaintiffs' claim is that Apopka has intentionally maintained a racially and geographically segregated system of municipal services as a result of which the disparities in the provision of street paving, water distribution, and storm drainage facilities have reached constitutional proportions. Discriminatory intent is not synonymous with a racially discriminatory motive, *Palmer v. Thompson*, 403 U.S. 217, 224, 91 S.Ct. 1940, 1944, 29 L.Ed.2d 438 (1971). Neither does it require proof that racial discrimination is the sole purpose, *McGinnis v. Royster*, 410 U.S. 263, 276–77, 93 S.Ct. 1055, 1062, 35 L.Ed.2d 282 (1973), behind each failure to equalize these services. It is, rather, the cumulative evidence of action and inaction which objectively manifests discriminatory intent. *United States v. Texas Education Agency*, 564 F.2d 162, *passim* (5th Cir.1977). *See also United States v. Texas Education Agency*, 579 F.2d 910, 914 (5th Cir.1978) (remarks on denial of rehearing).

Although the fluid concept of discriminatory intent is sometimes subtle and difficult to apply, there is ample evidence in this case of the correlation between municipal service disparities and racially tainted purposiveness to mandate a finding of discriminatory intent. Nearly every factor which has been held to be highly probative of discriminatory intent is present.

First, the magnitude of the disparity, evidencing a systematic pattern of municipal expenditures in all areas of town except the black

---

community was so inadequate that at many times of the day there was insufficient water for such normal purposes as bathing. 511 F.Supp. at 1379–81.

[4] For example, the city asserts that the unpaved streets are really "alleys" or "private driveways." But the district court properly found, after analysis of soil samples showing municipal road grading and intermittent repair, that there was sufficient evidence of municipal maintenance for the streets to be deemed dedicated to the City of Apopka by operation of Fla. Stat. § 95.361. *See* 511 F.Supp. at 1379.

The city claims that the water distribution problem results from inadequacies in the privately owned water pipes running from the city's main supply lines to indoor plumbing facilities. But the district court properly found that the source of the water scarcity lies in the fact that the city's main lines are inaccessible to many residences because, unlike the situation in the white community, many streets in the black community are not serviced by municipal main lines so that special "service lines" must be run from main lines on remote streets to as many as sixteen black residences. *See id.* at 1380–81.

Finally, the city argues that storm water drainage is a problem throughout the municipality. However, the district court properly found that while the white community is substantially serviced by a curb and gutter system, the "alternate" drainage system in the black community consists only of ditches dug along the sides of the street which function improperly because they are not regularly maintained. *See id.* at 1380.

community, is explicable only on racial grounds. *Arlington Heights v. Metropolitan Housing Corp.*, 429 U.S. 252, 266, 97 S.Ct. 555, 564, 50 L.Ed.2d 450 (1977); *see Washington v. Davis*, 426 U.S. at 242, 96 S.Ct. at 2048 (1976). Second, the legislative and administrative pattern of decision-making, extending from nearly half a century in the past to Apopka's plans for future development, indicates a deliberate deprivation of services to the black community. A municipal ordinance restricting blacks to living only on the south side of the railroad tracks remained in force in Apopka until 1968. The ordinance contributed to the ghetto-like qualities of the black residential area. Blacks continue to be significantly under-represented in administrative and elective positions, and their requests for improved municipal services continue to be ignored while substantial funds are expended to annex and develop the new predominantly white sections of town. Third, the continued and systematic relative deprivation of the black community was the obviously foreseeable outcome of spending nearly all revenue sharing monies received on the white community in preference to the visibly underserviced black community. While voluntary acts and "awareness of consequences" alone do not necessitate a finding of discriminatory intent, *Personnel Administrator v. Feeney*, 442 U.S. 256, 279, 99 S.Ct. 2282, 2296, 60 L.Ed.2d 870 (1979), "actions having foreseeable and anticipated disparate impact are relevant evidence to prove the ultimate fact, forbidden purpose," *Columbus Board of Education v. Penick*, 443 U.S. 449, 464, 99 S.Ct. 2941, 2945, 61 L.Ed.2d 666 (1979).

Although none of these factors is necessarily independently conclusive, "the totality of the relevant facts," *Washington v. Davis*, 426 U.S. at 242, 96 S.Ct. at 2048, amply supports the finding that the City of Apopka has engaged in a systematic pattern of cognitive acts and omissions, selecting and reaffirming a particular course of municipal services expenditures that inescapably evidences discriminatory intent. *See Columbus Board of Education v. Penick*, 443 U.S. at 456, 99 S.Ct. at 2946; *Personnel Administrator v. Feeney*, 442 U.S. at 279, 99 S.Ct. at 2296. The finding of discriminatory intent by the district court is not clearly erroneous and therefore is affirmed.

NOTES AND QUESTIONS

1.   *Hawkins v. Town of Shaw and the Right to Equal Services.* In the landmark decision in Hawkins v. Town of Shaw, 437 F.2d 1286 (5th Cir.1971), *aff'd en banc on rehearing*, 461 F.2d 1171 (5th Cir.1972), the court found that the town's virtually complete failure to provide basic public services, such as street paving and sewer hook-ups, to African-American neighborhoods, while providing such services to white neighborhoods, constituted racial discrimination in violation of the Equal Protection Clause. The Fifth Circuit acknowledged the absence of direct evidence of intent to discriminate, but found the enormous disparities in service provision

sufficient to establish unconstitutional racial discrimination. The Supreme Court specifically disavowed *Hawkins*'s reliance on racially discriminatory effects in Washington v. Davis, 426 U.S. 229, 245 (1976). The Supreme Court held that proof of discriminatory intent was necessary to establish racial discrimination in violation of the Equal Protection Clause.

Since *Washington v. Davis*, several lower federal courts, based on evidence similar to the facts of *Hawkins*, applied the discriminatory intent standard and found constitutional violations in the grossly disparate provision of municipal services. *E.g.*, Ammons v. Dade City, 783 F.2d 982 (11th Cir.1986) (racially discriminatory intent in drainage, street paving, and street repairs); Baker v. Kissimmee, 645 F.Supp. 571 (M.D.Fla.1986) (same). Plaintiffs have relied more heavily on Title VI of the Civil Rights Act, which prohibits discrimination on the base of "race or color or national origin" in any "program or activity" receiving federal funds. 42 U.S.C. § 2000d. The case after these notes illustrates that trend.

2. *A Right to Equal Services?* Certain bases for the allocation of services, such as racial discrimination, are clearly unlawful, but should we assume that as a general rule a locality must provide services of equal quantity and quality to each of its neighborhoods or groups of constituents? Would it be wrong for a government to allocate services according to willingness to pay, so that a neighborhood willing to pay extra taxes would receive more or better services? Could a government use the provision of services as a reward to loyal political supporters? Could it favor taxpayers who might otherwise move elsewhere in order to persuade them to remain within the jurisdiction? More generally, instead of establishing legal requirements, should we assume that the greater capacity for political participation at the local level plus the opportunities for exit to other communities provide sufficient controls on local government service allocation decisions?

Professor Frug, in City Services, 73 N.Y.U.L.Rev. 23 (1998), argues strenuously in favor of the equality norm in municipal services, asserting that all citizens, regardless of wealth, should receive the same level of service. Professor Frug notes that many services and government activities, such as admission to public schools or parks, voting rights, jury duty, and military service, are available to all irrespective of income or wealth. Moreover, he argues that the larger community's self-interest is better protected by a system that provides equal services to all because it is only in this way that the local government can fulfill its role in building communities.

Can we assume that all groups can protect their interests through the political process or by relocation? "Those without property have consistently occupied the bottom, not the top, in the fight for political influence. Even when they possess an equal vote, those without wealth often are not able to exert the political power and influence necessary to ensure equality in the provision of municipal services." Kessler v. Grand Central District

Management Association, 158 F.3d 92, 129–30 (2d Cir.1998) (Weinstein, J., dissenting).

Whatever the merits of the arguments, courts have been extremely reluctant to create a right to equal service. Professor Sklansky finds three reasons for this: (1) courts do not have the information necessary to make budgetary decisions on public spending; (2) standards of adequacy in public services are elusive; and (3) elected officials have strong incentives to respond to public demands for services. *See* David A. Sklansky, The Private Police, 46 U.C.L.A. L. Rev. 1165, 1283 (1999).

3. *Defining Equality.* One reason why courts may be cautious about creating a right to equal services is the difficulty of determining what equal service provision means:

> There are three general theories of justice that figure prominently in discussions about equity. The oldest and most prominent is Aristotle's *equity principle*, which states that goods should be divided in proportion to each claimant's contribution. * * *
>
> A second theory of justice is classical utilitarianism, which asserts that goods should be distributed so as to maximize the total welfare of the claimants (the *greatest good for the greatest number*). * * *
>
> A third approach to social justice * * * is due to John Rawls. * * * [His] central distributive principle may be simply stated: the least well-off group in society should be made as well off as possible.

H. Peyton Young, Equity: In Theory and Practice 9–10 (Princeton Univ. Press 1994).

Does this analysis suggest that a city's decision to rely on special assessments to pay for many services is consistent with a theory of equality, even if that means that neighborhoods with a greater ability and willingness to pay more assessments receive more services? Could a city also argue that targeting services to taxpayers considered most likely to otherwise leave the jurisdiction is also consistent with equality?

Would equality require that more money be spent in poorer neighborhoods than in more affluent ones if that is necessary to assure comparable levels of service quality? In Beal v. Lindsay, 468 F.2d 287 (2d Cir.1972), individual black and Puerto Rican residents sued New York City, alleging racial discrimination in the maintenance of city parks. They presented evidence to show that the park in their neighborhood had become a wasteland, with inoperable equipment, litter, abandoned cars, and frequent criminal activity. In contrast, city parks in predominantly white areas were safer and well maintained, equipped, and patrolled. The court rejected the claim, finding that the city spent equal amounts of money on all parks. In the court's view, the city had met its constitutional obligation with equal inputs of resources, even though it had not achieved equal results. *Accord*, Alexander v. Chicago Park District, 709 F.2d 463 (7th Cir.1983) (noting that disparity in park quality could be due to many factors such as greater vandalism or higher rates of usage caused by larger numbers of children in neighborhood).

Is equality of inputs enough even if that fails to assure equality of outputs? Is a municipality providing equal services if the size and frequency of its police patrols are the same in low crime and high crime areas? What is the nature of the municipality's service obligation?

NEW YORK URBAN LEAGUE, INC. V. STATE OF NEW YORK

United States Court of Appeals
71 F.3d 1031 (2d Cir.1995)

PER CURIAM:

Plaintiffs filed this action on October 20, 1995, challenging the allocation by the State of New York and the Metropolitan Transportation Authority ("MTA") of funds for mass transit in New York City and surrounding suburban communities. Plaintiffs claim that riders of the New York City Transit Authority ("NYCTA") subway and bus system, the majority of whom are members of protected minority groups, pay a higher share of the cost of operating that system than commuter line passengers, who are predominantly white, pay to support the commuter rail system, and that U.S. Department of Transportation ("U.S.DOT") regulations promulgated under Title VI of the Civil Rights Act of 1964 proscribe such a result. Upon filing their complaint, plaintiffs moved for preliminary injunctive relief barring the implementation of a proposed 20% fare increase for subway and bus riders. The United States District Court for the Southern District of New York (Robert P. Patterson, Jr., Judge) granted a preliminary injunction against the MTA on November 8, 1995. This court entered a stay the following day.

This appeal presents the narrow question of whether plaintiffs have made the requisite showing for preliminary injunctive relief barring the MTA from imposing the fare increase on the NYCTA lines. To justify such an injunction, plaintiffs must show irreparable harm in the absence of injunctive relief and a likelihood of success on the merits of their underlying claim. We conclude that they have not. * * *

I.   BACKGROUND

A.   Facts

At the heart of this case are the complex systems of public transportation serving New York City and surrounding suburban communities. The following facts are not in dispute. The New York City Transit Authority ("NYCTA") administers the subway and bus system within four boroughs of New York City, transporting some 1.5 billion passengers per year on twenty-five subway lines and 231 bus routes. The Long Island Railroad ("LIRR") and the Metro-North Commuter Railroad

("Metro-North") (collectively, the "commuter lines") carry 135 million passengers per year to some 250 stations located along nineteen lines. The NYCTA has annual operating expenses of $3.1 billion, while the commuter lines have annual operating expenses of $1.4 billion.

Both the NYCTA and the commuter lines operate under the umbrella of the Metropolitan Transit Authority ("MTA"), a public benefit corporation created under New York law. *See* N.Y. PUB.AUTH.LAW §§ 1263(1)(a), 1264 (McKinney 1982 & Supp.1995). * * *

Under New York law and applicable bond covenants, the MTA must be self-sustaining with respect to the combined operating expenses of the MTA and its subsidiary corporations, including the commuter lines. *Id.* § 1266(3). Similarly, the NYCTA must be self-sustaining with respect to its operating costs. *Id.* § 1202(1). Because the revenues derived from fares do not meet the operating costs of the NYCTA or the commuter lines, each depends upon funding from federal, state, and city sources to pay a percentage of its costs. * * *

In August 1995, the MTA projected that the NYCTA's operating costs would exceed its operating revenues (including income from fares and federal, state, and local subsidies) by $167 million in 1995 and $316 million in 1996. For the commuter lines, the MTA projected a slight surplus for 1995 and a deficit of $72 million for 1996. In response to these projections, the MTA board considered and adopted a funding package involving cost-cutting measures and fare increases for the NYCTA and the commuter lines. The MTA calculated that a 20% fare increase for the NYCTA would generate $45 million in additional revenue in 1995 and $274 million in additional revenue for 1996; and that a fare increase of 8.5% for the commuter lines would generate $5.6 million in 1995 and $33.5 million in 1996.

B. Procedural History

The thrust of the underlying complaint in this action is that riders of the New York City subway and bus system, compared to passengers on the commuter lines, bear a disproportionately high share of the cost of operating the transportation system they use.

Plaintiffs contend that, inasmuch as the NYCTA serves a predominantly minority population and the commuter lines serve an overwhelmingly white population, the disparity in the share of costs borne by the two groups of passengers violates U.S. DOT regulations promulgated under Title VI of the Civil Rights Act of 1964. * * *

II. DISCUSSION

A. Likelihood of Success on the Merits

Section 601 of Title VI of the Civil Rights Act of 1964 provides:

No person in the United States shall, on the ground of race, color, or national origin, be excluded from participation in, be denied the benefits of, or be subjected to discrimination under any program or activity receiving Federal financial assistance.

42 U.S.C. § 2000d.

In *Guardians Association v. Civil Service Commission*, 463 U.S. 582, 103 S.Ct. 3221, 77 L.Ed.2d 866 (1983), the Supreme Court held that this provision only prohibits *intentional* discrimination, not actions that have a disparate impact upon minorities. *See id.* at 610–11, 103 S.Ct. at 3236–37 (opinion of Powell, J., in which Burger, C.J., and Rehnquist, J., joined); *id.* at 612, 103 S.Ct. at 3237 (opinion of O'Connor, J.); *id.* at 641–42, 103 S.Ct. at 3253 (opinion of Stevens, J., in which Brennan and Blackmun, JJ., joined). Nonetheless, the Court concluded that Title VI delegated to federal agencies the authority to promulgate regulations incorporating a disparate impact standard. *See id.* at 584, 103 S.Ct. at 3223 (opinion of White, J.); *id.* at 623 n. 15, 103 S.Ct. at 3244 n. 15 (opinion of Marshall, J.); *id.* at 643, 103 S.Ct. at 3254 (opinion of Stevens, J., in which Brennan and Blackmun, JJ., joined); *see also Alexander v. Choate*, 469 U.S. 287, 293 & nn. 8–9, 105 S.Ct. 712, 716 & nn. 8–9, 83 L.Ed.2d 661 (1985).

The U.S. Department of Transportation has promulgated regulations under Title VI prohibiting actions with a disparate impact upon minorities. 49 C.F.R. § 21.5(b)(2) provides:

A recipient, in determining the types of services, financial aid, or other benefits, or facilities which will be provided under any such program . . . may not, directly or through contractual or other arrangements, utilize criteria or methods of administration which have the effect of subjecting persons to discrimination because of their race, color, or national origin. . . .

* * * A plaintiff alleging a violation of the DOT regulations must make a prima facie showing that the alleged conduct has a disparate impact. Once such a showing has been made, the burden shifts to the defendant to demonstrate the existence of "a substantial legitimate justification" for the allegedly discriminatory practice. * * * If the defendant sustains this burden, the plaintiff may still prove his case by demonstrating that other less discriminatory means would serve the same objective.

The underlying complaint in this case alleges that actions of the State of New York and the MTA have "placed a disproportionate amount of the cost of operating the MTA upon the predominantly minority riders of the NYCTA"—*i.e.*, that riders of the city subways and buses pay a higher percentage of the operating cost of the NYCTA than commuter rail passengers pay of the operating costs of the commuter rails. Complaint at 17. Plaintiffs do not dispute that (1) the allocation of subsidies to the

NYCTA and the commuter lines is commanded by state law; and (2) both the NYCTA and the commuter lines (or, more precisely, the MTA with respect to the commuter lines) are required to operate on a self-sustaining basis with respect to their operating costs. If the State chooses to allocate funds in a certain manner (or, for that matter, if the City decides to withhold funds from the NYCTA), and, as a result, sufficient funds are not available to meet the NYCTA's operating expenses, the NYCTA board (also the board of the MTA) has no choice within the framework of state law but to respond, either by adjusting the level of revenue taken in by the NYCTA or by taking other actions, such as cutting service. The plaintiffs ultimately object to and seek to alter the allocation of subsidies as between the NYCTA and the commuter lines.

The district court concluded that (1) plaintiffs had made a prima facie showing that the proposed fare increases, taken together, would have a disparate impact upon members of protected minority groups; and (2) the MTA had failed to demonstrate a substantial legitimate justification for its conduct. In so doing, the district court assessed the impact of the NYCTA and commuter line fare increases without examining the larger financial and administrative picture of which those fare increases are a part. We conclude that the district court made insufficient findings to support either of its conclusions.

* * *

1.   *Prima Facie Showing of Disparate Impact*

The district court's conclusion that the plaintiffs had made a prima facie showing of disparate impact was based primarily upon a comparison of the so-called "farebox recovery ratios" of the NYCTA and the commuter lines. The farebox recovery ratio measures the percentage of each system's operating cost—adjusted to include certain interest payments, depreciation, and the cost of police services—that is recovered through fare revenues. The district court found that the NYCTA fare increase would lead to a significant (12.2%) increase in the farebox recovery ratio for the subway and bus system, while the commuter line fare adjustment would lead to smaller increases (2.6% and 2.2%) in the respective farebox recovery ratios of Metro-North and LIRR.

Because the underlying claim challenges the total allocation of subsidies to the NYCTA and the commuter lines, the district court should have first assessed whether any measure or combination of measures could adequately capture the impact of these subsidies upon NYCTA and commuter line passengers. The MTA contends that the relative costs borne and benefits received by passengers of the two systems cannot be measured at all, because users of the NYCTA derive significant but difficult-to-quantify benefits from the subsidization of the commuter lines, including a reduction in traffic congestion, pollution, and other adverse effects that would accompany an increased use of cars by those commuting from the suburbs. The MTA also argues that, to the extent that the relative costs and benefits of the two systems can be measured at all, statistics other than the farebox recovery ratio are more appropriate, including: (1) the percentage of mean household income that NYCTA and commuter line passengers spend on commuting; (2) a comparison of the relative population of the areas served by the two systems and the relative subsidies flowing to each system; and (3) a measure reflecting relative capital subsidies to each system.

* * *

In our view, the farebox recovery ratio is not a sufficient basis for a finding of disparate impact. While for some purposes the farebox recovery ratio may be a convenient measure of the share of costs borne by different groups of passengers, the ratio ignores financial reality in an important respect. It does not reveal the extent to which one system might have higher costs associated with its operations—costs stemming from different maintenance requirements, schedules of operation, labor contracts, and so on. There is no reason to assume that the expenses of each system would bear any sort of proportionate relationship, particularly when those systems are fundamentally different in terms of how they carry passengers, frequency of stops, and operating schedules. The different costs associated with the two systems can, in effect, obscure the level of subsidies provided to each. The farebox recovery ratio thus says very little about the overall allocation of funds to the two systems, which is the focus of the complaint in this action. Without further factual findings supporting its selection as an appropriate statistical measure of the subsidization of transportation systems, the farebox recovery ratio itself is insufficient to support a conclusion that the total allocation of subsidies has a disparate impact upon minority NYCTA riders—a conclusion essential to a determination of plaintiffs' likelihood of success on the merits.

2. Substantial Legitimate Justification

Even if there were a sufficient basis on this record for a finding that plaintiffs had made a prima facie showing of disparate impact, the district court's conclusion as to the second prong of the analysis—whether the defendants have shown a substantial legitimate justification for the challenged conduct—is likewise unsupported. The district court found that, "absent State appropriations or a substantial cutback in personnel with consequential cutbacks in operations, a fare increase for the NYCTA *is a business necessity in the near future.*" New York Urban League, Inc. v. Metropolitan Transp. Auth., 905 F.Supp. 1266, 1278 (S.D.N.Y.1995) (emphasis supplied). Nevertheless, the district court ultimately concluded that the MTA had not provided a legitimate justification for the NYCTA fare increase. In so concluding, the district court reasoned that * * * even though an NYCTA fare increase will be necessary in the near future, there is no reason for the relative NYCTA and commuter line fare increases to lead to a disparate impact * * *.

The district court's * * * observation—that there is no reason for the NYCTA and commuter line fare increases to result in a disparate impact—is unsupported. The district court's reasoning seems to suggest that the MTA could meet its revenue goals through an equal fare increase for the NYCTA and the commuter lines. Even if the MTA could shift fare revenues from the commuter lines to the NYCTA, the district court made no finding that the availability of commuter line revenues would significantly affect the necessity for the 20% increase on the NYCTA. Indeed, the MTA offered testimony that raising the equivalent revenues through an equal percentage increase on each system would result in a 22 cents increase of the NYCTA fare, likely to be rounded to 25 cents (or 20%). In the alternative, the district court's reasoning suggests that plaintiffs' legal claim would be resolved if the MTA were to increase the commuter line fare by 20%, or by whatever amount would yield the same farebox recovery ratio as that projected for the NYCTA. But the district court made no finding that a greater increase in the commuter fare would provide a means for increasing the NYCTA's revenues, or eliminate the justification for the NYCTA raise. * * *

Thus, the district court made insufficient findings to reject the MTA's stated justification for a fare increase. Indeed, the district court did not properly frame the question: the focus of the plaintiffs' complaint is the total allocation of subsidies to the NYCTA and the commuter lines, but the district court did not consider, much less analyze, whether the defendants had shown a substantial legitimate justification for this allocation. The MTA and the State identified several factors favoring a higher subsidization of the commuter lines. By encouraging suburban residents not to drive into the City, subsidization of the commuter rails minimizes congestion and pollution levels associated with greater use of automobiles in the city; encourages business to locate in the City; and provides additional fare-paying passengers to the City subway and bus system. In these respects and in others, subsidizing the commuter rails may bring material benefits to the minority riders of the subway and bus system. The district court dismissed such factors, concluding that the MTA board did not explicitly consider them before voting on the NYCTA and commuter line fare increases. That finding is largely irrelevant to whether such considerations would justify the relative allocation of total funds to the NYCTA and the commuter lines.

* * *

CONCLUSION

We conclude that plaintiffs are not entitled to an injunction on the grounds articulated by the district court. The district court's conclusion that plaintiffs were likely to succeed on the merits of their claim was based upon insufficient findings that a disparate impact exists or that the defendants' proffered justifications were inadequate. * * *

Accordingly, we vacate the injunction and remand the cause for further proceedings consistent with this opinion.

NOTES AND QUESTIONS

1. *Establishing Discrimination.* Leaving aside the question of whether any differences in subsidy levels are justified, why wasn't the plaintiffs' showing that commuter rail passengers were more heavily subsidized by state aid, so that they paid a lower share of the cost of a transit ride than did city transit passengers, enough to make out a prima facie case of disparate impact? Suppose that in one system the passengers are paying sixty percent of the cost of a ride (with tax dollars making up the difference) while in the other passengers are paying eighty percent of the cost of a ride. Isn't the first set of riders receiving more favorable treatment? The court relies on the fact that the more heavily subsidized system might have higher costs. But higher costs are likely to result from either higher quality services or system inefficiencies. Would either of those factors justify a higher level of subsidy?

Before the district court, plaintiffs had presented various types of statistical evidence to support their claim that the funding system discriminated in favor of the commuter lines. In addition to the farebox recovery ratio, the plaintiffs compared the two transit systems in terms of (a) the ratio of passengers to subsidies; (b) subsidies per passenger; (c) subsidies per vehicle mile (per subway car, train car, or bus); and (d) subsidies per revenue passenger mile. New York Urban League, Inc. v. Metropolitan Transp. Authority, 905 F.Supp. 1266, 1275, *rev'd on other grounds*, 71 F.3d 1031 (2d Cir.1995). Under the Second Circuit's approach would any of these be an appropriate basis for inter-system comparison? For a history of subsequent developments in the case, *see* Kevin L. Siegel, Discrimination in the Funding of Mass Transit Systems, 4 Hastings W.-N.W.J.Envtl.L. & Pol'y 107, 110 (1997).

2. *Establishing Discriminatory Impact.* The complicated financial structure and funding formulas of the two transit lines in the main case made it difficult to establish whether the system actually discriminated against users of one of them. In many other Title VI cases, discrimination is much easier to establish, but plaintiffs must overcome the hurdle of proving that the discrimination has an impact on the basis of their membership in a protected class. In Sandoval v. Hagan, 197 F.3d 484 (11th Cir.1999), *rev'd on other grounds sub nom.*, Alexander v. Sandoval, 532 U.S. 275 (2001), for instance, the plaintiffs filed a Title VI challenge against Alabama's decision

to provide drivers' license testing only in English. Although the policy was easily found to discriminate against non-English speakers, the plaintiffs then had to prove discrimination against a class protected by Title VI—that is, that the English-only policy created a disparate impact based on national origin. Thus, the analysis focused on whether non-English speakers are also predominantly of non-U.S. origin. *See also* Flores v. Arizona, 48 F.Supp.2d 937 (D.Ariz.1999) (noting that plaintiffs must establish that alleged discrimination in school funding creates a discriminatory impact on the plaintiffs "because of their membership in a protected group, not because they are poor or because they reside in lower wealth school districts." *Id.* at 954).

3.   *Justifying Discriminatory Impact.* As the *New York Urban League* court noted, once a Title VI plaintiff establishes discriminatory impact, the burden then shifts to the defendant to demonstrate a "substantial legitimate justification" for its conduct. What flaw did the Second Circuit find in the district court's analysis? The appellate court indicated that commuter rail's ability to encourage suburbanites to take public transportation provided "material benefits" to the New York City transit riders. Is the court suggesting that a greater subsidy for the wealthier suburban riders may be justified because the commuters will drive their cars if the fare is raised? Lower subsidies for city residents, however, many of whom have no alternative to public transportation, will not produce the same decrease in ridership. How can the discriminatory impact be justified by a fact that is itself based on inequalities?

What standard should apply to evaluate the defendant's justification for discriminatory programs and services in a Title VI challenge? Although the Supreme Court has not spoken directly on this question, lower courts have applied the standard applicable to employment discrimination cases under Title VII of the Civil Rights Act—that is, they have required the government defendant to establish that the challenged discriminatory practice has a "manifest relationship" to a legitimate governmental goal. *See, e.g.,* Larry P. v. Riles, 793 F.2d 969 (9th Cir.1984).

4.   *Private Right of Action for Discriminatory Impact.* In 2001, the Supreme Court reversed the *Sandoval* decision discussed in Note 2, holding that private individuals may not sue to enforce the disparate impact regulations promulgated under Title VI. *See* Alexander v. Sandoval, 532 U.S. 275 (2001). The Court, in an opinion by Justice Scalia, determined that as a matter of statutory interpretation only the federal agencies providing financial assistance are authorized to enforce the regulations that forbid the recipients of federal funding from utilizing criteria or methods of administration that have a racially disparate impact. The Court noted that one important enforcement mechanism available to agencies is the termination of program funding, although such termination is subject to a variety of procedural restrictions, including notification of the appropriate congressional committees and the possibility of judicial review. Thus, without disturbing its precedent that regulations promulgated under Title VI may

adopt a disparate impact standard for defining discrimination, the Court may have significantly curtailed local government liability for such discrimination. Nevertheless, at least until the Court holds otherwise, the federal government is still able to use the threat of loss of federal funds to enforce the discriminatory impact standard under Title VI. In addition, state civil rights laws may authorize discriminatory impact challenges to public services. *See* Darensburg v. Met. Transp. Comm., 636 F.3d 511 (9th Cir. 2011) (rejecting discriminatory impact challenge under state law to funding allocation between bus and rail in San Francisco).

For an analysis of judicial application of the discriminatory effects test under Title VI prior to *Sandoval, see* Charles F. Abernathy, Legal Realism and the Failure of the "Effects" Test for Discrimination, 94 Geo.L.J. 267 (2006). In this piece, the author concludes that the test did not provide a "judicially manageable tool for reviewing state and local practices having a disparate effect on racial minorities," *id*. at 270. His evaluation of the caselaw led to this sweeping conclusion: "The results are so overwhelmingly condemnatory of the effects test as a useful tool for judges that if this had been a clinical trial of a new medicine, it would have been deemed unethical to continue." *Id.*

B. TORT LIABILITY

This section explores the state rules of municipal tort liability and the ways in which courts and legislatures have defined the ability of individuals to recover for damages they suffer as a result of municipal action. The role of federal law in creating state and local liability, especially 42 U.S.C. § 1983 and other civil rights statutes, is beyond the scope of this Section's coverage. The doctrine of state sovereign immunity was firmly rooted and universally accepted by the states when they framed their constitutions. Municipal immunity, in contrast, was subject to much greater variation in acceptance. The principle of municipal immunity may be traced to the early English decision of Russell v. Men of Devon, 100 Eng. Rep. 359 (K.B. 1788). For a thorough discussion of the history of governmental immunities under state tort law, *see* F.W. Harper, F. James, Jr., and O.S. Gray, 5 The Law of Torts § 29.1–.6 (2d ed. 1986).

Beginning in the 1950s, and extending through the 1970s, widespread judicial and legislative activity resulted in modification or outright abolition of municipal immunity from tort liability. The rationale of the Illinois Supreme Court is illustrative:

> The original basis of the immunity rule has been called a 'survival of the medieval idea that the sovereign can do no wrong,' or that 'the King can do no wrong.' . . . . [H]ow immunity ever came to be applied in the United States of America is one of the mysteries of legal evolution. And how it was then infiltrated

into the law controlling the liability of local governmental units has been described as one of the amazing chapters of American common-law jurisprudence. 'It seems, however, a prostitution of the concept of sovereign immunity to extend its scope in this way, for no one could seriously contend that local governmental units possess sovereign powers themselves.' As was stated by one court, 'The whole doctrine of governmental immunity from liability for tort rests upon a rotten foundation. It is almost incredible that in this modern age of comparative sociological enlightenment, and in a republic, the medieval absolutism supposed to be implicit in the maxim, 'the King can do no wrong,' should exempt the various branches of the government from liability for their torts, and that the entire burden of damage resulting from the wrongful acts of the government should be imposed upon the single individual who suffers the injury, rather than distributed among the entire community constituting the government, where it could be borne without hardship upon any individual, and where it justly belongs.' Barker v. City of Santa Fe, 47 N.M. 85, 136 P.2d 480, 482. Likewise, we agree with the Supreme Court of Florida that in preserving the sovereign immunity theory, courts have overlooked the fact that the Revolutionary War was fought to abolish that 'divine right of kings' on which the theory is based.

Molitor v. Kaneland Community Unit District, 163 N.E.2d 89, 93–94 (Ill.1959)

During the 1980s, the pendulum swung back in favor of some municipal immunity. Two facts fueled the backlash: some governments were hit with very large damages awards; and a well-publicized insurance crisis made the cost of liability insurance a top legislative concern. The resulting landscape in the early 21st century is a patchwork of state constitutional provisions and state tort liability and immunity statutes. Flexible, judicially created doctrines, along with frequent statutory modification, expand and contract the limits of governmental immunity as public sensibilities change. The cases that follow explore the different components that currently shape the law of municipal tort liability. Each individual state, of course, will have its own particular combination of legislative enactments and judicial doctrine. Remember, too, that just because a government may not enjoy immunity from tort liability in any given case, a plaintiff must still establish liability under the relevant state tort law principles. As a practical matter, though, a finding of no immunity may make a government far more likely to settle a case.

As you study the specific immunity principles and defenses to liability discussed in the following pages, it is important to keep in mind the overarching policy contours of the immunity debate. Those who favor broad municipal immunity argue that wide ranging liability will cripple state and local governments and inhibit their willingness to respond to new social problems. Moreover, the absence of immunity means that courts, rather than local elected decision-makers, play a key role in the allocation of municipal funds and services. Critics of municipal immunity, in contrast, argue that liability will merely make government more responsible and will properly compensate citizens who suffer harm at the hands of their government. They argue that neither grass-roots political participation nor ease of exit from localities is sufficient to deter negligence in the provision of public services. A basic question is whether the law should treat governmental service providers any differently than their private sector counterparts. Is there a distinctive public interest in the decision-making autonomy of local government bodies?

1. GOVERNMENTAL IMMUNITY

LITTLE V.
MISSISSIPPI DEPARTMENT OF TRANSPORTATION
Supreme Court of Mississippi
129 So. 3rd 132 (2014)

On the evening of November 26, 2004, Floyd Little, Roger Pierce, and Kelly Sykes were operating separate vehicles on Highway 26 in George County. Unbeknownst to them, a large pine tree had fallen across the highway. Little was traveling east on Highway 26, and he collided with the tree first. Pierce was coming from the opposite direction and ran into the other side of the tree. Sykes then collided with the rear of Pierce's vehicle. All three incurred property damage; Little and Pierce sustained personal injuries. Little, Pierce, and Sykes (collectively "Little") filed a complaint against the Department. Little alleged that the Department was negligent in the following respects: (1) failing to adequately maintain, repair, and inspect the highway; (2) failing to remove dead or dangerous trees near the road; and (3) failing to properly patrol, find, and remove the leaning tree before it fell.

* * * [T]he circuit court concluded that the Department was entitled to discretionary-function immunity and granted the motion to dismiss. Little appealed, and the Court of Appeals affirmed.. Little filed a petition for writ of certiorari, which we granted.

* * * The application of the Mississippi Tort Claims Act (MTCA) is a question of a law that is reviewed *de novo*. * * *

Under the MTCA, a government entity and its employees are immune from liability for claims arising from "the exercise or performance or the failure to exercise or perform a discretionary function or duty [.]" Miss.Code Ann. § 11–46–9(1)(d) (Rev.2012). The language of

Section 11–46–9(1)(d) requires us to look at the *function* performed—not the *acts* that are committed in furtherance of that function—to determine whether immunity exists. * * * If the function is ministerial, rather than discretionary, there is no immunity for the acts performed in furtherance of the function. A ministerial function is one that is "positively imposed by law." *Pratt,* 97 So.3d at 72. The function at issue here is right-of-way maintenance, which is a ministerial function required by law. The decision of whether to cut down a tree is not a function, but rather an act performed in furtherance of the ministerial function of maintaining highway rights-of-way.

In the instant case, the Court of Appeals held that right-of-way maintenance was a discretionary function, thus, the Department was immune from liability. *Little,* 129 So.3d at 196. The Court of Appeals's holding is in direct conflict with language this Court used recently in *Mississippi Transportation Commission v. Montgomery,* 80 So.3d 789 (Miss.2012). In that case, the issue was whether the maintenance of traffic control devices was a discretionary function for the Mississippi Transportation Commission (the Commission). (discussing Miss.Code Ann. § 63–3–305 (Rev.2004)). We wrote:

> Ordinarily, where a statute mandates the government or its employees to act, all acts fulfilling that duty are considered mandated as well, and neither the government nor its employees enjoys immunity. Occasionally, however, the Legislature will mandate that a political subdivision fulfill some particular function, but then specifically set forth that some portion or aspect of that function is discretionary. When that happens, acts fulfilling the discretionary portion of the governmental function enjoy immunity.

> Here, Section 65–1–65 imposes a statutory duty on the highway department to maintain all state highways. *See* Miss.Code Ann. § 65–1–65 (Rev.2005). Were this the only statutory provision at issue, we would find that the Commission is not immune for the acts carrying out that function. The Legislature, however, carved out a portion of the function mandated by that statute, and made it discretionary. Section 63–3–305 gives local authorities discretion in placing and maintaining traffic devices "as they may deem necessary to indicate and [to] carry out the provisions of this chapter. . . ." Miss.Code Ann. § 63–3–305 (Rev.2004). Although the Commission's duty to maintain highways is not discretionary, the placing of warning signs is, because the Legislature has provided specific language in the statute extending discretion to those acts. Otherwise, the Commission would not enjoy immunity.

Montgomery, 80 So.3d at 798. According to *Montgomery,* there is no immunity for maintenance of state highways unless a statute carves out a particular exception for a certain activity, such as traffic control devices. *Id.* Addressing *Montgomery* in the instant case, the Court of Appeals wrote:

> Our [S]upreme [C]ourt has long held that road maintenance and repair are discretionary, rather than ministerial functions. *See, e.g., Mohundro v. Alcorn Cnty.,* 675 So.2d 848, 854 (Miss.1996) *Coplin v. Francis,* 631 So.2d 752, 754–55 (Miss.1994); *State ex rel. Brazeale v. Lewis,* 498 So.2d 321, 323 (Miss.1986). However, in *Montgomery,* the [C]ourt . . . seemed to deviate from its long-standing and bright-line rule that road maintenance and repair implicate a discretionary function. . . .
>
> Here, unlike in *Montgomery,* no additional statute is involved. Nevertheless, we note that the [C]ourt in *Montgomery* did not expressly overrule its prior decisions holding that road maintenance and repair are discretionary functions. * * *
>
> In *Lewis,* the [C]ourt held that a clearly ministerial duty may require the exercise of discretion in the discharge of the otherwise ministerial function. *Lewis,* 498 So.2d at 323. In such a case, the government actor would be immune from suit for injuries arising out of the exercise of his discretion in the discharge of what is otherwise a ministerial function. Therefore, we are constrained to hold that our [S]upreme [C]ourt did not intend to change existing law regarding its earlier holdings that road maintenance and repair are discretionary functions.

Little, 129 So.3d at 195. The Court of Appeals was correct that *Montgomery* indicated a change in the law, and such was the Court's intention. However, because we did not overrule prior, contrary cases in *Montgomery,* confusion on the part of the lower courts is understandable. To the extent that *Montgomery* failed to overrule conflicting cases, we do so today.

Previously, we have said that, while a certain act may be mandated by statute, *how* that act is performed can be a matter of discretion. *See, e.g., McQueen v. Williams,* 587 So.2d 918, 922 (Miss.1991) (although sheriff had a statutory duty to keep prisoners in jail, "personal deliberation, decision, and judgment" were involved in performing that duty, therefore, it was "discretionary in nature"); *Brazeale v. Lewis,* 498 So.2d 321, 323 (Miss.1986) (even if board of supervisors had ministerial duty to maintain the roads, "making the determination as to which roads should be the better maintained under such conditions would be a discretionary matter"). It is the *function* of a governmental entity—not the *acts* performed in order to achieve that function—to which immunity does or does not ascribe under the MTCA. Today we make it clear that, pursuant to *Montgomery,* the line of cases holding otherwise is overruled. We hold that, "where a statute mandates the government or its employees to act, all acts fulfilling that duty are considered mandated as well, and neither the government nor its employees enjoys immunity." *Montgomery,* 80 So.3d at 798.

Because Section 65–1–65 requires the Department to maintain and repair state highways, that duty—and all acts in furtherance of that duty—are ministerial unless, as in *Montgomery,* another statute makes a particular act discretionary. * * * The Department is not entitled to discretionary-function immunity for failure to properly maintain and repair highways because that function is ministerial. Therefore, the circuit court erred in granting the Department's motion to dismiss on that basis, and we reverse and remand for further proceedings consistent with this opinion.

The dissent continues to toe the line of cases that we eroded in *Montgomery* and overrule today. In truth, the dissent's explication of our caselaw ascribing immunity to acts rather than functions does even more to highlight the extent to which our precedent has strayed from the language of the MTCA itself. As we note above, it is the *function,* not the act, to which the MTCA grants or denies immunity. We—the judicial branch of government—should not place ourselves in the position of changing the substantive law enacted by the Legislature, and unfortunately the cases upon which the dissent relies reveal that, in the area of functional immunity under the MTCA, we have been doing just that. Today, we provide a much-needed correction. If the Legislature, as the state's policy-making body, wishes to ascribe immunity to acts rather than functions, it is certainly free to do so, but it has not done so yet.

The Department's duty to maintain and repair highway right-of-way is a ministerial function. Therefore, the Department is not entitled to discretionary-function immunity for the acts, or the failure to act, associated with that function, and the circuit court erred in granting the Department's motion to dismiss on that basis. The judgments of the George County Circuit Court and the Court of Appeals are reversed, and the case is remanded to the circuit court for further proceedings consistent with this opinion.

WALLER, CHIEF JUSTICE, dissenting:

I agree that the Mississippi Department of Transportation ("MDOT") is required to inspect and maintain state highways; however, the implementation of maintenance is discretionary because it involves decisions made by employees which must be based on considerations of public policy. Because of this Court's longstanding bright-line rule that road maintenance and repair is discretionary, I respectfully dissent.

* * * This Court and the Court of Appeals repeatedly have held that road maintenance and repair are discretionary as opposed to ministerial functions. * * * [T]he duty to maintain highways and right-of-way under Section 65–1–65 is a discretionary function, which necessarily involves economic and policy considerations.

Under the Mississippi Torts Claims Act ("MTCA"), a governmental entity and its employees are immune from liability for claims arising from "the exercise or performance or the failure to exercise or perform a discretionary function or duty[.]" Miss.Code Ann. § 11–46–9(1)(d) (Rev.2012). A two-prong analysis is required to determine whether governmental conduct is discretionary: "(1) whether the activity involved an element of choice or judgment; and if so, (2) whether the choice or judgment . . . involves social, economic or political policy alternatives." *Doe v. State ex rel. Miss. Dep't of Corrections,* 859 So.2d 350, 356 (Miss.2003) (quoting *Bridges v. Pearl River Valley Water Supply Dist.,* 793 So.2d 584, 588 (Miss.2001)). A governmental duty is ministerial if "the duty is one which has been positively imposed by law . . . its performance required at a time and in a manner or upon conditions which are specifically designated. . . ." *L.W. v. McComb Separate Mun. Sch. Dist.,* 754 So.2d 1136, 1141 (Miss.1999). *See also City of Jackson v. Doe ex rel. J.J.,* 68 So.3d 1285 (Miss.2011) (operation of a city park was a discretionary function because no regulations dictated the manner in which a city park should be operated).

Section 65–1–65 provides in part, "it shall be the duty of the director, subject to the rules, regulations and orders of [MDOT] . . . to organize an adequate and continuous patrol for the maintenance, repair, and inspection of all of the state-maintained state highway system [.]" Miss.Code Ann. § 65–1–65 (Rev.2012). With regard to the first prong of the test, Section 65–1–65 clearly involves an "element of choice or judgment," because it gives discretion to MDOT to determine how the highways are to be maintained by setting rules and organizing patrols throughout the state's thousands of miles of highway.

Regarding the second step for determining discretionary-function immunity, this Court reasoned, as it pertained to road maintenance by a member of a board of supervisors in *Brazeale:*

> [W]e recognize that, for various reasons, at least some roads may be in a state of disrepair from time to time, particularly due to the lack of funds, which would, of course, require that the main, heavily-traveled roads receive the supervisor's immediate attention. Certainly, making the determination as to which roads should be the better maintained under such conditions would be a discretionary matter. . . .

Brazeale, 498 So.2d at 323. Following this rationale, Court of Appeals wrote in *Lee v. Mississippi Department of Transportation*: "We recognize that MDOT has a limited number of funds to disperse in the maintenance and upkeep of the State's highways. Therefore, MDOT *must* use its discretion and judgment when determining the order in which roads will be resurfaced or repaired." *Lee,* 37 So.3d at 78.

Section 65–1–65 does not specify in what manner or under what conditions maintenance is to be performed, thus calling for discretion and judgment on the part of MDOT. Further, highway maintenance by MDOT involves policy and economic considerations through the exercise of MDOT's discretion in determining which highways or roads should be repaired first and which maintenance issues are most important.

I would affirm the Court of Appeals decision and the judgment of the trial court and follow the precedent this Court has established since the Mississippi Torts Claims Act was adopted in 1984. I would find that MDOT's duty to maintain, repair, and inspect highways is discretionary, and MDOT is entitled to discretionary function immunity under Mississippi Code Section 11–46–9(1)(d).

TRUMAN V. GRIESE
Supreme Court of South Dakota
762 N.W.2d 75 (2009)

Monny Truman (Truman), individually and as special administrator of his wife Patricia's estate, and Steven and Dee Ann Rounds sued Darren Griese (Griese), in his official capacity as South Dakota Department of Transportation (DOT) Pierre Region Traffic Engineer, and employees of the DOT as John Does after a car accident forty miles west of Pierre. Griese moved for summary judgment based on sovereign immunity. The trial court granted Griese's motion. Truman appeals. We affirm.

FACTS

The accident occurred at the intersection of three highways: South Dakota Highway 34, South Dakota Highway 63, and United States Highway 14. This intersection is also known as "Four Corners." The traffic design of this interchange is not easily conveyed in words. S.D. Highways 63 and 34 meet at a "T" intersection. S.D. 34 forms the top of the "T," running east-west. S.D. 63 forms the bottom of the "T," north-south, but continues west along the top-*left* part of the "T," merging at a right angle with S.D. 34.

U.S. 14 travels across top-*right* part of the "T," east-west with S.D. 34, then continues north-south with S.D. 63. However, U.S. 14 does not continue to a stop at the right angle intersection of the "T." Instead, U.S. 14 curves between the two roads, just southeast of the "T." This curved route creates two "Y" intersections at the junctions of U.S. 14 and S.D. 63 (south of the "T" intersection), and U.S. 14 and S.D. 34 (east of the "T" intersection). As a result of this design, the through-traffic on U.S. 14 does not stop to make the direction change.

On February 13, 2004, Monny and Patricia Truman, Dee Ann Rounds, twelve-year-old Ciara Rounds, and eight-year-old Zachary Rounds were driving in Truman's vehicle from Pierre to Rapid City. They traveled west-bound on U.S. 14/S.D. 34. Truman approached Four Corners and followed U.S. 14 along the south-bound curve.

At the same time, Richard Giago was driving north on S.D. 63/U.S. 14 (The bottom of the "T"). Giago's wife, Sue Ann, and son, Jayden, were passengers in his vehicle. When Giago reached the point where S.D. 63/U.S. 14 diverge, he continued northward on S.D. 63, across the "Y" junction.

The vehicles collided almost head on. The results were devastating. Truman suffered broken bones, a skull injury, and permanent vision loss in his right eye; Patricia was killed; Dee Ann suffered severe head injuries and multiple broken bones; Dee Ann and Steven lost their unborn child, Jesse; Ciara and Zachary suffered minor injuries; Giago and Jayden both suffered severe injuries and were hospitalized; Sue Ann was killed.

Truman brought claims against Griese for negligence, wrongful death and loss of consortium. Truman alleged Griese violated duties imposed by SDCL 31–28–6 by failing to post additional traffic control signs at Four Corners. Griese filed a motion for summary judgment on the basis of sovereign immunity. The trial court entered an order in favor of Griese's motion.

Truman appeals the following issue:

Whether Truman's claims under SDCL 31–28–6, regarding the necessity for and placement of highway warning signs, are barred by sovereign immunity under the facts of this case.

ANALYSIS AND DECISION

No one can look at the facts surrounding this litigation without a sense of sorrow. Lives were lost and lives were damaged. Yet our task is a narrow one—to determine if the State of South Dakota's sovereign immunity applies. * * * Because we conclude that Griese's duties under SDCL 31–28–6 are discretionary, sovereign immunity applies and the trial court is affirmed. * * *

Sovereign Immunity: Ministerial and Discretionary Duties

Shortly after the adoption of Article III, section 27 of our State Constitution, this Court first recognized that sovereign immunity applied to the construction and maintenance of highways. *Bailey v. Lawrence County,* 5 S.D. 393, 59 N.W. 219 (1894).

> [W]hile it is true that the legislature has imposed upon counties the duty of keeping in repair the bridges on the public highways, and provided the method for raising revenue by taxation requisite for such purpose, yet to hold that the counties are thereby made liable for injuries caused by defects in such bridges, in the absence of legislation making them so liable, would be a species of judicial legislation.

Id. at 221.

Shortly thereafter, we concluded that sovereign immunity applied to discretionary governmental duties but not to ministerial ones. *State v. Ruth,* 9 S.D. 84, 68 N.W. 189 (1896). In *Ruth* we defined a ministerial duty as a narrow one. It is where a governmental employee "disregarded a plain provision of the law[.]" *Id.* at 191. All other duties that fell outside that definition were discretionary. We also noted that "[i]t is the nature of the particular duty, and not the character of the office, which determines whether or not a duty is ministerial." *Id.*

> [A] ministerial act is defined as *absolute, certain, and imperative,* involving merely the execution of a specific duty arising *from fixed designated facts* or the execution of a set task imposed by law prescribing and *defining the time, mode and occasion of its performance with such certainty that nothing remains for judgment or discretion,* being a simple, definite duty arising under and because of stated conditions and imposed by law. A ministerial act envisions direct adherence to a *governing rule or standard* with a compulsory result. *It is performed in a prescribed manner without the exercise of judgment or discretion as to the propriety of the action.*

Hansen, 584 N.W.2d at 886.

In order to find a duty "ministerial," we must find a "governing rule or standard" so clear and specific that it directs the government actor without calling upon the actor to ascertain how and when to implement that rule or standard. Moreover, in *Hansen,* we reviewed the duties of that DOT official and noted "one could not pluck an ordinary citizen off the street and expect they could successfully execute the duties of [this office]." 584 N.W.2d at 887–888.

Nature of the Duties Under SDCL 31–28–6

SDCL 31–28–6 provides:

> The public board or officer whose duty it is to repair or maintain any public highway shall erect and maintain *at points in*

> *conformity with standard uniform traffic control practices* on each side of any sharp turn, blind crossing, or other point of danger on such highway, except railway crossings marked as required in § 31–28–7, a substantial and conspicuous warning sign, which sign shall be on the right-hand side of the highway approaching such point of danger. A violation of this section is a Class 1 misdemeanor.

(Emphasis added.) Truman alleges that the omission of warning signs at Four Corners is a violation of a *ministerial* duty under SDCL 31–28–6. We disagree.

Under SDCL 31–28–6, the "governing rule or standard" is not the mere presence of a "sharp turn, blind crossing, or other point of danger," but the existence of "standard uniform traffic control practices." *See id.* Contrary to Truman's position presented at oral argument, the language "in conformity with standard uniform traffic control practices" does not refer to the characteristics of the "substantial and conspicuous warning sign." Instead, this phrase, "in conformity with standard uniform traffic control practices," plainly modifies the "points" at which signs "shall" be located. Therefore, any ministerial duties pertaining to the placement of traffic control signs under this statute must be required by standard uniform traffic control practices.

The placement of signs in situations that have neither standard nor uniform practices must *necessarily* be outside any ministerial requirements of SDCL 31–28–6. We have previously held that such sign placement, per SDCL 31–28–6, requires "the exercise of judgment or discretion as to the propriety of the action." *Hansen,* 584 N.W.2d at 886. Therefore, in order to establish a ministerial duty under this statute, "standard uniform traffic control practices" must exist and delineate at which specific points signs must be erected at this type of intersection. *See* SDCL 31–28–6. * * *

The dissent makes much of the word "shall" as a mandatory directive as it is found in the text of SDCL 31–28–6. However, "[s]tatutes and court rules must be construed in their entirety. The effect of the word 'shall' may be determined by the balance of the text of the statute or rule." *Discover Bank v. Stanley,* (citations omitted). In an examination of the text of SDCL 31–28–6, it is only when that public official in the exercise of his or her discretion determines that the public highway contains "any sharp turn, blind crossing or other point of danger on such highway" based upon "standard uniform traffic control practices" that he or she "shall erect and maintain . . . a substantial and conspicuous warning sign . . ." * * *

Ultimately, Truman argues that Four Corners contains a design that he believes is unsafe. Because of its non-standard design, he is unable to establish standard uniform traffic control practices regarding the placement of warning signs. Without standard uniform traffic control practices, the placement or omission of signs by government actors is discretionary under SDCL 31–28–6. * * *

CONCLUSION

One can only imagine the reaction of an average citizen if he or she * * * were "plucked off the street" and informed it was now his or her legal duty to place "substantial and conspicuous warning signs" at any "sharp turn, blind crossing or other point of danger" as defined by "standard uniform traffic control practices" on every highway in this state. How much stronger would their reaction be when they realize that the failure to place a sign in every conceivable place would result in their being subjected to suit and criminal charge simply based on a plaintiff's pleading disagreeing with the initial placement decision, and a jury being allowed to "Monday morning quarterback" his or her conclusions about what is a "sharp turn, blind crossing or other point of danger," even if he or she somehow followed "standard uniform traffic control practices?" There is a reason that the duty to select appropriate places for warning signs was entrusted to defendant Griese, who happens to be the Pierre Region Traffic Engineer of the South Dakota Department of Transportation. Given the thousands of miles of highways in this state that run over all kinds of terrain, such an undertaking is not a ministerial task for amateurs; it calls for a person with professional training to exercise professional discretion in the performance of his or her duties under SDCL 31–28–6.

SDCL 31–28–6 requires appropriate warning signs in places where "standard uniform traffic control practices" indicate or where the exercise of the engineer's discretion determines a "sharp turn, blind crossing or other point of danger" exists. Thus, there are basically three options when one looks at SDCL 31–28–6: signs everywhere, signs nowhere, or signs at some points placed there by the exercise of the collective discretion of experts as expressed in uniform standards and the individual discretion of experts in non-standardized situations. Under our settled law, absent applicable uniform standards, the individual expert's decisions are protected by sovereign immunity until the Legislature decides otherwise. * * *

SABERS, RETIRED JUSTICE (dissenting).

I respectfully dissent. Griese argues and the trial court declared that summary judgment was appropriate because "the duty under [SDCL] 31–28–6 is a discretionary duty and therefore . . . sovereign immunity applies." I disagree. In fact, I believe that when certain factual circumstances exist, the duty mandated by SDCL 31–28–6 is ministerial. Additionally, there are at least eight reasons why summary judgment should not have been granted by the trial court and affirmed by the majority of this Court in this case.

A dichotomy exists: ministerial or mandatory acts are provided no immunity, while discretionary acts are immunized. The difficulty arises in distinguishing the discretionary acts from those that are ministerial. South Dakota case law has identified factors helpful in drawing this distinction. These factors include:

(1) The nature and importance of the function the officer is performing;

(2) The extent to which passing judgment on the exercise of discretion by the officer will amount necessarily to passing judgment by the court on the conduct of a coordinate branch of government;

(3) The extent to which the imposition of liability would impair the free exercise of his discretion by the officer;

(4) The extent to which the ultimate financial responsibility will fall on the officer;

(5) The likelihood that harm will result to members of the public if the action is taken;

(6) The nature and seriousness of the type of harm that may be produced;

(7) The availability to the injured party of other remedies and other forms of relief.

King v. Landguth, 726 N.W.2d 603, 607. Upon applying these factors to this case, it is important to recognize that liability will not fall upon the officer exercising his duty, the likelihood of harm to the public is great, and the nature and seriousness of the harm is extremely grave. Moreover, passing judgment on the officer's discretion will not be passing judgment upon a separate branch of government and there is no real availability of relief to the injured parties. Therefore, these factors favor the conclusion that the act at issue was ministerial, not discretionary. * * *

Common sense and South Dakota law directs that the highway officer shall erect and maintain substantial and conspicuous warning signs under these circumstances. * * * By affirming the trial court's grant of summary judgment, this Court violates the plaintiff's state and federal constitutional rights to a jury trial, and undoubtedly, offends traditional notions of justice. * * *

Chief Justice Gilbertson concludes with the argument that "one can only imagine the reaction of the average citizen if he or she" were "plucked off the street" and required to perform the duties of the engineers of the State Highway Department. I submit he is missing the whole point. The State Highway Department has over a thousand employees who are educated, trained, and equipped to do the jobs the Legislature has mandated them to do. Moreover, the average citizen as a juror continually makes determinations on others' competence, skill, or lack thereof, or outright negligence.

In contrast, I submit that any right-thinking average citizen would be "shocked" to be presented with the substantial injuries, damages, hospitalizations, and the deaths of three people caused by the failure of this highway engineer to do his duty as mandated by the South Dakota Legislature, and then to be told by the majority of this Court that there is no remedy for these injuries and deaths, even though caused by "the want of ordinary care or skill." * * *

Incredibly, under the majority's view, the Highway Department could arbitrarily, unreasonably, and capriciously design the busiest, most dangerous intersection in South Dakota without stop signs or signage of any kind and never be accountable, despite numerous injuries and deaths year after year.

* * * I am not suggesting a directed verdict on liability, but rather a reversal and remand for a jury trial on the merits of this case in accordance with the state and federal constitutions.

NOTES AND QUESTIONS

1.   *Defining Discretionary Function.* These two cases illustrate very different interpretations of discretionary function immunity. *Little* takes what it describes as a functional approach, whereas the *Truman* court falls back on whether the "average citizen" would have the required professional training to exercise the action that forms the basis of the personal injury lawsuit. In addition, the dissenting judges in both cases offer alternative analytical approaches, which may be more persuasive to you than their respective majority opinions.

Can the *Little* court's functional approach be squared with the statutory language, which establishes immunity for claims arising from "the exercise or performance or the failure to exercise or perform a discretionary function or duty"? Doesn't the court remove the possibility that the exercise of a duty can qualify as discretionary and thus immune? What could the term "discretionary duty" mean anyway?

The *Truman* court's "average citizen" seems a bit off the mark as well. Does the fact that ordinary citizens can't perform an action without the specialized training given to government employees make that action discretionary? Surely there are many ministerial duties that ordinary, untrained citizens would be unable to perform; is the court suggesting they are all now immune?

Both courts refer to legislative prerogative to decide the immunity question. With the functional test, the burden is on the legislature to grant immunity to otherwise ministerial acts; for the *Truman* court, however, the legislature must act to remove immunity if it believes that the court has improperly protected a particular government action. Which approach strikes a better balance between legislative and judicial powers? In your opinion, which test better draws the line between the need for government accountability for its actions and the need for government to act to protect the public health, safety, and welfare without the "Monday morning quarterbacking" mentioned by the court in *Truman*? Can one or both of the tests be criticized as imposing an unreasonable burden on the legislature to anticipate too many unpredictable chains of events?

2. *Discretionary vs. Ministerial in Other States.* The discretionary vs. ministerial test is widely used and hard to articulate. See if any of the following judicial definitions seem more persuasive and/or workable. Apply them to the facts of the cases described in Note 3 below.

New York: "Discretionary . . . acts involve the exercise of reasoned judgment which could typically produce different acceptable results whereas a ministerial act envisions direct adherence to a governing rule or standard with a compulsory result." Tango v. Tulevech, 459 N.E.2d 182, 185 (N.Y.1983).

Washington: "(1) Does the challenged act, omission, or decision necessarily involve a basic governmental policy, program, or objective? (2) Is the questioned act, omission, or decision essential to the realization or accomplishment of that policy, program, or objective as opposed to one which would not change the course or direction of the policy, program, or objective? (3) Does the act, omission, or decision require the exercise of basic policy evaluation, judgment, and expertise on the part of the governmental agency involved? (4) Does the governmental agency involved possess the requisite constitutional, statutory, or lawful authority and duty to do or make the challenged act, omission, or decision? If these preliminary questions can be clearly and unequivocally answered in the affirmative, then the challenged act, omission, or decision can, with a reasonable degree of assurance, be classified as a discretionary governmental process and nontortious, regardless of its unwisdom. If, however, one or more of the questions call for or suggest a negative answer, then further inquiry may well become necessary, depending upon the facts and circumstances involved." Evangelical United Brethren Church of Adna v. State, 407 P.2d 440, 445 (Wash.1965).

Wisconsin: "A public officer's duty is ministerial only when it is absolute, certain and imperative, involving merely the performance of a specific task when the law imposes, prescribes and defines the time, mode and occasion for its performance with such certainty that nothing remains for judgment or discretion." Lister v. Board of Regents, 240 N.W.2d 610, 622 (Wis.1976).

3. *Problems.* The following examples illustrate some of the many circumstances in which local governments are sued in tort. Decide whether the local government should be immune in each of the following situations, basing your answer on application of the ministerial vs. discretionary function test. Remember that a judicial refusal to find immunity does not result in automatic governmental liability; the plaintiff will still need to establish all elements of a cause of action in tort.

(a) Edwin Hill owned two pit bull dogs with a history of violent incidents. The city had received several complaints; subsequently, it held hearings but determined that the dogs were not subject to seizure as vicious dogs. The city informed Hill, however, that it had determined that his dogs were dangerous. It ordered Hill to repair his property's fences and to enroll the dogs in obedience training programs. Hill did not comply with the order; the city failed to monitor the situation. Five months later, Betty Lou Stidham was mauled to death by the dogs. Her estate sued the city. Chase v. City of Memphis, 971 S.W.2d 380 (Tenn.1998).

(b) John Taillon was killed when the vehicle he was driving was struck by a vehicle driven by Ioanis Grigas at a hazardous intersection where 17 accidents had occurred in the previous eight years. Grigas had not seen the large "Slow" sign at the approach to the intersection. Several years before the accident, the city had asked the state Department of Transportation to install flashing beacons to warn drivers; the state responded that such a device was not warranted. The estate of John Taillon sued the city and the state; it alleged that the city should be liable for its failure to monitor the intersection and to report the numerous accidents to the state. Bergeron v. City of Manchester, 666 A.2d 982 (N.H.1995). Although most state courts grant discretionary function immunity to decisions on the placement of traffic signals, the Minnesota Supreme Court refused to follow that trend in Nusbaum v. County of Blue Earth, 422 N.W.2d 713 (Minn.1988).

(c) Patrick Denais was a patient of the Hennepin County Mental Health Center. On July 23, he told a doctor at the center that he was contemplating suicide and asked to be hospitalized. The doctor evaluated him, but concluded that he had sufficient self-control and did not require hospitalization. Denais began to take two medications for depression and met with the doctor four days later. At that time, the doctor noted that Denais was continuing to feel depressed, but the doctor noted "no suicidal plan or intent." About two weeks later, Denais hanged himself in the bedroom of his home. His estate sued the county. Terwilliger v. Hennepin County, 561 N.W.2d 909 (Minn.1997). *Compare* Cairl v. State, 323 N.W.2d 20 (Minn.1982) (discretionary function immunity for releasing mentally handicapped individual from residential facility for Christmas home visit; patient subsequently set fire that killed one person).

(d) In 1972, Wilbert Landwehr received a permit to construct a home on land across the street from a ditch that formed part of the city's storm sewer drainage system. At that time, several city officials expressed concern about possible flooding. The house sits at one of the lowest points in the area. In 1979, the city engineer reviewed the city's storm sewer system and recommended numerous improvements to the area around Landwehr's home. No action was taken on the report. In 1983, the property was flooded during heavy rains, causing more than $53,000 in damage. The current homeowners sued the city. Chabot v. City of Sauk Rapids, 422 N.W.2d 708 (Minn.1988).

(e) Joseph Giacomantonio, a police officer, is involved in the production of a television program called "Keeping Greater Portland Safe." The program broadcasts names and photographs of individuals with outstanding arrest warrants. Giacomantonio mistakenly placed Charles Carroll on the list of those wanted for theft. Carroll had been cited recently for driving under the influence of alcohol; Giacomantonio had apparently copied his name from the wrong list. Carroll sued the city, alleging defamation and negligent and intentional infliction of emotional distress. Carroll v. City of Portland, 736 A.2d 279 (Me.1999).

4. *Influence of the Federal Tort Claims Act.* Though many state courts use the discretionary vs. ministerial standard for determining the scope of local government tort immunity, another group follows the lead of the federal courts' interpretation of the Federal Tort Claims Act, 28 U.S.C. § 2680(a). That statute authorizes tort claims against the federal government and provides immunity for "the exercise or performance or the failure to exercise or perform a discretionary function or duty." In a series of cases, the Supreme Court has developed a distinction between planning decisions, which are immune, and operational decisions, which are not. Applying that categorization to its own government tort liability statute, the Iowa Supreme Court has made immunity available only to "those decisions based on political, social, or economic policy considerations which cannot be assessed by customary tort standards." Messerschmidt v. Sioux City, 654 N.S.2d 879, 883 (Iowa 2002). The court has refused immunity in cases alleging injuries resulting from: a school district's hiring, retention, and supervision of a middle-school teacher, *see* Doe v. Cedar Rapids Comm. Sch. Dist., 652 N.W.2d 439 (Iowa 2002); a building inspector's issuance of an occupancy permit, *see* Madden v. City of Eldridge, 661 N.W.2d 134 (Iowa 2003); city adoption of a particular timing sequence for traffic lights, *see* Graber v. City of Ankeny, 656 N.W.2d 157 (Iowa 2003); a school teacher's choice of discipline for infraction of school rules, *see* Ette ex rel. Ette v. Lin-Mar Comm. Sch. Dist., 656 N.W.2d 62 (Iowa 2002); a city's removal of a road barricade during a parade, *see* Messerschmidt v. Sioux City, 654 N.W.2d 879 (Iowa 2002); and a teacher's failure to supervise activities of her students, *see* City of Cedar Falls v. Cedar Falls Comm. Sch. Dist., 617 N.W.2d 11 (Iowa 2000).

The court's opinion in Schmitz v. City of Dubuque, 682 N.W.2d 70 (Iowa 2004) held that the city's decision to not grade trail shoulders in a park was not an immune discretionary function. The court concluded that no "social, economic, [or] political policy" was involved, and that cost alone would be an insufficient basis for immunity. 682 N.W.2d at 75–76. Why does judicial rejection of a government's cost-benefit analysis not violate the court's admonition against second-guessing a government's social, economic, or political policy? It is not immediately apparent that the planning vs. operational distinction provides any better gauge of the proper scope of government immunity.

Other states using the planning vs. operational approach to government immunity include Florida, *see* Wallace v. Dean, 3 So. 3d 1035 (Fla. 2009); Alaska, *see* Angnabooguk v. State, 26 P.3d 447 (Ak. 2001); Tennessee, *see* Bowers v. City of Chattanooga, 826 S.W. 2d 427 (Tenn. 1992); Minnesota, *see* Schroeder v. St. Louis County, 708 N.W. 2d 497 (Minn. 2006); and Idaho, *see Jones v. St. Maries, 727 P.2d 1161 (Id. 1986).*

5. *Statutory Retention of Immunity.* Many state statutes establish a general rule of government liability for its negligent acts or omissions and then carefully carve out exceptions for immune discretionary activities. The Maine statute reproduced below, Me.Rev.Stat.Ann.tit. 14, § 8101 et seq., adopts the opposite default position:

§ 8103. Immunity from Suit

1. Immunity. Except as otherwise expressly provided by statute, all governmental entities shall be immune from suit on any and all tort claims seeking recovery of damages. When immunity is removed by this chapter, any claim for damages shall be brought in accordance with the terms of this chapter.

§ 8104–A. Exceptions to Immunity

Except as specified in section 8104–B, a governmental entity is liable for property damage, bodily injury or death in the following instances.

1. Ownership, maintenance or use of vehicles, machinery and equipment. A governmental entity is liable for its negligent acts or omissions in its ownership, maintenance or use of any:

    A. Motor vehicle . . .

    B. Special mobile equipment . . .

    C. Trailers . . .

    D. Aircraft . . .

    E. Watercraft . . .

    F. Snowmobiles . . . and

    G. Other machinery or equipment, whether mobile or stationary.

2. Public buildings. A governmental entity is liable for its negligent acts or omissions in the construction, operation or maintenance of any public building or the appurtenances to any public building.

§ 8104–B. Immunity notwithstanding waiver

Notwithstanding section 8104–A, a governmental entity is not liable for any claim which results from:

1.   Undertaking of legislative act. Undertaking or failing to undertake any legislative or quasi-legislative act, including, but not limited to, the adoption or failure to adopt any statute, charter, ordinance, order, rule, policy, resolution or resolve;

2.   Undertaking of judicial act. Undertaking or failing to undertake any judicial or quasi-judicial act, including, but not limited to, the granting, granting with conditions, refusal to grant or revocation of any license, permit, order or other administrative approval or denial;

3.   Performing discretionary function. Performing or failing to perform a discretionary function or duty, whether or not the discretion is abused and whether or not any statute, charter, ordinance, order, resolution or policy under which the discretionary function or duty is performed is valid or invalid;

4.   Performing prosecutorial function. Performing or failing to perform any prosecutorial function involving civil, criminal or administrative enforcement;

Me.Rev.Stat.Ann.tit. 14, § 8104–B

What advantages does a statute like Maine's have for local government defendants? Is § 8104–B necessary? Other states that take an approach similar to Maine's include California (Cal.Gov't Code § 815), Delaware (Del. Code Ann. tit. 10, §§ 4011–4012), New Jersey (N.J.Stat.Ann. § 59:1–1–:12–3 and Tennessee (Tenn. Code Ann. §§ 29–20–101 to –407).

6.   *Governmental vs. Proprietary Functions.* One of the earliest lines of demarcation in the history of municipal immunity was the distinction between governmental and proprietary functions. Even in the days of extensive municipal immunity, many state courts imposed liability for harm caused by local governments in the execution of their proprietary, as opposed to their governmental, functions. Much like the discretionary versus ministerial and planning versus operational tests, the governmental versus proprietary distinction is difficult to apply. Relevant factors include whether the municipality is generating a financial profit from the activity, whether the function is a traditional or historical governmental function, or whether the activity is mandatory or permissible. Not surprisingly, the cases reveal considerable inconsistency; one dissenting justice in Vermont lamented the court's unwillingness to abandon the distinction and cited several examples of "artificial distinctions and inconsistent results . . . For instance, as our law stands now, relief may be obtained from towns (1) when the plaintiff is injured because of ice caused by a leaking water main, but not because of ice

caused by water escaping from a fire hydrant . . . (2) when the plaintiff is injured during the construction of a public playground, but not during the operation of a mechanical rope ski tow in a municipal park . . . and (3) when the plaintiff is injured while driving over a hole caused by the town's repair of a sewer or water line, but not while driving over a hole caused by the town's repair of a street." Hillerby v. Colchester, 706 A.2d 446, 455 (Vt. 1997) (Johnson, J., dissenting). In that case, however, the majority justified its continued adherence to the distinction: "Municipalities perform governmental responsibilities for the general public as instrumentalities of the state; they conduct proprietary activities only for the benefit of the municipality and its residents." *Id.* at 447. A few other courts have maintained the common law distinction between governmental and proprietary functions, *e.g.,* Jean Moreau & Assoc. v. Health Center Comm. ex rel. County of Chesterfield, 720 S.E.2d 105 (Va. 2012) ("A function is governmental in nature if it is directly related to the general health, safety, and welfare of the citizens * * * in contrast, a function is proprietary in nature if it involves a privilege and power performed primarily for the benefit of the municipal corporation."); Williams v. City of New Haven, 707 A.2d 1251 (Conn.1998) (immunity for governmental function bars suit against city for injuries sustained by child injured by high speed stream of water from fire hydrant); City of Round Rock v. Smith, 687 S.W.2d 300 (Tex. 1985) (city's approval of subdivision plat is an immune governmental function).

In a personal injury case arising out of the World Trade Center bombing, the New York Court of Appeals held that the provision of security was a governmental function entitled to immunity. While recognizing that the Port Authority's responsibilities for keeping its buildings safe fall along a continuum, the court concluded that although the Port Authority would not be immune in a slip and fall case involving its alleged negligent failure to maintain a safe environment, the actions complained of in this case involved complex governmental decisions involving the strategic allocation of resources. *See* In re World Trade Center Bombing Litigation, 957 N.E.2d 733 (N.Y. 2011).

For a detailed critique of the governmental-proprietary rule as "elusive and unsatisfactory", *see* F.W. Harper, F. James, Jr., and O.S. Gray, 5 The Law of Torts § 29.6 (2d ed. 1986).

Some states have enacted legislation to abolish the distinction between governmental and proprietary functions; some explicitly remove immunity for both, *e.g.,* Idaho Code § 6–903; Iowa Code § 670.2; Mont. Code Ann. § 2–9–102; while some explicitly establish immunity for both, *e.g.,* Okla.Stat. tit. 51, § 152.1; Tenn. Code Ann. § 29–20–201. A few state statutes preserve the distinction, immunizing governmental functions, while making proprietary functions liable, *e.g.,* Mich.Comp.Laws § 691.1413; Va. Code Ann. § 15.2–4533. Remember, though, that irrespective of whether any particular state preserves the distinction between governmental and proprietary functions, the planning versus operational or discretionary versus ministerial distinction may still be important in defining the limits of municipal liability.

7. *Official Immunity for Government Officers and Employees.* Plaintiffs in local government tort cases may also sue the individual government officers and employees who were involved in the actions leading to the alleged injury. Although the inquiries in both instances will be substantially similar, the legal rules and standards for evaluating the potential immunity of the officials themselves may be quite different from the rules for the local government defendant. Actual recovery against a defendant employee or officer may take various forms, depending on the state's liability statutes: the individual official may be personally liable; the government as the employer may be vicariously liable under the doctrine of respondeat superior (*see* Watson v. Metropolitan Transit Commission, 553 N.W.2d 406, 414–15 (Minn.1996)); or state law may provide for government reimbursement of successful claims against government officials for actions deemed to be within the scope of the official's employment (*e.g.*, 51 Okla.St.Ann. § 162).

Although local government officers may enjoy immunities similar to their government employer, sovereign immunity does not form the doctrinal basis of official immunity. The supreme court of Wisconsin identified the different underlying policy rationales that support its doctrine of official immunity:

> (1) The danger of influencing public officers in the performance of their functions by the threat of lawsuit; (2) the deterrent effect which the threat of personal liability might have on those who are considering entering public service; (3) the drain on valuable time caused by such actions; (4) the unfairness of subjecting officials to personal liability for the acts of their subordinates; and (5) the feeling that the ballot and removal procedures are more appropriate methods of dealing with misconduct in public office.

Lister v. Board of Regents, 240 N.W.2d 610, 621 (Wis.1976).

In contrast to the approving tone of *Lister*, some state courts view official immunity in a more negative light. In Terwilliger v. Hennepin County, 561 N.W.2d 909 (Minn.1997), for instance, the court justified its refusal to extend official immunity to a psychiatrist in a county medical facility by noting that it would be unfair "to erect a shield against malpractice liability that is unavailable to private practitioners." *Id.* at 913.

In any attempt to establish the applicable legal standards of official immunity or liability, careful research into the doctrine of the relevant state is necessary. Nevertheless, some starting points can be identified. First, judicial and legislative officials are likely to enjoy absolute immunity for their official actions. Kimps v. Hill, 546 N.W.2d 151, 156 n. 6 (Wis.1996); Holytz v. City of Milwaukee, 115 N.W.2d 618, 625 (Wis.1962). Second, discretionary function immunity may be available to the official defendant, but its limits need not coincide with the discretionary function immunity of the government defendant. In some states, the individual official receives broader protection than the government defendant, while in others, the official's immunity may be more narrowly defined. *Compare* Nusbaum v. County of

Blue Earth, 422 N.W.2d 713, 718 n. 4 (Minn.1988) ("Discretion in the context of an employee's immunity was much broader than the type of discretion referred to in the discretionary function exception applicable in actions against governmental units") *with* Carroll v. City of Portland, 736 A.2d 279, 282 n. 3 (Me.1999) (under state tort claims act, "liability is the rule and immunity the exception for governmental employees, [while] immunity is the rule and liability the exception for governmental entities"). Finally, the defendant official's state of mind may be relevant to immunity: in many states, official immunity is lost if the officer's conduct was "malicious, willful and intentional." Kimps v. Hill, 546 N.W.2d 151, 156 n. 7 (Wis.1996). *See also* Shoemaker v. Smith, 725 A.2d 549, 560 (Md.1999) (actual malice needed to defeat official immunity defined as "an act without legal justification or excuse, but with an evil or rancorous motive influenced by hate"); City of Amarillo v. Martin, 971 S.W.2d 426, 429 (Tex.1998) ("employees' official immunity is waived only for more culpable conduct, such as gross negligence, bad faith, or willful or wanton conduct").

2. PUBLIC DUTY DEFENSE AND THE SPECIAL DUTY EXCEPTION

If a government tort defendant is not successful in its attempt to establish immunity from suit, the plaintiff's next challenge will be to prove the traditional elements of tort liability, namely, duty to the plaintiff, causation, and harm. The applicable legal principles generally mirror those used in private tort litigation and will not be repeated here. Unlike the private individual defendant, however, a government defendant is uniquely able to raise the public duty defense. Simply stated, "the rule declares government owes a duty of protection to the public, not to particular persons or classes." Tipton v. Town of Tabor, 567 N.W.2d 351, 357 (S.D.1997). The limits of the defense, its rationale, and the special duty exception to the defense, are discussed in the following cases.

GLEASON V. PETERS
Supreme Court of South Dakota
568 N.W.2d 482 (1997)

AMUNDSON, JUSTICE

Charles and Ann Gleason (Gleasons) on behalf of their son, Michael Gleason (Michael), appeal the grant of summary judgment in favor of Deputies Dave Smith (Smith) and Brian Dean (Dean) (often collectively referred to as officers), and Lawrence County. We affirm.

On December 31, 1994, Wayne Huck received permission from his father, David Huck (Huck), to have an underage drinking party on their leased premises located a few miles north of Whitewood, South Dakota. Kegs of beer were purchased and various students from Brown High School in Sturgis, South Dakota, were invited. As the students arrived, they were charged an entrance fee if they intended to drink the beer supplied by the Hucks.

It is undisputed that two Lawrence County police officers received an anonymous tip of a potential juvenile party near Whitewood. Deputy Smith was the first officer to arrive at the scene after noticing a bonfire. He drove through an unlocked gate on the Huck premises. At that time, Huck approached Smith's vehicle and the two conversed about the party. Smith then left the scene and met with other officers to discuss options regarding further investigation of the party. Smith initially spoke with Dean and then the two contacted the chief deputy for guidance. The chief deputy suggested using a spotting scope[1] to assist with the identification of the individuals in order to obtain probable cause. However, the officers were unable to do so, as they received a priority call regarding another matter to be investigated forthwith.

Meanwhile, Michael arrived at the Huck residence. He did not drink alcoholic beverages before or during the party. While there, Michael was attacked by Trevor Peters (Peters), Eric Johnson (Johnson), and Christopher Schleuning (Schleuning), other students attending the party. After being hit and kicked repeatedly, Michael was driven by a friend to his parents' residence. From there, he was taken to the emergency room at a hospital in Sturgis. As a result of the beating, Michael received two reconstructive surgeries on his face and incurred medical expenses in excess of $40,000.

Gleasons, on behalf of Michael, sued * * * Deputies Smith and Dean, and Lawrence County for failing to stop the party. The trial court granted summary judgment in favor of Smith, Dean, and Lawrence County based on the special duty test established in *Tipton v. Town of Tabor*, 538 N.W.2d 783, 787 (S.D.1995) (*Tipton I*). Michael appeals. * * *

I.   PUBLIC-DUTY RULE.

Gleasons argue that the public-duty rule should be abrogated, because it "has no place in South Dakota jurisprudence[.]" We disagree. We recently upheld the application of the public-duty rule in *Tipton v. Town of Tabor*, 567 N.W.2d 351, 358 (*Tipton II*), citing various reasons supporting the doctrine. One of these reasons is to promote "accountability for offenders, rather than police who through mistake fail to thwart offenses." 567 N.W.2d at 356. "Otherwise, lawbreaker culpability becomes increasingly irrelevant with liability focused not on the true malefactors, but on local governments." *Id.* This is particularly applicable to the case at hand, because to hold as Gleasons urge would be to hold the officers accountable for the unforeseeable actions of

---

[1]   [Editors' note: A spotting scope is a single barrel, high powered binocular. Its original use was in rifle competitions or target practice, to allow inspection of the placement of shots on a target. It is now used in some states by law enforcement personnel for close range observation.]

lawbreakers simply because the officers were unable to stop an underage drinking party. As we have stated, "[g]enerally, the law imposes 'no duty to prevent the misconduct of a third person.' " 567 N.W.2d at 357 (quoting *Cracraft v. City of St. Louis Park*, 279 N.W.2d 801, 804 (Minn.1979)).

Gleasons are essentially urging this Court to allow a cause of action against the county under a theory of strict liability. The facts in this case certainly do not warrant such a result. Therefore, we again decline the opportunity to open the floodgates of litigation and abrogate the public duty rule in South Dakota.

II. *TIPTON I* FACTORS.

Not having abrogated the public-duty doctrine, we address Gleasons' second argument on appeal. They argue that the trial court erred in determining there was no genuine issue of material fact as to whether Smith, Dean, and Lawrence County possess a special relationship with Gleasons.

The special duty rule provides that a plaintiff must show a breach of a duty owed to him/her as an individual rather than to the community at large in order to establish liability. * * *

> Ordinarily, a breach of the general duty to prevent criminal acts which police owe to the public does not impose liability upon the employing governmental unit for damages which particular citizens suffer as a result of the breach. Instead, only where a special duty, i.e., a duty particularized as to an individual, is breached by the police will the municipality be held liable for damages. . . . When the reliance element is either not present at all or if present, is not causally related to the ultimate harm, this underlying concern is inapplicable and the invocation of the special duty exception is then no longer justified.

Eugene McQuillin, Municipal Corporations § 53.04.50, at 179 (3rd Ed.1993) * * *

In *Tipton I*, this Court recognized that there may be certain circumstances in which a government entity possesses a special duty that results in liability. In order to properly examine those circumstances, we adopted four factors to be applied when determining whether a county "assumes to act for the protection of individuals":

> "1) the state's actual knowledge of the dangerous condition;
>
> 2) reasonable reliance by persons on the state's representations and conduct;
>
> 3) an ordinance or statute that sets forth mandatory acts clearly for the protection of a particular class of persons rather than the public as a whole; and

4)   failure by the state to use due care to avoid increasing the risk of harm."

Tipton I, 538 N.W.2d at 787. * * * "Strong evidence concerning any combination of these factors may be sufficient to impose liability on a government entity." *Id.* This was slightly modified, however, in *Tipton II*, wherein this Court held that meeting only one element, actual knowledge, is insufficient to establish a private duty. *Tipton II*, 567 N.W.2d at 363–64 (stating, "To impose tort liability upon local law enforcement for failure to protect an individual solely upon actual knowledge of imminent danger directly conflicts with the principal rationale behind the public duty rule[.]") Keeping this modification in mind, we address each of the four *Tipton I* factors in a light favorable to Gleasons.

A.   Actual Knowledge

According to *Tipton II*, " '[a]ctual knowledge' means knowledge of 'a violation of law constituting a dangerous condition.' Constructive knowledge is insufficient: a public entity must be uniquely aware of the particular danger or risk to which a plaintiff is exposed. It means knowing inaction could lead to harm." 567 N.W.2d at 358 (citations omitted). In addition, "actual knowledge denotes a foreseeable plaintiff with a foreseeable injury." 567 N.W.2d at 359. Therefore, in the case before us, the officers must have had actual knowledge that their failure to stop the party would lead to Michael being assaulted by individuals who attended the party.

Gleasons, however, merely argue there was substantial evidence that Smith was aware of juveniles consuming alcohol on the Huck premises. Assuming it is true that Smith knew juveniles were consuming alcohol at the party,* * * the actual knowledge element is not met, because Gleasons presented no evidence * * * that Smith knew there would be an assault and that a victim would be injured. In fact, a great leap would be required to show Smith knew an assault would occur. * * *

B.   Reasonable Reliance

Gleasons fail to include an argument or cite authority in their brief concerning the second factor, reliance on the police officers' conduct. "Failure to cite authority violates SDCL 15–26A–60(6) and constitutes a waiver of that issue." *State v. Phillips*, 489 N.W.2d 613, 616 (S.D.1992).

C.   Ordinance for Protection of Particular Class

As stated in *Tipton II*, "[t]his element 'permits recovery against a government entity for negligent failure to enforce its laws only when there is language in a statute or ordinance which shows an intent to protect a particular and circumscribed class of persons.' " 567 N.W.2d at 366 (quoting *Tipton I,* 538 N.W.2d at 786) (other citations omitted).

In their brief to this Court, Gleasons contend SDCL 7–12–4 applies to this element, which states:

> It shall be the duty of the sheriff to comply with all orders of the attorney general or his agents and at all times, whether on duty under the call of the attorney general or his agents or not, to see to it as far as may be possible that all the laws of this state and especially all laws relating to alcoholic beverages are faithfully executed and enforced.

* * * The clear language of this statute provides that officers are to enforce the law. This certainly means to enforce the law in order to protect the general public and not a particular class of individuals.

D.   Failure To Avoid Increasing Risk of Harm

This factor means the action of the officers must cause harm or expose Gleasons to a greater risk. *Tipton II*, 567 N.W.2d at 366–67. Gleasons argue this factor "has a strong presence in this case." However, they misinterpret the meaning of the element. Rather than demonstrate how the officers failed to avoid increasing the risk of harm, Gleasons simply argue the officers failed to use due care. Even if we assume it is true that the officers failed to use due care and were unable to decrease any possible harm to Michael, we have stated, "[f]ailure to diminish harm is not enough." *Id.* (citation omitted). It is undisputed that no affirmative action by the officers " 'contributed to, increased, or changed the risk which would have otherwise existed.' " 567 N.W.2d at 367 (quoting *Von Batsch v. American Dist. Telegraph Co.*, 175 Cal.App.3d 1111, 222 Cal.Rptr. 239, 246–47 (1985) (involving a killing by intruders after officers failed to find evidence of intruders)). All that is shown here is that the officers failed to eliminate the potential danger of an assault being committed on a juvenile at the party. The undisputed facts in this case disclose the officers exposed Michael to no greater a risk than that to which the public was exposed. Therefore, Gleasons fail to meet the requirements of *Tipton II*.

LAUER v. CITY OF NEW YORK

Court of Appeals of New York
733 N.E.2d 184 (2000)

KAYE, CHIEF JUDGE.

On this appeal we revisit a familiar subject: whether a member of the public can recover damages against a municipality for its employee's negligence. Here we answer that question in the negative.

Three-year-old Andrew Lauer died on August 7, 1993. That same day, Dr. Eddy Lilavois, a New York City Medical Examiner, performed an autopsy and prepared a report stating that the child's death was a homicide caused by "blunt injuries" to the neck and brain. Although the report indicated that the brain was being preserved for further examination, the following day a death certificate was issued stating that Andrew's death was a homicide. Based on the Medical Examiner's conclusion, the police began investigating what they thought was a homicide, focusing primarily on plaintiff, Andrew's father. Weeks later, on August 31, 1993, the Medical Examiner and a neuropathologist conducted a more detailed study of Andrew's brain. The report, prepared in October 1993, indicated that a ruptured brain aneurysm caused the child's death, thus contradicting the earlier conclusion. The Medical Examiner, however, failed to correct the autopsy report or death certificate, and failed to notify law enforcement authorities.

Meanwhile, the Police Department's investigation into Andrew's death continued. Some 17 months later, in March 1995, after a newspaper expose, the autopsy findings were revised, the police investigation ceased and an amended death certificate was prepared. As a result of this incident, the City Medical Examiner who had conducted the examination resigned. Plaintiff and his estranged wife subsequently commenced separate actions. * * *

In the present action seeking $10 million in damages against the City of New York, the Office of the Chief Medical Examiner, Dr. Lilavois and the Police Department, plaintiff alleges * * * both negligent and intentional infliction of emotional distress. He claims that defendants' conduct—including the Medical Examiner's negligent performance of the autopsy, failure to correct the erroneous report and death certificate, and failure to disclose that Andrew's death was not a homicide—"precipitated the destruction of [his] marriage * * * forced him to sell his home and leave his neighborhood, and caused him to become the object of public scorn, humiliation, ridicule, embarrassment, harassment and contempt throughout the City of New York." He further alleges that he "sustained severe and debilitating emotional distress, emotional anguish, anxiety and mental suffering."

* * * No one disputes that the Medical Examiner's misconduct here in failing to correct the record and deliver it to the authorities was ministerial. * * *

We do not agree with plaintiff that a ministerial breach by a governmental employee necessarily gives rise to municipal liability. Rather, a ministerial wrong "merely removes the issue of governmental immunity from a given case" * * *. Ministerial negligence may not be immunized, but it is not necessarily tortious. * * * There must still be a basis to hold the municipality liable for negligence. * * *

This brings us directly to an essential element of any negligence case: duty. Without a duty running directly to the injured person there can be no liability in damages, however careless the conduct or foreseeable the harm. * * * While the Legislature can create a duty by statute, in most cases duty is defined by the courts, as a matter of policy.

* * * To sustain liability against a municipality, the duty breached must be more than that owed the public generally * * *. Indeed, we have consistently refused to impose liability for a municipality in performing a public function absent "a duty to use due care for the benefit of particular persons or classes of persons" (*Motyka v. City of Amsterdam*, 15 N.Y.2d 134, 139, 256 N.Y.S.2d 595, 204 N.E.2d 635). Here, because plaintiff cannot point to a duty owed to him by the Office of the Chief Medical Examiner, his negligence claim must fail.

Pointing to New York City Charter § 557, plaintiff argues that the Office of the Chief Medical Examiner owed him a duty to communicate accurate information to authorities pertaining to his son's death. Section 557 charges the Chief Medical Examiner with examining "bodies of persons dying from criminal violence" or other suspicious circumstances, keeping "full and complete records in such form as may be provided by law," and promptly delivering "to the appropriate district attorney copies of all records relating to every death as to which there is, in the judgment of the medical examiner in charge, any indication of criminality."

Violation of a statute resulting in injury gives rise to a tort action only if the intent of the statute is to protect an individual against an invasion of a property or personal interest. * * *

New York City Charter § 557 * * * establishes the Office of the Chief Medical Examiner as part of the City's Department of Health, and requires performance of autopsies and preparation of reports for the benefit of the public at large. Significantly, the only individual to whom the Medical Examiner must by statute report is "the appropriate district attorney" (see, New York City Charter § 557[g]). Neither plaintiff, nor other members of the general public who may become criminal suspects upon the death of a person, are persons "for whose especial benefit the statute was enacted" (*see, Motyka v. City of Amsterdam, supra,* 15 N.Y.2d, at 139, 256 N.Y.S.2d 595, 204 N.E.2d 635). Permitting recovery here would rewrite section 557, radically enlarging both the responsibility of the Office of the Chief Medical Examiner and the potential liability of the City.

Nor do we find any duty to plaintiff derived from a "special relationship" with him. A "special relationship" requires:

"(1) an assumption by the municipality, through promises or actions, of an affirmative duty to act on behalf of the party who was injured; (2) knowledge on the part of the municipality's agents that inaction could lead to harm; (3) some form of direct contact between the municipality's agents and the injured party;

and (4) that party's justifiable reliance on the municipality's affirmative undertaking" (*Cuffy v. City of New York*, 69 N.Y.2d 255, 260, 513 N.Y.S.2d 372, 505 N.E.2d 937).

The "direct contact" and "reliance" requirements are particularly important, as they rationally define and limit the class of persons to whom the municipality's "special duty" extends (*id.*, at 261, 513 N.Y.S.2d 372, 505 N.E.2d 937).

Those requirements are not met here. The Medical Examiner never undertook to act on plaintiff's behalf. He made no promises or assurances to plaintiff, and assumed no affirmative duty upon which plaintiff might have justifiably relied. Plaintiff alleges no personal contact with the Medical Examiner, and therefore also fails to satisfy the "direct contact" requirement of the test. There is, moreover, no indication that the Medical Examiner knew that plaintiff, or anyone else, had become a suspect in the case. Nor do Medical Examiners generally owe a "special duty" to potential homicide suspects. Their function in this context is not as a law enforcement agency but solely to impart objective information to the appropriate authorities for the benefit of the public at large (*see, People v. Washington*, 86 N.Y.2d 189, 192–193, 630 N.Y.S.2d 693, 654 N.E.2d 967).

* * *

Here, in order for plaintiff's claim for negligent infliction of emotional distress to be successful, we would have to impose a new duty on the Office of the Chief Medical Examiner, which for the future would run to members of the public who may become subjects of a criminal investigation into a death. This we refuse to do. * * *

SMITH, J. (dissenting).

Because I believe that plaintiff Edward G. Lauer has adequately pleaded a prima facie case for negligent infliction of emotional distress, I dissent.

* * *

An investigation by the District Attorney focused almost immediately on plaintiff. On August 31, 1993, however, approximately three weeks after the initial autopsy, Dr. Angeline R. Mastri and Dr. Lilavois examined Andrew's brain and concluded that he died of natural causes from an aneurysm due to dysplasia of a branch of the left posterior cerebral artery. On that day, Drs. Lilavois and Mastri prepared a neuropathology report reflecting the accurate cause of Andrew's death. The report was filed with the OCME on October 14, 1993. Neither the New York City Police Department nor the District Attorney's office was apprised of the OCME's new findings regarding the true cause of Andrew's death. The Lauers were also not informed.

Police investigators allegedly attended Andrew's funeral, informing plaintiff's friends and family that plaintiff had "twisted his son's neck" and had "killed his son." Many of plaintiff's friends and family became openly hostile towards him, and his wife sued him for divorce. In addition, plaintiff was forced to sell his home because he was ostracized by his neighbors.

In March 1995, approximately 17 months after the OCME discovered the true cause of death, the New York Daily News began an inquiry into the status of the police investigation. The newspaper learned from the OCME that "coroners had long ago reclassified Andrew's death as natural." It was only upon the Daily News' expose that the authorities learned that Andrew's death was no longer considered a homicide. The OCME subsequently amended the autopsy report and prepared an amended death certificate.

* * *

In *Cuffy v. City of New York*, 69 N.Y.2d 255, 260, 513 N.Y.S.2d 372, 505 N.E.2d 937, this Court delineated the four elements of a special relationship, which are: "(1) an assumption by the municipality, through promises or actions, of an affirmative duty to act on behalf of the party who was injured; (2) knowledge on the part of the municipality's agents that inaction could lead to harm; (3) some form of direct contact between the municipality's agents and the injured party; and (4) that party's justifiable reliance on the municipality's affirmative undertaking."

These four factors are sufficiently alleged in this case. The OCME assumed control of Andrew's remains and undertook an affirmative duty, through its actions, to correctly determine the cause of death. Once labeling the death a homicide, Dr. Lilavois and the OCME knew that such characterization would prompt a police investigation. Setting an investigation into motion, the doctor and the OCME knew or should have known that any failure to come forth with exculpatory information could unnecessarily prolong the police investigation, causing harm to the limited number of individuals suspected of the crime. Significantly, Dr. Lilavois and the OCME exclusively possessed the exculpatory evidence.

The "direct contact" element, "which is closely related to the element of reliance, serves to rationally limit the class of persons to whom the municipality's duty of protection runs and exists" (*Kircher v. City of Jamestown*, 74 N.Y.2d 251, 257, 544 N.Y.S.2d 995, 543 N.E.2d 443). While direct contact is necessary, this Court has not been overly rigid in its application, taking the particularities of each case into consideration (*Cuffy v. City of New York*, 69 N.Y.2d, *supra*, at 261–262, 513 N.Y.S.2d 372, 505 N.E.2d 937). * * *

Here, plaintiff alleges that he had extensive contact with the OCME. While the extent of the contact is not clear from the record, this appeal is before us through a motion to dismiss. Given the procedural posture, plaintiff has been foreclosed up to this point from conducting discovery. Presumably, an agent from the OCME came to retrieve Andrew's body from plaintiff's home. However, what the record does establish is that Andrew's body came into direct contact with the OCME and that plaintiff is Andrew's next of kin. Under the circumstances of this case, Andrew's body, in which plaintiff maintained a cognizable property interest (*see generally, Darcy v. Presbyterian Hosp.*, 202 N.Y. 259, 95 N.E. 695), is another link between plaintiff and the OCME, and sufficiently distinguishes plaintiff from the public at large (*see, Kircher v. City of Jamestown, supra,* at 257–258, 544 N.Y.S.2d 995, 543 N.E.2d 443).

Finally, the key element of justifiable reliance is adequately alleged. Indeed, plaintiff had no choice but to rely on the OCME for an accurate assessment of Andrew's cause of death. Furthermore, plaintiff relied on the OCME to correctly report to the authorities any information in this regard. Even if defendant's initial conclusion regarding the nature of Andrew's death is shielded from liability, at a minimum, plaintiff had the right to rely upon the OCME to competently perform its statutorily mandated duties.

The conclusion that a special relationship exists does not mean that plaintiff may automatically recover. It remains a question for the trier of fact as to whether plaintiff has established the claims raised in the complaint.

* * * The record establishes that for 17 months plaintiff was erroneously suspected of the murder of his only son. Plaintiff's emotional injuries were allegedly the proximate result of Dr. Lilavois' failure to inform authorities that Andrew's death was caused by natural circumstances rather than homicide, as initially suspected. Believing that plaintiff was a murderer, his wife divorced him. His family, friends and neighbors shunned him. For close to two years, plaintiff needlessly lived under a cloud of suspicion, allegedly enduring depression and loss of weight caused by the nightmare he lived.

Under the circumstances presented, plaintiff should be given the opportunity to prove his allegations * * *.

NOTES AND QUESTIONS

1. *Availability of the Public Duty Defense.* State courts are divided over the availability of the public duty defense. A number of courts have abolished it outright, *e.g.,* Ficek v. Morken, 685 N.W.2d 98 (N.D. 2004); Natrona County v. Blake, 81 P.3d 948 (Wyo. 2003); Jean W. v. Commonwealth, 610 N.E.2d 305, 308 (Mass.1993); Maple v. City of Omaha, 384 N.W.2d 254, 257

(Neb.1986); Schear v. Board of County Commissioners of Bernalillo County, 687 P.2d 728, 730–31 (N.M.1984); Wilson v. Nepstad, 282 N.W.2d 664, 671 (Iowa 1979); Brennen v. City of Eugene, 591 P.2d 719, 724–25 (Ore.1979); Adams v. State, 555 P.2d 235, 241–42 (Ak. 1976).

Some courts, however, have been unwilling to abolish the rule, *e.g.*, Myers v. McGrady, 628 S.E.2d 761 (N.C. 2006) (public duty doctrine immunized state Division of Forest Resources from claim of negligence in managing forest fire); Beal v. City of Seattle, 954 P.2d 237 (Wash.1998) (retaining public duty defense but finding it inapplicable in case against 911 emergency operator); Ezell v. Cockrell, 902 S.W.2d 394 (Tenn.1995) (public duty defense preserved implicitly by state governmental immunity statute found to bar claim that police officer negligently failed to arrest drunk driver).

The Illinois Supreme Court went even further in its affirmation of the public duty defense, invalidating the special duty exception as an unconstitutional violation of separation of powers and as inconsistent with the constitution's abolition of sovereign immunity "[e]xcept as the General Assembly may provide by law." Zimmerman v. Village of Skokie, 697 N.E.2d 699 (Ill.1998). In an opinion nearly 25 years later, though, the same court held that a school district had a duty to children of another school district, which meant that plaintiffs could proceed with their claim that the defendant district had willfully and wantonly "passed on" a known sex offender to another district without revealing his past. The court found that the public duty rule was "of no moment in this case," thus leaving the status of the defense uncertain. *See* Jane Doe-3 v. McClean County Unit Dist. No. 5, 973 N.E.2d 880, 893 (Ill. 2012). That statement provoked a strenuous dissent, and a concurrence urging the court to "clearly pronounce the public duty rule dead or alive."

The courts hostile to the special duty rule reason that its continued application is inconsistent with legislative abolition of sovereign immunity. Do you agree? Is it meaningful to provide that governments can be liable in tort for their misconduct but then to use the defense to shield them when the government can establish that its duty runs to the public as a whole rather than to individual plaintiffs?

Remember that the state legislature retains the ultimate authority to shape the contours of governmental tort liability. *See, e.g.*, Brum v. Town of Dartmouth, 704 N.E.2d 1147, 1153–54 (Mass.1999) (Ireland, J., concurring) (discussing legislative response to court's abolition of the public duty rule in *Jean W. v. Commonwealth, supra; see* Mass.Gen. Laws ch. 258, § 10(d)–(j) (reinstating governmental immunity for wide range of behavior previously protected by public duty defense); Alaska Stat. § 09.65.070(d)(1) (reestablishing public duty rule for government inspections in response to *Adams v. State, supra*). The public duty rule is a creature of the judiciary, generally traced to the Supreme Court's decision in South v. State of Maryland, 59 U.S. (18 How.) 396, 403 (1855) (refusing to impose tort liability on sheriff for failing to protect a kidnapping victim on the basis of the sheriff's "public duty, for neglect of which he is amenable to the public, and punishable by indictment only"). Does that make deference to legislative prerogative less persuasive?

2.   *Continuing Justifications for the Public Duty Defense.* Consider this excerpt from an opinion by the Tennessee Supreme Court:

> One policy consideration frequently expressed is that individuals, juries and courts are ill-equipped to judge governmental decisions as to how particular community resources should be or should have been allocated to protect individual members of the public. Some courts have theorized that severe depletion of those resources could well result if every oversight or omission of a police official resulted in civil liability. They have also observed that such a rule would place police officials in the untenable position of insuring the personal safety of every member of the public, or facing a civil suit for damages, and that the public duty doctrine eliminates that dilemma. *See* Landis v. Rockdale County, 212 Ga.App. 700, 445 S.E.2d 264, 268 (1994) (where the Georgia Court of Appeals applied the public duty doctrine and stated that "[a] policeman's lot is not so unhappy that he must choose between being charged with dereliction of duty if he does not arrest when he has probable cause or being mulcted in damages if he does.").

> Another policy consideration justifying recognition of the public duty doctrine is that police officials often act and react in the milieu of criminal activity where every decision is fraught with uncertainty. Illustrative of that approach was the Connecticut Supreme Court's endorsement of the public duty doctrine in a failure-to-arrest case: [t]he adoption of a rule of liability where some kind of harm may happen to someone would cramp the exercise of official discretion beyond the limits desirable in our society. Should the officer try to avoid liability by removing from the road all persons who pose any potential hazard, he may find himself liable in many instances for false arrest. We do not think that the public interest is served by allowing a jury of laymen with the benefit of 20/20 hindsight to second-guess the exercise of a policeman's discretionary professional duty. Such discretion is no discretion at all. Shore v. Town of Stonington, 187 Conn. 147, 444 A.2d 1379, 1384 (1982).

> Finally, many courts subscribing to the public duty doctrine have emphasized that mechanisms, other than civil negligence actions, exist wherein individual officials may be held accountable for dereliction of duty, for instance, internal disciplinary proceedings or formal criminal prosecutions. Such courts have concluded that, on balance, the community is better served by a policy that both protects the exercise of law enforcement discretion

and affords a means of review by supervisory personnel who are best able to evaluate the officer's alleged negligent behavior.

Ezell v. Cockrell, 902 S.W.2d 394 397–98 (Tenn.1995).

Are you persuaded by these reasons? Do you think that the public duty rule is merely a backhanded exercise of judicial power to reinstate sovereign immunity, or can you identify different rationales and scopes of coverage for the two principles? Would abolition of the public duty rule make local governments less likely to adopt new regulatory schemes? Isn't there an independent value served by statutory regulation, in that presumably law-abiding citizens will seek to comply with the legal standard, irrespective of the government's ability to police compliance in each and every instance? Or should the government be encouraged to refrain from adopting ever more regulation unless it is prepared to enforce it properly?

3.   *Defining Special Duty.* Contrast the definitions of the special duty exception offered by the courts in the two main cases, focusing specifically on the state of mind required of both the citizen and the government official. Can you articulate a principle that would prefer one approach over the other? Can you identify some vagueness in the South Dakota court's definition? Is that a positive or negative aspect of the court's rule? For additional renditions of the special duty test, *see, e.g.,* Day v. State, 980 P.2d 1171, 1175 (Utah 1999) ("A special relationship can be established (1) by a statute intended to protect a specific class of persons . . . from a particular type of harm; (2) when a government agent undertakes specific action to protect a person or property; (3) by governmental actions that reasonably induce detrimental reliance by a member of the public; and (4) under certain circumstances, when the agency has actual custody of the plaintiff or of a third person who causes harm to the plaintiff"); Powell v. District, 602 A.2d 1123, 1130 (D.C.Ct.App.1992) (adopting two prong test: "1) a direct contact or continuing contact between the victim and the governmental agency or official; and 2) a justifiable reliance on the part of the victim"). Can you devise a preferable test?

4.   *Special Duty and Emergency Service Responses.* Notwithstanding the many instances in which courts apply the public duty rule to bar plaintiff recovery, they have seemed less resistant to finding a special duty between injured members of the public and their local government emergency services providers.

In Day v. State, *supra,* the court determined that police officers owe a special duty of care to public highway users and held that the public duty defense was unavailable to protect the government from liability for a death caused in a high speed police chase of a fleeing criminal. The court cited numerous similar decisions from other states and concluded that the overwhelming majority recognize potential governmental liability for injuries to third parties injured during police chases. The Washington Supreme Court, in Beal v. City of Seattle, 954 P.2d 237 (Wash.1998), was similarly receptive to the plaintiff's attempt to establish a special duty in a wrongful death action brought against the city for its long delay in responding to a 911 call for help. The majority concluded that tort liability could be based on the municipality's express assurances of police protection when a woman called for protection from her estranged husband. In Nelson v. Driscoll, 983 P.2d 972 (Mont.1999), the court concluded that plaintiff had alleged sufficient facts to establish a special duty in a lawsuit against a county sheriff who had ordered the deceased to park her car and walk because she had been drinking. The woman was later killed by another intoxicated driver. *Compare* Valdez v. City of New York, 960 N.E.2d 356 (N.Y. 2011) (no special relationship exists between plaintiff and police officer who reassured her that boyfriend would be arrested immediately, so that she could return home); Cubit v. Mahaska County, 677 N.W.2d 777 (Iowa 2004) (granting emergency response immunity to dispatcher trainee's failure to notify state trooper that a motorist intended to commit suicide by crashing into a police vehicle).

3. GOVERNMENT LIABILITY IN THE ISSUANCE OF PERMITS AND LICENSES

QUALITY COURT CONDOMINIUM ASSOC. V. QUALITY HILL DEVELOPMENT CORP.

Supreme Court of Rhode Island
641 A.2d 746 (1994)

MURRAY, JUSTICE.

This case came before this court on the appeal of the defendant, the city of Pawtucket (city), from a judgment on a Superior Court jury verdict in favor of the plaintiff, Quality Court Condominium Association (Quality), in the amount of $69,463.

The facts underlying this dispute are as follows. In August 1988 Quality filed a complaint against several defendants in Superior Court, seeking damages associated with the improper construction of certain condominiums located in the city. * * *

In its complaint Quality alleged that the condominiums were not constructed in a workmanlike manner and that defendants failed to repair damage that Quality had requested be fixed. Quality also asserted that the building inspectors for the city were negligent in failing to inspect the condominiums properly and in approving construction work that was in violation of state building-code requirements. * * *

Several condominium owners testified at trial regarding a myriad of problems that they experienced with their units soon after their purchase. Elizabeth Healy (Healy) testified that she purchased her unit in August 1986 for $92,000. She stated that her problems began the day before the closing, when she discovered water in her basement. In February 1987 she came home one evening and "my dining room table * * * was covered with water. * * * I put the light on and the water was pouring out of my light fixture and you could hear the water running right in the walls like a waterfall * * * and water was coming out [of] the light fixture at the front door." These water problems also surfaced in other areas. She described "drastic" leaks in her roof, from which leaking water damaged carpets, ceilings, and closets. Healy also stated that the floor in her unit tilts downward and that a supporting wall had to be installed across the middle of her basement to prevent further damage. She described cracks in her ceilings, walls, and kitchen formica. She added that her unit has been repainted on three occasions, yet water damage is still visible.

Robert Girouard (Girouard) testified that he also purchased his unit in August of 1986. Girouard testified that he had many concerns regarding the construction of his unit. He stated that he spoke to Todd Olbrych (Olbrych), a city building inspector, when Olbrych was inspecting Girouard's unit in November 1986. Girouard testified that Olbrych informed him he was at the site to "issue letters of certificates of occupancy." Girouard also averred that Olbrych informed him it was "obvious" that the city could not issue a certificate of occupancy because the "unit was not ready." Girouard testified that he pointed out to Olbrych problems with the floor joists in the basement, water leaks, ceiling stains, and joist spans in excess of fourteen feet. Girouard testified that in spite of his pointing out the problems and Olbrych's initial comments, Olbrych stated that "the plans were stamped by the architect and that * * * he [had] to go by the stamp of the architect." * * *

Olbrych testified that as the city building inspector one of his responsibilities was to enforce the Rhode Island State Building Code. He testified that he inspected the Quality Court Condominiums. He stated that he was concerned about the span of the joists that Girouard had pointed out; however, "[i]t was approved by the architect as being structurally sound." He averred that the building code requires that the city "take the architect['s] stamp; so we did." He stated that on the day he inspected Girouard's unit, he did not find any "serious" code violations.

Robert Hunt (Hunt), a state building official, did not agree with Olbrych's view of the premises or his understanding of the responsibilities of a municipal building inspector. Hunt testified that one of the responsibilities of a municipal building inspector is to issue building permits to ensure that the plans for construction meet the requirements of the state building code. If the inspector finds a violation of the state building code, Hunt explained, it is his or her responsibility to notify the building's owner of the violation. Hunt explained that an architect's stamp signifies that an architect is duly qualified and licensed to make architectural drawings. Hunt explained that a building inspector does not rely on the stamp "for anything."

As a result of a complaint filed by Quality with the Attorney General's office, Hunt made an inspection of the condominiums in July 1987. He testified that he made his inspection along with a representative from the Attorney General's office, a representative of the city building inspector's office, the city's director of public works, and several of the unit owners. He testified that he inspected about six to eight units. He stated that he found at least seven separate building-code violations that were common to all the units that he inspected. He found that the building was constructed too low in the ground, that the floor framing was overstressed, and that although the maximum stress level of the floor joists was fourteen feet, the joists were overstressed to seventeen feet. He also testified that he found other violations that were unique to specific units. By letter, Hunt notified the Attorney General's office and the city of the building-code violations.

* * *

According to the public-duty doctrine, Rhode Island government entities enjoy immunity from tort liability arising out of their discretionary governmental actions that by their nature are not ordinarily performed by private persons. *Haley v. Town of Lincoln*, 611 A.2d 845, 849 (R.I.1992). The rationale behind the public-duty doctrine is "to encourage the effective administration of governmental operations by removing the threat of potential litigation." *Catone v. Medberry*, 555 A.2d 328, 333 (R.I.1989). * * * In cases in which this court has acknowledged the existence of a special duty, the plaintiffs have had some form of prior contact with state or municipal officials "who then knowingly embarked on a course of conduct that endangered the plaintiffs, or they have otherwise specifically come within the knowledge of the officials so that the injury to that particularly identified plaintiff can be or should have been foreseen." *Knudsen v. Hall*, 490 A.2d 976, 978 (R.I.1985).

A further erosion of the government's immunity occurs when the state or the municipality embarks on a course of action that is "egregious." "[T]he state is not immune from liability even though no special duty has been shown 'when the state has knowledge that it has created a circumstance that forces an individual into a position of peril and subsequently chooses not to remedy the situation.'" *Haley*, 611 A.2d at 849.

At the outset we note that the activities and the inspections that are required to ensure compliance with the state building code cannot be engaged in by private enterprise. Consequently, the action we review falls within the ambit of conduct covered by the public-duty doctrine. * * *

The record reflects that Olbrych met with Girouard, and Girouard specifically identified problems with his unit. Olbrych thus had specific knowledge of certain irregularities with respect to Girouard's unit. We emphasize that a single inspection of a premises by a building inspector would not support the requirements for the creation of a special duty on behalf of the city. However, the record reflects additional factors that created a special duty.

Hunt testified that a representative of the city's building inspector's office was present at the site when he made his inspections and noted the violations. Olbrych testified that he was present at the meeting with a representative of the Attorney General's office to discuss alternatives in remedying the problems with the condominiums. The architect testified that he met with the seller of the condominiums, the "[b]uilding [i]nspector for the [c]ity," and several of the unit owners to resolve the problems. Additionally the city received written notice from Hunt of the specific building-code violations observed and recorded in his July 1987 inspection. Olbrych specifically testified that he returned to the condominiums on "several occasions" to view the repair work. Subsequently, in December 1987, he wrote a memo to his superior informing him that all the units were in compliance with the building code. This second assertion of compliance was contradicted at trial by several witnesses.

This court is persuaded that the specific events listed above brought the individual unit owners " 'specifically into the realm of [the city's] knowledge.' " *Barratt v. Burlingham*, 492 A.2d 1219, 1223 (R.I.1985) (Kelleher, J., concurring). This was not an instance in which the potential "victim" was unknown to the city. . . . After the meeting with a representative of the Attorney General's office the city's duty was to the individual owners of the condominium's units and "not to some amorphous, unknown 'public.' " *Barratt*, 492 A.2d at 1223. Olbrych had continued contact with Quality during 1987. Olbrych clearly appreciated the seriousness of the violations since he returned on a number of occasions to ensure that the proposed corrective measures were taken. The city was acutely aware of a threat to the specific plaintiffs and in fact took some action to ensure remedy of the code violations. The city " 'knew or reasonably should have known of a threat to the specific plaintiff[s].' " *Id.* Consequently the city owed Quality a special duty.

We emphasize that a building inspector's visiting a site to ensure compliance with a building code would not be sufficient to establish a special duty. A municipality should not be the general insurer of every construction project within its limits. If it were, the resulting exposure to liability would be insurmountable and would dissuade municipalities from enacting or enforcing building codes. As a general rule building codes or ordinances impose an obligation on behalf of the municipality to the public at large. However, in this instance the actions of the city brought Quality into the realm of its specific knowledge and thereby created a special duty. Consequently, because we find that a special duty existed, the trial justice did not err in denying the city's motion for a directed verdict. * * *

LaFond v. Vermont Department of Social and Rehabilitation Services

Supreme Court of Vermont
708 A.2d 919 (1998)

MORSE, JUSTICE.

On May 7, 1992, plaintiffs' infant son died when he became entangled in a curtain cord while in his crib at Kiddie Kare Day Care, a licensed day-care center. In a lawsuit against defendant Vermont Department of Social and Rehabilitation Services, plaintiffs alleged that their son's death was caused in part by the Department's negligent inspection and supervision of the day care facility. The trial court denied the Department's motion for summary judgment based upon a claim of sovereign immunity, and we allowed an interlocutory appeal. V.R.A.P. 5(b). We now hold that the trial court erred in denying the Department's motion for summary judgment, and therefore reverse.

I.

Kiddie Kare had been licensed by the Department as a day-care facility since 1981. In 1989, plaintiffs enrolled their two daughters there, and the following year enrolled their son Tyler, who attended until his death in May 1992. Prior to enrolling their daughters, plaintiffs, who were eligible for a child-care subsidy, inquired of a Department employee whether Kiddie Kare was a covered facility and whether it was a good day-care center. The employee responded that she had nothing bad on file about Kiddie Kare and that the Department would provide the subsidy. Plaintiffs also visited the center before enrolling their daughters.

On May 4, 1992, a Department employee inspected Kiddie Kare as part of an annual relicensing requirement. Three days later, on May 7, 1992, plaintiffs' son Tyler became entangled in a curtain cord while in his crib at the Kiddie Kare center. Strangulation from the cord caused suffocation and death. The inspector had not observed a curtain cord hanging down from the window next to the crib in which Tyler died. Department regulations did not prohibit or restrict curtain cords at the time of Tyler's death, although information about the risk of strangulation by such cords had been publicly available from the United States Consumer Product Safety Commission since 1985, and the inspector acknowledged that she would have inquired about its proximity to the crib if she had seen it. * * *

II.

The death of a child under the grievous circumstances presented here evokes profound sympathy for the child's family, especially his parents, whose pain and anguish can scarcely be imagined. Our duty, however, is to determine whether, as a matter of law, the doctrine of sovereign immunity bars plaintiffs' tort suit for damages against the Department. Analyzed dispassionately, the law dictates that sovereign immunity applies. The licensing and inspection of day-care facilities are inherently *governmental* functions which find no private analog or duty of care in our common law. Accordingly, under the Vermont Tort Claims Act, 12 V.S.A. §§ 5601–5606, and the relevant case law plaintiffs' action is barred.

Sovereign immunity protects the state from suit unless immunity is expressly waived by statute. *LaShay v. Department of Social & Rehabilitation Servs.,* 160 Vt. 60, 67, 625 A.2d 224, 228 (1993). The State of Vermont has waived its immunity to certain suits under 12 V.S.A. § 5601(a), which in pertinent part provides:

> The state of Vermont shall be liable for injury to persons . . . caused by the negligent or wrongful act or omission of an employee of the state while acting within the scope of employment, under the same circumstances, in the same manner and to the same extent as a private person would be liable to the claimant. . . .

Thus, the general rule is that "[t]he government remains immune . . . for governmental functions for which no private analog exists." *LaShay,* 160 Vt. at 68, 625 A.2d at 229. * * *

The question whether the State may be liable in tort for its allegedly negligent inspection of private facilities is not one of first impression in Vermont. Indeed, we recently addressed a claim similar to plaintiffs' in *Andrew v. State,* 165 Vt. 252, 682 A.2d 1387 (1996). There, the assertion was that a State inspection under the Vermont Occupational Safety and Health Act (VOSHA), 21 V.S.A. §§ 201–264, had negligently failed to discover and remedy "a conspicuous hazard that violated an OSHA regulation," resulting in injury to the plaintiffs. *Id.* at 254, 682 A.2d at 1388. There, as here, the plaintiffs claimed that the State's regulatory and inspection scheme created a duty analogous to the duty imposed upon private parties under Restatement (Second) of Torts § 324A (1965), which provides as follows:

> One who undertakes, gratuitously or for consideration, to render services to another which he should recognize as necessary for the protection of a third person or his things, is subject to liability to the third person for physical harm resulting from his failure to exercise reasonable care to protect his undertaking, if

(a) his failure to exercise reasonable care increases the risk of such harm, or

(b) he has undertaken to perform a duty owed by the other to the third person, or

(c) the harm is suffered because of reliance of the other or the third person upon the undertaking.

In support of their argument that Restatement § 324A established a private analog for their claim against the State, the plaintiffs in *Andrew* relied on this Court's decision in *Derosia,* 155 Vt. 178, 583 A.2d 881. There, we held that a private insurance carrier that had voluntarily assumed the duty of ensuring the safety of its insured's workplace through periodic inspections could be held liable to an injured employee under § 324A. We rejected the comparison to *Derosia* in *Andrew,* however, holding that VOSHA's regulatory scheme was not designed as an undertaking of service to the employer. Unlike *Derosia,* we noted, a government safety inspection "does not involve a consensual or contractual relationship between the inspector and the employer," nor was it a situation in which the "employer lacked safety expertise and [the] insurer offered to fill that gap." *Andrew,* 165 Vt. at 258, 682 A.2d at 1391. Rather, the relationship between the government and the employer, "refute[d] any suggestion that the State ha[d] undertaken the employer's duty to provide a safe workplace." *Id.* As we explained:

> § 324A's threshold requirement that there be an undertaking of services is not met here, as a matter of law. . . . [T]he State is not undertaking a service for the employer or its employees, but rather is policing the employer's compliance with the law. To be sure, VOSHA is intended to protect the public, but the statute is not intended to shift the burden of protecting workers and compensating them for their workplace injuries from the employers and their workers' compensation insurers to the State.

Id. at 260, 682 A.2d at 1392.

* * * Like VOSHA, the purpose of the State's day-care regulatory scheme is to ensure a safe environment, 33 V.S.A. § 3502(d). Also like VOSHA, the State's regulations expressly provide that *"[t]he licensee* shall be responsible for compliance with these" standards. Agency of Human Services, Children's Day Care Licensing Regulations for Early Childhood Programs, § A.1, 4 Code of Vt. Rules, 13–162–008–4 (1989) (emphasis added). * * *

Thus, like the employer under VOSHA, it is the *day-care facility* that "retains primary responsibility for ensuring . . . safety. . . . In contrast, the State is given a regulatory enforcement role. . . ." *Andrew,* 165 Vt. at

257, 682 A.2d at 1391. Indeed, as we noted with respect to VOSHA, the State's relationship with the day-care provider "is often adversarial" in nature. *Id.* Day-care providers must permit inspections and examinations of records by the Department, 33 V.S.A. § 306(b)(2). The State may sue the provider for injunctive relief or civil penalties for operating without a license, *id.* § 306(b)(5), (6), and day-care licenses may be revoked or suspended by the Department for violations that imperil health and safety. *Id.* § 306(b)(3). The day-care facility may appeal any licensing action by the Department to the Human Services Board, and ultimately to the Supreme Court. 3 V.S.A. § 3091(a), (f).

Thus, the primary purpose of the Department's inspection is to enforce compliance with the law, not to render services to the day-care center. *See Andrew,* 165 Vt. at 257–58, 682 A.2d at 1391.

The fact that Department inspectors may offer guidance to a day-care provider on how to improve its facility does not, contrary to plaintiffs' assertion, establish that the State has undertaken the provider's duty of care toward the children under its supervision. * * * Nor, as plaintiffs urge, does the statutory requirement that day-care facilities post a notice of health and safety violations, see 33 V.S.A. § 306(b)(7), somehow suggest an undertaking by the Department to assume the day-care center's duty of care. * * *

In sum, we are not persuaded that the State's enforcement scheme for ensuring adequate health and safety standards in day-care centers creates an actionable duty to plaintiffs, any more than the VOSHA provisions aimed at ensuring workplace safety shift the responsibility for workplace safety from the employer to the State. "In reality," as we observed in *Andrew,* "plaintiffs' cause of action amounts to a claim of negligent enforcement of safety standards under a regulatory statute. There is no private analog for such an action." 165 Vt. at 260, 682 A.2d at 1392. * * * Absent an express legislative directive to the contrary, we are not prepared to make the State and its officers effectively the liability insurer of day-care providers, or any other licensed industry.

Indeed, the number and variety of licensing and inspection programs conducted by state and local governments is staggering. Vermont statutes provide, for example, for the inspection of inpatient mental health facilities, 18 V.S.A. § 7313, nursing homes for the elderly, 33 V.S.A. § 7108, food and drug manufacturing facilities, 18 V.S.A. § 4070, hazardous waste storage facilities, 10 V.S.A. § 6609, milk production facilities, 6 V.S.A. § 2741, maple syrup processors, 6 V.S.A. § 484, frozen food manufacturers, 6 V.S.A. § 443, livestock dealers, 6 V.S.A. § 768, agricultural nurseries, 6 V.S.A. § 4023, fertilizers, 6 V.S.A. § 367, insecticides, 6 V.S.A. § 915, sewage treatment facilities, 24 V.S.A. § 3502, and all plants and facilities subject to the supervision of the public service board, 30 V.S.A. § 29, to name a few.

Nearly every resident or visitor to Vermont has daily contact with one or more entities licensed and inspected by the state. To recognize a tort duty of care arising from a day-care licensing and inspection scheme would thus have broad fiscal and policy ramifications for state and local governments, well beyond the parameters of this particular case. The creation of such a cause of action, in our view, is a matter more properly addressed by the Legislature. * * *

NOTES AND QUESTIONS

1. *Comparing the Applicable Legal Rules*. Note that the two cases differ not only in the results they reach, but also in the rule applied. As between the public duty rule (with its special duty exception) and the theory of governmental function immunity, which is more protective of governmental immunity? Which more properly strikes the balance among the interests of the plaintiff, the government and its taxpayers, and the general society?

2. *Government Liability for Inspections*. The potential governmental liability from allegedly deficient inspections is enormous. Most courts have refused to impose government liability for damages resulting from conditions that violated applicable laws but went undiscovered or unreported by government inspectors. Some courts apply the rule to bar recovery against state, but not local, inspectors. *See, e.g.*, Stone v. North Carolina Department of Labor, 495 S.E.2d 711 (N.C.1998) (public duty rule prevents recovery against government for deaths and injuries sustained in fire at food products plant, even though government never inspected plant for compliance with health and safety regulations; inspection would have discovered that fire exits were unmarked, blocked, and otherwise inaccessible); Tipton v. Town of Tabor, 567 N.W.2d 351 (S.D.1997) (city grant of license to owners of wolfdog hybrids did not create special duty to child who was mauled); Corbin v. Buchanan, 657 A.2d 170 (Vt.1994) (though local law required smoke detectors, government's failure to properly inspect buildings and enforce orders to correct dangerous condition did not remove government's protection under public duty rule from liability for tenant's death from smoke inhalation); Island Shores Estates Condominium Assoc. v. City of Concord, 615 A.2d 629 (N.H.1992) (public duty rule protects city from liability for allegedly negligent misrepresentation in implementation of its building inspection program); Benson v. Kutsch, 380 S.E.2d 36 (W.Va.1989) (city not liable for failure to inspect premises to determine compliance with smoke detector regulations); Trianon Park Condominium Assoc., Inc. v. City of Hialeah, 468 So.2d 912 (Fla.1985) (city not liable for damages suffered by owners as a result of severe roof leakage and other building defects, although city had issued certificate of occupancy). At least three state supreme courts have rejected the public duty doctrine in local inspection cases. *See* Thompson

v. Waters, 526 S.E.2d 650 (N.C. 2000) (notwithstanding holding in Stone, cited above, the court declined to apply the public duty defense to bar plaintiff's claim against local building inspectors for allegedly negligent inspections); Wood v. Guilford County, 558 S.E.2d 490 (N.C. 2002) (limiting public duty defense to law enforcement agencies and state, but not local, agency inspections); Ficek v. Morken, 685 N.W.2d 98 (N.D. 2004) (refusing to apply public duty doctrine to immunize local government's issuance of certificate of occupancy).

3.   *Government Liability for Licensing.* Government liability for injuries caused by individuals who have received a government-issued license could lead to similar or greater consequences than liability stemming from permits. From drivers licenses, *see* Johnson v. Indian River Sch. Dist., 723 A.2d 1200 (Del. Super. Ct. 1998), to firearms licenses, *see* Blatt v. N.Y. City Housing Auth., 506 N.Y.S.2d 877 (N.Y. A.D. 1986), to the numerous professions licensed by governments, *see, e.g.,* Collins v. State, 617 N.Y.S.2d 1010 (N.Y. Ct. Cl. 1994) (boxers); Barber v. Williams, 767 P.2d 1284 (Kan. 1989) (fortune-tellers), a large number of private activities require government licenses. If the public duty defense is not available in these contexts, what limits would you suggest to government liability?

The courts that apply the public duty defense to immunize government licensing from tort liability stress that "governments must be able to enact and enforce laws without creating new duties of care and corresponding tort liabilities that would, in effect, make the governments and their taxpayers virtual insurers of the activities regulated." *Trianon Park, supra,* 468 So.2d at 922. The Supreme Court of Minnesota reached a result contrary to the Vermont court's decision in *Lafond* and held that the county had a special duty to children injured by a licensed day care provider. Andrade v. Ellefson, 391 N.W.2d 836 (Minn.1986). The *Andrade* court found a special duty solely on the basis of the government's actual knowledge of the daycare provider's cruel and unsafe actions. Reliance by the plaintiffs was not established. In contrast, the *Quality Court* opinion removed the public duty defense, but only after it concluded that the plaintiffs had actually relied on the government's inspections. Which approach is better? Should governmental liability for negligent licensing and inspections depend on whether the injured party relied on the government's actions? Should citizens be able to assume that a government license or permit makes some sort of assurance about the quality of the enterprise that is licensed? Do the differences between the licensing/inspection cases and the facts of *Gleason* and *Lauer* suggest that the special duty rule ought to apply differently in those two situations?

4.   *Statutory Codifications of the Public Duty Rule.* Just as we saw in the context of the discretionary function exemption, some state legislatures have codified the public duty rule. The statutes fall into one of two main categories: some state laws explicitly immunize governments from liability in licensing or inspecting, *see, e.g.,* W.Va.Code, 29–12A–5(a)(9); others explicitly provide for government liability if the licensing or permitting power is

"exercised in a grossly negligent manner." *See* S.C.Code Ann. § 15–78–60(12). Do you see any relevant differences between the two approaches?

C. MAINTAINING ORDER

Governmental attempts to preserve order and maintain a safe community inevitably collide with individual citizens' desires to act and move about freely. Most of the rules governing public order are contained in federal and state criminal laws and are beyond the scope of this text. Nevertheless, local governments frequently enact regulations to curb behavior perceived as detrimental to the general interest in community peace, safety, and tranquility. "Order maintenance" regulations (as opposed to typical state and federal "law enforcement" statutes) are designed to improve the quality of life in public spaces. They include: anti-loitering ordinances targeting gang behavior, drug dealing, and prostitution; juvenile curfews; and local laws "prohibiting aggressive panhandling, unlicensed street vending, graffiti scrawling, public drinking and urinating, and loitering in vicinity of automated teller machines." Debra Livingston, Police Discretion and the Quality of Life in Public Places: Courts, Communities, and the New Policing, 97 Colum.L.Rev. 551, 555–56, 558 n.20 (1997).

Order maintenance regulations address behavior that makes public areas less inviting and reduces the community's sense of safety and pride of neighborhood. Professor Robert Ellickson describes the target of local order maintenance regulation as "chronic street nuisances," which he defines as behavior that "(1) violates community norms governing proper conduct in a particular public space (2) over a protracted period of time (3) to the minor annoyance of passersby." Robert C. Ellickson, Controlling Chronic Misconduct in City Spaces: Of Panhandlers, Skid Rows, and Public-Space Zoning, 105 Yale L.J. 1165, 1175 (1996).

Order maintenance rules raise serious questions concerning their vagueness in describing prohibited behaviors and the discretion given to the police enforcement authority. The following cases illustrate the wide range of issues that arise when a local government decides to restrict individual movement and associational behavior for the benefit of the greater common good and the tranquility of community space.

1. CURFEWS

SCHLEIFER V. CITY OF CHARLOTTESVILLE
United States Court of Appeals
159 F.3d 843 (4th Cir.1998)

WILKINSON, CHIEF JUDGE:

This appeal involves a challenge to the constitutionality of a juvenile nocturnal curfew ordinance enacted by the City of Charlottesville. The district court held that the ordinance did not violate the constitutional rights of minors, their parents, or other affected parties and declined to enjoin its enforcement. We agree that the ordinance is constitutional and affirm the judgment of the district court.

I.

On December 16, 1996, the Charlottesville City Council, after several months of study and deliberation, amended Section 17–7 of the City Code to enact a new juvenile nocturnal curfew ordinance. * * *

Effective March 1, 1997, the ordinance generally prohibits minors, defined as unemancipated persons under seventeen, from remaining in any public place, motor vehicle, or establishment within city limits during curfew hours. The curfew takes effect at 12:01 a.m. on Monday through Friday, at 1:00 a.m. on Saturday and Sunday, and lifts at 5:00 a.m. each morning.

The ordinance does not restrict minors' activities that fall under one of its eight enumerated exceptions. Minors may participate in any activity during curfew hours if they are accompanied by a parent; they may run errands at a parent's direction provided that they possess a signed note. The ordinance allows minors to undertake employment, or attend supervised activities sponsored by school, civic, religious, or other public organizations. The ordinance exempts minors who are engaged in interstate travel, are on the sidewalk abutting their parents' residence, or are involved in an emergency. Finally, the ordinance does not affect minors who are "exercising First Amendment rights protected by the United States Constitution, such as the free exercise of religion, freedom of speech and the right of assembly." *Id.* § 17–7(b)(8).

The ordinance sets forth a scheme of warnings and penalties for minors who violate it. For a first violation, a minor receives a verbal warning, followed by a written warning to the minor and the minor's parents. For subsequent violations, the minor is charged with a Class 4 misdemeanor. The ordinance also makes it unlawful for certain other individuals, including parents, knowingly to encourage a minor to violate the ordinance. The full text of the ordinance is included as an appendix to the opinion. * * *

Plaintiffs brought this action for declaratory and injunctive relief, alleging that the ordinance violates their rights under the First, Fourth, Fifth and Fourteenth Amendments. At trial, plaintiffs dismissed their Fourth Amendment claims. Following trial, by order dated May 20, 1997, the district court rejected plaintiffs' remaining claims and denied their motion for a permanent injunction. Plaintiffs now appeal.

II.

Initially we must consider the level of scrutiny appropriate to this case. * * *

In light of the case law, two things seem clear. First, children do possess at least qualified rights, so an ordinance which restricts their liberty to the extent that this one does should be subject to more than rational basis review. Second, because children do not possess the same rights as adults, the ordinance should be subject to less than the strictest level of scrutiny. We thus believe intermediate scrutiny to be the most appropriate level of review and must determine whether the ordinance is "substantially related" to "important" governmental interests. We also conclude, however, that the ordinance survives constitutional attack under either a substantial or a compelling state interest standard. The narrow means chosen by the City in the ordinance serve strong and indeed compelling public needs.

III.

A.

The text of the Charlottesville curfew ordinance identifies three legislative purposes: (1) to reduce juvenile violence and crime within the city; (2) to protect juveniles themselves from being swept up in unlawful drug activities and from becoming prey to older perpetrators of crime; and (3) to strengthen parental responsibility for children. These enumerated purposes represent important and compelling governmental interests. * * *

The City contends that its curfew ordinance was passed to combat the marked growth in the rate of juvenile crime both nationwide and within Virginia. * * * In fact, the City produced evidence of a twenty-five percent increase in the delinquency caseload of Charlottesville's Juvenile and Domestic Relations Court between 1991 and 1996. Given the projected increase in the nation's juvenile population between 1995 and 2005, the problem of juvenile crime was unlikely to abate.

In addition, the City has documented two troubling features of the juvenile crime phenomenon. First, the City's evidence on nationwide trends indicated a high rate of recidivism among juveniles and a correlation between juvenile delinquency and adult criminal activity. Thus reducing juvenile crime was a pressing first step in reducing the overall impact of crime on the community. Second, Charlottesville's City Council was concerned about the marked increase in the violence associated with juvenile crime. As the City's expert Dr. Ruefle stated in an affidavit submitted to the district court, "[j]uveniles in Virginia now commit serious property crimes at twice the rate of those 18 years of age and older, and since 1990, they also commit serious violent crimes at a higher rate than adults." In light of this evidence, Charlottesville's first stated purpose is undeniably compelling.

Likewise, the City's strong interest in fostering the welfare of children and protecting the youngest members of society from harm is well-established. * * * Each unsuspecting child risks becoming another victim of the assaults, violent crimes, and drug wars that plague America's cities. Given the realities of urban life, it is not surprising that courts have acknowledged the special vulnerability of children to the dangers of the streets. Charlottesville, unfortunately, has not escaped these troubling realities. Two experienced City police officers confirmed to the district court that the children they observe on the streets after midnight are at special risk of harm.

Charlottesville's third purpose—strengthening parental responsibility for children—is also a significant interest. The City shares with parents and guardians a responsibility to protect children. State authority complements parental supervision, and "the guiding role of parents in the upbringing of their children justifies limitations on the freedoms of minors." *Bellotti II*, 443 U.S. at 637, 99 S.Ct. 3035. * * * Therefore, like the City's two preceding interests in reducing the incidence of juvenile crime and juvenile victimization, the City's third aim constitutes an important governmental purpose.

B.

Conceding for the sake of argument that the curfew's stated ends are sufficiently compelling, plaintiffs train their attack on the means by which the ordinance seeks to achieve its goals.

We agree with plaintiffs that the curfew must be shown to be a meaningful step towards solving a real, not fanciful problem. * * *

Charlottesville was constitutionally justified in believing that its curfew would materially assist its first stated interest—that of reducing juvenile violence and crime. The City Council acted on the basis of information from many sources, including records from Charlottesville's police department, a survey of public opinion, news reports, data from the United States Department of Justice, national crime reports, and police reports from other localities. On the basis of such evidence, elected bodies are entitled to conclude that keeping unsupervised juveniles off the streets late at night will make for a safer community. The same streets may have a more volatile and less wholesome character at night than during the day. Alone on the streets at night children face a series of dangerous and potentially life-shaping decisions. Drug dealers may lure them to use narcotics or aid in their sale. Gangs may pressure them into membership or participation in violence. * * * Those who succumb to these criminal influences at an early age may persist in their criminal conduct as adults. Whether we as judges subscribe to these theories is beside the point. Those elected officials with their finger on the pulse of their home community clearly did. In attempting to reduce through its curfew the opportunities for children to come into contact with criminal influences, the City was directly advancing its first objective of reducing juvenile violence and crime. * * *

Charlottesville's City Council concluded that a nighttime curfew might help curb this rising trend of juvenile crime. In making this decision, the City relied on the experience of cities like Lexington, Kentucky, where eight months of enforcing a nighttime juvenile curfew effected an almost ten percent decrease in juvenile arrests for the serious crimes of homicide, assault, robbery, rape, burglary, larceny, auto theft and arson. And the district court heard testimony that a curfew has the greatest chance of reducing juvenile crime in a smaller city like Charlottesville, where juvenile crime, though a serious problem, has not yet become totally uncontrollable. Fundamentally, however, this dispute about the desirability or ultimate efficacy of a curfew is a political debate, not a judicial one. If local communities conclude that curfews are ineffective in reducing crime, too onerous to enforce, or too intrusive on the liberties of minors, then they are free to discontinue them. Yet local legislative bodies are entitled to draw their conclusions in light of experience with a curfew's operation, and not have their efforts at reducing juvenile violence shut down by a court before they even have a chance to make a difference. * * *

Finally, plaintiffs dispute the City's claim that the curfew will support the parental role in child-rearing, its third stated goal. They focus exclusively on the testimony of the parent plaintiffs, who clearly do not appreciate the curfew and do not welcome it as an enhancement of their authority. The City was entitled to believe, however, that a nocturnal curfew would promote parental involvement in a child's upbringing. A curfew aids the efforts of parents who desire to protect their children from the perils of the street but are unable to control the nocturnal behavior of those children. And a curfew encourages parents who ignore their children's nighttime activities to take a more active role in their children's lives. Finally, the curfew assists the efforts of parents who prefer their children to spend time on their studies rather than on the streets. City law enforcement officers related anecdotal evidence that some parents actively welcome the support of the authorities in establishing baselines for their children and in enforcing reasonable limits on the freedom of their children to wander the streets in the middle of the night. And the City Council acted on the basis of surveys and testimony at public hearings reflecting widespread approval of the curfew and the support it offers to parents' efforts to discipline their children. * * *

V.

Finally, we consider plaintiffs' claims that various exceptions to the ordinance are unconstitutionally vague. A law is not void for vagueness so long as it "(1) establishes 'minimal guidelines to govern law enforcement,' and (2) gives reasonable notice of the proscribed conduct." *Elliott v. Administrator, Animal and Plant Health Inspection Serv.*, 990 F.2d 140, 145 (4th Cir.1993) (citation omitted). * * *

Striking down ordinances (or exceptions to the same) as facially void for vagueness is a disfavored judicial exercise. Nullification of a law in the abstract involves a far more aggressive use of judicial power than striking down a discrete and particularized application of it. Of course there will be hard cases under any law. And of course all the particular applications of any general standard will not be immediately apparent. That is no reason, however, for courts to scrap altogether the efforts of the legislative branch. It is preferable for courts to demonstrate restraint by entertaining challenges to applications of a law as those challenges arise.

The Charlottesville ordinance provides an exception for those minors who are "exercising First Amendment rights protected by the United States Constitution, such as the free exercise of religion, freedom of speech and the right of assembly." Charlottesville, Va., Code § 17–7(b)(8). Plaintiffs insist that this exception accords standardless discretion to law enforcement officers to decide whether or not the exception applies. According to plaintiffs, it also forces citizens to learn a complex body of constitutional law in order to comprehend its scope.

We decline to punish the City for its laudable effort to respect the First Amendment. *See CISPES (Committee in Solidarity with the People of El Salvador) v. FBI*, 770 F.2d 468, 474 (5th Cir.1985). A broad exception from the curfew for such activities fortifies, rather than weakens, First Amendment values. Plaintiffs basically attempt to place city councils between a rock and a hard place. If councils draft an ordinance with exceptions, those exceptions are subject to a vagueness challenge. If they neglect to provide exceptions, then the ordinance is attacked for not adequately protecting First Amendment freedoms. It hardly seems fitting, however, for courts to chastise elected bodies for protecting expressive activity. The Charlottesville ordinance is constitutionally stronger with that protection than without.

The First Amendment exception also does not accord unfettered discretion to law enforcement officials. Every criminal law, of course, reposes some discretion in those who must enforce it. The mere possibility that such discretion might be abused hardly entitles courts to strike a law down. * * *

The First Amendment exception provides adequate notice to citizens. It is perfectly clear that core First Amendment activities such as political protest and religious worship after midnight would be protected. It is equally clear that rollerblading would not. Between these poles may lie marginal cases, which can be taken as they come. * * *

The ordinance also creates an exception in cases where a minor is involved in an emergency. Without citation to authority, plaintiffs pose a variety of hypothetical situations in which this exception may or may not apply. For example, they wonder whether the exception would include the need to go to a store to purchase cough medicine or a thermometer. Once again, the existence of questions at the margins does not justify striking down the exception altogether. A brief review of the exception illuminates many situations to which it plainly applies. The ordinance specifically defines emergency as "refer[ring] to unforeseen circumstances, or the status or condition resulting therefrom, requiring immediate action to safeguard life, limb or property." Charlottesville, Va.Code § 17–7(a). It further details that "[t]he term includes, but is not limited to, fires, natural disasters, automobile accidents, or other similar circumstances." *Id.* While "[t]here is little doubt that imagination can conjure up hypothetical cases" to test the meaning of emergency, these speculative musings do not render this term unconstitutionally vague. *American Communications Ass'n v. Douds*, 339 U.S. 382, 412, 70 S.Ct. 674, 94 L.Ed. 925 (1950).

Plaintiffs' vagueness claims threaten to make the drafting of a curfew ordinance an impossible task. The practical exceptions to the City's curfew shall not provide the cause of its demise.

* * * Accordingly, we affirm the judgment of the district court. We do so in the belief that communities possess constitutional latitude in devising solutions to the persistent problem of juvenile crime.

NOTES AND QUESTIONS

1. *Minors as a Class?* Juvenile curfew ordinances have been successfully challenged on equal protection grounds. Like the *Schleifer* court, other courts employ intermediate scrutiny. The Second Circuit described the standard: "If a municipality wishes to single out minors as a group to curtail a constitutional freedom . . . then the municipality must satisfy constitutional requirements by tying their policies to the special traits, vulnerabilities, and needs of minors." Ramos v. Town of Vernon, 353 F.3d 171 (2d Cir. 2003). What "constitutional freedom" is the *Ramos* court referring to? Can you think

of constitutional provisions in addition to the First Amendment that are implicated by juvenile curfew ordinances?

2. *Why Intermediate Scrutiny and What Does It Mean?* Applying this relatively stringent standard of review is not necessarily intuitive in constitutional challenges to juvenile curfew ordinances. Perhaps courts believe that something more than rational basis review is required because "[j]uveniles lack the right to vote, and without an independent voice in legislative decision[-]making, minors must rely on others to ensure adequate protection of their rights" and minors are placed "outside those political processes that ordinarily protect minorities." *Ramos* (citing United States v. Carolene Prods. *Co.,* 304 U.S. 144 n. 4 (1938)). Furthermore, intermediate scrutiny requires that the curfew be "substantially related" to "important" governmental interests. To survive intermediate scrutiny, the municipality cannot rely on "stereotypes and assumptions," but must show that the *particular* ordinance is the product of "reasoned analysis." This can be a difficult standard to meet requiring particularized proof of seemingly obvious facts. *See Ramos v. Town of Vernon,* 353 F.3d 171 (2d Cir. 2003) (invalidating a juvenile curfew where the municipality failed to show that crime was committed at night and that minors were either committing the crimes or being victimized).

3. *Juvenile Curfews and Vagueness.* As you will see in the next case, the Supreme Court's invalidation of Chicago's gang loitering ordinance was based on its conclusion that the law was impermissibly vague. Perhaps as a result of that opinion, the vagueness challenge has received renewed attention in juvenile curfew cases. In fact, several courts have invalidated juvenile curfews on the grounds that they were impermissibly vague. *See, e.g.,* City of Sumner v. Walsh, 61 P.3d 1111 (Wash. 2003) (invalidating as vague the prohibition making it "unlawful for any juvenile to remain in any public place or establishment within the city of Sumner during curfew hours;" defining "remain" as "to linger or stay"); Betancourt v. Town of West New York, 769 A.2d 1065 (N.J. A.D. 2001) (invalidating ordinance for use of undefined terms such as "social events", "cultural events", "direct transit", and "errand involving a medical emergency"). The Washington court concluded that the ordinance's language did not "provide ascertainable standards for locating the line between innocent and unlawful behavior," *Sumner,* 61 P.3d at 1115. Similarly, the New Jersey court found that the ordinance failed to define its crucial terms "with sufficient definiteness that ordinary people can understand what conduct is prohibited," and also that its vague language encouraged "arbitrary and discriminatory enforcement," *Betancourt,* 769 A.2d at 1070. The Alaska Supreme Court reached the opposite result, rejecting vagueness challenges to a municipal curfew, Treacy v. Anchorage, 91 P.3d 252 (Ak. 2004). After you have read *Morales* in the next Section, ask yourself which approach seems more faithful to the standards the Court articulated in that case.

4. *The Appropriate Level of Judicial Review.* Judicial opinions disagree on the correct standard of review to apply to curfew challenges, primarily

because the courts have different attitudes about the level of freedom to which juveniles are generally entitled and about the extent to which the parent or the government should be in charge of children's nighttime activities. For cases discounting the importance of juvenile rights and applying minimal scrutiny, *see, e.g.,* Sale v. Goldman, 539 S.E.2d 446 (W.Va. 2000); City of Panora v. Simmons, 445 N.W.2d 363 (Iowa 1989). In addition to the two main cases, intermediate scrutiny was applied by the court in Hodgkins v. Peterson, 175 F.Supp.2d 1132 (S.D. Ind. 2001), *rev'd on other grounds*, 355 F.3d 1048 (7th Cir.2004). Strict scrutiny, the most protective of juvenile liberties and the most restrictive of government discretion, was applied in Commonwealth v. Weston W., 913 N.E.2d 832 (Mass. 2009); State v. J.P., 907 So.2d 1101 (Fla. 2004); and Nunez v. City of San Diego, 114 F.3d 935 (9th Cir.1997). For an analysis of the judicial inconsistency on this point, *see* Calvin Massey, Juvenile Curfews and Fundamental Rights Methodology, 27 Hastings Const. L.Q. 775 (2000).

    5.   *Juvenile Curfews in State and Federal Courts.* Juvenile curfews such as the one challenged in *Schleifer* have become extremely common. It is estimated more than 75% of U.S. cities with populations over 200,000 have enacted some type of curfew. Lawsuits asserting abridgement of various constitutional protections of minors and their parents, similar to the arguments raised in *Schleifer*, have been filed in many state and federal courts. The cases are split, showing different judicial attitudes about the rights of juveniles, the interests of local communities, and the proper level of judicial review. *Compare* Anonymous v. Rochester, 915 N.E.2d 593 (N.Y. 2009); Nunez v. San Diego, 114 F.3d 935 (9th Cir.1997); City of Sumner v. Walsh, 61 P.3d 1111 (Wash. 2003); Maquoketa v. Russell, 484 N.W.2d 179 (Iowa 1992); Betancourt v. Town of West New York, 769 A.2d 1065 (N.J. A.D. 2001); *and* K.L.J. v. Florida, 581 So.2d 920 (Fla.App.1991) (invalidating juvenile curfews on basis of state and federal constitutional law principles) *with* Commonwealth v. Weston, 913 N.E. 2d 832 (Mass. 2009); Sale v. Goldman, 539 S.E.2d 446 (W.Va. 2000); Hutchins v. District of Columbia, 188 F.3d 531 (D.C.Cir.1999); Qutb v. Strauss, 11 F.3d 488 (5th Cir.1993); In re Maricopa County, 887 P.2d 599 (Ariz.App.1994) (juvenile curfews held constitutional). For discussion of the case law and the articulation of the argument that broader, multi-dimensional strategies would produce clearer reductions in juvenile crime than restrictive measures such as curfews, *see* Brian Privor, Dusk 'Til Dawn: Children's Rights and the Effectiveness of Juvenile Curfew Ordinances, 79 B.U.L.Rev. 415 (1999). Under what circumstances might a curfew for all ages survive constitutional challenges? *See* Embry v. City of Cloverport, Ky., 2004 WL 191613 (W.D. Ky.) (invalidating general curfew on grounds of vagueness and overbreadth). How about a juvenile curfew in rural areas, as opposed to the more common urban setting?

2. LOITERING AND EXCLUSION

CITY OF CHICAGO v. MORALES
Supreme Court of the United States
527 U.S. 41 (1999)

JUSTICE STEVENS announced the judgment of the Court and delivered the opinion of the Court with respect to Parts I, II, and V, and an opinion with respect to Parts III, IV, and VI, in which JUSTICE SOUTER and JUSTICE GINSBURG join.

In 1992, the Chicago City Council enacted the Gang Congregation Ordinance, which prohibits "criminal street gang members" from "loitering" with one another or with other persons in any public place. The question presented is whether the Supreme Court of Illinois correctly held that the ordinance violates the Due Process Clause of the Fourteenth Amendment to the Federal Constitution.

I

Before the ordinance was adopted, the city council's Committee on Police and Fire conducted hearings to explore the problems created by the city's street gangs, and more particularly, the consequences of public loitering by gang members. Witnesses included residents of the neighborhoods where gang members are most active, as well as some of the aldermen who represent those areas. Based on that evidence, the council made a series of findings that are included in the text of the ordinance and explain the reasons for its enactment.

The council found that a continuing increase in criminal street gang activity was largely responsible for the city's rising murder rate, as well as an escalation of violent and drug related crimes. It noted that in many neighborhoods throughout the city, "the burgeoning presence of street gang members in public places has intimidated many law abiding citizens." 177 Ill.2d 440, 445, 227 Ill.Dec. 130, 687 N.E.2d 53, 58 (1997). Furthermore, the council stated that gang members "establish control over identifiable areas . . . by loitering in those areas and intimidating others from entering those areas; and . . . [m]embers of criminal street gangs avoid arrest by committing no offense punishable under existing laws when they know the police are present. . . ." *Ibid*. It further found that "loitering in public places by criminal street gang members creates a justifiable fear for the safety of persons and property in the area" and that "[a]ggressive action is necessary to preserve the city's streets and other public places so that the public may use such places without fear." Moreover, the council concluded that the city "has an interest in discouraging all persons from loitering in public places with criminal gang members." *Ibid*.

The ordinance creates a criminal offense punishable by a fine of up to $500, imprisonment for not more than six months, and a requirement to perform up to 120 hours of community service. Commission of the offense involves four predicates. First, the police officer must reasonably believe that at least one of the two or more persons present in a "public place" is a "criminal street gang membe[r]." Second, the persons must be "loitering," which the ordinance defines as "remain[ing] in any one place with no apparent purpose." Third, the officer must then order "all" of the persons to disperse and remove themselves "from the area." Fourth, a person must disobey the officer's order. If any person, whether a gang member or not, disobeys the officer's order, that person is guilty of violating the ordinance. *Ibid.*

Two months after the ordinance was adopted, the Chicago Police Department promulgated General Order 92–4 to provide guidelines to govern its enforcement. That order purported to establish limitations on the enforcement discretion of police officers "to ensure that the anti-gang loitering ordinance is not enforced in an arbitrary or discriminatory way." Chicago Police Department, General Order 92–4, reprinted in App. to Pet. for Cert. 65a. The limitations confine the authority to arrest gang members who violate the ordinance to sworn "members of the Gang Crime Section" and certain other designated officers, and establish detailed criteria for defining street gangs and membership in such gangs. *Id.*, at 66a–67a. In addition, the order directs district commanders to "designate areas in which the presence of gang members has a demonstrable effect on the activities of law abiding persons in the surrounding community," and provides that the ordinance "will be enforced only within the designated areas." *Id.*, at 68a–69a. The city, however, does not release the locations of these "designated areas" to the public.

II

During the three years of its enforcement, the police issued over 89,000 dispersal orders and arrested over 42,000 people for violating the ordinance. In the ensuing enforcement proceedings, two trial judges upheld the constitutionality of the ordinance, but eleven others ruled that it was invalid.

* * * [In a case consolidating numerous challenges to the ordinance, the Illinois Supreme Court held]: "that the gang loitering ordinance violates due process of law in that it is impermissibly vague on its face and an arbitrary restriction on personal liberties." 177 Ill.2d, at 447, 227 Ill.Dec. 130, 687 N.E.2d, at 59.

* * * We granted certiorari, 523 U.S. 1071, 118 S.Ct. 1510, 140 L.Ed.2d 664 (1998), and now affirm. Like the Illinois Supreme Court, we conclude that the ordinance enacted by the city of Chicago is unconstitutionally vague.

III

The basic factual predicate for the city's ordinance is not in dispute. As the city argues in its brief, "the very presence of a large collection of obviously brazen, insistent, and lawless gang members and hangers-on on the public ways intimidates residents, who become afraid even to leave their homes and go about their business. That, in turn, imperils community residents' sense of safety and security, detracts from property values, and can ultimately destabilize entire neighborhoods." The findings in the ordinance explain that it was motivated by these concerns. We have no doubt that a law that directly prohibited such intimidating conduct would be constitutional, but this ordinance broadly covers a significant amount of additional activity. Uncertainty about the scope of that additional coverage provides the basis for respondents' claim that the ordinance is too vague. * * *

Vagueness may invalidate a criminal law for either of two independent reasons. First, it may fail to provide the kind of notice that will enable ordinary people to understand what conduct it prohibits; second, it may authorize and even encourage arbitrary and discriminatory enforcement. *See Kolender v. Lawson*, 461 U.S., at 357, 103 S.Ct. 1855. Accordingly, we first consider whether the ordinance provides fair notice to the citizen and then discuss its potential for arbitrary enforcement.

IV

"It is established that a law fails to meet the requirements of the Due Process Clause if it is so vague and standardless that it leaves the public uncertain as to the conduct it prohibits. . . ." *Giaccio v. Pennsylvania*, 382 U.S. 399, 402–403, 86 S.Ct. 518, 15 L.Ed.2d 447 (1966). The Illinois Supreme Court recognized that the term "loiter" may have a common and accepted meaning, 177 Ill.2d, at 451, 227 Ill.Dec. 130, 687 N.E.2d, at 61, but the definition of that term in this ordinance—"to remain in any one place with no apparent purpose"—does not. It is difficult to imagine how any citizen of the city of Chicago standing in a public place with a group of people would know if he or she had an "apparent purpose." If she were talking to another person, would she have an apparent purpose? If she were frequently checking her watch and looking expectantly down the street, would she have an apparent purpose?

Since the city cannot conceivably have meant to criminalize each instance a citizen stands in public with a gang member, the vagueness that dooms this ordinance is not the product of uncertainty about the normal meaning of "loitering," but rather about what loitering is covered by the ordinance and what is not. The Illinois Supreme Court emphasized the law's failure to distinguish between innocent conduct and conduct threatening harm. Its decision followed the precedent set by a number of state courts that have upheld ordinances that criminalize loitering combined with some other overt act or evidence of criminal intent. However, state courts have uniformly invalidated laws that do not join the term "loitering" with a second specific element of the crime.

The city's principal response to this concern about adequate notice is that loiterers are not subject to sanction until after they have failed to comply with an officer's order to disperse. "[W]hatever problem is created by a law that criminalizes conduct people normally believe to be innocent is solved when persons receive actual notice from a police order of what they are expected to do." We find this response unpersuasive for at least two reasons.

First, the purpose of the fair notice requirement is to enable the ordinary citizen to conform his or her conduct to the law. * * * Although it is true that a loiterer is not subject to criminal sanctions unless he or she disobeys a dispersal order, the loitering is the conduct that the ordinance is designed to prohibit. If the loitering is in fact harmless and innocent, the dispersal order itself is an unjustified impairment of liberty. If the police are able to decide arbitrarily which members of the public they will order to disperse, then the Chicago ordinance becomes indistinguishable from the law we held invalid in *Shuttlesworth v. Birmingham*, 382 U.S. 87, 90, 86 S.Ct. 211, 15 L.Ed.2d 176 (1965). Because an officer may issue an order only after prohibited conduct has already occurred, it cannot provide the kind of advance notice that will protect the putative loiterer from being ordered to disperse. Such an order cannot retroactively give adequate warning of the boundary between the permissible and the impermissible applications of the law.

Second, the terms of the dispersal order compound the inadequacy of the notice afforded by the ordinance. It provides that the officer "shall order all such persons to disperse and remove themselves from the area." App. to Pet. for Cert. 61a. This vague phrasing raises a host of questions. After such an order issues, how long must the loiterers remain apart? How far must they move? If each loiterer walks around the block and they meet again at the same location, are they subject to arrest or merely to being ordered to disperse again? * * *

Lack of clarity in the description of the loiterer's duty to obey a dispersal order might not render the ordinance unconstitutionally vague if the definition of the forbidden conduct were clear, but it does buttress our conclusion that the entire ordinance fails to give the ordinary citizen adequate notice of what is forbidden and what is permitted. The Constitution does not permit a legislature to "set a net large enough to catch all possible offenders, and leave it to the courts to step inside and say who could be rightfully detained, and who should be set at large." *United States v. Reese*, 92 U.S. 214, 221, 23 L.Ed. 563 (1876). * * *

V

The broad sweep of the ordinance also violates "'the requirement that a legislature establish minimal guidelines to govern law enforcement.'" *Kolender v. Lawson*, 461 U.S., at 358, 103 S.Ct. 1855. There are no such guidelines in the ordinance. In any public place in the city of Chicago, persons who stand or sit in the company of a gang member may be ordered to disperse unless their purpose is apparent. The mandatory language in the enactment directs the police to issue an order without first making any inquiry about their possible purposes. It matters not whether the reason that a gang member and his father, for example, might loiter near Wrigley Field is to rob an unsuspecting fan or just to get a glimpse of Sammy Sosa leaving the ballpark; in either event, if their purpose is not apparent to a nearby police officer, she may—indeed, she "shall"—order them to disperse.

Recognizing that the ordinance does reach a substantial amount of innocent conduct, we turn, then, to its language to determine if it "necessarily entrusts lawmaking to the moment-to-moment judgment of the policeman on his beat." *Kolender v. Lawson*, 461 U.S., at 359, 103 S.Ct. 1855 (internal quotation marks omitted). * * * [T]he principal source of the vast discretion conferred on the police in this case is the definition of loitering as "to remain in any one place with no apparent purpose."

As the Illinois Supreme Court interprets that definition, it "provides absolute discretion to police officers to determine what activities constitute loitering." 177 Ill.2d, at 457, 227 Ill.Dec. 130, 687 N.E.2d, at 63. We have no authority to construe the language of a state statute more narrowly than the construction given by that State's highest court. * * *

Nevertheless, the city disputes the Illinois Supreme Court's interpretation, arguing that the text of the ordinance limits the officer's discretion in three ways. First, it does not permit the officer to issue a dispersal order to anyone who is moving along or who has an apparent purpose. Second, it does not permit an arrest if individuals obey a dispersal order. Third, no order can issue unless the officer reasonably believes that one of the loiterers is a member of a criminal street gang.

Even putting to one side our duty to defer to a state court's construction of the scope of a local enactment, we find each of these limitations insufficient. That the ordinance does not apply to people who are moving—that is, to activity that would not constitute loitering under any possible definition of the term—does not even address the question of how much discretion the police enjoy in deciding which stationary persons to disperse under the ordinance. Similarly, that the ordinance does not permit an arrest until after a dispersal order has been disobeyed does not provide any guidance to the officer deciding whether such an order should issue. The "no apparent purpose" standard for making that decision is inherently subjective because its application depends on whether some purpose is "apparent" to the officer on the scene.

Presumably an officer would have discretion to treat some purposes—perhaps a purpose to engage in idle conversation or simply to enjoy a cool breeze on a warm evening—as too frivolous to be apparent if he suspected a different ulterior motive. Moreover, an officer conscious of the city council's reasons for enacting the ordinance might well ignore its text and issue a dispersal order, even though an illicit purpose is actually apparent.

It is true, as the city argues, that the requirement that the officer reasonably believe that a group of loiterers contains a gang member does place a limit on the authority to order dispersal. That limitation would no doubt be sufficient if the ordinance only applied to loitering that had an apparently harmful purpose or effect, or possibly if it only applied to loitering by persons reasonably believed to be criminal gang members. But this ordinance, for reasons that are not explained in the findings of the city council, requires no harmful purpose and applies to non-gang members as well as suspected gang members. It applies to everyone in the city who may remain in one place with one suspected gang member as long as their purpose is not apparent to an officer observing them. Friends, relatives, teachers, counselors, or even total strangers might unwittingly engage in forbidden loitering if they happen to engage in idle conversation with a gang member.

VI

In our judgment, the Illinois Supreme Court correctly concluded that the ordinance does not provide sufficiently specific limits on the enforcement discretion of the police "to meet constitutional standards for definiteness and clarity." 177 Ill.2d, at 459, 227 Ill.Dec. 130, 687 N.E.2d, at 64. We recognize the serious and difficult problems testified to by the citizens of Chicago that led to the enactment of this ordinance. "We are mindful that the preservation of liberty depends in part on the maintenance of social order." *Houston v. Hill*, 482 U.S. 451, 471–472, 107 S.Ct. 2502, 96 L.Ed.2d 398 (1987). However, in this instance the city has enacted an ordinance that affords too much discretion to the police and too little notice to citizens who wish to use the public streets.

Accordingly, the judgment of the Supreme Court of Illinois is

Affirmed.

JUSTICE O'CONNOR, with whom JUSTICE BREYER joins, concurring in part and concurring in the judgment.

It is important to courts and legislatures alike that we characterize more clearly the narrow scope of today's holding. As the ordinance comes to this Court, it is unconstitutionally vague. Nevertheless, there remain open to Chicago reasonable alternatives to combat the very real threat posed by gang intimidation and violence. For example, the Court properly and expressly distinguishes the ordinance from laws that require loiterers to have a "harmful purpose," see *id.*, at 1862, from laws that target only gang members, see ibid., and from laws that incorporate limits on the area and manner in which the laws may be enforced, see *ante*, at 1862. In addition, the ordinance here is unlike a law that "directly prohibit[s]" the " 'presence of a large collection of obviously brazen, insistent, and lawless gang members and hangers-on on the public ways,' " that " 'intimidates residents.' " *Ante*, at 1856 (quoting Brief for Petitioner 14). Indeed, as the plurality notes, the city of Chicago has several laws that do exactly this. *See ante*, at 1857, n. 17. Chicago has even enacted a provision that "enables police officers to fulfill . . . their traditional functions," including "preserving the public peace." *See post*, at 1883 (THOMAS, J., dissenting). Specifically, Chicago's general disorderly conduct provision allows the police to arrest those who knowingly "provoke, make or aid in making a breach of peace." *See* Chicago Municipal Code § 8–4–010 (1992).

In my view, the gang loitering ordinance could have been construed more narrowly. The term "loiter" might possibly be construed in a more limited fashion to mean "to remain in any one place with no apparent purpose other than to establish control over identifiable areas, to intimidate others from entering those areas, or to conceal illegal activities." Such a definition would be consistent with the Chicago City Council's findings and would avoid the vagueness problems of the ordinance as construed by the Illinois Supreme Court. *See* App. to Pet. for Cert. 60a–61a. As noted above, so would limitations that restricted the ordinance's criminal penalties to gang members or that more carefully delineated the circumstances in which those penalties would apply to nongang members.

JUSTICE KENNEDY, concurring in part and concurring in the judgment.

JUSTICE BREYER, concurring in part and concurring in the judgment.

JUSTICE SCALIA, dissenting.

The citizens of Chicago were once free to drive about the city at whatever speed they wished. At some point Chicagoans (or perhaps Illinoisans) decided this would not do, and imposed prophylactic speed limits designed to assure safe operation by the average (or perhaps even subaverage) driver with the average (or perhaps even subaverage) vehicle. This infringed upon the "freedom" of all citizens, but was not unconstitutional.

Similarly, the citizens of Chicago were once free to stand around and gawk at the scene of an accident. At some point Chicagoans discovered that this obstructed traffic and caused more accidents. They did not make the practice unlawful, but they did authorize police officers to order the crowd to disperse, and imposed penalties for refusal to obey such an order. Again, this prophylactic measure infringed upon the "freedom" of all citizens, but was not unconstitutional.

Until the ordinance that is before us today was adopted, the citizens of Chicago were free to stand about in public places with no apparent purpose—to engage, that is, in conduct that appeared to be loitering. In recent years, however, the city has been afflicted with criminal street gangs. As reflected in the record before us, these gangs congregated in public places to deal in drugs, and to terrorize the neighborhoods by demonstrating control over their "turf." Many residents of the inner city felt that they were prisoners in their own homes. Once again, Chicagoans decided that to eliminate the problem it was worth restricting some of the freedom that they once enjoyed. The means they took was similar to the second, and more mild, example given above rather than the first: Loitering was not made unlawful, but when a group of people occupied a public place without an apparent purpose and in the company of a known gang member, police officers were authorized to order them to disperse, and the failure to obey such an order was made unlawful. *See* Chicago Municipal Code § 8–4–015 (1992). The minor limitation upon the free state of nature that this prophylactic arrangement imposed upon all Chicagoans seemed to them (and it seems to me) a small price to pay for liberation of their streets.

The majority today invalidates this perfectly reasonable measure by ignoring our rules governing facial challenges, by elevating loitering to a constitutionally guaranteed right, and by discerning vagueness where, according to our usual standards, none exists.

* * *

The fact is that the present ordinance is entirely clear in its application, cannot be violated except with full knowledge and intent, and vests no more discretion in the police than innumerable other measures authorizing police orders to preserve the public peace and safety. As suggested by their tortured analyses, and by their suggested solutions that bear no relation to the identified constitutional problem, the majority's real quarrel with the Chicago Ordinance is simply that it permits (or indeed requires) too much harmless conduct by innocent citizens to be proscribed. * * *

But in our democratic system, how much harmless conduct to proscribe is not a judgment to be made by the courts. So long as constitutionally guaranteed rights are not affected, and so long as the proscription has a rational basis, all sorts of perfectly harmless activity by millions of perfectly innocent people can be forbidden—riding a motorcycle without a safety helmet, for example, starting a campfire in a national forest, or selling a safe and effective drug not yet approved by the FDA. All of these acts are entirely innocent and harmless in themselves, but because of the risk of harm that they entail, the freedom to engage in them has been abridged. The citizens of Chicago have decided that depriving themselves of the freedom to "hang out" with a gang member is necessary to eliminate pervasive gang crime and intimidation—and that the elimination of the one is worth the deprivation of the other. This Court has no business second-guessing either the degree of necessity or the fairness of the trade.

I dissent from the judgment of the Court.

JUSTICE THOMAS, with whom THE CHIEF JUSTICE and JUSTICE SCALIA join, dissenting.

The duly elected members of the Chicago City Council enacted the ordinance at issue as part of a larger effort to prevent gangs from establishing dominion over the public streets. By invalidating Chicago's ordinance, I fear that the Court has unnecessarily sentenced law-abiding citizens to lives of terror and misery. * * *

I

The human costs exacted by criminal street gangs are inestimable. In many of our Nation's cities, gangs have "[v]irtually overtak[en] certain neighborhoods, contributing to the economic and social decline of these areas and causing fear and lifestyle changes among law-abiding residents." U.S. Dept. of Justice, Office of Justice Programs, Bureau of Justice Assistance, Monograph: Urban Street Gang Enforcement 3 (1997). Gangs fill the daily lives of many of our poorest and most vulnerable citizens with a terror that the Court does not give sufficient consideration, often relegating them to the status of prisoners in their own homes. * * *

The city of Chicago has suffered the devastation wrought by this national tragedy. Last year, in an effort to curb plummeting attendance, the Chicago Public Schools hired dozens of adults to escort children to school. The youngsters had become too terrified of gang violence to leave their homes alone. Martinez, Parents Paid to Walk Line Between Gangs and School, Chicago Tribune, Jan. 21, 1998, p. 1. The children's fears were not unfounded. In 1996, the Chicago Police Department estimated that there were 132 criminal street gangs in the city. Illinois Criminal Justice Information Authority, Research Bulletin: Street Gangs and

Crime 4 (Sept.1996). Between 1987 and 1994, these gangs were involved in 63,141 criminal incidents, including 21,689 nonlethal violent crimes and 894 homicides. *Id.* at 4–5. Many of these criminal incidents and homicides result from gang "turf battles," which take place on the public streets and place innocent residents in grave danger.

Before enacting its ordinance, the Chicago City Council held extensive hearings on the problems of gang loitering. Concerned citizens appeared to testify poignantly as to how gangs disrupt their daily lives. Ordinary citizens like Ms. D'Ivory Gordon explained that she struggled just to walk to work:

> "When I walk out my door, these guys are out there. . . . They watch you. . . . They know where you live. They know what time you leave, what time you come home. I am afraid of them. I have even come to the point now that I carry a meat cleaver to work with me. . . . I don't want to hurt anyone, and I don't want to be hurt. We need to clean these corners up. Clean these communities up and take it back from them." Transcript of Proceedings before the City Council of Chicago, Committee on Police and Fire 66–67 (May 15, 1997) (hereinafter Transcript).

II

* * *

B

The Court concludes that the ordinance is also unconstitutionally vague because it fails to provide adequate standards to guide police discretion and because, in the plurality's view, it does not give residents adequate notice of how to conform their conduct to the confines of the law. I disagree on both counts.

1

At the outset, it is important to note that the ordinance does not criminalize loitering per se. Rather, it penalizes loiterers' failure to obey a police officer's order to move along. A majority of the Court believes that this scheme vests too much discretion in police officers. Nothing could be further from the truth. Far from according officers too much discretion, the ordinance merely enables police officers to fulfill one of their traditional functions. Police officers are not, and have never been, simply enforcers of the criminal law. They wear other hats—importantly, they have long been vested with the responsibility for preserving the public peace. *See, e.g.,* O. Allen, Duties and Liabilities of Sheriffs 59 (1845) ("As the principal conservator of the peace in his county, and as the calm but irresistible minister of the law, the duty of the Sheriff is no less important than his authority is great"); E. Freund, Police Power § 86, p. 87 (1904) ("The criminal law deals with offenses after they have been committed, the police power aims to prevent them. The activity of the police for the prevention of crime is partly such as needs no special legal authority"). Nor is the idea that the police are also peace officers simply a quaint anachronism. In most American jurisdictions, police officers continue to be obligated, by law, to maintain the public peace.

* * *

In order to perform their peace-keeping responsibilities satisfactorily, the police inevitably must exercise discretion. Indeed, by empowering them to act as peace officers, the law assumes that the police will exercise that discretion responsibly and with sound judgment. That is not to say that the law should not provide objective guidelines for the police, but simply that it cannot rigidly constrain their every action. By directing a police officer not to issue a dispersal order unless he "observes a person whom he reasonably believes to be a criminal street gang member loitering in any public place," App. to Pet. for Cert. 61a, Chicago's ordinance strikes an appropriate balance between those two extremes. Just as we trust officers to rely on their experience and expertise in order to make spur-of-the-moment determinations about amorphous legal standards such as "probable cause" and "reasonable suspicion," so we must trust them to determine whether a group of loiterers contains individuals (in this case members of criminal street gangs) whom the city has determined threaten the public peace. * * *

In concluding that the ordinance adequately channels police discretion, I do not suggest that a police officer enforcing the Gang Congregation Ordinance will never make a mistake. Nor do I overlook the possibility that a police officer, acting in bad faith, might enforce the ordinance in an arbitrary or discriminatory way. But our decisions should not turn on the proposition that such an event will be anything but rare. Instances of arbitrary or discriminatory enforcement of the ordinance, like any other law, are best addressed when (and if) they arise, rather than prophylactically through the disfavored mechanism of a facial challenge on vagueness grounds. * * *

2

The plurality's conclusion that the ordinance "fails to give the ordinary citizen adequate notice of what is forbidden and what is permitted," *ante*, at 1861, is similarly untenable. There is nothing "vague" about an order to disperse. While "we can never expect mathematical certainty from our language," *Grayned v. City of Rockford*, 408 U.S. 104, 110, 92 S.Ct. 2294, 33 L.Ed.2d 222 (1972), it is safe to assume that the vast majority of people who are ordered by the police to "disperse and remove themselves from the area" will have little difficulty understanding how to comply. App. to Pet. for Cert. 61a. * * *

As already explained, *supra*, at 1881–1883, the ordinance does not proscribe constitutionally protected conduct—there is no fundamental right to loiter. It is also anomalous to characterize loitering as "innocent" conduct when it has been disfavored throughout American history. When a category of conduct has been consistently criminalized, it can hardly be considered "innocent." * * *

The plurality also concludes that the definition of the term loiter—"to remain in any one place with no apparent purpose," see 177 Ill.2d, at 445, 227 Ill.Dec. 130, 687 N.E.2d, at 58—fails to provide adequate notice. "It is difficult to imagine," the plurality posits, "how any citizen of the city of Chicago standing in a public place . . . would know if he or she had an 'apparent purpose.'" *Ante*, at 1859. The plurality underestimates the intellectual capacity of the citizens of Chicago. Persons of ordinary intelligence are perfectly capable of evaluating how outsiders perceive their conduct, and here "[i]t is self-evident that there is a whole range of conduct that anyone with at least a semblance of common sense would know is [loitering] and that would be covered by the statute." *See Smith v. Goguen*, 415 U.S. 566, 584, 94 S.Ct. 1242, 39 L.Ed.2d 605 (1974) (White, J., concurring in judgment). Members of a group standing on the corner staring blankly into space, for example, are likely well aware that passersby would conclude that they have "no apparent purpose." In any event, because this is a facial challenge, the plurality's ability to hypothesize that some individuals, in some circumstances, may be unable to ascertain how their actions appear to outsiders is irrelevant to our analysis. Here, we are asked to determine whether the ordinance is "vague in all of its applications." *Hoffman Estates*, 455 U.S., at 497, 102 S.Ct. 1186. The answer is unquestionably no.

* * *

Today, the Court focuses extensively on the "rights" of gang members and their companions. It can safely do so—the people who will have to live with the consequences of today's opinion do not live in our neighborhoods. Rather, the people who will suffer from our lofty pronouncements are people * * * who have seen their neighborhoods literally destroyed by gangs and violence and drugs. They are good, decent people who must struggle to overcome their desperate situation, against all odds, in order to raise their families, earn a living, and remain good citizens. As one resident described, "There is only about maybe one or two percent of the people in the city causing these problems maybe, but it's keeping 98 percent of us in our houses and off the streets and afraid to shop." Tr. 126. By focusing exclusively on the imagined "rights" of the two percent, the Court today has denied our most vulnerable citizens the very thing that JUSTICE STEVENS, *ante*, at 1858, elevates above all else—the "freedom of movement." And that is a shame. I respectfully dissent.

VIRGINIA V. HICKS

Supreme Court of the United States
539 U.S. 113 (2003)

JUSTICE SCALIA delivered the opinion of the Court.

The issue presented in this case is whether the Richmond Redevelopment and Housing Authority's trespass policy is facially invalid under the First Amendment's overbreadth doctrine.

I

A

The Richmond Redevelopment and Housing Authority (RRHA) owns and operates a housing development for low-income residents called Whitcomb Court. Until June 23, 1997, the city of Richmond owned the streets within Whitcomb Court. The city council decided, however, to "privatize" these streets in an effort to combat rampant crime and drug dealing in Whitcomb Court—much of it committed and conducted by nonresidents. The council enacted Ordinance No. 97–181–197, which provided, in part:

> "'§ 1. That Carmine Street, Bethel Street, Ambrose Street, Deforrest Street, the 2100–2300 Block of Sussex Street and the 2700–2800 Block of Magnolia Street, in Whitcomb Court . . . be and are hereby closed to public use and travel and abandoned as streets of the City of Richmond.'" App. to Pet. for Cert. 93–94.

The city then conveyed these streets by a recorded deed to the RRHA (which is a political subdivision of the Commonwealth of Virginia). This deed required the RRHA to "'give the appearance that the closed street, particularly at the entrances, are no longer public streets and that they are in fact private streets.'" *Id.,* at 95. To this end, the RRHA posted red-and-white signs on each apartment building—and every 100 feet along the streets—of Whitcomb Court, which state: "'NO TRESPASSING[.] PRIVATE PROPERTY[.] YOU ARE NOW ENTERING PRIVATE PROPERTY AND STREETS OWNED BY RRHA. UNAUTHORIZED PERSONS WILL BE SUBJECT TO ARREST AND PROSECUTION. UNAUTHORIZED VEHICLES WILL BE TOWED AT OWNERS EXPENSE.'" Pet. for Cert. 5. The RRHA also enacted a policy authorizing the Richmond police

> "'to serve notice, either orally or in writing, to any person who is found on Richmond Redevelopment and Housing Authority property when such person is not a resident, employee, or such person cannot demonstrate *a legitimate business or social purpose* for being on the premises. Such notice shall forbid the person from returning to the property. Finally, Richmond Redevelopment and Housing Authority authorizes Richmond

Police Department officers to arrest any person for trespassing after such person, having been duly notified, either stays upon or returns to Richmond Redevelopment and Housing Authority property.'" App. to Pet. for Cert. 98–99 (emphasis added).

Persons who trespass after being notified not to return are subject to prosecution under [Virginia's trespass statute.]

B

* * * [T]he RRHA gave [respondent Kevin Hicks, a nonresident] written notice barring him from Whitcomb Court, and Hicks signed this notice in the presence of a police officer. Twice after receiving this notice Hicks asked for permission to return; twice the Whitcomb Court housing manager said "no." That did not stop Hicks; in January 1999 he again trespassed at Whitcomb Court and was arrested and convicted under § 18.2–119.

At trial, Hicks maintained that the RRHA's policy limiting access to Whitcomb Court was both unconstitutionally overbroad and void for vagueness. * * * [T]he Virginia Supreme Court concluded that the RRHA policy was unconstitutionally overbroad. While acknowledging that the policy was "designed to punish activities that are not protected by the First Amendment," 264 Va. 48, 58, 563 S.E.2d 674, 680 (2002), the court held that "the policy also prohibits speech and conduct that are clearly protected by the First Amendment," *ibid.* The court found the policy defective because it vested too much discretion in Whitcomb Court's manager to determine whether an individual's presence at Whitcomb Court is "authorized," allowing her to "prohibit speech that she finds personally distasteful or offensive even though such speech may be protected by the First Amendment." *Id.,* at 60, 563 S.E.2d, at 680–681. We granted the Commonwealth's petition for certiorari. 537 U.S. 1169, 123 S.Ct. 990, 154 L.Ed.2d 910 (2003).

II

A

Hicks does not contend that he was engaged in constitutionally protected conduct when arrested; nor does he challenge the validity of the trespass *statute* under which he was convicted. Instead he claims that the RRHA *policy* barring him from Whitcomb Court is overbroad under the First Amendment, and cannot be applied to him—or anyone else. The First Amendment doctrine of overbreadth is an exception to our normal rule regarding the standards for facial challenges. *See Members of City Council of Los Angeles v. Taxpayers for Vincent,* 466 U.S. 789, 796, 104 S.Ct. 2118, 80 L.Ed.2d 772 (1984). The showing that a law punishes a "substantial" amount of protected free speech, "judged in relation to the statute's plainly legitimate sweep," *Broadrick v. Oklahoma,* 413 U.S. 601,

615, 93 S.Ct. 2908, 37 L.Ed.2d 830 (1973), suffices to invalidate *all* enforcement of that law, "until and unless a limiting construction or partial invalidation so narrows it as to remove the seeming threat or deterrence to constitutionally protected expression," *id.,* at 613, 93 S.Ct. 2908. * * *

We have provided this expansive remedy out of concern that the threat of enforcement of an overbroad law may deter or "chill" constitutionally protected speech—especially when the overbroad statute imposes criminal sanctions. * * *

As we noted in *Broadrick,* however, there comes a point at which the chilling effect of an overbroad law, significant though it may be, cannot justify prohibiting all enforcement of that law—particularly a law that reflects "legitimate state interests in maintaining comprehensive controls over harmful, constitutionally unprotected conduct." 413 U.S., at 615, 93 S.Ct. 2908. For there are substantial social costs *created* by the overbreadth doctrine when it blocks application of a law to constitutionally unprotected speech, or especially to constitutionally unprotected conduct. To ensure that these costs do not swallow the social benefits of declaring a law "overbroad," we have insisted that a law's application to protected speech be "substantial," not only in an absolute sense, but also relative to the scope of the law's plainly legitimate applications, *ibid.,* before applying the "strong medicine" of overbreadth invalidation, *id.,* at 613, 93 S.Ct. 2908. * * *

C

The Virginia Supreme Court found that the RRHA policy allowed Gloria S. Rogers, the manager of Whitcomb Court, to exercise "unfettered discretion" in determining who may use the RRHA's property. 264 Va., at 59, 563 S.E.2d, at 680. Specifically, the court faulted an "unwritten" rule that persons wishing to hand out flyers on the sidewalks of Whitcomb Court need to obtain Rogers' permission. *Ibid.* This unwritten portion of the RRHA policy, the court concluded, unconstitutionally allows Rogers to "prohibit speech that she finds personally distasteful or offensive." *Id.,* at 60, 563 S.E.2d, at 681.

Hicks, of course, was not arrested for leafleting or demonstrating without permission. He violated the RRHA's *written* rule that persons who receive a barment notice must not return to RRHA property. The Virginia Supreme Court, based on its objection to the "unwritten" requirement that demonstrators and leafleters obtain advance permission, declared the *entire* RRHA trespass policy overbroad and void—including the written rule that those who return after receiving a barment notice are subject to arrest. Whether these provisions are severable is of course a matter of state law, see *Leavitt v. Jane L.,* 518 U.S. 137, 139, 116 S.Ct. 2068, 135 L.Ed.2d 443 (1996) *(per curiam),* and the Virginia Supreme Court has implicitly decided that they are not—that all components of the RRHA trespass policy must stand or fall together. It could not properly decree that they fall by reason of the overbreadth doctrine, however, unless the trespass policy, *taken as a whole,* is substantially overbroad judged in relation to its plainly legitimate sweep. *See Broadrick, supra,* at 615, 93 S.Ct. 2908. The overbreadth claimant bears the burden of demonstrating, "from the text of [the law] and from actual fact," that substantial overbreadth exists. *New York State Club Assn., Inc. v. City of New York,* 487 U.S. 1, 14, 108 S.Ct. 2225, 101 L.Ed.2d 1 (1988).

Hicks has not made such a showing with regard to the RRHA policy taken as a whole—even assuming, *arguendo,* the unlawfulness of the policy's "unwritten" rule that demonstrating and leafleting at Whitcomb Court require permission from Gloria Rogers. Consider the "no-return" notice served on nonresidents who have no "legitimate business or social purpose" in Whitcomb Court: Hicks has failed to demonstrate that this notice would even be given to anyone engaged in constitutionally protected speech. Gloria Rogers testified that leafleting and demonstrations *are* permitted at Whitcomb Court, so long as permission is obtained in advance. App. to Pet. for Cert. 100–102. Thus, "legitimate business or social purpose" evidently includes leafleting and demonstrating; otherwise, Rogers would lack authority to permit those activities on RRHA property. Hicks has failed to demonstrate that *any* First Amendment activity falls outside the "legitimate business or social purpose[s]" that permit entry. As far as appears, until one receives a barment notice, entering for a First Amendment purpose is not a trespass.

As for the written provision authorizing the police to arrest those who return to Whitcomb Court after receiving a barment notice: That certainly does not violate the First Amendment as applied to persons whose postnotice entry is not for the purpose of engaging in constitutionally protected speech. And Hicks has not even established that it would violate the First Amendment as applied to persons whose postnotice entry *is* for that purpose. Even assuming the streets of Whitcomb Court are a public forum, the notice-barment rule subjects to arrest those who reenter after trespassing and after being warned not to return—*regardless* of whether, upon their return, they seek to engage in speech. Neither the basis for the barment sanction (the prior trespass) nor its purpose (preventing future trespasses) has anything to do with the First Amendment. Punishing its violation by a person who wishes to engage in free speech no more implicates the First Amendment than would the punishment of a person who has (pursuant to lawful regulation) been banned from a public park after vandalizing it, and who ignores the ban in order to take part in a political demonstration. Here, as there, it is Hicks' nonexpressive *conduct*—his entry in violation of the notice-barment rule—not his speech, for which he is punished as a trespasser.

Most importantly, both the notice-barment rule and the "legitimate business or social purpose" rule apply to *all* persons who enter the streets of Whitcomb Court, not just to those who seek to engage in expression. The rules apply to strollers, loiterers, drug dealers, roller skaters, bird watchers, soccer players, and others not engaged in constitutionally protected conduct—a group that would seemingly far outnumber First Amendment speakers. Even assuming invalidity of the "unwritten" rule that requires leafleters and demonstrators to obtain advance permission from Gloria Rogers, Hicks has not shown, based on the record in this case, that the RRHA trespass policy as a whole prohibits a "substantial" amount of protected speech in relation to its many legitimate applications. That is not surprising, since the overbreadth doctrine's concern with "chilling" protected speech "attenuates as the otherwise unprotected behavior that it forbids the State to sanction moves from 'pure speech' toward conduct." *Broadrick*, 413 U.S., at 615, 93 S.Ct. 2908. Rarely, if ever, will an overbreadth challenge succeed against a law or regulation that is not specifically addressed to speech or to conduct necessarily associated with speech (such as picketing or demonstrating). Applications of the RRHA policy that violate the First Amendment can still be remedied through as-applied litigation, but the Virginia Supreme Court should not have used the "strong medicine" of overbreadth to invalidate the entire RRHA trespass policy. Whether respondent may challenge his conviction on other grounds—and whether those claims have been properly preserved—are issues we leave open on remand.

* * *

For these reasons, we reverse the judgment of the Virginia Supreme Court and remand the case for further proceedings not inconsistent with this opinion.

JUSTICE SOUTER and JUSTICE BREYER concurred in the judgment.

JOHNSON V. CITY OF CINCINNATI

United States Court of Appeals
310 F.3d 484 (6th Cir.2002)

BOYCE F. MARTIN, JR., CHIEF JUDGE.

The City of Cincinnati appeals the decision of the district court declaring the City's drug-exclusion ordinance, Cincinnati Municipal Code § 755, unconstitutional on its face, and unconstitutional as applied to plaintiffs Patricia Johnson and Michael Au France, and awarding plaintiffs attorney fees. For the reasons set forth below, we AFFIRM the judgment of the district court.

I.

A.

On August 7, 1996, the City enacted the Ordinance to enhance the quality of life and protect the health, safety, and welfare of persons in neighborhoods with a "significantly higher incidence of conduct associated with drug abuse than other areas of the City." Cincinnati, Ohio, Ordinance No. 229–1996, § 1(A), (D) (Aug. 7, 1996). To advance this goal, the Ordinance excludes an individual for up to ninety days from the "public streets, sidewalks, and other public ways" in all drug-exclusion zones if the individual is arrested or taken into custody within any drug-exclusion zone for one of several enumerated drug offenses. Cincinnati Municipal Code § 755–5. The Ordinance extends this exclusion for a year if the individual is convicted. *Id.* The Ordinance defines drug-exclusion zones as "areas where the number of arrests for . . . drug-abuse related crimes for the twelve (12) month period preceding the original designation is significantly higher than that for other similarly situated/sized areas of the city." *Id.* § 755–1.

Excluded persons who violate the Ordinance are subject to prosecution for criminal trespass, a fourth-degree misdemeanor. *Id.* The City's chief of police, however, must grant a variance to any person who proves that he or she (1) resided in the drug-exclusion zone prior to receiving the exclusion notice, or (2) was employed by, or owned, a business located in a drug-exclusion zone prior to receiving the exclusion notice. *Id.* § 755–11(2)(b). Provided they have written regulations prohibiting "drug abuse-related activities by their clients and which have entered into a written agreement with the police division concerning the applicability of those rules," social service agencies may also grant variances "for reasons relating to the health, welfare, or well-being of the person excluded, or for drug abuse-related counseling services." *Id.* Variances must be in writing and the individual must keep the variance with him or her at all times within a drug exclusion zone. *Id.* § 755–11(2)(c). The variance becomes void if the holder violates its terms or is subsequently arrested for a drug offense. *Id.* § 755–11(2)(c), (d)(4). * * *

In September 1998, the City Council designated Over the Rhine—a mixed residential/commercial neighborhood located immediately north of the City's downtown business district—a drug exclusion zone. The City's designation of Over the Rhine followed a police report examining City-wide drug arrests from June 1996 to May 1997. The report, which was subsequently incorporated into the Ordinance's factual findings, detailed that 18.7% of City drug arrests occurred in Over the Rhine. According to the report, reducing the number of drug offenses in Over the Rhine was extremely difficult because many arrested individuals returned to the neighborhood immediately upon release. Citing Portland, Oregon's 38% crime reduction in certain neighborhoods following the establishment of a drug exclusion ordinance, the police report characterized a drug-exclusion ordinance as an additional tool to reduce crime and improve the quality of life in Over the Rhine.

In 1998, the City amended the Ordinance to provide that the ninety-day exclusion period terminates upon acquittal, dismissal of charges, or failure to prosecute. * * *

B.

Johnson was arrested on March 18, 1998, for a marijuana trafficking offense in Over the Rhine. At the time of her arrest, she variously lived with Katrina Chambers and Frank Johnson, two of her adult children. Marquisa Harmon, Johnson's other adult daughter, resided in Over the Rhine. Johnson did not reside with Harmon, but she helped care for Harmon's five minor children and regularly took two of the children, Tania and Jaquanna, to school.

As a result of her arrest, Johnson received an exclusion notice prohibiting her from entering Over the Rhine from March 24, 1998, until June 22, 1998. Because she was not a bona fide resident of, or employed in, Over the Rhine, Johnson did not qualify for a variance, and she did not appeal her exclusion notice. * * *

[Editor's Note: A similar challenge was brought by Michael Au France, a homeless man who "regularly sought food, clothing, and shelter from social service organizations located in Over the Rhine," and whose attorney's office is located in the same area.

In its analysis, the court first held that the Fourth Amendment's protection against unreasonable searches and seizures was inapplicable. Subsequently, it concluded that the ordinance implicated a constitutionally protected "right to travel locally through public spaces and roadways." In the next section, the court held that the ordinance affected Ms. Johnson's and Mr. Au France's first amendment rights of association. In Ms. Johnson's case, the ordinance prevented her from visiting her grandchildren, and for Mr. Au France, the prohibition meant that he could not visit his attorney's office nor the many social service offices located in the area.]

VI.

Having addressed the existence of the relevant rights, we now turn to whether the Ordinance infringes on those rights, and if it does, whether it is nevertheless sufficiently tailored to allow the Ordinance to pass judicial scrutiny.

A.

1.

* * * [W]here a fundamental liberty interest protected by the substantive due process component of the Fourteenth Amendment is involved, the government cannot infringe on that right "unless the infringement is narrowly tailored to serve a compelling state interest." *Glucksberg,* 521 U.S. at 721, 117 S.Ct. 2258 (citation omitted); *Lakewood, Ohio Congregation of Jehovah's Witnesses, Inc. v. City of Lakewood,* 699 F.2d 303, 309 (6th Cir.1983).

2.

We agree with the district court's conclusion that the City's interest in enacting the Ordinance—to enhance the quality of life in drug-plagued neighborhoods and to protect the health, safety, and welfare of citizens in those areas—represents a compelling government interest. The question, then, is whether the Ordinance is narrowly tailored to serve that interest.

To determine whether the Ordinance is narrowly tailored to achieve the City's compelling interest in reducing drug abuse and drug-related crime, we (1) assess whether the Ordinance implicates an individual's interest in localized travel with specific reference to the precise nature of the infringement and (2) determine whether the Ordinance is the least restrictive means to accomplish the City's goal. In making this latter inquiry, we ask whether any other methods exist to achieve the desired results of enhancing the quality of life and protecting the health, safety, and welfare of citizens in high drug-crime neighborhoods. "[I]f there are other, reasonable ways to achieve those goals with a lesser burden on constitutionally protected activity, a State may not choose the way of greater interference. If it acts at all, it must choose 'less drastic means.'" *Dunn,* 405 U.S. at 343, 92 S.Ct. 995.

The Ordinance bars excluded individuals from each and every public space and roadway in Over the Rhine. In our view, the right to travel locally through public spaces and roadways is essentially a right of access. By blocking affected individuals' access to an entire metropolitan neighborhood of 10,000 people, the Ordinance therefore plainly infringes on the right to localized travel through the public spaces and roadways of Over the Rhine.

In denying access, the Ordinance initially presents constitutional tailoring problems because it broadly excludes individuals from Over the Rhine without regard to their reason for travel in the neighborhood. Thus, the Ordinance prohibits Johnson from engaging in an array of not only wholly innocent conduct, but socially beneficial action like caring for her grandchildren and walking them to school. Likewise, the Ordinance bans Au France from seeking food, shelter, social services and meeting with his attorney in the Over the Rhine, at the same time it bans him from pursuing illegal drugs in Over the Rhine.

The broad sweep of the Ordinance is compounded by the fact that the Ordinance metes out exclusion without any particularized finding that a person is likely to engage in recidivist drug activity in Over the Rhine. * * *

3.

With respect to less restrictive alternatives, the City contends that the Ordinance is narrowly tailored because the City's "other attempts to curb the incidence of drug crime failed." In support of this assertion, the City argues that drug and prostitution activity remained constant in Over the Rhine, notwithstanding "an effort to increase police presence in the area through the use of foot patrols, bicycle patrols, and use of the District One Criminal Apprehension Team." Similarly, the City cites the report's statement that, "In July of 1995, several covert operations resulted in the arrests of 16 persons for soliciting prostitution, as well as 5 persons for felony drug violations. Even though covert operations continued on a monthly basis, seven months later, efforts in February and March of 1996, still resulted in 21 soliciting arrests and 50 various drug arrests."

We, of course, "do not demand of legislatures scientifically certain criteria of legislation." *Ginsburg v. New York,* 390 U.S. 629, 642, 88 S.Ct. 1274, 20 L.Ed.2d 195 (1968) (internal quotations omitted). But when constitutional rights are at issue, strict scrutiny requires legislative clarity and evidence demonstrating the ineffectiveness of proposed alternatives. *See Grutter v. Bollinger,* 288 F.3d 732, 749–51 (6th Cir.2002). Thus, the City would have to provide some detail on the "use of foot patrols, bicycle patrols, and use of the District One Criminal Apprehension Team," and put forth some evidence demonstrating these efforts were ineffective in reducing drug-related crime in Over the Rhine. Similarly, while we credit the City's statistical evidence regarding covert operations, such evidence does not demonstrate the ineffectiveness of other law enforcement operations.

The City's citation to the experiences of Portland, Oregon is also misplaced in considering narrow tailoring. Even if we were to extrapolate that what worked in Portland would likely work in Over the Rhine, this fact would not sustain the Ordinance. In considering whether a government regulation is narrowly tailored, it is not enough that the regulation achieves its ostensible purpose, it must do so without unnecessarily infringing upon constitutionally protected rights.

Beyond its conclusory claims that other efforts to combat drug crime were unsuccessful, the police department's report does not contain any indication that the City or its police department evaluated alternatives to the Ordinance. Faced with such a record, we cannot conclude that other alternatives could not achieve the same intended goals of the Act. While we are prepared to accept the legislative judgment of the City regarding potential alternatives, *see Grutter,* 288 F.3d at 751, the City nevertheless bears the burden of identifying potential alternatives. Given the nature of the right at issue—indeed, the Ordinance itself proclaims that "[i]ndividuals have a significant private interest in being able to travel and associate freely in all areas of the city"—the City must do more to consider potential alternatives. It is, of course, possible that a regulation like the Ordinance might be the narrowest method of addressing a seemingly uncontrollable drug and crime epidemic. But without some affirmative evidence that there is no less severe alternative, we cannot conclude that the Ordinance, in its present form, survives constitutional scrutiny. * * *

C.

In striking down the Ordinance, we do not foreclose the possibility that a narrower version of the Ordinance, supported by a clearer record, could withstand strict scrutiny. Temporary exclusion is an extreme measure, but we recognize that municipalities like the City of Cincinnati face formidable challenges in improving the safety and well-being of its citizens in high crimes areas. While we have every confidence that the City acted in the utmost good faith and with the best intentions in enacting the Ordinance, the Ordinance, in its present form, does not withstand constitutional scrutiny. * * *

[The holding triggered a lengthy and sharply worded dissent. *See* 310 F.3d at 506–519 (Gilman, J., dissenting). Judge Gilman argued that the majority had improperly created a fundamental right to intrastate travel and that it had wrongly concluded that the ordinance infringed on plaintiffs' constitutional freedoms of association.]

NOTES AND QUESTIONS

1. *Chicago's New Gang Loitering Ordinance.* Perhaps predictably, soon after the Court's decision in *Morales,* the City of Chicago passed a new gang loitering ordinance that tracked the language suggested by Justice O'Connor in her concurrence. Consider the city's new definition of gang loitering: "remaining in any one place under circumstances that would warrant a reasonable person to believe that the purpose or effect of that behavior is to enable a criminal street gang to establish control over identifiable areas, to intimidate others from entering those areas, or to conceal illegal activities." Chicago Mun. Code § 8–4–015. Notwithstanding its fealty to Justice O'Connor's guidance, at least one commentator suggested that the replacement ordinance may also be unconstitutional. *See* William J. Stuntz, Local Policing After the Terror, 111 Yale L. J. 2137, 2154 n.55 (2002). Do you agree?

2.   *Order Maintenance and Privatization.* In *Hicks*, the Supreme Court paid little attention to the fact that the city of Richmond was able to accomplish its goal by "privatizing" formerly public space. Why is the property private if it is owned by the Richmond Redevelopment and Housing Authority, a political subdivision of the state? Does privatization allow the Housing Authority to impose even more stringent controls on the comings and goings of residents, their guests, and the general public? Is the policy defensible on the grounds that it merely creates a publicly owned analogue to the increasingly popular phenomenon of gated communities? Can you identify a constitutionally persuasive difference between "remaining in any one place with no apparent purpose" and "demonstrating a legitimate business or social purpose for being on the premises"? Does it matter that *Morales* dealt with a legislatively adopted ordinance while *Virginia v. Hicks* upheld a policy adopted by the housing authority? In contrast to the gang loitering ordinance invalidated in *Morales*, the trespass policy in *Virginia v. Hicks* was strenuously opposed by the tenants themselves. Is that relevant? The Supreme Court has been protective of public housing authorities' attempts to preserve order in their complexes. In Department of Housing and Urban Dev. v. Rucker, 535 U.S. 125 (2002), the Court unanimously upheld a federal law that requires housing authority leases to provide for termination if a member of the household or guest in the unit engages in drug-related activity, even if the tenant was unaware of the activity. For critical analysis of housing authority trespass policies and review of possible legal challenges, *see* Elena Goldstein, Note, Kept Out: Responding to Public Housing No-Trespass Policies, 38 Harv. C.R.-C.L. L. Rev. 215 (2003). On remand in *Virginia v. Hicks*, the Virginia Supreme Court rejected Mr. Hicks' remaining challenges of vagueness and governmental violation of an asserted right of intimate association. Commonwealth v. Hicks, 596 S.E.2d 74 (Va. 2004).

3.   *Drafting a Constitutional Exclusion Ordinance.* Though *Morales* is a vagueness opinion and *Johnson* is based on the excluded individuals' substantive rights of travel and association, does the Supreme Court's opinion provide any evidence about how the Justices might react to an exclusion ordinance? For the *Johnson* court, one of the ordinance's crucial flaws was the absence of an individualized determination as a prerequisite to an exclusion order. Suppose that Cincinnati amended its ordinance to provide for particularized determinations whether the individual's reasons for entering the area are "wholly innocent [or] socially beneficial action." Would the amended ordinance possibly run afoul of *Morales'* vagueness concerns? If so, how can the city steer a constitutional course between the two opinions? For the *Johnson* court, the second major defect in the Cincinnati ordinance was the city's failure to establish that it had considered less restrictive alternatives. The court is quite specific in its discussion of the type of evidence that would establish that the city had narrowly tailored the ordinance in the manner that is the least restrictive of the identified constitutional rights. Is this simply a matter of proof? Is it a reasonable burden to impose on local law enforcement departments?

4. *Exclusion in State Court*. Two years prior to *Johnson*, in 2001, the Ohio Supreme Court invalidated the same Cincinnati ordinance under both the Ohio and the U.S. Constitutions. Its opinion in *State v. Burnett*, 755 N.E.2d 857 (Ohio 2001), is similar to *Johnson* in that the state court found a federal constitutional right to intrastate travel, and concluded that the ordinance impermissibly infringed on that right. Unlike *Johnson*, it rejected the challenger's freedom of association argument. Notwithstanding the state court's invalidation of the ordinance, the federal appellate court concluded that the dispute over attorneys fees meant that the case was not moot.

5. *Double Jeopardy and Exclusion Ordinances*. In separate cases, the Oregon courts upheld two different exclusion ordinances adopted by the city of Portland. In one case, the city had adopted a drug exclusion ordinance like the Cincinnati ordinance invalidated in the main case. *See* State v. James, 978 P.2d 415 (Or. Ct. App. 1999). The other involved an ordinance that excluded convicted prostitutes from designated "prostitution-free" zones. *See* State v. Lhasawa, 55 P.3d 477 (Or. 2002). The courts rejected the challenge that the exclusion ordinances violated criminal defendants' double jeopardy rights by subjecting them to multiple punishments for the same offense. Rather, they found that the ordinances did not impose a public stigma on the individual subject to the exclusion orders, and concluded that they complied with the Supreme Court's double jeopardy standards. Would the Sixth Circuit find the prostitution exclusion ordinance to be invalid on the same grounds as the drug exclusion ordinance it invalidated in *Johnson*? Is there any basis for distinguishing between the two types of ordinances?

6. *Exclusion and Retroactivity*. Refer back to *City of Northglenn v. Ibarra* in Chapter IV, in which the supreme court of Colorado found a local sex offender registration ordinance preempted by state law. Like the drug and prostitution zone exclusions, restrictions on where sex offenders may live ostensibly seek to remove them from areas where their criminal behavior is deemed more likely to occur. At the same time, though, the laws may make it difficult or impossible for former prisoners to find residential homes in their communities. In Hyle v. Porter, 882 N.E.2d 899 (Ohio 2008), the Ohio Supreme Court considered the applicability of a 2003 Ohio law, which prohibited convicted sex offenders from living within 1000 feet of any school, to an individual who had lived in his house with his wife since 1991. The court concluded that the Ohio legislature had not intended to apply the law to those whose criminal detentions pre-dated its enactment. As a result, the court was able to avoid the more difficult question of how the Ohio Constitution's general prohibition of "retroactive laws" would apply. Under Ohio caselaw, "a retroactive statute is unconstitutional if it retroactively impais vested substantive rights, but not if it is merely remedial in nature." State v. Consilio, 871 N.E.2d 1167 (Ohio 2007). As you might suspect, this has not proved to be an obvious distinction.

The Supreme Court has upheld a federal sex offender registration law. *See* U.S. v. Kebodeaux, 133 S.Ct. 2496 (2013) (allowing Congress to require registration of former military who had been convicted of a sex offense).

Similarly, three federal circuits have upheld state sex offender registration laws. *See* Mueller v. Raemisch, 740 F.3d 1128 (7th Cir. 2014); Doe v. Bredesen, 507 F.3d 998 (6th Cir. 2007) (upholding Tennessee's registration and monitoring laws for sex offenders against federal ex post facto challenge); Weems v. Little Rock Police Dept., 453 F.3d 1010 (8th Cir. 2006) (rejecting an array of federal constitutional challenges to an Arkansas law prohibiting convicted sex offenders from living within 2000 feet of a school or daycare center). Are drug and prostitution exclusion zone laws vulnerable on retroactivity grounds?

How far might these regulations of convicted sex offenders go? In Doe v. Prosecutor, Marion County, Indiana, 705 F.3d 694 (7th Cir. 2013), the court invalidated an Indiana law prohibiting registered sex offenders from using social media sites and instant messaging, concluding that it was not narrowly tailored to serve a significant government interest.

7. *Judicial Responses to Local Order Maintenance Regulation.* The Court's holding in *Morales* is consistent with its modern tradition of invalidating vagrancy and loitering laws. *See, e.g.*, Kolender v. Lawson, 461 U.S. 352 (1983); Papachristou v. Jacksonville, 405 U.S. 156 (1972); Shuttlesworth v. Birmingham, 382 U.S. 87 (1965). Justice Stevens, however, was able to attract majority support only for that part of his opinion in which he concluded that the Chicago law did not contain adequate enforcement guidelines. The Court's opinions, taken in their entirety, appear to offer guidance for communities seeking to enact anti-gang loitering ordinances that will survive constitutional challenge. Justice Stevens' opinion, for instance, explicitly approved of laws that prohibit loitering that is done in conjunction with an "overt act or evidence of criminal intent." 527 U.S. at 57. *See, e.g.*, Tacoma v. Luvene, 827 P.2d 1374 (Wash.1992), referred to approvingly in Justice Stevens' *Morales* opinion, 527 U.S. at 57 n.25, in which the Washington Supreme Court upheld a loitering ordinance that required a finding that the defendant intended to engage in illegal drug activity. Moreover, Justice O'Connor's concurrence provides specific syntactic guidance for language that would, in her view, withstand constitutional challenge on vagueness grounds.

Judicial disagreement over order maintenance regulations persists. *Compare* Silvar v. Eighth Judicial Dist. Court ex rel. County of Clark, 129 P.3d 682 (Nev. 2006) (prostitution loitering ordinance invalidated as vague and overbroad) *and* E.L. v. State, 619 So.2d 252 (Fla.1993) (invalidating ordinance that prohibited loitering "in a manner and under circumstances manifesting the purpose to engage in drug related activities" as vague, overly broad, and a violation of substantive due process) *with* Ford v. State, 262 P.3d 1123 (Nev. 2011) (upholding and distinguishing state statute adopted in the wake of *Silvar*), Tacoma v. Luvene, 827 P.2d 1374 (Wash.1992) (upholding ordinance similar to one in *E.L. v. State* against similar challenges). Anti-"teen cruising" ordinances have been upheld, *e.g.*, Brandmiller v. Arreola, 544 N.W.2d 894 (Wis.1996) and invalidated, *e.g.*, State v. Stallman, 519 N.W.2d 903 (Minn.Ct.App.1994). An Alabama appellate court invalidated an ordinance prohibiting sleeping in cars, *see* Horn v. Montgomery, 619 So.2d 949 (Ala.Cr.App. 1993), concluding that the discretion needed to apply the ordinance to prevent its application to, for example, a person who pulled off the road for a quick nap, rendered the ordinance fatally vague and discriminatory. In contrast, the Ninth Circuit upheld a Seattle ordinance that prohibited lying on the sidewalk in commercial zones during working hours, *see* Roulette v. Seattle, 97 F.3d 300 (9th Cir.1996). A number of cities, primarily in California, have used the doctrine of public nuisance to enjoin gang-like congregations. *See* Christopher S. Yoo, Comment, The Constitutionality of Enjoining Criminal Street Gangs as Public Nuisances, 89 Nw.U.L.Rev. 212 (1994). The California Supreme Court upheld the practice in People ex rel. Gallo v. Acuna, 929 P.2d 596 (Cal.1997).

Professor Ellickson identified three critiques: First, what he calls the "hyper-egalitarian" approach excuses the targeted behavior on the grounds of poverty and duress; second, the First Amendment critique ignores the anti-social effects of the behavior and focuses exclusively on the expressive freedom and associational liberty that are denied; third, the criminal law approach argues that the prevalent vagueness of local order maintenance regulation improperly protects abusive police practices. Ellickson regrets that none of these approaches considers the effect of leaving the behavior unregulated on America's urban areas. He denounces the "excessive federal constitutionalization of street law," and argues that viable cities must have the authority to preserve "a basic minimum of decorum in downtown public spaces. . . ." Robert C. Ellickson, Controlling Chronic Misconduct in City Spaces: Of Panhandlers, Skid Rows, and Public-Space Zoning, 105 Yale L.J. 1165, 1170–72 (1996). Ellickson argues that the "best solution to the problem of street misconduct would be the maintenance of a trustworthy police department whose patrol officers would be given significant discretion in enforcing general standards against disorderly conduct and public nuisances." *Id.* at 1245. His alternative proposal is that cities should adopt public space zoning schemes that prohibit street nuisances in some parts of the city, tolerate limited occurrences in others, and authorize them in yet other parts. *Id.* at 1225.

8.   *Void-for-Vagueness and Street Disorder.* As *Morales* illustrates, the void-for-vagueness rationale is one of the most successful challenges to order maintenance regulations. Professor Debra Livingston—now a federal appeals court judge—argued strenuously that the courts have generally misapplied that principle. While recognizing an understandable judicial skepticism of local laws that are similar to those used in the 1950s and 1960s in racially discriminatory ways, she argues that the vagueness doctrine is an inappropriate and ineffective tool for reining in abusive police practices:

> Even when local laws and ordinances regulating minor forms of street misconduct establish quite specific substantive criteria to govern their enforcement, as many recently enacted public order laws do, the police officer on the street still retains significant

discretion: to find the facts in one-on-one encounters (at least initially, and often without any subsequent review); to apply the law to the facts (honestly or dishonestly, with prudence or abandon); to enforce the law with citation or arrest; to use the law as a basis for informal resolution of a street order problem; or to ignore its violation altogether. The police department also retains significant discretion: whether to establish policies regarding the enforcement of laws regulating street misconduct; whether to allocate its officers to neighborhoods where infractions are likely to be observed. Limiting the discretion that police exercise on the street simply by demanding specificity in the laws that they enforce is . . . hopeless.
. . .

Debra Livingston, Police Discretion and the Quality of Life in Public Places: Courts, Communities, and the New Policing, 97 Colum.L.Rev. 551, 593 (1997).

Livingston notes at least two negative consequences of judicial invalidation of order maintenance regulation on vagueness grounds: It increases the prevalence of private sector security forces and it increases the likelihood that the police will "operate at the boundaries of lawful practice, misusing other laws as a basis for arrest or otherwise abusing their position." *Id.* at 633. Livingston echoes Ellickson's call for greater police discretion and argues that local administrative procedures, both within the police department and in the form of community review boards, are far more effective ways to manage police discretion than judicial invalidation of order maintenance regulations. *Id.* at 645–667.

9. *Community Policing and the Case for Enhanced Discretion.* The now widely accepted principles of "community policing" have transformed the focus of local law enforcement practices, establishing a more comprehensive attempt to help preserve neighborhood stability, liveable communities, and "neighborhood wellness" in urban areas. Order maintenance regulations are an important component of this approach.

The profound shift in policing practices can be traced to a 1982 article by James Q. Wilson and George L. Kelling, now known simply as *"Broken Windows."* According to Jeremy Travis, director of the National Institute of Justice, research arm of the U.S. Department of Justice, the article "has had a greater impact than any other article in serious policing." In it, the authors argued that police officers should be more present in the neighborhoods they patrol, and that they should concentrate more of their efforts on reducing street disorder. Wilson and Kelling offered the following rationale:

. . . [D]isorder and crime are usually inextricably linked, in a kind of developmental sequence. Social psychologists and police officers tend to agree that if a window in a building is broken and is left unrepaired, all the rest of the windows will soon be broken. . . .

We suggest that 'untended' behavior also leads to the breakdown of community controls. A stable neighborhood of families who care for their homes, mind each other's children and confidently frown on unwanted intruders can change, in a few years or even a few months, to an inhospitable and frightening jungle. A piece of property is abandoned, weeds grow up, a window is smashed. Adults stop scolding rowdy children; the children, emboldened, become more rowdy. Families move out, unattached adults move in. Teenagers gather in front of the corner store. The merchant asks them to move; they refuse. Fights occur. Litter accumulates. People start drinking in front of the grocery; in time, an inebriate slumps to the sidewalk and is allowed to sleep it off. Pedestrians are approached by panhandlers. . . .

Though it is not inevitable, it is more likely that here, rather than in places where people are confident they can regulate public behavior by informal controls, drugs will change hands, prostitutes will solicit and cars will be stripped. That the drunks will be robbed by boys who do it as a lark, and the prostitutes' customers will be robbed by men who do it purposefully and perhaps violently. That muggings will occur.

James Q. Wilson and George L. Kelling, Broken Windows: The Police and Neighborhood Safety, Atlantic Monthly, March 1982 at 29, 31–32, available at www.theatlantic.com/politics/crime/windows.htm. *See also* George L. Kelling and Catherine M. Coles, Fixing Broken Windows: Restoring Order and Reducing Crime in Our Communities (Simon & Schuster, Inc. 1996). Some empirical legal scholarship challenges the fundamental basis of the *Broken Windows* hypothesis. The authors found "no empirical evidence to support the view that shifting police towards minor disorder offenses would improve the efficiency of police spending and reduce violent crime." Bernard E. Harcourt and Jens Ludwig, Broken Windows: New Evidence from New York City and a Five-City Social Experiment, 73 U.Chi.L. Rev. 271, 315 (2006).

Nowhere is the debate over *Broken Windows* more heated than in New York City, where the current police chief has encouraged his force to engage in practices based on the theory. The 2014 death of Eric Garner, an unarmed African American man who caught the police's attention because of an alleged illegal sale of cigarettes on the street, has led to public outcry and opposition. According to the critics, this style of policing is based on overly aggressive police tactics and racial profiling. As Derrick Z. Jackson put it in a 2014 Boston Globe opinion piece, "Few people want petty criminals ruling the corners, but neither do they want them executed." Boston Globe, Dec. 29, 2014.

10. *Civil Liberties and Community Policing.* In contrast to Professors Livingston and Ellickson's general endorsement of order maintenance regulations, other scholars are more critical. *See, e.g.,* Bernard E. Harcourt,

Reflecting on the Subject: A Critique of the Social Influence Conception of Deterrence, the Broken Windows Theory, and Order-Maintenance Policing New York Style, 97 Mich.L.Rev. 291, 308–331 (1998). Professor Harcourt concludes that the *Broken Windows* theory is a superficial and incomplete proposal for a problem that extends far beyond the maintenance of public order to more deeply rooted problems of racism and poverty. Other commentators have raised important concerns about abuse of police discretion and discriminatory impact on minority residents. *See, e.g.*, David Cole, Discretion and Discrimination Reconsidered: A Response to the New Criminal Justice Scholarship, 87 Geo.L.J. 1059 (1999); Dorothy E. Roberts, Foreword: Race, Vagueness, and the Social Meaning of Order-Maintenance Policing, 89 J.Crim.L. & Criminology 775 (1999). Professor Roberts argues that order maintenance regulations reinforce racial stereotypes and give legitimacy to police harassment. Similarly, Professor Cole criticizes the "New Discretion" on five grounds: (1) it ignores the extensive discretion the police have even in the absence of order maintenance regulations; (2) it minimizes the existence of racial discrimination in our criminal justice system; (3) it overlooks the inability of the political process to protect inner city residents; (4) it unwisely accepts the resulting increase in public (police) interference with private lives in exchange for a decrease in private (criminal) interference with the lives of community residents; and (5) it ignores the illegitimacy that attaches to widespread police discretion in the aftermath of high profile incidents such as the beating of Rodney King and the killing of Amadou Diallo. 87 Geo.L.J. at 1070–1092. How would the proponents of order maintenance respond to those criticisms? How can a court properly assess whether, in Professor Roberts' words, "the disproportionate arrest of people of color under the [Chicago gang-loitering law is] evidence of racial discrimination, or evidence that the Chicago Police Department is finally starting to protect the city's minority communities against internal disorder?" 89 J.Crim.L. & Criminology at 779.

11. *An Equal Protection Right to Community Policing?* The City of Chicago's Deputy Corporation Counsel Lawrence Rosenthal, who argued the *Morales* case before the Supreme Court, suggests that the Equal Protection Clause should be interpreted as including, not merely a prohibition of certain types of governmental powers, but also as recognizing an affirmative right to "security against lawbreakers." Under that view, the inquiry shifts from a focus on whether the tactics employed by the police meet the substantive equality norm and asks whether all segments of the community have received equality of protection. Recognizing that poorer, disproportionately minority neighborhoods in urban areas have less stability and higher crime rates than other neighborhoods, Rosenthal argues that the standard, reactive conventional policing tactics, applied equally throughout the city, provide but an illusion of equality. In response to the critique that community policing practices are applied discriminatorily to members of minority groups, he argues that the answer is to improve rather than to abandon the techniques: "The answer to racial discrimination in law enforcement is improved training, supervision, discipline for misconduct, and judicial oversight, rather

than confining the police to tactics that have no hope of affording the residents of disadvantaged neighborhoods the same security enjoyed by the wealthy." *See* Lawrence Rosenthal, Policing and Equal Protection, 21 Yale L. & Pol'y Rev. 53, 101–02 (2003).

INDEX

References are to Pages